The Investment Manager's Handbook

The
Investment Manager's
Handbook

Edited by

SUMNER N. LEVINE

State University of New York
Stony Brook, New York

DOW JONES-IRWIN
Homewood, Illinois   60430

ISBN 0-87094-207-7
Library of Congress Catalog Card No. 79–53965
Printed in the United States of America

1 2 3 4 5 6 7 8 9 0 K 7 6 5 4 3 2 1 0

Preface

This handbook is intended for professional investment managers responsible for the performance of pension funds, mutual funds, trusts, endowments, and the internal portfolios of savings institutions and insurance companies.

The past decade has witnessed an enormous growth in the range and sophistication of knowledge required by portfolio managers. This handbook has been designed to meet the resulting need for a convenient and comprehensive reference. In order to provide authoritative coverage of the extensive range of material contained herein, some 40 experts—both practitioners and academics—were invited to contribute. Throughout, an effort was made to balance practice and theory.

Part One is devoted to fundamentals—administrative and theoretical—of investment management. Part Two surveys management strategies as applied to passive and active equity portfolios, real estate and fixed income portfolios, international diversification, and stock options. Measuring and monitoring performance are dealt with at length in Part Three, while equally important legal and regulatory matters are discussed by the contributors in Part Four. Management by type of portfolio—pensions, trusts, banks, insurance, and so on—is discussed in Part Five, and money market portfolio management is covered in Part Six. Part Seven comprehensively surveys computer services in constructing, managing, and monitoring portfolios.

Security analysis is covered extensively in the *Financial Analyst's Handbook, 1: Portfolio Management* (Dow Jones-Irwin, 1975), and therefore has not been included here.

It has been a great pleasure serving as editor of this handbook. Certainly the job could not have been accomplished without the valuable guidance of and suggestions by the Editorial Advisory Board and the splendid cooperation of the contributors. To all the participants, I wish to express my thanks and appreciation.

March 1980   ***Sumner N. Levine***

Contributors

Keith P. Ambachtsheer Partner and Director of Research, Canavest House Ltd., Toronto, Canada.

W. Scott Bauman The Colgate Darden School of Business Administration, University of Virginia, Charlottesville, Virginia.

Philip W. Bell William Alexander Kirkland Professor of Accounting and Economics, Jesse H. Jones Graduate School of Administration, Rice University, Houston, Texas.

Thomas P. Bleakney Vice President and Consulting Actuary, Milliman & Robertson, Inc., Seattle, Washington.

John R. Boyd Vice President, Seattle First National Bank, Seattle, Washington.

Eugene D. Brody Vice President, Oppenheimer Capital Corp., New York, New York.

John L. Casey Senior Vice President-Law, Scudder, Stevens & Clark, New York, New York.

William J. Chadwick Counsel of Paul, Hastings, Janofsky & Walker, Los Angeles, California.

Charles D. Ellis President, Greenwich Research Associates, Greenwich, Connecticut.

Edwin J. Elton Graduate School of Business Administration, New York University, New York, New York.

J. Robert Ferrari Vice President and Chief Economist, Prudential Insurance Company of America, Newark, New Jersey.

H. Russell Fogler College of Business Administration, University of Florida, Gainesville, Florida, and Capital Market Consultant, Frank Russell Company, Tacoma, Washington.

John G. Gillis Partner, Hill & Barlow, Boston, Massachusetts.

Martin J. Gruber Graduate School of Business Administration, New York University, New York, New York.

Roger G. Ibbotson Graduate School of Business, University of Chicago, Chicago, Illinois.

Charles D. Kuehner Director, Security Analysis and Investor Relations, American Telephone and Telegraph Co., New York, New York.

Morton Lane President, Discount Corporation of New York Futures, Chicago, Illinois.

Martin L. Leibowitz General Partner and Manager of Bond Portfolio Analysis Group, Salomon Brothers, New York, New York.

Donald R. Lessard   Sloan School of Management, Massachusetts Institute of Technology, Cambridge, Massachusetts.

Sumner N. Levine   State University of New York, Stony Brook, New York.

Vinay V. Marathe   Barr Rosenberg Associates, Orinda, California.

Edmund A. Mennis   Chairman of the Board, Security Pacific Investment Managers, Inc., Los Angeles, California.

Norton H. Reamer   President, The Putnam Management Company, Inc., Boston, Massachusetts.

Patrick J. Regan   Vice President, BEA Associates, Inc., New York, New York.

Fred B. Renwick   Graduate School of Business Administration, New York University, New York, New York.

Edward M. Roob   Senior Vice President, First National Bank of Chicago, Chicago, Illinois.

Paul Sack   The Rosenberg Real Estate Equity Funds, San Francisco, California.

Paul R. Samuelson   Director of Portfolio Analysis, The Ford Foundation, New York, New York.

Hazel A. D. Sanger   Vice President, Thorndike, Doran, Paine & Lewis, Atlanta, Georgia.

Keith V. Smith   Dean, Krannert Graduate School of Management, Purdue University, Lafayette, Indiana.

Marcia Stigum   Money Market Consultant, New York and London.

Dennis A. Tito   President, Wilshire Associates, Santa Monica, California.

Thomas A. Vaughn   Vice President, First National Bank of Chicago, Chicago, Illinois.

James R. Vertin   Senior Vice President, Wells Fargo Investment Advisors, San Francisco, California.

Wayne H. Wagner   Vice President, Wilshire Associates, Santa Monica, California.

James L. Walters   Vice President and Counsel, Wellington Management Company, Boston, Massachusetts.

Arthur Williams III   Vice President, Merrill Lynch, Pierce, Fenner & Smith, New York, New York.

J. Peter Williamson   The Amos Tuck Graduate School of Business, Dartmouth College, Hanover, New Hampshire.

Lawrence Zamos   Senior Associate, Wilshire Associates, Santa Monica, California.

Arthur Zeikel   President, Merrill Lynch Asset Management, Inc., New York, New York.

Karl Zerfoss, Jr.   First Vice President, Kemper Financial Services, Inc., Chicago, Illinois.

Contents

PART ONE
BASIC ASPECTS

1. **Overview of Investment Management,** *W. Scott Bauman* **3**

   The Objectives and Requirements of the Investor. The Environment for Investments. Portfolio Plans or Policies. Control of the Investment Programs. Professional Qualifications for Investment Managers: *The C.F.A. Competency Standards.* Types of Portfolios or Investment Accounts: *Individual/Family-Type Investors. Formal Retirement Funds. Insurance Companies.*

2. **Structures of Investment Management Organizations,** *W. Scott Bauman* **32**

   Operational Functions of the Organization: *Economic and Capital Market Research. Industry and Security Research. Statistical Research Systems. Account Management. Transactions and Records Management.* The Decision-Making Structure. General Characteristics of the Organizational Structure: *Scope and Diversity of Functions. Structure of the Organization. Size of the Organization.* Types of Institutions: *Investment Counsel Firm. Investment Companies. Bank Trust Investment Division. Insurance Company Investment Operation. Brokerage Firm Investment Advisory Department. Pension Fund Portfolio Management. Published Investment Advisory Services.*

3. **Setting Investment Objectives,** *Charles D. Ellis* **61**

   Investment Counseling. Controlling Risk: *Evaluating Policy and Operations.*

4. **The Efficient Market-Random Walk Debate,** *Charles D. Kuehner and Fred B. Renwick* **70**

   Introduction. Requirements for an Efficient Market: *1. Effective Information Flow. 2. Fully Rational Investors. 3. Rapid Price Change to New Information. 4. Low Transaction Cost. 5. Continuous Trading.* Situation Prior to Emergence of the Efficient Market Concept: *Technical Analysis. Fundamental Analysis.* Three Forms of the Efficient Market-Random Walk Hypotheses: *1. The Weak Form. 2. The Semistrong Form.*

3. *The Strong Form.* The Weak Form of the Efficient Market-Random Walk Hypotheses: Survey of Evidence: *Overview. Analysis of Studies.* The Semistrong Form of the Efficient Market-Random Walk Hypotheses: Survey of Evidence: *Overview. Analysis of Studies.* The Strong Form of the Efficient Market-Random Walk Hypotheses: Survey of Evidence: *Overview. Analysis of Studies.* Implications, Challenge, and Conclusion: *Implications. Challenge to Security Analysis. Conclusion.*

5. **Modern Portfolio Theory,** *Edwin J. Elton and Martin J. Gruber*   **160**

Overview. The Portfolio Choice Problem. Mean Return and Risk: *The Mean Return. A Measure of Risk. Variance of Combinations of Assets. Characteristics of Portfolios.* The Efficient Frontier with Riskless Lending and Borrowing. Implementation of Theory: *The Inputs to Portfolio Analysis. Single Index Models—An Overview. Other Models of Why Stocks Move Together. Simple Portfolio Selection Criteria.* Conclusion.

6. **Portfolio Beta Prediction,** *Vinay V. Marathe* **202**

Overview. The Capital Asset Pricing Model. The Traditional Method of Estimating Betas. Estimation Error and Bayesian Adjustment. A Multiple-Factor Model of Security Returns: *Common Factors of Security Returns. Implications for Predicting Portfolio Betas. Implications for Predicting Portfolio Residual Risk. Implications for Performance Attribution and Analysis.* Improved Prediction of Beta from Investment Fundamentals. Conclusion. Appendix.

PART TWO
MANAGEMENT STRATEGIES

7. **Active Equity Management Strategies,** *Arthur Zeikel* **225**

Active Investment Tactics. Security Analysis and Common Stock Evaluation. Evaluation Models. Business Cycles and Investment Timing. Timing and Technical Analysis. Dow Theory and Price Charts: *Price Chart Patterns. Bar Charts. Moving Averages.* Critique of Technical Analysis: *Coping Better.*

8. **Passive Equity Management Strategies,** *James R. Vertin* **282**

Passive versus Active Management: *Some Issues. The Question of Market Efficiency. Transaction Costs. Management Fees. Risk-Return Considerations. Passive Management Performance.* Managing Passive Portfolios: *Choosing an Index. Portfolio Construction—Duplication or Sampling? Trading Strategies. Pooled versus Individual Portfolios.* Passive Equity Management Strategies: *Core-Noncore (Passive-Active) Portfolios. How Much Passive Management? Asset Allocation Assistance. Market Inventory Fund. Other Passive Possibilities.*

9. **Management of Bond Portfolios,** *H. Russell Fogler* **305**

Evolution and the Multiperiod Problem—An Overview. Management Strategies: *The Benchmark Yield Curve. The Expected Return—The Start-*

ing Point. Interest Rate Anticipation. Sector-Quality-Coupon (SQC) Selection. Swapping. Economic and Credit Analysis. Maturity Structure Strategies. Objectives and Risk: *A Balance Sheet Approach. Price Volatility. Interest Rate Cycle Risk. Yield Volatility. Call Risk. Default Risk. Reinvestment Risk.* Price versus Reinvestment Risk—Offsetting Forces and Immunization: *Portfolio Immunization. Duration and Immunization. Caveats on Immunization and Duration. Summary on Immunization.* Empirical Studies: *Return Functions. Dumbbells versus Laddered Portfolios. The Search for a "Bond Beta"—and the Nonlinearity Dilemma. Immunization Studies. Procedures for Detecting Bankruptcy.* Summary. Appendix: *Duration and Immunization Mathematically.*

10. **Management of Real Estate Portfolios,** *Paul Sack* **345**

Why Invest in Real Estate? *The Liquidity of Real Estate Investments. Incremental Value in Real Estate. Characteristics of High Quality Properties. Characteristics of Higher Risk Properties. Determining Intrinsic Value. Leverage.* How to Invest in Real Estate: *Commingled Funds: Open-End versus Closed-End. Selecting a Real Estate Manager, Fund Manager, or Consultant.* Evaluating Performance. Summary.

11. **International Diversification,** *Donald R. Lessard* **359**

Introduction. The Potential Advantages of International Diversification: *Expected Returns and Gains from International Diversification.* Obstacles to International Investment: *Currency Risk. Political or Sovereign Risk. Limited Size and Depth of Foreign Markets. Relative Efficiency of Foreign Markets. Taxes, Restrictions on Ownership, and other Institutional Obstacles. Conclusions Regarding Obstacles to International Investment.*

12. **Option Strategies,** *Eugene D. Brody* **384**

The Language of Options. Strategy and Technique: *Accumulation of a Position. Using Options as an Extension of Investment Policy. Buy Call and Treasury Bill. Buy and Write. Overriding. Selling Puts. Conversion.*

13. **Techniques of Portfolio Adjustments,** *Edmund A. Mennis* **399**

Changes in Portfolio Objectives: *Statement of Objectives. Investment Results Expected. Risk Tolerance. Investment Time Horizon.* Changes in Portfolio Objectives. Changes in Asset Mix: *Asset Mix Defined. Causes of Changes in Asset Mix. Factors Affecting Expected Returns. Predicting Expected Returns. Determination of Asset Mix.* Changes in the Composition of Fixed-Income Portfolios: *Maturity. Quality. Coupon. Sector. Techniques Contrasted.* Changes in the Equity Portfolio: *Alternative Styles of Equity Management. Industry Portfolios. Determination of Industry Weights. Company Selection. Sector Portfolios.*

14. **Investment Returns on Stocks, Bonds, and Bills,** *Roger G. Ibbotson* **420**

The Risks and Rewards. Measurement of the Five Series: *Common Stocks. Long-Term Corporate Bonds. Long-Term Government Bonds. U.S. Treasury Bills. Consumer Price Index.*

15. **Historical Returns of Real Estate Equity Portfolios,** *Keith V. Smith*   **426**

Index Trends. Real Estate Investment Trusts. Index Appreciation. Comparisons of Samples. Traditional Performance Evaluation. Risk-Adjusted Performance Evaluation.

PART THREE
MEASURING AND MONITORING PERFORMANCE

16. **Equity Portfolio Performance,** *Dennis A. Tito and Lawrence Zamos*   **445**

The History of Performance Measurement. Examining Performance: *Why Monitor Performance? Who Is Concerned? Meeting Sponsor Objectives. Subdivision of Funds. Period of Performance. The Analyst.* Basic Measurements of Performance: *Return. Risk. Other Important Measures of Performance.* Evaluating Performance: *Achieving Objectives. Benchmarks for Comparative Analysis. Comparative Analysis of Returns. Risk and Return—Using the Capital Market Line. Return and Diversification Relationship. Management Trends.* Correcting Performance: *Trade-off Analysis. Simulation. Optimization. Control.*

17. **Trends in Bond Portfolio Management,** *Martin L. Leibowitz*   . . . **474**

The Evolution of Active Bond Management: *The Scope of Bond Management Activity. Prospective Problems in Rate Anticipation.* The Baseline Method for Relating Short-Term Performance to Long-Term Goals: *The Yardstick of Total Return. The Baseline Portfolio. Management Activity Relative to the Baseline Portfolio. Evaluating Proposed Departures from the Baseline. Sources of Return. Communication between Sponsor and Manager.*

18. **Monitoring Executions,** *Wayne H. Wagner* **507**

Why Monitor Execution Costs? Explicit and Implicit Trading Costs. A Simple Model for Execution Evaluation. Pitfalls in Measuring Execution Costs. Reducing the Cost of Transacting. Conclusion. Appendix.

19. **Evaluating the Quality of Research Information,**
Keith P. Ambachtsheer **521**

What is Research Information? *Why Does this Question Deserve an Answer?* Key Factors in Predictive Ability Measurement: *The Diefenbach Study. The Korschot Study. The Value Line Method.* Information Coefficient Analysis. Case Studies Using Information Coefficient Analysis. Using Information Coefficient Analysis in Portfolio Management. Information Coefficient Analysis: Is It Ideal? Concluding Comments.

20. **Measuring and Reporting on Performance,** *Philip W. Bell* **543**

Concepts and Measures Needed for the Evaluation of Performance: *Objectives: Comparability and Necessary Conditions for Comparability in Performance Measures. Formulating the Data: A Basic Worksheet Tabulation. Current Value Income and Comparative Position Statements, Reconcilia-*

tion with Historical Cost Statements, and Weaknesses of the AICPA Recommendation. Changes in the General Price Level, Inflation Accounting,
and Performance Evaluation. Tax Considerations, the Timing Problem,
and Interpretation of the Data: *Tax Considerations and Performance Reporting. The Timing Problem and Interpretation of the Data.*

**PART FOUR
REGULATORY ASPECTS**

21. **An Overview of Fiduciary Law,** *James L. Walters* **567**

The Standard of Reasonable Care. The Duty of Loyalty. The Effect of
Public Interest on Fiduciary Duty. Preventive Steps for the Fiduciary:
*Knowledge of Specific Laws or Rules affecting the Client. Exculpatory
Clauses. Investment Objectives. Disclosure and Consent. Documenta-
tion.*

22. **ERISA and the Portfolio Manager,** *William J. Chadwick* **583**

Introduction. Fiduciary Responsibility: *Coverage. Structure and Content.
Fiduciary Duties. Liability for Fiduciary Breaches. Exculpatory Provisions.* Prohibited Transactions: *Overview. Prohibited Transaction Restrictions. Statutory Exemptions. Transitional Rules. Administrative Exemptions.* Conclusion: Transactional Analysis.

23. **Regulation of Investment Managers under Federal Securities Laws,**
John G. Gillis **603**

Introduction. Investment Advisers Act: *Background. Who Is an Investment Adviser. Registration and Qualifications.* Books and Records:
*Required by Section 204. Other Requirements—ERISA. Institutional In-
vestment and Beneficial Ownership Disclosure.* Investment Advisory Contracts: *Topics Covered. Investment Objectives and Restrictions.* Fees for
Investment Advisory Services. Marketing Investment Advisory Services—
Disclosure: *Advertising. Brochure Rule and Revised Form ADV. Requirement to Revise Form ADV. Disclosure of Brokerage Placement Practices.*
Relationships with Brokers: *Broker Referrals and Continuing Relationships. Cash Payments for Referrals.* Prohibited Transactions—Fraud:
*General. Dealing with a Client as Principal or Broker. Custody or Posses-
sion of Clients' Funds or Securities. Adviser and Personal Securities Transactions. Inside Information. Corporate Projections.* Liability: *Implied Private Actions under the Investment Advisers Act. SEC Administrative
Powers.*

24. **Legal Limits on Investing: with Reference to State Regulations,**
John L. Casey **650**

Approaching a Common Type of Trust: *What is a Trust? Making the
Review.* The Base Case: *What are the Investment Powers?* Balance, Diversification, Concentration: *A Balanced Portfolio. Diversification. Concentration and Indexing. Individual Security Selection and Portfolio Construc-*

tion. When Trustees Retain a Professional Investment Manager. Family Objectives and the Investment Vehicles in the Cosmo Trust: *Family Objectives. Reserves. Long-Term Municipals. Discriminating between Issues of Securities; Mutual Funds. Stocks Generally. The Local Business. Deliberate Retention or Sale. Investment Recommendations. Broker Selection. Advisory Fees or a Small Business. Deferred Compensation. Real Property as a Trust Investment.* Specific Investment Restrictions for Other Funds Including Institutions: *New York Trustees. Public Retirement Funds and Investment Companies. Insurance Companies and other Savings Institutions. Dividend Limits. Foreign Investments. Retention of Securities which Do Not Meet Standards for New Investments: Unrealistic Assumptions.* New Restrictions: Social-Impact Investing: *Background. Current Issues. Corporate Responses. Shareholder Response. The Investment Manager's Response.*

25. Professional Self-Regulation, *W. Scott Bauman* **687**

Educational Standards. Standards of Professional Conduct: *Code of Ethics. Standards of Professional Conduct.* Enforcement of Standards. Continuing Education.

PART FIVE
MANAGEMENT BY TYPE OF ACCOUNT

26. Management of Pension Fund Portfolios, *Patrick J. Regan* **697**

The Size and Growth of Pension Assets. Questions for the Investment Manager: *1. Is the Plan Sponsor a Government Entity, a Labor Union or a Corporation? 2. Is It a Defined Benefit or a Defined Contribution Plan? 3. How Mature Is the Plan and How Will This Change in the Coming Years? 4. How Conservative Are the Funding Methods and Actuarial Assumptions Used to Compute the Pension Costs and Liabilities?* Summary. Appendix.

27. Municipal and State Pension Plans, *Thomas P. Bleakney* **709**

Funding. Investments Held by Public Systems. Investment Trends. Investment Powers. Political Considerations. Socially Useful Investing.

28. Life Insurance Company Investments, *J. Robert Ferrari* **725**

Life Insurance and Savings. Sources of Funds for Investment. Investment Objectives: *Distribution of Assets and Liabilities. Basic Investment Characteristics. The Risk-Return Trade-Off.* Investment Risk: *Insolvency Risk. Liquidity Risk. The Special Problems of Inflation.* Company Organization. Regulation of Life Insurance Investments: *Qualitative Restrictions. Quantitative Restrictions.* Life Insurance Company Taxation. Special Features of Life Insurance Investments: *Forward Commitments. Private Placements.* Historical Investment Behavior: *General Account Investments. Separate Account Investments.*

29. Fire and Casualty Portfolios, *Karl Zerfoss, Jr.* **750**

The Environment. General Approach. Investment Objectives. The Mix of Assets. Investment Principles: *Bonds Should Be Actively Managed. Tax Management. Realize Common Stock Gains. Diversification and Quality.* Organizing the Investment Function.

30. Portfolio Management—Guidelines for a Commercial Bank,
** *Edward M. Roob and Thomas A. Vaughn*** **761**

Investment Objectives and the Constraints: *Assess the Bank's Overall Risk Position. Study Liquidity Requirements versus Income Needs. Analyze the Pledging Requirements to Secure Public Funds. Evaluate the Bank's Overall Tax Position, Both Current and Future.* Portfolio Strategies: *"Three-Part" Portfolio Strategy. Type of Investment, Diversification, and Quality. Portfolio Maturity Structure. The "Dumbbell" or "Hour-glass" Portfolio. The "Cyclical" Portfolio.* Swapping: *Yield Pick-Up Swap. The Substitution Swap or Replacement Swap. The Intermarket Swap. The Yield Anticipation Swap. Tax-Loss Trading. Gain Trading. Open-Ending.* Improving Returns on Government Securities Portfolios: *Repurchase Agreements ("Repos"). Resale Agreements ("Resales"). Lending of Government Securities. Liability Management.* Authority and Control Procedures: *Reasons for Having a Written Policy. The Elements of an Investment Policy.*

31. Interest Rate Futures and the Management of Bank Portfolios,
** *Morton Lane*** **777**

Existing and Planned Financial Instrument Futures—How the Contract Markets Work: *Chicago Mercantile Exchange (International Monetary Market—IMM—subdivision). Chicago Board of Trade (CBOT). American Commodity Exchange at the Amex (American Commodities Exchange or ACE).* Examples of Hedging Situations for Commercial Banks: *Asset Portfolio. Liability Portfolio. A Numerical Example; Asset Portfolio. A Numerical Example; Liability Portfolio.* Arbitrage.

32. Personal Trust Management, *John R. Boyd* **789**

Trust Institutions. Types of Personal Trust. Organizational Structure of Trust Departments: *1. The Trust Administrator. 2. The Portfolio Manager. 3. The Security Analyst. 4. The Securities Trader.* Investment Standards for Trustees. Custodial and Record Keeping Services. Case Studies: *Case 1. Case 2.*

33. Managing Investment Company Portfolios, *Norton H. Reamer* . . . **801**

What is an Investment Company? Variety of Objectives and Types. Features and Services of Investment Companies. Legal, Tax, and Regulatory Issues. Investment Management of Investment Companies. Types of Organizations. Investment Styles. Risk Control and Modern Investment Techniques. Selecting an Investment Company.

34. **Educational Endowment Funds,** *J. Peter Williamson and*
     Hazel A. D. Sanger 827

     Introduction. Organization and Decision Making. Setting Investment Objectives: *Real Total Return. Spending. Gifts. Educational Inflation Premium.* Spending Policy. Asset Structure.

PART SIX
MONEY MARKET PORTFOLIOS

35. **The Mathematics of Interest Rates, Swaps, and Futures,**
     Sumner N. Levine 853

     Expressions for Rates: *Interest as a Discount. Interest Paid on Maturity. Relationship between Discount Rate and Rate at Maturity. Compound Rates. Converting a Discount Rate into a Compound Rate (Bond Equivalent Yields).* Bond Rates: *Return when Coupon Payments are Not Reinvested. Return when Coupon Payments are Reinvested. Yield to Maturity.* Analysis of Money Market Investments: *Break Even Analysis.* Analysis of Bond Swaps. Interest Rate Futures.

36. **Managing a Liquidity Portfolio,** *Marcia Stigum* 867

     Part 1—The Instruments in Brief: *Dealers and Brokers. U.S. Treasury Securities. T-Bill Futures Market. Federal Agency Securities. Federal Funds. Eurodollars. Certificates of Deposit. Eurodollar Certificates of Deposit. Commerical Paper. Bankers' Acceptances. Repurchases and Reverses. Municipal Notes.* Part 2—The Market Makers: Dealers and Others: *The Dealers. Dealer Financing. Interest Rate Predictions. Confidence Level in Positioning. The Maturity Choice. Strategies to Earn Position Profits. Arbitrages. The Clearing Banks. The Brokers. Communications.* Part 3—The Investors: Running a Short-Term Portfolio: *Contrast of a Portfolio Manager with a Dealer. The Parameters. Managing a Liquidity Portfolio. The Way It's Done.*

PART SEVEN
COMPUTER TECHNIQUES

37. **Computer Construction of Optimal Portfolios,** *Paul R. Samuelson*   921

     The Construction of an Optimal Portfolio at a Single Point in Time. The Revisions of an Optimal Portfolio through Time.

38. **Commercially Available Computer Services,** *Arthur Williams III*   939

     Organization: *Economics. Portfolio Strategy. Common Stock Analysis and Management. Fixed Income. International. Accounting. Performance Measurement and Portfolio Audit. News and General Business Information Services. Real Estate.* List of Commercially Available Computer Services: *I. Economics. II. Portfolio Strategy and Simulation. III. Common Stock Analysis and Management. IV. Fixed Income Securities Analysis and Management. V. International Information. VI. Accounting. VII. Performance Measurement and Portfolio Audit. VIII. News & General Business Information Services. IX. Real Estate. List of Firms and Services.*

PART EIGHT
STOCK MARKET INDEXES

39. Stock Market Indexes, *Sumner N. Levine* 979

GLOSSARY 991

Index 1025

Part One

Basic Aspects

Chapter 1

Overview of Investment Management

W. SCOTT BAUMAN
The Colgate Darden School of Business Administration
University of Virginia
Charlottesville, Virginia

Because investment management is an important and vast subject, it is indeed an appropriate subject for a handbook. In order to provide the reader with an overall understanding and appreciation of the subject, this chapter is intended to furnish a broad review of the functions and responsibilities frequently associated with investment management. Major functions, knowledge, and methods employed by investment managers discussed here will be considered in greater depth in succeeding chapters.

Simply stated, investment management consists of the tasks of planning, implementing, and controlling an investment program for an individual or institutional investor. These tasks entail integrating three important elements that lead to the construction and maintenance of an optimal portfolio for an investor. One element in the investment management process is the selection of suitable portfolio goals and constraints for a given investor in terms of the investment returns sought and the level of risks deemed acceptable. A second element is the analysis of forces in the socioeconomic and investment environments that may affect risks and returns of capital in economic sectors and security markets. A third element is the selection of categories of assets and of individual assets that possess investment characteristics considered to be optimal for a particular portfolio. (The type of assets to be considered here will be primarily, although not exclusively, investment securities.) Consequently, the investment manager is at, or at least near, the center of the whole investment decision-making process.

3

The remainder of this chapter will amplify on the major tasks and elements of investment management.

THE OBJECTIVES AND REQUIREMENTS OF THE INVESTOR

A major responsibility of the manager is the development of appropriate performance objectives for each portfolio. The investment manager should personally analyze the financial expectations and needs of an investor because the investor may overlook or not fully understand important future financial needs, or the investor may not clearly articulate those needs. By personally analyzing the investor's requirements, the manager will have a better appreciation and clearer understanding of them. Relevant financial objectives and requirements of the investor should be translated into clearly stated portfolio performance objectives and constraints. These should be reduced to writing in order to avoid misunderstandings as to what performance is to be expected, and to avoid unintentional portfolio performance digressions. These objectives may be stated in subjective, descriptive, or quantitative terms. The advantages of quantitatively stated performance objectives are that they are less ambiguous and that they can be more easily compared to subsequently realized portfolio performance. Here are several examples of quantitatively stated portfolio objectives:

To outperform the Standard Poor's 500 (S&P 500) Stock Index by at least one percentage point.

To outperform the S&P 500 Stock Index on a risk-adjusted basis.

To outperform the mean return of a selected sample of comparable (pension fund or mutual fund) portfolios.

To achieve a return of at least 9 percent.

To achieve a return at least equal to a minimum actuarial assumption of 6 percent.

To achieve a return at least equal to the inflation rate plus 3 percent.

Statements of investment objectives are incomplete unless they are expressed in terms of both returns and risk. The return variable can be stated in different ways, i.e.: *(a)* in terms of size of mean or minimum expected rate of return, possibly subdivided into investment income and capital growth components; *(b)* in terms of time horizon over which objectives are to be achieved; *(c)* in comparative terms to the returns on similar portfolios or market indexes, possibly on a risk-adjusted basis; or *(d)* in terms of after-tax returns or tax sheltered returns. The risk variable can be stated on the basis of a maximum limit on the fluctuation over time of the portfolio's return in terms of volatility, standard deviation, mean absolute deviation, or portfolio beta; and in terms of liquidity reserve requirements. Empirical evidence suggests that the return variable and risk variable are related to one another in the form of a positive risk-return trade-off; that is, the amount of expected return and the amount of risk available from individual securities are positively correlated. Therefore, performance objectives should be consistent with an investor owning an efficient portfolio.

An *efficient portfolio* is one that offers the highest available return for a given amount of risk, or one that assumes the lowest amount of risk for a given level of return. Performance objectives are optimal for a given investor if an efficient portfolio is selected that conforms to the investor's risk-return trade-off preference.

Clients share a responsibility with the investment manager in formulating suitable performance objectives in harmony with their own psychological temperament or tolerance toward risk. Investment managers are in the business of selling their services to investors. Because they are not only in competition with one another but in competition with other savings and investment market channels, they have a task of attracting and retaining the funds of clients. Like hair styles and hemlines, what a business is able to sell sometimes depends in part on what fashions are currently in demand. Consequently, some managers are tempted to pursue objectives which might convey a currently favorable image, but which are not realistic or in the best long-term interests of clients.

The optimistic and flamboyant portfolio performance objectives of the 1920s and 1960s were associated with speculation in short-term trading profits, in stocks of young risky companies and unseasoned managements, in stocks priced at speculative levels, and with high portfolio turnover rates. The popularity of these aggressive performance goals suddenly gave way with the sharp market corrections of the 1930s and 1970s.

With confidence shaken by the Depression and perpetuated by the upheavel of World War II, prudent and even ultraconservative investment policies were in fashion in the 1930s, 1940s, and early 1950s. Consequently, investment objectives and portfolios in that era needed to convey an image of strength. Portfolio strategies which were popular during a part of that era were associated with preservation of principal, adequate and stable income, balance between bonds and stocks, very extensive diversification, and portfolio window dressing with securities of large, entrenched companies having well-known names.

After two decades of stock market returns below the interest rate on high grade bonds, performance objectives and policies in the late 1970s are once again sober and conservative in which many portfolios emphasize bonds, broad diversification, stock market indexing, passive portfolio management, large companies, and dividend yields. This recurring reversal of portfolio performance objectives and policies from one decade to another can be detrimental to long-term portfolio performance inasmuch as it appears somewhat analogous to the farmer who locks the barn door after the horses are stolen or to the generals who prepare for the next war on the basis of successful strategies used in the previous war. We should guard against inappropriate performance objectives which are either too ambitious or needlessly conservative. In conclusion, portfolio performance objectives should be adequately supported by an optimal combination (1) of what an investor financially or psychologically wants or needs, (2) with what is available in the securities markets, and (3) with what the investment manager is capable of producing.

THE ENVIRONMENT FOR INVESTMENTS

Once performance objectives are devised for a portfolio, the investment manager must implement them in the prevailing economic environment or securities market setting. Inasmuch as broad forces in the investment environment can have a dominant influence on the performance of a portfolio, the manager needs to develop necessary long-term and short-term portfolio plans or strategies that capitalize as favorably as possible on these forces. To do this, the manager needs to study these forces and formulate expectations regarding their probable direction and effects on different securities markets.

There are many economic, business, political, social, technological and psychological forces that affect investment returns. These forces affect the financial ability of security issuers to pay interest and dividends, affect the interest rate structure, affect the purchasing power of the dollar, affect the expectations of investors, and ultimately affect the market prices of stocks and bonds. Some forces may affect all security markets such as major civil unrest or interest rate changes, while some forces simultaneously affect one security market sector favorably and another sector adversely such as industrial wage increases and government regulation. The investment manager needs to analyze the outlook for these forces and their probable effects in order to determine how best to allocate the funds in a portfolio among the different securities market sectors.

Based on performance objectives, the amount of funds allocated to bonds will depend on the outlook for interest rates, inflation, and possibly the relative attractiveness of the stock market. When the outlook for such forces changes, the manager may shift funds between the bond market and the stock market. The outlook for interest rates will depend on supply and demand conditions for loanable funds, and on business conditions, monetary policy, and investor expectations.

Where portfolio funds will be allocated in the bond market depends on: the yield curve for bonds with different maturities; yield spreads between bonds in different credit risk classes; need for liquidity, safety, and diversification; and the desirability of various bond features such as call protection, convertibility, discounts, high coupons, foreign bonds, tax-exemption, etc.

Within the guidelines of the investor's risk and return objectives, the amount of funds allocated to common stocks will depend on the short and long term outlook for broad economic forces that will affect the earning power and dividend paying ability of corporations, the outlook for inflation and interest rates which affect the earnings capitalization rates for common stocks, and the prevailing expectations of investors in the stock market. All of these factors have a significant influence on the risks and returns available in the stock market. If the investment manager believes that the expected returns in the stock market will now be more attractive relative to the risks, for example, because he or she believes that corporate earning power will be improving, inflation and interest rates will be decreasing, or investor expectations will be shifting from pessimism to optimism, then the manager will wish to allocate more funds to common stocks in a portfolio than would otherwise be the case. It is important for the manager to look ahead inasmuch as the stock market tends to anticipate fluctuations and trends in corporate earning power and dividend rates and to anticipate fluctuations in earnings-dividend capitalization rates.

Once it is determined how much is to be allocated to common stocks, stock market sectors need to be selected in which to invest. Although the market prices and earnings of most stocks tend to go up and down together with the stock market and business cycle, the prices and earnings of stocks in various sectors or homogeneous groupings tend to diverge somewhat from the overall stock market trend. The stocks within these individual sectors tend to perform somewhat similarly. Investment managers use different systems for identifying stock market sectors. One system assigns stocks to sectors on the basis of investment risk or quality such as high, medium, and speculative quality. Another system classifies stocks on the basis of their historical market volatility such as the beta coefficient which measures the degree to which the historical return of a stock was sensitive to the return of a stock market index. If the investor's performance objectives allow, the investment manager may increase the allocation to lower quality and higher beta (less stable) stocks, for example, if the manager anticipates an expanding phase of the business cycle or stock market cycle.

Other systems of classifying stock sectors is on the basis of growth versus income-yield type stocks, cyclical versus stable or defensive type stocks, large versus small companies, etc. The manager will allocate funds to these sectors that are compatible with the investor's objectives and tax bracket, and that have anticipated favorable return and risks characteristics in the market place.

PORTFOLIO PLANS OR POLICIES

Once the performance objectives of an investor are determined and the investment environment is analyzed, portfolio plans need to be devised by the investment manager that are consistent with these objectives and compatible with the environment for security investments. In addition, the portfolio plans or policies selected need to be those that the investment manager and his organization have the capability of being able to execute with a reasonable likelihood of success.

In order to achieve a satisfactory investment performance, some types of portfolio plans are more demanding than other types on an investment management organization in terms of the time, skills, and effort required. More active and higher risk investment strategies require greater precision (or luck) in decision making than more passive and more conservative strategies. Although the subject of investment management is widely considered to be a disciplined field of study, it is recognized as embracing more of the characteristics of an art than of a science. Consequently, it is not rare for two investment managers to recommend two somewhat different types of portfolio plans for the same investor. Such differences can be attributed to different management capabilities or different judgements about the outlook for the investment environment.

These differences are brought into sharp focus by debate over the *efficient market hypothesis* (EMH), and the *capital asset pricing model* (CAPM). The EMH asserts that the market prices of all securities are in equilibrium, that is, the prices properly reflect all relevant available information and therefore an investment manager is unable to buy an undervalued security (i.e., its market price is less than its true or correct value) and is unable to realize an excess or superior return other than by luck. Empirical evidence suggests that some or many managers are unable to produce superior returns with any consistency, while some managers contend that they have been able to do so. The CAPM asserts that an efficient portfolio of common stocks is one that is very widely diversified such that the risk and return of the portfolio is comparable to the stock market as a whole. Such a portfolio is sometimes referred to as the *market portfolio* or an *index fund*. Because the risks associated with any one stock or corporation are substantially diversified away in the market portfolio, the paramount risk that remains is that of the stock market and the economy as a whole, which is sometimes called *market risk* or *systematic risk*. The market risk in such a portfolio can be increased by the use of financial leverage (such as using margin), or it can be reduced by investing a portion of the portfolio's assets in fixed-income securities (such as U.S. Treasury Bills). The extent to which investors and managers accept or reject the EMH and the CAPM will obviously determine what portfolio plans are selected.

The investment manager for a conservative client, who believes he is either unable to select undervalued securities or who is unsure he can, will employ a *passive portfolio* plan. Such a portfolio will tend to maintain (1) a stable long-term asset mix between stocks, long-term bonds, short-term bonds, and liquid reserves, (2) broad diversification among stocks (an extreme example is an *index fund* portfolio with diversification comparable to a stock market index, such as the S&P 500 Index), and (3) a low portfolio turnover rate (that is, engage in very few switches between securities in the market).

In contrast, the investment manager for a less risk-averse client, who believes he can identify undervalued market sectors and undervalued securities, will employ an *active portfolio* plan. Such a portfolio strategy may consist of one or more of the following: (1) cyclical timing by altering the asset mix during cycles in the stock market and the bond market, (2) shifting between different categories of stocks (such as various risk or beta levels, different industries, low price-earnings ratio stocks, stock options, etc.), (3) buying stocks that appear to be undervalued, selling stocks that appear overvalued, and (4) generally concentrating in those securities which appear to offer superior expected returns.

In order to implement portfolio plans, the investment manager needs to continually obtain, analyze, and critically evaluate extensive research information regarding economic and business conditions, financial markets, industries, and companies. Successful investment decisions are dependent on a thorough and timely research analysis of relevant sources of information. This research effort is so vast that part of the task is performed by investment managers and part of it by other specialists including economists and industry research analysts.

CONTROL OF THE INVESTMENT PROGRAMS

The final task of investment management is to exercise control over the investment programs of investors in order to be assured that objectives are being achieved. Control over investment performance can be strengthened when management systematically and regularly monitors the effectiveness of every major phase of investment operations. Therefore, the investment management needs to review the suitability of portfolio performance objectives in terms of the circumstances of the investors; to evaluate the results of portfolio plans and policies in terms of successfully meeting objectives; to evaluate the securities research system, including the quality of research sources; and to review the other aspects of the portfolio management system. By monitoring each phase, management can take corrective action or make improvements on a timely basis. Such actions include redirecting budget resources to those phases or efforts in the investment operations that offer the greatest promise for achieving performance objectives. The evaluation of the quality of brokerage firm research, for example, may be used in determining an optimal allocation of brokerage commissions.

Because the past is so often a prologue for the future, the investment manager should review his or her portfolio performance as well as that of others during various past periods in order to gain insights into how portfolio performance can be altered and improved in the future. Past performance should be measured over a sufficiently long period in order to observe different investment environments and phases of security market cycles. Some managers and strategies perform relatively better during bull markets, for example, while others do better under adverse market conditions. In evaluating a particular portfolio plan or strategy, the investment manager should determine whether a comparatively less desirable performance during one type of market environment is more than offset by a much more favorable performance in another environment such that longer term objectives are being achieved.

The portfolio approach taken in evaluating the past performance of a specific portfolio may be determined in part by the portfolio plan that has been followed. For example, portfolios with active type plans can be, and perhaps should be, evaluated differently from portfolios with passive type plans. A cyclical timing strategy can be evaluated by observing the portfolio's asset mix near major market turning points and comparing the change in asset mix between market bottoms and tops in order to determine whether performance is being enhanced by timely portfolio asset shifts. Other active plans can be evaluated by determining whether portfolio asset turnover and transaction costs were more than offset by improved investment performance. The performance of individual securities and classes of securities purchased may be compared to the performance of those sold. The performance of a portfolio can be compared with stock market and bond market indexes, and with other portfolios having similar objectives and strategies.

Portfolio evaluations can generate many questions to which explanations should be sought. Does the past performance of a portfolio reflect risks taken, superior management, luck, or mistakes in judgement? When a mistake or poor decision is recognized, remedial action should be taken to minimize its recurrence. Investment management is a sufficiently difficult job that if a manager claims he has never made a poor decision, he is either fooling himself, is a liar, or is not human.

PROFESSIONAL QUALIFICATIONS FOR INVESTMENT MANAGERS

Based on the foregoing description of the functions and the process of investment management, it can easily be seen that an investment manager needs to have both a broad and a specialized professional background. Although the specific duties of investment managers can vary depending on the particular structure of an organization, we normally think of these people as managers of portfolios and as professional advisors to individual investors. In addition, many of them have responsibilities of managing their organization's investment operations. The professional qualities which are believed to have a bearing on the effectiveness of investment managers will now be discussed.

The field of investment management is broad in scope, complex in subject matter, challenging in application, and demanding in responsibilities. A survey was conducted in 1978 of a significant sample of over one thousand investment managers and security research analysts in order to learn about their backgrounds and professional attitudes.[1] More than 37 percent had one college degree and another 59 percent had two or more degrees.

Specialized or professional education is also considered to be important in the field. Over 40 percent of the portfolio managers in the sample are Chartered Financial Analysts (C.F.A.s). The C.F.A. is a professional designation that has been awarded to 5,570 analysts and managers over the 1963–78 period by The Institute of Chartered Financial Analysts. In order to be awarded the C.F.A., a candidate must meet several requirements, including completion of four years of occupational experience, mastery of a recognized common body of knowledge, successful completion of three annual examinations taken sequentially, and compliance with stipulated standards of professional conduct. The significant number of C.F.A.s in the field is a reflection of the character of the occupation and the perceived desirability of mastering a professional body of knowledge. Although the C.F.A. program is voluntary, its requirements are somewhat similar to other recognized professions that submit themselves to examinations of competency as evidenced by state medical examinations, bar examinations, and the Certified Public Accountant (C.P.A.) examinations.

---

[1] *Professional Standards in Investment Management,* W. Scott Bauman. This survey and study was sponsored by The Financial Analysts Research Foundation, Charlottesville, Virginia. The study is based on a survey of a random sample of 1,044 members of The Financial Analysts Federation, an association composed of practicing investment managers and security research analysts in the United States and Canada.

What is the nature of the body of knowledge that an investment manager needs to know? This question can be answered, at least in part, by reviewing the topics and knowledge specified for the C.F.A. candidate study program and as suggested by the tasks and responsibilities described thus far in this chapter. In referring to the C.F.A. competency standards, a candidate needs to have a reasonable mastery of seven major topics: economics, financial accounting, quantitative techniques, fixed-income securities analysis, equity securities analysis, portfolio management, and standards of professional conduct. These topics and knowledge are described in greater detail below in excerpts from *The C.F.A. Announcement*[2]:

The C.F.A. Competency Standards

Representing a dynamic profession, the subject matter and skills needed by a C.F.A. continue to evolve. The principal areas and topics to be mastered by C.F.A. candidates are summarized in the Topic Areas described below and shown in the *General Topic Outline.* Of the seven broad subject areas, the first three are the basic fields of *Economics, Financial Accounting,* and *Quantitative Techniques.* The next three areas are the two techniques of analysis—*Fixed-Income Securities Analysis* and *Equity Securities Analysis*—and *Portfolio Management.* The seventh topic relates to *Ethical and Professional Standards.* The candidate study program emphasizes the continuity of required subject matter over the three different levels, as well as a progression to higher levels of sophistication involving more complex financial problems. In addition, at the progressively more advanced levels, the experienced candidate is expected to deal with an expanded number of topics. In summary, the three candidate levels of the C.F.A. Program are recognized as a basic part of the professional career development of the investment and financial analyst.

Area One—Economics

Pre-Candidate Requirements

The candidate should be familiar with the basic principles of macroeconomics and the monetary system. The analyst should have minimum knowledge equivalent to one academic year of principles of economics as reflected in an elementary economics college textbook. C.F.A. examinations, it should be stressed, emphasize the practical application of economic concepts rather than abstract economic and monetary theories.

Candidate Level I

The candidate should be familiar with the tools of economic analysis and forecasting, have a perspective of historical trends of economic cy-

---

[2] Published annually by The Institute of Chartered Financial Analysts, Charlottesville, Virginia.

cles, and understand the structure of money and capital markets. Primary emphasis is placed on the relevance and application of economics to the analysis of investment securities.

Candidate Level II

The candidate should be able to apply basic economic concepts and techniques, studied under Candidate Level I, to an evaluation of specific companies and industries. Emphasis is placed on forecasting broad economic trends and their implications for projections of interest rates, aggregate corporate earnings, and security price changes.

Candidate Level III

The candidate should be able to analyze economic conditions, domestic policies and government actions, and their effects on the economy, inflation, and employment. The analyst should understand the implications of these policies and conditions and be able to relate these in a comprehensive analysis of aggregate corporate earnings, earnings trends in specific industries and companies, interest rates, and security prices. This analysis will aid in the formulation of investment policy decisions.

Area Two—Financial Accounting

Pre-Candidate Requirements

The candidate should understand the principles of accounting equivalent to at least one academic year of accounting as reflected in an elementary college accounting text.

Candidate Level I

The candidate should be able to apply accounting principles and techniques to financial analysis. Emphasis is placed on skill in using published accounting data, including corporate financial statements and reports, in a meaningful analysis of companies.

Candidate Level II

The candidate should have a sufficiently thorough understanding of financial accounting—including such areas as mergers and acquisitions, inventory and plant valuation, foreign exchange gains and losses, pension plans and leases—to interpret financial statements for use in the proper evaluation of companies and securities. Candidates are expected to be familiar with the statements and interpretations of the Financial Accounting Standards Board, as well as the opinions and decisions of regulatory authorities and the former Accounting Principles Board.

Candidate Level III

In addition to knowledge of accounting procedure and techniques, the candidate is expected to be able to relate accounting data to the investment decision-making process with emphasis on portfolio management.

Area Three—Quantitative Techniques

Pre-Candidate Requirements

The candidate should have some familiarity with elementary statistics and basic mathematics.

Candidate Level I

The candidate should have a sufficient understanding of elementary statistics and the mathematics of finance to be able to work with statistical data and to apply a knowledge of statistical techniques to basic problems in finance and financial analysis.

Candidate Level II

In addition to the knowledge of Level I, a candidate is expected to be familiar with more advanced techniques—such as probability theory, hypothesis testing, and simple and multiple regression and correlation analysis—and to be able to apply these techniques to problems of financial projections, portfolio analysis, security valuation, and risk.

Candidate Level III

At this advanced level, the candidate is expected to understand the application of more sophisticated statistical techniques and systems to problems in financial analysis, capital markets, and portfolio management.

Area Four—Fixed-Income Securities Analysis

Pre-Candidate Requirements

The candidate should have the equivalent of two years of college study in business administration—including business finance, corporate financial analysis, and money and banking (or money and capital markets).

Candidate Level I

The candidate is expected to be able to understand and analyze the basic characteristics (coupon, maturity, call, conversion, sinking fund, etc.) of fixed-income instruments, including corporate bonds, national and local government bonds, straight preferred stocks, and convertible debentures and preferreds. The analyst should be able to determine the basic investment quality of fixed-income securities in terms of the bond form (mortgage, debenture, pass-through, income bonds, etc.) and the risk of corporate illiquidity or insolvency. The candidate should understand the basic concept of yield and bond price determination and the attendant risks of interest rate and purchasing power.

Candidate Level II

At this level the candidate should have an understanding of the financial and investment implications of the elements and characteristics of fixed-income securities. The analyst should be able to analyze in depth government and corporate issuers and their fixed-income securities. The candidate should understand the implications of yield, the interest rate structure, yield spreads, the yield curve, and comparative returns of bonds and stocks.

Candidate Level III

The candidate should be able to formulate portfolio policy, understand the mechanics of bond management including analysis of bond swaps, and evaluate performance. Emphasis at this level is placed on the management of fixed-income securities in a portfolio situation and their suitability to both objectives and constraints of different investors under changing economic and market conditions.

Area Five—Equity Securities Analysis

Pre-Candidate Requirements

The candidate is assumed to have the equivalent of two years of college study in business administration—including business finance, corporate financial analysis, and money and banking (or money and capital markets).

Candidate Level I

The candidate should be able to appraise industries and companies from a financial and investment point of view. The analyst should be able to understand and interpret ordinary types of financial data and thereby demonstrate an ability to appraise the value and risks of common stocks.

Candidate Level II

Emphasis is placed on a complete appraisal and evaluation of industries and companies. The current position and outlook for common stocks and other equities as well as the investment implications for different investors are examined. The candidate should be able to apply the techniques of security analysis, including measures for valuation and risk, to individual companies and also to a group of companies within the same industry.

Candidate Level III

Emphasis at this level is on the analysis and selection of common stocks, in line with the financial circumstances of different types of individual and institutional investors and consistent with changing economic and market environments.

Area Six—Portfolio Management

Pre-Candidate Requirements

Because the task of portfolio and investment management involves the integration of economics, financial accounting, quantitative techniques, and fixed-income and equity security analysis, the pre-candidate requirements are the same as for those topic areas.

Candidate Level I

The candidate is expected to understand the financial circumstances of different individual and institutional investors, to be able to formulate appropriate portfolio account objectives and constraints, and to be able to select specific investment instruments suitable for such portfolios.

Candidate Level II

At this level, the candidate should be able to construct portfolios and to formulate portfolio strategies based on an analysis of the outlook of the economy and of conditions in the securities markets. Emphasis is placed on security selection within the concepts of diversification, risk, return, and modern portfolio theory.

Candidate Level III

Based on knowledge gained at previous levels and in the other topic areas, the candidate is expected: (1) to interrelate economic and market conditions, securities analysis, analysis of the requirements of individual and institutional investors, and portfolio concepts; (2) to develop suitable investment policies; and (3) to construct appropriate portfolios. The candidate should have an understanding of the investment management process, including how to organize and implement the security analysis and portfolio management effort and how to evaluate the results.

Area Seven—Ethical and Professional Standards

Pre-Candidate Requirements

Candidates are required to show evidence of sound character and to agree, in writing at the time of registration, to abide by the I.C.F.A. Code of Ethics, Standards of Professional Conduct, and related rules. Character references are an integral part of the registration requirements. Violation of professional standards may result in suspension from the candidate program or revocation of the charter.

Candidate Level I

The candidate should be familiar with the general purpose and content of the basic security laws and regulations that pertain to the investment field, including the structure of the principal regulatory bodies (SEC, N.A.S.D., N.Y.S.E., etc.) that administer these regulations. The candidate should be familiar with the purpose and administrative organization of the F.A.F./I.C.F.A. self-regulation programs. The candidate is expected to be aware of the general content of the Code of Ethics, the Standards of Professional Conduct, the Rules of Procedure, and Article VIII (Sections 4, 5, and 6) of the I.C.F.A. by-laws. It is essential that each candidate be knowledgeable of one's personal obligations and liabilities as they relate to membership in the Federation and/or the Institute.

The C.F.A. Candidate Study Program—General Topical Outlines

	Candidate Level				Candidate Level		
	I	II	III		I	II	III

Economics

Tools of analysis and
  forecasting:
  —National income accounts
  —Flow of funds and money
    supply indicators
  —Input-output analysis
  —Leading indicators
Historical and structural
  perspective:
  —Economic trends and cycles
  —Flow of funds and relation-
    ship to national income
    accounts
  —Economic price indexes
  —Aggregate profit trends by
    types
  —Trends and cycles in stock
    prices and interest rates
Forecasting broad economic
  forces:
  —Quantitative and qualita-
    tive aspects of forecasts
  —Implications for forecasts
    of:
      interest rates and the
        structure of interest
        rates
      corporate profits and
        earnings of stock price
        indexes
      aggregate equity price
        indexes
      industry and company
        prospects
Economic policy:
  —Government policies and
    actions regarding:
      growth, inflation and
        employment
      monetary and fiscal
        policies
      social goals
      antitrust and industry
        regulation
      international policy, in-
        cluding balance of
        payments
  —Implications of policy
    decisions for:
      profit outlook
      interest rates
      equity prices
      industry and company
        analysis

Financial Accounting

Principles and construction of
  accounting statements:
  —Income statements
  —Balance sheets
  —Sources and uses of funds

Content and usefulness of
  accounting reports to regulatory agencies

Financial analysis of accounting
  statements:
  —Adjustments for
    comparability
  —Ratio analysis
  —Adjustments for sub-
    sidiaries, affiliates and
    foreign operations
  —Stock splits and dividends
  —Rights, warrants and
    convertible securities
  —Effect of price level
    changes

Areas of judgment:
  —Inventories
  —Depreciation
  —Tax treatment
  —Intangibles
  —Consolidation
  —Acquisitions and mergers
  —Deferred assets and
    liabilities
  —Off balance sheet financing
  —Pension plans

Current accounting principles
  and practices:
  —AICPA and FASB opinions
  —Regulatory decisions

The C.F.A. Candidate Study Program *(continued)*

Candidate Level
I   II   III

Candidate Level
I   II   III

Application of Quantitative Techniques

Elementary statistics:
—Averages and measures of dispersion
Mathematics of finance:
—Compound growth
—Present value of stocks and bonds
—Performance measurement techniques
Probability theory:
—Expected values
Strategies
Hypothesis testing:
—Sample testing and confidence limits
—Analysis of variance
Simple and multiple regression and correlation
Matrix algebra
Mathematical programming in portfolio theory
Applications of computer systems to financial analysis

Techniques of Analysis— Fixed Income Securities

Classification of fixed income securities:
—By issuer
—By maturity, if any
—By security
—By contractual obligation
—By tax status
—Convertible features, if any
Special characteristics:
—Call features
—Sinking fund provisions
—Security
—Protective covenants
—Taxable features
Fixed income security selection and management:
—Quality ratings
—Interest or preferred dividend coverage, past and future
—Coupon and maturity
—New issues, discount and premium bonds
—The yield curve and interest rate structure
—Marketability
—Bond swaps

Techniques of Analysis— Equity Securities

Sources of information

Financial instruments:
—Stocks, warrants, rights, options

Industry appraisal and evaluation:
—Interindustry competition, supply-demand, product prices, costs and profits
—Security market evaluation of profits, historical and projected

Company appraisal and evaluation:
—Sales volume, product prices, product research, intraindustry competition
—Ratio analysis-balance sheet and income statement and analysis of corporate profitability, liquidity, solvency, operating and financial leverage
—Management appraisal
—Earnings and dividend evaluation and projection, near and long-term
—Valuation techniques, long and short-term:
    discounted cash flow earnings multiples, absolute and relative growth stock valuation
—Risk analysis-quantitative and qualitative
—Efficient capital market hypothesis

The C.F.A. Candidate Study Program *(continued)*

Candidate Level
I   II   III

Candidate Level
I   II   III

Objective of analysis—
Portfolio Management

Investor objectives and
constraints:
—Individuals
—Institutions:
  investment companies
  foundations and endow-
    ment funds
  pension funds and profit
    sharing plans
  trust funds
  property and liability
    insurance companies
  life insurance companies
  commercial banks

Portfolio strategy and construction
—Policy inputs:
  assumptions regarding
    the short and long-
    term outlook for the
    economy and the
    securities markets
  types of investments to
    be used regarding
    quality, liquidity, risk
    and other characteris-
    tics
  portfolio diversification
    by type of investment
    and diversification by
    industry
—Account objectives and
  constraints:
  specific definition of ob-
    jectives, e.g., risk and
    return, liquidity re-
    quirements, legal and
    regulatory constraints
  the time horizon for the
    investment
  aggressive and specula-
    tive properties
—Investment selection:
  selection of specific
    investments suitable
    for objectives
  comparative evaluation
    of alternative invest-
    ments
—Modern portfolio theory
  and the construction of
  "efficient portfolios"
—Tax planning
—Execution of purchases and
  sales
—Evaluation of account
  performance

Conduct of Analysis—
Ethical and Professional
Standards, Securities Laws
and Regulations

Ethical standards and profes-
sional responsibilities:
—Public
—Customers and clients
—Employers
—Associates
—Other analysts
—Corporate management
—Other sources of informa-
  tion

Treatment of ethical issues:
—Identification of ethical
  problems
—Administration of ethical
  policies
—Changing structure of
  financial markets and the
  participants therein and
  the consequent develop-
  ment of new ethical issues

Security laws and regulations:
—Nature and applicability
  of fiduciary standards
—Pertinent laws and regulations
—Treatment of insider
  information

Candidate Level II

The candidate should be able to recognize unprofessional practices and violations of standards in more sophisticated areas, including conflicts of interest and use of insider information, and to understand appropriate corrective actions.

Candidate Level III

The candidate should understand how to administer a program of professional and ethical standards within an organization in terms of internal disciplinary controls as well as compliance with security laws, regulations, and I.C.F.A. standards and rules. The candidate should understand the full meaning of the public interest, the professionalism of financial analysts, and ethical issues associated with changes in the financial system.

The organizations that employ investment managers consider it highly desirable for their managers and analysts to continue their education and professional development. Based on the survey previously cited, at least 80 percent of employer organizations financially support its professional staff in each of the following educational activities: pay expenses for attendance at analysts' society luncheons; pay the travel and/or registration expenses for selected professional conferences, seminars, and courses; allow time off from work to attend such professional meetings; pay part or all of the expenses for the C.F.A. candidate program; and pay membership dues for the local society and/or the I.C.F.A.[3] Taking all of these activities into account, 96.4 percent of those surveyed received support for one or more (but not all) of these activities.

This education, coupled with on-the-job training and experience gained through practice, is essential for investment managers to be able to organize and apply their knowledge to the analysis of investment problems, to the formulation of solutions, and to the making of policy and investment decisions. These skills of application in investment management are developed by on-the-job training and by work experience in the investment field. The development of these skills and mature judgment are partly a result of exposure to problems and problem solving tasks in the investment field as well as in life. The investment manager's experience and seasoning is reflected by age, by the number of years one has engaged in responsible investment research and management work, by the reputation of the people and organizations one has worked with, and by the professional reputation or technical record which one has established in the performance of his tasks.

Perhaps the most important single qualification for a manager has

---

[3] Bauman, *Professional Standards in Investment Management.*

to do with intelligence and judgment. Because successful investment management is considered to be intellectually challenging, a good level of intelligence is necessary. There are different kinds of intelligence or aptitudes. Investment management stresses a research aptitude for gathering, absorbing, and retaining large amounts of diverse items of information, of being able to identify relevant information, and of fitting it together in forming an efficient portfolio. The investment manager should be able to recognize and understand cause and effect relationships in verbal and numerical terms. Such aptitudes are used to formulate portfolio performance objectives based on an appraisal of the client's financial requirements, to devise appropriate strategies, to select portfolio policies based on an appraisal of the investment environment, and to select securities based on these policies and based on the financial analyses of securities.

An important, though sometimes subtle, ingredient to professional performance is an investment manager's attitudes and motivation. Those who successfully achieve performance objectives frequently seem to have several desirable personality characteristics. They seem to be highly dedicated and stimulated by their work; they pride themselves in serving the best interests of their clients; they are energetic, ambitious, and strongly motivated to be competitive and have a determination to succeed; they seek new and challenging experiences; and they have a positive and constructive attitude. They seem to be self-disciplined and emotionally mature. A manager's degree of stability may be revealed by how one reacts to important changes in the investment environment, changes in security prices, and changes in market sentiment. If one overreacts, makes extreme or excessive changes in portfolio policies, has a high portfolio turnover, gets swept away with the prevailing market psychology, or becomes preoccupied with minor daily news items, one probably will not be successful as an investment manager.

Because the functioning of portfolio management depends on the efforts of a number of people, it is desirable for the investment manager to have the personal skills to work effectively with these people in order that the portfolio may derive the greatest possible benefits from the talents offered by these people.

The investment manager is dependent on the services and cooperation of people who are subordinates, superiors, and peers within the organization and of people who are outside the organization. These people assist by supplying the manager with research information, by reviewing one's work and making constructive suggestions, and by executing portfolio transactions. Therefore, if one has the skill to draw out the best talents of these people, individually and in groups and committees, who are sometimes working under stress conditions, then the performance of the portfolio can benefit. In addition, it is helpful to have a close and harmonious relation with the client. In this way, the portfolio manager may have a better insight into the financial requirements and temperament of the client which serve as a basis for the formulation of performance objectives, and the client will have greater confidence in the portfolio manager and a better understanding of the stated objectives.

TYPES OF PORTFOLIOS OR INVESTMENT ACCOUNTS

The institutional characteristics of portfolio accounts have an important bearing on the nature of the relationship between the investment manager and the investor as well as on the nature of portfolio objectives and plans. The major categories of accounts administered by investment managers will be identified and briefly discussed in this section.

Individual/Family-Type Investors

The seven classes of portfolios in this major category represent investment funds supplied separately by individual investors, families, or household units.

Advisory Account. Under this arrangement, an individual investor employs an investment advisor or advisory firm who furnishes investment recommendations on what securities to buy and sell and when to buy and sell them. The advisor tailors this advice to the particular goals and requirements of each client's circumstances. For this advice the client pays a quarterly fee, usually determined as a percent of the portfolio's market value. The client has the freedom of accepting and implementing the advice or not. If the client frequently does not follow the recommendations, the advisory relationship is usually terminated. The client retains the responsibility of placing security transaction orders with a brokerage firm. The minimum size account is usually $100,000 to $200,000. The portfolio goals and constraints vary widely among clients.

Investment organizations which provide this service are unincorporated or incorporated investment counsel firms, investment advisory departments of broker-dealer firms, financial publishing houses, and trust investment departments of banks.

Management Account. This account is quite similar to advisory accounts, described above, and indeed, even the titles used for such classes of accounts vary from one investment organization to another. The term *agency* account is sometimes used.

The primary difference between an advisory account and a management account is that in the latter case the investment organization acts more as a portfolio manager than as an advisor, in which the portfolio manager has complete discretion to make, implement, and execute portfolio decisions. Once the manager decides to make a port-folio change in a management account, the manager or his or her security trader places security orders directly with broker-dealers for execution, without the prior approval of the client. Obviously, the portfolio manager of a management account has inherently greater control over making investment decisions than an advisor of an advi-sory account. Because investment decisions in a management account are not reviewed and approved by the client prior to implementation, the client has, in effect, placed a higher level of confidence in the professional judgement of the portfolio manager. In the case of both management and advisory accounts, however, the client is kept in-formed regarding transactions and the status of the portfolio on a peri-odic basis. As in the case of advisory accounts, portfolio goals and con-straints vary widely according to the circumstances of each client.

No-Load Mutual Fund. This class of portfolio (and load mutual funds and closed-end funds described below) are defined as investment companies. As such, their assets represent a portfolio of marketable securities, and their source of capital is primarily from individual inves-tors who own securities, mostly common shares, which have been is-sued by the investment company. Portfolio objectives and policies vary widely among investment companies.

No-load mutual funds and load mutual funds (described below) are called open-end investment companies because their common stock capital structure is "open" in the sense that mutual funds are generally prepared to issue new common shares directly to new investors and to retire or redeem existing common shares directly from current shareholders during each business day. Consequently, these portfolios experience either a net cash inflow or a net cash outflow during any given time period depending on whether more shares or less shares are issued than old shares are redeemed. Because a net cash outflow may occur due to a net reduction of mutual fund shares outstanding, such a portfolio has a greater need for marketability and possibly liquid-ity as well.

An investor in most no-load mutual funds pays no sales charge (load or commission) when he purchases fund shares nor a redemption fee when he liquidates his shares. As a result, the investor does not purchase shares through a sales representative or a broker-dealer firm, but rather deals directly with the mutual fund home office or an affiliated distribu-tor firm. Because a no-load mutual fund utilizes no sales force, it usually generates fund share sales in one of three ways: (1) by advertising, (2) by being affiliated with an investment organization which has con-tact with the public such as a broker-dealer firm or an investment counsel firm, and/or (3) by its reputation in terms of portfolio perfor-mance.

In this last instance, large sales of fund shares sometimes result for a mutual fund with a substantial portfolio performance, because of wide publicity given by several financial publishers of mutual fund performance ratings. A portfolio management who attracts investors on the basis of performance publicity is economically motivated (or is under considerable pressure, when carried to an extreme) to achieve a successful future performance. A portfolio management which fails to deliver this expected performance will lose a source of new business and, possibly worse yet, may experience substantial share redemptions. The volume of redemptions in a no-load fund could be more volatile because individual shareholders incur virtually no direct transaction costs. Because the client tends to take the initiative to select and purchase the shares of a no-load fund, one tends to be more sophisticated or to take a more active interest in investment matters than the client of a load fund.

Load Mutual Fund. A load mutual fund is, of course, quite similar to no-load mutual funds, described above. The greatest difference is that investors pay a loading charge or sales commission, usually about 8½ percent of their investment, when they purchase shares of a load fund. Usually no redemption fee or commission is charged when shares are liquidated by investors in a load or no-load fund. The loading charge serves as an inducement or compensation for salespeople and dealers to solicit purchase orders from prospective mutual fund investors. It is difficult to generalize about the investment requirements of clients of load funds because there are so many funds with a wide range of different portfolio objectives and policies and they employ different appeals to attract and retain investors.

Closed-end Fund. A closed-end fund is an investment company. The major difference between a mutual (open-end) fund and a closed-end company is that the latter has a somewhat permanent capital structure. Its capital structure, therefore, resembles some of the characteristics of the capital structure of a typical corporation. The common shares of the fund are traded in the secondary market, either on an exchange or in the over-the-counter market. A few funds employ leverage in their capital structure by the use of preferred stocks and debt capital.

Some special purpose close-end companies which emphasize investment in private placements and in small closely-held growth-oriented companies, are called *venture capital* funds. Some closed-end funds, called *dual purpose* funds, have two special classes of common stock type shares: (1) income shares, which are entitled to the net investment income from the total portfolio; and (2) capital shares which have a claim on the appreciation from the total portfolio.

Because of the closed capital structure, the portfolio of the conventional closed-end fund needs less marketability; likewise, the fund has inherently a stronger tenure of investment management which permits the portfolio management either to be more lax about performance or to place more emphasis on performance with a longer term time horizon. Portfolio policies tend to vary among closed-end funds. Because most of these funds have operated for several decades or more, their policies tend to be traditional in nature. Closed-end fund shares trade in the open market, frequently at discounts from their underlying asset values. The shareholders tend to be passive investors though sometimes more affluent than load share fund shareholders.

Personal Trusts. A personal trust is an agreement made by a person (called a trustor, creator, or grantor) who supplies assets (called the corpus) to a person or bank who administers the assets as trustee. The trustee ordinarily has custody of the assets, manages them, and disburses funds to beneficiaries. The agreement specifies when and over what period of time the income from the trust is to be disbursed and to whom it is to be paid. The recipient of the income is called the income beneficiary or life tenant. The agreement also specifies when the principal is to be disbursed and to whom it is to be paid. The recipient of the principal is called the remainderman or the beneficiary of the principal. Regarding portfolio objectives and policies, the trust agreement (1) may provide explicit instructions, (2) may grant full discretion to the trustee in regard to investment matters, or (3) may be silent. If it is silent, it is called a legal trust and the assets are to be invested in accordance with the laws of the state. The laws of some states specify a *legal list* which defines what investments are legal or permissable for legal trusts. The majority of states, however, require personal trusts to be invested in accordance with the *prudent-man rule,* i.e., in a manner that a responsible and prudent person would act. In most modern trusts, the agreement grants the trustee full discretion, and the trustee is free to adopt investment objectives and portfolio policies which best meet the requirements of beneficiaries; in accordance with the prudent-man philosophy.

Personal trusts may be classified into two major categories, testamentary trusts (discussed in the section below), and living trusts, sometimes called inter vivos trusts. Living trusts are established while the creator is alive. Living trusts are of two types: revocable and irrevocable.

The Revocable Living Trust. The revocable living trust is distinctive from most other personal trusts in that the creator retains the power, while alive, to terminate the trust agreement and repossess the corpus. Because the creator retains ultimate control, the tenure of investment management of the trustee is weaker. Clients usually have several reasons for creating revocable living trusts, such as to delegate the responsibilities of asset administration and investment management while they are living and to avoid probate. However, another possible reason for a revocable agreement is for the creator to evaluate the effectiveness of the trust arrangement and the effectiveness of the portfolio management. If the creator is not satisfied, one may revise the trust agreement or appoint a new trustee. Consequently, trustees and trust investment officers are usually sympathetically responsive, within reason, to the wishes of creators.

Irrevocable Personal Trust.   A brief background description of personal trusts and living trusts was presented in the section above. This section deals with both irrevocable living trusts and testamentary trusts together because of a similarity of relationship between the trustee and the beneficiaries.

A *testamentary trust* becomes operational under the terms of the last will and testament upon the demise of the estate owner, who is called the testator. The trust receives its corpus from the estate when the estate is settled by probate court. Such a trust may be subject to federal personal income taxes as a separate entity.

An *irrevocable living trust* becomes operational when a trust agreement is approved by the creator or trustor and the trustee accepts the corpus. If the trustor permanently and fully relinquishes all control over the trust, in effect, a gift has been made such that the property may be subject to federal gift taxes, but not subject to federal estate taxes upon the death of the creator. In addition, the trust may be subject to federal personal income taxes as a separate entity.

When the irrevocable living trust and the testamentary trust become operational, both trusts become irrevocable inasmuch as the trust instructions, or agreement cannot be changed except in extenuating circumstances, and only then by formal court proceedings. Consequently, the trustee and portfolio management is guided by the trust agreement, the law, and court orders. As stated above, the trust agreement (1) may provide explicit instructions regarding investment objectives and portfolio policies, (2) may grant the trustee full discretion in such matters, or (3) may say nothing. If it says nothing, then it is a legal trust. Most modern trusts give the trustee full discretion in which case he is able legally to adopt prudent portfolio policies aimed at best serving the interests of the beneficiaries.

Within the confines of legally determined fiduciary constraints, the trustee holds a strong tenure of investment management. Because fiduciary constraints embrace a prudent philosophy and because of the strong tenure of the trustee, portfolio management of irrevocable personal trusts tends to be conservatively oriented. Beyond the confines of these constraints, the portfolio manager should adopt policies which seek to achieve a performance that satisfies the financial requirements of the beneficiaries. A trust may have two or more beneficiaries with different life tenants and remaindermen having conflicting financial interests and goals. Consequently, the investment management may find itself with one or more clients who want or need maximum income and one or more clients who want maximum growth. This frequently leads to a compromise in portfolio policy which fails to please fully any of the beneficiaries.

Formal Retirement Funds

Formal retirement funds consist of portfolios whose primary explicit purpose is to finance, partially or totally, the family consumption requirements of individuals or couples during their retirement years. Contributions into the most popular retirement fund programs are exempt from federal income taxes, as well as the income earned on the portfolio. Income taxes are normally paid by the pensioner upon receiving cash disbursements; if one is retired, the tax paid is usually less because it is based on lower income and therefore is taxed at lower progressive rates.

The beneficiary client is the current or future cash recipient from the fund and will be referred to simply as the pensioner. Perhaps because of the contemporary origin of group employee retirement funds, which under most plans are presently accumulating capital, no major investment policy distinction is usually made by investment management between gainfully employed (future) pensioners for whom current and previous contributions are retained in the fund (for later disbursement) and retired pensioners who are recipients of current cash benefits. The obligations of the portfolio differ between retired pensioners and future pensioners in terms of the investment time horizon and in terms of current financial dependency on the portfolio by the pensioner. That is to say, a young person faces a long time horizon and virtually no current financial dependency on the pension portfolio. Retired pensioners, however, who may be in their middle sixties or older have a considerably shorter investment time horizon and possibly a very heavy dependency on the pension fund.

We frequently minimize the importance of this dependency on the pension portfolio because the employer (company or employment institution) or life insurance company is usually legally liable for pension payments and, in a growing or stable pension fund, new deposits and cash investment income are available to meet current pension disbursements. Nevertheless, if a pension fund program matures and the employer organization should decrease its work force and scale of operations, current pension disbursements may place an unexpected burden on the funds in the portfolio. More clearly in the case of variable annuities and mutual funds, adverse portfolio performance has a direct and relatively immediate effect on the size of the cash payments or withdrawals and in turn, on the consumption level of retired annuitants or shareholders with short time horizons, while the adverse effect on the consumption level of future pensioners is deferred and possibly averted with a cyclical market recovery.

Trusteed Pension. Trusteed pension programs are sometimes called noninsured plans because they are usually funded through a trust agreement in contrast to an insured annuity program which is funded through a life insurance company annuity policy contract.

As in the case of personal trusts discussed in the sections above, a considerable number of alternative terms and arrangements may be adopted in any given trusteed pension agreement. The parties to the agreement, as a minimum, are the employer organization, the employees, and the trustee. Trust administration includes the responsibilities for the receipt of contributions from the employer, disbursement of benefits to employe pensioners, maintenance of records, custody of trust assets, and quite often portfolio management. Most of these functions may be performed by one organization, such as a bank, or they may be assigned to two or more different organizations, such as a management-employe committee, a bank, or an investment counsel organization.

Noninsured pension plans have become very popular. Because of the wide number of possible variations in these plans, we will discuss only the most common types of arrangements, giving emphasis to portfolio performance requirements.

Under the typical pension plan, the employer agrees to pay stipulated amounts at periodical intervals to individual employes, commencing at retirement and continuing for life. This employer liability is usually discharged by periodic employer pension contributions, by funds representing previous employer contributions, and by the profit performance of the pension portfolio. Ideally, the investment requirements of any given portfolio are satisfied by a risk and return performance in which the portfolio return minimizes the employer's future pension costs, and the portfolio risk level protects the interests of pensioners and, at the same time, does not exceed the client's risk tolerance level.

From the standpoint of pensioners, investment portfolio risk policies may be less constrained when the employer organization is in a relatively strong business and financial position, the pension fund is in an accumulation phase (i.e., employer pension contributions and investment income exceed pension benefit disbursements), and the pension fund is *fully funded* (i.e., fund assets equal the incurred liabilities for past services, actuarially discounted).

The investment management responsibility for a pension fund portfolio, as distinct from general pension trust administration, may be assumed by an employer or union pension committee, a bank trust investment department, an investment counsel firm, or other portfolio management organization. The portfolios of many noninsured pensions are managed by bank trust investment departments. The portfolios of larger pension funds are sometimes split among two or more investment management organizations for purposes of diversifying against the risk of mediocre portfolio performance. In order to gain the investment management benefits of a larger portfolio, the assets of small pension funds are sometimes commingled in a single portfolio managed by a bank, which is called a *pooled pension common trust fund*.

The investment management powers granted to the pension fund portfolio manager by the employer can vary. The instructions may grant complete investment discretion, may grant discretion limited by the prudent-man rule, may require that investment changes be approved in advance by an employer committee or officer, or may grant discretion within certain stipulations. Typically, portfolio managers have complete discretion in investment matters within broad guidelines.

Pension portfolio performance requirements should stress a maximum long-term rate of return with less concern for the risk of principal volatility during the accumulation stage. Based on a rough rule of thumb, each percentage point of the annual rate of return earned on contributed funds should be equivalent to 20 percent of the annual cost of pension benefits to the employer company.

Insurance Companies

Life Insurance Company Programs. These types of programs are perhaps the oldest and best known formal devices used to fund retirement. An individual saver or policy holder may purchase a deferred annuity or an immediate annuity from an annuity guarantor, which is a life insurance and annuity company. A *deferred fixed annuity* is a contract which guarantees to pay the policy holder or annuitant a fixed number of dollars each month or each year for life commencing at some future date, say when one retires at 65. An *immediate fixed annuity* is a contract which guarantees to pay the annuitant, who is usually already retired, a fixed number of dollars each month or each year for life, in which payments are now being disbursed to the annuitant.

Annuities may be purchased by an individual under a single policy or for a group of individuals (such as for an employe group) under a group policy contract. In either type of contract, the policy premium (annuity purchase price) and portfolio performance requirements are somewhat similar for the annuity company. The premium paid for a group contract may be less per annuitant than for a single contract because of administrative and market cost savings due to economies of large scale. Deferred annuities may be purchased by a single premium payment or by a series of monthly or annual premium payments made over a period of years.

Because the principles and purposes of annuities can be and frequently are intertwined with life insurance (more precisely called death insurance), annuities are sold by life insurance companies, and their features are commonly incorporated in life insurance contracts. In fact, all permanent life insurance policies (whole life, limited payment life, and endowment life insurance) but not term insurance, have annuity settlement or conversion options available to the insured (the person whose life is insured). The conceptual relationship between life insurance and annuity insurance might be tersely summarized thusly: life insurance financially protects those who are dependent on the insured against the risk of premature death; while annuity insurance protects the annuitant, and possibly a spouse, against the risk of living too long, that is, outliving one's retirement savings. A portion of the cash premium payment for permanent life insurance provides for the gradual accumulation of assets, called cash surrender value (C.S.V.), in the insurance company which are held for the future benefit of the insured. This portion of the life insurance premium is conceptually a premium for a deferred annuity contract. If the insured lives to retirement age, the policy matures, or may be cancelled. In either case, the C.S.V. may be left on deposit with the insurance company or withdrawn in cash, or the policy may be converted to an immediate annuity, in which case the C.S.V. is used, in effect, as the purchase price (single premium) for the annuity.

Based on mortality experience and the law of averages, an actuarially calculated minimum required rate of return on policyholder reserves is determined which, if realized, will meet the annuity obligations or policyholder liabilities of the insurance company. Because the portfolio performance requirement under a deferred fixed annuity (and CSV arrangements) is both fixed in terms of dollar amounts and long term, covering of a significant time span of human life, portfolio management seeks investments which provide assurance of meeting minimum long-term rate of return requirements in fixed dollar terms. From the standpoint of portfolio performance requirements, the investment time horizon is generally quite long for policyholder reserves of young, deferred annuitants. If the insurance company is mutual (owned by the policyholders) or the insurance contract is participating, then the benefits of superior portfolio performance accrue to the policyholders; otherwise such benefits accrue to the insurance company and its stockholders. In addition to client requirements, the general operations of insurance companies, including investment management, are subject to special and technical tax and legal constraints.

Immediate Fixed Annuity. Because of the fixed dollar nature of the contractual obligations to annuitants, the portfolio performance requirements of a life insurance and annuity insurer (company) in respect to immediate annuitants is quite similar to deferred annuitants. The primary difference is the timing of cash flows into and out of the annuity fund. In the case of immediate annuitants, cash benefits are currently being disbursed on a periodic basis during the lifetime of the beneficiaries. Therefore, sufficient liquid reserves need to be available to meet near-term disbursements. Because surplus reserves are usually small in comparison to annuity liabilities, little impairment of principal can be tolerated. Under participating annuity contracts (those issued by mutual insurers and participating contracts issued by stockholder owned insurers), annuity benefits may be increased above the guaranteed amount when the portfolio rate of return exceeds the assumed actuarial rate of return. Under nonparticipating contracts, superior portfolio performance accrues to the benefit of the stockholders of the insurer.

Property and Casualty Portfolios.   The primary business of a property and casualty insurance company is to insure policyholders against the risk of loss due to property damage, and to accidents and illnesses of individuals. This is the underwriting part of the insurance business. In the course of underwriting risks, underwriting premiums flow into the company which are used to pay operating expenses and to purchase investments. The investment part of the insurance business can become a sizable operation. The investment portfolio is available to meet insurance claims and expenses for processing claim settlements and to produce an investment return.

Insurance carriers are either mutual or stockholder-owned companies. The underwriting and investment profits, if any, accrue to the benefit of policyholders who are owners of mutual companies, or they accrue to the benefit of stockholders in stockholder-owned companies.

In serving the interest of policyholders and stockholders, the portfolio performance requirements are to meet the short-term liquidity needs of insurance claim settlements, to minimize the risk of principal impairment which could jeopardize the interests of policyholders and stockholders, and to optimize investment returns for the benefit of the company owners. The need for liquidity and for marketability in the portfolio depends on the stability or predictability of aggregate insurance claims and on the ratio of policyholders' surplus (capital and interest) to total liabilities. Portfolio objectives can be more aggressive given a larger ratio and/or greater predictability of underwriting losses. An insurance company is subject to the same federal income tax constraints as ordinary corporations, so that tax-exempt bonds and preferred stocks in the portfolio receive tax shelter.

Several of these types of portfolio are discussed in greater detail in this book.

Chapter 2

Structures of Investment Management Organizations

W. SCOTT BAUMAN

The Colgate Darden Graduate School of Business Administration
University of Virginia
Charlottesville, Virginia

Although the performance of a portfolio account is greatly influenced by the abilities of and decisions made by the investment manager in charge of the account, a point often overlooked is that the internal support and operating environment within the investment management organization can also have an important bearing on the professional effectiveness of the services rendered by the account manager. The effectiveness of the manager can be enhanced by an organization that provides a stimulating environment, incentives, high quality research information, administrative support, intelligence policy direction, and other appropriate guidance. Conversely, an organization can impede or inhibit the effectiveness of the manager. For these reasons, an examination of the structure and operations of the investment organization is a relevant subtopic to the overall subject of investment management. Moreover, some investment managers are responsible for the administration of their organizations in addition to the management of portfolios. Consequently, this chapter will briefly discuss the types of organizational structures, systems, and institutions within which investment managers operate.

OPERATIONAL FUNCTIONS OF THE ORGANIZATION

Each of the major professional and administrative functions performed by or for an investment management organization will be briefly discussed here. Each of these functions will be covered under separate headings for purposes of clarity even though the same person is frequently involved in more than one of them.

32

Economic and Capital Market Research

The investment performance of portfolios is significantly affected by major socio-economic forces and by supply and demand conditions in the capital markets. Therefore, an important function that needs to be performed either by or for the investment management organization is economic and capital market research. Because a great deal of work is conducted in this important area, many organizations rely on a number of external research sources in addition to their own internal studies. Depending on the size of the organization, the staff may include economists, financial economists, and market analysts who devote part or all of their time to analyzing and forecasting trends in economic demand, industrial production, employment, government fiscal policy, monetary policy, government regulations, inflation, long- and short-term interest rates, aggregate corporate profits, capital and consumer spending, and other conditions affecting international and domestic capital market cycles.

Some organizations have an investment policy or market strategy committee which regularly interprets these trends and cycles in order to formulate basic portfolio policy guidelines to be applied to the various classes of portfolios according to account objectives. In other organizations, the account manager assumes this responsibility. Periodic revisions in policy guidelines would pertain to shifts in portfolio asset mix between stocks and bonds; to shifts between bonds of different maturities, credit classes, and sectors; and to shifts in equities between different risk classes, growth and income characteristics, and industry sectors.

Industry and Security Research

Although it may sometimes be difficult to make clear demarcations between the functions of capital market research, formulation of portfolio policy guidelines, and security research analysis because of their mutual interdependency or interaction within the decision-making process, each of these functions is sufficiently unique to be considered separately. While capital market research and portfolio policies determine the types and characteristics of broad categories of securities to be held in portfolios with different account objectives, industry and security research analysis determines which specific issues within these categories are most suitable for specified investment purposes.

The selection of specific issues will, of course, have an effect on portfolio performance, and indeed even in well-diversified portfolios, a handful of individual issues with extraordinary gains or losses have a significant affect on an account's overall performance.

Investment managers must rely at least in part on the security research conducted by others, inasmuch as they do not personally have the time to analyze in depth dozens of industries and hundreds of companies and securities. Consequently, this function is assumed by bond analysts and industry research analysts, each of whom analyzes companies and securities in one or a few specific industries. While smaller investment management organizations rely on the securities research conducted by several external sources, particularly from research departments of brokerage firms, larger management organizations rely on their own staff of research analysts augmented by external sources. The depth and frequency of research conducted on a particular security and the speed by which new information is transmitted to portfolio managers is dependent on the dollar value of the investment interest, the volatility or riskiness of the security, and frequency of activity of the portfolio strategies for which the particular security is intended to serve. For example, price changes and trading volume of a security may be reviewed several times a day, industry and company news items studies several times a week, the company contacted monthly, and a detailed analysis made quarterly for a major speculative holding, in which all significant news is transmitted within an hour to managers of accounts employing active strategies with high performance objectives.

Statistical Research Systems

With the development of modern capital market theory (sometimes called modern portfolio theory) and readily available computers and data banks, a quantitative revolution has occurred in investment research methods. Quantitative models are being developed to select securities on the basis of expected returns and estimated risks, to construct efficiently diversified portfolios, and to estimate portfolio returns and risks on the basis of stock market and bond market trends. Because these capital market models are quantitatively explicit, they are intended to assist investment decision-makers by making their analysis and thinking process more rigorous and better disciplined.

The quantitative approach encompasses a number of different theories, models, and techniques, such as portfolio theory, the capital asset pricing model, linear regression and correlation analysis, present value theory, quadratic programming, and optimizer models. These research systems have developed so rapidly and so extensively that investment quantitative specialists are being employed by investment management organizations and by consulting firms who develop and operate these systems. Most of the models and systems are not intended to make final investment decisions but rather to assist and complement traditional fundamental analysis and human judgment.

Account Management

The responsibilities for the investment administration of each portfolio or client account is normally assigned to one individual. This individual is the portfolio manager or account manager for that particular fund. The amount of investment authority, control, and supervision-time that this manager has for a particular account varies considerably depending on organizational policies and the authority retained by the fund owner. In any event, the account manager needs to be a coordinator by being sure that client instructions are carried out, that the client is adequately informed on the status of the account, and that portfolio plans are being properly executed. Depending on what responsibilities and authority are assigned to the account manager in the portfolio management process, he or she may have the discretion to make portfolio changes without obtaining prior approval. If one does not have this authority, the manager is still normally responsible for being alert to investment problems or opportunities that are unique to the account and for making recommendations to improve the financial position of the portfolio.

Regardless of the degree of independent authority the account manager has, one is still dependent on significant services rendered by other investment functions. The time and care the manager is able to devote to an account depends on the number and size of other accounts he or she manages, how similar and demanding the objectives are among these accounts, and what other functional responsibilities the manager has in the organization.

Transactions and Records Management

Executing security transactions, receiving and disbursing funds, and maintaining account security records are necessary—though sometimes time-consuming—functions, particularly in the case of a large number of small accounts. In order to improve efficiency and to conserve on the time of portfolio managers, these functions are frequently consolidated in specialized support units in the organization.

Security market orders in many organizations, particularly the larger ones, are processed through trading specialists at a market trading desk or department. The trading specialist or trader may be given specific instructions or may have discretion regarding market price limits and time duration within which to execute orders. A knowledgeable and skillful trader can frequently execute orders at more attractive prices and save on transaction costs, particularly on large orders. The trading department may be responsible for carrying out a brokerage allocation plan which allocates orders and commissions among various brokers on the basis of good investment research services and efficient execution services rendered to the organization.

Accurate, complete, and up-to-date account records, which include current market values, are helpful to the portfolio manager in supervising the account in accordance with investment policy objectives and constraints. Particularly when a large number of accounts are under management, computerization of records serves to reduce costs and to increase the speed by which portfolios can be reviewed and changes implemented. Record keeping services provided by the organization can be useful in keeping clients informed on the investment status of their accounts and in providing them with information for their tax returns.

THE DECISION-MAKING STRUCTURE

The lines of authority, the lines of communication, the management style, and the roles played by the professional members vary considerably from one investment management organization to another. The nature of professional staff relationships in an organization is determined in part by management's attitudes and philosophy, by characteristics of the clients, by portfolio objectives and constraints, and by qualities of the staff. Five variations of internal interrelationships will be identified and briefly described here.

The *chain of command system* is one in which investment decisions are the responsibility of department heads and other group administrators. This arrangement resembles that of a government, bureaucratic, or authoritarian organization. A junior portfolio analyst submits analyses and recommendations to a senior portfolio manager for review and approval. Within certain prescribed limits, the senior portfolio manager may have the authority to effect a portfolio change. Decisions of greater importance are submitted by the senior portfolio manager to the head of the portfolio management division within which this portfolio is assigned. Within certain limits, the division head can authorize a portfolio action, otherwise a report is forwarded with a recommendation of action to the superior, who may be the head of the department or of a group of divisions. If the person has the authority, the recommendation is approved and implemented. If, however, it involves a major policy change, approval from a senior executive may be needed. The advantage of such a system is that members of management maintain clear control over plans and decision making. The lines of communication and lines of authority and responsibility are clearly identified. If these administrators are good leaders, work closely with the people around them, and professionally are well qualified, good and timely decisions can be made. If these conditions are not present, if too much authority is centralized at the top, or if there are too many layers of management through which recommendations must be approved, then initiative and incentives among the professional staff can be stifled, and important decisions delayed too long.

A second type of management is the *committee system.* The number of committees and the extent of their responsibilities in an investment organization can vary. An organization with a strong committee system can have committees which are responsible for making many decisions and for reviewing the decisions of other committees. The securities which are added to and dropped from the organization's approved list or buy list may be decided by a securities committee. Changes in common stock portfolio policies may be made by a common stock policy committee, changes in bond portfolio policy can be handled by a bond policy committee, and general investment policy may be made or reviewed by a senior investment committee. The portfolio policies and security holdings and changes thereto for each investment account may be reviewed and approved by an account review committee.

The strength of this system is that each decision receives the scrutiny and benefit of group deliberation. This attitude is supported by the cliché that two heads are better than one, or that a whole group is greater than the sum of its individual parts. Undoubtedly, some committees are very productive.

In evaluating the effectiveness of a committee, several questions are pertinent. How often does it meet? Does it meet often enough to deal with changes in a timely fashion? If significant new information suddenly becomes available which should be acted on promptly, can the committee be quickly assembled? If not, are certain individuals empowered to act? Is the committee encumbered by too many members? Are meetings well organized, or do they ramble, absorbing a lot of valuable work-hours? What is the role of the committee? To exchange views and information, to review or critique previous staff decisions, or to make decisions? A committee is better suited to perform certain kinds of roles. Committees appear better suited for formulating policies, broad guidelines, and basic objectives, rather than for making rapid and frequent individual security decisions. If decisions are made by a committee, how are they made? By majority vote, by consensus, by the chairperson, or by the senior members? Do the most able members have the greatest influence in the committee and do the best ideas have the greatest likelihood of being accepted? Or are decisions influenced by office politics, by people who have the greatest bureaucratic power, or by people who are the most articulate, manipulative, or vociferous? Depending on how the committee operates, it can draw out the best ideas of the individual members; procrastinate; lead to

indecisive, confusing, or poorly compromised actions; or make mediocre decisions by averaging out the best and poorest ideas.

One variation on the chain of command and committee systems is
the *rule system* in which the organization operates under a well-defined
set of portfolio policies and investment rules. Under this arrangement,
a portfolio manager is free to make investment and policy decisions
in respect to a given portfolio account insofar as they are not inconsistent with the organization's approved portfolio policies and investment
rules. The effectiveness of this system depends on the quality of the
rules, how rigid or flexible they are, how much discretion or judgment
is left up to the portfolio manager, how frequently the rules are reviewed, how easy it is to change them, and how easy it is to authorize
exceptions to the rules. Carefully established policies and rules sometimes avoid investment decisions based on emotional impulses of the
moment or on occasional poor judgment.

A fourth approach is the *team system.* Each portfolio is assigned
to a team of portfolio managers, usually consisting of a group of two
to four people, in which one member of the team has primary responsibility for the assigned portfolio. The team is like a committee in the
sense that the members exchange views and information and engage
in friendly arguments. However, it differs from that of the usual committee. The working relationship of the team members is informal,
with uninhibited give-and-take and close continual contact. Decisions
are not formalized or finalized by the team as a whole. The team
member who has primary responsibility for a portfolio has sole authority and responsibility for all decisions. If a significant development
occurs which requires prompt action, and the primary manager is
not available, then the team member with secondary responsibility
takes the necessary portfolio action.

In comparison to the previous systems, the team approach provides
greater simplicity, greater flexibility and freedom, and a framework
within which to make decisions more rapidly. This system can be quite
effective if the team members are well qualified, especially the primary
member, if they work cohesively, and the abilities of each member
complement those of the other members such that the team is balanced
and has a well-rounded background. If these conditions are not met,
then this arrangement can be less satisfactory.

The fifth arrangement is the *decentralized system* which includes
the so-called superstar system. The decentralized arrangement is one
in which a portfolio manager has sole and complete discretion in the
management of the assigned portfolio. As compared to the previous
four systems, this one has the simplest and most flexible management
arrangement. It is similar to the team system except that the portfolio
manager does not work continually with other portfolio managers in
reference to any one specific portfolio. In arriving at decisions, the

manager is free to use whatever source of research and other information she or he wishes.

This can be a satisfactory arrangement if the portfolio manager is highly proficient and conscientious, if one has ready access to and uses high-quality research information with sufficient breadth of coverage, and if one is familiar with the portfolio performance objectives of the client. There should be a back-up system so that when the portfolio manager is away from the office on trips or because of illness or a vacation, another professional member of the organization is able to follow through with portfolio responsibilities.

The superstar system may be considered as one subtype under the decentralized system. The merits of the superstar arrangement have provided considerable debate in the investment community. Under this system, one portfolio manager has sole authority over a portfolio account; in addition, however, one is ordinarily expected (1) to achieve high short-term rates of return, (2) to achieve a short-term rate of return which is above the average return in the stock market, or (3) to achieve a short-term rate of return which is above that of other selected portfolios. One who succeeds, is subsequently and periodically rewarded by additional compensation, and/or the organization is assigned additional funds to manage. This system gained considerable popularity in the latter half of the 1960s, particularly among corporate pension funds using split funding, among performance mutual funds, and hedge fund partnership type accounts. This system seemed to succeed during the rising phase of stock market speculation, in part because a number of these portfolios concentrate in stocks with volatile prices and with thin markets. With stock market declines in the 1970s, many superstarred portfolios underperformed the market. The controversy surrounding the superstar system seems to focus on questions as to whether portfolio performance objectives were set too high and time horizons set too short, and whether portfolio managers were tempted or pressured into adopting speculative strategies which were unfeasible and inconsistent with the proper investment requirements of clients. Less acrimonious discussion is associated with the merits of the basic decentralized system.

In describing these five types of professional internal interrelationships, many portfolio management organizations employ combinations of parts of two or more of these systems. Moreover, the success of these systems is dependent in part on the abilities of the professional staff and the willingness of the staff to make the system work effectively. Any carefully designed system will break down if key members of the organization abuse, resist, or fight the system. The system should be compatible with the particular requirements of the total portfolio management system, which includes performance objectives, strategies, and qualities of the professional staff.

GENERAL CHARACTERISTICS OF THE ORGANIZATIONAL STRUCTURE[1]

The basic characteristics of the structure of an organization, within which the investment management system operates, have both obvious and subtle influences on the type of portfolio performance which might be expected. The size, complexity, scope, and diversity of an organization have a bearing on the extent to which an investment management system successfully achieves portfolio performance objectives. Let us consider each of these facets.

Scope and Diversity of Functions

In evaluating the portfolio management system, the question is sometimes raised as to whether the system operates best in a specialized, single-purpose organization or in a diversified, multipurpose one.

Multipurpose Organization.   Let us examine the case for the multipurpose organization. Examples of such organizations are commercial banks with trust departments, insurance companies, broker-dealer firms with investment advisory departments, employer organizations with a pension fund portfolio management department, and foundations and universities with an endowment fund portfolio management department.

One argument in support of the multipurpose or integrated organization is the reduction of total operating expenses achieved by having two or more different functions sharing common facilities and personnel. The trust investment division, for example, may be able to gather some of its economic, industry, and security market data for the investment management system at little or no cost from the bank's portfolio bond department, economics department, bond underwriting department, and correspondent banks. The bank's securities trading department may process security transactions for the trust department as well as for the bank's portfolio, correspondent bank portfolios, and the underwriting department. The bank's computer data processing system may maintain the portfolio records of the trust department and perhaps service the statistical and analytical requirements of investment research. The bank's legal and tax staff may render advice on tax problems for client portfolios. The marketing cost and effort in attracting new clients for the trust investment division can be shared with the trust department and commercial bank departments.

The investment research department in a broker-dealer firm could have its costs shared by the brokerage sales department, the underwrit-

---

[1] This section is taken from Sumner N. Levine ed. *Financial Analyst's Handbook* (Homewood, Ill.: Dow Jones-Irwin, 1975), pp. 1166–78. © 1975 by Dow Jones-Irwin, Inc.

ing department, as well as the portfolio management department. By sharing common costs, banks and brokerage firms are presumably able to provide clients with more or better services at the same or at a lower cost than otherwise.

Another advantage of some multipurpose organizations is the convenience to customers of having two or more needs met by the same organization. A bank, for example, can provide an investor with a wide range of services, including trust, estate, investment advisory, security custodial, record keeping, tax, checking account, and savings account services. In addition, the bank can service some of the client's business needs, such as corporate pension fund management and business credit. The customer can get to know the bank people better and save time by doing business with this one-stop financial service center rather than dealing with two or more separate organizations.

This same advantage might be said to apply to insurance companies where a customer's permanent life insurance policy, for example, provides for protection against the risk of premature death and provides for an income producing savings fund and a retirement income annuity. An insurance company may meet a number of other financial needs for a client, such as mutual funds, variable annuities, corporate group employee insurance and pension plans, variable life insurance, and separate accounts. If the customer has a small investment account or small portfolio to manage, the multipurpose organization may be willing to accept this unattractive account and to manage it well when the customer is using other services which are more profitable to the organization.

A third argument for the integrated multipurpose organization is that senior management may have greater control over the effectiveness of an in-house portfolio management system and may derive benefits at a lower cost than if these services were contracted from an outside organization. This argument is used by corporations, unions, and government agencies as justification for having their own in-house employee pension fund portfolio management department, by universities and foundations for managing their own endowment funds, and by insurance companies for managing their own insurance portfolios.

A fourth possible advantage of the multipurpose organization is the continuity and stability of support provided to the investment management system. For example, a diversified corporation is better equipped to transfer funds generated from strong and prospering units and to supply additional support to the investment management system if or when it is subject to the loss of key professional personnel, subject to severe competitive pressures, or subject to other temporary adverse conditions in the securities industry.

What might be the disadvantages of the multipurpose organization? Four potential disadvantages will be cited here.

First, in the multipurpose organization, the investment management system competes with other functions for support from the same budget source. The trust investment division competes with the rest of the trust department and the rest of the commercial bank for funds to support the investment management system. In insurance companies, the investment department competes with the underwriting and sales departments. The same is true of other in-house investment management departments, such as for a university's endowment fund portfolio, for a corporation's pension fund, and for a broker-dealer firm's investment management department.

In many multipurpose organizations, revenues generated by the investment management system can be identified or estimated. In addition, many direct expenses can be determined. However, senior management has the problem of determining what is a fair charge for overhead costs against the investment management function, what is a fair net return on the function, how much of this return should be plowed back, and how much of an outlay should be allocated by the organization to upgrade or expand the investment function. Given the competition for resources among the various functions of a multipurpose organization, such questions are not easy or simple for senior management to resolve. Because the investment management system may represent a relatively small component of a multipurpose organization, its requirements may be more easily neglected or overlooked.

The portfolio management system will likely have a high quality operation only if senior management assigns a proper priority to it, provides appropriate direction, and furnishes necessary support. One way to insulate the system from competition for resources within the multipurpose organization is to segregate it as a separate, autonomous department or subsidiary that is directly responsible to senior executive management. As a department it might not be insulated enough; on the other hand, as a subsidiary it may become too isolated in respect to tapping the benefits of a multipurpose organization.

A second possible problem, especially for horizontally integrated financial organizations, is a possible obligation to use the services available from other units in the organization regardless of their suitability or quality. The trust investment division, for example, may be expected to use services of the bank's economics department, correspondent bank relations, trading department, computer system, and marketing (new business development) department. Yet some of these services may be less suitable, more costly, or of less quality than services available to the investment division from outside the bank. In the case of the college endowment fund, the university portfolio management may be tempted to or be expected to accept the advise of professors of economics and finance regardless of their professional qualifications. In the case of the broker-dealer firm, the portfolio management department might be expected to use the facilities of its trading department and to use and accept the investment recommendations of industry research analysts in the securities research department or in the underwriting department, regardless of their quality or appropriateness.

Another possible disadvantage of the horizontally integrated financial organization pertains to the one-stop financial center concept. It is indeed fortunate for a customer to find that a single organization is well equipped to meet all personal and business financial needs. An informed observer knows that a diversified firm may have product lines of different quality. However, the less informed prospective customer may not be aware of this. If the multipurpose organization, for example, has a poor reputation for certain services, this may unfairly cast an unfavorable image on the portfolio management service, or vice versa. Consequently, the quality of each service provided by a multipurpose organization should be evaluated on its own merits.

A fourth possible problem of the multipurpose organization is that senior management may not be adequately qualified to organize and properly control a high-quality, in-house portfolio management system. In some instances, senior management may hire incompetent portfolio managers or approve poor portfolio policies. In other instances, senior management may exert pressure or influence on the in-house investment management system which inadvertently impedes portfolio performance. Undesirable influence, conflicts of interest, or other pressures frequently occur, for example, in corporate, union, and government employee retirement funds and in college and foundation endowment portfolios. If these pressures cannot be deflected by adequate internal controls, then they might be minimized by contracting for the portfolio management service of one or more outside investment management firms, and by maintaining arms' length, professional, and business-like relationships with such firms.

Specialized Organization. Let us now consider the investment performance characteristics of the independent, specialized portfolio management organization. The term *independent* is used here to mean an organization which is a completely separate, legal entity, and is not a department or subsidiary of any other organization. Examples of single-purpose portfolio management organizations are ones which manage only investment counsel accounts, mutual funds, and closed-end funds.

An advantage frequently associated with the single-purpose portfolio management firm is the incentive of the organization to assign its full energies to the exclusive business of achieving portfolio objectives for its clients or fund shareholders. The management is not distracted by any other priorities, functions, or services. The success and reputation of the organization rests solely on meeting portfolio objectives and satisfying portfolio clients. Therefore, if management wants to retain existing clients, obtain referrals from satisfied clients, and attract new clients, it is vital, if not crucial, for management to have an effective portfolio management system which achieves a record of successful investment performance.

Another possible advantage is that the relationship between the organization and the client tends to be simple, clear-cut, objective, and business-like. The relationship need not be cluttered or complicated by other commercial, political, or personal arrangements which may exist with a multipurpose organization or with an in-house portfolio management system. The relationship can be established or terminated in a relatively short time. If one has sufficient funds, the client may diversify investment management by spreading funds over two or more separate portfolio management organizations.

What are the possible disadvantages of the single-purpose organization? It is possible for the organization and the professional staff to become so specialized and to develop such a narrow perspective that the investment management system concentrates on daily events of only current interest and fails to recognize, analyze, and evaluate broad or diverse trends which are gradually unfolding in the broad business or social environment.

A second possible limitation is that the portfolio firm is dependent to a greater extent on the supporting services of outside organizations, such as industry and security research, information about economic and political developments, and legal, tax, and computer services. The firm is dependent on the existing quality and reliability of those services which are available to it. The cost of some of these external services may be higher than if they were in-house. On the other hand, the firm frequently has a wide choice of competing services from which to choose, and if or when such services become less attractive, there is no permanent obligation to continue them, so that they may be conveniently replaced with better ones.

From the standpoint of clients, a third possible disadvantage of the single-purpose firm is that the investment program and services are less integrated. For example, the bank trust department is able to offer trust executor and custodial services in conjunction with portfolio management. The insurance company is able to package death insurance benefits, savings, investment management, and annuity benefits together in an integrated contractual program, including variable annuities and variable life insurance. The client, who employs a single-purpose portfolio management firm, retains the responsibility of filling comprehensive needs by integrating, as best as possible, the financial services offered by two or more different specialized organizations.

A fourth possible problem is that the single-purpose firm may be inherently less entrenched and stable. If severe adverse forces impact on the investment management industry, such as occurred in the early

1970s for the mutual fund management business, this can lead to a more serious strain on the financial strength and operational effectiveness of a single-purpose portfolio management firm than on that of a diversified, multipurpose one. Conversely, if adverse forces affect one or more major lines of a multipurpose organization, this could lead to a reduction in support supplied to the portfolio management unit.

Finally, unlike multipurpose organizations, the senior professional staff of the single-purpose firm may not be subject to review or held accountable within the organization by a general executive management echelon. In a single-purpose firm, the occupational strength of the specialized professional staff is in management of portfolios rather than in the business management of an organization composed of personnel, budgets, office facilities, and equipment. The senior portfolio managers in many single-purpose firms, to be sure, have acquired the necessary skills to plan, organize, and control the operations effectively. However, in small, young, or rapidly growing organizations, the senior professional staff may not have gained the necessary skills to manage properly all aspects of the operations. In the absence of experienced business management, some employees may not be adequately trained or supervised, communications may break down, operating costs may get out of line, funds may not be properly controlled or safeguarded, and so on. Such organizational distractions could disrupt the performance of the professional staff.

Given the foregoing discussion, no clear conclusions can be drawn as to whether multipurpose firms as a class or single-purpose firms as a class have an inherently greater chance of providing an investment management system which will achieve portfolio objectives.

Structure of the Organization

In this section, we will consider the implications of organizational structure on portfolio performance in terms of four structural forms— the unitary system, the branch system, the correspondent system, and the parent-subsidiary arrangement. In the next section, we will consider the implications of organizational size.

The *unitary* organization is one which confines its whole investment management operations to offices in only one building location. Under such circumstances, all members of the professional investment staff are in one physical location rather than spread out in offices in different cities or communities. This arrangement tends to facilitate closer and frequent interaction and communication among members of the professional staff in regard to all aspects of the investment decision-making process, including investment research, formulation of portfolio policies, and review of client investment objectives and requirements. The professional staff in a unitary organization is able to be a closer knit group which can more fully share information and ideas from one another on a continuous and informal basis. With this type of interaction, each staff member has a greater opportunity of relating and tailoring duties and responsibilities to the entire investment decision-making process. In addition, it is easier for senior management to monitor, evaluate, and control all functions of the investment management system.

On the other hand, the unitary operation tends to be more remote to clients and prospective customers who reside in cities some distance from the unit headquarters. This situation may impede the development of clientele outside the headquarters city, may hamper communications and a close working relationship with distant clients, and/or may increase the costs of communications with such clients. The latter may entail a greater commitment in time and travel cost for the professional staff in visits to faraway clients. On the other hand, such geographic barriers appear to be breaking down. Given the convenience of long-distance telephone service, of a fully developed, fast, jet airline network, and of modern highways and car rental arrangements, geographic distances are becoming less significant in terms of client relations. Depending on the volume of accounts and of travel involved, the total costs may be less than would be incurred in maintaining a branch system. Nevertheless, psychological, political, or competitive pressures sometimes necessitate having investment management representation residing in the same city or region as the client.

The *branch* type of investment management organization is utilized by investment counsel firms and to varying degrees by bank trust departments. Under this arrangement, certain functions are centralized in the head office, while others are decentralized in branch offices. Investment research and formulation of basic portfolio strategies with respect to economic and security market conditions are usually conducted under the direction of senior management and a staff in the head office. The final approval of policies and security transactions for individual portfolios are made either by the senior or specialized staff in the head office or by client account advisors in the branch office, depending on the organization's procedures.

With a branch system, the overhead of the specialized functions of investment research and basic portfolio policy formulation may be spread over or absorbed by a larger number of client accounts at widely dispersed geographic locations. This overhead cost per account may be less, or alternatively, this potentially larger number of accounts are able financially to support a higher quality or a more fully developed investment management system. In addition, the branch account advisor is able to have a closer relationship and more frequent two-way communication with clients because of geographic proximity.

What are the possible disadvantages of the branch system? Some disadvantages, as might be expected, are the possible advantages of the unitary system. The branch account advisor is moderately or significantly removed from the investment management operations in the head office. Consequently, the advisor's function or duties may not be as closely integrated in the total decision-making system. If the authority for portfolio decisions rests with branch advisors, then decisions might not fully reflect all of the expert resources available in the head office, and senior head office management might not have as much control over the quality and suitability of investment selections or portfolio policy decisions when they are being made in the field.

If, on the other hand, final authority for portfolio investment decisions resides in the head office, this centralization might create other problems. One result is awkward procedures and delays in implementation of portfolio changes at a time when speed of action is desirable, that is, two separate levels of the organization at two different locations (the branch account advisor and the head office staff) may need to concur with each portfolio change. If advisors in branch offices are relied on as the primary contact with clients, it is possible that the head office staff may be so isolated from clients that they develop a somewhat impersonal, standardized, or routine approach to meeting portfolio requirements of various clients. If the head office has final authority, some of the decisions may not fully reflect the personal financial considerations and portfolio performance objectives of clients. A branch advisor who is insulated from head office investment operations, may be less effective as a communicator or intermediary between the client and the investment organization.

From a cost standpoint, does each branch pay for itself? A branch operation is, of course, justified if the organization is able to gain a sufficient number of accounts that it would not otherwise have if there were no branch at that location.

The *correspondent* or affiliate system is, in a sense, one step removed from the branch system. The correspondent system is used by many bank trust investment divisions and by some investment counsel firms. A correspondent relationship is one in which one (usually a large) investment counsel firm or one (usually a large) trust investment division furnishes, for a consideration, investment research reports and portfolio policy suggestions to another (usually a smaller) counsel firm or trust investment division. Both parties to the correspondent relationship are usually, although not always, separate and independent organizations. A correspondent system has some of the characteristics of both the unitary and the branch systems. The small investment organization has the freedom of movement and compactness of a unitary organization, but has a measure of dependency on the investment expertise from an outside operation at a distant location. The effectiveness of the small organization depends on the quality of the local staff, the

quality of the investment services of the correspondent, and the efficiency by which relevant information is transmitted between the two
organizations.

The final type of organizational structure is the *parent company-
subsidiary company* arrangement. A number of financial and industrial
firms, as parent or holding companies, have acquired or formed subsidiaries which function as portfolio management organizations. These
subsidiaries are wholly or partially owned by the parent corporation.
Business corporations, such as a rubber company and a merchandising
company, have acquired or formed portfolio management subsidiaries.
Financial firms, such as life insurance companies, bank holding companies, and broker-dealer firms, have acquired or formed such subsidiaries. Such subsidiaries operate as investment counsel firms, mutual fund
management companies, or both.

As to how much autonomy is exercised by the subsidiary's management depends on the arrangements with the parent company. Some
of the potential strengths and weaknesses in the subsidiary-type organization correspond to those previously cited above for the multipurpose
organization; however, because of the greater diversity of possible arrangements and combinations among different types of parent companies, fewer general comments can be made here. The opportunity
for synergism of a life insurance company and a mutual fund management company combination is obvious where, for example, the same
sales force may sell both life insurance and mutual funds; but the operational benefits are less for the combination of an industrial corporation
with a mutual fund. Therefore, in evaluating the investment management system in a subsidiary organization, one must not only appraise
the quality of the operations in the subsidiary but the nature of controls
and quality of support provided by the parent organization.

Size of the Organization

The size of the investment management organization has several
implications regarding portfolio performance. Is a large organization
inherently best, or is the small one better? We will primarily discuss
the advantages of each size organization. Factors considered advantages for larger organizations may, by inference, be considered as possible disadvantages for smaller organizations, and vice versa. The importance and relevance of these advantages and disadvantages to a given
investor depend on particular portfolio requirements and performance
objectives. One size organization may possibly be better suited to
achieve particular objectives than another size organization. It is possible that some investment management organizations are too small
and restrictive; and it is equally possible that the size of some organiza-

tions has exceeded the optimum economies of scale, such that the excess size has a neutral or possibly even a negative effect on the performance of some portfolios.

Let us first examine the possible inherent advantages of the large portfolio management organization, followed by a consideration of the advantages of the smaller organization.

One advantage of the large organization is its greater degree of corporate or organizational stability, consistency of management, and continuity of services over an extended period of time. Some of the large bank trust departments, insurance companies, investment companies, and investment counsel firms have been prudently managing portfolios for over half a century. A large organization has a likelihood of having management in depth, that is, management echelons with staggered ages so as to provide an orderly and gradual succession of seasoned management over extended periods of time. If a highly productive executive is suddenly terminated from the large organization, the disruption in the long-term effectiveness of the portfolio management system can be negligible.

The large organization is able to support a complete or an elaborate system of review and control of the investment decision-making process by two or more levels of management so that each portfolio receives a consistent quality of supervision. This continuity of quality management over extended intervals of time is of special importance to certain clients. For example, it is ordinarily not feasible or extremely awkward for beneficiaries to replace trustees of irrevocable trusts and estates. Consequently such portfolios may be under the same management for decades. Many life insurance policyholders, beneficiaries, and annuitants are dependent on and financially committed to the same life insurance company portfolio for over a whole generation or two. Continuity of quality investment management is, therefore, important to all individual and institutional clients who are not in a position to replace the organization. Clients might not become aware in a timely fashion of a deterioration in the performance of a smaller management organization because the clients lack the time, interest, or ability to monitor closely on a continuing basis the portfolio management system. The professional relationship between the organization and client is sometimes difficult to terminate on a timely basis because of other personal, psychological, or political reasons which tend to lock in an account.

This situation frequently exists where the relationship involves an in-house portfolio management system, which involves relatives or close friends and other business or political connections. Confrontations with the problem of replacing a portfolio manager tend to be avoided when a large and stable management organization is able, over long periods of time, to achieve the investment performance objectives which the client had expected at the time the professional relationship was established.

A second advantage of the large organization is its ability to support a relatively complete investment system within a single organization. Because of the volume or scale of operations, the organization can support a large staff with a wide range of different specialized professional talents, a large library of research materials, an expensive and an elaborate computer research system and computer data bank, and a fully developed trading department system and can acquire considerable institutional brokerage house research through a large volume of soft-dollar commissions. With a large staff of professional specialists, the economy, government policies, international conditions, stock and bond market conditions, and many industries and companies can be analyzed and evaluated in depth. This research can be channeled to portfolio policy and strategy committees, account review committees, investment committees, bond committees, and others, where the research and portfolio recommendations can be carefully monitored and evaluated by a group of seasoned professionals. In short, the management of a large organization is in a position to plan, direct, and control a comprehensive and in-depth portfolio management system.

Let us now turn to the potential advantages of the smaller investment organization. The smaller organization has a simpler structure and is easier to operate, control, and evaluate. There is no elaborate system of specialized departments, committees, tiers of management, head office with branch offices, or affiliates or subsidiary units. The professional staff is close-knit like the unitary organization, only more so because of its small size. It is easier for senior managers to be intimately familiar with and to be a significant part of the organization's investment management system and to exercise closer control over the quality of the system. There is considerably less delegation of authority and diffusion of responsibility by the top management. If a member of the professional staff misunderstands an assignment or is not performing as expected, this can be more quickly detected and corrected.

Given this greater centralization of authority, decisions and actions can still be taken more rapidly than in some large organizations which are only partially decentralized. If portfolio performance objectives are based on strategies which sometimes require rapid decisions, then the small and simpler organizational system may be well equipped to execute such strategies.

The smaller organization has less problems with marketability. Because of the smaller amount of funds under management, the organization is able to accumulate or liquidate security portfolio positions in many of their accounts more rapidly and at a possible lower market transaction cost than other firms with large dollar holdings. Because the amount of funds is smaller, diversified portfolio positions can be taken in corporations with smaller capitalizations and possibly offering higher returns without adversely disturbing the market price. Consequently, a wider selection of different investments is available, and the portfolio management system has a higher degree of market mobility. This type of flexibility can easily enhance investment performance.

The quality and motivation of the professional staff at the smaller and younger organizations can be quite high. The key managers frequently are owners or otherwise share in the profits of the organization; consequently their financial rewards relate to the success of the organization and to attracting and retaining satisfied clients. Therefore, portfolio managers and security analysts who are ambitious and confident of their abilities frequently obtain their initial training and experience as employees in a large organization, and later gravitate to the smaller organization where their individual energies have a clearer and greater impact on the investment management system and where their efforts have a more direct and immediate result in professional satisfaction and personal compensation.

In contrast, some of the less industrious, less able or less confident professionals seek shelter in the large, stable, and more secure bureaucracies. To the extent that a large organization has a staff composed of both highly qualified and less qualified individuals, the chance exists that the input of those who are most competent will be diluted through the system of departments, review committees, and echelons such that the net output is of mediocre or average quality. And of course one reason good people sometimes go to a smaller organization is because their abilities are not fully recognized, appreciated, or used by the larger one. Consequently, a group of outstanding people in a small organization may be better able to produce a superior performance than they could in a large organization, given its inherent institutional constraints.

In the smaller organization, each client and each portfolio tend to be of greater importance and have less chance of being neglected or lost in the shuffle. This is especially relevant to clients with smaller portfolios because these are the ones which can be more easily neglected.

Many clients are attracted to large organizations because they are very well known, have been in business for a long time, and have established a reputation based on past achievements, sometimes in the distant past. Because of this large and apparent easy inflow of new funds, some organizations will overload their portfolio managers with too many accounts and their security analysts with too many different holdings to analyze and research.

Because the top executives of the smaller organization are frequently the portfolio managers and account representatives, the prospective client is better able to meet and personally evaluate those who have the authority and responsibility for portfolio decisions. Then after a relationship is established, a client will continue to have greater access to the senior managers. Consequently, the client is able to be kept informed on portfolio management matters directly from those who are making the decisions; and when financial requirements change, the client is able to relay this directly to the portfolio manager for prompt action. This direct relationship with the portfolio manager, who is responsible for the account, increases the likelihood that the client will receive more individualized attention, that portfolio objectives will be more closely tailored to the client's specific requirements, and given this more personal relationship, that the manager will strive harder to achieve performance objectives.

The small portfolio management organization has some of the characteristics of the highly specialized organization cited previously. Both organizations lack a large staff of specialists with a diverse background of professional expertise.

The small organization can take the small steps to solve this problem as the specialized, single-purpose organization, namely to choose, on a selective basis, specialized professional services and research which are available from outside organizations and groups.

TYPES OF INSTITUTIONS

Many different types of institutions have investment management organizations. Seven different types of institutions are briefly described in this section. In examining each type of institution, their uniqueness should not be overemphasized inasmuch as the kinds of investment accounts serviced by each of these institutions have increased considerably in scope over recent decades. Many institutions have changed or are changing and broadening their investment management services, so that their once unique nature is tending to disappear. For example, securities portfolios of employe retirement plans are managed by bank trust departments, investment counsel firms, insurance companies, investment companies, investment advisory departments of broker-dealer firms, and nonfinancial corporations. Investment counsel firms provide advice on the management of bank and insurance company portfolios. Banks and brokerage firms have created or have acquired investment counsel departments and subsidiaries. Insurance companies and brokerage firms have acquired and manage mutual funds. This "department store of finance" approach reflects a significant institutional trend which will probably continue in the future.

Investment managers, portfolio managers, and investment advisers are employed primarily in a half dozen different types of institutions.

Based on a recent random survey of 630 managers in the industry, the listing below shows the percent employed by each type of institutional organization:

Investment counsel firm	34.1%
Investment Company	4.9
Bank trust investment	40.2
Insurance company investment	14.8
Brokerage firm advisory	2.4
Pension portfolio management	3.6
	100.0%

Bank trust investment organizations employ the largest proportion of investment managers, followed by investment counsel firms and insurance companies.

Investment Counsel Firm

Perhaps the simplest and most specialized type of portfolio management organization is the proprietorship and partnership forms of investment counsel firms (sometimes called investment management firms). In this instance, the owner or owners of the firm are usually the senior portfolio managers or senior investment advisors. The primary or sole purpose of the firm is to manage the securities portfolios of individual and institutional clients for a fee, usually determined by the total market value of the principal in the portfolios.

Because the primary purpose of the organization is to manage outside client portfolios, the reputation and success of the firm will depend on satisfying clients through the achievement of performance objectives. If the objectives are achieved, the firm's investment fees will tend to grow for two reasons. First, appreciation of the portfolios will automatically generate larger fees. Secondly, a favorable record of past performance and satisfied clients will provide testimonies, referrals, and endorsements that will attract new clients to the firm. Conversely, poor performance will jeopardize the retention of clients and repel prospective clients. Because a client has the freedom to commence and terminate portfolio management services on relatively short notice, the client-investment counsel relationship tends to be relatively personalized and interactive.

Investment Companies

The best known professionally managed portfolios are those of mutual funds and closed-end investment companies. These portfolios quite commonly are supervised under contract by a separate legal entity called a management company. The owners and portfolio managers of this latter company manage the portfolio of the investment company under a fee arrangement similar to that of an investment counsel firm.

Likewise, the organization of the management company can be quite similar to that of an investment counsel firm. Indeed, an investment company portfolio, in some respects, is a logical extension of the portfolio management services provided by investment counsel firms. (A counsel firm may manage the separate portfolios of clients with a minimum of $100,000 to $250,000, and encourage prospective clients with smaller sums to invest in shares of a mutual fund it manages.)

The mutual fund has a unique corporate structure in which the fund ordinarily stands ready at all times to sell new shares to or redeem (retire) existing shares at net asset value from mutual fund investors in the company. Because of cash flows into and out of the portfolio, a portfolio manager may at times be forced to liquidate sizeable portfolio holdings in declining security markets and at other times be expected to invest sizeable amounts of cash in rising markets. If the portfolio is concentrated in common stocks of risky, volatile companies, or in stocks of smaller companies with thin markets, then sizeable liquidations in weak markets or sizeable purchases in strong markets may well have adverse affects on the performance of the portfolio. Alternatives are available to avoid or minimize this consequence. One is for management to hold stocks that are more stable and have broader markets. This, of course, reduces risk and volatility but may also exclude certain investments that are potentially quite profitable. A second alternative is for the portfolio to hold larger amounts of cash and liquid short-term debt instruments in order to accommodate unexpected short-term cash outflows and inflows. This procedure may reduce the portfolio's total return, however, inasmuch as liquid assets frequently earn a lower return than equities. Still another alternative is for the portfolio to hold a larger number of issues with a smaller position in each.

In part because of uniform disclosure requirements, mutual funds are given considerable publicity by investment periodicals in terms of monthly, quarterly, and annual portfolio profitability and volatility rankings, and in terms of quarterly portfolio holdings and transactions. Those funds receiving high rankings frequently experience sizeable cash inflows, and those assigned low rankings sometimes experience sizeable redemptions. This type of competitive environment occurred in the late 1960s and early 1970s. Such an atmosphere places an added incentive or pressure on mutual fund portfolio managers to produce a performance that will receive a favorable short-term and long-term ranking. Healthy competition can encourage portfolio managers to strive toward the achievement of performance objectives. However, pressure for short-term performance can encourage some portfolio managements to seek substantial short-term gains by speculative strategies, investing in highly risky stocks, and by generating high portfolio trading turnover rates. Such approaches frequently lead to sizeable portfolio losses and high transaction costs.

Although the closed-end investment company has many similarities to a mutual fund, it has one important difference. The capital structure of a closed-end company resembles that of an ordinary corporation; that is, it has a fixed number of common shares outstanding and, in a few instances, has preferred stock and debt instruments in its capital structure. Because common shares of the company are not continuously offered for sale and are not redeemable on demand by shareholders, portfolio management does not have to contend with cash inflows and outflows. This type of organizational structure permits a wider latitude in the selection of performance objectives and in the selection of marketability and volatility characteristics of investment assets. Moreover, portfolio management is not subjected to the same type of competitive pressures as is the management of a mutual fund. Management has greater freedom and flexibility to pursue what it believes to be the best investment strategies for achieving long-run performance objectives.

Because management is more entrenched (some would say management has control of a "captive" portfolio), the inherent demands to achieve performance objectives are not so great in the closed-end company as in the mutual fund. However, the same might be said for the managements of business corporations. As in the case of other successful business enterprises, many portfolio managers strive to achieve performance objectives regardless of external pressures from investors or shareholders. Many investment company managements want to be associated with a successful record and with satisfied investors. In contrast to some other forms of investment management organizations, the portfolio performance record of investment companies is subject to broad dissemination and widespread public scrutiny.

Bank Trust Investment Division

Traditionally, the function of a trust investment division of a commercial bank is to conduct security research and portfolio management of personal trusts, estates, and agency accounts. These portfolio management services are normally furnished to the trust department which acts in the capacity of executor or administrator for estates, acts in the capacity of trustee for personal trusts, and in the capacity of agent for agency accounts. When a bank is named as executor or trustee by an estate owner in his or her last will and testament or in a trust agreement, the bank ordinarily takes custody or control of the designated assets, manages the assets, and makes distributions of income and principal to designated beneficiaries at specified times. Therefore, in terms of the total services provided to beneficiaries, the trust investment division furnishes only a part. That part involves the portfolio management of those assets in trusts and estates comprising marketable stocks, bonds, and money market instruments.

The traditional type of trust investment management operation represents a relatively small though essential part of the overall operations of many full line commercial banks. The quality and effectiveness of the investment management system varies widely among banks. It is determined by several factors: One is the priority of importance assigned to it by senior bank management which reflects the bank's desire to offer a competitively attractive portfolio management service to clients. A second factor is the type and investment sophistication of the trust clients attracted to the bank. If most clients turn their trust business over to the bank because of commercial banking relationships, or because of the general trust services as distinct from professional portfolio management services, then the primary determinant of attracting trust clients may be the existence of commercial banking arrangements and the availability of the general trust services rather than the quality and professional reputation of the trust investment management organization. Such attitudes and perceptions by senior bank management will play a part in determining the allocation of resources and size of budget support made available by the bank to the investment management operations. A number of banks, especially in financial centers, have developed a reputation for proficient investment management and have relatively large well-staffed and well-managed trust investment divisions.

The class of trust accounts managed by a bank is a third factor which sometimes determines the nature of investment management services rendered. The portfolios of estates, testamentary trusts, and small trusts sometimes receive less intensive investment management. The bank is frequently appointed to administer these accounts in which the appointment, from a practical standpoint, is considered to be permanent. This is not the case, however, with revocable living trusts and agency investment accounts. As a fourth factor, some evidence suggests that banks are economically unable to provide high quality portfolio management to trusts and estates because the management fee structure as established by statutes, courts, and customs is too low. In fact, some trust departments operate at a loss.

The legal system is a fifth factor through its effect on the determination of portfolio performance objectives. Regardless of the intentions of the estate owner or trust grantor, the portfolio objective pursued will tend to be conservative, defensive, and conventional. The portfolio performance of trusts and estates is reviewed by judges (who are usually unschooled in investment matters), generally in the light of the legal prudent-man rule. If a portfolio loss occurs, a beneficiary may sue in court for damages (called a surcharge). Whether or not the beneficiary wins the surcharge case, the publicity can be detrimental to the bank. Within this legal framework, investment management has more to gain by avoiding a portfolio loss than by achieving a superior return.

A common way to avoid exposure to a possible loss is to minimize risks. Many securities that offer a very low level of risk also offer a low total investment return. This type of constraint may be justified when the financial requirements of a trust beneficiary are compatible with a conservative performance objective. However, a conflict of sorts can arise when financial requirements justify a more enterprising performance objective.

Compared to some of the other forms of investment management organizations, banks and their associated trust investment management operations have stability, inherent financial strength, and durability. These factors can provide some assurance that a trust portfolio will be administered in a responsible, dependable, and consistent manner over an extended period of time, which is often required for such portfolios.

In recent years, many banks have reorganized or broadened the capabilities of their investment management system in order to meet the investment performance objectives of corporate pension portfolios and investment counsel type portfolios. The investment management system servicing these accounts is housed either in the trust investment division, in an entirely separate department, or in a corporate subsidiary or affiliate. The size of the investment management business from pension and investment counsel accounts has grown rapidly and has become substantial for many banks.

Because banks have taken a diverse organizational approach to the development of these relatively new forms of business, only limited generalizations can be drawn about the basic characteristics of their investment management organizations. Some of these investment operations have retained the organizational characteristics of a traditional trust investment division; some have acquired the characteristics of an investment counsel firm, while others are still in a state of transition.

Insurance Company Investment Operation

An insurance company (sometimes referred to as an insurance underwriter, insurance carrier, or insurer) performs two major functions: underwriting risks of loss of customers (called insureds), and investing a portion of the premium (the price paid by the insured for protection against a risk) in assets that are available as a reserve to meet future insurance claims of insureds. We are, of course, primarily interested in this second function; however, to understand the investment management function, we need to have some appreciation of the underwriting function.

Some insurance companies are stockholder companies (owned by stockholders, an arrangement which corresponds to that of other private, profit-making business corporations), while others are mutual companies (owned by the insureds). For competitive reasons, the port-folio management operation is similar in both types of companies.

The senior management tends to view company operations as con-sisting of three components: investment, underwriting, and marketing (the selling of insurance services to customers). In accordance with standard methods of accounting, the investment and underwriting (in-cluding marketing) components are treated as separate, though related, profit centers in the company. As in the case of other multipurpose organizations (such as banks discussed above), the form and proficiency of the investment management system depend on the order of the importance assigned to it by senior management. This order of impor-tance can vary widely among insurance companies. At one extreme, a management regards the firm primarily as an investment company, with the purpose of the underwriting department being to fund the investment portfolio with policyholder insurance reserves. Under such circumstances, management may support a strong and highly capable investment management organization. At the other extreme, a man-agement may place primary attention on the underwriting and market-ing functions and treat the investment operation as a necessary auxil-iary service. Given this attitude, the investment management organization could be a small and routine operation.

The characteristics of the investment management organization and the portfolio performance objectives are or should be determined by the type and quality of insurance risks underwritten. Some risks are associated with short-term insurance contracts such as property, health, and casualty risks. In these cases the quarterly or annual premium is collected and, within a year, the bulk of loss claims are paid. Sizeable portions of such reserves should be routinely invested in conservative and somewhat conventional liquid assets. In addition, if the insurer aggressively underwrites lower quality (preferred) risks and ones with elements of catastrophic risk, then a large portion of the portfolio should be invested in liquid type assets. Conversely, if the insurer underwrites high quality risks which adhere more closely to the law of averages and in which the loss ratio (settlement costs as a proportion of premium revenue) is stable and more predictable, then investment management has greater latitude in seeking to achieve more enterpris-ing portfolio performance objectives. Management also has greater investment latitude if the company has a larger stockholder surplus account.

Some insurance risks are associated with long-term contracts, such as permanent (ordinary) life and annuity insurance policies. Such con-tracts generate substantial policyholder reserves in the form of fixed dollar liabilities that remain invested in the portfolio for extended peri-ods of time. Under these circumstances, the investment management organization can have a large operation with a strong expertise in long-term investments, especially in debt instruments.

In recent years, life insurance companies have broadened the product line available to customers by the introduction of equity-type products. These include mutual funds, separate account corporate pension funds, variable annuities, and variable life insurance policies. These long-term programs are funded by portfolios concentrated in common stocks and are somewhat similar to portfolios in the mutual fund and pension fund industries. Consequently, the investment management operations in insurance companies are developing organizational characteristics resembling those in pension fund and mutual fund organizations.

Brokerage Firm Investment Advisory Department

Some security broker-dealer firms maintain an investment advisory department that manages customer portfolios on a discretionary basis for a fee. Portfolio managers function in about the same way as those in investment counsel firms, the primary difference being that the portfolio management service is usually of secondary importance to the broker-dealer firm, while it is the only business of an investment counsel firm. In larger brokerage firms, the portfolio managers may be working in this function on a full-time basis. In other instances, portfolio managers may spend a portion of their time in other departments of the firm, such as securities research, underwriting or sales.

The quality of the investment management organization is determined by the priority given to supporting the operations relative to other departments in the firm. In making portfolio changes, safeguards should be taken to avoid potential conflicts of interest with the underwriting and brokerage commission functions of the firm.

Most brokerage firms have no investment management department and, in those that do, the professional staff tends to be small. Although broker-dealer firms as a whole are not a major factor in the portfolio management industry, some firms are expanding such services.

Pension Fund Portfolio Management

Unlike the other organizations described above, the pension fund investment management system is not associated with any one specialized type of management organization. Although a substantial number of pension funds are managed by trust investment divisions and by investment counsel firms in which portfolio managers may be managing only pension fund accounts, a number of other types of organizations also manage pension funds. The term *pension fund* is used here in a broad sense to encompass all categories of group employee retirement funds, including: corporate profit-sharing funds, *separate accounts* and group variable and fixed annuity plans administered by insurance companies, and state and local government retirement funds.

In addition to the organizations already mentioned, pension fund portfolios are managed by broker-dealer firms, and, internally, by the employes' corporations, government employers, and labor unions. Some pension funds, especially smaller ones, are invested in conventional mutual funds and in commingled funds limited to small pension fund accounts. This latter type is a common trust fund administered by banks or by an investment management company. Thus, given the diversity of pension fund management arrangements, few generalizations can be made about this form of investment organization.

Published Investment Advisory Services

Several firms publish and distribute periodic investment advisory reports to subscribers as well as provide a portfolio advisory service. Frequently, this consists of publishing one or more recommended model portfolios, each intended for a different portfolio objective. Recommended changes in the model portfolios are then published in reports sent periodically to subscribers. The frequency of change in investment policies and in portfolio holdings is determined by the interval of time between published reports. Most services issue reports at fixed intervals, such as weekly, biweekly, or monthly. A service that issues reports weekly, for example, has subtly committed itself to the belief that (1) investment conditions may change significantly within an interval as short as a week and/or (2) investment performance can benefit by the timing of a portfolio switch within an interval of a week. If this were not the belief, then subscribers might otherwise question why they need to pay for a service that issues weekly reports. This questioning would more likely arise among subscribers if consecutively issued weekly reports expressed the opinion that no significant developments had occurred between weekly reports and recommended no change in portfolio policies and security holdings. In order to dispel such thinking, an advisory service is committed to finding material each week for its report, is tempted to magnify or enlarge on weekly events, and is tempted to recommend portfolio changes because of minor developments.

On the other hand, services which report biweekly or monthly will want to assure their subscribers that they have missed nothing since the last report. These reports will be slanted to uphold this viewpoint.

The size and quality of investment research operations in published advisory organizations will tend to be limited by subscription revenues. An exception is an organization which is also supported by other investment services, such as investment counsel accounts and mutual fund accounts.

Chapter 3

Setting Investment Objectives*

CHARLES D. ELLIS
President
Greenwich Research Associates
Greenwich, Connecticut

"If you don't know where you're going, any road will take you there" is a familiar expression that has all too much application to investment management as it is typically practiced in America today.

There is more than irony in the paradoxical fact that most investment managers devote most of their time, energy, and ability in an apparently futile effort to achieve an objective that appears unattainable and which, even if accomplished, would not be very important compared to a far, far easier task in which most investment managers could consistently achieve the intended objective. Even more significant, this relatively "easy" objective, when achieved, would really matter. Unfortunately, very few investment managers devote any serious time, effort, or talent to attain this objective.

The unimportant and very difficult task to which most investment managers devote most of their time with little or no success is to "beat the market." Realistically, to outperform the equity market by even one half of one percent each year would be a great success which few, if any, investment managers have achieved. In fact, during the last several market cycles (the only periods for which we have systematic and reliable measurements of portfolio performance) most major investment organizations have been unable to keep pace with the market averages. Moreover, it appears to be true that their very efforts to beat the market have been a main cause of their own underachievement.

---

* © 1979 by Charles D. Ellis.

The truly important, but not very difficult task would be to establish sensible investment policies with which to achieve realistic and specified investment objectives. An appropriate change of even quite modest magnitude in the basic asset allocation decision, for example, can capture an improvement in total return that would be significantly greater than the elusive increment sought in the "beat the market" syndrome.

The time-honored term for this important work is *investment counseling*. As Peter Drucker so correctly emphasizes, it's a great deal more important to be working on the really right things than to be doing even the nearly right things unusually well.

In investment management, the real opportunity to achieve superior results is in establishing and adhering to appropriate investment policies over the long term, and this can only be done by setting realistic investment objectives, which is the subject of this chapter.

Investment Counseling

Despite general acknowledgement of the importance of investment counseling in the abstract, the evidence is disturbing and overwhelming that investment counseling is used little, if at all, in practice. Both A. G. Becker and Greenwich Research Associates studies show there is virtually no significant difference in the basic asset allocations of such extraordinarily different kinds of employe benefit funds as defined benefit pension funds and profit sharing funds.[1] Nor does asset mix differ significantly with such theoretically compelling factors as to whether actuarial investment return assumptions are high or low, whether pension benefit obligations are underfunded or fully funded, what fraction of accrued benefit obligations are vested, the average age of the affected workforce, or the ratio of active versus retired participants.

The differences between the functions and needs of pension plans and profit sharing plans are profound and allegedly well understood. That their investments are not differentiated leads to the sobering conclusion that while investment counseling may be honored in theory, it is little used in practice.

Whether investment management is primarily an art or a science has long been a favorite topic for informal discussion among professional investors, perhaps because the discussions are typically resolved quite cheerfully by demonstrating that the practice of investment management is clearly not a science, and must therefore be an art. Investment management is neither art nor science. It is instead, a problem

---

[1] Both groups had 43 percent in equities; 42 percent in fixed-income investments; and 16 percent in cash equivalents in 1978 as reported in Greenwich Research Associates' Seventh Annual Report on Large Corporate Pensions (1979).

in *engineering*. (And quite simple when compared to many of the other engineering problems facing our society such as air traffic control, space probes, or increasing automobile mileage while reducing pollution emissions.) Moreover, recent advances in the availability of data and the important development of modern portfolio theory are providing investment managers—and their more sophisticated clients—with the tools and analytical frame of reference they need to understand the investment problem so it can be solved or managed.

Just as the development of such diagnostic devices as x-ray machines and modern pharmacology made it possible for medical doctors to transform medical practice, it is now possible to transform investment management. When doctors fully understand the causes and pathology of a disease, they usually find the cure usually requires effective impact on only one dominant factor, and is therefore both powerful and cheap. Before the real solution is discovered, doctors attempt to treat the disease with treatments that are not only unproductive, but are also quite costly.

CONTROLLING RISK

Similarly, in investment management it is becoming clear that the crucial factor is not how to increase rates of return, but rather *how to control risk,* and that risk control is not nearly as costly as is the conventional effort to boost rates of return. In fact, the rate of return obtained in an investment portfolio is a derivative of the level of systematic risk (nondiversifiable risk) that is assumed in the portfolio, the consistency with which that risk level is maintained through the market cycle, and the skill with which specific risk (which is disposable through diversification) is eliminated or minimized through portfolio diversification. In formulating policy and strategy in politics, war, business, or investing, the necessary first step is a realistic determination of the true nature of the environment in which operations will be conducted. It is essential that this assessment be very accurate, because no matter how astute the subsequent analysis may be, to the extent that the original assumption or promise is not relevant to the environment, the conclusions will be wrong. The greater the error in the original premise, the greater the error in the ultimate policy and strategy.

There are two quite different kinds of errors in assessment: (1) errors that overstate the importance of minor factors which would cause attention to be devoted to the wrong priorities, and (2) errors that cause misunderstandings of the causal relationships so that efforts to achieve the intended objective will be counterproductive.

What then is a realistic assessment of the rates of return in the equity market? The conventional answer is 9 percent. What an exquisite and extraordinary deception this is. If only it were simply mean-ingless! Alas, it has, for most investment managers and most of their clients quite considerable meaning. It is the average annual rate of return they expect from investments in common stocks. It is, in fact, the return to which they feel they are entitled in a typical year. How-ever, as everyone knows, the actual experience of equity investors has been nothing like "9 percent compounded" for quite a long time. In fact, for most of the past decade, investors have experienced not gains, but losses. What's wrong? Have equity markets and equity re-turns somehow changed from a favorable and sublime 9 percent to the violent and adverse? And if so, should the investment objectives of the past be replaced with new objectives? The answer to both ques-tions is "no"—but with one caveat. Inflation—and specifically a change in rate of inflation anticipated in the market—has caused an important change in the nominal rate of return required by equity investors, and this, in turn, has exerted a major effect on the level of stock prices. Simply put, equity investors continue to require about the same rate of return after offsetting inflation as they used to require when rates of inflation were far less. This means that nominal equity returns now must be higher than the nominal returns that were required when the expected rate of inflation was lower (2 percent in the 1950s versus 7 percent in the 1970s).

As a result of the change in the expected rate of inflation, the long-term average rate of return required by equity investors has increased from approximately 9 percent to approximately 14 percent, so the conventional 9 percent expectation is out-of-date. Even this quite sub-stantial change—from 9 percent to 14 percent is an increase of 56 percent—does not give a realistic measure of normal returns in the stock market because it does not describe the difference or distribution of the year-by-year returns. And as every investor now knows, the differences in year-to-year returns have been considerably more impor-tant than the similarities.

Without using statistical terminology, we can now estimate that the returns to the equity investor will—in two-thirds of the years ahead—be within the rather wide range of −9 percent to +37 percent. And we can estimate that in the other one-third of the years, the actual returns will be divided evenly between losses greater than 9 percent and gains greater than 37 percent. And finally, we can say that over the very long term, total rates of return will tend to approximate 14 percent compounded annually. Now it's a vastly different thing to say returns will be "14 percent plus or minus 23 percent two-thirds of the time," than to say simply "14 percent" and it matters greatly to those who are trying to specify appropriate investment objectives *or* to examine the feasibility of the investment policies through which the objective is to be achieved *or* to reappraise their established objectives in the light of actual experience *or* to assess the operating performance of an investment manager assigned to achieve the objective.

Instruction in the width of the dispersion of returns—23 percent plus 23 percent equals a "normal" range of 46 percent which is more than three times as large as the average amount of expected return—comes unfortunately for most investment managers in those most distressing circumstances when losses are particularly severe. As the losses are usually unexpected—because they have typically not been discussed in advance—they cause considerable alarm and provoke clients and managers to improvise hastily an ad hoc reappraisal of their investment policies and objectives.

Such reviews can be expected to result all too often in action that is easily described as "the wrong decision at the wrong time for the wrong reasons," and the consequences—typically a substantial shift from equities at currently depressed prices into bonds and other fixed-income investments that will not rise in capital value with the next cycle of the equity market—are predictably harmful to the long-term returns of the portfolio.

Comparable harm is also done when the recently past years' returns have been higher than should be expected, and investment managers and their clients shed the requisite caution and increase the amount of risk assumed in the portfolio. And then, after a few years of adversity of the sort that fall normally within the very wide range of the long-term distribution of annual returns, this extra portfolio risk will magnify the impact of the market's decline, magnify the normal investor anxieties, and lead to the ad hoc revisions that cause investors to "sell low" what they have previously "bought high."

Peter Bernstein has explained this altogether human phenomenon by pointing out that almost everybody dislikes it when stocks go down in price even though it is in their best interest to have stock prices go down—so they can buy more shares with their savings and receive more dividends both now and in the future. As Pogo would say, "we have met the enemy, and it is us."

Since investors and their investment managers are subject to human frailties and foibles, the setting of investment objectives—and the investment policies designed to achieve them—needs to be done with considerable care and extensive analysis of the nature of the investment environment not only so the appropriate objective will be selected, but also so the investors and their managers will be able to hold to that same, still appropriate objective and the still appropriate investment policies when the market has been strongly negative and both objectives and policies look most dubious. A curious idea continues to make the rounds that the investment objective for a particular portfolio should be set in whole or in part according to the funds the investor wants or needs to draw from the portfolio each year. Sometimes this shows up in pension funds where the actuarial rate of return assumption will be put forth as a guide to investment. Sometimes it shows up with college presidents insisting on higher endowment fund returns to make up for operating deficits. And sometimes it arises when personal trust funds are asked to finance a more expensive way of life.

This is nonsense. We now know that the return (per unit of risk) cannot be increased just because an investor wants a higher return with which to finance more spending. Specifically, the spending decisions of the investor cannot contribute to the formulation of sound investment policies and objectives: these must be determined in accordance with the discipline of the investment market. On the contrary, the spending decisions should most definitely be governed by the investment objectives and policies—and results. One qualification of this prescription is worth noting: when spending will exceed current income from dividends and interest, a reserve fund probably should be established and funded with regular percentage withdrawals from the portfolio's long-term invested assets. Otherwise withdrawal of capital will occur in a pattern that would be a harmful reversal of dollar costs averaging, i.e., would take a larger percentage of the portfolio's assets at market lows and a smaller percentage at market highs.

Time is the single most important factor that separates the appropriate investment objective of one portfolio from the appropriate objective of another portfolio. Specifically, it is the length of time over which an investor can and will commit the portfolio and evaluate investment results and the investment objectives and policies.

At the extremes, the importance of the investor's time horizon for investment objectives is clear: a one-day or one-week investment in anything but Treasury Bills (or the equivalent) would be virtually impossible to justify, and over a half century, it is easy to show that equities are the optimal investment for the entire portfolio.[2] (Note that this self-evident proposition fits with the core assertion that the priority objective in investment management is to control risk, not to maximize returns.)

The governing time horizon for each stratum of the investment portfolio—and it is a remarkably useful exercise to analyze the portfolio of assets in comparison to specified segments of actual or potential obligations as do the banks and insurance companies—will determine the nature of the investments that can and should be made and the investment objectives that should be chosen.

A good example of different time horizons warranting different investment policies will be found in the profit sharing plan of a corpora-

---

[2] The question of common stocks versus such other forms of equity investment as real estate will not be analyzed here.

tion whose participants have quite different expectations as to how long they will work at the company. An older worker may be quite near retirement, for example, and be particularly interested in preserving accumulated asset values during the last few years of a long career, while a younger worker may be planning to work (and continue investing through the profit sharing plan) for thirty or forty years into the future. The older worker's time horizon may call for a portfolio 100 percent in short- and intermediate-term fixed-income securities, while the younger worker's time horizon would call for 100 percent equities and growth investments. In recognition of these real differences, more and more companies are now providing employees with different time horizons an opportunity to elect different asset allocations and to change the asset allocation as their time horizons change over the years as they approach retirement.

The second major factor that separates investment objectives is the risk tolerance of the investor. As discussed above, the investor who is very well informed about the investment environment will know what to expect, and will be able to take in stride those disruptive experiences that may cause other less informed investors to overreact to either unusually favorable or unusually adverse market experience. Risk tolerance matters only at the market's extremes.

Investment managers and their clients can do a lot to improve portfolio returns by being sure they both are well informed about the realities of the investment environment in which the portfolio will be managed. (The risk tolerance of a corporate pension fund is not just the risk tolerance of the pension staff or even the senior financial officer: it is the risk tolerance of a majority of the board of directors at the moment of most severe market adversity.)

While most observers maintain that the exceptional liquidity of our capital markets is a considerable advantage, it may well be that less liquidity would be beneficial both to the formation of investment objectives and to their faithful implementation in all market conditions. Indeed, in investment management, if it must be done quickly, it is not fiduciary.

The dimensions on which investment objectives are set should always be relative to the market. Where absolute rates of return are appropriate, only fixed-income investments will apply. When investments are made in equities, the objective specified should always be relative to the equity market as a whole or to an agreed-upon sector of the equity market such as large capitalization-growth stocks, utility stocks, or stocks with low price-to-book value ratios. Specifically, an investment manager should not be asked to manage a portfolio of growth stocks and to have as an objective to match or exceed the year-to-year rate of return experienced in the overall stock market.

The level of systematic risk (described as portfolio beta) chosen for a particular portfolio will lead to a specific investment objective specified in terms of a relative-to-market average rate of return over a period of several years, but not in each and every year. In fact, the results achieved by a manager who is achieving superior results over the longer term may appear, in a single period, to be less than the average expected. This is because each manager's actual results (like the market's returns) form a probability distribution with an average return and a range of returns around that average. Consequently, investment objectives should be understood and specified in terms of the mean rate of return and a distribution around that mean.

Fortunately for investment managers and their clients, modern portfolio theory provides the tools with which such probabilistic patterns can be understood conceptually and specified in practice. And this means that the evaluation of the performance of an operating portfolio can be separated from the formulation of investment policies and the determination of investment objectives—with each open for rigorous examination and either modification or reaffirmation.

Such examination should be undertaken at least once each year to determine whether recent experience calls for a change in the long-term assessment of the investment environment or the investor's constraints, and hence in the appropriate investment objective.

Evaluating Policy and Operations

Having established investment objectives that are realistic in the market context and appropriate to the time horizon and risk preferences of the investor, it is appropriate to specify the specific investment policies to be followed by the investment manager in pursuit of the stated objectives. It is in comparison to these investment policies that the operational performance of the investment manager should be measured and evaluated. For example, as noted above, it would be both unfair and misinforming to attempt an evaluation of the operational performance of a portfolio of growth stocks (or utility stocks or foreign stocks or high yield stocks) by comparing its results to the market averages because such a comparison is evaluating both policy and operations which should be examined separately. Specifically, the operational performance of a growth stock portfolio should be critiqued in comparison to an index of growth stocks or portfolios of growth stocks, while the policy of investing in growth stocks would be critiqued by examining the behavior of portfolios of growth stocks in comparison to the behavior of the stock market as a whole.

The separate examination of operations and policy is important. Otherwise, it would not be possible to determine which is contributing to or detracting from investment success. All too often, a portfolio manager has been blamed for the adverse impact of policy over which she or he had no control. And in some cases, the portfolio manager has been credited with good performance when, in fact, his operational performance was a drag on the results that should have devolved from an effective policy.

If the policy is found inappropriate, it should be changed and the new policy made explicit to the portfolio manager. If the operating performance of the portfolio manager does not conform with policy, the manager should be replaced even if such deviation from stated policy resulted in a higher rate of return than would have been earned by following stated policy. (Of course, an incompetent portfolio manager would also be replaced, but this is a different issue.)

An important advantage arising from the separation of investment policy from portfolio operations is the opportunity to control portfolio managers who, because they are human, are tempted to move away from long-term policy—particularly at the high and low points in a market cycle—by reducing portfolio risk at the low point and accepting greater risk at the high point. Segregating responsibility for investment *policy* from responsibility for portfolio *operations* is essential to the work of managing the managers—removing the "what" and obliging them to concentrate entirely on the "how"—so their natural preoccupation with the present will not corrupt the portfolio's long-term policy.

The dimensions along which investment policies can be established include: stock-bond ratios; average maturity and quality ratings—both with high-low ranges—in the bond portfolio; portfolio turnover; whether to keep the equity portfolio fully invested or to engage in market timing;[3] how widely to diversify; what risk level to establish (and whether to vary the risk level, and if so, to what limits); and in what types of stocks to invest.

The tools developed out of modern portfolio theory now make it almost easy to quantify most investment policies and to measure portfolio operation to be sure it is in conformance with policy. This is an extraordinary advantage for the gifted investor and for the serious client. It makes genuine investment counseling possible, and should make it feasible for each portfolio manager to achieve excellent performance—when compared to the realistic investment policies he should be following to achieve the agreed upon objectives of the fund.

---

[3] There is no evidence that market timing works even though most investment managers engage in it. This is a good example of the need to "manage the managers" more fully.

The Efficient Market-Random Walk Debate*

CHARLES D. KUEHNER

Director, Security Analysis and Investor Relations
American Telephone and Telegraph Co.
New York, New York

FRED B. RENWICK

Graduate School of Business Administration
New York University
New York, New York

INTRODUCTION

In recent years, no single issue has split both the academic world and the financial community as much as has the efficient market-random walk debate. Since the mid-1960s, both groups have focused a great deal of attention on the *efficiency* of the securities markets. By efficiency they did not mean how efficiently stock certificates were moved from seller to buyer, or how promptly customers' bills were collected. Rather, they meant how efficient stock prices are in reflecting value.

> Efficiency in this context means the ability of the capital markets to function so that prices of securities react rapidly to new information. Such efficiency will produce prices that are "appropriate" in terms of current knowledge, and investors will be less likely to make unwise in-

---

* The views expressed herein are those of the authors and do not necessarily represent those of the organizations with which they are affiliated.

vestments. A corollary is that investors will also be less likely to discover great bargains and thereby earn extraordinary high rates of return.[1]

The idea that market prices embody what is knowable and relevant for judging securities and adjust rapidly to such information "was considered bizarre in 1960 but by 1970 was very generally accepted by academicians and by many important financial institutions.[2] The practical significance of the efficient market hypothesis to investors is simply this: To do unusually well in selecting investments, one must have superior insight and abilities to see into the murky future better than other investors.

As the efficient market concept has developed, there has been a noticeable movement of the academicians into the fold, the so-called "true believers." Paul Samuelson seems to reflect the general academic point of view. He did admit that certain institutional investors did perform better in certain years "and there were other years when they didn't."[3] He also noted that when investigators seek to identify either the portfolio managers or methods "endowed with superior investment prowess, they are unable to find them." Samuelson challenged those who doubt the random walk concept to "dispose of it by producing brute evidence to the contrary." To be sure, there were a number of exceptions in the academic community. For example, Downes and Dyckman stated that several studies exist "whose results are not consistent with the efficient markets hypothesis in, at most, its semistrong form. Unfortunately, these studies have been largely ignored by summarizers of the efficient markets literature."[4] In the main, practicing security analysts and portfolio managers, the "nonbelievers," have been seemingly unconvinced of the merits of the efficient market hypothesis. Even Ben Graham, one of the pioneers of fundamental security analysis, raised the caveat, "It may be that the professionally managed funds are too large a part of the total picture to be able to outperform the market as a whole."[5]

---

[1] James H. Lorie, "Public Policy for American Capital Markets," (Washington, D.C.: U.S. Dept. of Treasury, 1974), p. 3. Also, for several alternative interpretations of "efficiency," see Mark E. Rubenstein, "Securities Market Efficiency in an Arrow-Debreu Economy," *American Economic Review* (December 1975), pp. 812–24.

[2] James H. Lorie and Richard Brealey, *Modern Developments in Investment Management* (New York: Praeger, 1972) p. 101.

[3] Paul A. Samuelson, "Where Are The People Who Are Beating the Market?," *Institutional Investor* (November 1975), pp. 83–88.

[4] David Downes and Thomas R. Dyckman, "A Critical Look at the Efficient Market Empirical Research Literature as It Relates to Accounting Information," *The Accounting Review* (April 1973), pp. 300–317. One significant exception to this general lack of recognition is the "Symposium on Some Anomalous Evidence regarding Market Efficiency," published as a special issue of the *Journal of Financial Economics*, vol. 6 (June–September 1978), pp. 93–330.

[5] Benjamin Graham quoted in Leopold A. Bernstein, "In Defense of Fundamental Investment Analysis," *Financial Analyst Journal* (January–February 1975), p. 58.

On the other side of the coin, William Fouse, an advocate of the efficient market concept and an investment officer of a very large bank, stated that "it is high time" for investment management to evaluate its theoretical basis, and that "in my opinion our industry has drifted to a point close to conceptual and logical bankruptcy."[6] Indeed, the growing interest in *index funds* reflects pessimism concerning the ability of conventional money managers to perform as well as the market. In this environment, it was quite natural that a vast outpouring would ensue in the academic journals, financial periodicals, and textbooks, as well as on convention platforms.

The objective of this chapter is to examine virtually all the important writings relative to the efficient markets dialogue. By doing so it is hoped that the reader will be able to form an independent judgment with respect to the merits of the numerous issues involved.

REQUIREMENTS FOR AN EFFICIENT MARKET

Kenneth Arrow, Fischer Black, Harold Demsetz, Eugene Fama, James Lorie, and others have set forth the following various requirements for an efficient market.

1. Effective Information Flow

This means that news is disseminated quickly and freely across the entire spectrum of actual and potential investors. Thus investors can react rapidly and appropriately as new information develops. Requirements from the Securities and Exchange Commission (SEC) and other regulatory bodies concerning full disclosure of material information are embodied in this concept.

2. Fully Rational Investors

This embodies the three following requirements from investors:

1. *Rational choice* among risky ventures and in risk-taking situations. Rational investors must have "attitudes of risk-aversion," which means preference for certainty and liquidity, unless a sweetner— additional return—is promised and expected as compensation for bearing additional risk.[7]

---

[6] William L. Fouse, "Practical Applications of Economic, Market, and Portfolio Theory," Stanford University Graduate School of Business, 1972 Investment Management Program (July 1972), p. 2.

[7] Kenneth Arrow, "The Role of Securities in the Optimal Allocation of Risk Bearing," *Review of Economic Studies* (April 1964), p. 91. Reprinted as chapter four in Kenneth J. Arrow, *Essays in the Theory of Risk-Bearing* (Amsterdam: North-Holland Publishing Company, 1976), pp. 121–133.

2. *Rational expectations* regarding future returns. Expectations are "rational" in that they "are essentially the same as the predictions of the relevant economic theory."[8]
3. *Rational beliefs* regarding expected returns and risks associated with the proposed investment. This means putting your money where your mouth is: willingness and ability to act upon personal assessments of the situation at hand. For a rational person—*"all* uncertainties can be reduced to *risk"*[9] and all rational persons have a rate of substitution between belief and money.[10]

3. Rapid Price Change to New Information

Prices change in response to new information: "All the information needed to predict the expected value of the next price level is reflected in the current price."[11] "Such changes are sometimes considered to constitute excessive volatility . . . when price changes are in response to new information, public policy should facilitate, rather than impede them.[12] "It is worth emphasizing again that price continuity or stability is not in itself a desirable characteristic of an efficient market. It is both undesirable and unprofitable for a specialist or market maker to resist changes in the price of a stock."[13]

Demsetz sets forth a *comparative institutional* approach—an alternative to the majority view that economic efficiency requires an ideal norm: flexible pricing in free and perfectly competitive markets. Demsetz notes that real-world institutional arrangements are not necessarily inefficient solely because of discernable deviations or discrepancies from the ideal; but rather "Users of the comparative institution approach attempt to assess which alternative real institutional arrangement seems best able to cope with the economic problem; practitioners of this approach may use an ideal norm to provide standards from which divergences are assessed for all practical alternatives of interest and select as efficient that alternative which seems most likely to minimize the divergence."[14] Achieving economic efficiency through choice

[8] John Muth, "Rational Expectations and the Theory of Price Movements," *Econometrica* (July 1961), p. 315.

[9] Daniel Ellsberg, "Risk, Ambiguity and The Savage Axioms," *The Quarterly Journal of Economics* (November 1961), p. 645.

[10] Leonard J. Savage, "Elicitation of Personal Probability and Expectations," *Journal of the American Statistical Association* (December 1971), p. 784.

[11] Stephen F. LeRoy, "Efficient Capital Markets: Comment," *The Journal of Finance* (March 1976), pp. 139–41.

[12] Lorie, "Public Policy," p. 3.

[13] Fischer Black, "Toward a Fully Automated Stock Exchange," *Financial Analysts Journal* (July–August 1971), p. 35.

[14] Harold Demsetz "Information and Efficiency: Another Viewpoint," *The Journal of Law and Economics* (April 1969), pp. 1–20.

of appropriate institutional arrangement, according to Demsetz, includes granting of monopoly and tariff privileges by governments, which seems best able to cope with the economic problem at hand. Demsetz's approach, the *comparative institutional* approach to market efficiency, uses "an ideal norm to provide standards from which divergences are assessed for all practical alternatives of interest"; then that alternative is selected and declared efficient if it seems most likely to minimize the divergence or comes closest to the ideal. Demsetz's view is that real-world institutional arrangements and markets are not necessarily inefficient solely because they might be imperfect.

4. Low Transaction Cost

Sales commissions and taxes on securities should be low enough so as not to impede either potential buyers or sellers from implementing their investment decisions.

5. Continuous Trading

The investor who desires to buy or sell can do so immediately. This focuses on the viability of the market and the close proximity of "bid" and "ask" prices. Consequently, the execution of a small trade should not ordinarily change prices significantly, if at all.

Black holds that the market should be structured in a way that large investors are not disadvantaged in dealing with many small investors. Specifically, he opines that the trading cost to the large investor should be the same for a given size transaction, whether he is trading with one large investor or many small investors. Admittedly the cost of handling the latter would be higher. However, Black contends that the extra cost of handling many small orders should be borne by the small investors who are responsible for such costs.

In commenting on some of the preconditions for efficiency. Fama notes that these "are not descriptive of markets met in practice" but that "these conditions, while sufficient for market efficiency, are not necessary." For example, he states that as long as transactions take account of all available information, even large costs do not necessarily mean that when transactions do occur, prices will not fully reflect available information. Also, "even disagreement among investors as to the significance of given information does not imply market inefficiency unless some investors are consistently able to make better evaluation of such information than is implicit in market prices."[15]

Finally, Sullivan underscores Arrow's original proposition that effi-

---

[15] Eugene F. Fama, "Efficient Capital Markets: A Review of Theory and Empirical Work," *Journal of Finance* (May 1970), pp. 383–417 *and* Eugene F. Fama, *Foundations of Finance* (New York: Basic Books, 1976), pp. 133–68.

cient markets can—but not necessarily must—imply optimal allocations of economic goods and services. By optimal allocations we mean that resources are allocated in such a way that no other choice will make every individual better off.

Sullivan, after investigating stock price behavior of corporations possessing considerable market power, questioned the exact meaning of the term "efficient capital market," and concluded: "even if the capital market is efficient in that it correctly values shares based on all available information, . . . it does not imply that the existence of an efficient capital market is a sufficient condition for the overall optimum performance of the economy or even for the optimum allocation of capital within the economy." Therefore, the Capital Asset Pricing Model views the capital market as efficient in that it values the firm given all available information; it is not efficient in that it necessarily allocates capital to firms which will employ it in the socially optimum manner."[16]

SITUATION PRIOR TO EMERGENCE OF THE EFFICIENT MARKET CONCEPT

It would be helpful, before proceeding with a review of empirical research on the question of the efficient markets hypothesis to delineate it from the two basically different schools of stock price evaluation into which random walk emerged in the early 1960s.

Technical Analysis

Technical analysis is *internally* oriented. In this, technicians endeavor to predict future price levels of stocks by examining one or many series of past data *from the market itself.*

> The basic assumption of all the chartist or technical theories is that history tends to repeat itself, i.e., past patterns of price behavior in individual securities will tend to recur in the future. Thus the way to predict stock prices (and, of course, increase one's potential gains) is to develop a familiarity with past patterns of price behavior in order to recognize situations of likely recurrence.
>
> The techniques of the chartist have always been surrounded by a certain degree of mysticism, however, and as a result most market professionals have found them suspect. Thus it is probably safe to say that the pure chartist is relatively rare among stock market analysts.[17]

Pinches states that technical analysts "believe that the value of a stock depends primarily on supply and demand and may have very

---

[16] Timothy G. Sullivan, "A Note on Market Power and Returns to Stockholders," *The Review of Economics and Statistics* (February 1977), pp. 108–13.

[17] Eugene F. Fama, "Random Walks in Stock Market Prices," *Financial Analysts Journal* (September–October 1965), pp. 55–59.

little relationship to any intrinsic value."[18] He summarizes a general statement of technical analysis, including:

1. Market prices are determined by supply and demand.
2. At any moment, supply and demand reflect hundreds of rational and irrational considerations: facts, opinions, moods, and guesses about the future.
3. Disregarding minor fluctuations, market prices move in trends which persist over an appreciable length of time.
4. Changes in trend represent a shift in balance between supply and demand. However caused, these shifts are detectable "sooner or later in the action of the market itself."

As we will see below, chartists assume that successive price changes in individual securities are *dependent*. This means that future stock prices are importantly dependent upon patterns of past price changes reflecting the shift between supply and demand. Among the many techniques used by technical analysts are:

1. Charting—past prices, e.g., Dow theory.
2. Determining—major trends (the tides), intermediate corrections (the waves), and minor fluctuations (ripples).
3. Share volume trends—rising-falling, and so on.
4. Combined volume and price charts.
5. Point and figure charts—channels, wedges, head and shoulders, triple tops, triple bottoms, and so on.
6. Support areas versus resistance levels.
7. Breadth of market—advance-decline lines.
8. Odd lots—purchases versus sales.
9. Odd-lot volume related to round-lot volume.
10. Odd-lot short sales.

Charles Jones, Donald Tuttle, and Cherrill Heaton concluded that:

> Many of the technical indicators . . . are intuitively appealing. They all have followers who claim to have used them successfully. Yet they do not stand up well when subjected to rigorous, unemotional testing. In brief, we could not recommend investing a nickel on the basis of any single technical indicator or combination of indicators.[19]

Jerome Cohen, Edward Zinbarg, and Arthur Zeikel stated that:

> we can understand the characterization of technical analysis as "crystal ball gazing." But we consider this characterization to be rather unfortunate, for it casts aside the good with the bad. The more scholarly and

---

[18] George E. Pinches, "The Random Walk Hypothesis and Technical Analysis," *Financial Analysts Journal* (March–April 1970), pp. 104–10.

[19] Charles P. Jones, Donald L. Tuttle, Cherrill P. Heaton, *Essentials of Modern Investments* (New York: The Ronald Press 1977), p. 279.

sophisticated technical analyst uses his tools with a proper sense of pro-portion . . . if a stock looks attractive to him on technical grounds he probes into its fundamental . . . he is certainly not unmindful of earnings growth, of values, or of the impact of business cycles.[20]

The broad consensus of several different technical indicators may be helpful in understanding market psychology for whatever value that nebulous term might have. Roberts states:

Perhaps no one in the financial world completely ignores technical analy-sis—indeed, its terminology is ingrained in market reporting—and some rely intensively on it. Technical analysis includes many approaches, most requiring a good deal of subjective judgment in applications. In part these approaches are purely empirical; in part they are based on analogy with physical processes, such as tides and waves.[21]

Fundamental Analysis

Fundamental analysis is *externally* oriented. "The fundamentalist never measures the attractiveness of a stock by the fickle standards of the market place, but rather determines the price at which one is willing to invest and then turns to the market place to see if the stock is selling at the required price."[22] The fundamental analyst focuses on the intrinsic value of a stock.

The assumption of the fundamental analysis approach is that any point in time an individual security has an intrinsic value (or in the terms of the economist, an equilibrium price) which depends on the earnings potential of the security. The earning potential of the security depends in turn on such fundamental factors as quality of management, outlook for the industry and the economy, etc.

Through a careful study of these fundamental factors the analyst should, in principle, be able to determine whether the actual price of a security is above or below its intrinsic value. If actual prices tend to move toward intrinsic values, then attempting to determine the intrinsic value of a security is equivalent to making a prediction of its future price; and this is the essence of the predictive procedure implicit in fundamental analysis.[23]

Fundamental analysis embraces many facets of a company in devel-oping an evaluaton of intrinsic value. Among the factors considered are:

---

[20] Jerome B. Cohen, Edward D. Zinbarg, and Arthur Zeikel, *Investment Analysis and Portfolio Management* (Homewood, Ill., Richard D. Irwin, 1977), p. 586. © 1977 by Richard D. Irwin, Inc.

[21] Harry V. Roberts, "Stock Market Patterns and Financial Analysis: Methodological Suggestion," *Journal of Finance* (March 1959), pp. 1–10.

[22] Frank E. Block, "The Place of Book Value in Stock Evaluation," *Financial Analysts Journal* (March–April 1964), p. 29.

[23] Fama, "Random Walks," pp. 56–57.

1. Growth: revenues, expenses, net income, earnings per share, assets.
2. Management: record, innovation, motivation, plans, long-range objectives, and philosophy.
3. Earnings rates: on total capital, on equity capital, objectives.
4. Capital structure: policy, credit ratings, debt ratio objectives, fixed charge coverage.
5. Dividends: payment policy, past growth, percent pay out.
6. Accounting policies: reserves, inventory policies, depreciation policies, tax normalization versus flow through.
7. Ratios: acid test ratio, quick ratio, current assets to current liabilities.
8. Marketing: market share, short- and long-term strategy, competition.
9. Labor: labor relations policies and environment, labor cost trends, labor intensity.
10. Economic environment: inflation, sensitivity to business cycles, long-term trends of industry, raw materials situation.
11. Technology: research and development, plant obsolescence, patent protection, productivity.
12. Social and political environment: government regulatory environment, tax situation, geographic decentralization.
13. Earnings per share: growth rates, stability, outlook.
14. Market price per share: growth, volatility, price-earnings multiple.
15. Per share: cash flow, book value, intrinsic value.
16. Risk: subjective evaluation.

THREE FORMS OF THE EFFICIENT MARKET— RANDOM WALK HYPOTHESIS

We have already touched upon the efficient market concept and its preconditions, i.e., the requirements for its efficiency. In its present stage of development (1980), the efficient market hypothesis takes three different forms: weak, semistrong, and strong. Each form stems from a different level of information or knowledge concerning a stock:

1. The Weak Form

This is the oldest statement of the hypothesis. It holds that present stock market prices reflect all known information with respect to past stock prices, trends, and volumes. Weak form tests analyze whether trading rules based only on historical price and volume data can lead to unusual profits. It is asserted, such past data cannot be used to predict future stock prices.

Reflecting the historical development of this form, which focused on various statistical tests for random movement of successive stock prices, it has also been characterized as the *random walk hypothesis*. The weak form implies that knowledge of the past patterns of stock prices does not aid investors to attain improved performance. Random walk theorists view stock prices as moving randomly about a trend line which is based on rational expectations regarding fundamental factors.[24] Hence they contend that (1) analyzing past data does not permit the technician to forecast the movement of prices about the trend line and (2) new information affecting stock prices enters the market in random fashion, i.e., tomorrow's news cannot be predicted nor can future stock price movements be attributable to that news.

In its present context, the weak form of the efficient market hypothesis is a direct challenge to the chartist or technician. It was the earliest focus of interest and has received by far the greatest attention in the literature.

2. The Semistrong Form

This form holds that current market prices *instantaneously* reflect all publicly known information. Semistrong form tests analyze whether all publicly available information and announcements (quarterly financial reports, public disclosures, and the like) are quickly and fully reflected in market prices. The semistrong form holds that such data cannot be analyzed successfully to achieve superior investment results.

This form of the efficient market hypothesis reflects a substantially greater level of knowledge and market efficiency than the weak form. The second stage, or level, of information content includes all knowledge which is available from such publications as annual reports, quarterly reports, press releases, and news flashes on "the broad tape," i.e., the Dow Jones news wire service. The semistrong form holds that, since such public information is already embedded, i.e., fully discounted, in current stock prices, analyzing such data cannot produce superior investment performance.

The shift from the weak, i.e., random walk, form to the semistrong form of the efficient market hypothesis represented a quantum jump.

> This stronger assertion has proved to be especially unacceptable and unpalatable to the financial community, since it suggests the fruitlessness of efforts to earn superior rates of return by the analysis of all public information. Although some members of the financial community were willing to accept the implications of the weaker assertion about the randomness of price changes and thereby to give up technical analysis, almost no members of the community were too willing to accept the implications of the stronger form and thereby to give up fundamental analysis.[25]

---

[24] Sidney Robbins, *The Securities Markets* (New York: Free Press, 1966), pp. 44–47.

[25] James H. Lorie and Mary T. Hamilton, *The Stock Market—Theories and Evidence* (Homewood, Ill.: Richard D. Irwin, 1973), p. 81. © 1973 by Richard D. Irwin, Inc.

It is crystal clear that the semistrong form represents a direct challenge to traditional financial analysis based on the evaluation of publicly available data.

3. The Strong Form

This form holds that present market prices reflect all information that is *knowable* about a company, including all relevant information that might be developed by exhaustive study, including interviews with corporate managements, by numerous fully competent institutional security analysts.

Strong form tests investigate whether professional traders, insiders or professional forecasting services can develop unique insights or privileged information which can be used for earning significantly large profits. The strong form holds that consistently superior investment performance is not possible.

The strong form ratcheted the efficient market hypothesis up to a still higher level of information and knowledge. In large measure, the strong form reflects the intense competition that exists among the nation's leading financial institutions. These institutions have staffs of security analysts who are top graduates of the nation's leading business schools, are highly motivated, and are held to high standards of professional performance. Security analysts who can outperform their peers in this environment move to higher positions in the investment analysis and management hierarchy. Those who fail to meet these lofty standards tend to move to other pursuits.

> . . . even if half of the professional money managers outperform the maket as a whole, the market conforms to the strong form of efficiency as long as they do not generate superior results consistently. That is, in a strong form market, up to half of the time money managers could outperform the market as a whole, if only during the remainder of the time their performance was inferior to the general market.[26]

The strong form of the random walk hypothesis constitutes a direct challenge to the most knowledgeable segment of the investment community: the institutional investor.

This concludes our capsule review of the efficient market—random walk hypothesis. Its significance to the practicing security analysts is pointed up in the words of Lorie and Richard Brealey, two founding fathers of the efficient market hypothesis, who summarize their views in these words:

> It is extremely unlikely, in principle, that the efficient market hypothesis is strictly true, particularly in its strongest form. For example, as long

---

[26] See Dan Dorfman, "Why Can't Research Directors Hold Their Jobs?" *Institutional Investor* (October 1973), pp. 48–50 ff.

as information is not wholly free, one might expect investors to require some offsetting gain before they are willing to purchase it. Nor does the empirical evidence justify unqualified acceptance of the efficient-market hypothesis even in its weakest form. The important question, therefore, is not whether the theory is universally ture, but whether it is sufficiently correct to provide useful insights into market behavior. There is now overwhelming evidence to suggest that the random walk hypothesis is such a close approximation to reality that technical analysis cannot provide any guidance to the investment manager. When one turns to the stronger forms of the hypothesis, the evidence becomes less voluminous and the correspondence between theory and reality less exact. Nevertheless, the overriding impression is that of a highly competitive and efficient marketplace in which the opportunities for superior performance are rare.[27]

I

THE WEAK FORM OF THE EFFICIENT MARKET-RANDOM WALK HYPOTHESIS: SURVEY OF EVIDENCE

Overview

The earliest documentation in this century of the efficient market-random walk model was recorded in 1900 by Louis Bachelier in his Ph.D. dissertation, written under the guidance of the world-famous French mathematician, H. Poincaré.[28] Bachelier's work dealt primarily with commodity prices and government bonds, but the principles are readily adaptable to other securities such as stocks. Bachelier concluded that past price patterns provided no basis for predicting future price changes.

Except for the endeavors of Holbrook Working of Stanford University on commodity prices and Alfred Cowles and Herbert Jones on stock prices, the efficient market-random walk concept was largely neglected until the mid-1950s.[29]

The first work reviewed in this chapter is that of Kendall, written in 1953. Kendall focused on serial correlation in an effort to determine whether weekly changes in stock market prices could be predicted from past data. His findings were essentially negative. Subsequently, Weintraub tested serial correlation over shorter periods, i.e., daily

---

[27] James H. Lorie and Richard Brealey, *Modern Developments in Investment Management* (New York: Praeger, 1972), p. 102.

[28] Louis Bachelier, "Theory of Speculation," in Paul Cootner, *The Random Character of Stock Market Prices* (Cambridge: MIT Press, 1964), pp. 17–78.

[29] Holbrook Working, "A Random—Difference Series for Use in the Analysis of Time Series," *Journal of the American Statistical Association* (March 1934), pp. 11–24; and Alfred Cowles and Herbert F. Jones, "Some a Posteriori Probabilities in Stock Market Action," *Econometrica* (July 1937), pp. 280–94.

price changes. Weintraub concluded that, under certain assumptions used in his study, serial correlation did indeed exist. Contrariwise, M. F. M. Osborne, a distinguished astronomer at the United States Naval Research Laboratory in Washington, D.C., applied computer techniques to daily stock price changes and determined that stock prices changes comport to "Brownian movement of small particles suspended in liquid." (Osborne's theory of Brownian movement is discussed later in this chapter.)

Granger and Morgenstern attacked the serial correlation question with a sophisticated mathematical tool, spectral analysis. They likewise found that the simple random walk model obtained for most time bands. However, there were some indications of nonrandom behavior in time spans of 24 months or longer.

Fama, one of the most diligent students of the efficient market-random walk hypothesis, also tested serial correlation of stock price changes over a period ranging from one to ten days. His extensive work confirmed the negative findings of the earlier researchers. Roberts pioneered an interesting approach: constructing hypothetical stock price charts from random numbers. He found that the Dow Jones Index of 30 industrial stocks could be quite closely replicated from random numbers.

Cheng and Deets also tested the Dow Jones 30 industrials for successive price changes, using a portfolio "rebalancing" strategy. However, they concluded, even after critical comment by Goldman, that the random walk theory is not supported by the evidence, since their rebalanced portfolios exceeded random portfolios by a substantial margin.

Additional tests of the efficient market-random walk hypothesis were conducted by Fama using *daily* runs, i.e., successive price changes in a similar direction. Using the 30 individual stocks in the Dow Jones Industrial Index, he found overwhelming evidence of the random distribution of price changes. Shiskin also tested runs in the Standard & Poor's 500 (S&P 500) stock price index, using *monthly* data for the index as a whole. He concluded that the evidence does not support the random walk theory.

Alexander pioneered trading rules or *filters* for daily price changes and determined that prices were affected by something other than a random walk. Cootner also tested filters and found that stock prices behaved as a random walk "with reflecting barriers."

Levy tested the random walk theory, using a *relative strength* strategy for 200 New York Stock Exchange (NYSE) stocks. He concluded that "the theory of random walks has been refuted." Jensen and Bennington used the same approach for all NYSE stocks for a longer period and found to the contrary. Jen evaluated both of these relative strength studies. While essentially sympathetic to the random walk in the longer run, Jen declared that relative strength did capture the essence of market imperfections in shorter time spans.

Analysis of Studies

Kendall—Serial Correlation: The Next Move. Maurice Kendall tested the independence of weekly closing market prices of 22 indices of British industry groups, e.g., oil, iron, and steel, for the 1928–38 period. He determined that it was preferable not to attempt to eliminate long-term trends and examine only the residuals. He found that, broadly speaking, random changes from one week to the next "are so large as to swamp any systematic effect which may be present," and that "such serial correlation as is present in these series is so weak as to dispose at once of any possibility of being able to use them for prediction."[30] He noted, however, that

> it may be, of course, that a series of *individual* share prices would behave differently; the point remains open for inquiry. But the aggregates are very slightly correlated and some of them virtually wandering. Investors can, perhaps, make money on the Stock Exchange, but not apparently by watching price movements and coming in on what looks like a good thing. But it is unlikely that anything I say or demonstrate will destroy the illusion that the outside investor can make money by playing the markets, so let us leave him to his own devices.

Kendall ranked the various series according to the magnitude of first serial correlation—as a measure of internal correlation of each series. He noted that the "aggregate series," e.g., all classes of stock, total distribution, total manufacturing, had greater internal correlation and significantly greater serial correlation than the constituent series, i.e., the several piece-parts. In part, Kendall found that this could be attributed to lag correlations between different series in the aggregate series: "Whatever the reason, the existence of these serial correlations in averaged series is rather disturbing. The so-called "cycles" appearing in such series may not be due to internal elements or structured features at all, but to the correlations between disturbances acting on the constituent parts of the aggregative series."

Weintraub—Serial Correlation: The Next Move. Robert Weintraub, employing serial correlation, used Kendall's concept of "the next move," in part, but applied it to a variable time period within the next day. Weintraub noted that professional traders earned such substantial incomes from speculating on short-term price movements that seats for floor traders were valued at several thousand dollars. This he found difficult to reconcile with the random walk hypothesis.

---

[30] Maurice G. Kendall, "The Analysis of Economic Time-Series—Part 1: Prices," *Journal of the Royal Statistical Society* 96 (1953): 11–25.

"These men, in effect, earn their incomes by betting *against* the applicability of the random walk hypothesis to price moves of less than 5 percent."[31]

The specific techniques used by Weintraub may be explained by the following example. If a stock price moved up from the closing price on Monday to the closing price on Tuesday, the next move (on Wednesday) was assumed to be up (+). Conversely, if the Monday to Tuesday closing price showed a downtrend, the next move was assumed to be down (−). However, in an effort to match the real world speculator's opportunities and avoid the mechanical approach of using daily closing prices, Wednesday's prices were either the *highest* during the day if the Monday–Tuesday trend was up (+) or the *lowest* during the day on Wednesday if the Monday–Tuesday prices were down (−).

Thus, speculators betting on the existence of trends would buy at Tuesday's close when the Monday–Tuesday was up (+) and sell during the day on Wednesday at a higher price, hopefully the day's high. Alternatively, if they believe in a zig-zag pattern, they would sell short on Tuesday and cover during the day on Wednesday, hopefully at the day's low price.

Table 1 depicts data for one of the time periods cited by Weintraub. Weintraub summarized his results as follows:

1. Using Kendall's definition of the next move, serial correlation of 0.31 was found.
2. Using the definition of the next move that would be employed by speculators betting on a zig-zag pattern, i.e., against the trend, serial correlation was −0.61.
3. Using the definition of the next move that professional traders would use betting on a monotonic trend, serial correlation was 0.69.

Weintraub concluded:

> One of the implications of my results is that speculators have opportunity to make capital gains. A corollary implication is that it is an error to infer, as many have done, from the lack of lagged serial correlation between first differences of closing prices that speculations have little or no opportunity to win. Instead, it would appear that this lack of serial correlation between first differences of closing prices simply means that speculators who are supposed to smooth out price movements over time are doing their job well.[32]

Osborne—Brownian Motion. M. F. M. Osborne investigated whether stock price changes comport to Brownian movement. This is a law of the physical sciences governing movements of small particles suspended in liquids. He analyzed changes in daily closing prices of

[31] Robert E. Weintraub, "On Speculative Prices and Random Walks: A Denial," *Journal of Finance* (March 1963), pp. 59–66.

[32] Ibid., p. 66.

Table 1
"The Next Move" Calculated from Dow Jones Industrials (30 Common Stocks) Daily Prices for June 1–July 31, 1962

| | | | | | "The Next Move" | |
| | | | | | For Speculators' Betting | |
Date	High	Low	Close	Under Kendall's Definition	On Trend	Against Trend
June						
1	616.54	603.58	611.07	− 2.31*	—	—
4	608.82	591.37	593.68	−17.37	−19.68	2.23
5	603.37	584.12	594.96	1.28	− 9.56	9.69
6	611.82	595.50	603.91	8.95	16.86	0.54
7	608.14	599.27	602.20	1.71	4.23	− 4.64
8	607.30	598.64	601.61	−00.59	− 3.56	5.10
11	603.20	592.66	595.17	− 6.44	− 8.95	1.59
12	593.83	580.11	580.94	−14.23	−15.06	− 1.34
13	586.42	572.20	574.04	− 6.90	− 8.74	5.48
14	579.14	560.28	563.00	−11.04	−13.76	5.10
15	579.90	556.09	578.18	15.18	− 6.91	16.90
18	583.08	567.05	574.21	− 3.97	4.90	−11.13
19	575.21	566.59	571.61	− 2.60	− 7.62	1.00
20	574.59	561.28	563.08	− 8.53	−10.33	2.98
21	561.87	549.15	550.49	−12.59	−13.93	− 1.21
22	551.99	537.56	539.19	−11.30	−12.93	1.50
25	541.24	524.55	536.77	− 2.42	−14.64	2.05
26	548.61	533.46	535.76	− 1.01	− 3.31	11.84
27	539.28	528.73	536.98	1.22	− 7.03	3.52
28	559.32	541.49	557.35	20.37	22.34	4.51
29	569.06	555.22	561.28	3.93	11.71	− 2.13
July						
2	576.63	557.31	573.75	12.47	15.35	− 3.97
3	582.99	570.53	579.48	5.73	9.24	− 3.22
5	586.30	577.39	583.87	4.39	6.82	− 2.09
6	582.58	571.28	576.17	− 7.70	− 1.29	−12.59
9	582.28	569.65	580.82	4.65	− 6.52	6.11
10	599.02	583.50	586.01	5.19	18.20	2.68
11	590.94	580.36	589.06	3.05	4.93	− 5.65
12	596.59	586.68	590.27	1.21	7.53	− 2.38
13	592.99	583.87	590.19	− 0.08	2.72	− 6.40
16	591.23	582.41	588.10	− 2.09	− 7.78	1.04
17	588.77	576.59	577.85	−10.25	−11.51	0.66
18	577.39	568.02	571.24	− 6.61	− 9.83	− 0.46
19	578.68	568.98	573.16	1.92	− 2.26	7.44
20	579.86	570.78	577.18	4.02	6.70	− 2.38
23	582.24	574.50	577.47	0.29	5.06	− 2.68
24	579.31	572.02	574.12	− 3.35	1.84	− 5.45
25	567.55	568.10	574.67	0.55	− 6.02	2.43
26	582.87	574.08	579.61	4.94	8.20	− 0.59
27	586.80	577.14	585.00	5.39	7.19	− 2.47
30	593.03	583.87	591.44	6.44*	8.03	− 1.13
31	601.15	591.78	597.93	6.49*	9.71	0.34

* The first number in this column, −2.31, is not a number in the series termed "The Next Move under Kendall's Definition". But this number is the first number in the previous trend series. Conversely, the last number in this column, 6.49, is not a number in the previous trend series but is the last number in the series termed "The Next Move under Kendall's Definition." The last number in the previous trend series is the next to last number in this column, 6.44.

Source: After Weintraub, "On Speculative Prices," p. 65, Table 2.

all NYSE stocks and found them nearly normally distributed. Osborne concluded that "it may be a consequence of many independent random variables contributing to the changes in values.[33] This he attributed to the tradeoff of seller and buyer, with both making logical decisions in the market. He also tested price changes of stocks over longer periods: weekly, monthly, and so on, up to 12 years. He concluded that price changes were randomly distributed.

He then examined Cowles's stock price data, some of it going as far back as 1831. Osborne postulated a certain linkage in price changes for stocks akin to earlier studies of changes in commodities:

> To put it another way, the NYSE is a market for money in exactly the same sense that it is for the securities of any given corporation. Certainly for the era covered in the Cowles' data, a dollar represented a share in the assets of Fort Knox in exactly the same sense that a stock certificate of General Motors represented a share in the assets of that corporation. Under conditions of trading at statistical equilibrium, why should these changes in value not diffuse in the same way.[34]

Granger and Morgenstern—Spectral Analysis. Granger and Morgenstern used spectral analysis, a highly sophisticated statistical technique, to test the random walk hypothesis. They examined some 700 weeks of SEC price series for various industries, e.g., motor vehicles, utilities, air transport, for years 1939–61; American Tobacco, General Foods, American Can, Woolworth, Chrysler, and U.S. Steel for the period 1946–60; the S&P's 500 Stock Index 1915–61 and the Dow Jones industrials for 1915–61.

Their work indicated that, after eliminating trend, the simple random walk model is upheld "for the large majority of the frequency bands." However, "it thus seems that the model, although extremely successful in explaining most of the spectral shape, does not adequately explain the strong long run (24 months or more) components of the series. Nothing definite can be said about the business cycle component of these series as they cover too short a time span."[35]

In pursuing the business cycle question further, S&P's index was analyzed for the 1875–1952 period and the Dow Jones index for 1915–58. A small business cycle component was seen at 40 months, but was not found to be statistically significant. They also noted that "The whole problem of studying business cycle indicators (impact on stock prices) is bedeviled with the vagueness of the concept of the business

---

[33] M. F. M. Osborne, "Brownian Motion in the Stock Market," *Operations Research,* March–April 1959, pp. 145–73. Also, see M. F. M. Osborne, *The Stock Market and Finance from a Physicist's Viewpoint* (Temple Hills, Maryland: Dr. Osborne, 1977).

[34] Ibid., p. 165.

[35] Clive W. J. Granger and Oskar Morgenstern, "Spectral Analysis of New York Stock Market Prices," *Kyklos* (1963), pp. 1–27.

cycle movement of the economy and the huge inaccuracies known to exist in many series used to indicate cycles."[36]

It was also pointed out that,

> To the extent that stock prices perform random walks, the short term investor (ignoring transaction costs) engaged in a fair gamble, which is slightly better than playing roulette, since that game is biased in favor of the bank. For the long term investor, i.e., one who invests at the very minimum for a year, the problem is to identify the phases of the different long run components of the overall movement of the market. The evidence of "cycles" obtained in our studies is so weak that "cyclical investment" is at best only marginally worthwhile. Even this small margin will rapidly disappear as it is being made use of.[37]

Fama—Serial Correlation: 1 to 10 Days Lag. Eugene Fama tested the independence of successive price changes by measuring serial correlation for the 30 individual stocks in the Dow Jones Industrial Index in the five years ending 1962.[38] Thus, if a company's data showed a high degree of correlation, it would suggest systematic dependence and might be used to predict future prices. Contrariwise, a low correlation coefficient would indicate that prior price changes cannot successfully be used to predict future prices. Table 2 summarizes coefficients of correlation between successive price changes for each of the 30 companies.

Column 1 of Table 2 shows that the correlation coefficients are generally close to zero and in eight cases out of 30 it is negative. Since the successive one-day price changes were unrelated, Fama also tested for possible lagged correlation. Thus, the correlation for each day's price change with that following by two days is shown in Column 2; the three-day lag, in Column 3; up to a lag of 10 days—shown in Column 10. Statistically there is virtually no relationship in these daily price changes. The average serial correlation coefficient shown in the bottom of the table ranges from −.04 to .03.

Fama tested correlation of price changes for adjacent periods of 1, 4, 9, and 16 days each. Table 3 shows that there is no evidence of significant linear dependence of price changes between these days. The average serial correlation coefficients are −.04, −.05 and +.01. He notes that "Looking hard, though, one can probably find evidence of statistically significant linear dependence in the table. But, with 1,200–1,700 observations per stock on a daily basis, statistically significant deviations from zero covariance are not necessarily a basis for

---

[36] Ibid., p. 16.

[37] Ibid., p. 30.

[38] Eugene F. Fama, "The Behavior of Stock Market Prices," *Journal of Business* (January 1965), pp. 34–105.

Table 2
Correlation Coefficients: Daily Price Changes versus Lagged Price Changes for Each Dow Jones Industrial Company

					Lag in Days					
Stock	(1)	(2)	(3)	(4)	(5)	(6)	(7)	(8)	(9)	(10)
Allied Chemical	.02	−.04	.01	−.00	.03	.00	−.02	−.03	−.02	−.01
Alcoa	.12	.04	−.01	.02	−.02	.01	.02	.01	−.00	−.03
American Can	−.09	−.02	.03	−.07	−.02	−.01	.02	.03	−.05	−.04
AT&T	−.04	−.10	.00	.03	.01	−.01	.00	.03	−.01	.01
American Tobacco ...	.11	−.11	−.06	−.07	.01	−.01	.01	.05	.04	.04
Anaconda	.07	−.06	−.05	−.00	.00	−.04	.01	.02	−.01	−.06
Bethlehem Steel	.01	−.07	.01	.02	−.05	−.10	−.01	.00	−.00	−.02
Chrysler	.01	−.07	−.02	−.01	−.02	.01	.04	.06	−.04	.02
DuPont	.01	−.03	.06	.03	−.00	−.05	.02	.01	−.03	.00
Eastman Kodak	.03	.01	−.03	.01	−.02	.01	.01	.01	.01	.00
General Electric	.01	−.04	−.02	.03	−.00	.00	−.01	.01	−.00	.01
General Foods	.06	−.00	.05	.00	−.02	−.05	−.01	−.01	−.02	−.02
General Motors	−.00	−.06	−.04	−.01	−.04	−.01	.02	.01	−.02	.01
Goodyear	−.12	.02	−.04	.04	−.00	−.00	.04	.01	−.02	.01
Int'l. Harvester	−.02	−.03	−.03	.04	−.05	−.02	−.00	.00	−.05	−.02
Int'l. Nickel	.10	−.03	−.02	.02	.03	.06	−.04	−.01	−.02	.03
Int'l. Paper	.05	−.01	−.06	.05	.05	−.00	−.03	−.02	−.00	−.02
Johns Manville	.01	−.04	−.03	−.02	−.03	−.08	.04	.02	−.04	.03
Owens Illinois	−.02	−.08	−.05	.07	.09	−.04	.01	−.04	.07	−.04
Procter & Gamble ...	.10	−.01	−.01	.01	−.02	.02	.01	−.01	−.02	−.02
Sears	.10	.03	.03	.03	.01	−.05	−.01	−.01	−.01	−.01
Standard Oil (Cal.) ...	.03	−.03	−.05	−.03	−.05	−.03	−.01	.07	−.05	−.04
Standard Oil (N.J.) ...	.01	−.12	.02	.01	−.05	−.02	−.02	−.03	−.07	.08
Swift & Co.	−.00	−.02	−.01	.01	.06	.01	−.04	.01	.01	.00
Texaco	.09	−.05	−.02	−.02	−.02	−.01	.03	.03	−.01	.01
Union Carbide	.11	−.01	.04	.05	−.04	−.03	.00	−.01	−.05	−.04
United Aircraft	.01	−.03	−.02	−.05	−.07	−.05	.05	.04	.02	−.02
U.S. Steel	.04	−.07	.01	.01	.01	−.02	.04	.04	−.02	−.04
Westinghouse	−.03	−.02	−.04	−.00	.00	−.05	−.02	.01	−.01	.01
Woolworth	.03	−.02	.02	.01	.01	−.04	−.01	.00	−.09	−.01
Average	.03	−.04	−.01	.01	−.01	−.02	.00	.01	−.02	−.01

Source: After Fama, "Behavior of Stock Market Prices."

rejecting the efficient market model."[39] He noted that, with a standard error of approximately .03, a correlation of .06 implies that a linear relationship explains only .36 percent of the variation in price changes.

Roberts—Random Numbers.   Roberts noted that:

Technical analysis includes many different approaches, most requiring a good deal of subjective judgment in application. In part these approaches are purely empirical; in part they are based on analogy with physical processes, such as tides and waves. . . . it seems curious that there has not been widespread recognition among financial analysts that the patterns of technical analysis may be little, if anything, more than

---

[39] Eugene F. Fama, "Efficient Capital Markets: A Review of Theory and Empirical Work," *Journal of Finance* (May 1970), pp. 383–417.

Table 3
Correlation Coefficients for 1-, 4-, 9- and 16-Day Interval Price
Changes for Each Dow Jones Industrial Company

	Interval in Days			
Stock	*(1)*	*(4)*	*(9)*	*(16)*
Allied Chemical	.02	.03	−.09	−.12
Alcoa	.12	.10	−.11	−.04
American Can	−.09	−.12	−.06	.03
AT&T	−.04	−.01	−.01	−.00
American Tobacco	.11	−.18	.03	.01
Anaconda	.07	−.07	−.13	.20
Bethlehem Steel	.01	−.12	−.15	.11
Chrysler	.01	.06	−.03	.04
DuPont	.01	.07	−.04	−.06
Eastman Kodak	.03	−.01	−.05	−.02
General Electric	.01	.02	−.00	.00
General Foods	.06	−.01	−.14	−.10
General Motors	−.00	−.13	.01	−.03
Goodyear	−.12	.00	−.04	.03
Int'l. Harvester	−.02	−.07	−.24	.12
Int'l. Nickel	.10	.04	.12	.04
Int'l. Paper	.05	.06	−.00	−.01
Johns Manville	.01	−.07	−.00	.00
Owens Illinois	−.02	−.01	.00	−.02
Procter & Gamble	.10	−.01	.10	.08
Sears	.10	−.07	−.11	.04
Standard Oil (Cal.)	.03	−.14	−.05	.04
Standard Oil (N.J.)	.01	−.11	−.08	−.12
Swift & Co.	−.00	−.07	.12	−.20
Texaco	.09	−.05	−.05	−.18
Union Carbide	.11	.05	−.10	.12
United Aircraft	.01	−.19	−.19	−.04
U.S. Steel	.04	−.01	−.06	.24
Westinghouse	−.03	−.10	−.14	.07
Woolworth	.03	−.03	−.11	.04
Average	.03	−.04	−.05	.01

Source: After Fama, "Behavior of Stock Market Prices."

a statistical artifact. . . . one possible explanation is that the usual method of graphing stock prices gives a picture of successive *levels,* rather than of *changes,* and levels can give an artificial appearance of pattern or trend.[40]

Using a series of random numbers, Roberts developed random price changes for data with a mean of plus 0.5 and a standard deviation of 5.0. This represents a hypothetical year's price changes, i.e., data for 52 weeks were developed and plotted on Figure 1.

The numbers were then cumulatively added, starting from a level of 450—relatively close to the range of the Dow Jones Industrial Index

---

[40] Harry V. Roberts, "Stock Market Patterns and Financial Analysis: Methodological Suggestions," *Journal of Finance* (March 1959), p. 1.

Figure 1
Simulated Price Changes Based on Random Numbers

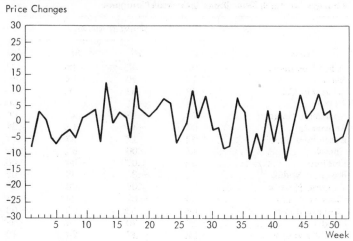

Source: After Roberts, "Stock Market Patterns."

Figure 2
Simulated Dow Jones Industrial Index Based on Random Numbers

Source: After Roberts, "Stock Market Patterns."

Figure 3
Actual Price Changes Dow Jones Industrial Index

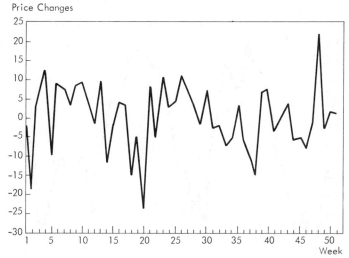

Source: After Roberts, "Stock Market Patterns."

at that time. This is shown in Figure 2. To a casual observer of the stock market, Figure 2 is quite realistic even to the head-and-shoulders top.

Figures 3 and 4 give the actual data for the Dow Jones Industrial Index for 1956. Roberts concluded that "the general resemblance between Figures 3 and 4 and Figures 1 and 2 is unmistakable."

Cheng and Deets—Rebalancing. Cheng and Deets tested the efficient market-random walk hypothesis by analyzing the independence of successive price changes for the 30 companies in the Dow Jones Industrial Index.[41] To do this, they compared the portfolio return under the buy and hold strategy (B&H) with the portfolio return under rebalancing strategy (RB) over a 31-year period 1937–69.

Under the B&H strategy, a fixed portfolio is purchased at the beginning of the period and held until the terminal period. Under RB strategy, a portfolio is purchased at an initial period and rebalanced at the end of each one-week holding period. Rebalancing means the selling of some portion of the securities that have experienced superior performance and replacing them in the portfolio with securities that have experienced a relatively inferior return. Thus, when rebalanced each of the 30 stocks will again constitute 1/30 of the total portfolio's value. As in Fama's earlier study (1972), Cheng and Deets assumed

---

[41] Pao L. Cheng and M. King Deets "Portfolio Returns and the Random Walk Theory," *Journal of Finance* (March 1971), pp. 11–30.

Figure 4
Dow Jones Industrial Index 1956

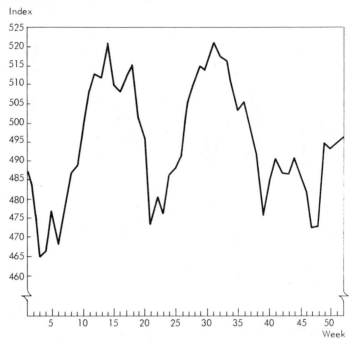

Source: After Roberts, "Stock Market Patterns."

no taxes or transaction costs "in order not to bias in favor of either strategy."

As shown by Table 4, they find that $1.00 equally distributed among the 30 Dow Jones industrial stocks in 1937 would have grown to $9.52 in 1969. However, with weekly rebalancing, the $1.00 would have grown to $22.76 in the same period.

After correcting errors which were noted by Barry Goldman regarding the original study, Cheng and Deets conclude even stronger than before that:[42]

1. The random walk theory is not supported by the evidence.
2. The buy and hold strategy is "overwhelmingly inferior to the rebalancing strategy."
3. There is a tendency for performance to improve as the frequency of rebalancing increases.

---

[42] Barry Goldman, "Portfolio Returns and the Random Walk Theory: Comment," and Pao L. Cheng and M. King Deets, "Reply," *The Journal of Finance* (March 1976), pp. 153–61.

Table 4

Return on Buy and Hold versus Rebalancing: 30 Dow Jones Industrial (1,625 weeks: 1937–69)

Frequency of Rebalancing	Weeks Holding Period	Portfolio Policy		
		Buy and Hold	Rebalancing	Difference
1,625	1	$9.52	$22.76	−$13.24
812	2	9.87	14.49	− 4.62
541	3	9.87	15.25	− 5.38
406	4	9.87	13.40	− 3.53
325	5	9.52	10.69	− 1.17
270	6	9.62	11.97	− 2.35
232	7	9.87	11.73	− 1.86
203	8	9.87	12.49	− 2.62
180	9	9.62	12.42	− 2.80
162	10	9.62	10.31	− 0.69
108	15	9.62	9.89	− 0.27
81	20	9.62	10.17	− 0.55
54	30	9.62	9.92	− 0.30
40	40	9.31	9.44	− 0.13
27	60	9.62	10.16	− 0.54
18	90	9.62	9.36	+ 0.26

Source: After Cheng and Deets, "Portfolio Return."

4. "In summary, the fact that rebalancing yields greater return than buy and hold indicates security prices are not independent."[43]

Fama—Runs in the Dow Jones 30 Industrial Index: Daily. Correlation coefficients may be dominated by a few unusual or extreme price changes. Hence, Fama designed a series of tests which focused on the directional signs of successive price changes to see if runs tended to persist.[44] In this series he used the 30 *individual companies* in the Dow Jones Industrial Index; daily price changes were designated as +, 0, or −, regardless of the amount of the change. For example: +++−−++0−− constitutes five runs. If successive price runs are found, i.e., if price changes tend to persist, the average length of runs will be longer and the number of runs will be less than if the series were random.

Table 5 summarizes Fama's data; the first column in the table, i.e., the actual daily runs for each company are compared with the second column showing the number of runs that would obtain with a perfectly random distribution. The data indicate a very slight tendency (760 versus 735) for the one-day runs to persist. As the test is extended for successive runs of 4, 9, or 16 days, the persistence disappears, and

[43] Ibid., p. 30.

[44] Eugene F. Fama, "Behavior of Stock Market Prices," in Lorie and Hamilton, *The Stock Market.*

Table 5
Runs of Consecutive Price Changes in Same Direction: Actual versus Expected for Each Dow Jones Industrial Company

Stock	Daily Changes		4-Day Changes		9-Day Changes		16-Day Changes	
	Ac- tual	Ex- pected	Ac- tual	Ex- pected	Ac- tual	Ex- pected	Ac- tual	Ex- pected
Allied Chemical	683	713	160	162	71	71	39	39
Alcoa	601	671	151	154	61	67	41	39
American Can	730	756	169	172	71	73	48	44
AT&T	657	688	165	156	66	70	34	37
American Tobacco	700	747	178	173	69	73	41	41
Anaconda	635	680	166	160	68	66	36	38
Bethlehem Steel	709	720	163	159	80	72	41	42
Chrysler	927	932	223	222	100	97	54	54
DuPont	672	695	160	162	78	72	43	39
Eastman Kodak	678	679	154	160	70	70	43	40
General Electric	918	956	225	225	101	97	51	52
General Foods	799	825	185	191	81	76	43	41
General Motors	832	868	202	205	83	86	44	47
Goodyear	681	672	151	158	60	65	36	36
Int'l. Harvester	720	713	159	164	84	73	40	38
Int'l. Nickel	704	713	163	164	68	71	34	38
Int'l. Paper	762	826	190	194	80	83	51	47
Johns Manville	685	699	173	160	64	69	39	40
Owens Illinois	713	743	171	169	69	73	36	39
Procter & Gamble	826	859	180	191	66	81	40	43
Sears	700	748	167	173	66	71	40	35
Standard Oil (Cal.)	972	979	237	228	97	99	59	54
Standard Oil (N.J.)	688	704	159	159	69	69	29	37
Swift & Co.	878	878	209	197	85	84	50	48
Texaco	600	654	143	155	57	63	29	36
Union Carbide	595	621	142	151	67	67	36	35
United Aircraft	661	699	172	161	77	68	45	40
U.S. Steel	651	662	162	158	65	70	37	41
Westinghouse	829	826	198	193	87	84	41	46
Woolworth	847	868	193	199	78	81	48	48
Averages	735	760	176	176	75	75	42	42

on average, the actual total conforms precisely with a random distribution.

Shiskin—Runs in the Standard & Poor's 500 Index: Monthly. Julius Shiskin made a test of the systematic nature of stock prices comparable to that used in economic series.[45] He noted that the _average duration of run_ is a generally accepted test of the systematic nature of economic series to determine whether month-to-month movements depart significantly from randomness. This concept focuses on the number of

[45] Julius Shiskin, "Systematic Aspects of Stock Price Fluctuations," University of Chicago, Seminar on the Analysis of Security Prices (May 1968).

consecutive months of change in the same direction. It takes into account only the direction of the change: $+++-+-$ and so on, not the amplitude. Shiskin stated that, for a purely random series, the expected average duration of runs is 1.5 (months, quarters, or whatever time unit is used). "For a random series of 120 observations, i.e., 10 years in monthly data, the average duration of run should be within the range of 1.36 to 1.75 about 95 percent of the time."

Shiskin examined the average duration of run for the S&P's 500 stock price index as a whole for 120 months. He found

> The average duration of run for stock prices is 2.37, well above the limits for a random series. Since stock prices had a pronounced upward trend from 1948 to 1966, the average duration of run was also computed for the series after the trend was eliminated. It proved to be 2.30, also well above the limits for a random series.[46]

Renwick—Explanable Outliers. Fred Renwick[47] noted that empirical samples of stock price changes typically reported by many different scholars usually contain larger fractions of extremely large values—"outliers"—than expected under normal random conditions. Invoking conclusions from *present value analysis,* he tested whether these extremely large price changes occur without special cause or explanation, that is, randomly.

Renwick's tests (see Table 6) consisted of:

1. partitioning a known sample—the Dow Jones 30 industrials—into two categories: *(a)* with (row I on Table 6) and *(b)* without (row II on Table 6) significantly large price changes over the time span studied, 1956 to 1962.
2. Computing whether a single proposed causal economic variable—average earnings growth rate divided by variance of growth—contributes significantly, as it should, to explaining differences between the two observed categories. The computation was a "chi-square" value, which measures the actual quantity observed in each cell compared to the quantity expected if no relationship exists between the row and column variables. Because three of the 30 companies posted negative average growth rates, 1956–62, only 27 companies were included in the final analysis.

Renwick's test results rejected, at a high level of significance, the proposition that the proposed economic explanatory variable is not useful in understanding the behavior of some price changes; or that extremely large changes in stock prices occur for no special cause,

---

[46] Ibid., p. 6.

[47] Fred B. Renwick, "Theory of Investment Behavior and Empirical Analysis of Stock Market Price Relatives," *Management Science* (September, 1968), pp. 57–71. © 1968 by The Institute of Management Sciences.

Table 6
Test Categories

Outlier Category	Explanatory Factor†		Total Number of Companies
	Over	*Under*	
Row I: Companies exhibiting excessively large price changes*	Allied Chem. Corp. American Can Co. American Telephone American Tobacco Dupont Excluding GM Eastman Kodak Company General Foods Corp. General Electric Co. General Motors Corp. Goodyear Tire & Rubber Johns-Manville Corp. Owens-Illinois Inc. Procter & Gamble Sears, Roebuck & Co. Standard Oil of Calif. Standard Oil of N.J. Woolworth (F.W.) Co.	Chrysler Corp. International Harvester Westinghouse Electric	20
Row II: Companies without significantly large changes in price	Texaco Inc. Union Carbide Corp.	Aluminum Co. of America Anaconda Co. International Nickel International Paper Swift & Company	7
Total number of companies	19	8	27

* "Excessively large" is defined to mean more than three standard deviation units away from the average change experienced over the time span studied.

† The explanatory factor is a ratio : average growth rate of income over the time span studied, divided by the variance of that growth.

Source: After Fred B. Renwick, "Theory of Investment Behavior."

explainable only by chance. For at least 27 of the Dow Jones 30, high and steady income growth was found to be associated nonrandomly with extremely large price changes, while low and variable income growth was found to be associated nonrandomly and significantly with the absence thereof.

The significance of the above finding was noted several years later by H. Russell Fogler who, in critically evaluating literature on random walk tests, wrote: ". . . accordingly, while randomness may be important as an explanator of daily price changes, this [Renwick's] evidence appears to support the hypothesis that large price changes are accounted for, at least partially, by changes in growth and variability of growth."[48]

---

[48] H. Russell Fogler, *Analyzing the Stock Market: Statistical Evidence and Methodology*, 2nd ed. (Columbus, Ohio: Grid, Inc., 1978), p. 37.

Alexander—Filters. Alexander pioneered trading rule techniques or *filters* for daily average closing prices to test independence of stock price changes. For example, with a 5 percent filter, if the price rises by 5 percent: buy; if it declines by 5 percent: sell. He used daily closing prices for the S&P's 425 industrials for the 1928–61 period.

According to Alexander, "the filter approach rather closely resembles, at least in spirit, the Dow theory. Stripped of its qualifications, the Dow theory consists of selling when the averages are a certain point off peak and buying when they are a certain distance up from the trough. The filter scheme can be described in precisely the same words."[49] Alexander's filters, however, differ from the Dow theory in that under the filter scheme, a certain distance is to be defined as X percent which is set in advance. Under the Dow theory a certain distance is determined by inspection of charts showing prices from swing to swing and at any point the key is the trough or peak of the preceding swing.

As shown below, Alexander found that brokerage commissions had a serious impact on the profitability of filters:

If a commission of 2 percent on each turnaround transaction had to be paid, however, the smallest filters would have incurred such substantial losses as to wipe out the initial capital. . . . Only the larger filters (21.7 percent or greater) show sizeable gains over commissions so as to approach "buy and hold," and only the very largest (over 40 percent) beat buy and hold by any substantial margin if commissions are deducted.

. . . I should advise any reader who is interested only in practical results, and who is not a floor trader and so must pay commissions, to turn to some other source for advice on how to beat buy and hold. . . . I maintain that neither commissions nor profits from "buy and hold" are relevant to the random walk issue. The case for exclusion of commissions is straightforward. Suppose that in a game of coin tossing, the bet is $1.00 a throw on heads, with the "house" charging a commission of $0.02 a throw . . . if after 10,000 bets you find you are $200 behind, it would be unreasonable to complain that the coin was not fair.

. . . As to the comparison with buy and hold—how is that relevant to the issue of whether stock prices follow a random walk? Buy and hold will be profitable when there is an upward movement of prices. If the uptrend is generated by a random walk with independent steps, there would be a certain expectation of profit from any given filter. It is a comparison of "observed" with "expected" profits that is relevant, rather than a comparison with buy and hold. For if, as we shall later see, from 1928–61 the filters were substantially more profitable than to be expected on a random walk hypothesis but sometimes more, sometimes less, profitable than buy and hold, we can still conclude, as I do, that something other than a random walk was at work.

The significant data of Table 7 may therefore be taken to be the

---

[49] Sidney S. Alexander, "Price Movement in Speculative Markets: Trends or Random Walks," in Cootner, *Random Character of Stock Market Prices* (Cambridge, Mass.: M.I.T. Press, 1964), pp. 338–72.

terminal capital assuming no commissions. Even the least profitable filter yielded a terminal capital 2.1 times the initial capital. Of course the number of transactions decline with increasing size of filter, so that the statistical reliability of the measure of profitability of the larger filters must be weaker, based as they are on eight or twelve transactions rather than the 1780 of the 1 percent filter. On the other hand, for "buy and hold" we have only one transaction, hence one observation.

The basic data are shown in Table 7.

Table 7
Filter Profitability 1928–1961

		Terminal Capital as Multiple of Initial Capital		
Filter Size	*Number of Transactions*	*If No Commissions*	*With Commissions*	*Buy and Hold*
1.0%	1730	41.3	0.0	5.1
4.0	418	10.7	0.0	5.1
8.2	142	14.8	0.9	5.1
12.5	88	4.0	0.7	5.1
17.0	54	2.1	0.7	5.1
21.7	32	6.4	3.4	5.1
29.5	20	5.3	3.6	5.1
34.6	16	4.8	3.5	5.1
40.0	12	6.2	5.0	5.1
45.6	8	10.6	9.2	5.1

Source: After Alexander, "Price Movement in Speculative Markets."

Alexander conducted several other filter tests and concluded with these remarks, "Taken all together the evidence runs strongly against the hypothesis that from 1928–61 the movement of the S&P Industrials is consistent with a random walk with drift. . . . maybe there just is a wee bit of persistence in the movement of stock price averages."

Cootner—Random Walk with Barriers. Paul Cootner commented that

> You can see why the idea (of a random walk) is intriguing. Where else can the economist find that ideal of his—the perfect market. Here is the place to take a stand if there is such a place.
>
> Unfortunately, it is not the right place. The stock market is not a random walk. A growing number of investigators have begun to suspect it and I think I have enough evidence to demonstrate the nature of the imperfections. On the other hand, I do not believe the market is grossly imperfect. . . . Even more interesting, is that my model is perfectly compatible with much of what I interpret Wall Street chart reading to be all about. Like the Indian folk doctors who discovered tranquilizers, the Wall Street witch doctors, without the benefit of scientific method,

have produced something with their magic, even if they can't tell you what it is or how it works."[50]

Cootner set forth the idea that, if professional investors held an idea of what was going to happen in the future, stock prices would behave as a random walk with reflecting barriers. Figure 5 shows how this concept operates.

Figure 5
Reflecting Barrier Concept

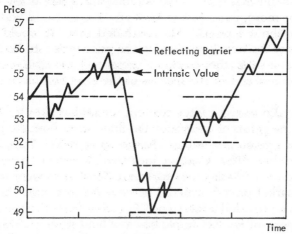

Source: Reprinted with permission from Charles D. Kuehner, in *Financial Analyst Handbook* (Homewood, Ill., Dow Jones-Irwin, 1975), p. 1251.

Thus, starting with the intrinsic value of 54, the hypothetical stock fluctuates randomly between 53 and 55. Subsequently, as new information is received, the stocks intrinsic value rises to 55, then down to 50, up to 53 and 56. The reflecting barriers, in part, express the fact that, because of transaction cost and so on, prices tend to move randomly about a central value. Cootner also noted that these barriers may be "soft and rubber like" since not all professionals held the same expectations. Also, that there is no reason to expect changes in the price expectation of professionals should occur in other than a random manner over the time dimension. Thus, over any substantial period of time, stock prices would be composed of a random number of trends each of which is a random walk within the reflecting barrier. Cootner notes that this concept has much random behavior, and it also has some implications which are strikingly different.

---

[50] Paul H. Cootner, ed., *Random Character of Stock Market Prices* (Cambridge, Mass., MIT Press 1964), pp. 231–52.

Cootner then noted that over *longer periods of time,* other factors, which may be relatively unimportant in the case of weekly changes, become much more significant. This is based on the assumption that stocks may have trends, or several trends, over longer periods of time, each with a reflecting barrier. This he contends implies that stocks would not be "as free to wander" as if the series were a random walk.

On this basis, Cootner studied 45 NYSE stocks, five of which had weekly price data for 10 years and 40 of which had data for five years, 1956–60. All data were adjusted for cash dividends, stock splits, and so on. He found that each of the 45 companies had at least one trend of a year or more, most had at least one longer trend and "very few stretches without a trend." He concluded that "It would seem as if the lengths of the trends involved in the price series studied, especially in conjunction with other evidence presented, *are significant evidence of nonrandomness,* but the analysis of the direction has much further to go.

Cootner also tested a filter concept somewhat akin to Alexander's. However, the points of measuring the filter were from the price *trend,* rather than a given percentage change up or down. Thus, in applying a 5 percent buy filter, Cootner measured 5 percent *from the trend line*—based on a 200-day moving trend. Short sales were made whenever the market price reached 5 percent *below* trend. The 5 percent decision rule provided a return of 18 percent (net of transactions costs) versus 10 percent for the simple buy and hold strategy. Cootner noted that the period studied was "peculiarly satisfactory for simple investment policies" and that the 45 stocks used were probably much closer to a perfect market than would be the case with smaller companies. As with similar research however, profits were not sufficient to cover transactions costs.

Levy—Relative Strength: 200 Stocks. Levy tested the random walk hypothesis using several different strategies based essentially on relative strength. His basic data were 200 NYSE stocks covering a 200-week period from 1960 to 1965. Stocks were selected from the S&P 425 Industrial Stock Index with representative sampling from each industry group. All stock price data were adjusted for splits, dividends, and rights. Three different inputs were computed:

1. *Relative Strength Data.* Computed for each stock using the formula: $C/A26$; or $C/A4$, in which C equals current week's price; $A26$ is average price over preceding 26 weeks; and $A4$ is average price over prior four weeks. These ratios were computed for each stock and ranked highest to lowest.
2. *Volatility Ranks.* Calculated for each set of prices using ratio of standard deviation to arithmetic means, i.e., the average closing price for the prior 26 weeks.

3. *Weekly Geometric Average.* For all 200 stocks to serve as the random portfolio. This has "the virtue of continually equalizing the dollars invested in each component stock."

The investment strategy was to use historical, i.e., 26- or 4-week average relative strength. Thus, upgrading continuously eliminated the weaker stocks from the portfolio and reinvested the proceeds in the strongest stocks. For example, under a 10 percent relative strength strategy, equal amounts were invested in each of the 20 strongest stocks. The portfolio would, however, not be changed until one or more stocks had declined in relative strengths to say rank 160 (from the top). Turnaround transactions costs of 2 percent were assumed.

Table 8 summarizes the data for several different cast-out rank strategies. It will be noted that the highest returns, i.e., the 21.8 percent gross or 19.1 percent net annual returns, are in the range of 150 castout rank. The random portfolio annual return was 10.6 percent, but this portfolio had a better, i.e., lower standard, deviation of four-week returns.

Table 8
Result of Portfolio Upgrading with 10 Percent Relative Strength Selection and Trades Based Upon Relative Strength Cast-Out Ranks

	Cast-Out Ranks						Geometric Average
Gross Results (percent)	*020*	*050*	*100*	*150*	*180*	*195*	
Annual return	14.20	20.30	21.10	21.80	19.30	13.80	10.60
Average of 4-week returns.....	1.08	1.47	1.54	1.59	1.45	1.09	0.83
Standard deviation of 4-week returns	4.79	4.85	4.35	4.39	4.53	4.60	3.52
Net Results (percent)							
Annual return	−3.20	11.10	16.30	19.10	17.80	13.20	10.60
Average of 4-week returns.....	−0.19	0.86	1.22	1.41	1.35	1.05	0.83
Standard deviation of 4-week returns	4.87	4.90	4.39	4.41	4.55	4.61	3.52

Source: Robert A. Levy, "Random Walks: Reality or Myth," Financial Analysts Journal (November–December 1967), p. 72.

Other strategies were tested, such as 10 stocks, i.e., 5 percent of 200 stocks, different relative strength selection, and different cast-out ranks. Additionally "balancing" of portfolios which had become too volatile was accomplished by introducing a bond component on a flexible basis. Thus, Levy's strategy called for movement out of bonds into stocks when the stock market was becoming relatively stronger and vice versa. The data indicate that this strategy permitted both a higher annual return on the relative strength portfolio than the random portfolio and a lower risk as measured by the standard deviations of the four-week returns.

Levy concluded that:

the profitability of portfolio upgrading variable ratio strategies over the 1960–65 period has been completely and reliably proven. Moreover, the large returns can be attained by incurring no more risks than would be incurred if a random investment strategy were pursued. . . . stock prices follow discernible trends and patterns which have predictive significance; and the theory of random walks has been refuted. . . . Of course, the empirical results presented herein must be interpreted in light of the specific time frame investigated. Therefore, an obvious extension of the study would be the performance of similar tests for different periods of time.[51]

Jensen and Bennington—Relative Strength: All NYSE Stocks. Michael Jensen and George Bennington endeavored to further test Levy's relative strength trading role.[52] They divided the years 1930–65 into seven nonoverlapping periods, e.g., 1930–35, . . . , 1960–65. Using all NYSE securities, they composed 29 separate samples of 200 stocks with an equal dollar amount invested in each, with dividends reinvested. Their results are shown in Table 9. Thus, before allowing for transaction costs, the 5 percent or 10 percent trading rules outperformed simple buy and hold, but failed to do so if such costs were included.

Table 9
Average Compound Returns—All Periods and All Portfolios

	Average Annual Return	
	Gross	Net of Transaction Costs
Buy and hold	11.1%	10.7%
10% rule	12.5	10.7
5% rule	12.4	9.3

Source: After Jensen and Bennington, "Random Walks and Technical Theories."

Jensen and Bennington also examined variations attributable to differences in risk calculated on the basis of difference in the standard deviation of monthly returns. Measures of systematic risk for each of the portfolios generated by the trading rules or buy and hold policy were reflected by comparison of the market return and the "riskless return." The latter measured by yield to maturity of U.S. government bonds due in five years, i.e., the portfolio holding period. They stated: "After explicit adjustment for the level of risk, it was shown that net

---

[51] Robert A. Levy, "Random Walks: Reality or Myth," *Financial Analysts Journal* (November–December 1967), pp. 69–77.

[52] Michael C. Jensen and George A. Bennington, "Random Walks and Technical Theories: Some Additional Evidence," *Journal of Finance* (May 1970), pp. 460–82.

of transaction costs the two trading rules (5 percent or 10 percent) as tested earned an average −3 percent and −2.4 percent less than the equivalent risk buy and hold policy."

Different portfolios were tested over several different time periods, including the 1961–65 period originally studied by Levy. Results for the latter are shown in Table 10.

Table 10
Average Compound Returns—1961–1965 Buy and Hold versus 10 percent Trading Rule

	Gross	Net of Transaction Costs	Beta
Buy and hold	10.1%	9.6%	0.96
Portfolio #1	14.6	12.9	1.09
2	10.5	8.7	0.96
3	12.0	10.1	1.30
4	8.1	6.3	1.09
5	12.3	10.3	1.02
Average portfolio	11.5	9.7	1.09

Source: After Jensen and Bennington, "Random Walks and Technical Theories."

Jensen and Bennington compared their own results with the 20–26 percent returns reported by Levy and conclude that "Levy's original high returns were spurious and probably attributable to selection bias." The authors attribute the latter to differences such as: their five portfolios included all stocks listed on the NYSE at the beginning of the period, whereas Levy's portfolio consisted of 200 stocks that were listed during the entire 1961–65 period. They also noted significant differences in risk, as reflected in the portfolio beta coefficients,

> Since the trading rules portfolios were, on the average, more risky than the buy and hold portfolios. This simple comparison of returns is biased in favor of the trading rules. . . . After explicit adjustment for the level of risk, it was shown that, net of transaction costs, the two trading rules (5 percent and 10 percent) we tested earned an average −0.3 percent and −2.4 percent less than the equivalent risk buy and hold policy.[53]

Jen—Relative Strength: Long Term versus Short Term. Another viewpoint was expressed by Jen who wrote

> . . . I am sympathetic to Jensen & Bennington's basic position that the random walk hypothesis will hold in a long run. J & B should, however, recognize that Levy's strategy may not be a statistical quirk, but actually represent a trading rule that works for a short period of time because the rule captures the essence of market imperfection at that period of time. On the other hand, the usefulness of Levy's rule is limited

---

[53] Ibid., p. 481.

to small traders only because a mutual fund of substantial size operating on Levy's 10 stocks ($X = 10$ percent) and 20 stocks ($X = 5$ percent) will most probably find that the market prices of the stocks will shift so much that the rules will no longer produce better returns.[54]

Jen also took exception to Jensen and Bennington's use of

the yield to maturity on five-year government bonds at the beginning of the period as the measure of riskless rates in their regressions. While government bonds are recognized traditionally as riskless bonds, they are only risk-free in a default sense, not in a price sense.

Jen concluded with the comment that:

As many writers including J & B have pointed out, most empirical evidence supporting the random walk hypothesis are of two kinds. The first kind is purely statistical in nature, that is, statistical procedures are applied to demonstrate that successive price changes over a short run in individual common stocks are very nearly independent for a long price series. The inference is then made that the market is efficient. The second kind of empirical tests involves the use of simple mechanical trading rules such as filters. While the evidence is largely consistent with the random walk hypothesis, it is again based on a long price series. Both kinds of tests can be criticized on the ground that the statistical procedure used cannot disprove the hypothesis that, for a *limited* period of time, price changes are not random for certain stocks or even a significant part of the market in response to some new information. Nor can they disprove the hypothesis that price changes are random for a long period but actually either mean or variance, or both, have shifted within that period in response to some new information.[55]

Kassouf—Legal Barriers to Efficient Markets.   Sheen Kassouf[56] investigated two of what he calls the "many legal impediments to optimal investment behavior on the part of trustees": (a) prohibition of the use of options as speculative devices, and (b) Federal Regulation T requirements that "when a short sale takes place, the client must deposit with the broker appropriate collateral consisting either of securities or cash.

Regulation T and prohibitions against short sales affect efficient pricing of securities via at least the two following mechanisms:

1. Failure to allow short sellers immediate use of the proceeds of a short sale, thereby creating a market imperfection which (according

---

[54] Frank C. Jen, "Discussion," *Journal of Finance* (May 1970), pp. 495–99.

[55] Ibid., p. 498.

[56] Sheen T. Kassouf, "Toward a Legal Framework for Efficiency and Equity in the Securities Markets," *Hastings Law Journal* (January 1974), pp. 417–34. Reprinted by permission of *Hastings Law Journal,* © 1974, Hastings College of the Law.

to Edward Miller[57]) completely "destroys the theoretical case for the random walk hypothesis."

2. Forbidding trustees to relinquish the custody of any of the assets in the trust, even though the trustees might be both willing and otherwise able to comply with collateral requirements.

Kassouf contends that: "Since trust law in many states forbids the trustee to relinquish the custody of any of the assets in the trust, short sales are a forbidden technique for trust investments" (pp. 431–433).

"The board was asked to allow brokers to execute short sales on behalf of National Bank Trust Departments if the trustee, in lieu of the required cash or securities, deposited with the broker a representation that the trustee held, and would continue to hold while the short position was not covered, the required collateral. This would not violate the intent of Regulation T: it would only change the location of the collateral required for the short sale" (pp. 432–433). "The board rejected this request citing 'possible evasions' which might occur" (p. 433).

Regarding the impact of legal barriers and prohibitions against trading Options as speculative devices, Kassouf wrote: "Absent a provision in the trust instrument allowing the selling of options, local law will control. Local law, either by statute or case law, ostensibly prohibits the use of options as speculative devices. This prohibition is based upon decisions involving questions of fact which have no present relation to the use of options as an instrument technique for bank trust departments. The irrationality of the Comptroller's stance can be seen by considering a simple example of a trust officer faced with the following two alternatives:

1. Buy 100 shares of Ford Motor Co. for a trusteed account. This non-controversial strategy is available to almost all trust officers. The common stock is presently on the "approved list" of most major bank trust departments.
2. Buy 100 shares of Ford Motor Co. and *simultaneously sell a call option on these shares.*

Assume that at the time these two alternatives are available, the price of the common stock is 60 and the premium that the seller of the option would receive for a six-month option is 7.5. The trust officer pursuing alternative (1) would realize a gain on this investment if the common stock moved up and would show a loss if the common stock fell in price. In contrast, the trust officer following alternative (2) would show no loss unless the common stock fell *more* than 7.5 points. (This example neglects all transaction costs.) Alternative 2 is superior to

---

[57] Edward M. Miller, "Risk, Uncertainty, and Divergence of Opinion," *The Journal of Finance* (September 1977), pp. 1151–68.

alternative 1 for every outcome where the common stock, six months from purchase, sells for less than 67.5.

Table 11 shows the profit or loss for each alternative, dependent upon the price of Ford Motor Co. common stock six months after purchase.

"Selling the call option reduces the variability of possible return, thus making the investment more stable than an outright purchase." Yet trust law prohibits the aforesaid feasible transaction.

Table 11
Legal Barriers to Efficient Markets

Final Price of Ford	Profit from Alternative 1	Profit from Alternative 2
45	−15	−7.5
50	−10	−2.5
55	− 5	+2.5
60	0	+7.5
65	+ 5	+7.5
70	+10	+7.5
75	+15	+7.5

Source: Sheen Kassouf, "Legal Barriers to Efficient Markets." Reprinted by permission of The Hastings Law Journal, © Copyright 1974, Hastings College of the Law.

Forbes—Dart Board Fund.   Noting that a chart of the Dow Jones Industrial Average over several recent years "looks like a profile of the Himalayas with its countless peaks and valleys," Malcolm Forbes and two associates threw darts at the stock market page in mid-1967 and "selected" a portfolio of 27 stocks. Table 12 shows the results of a $1,000 investment made in each stock. While there were wide differences between the best and worst performers, overall results were well above the S&P 500 and the Dow Jones Industrial Average.

In this study, no new stocks were bought nor were any of the original 27 stocks sold. However, where a merger eliminated a stock, the proceeds were reinvested in the acquiring company. Forbes commented ". . . . . we think this raises some interesting questions for the random walk theorists. . . . our experiment suggests that a sit tight philosophy, while it can test your patience, has a lot to recommend itself over constant buying and selling."[58]

Clarens—The Pause: The Rule.   Clarens[59] emphasizes the system-

---

[58] Malcolm S. Forbes "Dart It All!" *Forbes* (March 5, 1979), pp. 108–9. Reprinted by permission of *Forbes* Magazine.

[59] John Clarens, Private Communication (New York: Clarens Associates, Inc., 1978).

Table 12
The Dart Board Fund (below are the present holdings of the Dart Board Fund; The original portfolio has been affected by several mergers, a cash tender offer and a spin-off)

Present portfolio	Value of portfolio 12/31/77	Value of portfolio 2/5/79	Change in value since 12/31/77	Change in value since 6/30/67	Price 2/5/79	Shares presently held
Aguirre	$ 790.48	$ 756.70	− 4%	− 24%	14*	54.05
Arvin	1,658.56	1,363.20	−18	+ 36	15	90.88
Baker International	1,480.31	2,009.54	+36	+101	32¾	61.36
Bunker-Ramo—com.	143.55	258.39⎤	+32	− 11	20¼	12.76
—$1.50 preferred	531.14	631.62⎦			22	28.71
Carolina P&L	602.54	567.29	− 6	− 43	22⅛	25.64
Chase Manhattan	737.61	734.53	− 1	− 27	29¾	24.69
Checker Motors	1,208.39	2,166.78	+79	+117	32½	66.67
Crouse-Hinds	1,642.98	2,293.08	+40	+129	24¼	94.56
EMI	771.42	600.00	−22	− 40	2⅝	228.57
Fed Paper Bd—com.	417.10	702.48⎤			24	29.27
—$1.20 preferred	356.06	604.81	+46	+117	31	19.51
Rexham†	713.41	865.85⎦			17¾	48.78
Firestone Tire & Rub	719.04	578.60	−20	− 42	12⅞	44.94
Florida Steel	1,102.88	1,705.78	+55	+ 71	29	58.82
General Dynamics	622.87	1,134.82⎤	+69	+ 24	33¼	34.13
Houston Nat Gas‡	111.21	103.01⎦			25⅛	4.10
Helene Curtis	537.23	495.90	− 8	− 50	7½	66.12
INCO Ltd	462.20	485.82	+ 5	− 51	18	26.99
INCO (originally ESB)	1,095.83	1,151.82	+ 5	+ 15	18	63.99
International Paper	1,495.81	1,363.33	− 9	+ 36	39⅞	34.19
Interpace	1,008.95	1,321.46	+31	+ 32	18½	71.43
Ludlow Corp	301.50	567.83	+88	− 43	14⅛	40.20
MacAndrew & Forbes	1,360.53	1,823.69	+34	+ 82	15¾	115.79
Pacific Tin Consol	1,044.97	1,123.63	+ 8	+ 12	12½	89.89
JC Penney	1,118.25	988.31	−12	− 1	31⅜	31.50
Pittston	3,695.59	2,940.58	−20	+194	18½	158.95
Singer—common	179.31	124.74⎤	−22	− 67	14	8.91
—$3.50 preferred	244.92	205.92⎦			33	6.24
Standard Oil Indiana	2,539.35	2,879.21	+13	+188	56⅛	51.30
Sunbeam	579.47	565.25	− 2	− 43	19⅞	28.44
Texas Oil & Gas	8,258.49	9,476.95	+15	+848	35	270.77
Textron	714.97	687.99	− 4	− 31	25½	26.98
Total	$38,246.92	$43,278.91	+13	+ 55		
S&P's 500	95.10	98.09	+ 3	+ 8		
DJIA	831.17	823.98	− 1	− 4		

* Company being liquidated; last price NYSE.
† Shareholders of Riegel Paper received both Federal Paper Board common and preferred shares and Rexham common.
‡ General Dynamics divested Liquid Carbonic, which was subsequently acquired by Houston Natural Gas.
Source: Reprinted by permission of *Forbes* Magazine from the March 5, 1979 issue.

atic (in contrast with random) character of the Dow Jones Industrials Index, 1860–1978. According to Clarens' data. Figure 6, common stock prices typically move substantially sidewise for several years following gains to new high levels. In a perspective spanning one hundred years, the pause appears to be the rule.

Figure 6
The Pause: The Rule

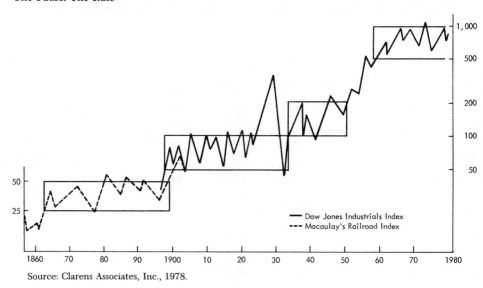

Source: Clarens Associates, Inc., 1978.

II
THE SEMISTRONG FORM OF THE EFFICIENT MARKET-RANDOM WALK HYPOTHESIS: SURVEY OF EVIDENCE

Overview

This form of the efficient market-random walk hypothesis centers on how rapidly and efficiently market prices adjust to new publically available information, including:

1. Expectations regarding contents of future financial reports from individual corporations. (For example, future changes in earnings, dividends, capital structure, sales, employment and the like). Current prices, according to the theory, should reflect rational expectations regarding these future realizations.
2. Incompatibilities between many competing published data series, and revisions of data series previously published, for example by governmental departments and agencies, particularly corporate profits and related data series. Efficiency implies, among other things, that the markets correctly expect and act now upon planned or possible future revisions of either published data or accounting method.
3. Increasing politicization of economic data, particularly price inflation-rate or cost-of-living data and unemployment rates.

The above matters have received relatively less attention in the literature.

Fama, Fisher, Jensen, and Roll tested the efficiency of the market prices in reacting to the announcement of over 900 stock splits involving NYSE listed firms. They ascertained that there is strong evidence that the market efficiently anticipates dividend increases. Ball and Brown conducted similar tests of the market's ability to correctly anticipate changes in earnings per share and likewise found that the market efficiently anticipates earnings changes of companies with rising earnings as well as those that decline.

Niederhoffer and Regan tested the promptness of news dissemination for 50 NYSE stocks experiencing the sharpest increase in earnings as well as the 50 with the sharpest declines. Their work revealed that news lags in reporting sharp earnings declines raises questions as to the efficient dissemination of significant news. Zeikel examined the efficiency of individual company stock prices in adjusting to new, significant information. His work suggests that market price reactions are not instantaneous, but may lag over a several month period.

Scholes tested the stock market's efficiency in absorbing secondary distributions. He analyzed some 345 secondaries and concluded that the market operates quite efficiently in adjusting to the news and that the size of the offer had no impact on market prices. He also demonstrated that secondary sales have different impacts on stock prices according to the type of institution or individual effecting the sale. Kraus and Stoll made similar studies for block trades. Their data largely confirm market efficiency. However, they did find some evidence that the size of the distribution tended to have an impact on stock prices.

Analysis of Studies

Fama, Fisher, Jensen, and Roll—Splits. Fama, Fisher, Jensen, and Roll conducted a test of the speed and accuracy of the market's reaction to the announcement of stock splits.[60] The tests embrace 940 splits of NYSE stocks in the 1927–59 period where the split increased shares outstanding by 25 percent or more. One objective of their study was to test the oft-heard theme that a stock split increases the total value of the share outstanding because investors are more inclined to purchase lower price shares.

Their analysis centered upon each stock's behavior in the period 30 months before and after the split. The way in which each stock price changed in relation to the overall market (eliminating the period

---

[60] Eugene F. Fama, Lawrence Fisher, Michael C. Jensen, and Richard Roll, "The Adjustment of Stock Prices to New Information," *International Economic Review* (February 1969), pp. 1–21.

adjacent to the split) was measured. Thus, one stock might, over the long run, have a tendency to rise 5 percent faster than the market and another stock to decline 5 percent relative to the market per year, and so on. Accordingly, the relationship of each stock's trend to that of the market during the period under study was eliminated. This would permit an unbiased calculation of whether prices of split stocks went up or down more than would rationally be expected by the split itself.

Figure 7 summarizes the price performance of all 940 stocks 30 months before and after each split. From the sharp upward trend of market prices prior to the split, it is suggested that the market was efficient in anticipating the pending split. Other data indicate that the mere fact a stock's price is rising sharply could have directly or indirectly been a causative factor in the split itself, i.e., most splits occur in rising markets and relatively few in depressed markets. After the 940 stock splits, prices on average did not change relative to the general market.

Another aspect of market efficiency is reflected in Figure 8. It shows the record of 672 stock splits where dividends were raised by an above-average amount within one year after the split. Prices did improve moderately in the several months following the split after which a generally flat pattern was evident.

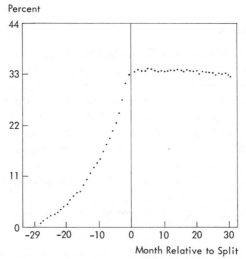

Figure 7
Relative Performance of 940 Stocks over the
Period of a Split

Percent

Month Relative to Split

Source: Fama, Fisher, Jensen, and Roll, "Adjustment of Stock Prices."

Figure 8
Relative Performance of 672 Stocks for Which
a Split Was Succeeded by a Relative
Increase in the Dividend

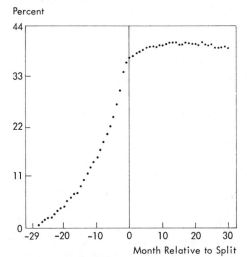

Percent

Source: Fama, Fisher, Jensen, and Roll, "Adjustment of Stock Prices."

Figure 9 traces the performance of 268 stock splits where no relative
increase in dividends occurred. Prices weakened in the several months
after the split and then trended sideways relative to the market as a
whole. Fama, et al., concluded that the market reflected disappoint-
ment in the dividend policy and prices drifted downward.

In conclusion, the authors cite these data as strong evidence that
the market is efficient both in anticipating the dividend increases and
in subsequently adjusting to dividend increases that were greater than
the market generally. Fama, et al., conclude: "On the average the
market makes unbiased dividend forecasts for split securities, and these
forecasts are fully reflected in the price of a security by the end split
of the month."

Ball and Brown: EPS Announcements. Ball and Brown conducted
a test of the stock market's ability to correctly anticipate changes in
annual earnings per share well in advance of the actual announcement
of the news.[61] They selected 261 large firms with complete earnings
data available in the S&P's Compustat tapes and complete information
in the University of Chicago's monthly price and dividend tapes. Prices
were adjusted for the general trend of the market. Each firm's actual

---

[61] Ray Ball and Philip Brown, "An Empirical Evaluation of Accounting Income, Number 5," *Journal of Accounting Research* (Autumn 1968), pp. 159–78.

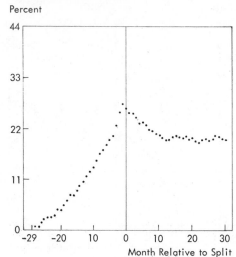

Figure 9
Relative Performance of 268 Stocks for Which a Split Was Not Succeeded by a Relative Increase in the Dividend

Percent

Month Relative to Split

Source: Fama, Fisher, Jensen, and Roll, "Adjustment of Stock Prices."

earnings per share were then compared to the forecast of earnings per share with the companies arranged in two groups:

1. Firms with "increased" earnings relative to forecast.
2. Firms with "decreased" earnings relative to forecast.

Figure 10 summarizes the key market price and earnings data. Stock prices of firms with *better* than expected earnings increased in the 12 months prior to the annual earnings announcement data and plateaued for the next six months. Stock prices of firms with *worse* than expected earnings declined in the 12 months prior to the announcement and then drifted essentially sideways.

Ball and Brown conclude that "most of the information contained in reported annual earnings is anticipated by the market before the annual report is released." In fact, the anticipation is so accurate that the announcement of the actual earnings does not appear to cause any unusual jumps in price relative to the market in the announcement month. They state that about 85–90 percent of the content of the annual earnings announcement is anticipated in advance of its announcement by other media, such as interim reports.

Neiderhoffer and Regan—News Reporting Lag. The efficient market concept depends importantly on prompt and widespread dissemi-

Figure 10
Stock Market Price Changes Attributable to Earnings Announcements

Percent Change

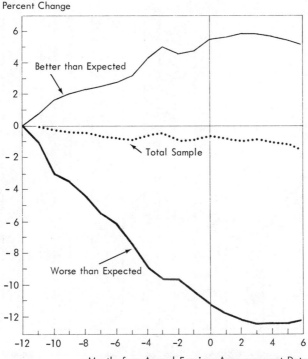

Months from Annual Earnings Announcement Date

Source: After Ball and Brown, "Empirical Evaluation of Accounting Income."

nation of all important news—good or bad. Neiderhoffer and Regan studied this question and found evidence which suggests that bad news is not reported as promptly as good.[62] They examined the time reporting interval for the 50 NYSE stocks that had the sharpest yearly increase in earnings as well as the 50 companies which had the sharpest declines in earnings. The data are summarized in Figure 11.

Some 88 percent of the top earning 50 companies reported their earnings within two months of the end of the fiscal year. In contrast, only 40 percent of the 50 bottom earning companies did likewise. Perhaps this underscores the old adage that "good news travels fast." However, it also raises questions with respect to market efficiency. For example, does the lack of earnings news convey a message of

---

[62] Victor Neiderhoffer and Patrick J. Regan, "Earnings Changes, Analysts Forecasts and Stock Prices," *Financial Analysts Journal* (May–June 1972), pp. 69–74.

Figure 11
Time Lag in Reporting Good News versus Bad News

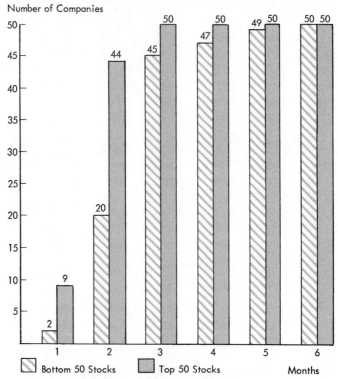

Source: After Niederhoffer and Regan, "Earnings Changes."

bad news to come? If so, do investors who act on that assumption gain an advantage over those who wait for the news?

Zeikel—Adjusting to New Information.   Zeikel examined the efficiency of the stock market in adjusting to new information. He stated that "Every industry, company and economic sector responds to a different set of business phenomenon, forces and critical factors. Every sound analytical approach requires that those factors be identified, isolated and followed on a consistent basis."[63]

Zeikel notes that critical factors are not confined to short-term movements, but include slower moving basic trend changes, social developments, new management techniques, new product introduction, changes in market share, and so on. He cited a number of specific case histories in which a significant new announcement caused pervasive market movement in stocks over a subsequent period lasting sev-

[63] Arthur Zeikel, at New York University Law School Seminar, "Legal Implications of Random Walk Hypothesis" (February 1974) and Merrill Lynch Asset Management Seminar (December 1978).

Figure 12
Curtiss Wright Corporation

• = Several articles in *New York Times* and other publications in December 1971 concerning its interest in U.S.
development of the Wankel engine.

eral months. He noted that substantial profit opportunities are available
in recognizing the significance of important news developments before
this is appreciated by the general market. For example, see Figures
12 and 13.

There appears to be a conflict here between the several months
of price stock prices apparently required to adjust fully to the news
and the random walk-efficient markets hypothesis that price adjustment to publicly announced news is instantaneous.

**Malkiel—Biases, Errors and Integrity of New Informa-
tion.** Integrity of publically disseminated data is another critical but
rarely discussed assumption underlying the efficient market concept
that "prices adjust rapidly and efficiently to all new information." Efficient markets theory makes no explicit allowance for systematic biases
or other distortions interjected knowingly into the systems widely used
for producing new and original source data.

Burton Malkiel warns that (. . . among other reasons . . .) because
"many of the numbers produced by the federal statistical system have
one use that extends well beyond their original purpose of monitoring
the economy,"[64] the system might well be doing violence to the assumed integrity of news. Examples are (1) inflation rate statistics and
(2) employment ratio-unemployment rate data, both being widely used

---

[64] Burton G. Malkiel, "Problems with the Federal Economic Statistical System and
Some Alternatives For Improvement," *The American Statistician* (August 1978), pp.
81–88.

Figure 13
Resorts International

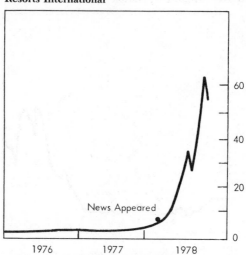

1976   1977   1978

• = State of New Jersey awarded license for casino
gambling to Resorts International, February 1978.

to (automatically) trigger contractual transfers of funds in both the
public and private sectors.

Scholes: Secondary Distributions. Scholes followed the methodology employed by Fama, Fisher, Jensen, and Roll to test market efficiency in secondary distributions.[65] These are sizable blocks of stock
that cannot be sold via the conventional channels but require special
sales effort because of the large amounts involved. He endeavored
to determine the effects of the secondary offering per se on price as
well as the price impact of the distributions informational content.
He analyzed some 345 secondary distributions in the 1961–65 period.
Scholes adjusted the prices of each security involved in a secondary
distribution for the normal relation of its price movement to the general market.

Figure 14 summarizes the relative price action of the 345 stocks
in the 40-day period surrounding the distribution. Scholes' data show
that prices declined about 1 percent in the 26 days prior to the actual
distribution with an approximately equal decline within six days after
the distribution was effective. Scholes pointed out that the SEC does
not require full identification of a secondary vendor until six days after
the distribution and that the decline in the six-day period indicated

---

[65] Myron G. Scholes, "A Test of the Competitive Market Hypothesis, the Market
for New Issues and Secondary Offerings," Ph.D. dissertation, University of Chicago,
1969; and Richard A. Brealey, *Security Prices in a Competitive Market* (Cambridge,
Mass.: MIT Press, 1971).

Figure 14
Stock Price Change Relative to Market

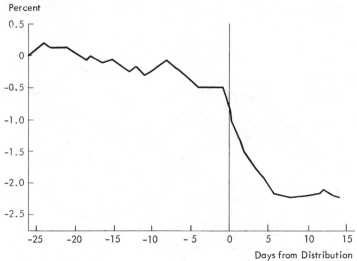

Days from Distribution

Source: After Scholes, "Test of Competitive Market Hypothesis"; and Brealey, *Security Prices*.

that the market anticipated this information in an efficient manner. Scholes also tested the impact of offering size, which ranged from less than $1 million to $100 million, on relative market price movement. There was no indication that size, either in dollar amount or in the percentage of a firm's shares involved, had a material impact on the market price.

Scholes examined other aspects of secondary offers to test market efficiency in interpreting corporate information, including the impact of the type of seller on subsequent market price performance. Figure 15 summarizes the relative price trends of secondary offers sold by various classes of investors.

As indicated in the chart, the informational content of the news of a secondary distribution causes price declines relative to the general market. However, sales by different types of investors experienced different market reactions. Sharpest immediate declines were made by shares sold by mutual funds and investment companies, and these declines continued for several months after the distribution. Shares sold by firms or officers reacted promptly with price declines, and this continued through most of the subsequent 18 months. Shares sold by individuals or for trust and estates had relatively less of an immediate price decline and, over the longer term, exhibited relatively less pressure than shares sold by institutions.

Many plausible interpretations can be made of these data. For exam-

Figure 15
Stock Price Change Relative to Market

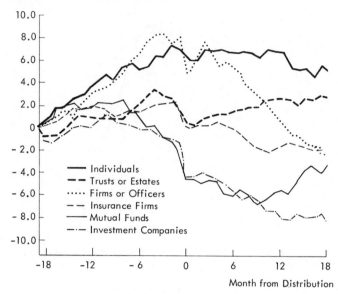

Relative Price Change (percent)

Individuals
Trusts or Estates
Firms or Officers
Insurance Firms
Mutual Funds
Investment Companies

Month from Distribution

Source: After Scholes, "Test of Competitive Market Hypothesis"; and Brealey, *Security Prices.*

ple, the market may recognize that sales by individuals or trusts and estates are frequently made to meet cash needs or to meet requirements for taxes in settling estates. Hence, this is not interpreted as bad news. Another interpretation is that mutual funds and investment companies, which have among the highest share turnovers of all institutions, may tend to sell shares promptly when bad news develops. Additionally, sales by corporate officers might signal to the market a concern by individuals who are rather well informed of a corporation's future outlook. Scholes thus concludes that price action is not attributable to the size of an offer as much as to the informational content of the sale. He cites this as further support for the efficient market hypothesis.

Kraus and Stoll—Block Trades. Alan Kraus and Hans Stoll also tested market efficiency—but on block trades.[66] These are blocks of 10,000 shares or more that can be traded in the normal course of a day's trading. They studied 2,199 block trades involving over $1 million each on the NYSE from July 1968 to September 1969. Basic data relative to these trades are shown in Table 13. Based on discussion with institutional traders, Kraus and Stoll concluded that it is "reasonably

---

[66] Alan Kraus and Hans R. Stoll, "Price Impact of Block Trading on the New York Stock Exchange," *Journal of Finance,* June 1972, pp. 569–88.

accurate to think of blocks on minus ticks as being initiated by sellers and blocks on plus ticks as being initiated by buyers."

In testing for market efficiency, they endeavored to measure the informational, distributional, and liquidity impact of plus ticks and minus ticks on subsequent prices. Prices were adjusted for the trend of the market as measured by the S&P's 500 Stock Index. The study covered the 20 days before and 20 days after the block trade. It involved 1,121 minus ticks and 345 plus ticks trades. Figure 16 summarizes data for minus ticks trades.

Table 13
Price Change of Block Trades Related to Prior Trade

	Tick		
Value of Block (millions)	−	*0*	+
$1–$2	603	425	247
$2–$5	421	171	99
Over $5	175	38	20
Total	1199	634	366

Source: After Kraus and Stoll, "Price Impact of Block Trading."

As Figure 16 indicates, closing prices on day zero averaged 2 percent below prices 20 days earlier. Also, a new (lower) level of prices tends to be established with a slight recovery by 10 days after the block trade with little shift thereafter.

Figure 17 points up price action, relative to the market, for 345 blocks on plus ticks. Closing prices on day zero averaged 5 percent above prices 20 days before the block trade. Also, prices tended to establish new higher levels.

Kraus and Stoll concluded that

> . . . these results do not show evidence of a change in rate of return subsequent to the block, reflected in a subsequent rise or fall of prices, that would support the existence of a distribution effect. Prices seemed to have experienced a once-and-for-all rise or fall depending on whether the block was purchased or sold. Such a pattern is consistent with the information hypothesis. However, further tests tend to support the liquidity cost version of the distribution hypothesis.[67]

In examining the latter, Kraus and Stoll tested the size of a block offered upon subsequent market price. If different securities are imperfect substitutes, relatively larger price changes would be associated with larger trades. Separate regressions were run for minus tick blocks and plus tick blocks relating size of block and size of price effect. The results show that:

[67] Ibid., p. 582.

1. Minus tick blocks had a heavier *negative* price impact as the size of the block increased.
2. Plus tick blocks had a corresponding *positive* price effect.

The results indicate that an increase of $1 million in block size had a price effect of 0.13 percentage points. For example, if a 20,000 share block of a $50 stock were increased to 100,000 shares, the price effect would be $0.25 per share.

Figure 16
Relative Price Performance for 1,121 Blocks on Minus Ticks

Relative Price Change (percent)

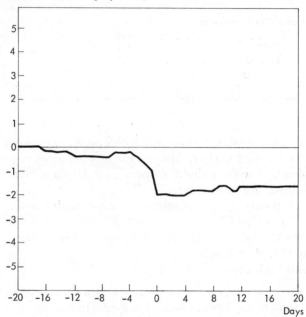

Source: After Kraus and Stoll, "Price Impact of Block Trading."

The authors conclude that, while the evidence is not uniformly strong, for trades on minus ticks the data indicated some form of distribution effect. This appears to be contrary to the findings of Scholes who found no relationship between size of secondary offering and price movement. In part, Kraus and Stoll concluded that this could be due to different institutional arrangements, such as commissions, for secondary distributions and block trades.

Figure 17
Relative Price Performance for 345 Blocks on Plus Ticks

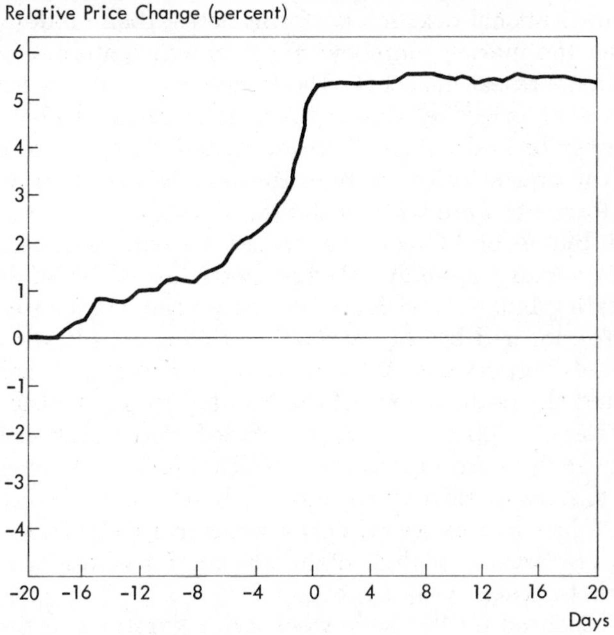

Relative Price Change (percent)

Days

Source: After Kraus and Stoll, "Price Impact of Block Trading."

III
THE STRONG FORM OF THE EFFICIENT MARKET-RANDOM WALK HYPOTHESIS: SURVEY OF EVIDENCE

Overview

The strong form of the efficient market–random walk hypothesis holds that even highly sophisticated research cannot produce consistently superior investment performance because present stock prices embody all that is known or knowable about a company.

Miller tested this question by analyzing low Price-Earnings (P/E) stock portfolios versus high over a 17-year period for over 300 companies. The evidence suggests that some bias exists in favor of low P/E companies, i.e., the market was not correctly evaluating their prospects for superior market performance in the test period. Breen performed a similar test, using low P/E stocks and randomly selected portfolios. He also found that low P/E stocks produce superior performance over a 14-year period.

The accuracy of security analysts' forecasts was analyzed by Diefenback, who examined over 1,200 specific buy or sell recommendations of institutional research firms. The results caused him to question whether institutional research performs better than random selection, or whether the market somehow reacts in anticipation of publication of institutional research reports. Niederhoffer and Regan analyzed the change in stock prices relative to earnings changes which were significantly higher or lower than those forecasted. They found substantial evidence of drastic price changes in cases where security analysts' earnings forecasts were wide of the mark.

Friend, Blume, and Crockett analyzed the performance of 136 mutual funds versus randomly selected portfolios of NYSE stocks with corresponding betas. They found mixed evidence with mutual funds being outperformed by the random portfolios with lower betas, and mutual funds outperforming the random portfolios with higher betas. Black tested the performance of the Value Line stock-ranking system covering some 1,400 stocks. He concluded that traditional methods of security analysis are superior to random selection. Kaplan and Weil also tested stock performance, but used beta as the control rather than the Value Line expected performance ranking. They concluded that the performance of their high beta portfolios supported the efficient market-random walk hypothesis.

Wallich focused on the wide stock price gyrations in the 1968–70 period and found such market swings were a challenge to the efficient market thesis that stock prices are efficiently determined. Kuehner found similar evidence for the 30 companies in the Dow Jones Industrial Index during the 1971–73 period.

Morton examined the relationship between risk and realized investor yields for some 400 companies. His data suggested that, using stock price fluctuations as a measure of risk, stocks with high risk showed no evidence of providing higher realized returns. Edesess tested the relationship between beta and total return for some 75 managed equity portfolios. He concluded that there was no reward for assuming higher risk or that historical beta was not a measure of risk. Fouse expressed the desirability of integrating conventional financial analysis with the efficient market theory for 500 companies. He found that in a 28-month test period, beta deciles did not predict returns, and he attributed this to the impact of relatively high interest rates. In a more recent 12-month period, however, there was a relatively strong relationship between realized yield and risk as reflected by beta.

Analysis of Studies

Miller—Low P/E Portfolios versus High. Paul Miller focused on low P/E multiple stocks versus high P/E multiple stocks.[68] His study

---

[68] Paul F. Miller, Jr., *Institutional Service Report—Monthly Review* (Philadelphia: Drexel & Co. Inc., November 1965).

raises questions about the efficiency of the market with respect to discounting future prospects. It covered annual data for the 1948–64 period for all companies in the S&P's Compustat tapes having sales over $150 million per year in any given year. The number of companies grew consistently in the period from 110 in 1948 to 334 in 1964.

P/E multiples were computed by using year-end stock market prices and calendar year (or fiscal year) earnings. The companies were ranked in five groups or quintiles for each year end. Table 14 summarizes the data and shows a strong tendency for price performance to vary inversely with the P/E multiple.

Table 14
Average Price Increase per Year

P/E Quintile	Price Increase
1st (high P/E)	7.7%
2d	9.2
3d	12.0
4th	12.8
5th (low P/E)	18.4

Source: After Miller, *Institutional Service Report.*

The lowest P/E quintile group had an average price performance which ranked first in 12 of the 17 years. In contrast, the highest P/E quintile group ranked last, i.e., fifth in 8 of the 17 years or 47 percent of the time. Distribution of the yearly results is shown in Table 15.

Table 15
Price Performance in Subsequent Year of Stock Ranked by Year-End P/E Multiple Quintiles (1948–64)

P/E Quintile	*Yearly Price Performance Ranking*				
	1st	*2d*	*3d*	*4th*	*5th*
1st (high P/E)	1	3	2	3	8
2d	1	1	2	11	2
3d	1	5	7	1	3
4th	2	7	4	2	2
5th (low P/E)	12	1	2	0	2
	17	17	17	17	17

Source: After Miller, *Institutional Service Report.*

Similar results were obtained for all three-year and five-year periods in the 1948–64 span. Miller concluded

> We think that the results of this study support our contention that price-earnings ratios are indeed an important consideration in portfolio management and research direction. However, much further work needs

to be done to determine why this bias has been so consistently present in favor of low price-earnings ratio groups.[69]

Breen—Low P/E Portfolios versus High. William Breen investigated performance of low price-earnings ratio stock portfolios against randomly selected portfolios, using the 1,400 company S&P's Compustat data for the 1953–66 period.[70] After eliminating all stocks with less than 10 percent compound growth in earnings per share for the prior five years, two test groups of ten stocks each were selected for January and sold the following January, i.e., a one-year holding period was used.

Return consisted of market price appreciation and dividends. Portfolio 1 consisted of the ten stocks with the lowest P/E multiples relative to the entire market. Portfolio 2 consisted of the ten stocks having the lowest P/E multiples in their respective industries. A control portfolio was made up of ten randomly selected stocks. The results are given in Table 16.

Table 16
Compound Return from Low P/E Portfolios (1953–1968)

Year	Low P/E Relative to Market		Low P/E Relative to Industry	
	Compound Return	Percentage Random Portfolio with Lower Return	Compound Return	Percentage Random Portfolio with Lower Return
1953	19.3%	95%	13.3%	95%
1954	57.5	95	92.8	95
1955	45.2	95	35.5	95
1956	19.4	90	7.7	65
1957	−9.9	45	−15.6	20
1958	112.6	95	72.6	95
1959	102.9	95	61.1	95
1960	13.7	90	12.1	90
1961	155.2	95	36.1	70
1962	−4.2	95	−19.8	35
1963	25.5	75	33.8	90
1964	26.1	80	26.7	80
1965	50.5	80	22.0	15
1966	3.4	85	6.1	90
Average	37.5	—	23.9	—

Source: After Breen, "Low Price-Earnings Ratios."

Breen concluded that "low price earnings multiples measured either relative to the whole population, or to industry classification, when combined with a control on average past growth in earnings, give portfolio performance which in most years is superior to the performance of randomly selected stocks.[71]

---

[69] Ibid., p. 5.

[70] William Breen, "Low Price-Earnings Ratios and Industry Relatives," *Financial Analysts Journal* (July–August 1968), pp. 125–27.

[71] Ibid., p. 127.

Dreman—Psychological Limitations on Efficient Market Hypothesis (EMH). David Dreman[72] challenges whether EMH, even if valid in theory, can be translated into operational realities, on the grounds that ". . . behavioral and interpretational problems prevent most professionals from outdoing the averages" (p. 252). According to Dreman, investors, on average, are far from being compulsively "rational" and instead:

1. Possess limited capacity to absorb, sort, and efficiently utilize "the mountains of available economic and financial data" regarding individual corporations and industry groups.
2. Follow "herd" and "groupthink" instincts in security selection.
3. Introduce psychological variables along with financial value and economic data when pricing purchases and sales of securities, including factors such as "tendency towards consensus," client pressure, job insecurity, respect for conventional expert opinion, and the like, which arise from high-pressure environments where many operating portfolio managers work.

Dreman contends that the market—the consensus of all investors—can be outperformed, through a strictly disciplined approach of buying and holding low P/E stock portfolios because ". . . the best chance an investor has is to stand apart from popular thinking. He must be able to forego the thrill of being in unison with the market, in agreement with expert opinion, and with the exciting, seemingly sure-fire ideas currently in vogue" (p. 271). Dreman's strategy for outperforming market averages includes "avoiding high-multiple growth and concept stocks" (p. 260), selecting shares of larger companies "currently out of market favor" as evidenced by their relatively low P/Es, and holding a diversified portfolio of twenty or more of these large size, low risk, low P/E stocks. Dreman contends that this strategy seems to work better than the alternative of applying judgment and reacting favorably to either expert or popular opinion.

As empirical evidence to support his psychological notion of stock price behavior, Dreman, with the assistance of William Avera and Clifford Atherton, computed price-earnings ratios for a sample consisting of more than one thousand NYSE stocks with 5-year records (May 1967 to August 1976) on the Compustat tapes. Dreman took the latest 12-month earnings to the end of a period from the Compustat tapes and the price two months thereafter to allow the latest quarter's earnings reports to be fully digested by the market.

The stocks in the study were divided into deciles, with each company's P/E determining its decile for each time period measured. Table 17 shows Dreman's results. The quarterly performance spread is most impressive, where, after buying and holding for one quarter, the lowest

---

[72] David N. Dreman, *Psychology And The Stock Market: Investment Strategy Beyond Random Walk* (New York: Amacom, 1977).

P/E decile averaged approximately 11 percent per annum more than the highest P/E decile.

The data on Table 17 are rates of return, compounded annually, from buying each P/E decile and switching the accumulated investment after each holding period to the commensurate decile throughout for holding periods of up to three years. Returns are also tabulated from buying and holding the original portfolios, without switching, for 9¼ years.

Dreman concluded that not only did the lowest P/E stocks outperform the high P/E ones, on average, over the May 1967 to August 1976 period; but in addition wrote: "our beta measurements indicated that the low P/E groups actually had moderately lower betas, thus making them less risky and slightly enhancing the overall results" (p. 292).

Table 17
Annualized Compound Rates of Return—May 1967 through August 1976 (full period of study)

Stocks Ranked by P/E Multiples Decile	Switching after Each				Holding Original Portfolios 9¼ Years
	Quarter	Six Months	One Year	Three Years	
1 (highest)	2.20	4.61	3.15	4.98	2.10
2	3.97	3.57	0.87	3.96	−.48
3	5.38	6.22	10.11	8.60	10.35
4	6.45	6.22	5.51	5.37	7.17
5	6.51	6.28	7.28	11.70	9.04
6	6.32	8.25	7.84	4.55	7.17
7	9.45	9.88	8.31	7.88	6.58
8	11.76	10.70	10.95	10.72	9.24
9	12.52	11.15	9.55	8.87	11.33
10 (lowest)	13.24	10.00	8.93	8.61	7.14

Source: David Dreman, *Private Communication* (New York, 1979).

Basu—Low P/E Stock Portfolios versus Random Selections. S. Basu[73] studied differences in mean annual return, for each of four categories of investors, between the lowest P/E stock portfolios and equal risk but randomly selected portfolios, net of all applicable portfolio-related costs, with approximately 500 companies, over 14 years, April 1957 thru March 1971. Basu's results are given in Table 18. (During this period low P/E portfolios earned higher absolute and risk-adjusted ratios of return than high P/E securities.)

Portfolio reallocators include investors who enter the securities market for some prespecified portfolio readjustment reason other than

---

[73] S. Basu, "The Investment Performance of Common Stocks in Relation to Their Price-Earnings Ratios: A Test of The Efficient Market Hypothesis," *The Journal of Finance* (June 1977), pp. 663–82.

Table 18
An Analysis of the Profitability of Investing in Portfolio E (low P/E Ratio) for Alternative Investor
Classes

	Random Portfolio*									
	(1)	*(2)*	*(3)*	*(4)*	*(5)*	*(6)*	*(7)*	*(8)*	*(9)*	*(10)*
I. Tax-Exempt Portfolio Reallocator $\bar{r}_d$†	0.0332	0.0372	0.0277	0.0254	0.0307	0.0247	0.0360	0.0280	0.0381	0.0284
II. Tax-Paying Portfolio Reallocator $\bar{r}_d$†	0.0247	0.0278	0.0203	0.0187	0.0229	0.0184	0.0269	0.0208	0.0285	0.0212
III. Tax-Exempt Trader $\bar{r}_d$†	0.0229	0.0269	0.0178	0.0149	0.0204	0.0145	0.0257	0.0182	0.0281	0.0180
IV. Tax-Paying Trader $\bar{r}_d$†	0.0111	0.0147	0.0060	0.0038	0.0088	0.0036	0.0135	0.0066	0.0158	0.0062

* Continuously compounded annual rates.
† $\bar{r}_d$ the mean return on E minus that on R, net of applicable portfolio-related costs.
Source: After Basu, "The Investment Performance of Common Stocks." p. 679.

speculation, for example, adjustment of portfolio beta and diversification. Traders, on the other hand, are speculators who wish to capitalize on the market's reaction to P/E information per se. Thus the distinction between reallocator and trader is important for evaluating the performance, particularly net of applicable portfolio-related costs, of low P/Es versus a randomly selected portfolio of equivalent risk" (p. 678).

Basu contends that "while the efficient market hypothesis denies the possibility of earning excess returns, the price-ratio hypothesis asserts that P/E ratios, due to exaggerated investor expectations, may be indicators of future investment performance" (p. 680).

Results on the first two lines of Table 18 show tax-exempt and tax-paying investors who entered the securities market with the aim of rebalancing their portfolios annually could have taken advantage of the market disequilibra by acquiring low P/E stocks. From the point of view of these investors a "market inefficiency" seems to have existed.

On the last two lines of Table 18, transactions and search costs and tax effects hindered traders or speculators from exploiting the market's reaction and earning net "abnormal" returns which are significantly greater than zero.

Basu concluded that ". . . publically available price-earnings ratios seem to possess 'information content' and may warrant an investor's attention at the time of portfolio formation or revision" (p. 681). ". . . The hypothesis that capital markets are efficient in the sense that security price behavior is consistent with the semistrong version of the 'fair-game' model cannot be rejected unequivocally" (p. 680).

Diefenback—Research Advice versus Performance. Robert Diefenback examined the one-year market performance of stocks previously recommended by the institutional research departments of 24 brokerage and advisory firms.[74] Some 1,200 specific buy recommendations

[74] Robert E. Diefenback, C.F.A., "How Good Is Institutional Brokerage Research?" *Financial Analysts Journal* (January–February 1972), pp. 55–60.

received in the November 1967–May 1969 period were evaluated by measuring market performance over the subsequent 52 weeks relative to the S&P Industrial Index. See Table 19.

Table 19
52-Week Market Performance of Buy Recommendations Received in November 1967–May 1969 Period

Broker or Investment Advisor	Number of Buy Recommendations	Mean Price Change	Percentage Outperforming S&P 425 Industrials	Mean Performance Differential from S&P 425 Industrials
A	12	+24.6%	75%	+25.9%
B	11	+ 6.7	36	+13.8
C	26	+ 1.8	54	+13.7
D	5	− 1.6	60	+11.8
E	12	+ 8.9	50	+11.6
F	288	+10.8	56	+ 9.8
G	49	+ 3.5	51	+ 6.9
H	192	+ 5.8	47	+ 5.9
I	13	+ 0.7	38	+ 5.7
J	91	+ 3.2	48	+ 4.3
K	59	+ 7.2	53	+ 4.0
L	24	− 1.5	50	+ 0.1
M	21	− 8.0	48	− 0.2
N	39	−13.9	46	− 1.6
O	147	−11.1	39	− 4.0
P	67	− 9.6	43	− 4.5
Q	39	−11.4	36	− 4.9
R	33	−10.7	39	− 6.3
S	14	−18.7	21	−11.1
T	23	−21.6	35	−11.7
U	9	−25.5	11	−13.4
V	8	−26.0	0	−19.3
W	9	−29.5	22	−21.3
X	18	−38.8	17	−25.3
Aggregate: All sources	1,209	− 0.3	47	+ 2.7

Source: After Diefenback, "How Good Is Institutional Brokerage Research?"

Diefenback concluded

> it is apparent that this group of investment recommendations did not in the aggregate provide a useful universe from which to select investment ideas. Whether or not these recommendations performed statistically better or worse than random selection is not demonstrated; but there would certainly seem to be little to choose between this group of recommendations and a random selection process.[75]

He also examined the relatively scarce number of sell recommendations received, which are summarized in Table 20. He also examined

---

[75] Ibid., pp. 58, 60.

six months' performance in the strong bull market of early 1968 and found buy recommendations averaged 16.5 percent better than the S&P 425. In contrast, buy recommendations averaged 2.6 percent in the six months ending in the market trough of May 1969.

Table 20
52-Week Performance of Sell Recommendations Received in November 1967–May 1969 Period

Broker or Investment Advisor	Number of Sell Recom- mendations	Mean Price Change	Percentage Out- performing S&P 425 Industrials	Mean Performance Differential from S&P 425 Industrials
H	4	−39.4%	0%	−28.1%
O	11	−27.4	9	−19.6
S	3	−24.4	0	−14.2
P	14	−16.6	36	− 9.1
D	3	−31.1	67	− 3.7
F	11	− 3.9	45	− 0.6
Aggregate: All sources	46	−18.7%	26%	−11.2%

Source: After Diefenback, "How Good Is Institutional Brokerage Research?"

Diefenback raised some fundamental questions, including:

1. Are the random walk theorists correct? Is it not possible to obtain above-average performance results by applying a sound sense of values, strong reasoning power and a well-disciplined mind to relevant facts?
2. Does the time required to prepare a good investment idea for market permit recognition to spread to the point where no value remains in the idea when it finally appears in finished form?

Renwick—Rational Expectations versus Realized Returns. Renwick[76] presented evidence, as shown in Table 21, that no significant difference exists between realized long-run market rates of return and properly formulated rational expectations of those returns.

Using present value models and no inside information—only data publicly available as of the date of the investment decision—Renwick computed expected future ten-year average rates of return and likelihood errors therewith associated for buy and hold periods on the S&P 500 stock composite portfolios, and compared these with after-the-fact (ex-post), realized returns.

The value of S&P 500 stock portfolios, a surrogate representing market value of aggregate corporate capital, was regressed against a single explanatory variable: next year's aggregate profits.

---

[76] Fred B. Renwick, *Introduction to Investments and Finance: Theory and Analysis* (New York: The Macmillan Company, 1971), pp. 285–300.

Using an estimated regression equation from data known as of the time of the investment decision, for example, 1908–50, and reasonable subjective estimates of future trendline slope of the explanatory variable, Renwick computed a range of rationally-expected rates of return on common stocks.

Table 21 shows the results. The actual return, 1950–60 was 16.8 percent per annum, compared with the ten-year prior expectation range between 12.0 and 24.1 percent per annum. Each of the five ten-year returns on Table 21 materialized within normal three standard deviation points around expected values. No significant deviation was found between ex-post realized returns and the ex-ante prior expectation.

One inference is that analysis is worthwhile. Returns do materialize without significant deviation from properly formulated expectations.

Table 21
Risks Using Assumed Regression Model

Regression equation (S and P portfolio 1908–50):
$V_t = 4.4109 + .467823$ (GNP) ± 3 (17.0526);
reduction in standard error = 56.04 percent; index of determination = .81

	Standard and Poor's 500 stock Composite Portfolios			
Years	*Minimum*	*Expected*	*Maximum*	*Actual*
1950–60	12.0	19.4	24.1*	16.8
1951–61	12.4	18.6	22.8	16.2
1952–62	12.4	18.6	22.2	14.2
1953–63	14.8	19.7	23.3	15.1
1954–64	14.1	18.5	21.8	14.5

Note: All numbers refer to return on shareholder investment (in percent, compounded annually.
* Numbers refer to 3σ limits.
Source: After Renwick, "Rational Expectations versus Realized Returns," p. 293.

Niederhoffer and Regan—EPS Forecasts versus Market Price Changes. Victor Niederhoffer and Patrick Regan state that "In their search for the philosopher's stone, security analysts have found that stock price fluctuations are closely linked to earnings changes."[77] This was brought out forcefully by Niederhoffer and Regan's examination of the 1970–71 market performance of 1,253 NYSE common stocks to test the linkage between EPS changes and market price changes. The 50 best and 50 worst companies in market price performance in 1970 are listed in Tables 16 and 17. The tables also show actual 1969 EPS and estimated EPS for 1970. The latter was the median

---

[77] Victor Niederhoffer and Patrick J. Regan, "Earnings Changes, Analysts' Forecasts and Stock Prices," *Financial Analysts Journal* (May–June 1972), pp. 65–71.

forecast of leading financial institutions as published in S&P's "Earnings Forecaster."

Niederhoffer and Regan concluded that the most important factor separating the best from the worst performers in market price was profitability, i.e, EPS changes. They noted that security analysts "consistently *underestimated* the earnings gains of the top 50 and just as consistently *overestimated* the same data for the bottom 50."

As shown in Figure 18, the security analysts' consensus had forecasted growth in earnings per share for the top 50 companies averaging 8 percent versus an actual increase of 21 percent. A subsequent rise in market price of 48 percent was recorded. The forecasts for the bottom 50 companies called for 15 percent growth in EPS versus an actual change of −83 percent. Market prices declined by 57 percent.

Tables 22 and 23 show the specific data for each of the 50 companies in the top group and the bottom group. In order to analyze the data on a more comparable basis and avoid statistical problems such as occur when the base year is small, the estimated EPS changes and actual EPS changes were normalized by price. Thus, earnings changes were expressed per $1 of market price. Hence, a rise of $.50 in EPS would be $.10 per $1.00 of price for a $5.00 stock but only $.01 for a $50.00 stock. Niederhoffer and Regan concluded that stock price changes were strongly influenced by EPS changes, both in absolute terms and relative to the consensus of security analysts' forecasts and that "it is clear that an accurate earnings forecast is of enormous value in stock selection."

Friend, Blume, and Crockett—Mutual Funds versus Random Portfolios. Irwin Friend, Marshall Blume, and Jean Crockett analyzed the

Figure 18
Median Changes: Forecasted Earnings, Actual Earnings, and Stock Market Prices

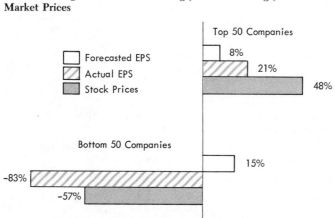

Source: After Niederhoffer and Regan, "Earning's Changes."

Table 22
Fifty Best Percentage Price Changes in 1970

		Earnings per Share				Stock Price, Actual % Chang
				Change per $ of Price		
	Actual 1969	Est. 1970	Actual 1970	Est.	Actual	
1. Overnight Transportation	$1.47	$1.47	$2.58	+.000	+.092	+125.0
2. Coca Cola Bottling, N.Y.	1.08	1.18	1.30	+.007	+.015	+ 84.2
3. Bates Manufacturing............	.02	NA	1.28	NA	+.163	+ 72.6
4. General Cigar	2.24	2.30	3.01	+.003	+.041	+ 70.5
5. Texas East. Transmission	2.40	2.50	2.70	+.003	+.009	+ 70.5
6. Credithrift Financial............	1.07	NA	1.15	NA	+.007	+ 63.6
7. Green Shoe Mfg.	1.93	2.20	2.60	+.014	+.085	+ 63.6
8. Pittston Co......................	1.11	1.67	2.20	+.021	+.040	+ 63.6
9. Campbell Red Lake Mining	.73	.65	.48	−.005	−.014	+ 62.3
10. Blue Bell	3.13	3.70	3.81	+.017	+.021	+ 60.0
11. Collins & Aikman	2.47	2.50	2.61	+.001	+.006	+ 50.2
12. Gamble-Skogmo.................	2.66	2.60	3.08	−.003	+.019	+ 57.1
13. Amerada Hess	2.41	2.55	3.22	+.005	+.027	+ 56.0
14. Giant Portland Cement	.71	NA	1.07	NA	+.042	+ 55.1
15. AMF, Inc.	1.85	2.00	2.05	+.008	+.011	+ 54.7
16. Rubbermaid, Inc.	1.28	1.40	1.44	+.005	+.007	+ 54.2
17. Cone Mills Corp.	.97	1.20	1.51	+.017	+.039	+ 58.6
18. Graniteville Co.	1.29	1.30	2.07	+.001	+.051	+ 52.5
19. Keebler	2.01	2.10	2.95	+.002	+.024	+ 51.8
20. Interco	3.13	2.80	3.31	−.012	+.007	+ 51.6
21. M. Lowenstein & Sons	2.69	2.75	2.58	+.003	−.005	+ 51.2
22. Maytag	1.62	1.70	1.70	+.004	+.004	+ 51.1
23. Cabot Corp.	2.75	2.95	3.83	+.007	+.019	+ 49.6
24. MAPCO	1.72	1.80	1.97	+.005	+.015	+ 48.9
25. Dr. Pepper	.50	.60	.61	+.003	+.004	+ 48.4
26. Pacific Intermt. Express	1.05	1.25	.94	+.013	−.007	+ 48.4
27. International Utilities	1.80	NA	2.40	NA	+.025	+ 47.2
28. U.S. Tobacco	1.69	1.95	2.04	+.014	+.019	+ 46.4
28. Russ Togs	1.02	1.30	1.47	+.019	+.030	+ 46.3
30. American Ship Building	1.10	1.25	1.42	+.006	+.017	+ 45.3
31. Liggett & Meyers	2.92	3.00	3.86	+.002	+.029	+ 45.2
32. Genuine Parts	1.40	1.57	1.73	+.007	+.018	+ 45.0
33. General Portland Cement	1.36	1.40	1.40	+.002	+.002	+ 44.9
34. Cudahy	1.77	NA	2.01	NA	+.019	+ 44.1
35. Cleveland Cliffs Iron	3.81	3.90	4.73	+.002	+.023	+ 43.8
36. Getty Oil	5.20	5.00	5.20	−.004	.000	+ 43.8
37. American Water Works	1.11	NA	1.29	NA	+.019	+ 42.7
38. Lone Star Gas	1.58	1.75	1.99	+.009	+.022	+ 42.5
39. Broadway Hale Stores	1.99	2.40	2.04	+.010	+.001	+ 42.3
40. Kings Dept. Store	.73	.73	.85	.000	+0.13	+ 41.9
41. Northwest Industries	d.23	1.40	2.21	+.132	+.197	+ 41.4
42. Weyerhaeuser	2.11	2.35	1.87	+.006	−.006	+ 41.4
43. Quaker State Oil	1.42	1.65	1.67	+.009	+.010	+ 41.1
44. Bucyrus Erie	1.84	1.70	1.72	−.007	−.006	+ 40.1
45. Louisiana Land & Explor........	2.80	2.90	2.93	+.002	+.003	+ 40.0
46. Copeland Refrigeration	2.30	2.40	3.50	+.003	+.081	+ 38.7
47. Philip Morris	2.58	3.00	3.36	+.012	+.022	+ 38.5
48. Kaufman & Broad	.80	1.00	1.12	+.004	+.007	+ 37.7
49. Helmerich & Payne	1.55	1.70	1.72	+.009	+.011	+ 37.5
50. Safeway Stores	2.01	2.10	2.70	+.004	+.028	+ 37.4

NA = not available.   d = deficit.

Source: Victor Niederhoffer and Patrick J. Regan, "Earnings Changes, Analysts Forecasts and Stock Prices"
Financial Analysts Journal (May–June 1972), p. 66.

Table 23

Fifty Worse Percentage Price Changes in 1970

	Earnings per Share			Change per $ of Price		Stock Price, Actual %
	Actual 1969	Est. 1970	Actual 1970	Est.	Actual	Change
1. Penn Central	$ .18	$ 2.00	$d13.67	+.064	−.490	−77.9%
2. University Computing	2.58	NA	d 1.28	NA	−.040	−77.7
3. Electronic Mem. & Mag.	.93	1.05	d 2.12	+.003	−.075	−76.9
4. Fairchild Camera...........	.23	1.00	d 4.40	+.008	−.050	−74.7
5. Scientific Resources	d .78	NA	d 1.40	NA	−.050	−72.7
6. Transcontinental Invest.	.60	1.30	d .62E	+.029	−.051	−72.5
7. FAS International	.92	1.10	.39	+.008	−.023	−71.1
8. Republic Corp..............	1.48	2.75	.23	+.046	−.045	−68.2
9. Sonesta	.27	NA	d 1.17	NA	−.112	−68.0
0. Automation Industries	.81	1.20	.22	+.032	−.049	−62.9
1. GAC Corp.	3.22	4.00	1.62	+.013	−.026	−62.9
2. Sprague Electric	.43	.75	d 1.78	+.012	−.063	−61.8
3. Memorex	1.87	2.50	.83	+.004	−.007	−61.0
4. Ward Foods................	1.84	NA	.40	NA	−.053	−60.6
5. Whittaker Corp.............	1.51	1.25	.28	−.014	−.067	−59.2
6. Ling-Temco-Vought	d .05	NA	d12.73	NA	−.500	−59.1
7. Dictaphone	1.09	1.15	d .74	+.003	−.079	−58.4
8. MEI Corp..................	d .19	NA	d .05	NA	+.012	−58.3
9. Smith International	1.63	1.75	.98	+.010	−.016	−58.2
0. Standard Pressed Steel	.73	.70	d 1.10	−.002	−.139	−58.1
1. High Voltage Engr..........	.21	.25	d 1.00	+.002	−.057	−57.4
2. Palm Beach Co.	1.01	NA	.10	NA	−.046	−57.2
3. Bourn's Inc.................	1.46	1.55	1.01	+.004	−.019	−57.1
4. Copper Range	6.80	10.00	4.07	+.050	−.042	−56.9
5. North American Phillips	2.49	2.65	1.00	+.003	−.027	−56.4
6. Deltec International	.96	NA	d 1.24	NA	−.198	−56.2
7. Control Data	3.08	2.50	d .40	−.005	−.030	−56.1
8. Faberge, Inc.	1.67	1.70	.41	+.001	−.038	−56.1
9. Hamilton Watch............	.68	NA	d 5.52	NA	−5.82	−55.8
0. Dillingham Corp............	1.15	1.25	d .51	+.004	−.063	−55.5
1. Berkey Photo ....'.........	1.13	1.00	.41	−.007	−.041	−55.4
2. Fuqua Industries	1.90	2.02	1.48	+.004	−.015	−54.8
3. Equity Funding	1.91	NA	2.21	NA	+.005	−54.7
4. Kentucky Fried Chicken	1.24	1.70	1.24	+.011	.000	−53.8
5. Seaboard World Air.	d .43	NA	d .32	NA	+.007	−52.8
6. Electronic Associates	d .85	NA	d 1.95	NA	−.110	−52.5
7. Athlone Industries	3.31	NA	1.33	NA	−.072	−52.1
8. Crowell-Collier	1.35	1.44	.55	+.003	−.081	−51.9
9. Microdot, Inc.	1.95	2.05	1.14	+.004	−.030	−51.9
0. Arlan's Dept. Stores	1.43	1.40	d 4.40	−.002	−.815	−51.4
1. National Cash Register	2.11	2.25	1.37	+.002	−.009	−51.1
2. Varian Associates	.93	1.00	.68	+.002	−.009	−51.1
3. Diversified Industries	1.33	1.80	.01	+.026	−.072	−50.7
4. Norlin Corp.	3.31	NA	2.20	NA	−.043	−50.7
5. Budget Industries	.96	1.50	d .41	+.016	−.040	−50.0
6. HCA Industries	d .15	NA	d 1.88	NA	−.804	−50.0
7. Boeing	.47	2.00	1.02	+.054	+.020	−49.3
8. Lionel	.21	.80	.08	+.086	−.015	−49.3
9. Callahan Mining............	.11	NA	d .06	NA	−.009	−49.1
0. Interstate Stores	1.70	2.00	.25	+.011	−.054	−49.1

NA = not available.   d = deficit.   E = preliminary earnings report.

Source: Victor Niederhoffer and Patrick J. Regan, "Earnings Changes, Analysts Forecasts and Stock Prices," *Financial Analysts Journal* (May–June 1972), p. 68.

performance of 136 mutual funds in the 1960–68 period in comparison with hypothetical portfolios made up of NYSE listed stocks.[78] The latter were selected randomly from NYSE stocks with betas corresponding to those in each of the mutual funds. Table 24 summarizes some of the key data from this extensive investigation.

The equally weighted portfolio assumes an equal dollar amount invested in each security included. Portfolio variant #1 was selected on the basis of each stock's probability of inclusion being proportional to the aggregate dollar amount of its shares outstanding. In one sense, this was a market-weighted portfolio because once selected, each stock was apportioned an equal amount of dollar investment. Variant #2 corresponds to #1 in selection of the securities. But, once selected, the amount invested was proportional to each stock's total market value.

This was, thus close to a market-value portfolio.

Among the key findings of this study were:

1. Low risk (beta 0.5–0.7). The randomly selected portfolios outperformed the mutual funds in all categories.
2. Medium risk (beta 0.7–0.9). Mutual funds outperformed two of the three random portfolios.
3. High risk (beta 0.9–1.1). Mutual funds outperformed two of the three random portfolios.

Table 24
Return from Dividends and Market Appreciation Mutual Funds versus Random Portfolios (1960–1968)

				Random Portfolios	
				Proportionately Weighted	
Risk Class	*Beta Coefficient*	*Mutual Funds*	*Equally Weighted*	*Variant #1*	*Variant #2*
Low	0.5–0.7	9.1%	12.8%	11.6%	10.1%
Medium	0.7–0.9	10.6	13.1	9.7	8.4
High	0.9–1.1	13.5	13.7	10.3	9.2

Source: Friend, Blume, and Crockett, *Mutual Funds.* © 1970 by McGraw-Hill Book Co.

On balance the evidence of mutual funds outperforming randomly selected portfolios differs from a number of earlier studies. To a large extent, such earlier studies were based on capital market theory which endeavors to equilibrate differences in risk—as measured by beta—as between the actual and hypothetical portfolios through the assump-

---

[78] Irwin Friend, Marshall Blume, and Jean Crockett, *Mutual Funds and Other Institutional Investors,* a Twenty Century Fund Study (New York: McGraw-Hill, 1970). © 1970 by McGraw-Hill Book Co.

tion of ending borrowing *risk-free* funds at the risk-free rate, i.e., government bonds. This assumption embodies an element of unreality and tends to achieve higher returns on the hypothetical portfolio that might actually be attained. This thesis is supported by recent research by Friend and Blume which indicates that the assumption of linearity between ex post returns and beta is not borne out by the improved evidence with respect to portfolios of stock and risk-free assets (government securities).[79] The data suggest that capital market pricing theory—on which a considerable body of research has been based—is not beyond question.

Black—Value Line Rankings versus Performance. Black tested the performance of the Value Line Investment Survey ranking system from 1965 to 1970 to determine if it support the random walk hypothesis.[80] In this ranking system, each of some 1,400 stocks is ranked according to expected performance for the next 12 months. Each stock is assigned a rank from I thru V as shown in Table 25.

Table 25
Distribution of Stocks by Expected Performance Ranking
Group

Expected Performance Ranking Group	Approximate Number of Stocks
I—Best	100
II—Above average	300
III—Average	600
IV—Below average	300
V—Poorest	100
Total	1,400

Source: Black, "Tests of Value Line Ranking System."

The rankings are based on a fundamental analysis of each company, including an evaluation of ten years of data in regard to earnings and market prices. Black noted that the rankings tend to assign high ranks to stocks with:

1. Low P/E ratios relative to past averages and to the markets' current P/E ratio.
2. Quarterly earnings have "upward momentum" relative to the market.
3. Upward price momentum.

---

[79] Irwin Friend and Marshall Blume, "A New Look at the Capital Asset Pricing Model," *Journal of Finance* (March 1973).

[80] Fischer Black, "Yes, Virginia, There Is Hope: Tests of the Value Line Ranking System," University of Chicago, Center for Research in Security Prices (May 1971).

Relative weights assigned each of the three factors are based on a cross-sectional regression past data. Using time-series tests to evaluate consistency of performance, Black found that Group I performed better than Group V in each of the five years and that "the probability of this happening by change is one in 32."[81]

Additional tests were made of the data on a monthly basis. This involved constructing portfolios of all stocks in each ranking group weighted equally. Then, at the end of each month, a portion of all stocks that had gone up were sold, while portions of stocks that had declined were purchased.

Revising the portfolio on a monthly basis produced about 10 percent better return for Rank I than annual revisions and some—10 percent less for Group V. A statistical test of significant (*t* test) indicated that "The possibility that this could have occurred by chance is one in 10,000 . . . the success of the rankings was very consistent over time." Interestingly, the average betas for the groups were Rank I: 1.11; II: 1.03; III: 0.98; IV: 0.96; and V: 1.03.

Black states

> In conclusion, it does appear that there is hope that traditional methods
> of portfolio management and security analysis can succeed. However,
> I must continue to maintain that it is a rather small hope. The Value
> Line Ranking System is one of only two or three clear examples I have
> seen that show significant performance over a reasonable period of time.

Figure 19 reflects the record of the five Value Line ranking groups in the 1965–78 period.

Kaplan and Weil—Beta versus Value Line Performance. Robert Kaplan and Roman Weil tested the beta risk measurement concept against the conventional performance concept in the Value Line stock selection contest.[82] The Value Line conducted a contest in which contestants selected a portfolio of 25 stocks from the Value Line List of 1,400 stocks. Contestants' portfolios were rated on the basis of the average percentage price increase of their 25 stocks in the six months ending in February 1973.

Kaplan and Weil said

> As believers in the efficient market theory, we did not think we can
> pick a portfolio of 25 stocks that will significantly and consistently outper-
> form other portfolios of equal risk. . . . Therefore, we chose to enter
> the contest with two portfolios, one from each end of the risk spectrum.

They reasoned that the high-beta portfolio should increase faster in a rising market. Conversely, if stock prices generally declined, the

---

[81] Ibid., p. 4.

[82] Robert S. Kaplan and Roman L. Weil, "Risk and the Value Line Contest," *Financial Analysts Journal* (July–August 1973), pp. 56–61.

Figure 19
Record of Value Line Rankings for Timeliness April 16, 1965–December 26, 1978
(without allowance for changes in rank)

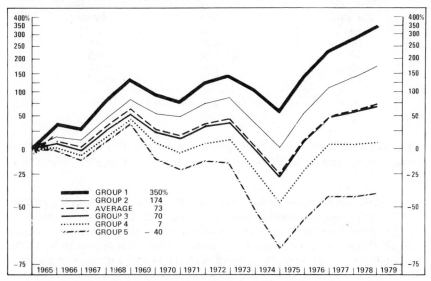

Source: Value Line "Selection and Opinion," July 2, 1979.

low beta portfolio would do relatively well. Kaplan and Weil's two portfolios were distributed as seen in Table 26.

Table 26
Expected Performance of Companies in High Beta and Low Beta Portfolios

Value Line Expected Performance Ranking Group	High Beta	Low Beta
I	1	2
II	7	7
III	10	9
IV	4	6
V	3	1
Total	25	25
Average ranking	3.04	2.88
Average beta	2.13	0.21

Source: After Kaplan and Weil, "Risk and Value Line Contest."

During the six month's contest period, the Value Line Index of some 1,400 stocks declined 8.8 percent. The Kaplan-Weil *low* beta portfolio increased 3.8 percent which placed it in the top 2.3 percent of the more than 89,000 contest portfolios. The *high* beta portfolio declined 22.9 percent and was in the lowest 0.6 percent of all portfolios.

Table 27
Performance versus Betas

Betas by Quintile	Average Beta	Average Price Change
1st	0.48	+ 1.4%
2d	0.79	− 2.8
3d	1.02	− 6.6
4th	1.29	−10.5
5th	1.82	−15.0

Source: After Kaplan and Weil, "Risk and Value Line Contest."

Kaplan and Weil noted that systematic risk is also reflected in the overall performance of all portfolios as shown in Table 27. They concluded

> that the performance of these five portfolios is consistent with their differing risks and the realized market return over the contest period. . . . Detailed investigation of individual securities does not appear to pay off. While such investigation may turn up stocks that appear to be mildly under- or overvalued, the overall performance of a diversified portfolio of stocks is dominated by the systematic risk of the portfolio and market movements.[83]

Bishop and Rollins—Lowry's Reports: A Denial of Market Efficiency? E. L. Bishop and J. R. Rollins[84] endeavored to test whether security price movements follows the random walk and efficient market concept, i.e., whether security price movements were independent of prior price patterns.

Their approach was to test "buy-sell-hold" recommendations of Lowry's Reports, a technical service. The key element in the Lowry approach is the linkage of daily up or down price changes with trading volumes of all listed stocks. Daily totals are aggregated in series of 15-day (short term) and 50-day (long term) series. The test was confined to five mutual funds believed to be a cross section of investment company objectives. The results of the tests are summarized in Table 28.

The authors concluded that: (1) funds with beta coefficients less than 1.0 produced trading returns inferior to a simple buy-and-hold strategy, (2) the S&P 500, as well as the funds, with a 1.0 Beta, produce trading returns virtually the same as buy-and-hold, and (3) *superior* performance was achieved with the higher beta funds.

It is then concluded that "if market returns are truly random, it will be impossible to capture favorable price movements over time by trading regardless of a portfolio's beta coefficients."

---

[83] Ibid., p. 60.

[84] E. L. Bishop, III and J. R. Rollins, "Lowry's Reports: A Denial of Market Efficiency?" *The Journal of Portfolio Management* (Fall 1977), pp. 21–27.

Table 28
Summary of Results of Lowry's Basic Trend Program and Simple Buy-and-Hold Program

Time Periods	Fund I Boston Fund (Beta: .563)		Fund II Dividend Shares (Beta: .730)		S&P 500 (Beta: 1.000)		Fund III National Investors (Beta: 1.010)		Fund IV Delaware Fund (Beta: 1.083)		Fund V Keystone S-4 (Beta: 1.800)	
	Buy and Hold	Trading Program	Buy and Hold	Trading Program	Buy and Hold	Trading Program	Buy and Hold	Trading Program	Buy and Hold	Trading Program	Buy and Hold	Trading Program
1950–75	1.062	1.061	1.083	1.079	1.097	1.102	1.106	1.111	1.083	1.086	1.084	1.153
1950–60	1.117	1.094	1.141	1.131	1.172	1.176	1.190	1.192	1.132	1.128	1.220	1.245
1950–65	1.105	1.093	1.136	1.130	1.158	1.156	1.161	1.176	1.123	1.130	1.180	1.205
1960–75	1.025	1.001	1.028	1.012	1.042	1.045	1.050	1.036	1.046	1.056	.996	1.090
1960–70	1.045	1.013	1.079	1.040	1.078	1.061	1.106	1.066	1.095	1.077	1.064	1.140
1960–65	1.082	1.061	1.118	1.110	1.118	1.102	1.109	1.115	1.099	1.105	1.102	1.134
1965–70	1.004	.970	1.047	.973	1.104	1.104	1.107	1.107	1.116	1.057	1.124	1.149
1965–75	.994	.968	1.010	.970	1.012	1.017	1.019	.990	1.028	1.035	.960	1.066
1970–75	.986	.967	.983	.960	.972	1.014	.947	.948	.954	1.011	.833	.996

Source: Bishop and Rollins, "A Denial of Market Efficiency," p. 25.

In light of the unusually high returns achieved by the Keystone S-4 Fund, additional statistical tests were made of its performance. Subsequently, Bishop and Rollings determined that (1) trading outperformed buy-and-hold in every test and (2) in the 25 years from 1950 to 1975, the trading program outperformed buy-and-hold in 15 of the individual 21 years when there was trading activity. They concluded that there was only a 4 percent probability that such performance resulted from mere chance.

On that basis, they stated "the trading program, has, in fact demonstrated a significant ability to out-perform a naive buy-and-hold program." Bishop and Rollins also pointed out that virtually all the many elaborate statistical tests of random price behavior published by academics have focused exclusively on price changes alone and that "price changes alone paint a unidimensional picture of market activity. *Volume* data combined with *price* changes show patterns of money flow into or out of the market and are thus a more complete picture of investor behavior." It is reasoned that stock prices may exhibit complete random behavior during extended periods of nonrandom behavior." It is concluded that "this study indicated that extraordinary gains can be achieved by sophisticated technical analysis using weak form data. This is a violation of both the efficient market and random walk theories."[85]

Beebower and Bergstrom—Pension Performance Consistency: 1966– 1970 versus 1971–1975. Gilbert Beebower and Gary Bergstrom analyzed the performance consistency of 148 pension and profit sharing funds over two five-year periods.[86]

They first selected unbiased samples of 148 portfolios from the Becker Funds Evaluation Service. This sample aggregated an investment of some $60 billion.

The several funds were ranked in ten groups. Thus, the top 15 funds in the 1966–70 period were designated as Group 1, the next 15 funds were placed in Group 2 and so on. The performance of the same ten groups were measured and ranked in the 1971–75 period. Performance was calculated by regressing the risk adjusted return of each group against the S&P 500. Beebower and Bergstrom reasoned that, "If the market is indeed efficient, the abnormal return on any portfolio will be insignificantly different from zero."

Table 29 shows key results for the two periods.

The authors found that the group of equity portfolios ranking highest in the 1966–70 period also did so in the 1971–75 period and that such consistency was not likely to result from chance. Also that such results

---

[85] Ibid., p. 27.

[86] Gilbert L. Beebower and Gary L. Bergstrom, "A Performance analysis of Pension and Profit-Sharing Portfolios: 1966–1975," *Financial Analysts Journal* (May–June 1977), pp. 3–12.

Table 29
Equity Portfolio Performance versus Standard & Poor's 500 Index

Portfolio Group	1966-70		1971-75	
	$\hat{\alpha}$	$\hat{\beta}$	$\hat{\alpha}$	$\hat{\beta}$
1	0.70	1.08	−0.27	1.10
2	0.38	1.03	−0.24	1.12
3	0.39	1.18	−0.48	1.17
4	0.16	1.20	−0.42	1.14
5	0.09	1.11	−0.18	1.12
6	−0.10	1.11	−0.46	1.13
7	−0.31	1.10	−0.36	1.13
8	−0.50	1.07	0.02	1.11
9	−0.55	1.12	−0.66	1.11
10	−0.89	1.15	−0.65	1.15
Group Average				
1–5	0.35	1.12	−0.32	1.13
6–10	0.47	1.11	−0.42	1.13

Source: After Beebower and Bergstrom, "Pension Performance."

could have resulted from differences in information, transaction costs, or other factors.

They noted that there appears to be (1) no relationship between group number and beta and (2) no relationship between alpha, or t-statistic of alpha, and any other statistic.

Wallich—Stock Price Gyrations versus Intrinsic Values. Henry Wallich expressed concern relative to the wide fluctuations in stock market prices in recent years. He noted that

> recent experience is a challenge to the "dart throwing" theory. It is an experience that confirms the wisdom of traditional investment policies, as I believe these policies are practiced by trust officers all over the country. . . . Recent extreme gyrations of some stocks, in my view, seriously question the assertion of the "dart throwing theory" that stocks always are valued at the price that the best analysis suggests.[87]

In reference to the 1968–70 price debacle, Wallich stated "on the contrary, such extreme gyrations seem to show that these stocks were not correctly valued and that the application of wisdom and good sense could discover this."

Charles Kuehner[88] noted that more recent evidence in support of Wallich's thesis is found in market gyrations in the 1971–73 period. The 30 companies included in the Dow-Jones Industrial Index are

---

[87] Henry C. Wallich, "Traditional vs. Performance Stock Valuation," *Commercial and Financial Chronicle* (February 18, 1971), pp. 1–5. Used with permission from Commercial and Financial Chronicle, 120 Broadway, New York, N.Y.

[88] Charles D. Kuehner, "Legal Implications of Random Walk Hypothesis" (New York University Law School Seminar, February 1974).

among the world's largest with assets and sales in the hundreds of millions up to several billions of dollars. These firms are widely held and closely followed. Thus, under the efficient market hypothesis, one might assume that prices of these stocks at any given time would provide valid evidence of each firm's "intrinsic value." Data in Table 30 raise question as to the market's ability to do so with any degree of stability. The table shows the price spread from low to high for each stock. Thus, if a stock's price ranged from a low of 30 to a high of 40, its price spread would be 33 percent. Price spreads in the table range from a minimum of 19 percent (General Motors in 1972) to a maximum of 173 percent (Chrysler in 1973). In 34 of the 90 cases, price fluctuations exceeded 50 percent and 80 of the 90 price fluctuations were 25 percent or more. This raises the question, did the underlying value of these well-known and established securities really fluctuate in accord with the gyrations in their market prices?

Morton—Relationship between Risk and Investor Returns. Walter Morton tested the efficiency of the market in discounting returns on

Table 30
Price Spread: Low to High Dow Jones 30 Industrials (1971–1973)

	1971	1972	1973
Allied Chemical	48%	29%	72%
Aloca	94	47	68
American Can	55	36	45
AT&T	32	30	21
American Brands	34	24	51
Anaconda	107	40	70
Bethlehem Steel	51	37	45
Chrysler	36	49	173
DuPont	22	28	40
Eastman Kodak	39	61	47
Esmark	57	31	95
Exxon	23	31	23
General Electric	43	25	38
General Foods	42	54	40
General Motors	24	19	89
Goodyear	29	26	155
Int'l. Harvester	47	51	76
Int'l. Nickel	86	25	40
Int'l. Paper	43	27	73
Johns-Manville	26	52	128
Owens Illinois	62	35	59
Procter & Gamble	45	48	35
Sears Roebuck	41	28	58
Standard Oil of Cal.	28	52	37
Texaco	34	34	73
Union Carbide	30	24	77
United Aircraft	84	71	123
U.S. Steel	44	27	43
Westinghouse	16	43	95
Woolworth (F.W.)	57	56	102

Source: Kuehner, "Legal Implications of Random Walk Hypothesis," New York University Law School Seminar (February 1974).

Figure 20
Realized Investor Yields versus Market Price Fluctuation for 400
Standard & Poor's Industrial Companies

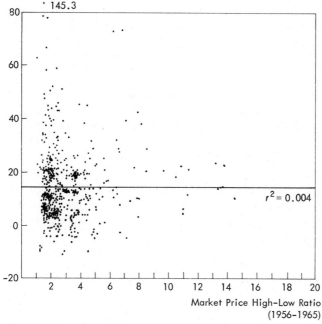

Average of Realized
Yields (1966–1968) (percent)

Source: Morton, "Market Price."

individual stocks over a future period of one, two, and three years.[89] For this purpose he studied 400 of the S&Ps 425 industrial companies for which complete data were available over the 12-year period 1956–68.

For the ten-year period 1956–66, an index of high-low market price fluctuations was calculated as a measure of instability or risk. Thus, a stock with a low average market price of 5 in 1958 and a high average market price of 10 in 1963 was assigned an index of 2, a high of 30 and a low of 10 was given an index of 3, and so on. Realized investor yields were measured by market appreciation and dividends over the 1965–68 period in six combinations of one-, two-, or three-year holding periods.

Figure 20 shows the relationship between average realized yield and market price instability for each of the 400 S&P companies. Morton observed that

the proposition that wide fluctuations mean high returns has no substance in theory or in fact. Investors must still rely on their knowledge and

[89] Walter A. Morton, "Market Price, Risk and Investor Return," *Commercial and Financial Chronicle* (June 3, 1971), pp. 1–5.

judgment about the reasonably expected dividends and capital gains for individual stocks based on their analysis of the firm and the industry. . . . The source of the error that high risks will yield high returns is an elementary intellectual confusion between the relation of risk to *ex ante*, or expected return, and relation of risk to *ex post*, or realized return. The first proposition that an investor does not take large risks unless he *expects* a large return is a matter of common observation confirmed by fact, logic and data. But the second proposition that the *actual* return realized by investors is necessarily commensurate with the risk taken is an elementary error unsupported by fact, logic or data.[90]

Edesess—Beta versus Portfolio Performance. Edesess noted that the capital asset pricing model holds that the expected portfolio return is linearly related to expected market returns, with the coefficient of market return in the linear equation expressed as beta.[91] However, he stated that estimates of beta which use data from more than one time period assume the validity of some form of the random walk theory. Being mathematically precise in using the capital asset pricing model, according to Edesess, tells "how to maximize expected *instantaneous* returns for a given value of the statistical variance of the *instantaneous* returns. That's all."

Figure 21
Managed Equity Portfolios: Total Returns versus Betas 1962–1972 (three cycles)

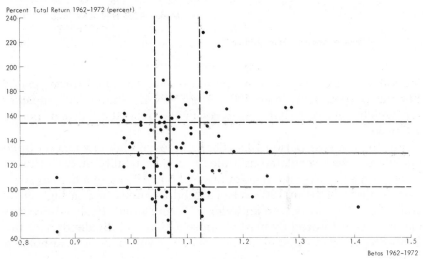

Source: After Edesess, "Resolved that Capital Asset."

[90] Ibid., p. 15.

[91] Michael Edesess, "Resolved that the Capital Asset Pricing Model Has Little Practical Value," University of Chicago, Seminar on the Analysis of Security Prices (October 1973).

Edesess raised two basic questions with regard to the capital asset pricing model.

1. The assumption that risk, which has many nuances and meanings, can be adequately measured by the statistical variance of the instantaneous return, or by beta.
2. The assumption that beta is constant over time.

He contends that investment management has not come to grips with the problem. Instead, Edesess said, it has "taken a leap to an abstract statement of the problem and, having leaped, we routinely accept our new situation as the starting point for all further work." He concluded that a major task facing investment management is to retreat from that leap.

Edesess studied 75 managed pension funds with regard to total return and historical beta over the 1962–72 period, which constitutes three market cycles (Figure 21), and 145 managed pension funds over the 1966–72 period, covering two market cycles (Figure 22).

Edesess concluded that based on both parametric and nonparametric tests of correlation there was "no evidence of correlation whatsoever" between beta and rate of return. Also he stated that "there was no reward for having had a higher historical beta." He added that either (1) there was no reward for assuming higher risk or (2) historical beta was not a proxy for risk.

Figure 22
Managed Equity Portfolios: Total Returns versus Beta 1966–1972 (two cycles)

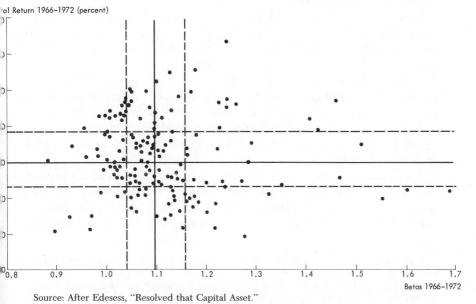

Total Return 1966–1972 (percent)

Betas 1966–1972

Source: After Edesess, "Resolved that Capital Asset."

Roll—Ambiguity When Performance Is Measured by the Securities Market Line. Roll probably ranks among the strongest of academic critics against efficient markets hypothesis and capital asset pricing theory. Roll contends that (a) betas and the securities market line criterion both fail to provide an unambiguous measure of risk, and can and will yield different judgements regarding performance of either securities or portfolios, depending upon which rational judge happens to employ the criterion,[92] and (b) "testing the asset pricing theory is difficult (and currently infeasible)."[93] His evidence is primarily theoretical; however the following paragraphs will summarize essential points of Roll's proof.

On the ambiguity of results when using beta or the securities market line as a criterion of performance, Roll argues:

> corresponding to every index, there is a beta for every individual asset (and thus for every portfolio); but these betas can be different for different indices and will be different for most. To consider the beta as an attribute of the individual asset alone is a significant mistake. For every asset, an index can be found to produce a beta of any desired magnitude, however large or small. Thus, for every asset (or portfolio) judicious choice of the index can produce any desired measured "performance," (positive or negative), against the securities market line (p. 1056).

Roll uses Figure 23 (A, B, C) to illustrate how three rational and reasonable judges can differ in assessing performance of 15 portfolios, where all parties agree that the securities market line is an appropriate criterion for performance evaluation.

Judge 1 chooses a market index "composed of equal weights in the individual assets" on the grounds that this, to him, "would be the most sensible portrayal of ignorance (regarding any better weighting scheme) and the fairest to all contestants."

Judge 2 "has studied asset pricing theory and argues that the appropriate index should have weights proportional to the aggregate market values of individual assets," and constructs an index accordingly.

Judge 3, "also a theorist, thinks that a good index should be mean-variance efficient in the sense of [Harry] Markowitz," and constructs an index accordingly.

Table 31 summarizes the properties of the three market indexes, and the resultant securities market line. All three indexes show the same mean return, 7.5 percent, with relatively small differences in variance of return. The slope and intercept of the three securities

---

[92] Richard Roll, "Ambiguity When Performance is Measured By The Securities Market Line," *The Journal of Finance* (September, 1978), pp. 1051–70.

[93] Richard Roll, "A Critique of the Asset Pricing Theory's Tests." *Journal of Financial Economics* (March, 1977), pp. 129–76.

Figure 23
Securities Market Lines and Positions of Selected Portfolios as Perceived by the Three Judges of the Contest*

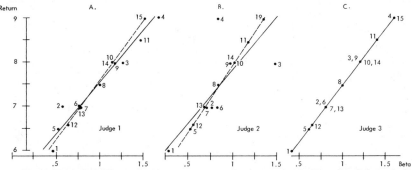

*The solid lines are ordinary least squares estimated securities market lines fitted through the fifteen contestants' portfolios. The dotted lines pass through portfolios 12–15, which were exactly mean/variance efficient ex post.
Source: Roll, "Ambiguity," p. 1056.

market lines differ ever so slightly; and all parties agree that "winners" and "losers" are correctly assessed by deviations from the line.

Each of the three judges concludes with a different set of assessments of performance of the 15 contestant portfolios, as shown on the rankings tabulated on Table 32 and graphed on Figure 23 (A, B, C). Roll then notes

> Although some contestants were similarly rated by both judges, (e.g., contestant 15 was ranked second by both and contestant 3 was ranked 14th by judge no. 1 and 15th by judge no. 2), other contestants were rated quite differently; (e.g., the number one winner according to judge no. 1 was a loser and ranked 13th out of 15 by judge no. 2) The rank correlation between the decisions of these two judges is only .0036 and the lack of agreement is clearly evident in the figure.
>
> As for judge no. 3, after calculating his securities market line and plotting the selected portfolios, he observes Figure 2(C). Every single

Table 31
Rankings of Contestants

			Judge No. 1							
Winners (best)→ (above the line)	2	15	14	5	10	/				
Losers (below the line)	6	13	9	8	7	12	4	11	3	1 ←(worst)
			Judge No. 2							
Winners (best)→	4	15	11	9	14	10	8	/		
Losers	13	1	12	7	5	2	6	3	←(worst)	

Source: Roll, Ibid., p. 1055.

Table 32
Indices and Securities Market Lines Used by the Three Judges in the Portfolio
Selection Contest

| | Composition of Index (percentage of index in security) | | | | Index | | Securities Market Line* | |
Judge	1	2	3	4	Mean Return	Variance of Return	Slope	Intercept
1	25	25	25	25	7.5	11.4	2.31	5.22
							(.119)	(.127)
2	10	40	40	10	7.5	13.0	2.40	5.46
							(.486)	(.444)
3†	18.2	37	21.5	23.3	7.5	11.0	2.57	4.93
							(0.)	(0.)

   * Standard errors are in parentheses. These lines were fitted cross-sectionally by ordinary least squares applied to mean returns and betas of the 15 portfolios in the contest.
   † Judge 3 actually specified more precise weights. The weights reported here have been rounded. (For example, the proportion of his index in asset 4 was actually 23.3214%). The exact weights were used in all calculations.
   Source: Roll, Ibid.

contestant is exactly on the line. Of course, this judge is unable to construct a ranking and can draw no inference about the relative abilities of contestants.

On past and potential testability of capital asset pricing theory, Roll contends, among other things, that "the theory is not testable unless the exact composition of the true market portfolio is known and used in the tests. This implies that the theory is not testable unless *all* individual assets are included in the sample" (p. 130).

"The market portfolio identification problem constitutes a severe limitation to the testability of the theory. No two investigators who disagree on the market's measured composition can be made to agree on the theory's test results" (p. 131).

Fouse—Integrating Fundamental Security Analysis with Efficient Market Theory. Fouse focused on practical applications of economic, market, and portfolio management theory.[94] He noted that economic theory holds that the value of a security is the discounted value of a future stream of dividends and that the widely used P/E model is a formulation of the traditional dividend model since the P/E is a function of EPS growth rate, payout ratio, and the appropriate discount rate. Fouse cited the need to reconcile conventional financial analysis with the efficient market theory: Given the consensus forecast for the stream of future dividends, common stocks will be efficiently priced in the market relative to the risk-free return plus a premium for risk

---

   [94] William L. Fouse, "Practical Applications of Economic, Market, and Portfolio Theory," Stanford University Graduate School of Business, 1972 Investment Management Program (July 1972).

that cannot be diversified away in portfolios. On this basis and using different proportions of risk, or a combination of stocks plus borrowing, "the market should tend to be so arbitraged that no net expected advantage should exist for one strategy over another."

In this arbitrage process, Fouse stated, the market, which is made up of a large number of well-informed buyers and sellers acting in their own best interest, discounts the future at an efficient rate. And as risk increases, these well-informed investors demand greater returns. On this basis he holds, given consensus expectations of the future, capital market theory provides a quantitative way to estimate market risks—historical beta is used as a proxy for future beta.

Working from this theoretical construct, security analysts in the Wells Fargo financial analysis department were asked to classify stocks as to risk developed from fundamental analysis. These ratings were arranged in eight groups from lowest to highest risk. Fouse found "a perfect match" between these risk ratings and the average betas of each group. Thus, it was concluded that traditional analysis, or accounting measures of risk, are embedded in the market price based risk measure, i.e. beta.

As a next step to incorporate this concept into portfolio management, a "market line" was developed to reflect the investors' required discount rate for each risk class. Thus, if the efficient market hypothesis is correct, there is a logical correspondence between implied earnings growth rates and actual forecast. Fouse tested the data for 25 major stocks, using growth estimates provided by a dozen large Wall Street firms. The five-year growth rates implied by the model averaged 10.4 percent. The Wall Street composite was 10.5 percent. R^2 was 0.90. On this basis, an ex ante market line was developed. Fouse pointed out that the realized return on each security would depend upon changes in perceived risk, changes in the market's price for risk, and changes in the consensus forecast of a security.

The concept was tested for 28 months using the beta deciles of the S&P 500. The relationship between the beta deciles and realized rate of return is shown in Table 33.

Table 33
Standard & Poor's 500 Stocks Relationship of
Beta Deciles and Realized Rate of Return over
28 Months

Relationship	Time Period (months)
Strong	16
Noticable	9
No relation	3
Total	28

Source: Fouse, "Practical Applications."

"However, for the 28-month period as a whole," Fouse stated, "beta deciles did not predict return. We think because excess return in stocks over borrowing rates [during this time span] were too small for beta to assert itself." The adoption of this concept by Wells Fargo has meant that "in the area of security analysis we have returned to fundamentals with a vengeance." Careful long-range forecasts are integrated into the market line, and conventional security analysis thereby has a direct interface with modern capital theory.

Fouse cited results of this approach in the 12 months ending July 1972 for some 270 common stocks, which is summarized in Table 34.

Table 34
Realized Rate of Return 12 Months: July
1971–July 1972

Risk Sector	Rate of Return
1	+ 7%
2	+ 9
3	+ 7
4	+15
5	+28

Source: Fouse, "Practical Applications."

Friend, Westerfield, and Granito—Integrating Expectations (Forecasts) into Tests of Market Efficiency.   The capital asset pricing model, according to William Sharpe,[95] "deals with predictions concerning a future period. It does not assume that the predictions or the implied relationships among them are stable over time. Nor does it assume that actual results will accord with such predictions, either period-by-period or, in any simple sense, 'on average.' All the econometric sophistication in the world will not completely solve the basic problem associated with the use of ex post data to test theories dealing with ex ante predictions" (p. 920).

Friend, Randolph Westerfield, and Michael Granito substitute ex ante (expected) for ex post (realized) measures of return in testing capital asset pricing theory.[96] They collected expected annual rates of return from commercial banks, insurance companies and investment counseling firms regarding NYSE stocks over $100 million in size, all for each of three dates as follows: August 1974, expectations on 66 stocks from 21 financial institutions; March 1976, expectations on 49 stocks from 33 institutions; February 1977, expectations on 56 stocks from 29 financial institutions.

[95] William F. Sharpe, "Discussion," *The Journal of Finance* (June 1978) pp. 917–20.

[96] Irwin Friend, Randolph Westerfield, and Michael Granito, "New Evidence on the Capital Asset Pricing Model" *The Journal of Finance* (June 1978) pp. 903–17.

The annual rate of return in a particular stock expected by a specific institution was obtained for each of the aforesaid years by adding a spot dividend yield (adjusted for the expected growth rate) to the annual growth rate in per share earnings expected over a five-year period and used by these institutions to estimate expected returns for purposes of their investment decisions.

Mean expected returns were computed for every stock for which at least five institutions regularly estimate the long-run, i.e., five years or longer, expected growth rate. In computing the mean expected return for each stock, equal weight was given to the estimate of each institution.

Armed with the above data Friend, Westerfield, and Granito computed linear regressions for each of the three aforesaid samples, to test whether capital asset pricing theory might be useful in explaining the observed phenomena in which we are interested, namely risky asset returns. Mean return for each stock was regressed on all three following explanatory variables:

1. The beta coefficient for each stock. The beta were based on monthly rates of return for the preceding five years. The market rate of return was assumed to be the return on the S&P 500 Index.
2. The residual standard deviation for each stock; based on monthly rates of return for the preceding five years and the S&P 500 Index (same as beta).
3. The standard deviation of the returns for that stock expected by the different institutions. This is basically a measure of the heterogeneity of expectations, an ex ante measure of the market's risk assessment.

To test the difference in explanatory power of risk factors on ex ante versus ex post returns, the authors also ran regressions using realized returns. "The ex post return used for each stock in each of the three periods covered was the monthly average for the 60-month period preceding the month of the year for which the ex ante return was estimated" (p. 908).

The results, which the authors published in the form of estimates of regression coefficients and associated statistics not reproduced here, "while not at all strong, support the view that the residual standard deviation of return and the related variance measures play fully as significant a role in the pricing of risky assets as the beta coefficient" (p. 908). That is, all three of the aforesaid explanatory variables were significant; not beta alone. The authors also note: "The explanatory power of the ex post regressions . . . is even lower than that for the ex ante regressions" (p. 908).

Malkiel and Firstenberg—Beating the Market Averages.   Malkiel and Paul Firstenberg[97] raised a fundamental question "How can the market be efficient and inefficient at the same time?" They then proceeded to answer that question.

They noted, "many studies indicate there is no evidence that professional firms can produce, on a sustained basis, above average returns from managing stock portfolios of equivalent risk." They attribute this to the efficiency of the stock market "where prices will generally reflect both the problems and opportunities" of any given stock. This condition results from the "countless security analysts thoroughly studying most securities," especially widely-held institutional-grade stocks.

Evidence to support the efficacy thesis was obtained from data published by Becker Securities Corporation of New York. Portfolio performance results for several hundred institutional common stock portfolios is shown in Table 35.

Table 35
Portfolios Outperformed by Standard & Poor's 500 Index

Holding Period	%
5 Years 1973–77	79
10 Years 1968–77	83
15 Years 1962–77	85

Source: After Malkiel and Firstenberg, "A Winning Strategy for an Efficient Market."

Malkiel and Firstenberg suggest "you can tell your random walker that this is an investment strategy that enables you to buy a broadly diversified portfolio of common stocks—but at a discount from net asset value in a closed-end investment company." Their strategy assumes (1) stocks and bonds in the closed-end fund do just as well on the market and (2) no widening of the discount from asset value. On this basis, performance is logically expected to out-perform the overall market.

They also note that closed-end funds tend to have less volatility and cited data for two groups of five funds each shown in Table 36.

They concluded that closed-end funds represent an opportunity to reduce investment risk and, since the shares are purchased at a discount, investors will earn larger returns that would be obtained by buying the shares in the underlying portfolio.

Friend, Baumol, and Murray—Efficiency Revisited. Friend stated "to much of the public, the stock market seems to be a legalized gambling casino. To many economists, the stock market seems endowed with an almost mystical degree of efficiency, even if what is meant

---

[97] Burton G. Malkiel and Paul B. Firstenberg, "A Winning Strategy for an Efficient Market," *The Journal of Portfolio Management* (Summer 1978) pp. 20–25.

Table 36
Volatility of Closed-End Investment Companies, January 1970–January 1978

	Historical Betas	
	Calculated from Movements of:	
	Net Asset Value	*Share Prices*
Closed-End Funds		
General American Investors	1.06	1.05
Lehman	1.04	1.08
Madison	0.88	0.99
Niagara	0.95	0.84
Tri-Continental.............................	1.06	0.87
Average	1.00	0.97
Dual Purpose Funds		
American Dual Vest	2.07	1.59
Gemini	2.25	1.62
Income and Capital	2.10	1.77
Putnam......................................	2.49	1.41
Scudder	1.59	1.34
Average	2.10	1.55

Source: After Malkiel and Firstenberg.

by efficiency is not always clear."[98] Which of these two extreme views is correct? Or does neither accord with reality, and the answer lie somewhere in between?

A broad overview of the past half century suggests that there have been numerous occasions when large bodies of investors have been emotionally affected by fads and fashions in Wall Street. Turning back the clock to late October 1929, one might have difficulty in asserting that, at that time, stock market prices were efficiently discounting the future. The same might have been said in March 1932 after the market had plunged by some 80–90 percent.

More recently, in early 1962, stock market ebullience even surpassed that of 1929, but it was relatively short lived. On May 28 a selling panic occurred with share volume reaching the highest level since 1929, thereby wiping out some $21 billion of market values in one day. Shares of many of the nation's leading firms dropped by one quarter to one third of their value in less than a week. Even a month later, after the dust had settled and stock prices had stabilized, market volumes reflected widespread disinterest in purchasing even the bluest of the "blue chips" at relative bargain prices.

A similar scenario occurred during the growth stock craze of 1967–68. At that time it was said that stock prices were not only discounting the future—they were discounting the hereafter as well. New issues of relatively unseasoned companies were eagerly gobbled up with

---

[98] Irwin Friend, "The Economic Consequences of the Stock Market," *American Economic Association Papers and Proceedings* (May 1972).

prices doubling and tripling or even more during the first week of trading. Many investors—large and small—operated on "the greater fool theory," i.e., to sell the shares later to other investors—whoever they might be. But this did not happen. In the ensuing 18 months, the stock market was hit by wave after wave of selling, much of it reaching panic proportions. As a result, by May of 1970, a pervasive state of disenchantment obtained. As before, shares of many of the nation's leading corporations were discounting not the hereafter but Armageddon. Within a year later most of these same securities were selling 25–50 percent higher and some even more.

By year end 1972 the P/E of the "nifty fifty" had zoomed to unprecedented levels, e.g., Xerox was selling at 46× earnings, Disney at 64× and Polaroid at 91×. Two years later, these same stocks had plummeted in value by 72 percent, 86 percent and 91 percent respectively.[99] How might we explain this apparently irrational behavior of a reputedly rational, all-efficient market?

Friend noted that "one important attribute of an efficient market in which investors are not indifferent to risk is that the risk as perceived by the investor when he is making his decision should correspond fairly closely to the risk which actually materializes." But he also observed that while such measures of risk as the relative stability of return on a stock tend to be reasonably invariant over time and that the empirical evidence generally points to a positive relationship between risk and return, "the results are by no means uniform or strong." After considering several other facets of the problem Friend concludes "it seems clear that no convincing case can be made for the position held by many economists that the stock market possesses a high degree of allocational efficiency, though the market does appear to transmit information rather rapidly."[100]

William Baumol noted that "we have all seen cases where the behavior of prices on the stock market has apparently been capricious or even worse, cases where hysteria has magnified largely irrelevant events into controlling influences."[101] Baumol also stated that while most analysis would doubtless agree that the price of a security should be determined, ultimately, by the companies' prospective earnings, "It is not clear, however, how closely the value of future earnings and share prices correspond in practice."[102]

Noting that there is not a sharp and well-defined conflict between

---

[99] Sanford Calderwood, "The Truth About Index Funds," *Financial Analyst Journal* (July–August 1977), p. 38.

[100] Friend, p. 218.

[101] Reprinted by permission of the publisher from *The Stock Market and Economic Efficiency* by William J. Baumol (New York: Fordham University Press, 1965), p. 7. © 1965 by Fordham University Press.

[102] Ibid., p. 35.

two extreme types of influences which account for stock prices, Baumol offers two possible explanations:

1. One explanation gives stock prices as being set systematically and rationally by an economic process which leads prices to approximate the economic value of the shares.
2. Another explanation envisions stock prices as essentially "a speculative and anticipatory phenomenon" in which "stock prices are what they are only because of what purchasers and sellers expect them to be."[103]

Roger Murray offered another essentially psychological explanation, "the financial community has a pervasive and highly developed talent for rationalizing its aberrations. When greed overcomes prudence, the arrival of a new era is proclaimed . . . concepts become a substitute for earning power. The compound interest table is banished as earnings growth is projected into the hereafter.[104]

IMPLICATIONS, CHALLENGE, AND CONCLUSION

After the random walk-efficient market hypothesis had been debated for over a decade, C. W. J. Granger stated

> there is still a great deal of controversy over the random walk model of stock market price movement. On the one hand, statisticians continue to provide evidence in favor of the model and, on the other hand, economists and financial analysts continue to state that they do not believe in the correctness of the model.[105]

Granger stated that this problem highlights

> the lack of contact between many of the academic workers and real financial analysts or market operators. One gets an impression of mistrust, partly due to the barrier formed by the different technical languages used by both sides. It is to be hoped that this gap will decrease as each side recognizes the advantages of closer cooperation.

He continued that the output of the academics often have important implications for analysts but that it must be properly understood and assimilated. On the other hand, he indicated that academics need to concentrate more on the actual problems of importance to analysts.

In this chapter an effort has been made to delineate the different points of view and sharpen up the thrust of the arguments on all sides

---

[103] Ibid., p. 36.

[104] Roger F. Murray, "Institutionalization of the Stock Market," *Financial Analysis Journal* (March–April 1974), p. 18.

[105] C. W. J. Granger, "What the Random Walk Model Does NOT Say," *Financial Analysts Journal* (May–June 1970), pp. 91–93.

of the spectrum. Regardless of whether one subscribes to the random walk-efficient market hypothesis, we must agree that the dialogue has served a useful purpose. Namely, it has helped to bring the academic and financial communities into closer appreciation of each other's points of view. It has also forced both the technician and the fundamentalist to rethink their premises and methods of evaluating securities. It has likewise posed certain implications and challenges for both.

Implications

Lorie and Hamilton, strong proponents of the efficient market-random walk hypothesis, summarize its implications in three different areas:[106]

1. Value of the Analyst. "The most general implication of the efficient market hypothesis is that most security analysis is logically incomplete and valueless." They asserted that for "true believers in efficient markets" an analyst's recommendation to buy or sell must be predicated on a significant difference between the analyst's views and those of other investors whose opinions have established the stock's current market price.

2. Economics of Scale in Security Analysis and Portfolio Management. The question of efficient allocation of human resources is also stepped up by increasing competition. Analysis of securities "costs about the same whether the amount available for investment is $1,000 or $1 billion." Thus if such endeavors could produce superior returns of, say, 0.5 percent, they state this would produce "additional returns of $5 on the investment of $1,000 and of $5 million on the investment of $1 billion." On this basis they conclude that security research "might make sense for large financial institutions having billions of dollars to manage, while it would not make sense for investors with smaller sums."

3. Consistently Superior Performance. Another implication of the efficient markets theory is "the extreme unlikelihood that one can consistently earn superior rates of return by analyzing public information in conventional ways." Thus, Lorie and Hamilton suggest that "the only hope for superiority in results like in seeking unique ways of forming expectations about the prospects for individual companies."

Challenge to Security Analysis

Another leading advocate of the efficient market-random walk hypothesis has specified two challenges to conventional security analysts:

1. Challenge to the Chartist. Fama states that

---

[106] Lorie and Hamilton, *The Stock Market.*

if the random walk model is a valid description of reality, the work of the chartist is of no real value in stock market analysis . . . the only way the chartist can vindicate his position is to show that he can *consistently* use his techniques to make better than chance predictions of stock prices. It is not enough for him to talk mystically about patterns that he sees in the data. He must show that he can consistently use these patterns to make meaningful predictions of future prices.[107]

2. Challenge to the Fundamental Analyst.   Fama also suggests that "if the random walks theory is valid and if security exchanges are 'efficient' markets, then stock prices in any point in time will represent good estimates of intrinsic or fundamental values." On this basis, he concludes that additional fundamental analysis is of value only when the analyst has information or new insights not already embedded in a stock's current market price. Thus, "if the analyst has neither better insights nor better information, he may as well forget about fundamental analysis and choose securities by some random selection procedure."[108]

Conclusion

This review has endeavored to objectively report on both sides of the efficient market-random walk debate. Virtually all the important literature in the field over the past quarter century has been evaluated and much of it distilled in this chapter.

The findings of the several studies capsulized in this report vary widely as to the efficient market-random walk question. Some studies accept the efficient market-random walk *in toto;* others reject it on all counts. In the main this is due to basic differences with respect to:

1. *Assumptions.* This includes such assumptions as "perfect markets." Malkiel,[109] for one, has commented that the random walk theory's key assumption is that at any given time stock prices sell at the best estimate of their intrinsic value but that "this line of reasoning is uncomfortably close to that used by the proponents of the greater fool theory." Other controversial assumptions center on whether beta truly measures the risk of a stock investment, and on how to measure beta and its future predictability.
2. *Time horizon.* The period covered by the several studies also appears to be crucial to the conclusions reached. For example, the basic

---

[107] Eugene F. Fama, "What Random Walk Really Means," *Institutional Investor* (April 1968), p. 40.

[108] Ibid.

[109] Burton G. Malkiel, *A Random Walk Down Wall Street* (New York, W. W. Norton, 1973).

market trend—whether it is a roaring bull market, a bear market, or a trendless sideways market—seems to affect the results obtained. Additionally, some studies use daily price change data, others use weekly, monthly, or annual data. This too seems to have affected the results. Thus, Fama[110] used price changes on a *daily* basis for the 30 individual companies in the Dow-Jones Industrial Average. On this basis he concluded there was no measurable pattern of "runs" in stock prices. On the other side of the coin, Shiskin[111] employed *monthly* price changes in the S&P 400 company index as a whole and concluded "runs" in stock prices clearly existed.

3. *Companies used.* Results were also affected by selecting fundamentally different sources of basic data input. A number of studies employed only companies above a certain size limit. Others used broad lists of companies, both large and small, such as the 1,400 companies published in the Value Line, or all 1,800 companies listed on the N.Y.S.E. Some studies employed individual companies. Other studies used composites ranging from 10 companies up to 300, or more, as a single item of input. This also impacted the results obtained.

4. *Factors evaluated.* Wide differences were found between the several studies with respect to the factors evaluated. Some studies focused on changes in market prices, others measured total returns, that is, dividend yield plus market price appreciation over one year or a span of several years. With regard to purchases and sales of stocks, some studies were conducted on the basis of no stock exchange commissions; others used the standard New York Stock Exchange Commission. On that point, Alexander[112] asserted that recognizing transaction costs seems to invalidate the outcomes of such studies. He noted that paying "the house" even a minimum commission on a "heads or tails" coin tossing gamble would serve to invalidate the 50–50 outcome universally accepted in this arena.

At the outset of this chapter (see footnote 5) it was noted that one of the early pioneers and leading advocates of fundamental security analysis, Benjamin Graham, had voiced doubts about the ability of professionally managed funds to outperform the market as a whole because such funds are too large a part of the total picture. More recently, William F. Sharpe, a leading pioneer in the capital asset pricing model on which the efficient market theory is based, has expressed "second thoughts about the efficiency of the market." He stated "I still believe the market is highly efficient, but I can no longer adhere to a hard-line view that the market is hyperefficient and never pro-

---

[110] Fama: *Behavior of Stock Market Prices,* supra.

[111] Shiskin: *Systematic Aspects of Stock Price Fluctuations,* supra.

[112] Alexander: *Price Movements,* supra.

cesses its information wrongly."[113] Sharpe also noted that "there has to be an incentive for people to do research, and in equilibrium there have to be some managers who can earn large enough returns (in excess of the market returns) to cover the costs of their research."[114] He concluded "The vast majority of active management is very conventional, and the record of the index funds versus the managers is a very serious indictment of them."[115]

In short, it is not possible to declare a "winner" or "loser" in the efficient market-random walk debate. Rather, weighing the total body of evidence, pro and con, the jury must render the identical verdict for both sides "SCOTCH VERDICT—NOT PROVED."

---

[113] William F. Sharpe quoted by E. F. Ehbar, *Fortune* (February 26, 1979), p. 105.

[114] Ibid., p. 106.

[115] Ibid., p. 107.

Chapter 5

Modern Portfolio Theory*

EDWIN J. ELTON *and* **MARTIN J. GRUBER**
Graduate School of Business Administration
New York University
New York, New York

OVERVIEW

If one picks up the daily press or reads the material from brokerage firms or banks, one continually sees references to modern portfolio theory. Modern portfolio theory refers to the theory that portfolio's can be selected on the basis of their mean return and risk. This chapter discusses modern portfolio theory. It is divided into four sections. In the first section we discuss how portfolios can be analyzed when mean return and risk determine their desirability. In the second section we discuss more precisely what is meant by the terms mean return and risk. In the third section we discuss the estimates needed to determine the preferred portfolios. Finally, in the last section, we discuss the techniques for selecting preferred portfolio from among all possible portfolios.

THE PORTFOLIO CHOICE PROBLEM

The assumption that portfolios can be selected on the basis of mean return and risk is the key assumption of modern portfolio theory. This means that we can pictorially represent the portfolio choice problem as shown in Figure 1.

---

* This chapter is based on a section of Edwin J. Elton and Martin J. Gruber, *Modern Portfolio Theory* (New York: John Wiley, forthcoming).

160

Figure 1
The Portfolio Choice Problem

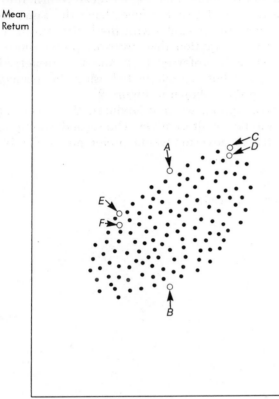

The dots represent the mean return and risk of different investments. Some of these dots are portfolios, some are individual securities. When one considers all the investments available and all the possible combinations that exist, then one realizes that we were conservative in representing alternatives and that Figure 1 should have many more dots.

To choose among the offerings, two assumptions allow the enormous number of choices represented in Figure 1 to be reduced to a manageable number of choices. These assumptions are:

1. Investors prefer more money to less money.
2. Investors are risk averse.

The assumption that investors prefer more to less money means that an investor would rather have $2,000 than $1,000. This very innocuous assumption leads to an enormous reduction in the number of portfolios that can be chosen. For example, in Figure 1 it means that portfolio *A* is to be preferred to portfolio *B*. Portfolios *A* and *B* have the same risk but portfolio *A* has higher mean return. If investors prefer more to less, then if two portfolios have the same risk, but different mean returns, the portfolio with the higher mean return is to be preferred. The assumption that investors prefer more to less allows us to say that *E* is preferred to *F*, and *C* is preferred to *D*. When all possible portfolios are eliminated using this principle, we reduce the choices to those shown in Figure 2:

With this one assumption, we have reduced the choice problem to a manageable number of alternatives. The second assumption, risk aversion, means that an investor would prefer not to gamble if by

Figure 2
Obtaining the Efficient Frontier

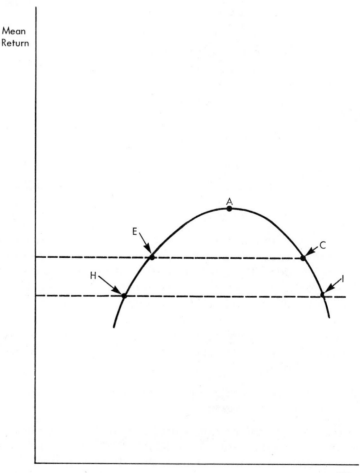

rejecting the gamble it does not affect average return. For example, assume an investor has the choice of a gamble that pays $1.00 if heads occurs and $0.00 if tails occurs, versus getting $.50 with certainty. Assume that the coin being flipped is fair. Thus, the investor taking the gamble would expect to earn $1.00 half the time and $0.00 half the time, or on the average the earning will be $.50. Thus, the average return of the gamble is $.50, the same as the return the investor earns without taking the gamble. Risk aversion implies that the investor would prefer $.50 with certainty. This assumption often bothers people and some further discussion might prove helpful. Risk aversion implies that on average, A rated bonds would be expected to offer a higher return than AAA bonds. This follows since if they offered the same return, all investors would prefer to hold the less risky AAA bonds and A rated bonds would not find a market.

The assumption of risk aversion means that portfolio *H* is preferred to portfolio *I* in Figure 2, and portfolio *E* is preferred to portfolio *C* since *E* and *H*, respectively, have less risk for the same mean return. The assumption of risk aversion reduces the portfolio problem to choosing among portfolios that lie on the curve *H, E,* and *A*. This is a manageable number of choices. Before going on, let's restate the analysis that allows reducing the choices from those shown in Figure 1 to those shown in Figure 2. Two assumptions were necessary: investors prefer more to less and investors are risk-averse. These assumptions implied the fundamental theorem of modern portfolio theory:

1. Given two portfolios with the same risk, investors prefer the one with the higher mean return.
2. Given two portfolios with the same mean return, investors prefer the one with the least risk.

The above theorem is the basis of modern portfolio theory. It allows the infinite number of possible portfolios that could be chosen to be reduced to a manageable number of alternatives. Throughout this section, we have been very ambiguous about the terms *mean return* and *risk*. It is time to be more precise.

MEAN RETURN AND RISK

The Mean Return

The concept of mean or average is standard in our culture. Pick up the newspaper and you'll often see figures on average income, batting averages, or average crime. The concept of an average is intuitive. If someone earns $11,000 one year and $9,000 in a second we say her average income in the two years is $10,000. If three children in a family are age 15, ten and five, then we say the average age is ten. A mean return or average is easy to compute. Consider the example shown in Table 1. If all outcomes are equally likely, then to determine the average, one adds up the outcomes and divides by the number of outcomes. Thus, for Table 1, the average is $(12 + 9 + 6) \div 3 = 9$. A second way to determine an average is to multiply each outcome by the probability that it will occur. When the outcomes are not equally likely, this facilitates the calculation. For Table 1 this is $(\frac{1}{3} \times 12) + (\frac{1}{3} \times 9) + (\frac{1}{3} \times 6) = 9$.

It is useful to express this intuitive calculation in terms of a formula. The symbol Σ should be read sum. Underneath the symbol we put the first value in the sum and what is varying. On the top of the symbol we put the final value in the sum. For example $\sum_{j=1}^{3}$ tells us to set $j = 1$ then $j = 2$ and then $j = 3$. If R_{ij} stands for the possible return of asset i and if the asset in question is the asset in Table 1, then the expected return on the asset in Table 1 can be expressed as:

$$\frac{\sum_{j=1}^{3} R_{ij}}{3} = \frac{R_{i1} + R_{i2} + R_{i3}}{3} = \frac{12 + 9 + 6}{3}$$

Using the summation notation just introduced and a bar over a variable to indicate average return, we have for the average return of equally likely returns:

$$\bar{R}_i = \sum_{j=1}^{N} \frac{R_{ij}}{N}$$

If the observations are not equally likely and if P_{ij} is the probability of the jth return on the ith asset then expected return is:

$$\bar{R}_i = \sum_{j=1}^{N} P_{ij} R_{ij}$$

This latter formula includes the formula for equally likely observations as a special case. If we have N observations each equally likely then the odds of any one occuring are $\frac{1}{N}$. Replacing the P_{ij} in the second formula by $\frac{1}{N}$ yields the first formula.

Table 1

Return	Probability	Event
12	1/3	A
9	1/3	B
6	1/3	C

A Measure of Risk

To measure risk we need a measure of how much the returns differ from the average.

Intuitively a sensible measure of how much the observations differ from the average is to simply examine this difference directly; that is examine:

$$R_{ij} - \bar{R}_i$$

Having determined this for each observation, one could obtain an over-all measure by taking the average of this difference. Although this is intuitively sensible, there is a problem. Some of the differences will be positive and some negative and these will tend to cancel out. The result of the cancelling out could be such that the average difference for a highly variable return need be no larger than the average difference for an asset with a highly stable return. In fact, it can be shown that the average value of this difference must always be precisely zero. The reader is encouraged to verify this with the example in Table 1. Thus, the sum of the differences from the mean tells us nothing about the size of these differences.

Since the square of any number is positive, we could eliminate this problem by squaring all differences before determining the average. This procedure is common in statistics and the average squared deviation has a special name.

The average squared deviation is called the variance and the square root of the variance is called the standard deviation. To illustrate the concept of the mean return and variances, we have presented some examples in Table 2. The variances of each of the return patterns for the assets in Table 2 are listed in Table 2. For example, for asset one the deviations are (15–9), (9–9), and (3–9). The squared deviations are 36, 0, 36 and the average squared deviation or variance is (36 + 0 + 36) ÷ 3 = 24.

To be precise, the formula for the variance of the return on the ith asset (which we will symbolize as σ_i^2) when each return is equally likely is:

$$\sigma_i^2 = \sum_{j=1}^{N} \frac{(R_{ij} - \bar{R}_i)^2}{N}$$

If the observations are not equally likely then, as before, we multiply by the probability of their occurrence. The formula for the variance of the return on the ith asset becomes:

$$\sigma_i^2 = \sum_{j=1}^{N} P_{ij} (R_{ij} - \bar{R}_i)^2$$

Table 2
Returns on Various Investments

	Asset 1		Asset 2		Asset 3		Asset 4		Asset 5	
	Market Condition	Return	Return	Market Condition	Return	Market Condition	Return	Rainfall	Return	Condition of market
	good	15	16	good	1	good	16	plentiful	16	good
	average	9	10	average	10	average	10	average	10	average
	poor	3	4	poor	19	poor	4	poor	4	poor
Mean return		9	10		10		10		10	
Variance		24	24		54		24		24	

The standard deviation is, of course, just the square root of the variance and is designated by σ_i.

The variance tells us that asset 3 varies considerably more from its average than asset 2. This is what we intuitively see by examining Table 2.

Variance of Combinations of Assets

This simple analysis can take us a long way toward a solution. However, the options open to an investor are not to simply pick between assets 1, 2, 3, 4, or 5 but also to consider combinations of these five assets. This ability vastly increases the number of options open to the investor and, hence the complexity of the problem; thus the need for portfolio theory. The risk of a combination of assets is very different from a simple average of the risk on individual assets. Most dramatically, the variance of a combination of two assets may be less than the variance of either of the assets themselves. In Table 2 there is a combination of asset 2 and asset 3 that is less risky than asset 2.

Let's examine this property. Assume an investor has $1.00 to invest. If one selects asset 2 and the market is good one will have at the end of the period $1.00 + .16 = $1.16. If the market's performance is average one will have $1.10 and if it's poor $1.04. These are summarized in Table 3 along with the corresponding values for the third asset. Consider an alternative. What if the investor invests $.60 in asset 2 and $.40 in asset 3. If the condition of the market is good, the investor will have $.696 at the end of the period from asset 2 and $.404 from asset 3 or $1.10. If the market conditions are average, asset 2 will pay $.66, and asset 3 $.44, for a total of $1.10. By now the reader might suspect that if the market condition is poor the investor still receives $1.10 and this is, of course, the case. If the market condition is poor the investor receives $.624 from the investment in asset 2 and $.476 from the investment in asset 3 or $1.10. These possibilities are summarized in Table 3.

This example dramatically illustrates how the risk on a portfolio of assets can differ from the risk of the individual assets. The deviations on the combination of the assets was zero because the assets had their highest and lowest returns under opposite market conditions. This result is perfectly general and not confined to this example. When two assets have their good and poor returns at opposite times, an investor can find some combination of these assets that yields the same return under all market conditions. This example dramatically illustrates the importance of considering combinations of assets rather than just the assets themselves. It also shows how the distribution of outcomes on combinations of assets can be different than the distributions on the individual assets themselves.

Table 3
Dollars at Period 2 Given Various Investments and Market Conditions

Condition of Market	Asset 2	Asset 3	Combination of Asset 2 and Asset 3
Good	$1.16	$1.01	$1.10
Average	1.10	1.10	1.10
Poor	1.04	1.19	1.10

The returns on asset 1 and asset 4 (from Table 2) have been developed to illustrate another possible situation. Asset 4 has three possible returns: which return occurs depends on rainfall. Assuming that the amount of rainfall that occurs is independent of the condition of the market, then the returns on the assets are independent of one another. Therefore, if the rainfall is plentiful we can have good, average, or poor security markets. Plentiful rainfall does not change the likelihood of obtaining any particular market condition. Consider our investor with $1.00 to invest and have him put $.50 in each asset. If rain is plentiful one receives $.58 from the investment in asset 4, and $.58 from the investment in asset 2 if the market is good, $.55 if it's average, and $.52 if the market is poor. This gives a total of $1.16, $1.13, or $1.10. Similarly, if the rainfall is average, the value of one's investment in asset 1 and 4 is $1.13, $1.10, or $1.07; and if rainfall is poor, $1.10, $1.07, or $1.04. Assume each possible level or rainfall is equally likely as is each possible condition of the market. Then there are nine equally likely outcomes. Ordering then from lowest to highest we have, $1.16, $1.13, $1.13, $1.10, $1.10, $1.10, $1.07, $1.07, and $1.04. Compare this to an investment in asset 2 by itself, the results of which are shown in Table 2. The mean is the same. However, the dispersion around the mean is less. This can be seen by direct examination and by noting how much less likely the extreme outcomes have become.

This example once again shows how the characteristic of the portfolio can be very different than the characteristics of the assets that comprise the portfolio. The example illustrates a general principle. When the returns on assets are independent such as the returns on assets 2 and 4, a portfolio of the assets can have less dispersion than either asset.

Consider still a third situation, one with a different outcome than the previous two. Consider an investment in assets 2 and 5. Assume the investor invests $.50 in asset 1 and $.50 in asset 2. The value of the investment at the end of the period is $1.16, $1.10, or $1.00. These are the same values one would have obtained if one invested $1.00 in asset 2 (or asset 5) directly (see Table 2). Thus, in this situation the characteristics of the portfolios were exactly the same as the characteristics of the individual assets.

We've analyzed three extreme situations. As extremes they dramatically illustrated some general principles that carry over to less extreme situations. When two assets tend to have their good and bad outcomes at different times (assets 2 and 3) then investment in these assets can dramatically reduce the dispersion obtained by investing in one of the assets by itself. If the good outcomes of asset 2 are not always associated with the bad outcomes of asset 4, but the general tendency is in this direction, the reduction in dispersion still occurs but the dispersion will not drop all the way to zero as it did in our example. However, it is still true that appropriately selected combinations of the two assets will have less risk than the least risky of the two assets.

Our second example illustrated the situation where the conditions leading to various returns were different for the two assets. More formally, this is the situation where returns are independent. Once again, dispersion was reduced but not in as dramatic a fashion. Note that investment in asset 2 alone can result in a value at period 2 of $1.04 and that this result occurs one third of the time. The same result can occur when we invested in equal amounts of asset 2 and 4. However, a combination of assets 2 and 4 has nine possible outcomes, each equally likely and $1.04 occurs only one ninth of the time. The difference is made up of returns between the average of $1.10 and the lowest of $1.04. Thus, with independent returns, the extreme observations can still occur. They just occur less frequently. Furthermore, these extreme observations are replaced by observations closer to the average so that the outcomes are less disperse.

Finally, our third example illustrated the situation where the characteristics of the portfolio were identical to the characteristics of the individual assets. In less extreme cases this is no longer true. Insofar as the good and bad returns on assets tend to occur at the same time, but not always exactly at the same time, the dispersion on the portfolio of assets is somewhat reduced relative to the dispersion on the individual assets.

We have shown with some simple examples how the characteristics of the return on portfolios of assets can differ from the characteristics of the returns on individual assets. These were artificial examples designed to dramatically illustrate the point. To reemphasize this point it is worthwhile examining some real securities.

Three securities were selected: IBM, General Motors, and Alcoa Aluminum. The monthly returns, average return, and standard deviation from investing in each security is shown in Table 4. In addition, the return and risk of placing one half of the available funds in each pair of securities is shown in Table 4.

Examining Table 4 clarifies how diversification across real securities can lead to tremendous reduction in risk for the investor.

The effect of diversification has been demonstrated by several authors. For example, Lorie and Fisher in the *Journal of Business* (April,

Table 4
Monthly Returns on IBM, Alcoa Aluminum, and General Motors (GM) (1975)

	R1	R2	R3	R4	R5	R6	R7	R8	R9	R10	R11	R12	$\bar{R}$	σ
IBM	12.05	15.27	-4.12	1.57	3.16	-2.79	-8.97	-1.18	1.07	12.75	7.48	-.94	2.95	7.15
Alcoa	14.09	2.96	7.19	24.39	0.06	6.52	-8.75	2.82	-13.97	-8.06	-0.7	8.80	2.95	10.06
GM	25.20	2.86	5.45	4.56	3.72	0.29	5.38	-2.97	1.52	10.75	3.79	1.32	5.16	6.81
½ IBM + ½ Alcoa	13.07	9.12	1.54	12.98	1.61	1.87	-8.86	0.82	-6.45	2.35	3.39	3.93	2.95	6.32
½ GM + ½ Alcoa	19.65	2.91	6.32	14.48	1.89	3.41	-1.69	-0.08	-6.23	1.35	1.55	5.06	4.05	6.60
½ GM + ½ IBM	18.63	9.07	0.67	3.07	3.44	-1.25	-1.80	-2.08	1.30	11.75	5.64	0.19	4.05	6.00

Correlation Coefficient: IBM & Alcoa .... .05
                           GM & Alcoa .... .22
                           IBM & GM .... .48

1970) considered the distribution of returns on portfolios of various sizes selected from NYSE stocks. They demonstrated how dispersion around the expected value declines dramatically as the portfolio size increases.

For example, they show that in 5 percent of the cases studied, investment of $1.00 in a single security resulted in a final wealth of less than $.663 in one year. Further, if the investor purchased two securities at the beginning of the year, one's wealth at the end of the year was less than $.746 5 percent of the time. Third, if the investor invests $1.00 in an eight-security portfolio, final wealth is less than $.831 5 percent of the time.

These results can also be used to examine the question of how frequently an investor will end up with less than invested. If the investor puts $1.00 in a single security, then one would have ended up with less than invested almost 40 percent of the time. On the other hand, if one invests in eight securities, this will occur less than 30 percent of the time. Once again, we see that the characteristic of the distribution of portfolios of securities can be quite different than the characteristics of individual securities.

Characteristics of Portfolios

The return on a portfolio of assets is simply a weighted average of the return on the individual assets. If R_p is the return on the portfolio and X_i is the fraction of the investor's funds invested in the ith asset and if R_i is the return on asset i, we have:

$$R_p = \sum_{i=1}^{N} X_i R_i$$

The expected return is also a weighted average of the expected returns on the individual assets. Taking the expected value (symbolized by E) of the expression just given for the return on a portfolio yields:

$$E(R_p) = E\left(\sum_{i=1}^{N} X_i R_i \right)$$

However, the expected value of the sum of various returns is the sum of the expected values. Therefore, we have:

$$\bar{R}_p = E(R_p) = \sum_{i=1}^{N} E(X_i R_i)$$

Finally, the expected value of a constant times a return is a constant times the expected return or;

$$\bar{R}_p = \sum_{i=1}^{N} X_i \bar{R}_i \tag{1}$$

This is a general formula and we will use it throughout. To illustrate its use, consider the investment in asset 2 and 3 discussed earlier. We determined that no matter what occurred, the investor would receive $1.10 on an investment of $1.00. This is a return of $\dfrac{.10}{1.00} =$ 10 percent.

Let's apply the formula for expected return. Recall that the expected return on asset 2 and asset 4 is 10 percent. Furthermore, $.60 was invested in asset 2 and $.40 in asset 4. Applying the formula for expected return yields:

$$\bar{R}_p = \left(\frac{.60}{1.00}\right)(.10) + \left(\frac{.40}{1.00}\right)(.10) = .10$$

The second summary characteristic was the variance. The variance on a portfolio is a little bit more difficult to determine than the expected return. Let's start out with a two-asset example. The variance of a two-security portfolio designated by σ_p^2 is simply

$$\sigma_p^2 = E(R_p - \bar{R}_p)^2 = E[(X_1 R_1 + X_2 R_2) - (X_1 \bar{R}_1 + X_2 \bar{R}_2)]^2$$
$$= E[X_1(R_1 - \bar{R}_1) + X_2(R_2 - \bar{R}_2)]^2$$

Squaring this expression yields

$$\sigma_p^2 = E[X_1^2 (R_1 - \bar{R}_1)^2 + 2X_1X_2 (R_1 - \bar{R}_1)(R_2 - \bar{R}_2) + X_2^2 (R_2 - \bar{R}_2)]$$

Since the expected value of the sum of random variables is the sum of the expected values

$$\sigma_p^2 = X_1^2 E(R_1 - \bar{R}_1)^2 + 2X_1 X_2 E(R_1 - \bar{R}_1)(R_2 - \bar{R}_2) + X_2^2 E(R_2 - R_2)^2$$

$E(R_1 - \bar{R}_1)(R_2 - \bar{R}_2)$ is called a covariance
If we let σ_{12} symbolize the covariance and recall that $E(R, -\bar{R})^2$ is a variance, we have,

$$\sigma_p^2 = X_1^2 \sigma_1^2 + X_2^2 \sigma_2^2 + 2X_1X_2\sigma_{12}$$

Notice what the covariance does. It is the product of two deviations, the deviations of the returns on security 1 from its mean $(R_1 - \bar{R}_1)$ and the deviations of security 2 from its mean $(R_2 - \bar{R}_2)$. In this sense it's very much like the variance. However, it is the product of two different deviations. As such it can be positive or negative. It will be large when the good outcomes for each stock occur together and when the bad outcomes for each stock occur together. In this case for good outcomes, the covariance will be the product of two large positive numbers which is positive. When the bad outcomes occur, the covariance will be the product of two large negative numbers which is positive. This will result in a large value for the covariance and a large variance for the portfolio. In contrast, if good outcomes for one asset are associated with bad outcomes of the other, the covariance is negative. It is negative because a plus deviation for one asset is associated with a minus deviation for the second and the product of a plus and a negative is negative. This was what occurred when we examined a combination of assets 2 and 3.

The covariance is a measure of how returns on assets move together. Insofar as they have positive and negative deviations at similar times, the covariance is a large positive number. If they have the positive and negative deviations at dissimilar times, then the covariance is negative. If the positive and negative deviations are unrelated, it tends to be zero.

For many purposes it is useful to standardize the covariance by dividing the covariance between two assets by the product of the standard deviations. This standardization produces a variable with the same properties as the covariance but with a range of −1 to +1. The measure is called the correlation coefficient. It is:

$$\rho_{ij} = \frac{\sigma_{ij}}{\sigma_i \sigma_j}$$

Dividing by the product of the standard deviations doesn't change the properties of the covariance. It simply scales it to have values between −1 and +1. Let's apply these formulas. First, however, it is necessary to calculate covariances. Table 5 shows the intermediate calculations necessary to determine the covariance between securities 1 and 2 and securities 2 and 3. The sum of the deviations between securities 1 and 2 is 72. Therefore, the covariance is $\frac{72}{3} = 24$ and the correlation coefficient is $\frac{24}{\sqrt{24}\sqrt{24}}$. For assets 2 and 3, the sum of the squared deviations is −108. The covariance is $\frac{-108}{3} = -36$ and the correlation coefficient is $\frac{-36}{\sqrt{24}\sqrt{24}}$. Similar calculations can be made for all other pairs of assets and the results are contained in Table 6.

Table 5
Calculating Covariances

Deviations Security 1	Deviations Security 2	Product of Deviations	Deviations Security 1	Deviations Security 3	Product of Deviations
(15–9)	(16–10)	·36	(15–9)	(1–10)	−54
(9–9)	(10–10)	0	(4–9)	(10–10)	0
(3–9)	(4–10)	36	(3–9)	(19–10)	−54
		72			−108

Table 6
Covariance and Correlation: Coefficients (in Brackets) between Assets

	1	*2*	*3*	*4*	*5*
1		24 (+1)	−36 (−1)	0 (0)	24 (+1)
2			−36 (−1)	0 (0)	24 (+1)
3				0 (0)	−36 (−1)
4					24 (+1)
5					

Earlier we examined an investor with $1.00 to spend and who put $.60 in asset 2 and $.40 in asset 3. Applying the expression for variance of the portfolio we have:

$$\sigma_p^2 = \left(\frac{.60}{1.00}\right)^2 24 + \left(\frac{.40}{1.00}\right)^2 54 + 2\left(\frac{.60}{1.00}\right)\left(\frac{.40}{1.00}\right)(-36) = 0$$

This was exactly the result we obtained when we looked at the combination of the full distribution. The correlation coefficient between securities 2 and 3 is −1. This meant that good and bad returns of assets 2 and 3 tended to occur at opposite times. When this situation occurs, a portfolio can always be constructed with zero risk.

Our second example was an investment in securities 1 and 4. The variance of this portfolio is

$$\sigma_p^2 = (1/2)^2\, 24 + (1/2)^2\, 24 = 12$$

In this case where the correlation coefficient was zero, the risk of the portfolio was less than the risk of either of the individual securities. Once again, this is general result. When the return patterns of two assets are independent so that the correlation coefficient and covariance are zero, a portfolio can be found that has a lower variance than either of the assets by themselves.

As an additional check on the accuracy of the formula just derived, let's calculate the variance directly. Earlier we saw there were nine possible returns when we combined assets 2 and 4. They were $1.16, $1.13, $1.13, $1.10, $1.10, $1.10, $1.07, $1.07, and $1.04. Since we started with an investment of $1.00, the returns are easy to determine.

The return is 16 percent, 13 percent, 13 percent, 10 percent, 10 percent, 10 percent, 7 percent, 7 percent, and 4 percent. By examination it is easy to see that the mean return is 10 percent. The deviations are 6, 3, 3, 0, 0, 0, -3, -3, and -6. The squared deviations are 36, 9, 9, 0, 0, 0, 9, 9, and 36 and the average squared deviation or variance is $\frac{108}{9} = 12$. This agrees with the formula developed earlier.

The final example we analyzed earlier was a portfolio of assets 1 and 5. In this case the variance of the portfolio is:

$$\begin{aligned}
\sigma_p^2 &= (1/2)^2\, 24 + (1/2)^2\, 24 + 2\,(1/2)(1/2)\, 24 \\
&= (1/4)\, 24 + (1/4)\, 24 + (1/2)\, 24 \\
&= 24
\end{aligned}$$

As we demonstrated earlier, when two securities have their good and bad outcomes at the same times the risk is not reduced by purchasing a portfolio of the two assets.

The formula for variance of a portfolio can be generalized to more than two assets. It is:

$$\sigma_p^2 = \sum_{j=1}^{N} X_j^2 \sigma_j^2 + \sum_{j=1}^{N} \sum_{\substack{k=1 \\ k \neq j}}^{N} X_j X_k\, \sigma_{jk} \qquad (2)$$

This formula is worthwhile examining closer. First, consider the case where all assets are independent and, therefore, the covariance between them is zero. This was the situation we observed for assets 2 and 4 in our little example. In this case $\sigma_{24} = 0$. Furthermore, assume equal amounts are invested in each asset. With N assets the proportion invested in each asset is $\frac{1}{N}$. Applying our formula yields:

$$\sigma_p^2 = \sum_{j=1}^{N} \left(\frac{1}{N}\right)^2 \sigma_j^2 = \frac{1}{N}\left[\sum_{j=1}^{N} \frac{\sigma_j^2}{N}\right]$$

The term in the brackets is our expression for an average. Thus our formula reduces to $\sigma_p^2 = \frac{1}{N}\,\overline{\sigma^2}$. As N gets larger and larger the variance of the portfolio gets smaller and smaller. As N becomes extremely large, the variance of the portfolio approaches zero. This is a general result. If we have enough independent assets the variance of a portfolio of these assets approaches zero.

In general, we are not so fortunate. In most markets the correlation coefficient and the covariance between assets is positive. In these markets the risk on the portfolio cannot reach zero but can be much less than the variance of an individual asset. Once again, consider equal investment in N assets. In this case, if bars over variables indicate averages we get[1]

$$\sigma_p^2 = \frac{1}{N}\overline{\sigma_i^2} + \frac{N-1}{N}\overline{\sigma_{ij}}$$

This expression is a much more realistic representation of what occurs when we invest in a portfolio of assets. The contribution to the portfolio variance of the variance of the individual securities goes to zero as N gets large. However, the contribution of the covariance terms approaches the average covariance as N gets large. Individual risk of securities can be diversified away but the contribution to the total risk caused by the covariance terms can't be diversified away. Table 7 illustrates how this relationship looks when dealing with U.S. equities.

The average variance and average covariance of returns were calculated using monthly data for all stocks listed on the NYSE. The average variance was 46.619. The average covariance was 7.058. As more and more securities are added, the average variance on the portfolio declines until it approaches the average covariance. Rearranging the previous equation clarifies this relationship even further.

$$\sigma_p^2 = \frac{1}{N}\left(\overline{\sigma_i^2} - \overline{\sigma_{ij}}\right) + \overline{\sigma_{ij}}$$

The first term is the difference between the variance of return on individual securities and the average covariance and the second term is the average covariance. This relationship clarifies the effect of diversification on portfolio risk. The minimum variance of the portfolio is the average covariance. As securities are added to the portfolio, the effect of the difference between the average risk on a security and the average covariance is reduced.

Having discussed what is meant by mean return and standard deviation, it is worthwhile reexamining the choice problem shown in Figure

---

[1] The proportion invested in any one asset is $\frac{1}{N}$ and the formula for the variance of a portfolio becomes:

$$\sigma_p^2 = \sum_{j=1}^{N}\left(\frac{1}{N}\right)^2 \sigma_j^2 + \sum_{j=1}^{N}\sum_{\substack{k=1\\k\neq j}}^{N}\left(\frac{1}{N}\right)\left(\frac{1}{N}\right)\sigma_{jk}$$

$$= \left(\frac{1}{N}\right)\sum_{j=1}^{N}\frac{\sigma_j^2}{N} + \frac{(N-1)}{N}\sum_{j=1}^{N}\sum_{\substack{k=1\\k\neq j}}^{N}\left(\frac{1}{N}\right)\left(\frac{1}{N-1}\right)\sigma_{jk}$$

Both of the terms in the brackets are averages. That the first is an average should be clear from the previous discussion. Likewise the second term in brackets is also an average. There are N values of j and $(N-1)$ values of k. There are $N-1$ values of k since k can not equal j so that there is one less value of k than j. In total there are $N(N-1)$ covariance terms. Thus the second term is the summation of covariances divided by the number in the summation and is thus an average. Replacing the summations by averages yields the expression in the text.

Table 7
Effect of Diversification

Number of Securities	Expected Portfolio Variance
1	46.619
2	26.839
4	16.948
6	13.651
8	12.003
10	11.014
12	10.354
14	9.883
16	9.530
18	9.256
20	9.036
25	8.640
30	8.376
35	8.188
40	8.047
45	7.937
50	7.849
75	7.585
100	7.453
125	7.374
150	7.321
175	7.284
200	7.255
250	7.216
300	7.190
350	7.171
400	7.157
450	7.146
500	7.137
600	7.124
700	7.114
800	7.107
900	7.102
1000	7.097
minimum	7.058

2. Figure 3 is such a representation. Figure 3 is the same as Figure 2, except that we have relabeled the axes to reflect more accurately what we mean by risk. Figure 3 represents the usual set of choices that are available. However, in some situations, the choices can be further simplified. It is to this task that we now turn.

THE EFFICIENT FRONTIER WITH RISKLESS LENDING AND BORROWING

Up to this point we have been dealing with portfolios of risky assets. The introduction of a riskless asset into our portfolio possibility set

Figure 3
Portfolio Choices

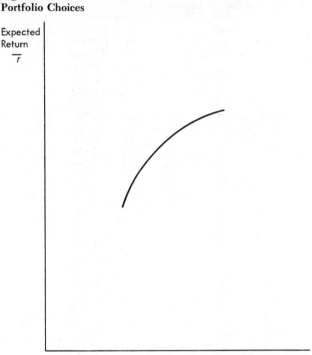

Expected
Return
$\bar{r}$

Standard Deviation=σ

considerably simplifies the analysis. We can consider lending at a risk-less rate as investing in an asset with a certain outcome (e.g. a short-term government bill or savings account). Borrowing can be considered as selling such a security short or simply borrowing at a riskless rate.

Let's call the certain rate of return on the riskless asset R_F. The standard deviation of the return on the riskless asset must be by defini-tion zero.

We will first examine the case where investors can lend and borrow unlimited amounts of funds at the riskless rate. Initially assume that the investor is interested in placing some funds in portfolio A and either lending or borrowing. Under this assumption we can easily deter-mine the geometric pattern of all combinations of portfolio A and lending or borrowing.[2] If the subscript C stands for a combination of

---

[2] Call X the fraction of original funds which the investor places in portfolio A. Remem-ber that X can be greater than one because the investor can borrow at the riskless rate and invest additional funds in portfolio A. If X is the fraction of funds which the investor places in portfolio A, $(1 - X)$ must be the fraction of the funds placed in the riskless asset. The expected return on the combination of riskless asset and risky portfolio is given by

asset A and the riskless asset, then the relationship between the returns on the combination and the risk of the combination is:

$$\bar{R}_C = R_F + \frac{(\bar{R}_A - R_F)}{\sigma_A} \sigma_C$$

Note that this is the equation of a straight line. All combinations of riskless lending and borrowing with portfolio A lie on a straight line in expected return standard deviation space.

The intercept of the line (on the return axis) is R_F and the slope is $\frac{\bar{R}_A - R_F}{\sigma_A}$. The line passes through the point $\bar{R}_A$. This line is shown in Figure 4.

Note that to the left of the point A we have combinations of lending and portfolio A while to the right of the point A we have combinations of borrowing and portfolio A.

The portfolio A we selected for this analysis had no special properties. Combinations of any security or portfolio and riskless lending and borrowing lie along a straight line in expected return standard deviation of return space. Examine Figure 5.

We could have combined portfolio B with riskless lending and borrowing and held combinations along the line R_F–B rather than R_F–A. Combinations along R_F–B are superior to combinations along R_F–A for they offer greater return for the same risk. It should be obvious that what we would like to do is to rotate the straight line passing through R_F as far as we can in a counterclockwise direction. The furthest we can rotate it is through point G.

Point G is the tangency point between the efficient frontier and a ray passing through the point R_F on the vertical axis. The investor can't rotate the ray further because by the definition of efficient frontier there are no portfolios lying above and to the left of point G.

$$\bar{R}_C = (1 - X) R_F + X \bar{R}_A$$

The risk on the combination is

$$\sigma_C = [(1 - X)^2 \sigma_F^2 + X^2 \sigma_A^2 + 2X(1 - X) \sigma_A \sigma_F \rho_{FA}]^{1/2}$$

Since we have already argued that σ_F is zero

$$\sigma_C = (X^2 \sigma_A^2) = X \sigma_A$$

solving this expression for X yields

$$X = \frac{\sigma_C}{\sigma_A}$$

Substituting this expression for X into the expression for expected return on the combination yields

$$\bar{R}_C = \left(1 - \frac{\sigma_C}{\sigma_A}\right) R_F + \frac{\sigma_C}{\sigma_A} \bar{R}_A$$

Rearranging terms yields the expression in the text.

Figure 4
Combinations of *A* and the Riskless Asset

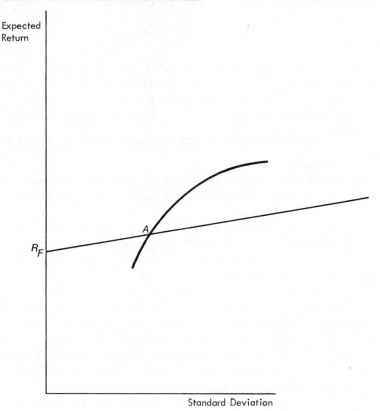

All investors who believed they faced the efficient frontier and risk-less lending and borrowing rates shown in Figure 5 would hold the same portfolio of risky assets—portfolio *G*. Some of these investors who were very risk-averse would select a portfolio along the segment R_F–*G* and place some of their money in a riskless asset and some in risky portfolio *G*. Others who were much more tolerant of risk would hold portfolios along the segment *G*–*H* borrowing funds and placing their original capital plus the borrowed funds in portfolio *G*. Still other investors would just place the total of their original funds in risky portfolio *G*. All of these investors would hold risky portfolios with the exact composition of portfolio *G*. Thus, in the case of riskless lending and borrowing identification of portfolio *G* constitutes a solution to the portfolio problem. The ability to determine the optimum portfolio without having to know anything about the investor has a special name; it is called the *separation theorem*.

Let's for a moment examine the shape of the efficient frontier under more restrictive assumptions about the ability of investors to lend and borrow at the risk-free rate. There is no question about the ability of investors to lend at the risk-free rate (buy government securities). If they can lend but not borrow at this rate, the efficient frontier becomes R_F–G–H. In Figure 6 certain investors will hold portfolios of risky assets located between G and H.

However, any investor who held some riskless asset would place all of his remaining funds in the risky portfolio G.

Another possibility is that investors can lend at one rate but must pay a higher rate to borrow. Calling this rate R'_F the efficient frontier would become R_F–G–H–I in Figure 7.

Here there is a small range of risky portfolios that would be optional for investors to hold. If R_F and R'_F are not too far apart, the assumption of riskless lending and borrowing at the same rate might provide a

Figure 5
Various Combinations of a Riskless Asset and a Risky Portfolio

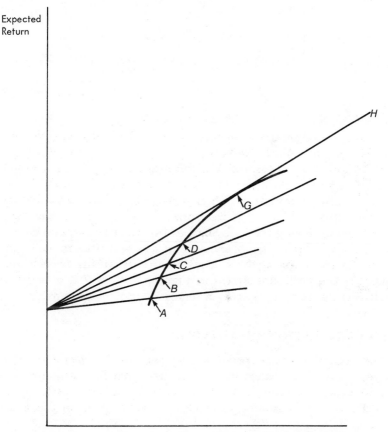

Figure 6
The Efficient Frontier when Lending Is Allowed but Borrowing
Is not Allowed

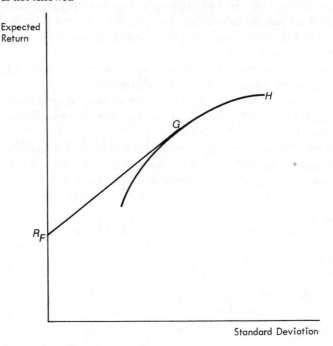

good approximation to the optimal range *G–H* of risky portfolios which investors might consider holding.

Having derived the set of portfolios to choose among it might be useful to discuss how it can be done. In general, obtaining the set of portfolios shown in Figures 5, 6, or 7, requires solving a mathematical programming problem. The exact procedures for solving it are beyond the scope of this chapter. (See Sharpe [14]* for a discussion.) However, if we can make some assumptions about why securities move together, we can simplify the analysis. Thus, before discussing procedures for obtaining the portfolios shown in Figures 5, 6, or 7 it is worthwhile discussing the manner by which securities move together.

IMPLEMENTATION OF THEORY

The theory we have presented so far was developed more than 25 years ago. The reader might well ask what has happened in the last 25 years. Similarly, one could ask why modern portfolio theory (M.P.T.) is only beginning to have a major impact on the financial

---

* Numbers in brackets refer to bibliography at end of chapter.

Figure 7
The Efficient Frontier when Lending Rates Are Lower than Borrowing Rates

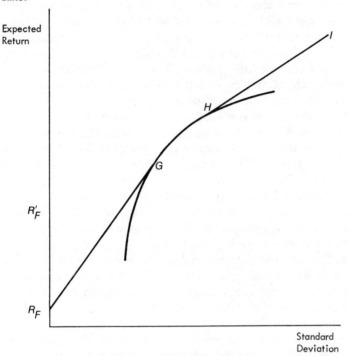

community. The answers to both these questions are closely related. Most of the research on M.P.T. for the past 25 years has concentrated on problems of implementation and simplification. It is only with the breakthroughs that have been made in these areas that firms are capable of and willing to use M.P.T. In the rest of this chapter we will be concerned with the implementation of portfolio theory. Breakthroughs in implementation fall into two categories. The first concerns a simplification of the amount and type of data needed to perform portfolio analysis. The second involves a simplification of the computational procedure needed to calculate optimal portfolios. As will soon become clear to the reader, these are not separate problems but rather are interdependent. The same methods which are used to simplify the inputs to portfolio analysis also lead to a simplification in calculating the efficient portfolio. Fortunately, they also lead to the portfolio selection problem being couched in terms which should be meaningful to the practicing security analyst and portfolio manager. Let's start our analysis by examining the inputs needed for implementing modern portfolio theory.

The Inputs to Portfolio Analysis

We now know that to define the efficient frontier we must find a set of portfolios such that no portfolio offers a greater return for the same risk and no portfolio offers less risk for the same return. Equations (1) and (2), discussed earlier in the chapter, define the input data necessary to perform portfolio analysis. From equation (1) we see that we need estimates of the expected return on each security which is a candidate for inclusion in our portfolio. From equation (2) we see that we need estimates of the variance of each security to be considered plus estimates of the correlation between each possible pair of securities in the population of stocks under consideration. This last requirement differs both in magnitude and in substance from the two previous requirements. Let's see why.

The principle job of the security analyst has traditionally been to estimate the future performance of those stocks she or he follows. At a minimum this should mean that the analyst produces estimates of expected returns on each stock followed.

With the increased attention that risk has received in recent years, more firms have employed analysts estimates of risk as well as return. The analyst who produces estimates of the expected return on a stock should also be in a position to produce estimates of the uncertainty of the return.

Correlations are an entirely different matter. Portfolio analysis calls for the analyst to produce estimates of the correlation between all possible pairing of stocks which are candidates for inclusion in a portfolio. Most firms organize their analysts along traditional industry lines. This means that one analyst might follow steel stocks or perhaps in a smaller firm all metal stocks, while a second analyst follows chemical stocks. But portfolio analysis calls for this analyst not only to estimate how a particular steel stock will move with another steel stock, it calls for the analyst to estimate how a particular steel stock will move with a particular drug company, a particular computer manufacturer, etc. There is no nonoverlapping organizational structure that allows such estimates to be produced.

The problem is made more complex by the number of the estimates involved. Most financial institutions follow 150–250 stocks. In addition to in-house portfolio analysis, the institution needs estimates of 150–250 expected returns and 150–250 variances. Let's see how many correlation coefficients it needs. If we let N stand for the number of stocks a firm follows then it has to estimate ρ_{ij} for all relevant values of i and j. The first index i can take on N values (one for each stock) the second can take on $(N-1)$ values (remember $j \neq i$). This would appear to give us $N(N-1)$ values for the correlation coefficient. However, note that since the correlation coefficient between stock i and j is the same as that between stock j and i, we only have half this many values of $N(N-1)/2$. The institution which follows 150–250 stocks needs between 11, 175, and 31,125 correlation coefficients. The sheer number of inputs is staggering.

It seems unlikely that analysts will be able to directly estimate correlation structures. Their ability to do so is severely limited by the nature of feasible organizational structures and the huge number of correlation coefficients which must be estimated. Recognition of this has motivated the search for and development of models to describe and predict the correlation structure between securities.

The models which have been developed for forecasting correlation structures fall into two categories—index models and averaging techniques. The most widely used technique assumes that the comovement between stocks can be captured by one influence or index. This type of model, appropriately called a single index model, will now be discussed.

Single Index Models—An Overview

Casual observation of stock prices reveals that when the market goes up (as measured by any of the widely available stock market indexes) most stocks tend to increase in price and when the market goes down, most stocks tend to decrease in price. This suggests that one reason security returns might be correlated is because of a common response to market changes and a useful measure of this correlation might be obtained by relating the return on a stock to the return on a stock market index.[3]

The return on a stock can be written as:

$$\overline{R}_i = \alpha_i + \beta_i R_M + e_i \qquad (3)$$

where α_i is the return expected on stock i when the market is flat

R_M is the rate of return on the market index—a random variable.
β_i is a constant which measures the change in R_i given a change in R_M
e_i is the return on stock i which is unexplained by α_i or R_M.

This equation simply breaks the return on a stock into two components, that part which is due to the market and that part which is independent of the market. β_i in the above expression measures how sensitive a stocks return is to the return on the market. A β_i of two

---

[3] The return on the index is identical, in concept, to the return on a common stock. It is the return the investor would earn if one held a portfolio with a composition identical to the index. Thus, to compute this return, the dividends that would be received from holding the index should be calculated and combined with the price changes on the index.

means that a stock return is expected to increase (decrease) by 2 percent when the market increases (decreases) by 1 percent. Similarly, a β of .5 indicates that a stock return is expected to increase (decrease) by .5 percent when the market increases (decreases) by 1 percent.

The model, as it has been presented, is often referred to as the *market model*. Up to this point we have made no simplifying assumptions about why stocks move together. The key assumptions of the single index model is that the only reason two stocks move together is because of common comovement with the market.[4] This is equivalent to assuming that the random component of return e_i for any stock i is unrelated (uncorrelated with) the random component of return for a second stock e_j. This means that the covariance between any two stocks i and j is equal to $\beta_i\beta_j\sigma_m^2$ where σ_m^2 is the variance of the market index. If we define σ_{ei}^2 as the residual risk of a security (that variation in the securities return that is unrelated to the market) we can write the expected return and variance of any portfolio as

$$E(R_i) \stackrel{=}{} \sum_{i=1}^{N} X_i \bar{R}_i = \sum_{i=1}^{N} X_i\alpha_i + \sum_{i=1}^{N} X_i\beta_i E(R_M) \qquad (4)$$

$$\sigma_p^2 \stackrel{=}{} \sum_{j=1}^{N} \sum_{j=1}^{N} X_iX_j\beta_i\beta_j\sigma_m^2 + \sum_{j=1}^{N} X_i^2\sigma_{ei}^2 \qquad (5)$$

There are many alternative ways of estimating the parameters of the single index model. From equation (4) and (5) it is clear that expected return and risk can be estimated for any portfolio if we have an estimate of α_i for each stock, an estimate of β_i for each stock, an estimate of σ_{ei}^2 for each stock and, finally, an estimate of both the expected return $(\bar{R}_M)$ and variance (σ_M^2) for the market. This is a total of $3N + 2$ estimates. For an institution following 150–250 stocks, this reduces the total number of estimates to 452–752. Compare this with the 11,457 to 31,620, discussed earlier, when no simplifying structure was assumed. Furthermore, note that there is no requirement for direct estimates of the joint movement of securities. This has been replaced with estimates of the way each security moves with the market. A nonoverlapping organizational structure can produce all estimates which are required.

The model can also be employed if analysts supply estimates of expected return for each stock, the variance of the return on each stock, the beta for each stock, and estimates of the expected return for the market and the variance of the market return. This is the same number of estimates $3N + 2$, as discussed above. However, this alternative set of estimates has the advantage that they are in more familiar terms. We've discussed means and variances before. The only

---

[4] A second necessary assumption of the single index model is that the size of the random error term in equation (3) is independent of the size of the market return.

new variable is beta. The beta is a measure of the sensitivity of a stock to market movements.

Before we leave this section we should discuss some more characteristics of the single index model.

Define the beta on a portfolio β_p as a weighted average of the individual β_is on each stock in the portfolio where the weights are the fraction of the portfolio invested in each stock. Then

$$\beta_p = \sum_{i=1}^{N} X_i \beta_i$$

Similarly define α_p as

$$\alpha_p = \sum_{i=1}^{N} X_i \alpha_i$$

Then equation (4) can be written as

$$\bar{R}_p = \alpha_p + \beta_p \bar{R}_m$$

If the portfolio p is taken to be the market portfolio (all stocks held in the same proportions as they represent in the market), then the expected return on p must be $\bar{R}_m$. From the above equation the only values of α_p and β_p which guarantee $\bar{R}_p = \bar{R}_m$ for any choice of R_m is α_p equal to zero and beta equal to one. Thus, the beta on the market is one and stocks are thought of as being more or less risky than the market, according to whether their beta is larger or smaller than one.

Let's look further into the risk of an individual security. The risk of the investor's portfolio could be represented as $\sigma_p^2 = \beta_p^2 \sigma_m^2 + \sum_{i=1}^{N} X_i^2 \sigma_{ei}^2$ Assume for a moment that an investor forms a portfolio by placing equal amounts of money into each of N stocks. The risk on the portfolio could be written as

$$\sigma_p^2 = \beta_p^2 \sigma_m^2 + \frac{1}{N^2} \sum_{i=1}^{N} \sigma_{ei}^2$$

Look at the last term. This can be expressed as $\frac{1}{N}$ times the average residual risk for a stock. As the number of stocks in the portfolio gets large, the importance of the residual risk—the non-beta risk diminishes drastically. In fact, as Table 8 shows, the residual risk falls rapidly so that most of it is eliminated on even moderately-sized portfolios.[5]

---

[5] To the extent that the single index model is not a perfect description of reality and residuals from the market model are correlated across securities, residual risk does not fall this rapidly. However, since the amount of positive correlation that is present in the residuals is quite small, residual risk does approach zero quite rapidly.

Table 8
Importance of Residual Risk

Number of Securities	Residual Risk Expressed as a Percent of the Residual Risk Present in a 1-Stock Portfolio
1	100%
2	50
3	33
4	25
5	20
10	10
20	5
100	1
1,000	.1

The risk that is not eliminated as we hold larger and larger portfolios, is the risk associated with the term β_p. If we assume that residual risk goes to zero, the risk of the portfolio becomes

$$\sigma_p = [\beta_p^2 \sigma_M^2]^{1/2} = \beta_p \sigma_M = \sigma_M \sum_{i=1}^{N} X_i \beta_i$$

Since σ_M is the same, regardless of which stock we examine, the measure of the contribution of a security to the risk of a large portfolio is β_i.

The risk of an individual security is $\beta_i \sigma_m^2 + \sigma_{ei}^2$. Since the effect of σ_{ei}^2 on portfolio risk goes to zero as the portfolio gets larger, it is common to refer to σ_{ei}^2 as diversifiable risk. However, the effect of $\beta_i \sigma_M^2$ on portfolio risk does not diminish as N get larger. Since σ_M^2 is a constant with respect to all securities, β_i is the measure of a security's nondiversifiable risk.[6] Since diversifiable risk can be eliminated by holding a large enough portfolio, β_i is often used as the measure of a security's risk.

The one question we have not answered about the single index model is where do betas come from. This will be taken up in Chapter 6. While we will not discuss the estimation of betas in this chapter we should say a few words about the performance of single index models in selecting efficient portfolios. The *single index model* employs a simplifying assumption about the way stocks covary. When this simplifying assumption is used it means that the model can not do a perfect job of reproducing the historical correlation between all stocks. However, it is possible that the model will lead to the better selection of optimal portfolios. This will be true if the historic correlation between securities contains a lot of random noise (seemingly relevant but actually irrelevant information) with respect to future correlations. Exten-

---

[6] An alternative nomenclature calls this market risk.

sive tests have been done on the single index model and they all indicate that the single index model does a better job of forecasting the future correlations between securities and leads to the selection of more efficient portfolios than does the historic correlation itself.[7] Having discussed the single index model let us discuss some other alternative representations of the input data needed for portfolio analysis.

Other Models of Why Stocks Move Together

The single index model assumes that the only reason stocks move together is because of common comovement with the market. The next logical step is to develop and incorporate in the model other influences (indexes) that might be important in explaining why stocks move together. Doing so increases the mathematical complexity of the model and the number and conceptual difficulty (of generating) the inputs to the problem. While increasing the number of indexes in a model will always allow the model to better explain the history of stock prices it will not necessarily lead to better forecasts or the selection of better portfolios. As we add more indexes we may be measuring influences which are unstable over time and to the extent this is true the model may lead to inferior rather than superior performance.

As an alternative to adding some indexes to a single index model, one may forecast future correlations by averaging over past correlations. This will no doubt result in smoothing out randomness in the data, however it may result in the loss of real information. In the rest of this section we shall discuss in more detail some multiindex models along with some averaging models.

Multiindex Models. The assumption underlying the single index model is that the only reason two stocks moved together is because of common movement with the market. Many researchers have found that there are influences beyond the market which cause stocks to move together. For example, as early as 1966, King [10] presented evidence on the existence of industry influences. Two different types of schemes have been put further for handling additional influences. We have called them the general multiindex model and the industry index model.

General Multiindex Models. Any additional sources of covariance between securities can be introduced into the equations for risk and return, simply by adding these additional influences to the general return equation. Let's hypothesize that the return on any stock is a function of the return on the market, the level of interest rates, and a set of industry indexes. If R_i is the return on stock i, then the return

---

[7] See Elton and Gruber [3], Elton, Gruber, and Urich [10], and Cohen and Pogue [1] for evidence.

on stock *i* can be related to the influences that affect it in the following way:

$$R_i = a_i + b_{i1} I_1 + b_{i2} I_2 + \cdots b_{iL} I_L + C_i$$

In this equation I_j is the actual level of index I_j, b_{ij} is a measure of the responsiveness of the return on stock *i* to changes in the index *j* and a_i is the expected return if all of the indexes were equal to zero (the unique return). The remaining term C_i is a measure of the differences that arise between actual returns and returns that would be predicted from the above equation. Since this equation is expected to predict returns correctly (on average), C_i has a mean of zero. Since the equation is not expected to produce perfect forecasts at any point in time, C_i has a positive variance which we shall call σ_{ei}^2.[8]

To use this model analysts must supply estimates of the expected return for each stock, the variance of each stock's returns, the index loading b_{ij} between each stock and each index and the means and variances of each index.[9] The number of inputs needed is $2N + 2L + LN$. As discussed at several points in this chapter, the inputs needed to perform portfolio analysis are expected returns, variances, and correlation coefficients. By having the analysts estimate means and variances directly, it is clear that the only input derived from the estimates of the multiindex models are correlation coefficients. We stress this point because later in this chapter we will evaluate the ability of a multiindex model to aid in the selection of securities by examining its ability to forecast correlations coefficients.

There is a certain type of multiindex model that has received a large amount of attention. These models restrict attention to market and industry influences. There are several models of this type which vary in the assumptions they make and, hence, the type and amount of input data needed. We will now examine the simplest of the models.

Industry Index Models. Several authors have dealt with multiindex models which start with the basic single index model and add indexes to capture industry effects. The early precedent for this work can be found in King [10] who measured effects of common movement between securities beyond market effects and found this extra market covariances was associated with industries. For example, two steel stocks had positive correlation among their returns, even after the effects of the market had been removed.[10]

---

[8] It proves convenient to construct this model so that the indexes are not correlated with each other. Sharpe [14] shows how any set of correlated indexes can be converted to a set of uncorrelated indexes.

[9] See Elton and Gruber [3] for a formal proof of this statement.

[10] King found that over the entire period studied, 1927–60, about half of the total variation in price was accounted for by a market index while an average of another 10 percent was accounted for by industry factors. In the latter part of the period, he studied the importance of the market factor dropped to 30 percent, while the industry factors continued to explain 10 percent of price movement.

If we hypothesize that the correlation between securities is caused by a market effect and industry effects our general multiindex model could be written as:

$$R_i = a_i + b_{im}I_m + b_{i1}I_i + b_{i2}I_2 + \cdots + b_{i2}I_2 + C_i$$

Where I_m is the market index

I_j are industry indexes which are constrained to be uncorrelated with the market and uncorrelated with each other.

The assumption behind this model is that a firm's return can be affected by the market plus several industries. For some companies this seems appropriate as their lines of business span several traditional industries. However, some companies gain the bulk of their return from activities in one industry and perhaps, of more importance, are viewed by investors as members of a particular industry. In this case the influences on the firm's return of all but the industry index (to which it belongs) along with the market index, are likely to be small and their inclusion may introduce more random noise into the process than the information they supply. This has prompted some authors to advocate a simpler form of the multiindex model. One that simply assumes that returns of each firm are only affected by a market index and an industry index. Furthermore, the model assumes that each industry index has been constructed to be uncorrelated with the market and with all other industry indexes. For firm i in industry j, the return equation can be written as:

$$R_i = a_i + b_{im}I_m + b_{ij}I_j + c_i$$

A logical question to ask at this point is how well multiindex models work. Its difficult to give a conclusive answer to this question for there are virtually an infinite number of possible multiindex models. Furthermore, the results on those multiindex models which have been tested are mixed. Elton and Gruber [3] tested the results of a general multiindex model and found that its performance was inferior to that of the single index model. Cohen and Pogue [1] tested an industry multiindex model and found that it did not perform as well as the single index model. On the other hand, Farrell [11] tested a version of the industry index model where indexes for groups of stocks (rather than traditional industries) were used and found his model outperformed the single index model.[11]

While the use of multiindex models holds great promise for the future, the results, to date, have been mixed. A natural question arises: If the addition of more indexes to a single index model can, at times, introduce more random noise than real information into the forecasting

---

[11] Farrell divided stocks into the following groups: growth, cyclical, stable, and petroleum.

process, might not a technique which smoothes more of the historic data lead to better results?

Average Correlation Models.   The idea of averaging (smoothing) some of the data in the historic correlation matrix as a forecast of the future has been tested by Elton and Gruber (3) and Elton and Gruber and Urich (10).

The most aggregate type of averaging that can be done is to use the average of all paired-stock correlation coefficients over some past period as a forecast of each paired-stock correlation coefficient for the future. This is equivalent to the assumption that the past correlation matrix contains information about what the average correlation will be in the future but no information about individual differences from this average. This model can be thought of as a naive model against which more elaborate models should be judged. We shall refer to this model as the overall mean model.

A more disaggregate averaging model would be to assume that there was a common mean correlation within and between groups of stocks. For example, if we employ the idea of traditional industries as a method of grouping, we would assume that the correlation between any two steel stocks was the same as the correlation between any other two steel stocks and was equal to the average historical correlation between steel stocks. The averaging is done across all paired-stock correlations between steel stocks in a historic period. Similarly, the correlation between any steel stocks and any chemical stocks is assumed to be equal to the correlation between any other steel stock and any other chemical stock and is set equal to the average of the correlations between each chemical and each steel. When this is done, with respect to traditional industry classifications, it will be referred to as the *traditional mean model.* However, the same technique has been used [3] with respect to pseudo industries.

The overall mean has been extensively tested against single index models, general multiindex models, and the historical correlation matrix itself. Tests have been performed using three different samples of stocks over a total of four different time periods. In every case, the use of the overall mean model outperformed the single index model, the multiindex model, and the historical correlation matrix. The differences in forecasting future correlation coefficients were almost always statistically significant at the .05 level. Furthermore, for most risk levels, the differences in portfolio performance were large enough to have real economic significance. Using the overall mean technique, as opposed to the best of the single index model, multiindex model, or the historical correlation model, often led to a 25 percent increase in return (holding risk constant).

The next logical question is what happens when we introduce some disaggregation into the results by using the traditional mean or pseudomean model. Here the results are much more ambiguous. Averaging models based on either traditional industries or pseudoindustries outperformed single index models, multiindex models and the historic correlation matrix both on statistical and economic criteria. However, their differences from each other and from the overall mean were much less clear. The ordering of these three techniques was different over different time periods and at different risk levels in the same time period. At this point all we can say is that, while it is worth continuing to investigate the performance of traditional mean and pseudomean averaging models, their superiority over the overall mean model has not yet been demonstrated.

Before ending this discussion, there is one more type of model which should be discussed. This type is a combination of the models discussed above. We'll call them mixed models. In a mixed model, the single index model is used as the basic starting point. However, rather than assume that the extra market covariance is zero, a second model is constructed to explain extra market covariance. This concept shouldn't be new to the reader. If we consider a general multiindex model, where the first index is the market, then we can consider all other indexes as indexes of extra market covariance. What is new is the way that extra market covariance is predicted. The most widely known model of this type is that described by Rosenberg [13]. Initial results with this type of analysis appear quite promising, although extensive tests of the forecast ability have not been performed.

Another approach which is worth exploring is to try the same type of averaging techniques discussed earlier directed to the extra market covariance. That is, instead of performing the averaging on the correlation coefficients themselves, perform the averaging on the correlations of the residuals from the single index model. For example, a traditional industry averaging scheme might be used. In this case, after removing the market influence, the residuals for each stock could be averaged within and between industries. Then the correlation between any two stocks would be predicted by combining their predicted correlation from the single index model with the extra market correlation predicted from the averaging model.

Simple Portfolio Selection Criteria

In the previous section we examined several models which were developed to simplify the inputs to the portfolio selection problem. Each of these models make a simplifying assumption about why stocks covary together. That is, each leads to a simplified structure for the correlation matrix or covariance matrix between securities. Each of these models was developed to cut down on the number of inputs and simplify the nature of the input needed to forecast correlations between securities. The use of these models was expected to lead to some loss of accuracy in forecasting correlations but the assumption was that the ease of using the models would offset the loss of accuracy. However, we have seen when applied with historic data, several of these simplifying models resulted in an increase, not a decrease, in forecasting accuracy. The models are of major interest because they both reduce and simplify the inputs needed to perform portfolio analysis and increase the accuracy with which correlations and covariances can be forecast. They both make it simplier to select portfolios and, lead to the selection of better portfolios.

There is yet another advantage of these models. Each allows the development of a system for selecting optimum portfolios that is so simple that it can often be performed without the use of a computer. Perhaps, even of more importance than the ease of computation, is the fact that the methods of portfolio selection described in this chapter make it very clear why a stock does or does not enter into an optimal portfolio. Each model of the correlation structure discussed in the previous section leads to a unique ranking of stocks, such that if a stock enters an optimal portfolio, any higher ranked stock must also enter the optimal portfolio. Similarly, if a stock does not enter an optimal portfolio, any lower ranked stock does not enter the optimal portfolio. This allows the analyst to judge the relative desirability of stocks even before the portfolio selection process is begun. Furthermore, as we shall see, the optimum ranking of stocks is in terms of concepts that are already familiar to security analysts and portfolio managers, as well as to readers of this book. This should minimize the institutional barriers to their adoption.

In this section we shall describe, in detail, the methods for selecting optimal portfolios which are appropriate when the single index model is accepted as descriptions of the covariance structure between securities. We make no attempt in this section to prove that there rules are optimum.

The mathematical sophistication needed to use these rules is considerably less than the mathematical sophistication needed to derive them. The reader who is interested in seeing where they came from should see Elton, Gruber, and Padberg [5]. In addition, in the interests of brevity we present only the rules for the case where the single index model is assumed appropriate and short sales are not allowed. The reader interested in the other cases is referred to the following articles:

1. Single index model short sales allowed, Elton, Gruber, and Padberg [4]
2. Constant correlation model short sales both allowed and disallowed [4]

3. Multigroup Model, Elton, Gruber, and Padberg [6]
4. Multiindex Model, Elton, Gruber, and Padberg [6] & [8]
5. Upper bound constraints on the faction of the portfolio which can be invested in any security, Elton, Gruber, and Padberg [9]

The Model. We will start this section by presenting the ranking criteria which can be used to order stocks for selection for the optimal portfolio. We will then present the technique for employing this ranking device to form an optimum portfolio, along with a logical explanation for why it works. After presenting the criteria for the composition of an optimal portfolio, we will demonstrate its use with a simple example. In this section we will assume unlimited borrowing and lending at the riskless rate; this is a mathematical convenience rather than a necessity. It is obvious that the full efficient frontier can be traced simply by selecting alternative values for the riskless rate of interest.

The Formation of Optimal Portfolios. The calculation of optimal portfolios would be greatly facilitated, and the ability of practicing security analysts and portfolio managers to relate to the construction of optimal portfolios greatly enhanced, if there were a single number which measured the desirability of including a stock in the optimal portfolio. If one is willing to accept the standard form of the single index model as describing the comovement between securities, such a number exists. In this case, the desirability of any stock is directly related to its excess return to beta ratio. Excess return is the difference between the expected return on the stock and the riskless rate of interest such as the rate on a Treasury bill. The excess return to beta ratio measures the additional return on a security (beyond that offered by a riskless asset) per unit of nondiversifiable risk. The form of this ratio should lead to its easy interpretation and acceptance by security analysts and portfolio managers for they are used to thinking in terms of the relationship between potential rewards and risk. The numerator of this ranking device is the extra return over the riskless asset we get from holding a security other than the riskless asset. The denomination is the nondiversifiable risk (the risk we can't get rid of) that we are subject to by holding a security rather than the riskless asset.

More formally, the index we use to rank stocks is *excess return to beta* or

$$\frac{\bar{R}_i - R_F}{\beta_i}$$

where,

$\bar{R}_i$ = the expected return on stock i
$\bar{R}_F$ = the return on a riskless asset
β_i = the expected change in the rate of return on stock i associated with a 1 percent change in the market return.

If stocks are ranked by excess return to beta (from highest to lowest) the ranking represents the desirability of any stock's inclusion in a portfolio. In other words, if a stock with a particular ratio of

$$\frac{\overline{R}_i - R_F}{\beta_i}$$

is included in an optimal portfolio, all stocks with a higher ratio will also be included. On the other hand, if a stock with a particular

$$\frac{\overline{R}_i - R_F}{\beta_i}$$

is excluded from an optimal portfolio, all stocks with lower ratios will be excluded (or if short selling is allowed, sold short.) When the single index model is assumed to reasonably represent the covariance structure then a stock is included or excluded, depending only on the size of excess return to beta ratio. How many stocks are selected depends on a unique cutoff rate such that all stocks with higher ratios of

$$\frac{\overline{R}_i - R_F}{\beta_i}$$

will be included and all stock with lower ratios excluded. We will call this cutoff rate C^*.

The rules for determining which stocks are included in the optimum portfolio is as follows:

1. Find the excess return to beta ratio for each stock under consideration, and rank from highest to lowest.
2. The optimum portfolio consists of investing in all stocks for which $(\overline{R}_i - R_F)/\beta_i$ is greater than a particular cutoff point C^*. (Shortly, we will define C^* and interpret its economic significance.)

The above procedure is extremely simple. Once C^* has been determined, the securities to be included can be selected by inspection. Furthermore, the amount to invest in each security is equally simple to determine and will be discussed shortly.

Ranking Securities. In Tables 9 and 10 we present an example that illustrates this procedure. Table 9 contains the data necessary to apply our simple ranking device to determine an optimal portfolio. It is the normal output generated from a single index or beta model, plus the ratio of excess return to beta. This same data could alternatively be generated by analysts' subjective estimates. There are ten securities in the tables. For the readers' convenience, we have already ranked the securities according to $(\overline{R}_i - R_F)/\beta_i$ and have used numbers that make the calculations easy to follow. The application of rule 2 (above) involves the comparison of $(\overline{R}_i - R_F)/\beta_i$ with C^*. Accept the $C^* =$

5.45 for the moment; we will shortly present a procedure for its calculation. Examining Table 10 shows that for securities 1 to 5 $(\bar{R}_i - R_F)/\beta_i$ is greater than C^* while for security 6 it is less than C^*. Hence, an optimal portfolio consists of securities 1 to 5.

Table 9
Data Required to Determine Optimal Portfolio $R_F = 5$

(1) Security Number	(2) Mean Return	(3) Excess Return	(4) Beta	(5) Unsystematic Risk	(6) Excess Return over Beta
i	$\bar{R}_i$	$\bar{R}_i - R_F$	β_i	σ^2_{ei}	$\dfrac{\bar{R}_i - R_F}{\beta_i}$
1	15	10	1	50	10
2	17	12	1.5	40	8
3	12	7	1	20	7
4	17	12	2	10	6
5	11	6	1	40	6
6	11	6	1.5	30	4
7	11	6	2	40	3
8	7	2	.8	16	2.5
9	7	2	1	20	2
10	5.6	.6	.6	6	1.0

Table 10
Calculations for Determining Cutoff Rate with $\sigma^2_m = 10$

(1) Security Number	(2) $(\bar{R}_i - R_F)/\beta_i$	(3) $\dfrac{(R_i - R_F)\beta_i}{\sigma^2_{ei}}$	(4) $\dfrac{\beta^2_i}{\sigma^2_{ei}}$	(5) $\sum_{j=1}^{i} \dfrac{(\bar{R}_j - R_F)\beta_i}{\sigma^2_{ej}}$	(6) $\sum_{j=1}^{i} \dfrac{\beta^2_j}{\sigma^2_{ej}}$	(7) C_i
1	10	2/10	2/100	2/10	2/100	1.67
2	8	4.5/10	5.625/100	6.5/10	7.625/100	3.69
3	7	3.5/10	5/100	10/10	12.625/100	4.42
4	6	24/10	40/100	34/10	52.625/100	5.43
5	6	1.5/10	2.5/100	35.5/10	55.125/100	5.45
6	4	3/10	7.5/100	38.5/10	62.625/100	5.30
7	3	3/10	10/100	41.5/10	72.625/100	5.02
8	2.5	1/10	4/100	42.5/10	76.625/100	4.91
9	2.0	.1/10	5/100	43.5/10	81.625/100	4.75
10	1.0	.6/10	6/100	44.1/10	87.625/100	4.52

Setting the Cutoff Rate *(C*).* As discussed earlier, C^* is the cutoff rate. All securities whose excess return to risk ratio are above the cutoff rate are selected and all whose ratios are below are rejected. The value of C^* depends on the characteristics of the securities which belong in the optimum portfolio. To determine C^*, it is necessary to calculate its value as if there were different numbers of securities in the optimum portfolio.

Since securities are ranked from highest excess return to beta to lowest, we know that if a particular security belongs in the optimal portfolio, all higher ranked securities also belong in the optimal portfolio. We proceed to calculate values of a variable C_i (the procedure is outlined below) as if the first ranked security was in the optimal portfolio ($i = 1$), and second ranked and the first ranked securities were in the optimal portfolio ($i = 2$), the first, second, and third ranked security are in the optimal portfolio ($i = 3$), etc. These C_1 are candidates for C^*. We know we have found the optimum C_i that is C^*, when all securities used in the calculation of C_i have excess returns to beta above C_i and all securities not used to calculate C_i have excess return to betas below C_i. For example, column 7 of Table 10 shows the C_i for alternative values of i. Examining Table 10 shows that C_5 is the only value of C_i for which all securities used in the calculation of i have a ratio of excess return to beta above C_i and all securities not used in the calculation of C_i have an excess return to beta ratio below C_i. C_5 serves the role of a cutoff rate in the way a cutoff rate was defined earlier. In particular, C_5 is the only C_i which used as a cutoff rate selects only the stocks used to construct it. There will always be one and only one C_i with this property and it is C^*.

Calculating the Cutoff Rate C^*. Recall that stocks are ranked by excess return to risk from highest to lowest. For a portfolio of i stocks C_i is

$$C_i = \frac{\sigma_m^2 \sum_{j=1}^{i} \frac{(\bar{R}_j - R_F)\beta_j}{\sigma_{ej}^2}}{1 + \sigma_m^2 \sum_{j=1}^{I} \frac{\beta_j^2}{\sigma_{ej}^2}} \tag{6}$$

where:

σ_m^2 = the variance in the market index

σ_{ej}^2 = the variance of a stock's movement that is not associated with the movement of the market index. This is usually referred to as a stock's nonsystematic risk.

This looks horrible. But a moment's reflection combined with a peek at the example below will show that it is not as hard to compute as it looks. While equation (6) is the form that should actually be used to compute C_i, this expression can be stated in a mathematically equivalent way which clarifies the meaning of C_i.

$$C_i = \frac{\beta_{ip}(\bar{R}_p - R_F)}{\beta_i} \tag{7}$$

where:

1. β_{ip} = the expected change in the rate of return on stock i associated with a 1 percent change in the return on the optimal portfolio.
2. all other terms as before

β_{ip} and $\bar{R}_p$ are, of course, not known until the optimal portfolio is determined. Hence, equation (7) could not be used to actually determine the optimum portfolio; rather, equation (6) must be used. However, this expression for C_i is useful in interpreting the economic significance of our procedure. Recall that securities are added to the portfolio as long as

$$\frac{\bar{R}_i - R_F}{\beta_i} > C_i$$

Rearranging and substituting in equation (7) yields

$$(\bar{R}_i - R_F) > \beta_{ip} (\bar{R}_p - R_F)$$

The right hand side is nothing more than the expected excess return on a particular stock based solely on the expected performance of the optimum portfolio. The term on the left hand side is the security analyst's estimate of the expected excess return on the individual stock. Thus, if the analysis of a particular stock leads the portfolio manager to believe that it will perform better than would be expected, based on its relationship to the optimal portfolio, it should be added to the portfolio.

Now let us look at how (6) can be used to determine the value of C_i for our example. While equation (6) might look complex, the ease with which it can be calculated is demonstrated by Table 10. Table 10 presents the intermediate calculations necessary to determine equation (6).

Constructing the Optimal Portfolio. Once the securities that are contained in the optimum portfolio are determined, it remains to show how to calculate the percent invested in each security. The percentage invested in each security is

$$X_i^0 = \frac{Z_i}{\sum\limits_{j=1}^{N} Z_j}$$

Where

$$Z_i = \frac{\beta_i}{\sigma_{ei}^2} \left(\frac{\bar{R}_i - R_F}{\beta_i} - C^* \right)$$

This expression simply scales the weights on each security so they sum to one and, thus, insure that we are fully invested. Note that the residual variance on each security σ_{ei}^2 plays an important role in determining how much we invest in each security.

Applying this to our example we have

$$Z_1 = \frac{2}{100}(10 - 5.45) = .091$$

$$Z_2 = \frac{3.75}{100}(8 - 5.45) = .095625$$

$$Z_3 = \frac{5}{100}(7 - 5.45) = .0775$$

$$Z_4 = \frac{20}{100}(6 - 5.45) = .110$$

$$Z_5 = \frac{2.5}{100}(6 - 5.45) = .01375$$

$$\sum_{i=1}^{5} Z_i = .387875$$

Dividing each Z_i by the sum of the Z_i we find that we should invest 23.5 percent of our funds in security 1; 24.6 percent in security 2; 20 percent in security 3; 28.4 percent in security 4; and 3.5 percent in security 5.

Let us stress that this is identical to the result that would be achieved had the problem been solved using the established quadratic programming codes. However, the solution can be reached in a small fraction of the time with a set of relatively simple calculations.

Notice that the characteristics of a stock that make it desirable and the relative attractiveness of stocks can be determined before the calculations of an optimal portfolio is begun. The desirability of any stock is solely a function of its excess return to beta ratio. Thus, a security analyst following a set of stocks can determine the relative desirability of each stock for inclusion in the optimal portfolio before the information from all analysts is combined and the portfolio selection process begun.

Up to this point we have assumed that all stocks have positive betas. We believe that there are sound economic reasons to expect all stocks to have positive betas and that the few negative beta stocks which are found in large samples are due to measurement errors. However, as pointed out in [4], negative beta stocks (and zero beta stocks) are easily incorporated in the analysis.

CONCLUSION

In this chapter we have both introduced the theory of modern portfolio analysis and have examined those recent breakthroughs which have turned modern portfolio theory into an implementable tool. The concepts we have outlined can be and have been used by firms to improve their investment performance.

BIBLIOGRAPHY

1. Cohen, Kalmon, and Pogue, Gerald A. "An Empirical Evaluation of Alternatives Portfolio Selection Models." *Journal of Business,* April 1967.

2. Elton, Edwin J. and Gruber, Martin J. *Modern Portfolio Theory.* New York: John Wiley, forthcoming.

3. ———. "Estimating the Dependence Structure of Share Prices." *Journal of Finance,* December 1973.

4. Elton, Edwin; Gruber, Martin J.; and Padberg, Manfred W. "Simple Criteria for Optimal Portfolio Selection." *Journal of Finance,* December 1976.

5. ———. "Simple Criteria of Optimal Portfolio Selection, Tracing Out the Efficient Frontier." *Journal of Finance,* June 1978.

6. ———. "Simple Criteria for Optimal Portfolio Selection, the Multiindex." *Journal of Financial and Quantitative Analysis,* September 1977.

7. ———. "Simple Rules in Optimal Portfolio Selection." *Journal of Portfolio Management,* Spring 1978.

8. ———. "Simple Criteria for Optimal Portfolio Selection Multiindex Case." *Management Science,* forthcoming.

9. ———. "Simple Criteria for Optimal Portfolio Selection with Upper Bound Constraints." *Operations Research,* November–December 1977.

10. Elton, Edwin J.; Gruber, Martin J.; and Urich, Thomas. "Are Betas Best?" *Journal of Finance,* December 1978.

11. Farrell, James. "Analyzing Covariance of Returns to Determine Homogeneous Stock Groupings." *Journal of Business,* April 1974.

12. King, Bernard. "Market and Industry Factors in Stock Price Behavior." *Journal of Business,* January 1966.

13. Rosenberg, Barr; Hought, Michel; and Marathe, Vanay. "Extra Market Components of Covariance among Security Prices." University of California, Berkley, 1973.

14. Sharpe, William F. *Portfolio Theory and Capital Markets.* New York: McGraw-Hill, 1970.

Portfolio Beta Prediction

VINAY V. MARATHE

Barr Rosenberg Associates
Orinda, California

OVERVIEW

The first section of this chapter reviews the capital asset pricing model and the possible applications of beta forecasts. The next section examines the shortcomings of the beta estimate obtained from a regression of the portfolio returns on the market returns. Next, a multiple-factor model of security returns based on economic theory, and its implications for portfolio beta and residual risk prediction, and performance measurement are discussed. Finally, some results on improved prediction of betas using investment fundamentals are presented.

THE CAPITAL ASSET PRICING MODEL

An investment manager's interest in a portfolio's beta stems from the impact of beta on the portfolio expected return and on portfolio risk. The capital asset pricing model (CAPM) of Sharpe [1964], Lintner [1965], and Mossin [1966] is a relation between equilibrium expected returns of assets and their betas.*[1] Based on some simple and unrealistic assumptions, they show that, in equilibrium, assets will be priced in the market such that expected returns are linearly related to betas according to the following equation:

---

* Where authors are listed with a data in brackets, see *References* at end of chapter.

[1] For a brief, nontechnical discussion and some empirical evidence, see Modigliani and Pogue [1974].

$$E(\tilde{R}_j) - R_F = B_j[E(\tilde{R}_M) - R_F], \tag{1}$$

where

$E(\tilde{R}_j) =$ expected total return, i.e., both capital gains and dividend, on asset j. The tilde ($\sim$) on R_j and on R_M is statistical notation for random variables, used here as a reminder that these returns are random (i.e., risky), as opposed to the certain return R_F for the riskless asset.

$E(\tilde{R}_M) =$ expected total return on the market portfolio[2]

$R_F =$ the riskless rate of return

$\beta_j =$ beta of asset $j = \dfrac{\text{COVARIANCE } (\tilde{R}_j - R_F, \tilde{R}_M - R_F)}{\text{VARIANCE } (\tilde{R}_M - R_F)}$

Considerable work has been done since the publication of the model in equation (1) and several theoretical models of equilibrium market prices of assets with somewhat more realistic assumptions have been developed. While these models result in slight modifications of equation (1), the linear relation between expected return and beta is preserved and borne out by empirical data.[3]

Portfolio excess return—i.e., return in excess of the riskless rate— is a weighted average of the excess returns on assets in the portfolio, with the weights corresponding to investment proportions—i.e., the portfolio excess return $\tilde{Z}_P$ is given by:

$$\tilde{Z}_P = h_1\tilde{Z}_1 + h_2\tilde{Z}_2 + \cdots + h_n\tilde{Z}_n = \sum_{i=1}^{n} h_i\tilde{Z}_i, \tag{2}$$

where $h_1, h_2, \ldots h_n$ are the investment proportions, and $\tilde{Z}_1, \tilde{Z}_2, \ldots \tilde{Z}_n$ are the excess returns on the n assets in the portfolio (i.e., $\tilde{Z}_i = \tilde{R}_i - R_F$).

Portfolio beta, β_P, from the definition following equation (1), is given by:

$$\beta_P = \frac{\text{COV}(\tilde{Z}_P, \tilde{Z}_M)}{\text{VAR}(\tilde{Z}_M)} = \frac{\text{COV}(h_1\tilde{Z}_1 + h_2\tilde{Z}_2 + \cdots + h_n\tilde{Z}_n, \tilde{Z}_M)}{\text{VAR}(\tilde{Z}_M)}$$

$$= \frac{h_1 \text{COV}(\tilde{Z}_1, \tilde{Z}_M) + h_2 \text{COV}(\tilde{Z}_2, \tilde{Z}_M) + \cdots + h_n \text{COV}(\tilde{Z}_n, \tilde{Z}_M)}{\text{VAR}(\tilde{Z}_M)} \tag{3}$$

$$= h_1\beta_1 + h_2\beta_2 + \cdots + h_n\beta_n = \sum_{i=1}^{n} h_i\beta_i$$

---

[2] In theory, the market portfolio consists of all risky assets in the economy in proportion to their outstanding capitalizations.

[3] For a more technical review of the modified capital asset pricing models, see Jensen [1972]. For empirical evidence, see Modigliani and Pogue [1974], Part II; Jensen [1972]; and Rosenberg and Marathe [1979].

Thus, the portfolio beta is a weighted average of the betas of the assets in the portfolio, with the weights being equal to the investment proportions.

From equation (2) it follows that the expected portfolio excess return is:

$$E(\tilde{Z}_P) = h_1 E(\tilde{Z}_1) + \cdots + h_n E(\tilde{Z}_n) = \sum_{i=1}^{n} h_i E(\tilde{Z}_i). \tag{4}$$

From equations (3) and (4) we see that if equation (1) holds for individual assets, it will also hold for all portfolios.

The capital asset pricing model is an ex ante model, so that all variables of equation (1), except the riskless rate R_F, are forecasts or expectations. Thus, to use equation (1) for identifying under- or overpriced assets—i.e., those assets whose expected returns are more (less) than the right-hand side of equation (1)—forecasts of expected returns on assets, $E(\tilde{R}_j)$, and on the market, $E(\tilde{R}_M)$, and of betas of assets, β_j, are needed.

Ex post, the return for a portfolio or asset will consist of a systematic component associated with the market return and a residual component, so that

$$Z_i = \beta_i Z_M + U_i. \tag{5}$$

Total excess return = systematic return + residual return.

The variability or variance of total return is a measure of the riskiness of asset or portfolio i. From equation (5), the variance of total excess return is given by

$$\text{VAR}(Z_i) = \beta_i^2 \, \text{VAR}(Z_M) + \text{VAR}(U_i). \tag{6}$$

Total risk = systematic risk + residual risk.

That part of the variability of return that is associated with comovement with the market, $\beta_i^2 \, \text{VAR}(R_M)$, is called systematic risk, and the remainder is residual risk. In equation (6), we do not have to account for the covariance between systematic return and residual return, since, by definition, residual return is that part of total return not associated with the market return.

Consider a portfolio with an investment proportion C in the riskless asset and the rest, i.e., investment proportion $(1 - C)$, in a market index fund. Then the expected return on the portfolio will be:

$$\begin{aligned} E(\tilde{R}_P) &= CR_F + (1 - C)E(\tilde{R}_M) \\ &= R_F + (1 - C)\,[E(\tilde{R}_M) - R_F]. \end{aligned} \tag{7}$$

For this portfolio, consisting of the riskless asset and the market index fund, the ex post return will be:

$$\begin{aligned} R_P &= CR_F + (1 - C)R_M \\ R_P - R_F &= (1 - C)(R_M - R_F) \\ Z_P &= (1 - C)Z_M \end{aligned} \tag{8}$$

So, the beta of the portfolio is $(1 - C)$, as expected, and portfolio risk, i.e., the variance of total excess return, is:

$$\text{VAR} \, (Z_P) = (1 - C)^2 \, \text{VAR} \, (Z_M) \qquad (9)$$

For this portfolio, the excess return is $(1 - C)$ times the excess return on the market portfolio $(R_M - R_F)$, both in terms of ex ante expectations and in terms of ex post realized returns. Although all of this is quite obvious for a portfolio invested in the riskless asset and the market index, it is helpful in clarifying some implications of the capital asset pricing model. Ex ante equation (1) holds for all portfolios, including the levered market portfolio (a portfolio with a short or long position in the riskless asset and a long position in the market index). Ex post, however, the residual return for the levered market portfolio is identically zero. Consequently, all the risk of the levered market portfolio is systematic risk, and its residual risk is zero. This is not surprising, since all the risk in a levered market portfolio comes from the portion in the market index.

The characteristics of the levered market portfolio also provide an explanation for the nature of the risk premium implied by the equilibrium relation of equation (1). In the market, if there is no compensation or premium in terms of higher expected return for riskier investments, the demand would fall far short of supply, and the prices for risky assets would drop until at equilibrium there is compensation in terms of higher expected return for riskier investments. In equation (1), the risk premium is related to β, i.e., to the systematic component of total risk as given by equation (6). The reason for this is that the residual risk can be completely eliminated or diversified away by investment in a levered market portfolio. Systematic risk, however, is intrinsic to the capital markets and cannot be avoided, thus requiring a risk premium to induce investors to invest in risky assets.

An investment manager needs to know the betas of assets to determine which assets are underpriced (overpriced), in that the manager's forecasted returns are higher (lower) in comparison to the equilibrium returns given by equation (1). She or he will then attempt to hold more (less) than the market proportions of under (over) priced assets. As his positions in risky assets become more extreme than the market proportions, the residual risk of the portfolio increases, and the manager will stop where the increase in residual risk just balances the increase in expected return due to stock selection.[4] Thus, residual risk in investment portfolios is a consequence of an attempt to exploit the ability to identify underpriced and overpriced assets. If an investment

---

[4] This is not necessarily so in the context of a multiple-factor model. Moving away from the market position or holding size in some asset starting from a portfolio that is not an index fund may actually reduce the portfolio risk due to reduced exposure to residual common factors, even though the exposure to the specific risk of the asset increases. For a detailed discussion of this, see Rosenberg and Marathe [1976].

manager feels she lacks this ability, she could, at much less effort, obtain a better risk/return trade-off by investing in a levered market portfolio.

The other reason why an investment manager may want to monitor the betas of assets, and therefore of the portfolio, is that the portfolio beta determines the expected systematic return and the accompanying systematic risk. Based on her forecast of the long-term return and risk in the market, she will choose a normal beta for the portfolio. (Figures of around 6 percent per annum in excess of the riskless rate and a standard deviation around 20 percent per annum for equities in the American capital markets are cited in many studies ranging over the past 50 to 100 years.) Then, based on short-term forecasts of market movements, she may want to increase or decrease the portfolio beta (market timing) by moving in and out of the riskless asset and/or tilting the equity component of the portfolio toward higher or lower beta assets.

THE TRADITIONAL METHOD OF ESTIMATING BETAS

Sharpe [1964] suggested one approach to estimating betas of assets. From the late 1960s until a little more than three years ago, most commercial services that provided beta estimates, and most financial institutions that computed their own betas for use in-house, used some slight variants of this approach. It is in this sense that the approach is labeled as the traditional method.

Sharpe suggested the estimation of beta by a least-squares regression of the ex post excess returns on the asset or portfolio on the ex post excess returns on the market index over a historical period. If we plot the returns on an asset against the returns on the market index, we obtain a scatter of points, as shown in Figure 1.

When a least-squares regression line is fitted to the data, the slope of the line is equal to $COV(R_i, R_M)/VAR(R_M)$, where both the numerator and denominator are sample estimates from the data to which the line is fitted.[5]

In Figure 1, each point corresponds to a pair of returns on the asset (or portfolio) and on the market over the same interval of time. (Monthly returns were used until quite recently, when weekly and daily prices became available on a large number of stocks traded on the exchanges in machine-readable form—i.e., on computer tapes.) If the regression estimate of beta—i.e., the slope of the regression line—is accepted, then estimates of the systematic return will fall on

---

[5] In statistical notation, the Greek letter β (beta) is generally used as a symbol for the slope, and α (alpha) is used for the intercept. Although Sharpe [1964] did not mention β or beta in suggesting this estimation procedure, he paved the way for the first Greek letter in investment jargon.

Figure 1
Estimation of Beta from Historical Returns Data

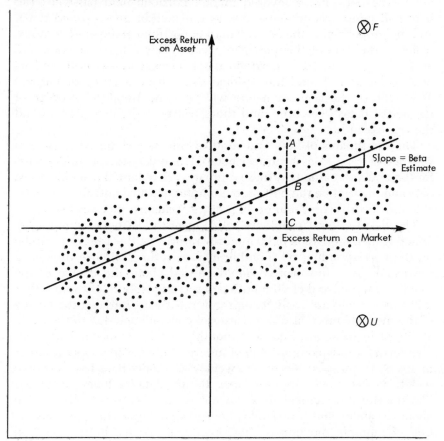

the line, and the vertical distance of the points from the line would be an estimate of the residual return. For example, when portfolio and market returns plot at point *A*, then *B-C* would be the estimate of systematic return over the month and *A-B* an estimate of residual return based on the slope of the regression line as an estimate of beta.

The scatter of points around the line is indicative of the residual risk. The variance of residual returns, also known as the standard error of the regression, is an estimate of residual variance or residual risk. For individual stocks, the scatter is very wide, reflecting the large residual risk. On the other hand, for portfolios, the scatter of points will be quite close to the line, since a large portion of the residual risk of individual assets is diversified away. For a levered market portfolio that is rebalanced every month to maintain a proportion *C* in the riskless asset, and therefore $(1 - C)$ in the market index, the points will fall on the line exactly, and its slope will equal $(1 - C)$ corresponding to the beta. For a levered market portfolio held passively, the beta will jump around somewhat as the market goes up and down and the proportion of the levered market portfolio in the market index, which is the beta of this portfolio, varies. (This will not happen if $C = 0$, in which case, the portfolio is the market index itself, and its beta will stay at 1, and the residual risk will be zero by definition.) The slope of the regression line will be some weighted average of the actual betas over time, and there will be a slight scatter around the regression line.

These estimates of beta and residual risk (as a standard deviation) will be referred to as historical beta ($H\beta$) and historical sigma ($H\sigma$) for the obvious reason that these estimates are obtained from historical data and may not be the best predictions for ex ante control of portfolio risk and security appraisal or ex post performance measurement.

There are several problems with the historical beta estimate obtained from a regression of 60 monthly returns on the asset or portfolio on the corresponding 60 monthly market returns. Before discussing the problems, a few words should be said about the choice of the monthly interval and of 60 monthly observations. Both of these rather arbitrary choices are really compromises. At least initially, the choice of the monthly interval was a matter of convenience due to the availability of month-end prices and monthly dividends in machine-readable form for easy computation of monthly returns on a large number of assets. In the past few years, weekly and daily data have become widely available on computer tapes. Return data for longer intervals, like quarterly or annual data, do not contain as much information about variability and covariability because of the smoothing or cancellation of monthly movements in opposite directions. Return data on shorter intervals, such as weekly or daily, has a much higher noise in the information due to untimely prices for less frequently traded assets. Thus, the monthly interval is a compromise to avoid the disadvantages of a too long or too short interval.

The choice of 60 monthly observations is again a compromise between a longer history for more observations to reduce the standard error of the beta estimate and a shorter history to avoid the use of outdated data. An ordinary least-squares regression assumes the slope and intercept are constant and also weights each observation equally. Implicit in this historical beta estimate are the assumptions that (1) the portfolio beta is constant over the five-year history and is a relevant forecast for the future, and (2) a monthly return five years ago has as much relevance for forecasting beta as the most recent monthly return (since all observations are equally weighted). At least three innovations have been tried to overcome these problems.

The first and natural approach is to obtain the beta estimate from a weighted regression, with declining weights on observations as one moves back in time, on the assumption that the more recent observations will provide more relevant information for a forecast. For individual assets, this seems theoretically sound, since the characteristics of firms—and therefore the riskiness of their securities—probably evolve gradually over time. However, even in this case, the weighting scheme is not at all clear and should probably be different from security to security, depending on the nature and characteristics of the firm. For a passive levered market portfolio, the beta will jump around as the market index goes up and down. For an actively managed portfolio, the problem is worse, since the investment manager may be willing to take more risk when he is more confident of his forecasts than otherwise, and the portfolio beta may not evolve gradually and smoothly in a systematic pattern justifying any particular weighting scheme.

The second approach seems, at first glance, to overcome all the problems simultaneously, but it introduces a new one and is actually counterproductive in that the final estimate is less accurate. This approach was used for a short while a few years ago by a commercial beta vendor, but it is not in use anymore. The idea was that if weekly data were used to construct overlapping four-week return observations, there would be 51 observations in a year. All the observations are quite recent and the noise-to-information ratio is low. However, non-overlapping return data have the very desirable property of absence of serial correlation. The use of overlapping four-week return observations introduces serial correlation, resulting in a less accurate estimate. In the actual procedure that was used, a correction for the serial correlation and estimation error was attempted, but the final estimate was less accurate.

The third approach is the use of a more sophisticated statistical procedure, known as varying parameter regression. As the name suggests, the regression parameters (i.e., the slope and intercept) are not assumed constant over time as in ordinary least squares. From a varying parameter regression it is possible to estimate the time pattern of the parameters and their variance over time as implied by the data. For the portfolio return, this implies the following model:

$$Z_{Pt} = \beta_{Pt} Z_{Mt} + U_{Pt}, \tag{10}$$

where

$$\beta_{Pt} = \phi_P \beta_{P,t-1} + b_{Pt}. \tag{11}$$

Subscripts t and $t-1$ indicate the time period. ϕ_P is a measure of how gradually the beta changes over time. If ϕ_P is not close to zero and the variance of b_{Pt}, the random change in beta, is small, then β_{Pt} will change gradually and smoothly over time. On the other hand,

Figure 2
Beta History for the Standard & Poor's New York City Bank Index Compared with Average Predicted Beta for New York City Banks

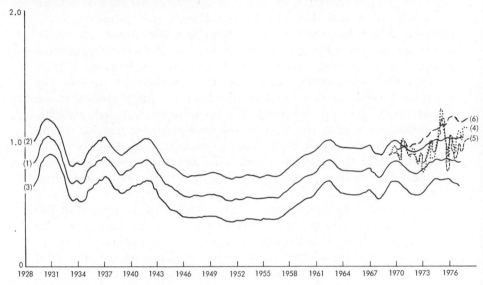

Key:
    (1) S&P mean beta.
    (2) S&P mean beta plus one standard error.
    (3) S&P mean beta minus one standard error.
    (4) Average predicted NYC Bank beta, all descriptors.
    (5) Average predicted NYC bank beta, selected fundamental descriptors.
    (6) Average predicted NYC bank beta, asset/liability descriptors.
Source: Rosenberg & Perry (unpublished paper).

if ϕ_P is close to zero and the variance of b_{Pt} is large, then β_{Pt} will change quite randomly over time. From the observations on Z_{Pt} and Z_{Mt}, the variance of U_{Pt} and of b_{Pt} and ϕ_P, and the time pattern of β_{Pt} (i.e., β_P values for all time periods) are estimated simultaneously. Since we are estimating all the variance components and the time pattern of β_P, a very long history of returns Z_{Pt} and Z_{Mt} is required. When the long history is available, it is possible to track variations in β_P quite accurately. However, as can be seen in Figure 2, when we use the additional information about the investment fundamentals of the company, it is possible to estimate the beta pattern more accurately over time.

ESTIMATION ERROR AND BAYESIAN ADJUSTMENT

Any statistical estimate has some estimation error. If the estimator is unbiased, then repeated application to different sets of observations will, on average, yield the true value, and the spread of estimates about this true value is a measure of the accuracy of the estimator and of the magnitude of estimation error for any one estimate.

In the context of beta estimation, the slope of the unobserved true relation between the portfolio return and the market return is what is sought. The residual returns obscure the true relation, and the slope can only be estimated probabilistically—i.e., a likely value and its standard error. For example, if something favorable but random happens to a firm in one month, we would obtain a point like F in Figure 1 for the firm's stock, with a large positive residual return. On the other hand, a random unfavorable outcome would result in a point like U. In a least-squares regression, the squared deviations from the fitted line are minimized, so a point like F would tend to tilt the line upward, and a point like U would tend to tilt it downward, thereby increasing or decreasing the estimate of beta (the slope of the line). The larger the estimate of $H\beta$, the more likely it is that there was large positive residual return, and the smaller the estimate of $H\beta$, the more likely it is that there was a large negative residual return. The regression also provides an estimate of the standard error of the slope, i.e., of $H\beta$.

Bayesian statistics suggest a procedure to combine two independent estimates to obtain a combined estimate that is more accurate than either estimate by itself. We have one estimate from the historical beta regression ($H\beta_j$) and its standard error ($\sigma_{\beta j}$). The other independent estimate is the fact that the average beta of all stocks is 1, and we can estimate its variance by subtracting the average estimation error variance of $H\beta$ of all stocks from the variance of estimated historical beta for all stocks. Let this be σ_β^2.

The best combined estimate ($\hat{\beta}_j$) weights the two estimates inversely in the proportion of their variance, so

$$\hat{\beta}_j = \frac{\sigma_{\beta j}^{-2} H\beta_j + \sigma_\beta^{-2} \, 1}{\sigma_{\beta j}^{-2} + \sigma_\beta^{-2}}$$
$$= \frac{\sigma_\beta^2 H\beta_j + \sigma_{\beta j}^2}{\sigma_\beta^2 + \sigma_{\beta j}^2}.$$

Let

$$k_j = \frac{\sigma_{\beta j}^2}{\sigma_{\beta j}^2 + \sigma_\beta^2}$$
$$\hat{\beta}_j = k_j + (1 - k_j) H\beta_j. \tag{12}$$

This procedure, well known in statistics for a long time, was applied to Bayesian adjustment of betas by Vasicek [1973]. Notice that k_j will be between 0 and 1, and if $H\beta_j = 1$, then the Bayesian adjusted beta, $\hat{\beta}_j = 1$. The more different $H\beta_j$ is from 1, the larger the Bayesian adjustment, and $\hat{\beta}_j$ will always be closer to 1 than $H\beta_j$.

A simplified version of this procedure has been used by Merrill Lynch to adjust their historical beta estimates. If one assumed the estimation error variance, $\sigma^2_{\beta j}$, is the same for all stocks, say S^2, then k_j will be equal for all stocks to $k = \dfrac{S^2}{S^2 + \sigma^2_\beta}$ and

$$\hat{\beta}_j = k + (1 - k)\mathrm{H}\beta_j. \tag{13}$$

The standard error of $\mathrm{H}\beta$ varies across stocks, and so (13) is an approximation to (12). The Bayesian adjusted betas as computed in (13) perform better than historical betas, in a predictive sense.

A MULTIPLE-FACTOR MODEL OF SECURITY RETURNS

One common misconception, which may perhaps be due to the procedure for estimating historical beta, is the existence of a causal relation between the market return and the returns on assets. Even though historical beta is estimated by a regression of the asset's returns on market returns, no causation is implied. Economic events influence the valuations of companies, and therefore of their securities, thus influencing their returns. The market return is a weighted average of returns on risky assets. The comovement between asset returns and market returns therefore arises due to the dependence of both on economic events.

Common Factors of Security Returns

Some economic events affect only firms within a particular industry. For example, the passage of the energy bill requiring better mileage performance from cars will affect the automobile industry. Because of increased costs, the value of automobile company stocks will decline. The month in which this news first reaches the market may result in a negative component of return to the stocks of automobile companies. This may be called an industry factor.

Other types of economic events may affect firms with certain characteristics across industries. Consider a possible crisis in the money markets precipitated by a contractionary monetary policy. Firms with high financial risk (as indicated in extreme leverage, poor coverage of fixed charges, and inadequate liquid assets) might be driven to bankruptcy. Most firms would suffer to some extent from higher borrowing costs and worsened economic expectations. Firms with higher financial risk would be affected more. Also, some industries, such as construction, might suffer more because of their special exposure to interest rates. On the other hand, such industries as liquor and tobacco might be unaffected. These types of events will result in some industry factors and some risk factors that impact firms to different degrees, depending on some characteristic of the firms, such as financial risk.

Finally, there are events that are specific to firms, such as labor disputes or the nationalization of assets abroad, which affect the valuation and therefore the returns of that firm alone. All of this reasoning may be summarized in an equation showing the components of excess return for a security in any month:

$$Z_j = \lambda_{1j}f_1 + \lambda_{2j}f_2 + \cdots + \lambda_{Kj}f_K + f_J + e_j, \tag{14}$$

where

$$f_J = \text{factor of return common to all firms in industry } J$$
(the industry of firm j) for the month
$$f_1, f_2, \ldots, f_K = K \text{ risk factors for the month}$$
$$e_j = \text{component of return specific to firm } j$$
$$\lambda_{1j}, \lambda_{2j}, \ldots, \lambda_{Kj} = \text{exposure of asset } j \text{ to the } K \text{ risk factors.}$$

Economic events are unexpected changes in the economy and, therefore, the common factors in security returns caused by them are random variables that could be positive, negative, or zero in any month.

Since the market return is a weighted average of returns on all assets, all of which have some exposure to the factors, we can expect the factors to have covariance with the market. We may decompose each factor into two portions—a portion related to the market and a residual factor—as follows:

$$f_k = b_k Z_M + g_k \tag{15}$$

and

$$f_J = b_J Z_M + g_J.$$

Substituting equation (15) into equation (14) and simplifying, we get:

$$Z_j = (\lambda_{1j}b_1 + \lambda_{2j}b_2 + \cdots + \lambda_{Kj}b_K + b_J)Z_M \tag{16}$$
$$+ \lambda_{1j}g_1 + \lambda_{2j}g_2 + \cdots + \lambda_{Kj}g_K + g_J + e_j$$
$$= \beta_j Z_M + U_j,$$

where

$$\beta_j = \lambda_{1j}b_1 + \lambda_{2j}b_2 + \cdots + \lambda_{Kj}b_K + b_J \tag{17}$$
$$U_j = \lambda_{1j}g_1 + \lambda_{2j}g_2 + \cdots + \lambda_{Kj}g_K + g_J + e_j. \tag{18}$$

The exposure coefficients of the asset $\lambda_{1j}, \lambda_{2j}, \ldots, \lambda_{Kj}$ would be expected to depend on the fundamental characteristics of the asset, such as earnings variability, leverage, asset growth, dividend payout, and many others. Market-based characteristics, such as historical beta, share turnover, trading volume, etc., may also contain some information for some exposure coefficients, i.e., λs.

Implications for Predicting Portfolio Betas

When a linear relation is hypothesized for the exposure coefficients, in terms of market-based and fundamental characteristics, and substituted in (17), we obtain a prediction equation for beta in terms of known fundamental and market-based variables. When this expression is substituted in equation (16), we obtain a cross-section time series regression equation that is valid for all assets in all months. This regression provides the coefficients for predicting beta from fundamental and market-based variables. The estimation procedure is discussed in detail in Rosenberg and Marathe [1975], and an intuitive discussion of why fundamentals may help in predicting beta, together with some examples, may be found in Rosenberg and Guy [1976]. As will be seen from the results in the next section, betas predicted from investment fundamentals have better predictive performance because of the additional information in the fundamentals and the larger weight on the current fundamental information. This allows the tracking of changes in portfolio betas due to both changing betas of assets in the portfolio and the changing portfolio composition.

Implications for Predicting Portfolio Residual Risk

As seen from equation (18), the residual return of securities (U_j) is made up of specific return (e_j) and the component due to residual factors. King [1966] showed that there were industry factors which explained covariances among assets over and above those attributable to the beta and market return. Farrell [1975] showed that growth, cyclical, stable, and oil stock tend to cluster, indicating additional factors. Rosenberg and Marathe [1976] estimate an extra-market covariance model through the estimation of the residual common factors of equation (18) $(g_1, g_2, \ldots, g_{45})$ for six risk indices and 39 industry factors) by monthly regressions. Then, from a history of monthly residual factors, their covariance matrix G is estimated. When a portfolio holding in some industry is different than that of the market, it is exposed to the risk in that factor. Similarly, when the portfolio's financial risk index is different from that of the market, it is exposed to the financial risk index factor. Thus, knowing the exposure to the residual common factors and the covariance matrix of residual factors, it is possible to predict and control residual risk due to common factor exposure.

Implications for Performance Attribution and Analysis

Many performance measurement services also use the regression of portfolio return on market return to measure performance. For a levered market portfolio with rebalancing to maintain constant proportion in the market, the intercept will be zero, and all the points will fall on the line. If the intercept is positive, it is argued that this is a result of selection of assets that, on average, have a positive residual return. In addition to the problems with beta estimation, and the resulting effect on the intercept (α), there are other problems with this approach. It cannot distinguish if the α was a result of market timing, stock selection, or sectoral policy (i.e., emphasizing certain industries or types of companies).

For instance, if a manager did no stock selection but was good at market timing by increasing or decreasing portfolio proportion in the index fund, he or she would have a positive α in the historical regression, since the regression will only estimate an average β and an α with respect to that. Using fundamentals and having the ability to track changes in portfolio β, and tracking changes in exposure to residual common factors allows an attribution of α each month to the market return, to sector policy, and to stock selection. A study of performance attributions over several month allows an analysis of the manager's strategy and its success with respect to market timing, sectoral policy, and stock selection. This approach to performance attribution and analysis is discussed in Rosenberg [1978].

IMPROVED PREDICTION OF BETA FROM INVESTMENT FUNDAMENTALS

This section summarizes the results of Rosenberg and Marathe [1975] on the predictive ability of fundamental descriptors (variables) for beta prediction and the predictive performance of the fundamental prediction compared to a Bayesian-adjusted prediction of the Merrill Lynch type. The study was conducted as follows.

At the beginning of each quarter, fundamental and market-based descriptors were computed from balance-sheet and income statements and market data available in machine-readable form at the time. The three monthly returns in the subsequent quarter are the dependent variables in the regression:

$$Z_{jt} = a + (b_0 + b_1 X_{1jt} + b_2 X_{2jt} + \cdots + b_N X_{Njt}) Z_{Mt} + U_{jt} \qquad (19)$$

Where Xs are the descriptors computed at the beginning of the quarter and Z_{jt} and Z_{Mt} are the three monthly excess returns on asset j and the market during the quarter. This process is repeated at the beginning of every quarter. The regression is performed on all assets in the 101 months from April 1966 (with 957 firms in that month) to August 1974 (by which time the number of firms had increased to 3,124). In all, there were 195,000 security-month observations.

Table 1 summarizes the results of simple prediction rules for β, using one descriptor at a time—i.e.,

$$\beta_j = b_0 + b_i X_{ij}.$$

Table 1
Individual Descriptors as Predictors of Systematic Risk

			Prediction of Beta	
Descriptor		Effect*	F-Statistic†	Order of Importance‡
			Market Variability	
Historical beta estimate	HBET	.243	2985	2
Historical sigma estimate	HSIG	.164	2405	7
Historical beta squared	BET2	.201	2593	3
Historical sigma squared	SGSQ	.168	2485	6
Historical beta times sigma	BTSG	.175	3510	1
Bayesian adjustment	BADJ	.180	2591	4
Share turnover, quarterly	STOQ	.129	1726	11
Share turnover, 12 months	STOA	.142	2193	9
Share turnover, five years	STO5	.159	1910	10
Trading volume/range of price	VLVR	.064	169	35
Current price	LPRI	−.067	83	43
Average monthly range, 12 months	ABRA	.211	2531	5
Average monthly range, five years	ARB5	.198	1362	15
Range, one year (log)	CMRA	.200	2364	8
			Earnings Variability	
Variance of earnings	VERN	.140	802	19
Extraordinary items	EXTE	.060	318	29
Variance of cash flow	VFLO	.130	752	20
Earnings of covariability	ABET	.127	402	27
Earnings/price covariability	BBET	−.015	7	52
			Unsuccess and Low Valuation of Earnings	
Growth in earnings/share	EGRO	−.001	13	49
Recent earnings change	DELE	.001	1	55
Relative strength	RSTR	−.057	109	34
Negligible earnings indicator	DMNE	.027	88	41
Book/price ratio	BTOP	−.020	48	45
Tax/earnings, five years	ATAX	.050	3	53
Dividend cuts, five years	CUTD	.036	170	33
Return on equity	ROEQ	−.005	0	56
			Immaturity and Smallness	
Total assets (log)	ASSI	−.108	383	28
Market capitalization (log)	CAPT	−.063	116	39
Market capitalization	OVAR		74	44
Market share	MKTS		2	54
Net plant/gross plant	NPGP	−.024	21	48
Gross plant/total assets	PTEQ	−.104	561	22
Real plant/equity	RPTE	−.094	503	23
Trading recency	TREC	.013	155	37
Indicator of earnings history	DMS5	−.044	85	42

Table 1 *(continued)*

Descriptor		Effect*	F-Statistic†	Order of Importance‡
			Prediction of Beta	
			Growth Orientation	
Payout last five years	PAYO	−.269	1406	14
Current yield	YILD	−.205	1421	13
Yield last five years	YLD5	−.204	1537	12
Indicator of zero yield	DMYL	.153	927	17
Growth in total assets	AGRO	.122	1177	16
Variance in capital structure	VCAP	.128	805	18
Earnings/price ratio	ETOP	−.042	116	40
Earnings/price normalized	ENTP	−.016	8	51
Earnings/price, five years	ETP5	−.090	427	26
			Financial Risk	
Book leverage	BLEV	.007	0	57
Leverage at market	MLEV	−.028	24	47
Debt/assets	DTOA	.110	481	24
Uncovered fixed charges	PNCV	.031	303	30
Cash flow	FLOW	−.180	588	21
Liquid assets/current liabilities	LIQU	−.003	9	50
Potential dilution	DILU	−.008	140	38
Adj. to earnings for inflation	PRDE	.045	202	31
Tax adjusted monetary debt	DTXO	−.095	463	25
Dummy variable/NYSE listing	DMNY	.017	34	46
Dummy variable/exchange list	DMEX	.058	162	36

* In this and all subsequent tables, the effects of the descriptors are reported as follows. For beta, the coefficient gives the adjustment to predicted beta for a unit change in the descriptor.

To make the effects of different descriptors comparable, the descriptors are standardized. For each descriptor, the capitalization-weighted average value for the S&P 500 is zero. Also, for each descriptor, the value of +1 is assigned to a firm that lies one standard deviation above this mean value. (For purposes of computing the standard deviation, the subpopulation of larger firms in the sample—those with capitalization greater than $50,000,000—is used.) Hence, a unit change in the descriptor corresponds to a movement of one standard deviation through the population of large firms. Most large firms therefore have values ranging between −3 and +3 on each descriptor. Smaller firms, for which fundamental data are typically more variable, frequently have values as extreme as +5 or −5.

Consequently, the reported effect for any descriptor is easily interpreted. For example, the value of .243 for the effect of the historical beta estimate on predicted beta implies that if a firm lies one standard deviation among the mean in its historical beta value, the prediction for beta should be adjusted upward by .243. Roughly 17 percent of large firms lie more than one standard deviation above the mean and therefore experience upward adjustments of this amount or more. Roughly 3 percent of large firms lie more than two standard deviations above the mean and experience upward adjustments of twice this amount or more. Symmetrically, about 17 percent (3 percent) of firms lie one (two) standard deviations below the mean and therefore experience adjustments as great as minus (twice) this amount.

† This is the F-statistic for the simple GLS regression in which the descriptor is the only information used to predict risk, with degrees of freedom (1,194955). The critical point for the 99.9 percent level of confidence is 10.64. The magnitude of the F-statistic is directly proportional to the variance in risk predicted by a linear function of the descriptor. The larger the F-statistic, the more important the simple predictive content of the descriptor.

‡ This is the rank of the descriptor, among all descriptors, in terms of explanatory power, with 1 being the highest.

Source: Rosenberg & Marathe (1975).

Table 2
Systematic Risk of Industries

Industry Number	Industry Name	Average Industry Values* Beta	Industry Risk Differences Not Explained by Other Fundamentals† Adjustment to Beta
1	Nonferrous metals	.99	−.142***
2	Energy raw materials	1.22	−.030
3	Construction	1.27	.062
4	Agriculture, food	.99	−.140***
5	Liquor	.89	−.165***
6	Tobacco	.80	−.279***
7	Apparel	1.27	.019
8	Forest products, paper	1.16	−.016
9	Containers	1.01	−.140**
10	Media	1.39	.124*
11	Chemicals	1.22	.011
12	Drugs, medicine	1.14	−.099***
13	Soaps, cosmetics	1.09	−.067*
14	Domestic oil	1.12	−.103*
15	International oil	.85	−.143*
16	Tires, rubber goods	1.21	.050
17	Steel	1.02	−.086*
18	Producer goods	1.30	.043
19	Business machines	1.43	.065
20	Consumer durables	1.44	.132*
21	Motor vehicles	1.27	.045
22	Aerospace	1.30	.020
23	Electronics	1.60	.155**
24	Photographic, optical	1.24	.026
25	Nondurables, entertainment	1.47	.042
26	Trucking, freight	1.31	.098
27	Railroads, shipping	1.19	.030
28	Air transport	1.80	.348***
29	Telephone	.75	−.288***
30	Energy, utilities	.60	−.237***
31	Retail, general	1.43	.073
32	Banks	.81	−.242***
33	Miscellaneous finance	1.60	.210**
34	Insurance	1.34	.103
35	Real Property	1.70	.339***
36	Business services	1.28	.029
37	Travel, outdoor recreation	1.66	.186**
38	Gold	.36	−.827***
39	Miscellaneous, conglomerate	1.14	.089*

* These are weighted averages, weighted by $1/\hat{\sigma}_n$.
† The estimated coefficients for industry dummy variables in GLS regressions, weighted $1/\hat{\sigma}_n$. The coefficients are tranformed to give the adjustment for that industry relative to the population of all firms. One asterisk indicates significance at the 95 percent level of confidence; two asterisks, significance at the 99 percent level; and three asterisks, significance at the 99.9 percent level.
Source: Rosenberg and Marathe (1975).

The F-statistic is a measure of the predictive content of that descriptor for beta. For detailed definitions of the descriptors, see Rosenberg and Marathe [1975].

Table 2 reports the average betas in industry groups and industry adjustments. If all we knew about a stock was the industry of the company, this is the best prediction. If we knew all the fundamentals in addition, then the industry adjustment is much smaller, as expected (the industry adjustment is additive to the prediction based on fundamentals). Detailed definitions of industry groups based on SIC codes are given in Rosenberg and Marathe [1975].

If all the descriptors are used together, a much better prediction of beta is obtained. The prediction rules using only fundamental descriptors and those using all the descriptors are not reported here but may be found in Rosenberg and Marathe [1975].

Table 3 shows the performance of prediction rules using various subsets of information relative to a Merrill Lynch type prediction rule $(\hat{\beta}_{nt} = .44 + .56H\beta_{nt})$ fitted to the same data base. It is an indication of the weakness of the historical beta estimate that, knowing the industry group alone, the performance is 91 percent of that due to the Bayesian-adjusted historical beta. The performance of beta, using fundamentals and industry adjustments (without using any historical return or market-based information) is 145 percent. This is impressive evidence of the predictive ability of fundamentals for beta. The predic-

Table 3
Unbiased Estimates of the Performance of Alternative Prediction Rules in the Historical Period (predicted variance as a multiple of the variance predicted by a widely utilized prediction rule*)

Information Used in Prediction	Prediction of beta
Market variability information only	
Benchmark†	1.00
Nonlinear function of the historical estimator	1.05
All market variability descriptors	1.57
Fundamental information only	
Industry adjustments only	.91
Industry adjustment and fundamental descriptors	1.45
Market variability and fundamental information	
All information except the historical estimator	1.79
All information	1.86
Chosen prediction rule	1.86

* The reported figure is the adjusted R^2 in the appropriate GLS regression for residual returns, $r_{nt} - r_{Mt}$, divided by the adjusted R^2 for the benchmark procedure.

† The benchmark prediction rule for beta is the fitted constant Bayesian adjustment, $\hat{\beta}_{nt} = .44 + .56H\beta_{nt}$, essentially identical to the Merrill Lynch prediction rule.

Source: Rosenberg & Marathe (1975).

tion based on all descriptors has a relative performance of 186 percent.

Figure 2 is taken from an unpublished study by Rosenberg and Perry. Lines marked (1), (2), and (3) are, respectively, the β estimate and $\beta \pm$ one standard error for the S&P NYC Bank Index estimated from the long history of monthly data from 1929 to 1977 by varying parameter regression. Lines (4), (5), and (6) are fundamental betas estimated using different subsets of fundamental variables. Notice the more precise tracking of beta variation using all fundamentals (4), compared to a smoothed-out pattern using asset/liability descriptors, which in turn is not as smoothed as the estimates from varying parameter regression. Standard errors for the fundamental estimates are not available but would be considerably smaller than those for the varying parameter regression estimates.

CONCLUSION

A theoretical rationale for, and empirical results on, improved prediction of beta from investment fundamentals is presented. The estimation of the underlying multiple-factor model also permits better predictions of portfolio residual risk and performance measurement.

APPENDIX

The variance of a random variable $\tilde{X}$ is a measure of the variability or the spread of possible outcomes for $\tilde{X}$.

$$\text{Variance} = E[\tilde{X} - E(\tilde{X})]^2 = \sigma^2(\tilde{X})$$
$$= \text{Expected value of the squared deviation about the mean (i.e., the expected value of } \tilde{X} = E(\tilde{X})).$$

Standard deviation is the square root of variance and has a more intuitive meaning. For a normally distributed random variable with mean (i.e., expected value of μ) and a standard deviation of σ, approximately two thirds of the outcomes lie between $\mu + \sigma$ and $\mu - \sigma$, and approximately 95 percent of the outcomes lie between $\mu \pm 2\sigma$.

The covariance between two random variables $\tilde{X}$ and $\tilde{Y}$ is a measure of their comovement and is defined as:

$$\text{COVARIANCE } (\tilde{X}, \tilde{Y}) = E[\{\tilde{X} - E(\tilde{X})\} \{\tilde{Y} - E(\tilde{Y})\}].$$

A more intuitive measure of comovement is the correlation coefficient, defined as:

$$\rho(X, Y) = \frac{\text{COV}(\tilde{X}, \tilde{Y})}{\sigma(\tilde{X})\sigma(\tilde{Y})}.$$

The correlation coefficient can take values between -1 and $+1$. A value of -1 means the two variables move exactly opposite; a value of ± 1 means the two variables move in the same direction. In either of these two cases, the two variables are perfectly correlated, and it is possible to predict, without error, the value of either variable by knowing the value of the other. When $\rho = 0$, the two variables are uncorrelated, and knowing one does not help at all in predicting the other. For other values between -1 and 1, the more different the value from 0, the better is the prediction of either variable based on the other.

REFERENCES

Farrell, James L. "Homogeneous Stock Groupings: Implications for Portfolio Management." *Financial Analysts Journal* (May–June 1975).

Jensen, M. C. "Capital Markets: Theory and Evidence." *Bell Journal of Economics and Management Science* (Autumn 1972).

King, Benjamin F. "Market and Industry Factors in Stock Price Behavior." *Journal of Business* (January 1966), pp. 139–90.

Lintner, John. "The Valuation of Risk Assets and the Selection of Risky Investments in Stock Portfolios and Capital Budgets." *Review of Economics and Statistics* 47 (February 1965), pp. 13–37.

Modigliani, Franco, and Pogue, Gerald A. "An Introduction to Risk and Return." *Financial Analysts Journal*, Part I (March–April 1974); Part II (May–June 1974).

Mossin, Jan. "Equilibrium in Capital Asset Markets." *Econometrica* 34 (October 1966), pp. 768–83.

Rosenberg, Barr. "Extra-Market Components of Covariances Among Security Prices." *Journal of Financial and Quantitative Analysis* 9, pp. 263–74.

———. "Performance Measurement and Performance Attribution." Working Paper no. 75. Research Program in Finance, Institute of Business and Economic Research, University of California, Berkeley, 1978.

Rosenberg, Barr, and Marathe, Vinay. "Prediction of Investment Risk: Systematic and Residual Risk." *Proceedings of the Seminar on the Analysis of Security Prices.* University of Chicago (November 1975).

———. "Common Factors in Security Returns: Microeconomic Determinants and Macroeconomic Correlates." *Proceedings of the Seminar on the Analysis of Security Prices.* University of Chicago (May 1976).

———. "Tests of Capital Asset Pricing Hypotheses." In *Research in Finance.* Edited by Haim Levy. Greenwich, Conn.: JAI Press, Inc., 1979.

Rosenberg, Barr, and Guy, James. "Prediction of Beta from Investment Fundamentals." *Financial Analysts Journal*, Part I (May–June 1976); Part II (July–August 1976).

Sharpe, William F. "Capital Asset Prices: A Theory of Market Equilibrium under Conditions of Risk." *Journal of Finance* (September 1964).

Vasicek, Oldrich A. "A Note on Using Cross-Sectional Information in Bayesian Estimation of Security Betas." *Journal of Finance* (December 1973).

Part Two

Management Strategies

Part Two

Chapter 7

Active Equity Management Strategies[*]

ARTHUR ZEIKEL

President
Merrill Lynch Asset Management, Inc.
New York, New York

Active portfolio management is a term used to describe what most investment professionals do to earn their living. It is the attempt to profit from stock selection, market timing or both. In capital asset pricing terms, it is an attempt to achieve investment returns that differ from those implied by the market line. Practicing portfolio managers employ a wide variety of investment philosophies and procedures. In fact, it has been frequently noted that there are perhaps as many methods of managing a portfolio as there are portfolio managers.

Some portfolio managers predicate the ebb and flow of their investments on business cycle analysis or the identification of technical trends (see Chapter 13). Others structure their equity portfolios to resemble closely the composition of a market index, such as the Standard & Poor's Composite, placing special emphasis on those industrial sectors believed to be particularly attractive—while at the same time limiting or eliminating those considered less attractive (see Chapter 8). Still others confine their efforts almost entirely to individual stock selection techniques.

According to Russell J. Morrison, two considerations are necessary for success in active portfolio management.[1] First, one must have a

---

Author's Note: Some studies indicate the transfer estimates used in Ellis' formula are high. However, even if they are, it would not affect the general premise substantially.

[*] Portions of material contained in this chapter are based on material from *Investment Analysis & Portfolio Management* (Homewood, Ill.: Richard D. Irwin, 1977), and *Guide to Intelligent Investing* (Homewood, Ill.: Dow Jones-Irwin, 1978), both written by Jerome B. Cohen, Edward D. Zinbarg, and Arthur Zeikel.

[1] Russell J. Morrison, "Speculation: Its Nature and Implications for Portfolio Management," *Financial Analysts Journal* (January–February 1976), p. 18.

good idea of how others view alternative investments. Second, one must disagree with the concensus—disagree as to direction or disagree as to amplitude of price movement. Thus, the task of the active portfolio manager is not to forecast returns accurately, but to forecast more accurately than the market. Moreover, the difference in expectations must be of sufficient magnitude to cover transaction costs and to allow for the error factor.

Active managers consider the holding period for portfolio securities to be temporary. Once the difference in expectation disappears, either because of the market's perception changes or because the manager is proven wrong, portfolio holdings are replaced by others which are believed to offer better returns than expected by the market. Active portfolio management requires either: *(a)* concentration in a fairly small number of issues with continuous reassessment of alternatives; or *(b)* moving in and out of well-diversified portfolios.

Charles D. Ellis, in an award-winning *Financial Analysts Journal* article, recently put an interesting perspective on the difficulty of out-performing the market by asking portfolio managers to solve "a simple but distressing equation."[2]

Assume:

a. Equities will return an average 9 percent rate of return.
b. Average turnover of 30 percent per annum.
c. Average costs—dealer spreads plus commissions—on institutional transactions are 3 percent of the principal value involved.
d. Management and custody fees total 0.20 percent.
e. The goal of the manager is to outperform the averages by 20 percent.

$$\text{Solve for } X \text{ percent: } (X)(9) - [.30(3+3)] - (0.20) = (1.20)(9)$$

$$X = \frac{1.8 + 0.20 + 10.8}{9}$$

$$X = \frac{12.8}{9}$$

$$X = 142\%.$$

In plain language, according to Ellis, the manager who intends to deliver *net* returns of 20 percent better than the market must earn a gross return before fees and transaction costs (liquidity tolls) that is more than 40 percent better than the market. If this sounds absurd, he points out, the same equation can be solved to show that the active manager must beat the market *gross* by 22 percent just to come out even with the market. In other words, for institutional investors to perform as well as, *but no better than,* the S&P 500, they must be

[2] Charles D. Ellis, "The Loser's Game," *Financial Analysts Journal* (July–August 1975), p. 19.

sufficiently astute and skillful to "outdo" the market by 22 percent. Frank E. Block of Bache Halsey Stuart Shields Incorporated put the problem this way:

> A second important point is that the market timers have to be right twice in a row in order to have success. It is not enough to sell near the high of a market move. One must also buy back at a lower price (adjusted for the compensating interest rate from the temporary cash investment and the transaction costs). Consider the probabilities of being right twice in a row. Let us assume that an investor has kept records on his opinions of the direction of the market for a number of years and found that they were correct 70 percent of the time. As his transaction will involve two decisions, the probability of being right two times in a row will be 0.70 times 0.70, which equals 0.49, or a 49 percent probability of success. A 70 percent batting average is not good enough to achieve average results in investment timing. It is important to remember that the pairs do not overlap. An error, either on the buy or the sell side, leaves the investor positioned so that he is not able to take advantage of the next turning point in the market. If he has made an error, at the next low he will be full invested and will have no cash to put in the market, or at the next high he will have no stock to sell because he is already at his maximum cash position. Thus the player of the timing game must have a batting average equal to the square root of 50 percent (about 71 percent) in order to have an expectation of breaking even.[3]

Ellis suggests four rules for those who are determined to win the "loser's game" despite the odds against them.

> First, be sure you are playing your own game. Know your policies very well and play according to them all the time.
>
> Second, keep it simple. Make fewer and perhaps better investment decisions. Simplify the professional investment management problem. Try to do a few things unusually well.
>
> Third, concentrate on your defenses. Almost all of the information in the investment management business is oriented toward purchase decisions. The competition in making purchase decisions is too good. It's too hard to outperform the other fellow in buying. Concentrate on selling instead.

---

[3] Frank E. Block, "Market Timing—Are Risk Free Assets Safe or Dangerous?" Institutional Research, Bache Halsey Stuart Shields Incorporated, June 28, 1978. Block also refers to William Sharpe's article "Likely Gains From Market Timing," *Financial Analysts Journal* (March–April), in which Sharpe determined that an 83 percent batting average would have to be necessary for active timers in order for them to break even when compared with a buy and hold strategy, assuming a 2 percent turnaround cost. Block notes that the 2 percent turnaround cost is too high today, now that we have negotiated rates, and the yields available on short-term risk-free assets are a good deal higher today than they were during the period studied. Thus the 83 percent batting average required to break even is probably a bit on the high side. Nevertheless, the true answer probably lies between our 71 percent and Sharpe's 83 percent, and the investor must do even better to achieve superior results.

Fourth, don't take it personally. The game is tougher than it looks, and lots of players accustomed to winning [other games] will lose at trying to beat the market.

Unfortunately, most "players" do not follow these, or their own, rules very well, and a large collection of historical evidence suggests that most professional portfolio managers are not very successful in their conduct of active management practices. More recently, however, the arguments against active management strategies are not so one-sided. Recently, for example, Harold B. Ehrlich of Bernstein-Macaulay, Inc., summarized some research findings which not only question the efficiency of the stock market, but seem to suggest the superiority of portfolio management—properly executed. In brief, Ehrlich points out: "The mathematical and statistical proofs of the 'efficient market-random walk' theories are not as sound as they have seemed. Fundamental research can produce private, special information which can be used to improve portfolio performance. Various stock prices and market forecasting techniques have yielded relatively superior results with a high degree of consistency. Certain filter screens have produced lists of stocks which have performed better than the market in general. A statistically meaningful number of large funds have shown consistently superior performance over the course of several market cycles."[4]

One of the more interesting bits of evidence to surface in the controversies over the benefits of active management versus passive strategies is a study completed by Computer Directions Advisers, Inc. (CDA), which suggests that, in the aggregate, portfolio changes made by mutual funds are not only productive but yield better results than those achieved by an index. According to the figures compiled by CDA, mutual funds (in the aggregate) have outperformed the S&P 500 by about three percentage points for the three quarters of 1978, by about 11 points over the last three years; and by about 15 points over the last five years. The top 75 mutual funds in the study did better by even wider margins.[5]

Perhaps the most damaging charge against capital market theory and the concept of efficient markets has been developed by the Value Line Investment Survey who claim that these general theories have been completely discredited by their own continual success at picking winners. According to statistics provided by Value Line, their stock selections between 1965 and mid-1978 have compounded at 20.2 per-

---

[4] Harold B. Ehrlich, "Can You Beat The Market After All?" Bernstein-Macaulay, Inc., April 1, 1978. See also the *Journal of Portfolio Management* (New York: Institutional Investors Systems, Fall 1977), an entire issue devoted to articles questioning the efficient market concept.

[5] Edward Kulkosky, "The Born-Again Mutual Funds?" *Financial World* (November 15, 1978), p. 43.

cent per annum. Value Line officials charge that because the concept of ranking stocks by price-earning ratios (relative to historical norms) and to the momentum of quarterly earnings has proved so successful, markets are not efficient and stock prices do not move in a random walk pattern. Their results also challenge the case for index funds that track the market.[6] Even proponents of the efficient market hypothesis have admitted that the results of the Value Line technique cast some doubt on the ability to reconcile such consistent performance over a long time period with generally accepted random walk theory.

Consequently, interest is once again developing among practitioners for the more effective use of active management strategies.

ACTIVE INVESTMENT TACTICS

Active investment decisions usually are classified under two broad headings: selection and timing. *Selection* asks what to buy or sell— bonds or stocks (and which bonds, and/or which stocks)? *Timing* asks when to buy or sell. As a practical matter, of course, these two categories are not mutually exclusive. The question of what to buy or sell is not made in a time vacuum. The real question is *what* to do with capital *now?* Granting the interlocking nature of selection and timing, however, it is useful to differentiate between them conceptually.

The traditional approach to the selection of investment has been that of security analysis, or evaluation. The essential goal of common stock evaluation is to determine the approximate trend line around which actual stock prices can be expected to fluctuate. At any given time, according to this approach, common stock analysts should have a reasonably clear idea whether stocks generally, and individual stocks in particular, seem underpriced or overvalued. This enables them to come to grips with both the what and when questions. For example, they may seek to buy issues which are relatively most underpriced, at a time when the market in general seems underpriced.

Value analysts assume that underpriced and overpriced situations ultimately will come into better balance. But they typically make little or no effort to predict when the corrective price movement will occur. Their reasons for ignoring efforts to predict are several. First, they argue that it is not possible to make predictions about turning points of prices with a better than chance probability of being accurate. This argument is supported by believers in the efficient markets hypothesis, who also doubt, however, that value analysis can be effective. Second, they point out that investors confront "a market of stocks rather than a stock market." By this they mean that efforts to predict the turning points of, say, the Dow-Jones Industrial Average are rather futile, since

---

[6] *Securities Week*, December 4, 1978, p. 8.

an average can go up or down but there is great disparity in the price movement of the individual component stocks of the average. Furthermore, they note with regard to attempts to predict the averages, most downturns during the postwar period have amounted to only some 10–20 percent. Certainly one cannot expect to be prescient enough to sell at the very peaks and buy back at the troughs. Assuming that even a good forecaster will make his or her sales at least 3–5 percent below the peaks, and that repurchases will be made 3–5 percent above the troughs, and making allowance for brokerage commissions and taxes of several percent on combined sale-repurchase transactions, the average price decline of 10–20 percent doesn't leave much, if anything, for profit. Moreover, there are very real dangers of being "whipsawed" by selling in anticipation of a price decline which fails to occur.

Timing decisions are usually classified into two broad categories, one considered the fundamental, or business cycle approach; and the other the technical, or market, approach. Business cycle analysis seeks to relate security price changes, both absolute and relative to the market, to general business developments and to the economic cycles of specific industries. Technical analysis focus attention (and dictates decisions) on internal developments within the security markets themselves. In other words, the active decision maker using the business

Figure 1
Portfolio Strategy Decision Matrix

Ability to Select Undervalued Securities ╲ Ability to Forecast Overall Market	*Good*	*Poor*
Good	1. Concentrate holdings in selected undervalued securities rather than diversify broadly. 2. Shift beta above and below desired long-term average, based on market forecasts.	1. Concentrate holdings in selected undervalued securities rather than diversify broadly. 2. Keep beta stable at desired long-term average.
Poor	1. Hold a broadly diversified list of securities. 2. Shift beta above and below desired long-term average, based on market forecasts.	1. Hold a broadly diversified list of securities. 2. Keep beta stable at desired long-term average.

Source: Adapted from Keith Ambachtsheer, "Portfolio Theory and the Security Analyst," *Financial Analysts Journal* (November–December 1972), p. 33.

cycle approach to common stock decisions deals with factors outside of the market itself—for example, industrial production, money supply, and the like. The technical manager, on the other hand, seeks to improve the basis of timing decisions by studying phenomena which are an integral part of the market mechanism—for example, prices and volume of trading. For this reason, technical analysis is often referred to as internal analysis or market analysis.

Figure 1 is a decision matrix, designed to place in perspective the investment tactics best suited to the forecasting and security selection abilities of the active manager. If decision makers believe they are good market forecasters, they should vary the stock-bond proportions of their portfolios quite often, in line with their forecasts. If they believe they are good stock or bond selectors, they should depart from the principle of broad diversification. If they are doubtful that they possess a high degree of either ability, they should concentrate on determining the most appropriate overall risk level for their portfolio and should proceed to create broadly diversified portfolios with constant risk (beta) levels that conform to their appraisals. The point is that active managers must decide what they think they are good at, and what they are not good at.

SECURITY ANALYSIS AND COMMON STOCK EVALUATION

Security analysis means, of course, fundamental analysis. This is the basic process of the evaluation of common stock by studying earnings, dividends, price-earnings multiples, economic outlook for the industry, financial prospects for the company, sales penetration, market share, and quality of management. Selecting the industry or industries which are likely to do best over the next three to five years and then choosing the company or companies within the selected industries which are likely to outperform their competitors—this is the essence of fundamental analysis.[7]

In general terms there are four aspects of any complete and concise analysis: *(a)* the sales analysis and forecast, *(b)* the earnings analysis and forecast, *(c)* the multiplier analysis and forecast, and *(d)* the analysis of management, a qualitative consideration.[8]

Basic to any estimate of earning power is a sales analysis and forecast. Growth of demand for a company's products is essential for common

[7] For an elaboration, see Jerome B. Cohen, Edward D. Zinbarg, and Arthur Zeikel, *Investment Analysis and Portfolio Management*, 3d ed. (Homewood, Ill.: Dow Jones-Irwin, 1977), Chapter 5. © 1977 by Dow Jones-Irwin, Inc. See Leopold A. Bernstein, "In Defense of Fundamental Analysis," *Financial Analysts Journal* (January–February 1975).

[8] For a detailed discussion of *(a)* and *(b)*, see Robert S. Schultz, "Sales Forecasting" and Edmund A. Mennis, "Forecasting Corporate Profits," in *Methods and Techniques of Business Forecasting*, William Butler, Robert Kavesh, and Robert Platt, eds. (Englewood Cliffs, N.J.: Prentice-Hall, Inc., 1974).

stock appreciation. While expanding production and sales do not guarantee rising profits, rising demand or the introduction of new products,
at least give a company an opportunity to earn a rising profit.

What the analyst is seeking is a working forecast of sales in order
to determine the profit implications of the sales forecast. But just as
a sales forecast is essential to an effective profits forecast, an economic
forecast is a preliminary prerequisite to the sales forecast. The starting
point of an effective industry and company forecast may be a GNP
forecast, with a breakdown of components. For example, a forecast
of sales for the automobile industry may be tied to the growth of
real GNP by using historic figures on the number of cars sold per
billion dollar increase in real GNP. Or, the analyst may use estimates
of prospective consumer durable goods expenditures, derived from
an econometric model of the composite economy and use this to forecast automobile sales. Or, the estimate may begin with a forecast of
personal disposable income for either the coming year or longer. Since
expenditures on automobiles are a relatively stable percentage of disposable personal income, a reasonable estimate of expenditures for
automobiles may be made. Since this will be an estimate for the entire
industry, market shares must be allocated to companies.[9]

Having obtained an estimate or range of estimates of prospective
sales growth rates the next step is to proceed to obtain an estimate,
or range of estimates, of prospective earnings growth rates. To achieve
this an analysis of earnings is necessary. One approach is to start with
the GNP forecast and derive from it a prospective corporate profits
trend for all industry. Then factor out a profits trend for the particular
industry under review, making such adjustments as special industry
characteristics suggest a greater or lesser rate of growth than that of
the total corporate profits series. From this develop a company estimate, again making adjustment for special company characteristics.

Or, one can start with the sales forecast developed earlier and relate
this to the company's profit margin, operating income, equity turnover,
rate of return on equity, earnings before interest and taxes, net income
after interest and taxes, return on total capital, and net earnings per
share. By dissecting the anatomical character of a corporation's profitability and measuring the impact of prospective changes on each element, it is possible to derive an estimate of a range of future earnings
from one to three years ahead.[10]

---

[9] See Jerome B. Cohen, Edward D. Zinbarg, and Arthur Zeikel, *Investment Analysis
and Portfolio Management*, 3d ed. (Homewood, Ill.: Dow Jones-Irwin, 1977), Chapter
6. © 1977 by Dow Jones-Irwin, Inc.

[10] Ibid., Chapter 7. Some newer analytic techniques for estimating earnings should
be mentioned. They include probabilistic forecasting, conditional forecasts, and com-
puter models for forecasting earnings. These have been excellently explained in J. Peter
Williamson, *Investments: New Analytical Techniques* (New York: Praeger Publishers,
Inc., 1970). See especially Chapter 5, "Security Analysis," and Chapter 6, "Stock-Selection
Techniques."

Once an earnings forecast, or a range of forecasts, is derived, it remains to develop and apply a multiplier, the price-earnings ratio. A variety of factors impinge upon and help determine a price-earnings ratio. Among these are the growth rate of earnings, actual and anticipated, the dividend payment, the marketability and volatility of the stock, the stability or volatility of earnings, and the quality of earnings and of management. Of these, perhaps, the growth rate of earnings is the most significant. In general, there seems to be a consensus that the higher the growth rate of earnings, the higher the price-earnings ratio.

The object of common stock evaluation is to obtain standards against which prevailing prices of stocks may be judged. It is assumed that investors as a whole are essentially rational over the long run (although their actions occasionally seem to border on the insane), and that rational individuals attempt to measure the economic, or going-concern values of the corporations whose stocks they buy and sell. Since there are millions of investors, there will exist vastly different ideas about the value of any given stock at any given time, and purchases and sales of the stock will be made in accordance with this multitude of ideas. Therefore, over an extended period of time, prices will fluctuate in a wide range, *but they will tend to fluctuate around some concensus of value.*

Furthermore, it is assumed that the normal tendency of the marketplace is to drive prices to extremes. When optimism is dominant, conceptions of value are liberalized, and prices rise steadily. Ultimately, it is recognized that the optimism was excessive, and prices react downward. As prices fall, caution turns to fear, and the price decline snowballs until it is finally recognized that the pessimism was overdone. At this point a price reversal occurs once again. Successful evaluators of common stocks, therefore, will try to avoid becoming overly optimistic or overly pessimistic. They will attempt to determine the approximate level around which the price tides will swell and ebb. The evaluation process can be described graphically, as follows:

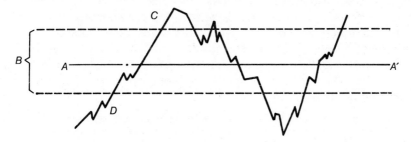

Where: *A–A'* is an objectively determined value line; *B* is a range allowed for errors which may have been made in the determination

of *A–A'*; *C* represents an area where prices would be considered too dear; and *D* represents an area where prices would be considered bargains. With regard to *A–A'*, we do not mean to imply that an evaluation must necessarily cover an extended span of time. The analyst may be content to make an estimate of any *point* on the line, near or distant.

From this brief summary of fundamental analysis, it should be clear that the modern approach to common stock evaluation centers on a two-part question. What is the potential growth of earnings and dividends of a company whose stock is being analyzed and what is a reasonable price to pay for that potential?[11]

EVALUATION MODELS

One of the more interesting portfolio management developments in recent years has been an enormous increase in the use and application of common stock evaluation models in the investment decision making process. Active managers, and their research suppliers, have become disappointed (and disenchanted) with the results obtained from traditional security analysis opinions covering the "value" of the individual stocks as well as the market itself. That is, opinions, from a diverse group of analysts, each working within a relatively narrow and isolated area, have not, in general, produced a value-added benefit to the portfolio manager's investment decisions. As a result, and in order to make more systematic a process of common stock evaluation, the use of evaluation models has gained in popularity. For example, Merrill Lynch, Pierce, Fenner & Smith, among others, now incorporate the findings of a common stock evaluation model into its bimonthly investment security perspective designed for institutional investors, pointing out that a valuation model is intended to serve two purposes: first, it serves as a quantitative benchmark for evaluating a current or expected level of stock prices on the basis of expectations and assumptions about such fundamental influences as economic growth, interest rates, dividends, earnings, and risk; second, it serves as a framework for understanding the interrelationships among those fundamental influences and the impact changes those influences have on the valuation of stocks. The fundamental model used by Merrill Lynch is essentially a dividend-valuation model, which contends that stock prices represent the investor's present valuation of an expected stream of dividends.[12]

---

[11] For a more detailed exposition of fundamental analysis, see Samuel S. Stewart Jr., "Corporate Forecasting," Chapter 32 in *Financial Analyst's Handbook*, vol. 1, Sumner N. Levine, ed. (Homewood, Ill.: Dow Jones-Irwin, 1975), © 1975 by Dow Jones-Irwin, Inc.

[12] For a more detailed explanation, see Cohen, Zinbarg, and Zeikel. *Investment Analysis*, Chapter 5. *See also* James C. Van Horne, *Financial Management and Policy*, 2d ed. (Englewood Cliffs, N.J.: Prentice-Hall, Inc., 1971).

The mathematic formula used to derive price on the basis of the dividend is

$$P = \frac{D_0(1 + G)}{(1 + K)} + \frac{D_0(1 + G)^2}{(1 + K)^2} + \frac{D_0(1 + G)^3}{(1 + K)^3} + \cdots + \frac{D_0(1 + G)^\infty}{(1 + K)^\infty}$$

in which dividends grow at rate G and are discounted at the investor's required rate of return K to derive a present value of the expected stream of dividends and D_0 is the current dividend. While the expected stream of dividends theoretically can be infinite under this formula, the low value of a dollar discounted two decades into the future means that for practical purposes it is the expectations of the first 20 years or so that determine the investment decision.

The equation above can be simplified as

$$P = \frac{D_0}{K - G}$$

That equation can be translated into a price-earnings multiple by dividing each side by E, or current earnings, as follows

$$P/E = \frac{D_0/E_0}{K - G}$$

The above result states that the calculated P/E_0 ratio (based on current earnings) equals the current pay out (D_0/E_0) divided by the difference between the investors expected rate of return (K) and the dividend growth rate (G). Note that if the payout ratio is constant, the dividend growth rate equals the earnings growth rate since (representing the pay-out ratio by R) we have

$$G = \frac{\Delta D}{D} = \frac{R\Delta E}{RE} = \frac{\Delta E}{E}$$

The growth rate can also be expressed in terms of the return on equity (ROE) when the growth in equity is financed only by retained earnings.[13] Representing a company's equity by Q we have

$$G = \frac{\Delta E}{E} = \frac{(E)}{(Q)} \frac{\Delta Q}{E} = \frac{E}{Q} \frac{(E - D)}{E} = (\text{ROE}) (1 - R)$$

Combining the last result with the earlier equation we have the final result

$$P/E_0 = \frac{R}{K - (\text{ROE})(1 - R)}$$

The quantity $1 - R$ is also called the reinvestment ratio.

The procedures for using the equation according to Merrill Lynch,

---

[13] Assumes balance sheet leverage is held constant.

is to project a theoretical market price by means of an intermediate-term outlook for earnings and the price/earnings multiple as developed from the model. The earnings outlook is generated from the projections of our analysts. The theoretical P/E can be derived by forecasting the payout ratio and required yield in a nine-step process:

1. forecast intermediate-term earnings;
2. forecast intermediate-term dividends;
3. derive a forecast of the payout ratio on the basis of steps 1 and 2;
4. forecast on an intermediate term basis the long-term interest rate for a relatively risk-free instrument;
5. evaluate the risk premium entailed in owning common stocks instead of bonds as a function of secular and cyclical risk influences; the risk premium is measured as a percentage of the interest rate;
6. derive total return required by investors for owning common stock by adding steps 4 and 5;
7. derive the nominal growth rate of dividends as function of return on equity using the reinvestment rate as a proxy for growth (ROE × reinvestment ratio);
8. subtract growth as determined in step 7 from required total return in order to derive required yield; and
9. determine the forecast of P/E by dividing step 3 by step 8.

Merrill Lynch qualifies their "model" work, and warns portfolio managers not to be too mechanical in the application of its findings by noting: "While a dividend evaluation model appears straightforward enough on the surface, it is usually in a static form. Application and the real world requires analysis and judgment within a dynamic framework. A purely mechanical approach to valuation will not work and should not be given an 'unjustified air of precision.' For example, in the early post-World War II period, the yields on stocks exceeded the yields on bonds, implying a very high risk premium and very low growth despite such favorable growth characteristics and rising cash flows. As market perceptions caught up with reality, total return was pushed up beyond the expectations that were based originally on the negative spread between bond and stock yields or the implied total return (9½–12 percent) as calculated from the stock yield (4–6 percent) and implied (retrospectively) growth (5½–6 percent) of the 1950–58 period. The risk premium ratio, which ranged from 317 percent to 185 percent, offered investors an excess return in light of growing prosperity and increasing confidence. Consequently, price-earnings multiples rose."[14]

In order to more directly incorporate the "fundamental" input of

---

[14] See *Investment Strategy*, Merrill Lynch, Pierce, Fenner & Smith, a bimonthly perspective, September–October 1979, p. 50–52.

the research analyst into the portfolio selection process, Merrill Lynch[15] has also introduced a relative valuation model of S&P industry groups that employs the techniques of modern portfolio theory. The purpose of this model is to combine an objective and impartial risk-return framework with analysts forecasts in order to assess the investment implications of earnings and dividend estimates and projections of future growth and profitability. The valuation procedure combines these forecasts with measures of business risk (company size and earnings variability), compares the projected future values of dividends and terminal prices to current prices, and provides expected investment returns implied by the fundamentals.

Using Merrill Lynch beta, a measure of stock price sensitivity to market moves, as a reasonable approximation of the market risk of the S&P groups, the portfolio model evaluates expected investment return within the context of investment risk. In order to distinguish this return from that implied by the analyst's estimates, Merrill Lynch calls it the "required return for Beta," or simply, the "required return."

After estimating an expected return and a return required for assuming risk in a portfolio context, Merrill Lynch then computes risk-adjusted returns for each S&P industry group. The difference between the analysts' implied return and the required return of portfolio theory is considered a measure of risk-adjusted relative return, also called forecast (or ex-ante) alpha, and allows investment managers to make several important decision making assessments. If, for example, alpha is significantly different from 0, either:

1. The analysts' estimates (right or wrong) are out of line with the market, or
2. Assuming the analyst estimates are reasonable, relative market values may be out of line with expectations.

The measure of surplus return, alpha is defined as: the rate of return implied by analyst estimates less the return required by the capital asset pricing hypothesis of portfolio theory. The implied return is a residual calculation, an internal rate of return determined by discounting a four year dividend stream and terminal price (calculated via the Gordon Model.[16]) The capital asset pricing hypothesis essentially says that returns required by investors are a function of risk, and that risk can be measured by beta.

---

[15] For a complete description of this new and innovative technique see Merrill Lynch, Pierce, Fenner & Smith Inc., *Investment Strategy* (March–April 1979), p. 13.

[16] In its simplest terms, the Gordon Model is an explicit recognition that the relationship between dividend (or earnings/price) yield and growth expectations is a smooth sloping tradeoff curve, and is not a straight line as implicity assumed by infinite growth valuation models.

Table 1
Industry Valuation Model

| | S&P 500 Weighting | Rank By ALPHA | Implied Return of Valuation Model | Required Return (risk adjusted) | Forecast ALPHA (surplus) Return | "Risk" (ML adjusted Beta) | Ratio of Alpha to Beta | Sustainable Dividend Yield | Forecast Earnings Growth | | | Equity Plowback Growth 4-Yr. Avg. | Relative P/E ÷ Relative 4-Yr. ROE |
									Near Term	3-5 Year	Next 5 Years		
Credit cyclicals	4.45	5	20.1	20.7	- 0.5	1.21	- 0.4	4.5	7.8	12.4	11.2	10.5	1.0
Heating and plumbing	0.15	29	21.0	20.7	- 0.3	1.21	- 0.2	4.8	15.3	11.2	11.6	18.1	0.6
Air conditioning	0.06	37	19.7	20.7	- 1.1	1.21	- 0.9	3.5	10.6	14.3	12.5	9.9	1.2
Cement	0.11	82	11.2	18.7	- 7.5	1.00	- 7.5	5.6	0.6	8.5	8.0	7.3	1.3
Roofing-wallboard	0.40	57	15.3	19.4	- 4.1	1.08	- 3.8	5.7	0.8	8.7	8.2	8.0	1.1
Mobile homes	0.04	77	18.3	24.5	- 6.2	1.61	- 3.9	4.2	6.4	11.8	12.0	8.9	1.2
Real estate	0.10	81	18.1	25.6	- 7.4	1.72	- 4.3	1.8	18.8	21.0	16.5	12.3	1.3
Savings and loan association	0.25	12	25.8	21.6	4.2	1.31	3.2	3.9	14.0	16.5	15.5	12.4	0.9
Finance companies	0.36	63	15.1	19.7	- 4.6	1.10	- 4.2	5.2	9.3	8.1	7.5	6.9	1.4
Forest product	1.57	62	17.2	21.7	- 4.5	1.31	- 3.4	3.6	16.5	12.7	11.7	10.7	1.2
Building miscellaneous	0.35	70	14.7	20.2	- 5.5	1.16	- 4.8	4.2	3.6	12.3	11.1	8.3	1.5
Property-casualty insurance	0.80	1	28.0	18.1	9.8	0.94	10.4	6.0	- 1.7	12.7	11.4	10.6	0.8
Finance miscellaneous	0.53	10	26.3	22.0	4.3	1.34	3.2	5.2	7.6	12.0	11.1	11.1	0.8
Consumer growth—mature	5.87	10	17.0	20.3	- 3.3	1.16	- 2.8	4.1	12.9	12.8	12.3	12.9	1.1
Cosmetics	0.90	64	16.0	20.7	- 4.7	1.21	- 3.9	4.4	11.5	12.4	11.9	12.5	1.1
Soft drinks	1.13	44	19.2	21.4	- 2.2	1.28	- 1.7	4.7	11.9	11.0	11.0	11.9	1.1
Drugs	4.38	58	15.5	19.7	- 4.2	1.11	- 3.8	3.7	12.5	13.4	12.7	12.7	1.2
Volatile consumer growth	5.92	11	17.5	20.8	- 3.4	1.22	- 2.8	3.2	12.5	13.5	13.1	18.8	0.9
Entertainment	0.58	54	18.0	21.7	- 3.7	1.31	- 2.8	2.7	9.1	14.6	14.1	19.2	0.8
Leisure time	0.22	42	20.8	22.6	- 1.8	1.41	- 1.3	3.7	8.7	12.5	11.8	17.7	0.8
Restaurants	0.50	56	18.6	22.6	- 4.0	1.40	- 2.9	1.5	15.3	15.7	13.6	19.9	1.1
Auto parts—after market	0.19	49	17.2	20.0	- 2.8	1.14	- 2.5	4.4	12.9	13.0	13.3	11.3	1.2
Radio-TV broadcasters	0.61	89	10.7	20.3	- 9.6	1.17	- 8.2	3.0	12.1	10.3	10.4	61.9	0.3
Publishing (newspapers)	0.53	36	18.5	19.5	- 1.0	1.08	- 0.9	3.5	14.9	14.6	14.5	18.2	0.8
Hospital supplies	0.51	85	14.0	22.2	- 8.2	1.36	- 6.0	1.8	16.0	17.8	16.8	11.9	2.1
Retail stores (drug)	0.18	87	11.7	20.9	- 9.2	1.23	- 7.5	2.6	13.1	14.5	13.4	15.9	1.2
Photography	1.44	16	23.2	20.8	2.5	1.22	2.1	4.9	9.8	10.4	10.0	8.8	1.3
Hospital management	0.20	60	19.4	23.7	- 4.2	1.52	- 2.8	1.8	23.2	21.2	19.0	13.8	1.8

Valuation Model Assumptions

Consumer cyclicals	9.29	1	21.0	18.6	2.3	0.99	2.3	6.1	−3.4	8.9	8.6	9.4	0.9
Textiles-apparel manufacturers	0.31	53	15.6	19.2	−3.5	1.05	−3.3	4.4	8.2	10.1	9.6	20.0	0.6
Textile products	0.19	48	15.8	18.2	2.4	0.95	2.5	7.2	1.1	6.7	6.4	5.8	1.3
Shoes	0.22	26	20.3	20.0	0.4	1.13	0.4	5.2	9.7	10.8	10.6	14.4	0.8
Vending and food service	0.07	73	14.4	20.2	−5.8	1.15	−5.0	5.2	11.0	9.4	9.4	9.1	1.2
Toys	0.03	90	14.0	24.3	−10.3	1.59	−6.5	2.7	16.0	13.2	12.6	10.2	1.4
Electric household appliances	0.39	33	21.7	21.7	0.1	1.32	0.1	5.3	6.8	14.1	13.1	8.7	1.3
Department stores	0.71	38	17.5	18.9	1.4	1.03	1.4	5.2	6.4	10.4	9.9	7.2	1.2
General merchandise chain	1.80	31	19.3	19.4	0.1	1.08	0.1	5.3	5.3	9.5	9.1	9.4	1.2
Small loans	0.09	35	19.1	19.7	0.6	1.10	0.5	6.6	11.3	7.9	7.9	8.5	1.0
Hotel-motel	0.24	66	16.2	21.4	5.2	1.28	4.1	2.7	14.1	16.4	13.0	9.6	2.0
Publishing	0.35	75	12.8	18.6	5.9	0.99	5.9	3.9	12.0	11.8	11.6	13.6	1.0
Air transport	0.45	19	23.6	21.6	2.0	1.31	1.5	2.4	7.5	16.7	13.4	8.3	1.1
Miscellaneous consumer cyclical	0.40	9	24.1	19.7	4.4	1.10	4.0	5.9	0.9	10.4	10.2	11.3	0.9
Automobile	3.22	3	23.8	17.0	6.8	0.82	8.3	7.8	−2.0	6.0	6.0	8.8	0.6
Auto parts—original equipment	0.37	8	22.8	18.2	4.6	0.95	4.9	6.0	5.5	11.7	11.0	10.2	0.8
Tire and rubber	0.32	40	16.3	17.9	−1.5	0.91	−1.6	7.8	−3.5	7.4	6.7	2.7	2.0
Home furnishings	0.42	21	20.7	19.3	1.5	1.06	1.4	3.1	29.5	19.2	18.4	17.8	1.1
Capital goods related	19.56	3	20.8	19.9	0.9	1.12	0.8	3.7	7.4	13.8	13.3	12.4	1.2
Office and business equipment—IBM	5.67	2	26.1	19.0	7.1	1.03	6.9	4.9	3.9	13.4	12.9	9.0	1.2
Oil well equipment and services	2.83	25	19.0	18.3	0.7	0.96	0.7	1.8	−0.7	18.3	17.2	21.0	1.0
Electronics (semi/components)	0.92	84	14.9	22.5	−7.6	1.40	−5.4	1.7	16.7	18.4	17.8	14.4	1.7
Electronics (instrumental)	1.11	88	11.2	20.5	−9.3	1.19	−7.8	1.5	19.1	16.5	16.4	13.6	1.8
Offshore drilling	0.19	94	9.8	21.4	−11.6	1.28	−9.0	2.3	−5.0	12.3	10.8	15.2	1.3
Office and business equipment	2.48	51	18.1	21.3	−3.1	1.27	−2.4	2.6	12.5	13.7	12.9	11.5	1.5
Pollution control	0.12	76	14.5	20.5	−6.0	1.19	−5.1	3.2	8.6	15.6	13.7	12.5	1.4
Electrical equipment	0.77	69	14.7	20.0	−5.3	1.13	−4.7	4.4	9.9	12.3	11.9	11.8	1.2
Machinery (construction, material handling)	0.89	11	24.0	19.6	4.3	1.10	3.9	3.9	0.9	15.5	14.3	14.4	0.9
Electronic major companies	1.96	15	23.4	20.7	2.6	1.21	2.1	5.2	8.3	10.4	9.9	10.3	1.1
Miscellaneous capital goods related	2.39	30	20.5	20.5	0.0	1.18	0.0	4.4	12.9	11.9	11.1	14.0	0.8

Table 1 *(continued)*

	S&P 500 Weighting	Rank By ALPHA	Implied Return of Valuation Model	Required Return (risk adjusted)	Forecast ALPHA (surplus) Return	"Risk" (ML adjusted Beta)	Ratio of Alpha to Beta	Sustainable Dividend Yield	Valuation Model Assumptions				
									Forecast Earnings Growth			Equity Plowback Growth 4-Yr. Avg.	Relative P/E ÷ Relative 4-Yr. ROE
									Near Term	3–5 Year	Next 5 Years		
Capital goods—diverse cycle	3.49	9	16.5	19.1	− 2.6	1.04	− 2.5	4.3	9.9	12.7	11.7	11.0	1.0
Miscellaneous auto original/aero related	0.29	5	25.4	19.0	6.4	1.03	6.2	5.6	10.6	12.7	12.6	15.5	0.6
Aerospace	1.32	32	18.1	18.2	− 0.1	0.95	− 0.1	4.1	13.9	14.6	12.6	10.3	1.0
Machinery (agricultural)	0.61	74	12.7	18.5	− 5.8	0.98	− 5.9	4.5	− 2.4	9.6	9.5	9.8	1.1
Machine tools	0.10	71	14.0	19.5	− 5.6	1.09	− 5.2	4.0	14.0	12.4	11.5	7.3	1.5
Machinery (industrial/specialty)	0.64	67	15.5	20.7	− 5.2	1.21	− 4.3	4.8	9.7	11.3	10.9	10.8	1.1
Railroad equipment	0.17	18	21.8	19.5	2.3	1.08	2.1	4.9	7.0	12.4	12.2	10.2	1.0
Basic industry and industrial commission	0.45	7	18.0	19.2	− 1.2	1.05	− 1.1	5.4	5.6	9.8	8.8	8.0	1.2
Aluminum	0.71	55	14.4	18.2	− 3.8	0.95	− 4.0	5.3	1.8	5.7	6.2	7.8	0.9
Paper	1.16	34	19.9	20.0	− 0.1	1.14	− 0.1	5.3	6.7	13.8	10.9	8.5	1.2
Containers (metal, glass)	0.43	17	19.6	17.2	2.3	0.84	2.7	5.5	5.8	10.9	9.7	8.4	1.1
Containers (paper)	0.15	80	10.5	17.9	− 7.4	0.91	− 8.1	4.3	10.5	11.1	9.9	8.2	1.4
Metals miscellaneous	0.89	92	8.5	19.0	−10.5	1.02	−10.1	3.7	17.4	5.7	5.7	5.5	1.8
Copper	0.36	72	12.7	18.3	− 5.7	0.96	− 5.9	3.5	12.4	6.4	6.2	0.2	4.5
Steel	0.86	79	12.4	18.8	− 6.4	1.01	− 6.3	7.1	1.4	4.4	4.4	3.2	1.8
Chemicals	2.58	14	23.5	19.8	3.7	1.11	3.3	5.8	2.0	12.4	10.7	9.8	1.1
Chemicals—miscellaneous	0.92	20	20.6	18.9	1.7	1.02	1.7	5.8	7.1	11.3	9.8	7.4	1.3
Metal fabricating	0.05	45	16.3	18.5	− 2.2	0.98	− 2.2	4.1	14.3	9.3	9.3	5.5	1.7
Lead and zinc	0.12	91	10.5	21.0	−10.5	1.24	− 8.4	4.4	12.6	8.2	8.1	6.4	1.7

Diverse intermediate cycle	3.30	8	16.1	18.6	− 2.5	0.99	− 2.5	3.9	8.7	12.8	13.5	9.7	1.4
Bituminous coal	0.24	50	18.7	21.7	− 2.9	1.31	− 2.2	4.5	7.2	11.7	21.9	12.6	1.5
Oil-crude products	0.83	86	9.7	18.8	9.1	1.01	9.0	1.8	12.7	15.5	13.8	11.5	2.1
Railroads	1.50	23	19.1	18.2	0.9	0.95	0.9	5.0	9.3	12.0	12.6	6.0	1.6
Auto trucks and parts	0.29	24	20.6	19.9	0.7	1.12	0.6	4.0	− 0.2	13.4	13.0	9.3	1.2
Fertilizers	0.26	47	13.5	15.8	− 2.3	0.69	− 3.3	4.5	7.6	12.5	11.0	14.4	1.0
Transportation miscellaneous	0.05	78	13.1	19.4	− 6.3	1.07	− 5.9	4.3	12.3	13.6	12.7	13.5	1.1
Truckers	0.18	83	11.5	19.1	− 7.6	1.04	− 7.3	3.6	6.0	10.7	10.5	18.6	0.7
Financial countercyclicals	4.39	2	22.0	20.2	1.8	1.16	1.6	4.8	11.0	11.4	10.8	9.7	1.0
Life insurance	0.73	46	17.5	19.8	− 2.3	1.12	2.1	4.0	4.5	11.8	10.9	9.8	1.2
Multi-line insurance	0.79	4	27.3	20.6	6.7	1.20	5.6	4.5	10.3	12.1	11.3	10.5	0.8
Banks New York City	1.22	13	23.9	20.2	3.8	1.15	3.3	5.6	12.7	10.5	10.0	8.7	1.0
Banks outside New York City	1.46	22	21.8	20.6	1.1	1.20	0.9	5.0	13.4	11.5	11.2	9.6	1.1
Gold mining	0.25	93	6.5	17.5	−11.0	0.88	−12.5	3.1	9.2	11.9	11.4	12.9	1.4
Defensive staples	7.20	6	17.3	18.1	− 0.8	0.94	0.9	5.1	9.4	11.0	10.5	10.7	1.0
Soaps	1.49	41	16.5	18.2	− 1.7	0.95	− 1.8	4.8	9.0	10.6	10.4	9.1	1.2
Distillers	0.44	52	15.1	18.6	− 3.4	0.99	− 3.4	4.9	8.3	11.2	10.5	7.4	1.6
Tobacco	1.38	6	22.8	17.3	5.5	0.85	6.5	5.0	13.6	13.9	12.8	14.5	0.8
Foods	3.36	39	16.8	18.1	− 1.4	0.94	1.5	5.4	9.7	10.4	10.0	10.7	1.0
Sugar refiners	0.04	59	11.1	15.3	− 4.2	0.64	− 6.5	5.4	6.8	12.2	10.8	6.9	1.6
Beverages: brewers	0.30	95	7.8	20.3	−12.5	1.16	−10.7	2.4	− 8.0	7.5	8.3	8.3	1.4
Miscellaneous defensive staples	0.19	61	13.3	17.8	− 4.5	0.91	− 5.0	6.4	9.2	7.4	7.2	8.1	1.0
Defensive-high liquidity	28.07	4	17.7	17.2	0.5	0.84	0.6	6.9	6.2	7.3	6.9	7.1	1.2
Telephone	6.27	7	21.0	15.8	5.2	0.70	7.4	8.8	0.8	6.0	5.9	4.8	1.2
Electric companies	3.81	28	17.2	16.9	0.3	0.81	0.4	10.2	2.6	3.6	3.5	3.5	1.1
Natural gas distributors	0.79	68	10.5	15.8	− 5.3	0.70	− 7.6	7.2	3.6	5.9	5.9	6.5	1.2
Natural gas pipe lines	1.34	65	12.7	17.8	5.2	0.91	5.7	5.5	13.3	8.7	8.5	10.4	1.0
Oil-international integrated	9.48	27	18.3	17.9	0.4	0.92	0.4	6.5	8.1	6.9	6.8	7.4	1.2
Oil-domestic integrated	6.91	43	15.7	17.7	− 1.9	0.89	− 2.1	3.9	10.3	11.5	10.0	10.5	1.3

Source: *Investment Strategy*, Merrill Lynch, Pierce, Fenner & Smith, September/October 1979, p. 58–59.

Forecast =   Implied Return   − Required Return
   Alpha   from Analysts Expectations   for Beta

Merrill Lynch's intentions are to reflect the investment implications of analysts in a common, objective framework. By doing so, the analysis provides an important fundamental input to investment strategy. In addition, even though the relative valuation display presents the projected industry total investment return over the holding period, our focus is on relative returns given a probable market scenario over the next three to five years, rather than on absolute returns.

The forecast alpha is simply the difference between the implied return and required return. Assuming the analyst's estimates are correct, alpha is an approximate indicator of "surplus" risk-adjusted returns: positive alphas generally indicate greater portfolio weight should be given to a stock or group; negative alphas imply underweighting.

The ratio of alpha to beta is also used as a ranking device of the desirability of surplus returns. As a measure of the surplus return per unit of risk, it is particularly appropriate for investors who can employ financial leverage or for those who adopt a defensive market posture but still wish to achieve the highest possible (low risk) returns.

Using the chemical industry as an example, the alpha rank is indicated as 14 in Table 1. Current prices imply a rate of return of 23.3 percent. Given the above-average risk (beta is 1.07) we require 20.0 percent return, compared to the market return of 19.3 percent. The difference between implied return and required return is the investor's additional compensation above the risk incurred, or alpha (3.3 percent). Beta of 1.07 tells us that the industry is slightly above average in risk relative to the S&P 500. Both yield and growth for this industry are the same as for the market; yield is 5.7 percent and expected growth is 9.5 percent.

These Merrill Lynch models have been developed to provide portfolio managers with a perspective as to the valuation of the market as a whole or for individual industry groupings. A corollary development to the increased use of such evaluation techniques has been the development of new analytical tools designed to provide portfolio managers with value judgments on individual securities. A good example of such development is a quarterly service offered by Goldman Sachs which estimates the potential returns available from common stocks within a framework of modern portfolio theory and investment risk analysis.[17]

---

[17] It is interesting to point out that the extension of modern portfolio theory to individual security evaluation is in direct conflict with the original intent of market line analysis. Conceptually, capital market theory asks investors to focus their attention on the risk of their portfolio as a whole rather than on individual security selection. The entire concept of an efficient market supposedly makes individual stock analysis fruitless. For a complete description of the underlying techniques, see Goldman Sachs, *Portfolio Strategy* (January 13, 1978), N.Y.

In effect, according to Goldman Sachs, "the product is a stock selection guide, with the intent to isolate those securities that may be over-/ or undervalued." Information given to portfolio managers and security analysts addresses itself to which stocks are attractively priced but does not provide guidelines as to how one should combine these securities in a portfolio (i.e., the appropriate weighting of each) to maximize the ratio of portfolio return to portfolio risk (consisting of systematic and residual risk).

On the basis of fundamental analysis, Goldman Sachs' analysts provide estimates for sustainable earnings growth and an average (normalized) dividend payout ratio over the next five years. In addition, a risk measure (beta) is estimated for each company that reflects the fundamental operating record as well as its price movement relative to the market (as measured by the S&P 500). From this data, a risk-adjusted excess return is derived for each security. Excess return is the difference between a security's implied return (based on earnings growth and dividend payout ratio) and a security's required return (a function of the security's beta).

Table 2 shows the first pages of a recent study showing estimated returns for 445 common stocks on the basis that the market's return is expected to be 15.7 percent. Table definitions are also given. The particular study used here for illustrative purpose assumed a required rate of return for the S&P 500 of 12.5 percent, consisting of a 9.0 percent AAA telephone bond rate and a 3.5 percent risk premium to compensate for the volatility of equity returns relative to long-term debt returns.[18] The market's risk-adjusted excess return, at the time of these calculations, was estimated at 3.2 percent (15.7–12.5); see column 7 for the S&P composite.

BUSINESS CYCLES AND INVESTMENT TIMING

Many portfolio managers assume that an accurate forecast of turning points in the business cycle will improve their ability to manage portfolios better. There is substantial evidence suggesting that an ability to foresee business cycle turning points for several months improves the ability to foresee major turning points in the general level of stock

---

[18] The equity risk premium is equal to the sum of estimated sustainable earnings growth (column 1) and the market's quarterly dividend yield (column 2) minus a forward-looking three-quarter moving average of the AAA-telephone bond (column 3). The assumption is that the market's price-earnings ratio is efficiently set over long periods of time (although at any point in time, it may be inefficiently set) and that investors expect the total return from equity investments to equal earnings growth plus dividend yield. The average risk premium between 1963:1 and 1977:3, based on our approach, has been 3.0 percent with a standard deviation around this average of 1.1 percent. That is, two out of three times the right premium has ranged between 1.9 percent and 4.1 percent.

Table 2
Ranking of Common Stock Risk-Adjusted Excess Returns

	(1) RANK BY RISK ADJ EXCESS ANNUAL RETURN	(2) PRICE (10/31/78)	(3) TREND GR RATE EPS (78-82)	(4) THEORETICAL PRICE (1982)	(5) GS3C LONG TERM BETA	(6) INTERNAL RATE OF RETURN CHANGE	(7) INDCTD ANNUAL RETURN (%)	(8) REOR'D ANNUAL RETURN (%)	(9) RISK ADJ EXCESS ANNUAL RETURN (%)	(10) NORMALIZED PE RATIO (1978)	(11) PE RATIO (1982)	
*S&P COMPOSITE AVERAGE ·	287	93.15	8	142	1.00	3.0	15.7	12.5	3.2	7.8	8.8	1
A C F INDS INC	291	32.00	6	44	0.57	3.2	14.8	11.8	3.0	7.6	8.3	2
AMF INC	314	16.13	5	23	1.43	3.5	17.0	15.4	1.6	6.4	7.6	3
ARA SVCS INC	281	37.75	10	71	1.59	3.4	20.2	16.7	3.5	7.3	9.5	4
ABBOTT LABS	206	31.75	16	60	0.95	2.5	18.9	12.2	6.7	14.2	14.7	5
AHMANSON H F & CO	115	19.63	10	47	1.40	3.7	26.8	15.1	11.6	5.4	9.0	6
AIR PRODS & CHEMS INC	355	24.75	11	38	1.21	3.1	12.3	13.8	-1.5	8.9	9.0	7
ALCAN ALUM LTD	349	32.63	6	45	1.11	3.6	12.3	13.1	-0.8	6.8	7.1	8
ALLIED CHEM CORP	158	30.63	8	57	0.87	3.6	20.7	11.8	8.9	5.9	8.1	9
ALLIED STORES CORP	127	22.75	9	48	1.24	3.5	24.8	14.0	10.8	6.3	9.4	10
ALPHA PORTLAND INDS	356	15.88	7	23	1.35	4.0	13.2	14.8	-1.5	5.5	6.3	11
ALUMINUM CO AMER	404	45.00	7	50	1.13	3.2	6.7	13.3	-6.6	8.4	7.2	12
AMERADA HESS CORP	106	23.25	7	56	1.36	4.5	26.9	14.8	12.1	3.2	5.9	13
AMERICAN BRANDS INC	330	47.75	5	57	0.63	3.3	11.6	10.8	0.7	7.7	7.7	14
AMERICAN BROADCASTING	371	35.25	10	53	1.49	3.3	13.3	15.9	-2.6	8.8	9.0	15
AMERICAN CAN CO	246	36.00	5	50	0.50	3.4	15.5	10.4	5.1	6.7	7.6	16
AMERICAN CYANAMID CO	178	24.50	8	41	0.59	3.4	18.8	10.7	8.0	7.1	8.8	17
AMERICAN EXPRESS CO	104	30.63	14	76	1.42	3.1	27.5	15.3	12.2	8.8	12.9	18
AMERICAN FLETCHER CORP	74	18.75	8	40	0.90	3.5	25.7	12.0	13.7	5.5	8.6	19
AMERICAN GEN INS CO	328	22.38	7	33	0.98	3.9	13.3	12.4	0.9	6.0	6.7	20
AMERICAN GREETINGS CP	345	10.88	9	18	1.49	3.5	15.3	15.9	-0.5	6.0	8.1	21
AMERICAN HOME PRODS CP	177	27.13	10	48	0.60	2.9	18.8	10.7	8.1	13.2	16.0	22
AMERICAN HOSPITAL SUPP	224	26.75	15	54	1.30	2.7	20.4	14.4	6.0	11.3	13.1	23
AMERICAN STD INC	413	41.63	8	46	1.07	3.4	15.3	12.9	-7.6	7.4	7.4	24
AMERICAN STORES CO	243	30.25	6	44	0.77	3.5	16.4	11.4	5.0	5.4	6.5	25
AMERON INC	430	16.75	1	12	0.97	4.5	1.7	12.3	-10.7	5.1	3.7	26
AMFAC INC	144	16.25	8	30	0.93	3.2	21.8	12.1	9.7	6.3	8.6	27
AMP INC	347	31.50	15	54	1.61	2.5	16.1	16.9	-0.8	13.8	13.5	28
AMSTED INDS INC	358	35.25	10	48	0.98	3.1	10.8	12.4	-1.6	10.7	9.9	29
ANGELICA CORP	101	5.50	10	14	1.34	3.9	27.0	14.7	12.3	5.0	8.6	30
ANHEUSER BUSCH INC	232	22.25	12	40	0.97	3.0	18.1	12.3	5.8	10.0	11.4	31

Table 2 *(continued)*

[1] Indicates the rank of the company by risk-adjusted excess annual return.

[2] Current price of the stock.

[3] Estimated trend growth rate in earnings per share for the next five years.

[4] The estimated justifiable price in 1982 based on normalized dividends (1978), earnings growth (1978–82), and sustainable return on equity (1978–82). Derivation of the theoretical price is detailed in Appendix A of our initial publication dated January 13, 1978.

[5] The estimated beta of the security, computed over the most recent 40-quarter interval. Developed by our portfolio strategy group, the betas include an adjustment to historical price betas by incorporating selected fundamental operating characteristics of the company relative to the S&P 500. The fundamental variables are company earnings variability relative to the earnings variability of the S&P 500 and a moving average of the dividend yield of the company relative to a moving average of the market's yield. A detailed explanation is available on request.

[6] The sensitivity of the security's internal rate of return to a one-percentage-point change in the estimated growth rate (column 3). For example, we are currently estimating an 8 percent trend rate of growth in earnings for the S&P 500 over the next five years. At its current price, the S&P 500 has an estimated 15.7 percent internal rate of return. If we assume a 10 percent growth rate, the internal rate of return is increased by 6 percentage points ($2 \times 3 = 6$ percent) to 18.9 percent. With the market's required return unchanged, risk-adjusted excess return is also increased by 6 percentage points. Column 6 permits the user to quickly compute security excess returns under different assumptions for trend growth in earnings.

[7] Indicates the internal annual rate of return for each security. This rate equates the current stock price to the sum of dividends over the next five years and the security's theoretical (1982) price.

[8] Indicates the required rate of return for each security, which is based on the company beta (systematic risk) and the required return assumed for the market. The derivation of required rate of return is given in Appendix B of our January 13, 1978 report.

[9] Risk-adjusted excess return is the difference between a security's internal rate of return (column 7) and its required rate of return (column 8).

[10] Current price divided by normalized earnings per share. Normalized earnings (1978) are derived as follows: prior five-year average return on equity is multiplied by book value per share in 1977 to get 1977 normalized earnings, which is then multiplied by the growth rate in column 3.

[11] Theoretical (1982) price, given in column 4, divided by normalized earnings in 1982. Normalized earnings (1982) are obtained by compounding the 1978 earnings per share at the rate given in column 3.

Source: Goldman Sachs Research, *Portfolio Strategy*, a quarterly service, (January 13, 1978).

Figure 2
Business Cycles and Stock Market Performance

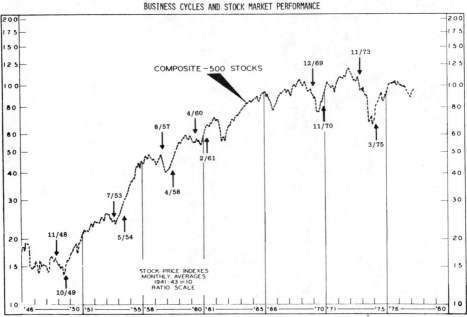

Note: Direction of arrows denotes beginning of recession (downward) or end of recession (upward) as defined by the National Bureau of Economic Research, Washington, D.C.
Source: Shearson Hayden Stone, *Equity Market Comments,* July 11, 1978.

prices. The evidence does not imply that every bear market must be accompanied by an economic recession, or vice versa. However, the tendency for this relationship to exist has been so pronounced, and the lead-lag relationship between the stock market and the business cycle has been so persistent, that if a recession or a slow-down of economic growth appears to lie ahead, the investor should consider that the odds are high it will be preceded by a significant stock market downturn some months in advance. Let's look at the record. Figure 2 shows movements of the S&P 500 Composite Stock Price Index with general business cycle turning points. Table 3 shows the relationship of recession to declines in the S&P 500 for the six business recessions following World War II. The pattern was essentially the same for prior periods.

It is essential to stress the fact that stock price peaks and troughs typically have preceded turning points of general business activity. Many investors are invariably surprised when, in the midst of rather dreary business news, stock prices rise, and in the midst of prosperity, stock prices fall. But such is the nature of the stock market.

Several theories have been offered to explain the stock market's

Table 3
Declines Associated with Recessions: Standard & Poor's 500 Composite Index (monthly averages)

First Month of Economic Decline	Length of Recession (months)	Lead Time of Stock Market Decline (months)	Percent Decline Before Recession Started	Total Length of Stock Market Decline (months)	Total Market Decline
December 1973..........	16	11	−20%	21	−41%
January 1970	11	13	− 8	17	−23
May 1960	10	10	− 8	15	−10
September 1957	8	14	−10	15	−15
August 1953	10	8	− 6	13	−11
December 1948..........	11	6	−10	12	−17

Source: Bache Halsey Stuart Shields Inc., "Economic Outlook and Investment," November 1978.

apparent forecasting ability. One is that investors, collectively, have good foresight, and that they act on the basis of what they think is going to happen to business activity rather than on the basis of what they currently see happening. Another argument is that investors act on the basis of current rather than anticipated future developments, but that the chief current indicators they watch—corporate profits and profit margins—tend to turn in advance of general business activity. Therefore, profit-oriented investors coincidentally bid stock prices up and drive them down in advance of general business activity. Yet a third theory is that stock price reversals help cause subsequent economic reversals by affecting consumer and business confidence and spending decisions. Finally, various monetary explanations for the stock price lead have been offered, as will be noted in later sections. Perhaps the truth lies closest to a combination of all these hypotheses.

Since an ability to foresee business cycle turning points normally would improve one's ability to foresee major turning points in the stock market as a whole, would it also improve one's ability to select the particular stocks to be most affected by the change in overall trend? The answer to this question is "sometimes yes, sometimes no." The relative price changes of individual stocks over short periods of time reflect many factors. These factors include relative changes in company sales, earnings, and dividends, but they also include the degree to which different stocks had been overpriced or underpriced prior to the turning point of the general market. To the extent that accurate forecasts of the overall economy can improve forecasts of relative changes in the prosperity of different industries, forecasts of relative price changes of stocks in different industries should be improved. Table 4 shows, for example, those S&P industry groupings which typically experience above-average price performance during years when overall profits decline.

Goldman Sachs provides institutional investors with a service which

Table 4
Standard & Poor's Industry Composites Registering Above-Average Price Performance during Years when Standard & Poor's Profits Decline

	Price										No. Years of Advance	No. Years Better Than S&P 500
	1975	1970	1967	1961	1960	1958	1957	1956	1952	1951		
S&P 500 Composite	+31.5%	+ 0.1%	+20.1%	+23.1%	− 3.0%	+ 38.1%	−14.3%	+ 2.6%	+11.8%	+16.5%	8	
Office and business equipment.........	+27.4	−17.5	+72.7	+46.8	+32.3	+ 76.5	+10.8	+56.1	+11.5	+14.2	9	6
Electric utilities	+38.7	+ 7.0	− 6.7	+25.2	+17.7	+ 33.4	+ 5.3	− 1.9	+13.8	+10.9	8	6
Small loans	+30.3	+ 8.2	− 7.6	+46.6	+28.4	+ 38.8	+10.7	− 7.3	+19.7	+30.2	8	7
Soft drinks	+59.2	+ 4.6	+39.4	+25.7	+45.3	+ 34.6	− 0.4	−18.4	+ 7.5	−10.8	7	6
Processed foods	+56.0	+ 4.6	+ 6.1	+42.8	+36.8	+ 50.8	+11.8	− 3.3	+15.2	− 7.1	8	7
Drugs	+ 2.8	− 4.4	+22.7	+23.6	+ 4.9	+ 66.8	+25.5	+12.7	−13.0	+18.7	8	7
Dairy products	+42.1	+ 7.3	+12.1	+19.1	+23.9	+ 26.6	+ 2.0	− 6.4	+15.8	+ 0.1	9	5
Finance companies	− 5.9	+10.3	+16.8	+45.3	+14.9	+ 27.2	+ 6.3	− 5.0	+32.2	+31.6	8	6
Oil (international)	+32.9	+14.4	+13.0	+25.3	−10.8	+ 20.9	− 9.3	+13.9	+ 7.1	+43.7	8	6
Tobacco	+15.6	+26.0	+19.8	+59.6	+32.5	+ 38.2	−12.4	− 5.4	+15.1	− 7.5	8	6
Coal	+38.7	+53.3	+48.6	+45.0	−22.6	− 29.8	−36.0	+40.0	+ 2.4	+15.3	8	5
Electronics*	+41.3	−29.3	+47.6	+ 8.5	+14.8	+116.5	− 5.2	+ 7.8	+19.8	+17.3	8	8
Soaps	+16.2	+ 3.4	+32.5	+34.1	+42.2	+ 36.5	+11.7	− 2.6	+ 4.0	− 5.9	8	5
Retail (food)	+33.2	+18.0	+ 3.9	+46.2	− 0.9	+ 49.8	+20.4	− 5.7	+20.9	− 5.5	8	8
Retail (department stores) ..	+74.3	+ 7.0	+36.5	+35.4	+ 2.5	+ 43.8	− 4.1	−14.5	+ 1.6	− 1.6	7	7
Natural gas distributors	+15.4	+24.0	+ 4.0	+29.0	+15.6	+ 33.4	− 4.2	+ 7.1	+ 5.7	+14.6	9	5
Machinery (steam gen.)	+30.8	+ 7.6	+37.1	+38.9	− 5.5	+ 11.5	−25.7	+34.2	+ 7.8	+ 0.3	8	5
Machinery (oil well serv.)....	+ 9.8	+ 4.4	+59.9	+27.6	−19.9	+ 15.5	−32.7	+62.9	+ 5.6	+35.4	8	5
Confectionery	+79.9	+ 3.3	− 0.5	+36.1	+36.7	+ 22.8	− 0.1	− 3.1	+ 3.4	− 1.7	6	5
Food (Canned)	+26.0	− 4.9	+24.7	+44.7	+48.4	+ 39.8	− 8.0	−13.0	− 1.1	− 5.5	5	5
Natural gas pipelines	+13.1	+28.4	+10.9	+10.7	+ 6.6	+ 42.1	−18.0	+18.0	+24.1	+30.6	9	6
Cosmetics.............	+37.3	− 0.9	+71.5	+67.2	+55.7	+ 76.7	N.A.	N.A.	N.A.	N.A.	5	5
Banks (regional)	+26.0	+ 2.5	− 1.9	+45.2	− 0.9	+ 35.1	−11.5	− 3.8	+14.4	+ 7.9	6	5
Banks (New York City)	+ 4.4	+ 3.8	+ 0.9	+48.4	− 9.4	+ 29.3	− 6.7	+ 1.4	+13.5	+ 7.5	8	4
Building—air conditioning ..	+56.3	− 1.6	+47.1	+32.5	+ 3.0	+ 41.1	−26.3	N.A.	N.A.	N.A.	5	5
Machinery (specialty)	+68.1	−12.9	+51.1	+ 0.8	+34.6	+ 42.7	−31.2	+36.9	+ 2.7	+ 5.6	9	6

* Electronics has been divided into two groups: Electronics-Instrumentation and Electronics-Semicondutors.
Source: Equity Research Statistical Analysis, Shearson Hayden Stone, New York, New York, December 1977.

compares the performance of broad market sectors (industry groupings of common stocks) for both the current economic cycle (dotted lines on Figure 3), and the average pattern experienced during the five previous·economic cycles (solid lines on Figure 3). Performance is measured relative to the S&P 500. The sector's price relative to the S&P 500 is indexed so that it always equals 1.0 at the economic trough. A number greater than 1.0 indicates that, at that point in the economic cycle, the sector's price relative to the S&P 500 is more favorable than it was (will be) at the economic trough. Conversely, a number less than 1.0 shows a less favorable relationship than that which existed (will exist) at the trough. Similarly, a rising line indicates that the group is outperforming the S&P 500, while a falling line indicates that the group is underperforming the index. In computing the sector's relative price, each of the S&P industry groups comprising the sector is weighted equally.

Figure 3, for example, shows that consumer durable related common stocks typically outperform the averages during the first year of an economic recovery, peak relative to the market in the second, and underperform as the expansion matures into the third year.[19]

Because recession years and the beginning stages of an economic recovery tend to be good periods of stock market performance,[20] substantial research efforts are directed towards identifying industry groups and individual stocks likely to outperform the broad market averages during the early stages of a new bull market. Merrill Lynch, for example, recently studied relative stock group performance during the first six months of bull market cycles and the last four months of bear market cycle. As a basis for this study, Merrill Lynch used industry classifications for the S&P 500 and the market cycle segments of 1966–67, 1970, and 1974–75. Industry groupings were categorized by the following performance characteristics:

(a) positive relative performance in the first six months of all three bull markets;

(b) positive relative performance in the first six months of all three bull markets and a superior performance, by at least 10 percentage points, in one or more of the three;

(c) positive relative performance by 15 or more percentage points in the first six months of two of the last three bull markets;

[19] "Analysis of Market Trends," *Portfolio Strategy*, Goldman Sachs Research (September 30, 1978).

[20] According to Goldman Sachs for example "The average level of the market in the 12 months subsequent to an economic trough has, since 1948, been higher than the average stock price level in the 12 months preceding an economic trough. For further details see "Investment Strategy Highlights *Update,*" Goldman Sachs Research, (December 1978).

Figure 3

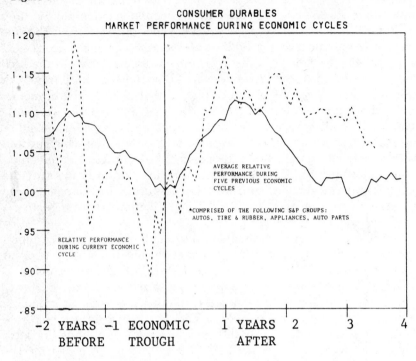

CONSUMER DURABLES
MARKET PERFORMANCE DURING ECONOMIC CYCLES

AVERAGE RELATIVE
PERFORMANCE DURING
FIVE PREVIOUS ECONOMIC
CYCLES

*COMPRISED OF THE FOLLOWING S&P GROUPS:
AUTOS, TIRE & RUBBER, APPLIANCES, AUTO PARTS

RELATIVE PERFORMANCE
DURING CURRENT ECONOMIC
CYCLE

-2 YEARS −1 ECONOMIC   1 YEARS 2   3   4
BEFORE   TROUGH   AFTER

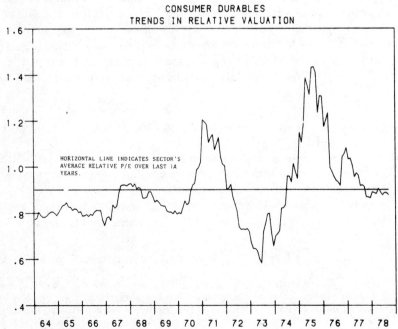

CONSUMER DURABLES
TRENDS IN RELATIVE VALUATION

HORIZONTAL LINE INDICATES SECTOR'S
AVERAGE RELATIVE P/E OVER LAST IA
YEARS.

* Comprised of the following S&P groups: autos, tire & rubber, appliances, auto parts.
Source: Goldman Sachs Research.

(d) negative relative performance in the first six months of all three new bull market cycles;

(e) positive relative performance in the last four months of all three bear markets;

(f) a high incidence of positive relative performance in both the first six months of all three bull markets and the last four months of all three bear cycles.

To better evaluate the historical record for current use, relative performance data was supplemented with information relating to market risk (beta); financial power (cash flow return on net assets, cash flow needs for dividends and capital spending in relation to cash flow generation); relative multiples; and prospects for relative earnings.[21]
The key findings were:

1. Industries that outperform the market in the early phase of a bull market are those that are characterized by superior growth qualities or that are especially sensitive to the expected turning of the business cycle. Credit-sensitive stocks, excluding utilities, stand out among those sensitive to the business cycle as beneficiaries of the anticipated decline in interest rates.

2. Industries that outperform other groups in the early phase of a bull market usually have high betas. Industries that outperform the average in the late phase of a bear market usually have low betas. The beta correlations are extremely high.

3. Basic industries are especially poor early bull-market performers, because they usually do not meet the criteria noted above.

Twenty-six S&P industry groups were found to have outperformed the S&P 500 in the first six months of the last three bull markets (1966, 1970, 1975). Among those superior performers, 11 groups exceeded the gain for the market by 10 percentage points or more each time—that is, an upside market move of 10 percent was accompanied by an increase of at least 20 percent in the group's price. Table 5 shows the above average performers and provides background data on value and future prospects. Table 6 shows industries that have outperformed the market by 15 percentage points or more in two of the last three bull markets.

Characteristics of the groups shown in Table 5 are as follows:

1. Prospects for superior growth of earnings and dividends are implied for many of the groups by above-average cash flow return on investment (ROI), generation of excess cash flow, and premium multiples. Appreciation represents a relatively high share of the total return expected of growth stocks. Hence the yields required for those issues

---

[21] Richard J. Hoffman and Steven R. Resnick, "Investment Strategy," Merrill Lynch, Pierce, Fenner & Smith, Inc. (May/June 1978).

Table 5
Good Early Bull-Market Performers

Economic Sector/ S&P 500 Group	(1) Positive Relative Strength in Early Phase of Each of Last 3 Bull Markets	(2) 1967	(3) 1970	(4) 1975	(5) 5-Year beta	(6) Relative P/E 3/78	(7) Average 10-Year Relative P/E	(8) Cash Flow ROI (1974–76)	(9) Ratio of Dividends and Capital Spending to Cash Flow (1974–76)	(10) 1978	(11) 1979	(12) Yield
			Relative Strength of 10 Percentage Points or More							Relative EPS		
Credit Sensitive												
Mobile homes	x		x	x	2.19	1.16	1.72	13.2%	68%	=	=	2.8%
S&L	x		x	x	1.54	0.51	0.77	11.9	NA*	+	+	4.7
Finance	x	x	x	x	1.07	0.97	1.08	NA	NA	=	=	7.2
Finance (small loans)	x	x	x		1.50	0.71	0.71	NA	NA	=	=	7.3
Building materials												
(roofing and wallboard)	x	x	x	x	1.14	0.79	1.01	11.8	106	+	−	5.5
Natural gas pipelines	x		x		0.95	0.81	0.71	13.8	125	+	+	5.7
Real estate	x	x	x	x	2.14	0.72	NA	NA	NA	+	−	1.7
Growth consumer staples												
Leisure time	x	x	x	x	1.78	NA	0.93	12.4	82	−	=	2.8
Entertainment	x	x	x	x	1.49	1.11	1.33	22.7	64	+	+	1.9
Beverages (soft drinks)	x	x		x	1.52	1.59	1.88	24.5	97	+	+	3.9
Drugs	x	x			1.09	1.53	1.88	21.6	78	+	+	3.5
Consumer staples												
Publishing	x	x	x		1.09	1.03	1.14	17.9	85	=	=	3.7
Publishing (newspapers)	x	x	x		1.19	1.26	1.28	27.8	60	+	+	3.1
Soaps	x				0.97	1.42	1.45	16.6	89	=	+	4.2
Consumer cyclicals												
Hotel-motel	x	x	x	x	1.68	1.17	1.37	12.3	165	+	=	3.1
Shoes	x	x	x	x	1.28	0.91	0.86	15.8	69	=	−	4.4
Retail stores (department stores)	x			x	1.19	0.95	1.22	12.1	113	=	+	4.9

Retail stores (drugs).............	x	x		x	1.69	1.31	1.51	19.2	53	+	+	2.0
Auto parts (after market)........	x	x			1.23	1.24	1.08	17.4	72	+	+	3.9
Intermediate goods and services											
Coal (bituminous)................	x	x		x	1.53	1.14	0.91	26.4	89	+	+	5.2
Capital goods											
Offshore drilling................	x	x			1.31	0.89	1.10	16.5	201	+	+	2.2
Machinery (steam generating).....	x	x	x		1.27	0.96	0.99	15.3	72	=	=	4.4
Oil well services................	x	x	x		0.98	1.16	1.23	23.0	89	+	+	2.1
Electrical equipment.............	x				1.31	1.28	1.30	17.5	79	+	−	4.1
Electrical (electronics)											
major cos.)...................	x	x		x	1.23	1.03	1.25	18.9	124	+	=	4.8
Vending and food service.........	x	x			1.28	0.92	1.44	19.1	88	+	=	4.6
S&P 500..........................					1.00	1.00	1.00	15.0	100	=	=	5.6

Note: Relative strength, P/E, yield, and relative EPS weighted by market value. Other measures are simple averages of the companies in each group, except for the case of telephone, which is market weighted. Yield is based on the indicated dividend rate of 4Q77 and the March month-end price. The S&P 500 yield is based on the indicated dividend rate of 1Q78 and the March month-end price. Relative P/E is based on future earnings.

* NA = Not available or not meaningful.

Source: Merrill Lynch, Pierce, Fenner & Smith, Inc.

Table 6
Groups Showing High Relative Strength during First Six Months of Two out of Three Bull Markets

	(1)	(2)	(3)	(4)	(5)	(6)	(7)	(8)	(9)	(10)	(11)	(12)
	Positive Relative Strength in Early Phase of 2 Out of 3 Bull Markets	Relative Strength of 15 Percentage Points or More			5-Year beta	Relative P/E 3/78	Average 10-Year Relative P/E	Cash Flow ROI (1974–76)	Ratio of Dividends plus Capital Spending to Cash Flow (1974–76)	Relative EPS		Yield
		1967	1970	1975						1978	1979	
Building materials (air conditioning)	x	x			1.52	0.88	2.75	10.9%	153%	+	–	4.1%
Hospital supplies	x	x			1.62	1.58	2.45	13.4	84	+	+	1.5
Textiles (apparel manufacturers)	x		x		1.20	0.69	0.72	10.8	63	–	=	4.5
Radio-T.V. broadcasters	x	x			1.40	0.89	1.07	26.0	65	+	=	3.6
Electrical household appliances	x		x		1.33	1.03	1.22	17.9	108	+	=	6.1
Fertilizers	x	x	x		0.61	0.90	0.79	24.0	146	–	+	5.8

Source: Merrill Lynch, Pierce, Fenner & Smith, Inc.

are lower than those required of the market. When the market yield required decreases because of a decrease in investors' total-return requirements, as occurs during the early phase of a bull market, growth stocks benefit more than does the market as a whole. For example, suppose that both a growth stock and the overall market offer a required return of 13 percent. The market may have a growth factor of 8 percent and a required yield of 5 percent. The growth stock may have a growth factor of 10 percent and a required yield of 3 percent. As total return declines to 11 percent, the impact of the decrease of 2 percent has a greater impact on the growth stock's required yield of 3 percent than on the market's required yield of 5 percent in the valuation formula, *price = dividends/required yield*. Most of the growth groups are in the growth consumer staples and capital goods sectors of the economy.

2. High sensitivity to the turning of the business cycle is implied by the dependence of many groups on interest rate trends and on consumer buying power and confidence. Hence, the early bull-market phase implies both a decrease in the risk premium and improvement in earnings expectations for those groups. Earnings expectations benefit from an expansion of margins as the result of lower unit costs, higher unit volume, or both. Most of the industries are in our credit-sensitive and consumer-cyclical groups. Industries that appear to fit the pattern are savings and loan associations, real estate, and leisure time companies.

3. Some groups, such as hotels-motels, are both growth and cyclically sensitive. Note that hotels-motels have a high beta and strong early bull-market performance records.

4. The growth and cyclical economic characteristics of the 26 groups have helped define a condition of relatively high market leverage. One approach to measuring that leverage is by means of beta. As might be expected, 23 of the 26 groups have betas above 1; the average beta is 1.37; and the lowest beata is 0.95. The average beta of the 11 groups that did particularly well in the last three bull markets was 1.51.

Industries with historical market patterns that suggest they should be underweighted in the early phase of a bull market are those that thrive in the economic environment of high capacity utilization usually created in the middle or late-middle stages of a recovery. In general, those industries are classified as intermediate goods and services, and they also tend to have minimal exposure to the capital spending cycle. Table 7 presents the historical data. In general, the industries comprise companies that have average betas. Profitability and the ratio of capital spending and dividends to cash-flow generation are somewhat below average; relative multiples, which are also somewhat below average.

Table 7
Poor Early Bull-Market Performers

	(1)	(2)	(3)	(4)	(5)	(6)	(7)	(8)	(9)	(10)	(11)	(12)
	Relative Weakness in Early Phase of Each of Last 3 Bull Markets	Relative Weakness of 10 Percentage Points or More			5-Year beta	Relative P/E 3/78	Aveage 10-Year Relative P/E	Cash Flow ROI (1974–76)	Ratio of Dividends plus Capital Spending to Cash Flow (1974–76)	Relative EPS		Yield
		1966	1970	1974						1978	1979	
Railroads	x				0.91	0.91	0.61	7.1%	134%	–	+	6.1%
Paper	x		x		1.08	1.01	0.92	15.9	115	–	–	5.5
Chemicals	x				1.15	1.10	1.01	18.9	126	–	–	5.9
Auto trucks and parts	x		x	x	1.00	0.66	0.86	12.0	118	–	–	5.7
Textiles (synthetic fibers)	x			x	0.95	1.26	0.86	13.6	119	–	–	7.0

Source: Merrill Lynch, Pierce, Fenner & Smith, Inc.

suggest that the market perceives them as lacking a growth factor. Among groups in the six economic sectors of our model portfolio, groups in intermediate goods and services had by far the greatest instance of underperformance.

Table 8 shows those industries which have shown relative strength in the last four months of each of the last three bear markets (1966, 1970, 1974). One element in tracking the development of a bull market is to watch for the cyclical group rotation at the end of the late bear market phase. The following groups fit a diversity of defensive profiles: high assured yield plus relatively low variability of total return (telephone, natural gas distributors, oils); a hedge against uncertainty and inflation (gold mining); and a combination of reasonable yield plus an assured growth factor (retail stores-food chains). Betas for those groups are usually well below average. Although return on investment is well above average for the integrated oils, secular growth problems can be perceived. Other groups such as electric utilities and tobacco have also tended to do well in the late bear market environment, but seclar problems have sometimes prevented their outperforming the market in all three late bear markets.

Curiously enough, four groups have outperformed the S&P 500 in the last four months of at least two of the last three bear markets and in the first six months of at least two of the last three bull markets (see Table 9). A possible explanation of the low relative downside risk is that the high yields of gas distributors and gas pipelines offer a hedge against declining prices while soap companies provide low variability of earnings. The dividends of the gas utilities are assured by good coverage ratios. The dividends of shoe manufacturers are assured by generation of excess cash flow. On the upside, gas pipelines and distributors benefit from declining interest rates; soap companies have benefited from identification as growth stocks; and shoe companies are helped by a high beta and exposure to increased consumer buying activity.

To sum up this part of the chapter, historical evidence suggests various investment strategies which may be employed profitably if investors develop an ability to forecast major economic turning points about four to six months in advance—or if they rely on the counsel of others who have such an ability. (Of course, many investors will adopt a buy-and-hold strategy, which ignores cyclical swings.) The precise implementation of these strategies depends on the aggressiveness, self-confidence, and flexibility of an investor. For example, large institutional investors are much less flexible than individual investors. Nevertheless, the general nature of the strategies are as follows:

1. If investors suspect that the prosperity phase of the business cycle is coming to an end but are not yet firmly convinced of the fact,

Table 8
Good Late Bear Market Performance

	(1)	(2)	(3)	(4)	(5)	(6)	(7)	(8)	(9)	(10)	(11)	(12)
	Relative Strength in Late Phase of Each of Last 3 Bear Markets	Relative Strength of 10 Percentage Points or More			5-Year beta	Relative P/E 3/78	Average 10-Year Relative P/E	Cash Flow ROI (1974–76)	Ratio of Dividends plus Capital Spending to Cash Flow (1974–76)	Relative EPS		Yield
		1966	1970	1974						1978	1979	
Natural gas distributors	x		x	x	0.61	0.90	0.61	10.5%	153%	–	+	7.3%
Telephone	x			x	0.50	0.81	0.81	10.8	165	–	=	6.9
Retail stores-food chains)	x				0.89	1.03	1.03	17.3	107	+	+	5.3
Gold mining	x	x		x	0.42	1.92	1.74	35.5	57	=	–	2.1
Oil (crude producers)	x	x	x		0.76	1.23	1.21	28.6	77	–	=	2.8
Oil (integrated domestic)	x			x	0.80	0.83	0.81	21.3	122	+	+	4.7
Oil (integrated international)	x		x	x	0.92	0.83	0.63	20.1	106	+	=	6.8

Source: Merrill Lynch, Pierce, Fenner & Smith, Inc.

Table 9
Good Late Bear-Early Bull Performers

	(1) Positive Relative Strength 1966–67		(2) 1970–1970		(3) 1974–75		(4)	(5)	(6)	(7)	(8)	(9) Relative EPS	(10)	(11)
	Bear	Bull	Bear	Bull	Bear	Bull	5-Year beta	Relative P/E 3/78	Average 10-Year Relative P/E	Cash Flow ROI (1974–76)	Ratio to Dividends plus Capital Spending to Cash Flow (1974–76)	1978	1979	Yield
Natural gas distributors	x		x	x	x	x	0.61	0.90	0.61	10.6%	152%	−	+	7.3%
Natural gas pipelines		x	x	x	x	x	0.95	0.81	0.71	13.6	125	+	+	5.7
Soaps	x	x		x	x	x	0.97	1.42	1.45	16.6	89	=	+	4.2
Shoes	x	x		x	x	x	1.28	0.91	0.86	15.8	69	=	−	4.4

Source: Merrill Lynch, Pierce, Fenner & Smith, Inc.

they might continue buying common stocks but confine purchases to companies whose sales are likely to be least vulnerable to recession and whose stocks' price-earnings ratios still seem relatively attractive.

2. When investors become convinced that a recession lies shortly ahead, even though the stock market is still strong, they should have the courage to stop making new common stock commitments. Investable funds should be kept liquid at this stage, however—that is, in bank time deposits or in short-term securities. Long-term bond investments probably are not yet appropriate, since interest rates are likely still to be rising. But the typical flat or downward-sloping shape of the yield curve at such times suggests that a good rate of return will be secured even on liquid investments.

3. When stock prices begin to weaken, in their classical lead relationship to general economic activity, it is time to institute quickly a net selling program with regard to common stocks. In particular, stocks of highly cyclical companies and stocks whose price-earnings ratios have risen to unrealistic levels should be eliminated from the portfolio. Proceeds from these sales still should be kept in liquid form.

4. When the recession gets under way, and stock prices are falling rapidly, interest rates are likely to be at a peak, and liquid funds should be shifted into high-quality bonds of long maturity. These are likely to appreciate most in value when the cyclical decline in interest rates takes place.

5. In the midst of the recession, yield spreads between high-quality and lower-quality bonds, and between bonds and mortgages, may become relatively wide. Income-oriented investors often find it worthwhile to shift funds from high-quality bonds to these higher yielding investments at such times.

6. When investors perceive the forthcoming end of the recession, a renewed stock buying program is in order—particularly the stocks of cyclical and glamour-growth companies which probably were severely depressed during the bear market. Profits on long-maturity bonds can be realized through sales, although some further rise in bond prices can be anticipated, with the proceeds of the sales to be invested in common stocks.

It must be recognized, of course, that the business cycle approach to investment timing has faults as well as virtues. First, since many full-time professional economists have only mediocre forecasting records, investors who are not economists cannot be expected to do very well in forecasting on their own—or in evaluating the forecasts of professionals. Second, even a consistent record of perfect six-month forecasts is unlikely to result in consistently correct investment timing.

For although the timing points have been reasonably stable, they have not been—and doubtless will not in the future be—unchanging. Consequently, many investors supplement business cycle analysis with the tools of technical analysis, described next.

TIMING AND TECHNICAL ANALYSIS

The business cycle approach to common stock timing deals with factors outside the stock market itself—for example, industrial production and money supply. The technical approach, on the other hand, seeks to improve the basis of timing decisions by studying phenomena which are an integral part of the market mechanism—for example, prices and volume of trading. For this reason, technical analysis is often referred to as internal analysis or market analysis.

Technical analysts study internal stock market data in an attempt to gain insight into what economists call the "supply and demand schedules" for a stock or for the stock market as a whole. They do this by looking for recurring patterns of price movement or recurring interrelationships between stock price movements and other market data. Since price movements reflect the opinions of millions of different people about everything having a bearing on stocks, it is unlikely that technicians can know in all cases why the discovered patterns occur. They may try to learn why—including in this effort an examination of relevant external information in addition to internal data—but the probability remains that many patterns and relationships will be unexplainable. Nevertheless, if the patterns are known to recur consistently, it seems sensible to take advantage of this knowledge even though the explanations remain unknown. After all, physicians do not know why aspirin works as well as it does, but they prescribe it nonetheless.

Technical analysts who are intellectually honest will be quick to admit that they have no hope of discovering foolproof methods of forecasting stock prices. Mistakes are bound to be made—often severe mistakes. But they also will argue that as long as their methods improve the probabilities of investment success, as long as they reduce the margin of error, they are worthy of serious consideration.

It should be noted that technical analysis is not a new, or even recent, development. In fact, it is considered by many to be the original form of investment analysis, dating back to the late 1800s. It came into widespread use before the period of extensive and fully disclosed financial information, which in turn enabled the practice of so-called fundamental research to develop. Its principal purpose was to help market technicians monitor the actions of informed investors. Many of the techniques used today have been utilized for over 50 years, although the use of computers has given rise to substantial modification of established methods.

The tools of the technical analyst are numerous,[22] and an elaborate and exotic jargon has been evolved. Technical factors examined and interpreted include odd-lot trading, the short interest, volume of trading indicators, breadth-of-market analysis, advance-decline lines, ratios and indexes, disparity measures, high-low indexes and ratios, moving average lines, the confidence index, and so on. The complete market technician's kit would also have to include chart jargon involving support and resistance, heads and shoulders, double tops and bottoms, line and saucer formations, V formations, measured move, first leg, the corrective phase, second leg, the coil or triangle, continuation patterns, reversal days, gaps, islands, bear traps, bull traps, fulcrums, duplex horizontals, inverse fulcrums, delayed endings, saucers, inverse saucers, compound fulcrums, and so on.

An example from a market letter reads as follows:

> The question is, of course, what we are to make of this phenomenon. The lows of mid-February and late February are, in all cases, close enough to each other so that if a rally were to continue from these levels, we would have a potential for a so-called "double bottom." The upside implications of that double-bottom base formation are not, at the moment, too terribly exciting, and we, for one, would prefer to see backing and filling around current levels so that a base suggesting a meaningful advance might be formed. The likelihood of such an event is strengthened by the fact that most of the averages have now moved above the downtrend channels projected from the year-end highs to their lows of last month.

A *Fortune* article on "The Mystique of Point-and-Figure" began "Question: Does this look like reaccumulation preparatory to a new upthrust? Answer: No—because fulcrum characteristics are not present."

This sort of jargon has convinced many observers that technical analysis is sheer rubbish. On the other hand, large numbers of Wall Street practitioners are equally convinced that price movements are not random and that technical analysis can improve one's chances of making correct timing decisions. One leading expert commented: "It is hard to find a practitioner, no matter how sophisticated, who does not believe that by looking at the past history of prices one can learn something about their prospective behavior, while it is almost as difficult to find an academician who believes that such a backward look is of any substantial value."

Technical tools are generally divided into three broad categories: general market analysis, contrary opinion, and price charts and stock selection techniques. Some of the subjects in each naturally overlap

---

[22] For a description of the basic tools and techniques involved in technical analysis see Chapter 13 of Cohen, Zinbarg, and Zeikel, *Investment Analysis and Portfolio Management,* and Chapter 34 of Levine, *Financial Analyst's Handbook,* vol. 1.

into other sections. For example, security credit is discussed as part of the theory of contrary opinion, but could just as accurately be considered an element in general market supply-demand analysis. Similarly, Dow theory is often considered as part of charting, because the philosophy underlying Dow theory is applicable to the study of individual stocks as well as to the overall market; it could just as well have been, however, a part of the market analysis section.

General market analysis covers a very long list of tools and techniques designed to determine the basic, general trend of stock prices. Technicians, and in fact most investors, consider it easier to select "up" stocks, that is, stocks which are expected to rise in price, if they have confidence that the general trend is favorable (bullish) as opposed to unfavorable (bearish).

Contrary opinion in the stock market is actually an attitude or intellectual process, not a tool of technical analysis. Further, it is difficult to define precisely the general theory without the use of ludicrous or silly-sounding statements. However, the general concept is to "go against the crowd." Humphrey Neill, generally considered the father of the theory, put it this way: "When everyone thinks alike, everyone is likely to be wrong," or "The crowd is usually wrong, at least in the timing of events."[23] Leslie Pollack stated it differently, by noting: "It is not the opinion of the majority, but the action of the minority which makes stock prices."[24]

This does not mean to imply that the majority is always wrong. Rather, that the majority is likely to be wrong when there is no real difference of opinion. Therefore, technicians have developed a series of tools and techniques designed to measure the status of popular opinion regarding the trend of stock prices, to determine when popular opinion is becoming too uniform, and, at that time, to take the opposite position in the market.

DOW THEORY AND PRICE CHARTS

Charles H. Dow is generally recognized as the father, if not the grandfather of technical analysis. His theories have been used for many years as a means of estimating the general trend of the market. Dow

---

[23] Over the years, Humphrey B. Neill has expressed these views many times, many ways, in many places. His most recent collection of thoughts and suggestions on contrary thinking are contained in *The Ruminator* (Caldwell, Ida.: Caxton Printers, Ltd., 1975).

Martin Zweig, one of the newer market technicians, holds the view "whenever non-professional investors become significantly one-sided in their expectations about the future course of stock prices, the market will move in the direction opposite to that which is anticipated by the masses." To support this contention he has published a comprehensive analysis on the tools of contrary opinion. *See* Martin Zweig, "Investor Expectations: Why They Are the Key to Stock Market Trends," *The Zweig Forecast,* (New York: Zweig Securities Advisory, Inc., 1975).

[24] Leslie M. Pollack, "Technical Analysis: A Basic Approach," Reynolds Co., N.Y. p. 3.

summarized his basic beliefs in three short sentences in an editorial published December 19, 1900, in *The Wall Street Journal,* the newspaper of which he was editor.[25] He stated: "The market is always to be considered as having three movements, all going at the same time. The first is the narrow movement from day-to-day. The second is the short swing, running from two weeks to a month or more; the third is the main movement, covering at least four years in its duration."[26] The trick, of course, is how to measure and determine each of these movements, assuming some validity of the general premise. Dow suggested a method in a series of *The Wall Street Journal* editorials, often commenting on the proper interpretation of each development.[27] Today, there are many versions of the Dow theory—perhaps as many versions as there are analysts who profess to use it. Therefore, it is unlikely that any description of the technique would command unanimous acceptance of what it is, much less how well it works. Nevertheless, aside from certain relatively unimportant details, what seem to be its essential characteristics can be outlined briefly.

As a major (primary) uptrend of the market averages proceeds, there are numerous intermediate (secondary) downward reactions, each of which retraces a substantial proportion of the preceding rise. After each reaction, price recovers and goes on to surpass the previous high. Dow theorists keep on the alert for a recovery which falls short of the previous high. If, following such an abortive recovery, a downward reaction pierces the low point of the last previous reaction, evidence is at hand that the market has gone into a major (primary) downtrend. This is illustrated schematically in Figure 4.

Most Dow theorists do not consider a signal of a new primary downtrend to be valid unless the pattern of "descending tops and bottoms" just described occurs in both the industrial and the transportation averages.[28] Since the industrials and transportations usually will not form the pattern simultaneously, the market may have a very sizable decline before a confirmed sell signal is given. Herein lies the principal

---

[25] Dow originally intended his index of stock prices to serve as a barometer of business trends, not a stock market timing tool.

[26] William Peter Hamilton, *The Stock Market Barometer* (New York: republished by Richard Russell Associates, 1960), p. 30.

[27] Ibid., contains several of these in their entirety, and makes for interesting reading.

[28] The transportation average used to include only railroads. The insistence on the "confirmation" of a signal by both the industrial and railroad averages originally was based on the idea that the industrials reflect productive processes and the railroads distributive processes. To have a healthy economy, both types of activities have to be sound. In recent times, the declining importance of railroads in the economy caused many critics to question the significance of railroad stock prices as a barometer. Even before the change to a more comprehensive transportation average, however, some technicians argued that railroad stock prices, if not a barometer of economic affairs, are at least a barometer of speculation in the stock market and therefore are of legitimate interest.

Figure 4
Schematic Diagram of a "Dow Theory" Bear
Market Signal

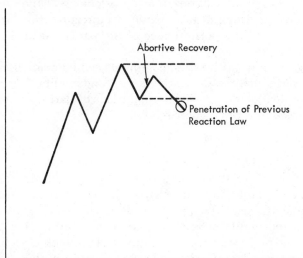

failing of the technique. In shallow bear markets, the signal usually comes shortly before the downtrend is about to reverse itself. Even this would not be too bad if the Dow theory promptly called the bottom of the market. A few percent saved is better than nothing. But to get a signal of a renewed uptrend the whole pattern previously described must repeat itself in reverse. That is, industrials and transportations must each trace out a pattern of ascending bottoms and tops. By the time they do, the investor who has acted upon the signals is likely to have been whipsawed.

Price Chart Patterns

The Dow theory deals with the market as a whole. But the underlying principle of ascending and descending tops and bottoms as symptoms of primary trend reversals also is applied to individual securities. Technical analysts keep hundreds of price charts on stocks in which they have an interest.

Since individual stocks have much more extensive cyclical swings in price than the market averages, it might be that a Dow-type approach produces generally favorable results. The trouble is that we simply have no statistically significant method of appraising the technique. For in addition to ascending and descending tops and bottoms, which are often referred to as "channels" and which are amenable to reasonably precise definitions, technicians refer to "heads and shoul-

ders" formations, "triangles," "rectangles," "flags and pennants," and
a host of other configurations with equally exotic names but with quite
imprecise definitions. A half dozen analysts looking at the same chart
will rarely give anything near a unanimous interpretation. We therefore end up testing the performance of the particular analyst rather
than the method.

Of course, somewhat the same comments can be made with regard
to intrinsic value analysis. Given the same "fundamental" information,
numerous evaluations are possible. But the lack of clarity seems particularly troublesome in price chart reading.[29]

Bar Charts

Technicians utilize three basic types of price charts: line charts,
bar charts, and point-and-figure charts. On both line and bar charts,
the horizontal axis represents time—days, weeks, or months—and the
vertical axis represents price. On a line chart, the closing prices of
successive time periods are connected by straight lines. On a bar chart,
vertical lines are drawn at each time period with the top and bottom
of each bar plotted at the high and low prices for the period. A small
horizontal line is drawn across the bar at the closing price level. Bar
charts of various market averages are published regularly in the financial sections of the newspapers. Most such charts include a vertical
scale at the bottom of the chart against which are drawn bars representing the volume of trading during each time period. Figure 5 contains
examples of this type of chart, each of which also shows a 200-day
moving averages of the daily closing price of the stock together with
summary data on earnings, dividends, and capital structure.

Moving Averages

Many technical analysts believe that a reversal in a major uptrend
of the price of an individual stock, or of the market in general, can
be detected in advance, or at least confirmed shortly after its occurrence, by studying the movement of current prices in relation to a
long-term moving average of prices. A moving average is designed
to reveal the underlying direction and rate of change of a highly volatile
series of numbers.[30] It is constructed by averaging a portion of the
series and then successively adding the next number of the series to
the numbers previously averaged, dropping the first number, and se-

---

[29] A study which attempts to define rigorously the specification of various patterns,
detect their existence and measure performance after breakouts finds "no evidence
of profitable forecasting ability." See Robert A. Levy, "The Predictive Significance of
Five Point Chart Patterns," *Journal of Business* (July 1971).

[30] Rates of change can also be analyzed by other procedures, ranging all the way
from simple year-to-year percentage changes to sophisticated methods involving calculus.

Figure 5
Illustrative Bar Charts of Stock Prices

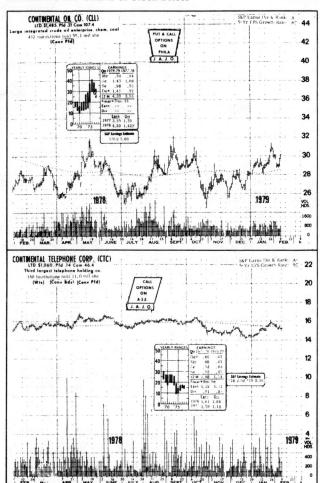

Source: Trendline division of Standard & Poor's Corp., Daily Basis Stock Charts.

curing a new average. For example, we could construct a five-day moving average of the daily closing of the Dow Jones Industrials as shown in Table 10.

Veteran technical analysts generally utilize a 200-day moving average of daily closing prices in their work,[31] which is usually graphed

---

[31] Many technicians take a short cut and use only one price a week for 30 or 40 weeks to construct a 200-day moving average. The Trendline chart service, a division of Standard Poor's, for example, computes its 200-day moving average by adding the closing price of 30 consecutive Thursdays, and dividing by 30. Each week the new figure is added, and the one for 30 weeks earlier is dropped. The resultant moving average then actually covers approximately 150 trading days.

Table 10
Five-Day Moving Average

Trading Day	Dow Jones Industrials	Five-Day Moving Total	Five-Day Moving Average
1	900		
2	902		
3	899		
4	894		
5	897	4,492 (sum of items 1–5)	898.4
6	896	4,488 (sum of items 2–6)	897.6
7	898	4,484 (sum of items 3–7)	896.8

(as in Figure 5) on regular stock price charts for easy comparison with daily or weekly price changes. Frankly, we have been unable to discover any evidence that a 200-day average—covering about 40 weeks of trading—produces any better results than some other long-term average, say 250 days (covering a year of trading). Be that as it may, the 200-day moving average is a usable technical tool, and is usually interpreted as follows:

Buy signals:

1. If the 200-day average line flattens out or advances following a decline, and the daily price of the stock penetrates that average line on the upside.
2. If the stock price is above the 200-day line and declines toward it, but fails to go through and instead turns up again.

Sell signals:

1. If the average line flattens out or declines following a rise, and the daily stock price penetrates that line on the downside.
2. If the stock price is below the average line and rises toward it, but fails to go through and instead turns down again.

A point-and-figure chart is quite different in concept and design from a line or bar chart. First, there is no time scale on such a chart—only a vertical price scale. Second, plots are made on the chart only when price moves up or down by a predetermined amount—typically 1 or 2 points in the case of medium-priced stocks, ½ point in the case of low-priced stocks, and 3 or 5 points for high-priced stocks. In addition to these differences, a point-and-figure chart provides no volume data unless the analysts work out some intricate schemes of their own, such as making their plots in different colors to represent different volumes. Most point-and-figure chartists take volume into account only indirectly.

The purpose of point-and-figure charting is to show a compressed picture of significant price changes. The analyst decides in advance that all movements of, say, ⅞ of a point or less will be considered as irrelevant. Thus, if price changes by ½ during a given day, no entry will be made on the chart. On the other hand, if price changes by 3 points in one day, three entries will be made on a 1-point chart. If time and facilities are limited, the analyst may work only with closing prices, but most serious chartists work with intraday prices as revealed by the ticker tape.

CRITIQUE OF TECHNICAL ANALYSIS

Readers of investments texts usually are led to think of stock market technicians in much the same way as scientists think of astrologers. To be perfectly candid, there are some understandable grounds for this attitude. The field of technical analysis has attracted large numbers of self-styled "professionals" who might be better classified as crackpots, or even charlatans.

Thus, we can understand the characterization of technical analysis as "crystal-ball gazing." But we consider this characterization to be rather unfortunate, for it casts aside the good with the bad. The more scholarly and sophisticated technical analysts use their tools with a proper sense of proportion. Typically, they use technical analysis as a guide to further study. If a stock looks attractive to them on technical grounds they probe into its fundamentals. While their decisions may be more heavily influenced by technical considerations, they are certainly not unmindful of earnings growth, of values, or of the impact of business cycles.

The honest technical analysts know that their approaches will not solve all investment problems. But they also know that no other single approach will either. They believe their tools can reduce the margin of error.

Moreover, while no single technical indicator can be expected to work every time, a useful picture may emerge when one follows several indicators which appear to be reasonably reliable, particularly in conjunction with the various economic indicators which have been discussed. Indeed, just as a diffusion index of a large number of economic indicators can be created, so too can a composite index of many technical indicators be constructed. A major advantage of a composite index is its stability, or infrequency of giving new signals. Hopefully, this lessens the chance of a whipsaw.

There are several commercial investment services which publish such a composite index on a subscription basis. Figure 6 shows the buy and sell signals that would have been given since 1965 by a composite of 12 technical indicators prepared by *Indicator Digest.* While we do not necessarily endorse the particular choice of indicators on which

Figure 6
Indicator Digest **Composite Index**

Source: *Indicator Digest* (Palisades Park, N.J., December 8, 1978), p. 5.

the chart is based, or the assigned weights,[32] the results are quite intriguing.

Technical analysis may be on the threshold of new discoveries. Economic statisticians are becoming increasingly interested in the subject of price fluctuations in the stock market. They have been investigating the so-called random walk hypothesis. The hypothesis states that stock prices respond quickly to new information as it becomes available and that new items of information enter the marketplace in random fashion. Therefore prices also move in random fashion. Specifically, periodic changes in price—hourly, daily, weekly, or monthly—are independent of the price changes during equivalent preceding periods.

The random walk hypothesis does not deny the possibility of forecasting stock prices. It accepts the principle that investment analysts who

---

[32] Since the interpretation of whether any particular component of the composite is favorable or unfavorable involves subjective judgments, the method is not as scientific as it appears at first glance.

can forecast company earnings and dividends accurately should do a fairly good job of forecasting stock prices. What it denies is that the analysis of past data, particularly past market price data, can produce better-than-chance price change forecasts.

Most of the statistical investigations of the random walk hypothesis confirm the belief that successive price changes are generally statistically independent. In our opinion, however, this fact does not necessarily warrant a conclusion that technical analyses of the type which have been described in this chapter are useless as methods of predicting future price movements. Several additional avenues of research appear to be called for. Among them are the following:

1. While successive changes in absolute prices may be independent, successive changes in relative prices may not be. For example, if a particular stock's price shows the sequence 50, 49½, 49, 49½, the direction of change is *down, down, up.* But suppose that at the same time the S&P Industrial Stock Price Index moves as follows: 90, 90.5, 91, 92.5. Relative to the market, the stock's price action is *down, down, down*—a different sequence from that revealed by absolute price data. Since the concept of relative strength plays so important a role in technical analysis, as indicated earlier in this chapter, it would be helpful if students of the random walk hypothesis would apply some of their tests (serial correlation, analysis of runs, spectral analysis, etc.) to relative price behavior.

2. Price patterns may become significant when interpreted in conjunction with other technical phenomena such as volume of trading and short selling. Furthermore, it may be that a statistical combination of technical and fundamental data will produce better clues to the future than either one used independently. Work done by Standard & Poor's Corporation and elsewhere suggests that past rates of change of profits offer good clues to subsequent stock price changes. This implies that there is a significant time lag between the market's receipt of fundamental information and the ultimate price response to that information. If so, statistical investigations of the interaction of technical and fundamental data may prove to be very fruitful.

3. Specific technical theories should be tested directly, as a supplement to the indirect approach which has characterized most of the research to date. Essentially, this involves *(a)* establishing trading decision rules which incorporate the premises of a technical theory, *(b)* simulating investment transactions based on these decision rules, and *(c)* observing whether these transactions produce better results, on average, than some sort of random investment policy. Such investigations may well prove that, say, the search for patterns of ascending or descending price tops or bottoms is a waste of time if the analyst is trying to predict future prices. But a proof obtained in this manner probably would be more convincing to investment practitioners than

a demonstration that any given period's price change is statistically independent of an equivalent previous period's price change.

Coping Better

Any discussion of active investment strategies must ponder the question: Why are so many investors wrong so much of the time?

Surely, one reason is that they accommodate change poorly. More for emotional than logical reasons, investors tend to base their expectations on visible and prevailing trends and patterns. But all too often, expectations based on such patterns fail to materialize. John Maynard Keynes, an outstanding investor of his day, put it this way: "The facts of the existing situation enter, in a sense disproportionately, into the formation of our long-term expectations: our usual practice being to take the existing situation and to project it into a future modified only to the extent that we have more or less definite reasons for expecting a change."

Investors compound the problem by tending to become overly protective of their own judgments. Not because they are right, or even likely to be right, but because they are their own. This in turn leads to an unwillingness to accept new information for what it's really worth. Frequently, it's worth a great deal and the reluctance to consider new information (change) with an open mind makes it harder to recognize the flaws which may exist in their operating investment premise.

Many investors work themselves into a significant loss position by failing to appreciate that a loss taken quickly is usually a minimal loss. Intelligent investors must learn to avoid the defensive rationalization of past bad judgments. They should recognize, rather, that when things change, they change. It is better to take the new events into consideration, admitting error and shifting investment posture, rather than fighting reality until conventional opinion converges on the new view and sweeps the old one away and with it the opportunity to prevent great loss.

In other words, information must be regarded by investors as a perishable commodity. The life cycle of new ideas steadily grows shorter. Change must be placed into its proper perspective much more quickly than heretofore. New developments are usually recognized, appreciated, and acted upon by a few. The new trend enjoys progressively wider recognition until it finally becomes the conventional wisdom, when it is extrapolated beyond its reasonable horizon. The First National City Bank Monthly Economic Letter recently noted: "The temptation to extrapolate events of the recent past into the indefinite future is strong, but it will lead to the wrong conclusion if the fundamental conditions that created these events are changing rapidly and significantly." The point is, they usually are.

Random Walk Revisited.   What we are suggesting is that the market is not totally efficient in its response to new developments. First, new and important information simply is not available simultaneously to all who might recognize or use it. Second, not all who have the information recognize it. Third, not all who recognize it are able immediately to translate that recognition into an evaluation of its worth in the market. That is, in any group of investors, some will exhibit the capacity to recognize and use information faster than others, and that capacity puts them at a competitive advantage.

The principal evidence supporting the random walk hypothesis has been based on the market's reaction to new information as supplied via corporate announcements such as earnings and dividends, stock splits, or secondary distributions; changes in Federal Reserve data; recommendations by brokerage firms and advisory services; and the periodic announcements of industry data. Little, if any, scientific testing has been conducted on the market's response to less obvious developments which affect the fortunes of a particular company or industry. Let us explain further.

The Market Is a Mirror. Generally speaking, the market is a mirror reflection of the forces that weave their way through our social, political, and economic systems. But the market—like the mirrors at amusement parks—tends to create distortions of the truth. These distortions create investment opportunities.

Long-term investment cycles in fact reflect structural economic shifts. For example, one can correlate the entire postwar bull market, up until the mid-1960s, with a persistent buildup of capital and the ability over the years to create wealth sufficiently in excess of basic needs to give rise to speculative tendencies. For most of the postwar period, an increasing number of families and corporations developed very large increases in their discretionary income.

Within that very long cycle, there have been fairly long subperiods which further illustrate the basic premise. The period 1946 to the mid-1950s was primarily one in which concern focused on corporate strength and on those strongly financed companies in basic industries capable of generating earnings progress; in other words, a period of industrial expansion. After the consumer and capital goods boom of the mid-1950s, investor emphasis shifted toward those companies which were considered impervious to the business cycle (the first of several growth stock phases). That period was followed by one in which investment attitudes began to concentrate on the maximizing of long-term returns in the new technologies.

Consider the two-tier market of late 1972–73.[33] It made sense as a legitimate response to a series of new problems—the much higher

---

[33] While the recollection of events during this period is fading among most professional practitioners, due to the passage of time and the unpleasantness of the experience, the classic nature of the investment environment at that time dictates we revisit the errors committed by many portfolio managers.

than anticipated inflation rate, a more competitive position of fixed income securities via long-term equity rewards, international balance of payment problems, and, perhaps most importantly, greater involvement by the government in heretofore private enterprise decisions. It became part of the conventional wisdom to assume that one way of avoiding these problems was to concentrate on those equities with a much higher than average growth rate, a much higher than average return on investment capital, a much lower labor content, and so forth. Common stocks in the first tier were held to have one dimension. That is, they required only a buy decision in order to provide above-average long-term rewards; they would not ever be considered for sale.

At this point the mirror became distorted. Investor response to new economic realities was overdone, and the opportunities that were so obvious to the early investors were not there for those who arrived late on the scene. Just about the time that one-decision growth stock investing reached its zenith of acceptance, fundamental business patterns changed dramatically to the detriment of investors following that approach. First, and perhaps most importantly, the economy started to shift from a consumer to a capital goods orientation. The market mechanism began to reallocate resources to those companies that needed capital to relieve shortages building up in the economic system—basic industries, whose stocks had not only been overlooked by investors, but actually were held in such low regard that many leading Wall Street research firms refused to cover these companies as part of their normal analytical effort.

Second, rapidly increasing worldwide inflation rates began to shrink consumer discretionary spending for nonessential items. Unit sales growth around the world declined (investors had forgotten that most growth companies earn much of their net income from foreign markets) and profit margins were squeezed as raw material companies were able to raise prices, due to shortages, faster than consumer oriented businesses. In short order, the worldwide inventory panic created by spiraling energy and other raw material costs produced the inevitable recession. Growth stocks proved to be particularly vulnerable to price weakness in a market made more nervous by increasing regulatory and legislative scrutiny of bank trust department investment practices. Bank trust departments, it may be recalled, had been the really big one-decision stock buyers of the period.

At the same time, some investors were rediscovering value. Their attention was directed to stocks of companies with highly depreciated plants being operated at high rates of utilization, selling at five to six times earnings, producing high current return from well-covered dividends and selling at substantial discounts from artificially low book values. The focus shifted to current dividend return from long-term price appreciation. Investors—large and small—began (and still are, as of this writing) selling the old-fashioned growth stocks at substantial losses to buy long-ignored investment values. And is it not equally predictable that the time will come when growth stocks are the rage once again?

Now, why did and why do investment trends change over time? Simply, or perhaps not so simply, because they reflect the changing needs, priorities, and requirements of an economic system in constant evolution. Over the longer-term, stock prices correlate with earning progress. Corporate earnings, in turn, are largely a function of the opportunities provided by changes in the overall economic system. Each new phase of economic movement creates earnings growth opportunities for some companies, while at the same time offering new problems for others. Stock price cycles, long and short, are a reflection, with varying lead and lag times, of these wavelike movements.

Critical Factors. Every industry, company, and economic sector responds to a different set of business phenomena, forces, and critical factors. Any sound analytical approach requires that these factors be identified, isolated, and followed on a consistent basis.

Change in these elements alters the profits outlook and immediately affects investment expectations. Consequently, stock price movements start to mirror these new developments long before it is generally recognized that they have taken place. Every effort must be made to interpret change swiftly and accurately. In today's market environment, the life cycle of a new idea is very brief, often as short as the first telephone call.

Early warning signals calling attention to a possible change may take the form of a new trend in a significant statistical indicator or a shift in the attitude of industry participants close to the point of critical action.

Critical factors are not limited to cyclical considerations nor confined to short-term movements, but include slower moving basic trend changes, social and environmental developments as well as internal corporate adjustments, the adoption of new management techniques, new product introductions, changes in market share, and so on.

These critical factors are not always, or even for the most part, obvious; if they were, anyone could successfully run a business. But they exist, are demonstrable, and—when properly understood—yield foresight. They may in some cases seem frivolous or seem in themselves to be the result of irrational behavior—say by the consumer or the government—but they submit to rational analysis.

Avon Products is a good case in point. Throughout 1972, the shares of this outstanding company moved in the forefront of the developing two-tier market. By early 1973, the price of Avon common stock has risen to $140 per share, from a low of $60 in 1970, and carried a price-earnings ratio (on estimated 1973 earnings of $2.45–$2.50 per share) of over 55. Institutional investors and research analysts alike were generally secure in their belief that earnings would continue to compound at a 15 percent annual rate and such a performance was adequate compensation for the lofty multiple on current earnings. In fact, so strong was the belief in the persistency of past earnings growth, that when the stock declined 40 points from its high, many regarded the development as another buying opportunity. Typical commentary ran as follows: "At its current price of $108, Avon common offers well-above-average longer-term appreciation potential. Chiefly responsible for our favorable opinion regarding Avon common is our optimism that over the foreseeable future the company's traditional business can record revenue gains of 14 to 16 percent annually."

Despite the prevalence of such views, largely based upon traditional analysis, the stock continued to drop and closed on December 31, 1973 at a little over $60 per share. Why? During the third quarter, management felt obliged to announce that the company was beginning to experience a sales slowdown in the United States. Contributing factors behind this unusual development can be cited in the words of management: "Dramatic increases in the price of food and other basic items and the prospects of further increases of this kind in the future have imposed a squeeze on the family's budget." As a visiting Englishman put it, "It was really quite predictable, if one had thought about it that way."

The point is, stock price movements will begin reflecting new developments long before it is generally recognized that they have taken place. In this regard, it has frequently been noted that new investment trends start with the belief of a few and end with the conviction of the many. In other words, some investors do recognize change more rapidly than others. How do they do it? A couple of rules are clear:

1. The ability to recognize an important change stems from an understanding of the fundamentals of a business and not from the gathering of statistical minutia.
2. The fundamentals of a business have to do with consumer needs and desires, on the one hand, and the methods employed to satisfy those needs—the key demand factors and the key supply factors.
3. Investors must conquer the urge to learn everything before making a decision.

Let's illustrate with a relatively simple example. In mid-1971, Gerber Products was selling between $45 and $50 a share, approximately 19.5 times the earnings of $2.40 per share reported for the March 1971 fiscal year. The stock had risen almost 60 percent during the prior 12 months (see Figure 7). On September 7, 1971 several leading newspapers carried headlines indicating that the "U.S. Birthrate Falls 15

Figure 7
Gerber Products: An Example of Critical Variable Analysis

Source: Trendline Division of Standard & Poor's Corp. Current Market Perspectives.

Per Cent," after the stock had already experienced a significant, but unexplained, correction. Sixteen months later the stock dropped to $24.50, its lowest price since 1966, after management reported a sharp decline in quarterly profits. The accompanying commentary indicated that the lower earnings reflected price competition and a decline in the number of births.

Now, the point of this narrative is not to elaborate on the obvious cause and effect relationship of the birth rate of Gerber's earnings. Rather, it is to support our view of how new information, which affected the stock's value, entered the marketplace's information system and started to change investor expectations of the future. Was it in September 1971, when a new study on birthrates received substantial publicity, or was it when the company's reported earnings finally reflected a trend that had been in force for some time? Furthermore, and also of importance, was the new information immediately discounted in the price of the stock? We think the answers to both questions are obvious.

As we all know, only too well, good investment decisions are rarely so easy, even in retrospect. The facts that govern the price action of securities are usually much more complex and much less easy to identify. Therefore, the general concept is worth exploring further with additional illustrations.

Illustration 1. During most of 1977, analysts and investors were concerned that deregulation and price cutting would seriously damage the profitability of most, if not all, passenger oriented airlines. In fact, *Business Week** on October 10, 1977 carried a transportation commentary "Why Price-Cutting Backfires in the Airline Industry."[34] Only four weeks later, the same magazine noted "A Flood of Travelers Boosts Airline Profits"[35] and noted: "The U.S. airline industry appears headed for a banner year, thanks to a spectacular surge in traffic that began in mid-September for many carriers. Thanks are also due to the Tax Reform Act of 1976, which allows airlines to offset 1977 income tax liability with available investment tax credits."[36] Six months later, after the stocks had risen quite substantially, as can be seen from the stock price charts in Figure 8, *Business Week* continued its coverage of industry developments by reporting "Airline Profits Are Taking Wing," and that "Second quarter earnings will not be available until late next month, but it is clear that revenues are rising much faster than expenses. The article continued "So long as cheap fares are drawing passengers who would otherwise not have traveled, revenue from discounts goes virtually intact to the bottom line because operating costs are relatively constant." It is fairly easy, and obvious, to relate the movement of airline stocks to returns of better business. But how many investors made the connection that the ultimate beneficiary of improved airline passenger business was the Boeing Company. Notice the compatible price action as shown in Figure 8.

Interestingly, after a relatively long period of superior airline stock price performance, and at a time when many analysts were expecting a continuation of good profit performance, *Business Week* carried another review of industry trends but this time warned investors "Why the Airlines' Record Profits Are Bound to Fade."[37] Notice that stocks "reacted" sometime earlier.

Illustration 2. Gaming industry (gambling) and related issues were a particular feature of the 1978 stock market. Many of the issues in this so-called industry category achieved spectacular market gains. Some of these are portrayed in Figure 9. Investor interest in the group commenced late in 1976 when New Jersey voters approved statewide

---

* Authors Note: Examples from *Business Week* were selected for several reasons. The magazine is widely read, inexpensively available, and an unusually good source of financial information of relative value to active investors. Undoubtedly similar information appeared earlier and with greater detail, in trade and industry publications. The *London Economist* is another particularly good, low-cost source of significant investment ideas.

[34] Page 116.

[35] "A Flood of Travelers Boosts Airline Profits," *Business Week* (November 28, 1977), p. 36.

[36] "Airline Profits Are Taking Wing," *Business Week* (June 26, 1978), p. 39.

[37] "Why the Airlines' Record Profits Are Bound to Fade," *Business Week* (September 18, 1978) p. 134.

Figure 8
Stock Prices, Critical Variables, and Public Information

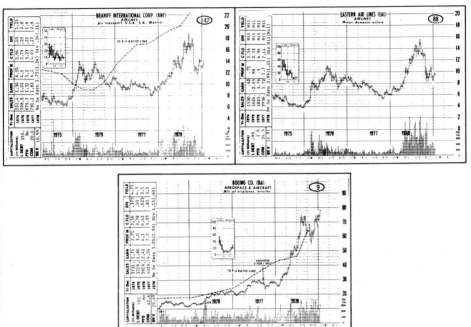

Source: "A Flood of Travelers Boosts Airline Profits," *Business Week* (November 28, 1977); and "Airline Profits Are Taking Wing," *Business Week* (June 26, 1978).

referendum allowing Atlantic City to issue casino licenses, the first of which went to Resorts International. Investors at the time appeared to have paid little attention to Resorts International common stock as its stock price experienced only gradual, but persistent, gain throughout 1977 and the early part of 1978. However, once investors became aware that operating results were likely to exceed even the most optimistic projections, stock prices reacted accordingly. General enthusiasm in the group seems to have reached a peak, at least as reflected in the stock price charts, at the precise time that *Business Week* contained a major article calling gambling "the newest growth industry."[38]

Perhaps the correlation between the items selected and the subsequent price action of the underlying common stock is accidental. Perhaps other factors were at work; they probably were. But there is a link between stock prices and basic information. These examples also stress another point. Intelligent investors must learn to make better use of widely available and low cost—but important—information. In addition to the daily media, there are many publications in each indus-

---

[38] "Gambling; The Newest Growth Industry," *Business Week* (June 26, 1978) p. 111.

Figure 9
Stock Prices, Critical Variables, and Public Information

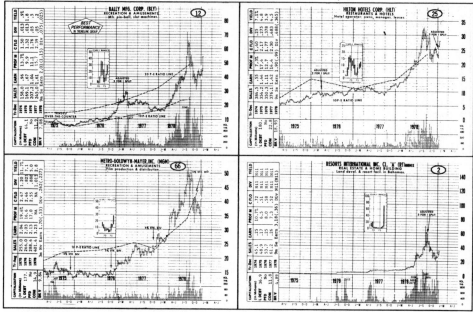

Source: "Atlantic City Wins Its Bet on Casinos," *Business Week* (November 5, 1976).

try which, if read and interpreted correctly, yield accurate accounts of new industry and company developments. Generally speaking, insufficient use is being made of them. Investors also have to develop a willingness to act on common sense and sometimes instinct, rather than on complete knowledge, when a change occurs. Henry Kissinger once remarked that foreign policy was "the need to gear action to the assessment that cannot be proved true when it is made." Often, investing is no different.

Portfolio planners of large capital pools must recognize that all stocks generally move together, but by different magnitudes. Furthermore, large size often prohibits the taking of effective action after new trends set in. Therefore, it seems appropriate that portfolio strategy be designed to incorporate what can be considered the principle of "spaced maturities." The portfolio as a whole should be viewed as a life cycle problem, containing the same stages of development that any new product, institution, or organism go through. In a broad categorical sense, the three important stages are inception, growth, and maturity. Decline, which is usually the last stage of the complete cycle, should—as much as possible—be eliminated.

Therefore, the portfolio should continuously include commitments which are passing through different stages of their investment life cycles. In this way, the portfolio as a whole would not be a static affair, but rather a living creation, with something coming in, something going out, something growing, and something maturing, all at the same time, as shown in the Figure 9.

It must also be recognized that investment commitments can move through the various stages of development at different paces of elapsed time. In other words, some ideas exhaust their potential very quickly, while others may prove productive over very long periods. Ideally, investors should pursue those stocks having the longest and relatively strongest estimated growth phases.

Mistakes often move from inception to decline quickly, frequently failing to pass through the two other stages (growth and maturity) of development, therefore, it is more important to keep track of where the commitment lies in the conceptual sense, rather than in terms of the actual holding period.

As a final thought, active investors must keep in mind, as they go about the problem of assessing change, that it is not whether conditions are good or bad that's important, but whether they are changing for the better or worse, relative to expectations, and whether the prospect is for recent trends to continue, or to change once again.

In the ultimate analysis, investment success is not as much a function of intelligence and ability but of personal conviction. In other words, are you willing to back your own judgment, especially if it means going against the crowd?

Chapter 8

Passive Equity Management Strategies

JAMES R. VERTIN

Senior Vice President
Wells Fargo Investment Advisors
San Francisco, California

The broadest definition of passive equity management is satisfied when neither the design of the portfolio nor its ongoing operation is based on any attempt to assess whether or not the underlying fundamentals of its holdings are reflected fairly in prices. Index funds designed to track the performance of a defined "market of stocks" such as is represented by the Standard & Poor's 500 Index constitute the only widely accepted current form of passive equity management. Although operational strategies for the accomplishment of the goal of index-matching are a phenomena of the 1970s, the idea of a formalized passive equity strategy was not new when Wells Fargo Investment Advisors created the first equity index portfolio in June 1971, a fund designed to track the performance of the New York Stock Exchange Composite Index on an equal-dollar-weighted basis. The conceptual basis for passive management originated from early-1950s work by Harry M. Markowitz concerning the construction of "optimal" and "efficient" investment portfolios, maximizing expected return at a given level of risk, investor risk preferences considered.[1] Extensions in the mid-1960s by Sharpe[2], Lintner[3], and Mossin[4], gave rise to the

---

[1] Harry M. Markowitz, "Portfolio Selection," *Journal of Finance,* vol. 7 no. 1 (March 1952) pp. 77–91. (Also, see Chapter 5 of this Handbook.)

[2] William F. Sharpe, "Capital Asset Prices: A Theory of Market Equilibrium under Conditions of Risk," *Journal of Finance,* vol. 19 (September 1964) pp. 425–42.

[3] John Lintner, "Security Prices, Risk and Maximal Gains from Diversification," *Journal of Finance,* vol. 20 (December 1965) pp. 587–616.

[4] Jan Mossin, "Equilibrium in a Capital Asset Market," *Econometrica,* vol. 34 (October 1966) pp. 768–83.

concept of the market portfolio as offering the highest level of return per unit of risk in an efficient market. This concept of a market portfolio, representing capitalization-weighted shares of all available types of risky assets, is the single most important theoretical notion underlying the use of passive investment management strategies.

Recognition of the economic value of indexing an equity investment portfolio occurred in the late 1960s in certain academic circles and spread to several investment management organizations about that time. Along with developments in portfolio theory, a growing body of analysis documenting stock market efficiency in the U.S. became available, supplemented by an expanding availability of portfolio performance data.[5] Several investment managers, utilizing increasingly more thorough analysis, identified the risk-return implications of passive investment management strategies vis-a-vis conventional portfolio management strategies. The severe decline of stock prices in the 1973–74 bear market, which was particularly injurious to poorly-diversified portfolios, together with a growing awareness on the part of pension plan sponsors of both the absolute and relative performance produced by their portfolio managers over time, led a number of plan sponsors to consider this alternative form of equity market exposure and to direct some of their equity assets into index funds. By 1978, at least $6 billion of institutional monies had been so placed and about 30 organizations were offering equity index fund management, usually based on the S&P 500 Index as their market proxy.

PASSIVE VERSUS ACTIVE MANAGEMENT

Some Issues

In choosing to track a market of stocks through a passive approach an investor either accepts the proposition that the benefits from trading stocks on the basis of forecasted future prices is not likely to consistently cover the higher management fees and transaction costs associated with active management, or the investor has been frustrated in attempting to identify—before the fact—which active managers will benefit from market inefficiencies. Also to be considered are the differences in management fees between passive and active management, the levels of stock selection skills believed to be possessed by active managers, the transaction costs associated with seeking to exploit assumed under- or overpricing through stock trading, and the statistical odds against successfully selecting a set of managers who, individually, will turn out to be superior performers.

---

[5] Eugene Fama, "Efficient Capital Markets: A Review of Theory and Empirical Work," *Journal of Finance,* vol. 25 (May 1970) pp. 393–417.

In the absence of demonstrated stock selection, market timing or other active management skills, and confidence in their persistence, passive management should be favored by a rational equity investor who prefers more wealth to less and who is normally risk-averse, since higher levels of risk-taking require higher levels of expected return and vice-versa. If the skill is not there, active management will simply incur higher costs without producing a compensating return. In addition, the typical actively-managed portfolio is more risky than a passive portfolio because uncompensated risk is being taken which could have been diversified away.

Since investors in the aggregate can not earn more return than the market itself produces, the stock market is said to be a "zero sum game." When one investor wins relative to the market, some other investor must have lost. In this sense, investors in the aggregate cannot have stock selection skill and, therefore, the average active investor should expect to lose relative to the market because the market does not incur management fees or transaction costs. With lower management fees and transaction costs, the passive portfolio should enjoy an advantage over the typical actively managed portfolio. How well the passive portfolio does relative to active management (i.e., what proportion of active managers will underperform the passive portfolio) depends on just how efficient the market is, on the size of the differential management fees and transaction costs, on how aggressively active portfolios are managed and over what time interval one chooses to measure the contest.

The Question of Market Efficiency

If an investor could routinely and consistently identify stocks which were underpriced and/or overpriced, he or she would regularly outperform the average active and passive investor. As long as this active investor maintained the secret of his or her success, he or she could continue to outperform. However, as soon as the secret became known, other investors would begin competing and the advantage would disappear. In a highly-developed, mature market there are few opportunities to identify and exploit insider information or to discover new ways to better evaluate publicly-available information. The net result of everyone trying to gain a performance advantage is to produce a market where existing prices tend to be fair prices. The stronger the competitive nature of the market, the more efficient the market will be. In the extreme, if the consensus expectation correctly discounts all information, stock prices will fluctuate randomly as they adjust to new information. Moreover, an upward trend in stock prices over time should be observed if earnings and dividends are upward-trending. If stock performance is a random walk about a trend, then actively managed portfolios will also exhibit this upward-trending characteristic over time.

The fact that active portfolios deliberately take on risk that can be diversified away will produce in any given year an outcome where some active portfolios (usually less than half) will outperform the market, even if the market is perfectly efficient. Of course, the winners will claim skill. Even over a succession of years, in an efficient market, some number of active portfolios can be expected to outperform the market every year. But, this would be expected to occur by chance. Tests of market efficiency have included examination of whether the proportion of actively managed portfolios which outperform the market over time is greater than the number one would expect to occur by chance alone. The results of such tests are discouraging for those who believe the U.S. equity market to be inefficient and, therefore, routinely "beatable" through the application of typical active management methods and skills.

Transaction Costs

An active portfolio manager who can identify "mispriced" stocks can only exploit that advantage by trading. Thus, the costs of acting on such information must be taken into account. These costs include not only the commission charged by the stock broker, but also the spread charged by the specialist for making a market in the stock. If a broker charges a $.125 per share commission on a $25 stock and the specialist employs a spread of 1/4 point, the transaction costs amount to a one-way minimum of 1.50 percent. In many cases the costs of trading will be even higher; for example, if the specialist employs a larger spread as in the case of an illiquid issue.

Management Fees

The fees for passive management are lower than for active management. A $20 million portfolio would typically incur an annual passive management fee of about 0.1 percent of market value, while a $20 million active portfolio will typically incur annual fees from 0.3–0.5 percent or more, depending primarily on the type of management organization employed. This is not a trivial difference for either the manager or the client to consider.

Risk-Return Considerations

Since active management incurs additional risk, compensating additional return beyond that required to cover higher fees and transaction costs is needed. In addition, since risk-averse investors demand to be compensated at an increasing rate for taking on additional risk, the size of the required gross compensating return level is again adjusted upwards. No such compensatory return requirements exist in the passive case.

We observe that higher management fees and higher transaction costs put the average active manager approximately 1 percentage point per annum behind the passive portfolio, assuming 25 percent sales turnover. In comparison, the additional return required to justify taking on the higher risk of active management is smaller. Given our estimate of the degree of risk aversion for the typical pension plan, for example, additional return in the area of 0.3 percent per annum is required to leave the plan as well off with an active as with a passive portfolio in terms of "utility." (This observation is based on our estimate that the average level of diversifiable risk found in institutionally managed portfolios reflects a residual standard error of 6 percentage points per annum.) In total, then, active management must generate at least 1.25 percentage points of gross additional return to break even with passive management. If turnover and/or risk is higher than found in the typical active portfolio case, then the required differential in return production will be greater than this 1.25 percentage point minimum.

Passive Management Performance

Between 1968 and 1977, according to the Becker Securities Funds Evaluation Service, the S&P 500 Index portfolio ranked on average in the 37th percentile of annual equity portfolio investment returns. In terms of cumulative ranking over the 1968–77 period, the S&P 500 Index portfolio was in the 17th percentile, which means that 83 percent of the managers surveyed failed to outperform the Index over this period. Because the survey permits additions to and deletions from the sample, the actual results of active management on a cumulative basis may be worse than those reported. The very interesting fact is that the S&P 500 Index portfolio improves its position as the time interval lengthens. Active managers are not consistently good or bad, year-to-year, and different portfolios come and go as better performers over time. Every year each manager must compete against the market where, on average, fewer than half will win. In the very long run, only a very few actively managed equity portfolios can hope to outperform the market if the market is reasonably efficient. Hence, the market portfolio will be an increasingly good performer over time.

MANAGING PASSIVE PORTFOLIOS

Choosing an Index

The original market-weighted index fund had as its performance benchmark the Standard and Poor's 500 Composite Stock Price Index.

This Index was selected because its composition includes almost 70 percent of the market value, on a capitalization-weighted basis, of all outstanding U.S. equity issues and because of the wide recognition accorded its movements as a standard of equity investment performance. Pragmatically, this Index provides a practical way to invest in a substantial portion of the capitalization-weighted equity market that is collectively owned by all investors and consists of approximately 5,000 exchange-listed and over-the-counter issues. Thus, the economics of the "zero-sum game" environment are captured in a form in which portfolio investment can be easily effected.

This form is also highly representative of aggregate institutional equity investment. Collectively, institutional market participants invest largely in the liquid sector of the total equity market generally represented by the S&P 500 Index. This can be seen in evidence compiled by the U.S. Comptroller of the Currency regarding domestic national bank trust departments and is illustrated in Figure 1.

Figure 1
Distribution of the Total Market Value of the S&P 500 Issues in the Composite Index versus Their Distribution in the Aggregate Bank Portfolio at Year-End 1976

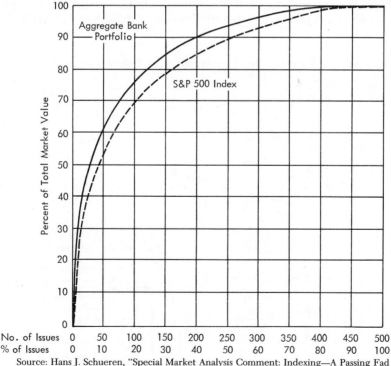

Source: Hans J. Schueren, "Special Market Analysis Comment: Indexing—A Passing Fad or an Evolving Trend?" Merrill Lynch, Pierce, Fenner & Smith, Inc., *Institutional Report* (July 1977).

Similar evidence involving insurance company equity portfolios is available. Thus, the S&P 500 Index can be considered as a good proxy for the market of stocks utilized in institutional portfolios. Any other index could, however, be used instead, depending on the characteristics desired. The larger the number of issues and the market value included in the index, the more representative of all stocks the sample will be.

Portfolio Construction—Duplication or Sampling?

Assume that the S&P 500 Index is chosen as the passive portfolio's benchmark. The operating objective is to duplicate as closely as possible the performance of the Index over any time period at the lowest possible cost to the investor. There are two general forms of portfolio construction employed in operating an index-matching fund; "full capitalization weighting" and "stratified Sampling." A choice must be made between them. Figure 2 shows the basic scheme of each approach for using the S&P 500 Index.

The *full capitalization weighting approach* is essentially a duplication of the actual S&P 500 Index construction. All S&P 500 issues, or as many as are deemed acceptable for investment purposes, are included and maintained in their respective market capitalization weightings,

Figure 2
Full Capitalization Weighting And Stratified Sampling Weighted Index Portfolios

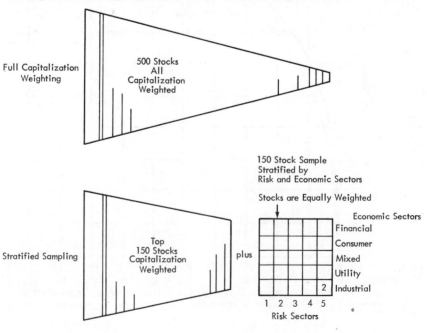

typically to the nearest round lot. The *stratified sampling approach* utilizes a smaller number of issues, typically a 200–300 issue sample of S&P issues, to track the performance of the Index. The sampling concept is to capture a significant portion of the market capitalization weight of the Index in a "core" portion which, in the illustration, comprises the largest 150 issues. These securities are maintained in their respective market weightings and represent perhaps 85 percent of the capitalization weight of the Index. The sampled portion of the portfolio will include a varying number of additional issues, depending generally on the asset size of the portfolio. The goal of the sampled portion is to reproduce the performance of those stocks in the Index which are not maintained in the core portion. The term *stratified* simply denotes the manner in which the stocks are grouped. The example in Figure 2 involves a 150-stock noncore sample stratified across five risk and economic sectors, which is the simplest way to reproduce that portion of the Index not captured in the core. Each stratified grouping, comprising a combination of one risk sector and one economic sector, is given a portfolio weight approximating the market capitalization weighting of that combination in the S&P 500 Index. Selection of issues for each grouping is not a random matter. Rather, after adjusting for the market capitalization weight of those issues held in the core portion, stocks are selected in descending order of capitalization weight to accommodate the capitalization requirement of each grouping and are typically equal-dollar-weighted in the portfolio. The diagram shows that after adjusting for the market capitalization weight of the core issues in the combination of risk sector 5, economic sector "Industrial," this noncore grouping will receive 2 percent of the portfolio's capitalization weight. The issues selected to populate this grouping will be those with the requisite general characteristics that also have the largest capitalization weights.

There are a number of important differences between these two basic approaches to the construction of passive portfolios. First and foremost, the full capitalization weighting approach tracks the performance of the Index with substantially better resolution than does any sampling approach. Since the use of the sampling technique naturally introduces divergence into the construction process, the sampled index portfolio will produce perhaps four times as large a tracking error (i.e., difference from the Index rate of return) as the full capitalization weighting approach.

There are at least five sources of tracking error associated with the operation of an index portfolio attempting to match the performance of the S&P 500. Of these, two are unique to the stratified sampling approach: the tracking error produced by the divergence discussed above, and that produced by the need for periodic portfolio rebalancing—both of which are inherent in the approach. The other three affect both approaches. First, the effect of recognizing monthly dividend income on the date each S&P stock goes "ex-dividend" (which, of course, is well before the payment is actually available for reinvestment) creates a cash drag that reduces fund performance relative to Index performance to the extent of the proportion of cash accrual to portfolio market value. Second, the brokerage cost of dividend reinvestment also represents a deduction from fund performance. Third, transaction costs associated with adjusting to changes in the composition of the Index itself represent another source of performance difference. Finally, if a "prudency screen" is utilized to provide a quality control element for the portfolio, the differences thus engendered in portfolio composition also create tracking error. These various sources of return deviation, index portfolio versus S&P 500, rank in severity in the following order: (1) sampling divergence; (2) cash drag effects; (3) rebalancing costs; (4) dividend reinvestment costs; and (5) prudency screen effects. Recent experience has shown that the magnitude of the tracking error resulting from sampling divergence can be as much as 150 basis points in a given year; the other effects are much less serious.

Table 1 illustrates the difference in tracking error that the two approaches produce. The first section of the table shows the monthly tracking results of the Wells Fargo Bank Index Fund (WFB) over the period January 1974–June 1975. During the period, the Fund employed a stratified sampling technique because its asset value was insufficient

Table 1
Comparison of Index Fund Management Methods Monthly Tracking Record

I. Period of Stratified Sampling*

Period	WFB Index Fund Return	S&P 500 Total Return	Return Difference
1974			
January	−0.89%	−0.84%	−.05%
February	0.07	0.03	+.04
March	−2.11	−2.00	−.11
April	−3.81	−3.73	−.08
May	−3.20	−2.92	−.28
June	−1.08	−1.10	+.02
July	−7.54	−7.58	+.04
August	−8.30	−8.52	+.22
September	−11.66	−11.70	+.04
October	16.22	16.69	−.47
November	−4.41	−4.45	+.04
December	−1.77	−1.80	+.03
1975			
January	12.60	12.47	+.13
February	6.56	6.70	−.14
March	2.14	2.23	−.09
April	4.67	4.88	−.21
May	4.92	5.07	−.15
June	4.50	4.65	−.15
Cumulative total return	2.80%	3.90%	−1.10%

Table 1 *(continued)*

II. Period of Full Capitalization-Weighting†

Period	WFB Index Fund Return	S&P 500 Total Return	Return Difference
1975			
July	−6.53%	−6.55%	+.02%
August	−1.51	−1.53	+.02
September	−3.24	−3.30	+.06
October	6.55	6.44	+.11
November	3.09	3.07	+.02
December	−0.92	−0.96	+.04
1976			
January	11.86	11.91	−.05
February	−0.59	−0.60	+.01
March	3.26	3.31	−.05
April	−0.94	−0.93	−.01
May	−0.76	−0.76	.00
June	4.30	4.33	−.03
July	−0.84	−0.71	−.13‡
August	0.16	0.14	+.02
September	2.41	2.43	−.02
October	−1.99	−2.02	+.03
November	−0.07	−0.06	−.01
December	5.41	5.44	−.03
1977			
January	−4.91	−4.91	.00
February	−1.49	−1.53	+.04
March	−1.26	−1.23	−.03
April	0.20	0.17	+.03
May	−1.52	−1.50	−.02
June	4.69	4.73	−.04
July	−1.52	−1.52	.00
August	−1.25	−1.26	+.01
September	−0.02	−0.04	+.02
October	−4.16	−4.15	.00
November	3.63	3.64	.01
December	0.58	0.55	+.03
1978			
January	−5.98	−5.99	+.01
February	−1.58	−1.59	+.01
March	2.67	2.69	−.02
April	8.74	8.76	−.02
May	1.35	1.35	.00
June	−1.62	−1.59	−0.3
July	5.67	5.68	−.01
August	3.35	3.36	−.01
Cumulative total return	25.13%	25.17%	−.04%

* Annual standard error (67 percent confidence) for period of stratified sampling: .47 percent.

† Annual standard error (67 percent confidence) for period of full capitalization weighting: .13 percent.

‡ In July .11 percent of the shortfall was incurred when the Index was revised to include the finance industry.

to attain full capitalization weighting. The second section provides the tracking results for July 1975–August 1978, the time period over which the Fund utilized the full capitalization weighting approach after having attained the size necessary for making the switch.

It is apparent that the Fund's monthly tracking errors (shown in the *Return Difference* column) are substantially smaller for the period of full capitalization weighting than for the earlier period of stratified sampling. The superiority of the full capitalization weighting approach is further evidenced through the standard error measurement, which shows the magnitude of the difference in the Fund's total return in relation to the return of the S&P 500 Index. The period of stratified sampling produced a one-standard-deviation estimate of .47 percent per annum from 18 monthly observations. This estimate indicates that 67 percent of the Fund's returns occurred within a range of ±.47 percent around the actual Index return, and that 95 percent of the returns occurred within a range of ±.94 percent of the Index return. The period of full capitalization weighting produced an annual standard error estimate of .13 percent from 38 monthly observations. Interestingly, if we remove the June 1976 observation, when S&P restructured the Index to include the finance industry, the estimated standard error falls to .10 percent per annum.

These results serve to illustrate the superiority of the full capitalization weighting strategy in achieving the operating objective of the fund. The goal of minimizing tracking error is extremely important because the magnitude of the error has a progressively increasing impact on investment results as the investment period lengthens. The following simulation demonstrates the effect of accepting increasing amounts of tracking error. The analysis was performed using return data on NYSE stocks for the period December 31, 1925–December 21, 1976. It illustrates the point that a sampled portfolio having the same average annual return as a fully-weighted portfolio will, because of tracking error, produce an inferior investment result over time. (Returns courtesy of Center for Research in Security Prices, University of Chicago.)

$1,000,000 invested December 31, 1925 proportionally by capitalization in NYSE stocks would have, on December 31, 1976, a value of:

 $50,552,000—with perfect tracking
 $50,276,000—with 1 percent additional return in even years
                   with 1 percent less return in odd years
 $49,554,000—With 2 percent additional return in even years
                   With 2 percent less return in odd years

Another difference between the two approaches is that stratified sampling will produce greater sales turnover than the full capitalization weighting approach. While the sampled portfolio must be rebalanced from time to time when cash inflows are insufficient to maintain the proper weightings, the full capitalization weighted portfolio remains automatically in proper balance. Considering trading liquidity, it is important to note that the construction of a full capitalization weighted portfolio maps directly into the natural liquidity of the marketplace. Since the contents of full capitalization weighted investment programs mirror the capitalization weighted image of the market, their total trading costs tend to be lower than those incurred in investing an equivalent amount of cash in a sampled portfolio. While a full capitalization weighted portfolio deploys the cash across the entire breadth of the Index, the sampled portfolio invests an equivalent amount of cash in a smaller number of issues. Thus, the larger individual trading lots required for a sampled portfolio's investment program exert greater pressure on stock prices. A good example of this occurs when the sampled approach requires purchase of a large block of a thinly-capitalized stock while the full capitalization weighted approach, requiring purchase of only a market-weighted position, perhaps utilizes only one or two hundred shares of the same issue.

The stratified sampling approach is, however, a less costly mode of operation for the manager than the full capitalization weighting approach. Since, on average, perhaps two hundred more issues are involved in each investment program and two hundred more dividends are collected quarterly, the internal costs of processing greater volumes of transactions for the full capitalization weighting approach must be absorbed by the managing institution. If the management fees charged to the investor are approximately the same, the manager utilizing the sampling approach will enjoy a wider operating margin even though, from the investor's standpoint, trading costs and tracking error considered, it is a more costly approach.

Trading Strategies

To understand and choose effective trading strategies for an Index-matching portfolio it is helpful to review the background of transactions and their associated costs in active as well as passive situations. The trading costs incurred in the normal course of value-added or active management stem from two sources: transaction costs and portfolio turnover. Active portfolio management depends upon the information content of its valuation process to produce portfolio trades. These trades are expected to help the manager "win." Specialists and market makers recognize that the information content of the trades in which they are asked to participate may be high enough to exert negative price pressures on their positions. They, therefore, introduce a spread based on position size and their assessment of the probable information content of the trade.

The cost of information-motivated transactions is divided into two

Figure 3
Transaction Costs

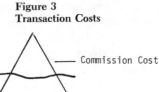

Total = 1.5 percent one-way.

parts. In Figure 3, the part of an individual trade depicted above the "water-line" is the visible commission cost. It is typically one-fifth the size of the additional cost that may be incurred through the market maker's spread, shown below the "water line." Estimates of typical one-way total transaction costs range from about .5–3 percent of transaction value. A reasonable single-point estimate derived from available studies would place the typical one-way transaction cost at about 1.5 percent.[6] The actual cost for a particular manager will generally depend upon the liquidity and block size of the stocks being traded and on the way the trades are packaged.

The trading motivation of a passive equity index fund is quite different than in the case of active management. The passive portfolio undertakes trades almost exclusively for "liquidity motivated" reasons. Not only is the specialist or market maker not exposed to information risk, but he usually deals in capitalization-weighted share quantities that reflect the natural liquidity of the marketplace as well. The liquidity motivation of the passive portfolio stems from the desire of the manager to acquire or sell pieces of the market portfolio with no regard for the relative valuation of any individual stock. Since the passive portfolio does not trade on particular information content of any kind, the market maker or specialist is not compelled to seek protection through introduction of a sizeable spread. He does, of course, continue to include a smaller spread to bear the risk of general market movements when taking a position with regard to the entire market.

In order to assess the total transaction costs involved in trading a capitalization weighted, S&P Index program of securities, we undertook a six-month analysis following the establishment of negotiated commission rates. The results of this analysis are shown in Figure 4. The test included 12 trading programs executed during the period

---

[6] Larry J. Cuneo and Wayne H. Wagner, "Reducing the Cost of Stock Trading," *Financial Analysts Journal* (November–December 1975), for example.

Figure 4
Index Fund Trading Costs Using Conventional Trading Methods

(*period of analysis* June to November, 1975—12 trading programs)

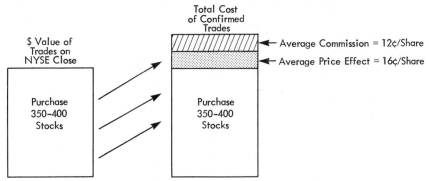

Total trading costs = 28¢ per share or .82 percent of contribution value.

of June–November 1975. Packages of 350–400 purchase orders were executed at the opening of the business day after being priced at the NYSE close of the prior day. The diagram demonstrates that the total transaction costs incurred in completing these trading programs averaged 28 cents per share or .82 percent of the value of the cash invested. Interestingly, the price effect or market maker's spread averaged 16 cents per share, which is quite consistent with the minimum pricing interval used by the brokerage community of ⅛ point or 12.5 cents for a liquid stock in the marketplace.

A variety of trading techniques are used by index fund managers, ranging from normal market order arrangements to "package" trading programs. The former technique is similar to conventional trading approaches; a package trading program (which may involve as many as 500 issues) is treated as if a single security transaction was being executed. Packaged programs may be executed by a broker on either a nonrisk basis or on an at-risk basis. The latter method involves the transfer of the price effect or market risk to the broker from the manager and, hence, from the investor, eliminating the price effect portion of the total transaction and leaving only the commission cost portion to be absorbed. While the commission cost is higher in such cases, the manager (and the investor) have, in effect, insured themselves against adverse short-term market moves during the period that the program is being executed. Figure 5 illustrates our experience in using the concept of the package program executed on an at-risk basis. Here, the purchase price of the package in each of 100 separate trading programs (involving 400–450 securities) was struck at the close of business on a designated day. The trades were actually executed on subsequent trading days at the risk of the selected broker. The cost of these package executions ranged from 8 to 12 cents per share and averaged

Figure 5
Index Fund Trading Costs Using Package Trading Procedure

Period of trading program experience: November 1975 to October 1978 (100 trading programs)

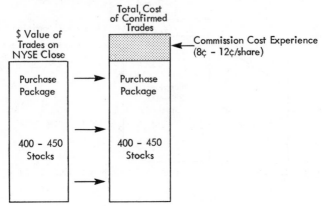

Total Trading Costs = 8¢ — 12¢ per share or .20 — .30 percent of contribution value.

an amount approximating 0.25 percent of the value of the invested cash.

Having established a basis for drawing comparisons between the trading costs of active and passive management strategies, the full effect of trading costs on expected portfolio return can be estimated by taking note of expected portfolio turnover. Conventionally-managed portfolio sales turnover averaged more than 30 percent per year in 1975–1976 before declining to 25 percent in 1977. Sales turnover rates for the WFB Index Fund are expected to be less than 1 percent per year. The resulting spread in incurred annual trading costs between these two forms of management is nearly .75 percent, assuming a 25 percent sales turnover level for an active account.

Trading Costs Comparison

Conventional equity portfolio sales turnover
  1977 .... 25.6%*
Total turnover
  Sales 25%
  Repurchases 25%
  Two-way .... 50% × 1.5% = Trading costs = .75%

Wells Fargo Bank Index Fund sales turnover
  1977 .... .07%
Total turnover
  Sales .... Less than 1%
  Repurchases .... Less than 1%
  Two-way .... Less than 2% × 0.25% = Trading Costs = .005%

  * Source: Becker Securities, Funds Evaluation Service, 1977. Courtesy of A. G. Becker Incorporated.

As can be seen from the illustration provided in footnote 7, a reasonable expected return estimate for the equity market at current levels is some 14 percent per year. Given this expected return, the effect of the differentially higher trading costs of active management can be evaluated:

Net Expected Return

	Index Fund (beta 1.0)	*Average Active Portfolio (beta 1.0)*
Expected return	14.00%	14.00%
Penalty for assuming diversifiable risk	—	−0.30
Trading costs	−0.005	−0.75
Management fee	−0.10	−0.30–0.50
Net expected return	13.89%	12.65–12.45%

After deducting the expected trading costs of each approach and their typical annual management fees, and the cost incurred from assuming (relative to market) diversifiable risk, it is clear that the average active manager must provide at least 1.25 percent per annum of added return to draw even with the passive approach.

The active-passive trade-off is further complicated by the fact that the typical active manager will underperform the average active manager. This means that choosing a manager at random carries with it less than a 50 percent chance that the manager's future results will be average or above. Just as individual stock returns are skewed to the left, so are stock portfolio returns skewed; the median, 50th percentile return will be below the average return. The limit on negative returns is (minus) 100 percent, but positive returns are not limited to (plus) 100 percent. One should expect the median portfolio to underperform the average portfolio by an estimated 20 to 30 basis points per year over time.

In retrospect, the economics of the marketplace as well as the published empirical evidence attest to the difficulty of outperforming the

---

[7] *Prospective return from U.S. Equity Market:*

Expected return equals current yield plus nominal growth assume:

Yield on market currently 5.5 percent
Expected inflation rate of 5 percent per year
Expected real growth of economy of 3.5 percent per year
Corporate America's share of GNP is static
Dividends grow proportionally with earnings

Then:

Expected return from equities will be 14.0 percent per year

$$(5.5 + 5.0 + 3.5 = 14.0)$$

Figure 6
Equities: Annualized Rates of Return for Periods Ending December 31, 1977

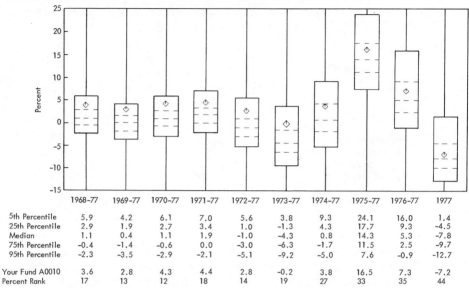

	1968–77	1969–77	1970–77	1971–77	1972–77	1973–77	1974–77	1975–77	1976–77	1977
5th Percentile	5.9	4.2	6.1	7.0	5.6	3.8	9.3	24.1	16.0	1.4
25th Percentile	2.9	1.9	2.7	3.4	1.0	-1.3	4.3	17.7	9.3	-4.5
Median	1.1	0.4	1.1	1.9	-1.0	-4.3	0.8	14.3	5.3	-7.8
75th Percentile	-0.4	-1.4	-0.6	0.0	-3.0	-6.3	-1.7	11.5	2.5	-9.7
95th Percentile	-2.3	-3.5	-2.9	-2.1	-5.1	-9.2	-5.0	7.6	-0.9	-12.7
Your Fund A0010	3.6	2.8	4.3	4.4	2.8	-0.2	3.8	16.5	7.3	-7.2
Percent Rank	17	13	12	18	14	19	27	33	35	44

Source: Becker Securities, Funds Evaluation Service, 1977. Courtesy of A. G. Becker Incorporated.

S&P 500 Index by the required amount. Figure 6 provides the range of annualized equity portfolio performance results for approximately 3,000 funds. The measurements were made for one- to ten-year cumulative periods ending December 31, 1977. The range of results is divided into quartile and other groupings, and the diamond-shaped figures denote the position of the S&P 500 Index performance result within that range. The percentile ranking of the S&P 500 within this range is provided in the row labeled "Percent Rank." Over the one-, five-, and ten-year periods shown, the annualized rate of total return of the median actively-managed equity portfolio underperformed the S&P 500 Index by a minimum of 0.6 percent and a maximum of 4.1 percent; in no year was there a positive difference in favor of the median active portfolio. In both the five- and ten-year periods, the S&P 500 outperformed more than 80 percent of the sample of some 3,000 portfolios.

Pooled versus Individual Portfolios

Passive equity portfolios are currently managed on either a pooled or an individual basis. The pooled approach provides several economies of scale to the investor that are unavailable on an individually invested basis. First, pooling enables a group of investors who, individually, would be unable to fund a full capitalization weighting portfolio approach, to avail themselves of the economic benefits of that approach at extremely low cost. Second, the combined cashflows of pooled participants create other cost-saving opportunities. As the dollar value of index fund investment programs increases, the transaction costs incurred as a percentage of the cash invested tends to decrease. This occurs generally because of cost economies available to the brokerage community in processing larger, as compared with smaller, share volume. In addition, when individual S&P 500 issues from an existing equity portfolio can be made available to an index fund for direct transfer, a significant portion of a total contribution may be absorbed "in kind" without incurring any transaction costs at all. (An "in-kind" transaction is effected with stock instead of cash, obviating any need to buy the issues involved.) Wells Fargo's experience over the past five years has been that between 35 percent and 70 percent of the dollar value of an existing equity portfolio presented for conversion to index fund participation can be accommodated through the in-kind transfer process. In fact, the pooled fund approach to indexing maximizes the proportion of an existing equity portfolio's value that can be accommodated in-kind, vis-a-vis the "stand-alone" index fund alternative. When the cash flow associated with a pooled index fund is combined with an existing equity portfolio, the larger total amount available for investment increases the purchase requirements for each stock in the index fund over what it would otherwise have been. This means that more shares of the existing equity portfolio can be accepted into the index fund through in-kind transfer. The size of this transfer is substantially greater than would be possible if a new stand-alone index fund was being created from the same existing-portfolio securities, absent the pooled fund's cash flow. In addition, the existence of cash inflows to the pooled portfolio may assist investors in incurring minimal transaction costs in exiting the fund.

In our view, there is no real economic reason to recommend a separate index portfolio vs. the pooled alternative. Two noneconomic reasons for individual or stand-alone portfolios may be encountered, however. First, the inventory fund concept requires the creation of an individual portfolio since legal considerations preclude the use of a pooled portfolio with multiple participants for this purpose. In addition, certain investors have a definite aversion to individual companies, types of companies, and even whole industries. If such issues must be dropped from the index being matched, then an individual portfolio excluding them is a necessity.

PASSIVE EQUITY MANAGEMENT STRATEGIES

Core-Noncore (Passive-Active) Portfolios

It is common in the case of large pension plans to hire a number of equity managers. Each manager, within a set of generally broad guidelines, is free to pursue an equity investment strategy. Each manager, usually implicitly, chooses a portfolio beta and a level of diversifiable risk (i.e., the risk associated with stock selection) for her or his individual piece of the whole. In the context of the total pension plan equity commitment, the aggregate portfolio beta is a weighted average of the individual portfolio betas. However, the level of diversification of the total equity portfolio is lower than the average of the individual portfolios because, collectively, the managers cancel out one another's positions to some extent. In many cases, the total portfolios of large multiple-manager pension plans resemble "closet" index funds. Unfortunately, because of higher management fees and trading costs, their performance will very likely fall short of that produced by a real index fund.

In addition, because managers tend to view their individual portfolios on a stand-alone basis, they introduce a conservative bias by overdiversifying their portfolios relative to the investment opportunities they perceive. Limitations on the size of holdings—by issue, industry, or market sector—and other constraints are common. In protecting the portfolio (as well as reducing personal business risk), the manager often fails to take full advantage of stock selection or other value-related judgments. In general, in multiple-manager plans, each manager individually could substantially increase the level of diversifiable risk in a separate portfolio with only a moderate increase in risk for the portfolio as a whole.

In this context, a passive portfolio can be useful not only in managing the risk of the equity portion of the asset base and in reducing overall management and trading costs, but also in providing active managers with a larger opportunity to more fully exploit their management skills. The idea is to establish a "core" passive portfolio as an addition to the manager set. The active portfolios would then represent the "noncore" position. The balance between the core and noncore portions would be specified, and the active managers instructed as to the desirable level of portfolio beta, the range of portfolio beta and the minimum and maximum levels of diversification to be attained. The set of portfolios then work in harmony, anchored by the passive portion, in compliance with the sponsor's plan objectives and goals.

How Much Passive Management?

A decision must be made as to the "optimal" size of the core portfolio. The critical inputs are judgments regarding the ability of the active managers to provide additional net return over the passive rate of return, and judgments regarding the client's risk-aversion and investment-planning horizon.

A typical pattern of core-noncore use which maximizes client satis-

Figure 7
Active-Passive Decision

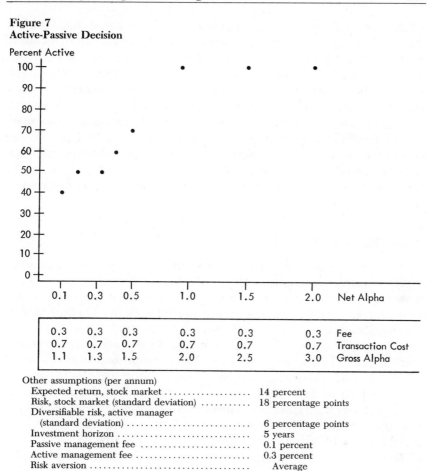

Percent Active

	0.3	0.3	0.3	0.3	0.3		0.3	Fee
0.7	0.7	0.7	0.7	0.7		0.7	Transaction Cost
1.1	1.3	1.5	2.0	2.5		3.0	Gross Alpha

Other assumptions (per annum)
Expected return, stock market .... 14 percent
Risk, stock market (standard deviation) .... 18 percentage points
Diversifiable risk, active manager
  (standard deviation) .... 6 percentage points
Investment horizon .... 5 years
Passive management fee .... 0.1 percent
Active management fee .... 0.3 percent
Risk aversion .... Average

faction is presented in the Figure 7. The optimal core-noncore balance is reported as "percent active" (rounded to the nearest 10 percent). The determination of the optimal core-noncore split is based on an application of modern portfolio theory, where estimates of return, risk, and client risk-aversion are employed in a Markowitz-type mean-variance model. The assumptions used in the analysis are listed. Given a net additional return (net alpha) of 0.5 percent per annum, the optimal size would be 70 percent active and 30 percent passive. Several important conclusions result from our work in this area. First, there is economic justification for mixing active and passive management under realistic sets of assumptions. Second, if a plan sponsor confidently expected to receive an additional net return from active management of more than 1 percentage point per annum, use of the passive alternative would generally not be warranted, assuming typical levels of diversifiable risk. Of course, if the expectation is that active management may not produce an additional net return, the economic conclusion would be that the entire equity portfolio should be managed passively. As noted earlier, the typical active manager can be expected to underperform the market while incurring higher risk. Moreover, if the stock market is reasonably efficient, it will be quite difficult for pension plan sponsors to identify and engage, in advance, that group of active managers who can be expected to consistently outperform by 1 percentage point or more per annum. Neither extreme is probably the right answer. Pragmatically, if the active managers can add as little as 0.1 percent net, then the solution calls for some inclusion of active management.

Asset Allocation Assistance

The single most important decision made in managing an institutional investment portfolio is the mix between alternative asset classes, principally stocks and bonds. Where changes in the mix employ timing procedures, use of a passive equity portfolio as the trading vehicle can significantly enhance performance. Large trading programs can very quickly move into and out of equities at a fraction of conventional trading costs. Importantly, this can be accomplished with no effect whatsoever on the existing actively-managed portfolios. Use of companion short-term and fixed-income funds in the hands of the passive manager can cover both sides of the mix change routinely. Thus, the passive manager can act as a balancing manager for the plan, efficiently adjusting the mix without interfering with any other manager.

To the extent the plan sponsor desires, the existing group of active managers can have a say in the asset mix decision. Or a special advisor can be hired to manage the asset mix decision. The special advisor may or may not be the organization that actually manages the passive portfolio.

Market Inventory Fund

The passive equity index fund is recognized as a significant development in the process of investment management. Both the economic value and the utility of the concept have been proven through operational experience and realized results. Encouraged by this, there has been a recent application of some of the elements of the passive equity index fund concept in a new form: the *market inventory fund*. This application combines some of the diversification and cost effectiveness associated with a standard index fund with the capacity to fulfill a market-making function among a group of affiliated active-equity managers.

The market inventory fund is generally an S&P 500 form of index fund which can, within limits, accommodate the trades of a pension plan's multiple-manager equity portfolio. The purpose of a market inventory fund is to act as an intermediary between active managers in order to eliminate situations where different managers purchase and sell the same stocks through an outside market maker during a quarterly time period. Long and short positions are created in the market inventory fund in relation to the composition of the S&P 500 Index in order that the portfolio can accept the sales of S&P 500 issues or fill the purchasing needs of the active managers in those issues. The importance of this concept is that the trading costs normally incurred when an active manager executes a transaction with an outside market maker can be completely eliminated in these specific situations. The impact of the concept on overall pension plan equity investment operations is two-fold. First, operating cost reductions are expected to occur since redundant trades are crossed within the plan's system, thereby eliminating the need to utilize the services of an outside broker or market maker. Second, since the trading costs incurred by the liquidity-motivated index fund are much smaller than those involved in information-motivated active management, the passive vehicle provides a more economically effective approach to clearing and resupplying the multiple manager system, as long as the brokerage community views inventory trading as being passive in nature. The market inventory fund is designed specifically to reduce turnover and trading costs within the system while delivering total return relative to the S&P 500 Index within a desired range of performance limits.

From a technical viewpoint, the market inventory fund concept appears to be a viable approach to reducing the costs of a pension plan's equity management activities. More study should be given to a possible problem, however, regarding the effect of information-motivated trades within the system since these trades may tend to produce results which are the reverse of those desired. Since active managers are engaged for their ability to employ special investment insights in their management activities, the presence of a sale (or purchase) order should generally indicate that the issue is expected to decline (or rise) in value following the transaction. The market inventory fund becomes underdiversified relative to the S&P 500 Index in order to accommodate these trades by taking positions while awaiting possible internal crossing transactions. Since the price impact stemming from the information content of these transactions will tend to force the value of the passive portfolio's long positions down and of its short positions upward, the process may result in negative bias to the tracking error for the portfolio or, more directly, financial losses for the total pension plan that could have been avoided. To the extent that the manager initiating a trade really has valuable information concerning the issue involved, failure to add (or subtract) the issue to (or from) the portfolio negates the value of the information to the fund.

The potential cost savings from a market inventory fund depend primarily upon the frequency with which active trades can be internally crossed through the plan's system. To date, there has been little published verification of the volume of such trades actually experienced by plans employing a market inventory fund. Moreover, the cost saving aspect depends upon the ability of market inventory funds to command the preferential transaction cost treatment normally accorded only to liquidity-motivated index fund trades. To the extent that information-motivated trades overflow the fund's capacity to inventory the issues involved, they may well be seen to be information-motivated trades in selected issues. It would be only logical to expect that at some point the brokerage community may refuse to accord the preferential treatment and, hence, cease to offer the cost savings by introducing trading spreads approximating those normally associated with the information-motivated trades of active management.

Other Passive Possibilities

The use of passive strategies need not be confined to domestic equity investment alone. Indeed, several managers have already extended the concept to the bond market and have also worked out management techniques for passive investment in the major foreign equity markets. Several closed-end real estate funds, passive once they are formed, also exist. In addition, strategies that utilize options written against passive equity portfolios are being discussed. In fact, there is no conceptual reason why any area of portfolio investment strategy should not be considered for application of passive portfolios. Such portfolios could be "yield-tilted" or "growth-tilted," for example, or take any one of a number of alternative forms—the concept is there, it works, and it lends itself to innovative utilization.

Chapter 9

Management of Bond Portfolios

H. RUSSELL FOGLER

Capital Market Consultant
Frank Russell Company
Tacoma, Washington
and
College of Business Administration, University of Florida
Gainesville, Florida

EVOLUTION AND THE MULTIPERIOD PROBLEM— AN OVERVIEW

Bond management has evolved greatly since the "100-year maturities and noncallable . . ." bonds of the late 1800s (Homer [17]).* In contrast to interest rates of 3–5 percent then, today's rates approach 8–10 percent. Undoubtedly, these high rates—versus the bleak 2.5 percent return of common stocks during 1966–77—are a major factor in the rise of active bond management. Active bond management implies both bond investment, as well as trading bonds whenever additional return can be obtained. The possibilities for both higher and lower return are well illustrated by Figure 1 which presents the results of bond portfolios of 78 banks during the period October 1970–December 1976, sketched on a volatility spectrum ranging from short liquid government securities (three-month U.S. Treasury Bills) versus the Salomon Brothers Long Term Corporate Bond Index.

Yet, despite active bond management, no comprehensive theory has evolved. In contrast to the fashionable speech of equity managers (e.g., "capital market theory," "mean-variance efficient portfolios," "minimal residual errors," etc.), bond managers only discuss "trading

---

* Numbers in brackets refer to References at end of chapter.

Figure 1
Returns of Bank Bond Portfolios, October 1970–December 1976

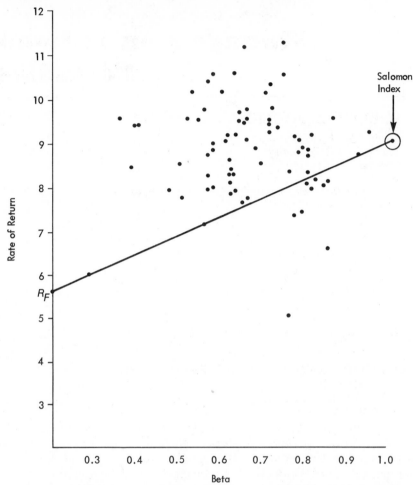

Note: Data contributed by Frank Russell Co. Volatility is calculated as the beta coefficient of each portfolio's return when compared to the return of the Salomon Brothers Long Term Corporate Bond Index.

strategies." *Why isn't there a theory?* One possible answer might be that bond returns (not yields) can be treated like stock returns, and thus bonds should be considered like stocks in capital market theory. Yet bonds are linked to interest rates, and thus the above answer is too simple; i.e., bond prices decline with stocks during inflation as interest rates rise, while they rise during depression offsetting stock returns. Another answer to why no theory has emerged may be that "there is a theory and it's the simple traditional one—viz., bonds are bought to meet fixed payments due at a future data." While such an answer is true, as well as elegant in its simplicity, unless the payments are in *nominal* dollars, inflation is a constant risk as evidenced by the tremendous growth in future pension fund obligations which are indexed to workers' pay scales in the final years of their employment.

Rather than the above two answers, the lack of bond portfolio theory is probably due to our present mathematical limitations—let me give a simple explanation, and then we will begin on practical state-of-the-art management approaches. If interest rates rise, and correspondingly bond prices fall this period, then the expected nominal return (yields) for next period will be higher. Thus, are we better off or worse off as a result of the interest rate rise? The answer is that "it depends on when you need to be liquid, now or later, and whether your payments vary with interest rates." This multiperiod aspect of the problem introduces interesting mathematical complexities (which are assumed away in stock-pricing models by assumptions of independence for future returns and the same time horizon for all investors). Yet, this multiperiod problem is at the heart of both management and performance measurement of bond portfolios.

The implications of the multiperiod impacts will be seen as this chapter proceeds from basic concepts (strategies, types of risk) to the more recent and advanced concepts (duration, immunization). These multiperiod impacts will be handled by three fundamental concepts: (1) the benchmark yield curve, (2) balance sheet risk, and (3) the juxtaposition of price versus reinvestment risk. Finally, near the end of the chapter, a review of the major empirical studies will be undertaken.

MANAGEMENT STRATEGIES

The Benchmark Yield Curve

Figure 2(A) illustrates a curve which plots two quantities: yield to maturity (vertical axis) versus maturity. Such a relationship is called the "yield curve." A *benchmark yield curve* is a yield curve against which all other yields will be compared. Thus, its relevance is whether it provides an easy, and generally accepted, standard for comparison. For example, the yield curve for all U.S. government securities might provide an appropriate benchmark since it provides a proxy for the time (i.e., multiperiod) cost of default-free money; however, constructing such a curve for current market rates would require some adjustment for bonds whose coupons (promised rate of interest payments) were different than the market (see "Interest Rate Anticipation" below, as well as the section on "Empirical Studies" and the Appendix, for some more technical aspects of yield curves and bond pricing). The *value of such a curve is that the additional return from each type*

Figure 2
Benchmark Yield Curve

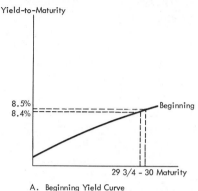

A. Beginning Yield Curve

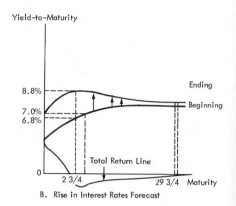

B. Rise in Interest Rates Forecast

of management strategy is seen as a special case caused by a change in some previous relationship to the curve.

The Expected Return—The Starting Point

Because so many managers are trying to buy and sell at the most favorable price, today's yields might be expected to reflect all information about supply and demand. If this were so, then a manager who buys a bond would expect his or her total return to reflect today's yield curve. Thus total return (R) would be equal to: (1) coupon income (C), (2) amortization (A) of premium or discount, and (3) repricing because of a higher or lower yield to maturity on the yield curve as the bond ages (slope effect), which has been coined the "roll effect" by Leibowitz [24]. Because coupon income (C) and amortization (A) are the components of yield to maturity (YTM), then

$$R = YTM + ROLL = C + A + \text{Roll}$$

For example, from Figure 2(A), the 30-year bond would have had a yield to maturity of 8.5 percent at the beginning of the period and 8.4 percent at the end of the period. If the bond had an 8 percent coupon, then over a horizon of one quarter:

Beginning price at 8.5 percent for 30 years = 94.60%
Ending price at 8.5 percent for 29.75 years = 94.59
Ending price at 8.4 percent for 29.75 years = 95.63
8 percent Coupon payment accrued   = 2.00%

Thus,

$$C = \frac{\text{Coupon Accrual}}{\text{Beginning Price}} = \frac{2.00}{94.60} = .0211$$

$$A = \frac{\text{Price Change on Level Curve}}{\text{Beginning Price}} = \frac{-.01}{94.60} = -.0001$$

$$ROLL = \frac{\text{Price Change Due to Slope}}{\text{Beginning Price}} = \frac{1.04}{94.60} = .0110$$

so that total return is[1]

$$R = .0211 - .0001 + .0110 = 3.20 \text{ percent}$$

Interest Rate Anticipation

One type of strategy to earn additional return is interest rate anticipation. This type of management strategy relies on the volatility characteristics of bonds:

1. *Bond prices are inversely related to the interest rate and depend upon the coupon rate.* If the market rate of interest *(i)* is equal to the coupon rate, then the bond will trade at its principal value. If the coupon rate is less than the market rate, the bond will trade at discount; conversely, the bond will trade at a premium if the market rate is lower than the coupon rate.
2. *The longer the maturity of the bond, the greater the price volatility* for a given change in the market rate.
3. *The volatility of a bond's price will increase, but at a diminishing rate, as the maturity is lengthened.* In fact, this nonlinearity is partially responsible for current curiosity about the concept of a bond's "duration" (to be discussed shortly), which is linear to price volatility, as well as incorporating the impact of coupon on price volatility.
4. *The volatility of a bond's price is inversely related to coupon,* for any given change in the market rate and for similar maturity bonds. This property is the feature that makes low coupon bonds (deep discounts) attractive for trading purposes if interest rate movements can be forecast.
5. *Bond price changes are not symmetrical against interest rate changes.* A decrease in the market rate of interest will increase

---

[1] Several questions may occur. First, the *C* and *A* effects add to 2.1, which is slightly less than one-fourth of 8.5 percent; this result is due to both rounding and the low amortization (noted below). Note that the amortization of the discount is not sufficient to offset the fact that, at 30 years even, the $4 coupon payment is made whereas, at 29¾ years, the coupon payment is three months away discounted at 8.5 percent. Also, the 1.1 percent roll effect is because of the hypothetical example of a slope change from 8.5 percent to 8.4 percent; in reality, such a large change would be unlikely for long maturities.

bond prices more than an equivalent increase in the rate will lower the prices.

These characteristics are explained further in Homer and Leibowitz [18], as well as being derived as theorems in a clear and concise mathematical form in Malkiel [26]; they can also be quickly verified with either a calculator or a yield book.

The above characteristics, plus a forecast of interest rates, is the basis for a strategy of interest rate anticipation. For example, let us assume that you forecast a rise in interest rates, as shown in the top two curves of Figure 2(B). Further, let us assume that you make a comparison between the previously considered 30-year 8 percent bond versus a three-year 8 percent bond.

	3-Year	30-Year
Beginning Yield (maturity 3, 30)	7.0	8.5
Beginning Yield (maturity 2¾, 29¾)	6.8	8.4
Ending Yield (maturity 2¾, 29¾)	8.8	8.7
Beginning Prices	102.66	94.60
Ending Prices (7.0 percent, 8.5 percent)	102.45	94.59
Ending Prices (6.8 percent, 9.4 percent)	102.95	95.63
Ending Prices (8.8 percent, 8.7 percent)	98.06	92.57
8 Percent Coupon Payment Accrued	2.00	2.00

Then,

$$C = \frac{\text{Coupon Accrual}}{\text{Beginning Price}} = \qquad .0195 \qquad .0211$$

$$A = \frac{\text{Price Change on Level Curve}}{\text{Beginning Price}} = \qquad -.0020 \qquad -.0001$$

$$ROLL = \frac{\text{Price Change Due to Slope}}{\text{Beginning Price}} = \qquad .0048 \qquad .0110$$

$$INT = \frac{\text{Price Change Due to Interest Shift}}{\text{Beginning Price}} = -.0476 \qquad -.0323$$

$$R = \frac{\text{Price Change and Coupon}}{\text{Beginning Price}} = \qquad -.0253 \qquad -.0003$$

Thus, the total return of each bond can now be viewed as

$$
R = \overbrace{C + A + ROLL}^{\text{Expected}} + \overbrace{INT}^{\text{Forecast}}
$$

where *INT* for the 3-year bond, for example, was calculated as $(98.06 - 102.95) \div 102.66$.

Based upon the above forecast, it would be desirable to stay with the 30-year bond relative to the three-year. This is because, although you are forecasting a rise in interest rates, the shape of the curve is forecasted to change such that intermediates will be hurt more than many longer bonds. How much you shift toward the 30-year maturity range would depend upon your confidence about your forecast, as well as the degree or risk aversion you or your client have for incorrect forecasts. Also, you might have chosen other maturities based upon either your liabilities or other considerations, and thus you might draw in a total return line such as at the bottom of Figure 2(B). Such a line would be calculated by performing the above analysis for many different maturities.

Sector-Quality-Coupon (SQC) Selection

As indicated in the section on the benchmark yield curve, the value of such a yield curve is that it allows you to examine each source of additional return from active management. The foregoing section showed two sources of return in addition to the expected return: viz., the negative return *(INT)* due to the rise in interest rates, as well as the additional return which active management could have earned by shifting toward the 30-year bond from the three-year bond. Now, the analysis will be extended to the concept of sector-quality-coupon selection.

The basic idea behind sector-quality-coupon selection *(SQC)* is that the yields vary by the corporate sector, quality rating, and coupon level of bonds. The yield spread for corporate sector is most likely a combination of both risk and the supply of issues (notice that the small supply of AA Railroads causes a very low yield, while the large supply of Utilities causes an opposite effect). Additionally, quality within a corporate sector is evaluated by various rating agencies such as Moody's, Standard and Poor's, and Fitch. The coupon effect is a result of both the differential tax on coupon income vs. capital gains, as well as the higher volatility of low coupon bonds (deep-discounts) during interest rate changes. Of course, both quality and coupon levels are along a continuous spectrum, but traders often create indexes based upon groups which have close characteristics (i.e., 4–4¼ percent Industrials, and so on).

Figure 3(A) shows a forecast which has two components: (1) a rise in interest rates; and (2) a narrowing of the sector-quality-coupon spread. The diagram uses the benchmark yield curve as the foundation on which the sector-quality-coupon spread is added. The hypothetical scenario is similar to relationships which often occur as interest rates for government securities rise when the Federal Reserve tightens money, but the rates on corporates rise less. In such a situation, the components of a bond's return can now be isolated by yield to maturity, roll, interest rate effect, and the change in the sector-quality-coupon

Figure 3
Sector-Quality-Coupon Analysis

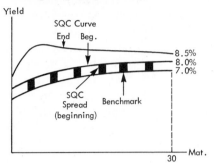

A. Benchmark plus SQC Spread

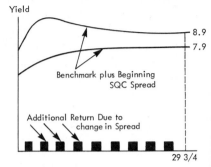

B. Interest Rate and SQC Effects

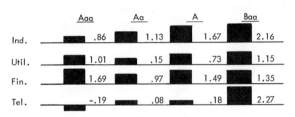

C. Return from Change in S/Q Spread – 1st Qtr. 1977

spread. To see how this is accomplished, as well as to show the impact of choosing the correct sector-quality-coupon category, the following analysis will look at the components of return for two 30-year 6 percent bonds, one being in the illustrated sector-quality-coupon category and one being in the benchmark category.

	SQC Category	*Benchmark Category*
Beginning Yield (30 years)	8.0%	7.0%
Beginning Yield (29¾ years)	7.9%	6.9%
Ending Yield of Benchmark Plus Beginning SQC Spread	8.9%	7.9%
Ending Yield of Benchmark Plus End SQC Spread	8.5%	7.9%
Beginning Prices	77.38	87.53
Ending Prices (8.0 percent, 7.0 percent)	77.41	87.55
Ending Prices (7.9 percent, 6.9 percent)	78.33	88.68
Ending Prices (8.9 percent, 7.9 percent)	69.84	78.33
Ending Prices (8.5 percent, 7.9 percent)	73.04	78.33
Coupon Accrual	1.50	1.50

Then,

$$C = \frac{\text{Coupon Accrual}}{\text{Beginning Price}} = \qquad .0194 \qquad .0171$$

$$A = \frac{\text{Price Change on Level Curve}}{\text{Beginning Price}} = \qquad .0004 \qquad .0002$$

$$ROLL = \frac{\text{Price Change Due to Slope}}{\text{Beginning Price}} = \qquad .0119 \qquad .0129$$

$$INT = \frac{\text{Price Change Due to Interest Shift}}{\text{Beginning Price}} = \qquad -.1097 \qquad -.1182$$

$$SQC = \frac{\text{Price Change Due to Spread Change}}{\text{Beginning Price}} = \qquad .0413 \qquad 0$$

$$R = \frac{\text{Price Change and Coupon}}{\text{Beginning Price}} = \qquad -.0367 \qquad -.0880$$

Thus, the total return of each bond can be viewed as

$$R = \overbrace{C + A + ROLL}^{\text{Expected}} + \overbrace{INT + SQC}^{\text{Forecasted}}$$

where SQC was calculated as the percentage price gain due to the spread narrowing—i.e., $(73.04 - 69.84) \div 77.38$.

Obviously, being in the right SQC-category bond can be profitable. In the above example, the correct choice would have resulted in a net gain of 5.13 percent. As can been seen, 0.85 percent occurred because of the lower overall price volatility, while 4.13 percent was due to be the favorable narrowing of the SQC yield spread. One way to view this result is shown in Figure 3(B), where the original SQC yield curve is shown with a corresponding yield curve if the spread had been constant, and the resultant return effect. The bottom of Figure 3(B) shows an approximately evenly-distributed return across maturities for the resultant change in the spread, and this has often been typical. While the foregoing example is fictitious, it should be realized that if correct selection is possible, gains of up to several percentage points are possible. For example, Figure 3(C) illustrates the average excess return by S-Q (but not coupon categories for bonds with over $50 million outstanding, compared against a benchmark of the U.S. government yield curve during the rise in interest rates during the first quarter of 1977.

As indicated earlier, one of the difficulties for practitioners has been the lack of a theory to date; yet, the basic ideas in trading strategy are becoming somewhat standardized, as can be seen by comparison of the above approach with Leibowitz's [24] approach for calculating sources of return (Figure 4). In his approach, for which computer pro-

Figure 4
Leibowitz's Approach to Yield Curve Analysis (sources of return)

Market Source	Components of Sector Return Model	Numerical Example	Major Risk Category
Yield Curve Accumulation Starting Yield Value at Associated Point on Yield Curve	Yield Curve Value	8.50%	
Sector Spread Accumulation Starting Sector Spread	+ Sector Spread	1.00	Rolling Yield 9.94%
Roll-Down Roll-Down the Yield Curve over the Horizon	+ (Horizon Volatility) × (Roll-Down in Sector Spread)	8.75 × 0.05 = 0.44	
Revaluation Expected Revaluation of Sector Leading to Change in Sector Spread Apart from Any Overall Market Movements	(Horizon Volatility) × (Revaluation in Sector Spread)	8.75 × 0.15 = 1.31	Revaluation 1.31%
Market Shift Overall Market Move	(Horizon Volatility) × (Market Shifts)	8.75 × 0.50 = 4.38	
Reshaping Yield Curve Reshaping Above and Beyond the Overall Market Move	(Incremental Reshaping Volatility) × (Market Shifts)	1.75 × 0.50 = 0.87	(Total Market Volatility) × (Market Shifts)
Sector Response Incremental Change in Sector Spread in Response to Overall Market Movement and Yield Curve Reshaping	(Incremental Sector Volatility) × (Market Shifts)	3.15 × 0.50 = 1.58	13.65 × 0.50 6.83%

Total Return 18.08%

Source: *Sources of Return in Corporate Bond Portfolios*, Martin L. Leibowitz, Solomon Brothers, 1978.

grams are available, three separate effects are considered: (1) rolling yield—which is equal to the previously discussed $C + A + ROLL$; (2) revaluation—which is any change in the SQC spread which is not related to shifts in the benchmark yield curve; and (3) total market volatility—which accounts for changes in the shape and level of the benchmark yield curve on the SQC yield curve, plus any additional changes in the SQC spread due to the changes in the benchmark yield curve. The first two measures require the investor to specify a horizon, and then the return volatility is calculated for each percentage point change in yield to maturity.

Swapping

In contrast to the above two strategies (interest rate anticipation and SQC selection) which concentrate on broad market movements, swapping strategies generally concentrate on highly specialized trading relationships. A commonly accepted method for classifying such swaps is Homer and Leibowitz's [18] four types: (1) pure yield pickup swap, (2) interest rate anticipation, (3) intermarket swap, and (4) substitution swap. Each of these types will be discussed below, but it is important to realize that the *expected return from any swap is usually based upon several motives not just one*—thus, these "types" of swaps are really just sources of return. Also, the first two of these swaps are often so related to portfolio policies or "styles" that labelling them as strategies seems more appropriate, and this has been done in this text as discussed below.

The *pure yield pickup swap* is similar to the analysis performed in the above section entitled "The Expected Return—The Starting Point." Basically, two bonds are examined to establish their difference in yield-to-maturity and roll, with a further adjustment to consider the impact of interim reinvestment of coupons at an assumed rate or return between now and the horizon date. Thus, such a trade merely requires selling the bond with the lower combination of yield to maturity-roll-and-reinvestment income, for purchase of the higher yield bond. This type of analysis does not consider any impact from changes in the level of interests rates overall, and it assumes that interim price volatility is not a consideration. In practice, unless there is some "free-lunch" aspect, one would assume some type additional risk must be taken on.[2]

---

[2] Obviously, this statement is founded in the *efficient market hypothesis*, which states that in a market with many smart traders, all looking for the best possible risk-return relationships, securities will be fairly and full priced. However, the markets need not be *perfect* in the sense of freely available information. Thus, some traders might have better and quicker information processing, thereby allowing them a gain (of course, if the market is efficient, then the extra gain would just provide them a fair return for their investment in the better information system). Another possibility is that there

The *interest rate anticipation swap* is the same as the example given in the above section entitled "Interest Rate Anticipation," where a 2.5 percent gain could be achieved by switching into the 30-year bond from the three-year bond. Basically, such a trade is precipitated by a forecasted change in the overall (benchmark) interest rates. As with the pure yield pickup, it seems reasonable to ask about the free-lunch possibilities. After all, if everybody forecasts a rise in rates, everybody will be trying to dump long-term bonds for short-terms, and therefore prices would be expected to adjust quickly enough to eliminate unwarranted profits. In fact, this type of logic is the basis for the *pure expectations theory* of the term structure discussed later in this chapter. Yet, it is interesting to notice that at least one market participant, and a large one at that, might be willing to go against the market; such a participant would be the Federal Reserve if it were trying to drain liquidity from the system by forcing short-term interest rates up and selling short-term bonds. Of course, it is only conjecture as to whether trading against the Federal Reserve would provide any significant return, but it is an interesting question.

In contrast to the above two swaps, which are really management strategies based upon overall market relationships, the *intermarket swap* works on trading between SQC categories, based upon a forecasted change in the yield spread between two different categories. This is similar to the "Sector-Quality-Coupon Selection" discussion, although that explanation was combined with an interest rate shift and the other sector was the benchmark sector. To see how this works, assume the yield spread were 25 basis points between AA-Industrial-High Coupons versus AAA-Industrial-High Coupons; if this spread were expected to widen, then the trader would swap from the AAs to the AAAs now, and then back to the AAs when the wider spread had occurred. During the widening of the spread, the prices of the AAs would decline *relative* to the AAAs, thereby providing a price gain via the swapping. How does one forecast such changes in the spreads? The most common forecasting method is to observe historical yield spreads at various points in the interest rate cycle, and then to adjust for current supply-and-demand effects. However, this is most difficult, as shown by the 1977–78 period of extremely narrow spreads between AAAs and U.S. government issues; many managers bought government issues early in 1977 expecting the spread to widen, only to have to

---

are not price takers at every price, as specified in a perfect market; such a case might arise when Property and Casualty Insurer's experience a catastrophe and must liquidate some of their bond portfolio. However, even in such a liquidation, this might be looked at as a sudden and temporary shift in the supply curve, with a corresponding temporary shift in the return (price)-risk relationship; admittedly, in such a situation, the temporary nature of the shift would be advantageous for institutions which had the ability to buy the bonds and assume the risk, although in a sense they are being given extra returns for providing liquidity, much as specialists on stock exchanges.

sit on their position through the next 18 months as both inflation and government spending continued unabated.

Finally, the fourth type of swap, the *substitution swap*, attempts to profit from a change in the yield spread between two nearly identical bonds. The logic of this type of swap is similar to the intermarket swap, except that the trade is based upon a forecast change in the yield spread between the two nearly identical bonds. The bonds could be issued by the same company, but with slightly different maturities and similar coupons; or the bonds could be between two different companies in the same SQC category. The forecast is generally based upon the past history of the yield spread relationship between the two bonds, with the assumption that any aberration from the past relationship is temporary, thereby allowing profit by buying the bond with the lower (higher) yield if the spread is to widen (narrow); this trade is later reversed leaving you in the original position, but with a trading profit from the relative changes in prices.

Economic and Credit Analysis

Rather than trying to forecast changes in market interest rate levels and yields spreads, economic and credit analysis examines the issuer's economic fundamentals (i.e., industry forecast, earnings projections, cost relationships and trends, financial ratios, variability of relationships, and so on). The purpose is to detect changes in the credit or bankruptcy risk of an issuer. For example, if the issuer's cost relationships were improving because of market share gains, and the bonds continued to trade at the historical spreads relative to other bonds, you might purchase the bond in anticipation of its price rising relative to other bonds as the market discovers that its risk has changed.

Can changes in a company's risk be picked up by economic analysis? The answer appears to be yes, based on studies indicating that changes in quality ratings are often preceded by the corresponding price (yield) change. Also, some interesting evidence exists for the ability of certain statistical techniques as prognosticators of rating changes. These studies will be discussed in the final section of this chapter, but now let's turn to the last type of strategy.

Maturity Structure Strategies

This type of strategy is mainly of theoretical interest at this stage. Several mathematical analyses, appearing in academic journals, have suggested that a "dumbbell" (i.e., shortest and longest bonds only) maturity strategy may provide the best risk-return trade-off, versus a more even distribution of securities. As with all strategies, a skeptic must question the free-lunch which is suggested, and such questioning has produced little concrete evidence in favor of a specific maturity strategy, unless a specific set of contractually fixed liabilities are to be paid in the future. The results of such questioning will be presented in the last part of this chapter, and the impact of future liabilities will be discussed throughout several of the sections beginning below with the topic of risk.

OBJECTIVES AND RISK

A Balance Sheet Approach

"WHAT IS RISK?" should be the first question for bond portfolio management. (For example, remember the earlier example about rising interest rates causing prices to drop, thereby raising future income from coupon reinvestment!) The strategies in the previous section were all trying to win additional return, but with little discussion of risk. Further, discussions with portfolio managers and corporate clients often uncover quite diverse and imprecise notions of risk. This void is especially troublesome when one is attempting to design a performance measurement system, since such measurement implicitly assumes risk-adjusted comparison between bond managers. But, of course, such confusion is to be expected in the absence of a comprehensive theory for bond management, and thus it is our task to clarify at least the separate elements of risk.

The approach presented here is to begin with the broadest view possible, before narrowing to more accepted doctrines. This approach is best presented by the hierarchial diagram in Figure 5.

Why take such an academic overview? Precisely because too narrow a focus leads to poorly-defined objectives for the portfolio manager. For example, what is the risk of bonds for a pension fund portfolio? Can this be answered without knowing if common stocks are also held?

Figure 5

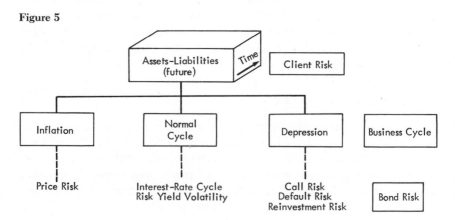

Whether the employee benefits are indexed to the CPI? Whether during a depression, salaries and final benefits decline? Should the pension fund's bonds be invested like a life insurance company's since they both have a long horizon—even though life contrasts are in fixed nominal dollars? Is the risk the same as for a bank's portfolio which liquidates its portfolio to make loans when interest rates are high? Thus, although it is not common practice yet, greater emphasis should be given to the *covariance* (i.e., the tendency to vary together) between the bond portfolio and other cash flows (i.e., future assets and liabilities) of the client. Without such broad analysis, how can a client specify how extra return should be obtained—certainly, incorrect interest rate timing might contain much greater or less risk than an incorrect forecast of yield spreads. The implications of this approach will become clearer later in this chapter when the concept of immunization is discussed. However, now the more standard classifications will be discussed.

Price Volatility

When interest rates rise, the prices of outstanding bonds fall. As indicated in the section on "Interest Rate Anticipation," the longer the maturity and the lower the coupon, the greater will be the price volatility for interest rate changes.

Whether price risk is important to the client depends on two factors: (1) the need for liquidity and (2) whether the client's future liabilities are indexed to the inflation rate. For example, in a bank portfolio which is liquidated to make loans, price volatility is a definite risk. For a life insurance company whose liabilities are in fixed nominal terms (i.e., not indexed to interest rates), price declines from higher interest rates represents a windfall gain from higher reinvested coupon income. For a pension fund, if the interest rate rise is from unanticipated inflation, versus normal business and interest rate cycles, then the price decline is a risk because it is equivalent to a loss in future purchasing power; this is equivalent to saying that the pension fund's liabilities are indexed to inflation, while a bond's payments are not. Notice that if the price decline is merely the result of the business cycle, not unanticipated inflation, then the pension fund has higher reinvestment income, and the price decline aspect seems unimportant unless management is concerned about the price variance of both stocks and bonds.

Interest Rate Cycle Risk

This is the same as price risk when inflation is not the cause of the interest rate rise. Obviously, risk would depend on the need for liquidity during such periods.

Yield Volatility

As discussed in the section on "Sector-Quality-Coupon Selection," yield spreads vary over time, and generally follow a pattern which is related to either a business cycle and/or an interest-rate cycle. The risk here is from two sources: (1) the need for liquidity and (2) the change in the probability of a state of economic depression. While the impact of liquidity needs is rather clear (i.e., if you are in a sector-quality-coupon category which performs poorly on a *relative* basis, your bond price declines more *relatively*), the second type of risk is less well understood and, thus, will be discussed next.

Suppose that during a credit crunch at the end of a business cycle, the yield spread of BAA bonds versus A bonds widens from 100 basis points to 300 basis points. If you buy these, and if subsequently no bankruptcies occur and the economy is not turned into a real depression, then during the next cycle as spreads reduce, the portfolio return will have been improved by the trade. However, such a favorable outcome depends on the assumption of a cycle, and, if an economic depression ensues instead of a cyclical recovery, then the results may well be different for the lower quality bonds. Should you undertake such cyclical swaps—it depends on the clients objectives, which depend on the overall risk posture of the client, as well as the overall covariance of the portfolio risk with the other asset and liability risks. Obviously, if the manager is told to undertake such risk, then the client should also measure how much of a manager's return comes from this type of risk.

The above discussion raises questions about the relationship between gains from trading on "normal cyclical relationships" versus what happens if the cycle ends in an abnormal economic event. Such an event could be either unanticipated inflation or unanticipated economic depression. Most likely, the cyclical change in the yield spreads results from the change in investors' subjective probabilities about the chance of either unanticipated inflation or unanticipated depression. If this is what happens, then the cyclical change in yield spreads will be a function of the four types of risk under each of these states in our previous diagram: price risk, call risk, default risk, and reinvestment risk. Because price risk has already been discussed, we will now consider the latter three risks.

Call Risk

Generally, bonds are issued with two types of provisions which allow the corporation to retire the bonds before maturity: call provisions and sinking fund provisions. Call provisions are generally written in the form of an option which allows the corporation to buy the bond back at some stated price, or prices, over par; if multiple prices are used, then the lower prices will be paid at times further into the future, and usually no call option is in effect during the first two to five years after issue. Sinking fund provisions require the issuer to retire some of the bonds before their maturity. Depending on the type of sinking fund provisions, the corporation may be either restricted to buying them at par or above, or alternatively, to purchase them in the open market. The actual wording of both types of provisions can be varied depending upon the supply and demand situation in the market at the time of issue, and is, in effect, adding a repurchase option to a standard present value contract.

These types of provisions create a risk to the portfolio if there is a substantial drop in interest rates.[3] Based upon the fact that a bond's price moves inversely to changes in the level of interest rates, during an economic depression with falling interest rates, bond values would be expected to rise. In fact, as will be shown in the section on duration and immunization, the rise can be sufficient to offset the lower income from reinvesting the coupons at the lower market rates. Unfortunately, such protection is lost if the issuer calls the bond out of your portfolio. Obviously, if the rest of the client's assets are his earning power and common stocks, which will presumably decline during an economic depression, then call risk can be a serious risk since all assets would be declining (covarying) together.

What is the price of better call protection? This is a difficult question because most new issues contain similar call provisions, thus not allowing a basis for a comparative analysis of return/call risk. Comparison with older issues is complicated by the impact of different coupon levels on the respective bonds' volatilities and treatment for income versus capital gains taxes. The best call protection will be with low coupon issues (because the issuer will not want to refund at current higher rates), as well as U.S. government issues which are either not callable or have their first call date further away than corporate issues.

Default Risk

The impact of default risk is well summarized by William Sharpe [29, pp. 252–53] in his analysis of his table which is included as Table 1:

---

[3] For sinking funds, the reverse can be true if market rates rise because, although bond prices will drop, the sinking fund creates a guaranteed demand for the bond. Further, if the bonds are bought at par or above from holders whose bonds were selected randomly, there is always a possible speculative gain from the sinking fund call, and thus the bonds will trade higher than other similar bonds without such a sinking fund.

What sort of experience might the long-run bond investor anticipate? And how is it likely to be related to the risk of the bonds held?

In a massive study of all large bond issues and a sample of small bond issues, Hickman attempted to answer this question. He analyzed investor experience for each bond from 1900 through 1943 to determine the actual yield to the date on which the bond matured, defaulted, or was called—whichever came first. He then compared this with the promised yield-to-maturity based on the price at time of issue. Every bond was also classified according to the ratings assigned at time of issue. [Table 1] shows the major results.

As one would expect, riskier bonds promised higher yields at time of issue. Moreover, a higher percentage of such bonds defaulted, in whole or in part, prior to maturity.

What about actual yield-to-maturity? As the table shows, in four out of five classifications it exceeded the promised amount, on average. Why? Because during the period studied, a substantial drop in interest rates made it attractive for issuers to call old bonds at premiums.

To see what might have happened had this not been the case, Fraine and Mills reanalyzed the data for large investment-grade issues. Their results are shown in [Table 1(B)]. The initial columns differ from those of [Table 1(A)] only because smaller issues are excluded. The major difference appears in the final column. It was obtained by substituting promised yield for realized yield whenever the latter was larger, thus removing the effects of most calls.

Both sets of results suggest that within the highest grades there were little if any difference in realized returns. Such bonds are all quite low in market risk and thus should carry similar (and small) risk premiums. Medium-grade (Baa) bonds performed somewhat better, which is consistent with a premium for this somewhat larger market risk. Low-grade bonds seem to have done even better on average, which is not surprising, given their substantial sensitivity to changes in anticipations about the economic climate.

Reinvestment Risk

Suppose you purchase a one-year, 8 percent bond at $1,000 today, in order to pay a debt of $1,081.60 one year from now. Because coupon payments are semiannual, your plan is sound enough *if* you can reinvest the semiannual $40 coupon at 8 percent.

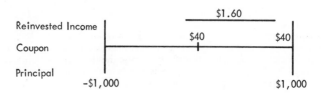

Table 1
Summary of Default Risk Statistics (actual and realized bond yields-to-maturity, 1900–1943)

A. All Large A Sample of Small Issues:

Composite Rating	Comparable Moody's Rating	Promised Yield-to Maturity at Issue (%)	Percent Defaulting Prior to Maturity	Actual-Yield-to-Maturity (%)
I	Aaa	4.5	5.9	5.1
II	Aa	4.6	6.0	5.0
III	A	4.9	13.4	5.0
IV	Baa	5.4	19.1	5.7
V-IX	below Baa	9.5	42.4	8.6

B. All Large Issues:

Composite Rating	Comparable Moody's Rating	Promised Yield-to Maturity at Issue (%)	Percent Defaulting Prior to Maturity	Actual-Yield-to-Maturity (%)
I	Aaa	4.5	5.1	4.3
II	Aa	4.5	5.1	4.3
III	A	4.9	5.0	4.3
IV	Baa	5.4	5.8	4.5

Sources: (A) W. Braddock Hickman, *Corporate Bond Quality and Investor Experience* (Princeton, N.J.: Published for the National Bureau of Economic Research by Princeton University Press, 1958). (B) Harold G. Fraine and Robert H. Mills, "The Effect of Defaults and Credit Deterioration on Yields of Corporate Bonds," *The Journal of Finance*, vol. 16, no. 3 (September 1961), p. 433. Adopted from: William F. Sharpe, *Investments* (Englewood Cliffs, N.J.: Prentice-Hall, 1978), pp. 252–53.

However, if interest rates drop by the semiannual payment time, then your reinvested income will be lower than $1.60. Thus, a drop in interest rates causes a decline in the *expected* income from investing interim coupon payments, and this is defined as *reinvestment risk.*

As with other risk, the impact of this depends on the client's need for reinvested income, as related to other future asset and liability flows. For an insurance company with whole life contracts in nominal dollars, the risk from a drop in interest rates can be substantial. For a pension fund, the risk might be less if benefit payments also declined (i.e., direct covariance of liabilities and reinvested income). For banks with short-term bonds, the effect might be minimal since their cost of funds could also be adjusted down with the interest rate decline (again direct covariance of future liabilities with interest rates).

Rather than present an extensive discussion of reinvestment risk here, the section below explains the details further. Placing this discussion in the next section is especially appropriate because the concept of *portfolio immunization can be viewed as the exact offsetting of reinvestment risk with price risk.*

PRICE VERSUS REINVESTMENT RISK—OFFSETTING FORCES AND IMMUNIZATION

Portfolio Immunization

The above example, about the reinvestment risk of your portfolio, introduces the fundamentals of the concept of portfolio immunization. *Immunization is a procedure which eliminates all reinvestment risk.*

To see how you would immunize a portfolio, examine Figure 6(A). Figure 6(A) is similar to the figure drawn in the section above on reinvestment risk, except for two changes: (1) the top line reads "Reinvestment Income Plus Price Change," and (2) the bond maturity has been extended to a maturity of 1½ years. To see the reason for these two changes, consider the case of interest rates dropping from 8 percent to 6 percent before the first payment period. Under such a situation, the first $40 coupon payment would be invested at only 6 percent rather than the anticipated 8 percent, thereby causing reinvested income to be $.40 lower than expected (six months at 6 percent is $1.20 versus the expected $1.60). However, at the liability payment horizon of one year, the price of the bond will be $1,009.70, or a windfall gain of $9.70 because of the last $40 coupon versus $30 on new 6 percent bonds. Thus, not only has reinvestment risk been wiped out, but a net gain of $9.30 has occurred!

Unfortunately, being in a no-free-lunch world, the above example would have caused a loss if interest rates had risen to 10 percent. Then, reinvestment income would have been up $.40, to $2.00, but the terminal bond price would have been $990.50, for a loss of $9.50, or a net loss of $9.10.

The above example illustrates what I will call

Offsetting Forces Principle: Unexpected price change always has the opposite sign from unexpected reinvestment income, if the investment horizon is sufficiently shorter than the bond's maturity.

Figure 6
The Basics of Immunization

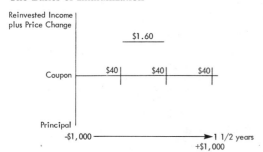

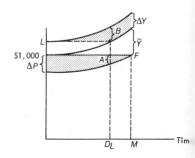

A. Reinvestment Effect of Lengthening Bond   B. Immunized Position

This statement is important because it leads to an important corollary statement below. For example, assume that, instead of a maturity of 1½ years, a bond of 13 months maturity had been chosen; then the price at the one-year horizon would have been either $1,001.50 or $998.10 (depending on whether rates fell or rose), whereby nearly exactly offsetting the change in reinvestment income. Obviously, by shortening the bond still more, at some point you could guarantee that, for given a change in interest rate, you would always be at least as well off as you expected, or:

> *Immunization Corollary:* There is always some maturity longer than the liability horizon for which the difference between unexpected price change minus unexpected reinvestment income will be zero.

Figure 6(B) illustrates the immunization corollary for a scenario of a rise in interest rates. Assume that a bond of maturity M was initially purchased at $1,000 in order to meet a liability of L dollars (with L equaling the sum of expected reinvested income, $\overline{Y}$, plus return of the fixed principal, F) at time D_L. The shaded areas represent the effect of the interest rate rise: i.e., unexpected reinvestment income (ΔY) is positive and price change (ΔP) is negative. Also, at the time of the liability payment (D_L), the price decline (amount A) is exactly equal to the higher reinvested income (amount B). Thus, this one bond-one liability portfolio is said to be immunized against interest rate changes.

Thus, *immunization is seen to be a simple positioning of bond payment streams against liability payment streams such that reinvestment income and price changes offset each other.* The logic of this procedure can be easily extended to whole portfolios as shown in the next subsection. However, such a procedure does not eliminate all risk as will be shown in the final subsection, and thus immunization may not be appropriate for many (most?) types of portfolios.

Duration and Immunization

In the above subsection, it was stated that immunization could be achieved if the ". . . investment horizon is sufficiently shorter than the bond's maturity." How can the exact maturity be selected? The answer is to obtain the *breakeven time* between the offsetting effects of coupon reinvestment and the final repayment of principal. The formula for this time is

$$D = \frac{\displaystyle\sum_{t=0}^{M} \frac{t\, C_t}{(1+i)^t}}{\displaystyle\sum_{t=0}^{M} \frac{C_t}{(1+i)^t}}$$

where D stands for duration as defined by Macaulay [25], C_t is the cash flow (coupon income and principal) in period t, and i is an interest rate (presumably, the bond's yield to maturity with an implicit assumption of this reinvestment rate being valid in the future).

As can be easily seen, the denominator is merely the present-value equation for the bond's price. The numerator is a similar term except that it is weighted by the time t. Thus, in the numerator, both coupon and time are weighted together and discounted, thereby producing an average present-valued time weighted factor, which when divided by the denominator's coupon-only weighted term, leaves an *average present-valued time.* This average means that both coupon reinvestment and principal repayment have been present-valued and averaged, thereby allowing D to represent the average (middle) time at which price risk and reinvestment risk are mutually offsetting.

To increase familiarity with the calculation of duration, it may be useful to consider Table 2, which contains the duration of various coupon/maturity variations under the assumption of a level yield curve at 7 percent. Several observations are relevant. First, the duration is always shorter than the maturity of a coupon bearing bond; this is expected because of the present valuing of the time subscript. Second, the rate of increase in duration is much less than the linear increase in maturity, and at some point reaches a peak. Third, it is difficult to get a duration of over 20 years, except from common stocks, whose duration can be calculated by another formula (see Macaulay [25]).

Table 2
Duration of Selected Coupon Bonds (level yield curve of 7 percent assumed)

	Maturity				
Coupon	*(1)*	*(5)*	*(10)*	*(20)*	*(50)*
.03	0.992	4.642	8.416	13.308	15.775
.05	0.988	4.458	7.798	11.872	14.764
.07	0.983	4.304	7.355	11.051	14.312
.09	0.979	4.174	7.022	10.519	14.058
.11	0.974	4.062	6.763	10.146	13.891

To relate this discussion to the previous example illustrated in Figure 6(B), it must be realized that, for a single payment contract, the duration and maturity of the contract are equal. Thus, in Figure 6(B), the maturity (D_L) of the liability was also its duration, and it can be proven that the correct bond to immunize the portfolio would also have had its duration calculated such that

$$D_A = D_L$$

where D_A represented the duration of the asset (bond) stream. The computational procedure for immunizing the portfolio is almost as simple as merely matching the duration of the portfolio assets to the duration of the portfolio liabilities, thereby balancing reinvestment versus price risks at the liability horizon. The actual procedure with references is discussed further in the Appendix, rather than slowing down the discussion here.

Thus, duration is useful for the immunization computation—but, its real fame is for another reason. Under certain theoretical conditions (to be studied shortly), a bond's duration provides a direct proportional scalar for its volatility to interest rate changes—thus, a bond with a duration of ten years will be twice as volatile as one with a duration of five years. This result is quite different than maturity; it can be easily checked with a yield book that the rate of price volatility declines as maturity increases. Further, because duration is calculated on both coupon and principal payments, it includes the impact of coupon level on volatility. Because of this proportion property, it has sometimes been suggested as a risk measure for price risk; however, as indicated both below and in the next section of this chapter, some reservations are in order before this would be an accurate price volatility measure.

Caveats on Immunization and Duration

Caveat 1. Immunization Requires That Future Asset and Liability Flows Exactly Offset Each Other. The basis for immunization, extended from the logic of Figure 6(B), is that: (1) initially the present-value of the portfolio's expected assets ($\Sigma \bar{A}$) equals the present-value of the portfolio's expected liabilities (ΣL) and (2) that all unexpected asset price changes ($\Sigma \Delta P$) and reinvested income changes ($\Sigma \Delta Y$) offset each other: i.e.,

$$\Sigma \bar{A} + \Sigma \Delta P + \Sigma \Delta Y = \Sigma \bar{L}$$

or, if ΣL is shifted over as a negative,

$$\Sigma \bar{A} + \Sigma \Delta P + \Sigma \Delta Y - \Sigma \bar{L} = 0$$

While this may initially seem like an innocuous requirement, let us look at five situations as set up in Table 3.

Table 3

Hypothetical Institutions	Arithmetic Sign			
	$\Sigma \bar{A}$	$\Sigma \Delta P$	$\Sigma \Delta Y$	$-\Sigma \bar{L}$
No. 1	0	−	+	0
No. 2	0	−	0	0
No. 3	0	−	0	−
No. 4	0	−	+	−
No. 5	−	−	+	−

The five types may be thought of as five types of financial institutions, and we will explain them below. Before beginning the explanation, let us assume that interest rates are positively correlated with inflation, and that the opposite of inflation is depression (thus, we are returning to our balance sheet scenarios in the earlier section of this chapter on risk).

The table contains the sign of the direction which each of the asset and liability flows might take as interest rates moved up or down. For example, No. 1 might be a "pure" life insurance company, with no contingent policy loans, and therefore it has the *perfect immunization configuration* $(0 - + 0)$; i.e., expected asset flows and liability flows both written in fixed nominal dollars have zero relation to inflation and interest rates, while its unexpected price change and reinvestment income can be positioned to offset each other.

Unfortunately, the other institutions are less immunizable. No. 2 cannot be immunized because a rise in interest rates causes a fall in price, with no offsetting changes. Such a case might be like a bank which liquidates its portfolio to make loans as interest rates rise; there is no corresponding period during which to reinvest at the higher rates. The case of a life insurance company with policy holder loans at low rates may be a combination of No. 1 and No. 2.

No. 3, which might be like a property and liability company, is also not immunizable if interest rates rise because of inflation, thereby simultaneously driving down the bond prices while claims in nominal dollars are rising (the sign is negative because the sign of ΣL is negative above). Also, because the period is too short to reinvest, reinvested income is unchanged. Of course, if current interest rates correctly incorporate inflation, then, on average, the loss will be zero but there will be some standard deviation risk from year-to-year.

No. 4 might be like a pension fund. It is similar to No. 3 in that its liabilities increase with inflation, but its horizon is long enough to allow some partial offset from higher reinvested income (although probably not enough to offset both negative signs). Although the impact of inflation can be factored into a modified formula for immunization (Vanderhoof [30]), it can be shown that such a result requires that at least some of the liabilities and expenses be less than proportionately affected by inflation, which may be a doubtful assumption for many institutions (see Fogler [13]).

Finally, No. 5 might be a portfolio like No. 4 except that it contains either common stocks or expected flows from corporate earnings. In such a case, these flows might be affected the same as the portfolio flows of No. 4 if unanticipated inflation is detrimental to common stock returns or corporate earnings.

In summary, the above is meant to illustrate that *simple* immunization procedures implicitly require three conditions: (1) that the scheduled payment date for portfolio liabilities is fixed; (2) liabilities are in fixed nominal dollar terms; and (3) that the only assets are bonds, and that these are default-free. These conditions were implicit in the analysis of Figure 6(B). Some more sophisticated immunization procedures have been advocated recently to relax the requirement of fixed nominal dollar liabilities; these procedures require shortening the portfolio's duration to hedge against inflation, and thus the portfolio may be exposed to reinvestment risk if *real* interest rates decline.

Caveat 2. For a Linear Relation Between Duration and Price Volatility, Macaulay's Duration Assumes a Level Yield Curve and Parallel Shifts. As can be seen in the duration calculation only one interest rate *(i)* was used, thereby implying a level yield curve which allows reinvestment at that rate. Obviously, this is an unrealistic assumption, but, as will be discussed later in the chapter, more sophisticated calculation schemes are available to avoid this assumption.

Also, for a bond with a ten-year duration to be twice as volatile as a bond with a five-year duration, it is necessary to have a parallel shift (this is also required if a level yield curve is the assumption). To see the necessity, simply think of the counterexample where the yield curve pivots on the five-year duration point, leaving the interest rate unchanged for a five-year duration. However, as mentioned above, the impact of this caveat may not be too great, and it will be discussed later.

Caveat 3. You Can Calculate an Average Duration, but not the Duration of an Average. In September 1973, the average characteristics of the original Kuhn Loeb Industrial Index were:

Average Price.................... 90.02
Average Coupon 6.77
Average Maturity 18.56
Average Yield to Maturity 8.00

By using these figures and a yield book, it can be ascertained that, if a bond had these characteristics, then its required maturity would be approximately 13 years. Obviously, one must be careful about the using of average characteristics, and these certainly should never be used to calculate the average duration. The proper procedure would be to calculate the duration of each bond, and then dollar weight these as Macaulay's duration is an additive measure mathematically.

Summary on Immunization

Despite the above caveats, immunization has an extremely important feature: it allows specification of a portfolio with zero reinvestment risk. Given the complex, multiperiod problem stated at the beginning of this chapter, such a feature is important in its ability to present the asset-liability positioning required to eliminate reinvestment risk (or conversely, price risk) due to interest rate movements which are not related to inflation. This may be a useful performance measurement benchmark against which to judge portfolio managers in institutions which approach the conditions of the No. 1 ("pure" life with fixed nominal liabilities); of course, the managers should first be informed that this is the zero risk benchmark, so that they are aware of what risks they are incurring. Certainly, because of this ability to capture multiperiod risk, immunization has potential as an analytical tool for bond portfolio management.

EMPIRICAL STUDIES

The purpose of this section is to report the results of some major studies about five areas of bond management: what causes returns, dumbbelled versus laddered portfolio, the search for a bond beta, the results of immunizing a portfolio, and the procedures available for detecting bankruptcy. Because of the many studies available, only a few major studies have been selected, and even then, only major results and conclusions are discussed.

Return Functions

The literature on the determinants of bond returns has two parts: (1) term structure theories and their testing and (2) analysis of risk premiums. The term structure questions are addressed to the linkage between the expected rates of return on bonds of different maturities. The *pure expectations hypothesis* argues that the return on a bond maturing in the future will be equal to the return that can be obtained from rolling over one-period bonds over the interim period. For example, if the present one-period rate (R_1) were .07 percent and if next period's rate $(_1\bar{r}_1)$ on a one-period instrument were expected to be .06 percent (i.e., a drop in rate), then the return on a two-period bond (R_2) would be found equal by

$$R_2 = [(1 + R_1)(1 + {}_1\bar{r}_1)]^{1/2} - 1.0$$
$$= [(1.07)(1.06)]^{1/2} - 1.0$$
$$= .063$$

In other words, if rates were expected to drop, the rate of return on the longer maturity bond would be less than on the shorter bonds today because the longer bonds provide their return for the whole two years.[4]

---

[4] Note that this example assumes away the problem of coupon reinvestment effects which requires additional adjustments.

The above logic is currently of interest because of the implications for deriving a market forecast of future interest rate movements. To see how this works, generalize the above equation to a bond of any maturity *(t)*, where the expected interim one-period rates starting at period *i* are $_t\bar{r}_1$ for i = 1, . . . , *t* − 1, as

$$R_t = [(1 + R_1)(1 + {}_1\bar{r}_1)(1 + {}_2\bar{r}_1) . . . (1 + {}_{t-1}\bar{r}_1)]^{1/t}$$

Now, if one wanted to know the forecast for interest rates one period from now, it would only be necessary to have R_2 and R_1, since the expected one period rate $_1\bar{r}_1$ would be the missing term: i.e.,

$$R_2 = [(1 + R_1)(1 + {}_1\bar{r}_1)]^{1/2} - 1$$

or

$$1 + {}_1r_1 = \frac{(1 + R_2)^2}{1 + R_1}$$

This is an easy sort of calculation since R_1 and R_2 are today's spot prices in the market, and once $_1\bar{r}_1$ is known, then using the spot price of R_3, $_2\bar{r}_1$ can be solved for, and so on.

Of course, the important question is whether the expected forward rates $_t\bar{r}_1$ are really accurate forecasts of what the market expects, as the pure expectations hypothesis suggests. Unfortunately, several studies suggest that such a simple equation may not be realistic. In particular, numerous studies have found that the forecasted rate was slightly below the subsequent actual rate, thereby suggesting that investors: may require a liquidity premium for investing in longer maturity bonds. However, the actual reasons for the liquidity premium are the subject of some conjecture. Recently a study by Eugene Fama [8] found that expected forward rates were accurate forecasts of future rates, after adjustment for a liquidity premium based upon the risk of changes in inflation. Studies such as the above generally accept the geometric mean model espoused by the pure expectations hypothesis, but modify it by a term for the liquidity premium. Such formulations are called the *liquidity premium theories* of the term structure. Finally, although there is less evidence, several papers have suggested that the liquidity premium may vary by maturity segments due to certain types of investors being unwilling to arbitrage away any unusual premiums if the bonds are outside their "preferred habitat" range of maturities. These latter studies, defining the market segmentation hypothesis (i.e., life insurance companies like long bonds, banks short, others in the middle) have received support from studies examining the differentials between long and short bonds relative to the supply of each, as well as some flow of funds studies of the impact of supply and demand by individual types of financial institutions. Overall, the evidence suggests some modification of the pure expectations hypothesis is appropriate, although the exact mechanism for doing this is not yet agreed on.

By contrast to the lack of conclusions above, the empirical studies of risk premiums are more unilateral in their theory about market demands. One of the earliest studies in this area was by Lawrence Fisher, who found that the following equation explained ". . . 81 percent of the total variance in the logarithm" of risk premiums:

$$X_0 = 0.262\ X_1 - 0.233\ X_2 - 0.469\ X_3 - 0.290\ X_4 + \text{a constant}$$

where

$X_0 =$ risk premium of the bond's yield to maturity minus the yield of a similar maturity government bond;

$X_1 =$ earning variability measured by the variance of earnings divided by the mean of earnings (coefficient of variation);

$X_2 =$ period of solvency;

$X_3 =$ equity-debt ratio with the equity at market value and debt at par value;

$X_4 =$ bonds outstanding at market value;

Coupon term = varied by each of the five dates studied (1927, 1932, 1937, 1949, 1953);

Sample size = varied from 45 industrial firms in 1932 up to 88 firms in 1953;

and all variables were measured in logarithms.

While Fisher didn't adjust for coupon differences, his results certainly indicate that the above measures are important in market pricing of risk premiums. Since this early study, other empirical research has verified the existence of various statistically significant relationships (e.g., see the later section on "Procedures for Detecting Bankruptcy"); thus, managers may find it useful to use such models as "screening devices," although if everyone follows such a procedure the advantage would be correspondingly reduced.

Dumbbells versus Laddered Portfolios

Various articles have suggested that dumbbell portfolios might be more risk-return efficient than laddered portfolios. A dumbbell (or barbell) portfolio concentrates in only very short and very long bonds, with no intermediates—hence the name. An evenly laddered portfolio has bonds of all maturity ranges, with about the same amount in each range.*

Why should dumbbells be better than other portfolios? The only possible reason seemed to be as a trading *tactic* when a future interest rate rise was expected to produce a yield curve with a "hump shape" in the intermediate range. As a long-term *strategy*, neither I nor others could offer any reason, and thus we had some doubt. This doubt was fostered by both the expectations hypothesis and the belief that the bond market is a high competitive arena (thereby approaching an efficient market). Thus, we undertook several studies to examine whether dumbbelled portfolios were more risk-return efficient.

In a study by Fogler with William Groves and James Richardson [11], it was found that the dumbbell strategy was always inferior on a risk-return basis, using a criterion of total holding-period returns and their variations. These results conflicted with the prior studies because: (1) the criterion in those studies ignored capital gains and losses unless realized, thereby favoring the longest bonds; (2) in Watson's study, transactions costs weren't included; and (3) large cash inflows and outflows were included in Watson's, thereby necessitating heavy liquidity and thus the shortest bonds. Thus, the maturity problem is certainly not a simple one, as indicated in the prior sections and the discussion on immunization.

More interesting research in this area is contained in another study by Fogler and William Groves [12]. In the course of the foregoing study, the most successful maturity strategy was found to be the *full-laddered strategy* (this was a strategy which kept a fixed percentage in the first three maturities and continually reinvested all proceeds in the longest bonds, holding them until they only had three years to maturity, and then buying long again—subsequently, renamed the buy-long-and-hold, or BLAH). We could still see no economic reason for the superiority of this strategy, and thus we decided to test this

---

* *Author's note:* The genesis of this area was in the attempt to correctly account for the multiperiod investment problem discussed at the beginning of this chapter. Such a problem can be viewed as a *decision-tree* over time, with the combination of early decisions and interest-rate changes "locking you in" at the later periods. The mathematical procedure for solving (optimizing) such a decision sequence is to start with the best decision at the last period, given each interest-rate scenario for that period, and to solve backwards (recursively) for the best initial starting-point portfolio. While the first attempt at solving this above problem was in the 1960s, Bradley and Crane [6] considerably expanded the size as well as implementing it on a computer in 1973, while Watson [31] simulated the problem for a bank. Unfortunately, the size of this type of problem expands so rapidly as more time periods are considered (i.e., the branches of the tree go up geometrically) that Bradley and Crane only included four periods. This effect by itself is sufficient to cause only four short and four long maturities to be held (which was their resulting solution) if transactions costs exist. However, Watson's very realistic simulation also indicated that a dumbbell of shortest- and longest-bonds was optimal.

strategy further, but this time both over a longer sample which included the 1930s Depression and combined with a portfolio of common stocks.

Table 4 shows the results of two sets of tests. The partial ladder strategy shown in Table 4(A) illustrates the results of testing a portfolio with 75 percent kept in stocks annually by yearend rebalancing. The bond portion invested the indicated percentages (out of 100 percent in bonds) equally over the maturities of 1, 2, and 3 years; the rest was invested in 20-year bonds that were reinvested five years later, when they had a maturity of only 15 years. Table 4(B) shows the results of a similar portfolio except the 1, 2, and 3 year maturities contained 15 percent total with the remaining 85 percent in intermediate bonds, as shown. The results suggest that the *risk-return measures of bond-stock portfolios were virtually insensitive to the maturity structure of the bond portfolio.* The Sharpe Index is a portfolio's return over a risk-free rate divided by its standard deviation, while the coefficient of variation is the standard deviation divided by total return—both show virtually no change for different bond policies.

Table 4
Combined Bond-Stock Portfolios

A. Partial Ladder Tests (stock-bond ratio = 75/25; 1926–1968):

	Short Maturity Allocation		
	27%	*21%*	*15%*
Rate of Return	9.08	9.09	9.09
Standard Deviation	17.63	17.63	17.63
Sharpe Index	.35	.35	.35
Coefficient of Variation	1.68	1.68	1.68

B. Shorter Portfolios (stock-bond ratio = 75/25; 1926–1968):

	Longest Maturity		
	10 years	*7 years*	*5 years*
Rate of Return	9.14	9.13	9.09
Standard Deviation	17.60	17.59	17.57
Sharpe Index	.35	.35	.35
Coefficient of Variation	1.67	1.67	1.68

Source: H. Russell Fogler and William A. Groves, "How Much Can Active Bond Management Raise Returns?" *Journal of Portfolio Management*, vol. 3 (Fall 1976), pp. 35–40.

What should one conclude from the above study? First, as with all studies, conclusions must be tempered by the data. The yield curve data from David Durand's classic study at the National Bureau of Economic Research were the basis for these results, but it is difficult to get better data. Also, we approximated the risk-free rate by a constant

3 percent when calculating the Sharpe Index. Nevertheless, until more careful studies are conducted, the above suggests that *the stock and bond markets may not be segmented, as some suggest*, and that, when viewed together, the linear risk-return relationship predicted by the capital asset pricing model may result. Indeed, the recent study by Friend, Westerfield, and Granito [14] found bonds were influenced by two market factors: an overall market factor, and some residual unique to bonds; although they interpreted this as evidence of segmentation, a more likely result is that the multidimensional nature of risk was rearing its head, and that it is present for both bonds and stocks.

The Search for a "Bond Beta"—and the Nonlinearity Dilemma

The combination of the theoretical underpinnings of the capital asset pricing model plus the linearity of beta has been able to revolutionize performance measurement in equity portfolios. The linear relationship allows a common sense risk adjustment procedure to account for the effect of highly volatile securities which move with the market. The simplistic gains bought by linearity have caused a desire for a bond beta. However, this is a difficult task because bonds are constantly maturing, and thus their risk is always changing (i.e., it is "nonstationary" in statistical terminology).

In addition to the problem of being nonstationary, nonlinearity in simple bond relationships is also a problem. Historical studies of bonds have always found a nonlinear relationship between risk and return as shown in Table 5. The results of Table 5 are based upon McCallum's study of Canadian Government bond prices from 1948–68, with the beta based upon a constructed bond index. As can be seen, total holding period return was a nonlinear function of maturity, standard deviation, and beta. Further, this finding is consistent with other studies which viewed return as related to the standard deviation of proxy bonds based on Durand's yield curves (Wilbur [33]), beta on U.S. governments (Yawitz and Marshall [35]), and duration (Dietz, Fogler, and Rivers [7]).

If the above findings are accurate, it is incorrect to impose a linear risk adjustment measure when comparing two portfolios of different risk. To see why this is so, consider Figure 7. If the real relationship is nonlinear, then bonds with less risk than the index will have returns above the line, while those with more risk will be below it. (Thus, to "win," a portfolio manager would always take less risk—note, however, that he is not beating the market, but only beating an incorrect measurement system.)

Why does the nonlinearity occur? Probably because a single risk measure is too simple to encompass the multiperiod covariance risk

Table 5
Nonlinearity of Return to Simple Risk Measures

A. Expected Returns for a Three-Month Holding Period:

Maturity in Months	Expected Return	Maturity in Months	Expected Return	Maturity in Months	Expected Return
3	.0075	42	.0094	132	.0061
6	.0085	48	.0094	144	.0059
9	.0088	54	.0091	156	.0063
12	.0091	60	.0090	168	.0055
15	.0094	66	.0087	180	.0048
18	.0094	72	.0088	192	.0045
21	.0097	84	.0080	204	.0049
24	.0096	96	.0074	216	.0055
30	.0103	108	.0073	228	.0048
36	.0103	120	.0066	240	.0045

B. Standard Deviations for a Three-Month Holding Period:

Maturity in Months	Standard Deviation	Maturity in Months	Standard Deviation	Maturity in Months	Standard Deviation
3	.0034	42	.0137	132	.0230
6	.0039	48	.0152	144	.0241
9	.0049	54	.0158	156	.0246
12	.0064	60	.0166	168	.0241
15	.0071	66	.0175	180	.0237
18	.0082	72	.0181	192	.0242
21	.0093	84	.0194	204	.0267
24	.0101	96	.0203	216	.0295
30	.0112	108	.0213	228	.0245
36	.0128	120	.0218	240	.0285

C. Beta's for a Three-Month Holding Period:

Maturity in Months	Beta Coefficient	Maturity in Months	Beta Coefficient	Maturity in Months	Beta Coefficient
3	.0000	42	.6932	132	1.2506
6	.0855	48	.7699	144	1.2503
9	.1699	54	.8066	156	1.3594
12	.2147	60	.9534	168	1.2724
15	.2845	66	.9005	180	1.2475
18	.3454	72	.9434	192	1.3367
21	.3875	84	1.0186	204	1.2148
24	.4371	96	1.0703	216	1.2877
30	.5419	108	1.1513	228	1.3509
36	.6268	120	1.1890	240	1.4707

Source: John S. McCallum, "The Expected Holding Period Return, Uncertainty and Term Structure of Interest Rates," *Journal of Finance*, vol. 30 (May 1975), Tables 1, 2, and 3.

Figure 7

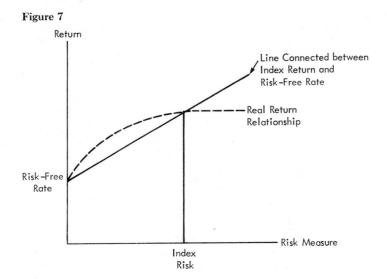

of the bond portfolio. As indicated in the Fogler and Groves study, bonds and stock returns may be connected in a more complex manner than presented to date.

Immunization Studies

The concept of duration has received increasing attention (e.g. see [34]) during recent years especially since a 1971 study by Fisher and Weil [10] showed that the expected ("promised") yield could be nearly attained by immunization. While Macaulay's original duration implicitly assumed both a level yield curve and a parallel shift in interest rates, both of these assumptions can be dropped. The recent works by Bierwag [5], Fisher and Weil [10], Ingersoll [19], and Khang [23] have all created adjusted duration formulas that relax these assumptions. The resulting calculations provide a time-based measure which can be matched against the same time measure of liabilities in order to ensure that reinvestment risk is eliminated.[5]

How well do these measures work? Table 6 contains part of the results of an interesting study by Kaufman, Loeffler, and Schweitzer [22]. In this study they used the original Macaulay duration measure (labelled *D1*), a measure developed by Fisher and Weil which modifies the Macaulay calculation by using different forward rates for the interest rates in each period *(D2)*, as well as two other measures for duration.

---

[5] Note that this does not mean that return would be linear to such measures. In fact, it is doubtful that this would be the case if other types of risk are still unaccounted for.

Table 6
Immunization Results for Ten-Year Planning Period (4 percent coupon rate assumed)

		Actual Yield			
Years	*Promised Yield*	*D1**	*D2*	*D3*	*D4*
1925–35	4.5105	4.4845	4.4845	4.4657	4.5198
1926–36	4.3999	4.3733	4.3734	4.3598	4.3976
1927–37	4.2998	4.2571	4.2572	4.2493	4.2697
1926–38	4.0499	3.9876	3.9877	4.0028	3.9558
1929–39	4.5444	4.4284	4.4286	4.4195	4.4451
1930–40	4.3999	4.2839	4.2841	4.2530	4.3440
1931–41	4.0549	3.9192	3.9196	3.8993	3.9591
1932–42	4.7214	4.5317	4.5325	4.4492	4.6980
1933–43	4.0511	3.8529	3.8541	3.7992	3.9675
1934–44	3.7363	3.5785	3.5799	3.5157	3.7117
1935–45	3.0906	2.9352	2.9366	2.8899	3.0347
1936–46	2.7456	2.5830	2.5840	2.5552	2.6451
1937–47	2.4740	2.3675	2.3687	2.3338	2.4441
1938–48	2.6863	2.5053	2.5058	2.4884	2.5428
1939–49	2.2642	2.1428	2.1433	2.1279	2.1768
1940–50	2.0388	1.9685	1.9692	1.9466	2.0181
1941–51	1.9675	1.9204	1.9212	1.8976	1.9715
1942–52	2.2398	2.1496	2.1500	2.1344	2.1841
1943–53	2.2200	2.1626	2.1630	2.1460	2.2004
1944–54	2.2834	2.2017	2.2020	2.1873	2.2320
1945–55	2.2199	2.1636	2.1640	2.1497	2.1933
1946–56	1.9534	1.9504	1.9506	1.9418	1.9665
1947–57	2.1357	2.1150	2.1149	2.1179	2.1048
1948–58	2.5978	2.5377	2.5379	2.5295	2.5539
1949–59	2.3732	2.3790	2.3794	2.3676	2.3995
1950–60	2.3496	2.3189	2.3187	2.3354	2.2774
1951–61	2.4119	2.4211	2.4209	2.4386	2.3785
1952–62	2.7299	2.7444	2.7443	2.7555	2.7159
1953–63	2.8973	2.8988	2.8988	2.9054	2.8803
1954–64	2.6790	2.6976	2.6974	2.7230	2.6381
1955–65	2.8138	2.8146	2.8143	2.8555	2.7215
1956–66	2.8707	2.8706	2.8702	2.9271	2.7447
1957–67	3.4999	3.4602	3.4597	3.5097	3.3528
1958–68	3.3401	3.3515	3.3509	3.4026	3.2419
1959–69	4.0619	4.0326	4.0323	4.0530	3.9915
1960–70	4.5782	4.5533	4.5532	4.5563	4.5461
1961–71	4.0455	4.0405	4.0405	4.0738	3.9762
1962–72	4.3300	4.3306	4.3312	4.3547	4.2864
1963–73	4.0174	4.0262	4.0266	4.1099	3.8705
1964–74	4.2658	4.2727	4.2737	4.3816	4.0746
1965–75	4.3380	4.3233	4.3250	4.4904	4.0215
1966–76	4.9014	4.8386	4.8413	5.0426	4.4770
1967–77	5.2229	5.0919	5.0961	5.3636	4.6124

* DI = Macaulay's duration.

Source: George G. Kaufman, Thomas A. Loeffler, and Robert L. Schweitzer, "Measuring Risk and Return for Portfolios of Coupon Bonds," working paper prepared for annual meeting of the Financial Management Association, 1978, Appendices.

The basic data were Durand's, with updating to 1977. As the results indicate, *D1*, *D2*, and *D3* achieved somewhat similar results and produced results closer to the promised yield. As can be seen, even during periods of large declines in interest rates such as the 1930s, realized returns were within at least 20 basis points of the promised yield. Thus, even though actual results differ slightly from promised (probably because of unexpected changes in the shape of the yield curve during interim reinvestment), the technique definitely minimizes reinvestment risk.

Procedures for Detecting Bankruptcy

In a summary of his recent article on bond prices, Weinstein [32] notes

> We find some evidence of price change during the period from 18 to seven months before the rating change is announced. We find no evidence of any reaction during the six months prior to the rating change. We also find little reaction, if any, during the month of the change or for six months after the change.

Also, traders claim that the market does anticipate such changes, and presently a number of credit analyses services are available from various investment firms. Thus, while earlier studies claim that prices don't anticipate rating changes (Katz [21], Grier and Katz [15], and Hettenhouse and Sartoris [16]), an open mind seems appropriate on this issue. Further, if such results are true, then portfolio managers should be aware of the types of research which might assist early detection of rating changes.

Probably one of the best known models for such types of analysis is Altman's [1] *discriminant analysis model.* This model (based upon the statistical technique called *discriminant analysis,* which puts events into two or more "groups") assigns a "Z-score" to each firm based on the equation

$$Z = 1.2X_1 + 1.4X_2 + 3.3X_3 + 0.6X_4 + 1.0X_5$$

where

X_1 = Working Capital/Total Assets
X_2 = Retained Earnings/Total Assets
X_3 = Earnings Before Interest and Taxes/Total Assets
X_4 = Market Value of Equity and Preferred/Total Liabilities
X_5 = Sales/Total Assets

Based upon the Z-score, a firm would be classified as either a bankrupt ($Z < 1.81$) or a nonbankrupt ($Z < 2.99$), with scores in-between not clearly assignable.

Is this model useful for credit analysis? The answer appears to be "a qualified yes." First, the user must be somewhat knowledgeable about the underlying statistical caveats which accompany such analysis when it is used to predict future bankruptcies (an excellent discussion is provided in references [2, 20]), but the model does appear to be useful in such prediction. Altman's original model was developed upon a sample of manufacturing firms in the asset size range of $1–25 million; more recently a seven variable model has been tested with both better results and a more general sample, and this would appear to be a more appropriate model [3]. Another qualification is that, while the above model is addressed to bankruptcy classification, classifying firms into groups by quality rating is a still more difficult task. Several discriminant models have been proposed [4, 28], but, after a very interesting comparative study of most other models, Altman [3] notes that, ". . . the accuracy of the various models is mediocre at best. . . ." Yet, as he emphasizes, the low cost operation of these models, as a screen to find companies which appear to be ripe for a change, argues for their use, as well as the insights which they provide about the dynamics of rating changes.

SUMMARY

Throughout this chapter, bond portfolio optimization models were not mentioned. Although several optimization models are available commercially at this time, using such a model requires two caveats: (1) acceptance of the measure of risk which is either implicitly and/ or explicitly used in the model; (2) necessity to have accurate estimates of the variance-covariance relationships between alternative types of bonds, as well as between bonds and stocks. Both of these caveats pose important problems presently. The limited definitions of risk have been explored in the body of this chapter; as to estimates of the variance-covariance relationships, data bases are much more limited than in common stocks. Thus, while such models can be used presently, extreme care must be exercised in interpreting their results in consideration of overall portfolio objectives and risk. No single model can serve all users until a more adequate theory of risk evolves.

Thus, in summary, the theory of risk requires further understanding, and this understanding will be the foundation of changes in the theory of bond portfolio management. The idea of simple, single dimensional measures of risk is likely to become obsolete. In the place of such measures, a multiperiod investment theory will be forthcoming, probably emerging from the concept of immunization, but in a much different form. Yet, until such a theory arrives, portfolio managers will need to develop their strategies with a fuller appreciation of the client's balance sheet risks as defined earlier in the chapter. Correspondingly, performance evaluation by clients will require a yardstick which is designed in consideration of their multiple objectives and risks.

APPENDIX

Duration and Immunization Mathematically

It was generally assumed throughout this chapter that readers are familar with the basic ideas of present value analysis, as well as the concept of bond pricing. These concepts, which can be found in Sharpe [29, Chapters 4 & 10], assist an understanding of duration.

Duration is most easily understood by examining the relationship of a bond's price to changes in the interest rate. Using the generally accepted present value formulation, the price *(P)* of a bond is a function of its coupon and principal payments at each future time period *(C_t)*, the market rate of interest *(i)*, and the number of periods till maturity *(n)*:

$$P = \sum_{t=1}^{n} \frac{C_t}{(1+i)^t} \tag{1}$$

where the final cash flow *(C_n)* includes both coupon and principal payments. Then, the change in the bond's price for a given interest rate change can be calculated as the *derivative* (from calculus), or rate of change (written *dP/di*) of equation #1, or

$$\frac{dP}{di} = \sum_{t=1}^{n} \frac{-tC_t}{(1+i)^{t+1}} \tag{2}$$

and finally, to obtain the percentage change in a bond's price *(dP/P)*, equation (2) is converted to the differential by multiplying both sides by *di*, and then the result is divided by *P*; thus,

$$\frac{dP}{P} = \frac{\sum_{t=1}^{n} \dfrac{-tC_t}{(1+i)^{t+1}}}{\sum_{t=1}^{n} \dfrac{C_t}{(1+i)^t}} \, di = - \left[\frac{\sum_{t=1}^{n} \dfrac{tC_t}{(1+i)^t}}{\sum_{t=1}^{n} \dfrac{C_t}{(1+i)^t}} \right] \frac{di}{(1+i)} \tag{3}$$

where the bracket term is equal to a Macaulay's duration. Thus, duration is a present-value weighted averaging of the time till maturity, and this average could be used to approximate the percentage price change for a given change in the interest rate.

As indicated in the chapter, immunization is usually viewed in the framework of Macaulay's duration. In this framework, each asset and liability is viewed as producing a series of cash flows (*A_t* for cash flows from assets in period *t*, and *L_t* for cash flows from liabilities). Immunization of the investment operation requires that the present value of the asset flows exactly equal to present value of the liability flow, or in commonly used notation:[6]

$$\sum_{t=0}^{T} A_t v^t = \sum_{t=0}^{T} L_t v^t \tag{4}$$

where v is the discount factor of $1/(1 + i)$, and T is the longest period of the cash flows from the present assets and liabilities. The necessary and sufficient mathematical conditions to immunize this operation against changes in value due to changes in i are obtained from setting the first and second derivatives with respect to i such that[7]

$$\sum_{t=0}^{T} t v^t A_t = \sum_{t=0}^{T} t v^t L_t \tag{5}$$

and

$$\sum_{t=0}^{T} t((t+1)v^t A_t > \sum_{t=0}^{T} t(t+1)v^t L_t \tag{6}$$

Finally, since $\Sigma A_t v^t = \Sigma L_t v^t$ by (4), dividing both of the derivatives in equations (5) and (6) by their respective magnitudes results in

$$D_A = D_L \tag{7}$$

and

$$D_A^2 > D_L^2 \tag{8}$$

respectively where D stands for duration as generally defined by Macaulay. Thus, the conditions for immunizing the firm's value against interest rate fluctuation would be to set the derivative of its assets flows equal to the derivative of its liability flows, while the second derivative of the asset flows is greater than the second derivative of the liability flows. The second order condition established by equations (6) and (8) insures that the value of the investment operation will increase regardless of the direction of the interest rate change.

REFERENCES

1. Altman, Edward I. "Financial Ratios, Discriminant Analysis and the Prediction of Corporate Bankruptcy," *Journal of Finance,* vol. 23 (September 1968): 589–609.

2. Altman, Edward, I. and Eisenbeis, Robert A. "Financial Applications of Discriminant Analysis: A Clarification." *Journal of Financial and Quantitative Analysis* 13 (March 1978): 185–95.

---

[6] Note that the words "investment operation" are chosen, rather than corporation. This choice is because if equation (4) held for a corporation, it would have no value. Also, if L_t were to include dividend payments to shareholders, then T for liabilities would approach infinity and immunization would be impossible since the longest asset flow must occur after the longest liability flow in order for the second order conditions to be fulfilled.

[7] It is, of course, assumed that neither any A_t or L_t is a function of i. However, this may not be true for many corporate liabilities which are related to inflation.

3. Altman, Edward I.; Avery, Robert; Eisenbeis, Robert; and Sinkey, Joseph, *Application of Classification Techniques in Business, Banking and Finance* (Greenwich, Connecticut: JAI Press, forthcoming 1980).

4. Ang, James S. and Patel, Kiritkumara. "Bond Rating Methods: Comparison and Validation." *Journal of Finance* 30 (May 1975): 631–40.

5. Bierwag, G. O. "Immunization, Duration, and the Term Structure of Interest Rates." *Journal of Financial and Quantitative Analysis* 12 (December 1977): 725–42.

6. Bradley, Stephen P., and Crane, Dwight B. "Management of Commercial Bank Government Security Portfolios: An Optimization Approach Under Uncertainty." *Journal of Bank Research* 4 (Spring 1973): 18–30.

7. Dietz, Peter O.; Fogler, H. Russell; and Rivers, Anthony U. "Bond Duration and Nonlinearity: An Empirical Note." Working paper under review.

8. Fama, Eugene F. "Forward Rates as Predictors of Future Spot Rates." *Journal of Financial Economics* 3 (October 1976): 361–78.

9. Fisher, Lawrence. "Determinants of Risk Premiums on Corporate Bonds." *Journal of Political Economy* 67 (June 1959): 217–37.

10. Fisher, Lawrence, and Weil, Roman L. "Coping with the Risk of Interest-Rate Fluctuations: Returns to Bondholders from Naive and Optimal Strategies." *Journal of Business* 44 (no. 4, October, 1971): 408–31.

11. Fogler, H. Russell; Groves, William A., and Richardson, James G. "Managing Bonds: Are 'Dumbbells' Smart?" *Journal of Portfolio Management* 2 (Winter 1976): 54–60.

12. Fogler, H. Russell, and Groves, William A. "How Much Can Active Bond Management Raise Returns?" *Journal of Portfolio Management* 3 (Fall 1976): 35–40.

13. Fogler, H. Russell. "Irving Fisher's Equation, Bonds, and Portfolio Immunization: A Generalization." Working Paper funded by the S. S. Huebner Foundation, University of Pennsylvania, 1979.

14. Friend, Irwin; Westerfield, Randolph; and Granito, Michael. "New Evidence on the Capital Asset Pricing Model." *Journal of Finance* 33 (June 1978): 903–17.

15. Grier, P., and Katz, S. "The Differential Effects of Bond Rating Changes Among Industrial and Public Utility Bonds by Maturity." *Journal of Business* 49 (1976): 226–39.

16. Hettenhouse, George, and Sartoris, W. "An Analysis of the Informational Value of Bond Rating Changes." *Quarterly Review of Economics and Business* 16 (1976): 65–78.

17. Homer, Sidney. "The Historical Evolution of Today's Bond Market." *The Theory and Practice of Bond Portfolio Management*, Peter Bernstein, ed. (New York: Institutional Investor Books, 1976), pp. 12–26.

18. Homer, Sidney, and Martin L. Leibowitz. *Inside the Yield Book* (Englewood Cliffs, N.J.: Prentice-Hall, 1970).

19. Ingersoll, Jonathan. "Duration and the Measurement of Risk." Report 7739, (University of Chicago, Center for Mathematical Studies in Business and Economics, July 1977).

20. Joy, O. Maurice, and Tollefson, John O. "Some Clarifying Comments on

Discriminant Analysis." *Journal of Financial and Quantitative Analysis* 13 (March 1978): 197–200.

21. Katz, S. "The Price Adjustment Process of Bonds to Rating Reclassifications." *Journal of Finance* 29 (1974): 551–59.

22. Kaufman, George G.; Loeffler, Thomas A.; and Schweitzer, Robert L. "Measuring Risk and Return for Portfolios of Coupon Bonds." Working paper prepared for the Annual Meeting of the Financial Management Association, 1978.

23. Khang, Chulsoon. "Bond Immunization When Short-Term Rates Fluctuate More Than Long-Term Rates." (University of Oregon, Center for Capital Market Research, 1977).

24. Leibowitz, Martin L. "Sources of Return in Corporate Bond Portfolios," Salomon Brothers, 1978.

25. Macaulay, Frederick R. *Some Theoretical Problems Suggested by the Movements of Interest Rates, Bond Yields, and Stock Prices in the United States Since 1856.* (New York: Columbia University Press for the National Bureau of Economic Research, 1938).

26. Malkiel, Burton G. "Expectations, Bond Prices, and the Term Structure of Interest Rates." *Quarterly Journal of Economics* 76 (May 1962): 197–218.

27. McCallum, John S. "The Expected Holding Period Return: Uncertainty, and the Term Structure of Interest Rates." *Journal of Finance* 30 (May 1975): 307–23.

28. Pinches, George E.; Singleton, J. Clay; and Jahankhani, Ali. "Fixed Coverage as a Determinant of Electric Utility Bond Ratings." *Financial Management* 7 (Summer 1978): 45–55.

29. Sharpe, William F. *Investments* (Englewood Cliffs, N.J.: Prentice-Hall, Inc., 1978).

30. Vanderhoof, Irwin. "Inflation, Expenses, Interest Rates and Benefits." Tokyo: transactions of the 20th International Congress of Actuaries, 1976.

31. Watson, Ronald D. "Tests of Maturity Structures of Commercial Bank Government Securities Portfolios: A Simulation Approach." *Journal of Bank Research* 3 (Spring 1972): 34–46.

32. Weinstein, Mark I. "The Effect of a Rating Change Announcement on Bond Price." *Journal of Financial Economics* 5 (December 1977): 329–50.

33. Wilbur, William L. "A Theoretical and Empirical Investigation of Holding Period Yields on High Grade Corporate Bonds," Ph.D. dissertation, Graduate School of Business Administration, University of North Carolina at Chapel Hill, 1967), pp. 22–23.

34. Wissner, Len., ed. "Immunization and Duration: State of the Art." *Proceedings of the Smith Barney Seminar,* Tarrytown, New York, October 1978.

35. Yawitz, Jess B., and Marshall, William J. "Risk and Return in the Government Bond Market." *Journal of Portfolio Management* (Summer 1977): 48–52.

Chapter 10

Management of Real Estate Portfolios

PAUL SACK

The Rosenberg Real Estate Equity Funds
San Francisco, California

This chapter will discuss equity investment in real properties. Emphasis will be on the goals of such investment, the types of properties best suited to attaining those goals, the special problems of acquisition and selecting an investment vehicle, problems of liquidity, the interrelated problems of leverage and risk. The characteristics of specific types of properties will not be discussed in detail but will be mentioned only to illustrate the types of expertise necessary for the actual selection of properties.

This chapter will not deal with mortgages, which are better regarded as part of the fixed income portfolio. Nor will the chapter deal with the tax and tax shelter aspects of real estate, except to the limited extent that they affect the tax exempt institutions whose managers are the major audience of the Handbook.

WHY INVEST IN REAL ESTATE?

The goals of investment in real estate are:

1. diversification;
2. to improve the stability of income and value of the portfolio;
3. to achieve current income;
4. protection from inflation of both income and principal.

These goals must be pursued in a manner consistent with the prudent manager's concern for safety of principal and requirements for liquidity.

345

1. Diversification. Real estate offers an opportunity to diversify into an investment whose values and current returns do not rise and fall on the same cycle as equity or fixed income securities. Moreover, as increasing numbers of portfolio managers make substantial investments in real estate, the ERISA mandate for diversification may ultimately be interpreted as requiring diversification into real estate.

For many years, it was believed that real estate values and yields moved with those of fixed income securities, but as investors have increasingly turned to real estate as an inflation hedge, the very forces which drive interest rates upward to build inflation into those rates have caused rates of return on real estate to decline. Investors have been willing to accept lower returns on properties offering inflation protection while they were demanding higher yields on fixed income securities. For example, 20 years ago the unleveraged return on real estate was consistently higher than the interest rate on mortgages, but the reverse is now the case. Thus rates of return on real estate equity investment and fixed income rates have moved in opposite directions over that period.

2. Stability of Income and Portfolio Value. Real estate values and rates of return are much less volatile than prices of equity or fixed income securities. Price movements in real estate are difficult to detect until they have progressed for a number of months, since prices are not quoted daily in newspapers. The market therefore recognizes changes in capitalization rates (yield) very slowly; and since leases are normally written for periods of years, current income also changes slowly. Thus, correctly chosen real estate investments can add to stability of portfolio values.

3. Current Income. Real estate investment can provide current income at a rate in excess of the dividend rate in most portfolios and comparable to (though currently less than) rates of return on fixed income securities. During 1978, for instance, current cash returns from real estate of investment quality and purchased on an unleveraged basis were 8–8.5 percent; returns on bonds rated Aa by Standard & Poor's averaged 8.9 percent, and dividends on the stocks which make up the Dow Jones Average represented a cash return of 6.0 percent based on prices of November 30, 1978.

4. Inflation Protection. A major purpose of diversification into real estate is to achieve protection against erosion by inflation of the real value of current income and principal. The investor in real estate hopes to achieve a current rate of return comparable with that on fixed income investments combined with significant inflation protection of that return.

Achieving inflation protection requires a careful analysis of lease maturities, favoring short-term over longer leases, and attention to the future competitiveness of the property in terms of location and design. Whereas 15 years ago, many investors considered the highest quality properties to be those leased for very long periods of time to tenants with top credit, the most highly-prized properties today are those with short-term leases which thus offer the possibility of increasing rents to offset inflation.

The Liquidity of Real Estate Investments

Real estate is essentially less liquid than most other forms of investment, and the financial structures which have been devised to give some promise of liquidity—the real estate investment trusts (REITS), for example—have almost uniformly been unsuccessful. While there is obviously a price at which a piece of property can be sold quickly to provide liquidity, the orderly exploration of the market and consummation of the sale of a property frequently take up to six months.

Portfolio managers should thus commit to real estate only that portion of the total portfolio on which liquidity is not required. For some portfolios, the need for 100 percent liquidity will totally rule out investment in real estate. For others with predictable positive cash flows, a prudent manager might well consider committing 5–20 percent of the portfolio to equity investment in real estate.

Funds invested in real estate should be considered committed for at least five and preferably ten years or longer. As will be seen below, leases turn over slowly; and it may take five to ten years for the increases in rental income, which were the original purpose of the investment, to materialize. Properties which promise excellent inflation protection over a holding period of ten years may show very little movement in current return and value for the first four to seven years, as the investor waits for leases to expire so that rents can be increased to reflect inflation.

Incremental Value in Real Estate

Real estate offers a highly capital-intensive investment in very durable, hard assets—bricks and mortar, etc. For several decades at least, the costs of construction have risen more rapidly than the general rate of inflation. As a result, the rents necessary to support the price of new construction have risen more rapidly than the general price indices.

Rents attainable in older buildings whose location and design allow them to compete with the new buildings have similarly risen to levels just below those commanded by the new structures. As potential rents have increased, value has increased; and as current leases expire and are rewritten at increased rents, the increments in the value of the property accrue to its owners.

Conversely, where long-term leases prevent the owner from increasing the rent to market levels, the incremental value lies with the tenant.

The properties which are most likely to yield increments in value and to provide inflation protection are clearly those whose design and location make it possible for them to compete with the new properties of the future. One of the cardinal rules in investing is thus to avoid paying for features which were built for the special purposes of the present tenant but for which future tenants might have no use—features such as walk-in refrigerators, extra-heavy electric power, etc.

Characteristics of High Quality Properties

Unfortunately, it takes an expert to recognize which properties are most readily rentable to future tenants and are therefore the most desirable investments. Some of the characteristics the experts look for will be cited in this section.

The three types of properties most sought as institutional investments are office buildings, industrial buildings, and shopping centers. To this list, some would add apartment buildings—others would not. Here is a quick catalog of what the experts look for in each of these types of property.

Office Buildings. Location should be in an area with other office buildings, convenient to transportation and highways, and close to such amenities as restaurants and at least convenience shopping.

Elevator service and air conditioning should be sufficient to serve the building, and there should be an adequate number of separate air conditioning zones so that different temperatures can be maintained in different areas of the offices. Ceiling heights of nine feet are preferred, but slightly lower ceilings are acceptable in many markets.

The configuration of the building should be such that the floors can be broken up into a great variety of shapes and sizes to suit the greatest number of possible future tenants. The distance from the hall to the window is crucial and varies from city to city as the average size of tenant varies. If the distance is too great, for instance, the average size tenant will be left with a long, thin office, with only a short frontage on the windows for executives and too much back space for clerical help. Floors with the elevators in the center core offer greater flexibility than those with elevators at one end of the floor.

Industrial Buildings. Location must be convenient to highways and, preferably, to a four-way highway interchange. Proximity to the airport and to a railway are important in most markets.

Warehouses should offer dock-high loading for trucks, with weather protection in certain climates; railroad access; good ceiling heights; automatic sprinklers; and no more than 15 percent office space.

Even though the building may now be occupied by a single tenant, the bay depths should be short enough that the building could be cut up for several tenants when the current lease runs out. There should be at least 100 to 120 feet of paved area for truck turn-arounds.

It is preferable if trucks can enter from one driveway and go out another.

In manufacturing buildings, one similarly looks for a configuration which will allow the space to be cut up for a number of tenants in the future. Mezzanine office space often has little value to a future tenant and should be heavily discounted. Adequacy of parking for present and possible future uses must be calculated.

Shopping Centers. Location must offer good access by automobile and, in some markets, public transportation. Purchasing power in the trading area is of almost equal importance, and careful attention must be paid to both present and possible future competition with which that purchasing power must be shared.

Bay depths should not be too deep for the average tenant. Most tenants prefer as much window space as possible, and small tenants can rarely make good use of a space more than 60 to 75 feet deep.

Layout of the center should make entry and exit easy for cars approaching from any direction. Every tenant's sign should be visible from the street. Parking should be laid out in such a way that cars to not back up in the main aisles as other cars enter or leave a space.

Apartment Buildings. Problems of management, fear of rent control, and competition from tax-oriented investors have caused many institutions to rule out investment in apartment buildings. Nevertheless, the ability to raise rents every year (or twice a year) gives apartment buildings the potential of better inflation protection than commercial or industrial properties whose leases are generally written for periods of years.

To be competitive, apartments should be located in good residential areas, reasonably convenient to the dominant modes of transportation and to shopping. Identification from a well-traveled artery reduces advertising costs.

One-bedroom units should contain at least 650 square feet and two-bedroom units 875 square feet; otherwise, they may have to compete on the basis of price rather than quality. Floor plans should allow for a variety of furniture arrangements, provide adequate closet space, etc.

In recent years, amenities such as landscaping (with mature trees, lakes, and streams), recreation buildings, swimming pools, saunas, whirlpools, pool tables, tennis courts, and views have become crucial to competitiveness.

Characteristics of Higher Risk Properties

One way to reduce risk is to purchase only existing properties which have already been leased and whose net income can be analyzed on the basis of actual leases, rent receipts, and operating history.

Vacant or Substantially Vacant Properties. A principal difficulty

in purchasing vacant or largely vacant properties is estimating the
ultimate income and expenses to determine net income and thus value.
If rents are projected at $6 per square foot, and only $5.50 proves
attainable, the overpayment for the property could prove substantial—
particularly if expenses turn out to be underestimated. For instance:

	Projected	*Actual*	*Percent Change*
Rents on 100,000 square feet	$ 600,000	$ 550,000	− 8.3%
Expenses	200,000	225,000	+12.5%
Net Income	$ 400,000	325,000	—
Value, capitalized at 8½%	$4,700,000	$3,800,000	−19.2%

Thus, an 8 percent overestimation of the potential rent combined with
a 12.5 percent underestimation of expenses lead to an overpayment
of 19 percent for the property.

To guard against such possibilities, some investors purchase only
substantially-occupied properties, where rents have been proven in
the open market and where expenses either are not the owner's responsibility or can be analyzed on the basis of past operating data.

Another way to protect one's self is to contract for purchase of a
substantially vacant property for a price which will vary in accordance
with the actual rents achieved when the property has been leased.
To do this, a contract is signed calling for progressive payments by
the purchaser to the developer-seller on the basis of leasing achievement. The price finally paid depends on the relationship of actual
leases and rents to the original projections.

Development Deals. New developments combine the necessity of
working with projected, rather than actual, rents and expenses with
additional uncertainty concerning the time required to bring the project onstream.

In recent years, as the Federal Reserve has resorted to periods of
tight and expensive money to control inflation, the nation has experienced several years of negative real growth in the economy, meaning
zero demand for additional commercial or industrial space. The result
has been a stretch-out of the time it takes to fully lease new developments. Time costs money—especially when money is tight and expensive. The result has been that new developments have oftentimes not
achieved projected profits, and returns have often been particularly
disappointing on a time-discounted basis.

The increased time required to lease up new properties was the
cause of the difficulties of many of the REITS, who had loaned money
to developers who were unable to pay the carrying costs when the
economy slowed up. Clearly, the rewards do not always justify the
risks in development deals.

Raw Land. While it is often possible to estimate that a given piece of raw land lies in the path of development and will improve in value, it is less easy to estimate the amount of time it will take for an increase in value to be realized; therefore, the time-discounted rate of return on raw land is extremely hazardous to forecast. The threat that environmentalists will downgrade potential uses also adds an element of uncertainty which it is difficult to measure. What, for instance, is a piece of raw land worth if it is rezoned for use as a park or "open space" ? The heir to 7,200 acres in Big Sur country in California was recently advised that environmental restrictions will allow subdivision into only three lots on each of which one house can be built.

Nevertheless, in a large real estate portfolio, there is room for a component of raw land—perhaps 5–10 percent of the total real estate portfolio.

Hotels and Motels. At first look, hotels and motels seem to offer excellent potential for inflation protection, because the rent can be renegotiated every night. The problem is that hotels and motels are less highly capital-intensive than the other real estate investments cited. Operating results depend on management skills, employee productivity, union negotiation, and marketing programs. Useful life of such properties may be severely curtailed by changes in fashion within the hospitality industry, requirement of a different amenity package, etc. Thus, investing in a hotel or motel is more like investing in a business than in a capital intensive piece of real property. Nevertheless, a properly-structured deal with a competent and financially capable manager could provide an attractive investment.

Restaurants and Other Special-Purpose Buildings. The incremental value in real estate stems from the usefulness of the property to other tenants in the future. Buildings specially designed to the specifications of one tenant—such as a fast-food chain—will obviously enjoy only the narrowest of markets if the original tenant moves out or, as is highly likely, if the design specifications of the original tenant change over time. Special purpose properties should be avoided.

Determining Intrinsic Value

The intrinsic value of a property is its replacement cost and constitutes the upper limit of value. Recall that the goal is to invest in well located, well designed properties which can expect to achieve increases in rents in the future matching the increases in market rents made necessary by increases in construction costs. If one pays no more than replacement cost at the time of purchase, the potential exists to share fully in the effects of inflation on market rents. If, however, one pays more than replacement cost, one has already given away some of the potential incremental value of the property. Often, a price above re-

placement cost seems justified by the net income of the property—
particularly if the rents reflect some special features built into the
property for the current tenant. Thus, it is important to estimate replacement cost independently before purchasing real property.

Leverage

Traditionally, tax-oriented investors have purchased real estate on
a highly leveraged basis with loans typically constituting 75–80 percent
of the purchase price. Leverage is necessary for these investors to
achieve a high ratio of depreciable assets to equity investment for
tax shelter. Such investors are typically less concerned with safety of
principal and stability of income than managers of institutional funds.

If one knew that rental income would always increase more rapidly
than expenses, it would obviously pay to be as highly leveraged as
possible. The problem is that rents do not always increase so rapidly,
and leverage works both ways.

For instance, consider the case of a building which has been foreclosed by a REIT because its 25 percent vacancy factor made it impossible for the investment to cover debt service. On an unleveraged basis,
the 25 percent vacancy factor would simply have reduced the operating return on equity from, say, 9.5 percent to approximately 6 percent—not the most desirable result but nothing near the disaster of
a foreclosure. Real estate leveraged with 75 percent debt typically
breaks even at 82 percent occupancy, while unleveraged properties
break even at occupancy of 40 percent or less.

Therefore, for institutional investors greatly concerned over preservation of principal and whose goals for real estate investment include
improving the stability of income and value for their portfolios, leverage in any significant degree seems inappropriate.

Moreover, even to tax-oriented investors, leverage was more attractive in the past when mortgage rates were lower than rates of return
on an unleveraged basis. In these times of "reverse leverage," borrowing reduces the rate of current income and increases the speculative
nature of the investment in a way that may be unsuited to the goals
of the managers of the fund. Managers will also want to consider the
net portfolio effect of borrowing on mortgages at rates which exceed
the interest rates being realized on the fixed income portion of their
own portfolio.

Furthermore, in most vehicles for investment in real estate by tax-
exempt institutions—including direct ownership—leverage will result
in unrelated business income subject to taxation, reducing rates of
return after taxes.

It seems safe to conclude, therefore, that most managers of institutional funds will purchase real estate on an unleveraged basis or will

be willing to accept only small amounts of leverage—particularly where properties can be acquired subject to old loans at low interest rates.

HOW TO INVEST IN REAL ESTATE

As should now be clear, considerable expertise is necessary to put together a real estate portfolio which will meet the goals and quality standards of institutional investors. Unfortunately, there are no rating services to label a property Aaa, A, or Baa. Every property is different, because no two locations can be exactly the same.

The ideal way to invest is through direct ownership, i.e., to acquire the necessary staff and then purchase and manage the properties in-house. For reasons of diversification and the difficulty of staffing, however, only a few of the very largest institutions will find this route feasible. For instance:

Diversification. Prudence dictates diversification into at least eight or ten properties. In order not to compete with small, tax-oriented investors, each property should be worth at least $2–$3 million. Thus, proper diversification would require a minimum investment of approximately $25 million. If the real estate portfolio is to be 20 percent of the total, then only a fund of at least $125 million can achieve adequate diversification through direct investment; if real estate is to be 5 percent of the total portfolio, only a fund of at least $500 million can consider direct investment.

Staffing. Acquiring staff with appropriate expertise will not be easy. Such persons are highly paid within the industry, are hard to attract and not easy to hold—especially for a one-time investment of only $25 million. Moreover, different expertise is required for industrial properties, office buildings, shopping centers, etc. Several staff thus will be required. Unless an annual program is contemplated of investing approximately $25 million per year for several years, it is doubtful an appropriate staff could be assembled. While theoretically the analysis might be delegated to real estate consultants, the expertise necessary to make the final decision on consultants' recommendations is not much different from that necessary to select from offerings by brokers. Thus, staffing requirements make direct investment feasible only for funds with assets in the range of $500 million and up.

All but a very few of the larger institutions, therefore, will elect to invest in real estate in combination with other institutions with similar goals and tax status, through the vehicle of commingled funds.

Commingled Funds: Open-End versus Closed-End

The most popular commingled vehicles are open-end funds. In the same manner as with open-end mutual funds, interests are continually offered to new investors. Current income from the properties as well as funds from new investors are available to buy out those who wish to sell, appearing to give real estate a measure of liquidity not usually attainable by direct ownership. If new investment exceeds withdrawals, the fund can expand, buy ever-larger properties, and offer greater diversification. There are two caveats:

1. If requests for withdrawal exceed the sum of cash flow and new investments, liquidity can be attained only by the fund's selling properties. Thus, the appearance of liquidity may be an illusion, especially if—as is likely—the market forces which cause one investor to decide to sell out cause many to make the same decision at the same time.

2. The second problem is the knotty one of appraising real estate. It is easy to set the price at which investors buy into or sell out of commingled pools of stocks or bonds; newspapers carry the market prices daily. But appraising real estate is either an art or a very inexact science. Two appraisers, using the same data and appraising for the same purpose, can differ by 15–20 percent in their appraisal of value. As most real estate owners will attest, the only time one knows what a property is worth is when one is walking away from the title company with a check after a sale—and even then one can't be sure the price might not have been higher.

Proponents of open-end funds argue that in a large portfolio, the errors cancel each other out, but that argument is unconvincing. The appraisals could easily have a constant bias—downward in the interest of prudence and conservatism or upward in the interest of improving performance measurements for the managers of the fund (who, after all, hire the appraisers).

One example of this problem involves a highly regarded institutional fund which boasted that it is conservative in its appraisals and that the only property it had ever sold went for 20 percent more than appraised value. The appraisal process thus transferred appreciation from the early investors to those who bought in later.

In another example, fund appraisers increased the value of the portfolio by $600,000 one year and then, because of reverses in some markets, reduced the value by $1.5 million the next year. Investors had sold out both years, so the appraisal process transferred capital from those who sold out the second year to those who sold out the first year. Whether they are willing to buy into and sell out of open-ended real estate portfolios on the basis of appraised values is something institutional managers will have to weigh.

Closed-end funds can be so structured that money does not change hands on the basis of appraisals. A fixed amount of money is received into the closed-end fund and is then invested in real properties on the basis of prices arrived at by negotiations at arm's length in the open market. When all the money has been invested, each investor owns a proportionate share of a pool of properties purchased at market prices rather than buying into the fund at values set by an appraiser, as in an open-end fund.

While an open-end fund receives new money for investment and grows over a period of years, the managers of closed end funds must periodically start a new fund—typically every year. Thus an open-end fund generally offers more diversification (more properties) than a single closed-end fund and, because the open-end fund can grow very large over time, is able to purchase larger properties than closed-end funds. However, it should be possible to achieve adequate diversification in a closed-end fund, provided it is large enough to purchase, say, a minimum of $20 million of properties; and there is no reason to believe that returns on the larger properties that lie beyond the means of closed-end funds are higher than returns on the size of property closed-end funds can buy without damage to their diversification plan.

Selecting a Real Estate Manager, Fund Manager, or Consultant

It is almost impossible to attend a one-day conference on real estate without hearing the word "entrepreneurial." Many believe that there is an entrepreneurial component to buying, as well as to developing, real estate and that the acquisition function cannot be institutionalized, i.e. carried out by a hierarchy of committees. In such hierarchies, the field work is generally done by the least experienced operative, and written reports travel upward through a series of two or three presumably increasingly expert committees. The experience of banks with REITS is often cited as evidence that such a decision-making structure may not work well in real estate.

On the other hand, there are large institutions which have been successful in real estate—notably some of the insurance companies. The people at the top of these programs are undeniably entrepreneurial and immensely knowledgeable about real estate. While they have not been able to filter all the bad properties out of the acquisition process, they have purchased some very good ones.

Decisions in real estate are not likely to be any better than the people who make them—up and down the decision-making line. It is an essential part of the process of selecting a real estate manager, therefore, to meet with and evaluate the people at all decision-making levels in the manager's shop. Careful attention should also be paid to the decision-making procedures.

Ideally, the selecting team would also visit a representative sample of properties already purchased by the manager.

Such an evaluation will itself require some real estate expertise. If this is available within the organization with which the investing fund is associated (as in the case of the pension fund of a corporation with a real estate department), so much the better. Otherwise, it will be wise to find an adviser who is knowledgeable about real estate and in whom the selection team has confidence. The role of such an adviser would not be to evaluate the proposed real estate strategy but only the knowledgeability of the experts being hired to carry it out.

Track records should be scrutinized if available, but they are unfortunately not so easy to interpret as one might hope. In the next section, "Evaluating Performance," it will be pointed out that increases in value may reflect the action of market forces over which the manager has had no control and that stabilized current income is a more meaningful measure of managers. In the cases of a closed-end fund or directly-owned properties, trends in current income are easily determined because the pool of properties is relatively fixed. On the other hand, in open-end funds where properties are continually being added to the portfolio (presumably bringing additional current income) and where portfolio values are changed quarterly on the basis of appraisals, it is not so easy to determine the track records of any single group of properties over time.

EVALUATING PERFORMANCE

Real estate is a long-term investment, because income and value change slowly. After all, one of the goals of diversifying into real estate is to add stability to the income stream and to portfolio value. Where six months seems a long time to investors in the stock market, six years is a short time in real estate.

For example, a property might be purchased because it is well located and competitively designed, its current rents are below market, and the current leases expire in six years. After six years, the investor could expect a very large increase in current income and capitalized value, including an increase in rents related to the rate of inflation over the six years following purchase. However, there would be no change in net income for six full years. Yet, it would be folly to give the manager low marks for failing to show increases in income while waiting for the current leases to expire. Real estate requires patience and cannot be evaluated on the basis of quarter-to-quarter operating results.

Most institutions, for reporting or other purposes, will want properties to be appraised independently every one or two years. Such appraisals will rely heavily on the income method of appraisal, in which current market rents will be factored in.

The formula for income value in real estate is the same as that for bonds, but the components are differently labeled:

$$\frac{\text{Stabilized net income}}{\text{Capitalization rate}} = \text{Value}$$

The *capitalization rate* is obviously akin to yield on bonds and is selected by the appraiser on the basis of her or his reading of the market. *Stabilized net income* is kin of dividends or interest payments, except that it has been adjusted for temporary aberrations in the rental market or rental program and for differences between rents received under current leases and market rents that could be achieved if those leases expired.[1] The appraisals thus can give a clue as to how the portfolio is progressing—bearing in mind, of course, that there is a 15–20 percent margin of error in appraisals.

The problem in evaluating performance on the basis of appraisals is that appraised values are heavily affected by changes in the capitalization rate, which is a function of market forces over which the manager has no control. For the past three years, for instance, real estate has been increasing in value, because capitalization rates have been declining by ½ percent (50 basis points) per year as investors have been willing to accept lower rates of return in the short run on investments which they believe offer protection against inflation. Obviously this kind of increase in value cannot be projected indefinitely into the future, as there is some minimum return greater than zero that investors will demand under any circumstances. Changes in value based on changes in the capitalization rate reflect not the performance of the real estate manager but the evaluation of real estate as an investment by financial markets.

Changes in the numerator of the value fraction, i.e., stabilized net income, are a better measure of how well the real estate manager has done in selecting properties and managing them, as stabilized net income is based on current market rents. Therefore, for the purpose of evaluating the real estate manager, it is useful to ask the appraiser for a separate set of values based on constant (year-to-year) capitalization rates.

SUMMARY

The goals of equity investment in real estate are diversification, stability of income and value, current income, and inflation protection.

---

[1] The appraiser handles the problem of the difference between rents under current leases and market rents which could be achieved if the current leases were not in force as follows:

Stabilized income under this method is net income which could be achieved if all rents at the property were current market rents. By the formula, stabilized net income would be divided by the capitalization rate to give the total value of the property, including both the owner's interest *and* the leasehold interests of the tenants. The appraiser would then calculate the annual estimated loss of rent resulting from the fact that rents under current leases are below market. The appraiser would then calculate the discounted present value of the stream of earnings losses resulting from the fact that rents under current leases are less than market rents, and that discounted present value would be the value of the leasehold interests. By deducting the value of the leasehold interests from the total value of the property determined by the formula, the appraiser would determine the value of the owner's fee interest in the property.

Real estate is less liquid than most other forms of investment, so managers should carefully consider the proportion of funds they can actuarially afford to commit.

Incremental value in real estate lies in those properties whose high quality of design and location will allow them to compete with new properties in the future. Since the cost of construction will rise with inflation, rents in new properties and those able to compete with them will also rise.

The type of properties deemed most suitable for institutional investment are shopping centers, office and industrial buildings. Apartments rank somewhat lower, followed by hotels and motels and raw land. There is disagreement as to whether development deals and special purpose buildings are suitable.

Leverage works both ways, increasing both potential returns and potential for loss. Leverage thus increases volatility and risk.

All but the largest institutions will invest in real estate through commingled funds, and the differences between open-end and closed-end funds should be carefully considered.

Measures of comparative performance of real estate and real estate managers are just beginning to be developed and will require understanding of the nature of real estate investment.

REFERENCES

Hoagland, H. E.; Stone, L. D.; and Brueggeman, W. B. *Real Estate Finance* (Homewood, Ill.: Richard D. Irwin, 1977).

Ring, A. A., and Passo, S. *Real Estate Principles and Practices* (Englewood Cliffs, N.J.: Prentice-Hall, 1977).

Wendt, P. F., and Cerf, A. R. *Real Estate Investment Analysis And Taxation* (New York: McGraw-Hill, 1979).

Wiley, R. J. *Real Estate Investment* (New York: Ronald Press, 1977).

Chapter 11

International Diversification*

DONALD R. LESSARD

Sloan School of Management
Massachusetts Institute of Technology
Cambridge, Massachusetts

INTRODUCTION

In contrast to many innovations in investment management, international diversification has appeal to individuals with a wide range of investment perspectives. To disciples of modern portfolio theory, it is a logical extension of the arguments made at the domestic level for holding passive, well-diversified portfolios. To active managers, who seek to outguess other market participants, it is a new frontier, where insightful analysis is likely to result in superior performance.

The potential advantage of international diversification is a better ratio of reward to risk than that obtainable with a purely domestic portfolio—a higher expected return for a given level of risk or a lower level of risk for a given return. While it is possible that this advantage can be gained by consistently investing in one or a few foreign markets which outperform the United States market on a risk-adjusted basis, it is more likely to follow from the fact that returns from common stocks in various countries do not move in lock step and thus the risk-return combinations available with an internationally diversified portfolio is likely to be superior to those of the individual stock markets.

Although there is extensive evidence that the comovement of returns across countries is low enough so that international diversification should result in an improved risk-return mix, individual and institutional investors, at least in the U.S., have shown considerable reluctance in committing substantial proportions of their assets abroad. Apparent

359

drawbacks to international investment which might explain this include concern over currency risks and political risks; perceived limitations on the size, depth, and efficiency of foreign markets; difficulties in obtaining information regarding foreign securities; and uncertainty regarding the prudence of foreign investment.

This chapter first reviews the evidence regarding the advantages of international diversification. It then examines the various perceived drawbacks to foreign investment.

THE POTENTIAL ADVANTAGES OF INTERNATIONAL DIVERSIFICATION

The concept underlying international diversification is the same one applying to diversification along any other dimension—whenever the returns of different assets are not subject to exactly the same risks, the risk of a diversified portfolio of these assets will be lower than the risk of the typical individual security (see Chapter 5 for a detailed discussion of diversification).

The proportion of the risk of individual investments that is diversifiable depends on the degree of correlation among the returns on these assets. Within the United States, the degree of synchronization or correlation between returns on shares of individual firms and a broad based market index typically is around .5. This means that on average, the undiversifiable or systematic risk of a security is 50 percent of its total risk. Figures for a variety of other countries are presented in Table 1.

In general, the proportion of risk of securities which is systematic in other countries is higher than in the U.S. This reflects the fact that these countries typically have a less diverse industrial base than the U.S. and, in some cases, a more volatile political environment. This

Table 1
Risk Reduction through Domestic Diversification (standard deviation of market portfolio relative to standard deviation of typical stock)

Country	Solnik 1966–1971	Lessard 1969–1973
France	.57	.68
Germany	.66	.66
Japan	—	.52
Netherlands	.49	.63
Switzerland	.66	.71
United Kingdom (England)	.59	.61
U.S.	.52	—

Note: Both papers use variance as the risk measure. Standard deviations are used in this chapter since the risk of portfolios typically is measured in these terms.

Sources: D. R. Lessard, "World, National, and Industry Relationships in Security Returns: Implications for Risk Reduction Through International Diversification," *Financial Analysts Journal* (January–February 1976), pp. 2–8; and B. H. Solnik, "Why Not Diversify Internationally Rather Than Domestically?" *Financial Analysts Journal* (July–August 1974), pp. 48–54.

Figure 1
Risk Reduction through National and International Diversification

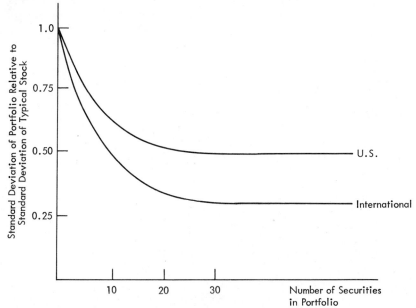

Source: B. H. Solnik, "Why Not Diversify Internationally Rather Than Domestically?" *Financial Analysts Journal* (July–August 1974), pp. 48–54.

is particularly true for less developed countries where there is much less room for risk reduction through domestic diversification.

When diversification is extended across national boundaries, a substantial proportion of the risk which is systematic within each country can be eliminated. Figure 1 shows this, comparing the risk reduction obtainable through diversification within the U.S. to that obtainable through international diversification. In the international case, portfolio risk drops to 33 percent of that of the typical stock, one-third less than the U.S. figure.

The reason for this additional diversification is that returns on diversified single-country portfolios display considerable independence. Many of the factors affecting share values are essentially domestic in nature. Differences among nations in tax laws, monetary policies, and general political climate are illustrative. Even factors that influence the world economy, such as the sudden increase of oil prices in 1973, can affect individual economies differently. This can be seen by examining the correlations between returns on the stock markets of seven major countries and the U.S. for different periods of time through 1977. (Table 2).

Are Correlations Increasing? Since low correlations among coun-

Table 2
Correlation of Major Foreign Markets with the U.S. Market* (selected periods†)

Country	1961–65	1964–68	1967–71	1970–74	1973–77‡	July 1971–June 1973	July 1973–June 1975	July 1975–June 1977
Canada	.828	.830	.813	.836	.727	—	—	—
France	.364	.016	.081	.349	.499	−.240	.683	.392
Germany	.563	.120	.343	.349	.431	.161	.487	.500
Japan	.181	.070	.224	.301	.396	.364	.293	.727
Netherlands	.695	.602	.570	.463	.609	.154	.671	.618
Switzerland	.559	.346	.532	.501	.629	.148	.689	.718
United Kingdom	.428	.187	.278	.483	.507	.312	.596	.256

* The S&P 500 is taken to represent the U.S. market.
† Based on monthly changes in value-weighted market indexes.
‡ Through June 1977, 54 observations.
Source: D. R. Lessard, "An Update on Gains from International Diversification," unpublished 1977, based on stock market data from *Capital International Perspective* (Geneva, Switzerland: Capital International, S.A.).

tries are key to diversification gains, an important question is whether markets are moving more closely together over time. It is well recognized that in recent years, the major nations of the world have become both politically and economically more interdependent. This has been reflected in higher correlation among stock markets in recent years, as shown in Table 2. However, they also have varied considerably from period to period. In the early 1960s correlations were nearly as high as in such recent periods as 1973–75 and 1975–77. They fell in the mid-1960s and continued at relatively low levels into the late 1960s as the level of activity in the U.S. and European economics diverged. Only in the case of Japan have the correlations with the United States increased steadily, as would be expected because of that country's increased industrial and financial integration with the world economy.

When the most recent periods are examined, an interesting pattern emerges. Correlations of major foreign security markets with the U.S. stock market were low from July 1971 to June 1973, reflecting major currency adjustments and divergent economic performance. From July 1973 to June 1975 they rose dramatically, reflecting the common impact of the energy crisis and subsequent developments and they remained relatively high for the July 1975–June 1977 period. The markets in the continental European Economic Community (EEC) countries have tended to move more closely together, with the exception of France, which has had a series of internal upheavals. The U.K. market has moved in and out of synchronization as international and domestic influences have varied in importance. The Japanese market also has varied in its degree of synchronization with others.

Given the increased interdependence of national economies, it is unlikely that the correlations will return to the low level of the mid-1960s but it is difficult to forecast whether they will stay at present levels. While there are strong international economic influences at work, there also are powerful political factors that are largely domestic in nature. Internal disruption, or even disagreement over economic growth versus income distribution, can cause returns in a particular country to fall out of synchronization with the rest of the world. Nevertheless, even during recent periods of relatively high market correlation, international diversification still would have reduced portfolio risk substantially.

Expected Returns and Gains from International Diversification

Although the degree of correlation indicates the extent to which risk can be reduced through international diversification, it does not provide a complete view of the advantages of international diversification, since it does not reveal exactly how domestic and internationally diversified portfolios will compare in terms of risk-adjusted returns.

This comparison requires knowledge about the expected returns in each market as well as the correlations.

However, because of the risk-reduction resulting from relatively low correlations, even relatively low expected returns on foreign markets would result in superior risk-adjusted performance by an internationally diversified portfolio compared to the U.S. market. This is best illustrated by example.

Minimum Expected Returns that Justify International Investment. The appropriate measure of the risk to a United States investor of a foreign holding is its contribution to the risk of one's total portfolio. Assuming that the domestic portfolio is well diversified, the contribution to the portfolio risk of the foreign investment is its β (beta) coefficient, technically the covariance of the security in question with the base portfolio divided by the variance of the base portfolio. (See Chapter 5 for a detailed discussion of β as a measure of security and portfolio risk.)

Taking the German market portfolio as a representative foreign holding, we note that it has an annual standard deviation of return of 20.4 percent compared to 18.5 percent for the U.S. and a correlation of .43 with the U.S. market. Thus the German stock market has a beta relative to the U.S. market portfolio of .47. As a result, a U.S. investor could consider the German market as attractive as the U.S. market if the expected return in excess of the risk-free interest rate was as little as one half the excess return expected from the U.S. market. Table 3 presents the results of similar calculations for the major foreign markets based on correlations and standard deviations measured over the 1973–77 period, and on the assumption that the U.S. investor demands (expects) a risk premium of 6.0 percent on the U.S. market portfolio that has a beta of 1.

Table 3
Risk and Required Return Measures for Foreign Market Portfolios (all figures estimated from data for 1973–1977)

Country	Annualized Standard Deviation of Returns (measured in U.S. dollars)	Correlation With U.S. Market (S & P 500)	Market Risk (beta) from U.S. Perspective	Minimum Risk Premium from U.S. Perspective
France	26.4	.50	.71	4.3
Germany	20.4	.43	.47	2.8
Japan	20.1	.40	.43	2.6
The Netherlands	21.9	.61	.72	4.6
Switzerland	22.7	.63	.77	4.7
United Kingdom	41.0	.51	1.13	6.8
United States	18.5	1.00	1.00	6.0

Source: D. R. Lessard, "An Update on Gains from International Diversification," unpublished, 1977.

Realized and Expected Returns. The past performance of foreign markets suggests the best of both worlds—lower risk and higher returns. Table 4 shows that realized total returns on most foreign markets have outstripped U.S. returns over most recent time periods. However, research findings for the U.S. and other markets show that past returns (unless perhaps for very long periods) provide little information regarding future returns. Further, at least part of the performance of foreign markets can be traced to circumstances that are unlikely to be repeated—the post-war economic recovery of Europe, its subsequent boom resulting from the common market, and the economic phenomenon of Japan propelled in part by a major increase in the degree of world economic integration. Structural shifts of this magnitude are unlikely to recur in the near future for mature industrialized countries, although any one of number of emerging nations may provide similar phenomena in the 1980s.

Table 4
Realized Total Rates of Return in U.S. Dollars (percent per year compounded)

	1959–78	1969–78
Japan	17.0	21.7
Austria	11.1	12.9
Germany	11.5	12.3
Switzerland	12.4	11.7
Denmark	8.4	10.8
Belgium	8.3	10.8
South African Gold Shares	12.5	9.4
Norway	8.4	8.5
Netherlands	8.5	7.6
France	5.8	6.9
Sweden	9.4	5.8
United Kingdom	9.3	4.7
Canada	6.5	4.4
United States (S&P 500)	6.5	3.2
Spain	7.8	2.4
Australia	8.3	1.8
Italy	−.2	−6.29

Source: Computed by the Putnam Companies from price index and dividend data from *Capital International Perspective*. All returns include reinvestment of estimated dividends and are adjusted to U.S. dollars at current exchange rates. Dividends are adjusted for source withholding taxes.

Nonetheless, analysis of fundamental economic conditions in various countries does provide a helpful point of departure in considering the growth of overall activity, corporate profits, and hence, share values. Savings rates and rates of capital formation in many countries, for example, continue to outstrip those of the U.S., as shown in Table 5.

The key question from an investor perspective, though, is the extent

Table 5
Saving and Capital Formation—Selected Countries, 1977

Country	Savings as Percent of Disposable Income	Gross Fixed Capital Formation as Percent of GNP
Canada	10.7	23.0
France	17.1	23.3
Germany	13.7	20.8
Japan	21.5	30.0
Netherlands	13.8	21.3
United Kingdom	14.2	18.0
United States	5.1	18.1

Sources: U.S. Department of Commerce, *International Economic Indicators* (December 1978) and International Monetary Fund, *International Financial Statistics* (December 1978).

to which these anticipated outcomes are capitalized in share values and the rate at which they are capitalized, that is, the expected rate of return given normal expectations of future economic outcomes. Some insight is provided by the current price-cash earnings multiplier—a crude measure of the market capitalization rate.[1] These ratios, shown in Table 6, suggest that unless investors in general expect poorer economic performance from countries other than the U.S., expected returns abroad are as high or higher than those for the U.S.

An alternative approach to estimating expected returns is to consider the implications of varying assumptions regarding domestic and international capital market equilibrium. The primary issue here is whether national markets are viewed as part of an integrated global market or as separate, segmented markets.

Capital Market Equilibrium and Expected Returns. If various national markets are completely isolated from each other, returns will be based solely on a domestic risk-return trade-off that reflects the total riskiness of a national portfolio and the risk preferences of domestic investors. In contrast, if capital markets are integrated into a single market, all securities will be priced in terms of their undiversifiable risk from a world perspective. If the capital asset pricing model applies in this world market, then investors presumably should hold the world market portfolio. A portfolio restricted to the U.S. market would not provide the maximum return for a given level of risk, since it implies bearing diversifiable, and hence uncompensated, risk.

A rough test of the desirability of international diversification under either extreme scenario—complete segmentation or complete integra-

[1] Cash earnings are defined by Capital International as reported earnings plus depreciation.

Table 6
Price-Cash Earnings Ratios for Major World Stock Markets

Country	December 29, 1978	Average each year-end 1974–1978
Singapore	12.1	10.0
Hong Kong	8.7	8.8
Italy	8.3	6.5
Japan	7.4	6.6
Australia	6.1	5.5
Canada	5.3	5.0
United Kingdom	5.1	4.6
United States	5.1	5.9
Belgium	5.0	4.1
Austria	4.1	4.2
Germany	3.9	3.8
Spain	3.5	6.2
Sweden	3.2	3.1
Denmark	3.1	3.4
France	3.1	2.8
Netherlands	3.1	3.1
Norway	2.6	3.8

Source: *Capital International Perspective,* January 1975–January 1979. Geneva, Switzerland.

tion—is possible if certain simplifying assumptions are made about the risk premiums that investors demand per unit of portfolio standard deviation. In the case of segmented markets, assume that investors in each country demand the same ratio of risk premium to total standard deviation (total risk). A test case using this assumption and employing as a basic yardstick the 6.0 percent risk premium assumed earlier for the U.S. market is illustrative.

Applying the assumption of complete segmentation and the 6.0 percent risk premium yardstick to Germany, the market risk premium needs to be greater than that for the United States (6.6 percent compared with 6.0 percent). This larger premium is necessary to provide the same risk-return ratio as demanded for the United States, since the standard deviation of the German market is greater than that of the U.S. market.[2]

The German risk-return situation changes significantly under the complete integration scenario. In an integrated world setting, the risk premium for the German market declines significantly for two reasons. First, the standard deviation of the world market portfolio is less than that for the U.S. market; accordingly, its risk premium must be less

---

[2] On the basis of the standard deviation figures from Table 3, the risk premium for the German market based on its total risk would be 6.6 percent.

$$6.6\% = \frac{20.4\%}{18.5\%} \times 6.0\%$$

Table 7
Expected Returns on Foreign Markets under Alternative Pricing Scenarios

Country	Segmented Pricing			Integrated Pricing		
	Annualized Standard Deviation	*Ratio of Standard Deviation to U.S.**	*Implied Risk Premium*	*Correlation With World Market Portfolio*	*National Risk (beta)†*	*Implied Risk Premium*
France	26.4	1.43	8.6	.67	1.09	6.1
Germany	20.4	1.10	6.6	.62	.78	4.4
Japan	20.1	1.09	6.5	.61	.75	4.3
Netherlands	21.9	1.18	7.1	.79	1.06	6.0
Switzerland	22.8	1.23	7.4	.78	1.09	6.2
United Kingdom	41.0	2.22	13.3	.69	1.74	9.9
United States	18.5	1.00	6.0	.93	1.06	6.0

* Standard Deviation.
† These betas are the product of the correlation of the national market times the standard deviation of the national market divided by the standard deviation of the world market.
Source: Follows approach outlined in D. R. Lessard, "World, Country, and Industry Relationships in Equity Returns: Implications for Risk Reduction through International Diversification," *Financial Analysts Journal* (January–February 1976), pp. 2–8, using correlations and standard deviations from 1973–77.

(5.7 percent compared with 6.0 percent under our assumptions).[3] Second, the German beta in terms of the world market portfolio is .78. Accordingly, the risk premium is 4.4 percent, (.78 × 5.7) which is well below the 6.6 percent risk premium under the assumption of complete segmentation. The risk premium of 4.4 percent, however, is higher than the minimum premium estimated earlier (2.8 percent in Table 3) necessary to make the risk-adjusted return on the German market equivalent to that of the U.S. market from the perspective of a U.S. investor who assigns a 6.0 percent risk premium to the U.S. market.

The similarly computed returns for each major foreign market under the two sets of assumptions are shown in Table 7. In either case, the computed returns for the foreign markets are above the minimum required from a U.S. perspective (Table 3) and, as a result, some international diversification would appear desirable.

To contrast the segmentation and integration views, the results can be interpreted as follows. If national stock markets are segmented, an international portfolio will have superior risk-adjusted performance because securities are priced in terms of their domestic systematic risk, some of which is diversifiable. If national markets are integrated, holding a solely domestic portfolio will imply inferior risk-adjusted

---

[3] The U.S. beta is 1.06 in terms of the world market. Accordingly, the risk premium for the world market is less than that assumed for the U.S. market.

$$\frac{6.0\%}{1.06} = 5.7\%$$

performance because the securities are priced to reflect only their global systematic risk. Thus, the purely domestic component of risk which is not diversified away will not be offset by any risk premium.

It is unlikely that principal national markets (and major stocks) are either completely segmented or integrated. There are substantial international investment flows and many shares are cross-listed on various exchanges. This fact would appear to ensure that comparative valuation is in terms of both national and international perspectives. Yet total integration does not appear to be the case given the home country bias in the portfolio holdings of virtually all investors. It is most likely that prices are determined in a relatively complex fashion because of the obstacles to international capital flows and because of differences in preferences and perceptions by domestic and international investors toward what to them are either local or foreign securities.

OBSTACLES TO INTERNATIONAL INVESTMENT

Currency Risk

The prime motivation for diversifying a portfolio internationally is to improve the reward-to-risk tradeoff by taking advantage of the relatively low correlation among returns on assets of different countries. However, since international investment implies investing in assets which provide returns in a variety of currencies whose relative values may fluctuate, it involves taking foreign exchange risks. A key question facing the investor, then, is whether these exchange risks are so large as to offset the benefits of international diversification. A related question is what, if any, special strategies should be followed to reduce the impact of foreign exchange risk. In dealing with these two questions, it is useful to consider why foreign exchange risk is singled out from the host of risks an investor takes when investing internationally.

The first response is simply that it is a new type of risk, at least for most U.S. investors, and therefore deserves special consideration. While undoubtedly true, this response provides little basis for action other than to call for investor education.

A more basic reason is that foreign exchange risk is perceived as a special type of risk which affects some investors but not others and hence does not fit into a normal reward to risk framework. It is a common perception that foreign exchange risks of investing, say, in the United Kingdom, affect U.S. but not U.K., investors. As a result, in contrast to the market risks of securities from a domestic perspective, it may be perceived that these risks will not be accompanied by a commensurate risk premium. If this is true, it has two important implications for passive international investment strategies: (1) investors will want to hedge some or all of the foreign exchange risks implicit in their foreign equity holdings; and (2) investors also may want to shift the weighting of their risky equity asset holdings toward a higher proportion of domestic shares and away from the world market portfolio. If, in contrast, exchange risk affects all investors equally, it will have no special implications for passive portfolio investment strategies.

With active strategies, of course, the existence of fluctuations in exchange rates means that the exchange dimension is a relevant one for making speculative bets. Whether these operations will be limited to outright currency speculation or will involve shifting equity portfolio weights across or within countries will depend on expected relationships between exchange rate and stock price movements.

The appropriate treatment of exchange risk depends on its nature— whether it is a risk which affects all investors equally or only certain investors—and its magnitude compared to other equity market risks. To understand the nature and importance of currency risk, it is necessary to take into account how exchange rates are related to returns on securities in relatively efficient markets. If security markets function reasonably well, anticipated future trends in exchange rates will be reflected in both interest rates and security prices. There will be uncertainty about these future currency values, but this uncertainty can, to a large extent, be avoided by hedging; i.e., borrowing or entering into forward currency contracts. Even if this uncertainty is not hedged, in most cases it will not increase significantly the volatility of foreign common stock returns from the standpoint of a U.S. investor relative to that of a local U.K. investor and, in the long run, will not cause the average returns from the two perspectives, if measured in real terms, to diverge.

Linkage between Exchange Rates, Interest Rates, and Price Levels. The key relationships to be considered are those among expected differences in inflation, differences in interest rates, expected changes in exchange rates, and forward rates. Four key relationships are illustrated in Figure 2. Since these interrelationships are consistent, any three of them determine the fourth. Similarly, if any one of them is violated, at least one other must be violated. Each of these linkages is reviewed below.

Expected Changes in (Spot) Exchange Rates and Expected Differences in Rates of Inflation. Theory and empirical evidence suggest that, over time, exchange rates do adjust to reflect relative rates of inflation. Therefore, in an efficient market, anticipations of relative inflation will lead to anticipation of corresponding changes in exchange rates.

Interest Rates and Expected Rates of Inflation. This linkage derives from the Fisher effect, which implies that nominal rates of interest in each country adjust to reflect anticipated inflation. As a result, the differences in interest rates will reflect the differences in expected rates of inflation.

Figure 2
Inflation, Interest Rates, Premiums, and Exchange Rates

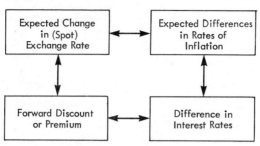

Interest Rates and the Forward Premium or Discount. For most currencies there are two types of exchange rates: spot rates, which are rates that apply to current transactions; and forward rates, which apply to exchange transactions at a particular point in the future. The forward discount or premium is the percentage difference between the current exchange rate and the forward rate, a rate at which future exchange transactions can be "locked in." The relationship between interest rates and the forward discount or premium rate is very powerful, since it is based on arbitrage. It must match exactly the difference in interest rates or investors will be able to profit without bearing any risk by borrowing in the country with the relatively low interest rate (including the cost of forward cover), investing in the money market in the country with the high rate, and removing exchange risk by covering in the forward market.

Anticipated Exchange Rates and Forward Rates. If forward rates differ from anticipated exchange rates, market participants will be induced to speculate on the difference between them, tending to move the forward rate toward the expected future spot rate.

Implications for the Relevance of Foreign Exchange Risks. With all these channels, there is little question that expected changes in exchange rates should be incorporated in interest rates and stock prices in a well-functioning market. In fact, if all these relationships were to hold exactly, anticipated currency fluctuations would be irrelevant for international investment strategies.

Of course, even if anticipated exchange rate changes are fully reflected in interest rates and stock prices, after-the-fact deviations from anticipated rates may have a significant impact on the relative performance of national stock markets.[4] Table 8 illustrates the relative importance of anticipated and realized exchange rate changes and stock market returns in local currency during 1978. Realized exchange rate

---

[4] Of the equilibrium tendencies discussed above, only that between interest rates and forward rates holds ex post. All others are ex ante relationships and realized outcomes are likely to deviate from them even in efficient markets.

Table 8
Stock Market Returns and Exchange Rate Changes for 1978 (in percent per year)

Country	Stock Market Return in Local Currency	Anticipated Change in Exchange Rate	Realized Change in Exchange Rate	Total Return in U.S. Dollars
Canada	+24.8	0.0	− 7.7	+15.3
France	+44.7	− 6.6	+12.7	+63.1
Germany	+ 4.6	+ 4.6	+15.8	+21.1
Italy	+34.4	−10.0	+ 5.1	+41.2
Japan	+21.6	+ 3.9	+23.5	+50.1
Netherlands	− 2.3	+ 1.0	+15.4	+12.7
Switzerland	− 4.3	+ 5.3	+23.6	+18.3
United Kingdom	+ 1.6	+ 0.5	+ 6.9	+ 8.6
United States	+ 0.4	—	—	+ 0.4

Sources: Market returns and realized exchange rate changes from December 31, 1977 to December 31, 1978 as reported in *Capital International Perspective*. Anticipated exchange rate changes are forward premiums/discounts as of January 3, 1978 from Citibank, *Foreign Exchange and International Money Markets*.

changes are large relative both to anticipated changes and stock market returns.

The effect of these changes on the relative performance of stock market investments in different countries from the perspective of U.S. investors diversifying abroad and foreign investors purchasing shares in the U.S., however, are symmetrical. In 1978, for example, the year-end value of a U.S. investor's holdings of Swiss shares (assuming he or she bought the "market") relative to the amount invested at the start of the year would have been 1.178 times that for the investor's U.S. holdings.[5] But from the Swiss investor's perspective, the relative

---

[5] The formula for computing the relative performance of U.S. and Swiss holdings for the U.S. investor is

$$\frac{1 + \$R_{sw}}{1 + \$R_{us}} = \frac{(1 + SfR_{sw})(1 + e)}{1 + \$R_{us}}$$

Where $\$R_{sw}$ and $\$R_{us}$ are the U.S. dollar percentage total returns (dividend plus capital gain) on the Swiss and U.S. markets respectively, SfR_{sw} is the total return on the Swiss market in Swiss francs and e is the percentage charge in the value of Swiss francs in terms of U.S. dollars.

$$\frac{.957 \times 1.236}{1.004} = 1.178$$

From a Swiss investors perspective, the formula is restated as

$$\frac{1 + SfR_{sw}}{1 + SfR_{us}} = \frac{1 + SfR_{sw}}{(1 + \$R_{us})(1 + e)}$$

where e is now the percentage change in the value of the U.S. dollar in terms of Swiss francs,

$$\frac{1}{1.236} - 1 \text{ or } -.191$$

$$\frac{.957}{(1.004)(.8091)} = 1.178$$

performance of the two markets would have been the same. With hindsight, both would have preferred Swiss shares. It is precisely this uncertainty about the relative returns in various markets that can be reduced by diversifying across countries.

Whether the interaction of stock prices and exchange rate changes magnifies the variability of relative returns across countries or not depends on the correlation between exchange rates and stock prices. These correlations in turn depend on a variety of factors including the nature of the currency movement—whether it was anticipated and whether it was in line with realized rates of inflation. They also include the circumstances of the firm in question—its distribution of net monetary balances denominated in various currencies and the exposure of its operating margins to changes in exchange rates. The only case in which the U.S. dollar price of foreign shares will move one for one with the value of foreign currencies is when share prices in those currencies are independent from exchange rate changes. This appears unlikely for individual firms, but may be approximately true for an entire stock market.

Managing Currency Risks. If a manager decides against bearing the risks of fluctuations in a particular currency, several routes are open. It is possible to hedge by borrowing in the currency in question in the same amount as the market value of the equity investment at that time or by entering into forward contracts for an equal amount. Either of these steps will offset the majority of the currency exposure of the equity portfolio.

The expected cost of hedging in the case of borrowing is the difference between the interest differential of the two currencies and the expected percentage change in the exchange rate. The cost of hedging through forward contracts is the difference between the forward discount or premium and the expected percentage change in the exchange rate. Barring controls on capital flows or on access to forward markets, these two costs will be identical through the interest rate parity relationship.

The cost of hedging is often incorrectly defined as the interest differential itself or the forward discount or premium, with no consideration of the expected change in exchange rates. This incorrect definition often leads to statements that hedging is "prohibitively expensive" and rests on the implicit assumption that foreign exchange markets are inefficient and do not reflect anticipations regarding a currency's future. Hedging occasionally is expensive, but substantial research shows that its cost ranges from 0.5 percent to 0.7 percent per year for most major currencies.

In addition to hedging currency risks, an active manager may occasionally wish to take a position in a currency to take advantage of a forecast of currency movements that differ from the general market expectation. Again, the alternatives include taking a money market position; that is, borrowing or lending, buying or selling forward exchange, or buying or selling stock. It should be clear, however, that buying shares in a particular country to take advantage of an expected currency appreciation involves assuming substantial additional uncertainty because equity returns are even more volatile than currency changes. If the forecast is limited solely to a currency movement, taking an equity position is an unreasonable strategy. By the same logic, selling equities to avoid a currency risk is also an unreasonable strategy. Forward contracts or borrowing and lending allow the manager to deal with exchange risk much more specifically.

Political or Sovereign Risk

Political or sovereign risk is viewed by many as a major obstacle to international investment. Clearly, political factors are a major determinant of the attractiveness for investment in any country. Countries viewed as likely candidates for internal political upheaval or with a pronounced trend toward elimination of the private capital sector will be unattractive to all investors, foreign and domestic alike; as a result, securities of these countries should be priced accordingly, and little new private real investment will take place. The general question of the impact of political risk on international investment strategies can be broken down into three specific questions: (1) Are political risks properly reflected in securities prices? (2) Do they differ from the perspectives of foreign and domestic investors and, (3) If so, what does this imply about international investment strategies? There is little research relating to any of these questions. Most research on sovereign risk focuses on the conflict between host governments and firms with direct investment; little has been directed at portfolio investment. Further, what little has been done relates primarily to bank loans to developing countries.

In judging whether political risks are properly reflected in prices, the only evidence is that relating to the overall efficiency of markets. The evidence suggests that information is reflected rapidly in major markets, and that realized returns, in general, bear a reasonable relationship to the risks taken.

The key consideration is that local investors as well as foreign investors typically are affected by these risks. There is no reason to believe that local investors will be systematically optimistic regarding their country's future. When political risks increase significantly, such investors will attempt to diversify out of the home market as rapidly as will foreigners. As a result, prices will fall until someone will be satisfied to hold the securities of a risky country.

Political risks are principally domestic phenomena that can be substantially diversified away internationally. As a result they will loom much larger to the domestic investor whose portfolio is concentrated in home assets. Accordingly, domestic shares might well be more attractive to foreign than domestic investors in periods of high perceived political risk.

Limited Size and Depth of Foreign Markets

A recurrent objection to international diversification is that the practical scope for foreign investing is limited. Many markets are perceived to be small, less liquid, and less efficient than those of the United States. Some investors question whether foreign markets are large enough and active enough to allow them to accumulate meaningful positions and realize profits from them. The fact is that foreign markets have come of age. Figures 3 and 4 illustrate the growth of these markets since 1966 in terms of capitalization and turnover, while Figure 5 provides further details. The growth of turnover in foreign markets is especially striking—increasing from 24 percent of the world total in 1966 to 53 percent in 1978. This view is further reinforced by an examination of the number of companies with market capitalizations in excess of $1.5 billion as shown in Table 9. About 48 percent are

Figure 3
Percentage Breakdown of World Stock Market Capitalization

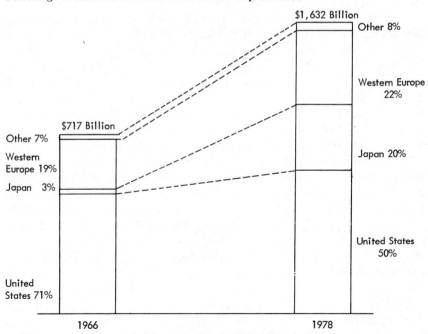

Source: *Capital International Perspective*, March 1976 and March 1979.

Figure 4
Percentage Breakdown of World Share Turnover

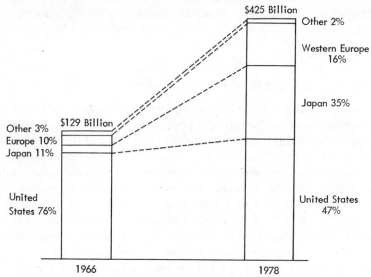

Source: *Capital International Perspective,* March 1976 and March 1979.

non-U.S. companies, and the breakdown by country closely parallels the size of each nations's stock market.

Undoubtedly, there are many foreign stocks whose total capitalization and turnover are too limited for them to be of interest to most U.S. institutional investors. Further, in many markets—particularly the Japanese and German—market capitalizations are often misleading indicators of an issue's marketability because a large proportion of the shares may be owned by banks, holding companies, or other concerns. However, these considerations do not imply that these markets are less attractive to foreign institutional investors than to local investors. In fact, just the opposite may be the case. Domestic investors who depend primarily on their own market for liquidity and diversification are likely to be more constrained by these limitations than international investors who, through diversification, can virtually eliminate the nonmarket risk unique to individual companies even if they hold only a small number of shares in each market. They also do not have to rely on any single market for liquidity and, as a result, can take a longer view in regard to each market and security, even though they will wish to realize profits within a reasonable period in each market and currency.

The constraints on diversification within a single market become apparent when one considers the degree of concentration within various markets. As shown in Table 10, a small number of shares account

Figure 5
Ranking the World's Equity Markets

This chart shows the total market value of each nation's publicly traded corporations. Even including smaller countries that don't make this top-ten list, U.S. shares account for nearly half of the world's quoted equity capital. The data are as year-end 1978 and include national, over-the-counter and regional stock exchanges.

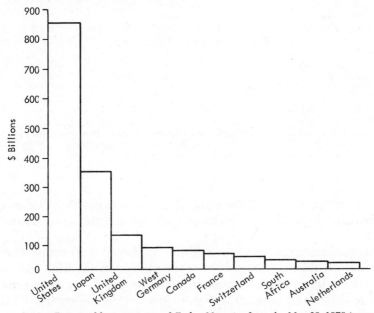

Source: Reprinted by permission of *Forbes Magazine* from the May 28, 1979 issue.

Table 9
Number of Companies with Stock Market Capitalization in Excess of $1.5 Billion in 1978

Country	Number	Percentage of Total
United States	84	51.5%
Japan	40	24.5
Germany	14	8.6
United Kingdom	10	6.1
Switzerland	7	4.3
Netherlands	3	1.8
Australia	1	0.6
France	1	0.6
Belgium	1	0.6
South Africa	1	0.6
Hong Kong	1	0.6
Spain	1	0.6
Total	163	100.0%

Source: *Capital International Perspective*, October 1978.

Table 10
Stock Market Concentration Ratios (1972)

Exchange	Percentage of Total Equity Capitalization Accounted for by 10 Largest Stocks	Least Number of Stocks Accounting for Half Total Equity Capitalization
Amsterdam	77.4	3
Brussels	50.7	10
London	26.4	100
Milan	48.0	11
Paris	21.2	48
Germany (all exchanges)	37.8	17
Zurich	76.0	3
Japan	17.0	10
New York	23.9	60

Source: Europe and United States—D. C. Corner and Stafford, *Open End Invest-ment Funds in the EEC and Switzerland* (Boulder, Colorado: Westview Press, 1977); Japan—B. Jacquillat, "International Portfolio Investment: Opportunities and Pitfalls," presentation to Stanford Investment Management Program, July 1975.

for a major proportion of the value of all shares in most smaller markets, such as Belgium, The Netherlands, and Switzerland, as well as in Germany.

Considering that 30 or more issues in about equal proportions are necessary to diversify away most of the specific (nonmarket) risk within a single national market, even a moderate sized domestic fund will find it difficult to achieve a high degree of diversification. This fact implies that domestic investors in such markets will want to hold foreign assets and that a substantial proportion of the shares of the dominant companies should be held by foreigners even if the systematic risk component of returns in the local economy is closely related to the world market index.

Since all shares must be held by someone, investors must be induced to accept the limitations imposed by the thinness and concentration of particular markets. It would appear that many of these limitations will be more severe for domestic than for international investors. As a result, the fact that certain markets are narrow may be a motivation for, rather than an obstacle to, international investment.

Relative Efficiency of Foreign Markets

A closely related concern is that of market efficiency. Although less efficiency may be desirable from an active investment manager's perspective because it implies that superior performance is possible, it may well put the international investor at a disadvantage relative to the domestic investor who has greater knowledge and better information.

The evidence on market efficiency is of three types: (1) direct tests of the randomness of stock price changes, (2) analyses of the relationship between realized returns and risk, and (3) tests of the actual performance achieved by professional managers. (See also chapters 4 and 5.)

Tests of the Random Walk Hypothesis. Most empirical research has focused on testing for the weak form of efficiency—whether sequences of price changes are related. Researchers have performed extensive tests of the major European markets, and recently these same tests have been extended to the major Asian markets. The studies find that price changes show greater serial correlation in foreign markets than in the U.S. market. However, the magnitude of these departures from randomness typically are not sufficient to yield gains from trading strategies based on past prices. (See also Chapters 4 and 5.)

Tests of the Risk Return Tradeoff. Two types of risk-return tests provide some basis for inferring the efficiency of stock markets. One is a test of the extent to which returns on various securities move together and how stable relationships among them are over time. The other is a test as to whether realized returns confirm that over the long run riskier securities provide higher returns.

The stability of betas for individual stocks is a test of the stability of the price relationship between individual issues and the stock market. Studies have found that betas for individual French and German securities were as stable as those for individual U.S. securities.

Regarding the relationship of realized returns to market risks, extensive tests for individual markets show that riskier securities, have in, fact provided higher realized returns. Further, the relationships between risk and return are more consistent when the international systematic risk as well as the purely domestic risk is taken into account. On balance, the risk-return trade-offs appear consistent with modern capital market theory and thus indicate relatively well-functioning markets.

Tests for Superior Performance. For the most part, performance measurement abroad is substantially less advanced than in the United States. In part, this is attributable to the difficulty of defining superior performance in the international context in which most European managers operate.

To be valid, tests of performance must compare portfolio results with benchmark results for the same universe of securities. If a study shows that domestically managed funds outperform the market index, care must be taken to ensure that their performance does not reflect foreign holdings or domestic securities not included in the benchmark index. Taking this into account, there appear to be no credible studies which show consistently superior performance by managed funds in any major foreign market. Since many European funds contain shares listed outside of the base country, foreign shares listed on the local exchange, and bonds, tests of efficiency for any single market are extremely difficult.

In summary, studies of foreign markets suggest that they generally can be considered to be efficient in the sense that prices adjust rapidly to new information and relationships between risk and return are consistent with those predicted by capital market theory. Whether they are efficient to the extent that most professional managers are unable to consistently outperform appropriate market benchmarks remains an open question. However, the results available suggest that the ability to consistently outperform the market is, at best, uncommon.

Taxes, Restrictions on Ownership, and other Institutional Obstacles

There exists a set of institutional obstacles that may make international investing costly, undesirable, or, in some cases, impossible. They include formal barriers to international transactions such as exchange controls that do not allow investors in one country to invest overseas or limit overseas investment to a fixed pool, as in the case of the United Kingdom,[6] double taxation of portfolio income for certain investors in particular countries,[7] and restrictions on ownership of securities according to the nationality of the investor. These obstacles also include informal barriers such as the difficulty of obtaining information about a market, differences in reporting practices that make international comparisons difficult, and, perhaps most important, subtle impediments to foreign investment based on traditional practice.

Many managers resist stepping into uncharted territory and may thus overestimate the risks associated with foreign investment. This resistance is reinforced by the fear that governmental rules (such as ERISA) will penalize managers for investing abroad if things go poorly, simply because such investments represent a departure from traditional practice.

Little research has been conducted on the impact of these institutional and governmental obstacles on either appropriate investment strategies or portfolio performance. One study of U.K. investment trusts found that they benefited little from international diversification and attributed this to the costs imposed by the U.K. foreign investment controls. Whether these costs were necessary or whether they reflected

---

[6] U.K. investors seeking to invest abroad must purchase currency from an investment currency pool. As a result, the £/$ exchange rate which must be paid to invest abroad is typically at a substantial premium to the regular exchange rate. On liquidation, a portion of the proceeds must be converted at the regular, typically less favorable, exchange rate.

[7] U.S. pension funds, for example, may have to pay a withholding tax on income from some foreign countries but have no U.S. tax against which it can be credited.

unnecessary trading remains an open question.[8] The U.S. interest equalization tax clearly hindered overseas investment by U.S. individual and institutional investors and, undoubtedly, the difficulty of buying into the Japanese market in the mid-1960s meant that its subsequent performance was academic to most U.S. investors.

A major implication of the existence of such obstacles is that even if one assumes an integrated, efficient world capital market, investors with different legal domiciles or tax situations may want to hold different portfolios. However, it is difficult to determine by how much such optimal portfolios should differ from the world market portfolio. This would depend on the balancing of the effect of the obstacles against the gains from more complete diversification. One theoretical study introduces obstacles into a model of capital market equilibrium under restrictive assumptions and shows that investors will not hold the world market portfolio.[9] Instead, investors will hold relatively high proportions of their home market portfolios and will weigh their holdings of foreign assets equally rather than by market values. More research, both in terms of quantifying specific obstacles and ascertaining their impact on capital market equilibrium, is required before optimum international portfolios can be specified for particular investors.

Conclusions Regarding Obstacles to International Investment

When examined closely, many of the obstacles to international investment are less serious than commonly thought. This does not mean that there are no difficulties, but it does appear that the advantages of diversification, when properly pursued, outweigh the drawbacks.

Regarding the major specific areas of concern, currency risks do not appear to reduce significantly the gains from broadly based diversification. There is little reason to believe that political risks are systematically ignored by local investors or that they weigh more heavily on foreign investors. Finally, major foreign markets are not as narrow or inefficient as generally may be perceived.

REFERENCES (BY TOPIC)

Correlations of Returns and Gains
from International Diversification

Bergstrom, G. L. "A New Route to Higher Returns and Lower Risk." *Journal of Portfolio Management* (Fall 1975).

---

[8] J. R. F. Guy, "An Examination of the Effects of International Diversification from the British Viewpoint on Both Hypothetical and Real Portfolios," *Journal of Finance* (December 1978).

[9] F. Black, "International Capital Market Equilibrium with Investment Barriers," *Journal of Financial Economics*, I, part 4 (1974).

Grubel, H. G. "Internationally Diversified Portfolios: Welfare Gains and Capital Flows." *American Economic Review* (December 1968).

Lessard, D. R. "World, Country, and Industry Relationships in Equity Returns: Implications for Risk Reduction through International Diversification." *Financial Analysts Journal* (January–February 1976).

Levy, H. and Sarnat, M. "International Diversification of Investment Portfolios." *American Economic Review* (September 1970).

Ripley, D. M. "Systematic Elements in the Linkage of National Stock Market Indices." *Review of Economics and Statistics* (September 1973).

Solnik, B. H. "Why Not Diversify Internationally Rather Than Domestically?" *Financial Analysts Journal* (July–August 1974).

Pricing of Securities in an International Context

Black, F. "International Capital Market Equilibrium with Investment Barriers." *Journal of Financial Economics* (1974).

Grauer, F. L. A.; Litzenberger, R. H.; and Stehle, R. E. "Sharing Rules and Equilibrium in an International Capital Market Under Uncertainty." *Journal of Financial Economics* 3 (1976).

Solnik, B. H. "The International Pricing of Risk: An Empirical Investigation of the World Capital Market Structure." *Journal of Finance* (May 1974).

———— "Testing International Asset Pricing: Some Pessimistic Views." *Journal of Finance* (May 1977).

Stehle, R. "An Empirical Test of the Alternative Hypotheses of National and International Pricing of Risky Assets." *Journal of Finance* (May 1977).

On Currency Risks

Cornell, B. "Spot Rates, Forward Rates and Exchange Market Efficiency." *Journal of Financial Economics* (December 1977).

Giddy, I. "An Integrated Theory of Exchange Rate Equilibrium." *Journal of Financial and Quantitative Analysis* (November 1976).

Kohlhagen, S. *The Behavior of Foreign Exchange Markets—A Critical Survey of the Empirical Literature.* New York University: Solomon Brothers Monograph 1978, no. 3.

Levich, R. N. "On the Efficiency of Foreign Exchange Markets: Review and Extension." In Lessard, ed., *International Financial Management* (Boston: Warren, Gorham, and Lamont, 1979).

Oldfield, G. C. and Logue, D. E. "What's So Special About the Foreign Exchange Market?" *Journal of Portfolio Management* (Spring 1977).

The Efficiency of Foreign Markets

Guy, J. R. F. "The German Stock Exchange." *Journal of Banking and Finance* (June 1977).

———— "The Performance of the British Investment Trust Industry." *Journal of Finance* (May 1978).

Lau, S. L.; Quay, S. T.; and Ramsey, C. M. "The Tokyo Stock Exchange and the Capital Asset Pricing Model." *Journal of Finance* (May 1974).

Solnik, B. H. "A Note on the Validity of the Random Walk for European Stock Prices." *Journal of Finance* (December 1973).

On the Performance of Internationally-Diversified Portfolios

Farber, A. L. "Performance of Internationally Diversified Mutual Funds." In E. J. Elton and M. H. Gruber, eds., *International Capital Markets* (New York: American Elsevier, 1975).

Guy, J. R. F. "An Examination of the Effects of International Diversification from the British Viewpoint on Both Hypothetical and Real Portfolios." *Journal of Finance* (December 1978).

McDonald, J. B. "French Mutual Fund Performance: Evaluation of International-ally Diversified Portfolios." *Journal of Finance* (December 1973).

Corner, D. C., and Stafford, D. C. *Open-End Investment Funds in the EEC and Switzerland* (Boulder, Colo.: Westview Press, 1977).

Chapter 12

Option Strategies

EUGENE D. BRODY

Vice President
Oppenheimer Capital Corp.
New York, New York

Standardized, exchange traded options have become part of the investment process at a growth rate not equalled by our fastest growing, high multiple companies. Despite the skepticism of nearly all investment professionals and the obstacles created by lawyers interpreting anachronistic legislation, the option pilot program has been an enormous success. The reasons for the success are manifold but the main one is that the option exchanges provide a vehicle that meets the need to reduce the risk of buyers and sellers in increasingly volatile environments. Options on stocks are not the only development reflecting this volatility phenomenon. All assets are subject to this volatility and uncertainty and in response new techniques and tools are being created to meet the threat to accumulated capital. Financial instrument futures are coming into increased use at banks and savings institutions because of the need to hedge against sharp changes in interest rates, both short- and long-term. Currency futures are being used as hedges by international corporations as the risk of floating exchange rates in an inflationary atmosphere becomes clearer. Commodity futures have been used for years for hedging purposes. All those whose function it is to protect the value of assets and earn fair returns should become familiar with risk transference tools.

THE LANGUAGE OF OPTIONS

The investment objectives of the use of options is to transfer risk in the form of reduced volatility. It is possible to increase returns while

384

reducing risk, but this is not guaranteed. There are also facilitation objectives in the use of options when they are used to accumulate or dispose of a position. Options can be used under certain circumstances as stock substitutes. Before discussing the various ways options can be used by the portfolio manager, a brief explanation of the following terms will be helpful in understanding the use of options.

Assignment: the process by which an option writer is selected to fulfill an option contract when an option is exercised by a holder. The exercise of an option takes place through the Options Clearing Corporation acting for the member firms of the corporation. If the member firm at which the options are short uses a first-in first-out selection process it is possible to determine how many options are ahead for assignment purposes.

Call: a contract giving the holder (buyer) the right to purchase 100 shares of a specific stock at a fixed price (striking price) for a fixed time period. The seller (writer) of the contract has the obligation to sell 100 shares of the stock anytime it is called (assigned, exercised) during the life of the contract.

Class of options: options of the same type (i.e., put—defined later—or call) covering the same underlying security.

Closing transaction: the purchase or sale of an option which offsets an existing position. The closing purchase of a call in the same series as one the writer has previously sold and not been assigned would cancel that outstanding obligation.

Conversion: the converting of puts to calls by the simultaneous purchase of the put, the purchase of stock, and the sale of a call. This is a virtually riskless transaction done by member firms and arbitrageurs who earn a small differential. Sometimes there is a windfall profit, i.e., stock is called and the converter is left with a "free" put. If the stock then declines he may realize a substantial gain. A reverse conversion is the purchase of a call, short sale of stock, and sale of a put. "Synthetic" puts are created by reverse conversions.

Covered call writer: the writer of a call who, as long as one is obliged as a writer, owns the underlying shares or securities convertible into those shares. It can also refer to a writer who owns calls for the same amount of shares written whose exercise price is equal to or lower than on the call written.

Covered put writer: a writer (seller) of a put who holds another put of equal or greater exercise price.

Custodian bank: bank whose escrow receipts are accepted by the Options Clearing Corporation. Custodian banks may issue escrow receipts on stocks whose aggregate market value is up to 10 percent of their capital. Many banks use the Depository Trust Corporation for this function as they are not limited by capital.

Escrow receipt: a document issued by a custodian bank to a broker as collateral for the sale of an option. The receipt guarantees that if the writer is called, the bank will deliver the stock.

Equivalencies: the relationship of options to stocks and to each other can be summarized as follows:

C = Call   St = Straddle
P = Put   + = Long
S = Stock (100 shares)   − = Short

(+P) = C+ (−S)   A long put equals a long call and short stock. If you are short stock, you have downside potential, but your upside risk is limited to the premium paid.

S = C+ (−P)   If you have a long position in a call and short position in a put you have the economic equivalent of owning a stock, since you own the upside potential through the long call and have the risk of ownership through the short put, i.e., stock will be put to you if it declines.

(+C) = (+S) + (+P)   A long call equals long stock and a long put. By being long a call, you have the upside potential of the stock, but you have paid a premium to limit loss.

(−C) = (−S) + (−P)   A short call equals short stock plus a short put. In this position, your profit is the premium on the call and your liability on the upside is unlimited.

(−P) = (+S) + (−C)   A short put equals long stock and a short call. If you are long stock and short its call you are in a covered writing position. This is equivalent to a short put, since you have limited your profit to the premium and have incurred the risk of ownership.

(−S) = (+P) + (−C)   Short stock equals a long put and a short call. In either case, you would profit from a decline in the price of the stock and suffer from a rise in price.

St = (+P) + (+C)   A straddle is equal to a long put and a long call.

St = (+C) + (+C) + (−S) *or* (+2C) + (−S)   A straddle equals two long calls and short stock. Seeing these two formulas together, one can understand that, since a put is equal to short stock and a long call, then a long straddle (put and call) is equal to short stock and two long calls. In either case, profits are made outside the range of the stock price plus or minus the premium. However, similarly:

St = (+S) + (+2P)   A straddle equals long stock and two long puts, since the implication remains that profit occurs outside a range.

(−St) = (−P) + (−C)   A short straddle equals a short put and a short call.

(−St) = (+S) + (−2C)   By substitution, we can also see that a short straddle equals long stock and two short calls. Similarly:

$(-St) = (-S) + (-2P)$ A short straddle is also equal to short stock and two short puts. In each of these last three cases, profit is earned when the stock stays within the range created.

In the money: an option is said to be in-the-money when the underlying stock's market price is higher than the striking price of a call or lower than the striking price of a put (see *Striking price*).

Expiration cycle: there are three cycles, January–April–July–October, February–May–August–November, and March–June–September–December. Three of the four months in each cycle are being traded at any one time. Trading begins on the most distant month in a cycle on the business day following an expiration date.

Expiration date: the date on which an option expires. This will be the Saturday following the third Friday of the expiration month as defined in the contract. Instructions to exercise an option must be given to the broker prior to 5:30 P.M., New York time, on the last business day preceding the aforementioned Saturday. Trading in expiring options stops at 3:00 P.M., New York time, on that same business day. Since the stock market is open another hour, many seemingly worthless options are repurchased to avoid the possibility of a sharp rise in the underlying stock in the final hour inducing an exercise.

Intrinsic value: the intrinsic value of a call is the amount the market price of the underlying stock exceeds the striking price of the call. The intrinsic value of a put is the amount the striking price of the put exceeds the market price of the underlying stock.

Neutral hedge: a stock-option or option-option position with no market bias, i.e., the long and short components of the position net out to zero exposure in stock equivalent. For example, long 100 *XYZ* and short 2 *XYZ* calls with a sensitivity (delta) of .50 would be a neutral hedge. Long 100 shares and short one of the same options would have a bullish bias of long 50 shares (long 1.00 short −.50) × 100, long 100 shares and short 3 of those options would have a bearish bias of short 50 shares (long 1.00, short −1.50) × 100.

Opening transaction: the initial purchase or sale of an option which does not offset any existing position.

Out-of-the-money: an option is said to be out-of-the-money when the striking price of a call (put) is higher (lower) than the market price of the underlying stock.

Option valuation: the value of an option is based on the following factors:

1. *Time left to expiration date*—it is self evident that other factors being equal, the longer an option has to run the more valuable it is.
2. *Relationship of striking price to market price*—it is also clear that the higher the ratio of market price of underlying stock to call

striking price the higher the value. It is also clear that the higher this ratio the less the leverage to the call buyer.

3. *Cost of money*—the level of interest rates plays an important role in option valuation since the buyer is purchasing the stock's volatility with limited capital. The covered call writer is being induced to assume the risk of ownership of the stock while foregoing the opportunity to earn interest on capital.

4. *Dividends*—since the call buyer does not receive dividends on the stock, when the stock trades ex-dividend the buyer's profit opportunity is reduced. The more dividends a stock goes "ex" during the life of a call, the less the value of a call on that stock.

5. *Volatility of underlying stock*—the more volatile a stock the more valuable the loss-limiting features of a call. Stocks with high volatility characteristics command high call premiums. The calculation of volatility is subjective. The distinguishing features of various probabilistic pricing models are their volatility calculation and shape of the probability distribution. The other factors in option valuation are fixed except for the cost of money but the differences there will not be great. Volatility measurement can vary widely and produce significant differences in option valuation. The efficacy of a pricing model depends on the volatility calculation. The underlying assumption of all these models is that historic volatility will approximate future volatility. This, of course, is not always true. Put valuation is a function of call value. Puts cannot get too far out of line with their corresponding calls since they can be created by selling stock short and buying calls (see *Equivalencies*).

Overvalued option: an option is considered overvalued when its market price is higher than its fair value as calculated by a probabilistic pricing model (see *Option valuation*).

Premium: the price paid for an option (Also used to describe excess over intrinsic value).

Put: a contract giving the holder (buyer) the right to sell 100 shares of a specified stock at a specified price over a given time interval.

Restricted option: options whose closing market price is more than 5 points out of the money and are selling for less than $.50 are "restricted." This means that opening transactions may not be made except by covered writers (or as part of certain spreads). The effect of this rule, which the SEC is under some pressure to eliminate, is to distort the market for these options.

Sensitivity (delta factor): the theoretical price move of an option when the underlying stock changes 1 point. If *XRX* common were to advance from 53 to 54 and *XRX* April 60s were expected to advance from 1 to 1¼ as a result, that option's sensitivity would be .25.

Series of options: options of the same class having the same exercise price and expiration time and the same unit of trading.

Straddle: a put and call on the same stock with the same expiration date and striking price. If any of the terms of the put and call are different, it is called a "combination."

Striking price (exercise price): the price at which a call buyer may purchase the stock or the price at which the put buyer may sell the stock. This price is not adjusted for cash distributions made out of "earnings and profits." However, when a stock splits, all option strike prices and the number of shares on which a call is outstanding are adjusted to reflect the change. For example, when IBM split 4 for 1, a call on 100 shares at 280 became four calls on 100 shares at 70. The aggregate striking price, $28,000, remained the same. When a stock dividend of other than a multiple of 100 is declared, the number of shares, as well as the striking price, is adjusted. For example, if a 20 percent stock dividend were declared on a stock, a call on 100 shares with a strike price of 60 would be adjusted to a call on 120 shares at 50. However, the price of the call quoted is per share so that if this call were trading at 4 the cost would actually be $480 (4 × 120) and not $400. When the numbers do not come out exactly even, the strike price is adjusted to the nearest one-eighth of a point.

Synthetic put: a put created by purchase of a call and the short sale of stock. For example, a stock is sold short at 43 and a call on that stock is purchased at 3½, then that position is equivalent to a put at 40 costing ½ point (see *Equivalencies*).

Taxes: gains or losses on options are capital transactions. Since one year options are not available, all results are short term. If a long call is exercised, then the holding period begins and the cost of the call is added to the cost basis (the exercise price) of the stockholder. If stock is called away, the premium received is added to the selling price and can be long term if the stock called was long term. In the case of a short put, an assignment reduces the purchase price of the stock and the holding period starts at exercise. If a put is purchased and stock is owned, then the holding period starts over after disposition of the put. If stock is already long term, then there is no effect on the holding period. If stock and put are purchased on the same date, and it is identified as a hedged position, then holding period begins on that date.

Uncovered writer: a writer of an option who is not a covered writer, i.e., he is not long the optioned security or its equivalent (see *Covered writer*). An uncovered writer is often referred to as a "naked" writer or as "being naked."

Underlying security: the security subject to being purchased or sold upon the exercise of an option.

Undervalued option: an option is considered undervalued when its market price is less than its fair value as determined by a probabilistic pricing model (see *Option valuation*).

Variable hedge (ratio writing)[1]: this strategy, which can be conservatively managed, involves the writing of more than one option per
100 shares of long stock. Since covered writing is basically a bullish
strategy because the position is always equivalent to net long, selling
more than one to one can reduce market exposure. Whether the market posture objective is to be bullish, neutral, or bearish, variable hedging has the flexibility to achieve the desired market exposure. The
term "variable" comes from the fact that the proper ratio of options
to stock (assuming no change in the desired exposure) varies as time
passes and/or the relationship of market price of the underlying stock
to striking price of the option changes. Therefore, the position must
be adjusted. The essence of this strategy is to create ranges of profitability and is equivalent to the sale of a straddle. In other words, variable
hedging is the sale of volatility. You are expecting a stock to remain
in a range but adjusting that range as necessary. For example, if *XRX*
were selling at 52 and *XRX* April 60s at $2, then the purchase of
stock and the sale of 3 April 60s at $2 each would produce a profit
range of 46–67 with maximum profitability at 60 at expiration.

STRATEGY AND TECHNIQUE

There are a number of option strategy techniques for portfolio managers depending on what they are trying to accomplish. These are
not mutually exclusive. Discussion by investment objective follows.

Accumulation of a Position

There are two ways to accumulate a position: (a) by purchasing
calls and (b) by selling puts.

Purchasing Calls.   Often it is possible to accumulate stock through
the option market. This is especially true around expiration dates since
long holders are selling and calls become available at a discount (less
than intrinsic value). Arbitrage operations cause markets in general
to be more liquid at these times. However, deep in-the-money calls
are especially illiquid and a careful buyer of these calls can effectively
pick up stock at bargain prices. Not only can one purchase at a discount
from parity, but the negotiated commission rate for the purchase of
calls plus the cost of exercise can often be less than the negotiated
rate per share of stock purchased on the stock exchange. If the option
being purchased is not near expiration, then the funds invested in
the call are less than would be invested in the stock and interest can
be earned on the difference. At the same time, risk of ownership is

---

[1] For a more complete discussion see Eugene D. Brody and Betsy L. Bliss, "Odds-
On Investing," (New York: John Wiley & Sons, 1978). © 1978 by John Wiley & Sons,
Inc. Reprinted by permission.

less. Care must be taken not to let a dividend pass without exercising the option because the rate of return advantage of the call plus the interest earning balance may disappear. It is not axiomatic that buying calls will be better than buying the stock. It is an alternative to be considered for relative cost of acquisition. Quite possibly, the broker through whom the portfolio manager is purchasing stock is using the option market to acquire the stock for him. The broker might even be shorting stock to the buyer against call purchases the broker has made, thereby creating a put for the broker (see *Equivalencies*) while earning interest on his short sale.[2]

Selling Puts. Selling uncovered puts on a stock that the portfolio manager wishes to own is a method of reducing the average cost of acquisition substantially. If the stock declines, remains the same, or goes up less than the put premium collected, the portfolio manager has clearly taken advantageous action. The risk in this procedure is that if the stock rises more than the put premium received, the portfolio's participation in that advance is limited to the put premium received, plus the interest earned on both the premium and the funds set aside for purchase of the stock at the put striking price. If there was an ex-dividend date during this period, that dividend would not be received by the put writer unless the writer was assigned on or before the ex-dividend date. This position is equivalent to buying stock and selling covered calls on it. For example, see Table 1.

Table 1

Stock Price In 90 Days	Sells 90 Day Put at 50 for $3*	Net	Purchase Stock at 50	Advantage of Put Sale
35............	−1,200 + 124.15	−1,075.85	−1,500	424.15
40............	−700 + 124.15	−575.85	−1,000	424.15
45............	−200 + 124.15	−75.85	−500	424.15
50............	+300 + 124.15	+424.15	—	424.15
55............	+300 + 124.15	+424.15	+500	(75.85)
60............	+300 + 124.15	+424.15	+1,000	(575.85)

* Assume interest at 9½ percent.

Using Options as an Extension of Investment Policy

1. Selling Calls. The flexibility that options offer is seen clearly when the portfolio manager can temporize a decision through the sale of calls. In the case of individual stocks, effective sales above the market can be made through the sale of calls as a result of premium

---

[2] Brokers earn interest on short sales. When interest rates are high it is particularly advantageous for the broker. There is a lending market for hedged short sellers who pay to borrow stock. The more long stock held in margin accounts (the "box") the more profitable short selling. This affects premiums since the short seller is also a call buyer.

over market for in-the-money calls or sale of out-of-the money calls where strike price plus premium equals the price objective. Once made, this decision can be easily unmade through repurchase of the call option written. Different calls can be sold, no calls sold or the stock sold. Naturally, if a call is sold and the stock declines, the call premium only partially compensates for the loss of market value in the stock. Substantial declines can be best avoided by sale of the stock. Since one doesn't know what will happen, a compromise is the sale of calls which is, in effect, a partial sale of stock.

Another effective way to use calls is to reduce the overall exposure of a portfolio to market risk. The sale of calls reduces beta. Should the market decline, the negative effect on the portfolio will be reduced. Should the market rise, the participation in the advance will be less than it would have been had the options not been sold. The effect on beta can be calculated and the portfolio beta adjusted. The relationship of option movements to underlying stock movements can be calculated by various option pricing models. This relationship is referred to as "sensitivity," i.e., the expected price movement of the option caused by a 1 point move in the stock. Sensitivity is not constant but changes as time passes and the relationship of the market price of the stock to the striking price of the option changes. As a general rule, the sensitivity of in-the-money options tends toward 1.00 as time passes and the sensitivity of out-of-the-money options tends toward zero as time passes. Sensitivity rises as the underlying stock rises and falls as the stock falls further from the striking price. Assume that a stock has a calculated beta of 1.20. An option with a sensitivity of .5 written against that stock will result in an effective beta of .6 (1.2 × .5) for that stock. As the stock rises its effective beta will decrease. The beta of the portfolio should be recalculated using the new beta of each option related position frequently to insure that the desired result is being achieved.

This effect of options on the beta of the portfolio allows the manager to increase the asset allocation for equities without increasing exposure to the stock market. Since the effect of the market on stocks can be reduced, then the proportion of stocks can be increased. For example, in a portfolio with a beta of 1.00 and a desired equity exposure of 50 percent, if beta is reduced to .8 then the equity exposure could be raised to 62.5 percent. If there is an expected incremental return on the increased equities and options over the expected return on the fixed segment, selling calls would clearly be an alternative to consider.

2. Buying Puts.[3]   The purchase of puts as a protective measure is

---

[3] For a complete discussion see Robert C. Pozen, "The Purchase of Protective Puts by Financial Institutions," *Financial Analysts Journal* (July–August 1978).

getting more attention recently. Since the ownership of a put guarantees sale at a fixed price, the portfolio is insulated from capital loss on the underlying stock during the life of the put. Dividends continue to be collected. In-the-money puts give the most protection but require relatively large cash outlays. At-the-money puts are pure premium (no intrinsic value). The most protection per dollar invested is usually gained from out-of-the money puts. They are analogous to deductible insurance policies. The cost is reduced by the fact that the owner of the asset is willing to bear some of the risk. What the owner wishes to avoid are the catastrophic losses. The purchase of out-of-the money puts as a form of deductible catastrophe insurance makes sense to anyone interested in capital preservation and/or reducing volatility. Since puts are not available on many stocks, consideration might be given to the purchase of out-of-the money puts on market type stocks whether or not they are part of the portfolio. This would tend to dampen volatility as in a call writing program but would allow for greater participation in strong markets. The upside has not been limited in this case but the downside exposure is reduced. Buying puts and owning stock is equivalent to buying a call. In a rising market, the cost of the puts would reduce the performance. In declining markets there would be substantial profits in the puts to offset the losses in market value of stocks owned. Buying puts as protection adds a contracyclical element to a portfolio just as an overriding program does. Different results will be achieved depending on the type of markets experienced and the prices received for calls paid for puts.

Buy Call and Treasury Bill[4]

This strategy (often 90 percent invested in T-Bills and 10 percent in calls) is based on the idea that calls have limited risk and the returns on the T-Bills or other cash equivalencies will almost equal or offset losses from calls expiring worthless or sold at a loss in flat to down markets. Gains in rising markets will be so large on the 10 percent invested in calls that the overall return will outperform the market averages and produce positive absolute returns. The theory is that losses will always be limited and capital protected. By avoiding large losses and participating in the advances the net result should be favorable. Keeping the asset base intact reduces the percentage gains required on shrunken assets to get back to a starting point, i.e. the need to go up 100 percent to recoup a 50 percent loss.

---

[4] For a more complete discussion see Robert C. Merton, Myron Scholes, and Matthew Gladstein, "A Simulation of the Returns and Risks of Alternative Option Portfolio Investment Strategies," Working paper (October 1976).

Buy and Write

The buy and write strategy, that is, the purchase of stocks in order to sell call options on them, has been successfully used by certain investment advisors who have been able to achieve incremental return and reduce volatility. The keys to a successful buy-write program are to limit the downside exposure of a stock position and to make the adjustments which reflect changes in the market price of the stocks. The buy-write strategist is accepting a known return (the premium), but the upside gain is limited. This limitation is offset by the advantage of losing less in down markets. Since the volatility of a buy-write program is less than that of a straight buyer of stocks, the buyer's return should be less. One also is probably taking more risk than a bond portfolio so, theoretically, the return should be higher than bonds and lower than stocks. Perhaps as a reflection of the types of markets experienced in recent years, the total returns of many buy-write programs have been higher than stocks or bonds.

The approaches to buy-write vary. Some buy-write strategists manage these portfolios as straight equity portfolios and sell options as their market outlook changes. The results will reflect that manager's judgment. At the other extreme, stocks are purchased only when there are overvalued options to be sold. The stock is regarded as an asset with certain volatility characteristics and that volatility can be sold for substantially more than it is intrinsically worth. Most buy-write managers fall in-between these two extremes. The successful buy-write program is dependent on earning good premiums in flat to up markets to offset the net losses on stocks in down markets. Since the covered writing position is a partially hedged position, (the long stock-short option position is always equivalent to a net long position), then it is clear that rising markets are where the returns are made for the buy-write strategy.

Overriding[5]

An overriding program is one where the option writer is not managing the underlying portfolio. The underlying portfolio may be unmanaged or managed by one or more advisors. The concept behind this strategy is that option writing is a distinct discipline and the option writer adds a contracyclical element to the investment process. The writer does not interfere with the portfolio investment decision. The overrider is constrained in that he must repurchase any outstanding options if the underlying stock is sold and if called, must replace the stock. In this way, the option writer's performance is kept separate

---

[5] For complete discussion of overriding see Eugene D. Brody, "Fear, Misinformation Keep Pensions From Big Option Market," *Pensions & Investments* (November 20, 1978).

from the performance of the underlying stock manager. The investment objective is to provide incremental return and reduce volatility. Overriding managers range from those who make market timing judgments on when to sell options to those who sell volatility in the form of overvalued calls. By instituting an overriding program, the portfolio will certainly achieve the objective of reducing volatility. The cost of that reduction will range from some give up in total return to some increment to total return, depending on the skill and methodology of the option writer.

Selling Puts

The buy-write program can be equivalent to an uncovered put selling program. The major difference is in the opportunities available. Since there are more stocks with calls traded than puts traded the opportunities are more limited. As the number of stocks on which puts are traded expands, that differential will diminish. Premiums on puts are generally less than on calls, and since the stock is not owned, there are no dividends. That is offset by the fact that interest is earned on the put premiums and the entire amount set aside for the stock purchase. Ideally, the portfolio should be able to have both alternatives open to it rather than one or the other (see Table 2).

Table 2

Stock Price In 90 Days	Sell 90 Day Put at 50 for $3*	Buy stock at 50—Sell Call at $4 for 90 days†
35	$424.15 - 1,500 = -1,075.85$	-1100
40	$424.15 - 1,000 = - 575.85$	$- 600$
45	$424.15 - 500 = - 75.85$	$- 100$
50	$424.15 + 0 = + 424.15$	$+ 400$
55	$424.15 + 0 = + 424.15$	$+ 400$
60	$424.15 + 0 = + 424.15$	$+ 400$

* Assume interest at 9½ percent. Note: Interest is based on the cash not invested in the stock ($5000) plus the cash from the put sale ($300).

† If there is a dividend paid to the shareholders during this time period then the buy-write is advantageous to the extent that the dividend exceeds the $24.15 put advantage in this example.

Conversion

In the definition of equivalencies it was stated that long call and short put is equivalent to owning stock. That being the case, it is often incrementally profitable to substitute that position for stock (assuming no tax consequences). If the interest earned on the proceeds exceeds the cost of establishing and reversing that position, it is an intelligent procedure. There are two major risks involved. The first occurs when the stock in question is at the striking price and the options are about

to expire. You have to decide whether to exercise your call or allow
your short put to be exercised. What you don't want is to end up
long twice as much stock as you started with or no stock at all. For
example, assume you affected this transaction on IBM using the 280
puts and calls. If the stock is below 280 on the last trading day prior
to expiration you expect stock to be put to you. After 3:00 P.M. when
trading stops in expiring options, the stock moves up to 280. You don't
know whether the put will be exercised so you are reluctant to exercise
the call lest you end up with 200 shares. For this reason it is generally
wise to close out the position a little early and establish a new one
or buy the stock back. The second risk is that stock is assigned (put
exercised) before enough interest is earned to offset transaction costs,
including the loss on the long call. Each potential position should be
examined on its own merits for rate of return and probability of success
before entering into such a transaction (see Table 3).

Table 3

	Cash Position	
	Decrease	*Increase*
Sell IBM for 275		$27,500.00
Sell IBM 280 put at 11		1,100.00
Buy IBM 280 call at 6	$600	
Net Credit		$28,000.00
Interest on $28,000 for 71 days at 11%		$ 620.52
Dividends to be paid on IBM until expiration......	$–0–	
Difference between $275 sales price and		
$280 strike price	500	
Net Profit before transaction costs		$ 120.52
Estimated transaction costs	$ 35	
Net Profit		$ 85.52
Incremental return annualized		1.57%

The strategies discussed here include all the basic option strategies
for institutional portfolio managers. There is no single "best" strategy
but there is enough flexibility in these strategies and their variations
to help portfolio managers achieve any stated investment objective.
Knowledge of the possibilities and understanding of the alternatives
of options can often help produce the desired results and reduce risk
at the same time.

BIBLIOGRAPHY

"As I See It; Options An Investment Tool—An Interview with Roger F. Murray," *Forbes* (October 1, 1975).

Black, Fischer. "Fact and Fantasy in the Use of Options." *Financial Analysts Journal* (July 1975).

Black, Fischer and Scholes, M. "The Valuation of Option Contracts and a Test of Market Efficiency." *Journal of Finance* (May 1972).

Bloch, Alan J. "An Option for the Age of Stability." *Journal of Portfolio Management* (Winter 1978).

Bracken, Jerome. "Models for Call Option Decisions." *Financial Analysts Journal* (September–October 1968).

Brody, Eugene D. "Options and the Mathematics of Defense." *Journal of Portfolio Management* (Winter 1975).

———. "Using Options in Bank Trust Portfolio Management." *Banker's Magazine* (Autumn 1977).

———. "Fear, Misinformation Keep Pension Funds From Big Option Market." *Pensions & Investments* (November 20, 1978).

Brody, Eugene D. and Bliss, Betsy L. *Odds-On Investing.* New York: John Wiley & Sons, 1978.

Daigler, Robert T. and Mullen, William T. *Structuring a Successful Covered Option Writing Program.* Memphis State University, 1977.

Gastineau, G. L. *Stock Option Manual.* New York: McGraw-Hill, 1975.

Galai, Dan and Masulis, Ronald W. "The Option Pricing Model and the Risk Factor of the Stock." *Journal of Financial Economics* (1976).

———. "On the Boness and Black-Scholes Models for Valuation of Call Options." *Journal of Financial and Quantitative Analysis* (March 1978).

Hart, James F. "The Riskless Option Hedge: An Incomplete Guide." *Journal of Portfolio Management* (Winter 1978).

Kassouf, N. "Optioned Equity Investing—Good Insurance for the Insurance Industry." *Best's Review Life/Health Insurance Edition* (April 1976).

Latane, Henry A. and Rendleman, R. J., Jr. "Standard Deviations of Stock Price Ratios Implied in Option Prices." *Journal of Finance* (May 1976).

Merton, Robert C. "The Impact on Option Pricing of Specification Error in the Underlying Stock Price Returns." *Journal of Finance* (May 1976).

———. "Option Pricing when Underlying Stock Returns Are Discontinuous." *Journal of Financial Economics* (March 1976).

———. "The Relationship Between Put and Call Option Prices: Comment." *Journal of Finance* (March 1973).

———. *Restrictions on Rational Option Pricing: A Set of Arbitrage Conditions.* (Cambridge, Mass.: The M.I.T. Press, August 1968), mimeographed.

———. "Theory of Rational Option Pricing." *Bell Journal of Economics and Management Science* (Spring 1973).

Muir, F. M. "How Block Traders Are Using Options." *Institutional Investor* (February 1977).

Parkinson, M. "Option Pricing: The American Put." *Journal of Business* (January 1977).

Pounds, Henry M. "Covered Call Option Writing: Strategies and Results." *Journal of Portfolio Management* (Winter 1978).

Pozen, Robert C. "The Purchase of Protective Puts by Financial Institutions." *Financial Analysts Journal* (July–August 1978).

Reiser, R. E. "Puts and Portfolio Strategy." *Trusts & Estates* (February 1977).

Rogalski, Richard J. "Variances and Options Prices in Theory and Practice." *Journal of Portfolio Management* (Winter 1978).

Schmalensee, Richard and Trippi, Robert R. "Common Stock Volatility Expectations Implied by Option Premia." *Journal of Finance* (March 1978).

Sharpe, William F. "Warrants, Options and Convertible Securities." In *Investments* (Englewood Cliffs, N.J.: Prentice-Hall, 1978).

Trippi, R. R. "Test of Option Market Efficiency Using a Random-Walk Valuation Model." *Journal of Economics and Business* (Winter 1977).

Wilburn, D. S. *A Model of the Put and Call Option Market.* (Cambridge, Mass.: Sloan School of Management, M.I.T., 1970). Unpublished thesis.

Chapter 13

Techniques of Portfolio Adjustments

EDMUND A. MENNIS

Chairman of the Board
Security Pacific Investment Managers, Inc.
(a subsidiary of Security Pacific Corporation)
Los Angeles, California

Portfolios of securities are rarely held over time without some changes or adjustments. The subject of the chapter is the nature of these adjustments, their causes and how they are made.

Two important ideas underlie this discussion:

1. A portfolio should have some objective or goal that it is designed to accomplish. Consequently, it should not be merely a repository of surplus cash but rather have some purpose, such as providing current income, or providing capital for some future need like retirement, college education, a future capital purchase, or the like.

2. A portfolio is not a miscellaneous collection of securities. Individual securities have different characteristics of risk and return. When combined into a portfolio, securities have a relationship to each other, so that the portfolio itself has characteristics of risk and return different from those of the individual components. Consequently, portfolio adjustments may be made on the basis of changes in the risk and return expectations for an individual security, but the impact of any such change on the total portfolio must be considered. Moreover, changes may be required in the structure of a portfolio that are caused not by changes in the characteristics of individual securities but rather by changes in the expected results and risk characteristics of the portfolio as a whole.

The types of portfolio adjustments to be discussed in this chapter fall into four clearly-defined categories:

1. changes in portfolio objectives,
2. changes in asset mix,
3. changes in the fixed-income portion of the portfolio, and
4. changes in the equity portion of the portfolio.

CHANGES IN PORTFOLIO OBJECTIVES

Establishing clear portfolio objectives is the key to a mutually satisfactory relationship between a client and an investment manager. Consequently, these objectives should be established early in the relationship and should be mutually understood and agreed upon. This task often is difficult, and the investment manager may have to take the initiative in order to help the client establish goals and determine whether those goals are realistic in the expected market environment. When agreement is reached, the objectives should be committed to writing to avoid possible future misunderstanding. This point may seem obvious, but frictions can easily develop if either the client or the manager is uncertain about what is expected, so that the manager often is changing directions or the client is unhappy because in some vague fashion the portfolio doesn't meet the client's expectations.

Statement of Objectives

Simply described, portfolio objectives are a statement, agreed upon by the client and the investment manager, of what the client expects and the constraints within which the investment manager may operate.

A statement of portfolio objectives generally covers three topics. The first is a general statement of the intent of the fund, that is, the purpose for which it was established. For an individual investor, the purpose could be to provide some level of income, or to develop a capital pool to meet some future need such as retirement income or some expected capital outlay. For a corporation, the purpose may be to provide future retirement benefits, or a reserve fund to provide near-term benefit payments, or an investment portfolio for some other corporate purpose.

The second topic usually covers investment constraints placed by the client on the manager. These constraints may include types of investments not permitted (for example, bonds rated less than A, foreign securities, options, real estate equities, stocks of a particular company or its competitors, etc.) or some limit to equity exposure (for example, equity exposure constrained between 40 and 60 percent of assets).

The third topic, and by far the most important, is a statement of the investment results expected and the risks that may be assumed in order to achieve these results.

Investment Results Expected

Expected investment results can be stated in a variety of ways. Most often results are expressed in *relative* terms, that is, the expected results for a reasonable period of time, usually three to five years, relative to some representative market average or some universe of portfolios of other investment managers. The Standard and Poor's 500 (S&P 500) stock composite and the Salomon Brothers or Lehman Brothers Kuhn Loeb bond indexes usually are used to measure stock and bond results, respectively.

The universe of portfolios of other managers varies. One widely-used measure is a broad group of funds with different objectives and asset mixes, such as the Becker universe. The difficulty with using such a universe is obvious: funds with different objectives and asset mixes are noncomparable, and certain types of funds will perform better than others in different market environments. Consequently, such comparisons are more useful if restricted to determining how segments of the portfolio, that is, the bond and stock portions, have performed relative to the bond and stock portions of other managers' portfolios. Nevertheless, even for stock and bond portfolios taken separately, objectives may differ and risk also should be considered as well as the return achieved.

Because of these limitations, many corporate investors and performance measurement services have created specialized universes of more restricted groups of funds of comparable size, objectives, and asset mixes.

Although relative performance measures probably are still the most commonly used method of establishing objectives and measuring results, their limitations are becoming more widely recognized. Past results are not necessarily an indication of future results. For example, the investment manager may have concentrated on a sector of the market that has been favored but subsequently may fall into disfavor, the results may be due to luck rather than skill, or the personnel or investment style of the manager may change. More importantly, good *relative* performance may not meet the needs of the client, especially in prolonged periods of adverse stock and bond market movements. The unhappy experience of many corporate pension fund sponsors during the past decade is clear evidence of this fact.

As a result, increased attention is being paid to expressing investment returns in *absolute* terms. The advantages of using absolute rather than relative return objectives are several: (1) it provides a clearly understood target for the manager to achieve; (2) holding the manager to an absolute rather than a relative return objective may avoid major contributions to a fund to make up for inferior absolute results; and (3) a quantification of results does not require the manager to forecast the standard and then attempt to agree with the client on what should be reasonable expectations for results better than the standard.

Absolute expected returns for a portfolio may be expressed in several ways. One is simply the absolute total return (income plus appreciation) expected over a given number of years. Alternatively, some income requirement, either for each year or an average for several years, may be imposed in addition to some total return expectation. Another way of stating absolute results is to consider the assets and the cash flows of a fund over time and set a period within which the fund should meet some asset target, say a given dollar amount or an amount equal to the vested or unfunded liabilities of a pension fund. Objectives stated in this manner have an implicit absolute return requirement, which can be computed, and it may be easier for the client to focus on objectives so stated.

Risk Tolerance

A major change in portfolio management during the past decade has been the inclusion of the concept of risk in any statement of portfolio objectives. The combination of wider understanding of modern portfolio theory and the unsatisfactory investment results of the past decade have focused the attention of clients and managers on this often-neglected area.

Risk tolerance can be defined in several ways. One way is to express risk in terms of portfolio volatility relative to the market, or portfolio beta. The current portfolio beta ordinarily is computed by using the beta of the individual securities in the portfolio weighted by the market value of each security in the total portfolio. Subsequent volatility of the portfolio itself may be somewhat different, but in well-diversified portfolios the differences should not be significant. Very often investment managers who use this concept of risk establish their clients' risk tolerance and then attempt to construct portfolios that will be "efficient," that is, portfolios that will produce the maximum return at some given level of risk.

One problem arises in this approach. Clients may have difficulty expressing their risk tolerances in terms of portfolio volatility. Even if they do so, subsequently they may find that their tolerance level expressed before the fact does not anticipate their tension level when subsequent results are adverse, even though it may be within the limits previously established. For a corporate pension fund, volatility may be an important consideration because failure to meet certain return objectives in a given year may require additional contributions to the fund. Use of the concept of portfolio volatility as a measure of risk therefore must be tailored to the requirements of the particular client.

Another approach to risk first states the desired level of return and then seeks to determine the minimum risk of failing to reach that desired return. The desired level of return can be expressed either explicitly, say an 8 percent return, or implicitly, say an objective of having assets equal to vested liabilities of a pension fund within a given time horizon, or pension fund contributions not to exceed 10 percent of payrolls. Risk can then be expressed in terms of the probabilities of not achieving the desired return, given either historical returns or expected returns for various types of assets plus the assumed asset mix of the portfolio.

Investment Time Horizon

One important caveat must be mentioned in discussing the statement of investment objectives. The investment time horizon over which results are to be achieved should be clearly stated. Because security markets are volatile, the shorter the time horizon over which results are measured, the lower are the probabilities of achieving an expected return from risky securities. Put another way, the standard deviation of expected annual returns is greater for one year than for five years. As the time horizon is shortened, either the expected return must be reduced or the probabilities of achieving it must be reduced. This point must be clearly understood if a satisfactory relationship between the client and the manager is to be maintained.

Changes in Portfolio Objectives

Thus far the discussion has dealt with establishing portfolio objectives, which was a base essential to a discussion of changes in these objectives. Portfolio objectives are set by the needs and circumstances of the client. These needs and circumstances generally are independent of the economic and market environment, although economic conditions may affect needs, just as changes in longer term expected returns from the securities markets may affect one's portfolio and require redefinition of objectives. Because the portfolio's objectives are set by the client's needs and circumstances and must be changed as the client's requirements change, the use of relative investment returns as an investment objective has obvious limitations.

For the individual investor, portfolio objectives might be changed as income needs change, or greater stability of principal is needed to meet a fixed and known obligation in the future. For a corporation, if a pension fund became frozen or if the work force matured, a different set of investment objectives would be needed. For a corporate pension fund, as assets cover a larger portion of liabilities, the desire for a more conservative and less volatile portfolio might require a change in objectives. Changes in tax laws or changes in the tax status of the client could require reevaluation of objectives.

How are changes in objectives made? Obviously the need for these changes can be discovered only through careful and continuing discussion between the client and the investment manager. Some discussion, however brief, should be an automatic part of every client meeting. Changes in objectives are the most fundamental factors affecting changes in the portfolio and they may require adjustments in asset mix, bond and stock diversification, and income production.

CHANGES IN ASSET MIX

In structuring a portfolio, the first consideration is the types of assets to be used in its composition. The assets may include a wide assortment of investment vehicles, from conventional securities such as bonds, stocks, and a variety of short-term money-market instruments, to other investments such as real estate mortgages and real estate equity, guaranteed income contracts, stock options, art, jewelry, stamps, coins, gold bars, and other stores of value. For the purpose of this chapter, the discussion will be restricted to marketable securities, such as bonds, stocks, and money market instruments. Other types of investments are of a more specialized nature; some of them, such as option and real estate, are considered in other chapters of this book.

In viewing asset mix, the total portfolio of the client will be considered. Some portfolios specialize in one type of asset, such as bonds or stocks, but ordinarily they are only a part of a total portfolio package.

Asset Mix Defined

Asset mix refers to the percentage weighting of various types of assets in a portfolio. Conventionally, a portfolio is divided between bonds and stocks; any cash equivalents held in money-market instruments are considered reserves, destined for bond and stock investment at the appropriate time.

Alternatively, cash equivalents can be considered as a viable investment alternative. When the concept of risk or volatility of return is added to the investment objectives, this latter approach has considerable merit. For example, an asset with a known return, such as Treasury Bills, is an investment where the principal has minimal fluctuations in value and the return varies with short-term interest rates. Other assets, fixed income and equity, provide expected returns and expected volatility that can be compared to the expected returns and minimal volatility of Treasury Bills. Portfolios then can be constructed that take into account the returns and volatility of three, rather than two, investment alternatives.

Causes of Changes in Asset Mix

Changes in asset mix are caused by fundamental factors that affect expected returns. These fundamental factors may be divided into three categories:

1. Changes in portfolio objectives, which may result in a change in the required return or the risk tolerance of the portfolio. These changes in portfolio objectives have been discussed earlier in this chapter.
2. Changes in the economic environment or the factors affecting an industry or a company, which cause changes in the expected returns for the various types of assets. For example, a change in the growth rate of earnings for a company will affect the expected return from its stock over time if the price has not yet adjusted to the change.
3. Changes in the market prices of assets, which will alter the expected returns. For example, a significant increase in the price of a stock portfolio with no change in the expected growth rate of earnings will have an effect on the expected return from that portfolio over time.

Factors affecting Expected Returns

As indicated above, expected returns for securities may be influenced either by economic forces or by market price changes.

Economic forces may be so broad in nature as to affect whole classes of assets. As examples, the rise in the rate of inflation during the past decade has had a significant effect on the expected returns of both stocks and bonds. Bond yields have risen to a level where, at certain times, the total expected returns from long-term bonds may be considered competitive or superior to the expected total returns from stocks. Past inflation rates have adversely affected the earnings and lowered the interest coverage of many electric utilities because their regulated rate structure has not permitted sufficiently rapid adjustment to rising costs. Consequently, expected returns have had to be reduced and bond quality has deteriorated. Inflation has adversely affected the trend of real profits and caused a major downward adjustment in the prices investors have been willing to pay for nominal earnings, thus substantially reducing the past return on common stocks and causing many to question future expected equity returns.

At other times, economic factors may affect expected returns for individual securities. A shift in consumer spending or in regulatory requirements may adversely affect the income stream of a particular company, lower its expected growth rate, decrease its interest coverage and threaten its ability to repay debt at maturity. The changing fortunes of particular companies in the automobile industry are examples of the effects of these shifts.

Price changes also can affect expected returns of both bonds and stocks. A change in the level of interest rates due to government policy or economic events can raise or lower bond prices, thus affecting the future investment return from fixed-coupon issues for a given dollar investment. Assuming no change in earnings growth rates, a change in the level of stock prices can affect both dividend yields and expected future price changes.

Within the broad moves of market prices, movements of particular sectors, industries, and individual securities may vary, thus altering the relationship of securities or groups of securities to each other. For example, a change in the slope of the yield curve will change the relationships to each other of the expected returns of bonds of different maturity but similar quality.

As an example of changes within the equity markets, at the end of 1974, the 10 percent of the stocks that had the greatest market weighting in the S&P 500 sold at a multiple that was 2.2 times that of the stocks in the lowest 10 percent of market weights and had a yield 5.34 percentage points less. Granted that the top 10 percent companies were larger, had better past and expected growth rates, and also had better fundamental financial characteristics, the question of their relative overvaluation and lower expected future returns should have been asked. These stocks were then considered "one decision" stocks, and growth was desirable at any price. As might be expected, the market pendulum swung to the opposite extreme. By March 1978, the top 10 percent companies had a price-earnings multiple less than, and a yield greater than, that of the bottom 10 percent. Again the expected return relationships were distorted and subsequently corrected in the market place.

Predicting Expected Returns

Because expected returns for different types of assets are so important in setting the asset mix for a portfolio, the determination of what returns to use is critical. Fortunately, data banks are now available giving historical returns for the three types of assets for extended periods, which encompass a panorama of historical events such as depressions, wars, booms and inflations. Averages of these historical returns, or returns for past periods expected to be comparable to future periods, may be used as inputs in predicting future returns. (Chapter 14 provides such historical returns.) Use of this approach requires good judgment in selecting the historically analogous period.

An alternative approach is to make projections of future economic and market conditions, which requires good judgment but also a different set of inputs. The starting point of estimating future expected returns ordinarily is one or more sets of economic assumptions, or scenarios, as they are popularly called. These scenarios are useful if they encompass a reasonable set of expected economic outcomes, if they are mutually exclusive and if not too many of them are used. One helpful procedure in making long-range and short-term economic forecasts is to use three forecasts, one of which is designated as "most probable."

Elsewhere I have discussed the types of economic inputs needed for use in investment analysis and also the process to derive expected returns.[1] Suffice it to mention here that, for each scenario, the following information is necessary:

1. estimates of short-term and long-term interest rates, which are either explicitly given or implicit in the forecast;
2. estimates of corporate profits;
3. relationship of these profits to expected earnings and dividends of some selected stock market indicator, e.g., S&P 500 or S&P 400; and
4. valuation models that will provide expected future values of these earnings, so that future equity returns can be projected.

Determination of Asset Mix

At this point, the investment manager has firmly in hand the investment objectives as set between the client and the manager and also several economic scenarios, each with an associated set of expected investment returns for three types of assets: bonds, stocks, and cash equivalents. The next step in the process of asset allocation is to estimate the probabilities of each economic scenario occurring. These probabilities are judgmental and can be established either by the manager subject to the client's review or by the client personally.

As discussed earlier, two other inputs to the process are needed. The investment time horizon to achieve the desired results must be established, keeping in mind that the shorter the time horizon the greater the variability in returns from risky assets and the lower the

---

[1] See Edmund A. Mennis, "The Practical Use of Economic Analysis in Investment Management," in *The Economic Framework for Investors* (Charlottesville, Va.: Financial Analysts Research Foundation, 1975), pp. 43–55, *and* Edmund A. Mennis, "Investment Management of Large Portfolios," in *Portfolio Management, Occasional Paper no. 7* (Charlottesville, Va.: Financial Analysts Research Foundation, 1978), pp. 1–18.

target return that can be achieved with any degree of assurance. The second additional input is given in the client's explicit or implicit statement of expected returns as stated in the investment objectives. The client must then, with the help of the manager, express a desired level of the probabilities of achieving this expected return. Various combinations also are possible. For example, the client's views can be expressed as a combination of a defensive or minimum target return that must be reached with a high degree of probability, and an aggressive return that must have a reasonable chance of success.

At this stage, the job of asset allocation can be accomplished most effectively by a computer, which can assimilate the expected returns and their probabilities of occurrence, the variability of such returns based on historical or assumed variance, and the current status and expected cash flow into the portfolio over the time horizon used. The output will be the combination of assets, that is, the proportions of the portfolio in cash equivalents, bonds and stocks, that will optimize the probabilities of achieving the expected return. If no asset mix can achieve the return under the risk constraints imposed, the required return or the risk constraints can be relaxed until an optimum solution is found.

When are changes made in the asset mix? As the earlier discussion indicated, changes in investment objectives or changes in the expected returns of the assets due to fundamental factors affecting the assets or significant price movements will require a review of the asset mix.

Changes in market price are the most frequent causes of a review of the asset mix, and the expected returns should be reviewed at regular intervals, expecially if market moves have been significant, in order to determine whether a change in asset mix is indicated. Less frequent reviews are necessary to check whether expected returns have been affected by changes in the factors affecting the economy and the assets themselves, but such a review should be made whenever a significant alteration is made in the economic forecasts.

Implicit in this process is the assumption that the investment manager can produce a portfolio that will meet or exceed the expected returns estimated for each type of asset included in the portfolio, net of commission costs and management fees. If this expectation is not reasonable, the manager should adjust the expected returns by whatever amount he or she expects to fall short, or else estimate market returns very conservatively.

The question is sometimes asked whether this approach is not a form of "market timing." Hopefully the discussion has suggested that it is not. Market timing attempts to predict market turning points and then to shift assets into or out of types of securities in order to take advantage of these predictions. These predictions are necessarily short-term in nature, and the volatility of and unexpected moves in market prices require superior predictive ability. A study by Sharpe[2] has suggested that better than an 80 percent predictive accuracy is necessary in order to be successful. Consequently, changes in asset mix are more likely to be successful if a longer investment time horizon is used and asset shifts are related more to fundamental factors than anticipating the next market turn.

CHANGES IN THE COMPOSITION OF FIXED-INCOME PORTFOLIOS

Adjustments in bond portfolios are made in an attempt to improve the return over time from fixed-income securities compared with those returns expected from those securities in the economic scenarios used. For many years bond portfolio management was essentially passive. Investments in bonds were made in approximately equal amounts, with maturity evenly spaced to the most distant maturity with which the investor was comfortable.

More recently, however, bond management has become more active as investment managers have sought to improve bond investment results.[3] The higher total returns available from bonds have made these investments a viable alternative to equities and not just a temporary haven for stock money. Moreover, as the frequency and amplitude of interest rate fluctuations have increased, the greater has been the price volatility, so that attempting to anticipate price fluctuations may be more rewarding. The bond portfolio composition at any particular time is primarily a function of expectations about future interest rate trends and yield spreads among various categories of bonds. The types of portfolio decisions required fall roughly into four categories: maturity, quality, coupon, and sector. Of these, maturity probably is most important.

Maturity

As a broad guideline, interest rate expectations are an important guideline for maturity selection. Maturities should be lengthened when interest rates are expected to fall and prices to rise, and maturities should be shortened when interest rates are expected to rise.

This general rule is, however, a considerable oversimplification, because portfolio moves must be made with a view to the total return to the account, including coupon income, reinvestment rates, and price

---

[2] See William F. Sharpe, "Likely Gains from Market Timing," *Financial Analysts Journal* (March–April 1975), pp. 60–69.

[3] For a more complete discussion of many of the techniques of active bond portfolio management, see Sidney Homer and Martin L. Leibowitz, *Inside the Yield Book* (Englewood Cliffs, N.J.: Prentice-Hall, Inc., and New York Institute of Finance, 1972).

volatility. Assumptions about the length and amplitude of bond price cycles are important. For example, if only a modest and gradual increase in interest rates were expected accompanied by a flattening of the yield curve, a higher total return might be derived from holding longer term bonds. As another example, in the higher yield ranges, price volatility of bonds with maturities of more than one or two years is very large and relatively larger for medium maturity bonds. Consequently, an investment manager sensitive to cyclical fluctuations in bond prices might be better off shifting from long bonds to cash equivalents or very short bonds rather than shifting to medium maturities if one expects interest rates to rise.

The maturity structure of a bond portfolio depends heavily upon cyclical forecasts of interest rates if a manager is going to engage in active bond portfolio management. Such forecasts should consider expected interest rates for various maturities and also the expected slope of the yield curve. Moreover, it seems hardly necessary to suggest that such forecasts should be reviewed frequently, as expected interest rates may change significantly due to changing economic expectations, Federal Reserve policy, and international considerations. Nevertheless, reasonable success in such forecasts can make the major contribution to successful bond portfolio management.

Quality

Quality diversification is another important consideration in constructing a bond portfolio. Ratings by Moody's and Standard and Poor's help the investor to differentiate between the quality of bonds, based on the ability of the borrower to pay interest and principal promptly when due. Uncritical acceptance of bond ratings is not advisable, however; these ratings have a tendency to lag behind changes in the financial characteristics of a company. Therefore, good bond research into the economic forces affecting an industry or a company as well as its financial position often can anticipate changes in credit quality and bond ratings and thereby provide investment opportunities. Even though a rating may not be changed, identifying companies near the upper or lower limits of a particular quality range can prove rewarding.

As a general statement, as the quality of a bond lessens, the interest rate that the issuing company must pay to its lenders increases. Because yield spreads between different quality bonds generally narrow during an economic recovery and widen during an economic contraction, high quality bonds should be purchased when the economy is expected to contract and lower quality bonds acquired when an economic expansion is expected.

However, high-grade bonds have tended to lead market turns. As prices of high-grade bonds begin to decline, investors who have an income requirement continue to purchase and thus support the prices of medium-grade issues. As a result, the peak in prices of medium-grade issues often is later in the market cycle than is the peak for high-grade issues. When investors do perceive a drop in bond prices of some duration and magnitude, prices of medium-grade bonds decline rapidly. At the trough of the bond price cycle, an upturn in prices of high-grade bonds precedes an increase in the prices of medium-grade bonds. Knowledge of these characteristics coupled with good interest rate forecasts can enhance the profitability of quality diversification as a bond management technique.

Coupon

Because of the downtrend and the wide fluctuations in bond prices during the past decade or so and the heavy volume of new issues, investors now have a wide selection of bonds with varying coupons, or rates of interest payments, stated in the bond indenture. The investor may select from high coupon bonds, ordinarily selling at a premium above par, current coupon issues at or about par and low coupon issues selling at discounts. High coupon bonds trading at or above their redemption price are often called "cushion" bonds. Although their potential for further price appreciation is restricted regardless of further declines in long-term interest rates, in a subsequent period of rising interest rates the high coupon provides a cushion against significant price declines. Yield and price relationships between bonds of different coupons change because of factors such as the supply of new issues, sinking fund activity, calls features, dealer carrying costs, and the general level and expected trend of interest rates.

Selecting the appropriate coupon for an investor can be a somewhat complex matter, depending upon the investment objectives previously established. The tax status of the investors is important; the investment return of a discount bond is higher for a taxpayer because of the lower capital gain tax incurred when the bond is paid at par at maturity. For a nontaxpayer, e.g., a corporate pension fund, the total return is a more important consideration. Consequently, selection of the appropriate issue would be influenced by the need for current income, the sensitivity to interim price fluctuations and interest rate expectations. For example, an investor seeking maximum income who is indifferent to price fluctuations ordinarily would select the high coupon bond. The investor seeking maximum total return would be influenced by expectations for future interest rates. If an investor expects interest rates to rise, but preferred to maintain a position in long-term bonds, high coupon issues would be one's first choice; if one expects interest rates to fall, the discount bonds would be preferable.

Again the significance of interest rate expectations in portfolio adjustments should be emphasized. These expectations involve not only identifying peaks and troughs but also the magnitude of the expected changes. This latter factor is important in selecting the appropriate coupon issue. For example, an interest rate decline to a level below the trough of the previous interest rate cycle can produce greater total returns from discount bonds than from high-coupon bonds, because price appreciation of the high-coupon bond would be limited by its redemption characteristics.

Sector

Sector transactions attempt to increase total return by anticipating changes in yield differentials between different categories of bonds, such as governments, industrials, utilities, and the like. These relationships change because of factors such as the relative supply of new issues and the outlook for specific areas of the economy. For example, the economic effects of inflation have caused general widening of yield differentials between utility bonds and many other sectors in the past several years. However, improvement in utilities' ability to cope with inflation through a more understanding regulatory environment and reduced requirements for new construction may affect their outlook favorably and cause yield differentials to narrow.

Techniques Contrasted

Several of the techniques for active bond portfolio management depend upon successful interest-rate forecasts. Maturity selection as well as quality and coupon selection fall within this category. Factors affecting sector selection also depend upon interest rate forecasts, but economic and financial analysis have a more important bearing on changes in this area.

Another technique used to guide changes in a bond portfolio is bond substitution or "swapping," in which portfolio adjustments are made in order to take advantage of temporary aberrations in the bond market due to supply and demand factors, such as long or short dealer positions and sinking fund requirements. Such swaps may result in exchanging bonds of similar quality, sector, coupon, and maturity at relatively favorable levels. These changes are made independent of interest-rate forecasts and depend upon opportunities ordinarily available only briefly. Active bond management in such transactions obviously requires that the investment manager be closely in touch with market conditions.

CHANGES IN THE EQUITY PORTFOLIO

Similar to changes in a bond portfolio, adjustments in an equity portfolio are made in an attempt to better the return that might be expected from the stock market generally. The factors that influence these changes will depend heavily upon the investment philosophy or style of the investment manager.

Alternative Styles of Equity Management

At least four different styles of equity portfolio management are in use at the present time.

1. The first and oldest treats a portfolio as a collection of individual securities. These securities are selected individually and with little consideration given to their interrelationships when they are combined into a portfolio. Selection may be made on the basis of their perceived undervaluation in the market place or alternatively because they have superior financial characteristics relative to the universe of stocks from which they were chosen. These superior financial characteristics are expected, over time, to lead to superior market performance. In a portfolio so constructed, changes are made in the portfolio either because of price changes (e.g., the security reaches a price target selected and is no longer undervalued) or because the perceived undervaluation is subsequently proved incorrect or because the fundamental financial characteristics change. Risk is rarely taken into account in this approach.

2. The second style embraces modern portfolio theory and concludes that the risk in individual securities (unique or specific risk as opposed to market risk) is not rewarded because the market is efficient and securities are rarely if ever mispriced. Therefore this unique risk should be diversified away by use of an index fund in which securities are held in proportion to their market capitalization weights. In such an approach, changes are made in the equity holdings in two circumstances. Changes in the composition of the index (e.g., changes in the securities of the S&P 500) would require a readjustment for new stocks and new stock weights. Also, on the grounds of fiduciary prudence, some stocks may be eliminated from the index.

3. In the third style, estimates are made of the risk and return expectations for individual securities. Ordinarily these expectations are for a period of time longer than one year. Then portfolio optimization models are used in order to construct an equity portfolio to give a required return at the lowest risk level or the highest return at a specified risk level. Portfolio adjustments are made either as prices change—thus altering the expected returns—or as the risk classification or the fundamental characteristics of the individual stocks change—thus altering their risk-reward expectations. This third approach uses some form of traditional security research to estimate returns and risk of individual securities. In contrast to an index fund, which diversifies away specific risk, this approach attempts to control portfolio risk. An

index fund approach is based upon the belief that inefficiencies are hard to find at the individual stock level and are not rewarded, at least after transaction costs. This approach attempts to take advantage of "found" inefficiencies in a controlled way.

4. The fourth approach is one that has been increasingly used in recent years. Portfolios are structured by classifying stocks into industries, with the weight in each industry either more than, equal to or less than comparable weights in each industry in the market portfolio. Several variants of this approach are discernable, and they are treated at greater length in the next section.

Industry Portfolios

The rationale for structuring portfolios by industries or economic sectors is based on the concept that broad economic trends and movements in major sectors of the economy can have an influence on stock price movements of industries and companies within these industries. Moreover, these broader trends are not as aggressively and efficiently analyzed as are individual companies, so that unique insights and market opportunities may be discovered. Some studies have indicated that the risk of a security is not just that of the market and the specific risk of the company but rather a market sector or industry risk is present as well.[4]

The first step in the construction of these portfolios is the determination of the appropriate industry groupings. Often these groupings are prepared judgmentally, in some instances based on various economic classifications or in other instances based upon financial characteristics of stock groupings, such as high growth, emerging growth, cyclical, regulated, etc. Another approach is to use the industry classifications of the S&P 500, although the large number of these industries can present problems in conceptualizing portfolio structure and in management of portfolio inputs. Consequently, the many S&P 500 industries often are grouped together in various related components.

Determination of Industry Weights

If portfolios are constructed by industries, what factors are used to determine the weight, or the percent of the equity portfolio, invested in each industry and how are these weights changed? Differences in market weights are essentially judgmental, using economic insights at the industry level that can be checked against insights into the

---

[4] See Benjamin F. King, "Market and Industry Factors in Stock Price Behavior," *Journal of Business* (January 1966), pp. 139–90; James L. Farrell, Jr., "The Multi-index Model and Practical Portfolio Analysis," *in Portfolio Management, Occasional Paper no. 4* (Charlottesville, Va.: Financial Analysts Research Foundation, 1976); and Miles Livingston, "Industry Movements of Common Stocks," *Journal of Finance* (June 1977), pp. 861–74. The last article has a good bibliography of other studies.

companies that comprise the industry. Positions are taken above or below comparable industry weights in the market portfolio where unique insights are believed to be available that are not yet reflected in market prices. Where no insights are available, a market weight is assumed.

In a more quantified and rigorous approach, the expected returns are prepared for each industry. The probabilities of achieving the expected return are used as a measure of the uniqueness of the insight, thus providing guidance for the degree of over- or underweighting. In many portfolios, the ability to mix the portfolio with riskless assets or to leverage the portfolio by borrowing is restricted by constraints imposed by the portfolio owner or by law. In this event, the expected price volatility relative to the market (beta) can be prepared for each industry and the equity portfolio weight of an industry would be a function of both expected returns and expected volatility. For example, the incremental weight taken for or against an industry with a low beta necessarily would be greater than for an industry with a high beta.

What would cause changes in industry weights? These changes would be made for several reasons. The first would be a change in the fundamental characteristics of the industry that would influence growth rates and expected investment returns. These expected investment returns also could be altered by a change in price or by a change in expected price volatility. In addition, changes in market price can change the relative attractiveness of one industry group to another. Frequent monitoring of the structure of a portfolio is necessary in order to assure the optimum portfolio mix.

An example of an industry change in the past few years may be illustrative of the process. In March 1975, the drug industry was viewed by the market as one of the few attractive groups in a relatively unfavorable market environment. The historical earnings growth rate of the industry in the previous five years was 13 percent per year compounded, and this rate was confidently expected to continue. The industry was selling at a price-earnings ratio of 23.3, or 2.4 times the market (S&P 500) multiple. Nevertheless, the economic environment abroad, especially in Europe, was deteriorating, thus threatening an important source of earnings. Moreover, the building of pressures on the dollar further threatened earnings due to currency losses. Not only was the earnings growth rate questionable, but a considerable increase in price volatility might have been expected as investors began to reevaluate a fundamental change in the industry's prospects. The industry then represented 8.81 percent of the S&P 500 and a position of a less-than-market weight seemed called for.

By July 1977, the industry had declined 20.8 percent in price, while the S&P 500 increased 18.6 percent. The industry then represented 4.44 percent of the market index, and the P/E ratio was 13.8, or 1.5

times the market P/E. At that time, however, prospects for the industry had improved. The regulatory environment was more favorable, and prospects for new product introductions had increased appreciably. The prospects for domestic profit improvement were much better, and the lower P/E ratios suggested investment opportunities for the next 12 to 18 months. Consequently, a reversal of the previously underweighted position seemed appropriate, and relative market performance subsequently was quite favorable. From July 1977 to July 1978, the industry appreciated 27.0 percent, relative to a gain of 1.9 percent in the S&P 500.

Company Selection

If an industry approach is used in portfolio construction, what process should be used to select companies to populate the industry? The method used most often is to select individual securities that are expected to outperform the industry. Assuming that this can be done successfully, the portfolio manager obviously has added value and incremental return. However, this method has some disadvantages. If individual stock selection is used, the portfolio is exposed to specific stock risk, and the advantages of economic and industry insights may be offset or lost. The stocks selected may be less subject to industry influences than other stocks but more affected by specific company characteristics. The weightings of the particular stock in the industry portfolio may vary from market weights, and again the industry effects may be offset. Moreover, the risk characteristics of the nonmarket weighted industry may differ from the industry risk characteristics.

An alternative procedure that can maximize the advantages of industry and economic insights and minimize the problem of specific risk would be to index the companies in each industry in proportion to their market weights in the industry. In effect, this approach diversifies away individual company risk at the industry level, takes advantage of insights gained from industry analysis and also is closer to effective industry analysis than the alternative of stock selection. Portfolio changes are reduced because changes are made only when industry expectations change rather than changed because of changing expectations for individual companies.

Sector Portfolios

Several problems are presented to the investment manager who decides to use industry groupings as an equity portfolio management technique. One first must decide what industry groupings to use. One then must determine whether the weighting of the industry groupings in the portfolio will be adjusted as a result primarily of changes in the characteristics of the companies within each industry or whether one also will attempt to integrate one's economic and market overview with one's evaluation of the outlook for individual industries. Should the manager choose the latter approach, relating macroeconomic variables to individual industries can be difficult. Security Pacific Investment Managers, Inc., has addressed both of these problems by the use of economic sector groupings that categorize industries by related financial and market characteristics and that also have meaningful relationships to economic variables.

The economic sector categories of industries were derived in the following way. First, the 500 stocks in the S&P 500 were classified by standard industrial classification numbers into 43 industry groups, and each group was tested to determine whether the price actions of the stocks in each group were similar. The second step was to aggregate the individual company financial data for each of the 43 industries and analyze key financial characteristics of each industry group, such as earnings and dividend growth, effects of leverage, and volatility of earnings growth.

By use of a statistical technique called cluster analysis, the industries then were sorted on the basis of their common key characteristics. These groupings were then refined and divided ultimately into sectors that related to their economic characteristics. As a last step, the price characteristics of each sector were analyzed and the past price movements of each sector were discovered to be significantly different with respect to trend, volatility and turning points, while within each group the price movements of the industries were quite similar. This analysis further reinforced the unique character of each sector and the opportunity to make significant market differentiations among them. The resulting economic sectors were as follows:

consumer discretionary durables,
consumer discretionary nondurables and services,
consumer nondiscretionary,
energy,
retail,
capital spending,
technology,
utilities,
finance, and
industrial commodities.

As a result of this approach, ten clearly defined economic sectors, each with its particular industry groupings, are available. Each sector is influenced by somewhat different economic forces, each has common financial characteristics and each has behaved differently in market price movements.

A distinct advantage of using this economic sector approach is the ability to examine an equity portfolio from a macro viewpoint, and to determine whether its characteristics are appropriate given the expected economic and market environment. For example, economic forecasts will indicate areas of strength and weakness in the economy, which can be directly related to the economic sectors of the portfolio described above. Market factors, such as cash available for investment by institutions and foreigners, margin debt, and price movements within types of stocks also can be included. We have found that a formal monthly review in this manner can add a valuable perspective to the construction of a portfolio and is an important first step before considering the details of portfolio construction by industry and company.

The sector weights are derived through two methods. The first is to add the weights for each industry and then cross check the results from an overall economic and sector perspective, making adjustments as needed. The second method is to check the resulting equity portfolio mix by using a portfolio optimization model that will provide the best sector mix, given the expected returns and volatility of each sector. In effect, ten sector funds can be created, with the investor having representation in each fund. The stocks in the industries in each sector are indexed to their proportionate market weight in that industry. The sector, which may have a weighting over, under, or equal to its market weight, will be comprised of industries so weighted as to provide the best opportunity to outperform that sector if it were market-weighted. Changes in such a portfolio would be made as the expected returns of the sectors and industries are altered due to fundamental factors or price movements. Moreover, if sectors are used, optimum portfolios of the ten sectors can be constructed adjusted to the client's risk tolerance by varying the sector weights depending upon each sector's expected return and volatility.

What are the advantages of this method relative to the more conventional use of industry weights? The approach is completely integrated, combining economic and market inputs at all levels with clients' expected returns and risk tolerance. Specific stock risk is reduced yet advantages are taken of unusual insights at both the sector and industry level. The blending of industry and economic sector viewpoints does not result in positions in particular industries massively different from market weights, but the cumulative differences for an entire portfolio can be significant.

CONCLUSION

The discussion in this chapter has indicated that portfolio adjustments are rather complex, may arise from a variety of causes, and may be necessary in a portion of the portfolio or in the entire mix of the portfolio. An investment manager who pays primary attention to being in or out of the equity market, or who tries to anticipate the next most attractive stock group, or who ignores a client's objectives in an attempt to deliver performance better than that of the market will run the grave risk of unhappy clients at some point. Moreover, changes in portfolio theory have been rapid in recent years, and ignoring them or failing to blend them into an investment style also runs the risk of unsatisfactory long-term results and dissatisfied clients. The profession of investment management is both demanding and ever-changing, and rarely can its practitioners rest on their past accomplishments for very long. The experience of the past must be joined with the best of modern research to provide the client with reasonable assurance of meeting reasonably attainable objectives.

Chapter 14

Investment Returns on Stocks, Bonds, and Bills

ROGER G. IBBOTSON
Graduate School of Business
University of Chicago
Chicago, Illinois

Our look at history consists of examining the returns of five capital market sectors. We measure total returns (capital gains plus income) on common stocks, long-term corporate bonds, long-term government bonds, U.S. Treasury Bills, and rates of inflation on consumer goods. Comparing the returns from the various sectors gives us insights into the returns available from taking risk and the relationships between capital market returns and inflation.

THE RISKS AND REWARDS

We display graphically the rewards and risks available from the U.S. capital markets over the past 53 years. Figure 1 shows the growth of an investment in common stocks, long-term government bonds, and Treasury Bills as well as the increase in the inflation index over the 53-year period. Each of the series is initiated at $1 at year-end 1925. The vertical scale is logarithmic so that equal distances represent equal percentage changes anywhere along the axis. The graph vividly portrays that common stocks were the big winner over the entire period. If $1 were invested in stocks at year-end 1925 and all dividends reinvested, the dollar investment would have grown to $89.59 by year-end 1978. This phenomenal growth was not without substantial risk, especially during the earlier portion of the period. In contrast, long-term government bonds (with a constant 20-year maturity) exhibited much less risk, but grew to only $5.34.

A virtually riskless strategy (for those with short-term time horizons)

420

Figure 1
Wealth Indexes of Investments in the U.S. Capital Markets 1926–1978 Assumed Initial Investment of $1.00 at Year End 1925 (includes reinvestment income)

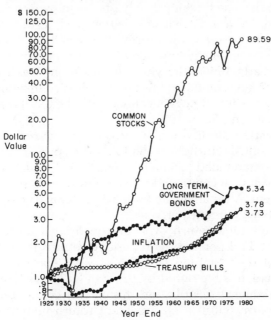

Source: Roger G. Ibbotson and Rex A. Sinquefield, *Stocks, Bonds, Bills, and Inflation: Historical Returns (1926–1978)* (Charlottesville, Va.: Financial Analysts Research Foundation, 1979).

Figure 2
Basic Series—Investment Total Annual Returns 1926–1978

Series	Geometric Mean	Arithmetic Mean	Standard Deviation	Distribution
Common Stocks	8.9%	11.2%	22.2%	
Long Term Corporate Bonds	4.0%	4.1%	5.6%	
Long Term Government Bonds	3.2%	3.4%	5.7%	
U.S. Treasury Bills	2.5%	2.5%	2.2%	
Inflation	2.5%	2.6%	4.8%	

-50%　　0%　　+50%

Source: Ibbotson and Sinquefield, *Stocks, Bonds, Bills, and Inflation.*

has been to buy U.S. Treasury Bills. However, Treasury Bills have had a marked tendency to track inflation, with the result that their real (inflation adjusted) return is near zero for the entire 1926–1978 period. Note that the tracking is only prevalent over the latter portion of the period. During periods of deflation (such as the late 1920s and early 1930s) the Treasury Bill returns were near zero, but not negative, since no one intentionally buys securities with negative yields. Beginning in the early 1940s, the yields (returns) on Treasury Bills were pegged by the government at low rates while high inflation was experienced. The government pegging ended with the U.S. Treasury-Federal Reserve Accord in March 1951.

We summarize the investment returns in Figure 2 by presenting the average annual returns over the 1926–1978 period. Common stocks returned a compounded (geometric mean) total return of 8.9 percent per year. The annual compound return from capital appreciation alone was 3.9 percent. After adjusting for inflation, annual compounded total returns were 6.2 percent per year.*

The average total return over any single year (arithmetic mean) for stocks was 11.2 percent, with positive returns recorded in nearly two thirds of the years (35 out of 53 years). The risk or degree of return fluctuation is measured by the standard deviation as 22.2 percent. The frequency distribution (histogram) counts the number of years the returns fell in each 5 percent return increment. Note the wide variations in common stock returns relative to the other capital market sectors. Annual stock returns ranged from 54.0 percent in 1933 to −43.3 percent in 1931.

A simple example illustrates the difference between geometric and arithmetic means. Suppose $1 were invested in a common stock portfolio that experiences successive annual returns of +50 percent and −50 percent. At the end of the first year the portfolio is worth $1.50. At the end of the second year, the portfolio is worth $0.75. The annual arithmetic mean is 0 percent, whereas the annual geometric mean (compounded return) is −13.4 percent. Naturally, it is the geometric mean that more directly measures the change in wealth over more than one period. On the other hand, the arithmetic mean is a better representation of typical performance over any single annual period.

The other capital market sectors also had returns commensurate

---

* Editor's note: Over the current decade the compounded growth rate for common stock with dividends reinvested has been considerably less than the long-term value of 8.9 percent. Thus from the beginning of 1969 to the end of 1978 the compounded growth rate has been 3.2 percent for common stock as compared to 5.8 percent for long-term corporate bonds and 5.9 percent for Treasury Bills. All figures neglect taxes. The inflation rate during this period was 6.7 percent. After inflationary adjustments and income taxes, it is evident that all of these investments resulted in a net loss in terms of real income. Assuming a 40 percent tax rate and a 6 percent inflation rate, investments must earn 10 percent before taxes to break even.

with their risks. Long-term corporate bonds outperformed the default-free, long-term government bonds, which in turn outperformed the essentially riskless U.S. Treasury Bills. Over the entire period the riskless U.S. Treasury Bills had a return almost identical with the inflation rate. Thus, we again note that the real rate of interest (the inflation-adjusted riskless rate) has been on average very near 0 percent historically.

MEASUREMENT OF THE FIVE SERIES

The returns were computed by compounding monthly returns, with no adjustments made for transactions costs or taxes. We describe each of the five total return series which are listed annually in Figure 3.

Common Stocks

The total return index is based upon Standard and Poor's (S&P) Composite Index with dividends reinvested monthly. To the extent that the 500 stocks currently included in the S&P Composite Index (prior to March 1957, there were 90 stocks) are representative of all stocks in the United States, the market value weighting scheme allows the returns of the index to correspond to the aggregate stock market returns in the U.S. economy.

Long-Term Corporate Bonds

We measure the total returns of a corporate bond index with approximately 20 years to maturity. We use Salomon Brothers' High Grade Long-Term Corporate Bond Index from its beginning in 1969 through 1978. For the period 1946–68 we backdate Salomon Brothers' index using Salomon Brothers' monthly yield data and similar methodology. For the period 1926–45 we compute returns using Standard and Poor's monthly high-grade corporate composite bond yield data, assuming a 4 percent coupon and a 20-year maturity.

Long-Term Government Bonds

To measure the total returns of long-term U.S. government bonds, we use the bond data obtained from the U.S. Government Bond File (constructed by Lawrence Fisher) at the Center for Research in Security Prices (CRSP) at the University of Chicago. We attempt to maintain a 20-year bond portfolio whose returns do not reflect the potential tax benefits, impaired negotiability, or the special redemption or call privileges frequently characterizing government bond prices and yields.

Figure 3
Basic Series, Indexes of Year-End Cumulative Wealth 1925–1978

Year	Common Stocks — Total Returns	Common Stocks — Capital Appreciation Only	Long-Term Government Bonds — Total Returns	Long-Term Government Bonds — Capital Appreciation Only	Long-Term Corporate Bonds Total Returns	U.S. Treasury Bills Total Returns	Consumer Price Index Rates of Inflation
1925.....	1.000	1.000	1.000	1.000	1.000	1.000	1.000
1926.....	1.116	1.057	1.073	1.039	1.074	1.033	0.985
1927.....	1.535	1.384	1.174	1.095	1.154	1.065	0.965
1928.....	2.204	1.908	1.175	1.061	1.186	1.099	0.955
1929.....	2.018	1.681	1.215	1.059	1.225	1.152	0.957
1930.....	1.516	1.202	1.272	1.072	1.323	1.179	0.899
1931.....	0.859	0.636	1.204	0.981	1.299	1.192	0.814
1932.....	0.789	0.540	1.407	1.108	1.439	1.204	0.730
1933.....	1.214	0.792	1.406	1.073	1.588	1.207	0.734
1934.....	1.197	0.745	1.547	1.146	1.808	1.209	0.749
1935.....	1.767	1.053	1.624	1.170	1.982	1.211	0.771
1936.....	2.367	1.346	1.746	1.225	2.116	1.213	0.780
1937.....	1.538	0.827	1.750	1.194	2.174	1.217	0.804
1938.....	2.016	1.035	1.847	1.228	2.307	1.217	0.782
1939.....	2.008	0.979	1.957	1.271	2.399	1.217	0.778
1940.....	1.812	0.829	2.076	1.319	2.480	1.217	0.786
1941.....	1.602	0.681	2.095	1.305	2.548	1.218	0.862
1942.....	1.927	0.766	2.162	1.315	2.614	1.221	0.942
1943.....	2.427	0.915	2.207	1.310	2.688	1.225	0.972
1944.....	2.906	1.041	2.270	1.314	2.815	1.229	0.993
1945.....	3.965	1.361	2.513	1.423	2.930	1.233	1.015
1946.....	3.645	1.199	2.511	1.392	2.980	1.238	1.199
1947.....	3.853	1.199	2.445	1.327	2.911	1.244	1.307
1948.....	4.065	1.191	2.528	1.340	3.031	1.254	1.343
1949.....	4.829	1.313	2.691	1.395	3.132	1.268	1.318
1950.....	6.360	1.600	2.692	1.366	3.198	1.283	1.395
1951.....	7.888	1.863	2.586	1.281	3.112	1.302	1.477
1952.....	9.336	2.082	2.616	1.262	3.221	1.324	1.490
1953.....	9.244	1.944	2.711	1.270	3.331	1.348	1.499
1954.....	14.108	2.820	2.906	1.325	3.511	1.360	1.492
1955.....	18.561	3.564	2.868	1.271	3.527	1.381	1.497
1956.....	19.778	3.658	2.708	1.164	3.287	1.415	1.540
1957.....	17.646	3.134	2.910	1.208	3.573	1.459	1.587
1958.....	25.298	4.327	2.733	1.097	3.494	1.482	1.615
1959.....	28.322	4.694	2.671	1.029	3.460	1.526	1.639
1960.....	28.455	4.554	3.039	1.124	3.774	1.566	1.663
1961.....	36.106	5.607	3.068	1.092	3.956	1.600	1.674
1962.....	32.955	4.945	3.280	1.122	4.270	1.643	1.695
1963.....	40.469	5.879	3.319	1.092	4.364	1.695	1.723
1964.....	47.139	6.642	3.436	1.084	4.572	1.754	1.743
1965.....	53.008	7.244	3.460	1.047	4.552	1.823	1.777
1966.....	47.674	6.295	3.586	1.036	4.560	1.910	1.836
1967.....	59.104	7.560	3.257	0.895	4.335	1.991	1.892
1968.....	65.642	8.139	3.248	0.846	4.446	2.094	1.981
1969.....	60.059	7.210	3.083	0.754	4.086	2.232	2.102
1970.....	62.465	7.222	3.457	0.791	4.837	2.378	2.218
1971.....	71.406	8.001	3.914	0.843	5.370	2.482	2.292
1972.....	84.956	9.252	4.136	0.840	5.760	2.577	2.371
1973.....	72.500	7.645	4.090	0.775	5.825	2.756	2.579
1974.....	53.311	5.373	4.268	0.748	5.647	2.976	2.894
1975.....	73.144	7.068	4.661	0.754	6.474	3.149	3.097
1976.....	90.584	8.422	5.441	0.815	7.681	3.309	3.246
1977.....	84.076	7.453	5.405	0.750	7.813	3.479	3.466
1978.....	89.592	7.532	5.342	0.682	7.807	3.728	3.778

Source: Ibbotson and Sinquefield, *Stocks, Bonds, Bills, and Inflation.*

U.S. Treasury Bills

For the U.S. Treasury Bill index, we again use the data in the CRSP U.S. Government Bond File. We measure one-month holding period returns for the shortest-term T-Bills not less than one month in maturity. Since U.S. Treasury Bills were not initiated until 1929, we use short-term coupon bonds whenever bill quotes are unavailable.

Consumer Price Index

We utilize the Consumer Price Index (CPI) to measure inflation. The CPI is constructed by the U.S. Department of Labor, Bureau of Labor Statistics, Washington, D.C.

Chapter 15

Historical Returns of Real Estate Equity Portfolios

KEITH V. SMITH*

Dean
Krannert Graduate School of Management
Purdue University
Lafayette, Indiana

Real estate is an important asset in the portfolios of the 50 million or so U.S. families and individuals who own their home. It also is an important asset in the portfolios of many institutional investors. Because of the dismal performance of the stock market during the past several years, equity investments in real estate have become recognized as a potentially useful asset to help investors hedge against the inflation that persists in our economy.

This chapter explores the achieved returns of real estate equity portfolios over the past 15 years. First, we compare indices of real estate activity with that for stocks and bonds. This leads to a discussion of some difficulties in evaluating real estate returns. Next we present and describe a sample of equity real estate investment trusts, as well as a sample of closed-end investment companies. Average returns for the two samples are then compared using both traditional and risk-adjusted performance measures. Implications of the findings and some additional difficulties are discussed in the concluding section.

INDEX TRENDS

To begin, it is useful to examine how real estate as an investment has fared over time, relative to other investment opportunities. On

---

* The author benefited from comments by Professors Fred Case, Frank Mittelbach, and David Shulman.

balance, a review of prior studies is not conclusive. An early study by Wendt and Wong [13] reported that investment returns for apartment houses *exceeded* stock returns over the 1952–62 period. Robichek et. al. [7] found that returns for farm real estate were less than that achieved by the Standard and Poor's Industrial Stock Price Index over the two decades, 1949–69. In an investigation of how real estate properties would fare alongside of common stocks in a portfolio construction exercise, Friedman [3] found that, using data for the 1963–68 period, real estate tended to dominate common stocks. Smith and Shulman [11] compared the returns for equity real estate investment trusts with that for closed-end investment companies over the period 1963–74 and found that the results are situational and depend on the particular horizon investigated. An overall conclusion by Roulac [9] is that there is no empirical evidence that real estate has outperformed common stocks.[1] Recently, however, Fama and Schwert [2] found that residential real estate is a better hedge against inflation than government and corporate securities.

Unfortunately, these studies were based on different types of real estate, different measures of return and risk, and different investment horizons. While there are a number of published indices that can be used to track the stock and bond markets over time, the same is not true for real estate. The problem, of course, is that the market for real estate is not nearly the same as that for the organized stock and bond markets. Real estate investments tend to have a local or regional character, while many companies reflected in the published stock market indices conduct their business on a national basis. There simply is not a real estate index comparable to the Dow Jones Industrial Average for the stock market.

A recent research report [10] presented return indices for fourteen different investment assets over the last 11 years, 1968–78. Based on that source, Exhibit 1 includes annual values of the indices for stocks (Standard & Poor's Composite Stock Price Index), bonds (Salomon Brothers Bond Index), and housing (median sales price of old homes in the United States as compiled by the National Association of Realtors®). The base year is 1968. The stock and bond indices reflect total returns, while the housing index does not include any income earned on each housing investment.

Nevertheless, we see that the housing index ended the decade almost twice as high as the stock index, and about a third higher than the bond index. The stock and bond indices experienced upward and downward moves in rather close parallel, while the housing index moved steadily upward. There thus was less variability in the housing index than there was in stock or bond indices. Other indices of real

---

[1] Further discussion is found in [12] (References at end of chapter).

Exhibit 1
Comparison of Return Indices for Stocks, Bonds, and Real Estate 1968–78
(1968 = 100)

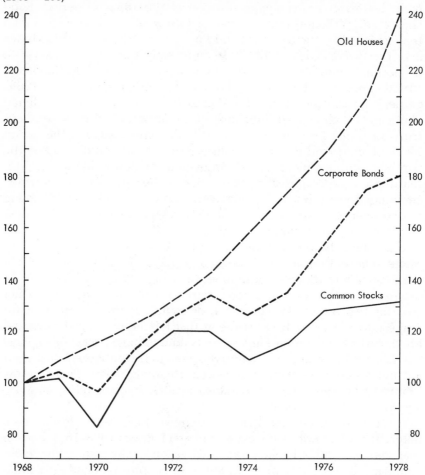

estate activity that were investigated confirm the general finding in Exhibit 1.

One difficulty with the comparison in Exhibit 1 is that the housing index represents only a segment of the total real estate market. In other words, it reflects the market prices of only old homes, and not of other investment opportunities such as land, apartment buildings, shopping centers, and industrial complexes. In addition, the housing index portrayed in Exhibit 1 shows only changes in market value for housing, and not any income which might accrue to an investor. If the housing index were to reflect total returns and thus be more comparable with the stock and bond indices, it is apparent that average investment would dominate average stock and bond investments even more. The dominance of real estate over common stocks also has been suggested in earlier studies [3, 4, 9].

REAL ESTATE INVESTMENT TRUSTS

A second difficulty with the comparison in Exhibit 1 is that market indices really do not represent investment opportunities for investors. Although an investor conceivably could have purchased shares in the 30 Dow Jones common stocks, it would have been almost impossible for an individual investor to duplicate either of the three indices reflected in Exhibit 1. For that matter, it is very difficult for most individual investors to invest in a portfolio of real estate directly.

A real estate investment trust (REIT) is a financial intermediary that allows widespread investment in real estate, albeit on an indirect basis. By providing a vehicle whereby many individuals can jointly own a portfolio of real estate investments, a REIT is similar to an investment company for corporate securities. In particular, the structure of a REIT is similar to that of a closed-end investment company, in that the shares of ownership are traded on the securities markets. The capital structures of REITs and closed-end companies are relatively fixed over time, and thus different from that of mutual funds which stand ready to buy and sell ownership shares from investors directly. Whereas REITs have not been in existence as long as investment companies, they have become an increasingly popular investment vehicle in recent years. Despite recent problems with some REIT investments, there were 218 REITs with total assets of $16.5 billion at the end of 1978.[2]

In order to receive the tax-exempt status necessary to facilitate their intermediary service, a REIT must have at least 75 percent of its assets invested in real estate; those assets must generally be operated in a passive manner; REIT income must be mostly derived from those assets; at least 90 percent of the REIT income must be distributed to the shareholders; and there must be one hundred or more shareholders.

The portfolios of REITs are invested in short-term construction loans, long-term mortgage loans, and equity positions in income-producing properties. REIT portfolios may be diversified both geographically and by the type of property which is held: hotels, shopping centers, townhouses, sports facilities, etc. A few REITs are self-administered by employees of the trust. More frequently, the REIT is managed by an independent advisor such as a commercial bank, a mortgage banker, a life insurance company, or other business organization. Typically

---

[2] A good source of institutional description of REITs plus industry data is found in [5]. An historical perspective on the development of the REIT industry was provided by Brewer [1]. Recent difficulties are documented in [6].

the advisor receives a management fee based on the size of the REIT portfolio, and frequently an incentive fee based on the portfolio performance of the REIT portfolio. A typical incentive fee might call for the REIT manager to receive an incentive fee (say 10–25 percent) of the amount by which the REIT income exceeds a designated (say 8–10 percent) of the average net worth of the REIT.

INDEX APPRECIATION

The National Association of Real Estate Investment Trusts (NAREIT) is a trade association for the REIT industry. It compiles and publishes a price index for a large sample of existing real estate investment trusts. Included are all REITs that are traded on the New York Stock Exchange, the American Stock Exchange, or on the national over-the-counter market. The index reflects market prices of the REITs, but not the income or capital gains distributions of the REITs. The index began in January 1972.

Exhibit 2 is a matrix of annual appreciation values based on the NAREIT Price Index over the period 1972–77. A matrix presentation allows observations of each subperiod within a total horizon. Each value along the main diagonal of Exhibit 2 is the average appreciation for the REIT universe for that year. Values above the main diagonal are the average annual appreciations for longer horizons. For example, the NAREIT Price Index experienced a 21.7 percent annual decrease during the 1972–73 horizon. For the total horizon, one is struck by the wide variability in average appreciation for the REIT sample. Not only are many of the values negative, but the numbers are quite large. The worst year was 1974, where the NAREIT Price Index experienced a 72.5 percent decline! For the total six-year horizon for which the NAREIT Price Index has been compiled, the average result is a 19.4 percent average annual decrease.

Exhibit 3 is a comparable matrix presentation for the Standard and Poor's Composite Stock Price Index. Dividends are not included so

Exhibit 2
Annual Appreciation for National Association of Real Estate Investment Trusts Share Price Index 1972–1977

Purchased at End of Year	Sold at End of Year					
	1972	1973	1974	1975	1976	1977
1971	2.5%	−21.7%	−44.8%	−34.9%	−24.6%	−19.4%
1972		−40.2	−65.3	−44.0	−30.2	−23.2
1973			−72.5	−45.8	−26.5	−18.2
1974				6.8	20.0	17.6
1975					34.9	23.5
1976						13.0

that comparisons can be made with the NAREIT Price Index in Exhibit 2. Although there are several negative values in the matrix, the S&P Index did not exhibit fluctuations as large as did the NAREIT Price Index. For the total six-year horizon, 1972–77, the S&P Index experienced a 0.9 percent decrease. Comparing the single year values from Exhibits 2 and 3, we see that the S&P Index exhibited higher values in each of the first four years, while the NAREIT Price Index had higher values during 1976 and 1977.

Exhibit 3
Annual Appreciation for Standard and Poors Composite Stock Price Index 1972–1977

Purchased at End of Year	Sold at End of Year					
	1972	*1973*	*1974*	*1975*	*1976*	*1977*
1971	18.5%	−2.2%	−12.2%	−2.8%	1.1%	−0.9%
1972		−19.3	−24.4	−8.9	−2.9	−4.4
1973			−29.2	−3.3	3.4	−0.3
1974				32.2	24.9	11.8
1975					18.0	2.8
1976						−10.4

COMPARISONS OF SAMPLES

Although the NAREIT Price Index provides a useful perspective, again it does not present a real investment opportunity for most investors. In order to obtain a more complete picture of real estate returns in recent years, it is desirable to examine particular investment opportunities. Exhibit 4 identifies 14 equity real estate investment trusts (EREITs). An EREIT is a real estate investment trust that specializes in equity investments. For the first eight EREITs, data was available over the extended horizon, January 1964 through June 1978. For the other six EREITs, data was only available for the period January 1971 through June 1978. The remainder of this chapter focuses on the achieved performance of this sample of EREITs. It is felt that the EREIT sample represents the best available picture of actual equity investments in real estate.

We see in Exhibit 4 that the common shares of the equity REITs are traded either on the organized stock exchanges or on the over-the-counter market. Asset size ranges from a low of $22 million to a high of $303 million. Annualized geometric mean return for each equity REIT is indicated for the two particular horizons. Here, and subsequently, return includes both appreciation and income. Price and dividend data were available on a monthly basis, but calculations were based on quarterly observations of return. The last column of Exhibit 4 presents the estimated value of systematic risk (i.e., "beta") for the

Exhibit 4
Selected Data for Sample of Equity Real Estate Investment Trusts (EREITs)

EREIT	Traded*	Asset Size†	Annualized Geometric Mean Return‡		Systematic Risk§
			Jan. 1964– June 1978	Jan. 1971– June 1978	
Denver Real Estate Investment Association	OTC	$ 32	8.8%	10.9%	.63
First Union Real Estate Equity & Mortgage Investment	NYSE	189	6.7	9.6	1.07
Franklin Realty Group	ASE	37	1.0	−3.9	1.98
GREIT Realty Trust	ASE	37	2.6	−4.3	1.22
Pennsylvania Real Estate Investment Trust	ASE	77	11.2	14.3	.74
Real Estate Investment Trust of America	ASE	48	5.3	2.3	.50
U.S. Realty Investments	NYSE	88	6.0	−4.4	1.18
Washington Real Estate Investment Trust	ASE	33	11.9	20.1	.37
First Fidelity Investment Trust	OTC	32		0.3	.73
General Growth Properties	NYSE	303		21.2	.99
Hubbard Real Estate Investments	NYSE	94		5.4	1.01
Realty Income Trust	ASE	80		11.9	1.99
Riviere Realty Trust	OTC	22		8.9	.42
Wisconsin Real Estate Investment Trust	OTC	36		−11.9	1.51

* NYSE = New York Stock Exchange; ASE = American Stock Exchange; OTC = Over-the-counter-market.
† As of year-end fiscal 1977 (in millions).
‡ Based on quarterly observations for indicated horizon.
§ Based on quarterly observations for horizon, January 1971–June 1978.

shorter horizon. Systematic risk ranges from a low of .37 to a high of 1.99, and averages 1.02 for the EREIT sample.

In order to compare equity real estate returns against achieved returns from the stock market, Exhibit 5 presents a sample of closed-end investment companies. They are chosen as a comparison sample because their organizational structure is similar to that for the EREITs. That is, both closed-end investment companies and real estate trusts are financial intermediaries whereby the investment assets of many individuals are pooled and a portfolio of investments (common stocks and real estate, respectively) is purchased and managed. The common shares of the closed-end companies also are traded on the organized stock exchanges. From Exhibit 5, we see that the asset size of the closed-end investment companies is considerably larger than that of the EREITs. The average size of the closed-end companies was $187 million, in contrast to an average $79 million asset size for the EREITs. Average value of systematic risk for the closed-end companies was 1.06, and thus virtually identical to that of the EREIT sample for the 7½ year horizon.

Exhibit 5
Selected Data for Sample of Closed-End Investment Companies

Closed-End Investment Company	Traded*	Asset Size†	Annualized Geometric Mean Return‡		Systematic Risk§
			Jan. 1964–June 1978	Jan. 1971–June 1978	
Adams Express Company	NYSE	$214	8.1%	6.9%	.68
Baldwin Securities Corporation	ASE	41	8.9	8.2	1.06
Carriers & General Corporation	NYSE	19	5.2	4.6	.94
Central Securities Corporation	ASE	49	2.2	−3.9	1.29
General American Investors Company, Inc.	NYSE	111	6.0	3.2	.99
Lehman Corporation	NYSE	435	4.6	1.0	1.18
Madison Fund, Inc.	NYSE	387	5.9	5.0	.99
National Aviation and Technology Corporation	NYSE	107	7.6	9.1	1.62
Niagara Share Corporation	NYSE	93	4.0	2.8	.83
Petroleum & Resources Corporation	NYSE	143	11.8	11.6	.64
Standard Shares, Inc.	ASE	105	9.2	9.3	1.35
Tri-Continental Corporation	NYSE	619	6.4	3.2	.92
U.S. and Foreign Securities Corporation	NYSE	111	4.8	9.4	1.23

* NYSE = New York Stock Exchange; ASE = American Stock Exchange.
† As of year-end fiscal 1977 (in millions).
‡ Based on quarterly observations for indicated horizon.
§ Based on quarterly observations for horizon, January 1971–June 1978.

Exhibit 6 presents additional information about the annual returns achieved by the EREITs. For each EREIT, the maximum and minimum annual values are presented along with the average annual value over the horizon for which data was available for each.[3] Again, considerable variability among the individual EREITs is noted. The highest annual value was 140.8 percent return for Wisconsin Real Estate Investment Trust in 1977. The lowest annual value was a 70.2 percent decrease in 1974 for the Realty Income Trust. The average annual value for the sample ranged from 5.8 percent to 32.7 percent. Recalling in Exhibit 2 the 72.5 percent average decrease for the NAREIT Price Index, it is evident that the EREITs as a sample did not do as badly as the overall universe of REITs then in existence. Still, investors who chose to invest in real estate via EREITs were exposed to a wide variety of investment experience over the last few years.

TRADITIONAL PERFORMANCE EVALUATION

A matrix presentation allows a more complete analysis of achieved returns because all possible horizons are treated. Exhibit 7 includes

---

[3] The average value for each EREIT in Exhibit 6 is a simple arithmetic average of the annual observations that were available. This is in contrast to the geometric mean returns reported in Exhibit 4.

Exhibit 6
Maximum, Minimum, and Average Annual Returns for Equity Real Estate Investment Trusts (EREITs) 1965–1977

EREIT	*Maximum*		*Minimum*		*Average*
Denver Real Estate Investment					
Association	33.8%	(1968)	−21.2%	(1969)	9.1%
First Fidelity Investment					
Trust	99.9	(1975)	−39.6	(1972)	14.1
First Union Real Estate Equity &					
Mortgage Investment	72.1	(1975)	−29.2	(1974)	10.7
Franklin Realty Group	135.5	(1976)	−50.3	(1974)	9.8
General Growth Properties	56.5	(1976)	−27.8	(1973)	14.1
GREIT Realty Trust	54.9	(1968)	−50.7	(1973)	8.2
Hubbard Real Estate					
Investments	58.0	(1976)	−35.9	(1974)	11.7
Pennsylvania Real Estate					
Investment Trust	57.3	(1976)	−30.4	(1974)	14.1
Real Estate Investment Trust					
of America	35.9	(1968)	−21.2	(1969)	6.6
Realty Income Trust	112.6	(1976)	−70.2	(1974)	32.7
Riviere Realty Trust	27.5	(1972)	−23.6	(1977)	5.8
U.S. Realty Investments	85.5	(1977)	−68.5	(1974)	11.1
Washington Real Estate					
Investment Trust	74.4	(1976)	−15.3	(1966)	15.6
Wisconsin Real Estate					
Investment Trust	140.8	(1977)	−68.8	(1974)	12.9

average annual returns for the sample of EREITs over the horizon 1965–77. Each value in the matrix is the average internal-rate-of-return to an investor for the sample of EREITs for that particular horizon. The internal-rate-of-return is that rate of return that causes the discounted present value of all cash distributions to the investor during the horizon, plus the sale of the EREIT common share at the end of the horizon to equal the purchase price of the EREIT common share at the beginning of the horizon. The calculations reflect discounting on a quarterly basis. It also should be noted that the averages in Exhibit 7 are based on only eight EREITs for the earlier years and 14 EREITs for the latter part of the total horizon.

Exhibit 8 is a comparable matrix for the sample of closed-end investment companies. All values in Exhibit 8 reflect the experience of 13 closed-end investment companies. A comparison of the individual values in Exhibits 7 and 8 reveals no particular dominance of one sample over the other. For the total horizon 1964–77, the average return on the EREIT sample was 7.4 percent—in contrast to only 6.6 percent for the closed-end sample. For certain subperiods, the EREITs clearly outperformed the closed-end companies. But for others, just the opposite result was experienced.

Exhibit 9 takes a closer look at performance for particular subperiods. The left part of Exhibit 9 compares EREIT returns with that

Exhibit 7
Average Annual Returns for Sample of Equity Real Estate Investment Trusts (EREITs) 1965–1977*

Purchased at End of Year	Sold by End of Year												
	1965	1966	1967	1968	1969	1970	1971	1972	1973	1974	1975	1976	1977
1964	14.7%	5.4%	14.6%	19.0%	12.1%	9.4%	9.4%	9.7%	7.2%	4.8%	6.4%	7.6%	7.4%
1965		−3.6	14.6	20.8	11.4	8.1	8.1	8.6	5.6	3.0	4.9	6.4	6.3
1966			38.4	37.5	18.2	12.1	11.5	11.7	7.7	4.4	6.6	8.2	8.1
1967				37.6	8.3	3.2	4.3	5.7	1.6	−1.7	1.4	3.7	3.9
1968					14.9	11.6	5.9	−2.0	−5.6	8.6	−4.2	−1.0	−0.4
1969						−6.4	0.4	3.9	−2.3	−6.7	−1.5	2.1	2.4
1970							8.5	10.2	−0.5	−6.7	−0.2	4.0	4.2
1971								13.3	−4.4	−11.7	−2.5	3.1	3.4
1972									−20.1	−23.2	−7.9	0.5	1.3
1973										−25.5	0.9	10.5	9.3
1974											41.4	37.9	26.9
1975												36.0	20.1
1976													5.5

* Each value is the average internal-rate-of-return to an investor for the sample of EREITs.

Exhibit 8
Average Annual Returns for Sample of Closed-End Investment Companies 1965–1977*

Purchased at End of Year	Sold at End of Year												
	1965	1966	1967	1968	1969	1970	1971	1972	1973	1974	1975	1976	1977
1964	10.5%	−1.8%	−4.4%	2.1%	3.1%	5.3%	8.5%	8.4%	6.0%	3.3%	4.3%	6.0%	6.6%
1965		−11.8	−10.9	−0.3	1.5	4.4	7.7	7.7	5.0	1.8	3.1	5.0	5.9
1966			−5.3	7.9	7.5	10.1	12.7	12.0	8.3	4.3	5.6	7.7	8.5
1967				36.6	24.9	24.3	10.3	9.9	5.6	1.0	2.8	5.5	6.6
1968					16.6	19.8	3.3	4.3	0.1	−4.8	−2.2	1.4	3.0
1969						26.5	10.8	9.8	3.0	−3.8	−0.7	3.5	5.2
1970							10.7	9.5	0.2	−8.0	−3.5	1.9	4.2
1971								8.6	−4.9	−14.4	−7.4	−0.1	2.9
1972									−16.5	−24.6	−12.5	−2.2	1.7
1973										−31.5	−9.2	4.5	8.4
1974											27.3	35.5	32.0
1975												52.3	38.8
1976													27.8

* Each value is the average internal-rate-of-return to an investor for the sample of closed-end investment companies.

Exhibit 9
Comparison of Average Annual Returns for Sample of Equity Real Estate Investment Trusts (EREITs) and Closed-End Investment Companies 1965–1977*

Single-Year Investment Horizon	*EREITs*	*Closed-Ends*	*Multiple-Year Investment Horizon*	*EREITs*	*Closed-Ends*
1965	14.7%	10.5%	1965–77	7.4%	6.6%
1966	−3.6	−11.8	1966–77	6.3	5.9
1967	38.4*	−5.3	1967–77	8.1	8.5
1968	37.6	36.6	1968–77	3.9	6.6
1969	14.9	16.6	1969–77	−0.4	3.0
1970	−6.4	26.5*	1970–77	2.4	5.2
1971	8.5	10.7	1971–77	4.2	4.2
1972	13.3	8.6	1972–77	3.4	2.9
1973	−20.1	−16.5	1973–77	1.3	1.7
1974	−25.5	−31.5	1974–77	9.3	8.4
1975	41.4	27.3	1975–77	26.9	32.0
1976	36.0	52.3	1976–77	20.1	38.8*
1977	5.5	27.8*			

* Average sample value is significantly larger (at $\alpha = 5\%$) than that for the other sample.

of closed-end companies for individual years. The average EREIT return was greater for seven individual years, while the average closed-end return was higher for the other six years. An asterisk is used to indicate a particular value for one sample that is significantly larger (on a statistical basis) than that for the other sample. In each case, a *t*-statistic was used to test whether the mean return of one sample was significantly different from the mean return of the other sample. Because of the rather small sample sizes that are involved, it takes a rather large difference between the average sample returns in order for one sample to be judged significantly larger than the other. We see that the EREIT sample was significantly larger in 1967, while the closed-end sample was significantly larger in 1970 and again in 1977.

The right-hand side of Exhibit 9 makes comparisons for each longer subperiod ending with 1977. The EREIT sample was larger for five of the horizons, the closed-end companies were larger for six of the horizons, and the average values were identical for the 1971–77 horizon. Only in the last two-year horizon, 1976–77, did one sample significantly outperform the other—in this instance the closed-end companies had a higher average annual return. As mentioned above, the EREITs averaged 7.4 percent, while the closed-end investment companies had an average annual return of 6.6 percent for the total 1965–77 horizon. That difference was not significant statistically.

RISK-ADJUSTED PERFORMANCE EVALUATION

The final comparison is presented in Exhibit 10. Two additional dimensions are reflected. First, performance comparisons are made

Exhibit 10

Performance Comparisons of Equity Real Estate Investment Trusts (EREITs) with Closed-End Investment Companies, Selected Horizons*

Investment Period	Horizon Dates	Geometric Mean Return, G	Market Comparison, A	Systematic Risk, B	Diversification Level, D
1. Entire Horizon	1/64 thru 6/78	(6.0%)			
8 Equity REITs		6.7	3.1%	.83	.29
13 Closed-Ends		6.5	1.8	1.04	.52†
2. Entire Sample	1/71 thru 6/78	5.0			
14 Equity REITs		5.7	5.5†	1.01	.32
13 Closed-Ends		4.7	1.1	1.05	.61†
3. 1st-Half Horizon	1/64 thru 3/71	8.5			
8 Equity REITs		9.9	3.5	.62	.27
13 Closed-Ends		9.7	2.6	1.00†	.43†
4. 2nd-Half Horizon	4/71 thru 6/78	3.7			
14 Equity REITs		3.9	5.1†	1.01	.30
13 Closed-Ends		3.4	1.3	1.06	.60†
5. Trough-to-Trough	10/66 thru 12/74	1.6			
8 Equity REITs		-0.4	-1.3	.76	.30
13 Closed-Ends		1.0	1.8	1.15†	.56†
6. Peak-to-Peak	1/69 thru 12/72	5.9			
8 Equity REITs		4.6	0.0	.75	.36
13 Closed-Ends		-1.3	-5.7	1.08†	.53†
7. Trough-to-Peak	1/64 thru 12/68	12.2			
8 Equity REITs		11.7	4.3	.45	.16
13 Closed-Ends		18.0†	8.0	.79†	.28
8. Peak-to-Trough	1/73 thru 12/74	-21.5			
14 Equity REITs		-28.4	-14.3	.74	.28
13 Closed-Ends		-23.7	8.1†	1.27†	.64†
9. Flat	1/76 thru 6/78	8.6			
14 Equity REITs		34.6†	32.5†	.50	.16
13 Closed-Ends		17.3	9.3	.87†	.44†

* For each horizon, the geometric mean return (in parenthesis) is that for the Standard and Poor's Composite Index.
† Average sample value is significantly larger (at α = 5%) than that for the other sample.

for additional investment subperiods based on the type of market encountered. Comparisons are made for nine investment periods. The first is for the period January 1964 through June 1978. The second is for the shorter period for which data was available for the entire sample of 14 EREITs. The third and fourth horizons are roughly half of the entire horizon. The other five horizons are for particular types of markets as indicated.

The second dimension in Exhibit 10 is that risk-adjusted performance measures are included as well. Geometric mean return is the traditional performance measure, while the next column presents achieved performance above or below the market on a risk-adjusted basis. The values shown are the average sample values of the intercept (sometimes called "alpha") of the estimated characteristic line for each portfolio. The characteristic line for a portfolio is a "best fitting" line that relates periodic returns on the portfolio to periodic returns on a market benchmark. Here, characteristic lines were estimated (using least-square regression) from quarterly observations of returns for the EREIT or closed-end company portfolio and returns on the S&P Composite Stock Price Index. Systematic risk for a portfolio is just the slope of its estimated characteristic line. The final column of Exhibit 10 presents average values of the coefficient of determination for the least square regressions which were used to estimate systematic risk and market-related performance. The coefficient of determination is often used as a measure of how well diversified a particular portfolio was during a particular investment horizon. The four performance measures in Exhibit 10 were described and used in an earlier study which compared EREITs with closed-end investment companies [11].

By examining the significant values in Exhibit 10, one can readily see differences in the two samples. For example, the diversification level of the closed-end sample was significantly greater than that of the EREIT sample in eight of the nine investment periods. In other words, closed-end portfolios were better diversified than were the equity real estate portfolios, when measured relative to the S&P Index. In part, this may be due to the larger number of individual investments reflected in the portfolios of the closed-end companies. For many EREITs, the portfolio is dominated by a few extremely large investments. Moreover, the closed-end sample exhibited a higher average value of systematic risk in each of the nine horizons, and is significantly higher for six horizons. This means that the EREITs were less susceptible to swings in the overall stock market over time. Different estimates of systematic risk and diversification would be expected, of course, if a total asset index were used instead of just a stock market index.

In terms of achieved returns, however, we see that there are only two significant values in the geometric return column. The closed-end companies had a significantly higher average return for the trough-to-peak horizon (in the mid-to-late sixties). Conversely, the EREITs had a significantly higher average return during the last 30 months for which data was available, and which was a rather flat stock market. In terms of risk-adjusted performance related to the market, the EREITs had a significantly larger return in three horizons, while the closed-end companies had a significantly higher value in only one horizon.

CONCLUSION

It is well known that many of the large fortunes in this country have been built on equity investments in real estate. For many individuals and families in the U.S., it is also likely that a large proportion of their total wealth is represented by the equity investment in their own home. In this chapter, we have examined equity real estate investments that are available to individuals and families of modest means, beyond that in their own homes.

Although a cursory look at selected indices of real estate activity suggests that investment in real estate has dominated investment in securities, the achieved experience of real estate investment trusts over time is quite mixed. Comparison with the achieved experience of closed-end investment companies reveals no sense of dominance of either real estate or common stocks. For the total 1965–77 horizon investigated, the EREIT sample experienced an average annual return of 7.4 percent in contrast to 6.6 percent for the closed-end sample. A subsidiary finding is that the EREIT portfolios were less risky, but also less well-diversified, than their common stock counterparts. One important observation is that the experience of individual EREITs shows wide variation in annual returns over time. This is in direct contrast to the view of the real estate industry as offered by some of the real estate indices that have been constructed and reported.

As with any empirical study, there are limitations that should be mentioned. The samples of EREITs and closed-end companies are small, even though they represent large proportions of their respective universes. Moreover, EREITs are only a small part of the equity-type opportunities that are available in the total real estate industry. Another limitation is that the historical returns in each instance are based on purchase at the beginning of a particular quarter and sale at the end of a subsequent quarter. No transaction costs were reflected in either the purchase or the sale, and thus the reported returns to investors are somewhat overstated.

Furthermore, the estimates of systematic risk and market-related performance (in Exhibit 10) are based on the capital asset pricing model, which has come under serious question in recent months. For example, Roll [8] has demonstrated the ambiguity that may result when performance is measured on a risk-adjusted basis relative to a given stock market index. Another limitation, especially in terms of how the findings are extrapolated toward the future, is that the historical experience for the EREITs—unlike that of the closed-end investment companies—includes the period of property acquisition and gradual development into an industry. The early years in the development of an EREIT generally would be characterized as active portfolio management, in contrast to a mature EREIT, or closed-end investment company, where portfolio management would be more passive. Finally, the comparison of EREITs and closed-end companies does not reflect the fact that most of the EREIT portfolios are managed under an incentive compensation scheme that may cause their portfolio managers to invest in more risky properties, as well as to take on more risky debt financing.

Nevertheless, the likely continuation of inflation should cause the findings presented here to be of interest to individual investors. For institutional investors, the diversification requirements of ERISA comprise an additional motivation for considering investment opportunities other than stocks and bonds. On balance, the findings presented here suggest that, at minimum, equity investments in real estate ought to be potentially valuable as part of large, multiasset portfolios.

REFERENCES

1. Brewer, Robert E. "REITs in Transition." *Appraisal Journal* (July 1974).
2. Fama, Eugene F. and Schwert, G. William. "Asset Returns and Inflation." *Journal of Financial Economics* (November 1977).
3. Friedman, Harris. "Real Estate Investment and Portfolio Theory." *Journal of Financial and Quantitative Analysis* (March 1971).
4. Kelleher, Dennis G. "How Real Estate Stacks Up to the S&P 500." *Real Estate Review* (Summer 1976).
5. *REIT 1977 Factbook* (Washington, D.C.: National Association of Real Estate Investment Trusts, 1977).
6. Robertson, Wyndham. "How the Bankers Got Trapped in the REIT Disaster." *Fortune* (March 1975).
7. Robichek, Alexander A.; Cohn, Robert A.; and Pringle, John J. "Returns on Alternative Investment Media and Implications for Portfolio Construction." *Journal of Business* (July 1972).
8. Roll, Richard. "Ambiguity When Performance Is Measured by the Securities Market Line." *Journal of Finance* (September 1978).
9. Roulac, Stephen E. "Can Real Estate Returns Outperform Common Stocks?" *Journal of Portfolio Management* (Winter 1976).
10. Salomon, R. S., Jr. "Stocks Are Still the Only Bargain Left." Salomon Brothers Research Department Report, July 1978.
11. Smith, Keith V. and Shulman, David. "Institutions Beware: The Perfor-

mance of Equity Real Estate Investment Trusts." *Financial Analysis Journal* (September–October 1976).

12. Utt, Ronald D. "Some Findings on the Profitability of Real Estate Investments." *REITs Quarterly* 4 (1977).

13. Wendt, Paul F. and Wong, Sui N. "Investment Performance: Common Stocks versus Apartment Houses." *Journal of Finance* (December 1965).

Part Three

Measuring and Monitoring Performance

Chapter 16

Equity Portfolio Performance

DENNIS A. TITO

President
Wilshire Associates
Santa Monica, California

LAWRENCE ZAMOS

Senior Associate
Wilshire Associates
Santa Monica, California

Investors believing in the long term prospects of the economy generally look to equity capital as a means of participating in the anticipated growth in economic wealth. Sponsors and managers of pension plans, mutual funds, insurance company funds, trust funds, endowment funds, and individuals seeking personal gain invest in equity issues as a means of meeting future needs and obligations. Sponsors and investors are concerned with the adequacy of their investment strategies to generate the performance that will achieve the results to meet their long-term commitments. But sponsors of pension funds, regulated by the Employee Retirement Income Securities Act of 1974 (ERISA), are required to pay particular attention to the results of investment activities. Corporate executives are specifically concerned because of their increased fiduciary responsibilities as well as the implications of increased liabilities on long-term corporate financial planning.

The fundamental reason for monitoring performance of an investment portfolio is to provide the insights necessary to take future actions that enhance the probabilities of achieving investment objectives. There is no point in monitoring performance unless the decision maker is willing to do something about it.

Prudent investors and managers of investment funds are all con-

445

cerned with the performance of their portfolios, but the degree of sophistication, the frequency of review, and the qualifications of the personnel performing the analyses vary greatly.

In recent years, the measurement of equity portfolio performance has moved from a casual, intuitive approach toward a very precise, quantitative, almost scientific process. The factors that have influenced this movement include:

1. The rapid growth in size of institutional investment portfolios, especially pension plans sponsored by corporations that channel tax-exempt dollars into retirement systems to attract and retain employees.
2. The legal implications of ERISA, which imposes new responsibilities on the corporate sponsors of pension plans for fund liabilities, thereby increasing the demands and constraints on corporate assets.
3. Increased complexity of investment as less traditional investments (real property, foreign securities, passive investments, etc.) begin to challenge the traditional cash, equity, and fixed-income securities for investment dollars.
4. Rapid expansion of investment and computer technology that has provided practical cost-effective means to implement analytic systems now in use to track and review investment performance.
5. Enlarged ranks of business school graduates and corporate executives who are trained in analytic techniques and can utilize the analytical methods for performance measurement.

In simplest terms, the results of investing capital are measured by return or gain on employed assets: total return is the sum of cash earnings plus changes in market values less operating costs and fees. The market value of a security at any point in time can be viewed as the combined opinion of investors of the probable or expected value of the stream of future earnings. Therefore, value depends on the investors' perceptions of the future, which are uncertain. Wherever there is uncertainty in predicting the future, there is risk. Risk is reflected in market values by discounting future expectations. The greater the uncertainty, the greater will be the discount and the lower the present value associated with future earnings. Thus, monitoring portfolio performance implies an understanding both of return on investment and the level of risk taken.

Modern portfolio theory (MPT) (see chapter 5) has produced a body of analytical tools that allow an objective, quantitative view of the relationships between risk and return and, thereby provide a basis for future action. Used as a tool, MPT gives the decision makers additional insights into the investment environment and better control over invested assets. Among all the facets of investment management, MPT has gained the greatest acceptance in the area of performance measurement, yet acceptance is by no means universal. The majority of the investment community is seeking further proof that the evaluator-decision maker can use MPT tools to better understand the dynamics of the marketplace and thereby increase the investment performance of capital assets.

Regardless of whether or not investment managers accept modern portfolio theory, they are taking risks in anticipation of gains. MPT provides a useful method of analyzing investment risk and return in quantitative terms. Risks and returns can be related to investment objectives and other standards of comparison for evaluation and diagnosis of performance results.

THE HISTORY OF PERFORMANCE MEASUREMENT

Prior to the early 1960s, monitoring investment performance was limited to simple—and frequently incorrect—measures of change in market and/or book value. For example, portfolio returns including dividends were often compared to indexes that measured only changes in market value. Further, the effects of contributions and withdrawals were handled inconsistently. Risk was neither measured nor accounted for.

In the early 1950s Harry M. Markowitz [6] published papers on the utility of wealth and portfolio selection. This work became the basis for William F. Sharpe's [8] model of the characteristics of market portfolios that is now used extensively in performance measurement. Both Sharpe and Jack L. Treynor [9] derived measures of portfolio performance based on portfolio theory. By studying mutual fund data, Michael Jensen [4] provided early demonstration of these techniques, and later Eugune Fama [3] developed a method for analyzing total performance in terms of various management effects. These early works, along with many other academic studies, have become the foundation for risk-adjusted performance measurement, now in widespread use in monitoring portfolio performance.

Perhaps most noteworthy, in 1968 the Bank Administration Institute (BAI) organized a task force of bankers and academicians to prepare recommendations for measuring investment performance. Relying heavily on earlier work by Peter O. Dietz [2] and embryonic developments in MPT, the BAI published *Measuring the Investment Performance of Pension Funds,* which became a standard reference for computational techniques and analysis of investment performance. The BAI study established useful procedures for measuring rates of return, estimating risk and classifying and valuing assets. A technique was provided whereby the computations could readily be implemented on the computer. By the early 1970s the theory was reduced to commercial practice.

BAI's recommended approach to quantitative measurement has become the model for performance measurement and comparative analysis, while MPT provides the methods for evaluation and diagnosis of results. Brokerage firms, banks, and investment consultants now produce analytical data for clients. Comparative return and quantitative risk measurement, as well as diagnostic tools, are readily available and widely used.

The use of these standards by pension fund sponsors and trustees has recently accelerated as a result of the 1974 government regulation of employee pension funds. The ERISA definition of prudence, ". . . acting in like capacity and familiar with such matters used in conduct of an enterprise of a like character with like aims" implies a need to compare results with those of other similar funds. The need for compliance with government regulations and reporting requirements has caused many managers of corporate pension funds to utilize concepts described in later sections of this chapter.

EXAMINING PERFORMANCE

Why Monitor Performance?

Monitoring performance implies more than just a routine critique of results. Measuring portfolio performance should provide the monitor with a basis for control over the future performance of invested capital.

To appreciate the significance of portfolio performance evaluation, consider a simple example: assume a sponsor produces and sells 1,000 units per year, with a net profit of 10 percent (or 100 units based on 1,000 units of assets employed). Further, assume that this sponsor has a pension fund liability equal to 30 percent of corporate assets (300 units), with funded assets amounting to 200 units. A 10 percent annual rate of return on the funded assets equates to 20 units, and a 10 percent improvement in investment performance on the funded assets would equate to two units. If two units in funded assets had to be made up through contributions generated by increased sales of the sponsor's product, 20 units would have to be produced and sold to net the two units to the pension plan. In this case, a 10 percentage point difference in fund performance is equivalent to a 2 percentage point difference in sales and production. For a firm with $100 million annual sales volume, a 10 percent improvement in the fund's investment performance in this example would have required $2 million in sales revenue to produce the equivalent cash flow into the assets of the pension plan.

Small improvements in large portfolios can have significant effects on use of sponsor assets. Quantitative performance analysis of equity portfolio provides valuable data to both sponsor and money manager that can be used in the management control function. Knowledge of how the portfolio manager performed and insight into the factors underlying those achievements should lead the decision maker towards better alternatives.

Who is Concerned?

A wide range of performance measurement parameters can be developed to analyze a portfolio. The degree of sophistication and complexity of calculations depends on the individual user's evaluation of the trade-off between potential value gained and the cost of analysis. For example, an executive with total corporate responsibility would consider results in the context of fundamental corporate objectives such as fund growth, impact on cash flow, demand on corporate assets, etc. The fund administrator may be more concerned with meeting fiduciary responsibilities, investment policy, contribution levels, and liabilities. Money managers will be concerned with producing results, meeting sponsor objectives, and performance relative to other managers. They will also be concerned with alternative methods of attaining investment results, including portfolio structure, asset mix, diversification analysis, and risk-return optimization. Table 1 summarizes the concerns of executives at different functional levels.

Meeting Sponsor Objectives

From the sponsor's point of view, the primary emphasis should be placed on measuring the performance of the entire fund. The performance of the total fund determines the ability of the sponsor to meet its obligations and indicates how well overall sponsor objectives were achieved. The significant measures include size, cash flow, rates of return, levels of risk, and diversification. These parameters are indicators of the ability of the sponsor to meet liabilities and obligations. They show how well the fund is performing with respect to the established objectives such as asset mix, portfolio risk, growth concentration, etc., and demonstrate the effectiveness of overall planning.

Subdivision of Funds

Subdivision or segmentation is useful in monitoring and diagnosing the sources and nature of investment results. The monitor may wish to see results presented either organizationally (i.e., account, money manager, industry or directed vs. unrestricted funds); by asset category (i.e., equity, fixed, cash, and other investment categories); or, by management type and/or style (e.g., equity, fixed, balanced, indexed, ag-

Table 1
Concern for Portfolio Evaluation

Level	Point of View	Nature of Concern or Impact
Board of Directors Executive Officers	Corporate objectives	Corporate cash flow Corporate capital structure Employee motivation Government regulations
Investment Committee Fund Director Fund Administrator	Fund objectives	Corporate liabilities Corporate cash flow Fund investment policy
	Money management	Overall results Asset mix Comparison with standards Comparison with objectives Manager selection Cost to operate
	Prudence	Level of risk Extent of diversification Concentration
	Reporting	Government regulations Corporate overview
Money Managers	Merit	Results Client satisfaction Reputation
	Effectiveness	Compared to objectives Compared to other managers Compared to index Explanation of results Cost of production
	Alternatives	Portfolio structure Asset mix Portfolio optimization Style change

gressive, conservative). The appropriate measurements are the same as those for the entire fund, plus additional measures that help differentiate manager skills.

Careful review of performance results by manager and asset type should lead to an understanding of the individual manager's style, areas of particular effectiveness, compliance with direction, adherence to stated investment approach, and ranking amongst peers. The degree of activity can be monitored by looking at the turnover rate. The ability to anticipate and time market movements can be assessed by observing the timing of changes in risk-return characteristics in relation to market changes. The aptitude for selecting higher performing securities is reflected in the difference between the risk adjusted expectations and actual results. Effectiveness of current actions can be monitored by comparing the actual result to the results that would have attained from holding the beginning portfolio unchanged. The degree to which performance is likely to deviate from index results may be examined by looking at returns in conjunction with risk and diversification statistics. In all cases, results can be compared with stated objectives, market behavior, other similar funds, or optimized sets. The comparisons will indicate the degree of success compared to reasonable expectations and point toward alternatives that may be available.

Period of Performance

The period of performance or the time span for calculating and analyzing results depends upon the type of fund and user needs. In the limit, results could be calculated as prices change, transaction by transaction, in the marketplace. This would be extremely costly and tell the observer little about long-term results. Transaction to transaction—or even day to day—price movements are accurately described as a random walk. As a result, any effort to analyze short-term performance presents the difficulty of segregating random price movements from true management skills. Random fluctuations do not compound, while persistent management effects do. Therefore, longer periods are necessary to provide an understanding of the capabilities of a manager. Large pension funds usually calculate results monthly, evaluate performance quarterly, and perform an in-depth analysis at least once a year. Most observers prefer to concentrate on performance achieved over fixed time spans such as one, three, or five years. Others feel that results over complete market cycles or since the inception of the fund are most relevant. Analyses over the longer periods are necessary to evaluate the overall investment style and assess performance of a portfolio manager, while quarterly reviews indicate potential problems and provide signals that might suggest the need for greater depth of analysis or closer tracking in the future.

Fund sponsors who have replaced investment managers have found that it can be very costly to continually change the management or direction. Conversely, it would be just as unsound to wait a long while to consider a change when indicators had suggested that change was desirable. Taking action should not automatically imply a requirement to change managers. Poor performance could suggest the need to review or change objectives, strategy, tactics, or may suggest the need to improve communications between sponsor and manager. For example, in a large fund with many managers of different styles, the plan sponsor has the option to channel higher portions of new contributions to better performers with the effect of increasing the expected returns for the entire fund without disrupting the operations of the money manager and incurring significant increase in cost.

The Analyst

The depth of analysis, degree of sophistication, and frequency of reporting are dependent upon the point of view of those who want to see the results, and the nature of their concern. As the requirement for detailed understanding increases, so does the requirement for specialized skills of analysis. The analysis may be performed by the sponsor, a trustee, money managers, an outside consultant or a combination of analysts. If the fund is small or detailed information is not desired, the sponsor may perform only a cursory review. In contrast, very large funds may hire full time specialists and maintain the large data bases required to analyze multimanager portfolios. If a sponsor relies on a master trustee to administer the fund, the sponsor might look to the trustee for performance results and analysis. Sometimes the trust bank or money manager may develop performance data or subscribe to a monitoring service for quantitative results.

Frequently sponsors, trustees, and money managers subscribe to one or more professional consulting services to gain unbiased specialized reports for the analysis of fund performance. The consulting services are generally specialized and skilled in the qualitative and quantitative methods of performance measurement and are able to maintain the large data bases required for comprehensive evaluation. Some consulting firms are skilled in a particular discipline (i.e., pension planning, manager selection, portfolio optimization, etc.) while others have very broad range and can help in a number of areas. Consultant support may involve one-time studies (such as helping the sponsor set objectives or select a money manager), or be an ongoing service to the client for an extended period of time (such as continuous monitoring of performance). A long term relationship is important in evaluating performance because it provides the time for a consultant to develop the insights into the sponsor's needs comparable to that of an in-house analyst.

BASIC MEASUREMENTS OF PERFORMANCE

The objective of performance measurement is to provide meaningful comparisons of results obtained through active portfolio management with objectives and standards, and to diagnose results and identify appropriate alternatives. Return is the primary aspect of performance, but the implications of risk must be understood. In this section, the commonly used measures of return and risk will be identified.

Return

Return on investment is the net gain, including change in market value and cash income received, during the period. Usually return is expressed as a rate of return over a period on the average value of assets invested. Since the rate of return for a portfolio will vary with the fund's cash flow as well as from appreciation, dividends, and transactions, the effect of contributions must be considered and understood.

Two different methods are used to measure portfolio return: the time-weighted and the dollar-weighted rate of return. The time-weighted rate of return is more indicative of the manager's contribution to the investment performance of the fund. The dollar-weighted rate of return indicates the effects of contributions to and withdrawals from the fund, along with the manager's performance. The dollar-weighted rate is also known as the internal rate of return, and is equivalent to the rates of return stated as yields on bonds or savings accounts.

Time-weighted rate of return (TWR) is the primary measure of the results of investment management, since it is unaffected by the fund's external cash flow pattern. It is a measure of the return on the amount of money actually committed to the portfolio at any given time.

Calculating exact time-weighted rates of return requires evaluation of the fund each time a contribution or withdrawal occurs. If fund valuations are not available or too costly to provide for each date of the cash flow, an approximation can be made on a monthly basis to estimate the true time-weighted rate of return. The Dietz method for approximation is generally used for computation of single period time-weighted rate of return. TWR is computed as the change in value adjusted for cash flow,* divided by the average portfolio market value over the period:

$$TWR = \frac{V - (V_0 + C)}{V_0 (T \times C)}$$

where

V = the value at the end of the month
V_0 = the value at the beginning of the month
C = the cash flow during the month
T = the portion of the month that the cash is used.

Example:
Let
V = \$120,000
V_0 = \$100,000
C = \$5,000 from contributions and dividends to fund
T = (cash flow on the 15th of the month)
= 15/30 = ½

then

$$TWR = \frac{120,000 - (100,000 + 5,000)}{100,000 + (½ \times 5,000)}$$

TWR = 14.6 percent for the month

---

* Cash flows into the fund are taken as positive and out of the fund as negative.

Time-weighted rates for multiple periods are measured by compounding (linking) the returns of each period during the interval:

$$(1 + TWR) = (1 + TWR_1)(1 + TWR_2)(1 + TWR_3)\ldots\ldots(1 + TWR_n)$$

Annual rates of returns are easily obtained by linking 12 monthly or four quarterly rates. The geometric average rate of return $(\overline{TWR})$ is

$$\overline{TWR} = [(1 + TWR_1)(1 + TWR_2)(1 + TWR_3)\ldots(1 + TWR_n)]^{1/n} - 1$$

Dollar-weighted rate of return (DWR) measures the impact of both actual investment decision and such external factors as the timing and magnitude of contributions to and withdrawals from the fund. The dollar-weighted rate of return summarizes the growth rate of the fund and is helpful in assessing the adequacy of the total fund to meet its obligations.

Calculating exact dollar-weighted rates of return requires the market value at the beginning and end of the evaluation period, along with the date and amount of each cash flow during the measurement period.

The dollar-weighted rate of return is calculated by determining the equivalent rate of return which, when applied to the dollar values invested for each period, would produce the final dollar value. It is evaluated by iteratively solving the following expression for DWR.

$$P = P_0 + \sum_{n=1}^{n} \frac{C_k}{(1 + DWR)^k}$$

where

$P =$ the value of the portfolio at the end of the *nth* interval,
$P_0 =$ the initial value of the portfolio,
$C_k =$ the cash flow occurring in the time interval k.

Solving this expression requires assuming a value for DWR, computing P, and reestimating DWR until the value calculated converges on the actual value. The solution becomes increasingly difficult as the number and/or frequency of contributions increase.

To illustrate different rates of return consider the following example. A hypothetical fund starting with one hundred units which increases (or decreases) in value as a result of investment management and has contributions and withdrawals to the fund from time to time. For simplicity, cash flow occurs at the end of each period.

A summary of fund value, return and cash flow for three months is given below.

Period	Beginning Value	End Value	Return	Rate of Return (%)	Cash Flow
1	$100	$110	$ 10	10%	$ 10
2	120	114	−6	−5%	−14
3	100	106	6	6%	0
Quarter	$100	$106	$ 10		$− 4

Looking at the typical balance sheet:

```
Beginning balance ...... $100
Cash flow ..............  − 4
Return ................    10
Ending balance ........  $106
```

From the balance sheet it appears the fund grew by 6 percent, from $100 to $106 over the quarter. The total return was $10 and net cash flow was $4 withdrawn. Using the equations given above, the quarterly time-weighted rate of return compounded monthly was calculated as 10.77 percent. The dollar-weighted return, which measures average growth of all funds invested during the evaluation time period, was computed to be 9.80 percent for the quarter. The dollar-weighted return, which includes the effects of cash flows, was 0.97 percent, less than the time-weighted return, indicating that the impact of cash flow on the fund was negative. That is, if timing of contributions and withdrawals were different, the fund may have realized a greater total return. For example, if cash flow had been a single $4 withdrawal at the end of the quarter, the ending balance would have been $106.77. It should be noted that in order to achieve this higher dollar-weighted return the sponsor would have had to control the timing of cash flows and predict the movement of the market to take advantage of periods when return was relatively high.

Risk

It is not sufficient to compute only the rate of return that a manager achieved. Positive returns in a bull market may represent poor performance and loss in a bear market may represent good relative performance. Only when the degree of risk incurred is taken into consideration is it possible to properly assess the achievements of a portfolio manager.

Risk as measured by uncertainty or variability of return is generally viewed by investors as undesirable. An investor who assumes a high level of variability therefore demands to be compensated for increased exposure to risk with a comparably higher expectation of return. Since different portfolios have different policies or attitudes toward risk, both risk and rate of return must be measured to permit valid comparisons of the investment skill exhibited by their managers. A superior fund manager is one who obtains, on the average, a high rate of return relative to the degree of risk permitted by policy or agreement to assume in investments.

Risk is a subjective concept: there is no straightforward, objective definition. In the field of finance, extensive testing on the variability of returns for different investment categories such as stocks, bonds, and real estate reveals differences in variability that tend to persist from one time period to the next. This suggests that usable estimates of risk can be gauged from past measures of volatility.

The proposition that risk and variability in rates of return are equivalent is generally accepted and is basic to modern portfolio theory. Total risk of a portfolio is thus measured as the standard deviation of a portfolio over time and referred to as sigma (σ). MPT breaks total risk into two components: (1) market or systematic risk (beta), which is that portion of risk related to market movements; and, (2) nonmarket or unsystematic risk (standard error) which is the portion of risk unrelated to market movement.

Market sensitivity (beta) is the measure of the sensitivity of a stock's return or a portfolio's return compared to the return of the entire market. Volatility or sensitivity are terms often used to describe market risk.

Historical beta coefficient is the empirical relationship between the return of a given security or portfolio and the return of the entire market. The historical beta is derived by computing the relationship of the periodic return of a security or portfolio relative to the returns of the market over a time span up to five years. The S&P 500 index is frequently used as typical of market behavior. Figure 1(A) shows a typical distribution of periodic observations of a security's return versus market return. Each dot on the chart represents the observed security and market return for a month. The characteristics of the security or portfolio's behavior are determined by linear regression techniques to derive the characteristics and statistics shown in Figure 1(B). The characteristic line, slope, or beta coefficient, and the standard error are noted. The standard error is represented by the band about the characteristic line. This band, also referred to as the certainty range, is the band within which approximately two-thirds of the observations can be expected to occur.

The market value of a portfolio with beta equal to 1.0 would be expected to increase or decrease at the same rate as the market. If the beta were equal to 1.2, the value of the portfolio would be expected to increase (or decrease) at a rate 20 percent greater than the market.

Cross-sectional beta is calculated as the dollar-weighted average of the beta coefficients of the individual securities making up the portfolio. Since it is measured at the end of each performance measurement

Figure 1
Portfolio-Market Relationship

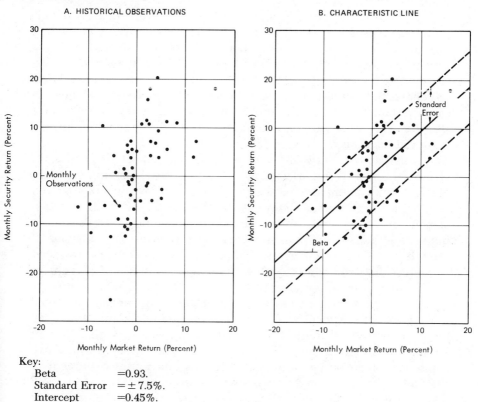

Key:
Beta	=0.93.
Standard Error	=± 7.5%.
Intercept	=0.45%.
Diversification	=0.29.

period, the weighted-average beta is a measurement of the instantaneous market sensitivity of the portfolio. The cross sectional beta is frequently used for portfolio performance since it reflects the changing expectations that result from the managers decisions to change portfolio risk.

The manager-generated portfolio beta is often related to an objective or reference beta specified as a goal by the sponsor or portfolio manager. The objective represents the long term market risk tolerance level desired by the sponsor of the individual account. The objective or reference beta coefficient is used as a standard of comparison to indicate how closely the manager is meeting sponsor objectives for risk tolerance.

A security beta coefficient computed from historical returns provides an adequate measure of the past volatility over the period of observation. Because the value of beta does vary over time, as shown in Figure

2, the estimate of historical beta does not always provide a good estimate of current value.

Fundamental beta coefficient is considered a better measure of current sensitivity and predictor of future near-term risk. A prediction formula, developed by Barr Rosenberg [7] through extensive academic research, is used to provide a short term forecast of fundamental security beta for the coming quarter. Forty-eight variables measuring different characteristics of the firm are included in the prediction equation as important predictors for the future level of systematic risk of a security. The set of variables are calculated from fundamental investment data and historical security return data.

Nonmarket risk (standard error) is the second important component of portfolio risk. Nonmarket risk is that portion of risk independent of market movement and may be categorized into two factors: common factor risk and individual factor risk. *Common factor risk* is that portion of nonmarket risk that can be attributed to groups of stocks such as industry effects or broad sector influences such as the behavior of growth stocks in recent years. *Individual factor risk* is represented by factors that are unique to a firm such as labor strikes, management errors, inventions, advertising campaigns, shifts in consumer taste, etc.

The standard error measures the probable range of rate of return deviations from expectations, given the portfolio beta and the movement of the overall market. For example, a portfolio with a beta of 1.0 and a standard error of 6 percent would be expected to achieve a rate of return somewhere between plus and minus 6 percent of the S&P 500 return roughly two observations out of three. If the S&P 500 return were 20 percent, the portfolio return would be expected to fall between 14 percent and 26 percent, 66 percent of the time.

Diversification is a measure of the degree to which portfolio returns can be explained by concurrent moves of the market. The S&P 500

Figure 2
Changing Risk Characteristics with Time

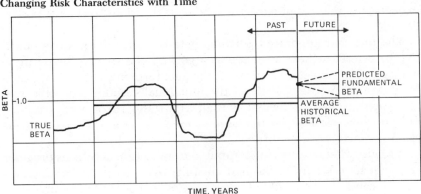

TIME, YEARS

Index is considered to be perfectly diversified, therefore, a portfolio with perfect diversification would move identical to or in direct proportion to the S&P 500. The portfolio coefficient of determination, commonly called R^2, is a measure of diversification that is related closely to standard error of the portfolio. By definition, the S&P 500 has an R^2 of 1.0 and a standard error of 0. An index fund will have an R^2 of .99 while a managed portfolio typically will have an R^2 ranging from .80 to .97. It is important to note that a high R^2 (and hence low standard error) minimizes the likelihood of a significant deviation from the market return.

Cash equivalents or similar investments that have no systematic relationship to the S&P 500 have a diversification of 0. The typical individual security has a diversification value of between .30 and .50.

Other Important Measures of Performance

A number of other parameters may be calculated that present meaningful information to investors.

Account balance. It is useful to examine the fund's balance as an overall check to minimize accounting errors. This can be done by adding or subtracting contributions and withdrawals, interest and dividends, and accounting for transactions during the period and changes in value of individual issues. The book value and cash on hand should be reconciled with reported value of the fund at the end of the period. This type of quality control procedure also serves to assure that performance results are not misstated for a period.

Allocation is the distribution of assets by classification. Asset allocation or mix is the percentage of assets in each category (i.e., equity, fixed income, cash, etc.). The asset mix indicates how closely the investment meets sponsor objectives, as well as revealing how the manager is responding to market trends. Funds can be classified as equity or fixed income, or as balanced funds—which contain both.

Cash flow for the total account represents the sum of contributions to the fund less the sum of withdrawals from the fund. Cash flows of a specific portfolio manager also show securities transactions, dividends, and interest as well as contributions from sponsor and fees.

Cash flow impact can be measured as the time-weighted rate of return less the dollar-weighted rate of return. Since the dollar-weighted rate indicates the effects of investment performance and cash flows, while the time-weighted rate indicates only investment performance, the difference between those two rates provides an indication of the impact of short term timing on the return experience of the total account.

While the manager does not control contributions and withdrawals, she or he normally does exert influence over the amount of funds placed in the stock market, the bond market, and other market segments. A positive cash flow impact for a segment indicates that the manager directed the flows into or out of favorable segments of the market at well-chosen times.

Concentration can be examined by looking at the total number of securities in a portfolio and the percent of the total dollar value represented by any single security or market sector. Sponsors may impose limits on maximum holdings for a portfolio.

Total dollar value of the fund, at the beginning or the end of the performance period, as well as the size of individually managed components, should be identified. Size itself is not a performance measure. However, for the purpose of comparative analysis, it is often desirable to compare funds of similar size and purpose.

Turnover is calculated as the lesser value of security purchases or sales divided by the average market value of the assets for the period. Although many investment managers provide information on the portfolio's turnover rate, an outside measure of turnover may be desired. Examined alone, the rate of turnover is not very illuminating. However, when considered in light of a fund's performance, it can become very useful. Turnover is an indicator of management activity. For example, if the portfolio's performance is relatively poor, a low rate of turnover may indicate a lack of sufficient attention to the management of the portfolio. On the other hand, a very high rate of turnover could result from overreaction to short term movements in the market.

Transaction costs include management and brokerage fees and are discussed in detail in Chapter 20.

EVALUATING PERFORMANCE

The evaluation of portfolio performance involves (1) comparing measures of performance against standards to determine the relative effectiveness, (2) diagnosing results to determine factors underlying performance, and (3) assessing alternatives available for improvement. Results might be evaluated relative to the sponsor's and investment manager's objectives, accepted performance benchmarks, other similar funds, or the investment universe. The data can be examined for a particular span of time or as trends over a number of evaluation periods. Diagnostic tools include allocation and optimization techniques for analyzing sponsor objectives, asset mix, and portfolio structure.

The relationship between risk and rate of return is basic to understanding and evaluating equity portfolios. Since investors as a group are averse to risk, riskier stocks command higher required rates of return. Figure 3 illustrates the trade-off between rate of return and market risk identified by MPT. The line showing the relationship between risk and rate of return is defined as the capital market line.

Figure 3
Capital Market Line

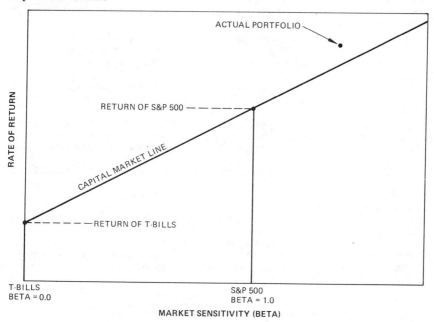

The intercept of the capital market line is the riskless rate of return, generally taken as the return on U.S. Treasury securities. Since returns on riskless securities are relatively fixed or constant over the measurement period, they do not move at all with changes in the market. Thus, riskless securities have beta coefficients of 0. Another significant performance comparison would be against the return on a perfectly diversified portfolio. The S&P 500 is a well diversified portfolio with a beta of 1 and is generally accepted as the basis for constructing the capital market line. The capital market line serves as a means of calculating expected return for a particular portfolio, and for comparison with other portfolios whose characteristics are known or can be estimated.

Achieving Objectives

The primary basis for evaluating performance is the achievement of stated objectives. Perhaps the most difficult problems associated with monitoring or managing a portfolio are establishing and articulating investment philosophy in terms that managers can translate into specific action. For example, terms like "passive" and "aggressive" have different meanings to different parties. A sponsor may hire an active money manager and pay relatively high fees in anticipation of

Figure 4
Individual Equity Manager Guidelines

Policy Guidelines

1. The securities that make up the total portfolio should be on a weighted-average basis _____ more/less volatile than the Standard & Poor's 500 Stock Average (S&P 500). This volatility requirement indicates the degree of market risk to be undertaken and may be represented by an average beta coefficient of _____.
2. Permitted variation from the desired average portfolio volatility level of _____ will be delimited by a range which has a low volatility bound of _____ and a high bound of _____.
3. Diversification of the portfolio will be such that at least _____ of the portfolio returns can be associated with movements in the S&P 500. This implies a minimum R^2 (square of the correlation coefficient between the portfolio and the S&P 500) of _____ at all times.
4. There are any number of differing percentages of equities, bonds and short-term investments that can be combined to achieve the average volatility/minimum portfolio diversification characteristics over the performance measurement horizon specified below. For example, one such portfolio mix which would fit the criteria would be 95 percent equities having an average beta coefficient of _____ combined with 5 percent short-term investments.
5. Because contributions and income will exceed benefits for the next several years, there is no specific requirement to maintain a liquidity reserve, and the existence of any such reserve should be viewed in the context of achieving the average desired volatility levels.

Investment Objectives and Measurement Horizon

1. Portfolio volatility and diversification levels will be monitored on a frequent basis, and it is expected that the above policy parameters will be adhered to and neither of the extreme ends of the volatility ranges will show up for more than two consecutive quarters.
2. It is anticipated that over the next three to five years the implementation of this particular policy should produce a minimum expected compound rate of return (net of investment management fees and time-weighted to adjust for external cash flows) equal to the rate of return of an unmanaged portfolio at the average volatility level of _____.
3. In addition to this minimum expected return, an incremental return of _____ percent per annum should be added as a result of the manager's ability to correctly anticipate overall market behavior (timing) and/or select undervalued securities (selection). The incremental return attributable to timing and/or selection will be monitored on a quarterly basis. The results of this analysis will be reviewed with each investment manager.

superior performance only to find that the manager operates portfolios that do not substantially differ from an index fund. Figure 4 is an example of an agreement that might be used by sponsors and portfolio managers to establish management objectives. Specifying objective levels and tolerances in allowable market risk, diversification, asset mix, and expected returns, along with time spans for evaluation, provides a meaningful set of criteria for performance evaluation.

Benchmarks for Comparative Analysis

There are a great many benchmarks or indices used for comparative analysis. The rate of return of Treasury Bills and the S&P 500 are perhaps used most frequently as indicators of longer term performance of capital markets, and they are generally the basis for establishing risk statistics.

A summary of commonly used indices is presented below.

T-Bills—the rate of return on 90-day Treasury Bills, which is used as a risk-free proxy in the calculation of market-related return.

Standard and Poor's Composite 500 Stock Index—an index whose value varies with the aggregate value of the common equity of 500 companies.

Standard and Poor's Composite 500 Stock Index, Equal-Weighted—an index comprised of equal investment in each security in the S&P 500. In the equal-weighted index, all security attributes such as rate of return or beta are given equal weighting. This index obviously places greater emphasis on the characteristics of smaller companies.

Standard and Poor's 400 Industrial Index—an index whose value varies with the aggregate performance of the common equity of 400 industrial companies.

Becker Securities Corporation 750—the 750 most widely held stocks in all portfolios subscribing to Becker's Funds Evaluation Services.

New York Stock Exchange Composite Index—an index whose value varies with the aggregate value of the common equity of all companies listed on the NYSE.

Value Line Composite Average—an index whose percent change is the unweighted geometric average of the percent changes of the 1,560 stocks included. More than 90 percent are NYSE-listed. Since no portfolio could be constructed that achieved the rates of return of this index, its use as an unbiased performance benchmark is questionable.

Wilshire 5000 Equity Index—established as a comprehensive indicator of the market, this index reports the market value of the outstanding equity of all securities for which daily pricing is available.

Dow Jones Industrial Average—an index whose value is proportional to the sum of the per-share prices of the 30 stocks included.

Kuhn-Loeb-Bond Index—is a portfolio comprised of approximately 3,900 nonconvertible industrial, utility, and financial bond issues. The value of the index varies with the aggregate value of all issues included.

Salomon Brothers Corporate Bond Index—is a portfolio comprised of approximately 4,000 corporate bond issues including utilities, industrials, finance companies, and banks.

Comparative Analysis of Returns

Returns can be evaluated in comparison to sponsor needs and goals or compared to indices. The results can be presented for evaluation in either tabular or graphic form. Figure 5 gives a comparison of returns for a given time period for a variety of comparative indices. The exam-

Figure 5
Rate of Return, Comparison with Standards

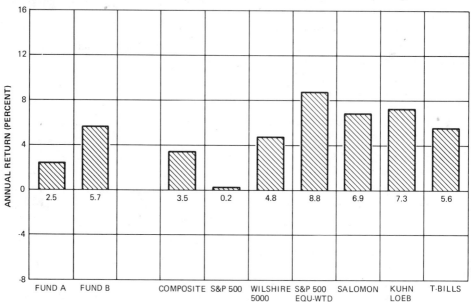

ple shows that the composite as well as both managed funds outperformed the market for the period; however, only fund *B* exceeded T-Bill returns.

Often it is desirable to display the relationship of the fund manager's results to other managers. This may be done statistically to indicate how the manager ranks with others. Figure 6 shows fund performance for different time periods compared to statistical results of other funds.

The rectangles indicate the overall range for the rates of return for several hundred mutual funds. The broken lines within the rectangle indicate the 75th and 25th percentiles while the solid line shows the 50th percentile, i.e., half of the portfolios have a return greater and half less than the indicated values. This type of display gives an indication of ranking or relative performance. This type of display would also be useful in presenting other performance measures (e.g., risk, diversification, management effects, allocation, etc.) for comparative purposes.

Risk and Return—using the Capital Market Line

The first step in evaluation is to compare performance to objectives or management strategy. The objectives set by the sponsor establish

Figure 6
Rate of Return, Statistical Comparisons

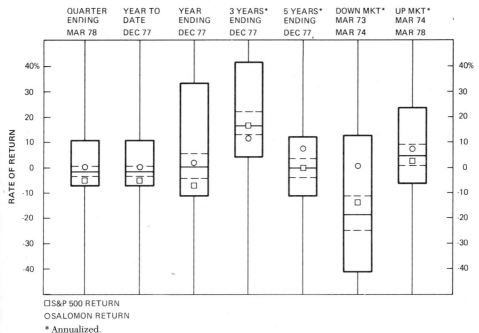

☐ S&P 500 RETURN
O SALOMON RETURN
* Annualized.

an objective risk level or a reference for comparison, which is shown in Figure 7. The difference between the actual results achieved by the money manager and the expected return of a portfolio at the objective or reference risk level is called the *net management effect.*

Differences between the results of the actual portfolio and established benchmarks or management objectives reflect management style and decisions made over the period. If the manager can shift portfolio market sensitivity or select undervalued securities in anticipation of major market moves, he or she may be able to achieve better performance. Results of the first type are termed *market-timing effects* and results of the second type are termed *security-selection effects.*

Market-timing effect is assessed by observing the level of market volatility—the actual portfolio beta coefficient—over the evaluation period. Superior market timing is suggested by low values or downward shifts in the beta coefficient prior to market downturns, and high values or upward shifts prior to market upturns. By maintaining the average beta coefficient higher than the reference beta coefficient, the manager who forecasts an upturn is able to participate in the rising market. In the example in Figure 8, the S&P 500 return is greater than the Treasury Bill return. Thus, the manager is credited with a positive timing effect equal to the difference between the expected return at

Figure 7
Net Management Effect

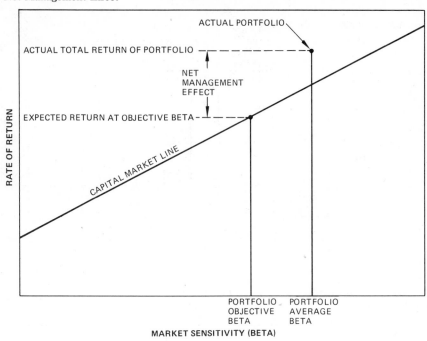

Figure 8
Market Timing Effect

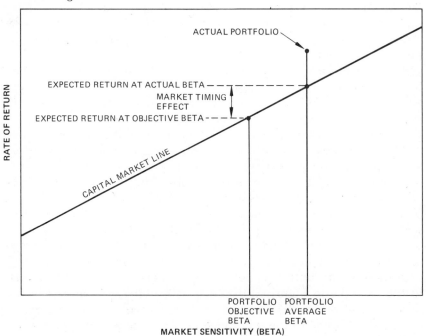

the average or actual portfolio beta and the expected return at the objective or reference beta.

Security-selection effect is determined by examining the actual return on the portfolio during the period. The actual portfolio return plotted on Figure 9 differs from the return that would be expected given the average beta of the portfolio. The selection effect is attributed to the manager's choice of specific securities. The sum effectiveness of the manager's application of market timing and security selection is indicated as an estimate of the total *net management effect* contributed by the manager to the performance of the account (shown in Figure 7):

Other management effects that can be analyzed are trading and indexing alternatives, shown in Figures 10 and 11. The trading effect can be examined by comparing the actual returns with the expected return that would have been achieved by the portfolio that existed at the beginning of the period, usually called a buy-and-hold portfolio. Another comparison is of the actual portfolio return to the return of an index fund; this provides an overall view of effectiveness of the manager. Since management of index funds is passive, the sponsor would expect superior performance from an actively managed fund.

Comparisons of various indices or funds with the capital market

Figure 9
Selection Effect

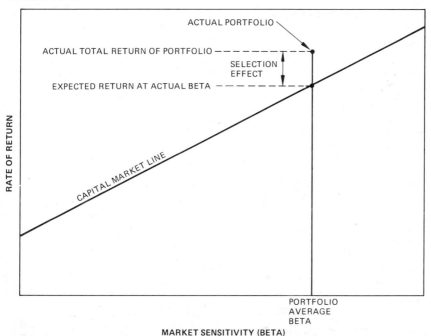

Figure 10
Trading Effect

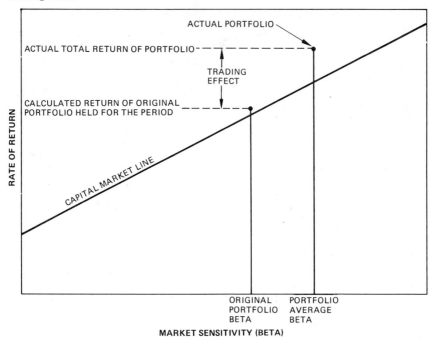

Figure 11
Effect of Active Management

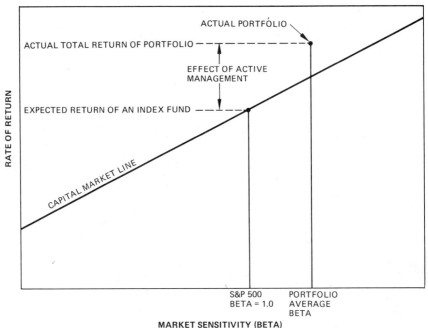

Figure 12
Performance Comparisons of Mutual Funds, Bank Pooled Funds, and Market Indices

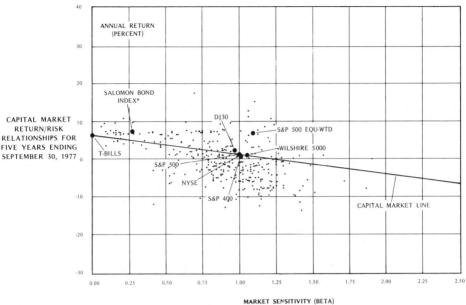

MARKET SENSITIVITY (BETA)

* Return-risk relationship calculated by Wilshire Associates using monthly performance results supplied by Salomon Bros.

line is frequently used as a basis for a risk-adjusted comparison between various funds and the investment universe. This indicates to the evaluator how a particular portfolio is performing relative to others. Figure 12 shows the capital market return-risk relationships for two years ending September 30, 1977. The return-risk relationship is calculated by using monthly performance results for mutual funds, bank pooled funds, and market indices. Similar charts showing relationships between return and total risk are also frequently used for comparison of performance. The negative market line slope shown in Figure 12 is due to the return of riskless T-Bills outperforming the S&P 500 during the period.

Two measures of risk-adjusted returns should be mentioned here. One, proposed by Sharpe, is the portfolio geometric mean return $(\bar{R}_p)$ less the risk free rate (R_f) divided by the standard deviation of the portfolio returns (σ_P):

$$S = \frac{\bar{R}_p - R_f}{\sigma_p}$$

The other measure suggested by Treynor is:

$$T = \frac{R_p - R_f}{\beta_p}$$

where β_p is the portfolio beta obtained by regressing the portfolio returns against the returns of the market index.

Return and Diversification Relationship

While the previous figures show pinpoint estimates for expected returns, they are in fact only the most likely estimate out of a range of possibilities. Portfolios with higher standard errors will exhibit more period-by-period variability than better diversified funds. To achieve statistically significant superior performance, less diversified portfolios must produce higher magnitudes of management effects.

The degree of diversification of the portfolio is a key indicator of management style. Less well-diversified portfolios place greater reliance on security selection as a means of improving portfolio performance over subsequent periods. More highly diversified portfolios are indicative of greater dependence on the overall market for achieving a desired level of portfolio return.

If two funds have the same beta, the one with the higher diversification will be subject to less fluctuation and therefore the expected return should be closer to the index. As the performance of an actively managed fund approaches that of the index, the question of investment objectives can be raised. Sponsors who pay a high premium for active portfolio management yet achieve index-like results should consider a lower cost index fund. Those who desire higher performance must expect their managers to undertake higher risk.

Management Trends

It is easy to partition the total return into components such as riskless return, market related, nonmarket related, management effects, timing, selection, etc. However, it is very difficult to differentiate between luck and skill of the investment manager in the short run. The skill level of an investment manager can be established by plotting specific monthly or quarterly effects and examining the trend history for consistency of management skill.

The significance of actual portfolio results can be measured using the standard error statistics to assess whether the actual performance is a likely or an unlikely event. Figure 13 shows quarterly security selection effects. The boundaries between statistically significant and insignificant are computed as a multiple of the portfolio standard error to express a stated level of statistical confidence.

CORRECTING PERFORMANCE

As stated at the beginning, the primary reason for analyzing the performance of investments is so that the decision maker can do some-

Figure 13
Trend Comparison

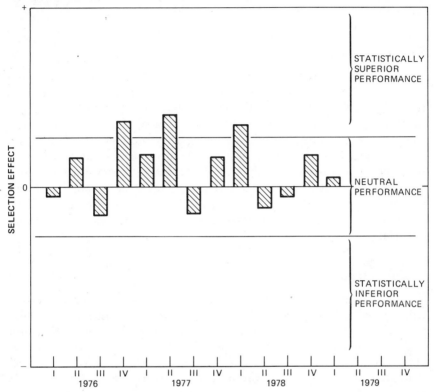

thing about it. This should not imply that the decision maker should continually change direction, even in the presence of poor performance. If total return is not sufficient to cover liabilities, the sponsor may want to reevaluate basic planning or objectives in fund management. A great variety of analytical techniques and tools such as trade-off analysis, simulation, and optimization programs can be used to better understand the options available.

Trade-off Analysis

Trade-off analysis implies an examination of the cost and benefit relationship of various alternatives to determine the desired course among action alternatives. Quantitative measures of performance can be calculated for each alternative under consideration. Comparing expectations of risk and return, along with management and transaction cost estimates, provide a basis for making more informed decisions on policy or operations. The benefits—and therefore payout and liabilities—may not be commensurate with the cost. Perhaps the sponsor may wish to take more or less risk, depending on the circumstances. The sponsor may also want to take a more active role by directing contributions or restating manager guidelines.

Simulation

In many cases, the sponsor does not have clearly defined or stated objectives. Simulation techniques can be used to analyze the interrelationships between contractual pension plan liabilities and investment portfolio performance into the future. Typical simulators allow the user to test assumptions by projecting the implications of risk and return characteristics in light of probable future economic characteristics. These tools are generally used to gain insight into future demands on sponsor assets under varying assumptions. Understanding future demands can help the sponsor set strategic objectives for risk as well as for return, asset mix, manager mix, and performance monitoring criteria.

Optimization

The manager charged with implementing quantitative objectives will find MPT-derived tools of risk measurement and optimization helpful. Optimization is a process that derives a mix of resources that best suits a particular set of objectives and constraints. Given a set of desirable portfolio characteristics, optimization techniques construct a portfolio that meets these conditions yet maximizes diversification. For example, if a portfolio manager is trying to achieve a high level of market sensitivity (beta of 1.1) while maintaining a modest risk (diversification of .95), it is possible to optimally select a portfolio that will provide these levels. If a portfolio already exists, optimization techniques can be used to determine the best tactics to maintain risk-return objectives while minimizing the transaction costs associated with the process of porfolio adjustment.

The manager desiring to improve performance may wish to increase or decrease portfolio risk as market conditions change, or may wish to improve adherence to goals by optimizing the portfolio to come closer to stated objectives.

Control

Management control over portfolio performance suggests that the decision maker has a stated objective, a strategy or action plan, a criteria for success, a means to measure performance, and alternatives if goals change or are not achieved. This implies that measuring investment performance is a continuing process. A sponsor—as well as a manager of portfolios—needs to know what results were obtained and how they were achieved. Such information can be used to alter the objectives stated for the account, the constraints placed on a manager, the cash flow of the fund, or the amount of money allocated to each manager. Perhaps more important: by measuring performance in specified ways, a sponsor has an effective means of communicating objectives to an investment manager.

It is difficult to separate performance due to skill from that due to luck, especially in the short run. Therefore performance monitoring should be done with great care. Performance can suggest areas for more detailed analysis and discussion. Superior performance due to good luck cannot be expected to continue in the future. Unsatisfactory performance may be the result of bad luck or may be the result of poor timing, excessive turnover, high management fees or execution costs, or from unreasonably high nonmarket risk. If so, detailed performance diagnosis may identify areas in which changes can improve performance.

REFERENCES

1. Davanzo, Lawrence. "A Review of Performance Measurement Services." *EM&R Report* (Endowment Management & Research Corporation, 1977).
2. Dietz, Peter O. "Pension Funds: Measuring Investment Performance." *New York Free Press* (1966).
3. Fama, Eugene. "Components of Investment Performance." *Journal of Finance*, 27 (June 1972): 551–67.
4. Jensen, Michael C. "The Performance of Mutual Funds in the Period 1945–1964." *Journal of Finance*, 23 (May 1968): 389–416.
5. Lorie, James H. (chairman), et al. "Measuring the Investment Performance of Pension Funds for the Purpose of Inter-Fund Comparison." *Bank Administration Institute* (1968).
6. Markowitz, Harry. "Portfolio Selection." *Journal of Finance* 7 (March 1952): 77–91.
7. Rosenberg, Barr and Guy, James. "Prediction of Beta from Investment Fundamentals." *Financial Analysts Journal* (May–June 1976, July–August 1976, September–October 1976).
8. Sharpe, William F. *Investments* (Englewood Cliffs, N.J.: Prentice-Hall, Inc., 1978).
9. Treynor, Jack. "How to Rate the Management of Investment Funds." *Harvard Business Review* (January 1965).
10. Weston, J. Fred and Brigham, Eugene F. *Managerial Finance*, 5th Ed. (New York: Dryden Press, 1975).

Chapter 17

Trends in Bond Portfolio Management

MARTIN L. LEIBOWITZ

General Partner and Manager
of Bond Portfolio Analysis Group
Salomon Brothers
New York, New York

The last decade has witnessed a revolution in the management of bond portfolios. There has been an explosion in the variety of fixed income securities as well as in the range of available trading techniques. Within the ranks of the larger fee-based management organizations, "active bond management" has progressed from the status of a novelty to that of the norm.

The first part of this article will attempt to explore both the nature and the evolution of the forces that led to the remarkable transformation of what was formerly thought to be a bastion of rather staid (if not stuffy) conservatism.

As one comes to understand these new markets and competitive forces, one realizes that they are not an unmixed blessing. The drift away from the older fundamentals has created a potentially dangerous separation between goals and practice. Active bond management does not by itself automatically insure progress in the direction of the portfolio's basic objectives. Indeed, in some instances, the hot pursuit of total return may be inconsistent with the reasons for the original allocation of the funds to the fixed income area.

In the second part of the article, the "baseline" approach is set forth as one practical way to blend modern management techniques with the earlier, more fundamental view of the bond portfolio function. By harnessing the short-term total-return focus of the active manager to the fund's longer-term objectives, the baseline method can provide concrete guidelines for the goal-oriented management of bond portfolios.

THE EVOLUTION OF ACTIVE BOND MANAGEMENT

The Scope of Bond Management Activity

The modern bond portfolio manager has a wide selection of both strategic and tactical options available every day. One can select from coupons ranging from 2½ percent to over 10 percent. One can choose from a spectrum of maturities ranging from one day to distant dates deep into the next century. One can select issuers with names known and respected around the world, or move into obscure situations requiring specialized credit analysis. One can move, in many ways, toward greater protection from the threat of a refunding call, or can be paid for accepting greater call risks. One can reach for the accelerated payback and market strength of a strong sinking fund or a pass-through security, or can elect for a longer "lock up" of an attractive initial yield.

The manager can structure a portfolio to maximize returns over any time horizon from the very short term to very long term. One can split a portfolio into two segments; one segment focused on maximum yields with minimum management, and the other segment kept in highly marketable securities and earmarked for intensive short-term management.

One can manipulate the timing of commitment of new money flows.

One can try to anticipate overall changes in the long interest rates by adjusting the volatility of the portfolio.

One can try to take advantage of changing yield curves.

One can try to take advantage of the changing yield spread relationships between market sectors differentiated by quality, by coupon, by type of issuer, by type of issue, etc.

One can trade one bond for a closely-related issue at an apparently attractive spread. One can monitor the markets for the opportunity to reverse a trade and swap back into an original holding. Or one can make a further spread move into a third bond and begin a whole chain of swaps.

A manager can construct package swaps which combine two or more bond holdings in order to offset the impact of some specific factor, e.g., matching capital losses with capital gains, maintaining a given volatility, keeping a given maturity structure, sustaining existing levels of current yield, etc.

One can consolidate a large number of fragmented holdings by swapping them for a highly marketable set of issues. One must then recognize an obligation to make these marketable securities pay their own way. One pays a certain cost premium for marketability. If the potential value of this marketability is not utilized in some way, then this cost premium is just being wasted.

If the portfolio is subject to taxation, then the portfolio manager can and should thoroughly address the process of tax liability management.

These options are most fully available to the manager of a long-term portfolio. However, the thoughtful manager of a short-term portfolio can take partial advantage of many of these same options, especially where one is free to incorporate long-term instruments into a portfolio on a controlled-risk basis.

These are only a sampling of the many possible courses of action available to today's bond portfolio manager. None of them carries a guarantee. Each course of action entails a certain degree of risk. The level of risk varies widely, from the relative safety of a constant volatility like-for-like swap to the all-out risk of a major maturity restructuring.

One of the problems is that the terms "active bond management" and "bond swapping" have been used indiscriminately to cover a range of very different market activities. To help provide a structure for this bewildering variety of possible market activities, the following broad classification scheme has been proposed [1]:*

1. Pure yield pick-up swaps
2. Substitution swaps
3. Sector (or intermarket spread) swaps
4. Rate anticipation

In the subsequent sections, these four swap categories will be described in the context of their role in the historical evolution of modern bond portfolio management.

In one sense, active bond management is not a new phenomenon. A certain number of U.S. investment managers have been using the most sophisticated "modern" techniques for many years. However, outside this relatively small circle, bond management activity consisted primarily of allocating the portfolio's new cash flow among new long issues. Figure 1 shows the general pattern of long-term interest rates over recent years. The rise in long corporate yields in the late 1960s provided bonds with a respectable level of return and helped to spark a broader interest in bond portfolio management. In these early days, when managers talked about a bond swap, they usually meant a traditional pure yield pick-up swap.

The Pure Yield Pick-Up Swap and Loss-Constrained Portfolios.   In a *pure yield pick-up swap,* a portfolio bond is replaced by a higher-yielding bond similar in all characteristics important to the fund (e.g., quality, maturity). The objective is to increase the total contractual return over the bond's life.

In practice, one of the major sources of pure yield pick-up swap

---

* Numbers in brackets refer to References at end of chapter.

Figure 1
New AA Utility Yields

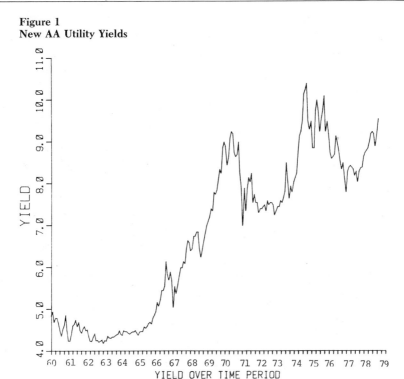

YIELD OVER TIME PERIOD

opportunities has been the combination of the long term secular rise in interest rates together with various portfolio constraints against realizing book losses [7]. These constraints forced many portfolios to carry positions of relatively low-yielding bonds long beyond the point where they represented appropriate holdings for the portfolio. As these constraints were then gradually relaxed, the managers of these previously-frozen portfolios found themselves presented with many swap opportunities that improved the overall portfolio structure and, at the same time, achieved significant pick-ups in yield. In order to appreciate how this situation came about, one first must understand the pervasive and corrosive effects of the accounting fiction which might be termed "loss constraint."

Many large bond portfolios are limited, in one way or another, in their ability to sustain book losses. This problem afflicts portfolios of virtually all types—pension funds, insurance companies, casualty companies, commercial banks, mutual savings banks, savings and loan associations, corporations, etc. Loss constraint encumbers both very small portfolios and many multibillion dollar portfolios. The operational and accounting rationale that dictate this policy differ from one institution to the next. But the net effect is the same. All holdings where the current market price is below the book cost, i.e., holdings carried at an unrealized loss, become essentially unsaleable. Such holdings therefore constitute frozen assets no matter how liquid or how marketable the securities themselves may be. The real problem is that these loss-frozen holdings must then be retained even when they have become quite inappropriate to the portfolio's current objectives.

Because of the extraordinary rise in interest rates over the past 20–30 years, any portfolio which has been a regular purchaser of long-term bonds will naturally find many of its holdings locked in by losses. It would be very surprising if all these older holdings remained totally suitable to the portfolio's new goals. Inevitably, in any loss-constrained portfolio, one can find a number of glaring examples of loss-locked, inappropriate security holdings. With the passage of time since their purchase, the market role in these securities has somehow changed, so that they are now in dissonance with the fund's basic purpose.

These dissonant securities may be perfectly valid investment vehicles—for some other portfolio! In fact, this may be the source of their problem. When certain securities have a strong special appeal for one class of investors, their market prices will be bid up above normal levels for bonds of similar quality, maturity, etc. These securities will then provide a relatively low market yield, and consequently will not pay their own way in portfolios which cannot make use of their special features. This creates the classic situation for pure yield pick-up swaps.

The so-called "flower bonds" are a prime case in point. These are U.S. Treasury bonds floated in the period 1953–63 and bearing coupons ranging from 3–4¼ percent. Their special feature is that when used to pay off estate taxes, their value is assessed at par. Because of this special feature, the market for flower bonds is chronically priced well above normal levels for current coupon Treasury bonds of comparable maturities. This enhanced price level translates into a yield disadvantage. On March 15, 1979, the 3½s of 1998 were priced around 77 for a yield-to-maturity of 5.42 percent. By comparison, current coupon long Treasuries (affording essentially the same degree of call protection) were priced to yield about 9.00 percent, i.e., over 350 basis points more than the flower bond.

Other examples of inappropriate holdings which often underyield the market can be found among short- and intermediate-term discount bonds—both corporates and Treasuries. Because of the large capital gain component in their return, these bonds have a special appeal to certain taxpayers. (The appeal is particularly strong for many taxpayers who have a sufficient supply of potential tax losses to assure an effective capital gains tax rate of 0 percent!) [11]

Discount bonds with strong sinking funds are another example of dissonant holdings in certain loss-constrained portfolios. These bonds have a special appeal both for defensive investors and for professional managers interested in the sinking fund "play." The issuer of these bonds must enter the open market periodically to buy bonds to satisfy its sinking fund requirement. As time progresses, there is a tightening in the available supply of bonds, and the price naturally rises. In addition, some portfolio managers may try to collect these bonds in order to further capitalize on the periodic surges of demand from the issuer. This collection process can lead to an even higher price level being established. As a result, collected sinking fund bonds may provide a market yield-to-maturity that is far below the general level for comparable securities.

The collector's basic hope is that the issuer will at some point find it necessary to pay a particularly good price for their whole collection. Other investors interested in the sinking fund play may hope to pick up capital gain on the collector's coattails, so to speak.

However, for loss-constrained portfolios, where these bonds were originally purchased near par, even a very attractive bid would still entail accepting a sizeable book loss. Consequently, the stringently loss-constrained manager is not likely to have the flexibility required to really benefit from the issuer's open market purchases. In fact, many sinking fund players make a point of examining how an issue is distributed among various types of institutions. Those bonds held by institutions thought to be severely loss-constrained—e.g., insurance companies—are then excluded from their estimate of the "floating supply." In other words, these sinking fund players actually count on insurance companies being totally unable to part with their bonds at any price below par. (There may be some surprises here.)

The lowest yielding holding may not always be the best candidate for a pure yield pick-up swap. First of all, it may carry a deep book loss with the attendant low ratio of proceeds-generated-per-loss-taken. Second, a low market yield by itself is not necessarily evidence of a security's dissonance relative to the portfolio's objectives. Deep discount long Telephones often provide a relatively low yield. However, these securities could function as uniquely valuable components of a well balanced portfolio for certain types of funds. For example, suppose a growing pension fund were concerned about the possibility of a secular downtrend in interest rates. A sustained downtrend would indeed reduce the coupon reinvestment rate of the existing portfolio, lower the rollover rate of maturing proceeds, perhaps lead to refunding calls of the higher coupon bonds, force the flow of net new contributions into relatively low-yielding investments, and even reduce the nominal dollar amount of the annuity that could be purchased for each dollar of future asset value [3]. For a fund concerned with this potential deterioration in overall return, deep discount long Telephones (or any deep discount high-grade corporate) might be an excellent counterbalance.

During the late 1960s and early 1970s the prohibitions against realizing book losses were gradually lifted for a number of state and city pension funds. In some cases, the book loss constraint was removed altogether and the portfolio manager was granted the flexibility to make investment decisions based solely upon market considerations. More frequently, the authorization to realize losses was limited by some requirement that sufficient incremental cash flow be gained in the swap to "recover" the book loss. A veritable garden of accounting fictions sprung up reflecting various formulas for determining loss recovery times and/or for amortizing realized losses as a charge against the portfolio's future income stream. Many of the formulas were inconsistent or flawed from a pure investment viewpoint. For example, they often failed to deal correctly with the reinvestment and compounding process in growing portfolios [5]. Nevertheless, virtually all these loss recovery formulas could be satisfied with a sufficiently large improvement in yield-to-maturity. The preceding years of total loss constraint insured that many portfolios contained ample opportunities for sizeable yield improvements. This led to increasing levels of pure yield pick-up swapping. Some of the older pension funds spent years moving out of massive holdings of low-yielding Treasury and corporate bonds that they had accumulated over the years.

While many portfolios were by-passed and, in fact, many still remain frozen today, the trend towards greater flexibility advanced further in the early 1970s. A new breed of active managers then came into view. They recognized that most high-grade bond portfolios contained large holdings of highly liquid, marketable bonds. Naturally, this liquidity had an associated cost in the form of generally lower yields. This new breed was determined to make this liquidity pay for itself on an on-going basis.

The Substitution Swap and the Give-Up of Nominal Yield. This determination led to an increasing focus on short-term trading activity in general, and to the rapid development of "substitution swapping" in particular. In a *substitution swap*, the portfolio manager tracks the yield spread relationships among groups of similar "substitutable" bonds. When the spread between any two like bonds reaches some extreme limit, presumably as a result of transient market imbalances, a swap is executed in the hope of obtaining a profitable reversal as the spread later returns to more normal levels.

The rewards from a successful chain of substitution swaps could be very clear and dramatic, especially when it consisted of a significant takeout of dollars combined with a return to the original portfolio holding. Moreover, to the extent that truly substitutable bonds were involved, the incremental risks were very small. For many managers, a cleanly executed string of substitution swaps paved the way towards greater investment flexibility. In particular, it demonstrated the importance of permitting the manager to swap in the direction of giving up yield-to-maturity.

This freedom to *give up* yield is a crucial, and yet sometimes a very difficult, step for many portfolios. To individuals outside the bond community (and this includes many members of the investment committees who set fund policy), to give up yield on a swap seems tantamount to willingly giving up return. Of course, just the opposite is true: such swaps give up long-term nominal yields with the intention of increasing real returns over somewhat shorter time frames. However, unless the manager obtains authorization for yield give-up trades, one's portfolio would be condemned to a one-way street which, at best, would result in a refrozen portfolio at some higher yield level, and at worst, would lead to an ill-structured portfolio vulnerable to call and possibly filled with significant credit risk.

While substitution swapping proved one way to tap the liquidity resources of bond portfolios, it soon became clear that it could not, by itself, constitute a comprehensive approach to bond management. First of all, the initiative for substitution swaps rests more with the marketplace than with the manager. Second, while such swaps could be highly profitable in absolute dollars and in terms of return on the specific holdings involved, they could have only a limited impact on total portfolio returns (except perhaps for smaller funds). Finally, the more intensive substitution swapping had become concentrated on a relatively small number of high-grade, widely-held, marketable issues. As the swap activity increased within this limited field, the extent of the aberrations became less and less, and consequently, there were fewer and fewer dramatic opportunities.

The substitution swap still remained a worthwhile activity, especially for the manager who was organized to carry it out on a low-cost, low-effort basis. But it could no longer justify being the sole focus of the manager's attention.

The Sector Swap and Professional Market Insight. In 1972, the sector swap began to be "rediscovered." In the *sector swap* (or *intermarket spread swap*), the manager tries to take advantage of the changing yield spread relationships between market sectors differentiated by quality, by coupon, by type of issuer (e.g., utility to industrial to finance to Canadian to Treasuries to Agencies), by type of issue (e.g., private versus public, strong sinking fund versus weak sinking fund), etc. As with all these techniques, the sector swap had been continuously and artfully practiced for decades by certain U.S. managers. However, its following among the newer breed of managers seemed to develop after the "squeezing out" of the substitution swap.

The sector swapper's professionalism and flexibility provide a definite edge. One is continually studying yield spread relationships among different sectors in the market. When one detects what appears to be a transient aberration, one can dig deeper into the fundamental sources of this aberration. The swapper's market experience and widespread daily contacts will aid in this effort. One's knowledge and insights into market forces will count here. This can put one in a position to make the key judgment as to whether the existing sector relationship is, in fact, a transient aberration which will revert to more normal levels over time—or whether it is the first signalings of a new trend and a new market structure. This approach to the marketplace does not belong equally to everyone. Here, the truly professional portfolio manager should have an edge.

Another advantage of sector swaps is that they can be initiated across significant portions of the overall portfolio. They can involve major swap programs. They can impact the overall portfolio performance.

While clearly riskier than substitution swaps, sector swaps can, by and large, keep the portfolio within the general confines of the long-term debt market, or more broadly speaking, within the confines of the portfolio's original maturity structure. Consequently, the manager can fairly well control the incremental risk entailed in a sector swap relative to the prior risk level established by the portfolio's basic structure.

In 1972 and 1973, there were a number of unusually clearcut examples of sector swap situations. One of the classic situations occurred in the Fall of 1973 when the yield of GNMA pass-throughs rose to unprecedented levels relative to both corporate and other Agency issues. Delving behind the statistics, the underlying cause could easily be traced to a drying up of new investable funds among thrift institutions. These had been the primary buyers of the then relatively new pass-through instrument. Because of their apparent complexity relative to straight bonds, the pass-throughs had not yet established a wide following among pension fund managers. (Actually, the evaluation of the probable true yields of the pass-throughs is far more complex— and more important—than is generally recognized even today.) However, at the extraordinarily attractive nominal yields that then prevailed (and the even more attractive probable cash flow yields), it was fairly likely that some major pension fund managers would soon overcome their initial problems with GNMA pass-through analysis and accounting. In fact, this is precisely what occurred. The bond manager who moved quickly and massively into pass-throughs reaped considerable rewards as the spread relative to corporates narrowed by over 75 basis points in the course of the next six months.

The GNMA example also illustrates the "new vehicle" type of sector swap. A portfolio manager who recognizes the value in a newly introduced sector may then reap sizeable rewards as the sector becomes increasingly accepted by the marketplace at large. (A particularly clear example of this new vehicle sector swap was the introduction of "Yankee" bonds in 1976).

Another classic example of a sector swap opportunity presented itself both in 1972 and early 1973. By giving up as little as 15 basis points, one could have swapped out of A Utilities into the very highest grade AAA Telephone issues. Even without the benefit of hindsight, this would have seemed like a very narrow give-up at the time. Once again, by delving behind the historical yield spreads, the manager could have determined that this narrow spread arose in part from an unusually forceful "reaching for yield" by many major market participants. It was not too difficult to expect that this special condition would abate at some point in the future, and that quality differentials would consequently widen. During this time, a number of portfolio managers actually implemented very sizeable swap programs into the higher quality corporates. (In certain cases, these managers found themselves having to continually defend the resulting give-ups in yield.) Such sector swaps proved *enormously* profitable over the ensuing months, probably far more so than could have reasonably been expected.

The sector swap has many appealing aspects, and it is thought by many to be one of the most professional forms of the bond manager's art.

At times in 1973, the field of bond portfolio management seemed ready to embark upon a grand new era of sector swapping.

Then performance measurement came to the bond market.

The Rise of Performance Measurement. From the end of 1972 through the Fall of 1974, interest rates on new AA long Utility issues rose by over 300 basis points. A typical portfolio of long corporates had its market value eroded by 6 percent over calendar 1973, and by a further 16 percent in the first nine months of 1974. The resulting effect upon the asset value of bond portfolios is well known. The enduring effects of these markets upon bond portfolio management may not be quite so evident.

These market problems came at a time when bond portfolio management was becoming increasingly competitive. Bond portfolios were beginning to be subjected to the same type of short-term performance measurement as had been applied to equity portfolios. The performance results of successful bond managers were being rapidly incorporated into the process for marketing their services.

Since calendar years constitute regrettably important time frames in the world of investment performance, the results of calendar 1973 loomed particularly large. Unquestionably, the 1973 markets gave a great boost to the use of performance measurement in the bond world. In 1973 and most of 1974, anyone who believed that long rates would rise could move into the short-term markets and get an incentive yield to do so, because of the higher short rates relative to long rates. A number of major fund managers did believe this and acted accordingly. Large reserve positions were accumulated. Conversely, there were others who for various reasons, ranging from an uncertainty to a conscious philosophy, kept investing their cash flows into the long-term markets. This sequence of events led to a great gulf between the short-term performances obtained by managers who followed one point of view versus those who followed the other. The magnitude of this gulf led to a trumpeting and comparison of performance results that may have significantly accelerated the incursion of the performance concept into the bond market.

It also led to very difficult times for those bond managers who remained in the long market. No matter how meticulously and profitably they may have executed pure yield pick-up swaps, substitution swaps, or sector swaps, their performance results were disastrous when compared with the managers who stayed in the short term market.

These effects are clearly shown by the Salomon Brothers Total Return Index for the high-grade long-term corporate bond market. This Index was developed in 1973 (with results backdated to 1969) [4]. Figure 2 shows how a $100 investment in the Index on January 1, 1969 would have grown, assuming full reinvestment of coupon income, to a cumulative value of $180 by the beginning of 1979.

Figure 3 provides a somewhat more sobering picture, at least for the bond portfolio manager. The year-by-year Index returns are compared with the assured annual returns available in one-year Treasury Bills.

Figure 2
Salomon Brothers High-Grade Long-Term Corporate Rate-of-Return Index—
Cumulative Change in Market Value of Rate-of-Return Index (including reinvestment)

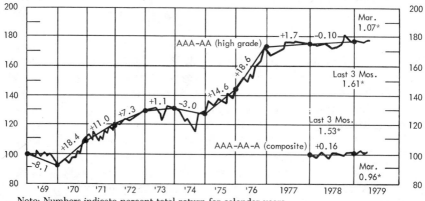

Note: Numbers indicate percent total return for calendar years.
* Nonannualized.
Source: © Salomon Brothers 1979.

Figure 3
Annual Total Returns: Long Corporates versus One-Year Treasury Bills

Year	One-Year Treasury Bills	Salomon Brothers High-Grade Long-Term Corporate Rate-of-Return Index	Incremental Return from High-Grade Long-Term Corporates
1969	6.55%	−8.10%	−14.65%
1970	8.09	18.38	+10.29
1971	4.89	11.02	+6.13
1972	4.13	7.26	+3.13
1973	5.68	1.14	−4.54
1974	7.21	−3.04	−10.25
1975	7.07	14.64	+7.57
1976	6.31	18.64	+12.33
1977	4.82	1.70	−3.12
1978	6.93	−.10	−7.03
Ten-Year Period	6.16%	5.79%	−.37%

While volatile bond markets did not originate with the 1973–74 debacle, this was the first time that such horrendous results were accompanied by widespread tracking of portfolio performance. The sorry returns of 1974 (or perhaps "nonreturns" would be a more apt expression) led to several important changes in the perception and practice of bond portfolio management.

One immediate effect was to put to rest the myth that the corporate bond market could be viewed as an essentially low-volatility haven for balanced portfolios. Over the years, many fund sponsors had come to view their portfolio allocation in terms of two components: (1) a risky, volatile equity portion, and (2) a safe, reliable (and usually dull) bond portion. In essence, this meant that the key decision was to determine the equity fraction, with the remainder being tacitly assigned to the "nonequity" asset—bonds. As Figure 3 shows all too clearly, while bonds may not be able to match the historical return volatility of common stocks, today's bond market has a significant wild streak all its own. For sponsors seeking reductions in their fund's overall level of volatility risk, this clearly implied a greater focus on the intermediate and shorter maturity areas of the fixed income markets. This may have led to a shortening in the average maturity of many bond portfolios whose purpose was to provide this "nonequity" alternative.

A different effect was felt among the more fully managed bond portfolios. With these funds, the primary objective was to achieve the maximum rate-of-return within the fixed income market. Given this objective, the most successful managers were those who had foreseen the 1973–74 surge in interest rates and had acted to restructure their portfolios into the shorter maturities. These were the managers who had successfully engaged in the first step of the fourth form of swap activity—the rate anticipation swap. The overt and well-advertised success of these managers who had "gone to cash" in the 1973–74 period forced many other portfolio managers to give more serious consideration to the benefits of rate anticipation. In particular, it led to a more open view regarding opportunistic departures from the long term maturity area that many managers had previously considered to be the "natural" arena for their fixed income assets.

In fact, at times in 1974, the short-term market looked almost too good to many investors. Some managers began to question whether long-term bonds were ever worth the extra risk relative to the assured return available in the then higher yield short-term market. There was a tendency to forget that the short-term market had its own type of risk. This particular overswing of the pendulum was dramatically corrected by the events of 1975 and 1976.

In 1975 and 1976, interest rates turned lower. As Figure 2 shows, the long-term corporate bond market provided outstanding levels of total return in 1975 (14.6 percent) and again in 1976 (18.6 percent). This turnaround confirmed the total return viability of the long-term market. Moreover, as seen in Figure 3, this was accompanied by reductions in the returns available in the short-term market.

Over this four-year period from 1973 to 1976, the best performance was achieved not by constant adherence to the long-term market nor by continually rolling over short maturities. Rather the managers with outstanding performance were those few who had "gone to cash" during the 1973–74 period and then had been able to reinvest themselves into the long market in time to participate in the 1975–76 rally. This underscored the "round trip" character of successful rate anticipation. One good timing decision is not enough. To be effective, the rate anticipator must not only "go to cash" at the right time, but must then subsequently choose the right time to "go long" again.

In 1977 and 1978, the bond market turned sour once again. The High-Grade Index provided returns of +1.7 percent and −.1 percent, respectively, in each of these years. The year 1978 ended with an inverted yield curve that was reminiscent of the 1974 era. These combined events demonstrated in practice what had been obvious in theory: when interest rates exhibit a strong cyclic pattern that dominates any secular trend, then consistently superior portfolio returns can only be found through successful "riding of the cycle," i.e., through rate anticipation.

Rate Anticipation and the Yield Illusion. The rate anticipation swap can be the most productive bond portfolio action; it is also the riskiest.

The key to successful rate anticipation is correct timing judgment.

With effective timing being such a critical element, it is most important that the portfolio manager avoid having one's judgment distracted or biased by secondary or tertiary factors. Unfortunately, the traditional instinct toward yield improvement can often exercise just such a distractive influence on the rate anticipation swapper. For example, high levels of interest rates are often accompanied by inverted yield curves. Under such conditions money market rates exceed the yields of long-term bonds and it is very natural for a bond portfolio manager to feel comfortable having a large reserve portion of funds "parked" in the short-term market. Even if one expects long-term rates to peak out at some point during the next several months, the higher yields earned on the reserve funds can be quite enticing. Indeed, with the yields favoring the short-term market, it would only be human for one to feel somewhat more at ease with one's present portfolio structure, to be somewhat less anxious in tracking of the long-term market, and, therefore, to be somewhat less eager to initiate any extension process on an anticipation basis.

On the other hand, if short-term rates were to fall, especially if they were to decline rather precipitously, then this same portfolio manager might well shift one's orientation and begin to focus on the relative yield loss entailed in remaining short. This apparent opportunity cost might then make the manager more eager to invest one's reserve into the now higher-yielding long market. This sense of an opportunity cost might consequently influence one's timing judgments regarding the bottoming out of the long market.

In the first case, the portfolio manager feels secure with the reserve portion because of its high relative yield rate. In the second case, the manager is becoming more anxious because the reserve now represents a yield loss. In both cases, the portfolio manager could be making the very big mistake of being beguiled by the "yield illusion."

The nature of this mistake can be seen from the simple mathematics of total return. Over a period of months, the incremental return accumulated by being short under even a sharply inverted yield curve can be wiped out by a very minor movement in the long-term market. Figure 4 shows the yield moves in the long market required to wipe out the accumulated return from having funds "parked" in the higher yielding market for a prescribed period of time. For example, with short rates at 10.00 percent and long rates at 8.50 percent, the accumulated yield advantage of being short for three months would be wiped out if long rates suddenly moved downward by as little as 4 basis points.

The key point here is that the portfolio manager should not allow timing judgments to be unduly influenced by the level of return available in the short-term "parking lot." This is not to say that the short-term market should be ignored. The action of short rates will, of course,

Figure 4
Basis Point Move in Long Rates (30-year 8.50 percent par bond)
Required to Offset Accumulated Yield Gain or Loss in Short Market

Short Rates	Time Invested at Short Rate			
	3 Months	6 Months	9 Months	12 Months
11.00%	−6	−12	−17	−23
10.50	−5	− 9	−14	−18
10.00	−4	− 7	−11	−14
9.50	−3	− 5	− 7	− 9
9.00	−1	− 2	− 4	− 5
8.50	+0	+ 0	+ 0	+ 0
8.00	+1	+ 2	+ 3	+ 5
7.50	+2	+ 5	+ 7	+ 9
7.00	+3	+ 7	+10	+14

Note: Short rates are quoted on simple annualized returns and no reinvestment is assumed for the long bond.

influence the long market and might even provide clues regarding a turn in the long market. However, this role of the short-term market as a possible signal should be distinguished from consideration of the short-term market as a relatively attractive or unattractive haven for waiting funds. These conclusion depends on the waiting period being measured in months, not years. For the portfolio manager who believes that the long bond market is in for a sustained slide and that any turnaround will be years in coming, then the level of available short (and intermediate) rates must, of course, enter more significantly into the manager's risk-reward equation.

For the portfolio manager engaged in rate anticipation, the crucial focus must be on effective round trip timing of entries into and exits from the long market. The manager cannot become distracted by the changing level of short rates. The relative yield advantage or yield loss on the reserves temporarily placed in the short market will have a miniscule impact on performance compared with even a modest movement in the long market. If the market situation follows the manager's scenario, then the superior performance will be accorded to the manager who correctly anticipates the turning point—not just verbally—but in terms of a well-timed and well-implemented restructuring of a significant portion of "parked" reserve funds.

Yield Curve Anticipation: Snap-Ups and Snap-Downs. The preceding discussion placed the primary emphasis on effective timing. This is particularly true for a long-term fund. However, it tacitly implied that there is only one method of reentering the long market—direct investment in long-maturity instruments. In light of how the 1974–75 market evolved, there are a number of alternative "reentry" techniques that are worthy of serious consideration. For example, Figure 5 shows the Treasury yield curves on September 1, 1974 and March

Figure 5
Historical Yield Curves

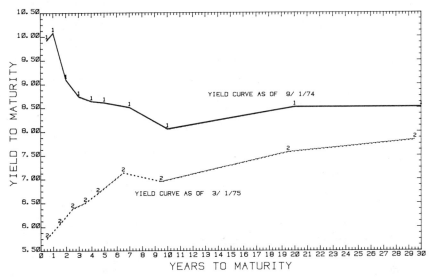

1, 1975. Over this six-month period, rates not only declined, but the yield curve "snapped down" from an inverted shape to a mildly positive shape. This "snap down" effect resulted in intermediate maturities undergoing a much greater downward movement in yield than the longs. For example, the five-year maturity declined by 170 basis points, almost 2½ times greater than the 68 basis point improvement at 30-years. Moveover, an investment in the five-year maturity on September 1, 1974 would have "aged" to a 4½-year maturity over the six-month holding period, thus adding some further yield improvement. The combination of these factors is shown in Figure 6. Here, the vertical axis depicts the annualized total return obtained from a continuously held investment at the indicated maturity point. From Figure 6, one can see that the performance of the five-year investment came very close to that of the long end over this particular period.

This should not be interpreted as a general endorsement of the intermediate maturity. It merely indicates that the "snap down" from a peaking inverted curve can lead to surprisingly attractive intermediate returns. It should also be pointed out that in deteriorating markets, there can also be a "snap up" effect with the result that intermediates perform worse than longs. This "snap up" has burned numerous investors who believed that intermediates offered reduced price volatility relative to longs. (On "average," the intermediates probably do have less price volatility than longs. However, strongly inverted or strongly positive yield curve shapes are not reflective of "average conditions.")

A good example of the "snap up" occurred in the course of calendar

Figure 6
Annualized Historical Returns from September 1, 1974 to March 1, 1975

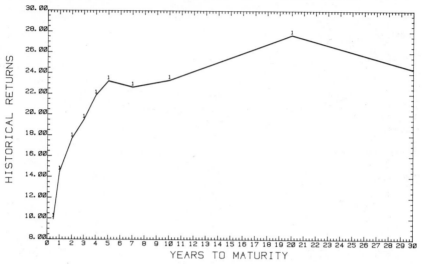

1978, when the Treasury yield curve changed significantly in both level and shape. As depicted in Figure 7, the change in the level of rates over 1978 ranged from approximately +100 basis points in 30-year maturities to over +350 basis points at the one-year point. These yield changes reshaped the yield curve. The moderately positive shape at the beginning of 1978 turned into a strongly inverted shape at the end of the year. One measure of this shape change is the spread of 30-year over one-year rates. This spread began the year at about +100 basis points and ended at over −150 basis points.

This was not a good year for reaping returns from the bond market. Figure 8 shows the total returns achieved over 1978 by investments along the yield curve. An investment in a 30-year Treasury security at the beginning of 1978 would have led to a market loss of some 9 points. The price loss would have more than offset the coupon income resulting in a negative total return over the one-year period. There is little surprise in the result that with such movements in rate levels, long-term bonds provided negative total return. However, many investors might be surprised to learn that any investment along the yield curve with a maturity of seven years or longer resulted in an essentially zero or negative return. In fact, for investments between seven and 30 years, the investment returns all fell within the narrow range of −2.0 percent to +.2 percent.

As a point of comparison with the corporate bond market, the Salomon Brothers Long-Term Bond Index provided a 1978 return of −.1 percent. In Figure 8, the Index return is plotted to correspond with

Figure 7
Yield Curves at Beginning and End of 1978

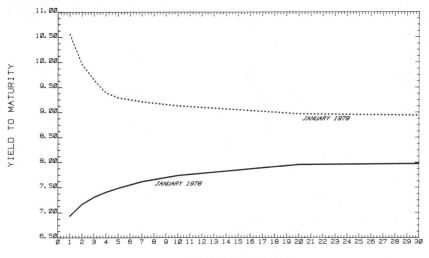

YEARS TO MATURITY

its average maturity of 24 years. As a second point of comparison, Figure 8 also shows the 1978 performance figure of 2.39 percent from the Salomon Brothers Total Return Index for Mortgage Pass-Through Securities [12].

Figure 8 clearly shows that, to have avoided the adverse effects of 1978, the bond portfolio manager with good hindsight would have needed to have been fully invested in maturities under three years (or even better yet, under one year!).

This pattern of returns of 1978, including the sorry behavior of the intermediate area, reflects the "snap up" in the shape of the yield curve that is evident from Figure 7. This provides an interesting contrast to the "snap down" effect over the six-month period following the peaking of rates in September, 1974.

In both periods, even though the market moved in opposite directions, the total return behavior of intermediates came significantly close to that of the longs. There were two reasons for this close comparability. First of all, the 1978 "snap up" and the 1974 "snap down" both resulted in intermediate yields changing considerably more than long rates. The second reason is that maturity is only a crude guide to price volatility. For example, even given the same movement in yield, a 30-year bond would only have a 50 percent greater price movement than a 12-year bond. The intermediates' much higher yield volatility compensated for their reduced price volatility to produce returns that were comparable with longs—over these two particular periods.

Figure 8
Historical Returns, (January 1, 1978–January 1, 1979)

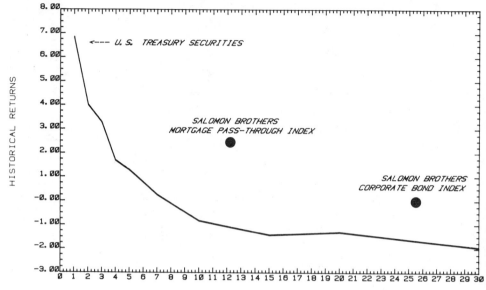

The prospects of yield curve reshaping can add an important refinement and balance to the rate anticipation process. For example, suppose a manager with a defensive short-term posture anticipates that the long market rates are approaching a peak. The manager must then determine the correct time to begin deploying at least a portion of short-term reserves. This action may be based either on the manager's definite belief that the peak level of rates is actually at hand or simply as a counterbalance to one's uncertainty as to when and how that peak will occur. In any case, once the decision has been made to commit some reserves, then the second decision must be to select the most appropriate maturity sector. If the manager believes that there is a good prospect for lower rates to be accompanied by a "snap down" in the yield curve, then intermediate maturities should be explored as an interesting reentry vehicle on a risk-reward basis. On the one hand, if rates improve and the yield curve does "snap down" to a more positive shape, then the right intermediate maturities can provide returns that are comparable to the long market. On the other hand, should long rates continue to rise (without a significant increase in the degree of inversion) then the shorter maturity of the intermediates will provide a certain protection against the full deterioration that would be experienced in the long market.

Finding the best distribution of maturities to take advantage of yield curve reshaping is no simple matter. In many instances, the proper balance of return may be available only with a rather narrow range of maturities. A number of analytic techniques have been developed to assist portfolio managers who wish to incorporate yield curve anticipation into their strategic process [6].

Productive use of yield curve judgments has a long history with commercial bank portfolios and other institutions with sizeable short-term portfolios. However, until recently, this approach has not found widespread use among managers of long-term pension funds. This appears to be changing, as pension fund managers become more aware of the important edge that yield curve anticipation can offer at certain points in the interest rate and yield curve cycle.

Prospective Problems in Rate Anticipation

In 1973, and even in 1974, there were relatively few bond portfolio managers who were significant rate anticipators.

However, over the subsequent four years, long-term interest rates followed a cyclic pattern (Figure 1) that was roughly similar to the 1970–74 experience. The resulting cyclic pattern of total returns (shown in Figure 2) underscored the potential of rate anticipation for bond managers who found themselves coming under increasing competitive pressure based upon performance comparisons. This proved to be an almost irresistible attraction, and more and more managers became partially or even totally committed to rate anticipation.

The tidal wave markets of 1973–78 seemed to sweep aside all the minutiae of what used to be called professional bond management. The incremental returns from yield pick-up, substitution, and sector swapping all appeared inconsequential in comparison with the massive effects of overall rate movements in the long market. The only question of import seems to be: whither long rates? Rate guessing, rate talking, rate anticipation have become the major and sometimes the sole preoccupation of many bond market participants.

This trend, if continued, would mean that only one form of active bond management would appear worthwhile—the rate anticipation swap.

This creates a number of basic problems for the practice of bond portfolio management.

First of all, many portfolio managers judge rates to be high or low based largely upon their experience with past rate cycles. For these managers, rate anticipation shares the danger in any cycle-related mode of investment that the manager's judgement may be biased by the belief (either explicit or implicit) that historical patterns will continue into the future.

Cycles do get broken. Aberrant events do occur. Debacles do take place. Secular trends do fade out and are sometimes reversed. Unforeseen problems do arise—in fact, frequently. yet the world manages to muddle through and even find new ways of coping with adverse trends and overcoming seemingly overwhelming obstacles.

For example, in 1973–74, the financial markets appeared to be discounting a variety of "horror scenarios." By and large, these disasters failed to materialize (at least right away), and there followed enormous rallies in both the bond and stock markets. On the one hand, one could read this lesson as a cyclic event supporting maximum market commitment at the point of deepest gloom and doom. On the other hand one could argue that the markets were basically correct in their assessment of the possibility of dire events—but that these horrors just didn't happen that particular time. (From this latter viewpoint, the lesson is that the financial markets attempt to reflect the full range of possible economic and political scenarios. Since only one of these possible scenarios can actually take place, the market's judgment can hardly be faulted in its perceptions just because all the other scenarios failed to occur. In other words, the market may not have been wrong in its grim judgment—the world may have been simply lucky!)

For an insightful discussion of some other facets of this "interest rate cycle risk," see Chapter 9, "Management of Bond Portfolios," by H. Russell Fogler.

All of this suggests that a superficial reading of the history of past cyclic events may prove a shaky guide for future action.

A second danger, related to the first, is that the very proliferation of rate anticipators could make rate anticipation much more difficult. During 1973–78, the force of economic events and market fundamentals overshadowed the role of bond portfolio managers. During this period, rate anticipators did not have to worry about other anticipators getting in their way and perhaps even preempting changes in the market's direction. However, as the rate anticipators crowd the market, this will in itself create a sizeable new element of uncertainty.

When there is widespread accumulation of anticipatory reserves, the problem of correct timing becomes much more difficult than usual. Once the market is perceived to be reaching a major peak, one can envision a torrent of funds being injected into the market within a concentrated period of time. Under such conditions correct timing must be interpreted as "anticipating the anticipators," and getting one's own funds largely invested before the market moves to new rate levels. In an environment where huge amounts of funds are poised to anticipate the next change in long-term rates, it is hard to see every money manager outperforming colleagues on a sustained round-trip basis by correctly calling (and implementing) each topping- and bottoming-out of the rate cycle.

Theoretically, one could envision so many funds engaged in rate anticipation that their activity could itself largely determine the level of the long-term bond market. The longer maturity area of the bond market would then tend to become delinked from the underlying economic cycle. Since any fundamental cyclic pattern could be fully anticipated and then discounted, one could ultimately see the disappearance of interest rate cycles as we know them today. Naturally, the closer the market approaches this theoretical point of full anticipation, the harder it will become to be a consistently successful rate anticipator.

A third general problem is that rate anticipation tends to overwhelm the incremental returns from any other form of bond management, even those that could prove more reliable on a year-after-year basis.

This third problem of rate anticipation is not a simple question of whether the portfolio manager should or should not try to forecast changes in long interest rates and act accordingly. In fact, it may be impossible for a manager not to be influenced by his or her own general market expectations. Moreover, one can legitimately argue that every form of swap activity is affected, to some degree, by overall movements in long rates. There is no relationship between two issues or two sectors which is totally free from the effects of a major market move. (As a result of the subsequent general deterioration in the long market after the Fall of 1973, even the classic sector swap involving GNMA passthroughs proved more successful than could have been anticipated on the basis of spread relationships alone.)

The question is not one of trying to stonily ignore one's market expectations, but rather a question of degree and intent. Ideally speaking, in substitution and sector swaps, the intention is to render a primary judgment on spread relationships and to factor out, to the extent possible, the impact of overall market movements.

Nor is the question one of trying to rule out rate anticipation swaps. This has proven enormously profitable for some portfolios, and no one should try to deny that success. A high degree of rate anticipation is embedded in the style of many very successful managers. Many managers devote great efforts, both individually and organizationally, to staying attuned to the latest public and private economic thinking. Rate anticipation is a perfectly legitimate form of swap activity, but it is characterized by a high potential payoff and an especially high risk.

By their nature, fixed income portfolios tend to be very risk-sensitive. The avoidance of risk often constituted the primary reason for the funds having been directed into the fixed-income markets in the first place. Consequently, any effort to obtain incremental return should be viewed through a prism reflecting the specific risk structure of the given portfolio.

The danger comes from lumping together all forms of bond management activity into one basket, without differentiation as to risk and intent. This danger is compounded when one crude performance yardstick is used to measure and compare portfolios and management efforts which differ widely in purpose and character. Without risk differentiation, the impact of rate movements would overwhelm all other forms of management activity. Without risk differentiation, the professional manager whose style runs more to substitution and sector swaps would, no matter how competent or successful, be deprived of both due credit and credibility. And all bond managers would be forced by these circumstances into concentrating solely on a continuing day-to-day frenzy of trying to anticipate an ever more anticipatory market, under a growing specter of serious performance and principal losses. This would be a most unfortunate state of affairs and one which would ultimately prove to be a no-win situation for professional bond management as a whole.

THE BASELINE METHOD FOR RELATING SHORT-TERM PERFORMANCE TO LONG-TERM GOALS

The Yardstick of Total Return

Many of the problems confronting today's bond portfolio manager can be traced to the sole reliance upon total return comparisons over short-term periods. Total return measurements do provide a useful yardstick of the extent to which the portfolio manager took advantage of general market opportunities during the measurement period. But this is only one factor in the complex process of portfolio management. A fundamental problem seems to arise when a single yardstick—total return measurement over short-term periods—is taken as the sole yardstick for all management activity.

This concentration on the single yardstick of total return can force dangerously simplistic comparisons among portfolios that may actually differ widely in function and purpose. In fact, the same level of achieved return may represent a very satisfactory result for one portfolio while having quite dismal implications for another portfolio with a different set of goals.

Moreover, even within a given portfolio, an overemphasis on short-term return can lead to conflicts with the long-term goals of the fund. For example, it could lead the portfolio manager into concentrating activity on catching short-term swings in interest rates. In turn, this excessive rate anticipation could lead to a frequent series of major portfolio shifts, thereby introducing considerable timing risk into the overall management process. The resulting volatility risk might be in direct contradiction to the original purpose of placing the funds into a fixed-income portfolio in the first place. This is just one instance of how an exclusive focus on maximization of total return over short periods can violate a fund's policy constraints and cause deviations from the fund's true long-term objectives.

These problems are particularly acute for fixed-income portfolios because of certain distinctive characteristics of the bond market. Much of the institutional investment in bonds is motivated by long-term, risk-avoidance purposes. These long-term purposes typically over-shadow any specific requirement for total return over short-term periods.

Thus, the ideal solution would be to find some concrete way of relating the returns achieved over short-term measurement periods to the fund's long-term goals.

We believe that such goal-oriented management is indeed possible through application of a technique which we call "the baseline portfolio." This technique combines the modern total return approach with a back-to-the fundamentals concept reminiscent of the pre-1970s style of bond portfolio management. [2]

The Baseline Portfolio

In theory, the portfolio mangement process can be viewed as consisting of the four major steps shown in Figure 9. The first step is to identify the long-term objectives of the fund. The second step commences with the manager's judgments regarding market prospects. At this point, the manager must make the broad decisions that relate

Figure 9
Overview of the
Portfolio Management
Process

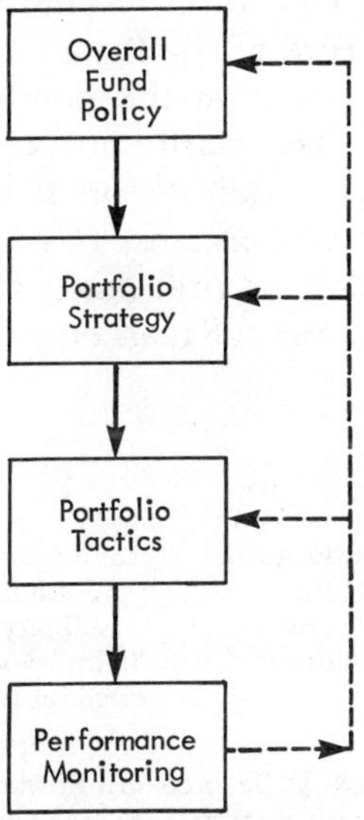

to portfolio strategy, i.e., to determine the portfolio's maturity structure. The rate and yield curve anticipation efforts would fall into this category of strategy decisions. Once this has been done, the third step consists of deciding upon the detailed portfolio tactics to be employed. These consist of selecting specific sectors to take advantage of perceived market opportunities. Sector and substitution swap activity would lie in this area of tactical decisions. The fourth step then consists of a continuing performance monitoring (in the most general sense) to ensure that the portfolio objectives are being fulfilled.

The first step is far more difficult than generally believed. It is no simple matter to identify a full set of portfolio objectives and then to define these objectives in a useful way. Such efforts tend to lead to either a frustratingly vague description of the objectives or an impossibly long collection of goals which mix the minor considerations in with the major ones.

For example, Figure 10 illustrates a partial list of the many objectives that could be ascribed to fixed-income portfolios. Moreover, any set of objectives are closely intertwined with an associated set of risk factors. (In this connection, risk is being defined in a far broader sense than the single volatility measure which has become traditional in many modern analyses. In the sense used here, risk entails all those potential events that could interfere with the portfolio being able to fulfill its long-term objectives.) When there are a large number of potential objectives and associated risk factors, it is no easy task to generate concrete guidelines for portfolio managers.

The purpose of the baseline portfolio is to provide a practical procedure for articulating the fund's long-term objectives in a concrete and useful fashion. The underlying idea is to take advantage of the relatively well-defined sector structure of the fixed income market.

An important characteristic of the bond market is the structural clarity of its asset classes. This clarity enables the return-risk relationships among the different market sectors to be relatively well-defined, especially over longer term horizons. The longer term motivation of investors and the market's structural clarity obviously fit hand-in-glove, allowing for the identification of market sectors that are particularly

Figure 10
Portfolio Objectives

Maximum Long-Term Nominal Return	Tax Liability Management
Maximum Long-Term Real Return	Liquidity Warehouse
Match Prescribed Liability Schedule	Stability of Principal
Reserve against Uncertain Liabilities	Stability of Income over Time
Earnings Contribution	Facilitate Corporate Flexibility
Earnings Management	Corporate Compliance

Aura of Balance and Prudence

well suited for serving the specific goals of a given fund. By selecting market sectors to match the fund's objectives and associated risk factors, one should be able to develop a portfolio structure which best suits the fund's long-term goals (see Figure 11). This is called the fund's Baseline Portfolio [10].

Since the baseline portfolio structure should be determined primarily by the long-range considerations, it should be relatively independent of the active manager's day-to-day market judgments. Thus, the baseline portfolio could be defined as the most balanced possible fulfillment of all of the fund's complex objectives and goals in the absence of an active market-related management activity. In other words, the baseline is that passive portfolio which carries the least risk relative to the fund's long-term goals.

Management Activity Relative to the Baseline Portfolio

From the vantage point of the baseline portfolio, one purpose of investment management is to take advantage of market opportunities. Active management can then be viewed as a series of strategic and tactical judgments such as those shown in Figure 12. These judgments

Figure 11
The Theoretical Baseline Portfolio

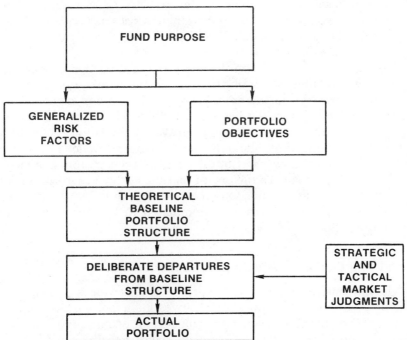

Figure 12
Active Bond Portfolio Management

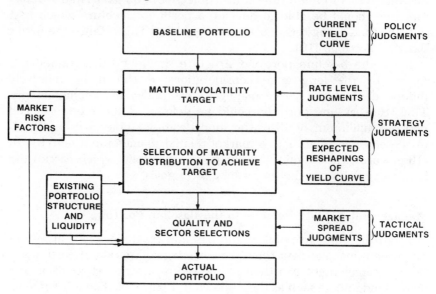

would lead to market-motivated departures from the baseline portfolio in an effort to achieve improved portfolio results. The resulting portfolio improvements—as well as the incremental risks incurred in achieving them—should theoretically be measured against the yardstick of the baseline portfolio itself.

The portfolio manager, in selecting the actual portfolio, clearly incurs an incremental risk in departing from the baseline portfolio. By so doing, one seeks an incremental return above and beyond what could be achieved with the baseline portfolio. Therefore, the benchmark for measuring the portfolio's return is the return that could have been achieved by simply holding the baseline portfolio. In essence, the baseline constitutes a sort of total return index customized to the fund's individual goals. To the extent that the achieved return exceeds the baseline return, the portfolio manager has added to the achievement of the portfolio goals as denominated in the currency of the Baseline Portfolio itself.

Evaluating Proposed Departures from the Baseline

The baseline portfolio can serve prospective as well as retrospective functions. At the beginning of each investment period, the baseline can help the portfolio manager to gauge—in a quantitative, objective fashion—the incremental risk incurred relative to these same goals.

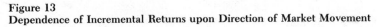

Figure 13
Dependence of Incremental Returns upon Direction of Market Movement

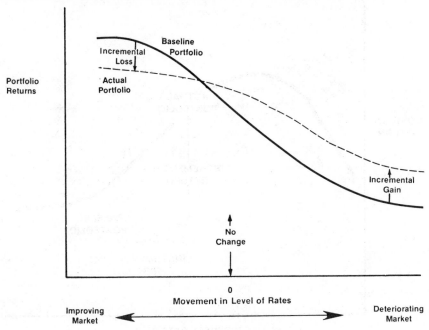

This prospective application of the baseline portfolio may be the most important one of all.

Figure 13 illustrates how a manager can compare one's actual portfolio's return profile to that of the baseline. Here the projected returns from the two portfolios are plotted across a range of potential movements in the overall level of interest rates. These "return vectors" [6] clearly show the nature of the tradeoffs involved in the departure from the baseline. The actual portfolio is considerably more defensive than the baseline; as long as the market stays at the same level or deteriorates (i.e., rises in yield level), the actual portfolio will outperform the baseline. There will be a loss relative to the baseline only under improving market conditions (i.e., declining yields). The choice of the actual portfolio suggests that the manager has a rather pessimistic outlook on the market, or feels that incremental performance is more important in dreary markets.

Another way of exploring this risk-return trade-off is for the manager to assign probabilities to the different rate movements. The expected returns (i.e., the probability-weighted average returns) can then be plotted as shown in Figure 14. The horizontal axis in Figure 14 represents some measure of portfolio aggressiveness—i.e., interest rate risk.

Figure 14
Market-Motivated Departures from the Baseline Portfolio

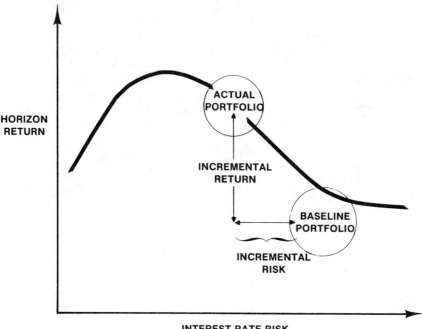

As noted earlier, the maturity structure is the most important decision made by an active portfolio manager. By varying the maturity
structure, one can control the amount of interest rate risk contained
in the portfolio. Various proxies for the interest rate risk of a portfolio
have been proposed—average maturity, historical variability, percentage price volatility, Macaulay's duration, horizon volatility, proportional volatility [8]. However, for any of these measures, the baseline
can be viewed as the reference point. To the extent that the active
manager departs from this baseline level of interest rate risk, one risks
falling below the baseline's performance.

This holds true for departures in both directions.

In the case of Figure 14, the manager is making a "defensive departure" from the baseline's risk level. By choosing a portfolio with less
interest rate sensitivity than the baseline, the manager hopes to obtain
a sizeable improvement in incremental returns, given a basically pessimistic outlook. However, the manager is exposing the portfolio to a
considerable shortfall in return relative to the baseline in the event
that this pessimistic outcome fails to materialize.

One should take note of the apparent paradox in the situation portrayed in Figure 14. The greatest risk here is the prospect of a stronger-

than-expected downward move in interest rates. This action would normally be viewed as an improving market. However, in this case, such a market improvement would lead to underperformance relative to the baseline portfolio, and hence would constitute the gravest threat to the fund's progress towards its long-term goals.

Figure 14 thus shows how a manager can gauge incremental interest rate risk relative to the baseline and, by implication, measure more generalized risk relative to long-term goals. There may be some controversy regarding what constitutes a satisfactory measure of interest rate risk. However, there is no disagreement that a greater level of risk consciousness needs to be introduced into the management process. Once any such volatility measure has been selected, the procedure implied in Figures 13 or 14 can be quantified, thereby providing the manager (and the sponsor) with a concrete, numerical indication of the incremental risk associated with a prospective portfolio strategy.

Sources of Return

This approach can be further refined by combining it with an analysis of the component sources of prospective return. In the first part of this article, we described four main categories of bond portfolio activity—pure yield pick-up, substitution swap, sector spread swaps, and rate anticipation. A given portfolio structure will typically contain (intentionally or not) some degree of each activity. By identifying the components of bond return, one can associate each category of management activity with its corresponding contribution to the return-risk characteristics of the overall portfolio. One such technique identifies eight component sources of return:

1. Yield curve accumulation,
2. Sector spread accumulation,
3. Rolling yield effect,
4. Revaluation in sector spread,
5. Market shifts,
6. Yield curve reshaping,
7. Sector response to yield curve changes, and
8. Specific issue spread action beyond that of the associated sector.

Another way of analyzing these return components is in terms of the kind of risks they represent. Thus, the combination of the first three components is simply the sector's rolling yield [9]. This rolling yield return is fairly well assured for sectors whose quality is not in doubt. In constrast, the revaluation return reflects a spread judgment that the sector is undervalued. There may be considerable risk surrounding any such projected revaluation.

The next three components of return, the resulting yield curve re-

Figure 15
Sector Returns for a Range of Market Shifts

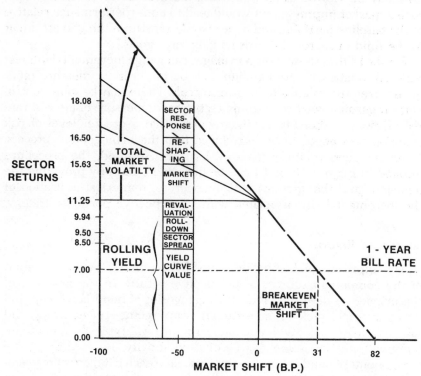

shaping, and the sector spread response, all depend on the magnitude of the overall market movement. It is useful to combine these three volatility factors into a measure of the sector's total market volatility.

Figure 15 provides a graphic representation of the relationships among these different return components and risk categories. A detailed explanation of this approach is contained in the author's study *Sources of Return in Corporate Bond Portfolios* [10].

These classification techniques have been developed to assist the investment manager in organizing and quantifying the many market judgements that are embedded in one's portfolio structure. The classification process also highlights the nature of the different risks incurred, as well as the differences in their portfolio impact over varying investment horizons. By analyzing the marketplace in terms of this same classification system, the manager may be better able to construct a portfolio having a desired set of characteristics. This classification procedure could also prove helpful in more precisely identifying the manager's motivation behind an intended departure from a goal-oriented baseline portfolio.

Communication between Sponsor and Manager

The baseline portfolio approach can facilitate the communication process between sponsor and manager.

At the outset, the baseline portfolio should itself be the result of discussions between the fund's sponsor and the manager. In these initial discussions, the sponsor must try to convey her sense of the fund's purpose, to define her overall objectives and their relative priorities, and to identify, and delimit, the risk factors that concern her. On the other hand, the manager contributes knowledge of the behavioral characteristics of the various asset classes, along with beliefs as to how they will function in the context of different portfolio structures. (At this point, the manager should try to put aside personal perceptions of immediate market value, and concentrate on the general long-term characteristics of the various market sectors.)

In all too many instances, this interchange tends to remain at a rather fuzzy level of generality, with both parties espousing the obviously desirable "Nirvana points," e.g., maximum return with minimum risk, highest yield without sacrifice of quality, minimum volatility with greatest stability of income, etc. If the discussion of goals ends at this point, then neither party has communicated a sense of the appropriate trade-offs. In a rather fundamental sense, no real understanding has been achieved.

However, a joint determination to specify a baseline portfolio can drive these discussions down to the concrete level. It will force the difficult choices to be made—and made jointly by both sponsor and manager. The sponsor must articulate the subtle priorities that can organize many objectives, and must develop a clear-cut structure by relating these priorities—with the manager's help—to choices between specific market sectors. The manager must rise above his or her active orientation to define the most balanced, passive portfolio structure matching the client's needs. In this fashion, both parties are able to merge and consolidate their different points of view. In essence, by specifying a baseline portfolio, they have come to agree on a practical, passive alternative to active management.

As with any real process of communication, these interactions may prove painful and arduous at the outset. However, once defined, the baseline can prove a mutual vantage point for interpreting the actual returns achieved over time. The all-too-common on-going confusion between conflicting short-term results and long-term goals will be reduced. Because of the sponsor's role in defining the baseline, the manager will no longer be quite so vulnerable to criticism for the many portfolio effects that are (in reality) mandated by the nature of the fund. In particular, having the baseline may considerably reduce artificial pressures on a manager with regard to high volatility, yield give-ups, particularly high- or low-quality postures, having the portfolio balanced away from the general market structure, or for deviations from the performance returns achieved by general market indices or theoretical peer groups.

Moreover, by concentrating the objective-setting in an initial phase shared with the sponsor, the baseline approach should allow the investment manager to focus more clearly on day-by-day market activities in the fund's behalf. At the same time, the fund sponsor will achieve the security of knowing that long term risk-return objectives are not being inadvertently compromised in the pursuit of short-term performance.

REFERENCES

1. Homer, Sidney, and Leibowitz, Martin L. *Inside the Yield Book.* Englewood Cliffs, N.J.: Prentice-Hall, Inc. and New York Institute of Finance, 1972.

2. Leibowitz, Martin L. "Goal-Oriented Bond Portfolio Management: The "Baseline" Method for Relating Short-Term Performance to Long-Term Goals." New York: Salomon Brothers, May 15, 1978. (Now Chapter 1, in *Total Return Management.* New York: Salomon Brothers, 1979).

3. Leibowitz, Martin L. "The Horizon Annuity: An Investment Measure for Linking the Growth and Payout Phases of Long-Term Bond Portfolio." New York: Salomon Brothers, 1976.

4. Leibowitz, Martin L., and Johannesen, Richard I., Jr. "Introducing the Salomon Brothers Total Performance Index for the High-Grade Long-Term Corporate Bond Market." New York: Salomon Brothers, November 2, 1973.

5. Leibowitz, Martin L. "New Tools in Bond Portfolio Management." *Trusts and Estates* (January 1973).

6. Leibowitz, Martin L. "Portfolio Returns and Scenario Analysis." New York: Salomon Brothers, March 20, 1978. (Now Chapter 5 in *Total Return Management.* New York: Salomon Brothers, 1979).

7. Leibowitz, Martin L. "Profits Losses, and Portfolio Objectives." New York: Salomon Brothers, June 15, 1976.

8. Leibowitz, Martin L. "The Risk Dimension." New York: Salomon Brothers, October 5, 1977. (Now Chapter 4, in *Total Return Management.* New York: Salomon Brothers, 1979).

9. Leibowitz, Martin L. "The Rolling Yield." New York: Salomon Brothers, April 21, 1977. (Now Chapter 2, in *Total Return Management.* New York: Salomon Brothers, 1979).

10. Leibowitz, Martin L. "Sources of Return in Corporate Bond Portfolios." Salomon Brothers, August 3, 1978. (Now Chapter 6, in *Total Return Management.* New York: Salomon Brothers, 1979).

11. Leibowitz, Martin L. "Total After-Tax Bond Performance and Yield Measures." New York: Salomon Brothers, June 1, 1974.

12. Waldman, Michael. "Introducing the Salomon Brothers Total Rate-of-Return Index for Mortgage Pass-Through Securities." Salomon Brothers, March 15, 1979.

Chapter 18

Monitoring Executions

WAYNE H. WAGNER
Vice President
Wilshire Associates
Santa Monica, California

WHY MONITOR EXECUTION COSTS?

When a pension fund sponsor selects a new manager or evaluates a current manager, a great deal of attention is focused on the ability of the research department to generate investment ideas and the portfolio manager's productive use of those ideas. Seldom is any attention paid to the trading desk, which nonetheless has been described as the "third leg of the stool" of successful investment management. Since poor execution can compromise or destroy the results of good investment research and portfolio management, this surprising lack of attention would seem to stem from a general feeling that trading costs are not controllable and/or insignificant. In addition, the evaluation of execution is not a trivial task, and a fairly complicated procedure may derive only ambiguous conclusions.

Yet the importance of evaluating execution costs should not be understated. Since the end of fixed commission schedules has unbundled commission costs, the trader can choose to purchase a variety of services with commission dollars, from bare bones execution to the acquisition of research material. It is imperative that the active investment manager understand the performance implications of execution-related costs. The Employee Retirement Income Security Act of 1977 (ERISA) recognized the importance of execution when it placed an explicit obligation on the investment manager to control and account for costs assessed during execution.

Total transaction costs include explicit brokerage fees, taxes and exchange fees, and implicit costs due to market maker spreads and market price impact. They also trigger higher administrative fees for trade accounting, auditing and performance monitoring. At first glance, these costs are detrimental to net portfolio performance. It has been suggested that these costs may, at times, more than offset the value of the information that prompted the trade to be executed. Transaction costs have been cited as the most probable underlying cause of "the institutional shortfall"—the amount by which the average managed portfolio has fallen short of stock market indices.

However, lowest cost execution does not necessarily represent best execution in every situation. The trader, after all, is fundamentally executing the desires of the portfolio manager who has reasons for desiring to purchase or sell a particular security in a particular amount at a particular time. The portfolio manager who feels he or she has a valuable insight into the probable future behavior of a stock may desire a very rapid execution that entails higher than average execution costs. Presumably, the higher trade cost will be more than compensated as the value of the manager's insight is manifest in the stock price. If the trade were not executed promptly, other investors may soon derive the same insight and destroy the information advantage by their trading activity. Conversely, at times the manager may trade to complete long term portfolio adjustments that are not based on short-term insights. Long term portfolio performance may be penalized if execution costs are excessive because the trader has not been made aware of the distinction between the two trading situations.

Thus the monitoring of execution must be kept in the proper context of total performance measurement. The proper question for execution evaluation is not "has the lowest possible execution cost been secured?" but "has the conduct of the trading function contributed to overall investment performance?"

EXPLICIT AND IMPLICIT TRADING COSTS

The evaluation of execution cost would be a trivial matter if the problem were one of simply totaling up the direct charges of brokerage commissions, exchange fees, taxes, and any other items that print on each trade ticket. Execution evaluation and trade cost measurement are complicated by indirect costs that derive from (1) the specific trade related services that the trader chooses to purchase, (2) nontrade related services purchased along with execution, and (3) the structural characteristics of the market in which securities trade.

As an example of a trade related service, assume that the trader desires immediate execution of an order. If no other investor is available at that moment to take the other side of the trade, the market maker may take an inventory position in the securities offered for trade, and charge a fee to compensate for his or her risk and the use of his or her capital. While this fee is never explicitly identified, traders who make consistent use of this facility may expect higher execution costs. Also consider the case where the number of shares being traded represent a significant portion of the normal daily trading activity in that particular stock. The broker will normally execute these orders using the firm's trading contacts to determine the extent to which other investors are willing to take the other side of the trade. Since this may represent a substantial commitment of skilled and well-compensated individuals, the trader should expect to pay extra for this accommodation.

Before fixed exchange rates were abolished, brokers would compete for the highly profitable commission business by providing other investment management related services (research) in addition to execution. The practice was particularly expensive—and annoying—to large volume institutional investors. They found that costs were disproportionate to the service provided and pressed for the abolishment of fixed rates. Old traditions die hard, however, and "paying up" for the purchase of nonexecution related services is still common. When evaluating execution, however, the value of these services must be considered. The appropriate question would seem to be: "Would I, as a manager or investor, pay the same amount for this service if I had to sign a check for it?"

The structural characteristics that complicate execution evaluation arise as follows. As the trader informs the broker of one's interest, the knowledge that an interested trader exists spreads inexorably through the brokerage and exchange community. The mere presence of an anxious buyer or seller is an item of significant information that will affect the near term future price of the stock: this is the equilibriating process whereby security value judgments are evaluated in the marketplace and security values established that represent the consensus perceived value of the security. When evaluating the execution, however, this represents a considerable complication: the cost of executing the trade is intrinsically intertwined with the value of the security being purchased or sold. Thus, changes in value may falsely be attributed to execution cost when, in fact, they represent simply changes in the consensus perception of the value of the stock.

Intrinsic, nonobservable trading costs are assessed through two primary channels. The first channel is the "spread" charged by exchange specialists, market makers, third market brokers, and other participants in the trading process. These participants earn their living on the spread between the average price at which they buy and the average price at which they sell. The market function served is one of intermediating the timing of orders since buy orders and sell orders seldom arrive in the market at the same time. This spread can be most directly observed in the over-the-counter markets, where the difference between the bid and asked prices represent the dealer's expected profits on small purchases and sales. Even though the spread cost of unlisted stocks is camouflaged by the ticker tape, each time an investor has a transaction with a market maker one incurs this cost in addition to the explicit commissions.

The second common channel of additional trading costs is the market impact of the trade. For example, if a manager attempts to accumulate quickly a large portion of a thinly traded stock, the force of that buying will drive the price up. It has been shown that the market responds to this type of information by an "information effect" that assesses the import of the trading activity, and by a very temporary "liquidity effect" that represents the cost of enticing other traders to take the other side of a large volume trade. Traders who accommodate anxious buyers or sellers may actually experience negative market impact.

Thus effective execution evaluation involves an analysis of the value of services received versus the cost of obtaining them. Some of the areas in which trading may be ineffective have been identified:

1. Incurring excessive trading costs by overestimating the value of the information.
2. Conversely, failing to capitalize on valuable insights by excessive concentration on low-cost execution.
3. Failing to capitalize on insight by divulging too much information during the trading process prior to completing the trade.
4. Failing to distinguish between these three situations and using one standard trading technique instead of adapting to the specific trade.
5. Failing to distinguish that different brokers have varying levels of skill in handling particular types of trading activity.
6. Displaying to the broker a lack of sensitivity to the level of trading costs.
7. Paying too much for nonexecution related services.

To summarize, the trading process involves the assessment of costs associated with a desire to change investment posture through the purchase and sale of securities. The costs represent the purchase of services such as (1) administrative costs of handling the paperwork associated with the exchange of the security, (2) some convenience services associated with the centralization of the trading process and the intermediation of the timing of purchases and sales, and (3) "paying up" for research services unrelated to the current execution. In addition to the direct costs of trading, the effects of nonobservable market spreads and trading impact must be evaluated. Finally, the evaluation of whether trading is good or bad depends upon the context; in proper context, the evaluation of executions is a part of the general problem of investment monitoring and performance attribution.

In the next section, the model most commonly used for execution evaluation will be presented and discussed. In the following section, the applicability of the model under various trading conditions will be assessed, and approaches other researchers have taken to improve the clarity of the observation will be discussed.

A SIMPLE MODEL FOR EXECUTION EVALUATION

In the abstract, the problem of evaluating implicit trading costs represents a comparison of what did occur to what would have occurred if this particular trade had not been executed. What might have been, of course, is clearly unobservable. The practical application, then, becomes a complicated problem of statistical inference wherein the actual trade price is compared to other prices that are (1) supposedly unaffected by this particular trading activity and (2) properly adjusted to account for the always-present market movements.

The transaction cost of a trade is operationally defined as the price impact of trading plus the commission. Total trade costs, then, are usually estimated by an equation similar to the following:

$$\text{Transaction cost} = \left[\frac{\text{Trade price} + \text{Dividend}}{\text{Adjusted benchmark price}} \right] - 1.0$$

Where

$$\text{Adjusted benchmark price} = (\text{benchmark price}) \cdot$$

$$\left\{ \left(\frac{\text{Security}}{\text{Volatility}} \right) \left[\frac{\text{Index value at trade time}}{\text{Index value at benchmark}} - 1.0 \right] + 1 \right\}$$

Sample computation:

Trade price	$17.50
Commission	.170
N.Y. state tax	.047
SEC fee	.001
Net price	17.282
Dividend	0
Previous close	17.625
Security beta	1.1
Index value at trade	95.53
Index value, previous close	95.57

$$\text{Adjusted benchmark} = 17.625 \left\{ 1.1 \left[\frac{95.53}{95.57} - 1.0 \right] + 1.0 \right\} = \$17.617$$

$$\text{Transaction cost} = \left(\frac{17.282 + 0}{17.617} \right) - 1.0 = -.0190 = -1.90\%$$

The adjusted benchmark price is computed from the anticipated change in the value of the security between execution time and some arbitrarily assumed benchmark. The benchmark time is chosen to represent a period during which the security price is unaffected by the particular trading activity. The index adjustment in the equation tends to improve the accuracy of the trading cost estimate by removing the estimated effects of market movement on the stock under analysis. The volatility parameter proportionally adjusts for the impact of typical market movement on this security, and is usually measured by the security beta factor.

The execution price includes the effects of all explicit commission costs and, by assumption, all implicit trading costs. (Estimated execution costs in the above formula will on average be positive for purchases and negative for sales).

Using a variety of different benchmark prices will also enable us to observe and interpret the market conditions under which trades are executed and how market conditions affect execution costs.

The dividend figure is a mechanical adjustment to remove the effects of any dividend paid between the benchmark time and the trade time.

When should the benchmark price be observed? The benchmark price will be most effective and efficient as an estimator of execution cost if it represents (1) a time in close proximity to execution at which both the stock price and the index price can be observed, yet (2) clearly represents a time at which this trade could not have affected the market price of the security. Because the selection of a benchmark price time is arbitrary and the results of the evaluation should be independent of the benchmark time, it is common to expand an evaluation by considering multiple benchmark prices and interpreting any differences in average estimated execution costs. An alternative is to use benchmarks computed from multiple prices, such as the average daily trading price or the high-low or open-closing prices average.

In the formula as shown, the benchmark price is assumed (by the location of the dividend adjustment) to occur before trade. Trade prices can also be compared to benchmark prices that occur after execution. These comparisons are particularly valuable when evaluating the interrelationships of portfolio management judgments and execution costs.

Even before discussing some common pitfalls associated with using this formula, it is clear that the benchmark price concept is a less than perfect information substitute for the price at which the security would have traded had the trade not been executed. The index adjustment, the volatility adjustment, and the distance in time between benchmark and execution price will all contribute statistical variability to the estimated trading cost. It follows, then, that the estimated trading cost of any particular trade will be subject to a great deal of estimation error. The effects of this unavoidable estimation error are reduced by sampling; that is, by averaging a great many executed trades to derive a better estimate of the average trading cost. Averaging is less subject to the errors implicit in any single observation. Most studies attempt to collect many hundreds of trades, even thousands, in order to overcome statistical estimation errors.

Trade prices are being altered constantly by other traders as they assess the impact of events real and inferred. These actions may sometimes reinforce the effects of the particular trade we are analyzing, thus possibly increasing the measured transaction costs. On other occasions, the actions will cancel some of the implicit trading costs, and the estimated costs will be less than would otherwise have been measured. The evaluator is then left with the statistician's hope that these effects are random and will cancel one another as sample size is increased.

Large sample sizes are particularly important if it is desired to hold constant certain factors that allegedly affect execution costs and measure the impact due to that factor. For example, we may wish to determine whether security sales imply higher or lower transaction costs than purchase orders.

Some categories that are frequently analyzed in trading studies include:

1. The size of the trade and its relation to market value.
2. Market movement and the direction of trade (e.g., buying into a falling market).
3. The discount level on the trade and the effect of fully negotiated commissions.
4. The effect of multiblock trades in the same issue over a short period of time.
5. The characteristics of the stock being traded such as liquidity, price, volatility, etc.
6. The mechanics of trading such as the type of order executed, the exchange, the manager ordering the trade, the broker executing the trade, etc.

These effects are commonly contrasted by partitioning the sample into trades that are affected by the factor and trades that are not affected by the factor. This permits a direct comparison of the factor effect and thus provides insight into conditions under which trading costs are higher, lower, or unaffected.

PITFALLS IN MEASURING EXECUTION COSTS

In order to view some of the difficulties of execution evaluation, let us join a researcher who has been assigned the task of conducting a study.

The researcher begins the trading cost study by discussing objectives with the head of portfolio management and the owner or trustee of the assets. Since interest in the topic is currently very high, one decides to proceed using historic trade data that already exists on the trading desk. While the ongoing monitoring process would obviously be beneficial, one argues that a study using historic data will have a more immediate impact, and guide in the design of an ongoing monitor. In addition, care must be taken to assure that the measurement process does not affect the results: neither the trader nor the broker should alter their behavior as a result of being monitored. The interest is in evaluating their performance, not in demonstrating that they effectively perform their jobs.

Having set the objectives of the study and secured approvals, the head trader is approached and asked to provide records of trades executed. The trader provides a stack of broker tickets or the trade blotter. These produce accounting-accurate records of all trades executed, prices paid, commissions and taxes, and the trade date. This is very helpful, of course, but the researcher would also like to know the time of the day the trade was executed to get an accurate estimate of the market at that point. One also requests the date and time that the trader was notified of the trade in order to select a benchmark price date that clearly antedates the trading activity. Because no one has studied trading costs, the trader has kept only the information necessary to settle the accounts.

Some of the information is impossible to get. On most occasions, traders can't match up executions with the ticker tape. The trades are executed over a period of hours, sometimes days. On a big order, the broker usually executes multiple small trades at various points in time, and only reports the final tally. Given today's commission rates, it is doubtful that the broker would be very interested in going through the extra effort and expense necessary to provide the additional information, even if asked.

At this point, the researcher notes the following considerations for an ongoing execution cost monitor:

1. Have the trader stamp the time and date on the order when it is first received by the trading department.
2. Time stamp the order again when broker informs trader that the trade is complete.

The trader may be willing to stamp the orders, but asks what to do about big blocks that may be parcelled out by the portfolio manager over a period of many days, perhaps even weeks or months. In some cases, banks have been active for over a year accumulating or liquidating a major position. How does one set a benchmark price for the trade instruction that effectively says, "take all you can get until I tell you to stop?" The researcher must add the following item to the checklist: Analyze multiple day trading programs by defining a trading program to be a period during which executions were made without more than an *"n"* day absence from the market.

As this little scenario indicates, performing a trading cost analysis involves making the best of a set of data that contains many impurities and complications that will frequently cause the final results to be stated with many qualifications and a great many caveats.

Not all of the potential pitfalls, of course, are related to the data collection. A robust evaluation of execution must also consider some issues such as the following.

To begin, the environment of the stock trader has changed rapidly since the advent of fully negotiated commissions. Processes and techniques that were acceptable to the brokerage community several years or even months ago may no longer be effective. The broker's willingness to cooperate will fluctuate from market to market and day to day dependent upon profitability and amount of business being handled. Elaborate techniques were devised to lower trading costs in a period of fixed commissions; they have little or no applicability to today's trading conditions. Thus, execution evaluation should be an ongoing process to detect changes in market conditions and how they affect trading practices.

One of the perpetual questions considered by institutional stock traders is whether execution costs for a large block will be lower if the block is parcelled out a bit at a time, and the broker is kept unaware of the size of the interest during the initial contact. But the broker has a vital financial interest in understanding the trading techniques of clients. If he believes there may be more stock behind the current order, due to his knowledge of accumulated positions and past trading practices, he will adjust his negotiations to protect his interests. Thus the cost of execution may begin as soon as the first call is made from the trade desk to a broker. The selection of an appropriate benchmark time thus will strongly affect the validity of the conclusions. For large trading packages, it may be necessary to establish benchmarks days or even weeks before the order is completed.

The trades executed may not be representative of the total activity of the trading desk. Consider the trades that fail to execute. The manager indicates that he or she would like to purchase a particular security, but is unwilling to pay more than some prespecified amount. Missed trades may represent an opportunity cost. The method used to express this trading interest to the trader or the broker may preclude valuable opportunities to improve portfolio performance. Again, the cheapest execution costs may not represent the most effective means of improving portfolio performance.

The equation for the estimated transaction cost included a volatility adjustment to allow for differential market effects of highly volatile stocks versus less volatile. Volatility coefficients, or betas, are known to be notoriously inaccurate for short periods of time and as predictors of the short term movement for an individual stock. Knowing the limitations of the beta coefficient, many researchers have chosen to ignore the volatility adjustment or use an adjustment estimated from industry or volatility fractile rather than individual stock betas.

One final cost that should not be forgotten in the evaluation of executions is the cost of operating the trading department itself. Trading procedures that require a great deal of time and/or highly trained staff will be more costly to maintain. While the cost of this increased activity will not be reflected in the direct estimates of execution costs, it will presumably be reflected in the management fee structure or the profitability of the investment management activity.

REDUCING THE COST OF TRANSACTING

While trading costs can be maddeningly difficult to pinpoint, institutional investors have for many years acted as though they were strongly in favor of reducing the costs of stock trading. Academic and business community studies have for years supported this desire. Performance measurement services have consistently shown that high turnover rates have resulted in poor performance, assuredly due to turnover costs. The Institutional Investor study report noted that ". . . a 10 percentage point increase in turnover rate would have reduced fund performance in the fund-average case by approximately 0.5 percent per month."

Banks and investment managers have been agitating for years for reduced costs and improved efficiency in stock trading. These pressures have led to the abolishment of the fixed commission schedule, and both the folklore and the evidence indicate that this has substantially reduced the total execution costs. Studies of execution costs during the era of fixed commissions indicate round trip trading costs in the range of 2½–4 percent. A recent study has derived trading cost estimates under 2½ percent ranging downward to below 1 percent. While the lower range of these numbers may not be generally available to all investors in a stable brokerage environment, the evidence clearly indicates a substantial increase in efficiency.

Another development that has shown the potential for reducing execution costs through effective organization of the trading activity is the index fund. The index funds have reduced their demands for specific brokerage services, and arranged their trading to provide maximum flexibility to the broker in terms of time of execution and even the stock being selected. They have made optimal use of low cost trading situations such as secondary offerings and automatic dividend reinvestment, and have established competitive bidding practices to award the entire trading package to the lowest bidder. In addition, index funds have carefully scrutinized the trading activity and made the broker aware of their sensitivity, even to the point of providing financial incentives to the broker for execution better than some preestablished benchmark. The value of these techniques have been appreciated by active managers, who have adjusted their trading strategies to capture some of the potential savings. Active investment managers have shown a heightened sensitivity to the cost of "anxious" trading and of the payment required for services extended.

Several multiple-manager trusts have implemented market inventory funds to reduce execution costs by having the index fund accommodate trades initiated by active investment managers operating under the same trust. By eliminating offsetting trades or substituting index fund trading techniques, trading costs can be eliminated or substantially reduced.

Finally, certain brokers, investment managers, and custodian banks have actively sought methods of reducing the costs associated with some of the antiquated practices of the brokerage and exchange community. There is continuing emphasis on substituting computer processing for labor-intensive hand processed orders. In addition, significant progress has been made to eliminate unnecessary security movement and avoid expensive clearance and settlement problems. Clearly, any procedure that reduces the broker's cost of executing and settling the trade will ultimately be reflected in lower cost execution, and the potential for cost reduction in this area has barely been tapped. As Dean LeBaron of Batterymarch has suggested, if a check can be cleared across the country for ten cents, why should it cost fifty dollars to execute a stock transaction?

CONCLUSION

In this chapter, execution evaluation has been identified as an important but somewhat perilous task. The scarcity of published papers describing practitioner experiences may indicate that the perils outweigh the import.

The Demsetz paper [6]* is the earliest publication on trading costs. During the time when abolishment of fixed commissions was being considered, the SEC funded several studies [7,8]. The organization of the Exchange and the economics of the brokerage function have attracted talented writers [1,4]. The effects of trading costs and the advisibility of alternate trading techniques have generated a few references [3,5,9,10]. Since the advent of negotiated commissions, however,

---

* Numbers in brackets refer to *Reference* at end of chapter.

only one paper has been published, of which the author is aware, that analyzes trade costs [2].

Why have so few papers been published? Can it be that most institutional investors have not studied or monitored execution costs? Or have these studies been too ambiguous (or too valuable!) to submit for publication? Perhaps the questions being addressed are too sensitive for publicity: value of research, broker-manager relationships, cost of paying up for research, etc. Nonetheless, those pension fund sponsors and institutional managers who have undertaken in-depth studies of the trading process have found valuable insights into organizing for better investment performance.

APPENDIX

A Checklist for Execution Evaluation

   I. Objectives of study
      A. Component of total performance
      B. ERISA compliance
      C. Evaluation of traders
      D. Evaluation of brokers
      E. Evaluation of trade technique
      F. Marketing support
      G. Other
  II. Period of analysis
      A. Start date
      B. End date
      C. Anticipated number of trades
      D. Description of market environment during period of analysis
 III. Data collection
      A. Trade data
         1. Ticker or CUSIP
         2. Buy or sell
         3. Shares traded
         4. Explicit trading costs
            a. Commission
            b. State tax
            c. SEC fee
         5. Trade date
         6. Submission time (if available)
         7. Trade time (if available)
      B. Benchmark data
         1. Security closing price
         2. Previous close

       3. Other benchmark prices (e.g., two days prior, closing price day after, five days after, ten days after)
       4. Index value as of benchmark price dates
  C. Market environment data
       1. Market volume
       2. Market index change
  D. Security environment data
       1. Volume
       2. Volatility measure
       3. Liquidity measure
       4. Industry group
  E. Trade factors
       1. Discount level
       2. Order type (e.g., market, limit)
       3. Exchange used
       4. Broker handling
       5. Manager requesting
       6. Trade reason (if available)
       7. Trade urgency (if available)
       8. Trader's estimate of degree of difficulty (if available)
  F. Other

IV. Factors to analyze
  A. Buys versus sells
       1. Direction of stock
       2. Direction of market
  B. Trade volume
       1. Size of order
       2. Percentage of stock daily volume
       3. Market volume
       4. Liquidity measure
  C. Trade mechanics
       1. Block orders
       2. Type of order
       3. Broker, exchange used
       4. Trade urgency
       5. Trade difficulty
       6. Discount level
  D. Contribution to overall performance
       1. Analyst recommendation
       2. Portfolio cash flow
       3. Subsequent performance

V. Conclusions and recommendations

REFERENCES

1. Bagehot, Walter. "The Only Game in Town." *Financial Analysts Journal.* (March–April 1971) p. 14.

2. Beebower, Gilbert L. and Priest, William W., Jr. "An Analysis of Transaction Costs in Equity Trading." Proceedings of the Seminar on the Analysis of Security Prices (November 1978). In *Financial Analysts Journal,* forthcoming.

3. Belliveau, Nancy. "Passive Trading Gets Active." *Institutional Investor.* (April 1977) p. 16.

4. Black, Fischer. "Toward A Fully Automated Stock Exchange." *Financial Analysts Journal.* (July–August 1971).

5. Cuneo, Larry J. and Wagner, Wayne H. "Reducing the Cost of Stock Trading." *Financial Analysts Journal.* (November–December 1975).

6. Demsetz, Harold. "The Cost of Transacting." *Quarterly Journal of Economics.* (February 1968) p. 40.

7. *Institutional Investor Study Report of the Securities and Exchange Commission.* U. S. Government Printing Office. 4 (1971):1728.

8. Kraus, Allan and Stoll, Hans R. "Price Impacts of Block Trading on the New York Stock Exchange." *Journal of Finance.* 27, 3:588.

9. Treynor, Jack L. "The Institutional Shortfall." *Financial Analysts Journal.* (November–December 1976) p. 43.

10. Wagner, Wayne H. and Zipkin, Carol A. "Can Inventory Index Funds Improve Active Equity Performance?" *Financial Analysts Journal.* (May–June 1978).

Chapter 19

Evaluating the Quality of Research Information

KEITH P. AMBACHTSHEER

Partner and Director of Research
Canavest House Ltd.
Toronto, Canada

Active portfolio management attempts to add value to performance results achievable through a passive buy-and-hold management approach. The success of active management is dependent on:

1. having research information which has predictive content, and
2. using the information effectively in the construction of security portfolios.

This chapter focusses on the necessary condition for successful active management: the availability of information with predictive value. Specifically, the chapter will discuss:

a. an appropriate definition of research information,
b. the key factors involved in effectively measuring the quality of research information,
c. different methods that have been used in published studies to measure predictive ability as well as the findings of these studies,
d. a new evaluation method called Information Coefficient Analysis (ICA).

WHAT IS RESEARCH INFORMATION?

A great deal of ambiguity can exist as to what constitutes research information. In the broadest sense, it is any information relevant to determining the absolute or relative value of individual securities or groups of securities. However, from a measurement point of view,

521

this is not a very useful definition. Recognizing that any valuation process involves three basic steps is helpful:

The Security Valuation Process

Input	*Evaluation*	*Output*
Facts about today and judgments about tomorrow	Transformation of the facts and judgments through formal or informal valuation models or standards	Expression of the valuation implications of the input and evaluation activity in quantitative or qualitative form

This chapter will focus on the evaluation of the output of any security valuation process. Specifically, how can its predictive content be measured?

Why does this Question Deserve an Answer?

It is intuitively obvious that active portfolio management can not be successful without valuation judgments that have at least some predictive content. It is equally obvious that the higher this content, the higher is the potential for superior portfolio performance.

Treynor and Black formalized the relationship between predictive ability and portfolio management theoretically some 6 years ago.[1] Brealey and Hodges[2] and Ambachtsheer[3] have published results which demonstrate the relationship between predictive ability and performance empirically. The implication of this theoretical and empirical work is that it is of crucial importance that investment managers have some idea about the predictive content of the research output they are using. Without this knowledge, an inefficient, if not misdirected, investment management process will result.

The predictive ability question is an important one not only to each investment management organization individually, but also in a much broader perspective. The efficient market hypothesis has gained a lot of credence over the last ten years. One form of the hypothesis states that when all information known (publicly and privately) is reflected in security prices, the market for such securities is "efficient." The implication is that there can be no predictive content in any valuation

---

[1] J. Treynor and F. Black, "How To Use Security Analysis To Improve Portfolio Selection," *Journal of Business* (January 1973). For further discussion of the Treynor-Black model, see R. Ferguson, "How To Beat The Index Fund," *Financial Analysts Journal* (May–June, 1975).

[2] S. Hodges and R. Brealey "Dynamic Portfolio Selection," *Financial Analysts Journal* (April–May, 1973).

[3] K. Ambachtsheer, "Portfolio Theory And The Security Analyst," *Financial Analysts Journal* (November–December 1972); "Profit Potential In An Almost Efficient Market," *Journal of Portfolio Management* (Fall 1974); and "Where Are The Customers Alphas?" *Journal Of Portfolio Management* (Fall 1974).

process that over- or undervalues securities in that type of market. Most studies which have tested the efficient market hypothesis through the performance of professionally managed U.S. pension and mutual funds have found that professional investment managers in aggregate have not been able to add value to the passive buy-and-hold approach. Therefore,the efficient markets hypothesis describes the real world (or at least the U.S. stock market). But is a test of the hypothesis through achieved portfolio performance necessarily a valid one? The answer must be no. It is entirely feasible that the average investment management organization is able to generate valuation judgments with some information content but then throw it away through faulty portfolio management techniques.

Direct measurement of predictive ability constitutes a much more powerful test of the efficient markets hypothesis. This theme will be developed further.

KEY FACTORS IN PREDICTIVE ABILITY MEASUREMENT

For meaningful predictive ability measurement to take place, a number of ingredients are ideally operative:

1. Most fundamentally, the valuation judgments must be explicit rather than implicit.
2. The judgments must be dated in a calendar time context (i.e. "October 31 1978").
3. The unit of account of the judgments (i.e. prescaled rankings, incremental return, or total return) should be consistent with the objective of the valuation approach. If that objective, for example, is to produce absolute valuation judgments, the valuation approach should provide intrinsic values or rates of return over some horizon. On the other hand, if the valuation approach is relative value oriented, then the rating approach should express relative value in a properly scaled, unbiased fashion.
4. While the evaluation period for predictive ability measurement should focus on a previously established "work out" period (i.e., one year), flexibility should be present to measure predictive content over periods longer and shorter than the expected "work out" period (i.e., six and 18 months).
5. The measurement approach should be amenable to standard tests of statistical significance. A corollary here is that large samples over many independent test periods are preferable to small samples over few test periods.
6. The research process under evaluation should be stable both with respect to methodology and people.
7. Predictive ability should be measured in such a way that the results

can be explicitly linked to the construction and rebalancing of portfolios (discussed later).

Before going on to describe a specific measurement methodology (ICA) which embraces most of these ideal ingredients, it is instructive to review three actual case studies performed with methodologies other than ICA.

The Diefenbach Study[4]

The study objectives were:

1. Make an overall assessment of the value of research recommendations received from the institutional research departments of 24 brokerage firms during an 80-week period from November 1967 to May 1969.
2. Obtain an objective comparison of the usefulness of the recommendations supplied by individual firms.

Study features included the following:

1. Measure the price performance (percent change) of each recommendation (designated as either a buy or a sell) over the 52-week period beyond forecast date.
2. Measure the S&P 425 Index performance (percent change) over the same 52-week period as for each buy or sell recommendation, and calculate the difference.
3. Overall, 1,255 "performance differentials" were created: 1,209 for stocks designated buy and 46 for stocks designated sell.

The findings are reproduced below in Table 1 and Table 2.

Relating this study and its findings to the ingredients for an ideal predictive ability measurement approach listed earlier, the following observations emerge:

1. The valuation judgments were explicit, being designated buy or sell.
2. Each judgment was calendar dated.
3. The unit of account (basically dividing the selection universe into "good" and "bad" stocks) is of questionable value if the purpose is to designate stocks into relative valuation categories (Why only two?). A related problem is the tremendous imbalance between stocks judged to be "good" (1,209) and stocks judged to be "bad" (46). Are the judgment makers intending to signal an overall market

---

[4] J. Diefenbach, "How Good Is Institutional Research?" *Financial Analysts Journal* (January–February 1972).

Table 1
52-Week Market Performance of Buy Recommendations (received during the 80 weeks ending November 11, 1967 through May 23, 1969)

Source	Number of Buy Recs.	Mean Price Change	Percent Outperforming S&P 425	Mean Performance Differential from S&P 425
1. A	12	+24.6%	75%	+25.9%
2. B	11	+ 6.7	36	+13.8
3. C	26	+ 1.8	54	+13.7
4. D	5	− 1.6	60	+11.8
5. E	12	+ 8.9	50	+11.6
6. F	288	+10.8	56	+ 9.8
7. G	49	+ 3.5	51	+ 6.9
8. H	192	+ 5.8	47	+ 5.9
9. I	13	+ 0.7	38	+ 5.7
10. J	91	+ 3.2	48	+ 4.3
11. K	59	+ 7.2	53	+ 4.0
12. L	24	− 1.5	50	+ 0.1
13. M	21	− 8.0	48	− 0.2
14. N	39	−13.9	46	− 1.6
15. O	147	−11.1	39	− 4.0
16. P	67	− 9.6	43	− 4.5
17. Q	39	−11.4	36	− 4.9
18. R	33	−10.7	39	− 6.3
19. S	14	−18.7	21	−11.1
20. T	23	−21.6	35	−11.7
21. U	9	−25.5	11	−13.4
22. V	8	−26.0	0	−19.3
23. W	9	−29.5	22	−21.3
24. X	18	−38.8	17	−25.3
Aggregate: All Sources	1,209	− 0.3%	47%	+ 2.7%
Mean: By Source	50	− 6.4%	40%	− 0.4%

Source: J. Diefenbach, "How Good is Institutional Research?" *Financial Analyst's Journal* (January–February 1972), pp. 56, 57.

Table 2
52-Week Market Performance of Sell Recommendations (received during the 80 weeks ending November 11, 1967 through May 23, 1969)

Source	Number of Sell Recs.	Mean Price Change	Percent Outperforming S&P 425	Mean Performance Differential from S&P 425
1. H	4	−39.4%	0%	−28.1%
2. O	11	−27.4	9	−19.6
3. S	3	−24.4	0	−14.2
4. P	14	−13.6	36	− 9.1
5. D	3	−31.1	67	− 3.7
6. F	11	− 3.9	45	− 0.6
Aggregate: All Sources	46	−18.7%	26%	−11.2%
Mean: By Source	8	−23.3%	26%	−12.6%

Source: J. Diefenbach, "How Good is Institutional Research?" *Financial Analyst's Journal* (January–February 1972), pp. 56, 57.

valuation judgment (i.e., bullish)? Given that the S&P 425 declined in value over the observation period, one would hope not!

4. By measuring the performance over only a single "work out" period (52 weeks), significant potentially valuable information is lost. For example, it is entirely possible much more powerful results could have been found over 13- or 26-week periods.
5. No formal tests of statistical significance were applied to the results.
6. Given the nature of the study, it was impossible to ensure stability in valuation methodology and people. However, the results were broken down by research firms. Had the experiment been repeated for one or more other nonoverlapping test periods, evidence of stability in the rankings of the 24 research departments could have been uncovered.
7. Given points 3–6 above, it is difficult to build an obvious bridge from the study to its portfolio management implications, although it seems wise to avoid stocks designated as sell by brokerage firm research departments.

The Korschot study[5]

This study differs fundamentally from the Diefenbach study in the sense that the focal point was inside rather than outside research information.

The overall objectives of this information measurement system are to:

1. define the analyst's role within the organization (the investment management firm of Waddell and Reed),
2. encourage analyst-portfolio manager communication, and
3. provide a basis for analyst incentive compensation.

The key features of the measurement system include:

1. The focal point is stock price action over a 12 to 18 month horizon beyond the forecast date in relation to a four point rating scheme (buy, hold, exchange, and sell).
2. Evaluation is carried out relative to:
   a. industry index performance over the same time period,
   b. total market index (S&P500) performance over the same time period (both in terms of return differential and in terms of "right" or "wrong" without regard to degree), and
   c. the effect the recommendations had on dollars made or saved in the actual portfolios.
3. The return differential results relative to the industry and market

---

[5] B. Korschot, "Measuring Research Analysts' Performance," *Financial Analysts Journal* (July–August 1978).

index performance are weighted (buys and sells received twice the weight of holds and exchanges, and new recommendations twice the weight of old recommendations) and then accumulated. The cumulative results are expressed as points allocated. Positive numbers are good; negative numbers are bad.

4. Study results are presented for seven (overlapping) forecast periods spaced six months apart from June 1974 to December 1977 for 12 analysts.

The overall results are presented in Table 3.

The cumulative results per analyst (performance versus S&P 500) are shown in Table 4.

Again relating this study to our previously enunciated features of an ideal measurement approach, the following observations can be made:

1. The valuation judgments were explicit, being expressed as buy, hold, exchange, or sell.

2. Each judgment was calendar dated and then accumulated with others until mid-year or end-of-year (whichever came first). The judgments were then priced out one year later. For example, all recommendations made during the first half of 1976 would be assigned both a recommendation price and an end-of-period price (June 30, 1977 in this case).

3. As with the Diefenbach study, the unit of account raises some question. While, for example, Korschot writes that his organization places greatest weight on selectivity within industry groups, the design of the measurement system hinders this purpose by allowing the analyst to potentially assign buys or sells to all stocks within given industry groups. Why not ask for unbiased relative value assignments within the groups and a separate value assignment on the group itself? The latter approach would permit relative value judgments within an industry group even though all stocks might be over or undervalued relative to those in another industry group.

4. The design of the measurement approach implies evaluation over a single work-out period for each recommendation somewhere between 12 and 18 months in length, depending on when the recommendation was made. As with the Diefenbach method, this approach leads to the loss of potentially valuable information with respect to when the judgments peak in terms of information content.

5. The approach does not lend itself to testing for statistical significance and no tests were reported in the study. A particular problem is the overlap of evaluation periods, with a new period starting before the previous one has run its course. Another problem is the point system, with different recommendations getting different (arbitrarily assigned) weights.

Table 3
Consistency of Performance (totals for all analysts)

Ending Period	6/30/74	12/31/74	6/30/75	12/31/75	6/30/76	12/31/76	6/30/77	12/31/77	Total
1. Performance versus Industry									
Points Allocated	−103	+ 97	+1,390	+1,523	+1,860	+437	+ 15	+ 16	+ 5,235
2. Performance versus S&P 500									
Points Allocated	+103	+869	+1,811	+3,687	+2,885	+932	+117	−1,700	+12,105
3. Total Right and Wrong Decisions versus S&P 500									
Right	66	133	314	288	177	156	158	209	1,501
Wrong	56	117	283	245	129	142	163	166	1,301
Net	+ 10	+ 16	+ 31	+ 43	+ 48	+ 14	− 5	+ 43	+ 200
Percent Right	54%	53%	53%	54%	58%	52%	49%	56%	54%
4. Dollars Made or Saved	Not measured	No	Yes	Yes	Yes	Yes	No	Yes	Yes

Source: B. Korchot, "Quantitative Evaluation of Investment Research Analysis," *Financial Analysts Journal* (July–August 1978), p. 45.

Table 4
Summary of Performance versus S&P 500 Stock Index

Analyst	Total Relative Points	Number of Times Evaluated	Number of Times With Positive Results	Per Cent Successful
1	4,368	8	7	88%
2	2,659	8	7	88
3	2,605	8	6	75
4	2,543	8	8	100
5	1,934	8	4	50
6	616	8	6	75
7	464	8	6	75
8	(470)	8	4	50
Sub Total	14,720	64	48	75%
9	(52)	2	1	50
10*	(746)	4	1	25
11	(894)	4	1	25
12*	(923)	3	0	0
Sub Total	(2,615)	13	3	23%
Total	12,105	77	51	66%

* No longer with the company.
Source: B. Korchot," Quantitative Evaluation of Investment Research Analysis," *Financial Analysis Journal* (July–August 1978), p. 46.

6. While the study made no reference to valuation methodologies employed, there was great stability in personnel over the test period. The results presented on a per-analyst basis suggest results which might well be of statistical significance (although no formal tests were carried out).
7. As with the Diefenbach approach, the Korschot method does not create a direct link to the portfolio building process. The results suggest that the analysts in aggregate are providing judgments with some information content; individually, some more so than others. However, portfolio managers are not left with any clear connection between analyst output, the evaluation system which monitors that output, and portfolio building rules.

The Value Line Method

The Value Line organization evaluates and publishes results of what it calls the Value Line One-Year Performance Rankings. These rankings (1 through 5) are assigned in a normally-distributed fashion to a universe of some 1,600 stocks.

The rankings are created through a predefined standard methodology drawn almost completely from published information about the earnings and price histories of the companies in the universe.

In order to demonstrate the effectiveness of its valuation methodol-

Table 5
Record of Value Line Rankings for Timeliness, April 16, 1965–July 5, 1978 (without allowance for changes in rank)

	1965*	1966	1967	1968	1969	1970	1971	1972	1973	1974	1975	1976	1977	1978†	1965 to mid 1978
Group 1 ...	+33.6%	− 3.1%	+39.2%	+31.2%	−17.7%	− 8.9%	+26.5%	+10.1%	−17.1%	−23.1%	+51.6%	+35.3%	+15.8%	+19.0%	+347%
Group 2 ...	+18.9	− 6.0	+31.9	+26.3	−16.3	− 4.0	+17.4	+ 7.5	−26.2	−27.8	+53.0	+36.3	+12.7	+16.5	+175
Group 3 ...	+ 8.9	− 9.7	+30.1	+21.4	−20.7	− 5.5	+12.2	+ 6.2	−27.0	−28.5	+52.9	+33.8	+ 5.2	+12.0	+ 74
Group 4 ...	+ .8	− 7.2	+25.1	+25.1	−26.8	−11.7	+14.2	+ 3.2	−29.1	−33.6	+48.4	+36.1	− .2	+ 9.0	+ 14
Group 5 ...	− 1.2	−12.4	+28.4	+25.9	−35.7	−13.1	+10.5	− 2.9	−43.1	−36.8	+42.1	+38.2	− 2.8	+ 9.8	− 37
Avg. all Stks.	+10.1	− 7.9	+29.9	+24.6	−22.1	− 7.5	+14.9	+ 5.5	−27.7	−29.6	+51.2	+35.1	+ 5.8	+12.5	+ 78
Dow-Jones Industrials															− 13
N.Y. Stock Exchange Composite															+ 9

* April through December.
† Dec. 28, 1977–July 5, 1978.

ogy, each year the Value Line organization calculates the return of equally weighted portfolios made up of all stocks in each of the five valuation categories, as well as the total universe performance and that of the popular stock indexes. The results of this evaluation approach are presented below in Table 5 and Figure 1.

Once again, relating this approach to our previously enunciated features of an ideal measurement approach leads to the following observations:

1. The valuation judgments were explicit, being expressed through rankings 1 to 5.
2. Each judgment is calendar dated. In the particular test outlined above, end-of-year judgments were evaluated.
3. The unit of account is unambiguous as a relative-to-the-universe expression of expected performance. The normalized allocation of rankings is consistent with the general shape of large sample relative return distributions. The five-point coding scheme is a reasonable compromise between the need to discriminate on one hand, and the recognition that detailed, exact discrimination is an impossibility on the other.
4. The one year evaluation period is a rigid one, as was the case in the two previously cited studies. Value Line also calculates performances based on changing the portfolios when the rankings change.

Figure 1
Record of Value Line Rankings for Timeliness April 16, 1965–July 5, 1978 (without allowance for changes in rank)

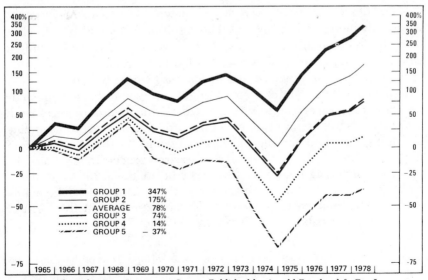

	GROUP 1	347%
	GROUP 2	175%
	AVERAGE	78%
	GROUP 3	74%
	GROUP 4	14%
	GROUP 5	− 37%

Source: *The Value Line Investment Survey.* Published by Arnold Bernhard & Co., Inc.

Performance differentials (before transaction costs at least) here tend to be more dramatic, indicating that "work-out" periods tend to typically be less than one year in length.

5. The approach lends itself easily to testing the results for statistical significance in the sense that the question "what are the chances that the published results could have been generated by a purely random process?" can be answered in any one of a number of ways. (As an aside, the answer to the question has almost always been: "Very, very small").[6]

6. While there might be personnel turnover, the Value Line organization has been using basically the same valuation methodology since the mid-1960s.

7. While the Value Line rankings do not provide a rigorous link to the portfolio building process, they are clearly useful. It is hard to disagree with Value Line when they say: "Concentrating in group 1 and 2 stocks, and doing so systematically, year in and year out, improves one's chances of outperforming the general market."

INFORMATION COEFFICIENT ANALYSIS

A simple, yet powerful, way of measuring predictive ability can be constructed through the appropriate use of standard regression-correlation techniques. In the most general form, this involves simply calculating the statistical association between two variables: forecasts (F) and actual outcomes (A). The resulting correlation coefficient can, in this context be called the information coefficient (or IC). Consider the three cases shown in Figure 2.

Case I depicts a situation of a perfect match between a set of forecasts (F) and the actual outcomes (A). The resulting IC would be 1.0. Case II implies some ability to forecast. In this case the measured IC might be 0.3. Finally, Case III shows a situation of no relationship between the Fs and As. The measured IC in this case would be 0.0.

In terms of what unit of account might the Fs and As be expressed? The general answer is: "to suit the situation at hand." If a research process leads to absolute rate of return projections, that would define the unit of account for the Fs. The As would be the actual rate of return outcomes. Alternatively, if the research process focused on relative valuation judgments, the Fs might be in the form of a 1 to 5 ranking scheme (as, for example, in the Value Line case). The actual relative performance results could also be expressed in the form of an identically distributed 1 to 5 ranking scheme. The information coef-

---

[6] See, for example, F. Black, "Yes, Virginia, There Is Hope: Tests of the Value Line Ranking System," proceedings of the Center for Research in Security Prices, University of Chicago, May 1971.

Figure 2

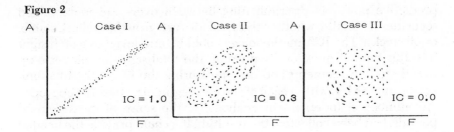

ficient in this case would be based on the correlation between the *F* and *A* rankings.[7]

It is often valuable to be able to measure predictive ability not just on the entire selection universe but on predefined components of the selection universe. For example, a typical research group of 12 analysts might follow a 200-stock selection universe broken down into 20 industry groups. Each of the analysts might be responsible for making relative value judgments within one or more of the 20 groups, employing an unbiased 1 to 5 rating scheme. Using a similar scheme, an investment policy committee might have the task of making relative value judgments across the 20 industry groups. The ICA methodology would permit predictive ability measurement as follows:

1. Within each of the 20 groups (although the implied small sample size would not permit drawing strong inferences until a considerable number of independent analyses had been taken).
2. By analyst (assuming that the analyst might cover more than one of the 20 groups). Again, the probable small sizes require patience in drawing strong conclusions from the resulting IC measures.
3. By intragroup judgments, taking all 200 stocks into account simultaneously.
4. By intergroup judgments, taking all 20 groups into account simultaneously.

A variant on this type of disaggregated analysis might be employed where a formal valuation methodology such as a form of the dividend discount model is employed. Does this methodology have the same

---

[7] Relative valuation judgments imply a cross-sectional measurement approach. The correlations (ICs) can be built up over time by collecting the results over multiple nonoverlapping time periods. Absolute valuation judgments (expressed, for example, as expected residual returns) should ideally be accumulated in a time series mode. Theoretically, this would permit the development of an IC per analyst per stock. Practically, of course, this latter approach creates great difficulty, in the sense that a great deal of time must elapse before meaningful IC measures can be developed. Discussions with Bob Ferguson of College Retirement Equities Fund have been helpful in clarifying this issue for us.

predictive power in discriminating between over- and undervalued securities no matter whether the securities are growth, cyclical, stable, or oil stocks? The ICA methodology could be employed to gain insight into this type of question by dividing the total selection universe up into these four segments and then measuring the IC for the total universe, and the ICs within each of the four segments. Once the appropriate number of independent analyses (in the sense of measurement periods) had been collected, the resulting ICs could provide the needed

Table 6
Information Coefficient Analysis (ICA) Uses

Measurement Application	*Comments*
1. Market predictions	Only one observation (one F and one A) per forecast period. A long period of time must pass before any serious analysis could be performed.
2. Major group predictions (i.e. growth, cyclical, oil, stable)	Only few observations per forecast period. As with market predictions, many years must pass before useful test data can be gathered.
3. Industry group predictions (i.e. drugs, autos, utilities, etc.)	As the number of items to be forecast per forecast period increases, relative judgments become both more feasible and desirable. For example, if 15 or more groups are defined, the Value Line-type 1–5 ranking scheme becomes very attractive. Each measurement period now generates a meaningful cross-sectionally derived IC. However, the sample size per measurement period would continue to be relatively small, implying the need for many independent analyses before meaningful inferences can be drawn.
4. Individual security predictions	Sample size per measurement period here is determined by exactly what is to be measured. A ranking scheme across a large security universe implies a correspondingly large sample size. A ranking scheme of group relative ratings could generate a larger or smaller sample size depending on whether all relative ratings are to be considered simultaneously or whether measurement is to take place within each group separately.
5. Comparative evaluations	Because ICA implies the computation of correlation coefficients on standardized sets of predictions, it lends itself to comparing the predictive power of differing valuation methods. Further standardization could be achieved by doing the comparative evaluation on identical selection universes over identical time periods.

information to answer this question. Table 6 provides a sample of ICA applications.

CASE STUDIES USING INFORMATION COEFFICIENT ANALYSIS

The first scattered results from ICA tests were reported in 1971–72. Richard Brealey[8] reported an average IC of 0.15 for a group of British money managers predicting relative one year group moves in the British stock market. This author reported a six-month IC of 0.17 for a research group making within group relative performance judgments on a 250-U.S. stock universe.[9]

By the fall of 1972, a commercial ICA software package developed by Canavest House had been introduced. A study was published in the fall of 1974, reporting on the measurement results achieved by investment management organizations using this commercial package.

The results are based on 40 rating sets, typically including 125 to 250 security ratings (i.e. *within* group ratings) and 15 to 30 group ratings. The ratings were prepared by 16 different investment institutions, typically at quarterly intervals, during the last two years. In analyzing the results, consider:

1. The correlations between the expectations and actual experience (i.e. the ICs) were calculated at regular one-month intervals beyond the forecast date (i.e. 1, 2, 3, . . . up to 12 months beyond the forecast date).
2. For each rating set the 1–3 month, 4–7 month, and 8–12 month ICs were average to smooth month-to-month fluctuations.
3. The appropriate *t* statistic is shown in brackets below each result. A value exceeding 2 implies the results are highly unlikely to be due to chance (e.g. less than one in 20).[10] See Table 7.

An investment counselling firm has been obtaining intra-industry group ratings using a 5 to 1 rating scheme from selected brokerage firm research departments for over three years now on 150-stock U.S. and Canadian selection universes. The firm uses these rating sets to construct a final rating set which is used to rebalance its U.S. and Canadian stock portfolios. The IC behavior of the two final rating sets is shown in Table 8.

As part of a recent study performed by Canavest House, College Retirement Equities Fund, and Citibank, the information coefficients of the output of two well-known valuation services were measured,

---

[8] Brealey, "Dynamic Portfolio."

[9] Ambachtsheer, see footnote 3.

[10] Keith Ambachtsheer, "Profit Potential In Almost Efficient Market," *Journal of Portfolio Management* (Fall 1974) p. 85.

Table 7
Average Information Coefficients

Number of Months beyond Forecast Date	1–3 Months	4–7 Months	8–12 Months
Average Security IC	0.17	0.16	0.09
("*t*" statistic)	(8.1)	(7.9)	(4.0)
Average Industry IC	0.07	0.18	0.11
("*t*" statistic)	(2.1)	(5.2)	(3.7)

Observations on Table 7:
a. The results indicate statistically significant predictive ability.
b. The degree of predictive ability is very modest.
c. The ICs peak well before the end of the 12-month forecasting horizon typically assumed.
d. No statistical difference between predicting relative security moves within groups and relative group moves existed. The results suggest security ICs peaked earlier than industry grouped ICs.
Source: Ambachtsheer, "Profit Potential."

specifically: Value Line's twelve-month performance rankings (based on historical price and earnings relationships and short term earnings surprise factors) and Wells Fargo's return differentials (based on the output of a dividend discount model and the security market line concept). In order to achieve maximum comparability, the return differentials were converted to a 1 to 5 ranking scheme as per Value Line. The test was carried out over six independent six-month periods commencing with the September 1973 forecasts, using an institutional type 200-stock universe. The universe was created by overlapping the Wells Fargo universe, the Value Line universe, and an actual client universe. There turned out to be 200 stocks common to all three. Test results are shown in Table 9.

Table 8

Rating Set Date	Canada			U.S.A.		
	Peak IC	(# mo.)	IC (12 mo.)	Peak IC	(Number months)	IC (12 months)
March 74	0.28	(6)	0.27	0.34	(9)	0.14
June 74	0.19	(6)	0.03	0.17	(5)	−0.01
September 74	0.23	(3)	−0.01	0.10	(2)	−0.01
December 74	0.15	(5)	0.12	0.03	(2)	−0.07
March 75	0.08	(9)	0.07	0.14	(2)	0.09
June 75	0.05	(8)	0.04	0.19	(3)	0.00
September 75	0.15	(3)	0.02	0.20	(4)	0.04
December 75	−0.01	(4)	NA	0.18	(2)	NA
March 76	0.12	(3)	NA	0.17	(6)	NA
Average	0.14	(5)	0.08	0.17	(4)	0.03

Source: Keith Ambachtsheer, "Where Are The Customers' Alphas?" *Journal of Portfolio Management* (Fall 1977), p. 54.

Table 9
Six-Month ICs

	Sept. 1973–Mar. 1974	Mar. 1974–Sept. 1974	Sept. 1974–Mar. 1975	Mar. 1975–Sept. 1975	Sept. 1975–Mar. 1976	Mar. 1976–Sept. 1976	Average	Standard Deviation
Wells Fargo	0.12	0.16	0.01	0.13	0.08	0.31	0.135	0.100
Value Line	0.17	0.04	−0.09	0.16	0.11	0.01	0.067	0.100

Observations on Table 9:

a. The Wells Fargo service delivered positive information six out of six times over the evaluation period on the 200 stock universe; the Value Line service five out of six times. These results would be highly unusual if the services actually had zero information content. Using the sample mean test of statistical significance, the t statistic for Wells Fargo is 3.3. For Value Line it is 1.7. At the 0.2 level of significance (5 degrees of freedom) the t value is 1.5, at 0.05 it is 2.6. The implication is that the Value Line results, if they were due to chance, would occur less than one out of five times, the Wells Fargo results less than one out of twenty times.

b. The ICA suggests considerable period-to-period variability in the IC for both valuation methodologies.

c. When a third set of rankings was created by weighting the Wells Fargo/Value Line rankings on a 2:1 basis. The IC pattern of the resulting combined rankings is shown in Table 10:

Table 10
Six-Month ICs

	Sept. 1973–Mar. 1974	Mar. 1974–Sept. 1974	Sept. 1974–Mar. 1975	Mar. 1975–Sept. 1975	Sept. 1975–Mar. 1976	Mar. 1976–Sept. 1976	Average	Standard Deviation
Combined	0.17	0.18	0.00	0.16	0.10	0.30	0.152	0.099

Note that when the judgments of two highly-independent methodologies are appropriately combined, the average IC increases while its period-to-period variability decreases.

USING INFORMATION COEFFICIENT ANALYSIS IN PORTFOLIO MANAGEMENT

Ranking systems reflecting over- or undervaluation judgments could be used directly by portfolio managers for portfolio rebalancing purposes. Such direct use is crude, however, in the sense that an ideal portfolio rebalancing approach maximizes incremental portfolio return at an acceptable level of incremental risk. This incremental return can only come from being overweighted in undervalued securities and underweighted in overvalued securities relative to their neutral (i.e. index) weights. The incremental risk comes from the possibility that the judgments will not be correct.

But what incremental return projections should be assigned to securities deemed to be undervalued? A ranking system can be used to approximate these projected return increments. Consider a 5-point ranking scheme with allocation rules shown in Figure 3 applied to a stock selection universe.

The rankings are essentially guesses about the relative performance of securities (or groups of securities) over some time horizon. Fortunately, quite a bit is known about the dispersion of nonmarket (or residual) returns (alphas) over various time horizons. Research performed by the author, for example, led to a finding that the average standard deviation of one year holding period residual returns over the 1971–75 period was 26 percent in both Canada and the U.S.A. This knowledge permits the transformation of the rankings into estimates of nonmarket return that would be achieved if the rankings were right and if 26 percent continues to be appropriate variability number. This transformation process is shown as step 2 in Figure 4.

Figure 3
A Ranking Scheme with Five Valuation Categories

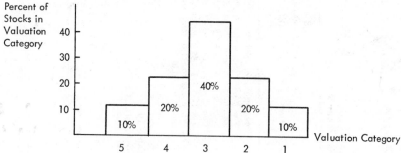

Figure 4

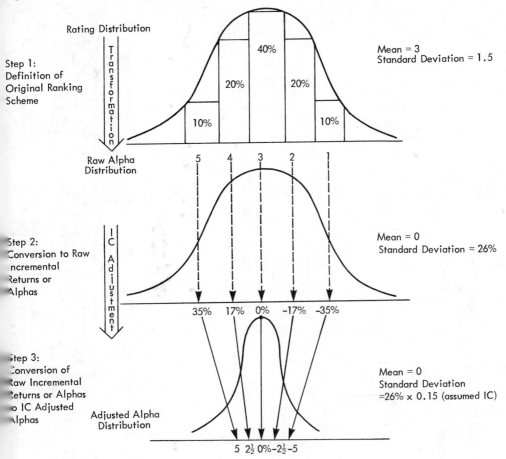

What IC (or correlation) can be expected between the forecast rankings and the actual rankings? If the answer to this question is "unity," then a historically-derived nonmarket return distribution can be substituted for the ranking distribution. If, more realistically, an IC assumption of 0.15 is employed, the raw nonmarket return forecasts must be adjusted to reflect this assumed level of predictive ability. This adjustment is shown as step 3 in Figure 4. The final result of the three-step process shown in Figure 4 is intuitively pleasing: the best stocks in the selection universe (i.e. the top 10 percent) are assigned a rating of 5. The actual average alpha of the top 10 percent in the selection universe is, on average, 35 percent. But the ratings are only forecasts. What will be the average performance of stocks forecasted to be in the top 10 percent? That depends on predictive accuracy. To the de-

Figure 5
Actual Ten-Category Ranking Scheme on 609 Stocks (December 31, 1976)

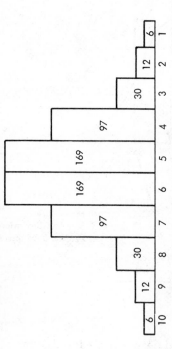

Information Coefficient Analysis for December 31, 1976–June 30, 1977

Ranking	10	9	8	7	6	5	4	3	2	1
No. of Stocks	6	12	30	97	169	169	97	30	12	6
Average returns for valuation categories had forecasts been perfect	81.8%	42.6%	23.9%	11.9%	2.3%	−7.2%	−15.7%	−23.7%	−30.2%	−38.3%
Average returns for valuation categories based on *actual* forecasts (measured IC = 0.19)	3.0%	5.3%	7.5%	2.2%	−0.7%	−3.5%	−3.4%	−1.6%	−7.6%	−16.0%

Observations:

1. The forecasts fall far short of perfection. For example, the performance gap between the actual best and worst six performers was 120.1 percent, while the performance gap between the forecasted best and worst six performers was only 19.0 percent.

2. Nevertheless, highly useful information was generated by the research process. Portfolios of securities ranked 10, 9, 8, and 7 would have outperformed portfolios of securities ranked 4, 3, 2, and 1 by 6 to 10 percent. Further, given the December 1976 IC assumption of 0.15, this result would approximately have been expected at the time the judgments were made through the derivation of adjusted alphas.

3. More generally, where adjusted alphas have been used to construct portfolios and where the adjustments were based on IC assumptions which were subsequently substantiated to have been realistic, realized portfolio alphas (or nonmarket) returns have

gree predictive accuracy is less than perfect, the realized alpha will be less than 35 percent. How much less? That depends linearly on the information coefficients. In the case of 0.15, the original 35 percent is reduced to 5 percent.

In the rating distribution, the ratings can be thought of as a variable with a mean of 3 and a standard deviation of, say, 1.5 rating points. The raw alpha distribution could reflect average experience over one-year holding periods of nonmarket returns for a universe of securities.

Again, it has a mean (0 percent) and a standard deviation (26 percent). Thus the 5 to 1 ranking scheme can be mapped onto this return distribution. Finally, the adjusted alpha distribution scales down the nonmarket returns to reflect a certain level of forecasting ability (reflected by an IC assumption of 0.15 in the example).

The adjusted alphas are more powerful numbers for portfolio rebalancing purposes than the original rankings. They now reflect realistic estimates of gains (and losses) that can be associated with a particular rating. These estimates permit a portfolio manager to judge if a contemplated change is worthwhile once implementation costs are considered. The adjusted alphas are also the appropriate input into portfolio optimization algorithms.

An actual example of this phenomenon is presented below. The example is based on the December 31, 1976 set of judgments on a 609-U.S. stock selection universe of a large U.S. investment institution. A 10 to 1 ranking scheme was employed to express under- or overvaluation judgments, with the 10 category representing the stocks judged to be most undervalued, and the 1 category the stocks most overvalued. The judgments were evaluated over a six-month "work out" period and were assumed to have an IC of 0.15. The actual (i.e., measured) information coefficient for the forecasts turned out to be 0.19. The returns shown in Figure 5 represent:

1. returns achieved by each valuation category if the forecasts had been perfect (i.e. IC = 1.0), and
2. returns achieved by each valuation category based on the December 31, 1976 judgments (i.e., assumed IC = 0.15, realized IC = 0.19).

INFORMATION COEFFICIENT ANALYSIS: IS IT IDEAL?

Previously, seven ingredients of an ideal predictive ability measurement approach were listed. The ICA approach is now evaluated in this context:

1. The approach forces explicit rather than implicit valuation judgments to be made.
2. Judgments must be related to a specific forecast date.
3. The unit of account in which the judgments are expressed can be

either in terms of returns directly or scaled through the use of a predetermined number of valuation categories. Further, the valuation categories can relate to the total selection universe or they can be disaggregated on a within and across security class (e.g. industry group) basis.

4. The approach permits evaluation over multiple "work out" periods. That is, ICs can be calculated to any date beyond the forecast date. This flexibility permits the assessment of IC patterns related to any time period beyond forecast date.

5. The approach is amenable to formal tests for statistical significance of the results.

6. The approach is flexible as it relates to people and methodologies under evaluation. For example, IC measures can be derived separately for different methodologies being employed to make valuation judgments on a given universe. Judgments made by specific individuals in a research group can also be tracked.

7. When the method of expressing valuation judgments and IC Analysis are appropriately alligned, the process leads to the generation of IC adjusted alphas. These expected return components can become direct inputs in the portfolio construction and rebalancing process.

CONCLUDING COMMENTS

Evaluating the quality of research information is a critically important component of an effective active investment management approach. Without knowledge of the predictive accuracy of valuation judgments, portfolio managers are flying blind.

This chapter set out seven key features of an ideal measurement method. A number of case studies were used to examine methods in actual use. The ICA method was found to be especially effective when evaluated against the seven characteristics of an ideal method.

As a by-product of the review of the case studies, considerable evidence was gathered to suggest that the U.S. and Canadian stock markets might not be as efficient as is believed today in some academic circles. Appropriately conceived research efforts do seem to generate useful information, albeit of modest quality. The challenge facing today's investment management organization is the appropriate use of research information of limited quality. A properly designed research quality measurement system is the ideal starting point from which to address this challenge. Such a system can not provide the definitive answer regarding the quality of today's valuation judgments in the future. It can, however, provide the basis for an informed view as to what that quality might be. And acting on informed views is what investing is all about.

Chapter 20

Measuring and Reporting on Performance

PHILIP W. BELL
William Alexander Kirkland Professor of Accounting and Economics
Jesse H. Jones Graduate School of Administration
Rice University
Houston, Texas

Although there would seem to be little agreement among investment managers about the nature, or even the feasibility, of developing reliable performance reports monitoring their work, practicing accountants and professional bodies concerned with audits of investment companies have reached a greater degree of consensus on what is required in the way of information for legitimately interested outsiders in this field than in almost any other. This consensus includes as one important element the provision of information on changes in current market values.

To many managers there is seemingly a certain mystique surrounding the handling of securities and/or other investments which often suggests that any attempt at objective measurement of performance in this field is impossible to effect, or at best will yield such faulty results as to be undesirable. Securities management in particular is an intuitive art to many of its practitioners, it would seem, like music and painting. Although reams of data are collected in this area of activity—in no other field of economic endeavor that we know of are prices, and quantities, and in particular current value (price times quantity) amounts so readily available and measurement of these so noncontroversial—securities managers, it is argued, simply cannot be subjected to a quantitative bottom line periodic appraisal like managers of other types of economic entities. Or at the very least one can say that there clearly is no agreement among investment managers (*a*) over what kind of test or tests might serve this purpose; or (*b*) over what time period some such test, if agreed upon, might be applied. It would seem that banks, brokerage houses, and others managing security portfolio accounts for individuals and even institutions simply do not believe in reporting rigorously on performance—do not really believe even in ordinary income statements, however constructed.[1]

In contrast to the seeming lack of consensus among managers of individual portfolio accounts as to what might constitute a reasonable measure to be used in evaluating performance the central professional body of practicing accountants in this country the American Institute of Certified Public Accountants (AICPA), through its Committee on Investment Companies, has so far singled out investments as the one area where the heated "historical cost vs. current value accounting" controversy is resolved. The committee's opinion is that current market values and changes in current market values not only can be but should be presented (along with traditional historical costs) in any set of financial reports subject to external audit.[2]

More recently, the Financial Accounting Standards Board (FASB), the now-dominant standards-setter for the accounting profession, has put out first an exposure draft (December 1978), then a final statement (September 1979), relating to the concerns of this chapter.[3] In these documents the Board outlines a plan whereby all U.S. corporations with more than $1 billion in total assets and/or more than $125 million in inventories plus gross plant assets must report for years 1979 forward, to become fully effective in 1980, "current cost/constant dollar" data as supplementary information in their financial statements. Such data on corporate earnings and position would be consistent with the standard for measuring and reporting on performance for individuals and companies managing securities which is suggested in this chapter. The latest effort of the accounting profession to establish new standards for a world of constantly changing specific prices around a norm of protracted and substantial inflation treats largely inventory and plant assets, leaving the older AICPA standards for marketable securities, and investment trusts, alluded to above, in tact.

We shall argue in this chapter that in the investment field accoun-

---

[1] See the author's "Portfolio Reports for Client and Manager," *Financial Analysts Journal* (May–June 1977), pp. 56–61, for some discussion, including examples, of the inadequacy of reports currently being turned out by banks, brokerage houses, private investment trusts, and others managing individual or institutional portfolio accounts. Many of these institutions do not submit any income statement to clients (surely the single most important performance measure), much less one such as that proposed here.

[2] See *Audits of Investment Companies* (New York: AICPA, 1973).

[3] See Financial Accounting Standards Board, Exposure Draft, Proposed Statement of Financial Accounting Standards, *Financial Reporting and Changing Prices* (Stamford, Conn.: FASB, 1978) and Statement of Financial Accounting Standards No. 33, *Financial Reporting and Changing Prices* (Stamford, Conn.: FASB, 1979).

tants are ahead of many managers in their thinking (or at least in their thinking about reporting on performance, for external as well as internal purposes). Income and comparative position statements based on measuring changes in current (market) values do, we feel, provide relevant measures which managers themselves need in order to practice their art effectively, in the same way that owners and others need them to evaluate the performance of the entity and of its management. We believe that the basic AICPA commitment to current value accounting in the general field of investments badly needs explanation, and requires some amendment in formulation and presentation. We further believe that were it not for the fact that taxation in this country is based on the realization of gains, rather than on the accrual or earnings of gains, there would be no reason to report income on a historical cost basis along with income on a current value accounting basis (as the AICPA recommends). Current income, and more particularly real current income, properly devised and dichotomized, can serve as the sole measure of performance, for insiders as well as outsiders, in this as in other fields. Realized income and/or Real Realized Income, in any of various forms including that reported in accordance with traditional accounting standards involving historical costs, or historical costs adjusted by some general purchasing power unit (PuPU for *Pu*rchasing *Po*wer *U*nit accounting) can, and ordinarily will be a most misleading measure of performance, hence should never be used for this purpose.

One last point before proceeding into the body of the chapter. Our aim here is to suggest measures that may be appropriate to monitor performance of entitites in the investments field. We believe strongly that information which is needed and important for evaluators of investment company performance is essentially the same type of information as that on individual firm performance needed by the managers of those investment companies for evaluation of their investments. The identical type of current value information which is needed to evaluate the performance of an investment firm is needed by the firm to evaluate the performance of others, i.e., of its investments. In this chapter we must restrict ourselves to considering the problem of measuring and reporting on the performance of investment entities, leaving to others, or perhaps to ourselves in another forum, discussion of the larger and more complicated issues involved in measuring and reporting on performance of business firms in such a way as to be useful to investors. The new Financial Accounting Standard Board effort (Statement No. 33) alluded to above is certainly a move in the right direction.[4]

---

[4] We have written extensively on the virtues of current value information in the evaluation of firms in general in Edgar O. Edwards and Philip W. Bell, *The Theory and Measurement of Business Income* (Berkeley: University of California Press, 1961),

CONCEPTS AND MEASURES NEEDED FOR THE EVALUATION OF PERFORMANCE

Objectives: Comparability and Necessary Conditions for Comparability in Performance Measures

Measurement normally involves quantifying the dimensions of something in terms of some unchanging unit of account, often in order to compare it with something else. Performance of an economic entity does not make much sense in absolute terms; absolute levels of performance, measured in some standard and unchanging unit of account, must be compared with something to have meaning, just as measures of heat and cold on a thermometer scale are generally compared to the freezing and boiling temperatures of water. Thus, we may compare actual performance with expected performance; actual performance this period with actual performances in previous periods; actual performance this period with actual performance of others, e.g., competitors, this period; or perhaps actual performance this period with the performance of some commonly accepted yardstick or measuring rod which also moves as measured in the stable unit of account—the yardstick in the investment field being perhaps Standard and Poor's (S&P 500) Index; the Dow Jones Average; or the AMEX, NYSE, or NASDAQ indexes.

The above suggests that perhaps the most important single quality a performance measure should have is that it should be such as to be *comparable* to other performance measures, and vice-versa. There have been many criteria suggested for the development of accounting information useful for the evaluation of decisions and performance—data must be objective, quantifiable, verifiable, free from bias, relevant, reliable, consistent, etc. But in fact all of these criteria will ordinarily be met if and only if data are comparable, one set with another, i.e., if the data produce identical reports of events when two sets of events are in fact identical, and if differences as given in reports of events reflect in some reliable, measurable fashion the nature of the differences in events that actually occurred, i.e., the measure of difference is reflected in some standard unit of account such as a degree on a thermometer scale.

---

especially Chapter 3, pp. 97–108, Chapter 7, pp. 220–32, and Chapter 8, pp. 264–69. See also Philip W. Bell and L. Todd Johnson, "Current Value Accounting and the Simple Production Case: Edbejo and Other Companies in the Taxi Business" in Robert R. Sterling and Arthur L. Thomas, eds., *Accounting for a Simplified Firm: Seventeen Essays Based on a Common Example* (Houston: Scholars Book Co., forthcoming). We have not yet published our thoughts in any detail about linkages between firm performance in current value terms and changes in the market value of the firm's securities on the exchanges; we are unhappy about many of the views expressed by others (especially "efficient market" addicts) on this matter and hope to contribute something constructive in the not-too-distant future, perhaps as part of a book in process on *Accounting for Economic Decisions.*

There are three underlying conditions that must be met if our comparability standard as expressed above is to be met—conditions that we hope will become clearer as we develop our framework and compare it with existing frameworks:

1. Our measure of performance must reflect actual events as they occur, that is the actual events of a period should be recorded to the exclusion of events which occurred in earlier periods or which may occur in future periods—*all* the events of a period *and only* the events of that period should be recorded to assess performance in that period.
2. The accounting model used to measure performance should be designed to classify change in such a way as to make clear why the change occurred in a period. In particular, the model should classify change into current operating income (e.g., dividend and interest earnings) on the one hand, and realizable holding gains due to a rise in the price of an asset while it is held. The two together comprise the change in the market value of the entity or total current income, before any distributions.
3. Current income and related comparative current position statements should be adjusted to take account of changes in the general price level and so record current income in "real" terms, i.e., in terms that reflect changes in the command over goods that occurred in a period. Basically these adjustments involve dividing nominal holding gains into fictional and real components (the "fictional" component being the gain that is necessary just to offset the rise in the general price level and so leave the owner of the asset no better or worse off in real terms).

Conditions 1 and 2 involve taking account of the effects of changes in specific prices of all assets owned and liabilities owed by the entity, something that historical cost accounting clearly does not do. Condition 3 involves an additional adjustment of these values to correct further for the effects of a change in the general price level in the economy, i.e., to put the nominal dollar market value gain or loss in purchasing power terms. For many years accountants, and users of accounting data, tended to think of these two types of adjustments as an either/ or matter; we will show that both types of adjustment are essential if one is to meet our central objective of having performance reports which allow comparability among different entities.

In manufacturing enterprises, and to a lesser extent in retail and wholesale trading enterprises, both condition 1 and condition 2 are important in the development of sets of data on performance which are comparable one to another. Defining clearly and reporting current operating income (revenues less all costs of operation at currently prevailing prices) as separate and distinct from holding gains—a distinction which lies at the core of condition 2—is of considerable significance, along with the appropriate temporal distribution of holding gains such that gains are reported as earned, not as realized (earned perhaps long ago), which is the central concern of condition 1.

In the case of investment entities, condition 2 concerns are of much less significance whereas condition 1 concerns are frequently very much more important than in the case of manufacturing and most other types of trading enterprises. There is no gains classification problem because there are no plant assets or inventories used in operations, hence no costs out-of-line in terms of current prices. Current operating income is simply the sum of dividends, interest, and perhaps rent earned, less some fee expenses (although some brokerage fees might legitimately be deducted from holding gains), and these are all already in terms of currently prevailing prices. On the other hand condition 1 considerations loom as very much more important concerns for investment enterprises, as compared with other types of firms. For investment enterprises, holding gains may be very large, and they may be erratic. The realization of gains involves sale, therefore the total value of an asset, rather than use and depreciation, hence a fraction of the value of the asset. (A realized holding gain in the case of a fixed asset is the excess of current cost depreciation over historical cost depreciation, i.e., it is a fraction of a fraction of an asset value.) Here, then, whether you report holding gains at the time they are earned, and become therefore realizable, or at the time they are realized as assets are sold (the gains having been earned perhaps in earlier periods) may make a significant difference in what is reported as income in measuring performance (during the period just finished).

One of our first tasks, then, is to develop a framework which will provide in particular for proper temporal distribution of gains, period-by-period. Our framework turns out to provide also for appropriate classification of gains, although that, we have argued, is not nearly so important in the case of investment entities as measuring and distinguishing between realizable and realized holding gains. The significance of condition 3, and how we work general price level adjustments into our analysis (as opposed to specific or relative price adjustments), and hence account for inflation, will be considered separately below. General price level adjustments might normally be accomplished as a separate exercise but not enter into basic accounting records, in contrast with specific price adjustments which might normally involve current-increment ledger accounts in the records and thus be built into the accounting information system in integral fashion.[5]

---

[5] For means of applying in fairly simple fashion both specific price and general price level adjustments to accounting records of business enterprises see Edgar O. Edwards, Philip W. Bell, and L. Todd Johnson, *Accounting for Economic Events* (Houston: Scholars Book Co., 1980), chap. 12.

Formulating the Data: A Basic Worksheet Tabulation

Table 1 involves worksheet data depicting a very simple case of an institutional portfolio (Mountain View College) managed by an individual investment counselor or by a firm (e.g., a bank or brokerage house). A similar worksheet could be developed for an investment company, like a mutual fund. All the information we need to develop reports to meet conditions 1 and 2, hence achieve comparability for such an entity, at least in the absence of general price level changes, is contained in Table 1.

The key to the Table 1 information lies in providing a separate line for any block of securities traded during the period; hence if some of a particular security has been purchased or sold during the period while other amounts of that security have been held continuously throughout the period, these two phenomena are registered on separate lines. The great difficulty with most comparative position statements or balance sheets presently being provided by investment houses to clients is that security holdings at the beginning and end of a period may combine two elements of change and report them as one (e.g., a holding gain, because of a rise in price of a security while held continuously during the period, may be combined with a change in amount due to a purchase or sale and the two together be reported as one figure). Thus, in Table 1 the market value of shares of General Electric Company Stock would be reported simply as $10,175,000 at the beginning of the period and $14,775,000 at the end of the period. The increase in value was actually due to a purchase of $4,712,000, a rise in value of these shares while held from purchase date to end of period amounted to $213,000, and a decline in value of other GE shares held throughout the period that amounted to $325,000 ($14,775,000 − $10,175,000 = $4,600,000 = $4,712,000 + $213,000 − $325,000). Similarly, 50 shares of Panhandle Eastern Pipe were purchased early in the period, increased in value, and were sold near the end of the period; 100 shares purchased at the same time were held to the end of the period (and continued to gain in value throughout the period held, in contrast to the GE shares purchased during the period). It is only a partial picture of events to report zero Panhandle values held at the beginning of the period and 100 shares, whose cost was $3,713,000, at a value of $4,400,000 at the end of the period. This understates gains earned from investing in Panhandle Eastern, for another $207,000 in addition to the $687,000 (=$4,400,000 − $3,713,000) was also involved. In the case of Panhandle investments, all of the gain realized during the period on this stock was earned (became realizable) this period. Not so of American Hospital Supply shares, where the realized gain from the sale of 200 shares this period had all accrued in earlier periods. Clearly, to report simply a market value of

Table 1
Worksheet for Mountain View College, Agency Account (December 31, 19X1–March 31, 19X2)

Security	Original Cost Information				Market Value Information				Realizable Gains (Losses)			Realized Gains (Losses)	
	Dec. 31, 19X1		Mar. 31, 19X2		Mkt. Value Dec. 31, 19X1	Purchases	Sales	Mkt. Value Mar. 31, 19X2	Operating Income	Holding Gain (Loss)	Total	Holding Gain (Loss)	Total
	No. Units	Cost	No. Units	Cost									
Stocks													
American Hospital Supply													
Held continuously	100	2,289	100	2,289	2,675	—	—	2,975	17	300	317	—	17
Traded	200	4,578	—	—	5,350	—	5,350 (1/12/X2)	—	-0-	-0-	-0-	772	772
Total	300	6,867	100	2,289	8,025	—	5,350	2,975	17	300	317	772	789
General Electric													
Held continuously	200	6,384	200	6,384	10,175	—	—	9,850	130	(325)	(195)	—	130
Traded	—	—	100	4,712	—	4,712 (2/10/X2)	—	4,925	-0-	213	213	—	-0-
Total	200	6,384	300	11,096	10,175	4,712	—	14,775	130	(112)	18	—	130
Heublein													
Traded + Total	200	4,796	—	—	5,775	—	5,625	—	-0-	(150)	(150)	829	829
Panhandle Eastern Pipe													
Traded	—	—	100	3,713	—	3,713 (1/12X2)	—	4,400	65	687	752	—	65
Traded	—	—	—	3,713	—	1,856 (1/12/X2)	2,063 (3/20/X2)	—	33	207	240	207	240
Total	—	—	100	3,713	—	5,569	2,063	4,400	98	894	992	207	305
Total, Stocks	18,047		17,098		23,975	10,281	13,038	22,150	245	932	1,177	1,808	2,053
Bonds													
Stockton, Calif. Unified School Dist., 5.2%, June 15, 1988;													
Held Continuously		5,000		5,000	5,070	—	—	4,880	130	(190)	(60)	—	130
Total, Marketable Securities		23,047		22,098	29,045			27,030	375	742	1,117	1,808	2,183

$8,025,000 invested in American Hospital Supply at the beginning of the period and $2,975,000 at the end of the period offers by itself no help in measuring and interpreting investment performance.

Current Value Income and Comparative Position Statements, Reconciliation with Historical Cost Statements, and Weaknesses of the AICPA Recommendation

Table 1 data, including as it does interest and dividend revenue, the historical (original purchase) cost of blocks of shares as well as their market values at beginning and end of period, and the market values at the time of purchase and/or sale of shares traded during the period, yield all the information we need to formulate current value income and comparative position statements in such a way that they can be compared with traditional historical cost statements as shown in Tables 2 and 3. A "Sources and Uses of Funds" statement, as shown in Table 4, helps reconcile and explain the other two statements as well as provide us with information on changes in liquidity in the account and on how and why the increased liquidity, as shown on the comparative position statement, came about during the period.

We stress at the outset of this section that we do not need the

Table 2
MOUNTAIN VIEW COLLEGE INVESTMENTS
Current Income Statement
December 31, 19X1–March 31, 19X2 (in thousands of dollars)

Revenues and Holding Gains (Losses)			
From Dividends		$245	
From Interest		170	
Total		$415	
Realized Holding Gains, this period	$1808		
Subtract Holding Gains realized this period which accrued in past periods	1751		
Equals Holding Gains accruing this period and realized this period		$ 57	
Add Holding Gains accruing this period but as yet unrealized		685	
Equals Realizable Holding Gains Accruing this Period		742	
Total Revenues and Holding Gains (Losses)			$1157
Operating Expenses			
Brokerage fees		$498	
Management fee		64	
Other		—	
Total Expenses			562
Current Ownership Income			$ 595
Contributions (Withdrawals)			(800)
Change in Ownership Equity			$ (205)

Table 3
MOUNTAIN VIEW COLLEGE INVESTMENTS
Comparative Current Position Statement
December 31, 19X1–March 31, 19X2

	March 31, 19X2		December 31, 19X1
Current Assets			
Cash	$ 210		$ 360
Savings	3,200		1,240
Total		$ 3,410		$ 1,600
Subtract Current Liabilities:			
Accrued Current Payables	–0–		–0–
Equals Funds		$ 3,410		$ 1,600
Add Marketable Securities			
At historical cost	$22,098		$23,047
Current cost increment	4,932		5,998
Total, Current Value		27,030		29,045
Equals Total Funds and Marketable Securities		$30,440		$30,645
Ownership Equity:			
Contributions	$17,900		$18,700
Retained Earnings	12,540		11,945
Total		$30,440		$30,645

historical cost and realized holding gain data in Tables 2 and 3 (the data do not affect the funds information in Table 4) for purposes of evaluating performance. Indeed they rather get in the way. We need realized holding gain data for tax purposes. But it is current income data which are essential for measuring the performance of our portfolio during this period and for comparing that performance with performance in earlier periods and with the performance of others in meaningful fashion. Current ownership income is the change in the market

Table 4
MOUNTAIN VIEW COLLEGE INVESTMENTS
Sources and Uses of Funds
December 31, 19X1–March 31, 19X2 (in thousands of dollars)

Sources:		
Dividends and Interest	$ 415	
Sale of Securities (Gross)	13,038	
New Contributions	–0–	
Total		$13,453
Uses:		
Purchase of Securities (Gross)	$10,281	
Payment of Operating Expenses	562	
Withdrawals	800	
Total		11,643
Increase (Decrease) in Funds:		$ 1,810

value of owners' interests in the portfolio independent of any new contributions or withdrawals during the period. As we have suggested above, that all-important figure of current ownership income is often missing from any existing manager reports to clients, which frequently provide simply a statement of the total market value of assets in the account at the beginning and end of the period, the amount at the end of the period including any new contributions and not including any new withdrawals during the period. In other words, what will be shown in many reports of managers to clients today is simply the $30,645,000 total for December 31, 19X1 and the $30,440,000 total for March 31, 19X2 (with some kind of detail on asset holdings), but not in effect the all-important breakdown of ownership equity in the two periods between total contributed capital (the dollars owners have at various times put into the account less what they have withdrawn from the account) and retained earnings (the cumulative market gains earned by the account over the years). The decrease of $800,000 in contributed capital between December 31, 19X1 and March 31, 19X2 as shown in Table 3 reflects the net withdrawals of the period as shown near the bottom on Table 2; the increase in retained earnings of $595,000 over the period as shown in Table 3 ($12,540,000 − $11,945,000 = $595,000) equals the current ownership income amount in Table 2. The two together yield the decline in ownership equity of $205,000 shown at the bottom of the income statement and as the difference in the total ownership equity amounts on the comparative position statement. Clearly the two components of the decline in ownership equity are essential in evaluating performance, or really the current ownership income component (i.e. the change in retained earnings on the comparative position statement) is what is vital in measuring and assessing performance—how well or badly the account did independent of new contributions and/or withdrawals.

Next consider the breakdown of current ownership income as between dividends and interest (which, if management fees and other current expenses are subtracted, yields a figure for current operating income) on the one hand, and realizable holding gains on the other. As is well known, the planned distribution of total gains between these two elements is a matter of policy, and may well be affected by tax and other considerations (see below). An income objective will often stress the former element, while a growth objective will often stress the latter element. But in fact, except for tax considerations and time-period considerations with respect to when gains are anticipated, the distinction between how the increase in total market value of the client is effected—whether through dividends and interest or holding gains—is immaterial. The best instructions a client who does not intend to withdraw amounts from the account can give a manager are: "Maximize the present value of future total after-tax increases in market value in the account over x years by whatever means you can—buying stocks and bonds which yield high dividends and interest which can be reinvested after payment of taxes but which are not expected to increase much in price, or buying 'growth stocks' which may be expected to rise in price but pay little in dividends, the increase in market value than being subject to capital gains taxation."

A still more important concern with respect to accumulating and reporting data on performance has to do with the definition of holding gains and how they are reported. The AICPA Committee on Investment Companies, in their industry audit guide recommendation, suggests an income statement along the following lines (using the data in Table 2).[6]

Statement of Operations (AICPA Committee Form)
(in hundreds of thousands of dollars)

Investment Income:			
Income from dividends and interest		$ 415	
Expenses (including brokerage fees[6]		562	
Total			($147)
Realized and Unrealized Gain (Loss) on Investments:			
Realized Gain (Loss)		$1,808	
Unrealized appreciation of investments			
Beginning of period	$5,998		
End of period............................	4,932		
Increase (decrease) in unrealized appreciation		(1,066)	
Net realized and unrealized gain (loss) on investments..............................			742
Total			$595

[6] See the AICPA Industry Audit Guide, p. 100 and elsewhere. The Committee on Investment Companies would seemingly report the historical cost of securities held at gross purchase price (thus never reporting the brokerage fee as an expense), and would report the value at time of sale as sale value less brokerage fee, thus not reporting the brokerage fee separately at time of sale either. In contrast, we would carry the historical cost value of securities at net purchase price, charging the brokerage fee as an expense, and we would then record the sale value as a gross value, before deducting the brokerage fee, and again charge the brokerage fee as an expense. The two methods may be contrasted by journal entries as follows, assuming no price changes:

At time of purchase:

AICPA		Our method	
Security A	$102	Security A	$100
		Brokerage fee	2
Cash	$102	Cash	$102

At time of sale:

AICPA		Our method	
Cash	$ 98	Cash	$ 98
Realized loss on sale	4	Brokerage fee	2
Security A	$102	Security A	$100

It seems to us that there is considerable value to a client-owner and manager in the separate reporting of brokerage fees, rather than in effect hiding them until sale and then reporting both purchase and sales fees as a realized capital loss. We have adapted the AICPA approach to accord with our preference on this matter.

The difficulty in the AICPA approach as we see it is that while it in effect can be adapted to arrive at the same figure for current owner-ship income as that following the format in Table 2, i.e., $595,000 (the AICPA format surprisingly does not actually provide the figure but shows only the two components—$147 and $742), it gives a mislead-ing impression of market performance in the period under consider-ation. The $1,066 decrease in unrealized appreciation does *not* mean that securities held by the firm have gone down in value over the period, as the casual interpreter might assume. That figure actually measures the decline in the *cumulative stock* of unrealized apprecia-tion in the account—a decline which could have been caused by new, as yet unrealized, decreases in value in securities held by the firm but also, by having realized gains through sale of securities which have risen in value since purchase, perhaps long ago. The AICPA's decrease in unrealized appreciation figure is a meaningless, composite figure consisting of adding any newly accrued unrealized gains this period ($685,000) and subtracting gains realized this period which had accrued in past periods ($1,751,000), the net decrease in *the stock* of unrealized appreciation in the account over the period then being $1,066,000. This figure, like the realized holding gain figure, contains information from past periods as well as from the present period, i.e., both violate condition 1 for they are not limited to reporting events of only the present period. The figure that you really want to use in measuring holding performance is the figure for realizable holding gains which accrued this period, which the AICPA method approaches by circu-itous, and we feel misleading, routing. As opposed to the gloomy picture that might be read from the AICPA report, the Table 2 approach suggests that managers did reasonably well in their holding activities this period. The account earned $742,000 in realizable holding gains this period, of which $57,000 was realized this period (along with $1,751,000 which was earned in past periods) and $685,000 is as yet unrealized (along with $247,000 unrealized gains carried over from previous periods). The emphasis is on, and we suggest below should be still more on, currently accruing realizable holding gains earned in the current period.

If one wishes to report realized holding gains (needed for tax pur-poses) on a comprehensive income statement, thus getting to an income figure consistent with historical costs, thereby conforming to generally accepted accounting principles ($415,000 + $1,808,000 − $562,000 = $1,661,000) we suggest that a statement such as that shown in Table 2 be formulated rather than a statement such as that suggested by the AICPA Committee on Investment Companies—Table 2 clearly showing the relationship between realized and realizable holding gains in meaningful fashion. We actually see little value in reporting realized holding gains in the body of the current income statement, however; it is not only absolutely worthless, it is misleading so far as evaluating events of this period are concerned. We would therefore relegate that figure to a footnote, subtracting that portion of realizable holding gains that is as yet unrealized from the realizable total and adding holding gains which were realized this period but which accrued in past periods to get the figure for total holding gains which were realized (hence are taxable) this period in the footnote. In effect we work backwards from realizable holding gains to realized holding gains (in a footnote to a true current income statement) rather than build from historical costs and present generally accepted accounting principles to current ownership income in the body of the income statement, even in the manner of Table 2 which we suggest as being far preferable to the AICPA Committee on Investment Companies approach.

Changes in the General Price Level, Inflation Accounting, and Performance Evaluation

Correcting accounts for specific price changes and reporting asset, equity, and income items in current value terms for investment entities, in the manner sketched above, goes far toward providing the essential data needed to evaluate the entity's performance in a given period. We cannot evaluate decisions and performance effectively in the face of data accumulated in accordance with traditional historical costs and the realization convention, for such data violate both conditions 1 and 2 above—condition 1 being the most important in the case of investment companies. You cannot effectively evaluate performance over a period on the basis of reports which (a) commingle data on events occurring in that period with events which occurred in other periods stretching back through time and which (b) do not include data for all the events which occurred in the period being evaluated—two critical defects of traditional historical cost accounting data which report gains on a realized basis rather than a realizable basis.[7] We can operate if we must, however, within a framework which adheres to the money convention of accounting (even though that violates condition 3 above). It would be better if we also made adjustments to put data into current value terms certain further adjustments

---

[7] Again, we should remind the reader that the defects of traditional accounting data, because of adherence to the realization convention, are still more serious than this in the case of manufacturing and other trading entities as compared with investment entities. For such entities realized holding gains are not even reported separately, but rather are bound up with current operating income in one reported "income from operations," because of the use of historical costs and arbitrary depreciation formuli in the case of fixed assets, and arbitrary "flow" concepts like FIFO and LIFO in the case of valuing inventory and the cost of goods sold. The classification of gains problem looms large in evaluating most other types of entities but is not really significant for investment entities. For further discussion of these matters, see Edwards, Bell, and Johnson, *Accounting,* chap. 11–13, and Edwards and Bell, *Theory of Income,* chap. 5–7.

which correct our data for the effects of changes in the general price level in the economy, thus expressing income and changes in ownership equity components in real terms and allowing comparisons in terms of general command over goods in the economy rather than in terms of nominal dollars (having possibly different purchasing powers). Many management decisions and many owner-evaluation decisions of management can, it is true, be effectively considered in terms of nominal dollar data. But this is not generally true for decisions and performance evaluations involving comparison of gains of a single entity as between different periods when the unit of account being used for measurement purposes—the dollar—differs for the two periods in terms of its command value over goods. And nominal dollar comparisons may even prove faulty when employed to compare events and performance between two entities in the same period, or over the same time-span.

The reader should be warned that general price level corrections are extremely tricky to apply in measuring entity performance—much trickier than in the case of adjustments necessary simply to express, say, growth of gross national product in real terms. Let us see why this is so, and how such adjustments may be effected. Then we can consider implications.

Let us assume first that the investment performance for Mountain View College depicted in Tables 1 and 2 for the first quarter of 19X2 was exactly duplicated, in nominal dollar terms, in the first quarter of 19X3. In the first quarter of 19X2 there was no change during the quarter in the general price level, i.e., inflation was nil. In the first quarter of 19X3, however, the general price level rose by 2½ percent. Was there a real gain or loss on Mountain View investments in the first quarter of 19X3? Let us assume the distribution of $800,000 was accomplished at the very end of the quarter. Then Mountain View would have needed total assets worth $30,645,000 × 1.025 = $31,411,125 before distribution at the end of the quarter to be just as well off as at the beginning of the quarter: a "fictional dollar gain" of $766,125,000 is needed simply to cover the effects of the general inflation. In order to refine our analysis we would have to adjust the various dollars of income earned by Mountain View over the period differentially to put each into end-of-period dollars to compare with this needed $766,125,000. If we assume, for purposes of simplification, that all price changes, including those on securities, occurred on the first day of the period, then clearly Mountain View, which has assets before distribution of only $31,240,000 at the end of the period, suffered a real loss during the first quarter of 19X3, in spite of showing positive current income as measured in nominal dollars. Clients and/ or owners need this information surely to judge management, but obviously management, too, needs to be made aware that in the first quarter of 19X3 Mountain View's investments were not keeping up with inflation, whereas positive real gains had been registered in the first quarter of 19X2.

The difficulty of adjusting for the effects of general price level changes in the accounts for, say, individual investment entities, as compared with, say, expressing growth in Gross National Product (GNP) in real terms, lies in the fact that holding (or capital) gains and losses are involved for firms but cancel each other out for the economy as a whole, one person's or entity's real holding gain being another person's or entity's real holding loss. Since the general price level is an average, any real gain because of a positive price differential must be offset by a real loss because of a negative price differential. A positive current operating income figure for a firm (GNP is simply the aggregate of all these) will normally imply a real gain, albeit it may be smaller or larger than the nominal gain if current operating income is expressed in other than current dollars—for example if gains are measured in end-of-period dollars but current operating income is expressed in average-of-period dollars. But a nominal holding gain may very well mean a real holding loss—this will be the case if the general price level rises over the period by a greater amount than the specific price of an asset. GNP adjustments to get measurements of real gains mean adjustments to income data; firm adjustments to get measurements of real gains mean adjustments to asset and liability amounts (in the case of holding gains) as well as income amounts (in the case of operating gains).

We have seen that what looked like equal nominal gains in two periods turned out to mean a real loss in one period compared with the nominal (equals real) gain in the other period. Temporal comparisons of single entity performances demand price-level corrections to data as well as adjustments for specific price changes with respect to assets held and liabilities owed by the firm. But so, too, surprisingly, do comparisons of performance between different firms in the same period, when both sets of data are subject to correction for the same inflation factor. Consider the Mountain View case for 19X3, with a growth in the general price level of 2.5 percent, as compared with the investment account of Desert Prairie College, whose income statement was identical to Mountain View's, but whose total assets were $10 million on December 31, 19X2 and $10,595,000 before distribution of the $800,000 on March 31, 19X3. Prairie View needed assets of $10,000,000 × 1.025 = $10,250,000 on March 31, 19X3 to leave it just as well off as on December 31, 19X2. It had more than enough, and therefore experienced a real gain. But Mountain View, with an identical nominal-value income statement suffered a real loss.

Comparability—over time and among firms—requires both individual price adjustments to express assets, equities, and income in current value terms and adjustments to these current value amounts to correct for the effects of inflation—increases (or decreases) in the general price level. It may be argued that it is up to the client or owner to make these adjustments. But the client seldom has the information to make the former adjustments. And in fact even general price level adjustments applied to data for individual firms ordinarily require considerably more information on the timing of purchases and sales, etc., than the client or owner has available. Making both kinds of adjustments should be relatively easy in the case of an investment entity for the firm itself to accomplish. And as indicated, managers really need both kinds of information to manage the investment account properly, to evaluate their own decisions. We believe that current value data are absolutely essential in the production of statements along the general lines discussed and illustrated above, and that further refinement of these data to express the information in a common unit of account—a price-level-adjusted dollar value—could be very helpful, to both managers and clients or owners. Such adjustments could be accomplished at very little effort and cost.[8]

Provision of a current income statement, a comparative current position statement, and a funds statement, or still better these plus a real current income statement and a comparative real current position statement as supplementary documents, along the lines sketched above, would be a major step toward supplying both insiders (managers) and outsiders (clients, owners, and others) the accounting information they need to evaluate individual decisions and overall performance in the investments field. Provision of this information would be consistent with the current thinking on external reporting of the Financial Accounting Standards Board (FASB), the central standards-setting body on professional accounting matters in the United States, as indicated earlier.

TAX CONSIDERATIONS, THE TIMING PROBLEM, AND INTERPRETATION OF THE DATA

We come finally to two complicating concerns not yet touched upon which deserve at least some mention. One concerns taxes, and how and where they may fit into the picture. The other concerns the timing problem; since securities as well as other investments are generally

---

[8] Actual procedures for adjusting for both specific price changes and for changes in the general price level for manufacturing firms, as well as finished statements, are discussed and illustrated in Edwards, Bell, and Johnson, *Accounting*, chap. 12. Whole books have been written about the process, but it is not that complicated, and adjustments for investment entities should ordinarily be considerably simpler than for manufacturing enterprises. Furthermore, the application of price-level-adjustments to current value data is a great deal simpler than application to historical cost data. We see no reason why both types of adjustments could not be readily applied to investment entities, with great benefits to all concerned.

subject to sharp cyclical price swings, is there ever an appropriate time period, long or short, over which performance can be fairly evaluated, i.e., will you not always look better if you start from a trough, worse if you start from a peak? This latter issue gets us finally into problems of interpretation of the information we have urged be reported.

Tax Considerations and Performance Reporting

Business entities whose main activity is the handling of investments for clients, beneficiaries, or shareholders—whether such entities consist of individual or institutional accounts, investment trusts, or investment companies like mutual funds, incorporated or not—generally pay no income taxes themselves as business entities, if they distribute all of their currently earned operating income (for example, dividends and interest) and realized holding gains. They are treated by tax authorities as conduits with the final recipients of the operating income and realized holding gains paying the full tax.

This means of course that the income and capital gains taxes paid on the distributed income will depend on the tax status of the recipients. Clearly where these recipients number more than one—the case in all investment entities except that of an account tailored to a single individual or institution—it is virtually impossible to assess, in the financial reports of the investment entity, the tax effects of the reported overall income earned.

For the individual managed account, on the other hand, approximate tax effects can normally be assessed in all likelihood, because the individual's general tax bracket is known. Thus, if an individual client is in, say, a 60 percent incremental tax bracket and considers income from investments to be supplementary to a normal salary income from which there is withholding—that is, he must think in terms of a 60 percent tax on securities income and a 24 percent tax on capital gains (60 percent of the 40 percent of the gain which is taxable at ordinary income tax rates)—a supplementary statement showing the tax effects of reported income could readily be drawn up. Most readers will immediately say, no doubt, that individual tax matters are up to the client and his or her tax accountant, not the manager of the investment account. But clearly management in making decisions on investments must be cognizant of the tax implications of these decisions on its client. To the extent possible it should assess its every move in terms of after-tax gains for its client.

Thus, assume Mountain View College used in the illustration above was an individual in a 53 percent incremental tax bracket. A management decision to sell the 300 shares of General Electric stock in the account on the grounds that it was not expected to appreciate in value over the next three years and buy stock XYZ with the proceeds, in the expectation that the XYZ stock would appreciate 10 percent over that period and pay the same dividends as the GE stock, might in fact be an unsound decision if events were as expected. The after-tax gain differential might be measured as follows:

Gross proceeds from sale of GE stock	$14,775
Brokerage fees	− 375
Net proceeds invested in XYZ stock	$14,400
Brokerage fees	− 360
Total	$14,040
Appreciation on XYZ stock	1,440
Capital gains tax on sale of GE stock	− 770
Accrued capital gains on XYZ stock	− 305
Total	$14,405

After-tax dividends would have been the same, but in effect management has here replaced assets worth $14,775 (stock at entry value) with assets less cash given up worth $14,405. And appropriately discounting the gains and losses in the transaction would make it worse. Nor would the decision be wise if the above was expected and in addition the XYZ stock purchased was expected to earn $400 more in dividends than the GE stock, for this would mean $188 in after-tax income to the client. Clearly these after-tax effects on our client in a 53 percent incremental tax bracket would differ from that of a client in a 65 percent incremental tax bracket, and both of these from that of a client in a 40 percent incremental tax bracket.

If taxes are important in decision-making, then taxes must be important in the evaluation of decisions and performance, and where feasible we believe some noting of the effects of income and capital gains taxes might be reported as supplementary information to current income and/or real current income financial statements. In this way the importance of tax effects will be kept in the forefront of thinking on the part of both manager and client.

The Timing Problem and Interpretation of the Data

One of the factors making managers of investments reluctant to report on performance in a systematic, rigorous, quantitative manner— a phenomenon alluded to above—has to do with the vagaries of the stock market, i.e., the variability of earnings from securities in general. As managers often see it, any formal report on their individual performance will inevitably be too much based on the behavior of the market as a whole. The manager of an account taken on during a peak in the cycle may look terrible for quite a while even though one may actually be managing well, at least given the presumption that one is to stay in the market.

The answer to this problem of course lies in comparing individual performance with standard performance indicators. What is desired is to compare the total change in market value, involving dividends and interest as well as realizable holding gains and/or losses, of the net assets, before contributions and withdrawals or dividends, for the individual investment entity with a comparable measure for the total change in market value of say, stocks in the Dow Jones Industrial Average, or of Standard and Poor's 500 companies as weighted in their index. Individual performances may also be usefully compared with performances of particular mutual funds and/or with an open-end fund average which is reported, along with the necessary data for the S&P 500, Dow Jones Industrials, and the consumer price index, in the *United Mutual Fund Selector* published bi-weekly by United Business Service. If, for example, it were found that between December 31, 19X1 and March 31, 19X2 the Dow Jones net asset value index rose by 3 percent, the comparable S&P Index by 7 percent, the comparable open-end mutual fund average by 10 percent, and the consumer price index by 2.5 percent, Mountain View College's account, whose net asset value increased by 5 percent over this period *(a)* bettered inflation, thus involving real gains, but *(b)* did not do as well as the S&P Index or the open-end mutual fund index. At least over this period Mountain View College might have been better off in an indexed fund or in an average open-end mutual fund, although of course differential costs among these various alternatives must be taken into account.

Beyond this lies the problem of the projected late-bloomer, the stock which presumably will blossom soon but the timing is uncertain. There are timing problems in evaluation over the short run of course. But these timing problems should not lead managers or client/owners to confuse subjective data on the future with objective data on the present and past in the evaluation process. Forecasted data may of course be useful in decision-making with respect to an uncertain future. The name of the game is to forsee "subjective goodwill" on the horizon—future dividend flows and/or realizable holding gains, i.e., projected increases in market value by one route or the other—that others do not forsee, and invest accordingly. But using such subjective data, perhaps along with objective data on the present and past, to evaluate past decisions and performance, as some discounted cash flows enthusiasts in accounting favor, can only cloud the issue. The "subjective goodwill" forseen—gains projected from in effect "outguessing the market"—must be turned into actual market value to complete the plan. The manager who continually makes promises but who does not produce results is not one to hire. Objective accounting data on the present and past are needed to evaluate past decisions and performance, and this evaluative process forms a vital element in the total decision-making process. Such accounting data may be of some direct use in predicting the future, but this possible use should not influence the nature of the data collected, in contrast to what some accountants seem to be arguing for these days. Objective accounting data on the present and past—involving current values in the manner we suggest in this chapter—are what are essential for both managers and interested outsiders in accomplishing their essential task of measuring and monitoring the performance of investment entities. In much investments work the evaluation task is often not undertaken systematically, still less often properly reported on. Clients and owners have a right to expect better.

Part Four

Regulatory Aspects

Chapter 21

An Overview of Fiduciary Law

JAMES L. WALTERS
Vice President and Counsel
Wellington Management Company
Boston, Massachusetts

An investment manager is a fiduciary to his or her clients. Basically, this means that the manager's activities are carried out subject to a standard of care and a duty of loyalty not required in other business relationships. Every action taken by an investment manager in one's role as a fiduciary bears the potential for later scrutiny if the correctness of one's conduct should be questioned. Therefore, it is important that an investment manager should possess a basic understanding of fiduciary principles and apply then in one's work. The purpose of this chapter is to examine the primary elements of a manager's fiduciary responsibility and provide a guide to understanding the law that may be of some practical use.

Investment management law is relatively new as a separate field of legal study, but it is evolving rapidly. This evolution is especially apparent with respect to the law defining a manager's fiduciary responsibilities, which has developed along with the relatively new profession of investment management. As one observer has noted,

> The birth of the prudent-man rule, the debate over its meaning, and the expansion of the duty of loyalty to cope with subtler situations than blatant self-dealing are all developments largely attributable to the changing character of investment management as trust administration became a business.[1]

Drawn from diverse and venerable sources, such as trust and agency law, these fiduciary concepts have recently emerged as key elements

---

[1] Reprinted by permission from *The Law of Investment Management*, Copyright 1978, Warren, Gorham and Lamont Inc., Boston, Mass. All Rights Reserved.

in modern specialized federal laws governing securities, investment companies, investment advisors, and employe benefit plans. Because of their newness, some of these federally imposed standards—such as in the Employee Retirement Income Security Act of 1974 (ERISA)—have yet to be interpreted by the courts, and their meaning and application are subjects of debate. The existence of these provisions, however, creates a likelihood that a more complete definition of fiduciary standards will be developed within a relatively short period of time. Investment managers should keep abreast of these judicial and administrative definitions, so their activities can remain consistent with current standards.

An investment manager's fiduciary responsibility is viewed by the law as consisting of two basic parts: reasonable care and loyalty. This analysis will follow that division, examining each of the two duties separately. An overview of this subject can do no more than present a broad outline. Subsequent chapters treat certain areas of the law more specifically, and will supplement the basic material presented here.

THE STANDARD OF REASONABLE CARE

The standard of reasonable care for investment managers is commonly referred to as "prudence." The law defining this duty to act prudently is less developed than that relating to the duty of loyalty. One reason for this, unfortunately, may be that the more refined issues of professional standards of care have had to wait their turn historically while the law dealt with the cruder questions of fraud and conflicting interests. Because of the increasing importance of professional money management, the law's attention is focusing on the required standard of care, and there are prospects for clearer definition in the future.

The law's lack of definiteness, however, is also largely due to the nature of the questions involved in determining the "prudence" of an investment manager's actions. An investment decision may be prudent in one situation and imprudent in another, depending upon the client, the client's objectives and the nature of the manager-client relationship. A case by case approach is more appropriate than specific rules because there are so many variables that enter into a determination of prudence. A recent description of the variety of factors upon which the standard of care may depend included the following:

> (1) the type of client and his ability to evaluate the recommendation (institutional or private, sophisticated or inexperienced), (2) the form in which advice is rendered (personal or nonpersonal), the extent of contact between the adviser and his client (whether in person or by publication), the ease with which the relationship can be terminated legally (agency or trust), and economically, whether the client can easily

replace the adviser with another or whether the client depends on the adviser for a smooth continued operation (investment company client), and (3) the fees that the adviser obtains. The amount of the assets managed may also dictate the expected degree of care; a small account bringing the adviser a small fee may not be reasonably expected to receive the same care and diligence as a much larger account, (4) the extent of the adviser's discretion, and finally, (5) the accessibility of relevant information to the adviser: if the adviser knew of the material fact and paid no attention, or if he could easily have discovered it but did not, or if a great deal of effort is required to discover the fact.[2]

Therefore, the standard of care to which investment managers are held will vary. The publisher of investment advice through a news letter is subject to a different standard of care to subscribers than a manager who provides advice to specific clients on a more direct basis. The highest standard of care is that expected of the professional investment counselor who professes to be capable of providing investment supervisory services for large accounts on a fully discretionary basis.

The law's general avoidance of rigid standards reflects a wisdom which should be appreciated rather than criticized. Although certain investment alternatives are foreclosed by the operation of law (such as the "legal lists" applicable to certain clients under some state laws), the investment manager is generally not subject to specific legal restrictions in selecting investments. If specific restrictions do exist for a particular client, the manager has a duty to be aware of them and not negligently or intentionally cause the client to violate applicable restrictions.

The more interesting questions arise in the much broader area where there are no specific rules to follow. For these questions, the law has created a flexible and objective standard of care which is largely determined by the professional investing community itself. The cornerstone of this standard is the often cited "prudent man rule," first articulated in 1830 in the Massachusetts decision, *Harvard College* v. *Amory:*

> All that can be required of a trustee to invest, is, that he shall conduct himself faithfully and exercise a sound discretion. He is to observe how men of prudence, discretion and intelligence manage their own affairs, not in regard to speculation, but in regard to the permanent disposition of their funds, considering the probable income, as well as the probable safety of the capital to be invested.

As applicable to investment managers, the prudent man rule has changed through court decisions and legislation in two important respects since the standard above was written. First, a professional money manager is likely to be judged not by how one would handle one's

---

[2] See Tamar Frankel, *The Regulation of Money Managers* (Boston: Little, Brown & Co., Inc., 1978), p. 669, vol. 2.

personal affairs, but by how other managers would act in a similar position with a similar client. This kind of flexible standard is reflected in ERISA, which defines prudence as being "how a prudent man acting in a like capacity and familiar with such matters" would have acted "in the conduct of an enterprise of a like character with like aims." Therefore, for example, an institutional money manager will be judged by the standards then prevailing among other institutional managers. This is often referred to as a prudent expert standard.

The second change in the prudence standard is that if there is a representation that the manager "has greater skill than that of a man of ordinary prudence, he is under a duty to exercise such skill."[3] Therefore, if a manager claims to be capable of rendering the kinds of services necessary to manage a particular type of account, one will be held to the standards of other managers handling that type of account.

The critical point to understand about the prudent man rule is that it provides a flexible and objective standard of care. The rule does not specify what is prudent, but, instead, specifies how prudence will be determined: a factual determination of the relevant standard of care then existing among others similarly situated. Because this process is objective, particular shortcomings, weaknesses or lack of ability of the manager in question are not considered in determining the standard. Thus, the language of the prudent man rule is meaningless without objective knowledge of the degree of care applied by other managers in similar circumstances. In this way, the law has a built-in flexibility, allowing it to adjust to changing types of relationships and standards in the profession.

The professional manager, even if one has full discretion, is not a guarantor of investment success. A manager's duty is to see that means used are reasonable as decisions will be judged as of the time they are made rather than with the benefit of later hindsight. If the process utilized by an investment manager represents the application of a reasonable standard of care, the resulting investment performance will not create a liability based on breach of fiduciary duty. A recent treatise on investment management law expresses this point well:

> Reasonable care asks whether an undertaking is carried on in a fashion which sufficiently tends to accomplish its aims. This does not mean that it must succeed or that failure proves lack of reasonable care. Reasonable care only requires that the teachings of experience be heeded so that unnecessary risks are avoided. For investment management, reasonable care normally translates into the use of methods and techniques which take into account principles, theories, customs and conventions generally observed by the investment management community . . . This does not imply that universal agreement about what should be done is necessary

---

[3] Restatement (Second) of Trusts Sect. 174 (1959).

. . . nor does it imply that new departures in method or technique are prohibited . . . Reasonable care is simply a balance between experience and enterprise. It requires that whatever the course chosen, there be due regard for what is generally known.[4]

Thus, questions as to the prudence of a particular investment method or approach are answered at any specific time with reference to general knowledge. Today, it may be clear that a manager who bases recommendations solely on extra-sensory perception or hallucinogenic visions is not applying a reasonable standard of care. However, as the collective knowledge of investment management develops and is applied, more traditional methods of investing may be challenged as well. For example, one legal commentator has urged that there should be a "presumptive prohibition" against the use of technical analysis on behalf of a client, to be rebutted only by express consent of clients given after receiving disclosure regarding "the limitations of technical analysis as a predictor of changes in stock prices." Basing his argument on the efficient market hypothesis, the same commentator would also restrict the use of fundamental analysis without the same kind of disclosure and express consent.[5] While this position may be extreme (and based on an exaggeration of market efficiency), it demonstrates that nothing is sacred in the continuing debate on the standard of care.

At the present time, except for extremes such as ESP, there are no clear answers to questions regarding the appropriateness of any particular method or approach. Nor are there definite answers to questions of degree, such as how much research a manager should do before making an investment decision. Again, these answers depend upon the nature of the relationship, what is represented, what is agreed to and what others similarly situated would regard as a minimal standard.

The fiduciary provisions of ERISA provide both a focus and a forum for answering these questions, and the definitions which evolve there will undoubtedly be extended to affect other fiduciary relationships with non-ERISA clients. In July, 1979, the Department of Labor adopted a regulation relating to the investment of employee benefit plan assets under ERISA's prudence rule. The regulation provides that a manager's duty to act prudently will be satisfied if, in making an investment decision, the fiduciary, "has given appropriate consideration to those facts and circumstances that, given the scope of such fiduciary's investment duties, the fiduciary knows or should know are relevant to the particular investment or investment course of action involved, including the role the investment or investment course of

---

[4] Reprinted by permission from *The Law of Investment Management,* Copyright 1978 Warren, Gorham, and Lamont Inc., Boston, Mass. All Rights Reserved.

[5] See Pozen, "Money Managers and Securities Research," 51 New York Univ. Law, Rev. 923 at 935 (1976).

action plays in that portion of the plan's investment portfolio with respect to which the fiduciary has investment duties." The regulation then goes on to list some factors which may be included in considering the role of an "investment or investment course of action":

(A) the composition of the portfolio with regard to diversification,
(B) the liquidity and current return of the portfolio relative to the antici-pated cash flow requirements of the plan, and
(C) the projected return of the plan investment portfolio relative to the funding objectives of the plan.[6]

It is interesting to note that these investment "guidelines" were designed to encourage an interpretation of the prudent man rule which is different from the traditional common law interpretation. The com-mon law approach has been to judge the prudence of a particular investment on its own merit, "without regard to the role that the investment plays within the overall investment portfolio." This tradi-tional standard developed because of a "need to resolve a basic conflict between the interests of the income beneficiary and the remainderman of a common law trust." Because employee benefit plans and most other institutional portfolios handled by investment managers do not have a conflict between income and principal beneficiaries, the law applicable to the management of such portfolios is expanding its focus to allow a "whole portfolio approach." The courts will be the final arbiter of this issue. However, in determining the prudence of a manag-er's decision, it is likely that a court will take into consideration factors relative to the entire portfolio that affected the specific decision at the time it was made. This result would probably have been reached by the courts without the Department of Labor's interpretation.

While the prudence guidelines present considerations such as diver-sification and projected return in a general way, they raise an interest-ing question regarding the role that investment technology may play in determining prudence. Investment technology attempts to provide quantitative measurements for these factors, and it is interesting to speculate on the effect that investment technology and a "whole portfo-lio approach" will have in defining fiduciary responsibilities.

As it develops and gains acceptance, investment technology will allow for some quantitative measurements to be applied in judging prudence. Investment technology provides a clear benchmark against which the activities, success, and expense of managers can be mea-sured. It also provides methods of quantifying and evaluating diver-gence from the benchmark.

The benchmark provided by investment technology is the market or index portfolio, which provides a point of comparison in the evalua-tion of such matters as investment performance, transaction costs, advi-

---

[6] Department of Labor, "Investment of Plan Assets under the Prudence Rule," July 23, 1979.

sory fees, and turnover. Recently, there was a flurry of interest in a law review article which suggested that fiduciaries might have a duty to "adopt a buy-the-market investment strategy" by indexing their portfolios.[7] Again, this position is likely based on an exaggerated view of market efficiency. This duty is probably better characterized as a duty to consider the index, especially relative to advisory fees and performance.

The quantitative measurement tools utilized in investment technology include beta (volatility relative to the market), r^2 (diversification of risk), expected return and covariance (the degree to which stock prices move together). With the index benchmark and these quantitative tools, it is possible to be much more specific in defining the degree of risk assumed by a manager in a client's portfolio. Thus, if the performance of a client's portfolio diverges from the benchmark, the manager who has incurred risk in the portfolio should be able to demonstrate in a rational fashion the reason for such risk taking and the expected effect of the risk upon the return of the portfolio.

The important point regarding investment technology is that as it develops and becomes accepted, the sophisticated quantitative measurements it provides may be applied in determining the prudence of a manager's actions whether or not the manager actually employed these tools. This does not require the use of investment technology, but there is the danger that a manager who is not familiar with these tools may expose clients to excessive risks which, had they been quantified, might have been avoided. Being aware of the quantitative measurements of portfolio decisions allows the manager to assess the strength of the rationale the manager is following. While small managers handling relatively small accounts may not be held to this degree of sophistication, a manager who claims the capability of handling an account such as a large employee benefit plan will likely find one's actions gauged quantitatively.

So far, this discussion of the fiduciary standard of care has begged the question of the client's investment objectives. It should be obvious, however, that because investment decisions are intended to carry out a client's objective, the context of such objectives is necessary in determining whether a manager has met the requisite standard of care. The manager's fiduciary responsibility may oblige one to consider not only the suitability of investments for a particular client in light of objectives, but also the appropriateness and reasonableness of the objectives themselves. This suitability doctrine is developing in the law, and goes further in some instances than the similar duty applied to broker-dealers.[8]

The duty of a manager to consider the specific objectives of a client

---

[7] John H. Langbein & Richard A. Posner, "Market Funds and Trust-Investment Law, *1976 American Bar Foundation Research Journal.* 1:11.

[8] See Bines, 4–1.

or to assist in developing those objectives will depend upon the nature
of the manager-client relationship and representations by the manager
as to what he will do. Investment managers to ERISA clients, for example, specifically have the responsibility to manage consistent with the
plan objectives and needs. Moreover, under ERISA, the manager cannot safely accept objectives given by a client without giving some
consideration to their appropriateness. As one commentator has noted,

> Investment managers may well face litigation challenging investment
> results which were achieved by adherence to deficient objectives set
> by plan sponsors. Therefore, both parties must be involved in the objec-
> tive setting process.[9]

A similar duty of suitability exists for managers who refer to themselves as investment counsel and provide investment supervisory services as defined in the Investment Advisers Act: "the giving of continuous advice as to the investment of funds on the basis of the individual
needs of each client." Further, any manager who has discretionary
authority will have some degree of responsibility for the reasonableness
of the objectives one is pursuing on a client's behalf. Even the nondiscretionary manager had some duty to make suitable investments, depending upon the reliance placed upon one's advice by the client
and the manager's access to information regarding the client.

It is unfortunate that the value and importance of setting investment
objectives is frequently overlooked by investment managers who are
otherwise very concerned about the prudence of their conduct. Without objectives, a manager has no guidelines regarding what investments
are reasonable, and investment rationale—one's best defense later on—
is without a real foundation. The development of reasonable and appropriate investment objectives, followed by the development of a rational
investment approach to achieve these objectives, is the safest course
for managers who wish to serve their clients well and avoid liability.
The fact that methods are available to articulate objectives in quantified
expressions of risk and return means that objectives should not be
unrealistic or too vague and subjective to be meaningful. Application
of these quantitative techniques to objective setting, as well as to the
investment process, should be an effective preventive legal step.

To conclude this overview of the standard of care, it is interesting
to speculate upon what may be considered within the realm of prudence in the future. The ability to approach a portfolio as an entity
and to quantify risks allows at least the consideration of investment
methods which were previously regarded as speculative. Already, investing in foreign securities markets is becoming recognized as an
effective means of diversifying a portfolio. Options and venture capital
are being added to institutional portfolios, though cautiously. Similarly,

---

[9] J. Hutchinson, "The Complete Fiduciary," *Pension World* (April 1978).

tomorrow's prudent investor may depart from the securities market altogether, adding real estate, art and other tangibles to one's portfolio. The wisdom of the law's flexible standard of prudence is that it can expand to include these and other investment media which may not even exist today.

THE DUTY OF LOYALTY

The fiduciary responsibility of an investment manager to a client includes a duty of loyalty. This means that the manager must give disinterested advice and that actions on a client's behalf must be carried out for the sole benefit of the client. Where more than one client is involved, the manager has a duty to treat each of them fairly. A manager's advice cannot be disinterested if the manager's range of discretion includes alternatives which, in some way, financially advantage the manager. A conflict will exist whether or not the client is actually harmed. In some instances, where managers have engaged in kinds of transactions which generally provide opportunities for abuse, managers have been found to have violated the duty of loyalty even though they gained no financial advantage and the client was not harmed.

This concept of loyalty is presented as an ideal, unlike the flexible prudent man rule which looks to see how others similarly situated are carrying out their responsibilities. The rationale that "everyone else was doing it" is a poor defense in questions involving the duty of loyalty. However, because the world of the investment manager is fraught with real and potential conflicts of interest, the practical reality is that the ideal of absolute loyalty cannot be obtained in every instance. While in some situations the law does demand an absolute loyalty, it has also recognized that some departures are inevitable and has established disclosure and consent standards and processes of regulatory review to protect clients where a conflict exists.

As with the duty of reasonable care, the duty of loyalty a manager owes a client will depend upon the nature of the relationship. The greater the opportunity for abuse, the higher the duty of loyalty required. Where a client places reliance on a manager, potential conflicts must be scrupulously considered and resolved. The investment manager who has full discretion with respect to a client's assets is subject to a high standard of loyalty.

Generally, the law is strict about conflicts of interest, and the courts appear to have been less charitable toward a manager's disloyalty than to a lack of investment acumen. The Supreme Court, exhibiting this sentiment, concluded in a "scalping" case that the Investment Advisers Act,

. . . reflects a Congressional recognition of the delicate fiduciary nature of an investment advisory relationship, as well as a Congressional intent to eliminate, or at least to expose, all conflicts of interest which might incline an investment adviser—consciously or unconsciously—to render advice which was not disinterested.

The various situations presenting real or potential conflicts for an investment manager are far too numerous to attempt to enumerate and discuss here. Moreover, the law does not provide clear guidelines to follow in many situations. Should a manager reduce personal expenses by use of a client's brokerage commissions to buy services, or should one buy those services directly? Should a manager direct commission dollars to a broker who brought him the account? An attractive stock is purchased, must it be allocated among all similar accounts? Can a manager recommend a stock she owns in her personal portfolio? Can a manager sell a stock he owns to an account he manages? Can a manager leave cash balances in clients' accounts with a bank that lends to the manager?

The range of possible conflict issues and fact situations is limited only by imagination. Thus, it is not difficult to understand why the law cannot develop clear rules of fairness for every potential conflict. Instead, the law approaches these problems in three general ways: prophylactic prohibition, statutory or regulatory standards and review, and disclosure and consent. To some extent, these approaches overlap, especially since most statutes designed to prevent abuse include a provision requiring disclosure.

The prophylactic approach avoids the abuses potentially caused by some conflicts by simply prohibiting certain kinds of transactions or behavior. An example is the prohibited transactions section of ERISA, where certain transactions (such as investments in employer securities) are precluded by law. Another example is Section 11(a) of the Securities Exchange Act of 1934 (as amended in 1975), which makes it unlawful, with certain exceptions, for a member of an exchange to execute a transaction on the exchange for an account with respect to which it exercises investment discretion. Further, the courts have adopted a prophylactic prohibition approach to "scalping," the practice of a manager's buying a stock before making a recommendation and selling it after the recommendation has had its effect on the market.

The point of these examples is to demonstrate that certain breaches of the duty of loyalty are simply unlawful, whether or not the manager has actually benefited or the client has actually been harmed. Thus, the prophylactic approach reflects a judgment in the law that certain transactions offer such a potential for abuse that they should be prohibited, regardless of the fairness or lack of fairness of the specific circumstances.

With respect to many conflict situations, the law does not prohibit a transaction, but provides for limits or procedures to prevent abuse. The extensive body of regulations and case law which has developed out of Section 17 of the Investment Company Act is an example of this approach. Section 17 prohibits certain transactions between an investment company and its manager, but also provides for an exemptive procedure under which transactions can be carried out once they have been determined by the Securities and Exchange Commission, upon prior application, to be fair. In such a situation, the regulatory agency is interposed in the transaction to assure, by overseeing fairness, that the manager maintains his or her duty of loyalty to the client.

Section 28(e), which was added to the Securities Exchange Act in 1975, represents a somewhat different approach. This Section addresses the very difficult conflict issues involved when a manager utilizes brokerage commissions from a client's portfolio to purchase research and brokerage services, sometimes paying commissions in excess of what might have been necessary without the extra services. The statute provides that a manager shall not have breached a fiduciary duty solely by paying excess commissions if the manager made a good faith determination that the amount of commissions paid was reasonable in relation to the value of the brokerage and research services received, "viewed in terms of either that particular transaction on his overall responsibilities with respect to accounts as to which he exercises investment discretion." Here, the fiduciary duty of the manager is highlighted and the requirement of a good faith determination is expressed. The point is that the law considers this a potential area for abuse but, rather than apply a prohibition or regulatory procedure, tells the manager what to consider. The actual protection afforded by Section 28(e) is debatable, but it is far from a safe harbor for fiduciaries.

Section 28(e) and the debate regarding paying up is also an example of the importance of disclosure where the underlying business situation has changed and the applicable law is unclear and developing. Since brokerage commissions became fully negotiated in 1975, some managers have refrained from seeking the lowest rates available. They contend that while the commission price may be low, the execution capability of discount firms is not adequate, and that the manager's executions would suffer over the long term to the detriment of clients. This argument for avoiding discount brokers may be true, but the fact that a manager also receives research or other services from firms it continues to use at higher commission rates ("paying up") raises potential conflicts. Full disclosure of brokerage commission policies, as well as the actual commissions paid, together with client consent, has been the best protection a manager could have during this difficult period of organic change in the securities industry.

Disclosure and consent are the most ready and effective tools with which an investment manager can resolve conflict of interest situations. They serve to restore an arm's length balance between the manager and client with respect to the particular matter affected by the manager's conflict of interest. The content and amount of disclosure and the requirement of an actual or implied consent depends on the facts and circumstances involved.

Disclosure and consent, however, are not sufficient to cause a transaction to be immune from challenge if it is not fair and reasonable on its merits. Moreover, disclosure is not adequate if it consists only of the barest facts and does not provide enough related information to allow the client to act knowledgeably. All information material to the transaction or situation must be given to the client, and the manager has a duty to assure that the disclosure is reasonably understandable for the client.

The Investment Advisers Act is primarily based on disclosure, unlike the Investment Company Act which regulates specific kinds of transactions. Carrying this concept forward, the Securities and Exchange Commission has adopted a comprehensive "brochure rule," requiring managers to provide clients and prospective clients with a written disclosure document containing specified information about the manager and the manager's activities. Managers would be well advised to prepare this document carefully, utilizing it to assure that clients have adequate information to understand the manager's way of handling the conflicts which are inevitable in the investment management profession. The advisory brochure should be approached as a fiduciary disclosure document rather than a sales piece.

Looking to the future, the law defining the fiduciary duty of loyalty is certain to continue to change and evolve. Similar to its effect upon the duty of reasonable care, ERISA provides a focus for future definition of the duty of loyalty through its "exclusive benefit" provision. The legal interpretation of the duty of loyalty, in ERISA or elsewhere, will be influenced by broader social standards of the times, as noted recently by an observer of this subject:

> . . . the problem of conflicts of interest is deeply rooted in very broad sociological and political developments which investment managers, their clients, and the courts cannot ignore. Just as we have seen enormous changes in what our citizens and our courts have regarded to be "due process," so it must be that as we move away from an individualistic competitive society to one deeply committed to consumer protection there will be new limits placed upon those whose business is "other people's money." Thus, I do not think any of us can intelligently discuss or analyze conflict of interest situations, duty of loyalty, fairness to all clients or "overreaching" without giving realistic recognition to the fact that both good business practice and the law are going to reflect sociological and political factors of the times.[10]

---

[10] D. Mercer, "Conflicts of Interest," Boston Security Analysts Society Educational Program, 1977.

THE EFFECT OF PUBLIC INTEREST ON
FIDUCIARY DUTY

While the sociological and political factors of our time are working to eliminate conflicts of interest, they are also, paradoxically, creating limits to an investment manager's fiduciary duty to pursue a client's best interest. Traditionally, a fiduciary has not been obliged to commit a crime to preserve or further the interest of a beneficiary. Today that limit has been extended on the basis of public policy to accommodate public interests such as the integrity of the securities markets. Another developing issue is whether a manager has a responsibility to vote shares held in a clients portfolio strictly in the interest of the client or according to an overriding interest of social responsibility.

The best example of the limits imposed by the public interest on a manager's duty is the prohibition against the use of material inside information. A manager must refrain from trading on the basis of information which has come from inside a company and is not publicly known. This restriction applies regardless of the potential gain or avoidance of loss for the client—a clear dilution of the duties of loyalty and reasonable care. The rationale for this rule is that it is in the public interest to preserve the capital market system by placing all investors on an equal footing with respect to available information.

Under certain circumstances, it may also be unlawful for a manager to base investment decisions on information which is not attributable directly or indirectly to the company or its insiders but which is "market" information, "third party" information or rumors, the origin of which is not clear. Presently, these kinds of information do not have a sufficient link to the issuing company to be prohibited on the same statutory basis as inside information. However, as the concept of the public interest expands, the manager may be prohibited from the use of such information if it is material. If this prohibition enters the law fully, it will represent a strengthening of the public interest as a rationale for limiting behavior; other limits upon fiduciaries may follow.

The issue of whether investment managers should consider social responsibility issues in making investment decisions or voting proxies is another area where the public interest may impose itself upon a manager's actions in clients' behalf. At present, most managers look to their clients for direction on social responsibility questions, but there is a disturbing trend for clients to delegate these issues to the manager. The law in this area is far from clear, but the fiduciary responsibility to pursue the best interest of clients likely outweighs any responsibility under a public interest rationale to further various causes through proxy voting or investment selection. Many institutions are currently under pressure to divest themselves of holdings considered objectionable on a social responsibility basis. A manager would clearly be violating fiduciary duty to a client if, without the client's express direction, the manager moved such securities from the portfolio and thereby reduced the return or increased the risk by underdiversifying the portfolio.

PREVENTIVE STEPS FOR THE FIDUCIARY

The following are some preventive steps which the fiduciary investment managers should consider in relationships with clients. These are presented only in summary fashion, and with a reminder that fiduciary standards depend on the facts and circumstances in each case.

Knowledge of Specific Laws or Rules affecting the Client

The investment manager should be aware of any specific laws affecting the client. For example, some institutional clients are restricted by state laws as to the types of investments that can be held in their portfolio. Investment companies are subject to both state and federal rules. Similarly, the manager should be aware of any restrictions which may exist in the client's underlying charter or other organizational documents. In establishing the manager-client relationship, it is good practice to obtain copies of any such documents, review them for investment restrictions and retain them with the client's file.

Exculpatory Clauses

Clauses in the investment manager's contract with the client which limit the manager's liability are worth including even though their effectiveness has diminished in recent years through court action and SEC interpretation. As a general rule, a manager cannot reduce liability by contract beyond the degree allowed by applicable law. As a practical matter, this means that a limitation on liability for bad faith or gross negligence will not be upheld.

Investment Objectives

The manager and the client together should develop investment objectives for the account, and these objectives should be in writing. Objectives should be reasonable and defined with as much specificity as possible with respect to risk, return, and expected portfolio characteristics.

Disclosure and Consent

The more disclosure the better. An express consent from a client should be obtained in advance of specific transactions or changes in procedure which potentially present conflict.

Documentation

The manager should be able to document one's decision process. With respect to both the duties of reasonable care and loyalty, a client-plaintiff has the burden of proof as to the appropriate standard to be applied. Once the standard is determined, however, the manager-defendant bears the burden of proving that any actions were consistent with that standard. The question then becomes an evidentiary one, and the ability to document why a particular action was taken is critical. This point is often misunderstood by managers, who believe that the purity of their motions will see them through. For example, in brokerage issues, the manager must be able to demonstrate why a particular broker was chosen over another, especially when the chosen broker provides additional services. The difficulty of proving negatives is great enough to sometimes preclude certain activity (i.e., proving that the choice of a particular broker was not made because that broker provides additional services).

CONCLUSION

This overview of fiduciary law is necessarily superficial, but is intended to outline the basic kinds of issues presented to investment managers and the approaches to these issues taken by the law. It is this writer's opinion that many people overcomplicate fiduciary issues and carry out their professional activities with only a murky understanding of the standards by which their actions will be measured. This generates anxiety and fear which, if reflected in overly-cautious investment decisions, can be harmful to one's clients. A common but unfortunate misunderstanding of the law is to look to the written language of the law for standards of care and the activities of others to resolve conflict issues. This is an exact reversal of the appropriate source for standards. The standard of care is largely determined by professional standards currently existing within the investment community. It is a flexible, objective standard. Looking for an answer from the written law is similar to concentrating on a Buddhist *koan,* an unsolvable riddle designed to explore the limits of a rational mind. Look to the community—are you employing what is "generally known"? Are you careful, skillful, diligent, and do your judgments have a sound basis?

The basic issues involved in the duty of loyalty are also straightforward. Is your advice disinterested, or do you have something to gain by choosing one course of action over another? Are your actions carried out for the sole benefit of your client, or will the benefit be diluted? Do you have to make choices among clients, and are you doing so fairly? Are you encountering conflicts which are specifically prohibited by the law? Most importantly, is your client fully aware of what you are doing, and can you demonstrate the client's acceptance?

In the coming years, we will see the law answer many fiduciary questions which are puzzling today and refine the definitions and standards within which professional investment managers carry out their activities on behalf of clients. But it is just as certain that new questions will arise and new issues present themselves. Involving as it does the exercise of care, skill, judgment, honesty and fairness, the investment management profession will continue to provide a focus for the development of fiduciary law.

Chapter 22

Erisa and the Portfolio Manager

WILLIAM J. CHADWICK

Counsel
Paul, Hastings, Janofsky & Walker
Los Angeles, California

INTRODUCTION

Part 4 of Title I of the Employee Retirement Income Security Act of 1974 (ERISA) has had and will continue to have a significant impact on the practices and procedures of portfolio managers responsible for the assets of ERISA covered pension and health and welfare plans. ERISA contains the legal framework within which all fiduciaries—a statutorily defined term encompassing portfolio managers—must conduct their affairs. The failure by a fiduciary to conduct its affairs within ERISA's framework may result in challenges through civil suits and liability for breaches of ERISA.

Both civil suits (i.e., challenges to fiduciary conduct) and liability (i.e., failure to meet the challenge) can be avoided if the portfolio manager appreciates the nature and scope of ERISA's legal framework and, of equal importance, acts in a manner reflecting its appreciation of ERISA. The ERISA-sensitive portfolio manager will develop procedures to ensure compliance and records to document the implementation of sound practices. Of course, to develop and implement procedures, the portfolio manager must understand ERISA's requirements.

ERISA contains both provisions relating to fiduciary responsibility and prohibited transaction restrictions. (See ERISA §§ 401–414.) The fiduciary responsibility provisions and the prohibited transaction restrictions are part of an integrated statutory scheme, which was designed to regulate the activities of, among others, portfolio managers.

However, these two sets of rules must be considered separately. The fiduciary responsibility provisions, for example, the prudent man rule, are "facts and circumstances" rules. A particular investment or investment course of action may or may not be prudent depending on the facts and circumstances. By comparison, the prohibited transaction restrictions are *per se* rules. For example, a portfolio manager is prohibited from acting on behalf of an adverse party. Such conduct is prohibited, and unless a statutory or administrative exemption from the prohibition is available, the portfolio manager may incur liability. The purpose of this chapter is to provide an overview of these statutory requirements.

ERISA's fiduciary responsibility provisions govern the structure and content of ERISA-covered pension and health and welfare plans. By analogy, ERISA's structural regulation is like the structural regulation of diversified open-ended management companies or mutual funds under the Investment Company Act of 1940. ERISA also governs the conduct of fiduciaries through the imposition of fiduciary duties, against which actual practices and procedures will be measured. ERISA's conduct regulation is similar to the regulation of trustees under the pre-ERISA common law of trusts. Of course, like under the Investment Company Act and the pre-ERISA common law, the failure by a portfolio manager to conduct its affairs consistent with ERISA may lead to liability.

ERISA's prohibited transaction restrictions prohibit fiduciaries from causing an ERISA-covered plan to engage in certain transactions. These prohibitions are absolute—fairness is not a defense. Even if a prohibited transaction does not result in an immediate loss to the plan, a participating portfolio manager may find itself "insuring" the plan against any subsequent loss until the transaction is corrected. No portfolio manager wants to place itself in such a position, particularly in the absence of insurance company type reserves.

Before proceeding to a more detailed analysis of ERISA's fiduciary responsibility provisions and its prohibited transaction restrictions, it is important to note that the Department of Labor is responsible for enforcement. Labor enforces the fiduciary responsibility provisions by reason of statutory authority contained in ERISA. However, its responsibility with respect to the prohibited transaction restrictions is a result of an Executive Reorganization. This does not mean that only the Labor Department's Regional and Area offices will conduct investigations and audits. The Internal Revenue Service (IRS) will continue to be very active in this regard. In addition, the Labor Department may delegate its investigative functions with respect to banks to the appropriate Federal banking agency. The Labor Department's authority to enforce the prohibited transaction restriction means that only the Labor Department can interpret the statute and grant exemptions from ERISA's restrictions. Either or both agencies (or the Comptroller of the Currency) may conduct investigations and audits.

FIDUCIARY RESPONSIBILITY

Coverage

Part 4 of Title I of ERISA applies, with certain exceptions which will be discussed below, to every employe benefit plan. (See ERISA §401(a).) The term employe benefit plan includes both pension plans and welfare plans. (See ERISA §3(3).)

The term pension plan includes any plan or program established or maintained by an employer or by an employe organization (e.g., a union) or by both if such plan or program provides retirement income to employes or results in a deferral of income by employees extending to the termination of covered employment or beyond. (See ERISA §3(2).) Under ERISA, tax-qualified pension, profit-sharing, thrift and savings, stock bonus and other similar plans, as well as many nonqualified plans, fall within the definition of the term pension plan.

It is important to note that the term pension plan as defined in ERISA is broader than the term pension plan as defined in regulations issued under the Internal Revenue Code of 1954 (the Code). Under the Code, the term pension plan only includes plans established and maintained by an employer to provide systematically for the payment of definitely determinable benefits to his employees over a period of years after retirement. (See Treasury Regulation, §1.401–1(b)(1)(i).) Even though a particular plan might not be a pension plan for tax purposes, it may still be a pension plan under ERISA. ERISA encompasses a wide variety of plans and programs.

On the other hand, certain types of plans do not fall within ERISA's definition of the term pension plan. For example, plans without employes, such as corporate plans and plans maintained by a sole proprietorship or a partnership (i.e., H.R. 10 plans) in which the only participant in the plan is the owner of the business, are not pension plans. (See Labor Regulations, §2510.3–3.) Other examples of noncovered pension plans include, but are not necessarily limited to, certain severance pay plans, bonus programs, individual retirement accounts or IRA's, and gratuitous pay plans.

As indicated above, welfare plans are also subject to Part 4 of Title I of ERISA. Like the definition provided for the term pension plan, the term welfare plan is broadly defined. The definition contained in ERISA includes any plan or program maintained by an employer or by an employe organization if such plan or program is maintained for the purpose of providing medical, surgical, or hospital care or benefits or benefits in the event of sickness, accident, death, or unemployment. (See ERISA §3(1).) Even if these types of benefits are provided through the purchase of insurance, the plan or program may be subject to ERISA.

However, certain types of welfare plans are not within the scope of ERISA's definition. For example, certain payroll practices, such as overtime pay, on-premise facilities, holiday gifts, hiring halls, remembrance funds, strike funds, industry advancement programs and certain group insurance arrangements are not subject to ERISA. (See Labor Regulations §2510.3–1.)

The fiduciary responsibility provisions only affect the activities of portfolio managers and other fiduciaries acting in connection with ERISA-covered pension and health and welfare plans. The portfolio manager should always identify such plans. Legally, the determination of whether a particular plan is subject to ERISA involves three steps. First, is the plan or program a pension or a welfare plan? (See ERISA §§3(1),(2).) Second, is the pension or welfare plan maintained by an employer or employee organization engaged in or representing employees engaged in commerce? (See ERISA §4(a).) Third, does a statutory exemption remove the pension or welfare plan from fiduciary coverage? (See ERISA §§4(b), 401(a).)

Structure and Content

Part 4 of Title I of ERISA contains structure and content provisions. (See ERISA §§402, 403.) Every pension and health and welfare plan subject to Part 4 of Title I of ERISA must satisfy these provisions. Some of these provisions are mandatory, while others are permissive in nature. However, in connection with the permissive provisions, it is important to note that certain activities can only be engaged in if the pension or health and welfare plan specifically contemplates the activity.

The mandatory plan provisions include the requirement that every pension and health and welfare plan must be established and maintained pursuant to a written instrument. This written instrument or instruments must either identify or establish a procedure for identifying one or more so-called named fiduciaries. (See ERISA §402(a)(1).) The named fiduciary or fiduciaries possess (or are deemed to possess) the authority to control and manage the operation and administration of the pension or health and welfare plan. (See ERISA §402(a)(2).) However, it is important to note that this authority does not mean that a plan's named fiduciary(s) possesses the authority to manage and control the assets of the plan. This authority generally rests with the trustee. (See ERISA §403(a).) Briefly stated, the authority for the management of a plan and the authority for the management (including the acquisition and disposition) of plan assets may be vested in different persons.

However, even though the named fiduciary(s) and the trustee may have authority with respect to different functions, the named fiduciary(s) may ultimately be held liable for the activities of the trustee.

In addition to the requirement that plans be established and maintained in writing and provide for one or more named fiduciaries, every pension and health and welfare plan must provide a procedure for establishing and carrying out a funding policy and method consistent with the objectives of the plan. (See ERISA §402(b)(1).) For example, a pension plan's procedure for establishing and carrying out a funding policy might provide that the plan's trustees will, at a meeting duly called for the purpose, establish a funding policy and method which satisfies the requirements of Part 3 of Title I of ERISA, relating to minimum funding standards, and shall meet annually at a stated time of the year to review such funding policy and method. It might further provide that all actions taken with respect to such funding policy and method and all reasons therefor shall be recorded in the minutes of the trustees' meetings. Since the purpose of the funding policy requirement is to enable plan participants and beneficiaries to ascertain that the plan has a funding policy that meets the requirements of Part 3 of Title I of ERISA, the type of procedure described above would satisfy the statutory requirement. On the other hand, a welfare plan in which the benefits are payed out of the general assets of the employer is not required to have a procedure for establishing and carrying out a funding policy. In such a case, there is no need to provide for such a procedure.

Other mandatory plan provisions require a pension or a health and welfare plan to specify the basis on which payments are made to and from the plan; describe any procedures under the plan for the allocation of responsibilities for the operation and administration of the plan; and provide a procedure for amending the plan, and for identifying the persons who have authority to amend the plan. (See ERISA §402(b)(2)–(4).) These requirements are just as important as the funding policy requirement discussed above. For example, a plan can only pay those types of benefits which are expressly provided for in the plan documents. However, plan documents can be amended to change the type of benefits to be provided.

The mandatory plan provisions are supplemented by permissive provisions. As indicated above, the permissive provisions are necessary if the activities described are to be engaged in. One permissive provision is that a pension or health and welfare plan may provide that any person may serve in more than one fiduciary capacity with respect to the plan. (See ERISA §402(c)(1).) For example, if a portfolio manager is to serve in more than one fiduciary capacity with respect to a pension plan, the pension plan must specifically sanction the dual fiduciary capacities in which the portfolio manager is serving. Another permissive provision permits a pension or health and welfare plan to provide that a fiduciary may employ another person or render advice with regard to the appointing fiduciary's authority and responsibility. (See ERISA §402(c)(2).) In the absence of such a provision, such employment would not be consistent with ERISA. One other permissive provision is particularly important to portfolio managers. Unless a pension or health and welfare plan permits a named fiduciary to appoint an investment manager, a statutorily defined term, such as appointment would be inconsistent with ERISA. (See ERISA §402(c)(3).) As a practical matter, this type of defect might leave the appointing fiduciary with the authority and responsibility it might otherwise have transferred to a duly appointed investment manager.

The mandatory and permissive provisions described above relate to the establishment of the plan. Additional provisions relate to the establishment of the trust. With certain exceptions, the assets of every pension and health and welfare plan must be held in trust by one or more trustees. As indicated above, the trustee or trustees possess the exclusive authority and discretion to manage and control plan assets. (See ERISA §403(a).) Of course, this authority and responsibility can be limited.

There are at least three ways to limit a trustee's authority and discretion with respect to plan assets. One way to limit a trustee's authority and discretion is to provide in the plan document that the trustee is subject to the direction of a non-trustee named fiduciary. (See ERISA §403(a)(1).) For example, a plan might provide that the trustee is subject to the direction of an investment committee appointed by the employer in connection with the plan. If a plan so provides, the trustee will be subject to proper directions by the committee provided such directions are consistent with ERISA and the terms of the plan. Of course, this procedure does not result in the complete removal of authority from the trustee. The trustee must still make certain that directions are, among other things, consistent with ERISA. Another way to limit a trustee's authority and discretion is to provide, in the plan document, for the appointment of one or more investment managers. (See ERISA §403(a)(2).) If the plan provides for the appointment of an investment manager and if the named fiduciary is prudent in making such an appointment, neither the named fiduciary nor the trustee should be held responsible for the decisions of the investment manager. A third way to limit the trustee's authority and responsibility is to provide for the direction of investments by plan participants. (See ERISA §404(c).) In the case of a pension plan which provides for individual accounts, such as a profit sharing plan, if a participant exercises control over the assets in his or her account, no person who is otherwise a fiduciary will be held liable under ERISA for any losses occasioned by the participant's exercise of control.

Once a portfolio manager determines that a particular pension or health and welfare plan is covered by ERISA it should check the plan documents, including the trustee agreement to ascertain whether they contain the mandatory provisions and the necessary permissive provisions. A simple checklist can be developed for this purpose.

Fiduciary Duties

ERISA contains six fiduciary duties and one exception to two of those duties. A fiduciary with respect to a pension or health and welfare plan must exercise duties with respect to such plan: (1) "solely in the interest" of participants and beneficiaries; (2) for the "exclusive purpose" of providing benefits to such participants and beneficiaries and defraying administrative costs; (3) with the care, skill, prudence, and diligence that a prudent man would use; (4) by diversifying plan investments; (5) in accordance with plan documents; and (6) by maintaining the indicia of ownership of plan assets within the jurisdiction of the courts. (See ERISA §404(a)(1),(b).) However, a fiduciary with respect to certain types of profit sharing and stock bonus plans, does not have to adhere to the diversification rule or to the diversification aspects of the prudence rule provided certain conditions are satisfied. (See ERISA §404(a)(2).) Each of these rules and the exception just mentioned, will be discussed below.

The "solely in the interest" and the "exclusive purpose" rules must be considered together. These rules impose the duty of undivided loyalty to participants and beneficiaries on all fiduciaries. They require fiduciaries to avoid conflicts of interest, and, in light of the purposes of ERISA, the words solely and exclusive must be interpreted literally. Obviously, they mean that a portfolio manager must scrupulously avoid any transaction if one of the purposes of the transaction is to benefit the employer maintaining the plan or the portfolio manager or an affiliate.

It is interesting to note that the exclusive purpose rule contained in ERISA and the exclusive benefit rule contained in the Code are not the same. (Compare ERISA §404(a)(1)(A) with IRC §401(a).) The exclusive benefit rule contained in the Code has not been interpreted literally by the IRS. The IRS has interpreted the rule contained in the Code so that exclusive really means "primary" for tax purposes. The ERISA rule, on the other hand, has been interpreted much more literally by the Department of Labor. ERISA is, in large part, a codification of trust law, not tax law.

The prudent man rule has probably generated more debate than all of the other rules combined. The importance of this rule to portfolio managers justifies quoting it here. The prudent man rule provides:

> A fiduciary shall discharge his duties with respect to a plan . . . with the care, skill, prudence, and diligence under the circumstances then prevailing that a prudent man acting in a like capacity and familiar

with such matters would use in the conduct of an enterprise of a like
character and with like aims. . . .

The prudent man rule is based on the common law rule adopted by
most states prior to ERISA, but there are some differences. For example, prior to ERISA most states required a trustee to exercise the skill
a person of ordinary prudence would exercise in dealing with his or
her own property. The courts interpreting this rule tended to focus
on each investment as opposed to the collective investments of the
trust or the whole portfolio, and they concentrated on the risk of loss
instead of evaluating return relative to risks incurred.

In enacting ERISA, Congress recognized that the rigid interpretation of the prudent man rule as developed by the state courts might
not be appropriate as applied to the various types of pension and welfare plans. The Conference Committee Report on ERISA provides
the following evidence of this recognition:

> The conferees expect that the courts will interpret [the] prudent man
> rule . . . bearing in mind the special nature and purpose of employee
> benefit plans. H.R. Rep. 93–1280, 93d Cong., 2d Sess. 302.

While this one statement may not seem to support a more flexible
interpretation of ERISA's prudent man rule than the similar common
law rules, there is additional legislative history to support just such
an interpretation. The legislative history developed in the late 1960s
supports the position that ERISA establishes a comparative, rather than
an absolute, standard of performance. The prudent man rule requires
the fiduciary possessing investment responsibility to invest as a prudent
person would invest the assets of a pension or a health and welfare
plan with a similar character and with similar aims or needs.

The prudent man rule does not mean that there is one standard
for all types of plans. There are different standards for large plans
and small plans, and for pension plans and welfare plans. These different standards are necessary since the characteristics and needs of a
pension plan are different than the characteristics of a welfare plan.
A pension plan trustee or investment manager may be able to justify
the accumulation of bonds with medium- and long-term maturity dates,
whereas a vacation plan trustee may have difficulty justifying such a
decision in light of the plan's liquidity needs.

A few aspects of the debate about ERISA's prudent man rule must
be focused on in this chapter. With the advent of modern portfolio
theory, among other things, portfolio managers have questioned
whether the prudent man rule requires that an investment should
be made by a fiduciary on the basis of the risk and anticipated return
attendant to that investment, with or without regard to the role that
it plays within the overall plan investment portfolio; what criteria
should be considered by fiduciaries in fulfilling their investment duties

pursuant to the prudent man rule; and whether specific investments are prudent.

The Department of Labor attempted to address these issues in the context of "safe-harbor" regulations. According to the Department of Labor, each investment will be judged with regard to the role it plays within the plan's portfolio. No particular investment is either prudent or imprudent. Certain investments that tend to be riskier than others (e.g., securities issued by new and small companies) may, depending on the circumstances, be prudent. The investing fiduciary should give appropriate consideration to: (1) the composition of the plan's portfolio with regard to diversification; (2) the liquidity and current return of the portfolio relative to the anticipated cash flow requirements of the plan; and (3) the projected return of the portfolio relative to the funding objectives of the plan.

The diversification rule requires portfolio managers to diversify a plan's investment portfolio so as to minimize the risk of large losses. However, ERISA does not establish a fixed debt-equity ratio or any other percentages. With respect to investments in other than employer securities and employer real property, ERISA merely directs a fiduciary not to invest the whole or an unreasonably large portion of the portfolio in a single security and cautions a fiduciary with respect to heavy investment concentration in geographical areas or industries. ERISA's diversification rule is very similar to the pre-ERISA common law rule.

The documents rule requires portfolio managers to act in a manner consistent with the plan documents. To this extent, the documents rule is similar to the pre-ERISA common law rule. However, ERISA's documents rule also provides that a fiduciary can only act in accordance with the plan documents to the extent that those documents are otherwise consistent with Part 4 of Title I of ERISA. Unlike the pre-ERISA common law rule, under ERISA the plan documents cannot override the otherwise applicable fiduciary duties. For example, if the plan documents direct the trustee to invest plan assets exclusively in equity securities and such an investment is or becomes imprudent, the trustee will not be shielded from liability on the basis of the plan documents. The prudent man rule overrides the plan documents.

The indicia of ownership rule requires a fiduciary to maintain the indicia of ownership of any plan assets within the jurisdiction of the courts, except as otherwise authorized by the Secretary of Labor. The Department of Labor has issued regulations which prescribe conditions permitting a fiduciary to maintain the indicia of ownership of plan assets outside the jurisdiction of the district courts of the United States. Under the regulations, if certain protective conditions are met, a plan may invest in foreign securities without incurring the costs which would be associated with the physical transfer of securities to and from the United States in order to satisfy the indicia of ownership rule.

The principal exception to one of the fiduciary duties discussed above is the individual account plan exception. The individual account plan exception permits individual account plans, such as profit sharing and stock bonus plans, to invest in employer securities and employer real property without regard to the diversification rule and the diversification aspects of the prudent man rule provided certain conditions are satisfied. To take advantage of this exception, the profit sharing or stock bonus plan must explicitly provide for the acquisition and holding of such assets.

In connection with the individual account plan exception, it is important to note that this exception only extends to the diversification rule and the diversification aspects of the prudent man rule. This exception does not extend to the solely in the interest rule, the exclusive purpose rule or the nondiversification aspects of the prudent man rule. Even if a profit-sharing plan explicitly provides for the acquisition and holding of employer securities or real property, such an investment may violate ERISA's exclusive purpose rule. While the acquisition and holding of employer securities or employer real property may not be inconsistent with ERISA at the time the investment is made, it may become inconsistent at a later date. In such a case, the portfolio manager may have an obligation to sell or otherwise dispose of the securities or real property even though the plan document may direct it to continue to hold this asset.

The portfolio manager must determine whether each investment or an investment course of action is consistent with the six fiduciary duties outlined above or within the one exception. This will require the portfolio manager to periodically review each account and, among other things, to document the reason or reasons for its investment conduct.

Liability for Fiduciary Breaches

The portfolio manager who breaches or violates any of the duties described above may be liable to the pension or health and welfare plan for any losses suffered by the plan and, if the portfolio manager has profited by reason of its breach, such portfolio manager may be required to restore such profit to the plan. In addition, the courts have authority to subject a breaching fiduciary to any appropriate equitable or remedial relief, including, but not limited to, removal of the fiduciary. (See ERISA §409(a).) In this regard, it is important to note the breadth of the courts' authority. The type of relief a court can grant in a particular case is only limited by the facts and circumstances and the creativity of the court and the plaintiff's attorney. A court finding a breach of responsibility by a fiduciary will most likely fashion relief so as to put the plan in the position that it would be in but for the breach. Relief may include recission of the transaction, reformation, including restoration of income lost as a result of the transaction and the income that would have been gained, but for the transaction, and removal of the portfolio manager from its position coupled with an injunction from serving in the same or similar capacity in the future with respect to the particular plan and perhaps with respect to other plans as well.

In addition to fiduciary liability, a portfolio manager may incur cofiduciary liability as a result of a breach of fiduciary responsibility by another fiduciary. (See ERISA §405(a).) For example, if a portfolio manager knowingly participates in a breach by a cofiduciary, he may incur personal liability. Similarly, if a manager has knowledge of a breach by a cofiduciary, he may incur personal liability unless he makes reasonable efforts under the circumstances to remedy the breach. According to the Department of Labor, a fiduciary with knowledge that a cofiduciary is about to breach its responsibilities must take all reasonable and legal steps to prevent the breach. Such steps might include preparation to obtain an injunction from a federal court, to notify the Labor Department or to publicize the action if the breach occurs. If the appropriate step or steps are taken, the nonparticipating fiduciary will not incur liability. However, mere resignation as a trustee, for example, will not suffice to avoid liability. In addition to participation in a breach or knowledge of a breach, a fiduciary may incur liability by reason of a breach by a cofiduciary, if a fiduciary's failure to fulfill its responsibilities permits a cofiduciary to commit a breach.

Exculpatory Provisions

A fiduciary cannot avoid its responsibilities or liability by the inclusion of an exculpatory provision in the plan document or the trust agreement. Exculpatory provisions have been declared void as against public policy. (See ERISA §410.) Even if such a provision is included in the plan document or in the trust agreement, it will not effectively shield a fiduciary from liability. Of course, even though exculpatory provisions are void, the allocation of responsibility between trustees is permissible. If particular responsibilities have been allocated to a co-trustee, the other trustee will not incur liability by reason of a breach of responsibility by such trustee provided it uses reasonable care to prevent a breach. In addition, if an investment manager is duly appointed by a named fiduciary, no trustee will be liable for the acts or omissions of such investment manager or be under an obligation to invest or otherwise manage any plan assets subject to the management of such investment manager.

While exculpatory provisions are void, ERISA does not prohibit a plan from purchasing insurance for its fiduciary or for itself to cover liability or losses occurring by reason of the acts or omission of a fiduciary. However, such insurance must permit recourse by the insurer against the fiduciary in the case of a breach of fiduciary responsibility. In addition, a fiduciary may purchase insurance to cover liability from and for its own account and an employer may purchase insurance to cover potential liability of persons who serve in a fiduciary capacity with respect to a pension or health and welfare plan. Certain forms of indemnification are also permissible.

PROHIBITED TRANSACTIONS

Overview

ERISA's prohibited transaction restrictions prohibit fiduciaries from causing an ERISA-covered plan to engage in certain transactions. (See ERISA §406.) These prohibitions are absolute—fairness is not a defense. The transactions prohibited include transactions involving a plan and a party-in-interest, a statutorily defined term.

The Code also contains prohibited transaction provisions. (See IRC §4975.) Violation of the Code's provisions results in the imposition of excise taxes on participating disqualified persons.

There are a number of differences between ERISA's prohibited transaction restrictions and the parallel provisions contained in the Code. First, ERISA's prohibited transaction restrictions apply to plan fiduciaries, while the parallel provisions contained in the Code apply to participating disqualified persons. The Code provisions do not apply to a fiduciary, such as a portfolio manager, where it is acting only as a fiduciary. Second, ERISA's prohibited transaction restrictions and the Code prohibitions relate to transactions between a covered plan and a party in interest or a disqualified person. The terms party in interest and disqualified person are defined in ERISA and the Code, respectively. The definitions provided for these terms are substantially identical. However, they are not identical. For example, under ERISA every employe of the employer maintaining the plan is a party in interest. However, under the Code, only highly compensated employes are parties in interest. Third, not every transaction prohibited under ERISA is prohibited under the Code. ERISA prohibits a fiduciary from acting in any transaction on behalf of a party whose interests are adverse to the interests of the plan or its participants and beneficiaries. This particular prohibition is not contained in the Code. However, the adverse representation prohibition is particularly important to portfolio managers. Fourth, the penalties under ERISA are in the form of civil penalties, while Code enforcement is through excise taxes.

Prohibited Transaction Restrictions

ERISA contains four types of prohibited transaction restrictions:

1. specific transaction restrictions;
2. a general transaction restriction;
3. fiduciary conduct restrictions; and
4. property restrictions. (See ERISA §§406,407.)

More than one type of restriction as well as more than one restriction of a particular type may apply to the same transaction or course of conduct. Because the statutory and administrative class exemptions do not necessarily provide relief from each applicable restriction, it is important to identify all of the applicable restrictions.

The specific transaction restrictions prohibit sales and exchanges as well as other dispositions of property between a covered plan and a party in interest. (See ERISA §406(a)(1)(A).) The specific transaction restrictions also prohibit leases of property between a plan and a party in interest; loans and other extensions of credit between a plan and a party in interest; and the provision of services between a plan and a party in interest. (See ERISA §§406(a)(1)(A)–(C).) These restrictions are referred to as specific transaction restrictions because they are phrased in terms of particular transactions.

The general transaction restriction prohibits the transfer of plan assets to any party in interest. (See ERISA §406(a)(1)(D).) This restriction is referred to as the general transaction restriction because it applies to any transaction involving the plan.

It is important to note the overlap between the specific transaction restrictions and the general transaction restriction. Almost all cases involving one or more of the specific transaction restrictions will also involve the general transaction restrictions. For example, if a plan purchases securities from a party in interest, the acquisition will be prohibited by reason of the specific transaction restriction relating to acquisitions of property. In addition, since the plan will transfer plan assets to pay for the securities, there will be a violation of the general transaction restriction.

The fiduciary conduct restrictions prohibit certain fiduciary activities. (See ERISA §406(b).) These restrictions are not transaction oriented, but conduct oriented. For example, ERISA prohibits a fiduciary, such as a portfolio manager, from dealing with plan assets in its own interest or for its own account. This is a specific conduct prohibition. A fiduciary may be engaging in this form of self-dealing even if the transaction is fair. This fiduciary conduct prohibition (as well as the other fiduciary conduct prohibitions) is absolute. In addition to prohibiting a fiduciary from dealing with plan assets in its own interest or for its own account, ERISA prohibits a fiduciary from acting in any transaction on behalf of a party whose interests are adverse to the interests of the plan and from receiving any consideration for its own personal account in connection with any transaction involving the plan.

The fiduciary conduct prohibitions are very important to portfolio managers. The fiduciary conduct prohibitions supplement the specific and general transaction restrictions. These particular prohibitions are designed to impose the duty of undivided loyalty to the plans for which they act as fiduciaries. Fiduciaries are prohibited from exercising their fiduciary authority when they have interests which may conflict with the interests of the plan for which they act.

It is important to note the breadth of the fiduciary conduct prohibitions. As indicated above, the specific and general transaction restrictions relate to transactions between a plan and a party in interest. The fiduciary conduct prohibitions, in a sense, are broader than the specific and general transaction restrictions. They prohibit a fiduciary from acting when it has an interest which may affect its best judgment as a fiduciary. A fiduciary may have a prohibited interest in the transaction even where the benefit is not derived by a party in interest. For example, it may be argued that a corporation affiliated with a corporation which is a fiduciary is not a party in interest by reason of the affiliation. However, if the fiduciary exercised its fiduciary authority so as to benefit its affiliate, the fiduciary may be acting in violation of ERISA's fiduciary conduct prohibitions. Again, it is important to note that, without regard to the fairness of the transaction, even the most subtle conflicts of interest may result in ERISA violations.

The property restrictions prohibit the acquisition and holding of employer real property and employer securities, unless certain requirements are satisfied. (See ERISA §§406(a)(1)(E), 406(a)(2), 407.) Pension plans are prohibited from acquiring or holding any employer security and any employer real property other than qualifying employer securities and qualifying employer real property. Even where the securities and real property are qualifying employer securities and real property, pension plan holding of these assets may not exceed 10 percent of the fair market value of the assets of the plan. A profit-sharing plan is generally subject to the same rules. However, such a plan is not subject to the 10 percent limitation if certain conditions are satisfied. If a profit-sharing plan explicitly provides for the acquisition and holding of qualifying employer securities or qualifying employer real property in excess of the 10 percent limitation.

The term qualifying employer security is defined in ERISA. It means an employer security which is stock or a marketable obligation. The term marketable obligation is also defined in ERISA. It means a bond, debenture, note, or certificate, or other evidence of indebtedness provided certain conditions are satisfied. One set of conditions relates to the price at which the obligation is acquired. Another set of conditions relates to plan holdings. For example, immediately following the acquisition of marketable obligations, not more than 25 percent of the aggregate amount of obligations issued in a particular issue and outstanding at the time of acquisition may be held by the plan and at least 50 percent of the aggregate amount must be held by persons independent of the issuer. In addition, immediately following the acquisition of the obligations by the plan, not more than 25 percent of plan assets may be invested in obligations of the employer or an affiliate of the employer.

The term qualifying employer real property is also defined by ERISA. Employer real property means real property which is leased to the employer maintaining the plan or to an affiliate of such employer. Qualifying employer real property means employer real property if a substantial number of the parcels are dispersed geographically, if each parcel of real property and the improvements are suitable for more than one use; and if the acquisition and retention of such property is consistent with the fiduciary responsibility provisions. One aspect of this definition is particularly troublesome. The plan must hold more than one parcel of qualifying employer real property and the parcels must be geographically dispersed. One parcel of employer real property does not constitute qualifying employer real property. However, with respect to the multiple parcel requirement, all of the parcels may be leased to one lessee.

In connection with the prohibited transaction restrictions, it is important to note the breadth of the definition provided for the term party in interest. (See ERISA §3(14).) The term party in interest includes any fiduciary; any service provider; each employer maintaining the plan; each union whose members are participants in the plan; and certain affiliates. For example, a subsidiary of a fiduciary with respect to a plan is a party in interest. In addition, an employee of a service provider is a party in interest. Since a fiduciary, such as a portfolio manager, is also a service provider, employee of the fiduciary are parties in interest.

The ERISA definition of the term party in interest is quite broad. It includes almost anyone with a relationship to a covered plan, almost without regard to remoteness. Portfolio managers must prepare party in interest rosters with respect to plans for which they have investment responsibilities.

The term fiduciary is also defined in ERISA. (See 3(21); 401(b).) The term includes anyone with discretionary authority or responsibility with respect to the management of a plan or with respect to the management of its assets. It also includes any person who renders investment advice for a fee or other compensation, direct or indirect. Most portfolio managers are fiduciaries and they must be sensitive to ERISA's prohibited transaction restrictions, particularly the fiduciary conduct restrictions.

Statutory Exemptions

The prohibited transaction restrictions prohibit a broad range of transactions. However, ERISA also contains statutory exemptions from the restrictions. (See ERISA §408(b).) It is important to note that the statutory exemptions do not necessarily cover all of the applicable restrictions. Many people make the mistake of proceeding on the basis of a statutory exemption which seems to describe the transaction in question. Unfortunately, in many cases, they subsequently realize that the statutory exemption does not remove all of the applicable restrictions.

The statutory exemptions from the prohibited transaction restrictions of particular importance to portfolio managers include (1) the service provider exemption, (2) a bank deposit exemption, (3) an ancillary service exemption, and (4) a collective fund exemption.

The service provider exemption is illustrative. Section 408(b)(2) of ERISA contains an exemption from the specific transaction restrictions and the general transaction restriction for the payment by a plan to a fiduciary for services if (1) the services are necessary for the establishment or operation of the plan, (2) the services are furnished under a contract or arrangement which is reasonable, and (3) no more than reasonable compensation is paid for such services. A service is necessary for the establishment or operation of a plan if the service is appropriate and helpful to the plan obtaining the service in carrying out the purposes for which the plan was established or maintained. The word necessary has not been interpreted literally. A contract or arrangement is reasonable if, among other things, it permits termination by the plan without penalty to the plan on reasonably short notice under the circumstances. However, a minimal fee and a service contract which is charged to allow recoupment of reasonable start-up costs is not a penalty.

It is important to note that the service provider exemption does not cover the fiduciary conduct restrictions. According to the Department of Labor, acts in contravention of the fiduciary conduct restrictions are separate transactions outside of the scope of section 408(b)(2). This means that a fiduciary, such as a portfolio manager, is prohibited from using its fiduciary authority to cause a plan to pay an additional fee to such fiduciary to provide a service. As a practical matter, any case involving the provision of multiple fiduciary services by a portfolio manager or by an affiliate, must be carefully scrutinized. Again, the mere statutory inclusion of a service provider exemption (or any other exemption) does not mean that complete relief from the prohibited transaction restrictions is available.

Transitional Rules

Because of the breadth of the prohibited transaction restrictions and the relatively narrow scope of the statutory exemptions, ERISA also contains transitional rules. The transitional rules grandfather certain transaction and conduct. In this regard it is important to note that, unlike the statutory exemptions, if a transaction is described in one of the transitional rules, all of the applicable prohibited transaction restrictions are not applicable until the expiration of the transitional rule. Complete relief is available if a transaction is described in a transitional rule. For example, one transitional rule covers the provision of services between a plan and a party in interest provided certain conditions are satisfied. The provision of services must be under a binding contract in effect on July 1, 1974. In addition, the party in interest providing the services to the plan must have ordinarily and customarily furnished such services on June 30, 1974 and the provision of such services must remain at least as favorable to the plan as an arm's length transaction with an unrelated party would be and if such provision of services was not, a prohibited transaction under Code section 503(b). This transitional rule expired on June 30, 1977. However, some of the other transitional rules do not expire until June 30, 1984 if the conditions are satisfied.

Administrative Exemptions

The Secretaries of Labor and Treasury are authorized to grant administrative individual or class exemptions from any and all of the prohibited transaction restrictions. As a result of an Executive Reorganization, the Department of Labor currently possesses this authority.

As indicated above, administrative exemptions from the prohibited transaction restrictions may be either individual or class exemptions. The difference is quite important. An individual administrative exemption only provides relief for the party or parties to whom the exemption was issued. Even if the facts are identical, another party may not proceed with a transaction on the basis of an individual administrative exemption. Of course, if an individual administrative exemption has been issued to one party, another applicant with identical facts would probably receive its own individual administrative exemption. Class administrative exemptions may provide relief to any fiduciary or party in interest which satisfies the conditions contained in the exemption. Class administrative exemptions are issued for a class of similarly situated parties.

A number of class administrative exemptions are important to portfolio managers. For example, class administrative exemptions have been issued with respect to transactions involving (1) employee benefit plans and certain broker-dealers, reporting dealers, and banks; (2) mutual fund in-house plans; (3) investment companies and plans; (4) insurance agents and brokers, pension consultants, insurance companies, investment companies and investment company principal underwriters, and employe benefit plans; and (5) insurance company pooled separate accounts.

It is important to note that, like the statutory exemptions from the prohibited transaction restrictions, class administrative exemptions from the restrictions do not always cover all of the applicable restrictions. Some of the class administrative exemptions are limited to the specific and general transaction restrictions, while other class administrative exemptions also extend to the fiduciary conduct restrictions. Portfolio managers must make certain that each applicable restriction is covered by the class administrative exemption. If one restriction is not exempted by reason of a statutory exemption or by reason of a class administrative exemption, the portfolio manager may incur liability.

CONCLUSION: TRANSACTIONAL ANALYSIS

Part 4 of Title I of ERISA is rather complex. No attempt has been made here to analyze every aspect of the fiduciary responsibility provisions and the prohibited transaction restrictions. Hopefully, this chapter provides an overview of the various statutory requirements.

Even though the fiduciary responsibility provisions and the prohibited transaction restrictions are cumbersome to work with, it is possible to analyze transactions involving plan assets to determine whether fiduciary problems are present. However, any such analysis must be structured to avoid overlooking subtle issues. In this regard, a six-step transactional analysis is helpful.

The first step in the transactional analysis requires an identification of the parties involved in any proposed transaction. The first part of this step is to determine whether the plan involved is an ERISA covered plan. If the plan is not subject to ERISA, it is not necessary to continue with the transactional analysis. However, if the plan is subject to ERISA, it is necessary to proceed to the second and third parts of the step. The second part of the first step involves the identification of parties in interest. Only transactions between an ERISA covered plan and one or more parties in interest are within the scope of ERISA's prohibited transaction restrictions. However, at least one party in interest will be involved in each transaction involving plan assets. In this regard, it is important to note that a fiduciary is a party in interest. The third part of the first step is to determine which parties in interest are fiduciaries. In effect, the portfolio manager must maintain two rosters in connection with each ERISA-covered plan for which it serves. One roster should identify all parties in interest, including fiduciaries, with respect to the plan. The other roster should separately identify each plan fiduciary.

The second step in the transactional analysis is to identify each applicable prohibited transaction restriction by type. If a transaction involves an ERISA covered plan and a party in interest, the portfolio manager should determine which of the four types (i.e., specific, general, fiduciary, and property) of the prohibited transaction restrictions apply. It is important to identify the restrictions by type because the statutory and class administrative exemptions do not always remove the taint of each type.

The third step in the transactional analysis is to determine whether a prohibited transaction is the subject of a statutory exemption from the applicable restrictions. Coverage by a statutory exemption in general is easy to determine. However, the determination of whether a statutory exemption covers all of the applicable prohibitions is more difficult. All of the statutory exemptions cover the specific transaction restrictions and the general transaction restrictions, but some of the statutory exemptions do not cover the fiduciary conduct restrictions. In addition, a statutory exemption may cover some but not all of the fiduciary conduct prohibitions. For example, a statutory exemption may provide relief from the restriction against a fiduciary dealing with plan assets in its own interest. However, the same statutory exemption may not provide relief from the adverse representation restriction or the kickback restriction. It is important to note that these distinctions in the scope of an arguably applicable statutory exemption are not readily apparent from the statutory language. The interpretive regulations issued by the Department of Labor must be read carefully to determine whether a statutory exemption is broad enough to cover all of the applicable prohibitions.

The fourth step in the transactional analysis is to determine whether a transitional rule provides the necessary relief. Unlike the statutory exemptions, if a particular transaction is the subject of a transitional rule, the transitional rule will afford complete relief provided its conditions are satisfied. However, the transitional rules are of limited duration.

The fifth step in the transactional analysis is to determine whether a class administrative exemption, which covers the transaction, has been granted. Like the analysis required in connection with a statutory exemption, a class administrative exemption must be read carefully to determine whether it covers both the specific transaction restrictions and the general transaction restriction and the fiduciary conduct restrictions. The Department of Labor has drawn the same distinctions in granting class administrative exemptions as it has in interpreting the statutory exemptions.

The sixth step in the transactional analysis requires a determination of whether the transaction is consistent with ERISA's fiduciary responsibility provisions. Many people tend to overlook this important step. In this regard, it is important to note that every transaction involving plan assets is subject to the fiduciary responsibility provisions. Even if a transaction is not prohibited or prohibited but exempt, the transaction must be analyzed in terms of ERISA's fiduciary duties. Neither the statutory exemptions nor the class administrative exemptions obviate the need to determine whether a transaction is, for example, solely in the interest of participants and prudent. The fiduciary responsibility provisions override the prohibited transaction restrictions.

If the six-step transactional analysis outlined above is followed, the portfolio manager should be able to spot issues and to deal with them effectively. ERISA is a highly technical statute and it must be dealt with in recognition of that fact. The only way to live in relative comfort under ERISA is to develop procedures to ensure compliance and records to document the implementation of sound practices.

Chapter 23

Regulation of Investment Managers under Federal Securities Laws

JOHN G. GILLIS
Partner
Hill & Barlow
Boston, Massachusetts

INTRODUCTION

The role of the investment manager in the process of the investment of funds in the capital markets has increased considerably in the last three decades. Investment managers in the United States are directly involved in the process of investment of billions of dollars. Coincident with the increase of assets to which investment managers have investment discretion or on which they advise, the numbers of investment managers and their skills have increased. Moreover, the function of investment managers has evolved into a profession where managers are subject not only to a variety of laws and regulations, but also subject to standards of professional conduct and practice developed by professional groups to which they belong.

As is well known, the securities markets in the United States have become increasingly institutionalized over the years. Institutional investors such as banks, insurance companies, employee benefit funds, investment companies (mutual funds), and nonprofit institutions have increased significantly their share of the securities markets. At the end of 1976, over 57 percent of the trading volume and over 70 percent of the value of shares traded on the New York Stock Exchange (NYSE) was effected by institutions. At the end of 1975 more than 33 percent of the shares listed on the NYSE were owned by institutions either on their own behalf or on the behalf of beneficiaries.[1] This is contrasted

---

[1] *New York Stock Exchange Fact Book* (1978). These statistics do not include bank administered personal trust funds, private hedge funds and nonbank trusts. It is estimated that if these were included "total institutional holdings would most likely be in the neighborhood of half the NYSE list." See also preliminary reports on the results of the SEC institutional investment disclosure rules effective in 1979. *Wall Street Journal*, March 27, 1979, p. 47.

with estimated holdings of about 13 percent in 1949 and 21 percent in 1966.[2] The Securities and Exchange Commission (SEC) estimates that at the end of 1976 over 40 percent of all common and preferred stock in the U.S. capital markets was held by institutions.[3]

At the same time that the role of institutional investors in the securities markets has increased the brokerage industry has been shrinking and developing more advisory service functions. Events of the last ten years have transformed the brokerage industry, starting with the decline in market prices in 1969, the back office problems in the late 1960s and early 1970s, the recession in 1973–75, and the abolition of the fixed commission structure on May 1, 1975. Numerous brokers have voluntarily ceased business, gone insolvent, or been absorbed by other firms. Even the largest of the brokerage houses have experienced mergers or consolidations with other large firms, as is readily evidenced by the combined names of many of the oldest and largest brokerage firms. The number of NYSE firms has declined.[4] As this development has been taking place, brokers have also been expanding the types of services available to customers and clients beyond the traditional execution of securities transactions to a wider range of services including investment advisory services.

With the increased institutionalization of the market, the role and responsibility of the financial intermediary has become a more significant aspect of the operation of the securities investment process.

The term investment manager refers to individuals involved in the investment decision-making process and also to the entities by which they are employed. These persons who have responsibility for advice on the investment of funds of others in the securities markets operate in a wide variety of contexts and for a wide variety of clients. Individual investment managers work for investment advisers and investment counselors who invest or advise on behalf of mutual funds, corporate accounts, individual accounts and employe benefit funds, among many others. As noted, brokers and dealers are increasing their investment advisory services and significant numbers of individual investment managers work in brokerage complexes. There are also a number of nonregistered investment advisers who, for different reasons, are not registered with the Securities and Exchange Commission. Banks, also exempt from registration, manage billions of dollars for several different types of clients. Employe benefit funds are becoming an increasingly large segment of the investing process. Of course, insurance companies have traditionally managed billions of dollars of assets not only generated from their insurance operations and pooled accounts, but

---

[2] *Institutional Activity on the NYSE,* Week of October 24–28, 1966, NYSE Research Department (1967).

[3] *Securities and Exchange Commission Annual Report,* 1976.

[4] *New York Stock Exchange Fact Book* (1979), p. 53.

also through their increased activity as investment advisers. Other institutions which employ investment managers include endowment funds, private foundations and public corporations.

Not only do individual investment managers work in a variety of contexts, but through their respective employers they are subject to a variety of laws. There are several federal securities statutes which may be applicable to investment management firms including the Investment Advisers Act of 1940, the Investment Company Act of 1940, the Securities Exchange Act of 1934, and the Securities Act of 1933. Moreover, investment manager entities are often subject to state securities laws, federal and state banking laws, state insurance laws, the Employee Retirement Income Security Act of 1974, (ERISA), the Internal Revenue Code and the common law of trusts and contracts.

As mentioned above, many individual and firm investment managers are subject to the standards of private professional organizations. One of these is the Investment Counsel Association of America, Inc. (ICAA) which is an organization of some 80 independent investment counsel firms. The term investment counsel, as defined by the Investment Advisers Act, means those investment advisers who are solely or primarily engaged in the business of providing continuous investment advice in managing clients' funds on the basis of the individual needs of each client.[5] They are independent in that they traditionally have been owned by individuals or others unconnected with an active securities broker or banks among others. The ICAA has established standards of practice as well as membership qualifications which apply both to the individual counsel firms and to their employees.[6] In the last few years the ICAA has established an accreditation program for persons to receive the designation Chartered Investment Counselor, which involves education and experience requirements as well as the passage of an examination. The ICAA also has issued from time to time policy statements on such matters as the reporting of performance.[7]

The Financial Analysts Federation (FAF), and its affiliated organization the Institute of Chartered Financial Analaysts, are professional organizations of individual securities analysts and investment managers. The FAF has 51 member societies, located in financial centers throughout the United States and Canada, as well as 15,000 individual members. It publishes a number of publications including the bimonthly *Financial Analysts Journal,* conducts regular seminars on areas of interest to its members, and holds an annual conference and several annual workshops in specialized educational programs. It is active in studying and commenting on developments in the securities

---

[5] Sections 208(c) and 202(a)(13).

[6] "Standards of Practice for Member Firms," January 8, 1976.

[7] "Standards of Measurement and Use for Investment Performance Data," 1976.

field relating to corporate disclosure, accounting, and government regulations, among others. Finally, it has established a private self-regulation program to which its members are subject, which include a Code of Ethics and Standards of Professional Conduct, and the enforcement thereof through a structure of disciplinary procedures.[8] (See Chapter 25.)

The Institute of Chartered Financial Analysts (ICFA), which is closely affiliated with the FAF, sponsors and administers a series of three annual examinations which, if successfully completed along with other requirements, entitles a person to the professional designation Chartered Financial Analyst. There have been over 6000 Chartered Financial Analyst designations awarded. Moreover, all new members of the FAF must pass the CFA I examination, and other requirements to be entitled to FAF membership. In addition to publications and educational activities, the ICFA also has a private self-regulation program with an identical Code and Standards to the FAF, as well as a structure to enforce it. The FAF and ICFA cooperate in disciplinary proceedings of members who are members of both organizations.[9]

Because this chapter of the Investment Managers Handbook is concerned with SEC regulation of investment managers, it will concentrate on the law applicable to entities known as investment advisers and counselors registered under the Investment Advisers Act of 1940. It will also include, as appropriate, brokers and dealers (or subsidiaries) who are also registered under the Securities Exchange of 1934. However, the subject of fiduciary responsibilities and standards will not be considered in any significant detail, except as it is reflected in the statutes analyzed, since this is the subject of another chapter of this Handbook.

The format of this chapter will be to review the Investment Advisers Act with refinements added by other statutes to which firm investment managers or their clients are subject. This Act has increasing impact as the number of SEC registered investment advisers has increased from 780 in 1945, 1,613 in 1965, and 4,798 in 1977 to 5,500 in 1978, now managing well over hundred billion dollars.[10]

INVESTMENT ADVISERS ACT

Background

The Investment Advisers Act of 1940 (Advisers Act or Act) was enacted as a part of a statute, Title I of which is the Investment Com-

---

[8] *See* The Financial Analysts Federation, *1979 Membership Directory.*

[9] *See* The Institute of Chartered Financial Analysts, *1979 Program.*

[10] Investment Company Institute, *Mutual Funds Forum,* October 1978.

pany Act, and Title II of which is the Investment Advisers Act. This was an outgrowth of a report by the Securities and Exchange Commission on the development of investment companies and investment advisers.[11] The Senate Report on the bill indicated that the emergence of the investment adviser as an important occupation or profession did not occur until after World War I. "However, it was not until after 1929 that investment adviser firms organized and increased rapidly." It was noted that firms for which information was obtained by the SEC managed, supervised and gave investment advice with respect to funds aggregating approximately $4 billion. It was felt that there was sufficient need for protection of the investing public and for the prevention of fraud to enact a statute regulating investment advisers as well as investment companies.[12]

While the Investment Company Act was quite comprehensive and detailed, the Advisers Act was much less so and has been altered in some important but not extensive respects since its enactment. However the SEC currently has under study the entire Advisers Act and rules thereunder (and the Investiment Company act), which may result in new or revised rules and proposed statutory amendments.

Who is an Investment Adviser

The Advisers Act defines an investment adviser broadly as:

> . . . any person who, for compensation, engages in the business of advising others, either directly or through publications or writings, as to the value of securities or as to the advisability of investing in, purchasing, or selling securities, or who, for compensation and as part of a regular business, issues or promulgates analyses or reports concerning securities . . . (Section 202 (a)(11))

To be subject to the Act the person or entity must (1) be an adviser within the definition of the Act and (2) make direct or indirect use of the mails or any instrumentality of interstate commerce in connection with his business as an investment adviser. (Sections 202(a)(14) and 203.)

The coverage of the Act is broad. It includes for example:

1. investment counselors who provide clients with investment advice based on individuals needs,
2. organizations which provide advice concerning the relative desirability of investing or not investing client's assets in securities even if no specific securities are recommended,

---

[11] Report of the Securities and Exchange Commission on Investment Trusts and Investment Companies (investment counsel, investment management, investment supervisory and investment advisory services), House Doc. 477 (1939).

[12] Senate Report no. 1775, Subcommittee on Banking and Currency, June 6, 1940.

3. persons who provide advice on foreign currency futures contracts,
4. persons preparing reports on securities or securities markets to assist investors in making their own investment decisions,
5. a wide variety of financial publications which are not bona fide newspapers, news magazines or business or financial publications of general and regular circulation including publishers of continuous services, articles or books to be used continuously by investors and used or sold indefinitely,[13]
6. persons who for fees conduct general instruction regarding development of investment programs, and
7. certain broker and dealers, among many others.

The Securities and Exchange Commission has recently reconsidered an earlier position regarding a single book, pamphlet or article of an investment advisory nature. It has concluded that registration "should not be required solely because a publication contains one or more formulas or guidelines intended to be used by investors in making determinations as to what securities to buy or sell or when to buy or sell them."[14]

There are several exclusions from the definition of investment adviser in the Act, including:

1. a bank or a bank holding company which is not an investment company,
2. any lawyer, accountant, engineer or teacher whose performance of advisory services is solely incidental to the practice of such profession,
3. any broker or dealer whose performance of such services is solely incidential to the conduct of the business as a broker or dealer and who receives no special compensation therefor,
4. the publisher of a bona fide newspaper, news magazine, or business or financial publication of general and regular circulation,
5. advisers on certain obligations issued or guaranteed by the United States, and
6. others as designated by the Commission by rule or order.

For example, Rule 202–1 excludes persons who offer investment advice to an employe benefit plan, as defined in the Employee Retirement Income Security Act of 1974 (ERISA), sponsored by such person's employer, if they are not in the business of being, or hold themselves out generally as, an investment adviser.

Moreover, the Act exempts certain investment advisers from registration. (Section 203(b).) These include (1) intrastate advisers whose

---

[13] After ten years of litigation the Wall Street Transcript was found to be a "bona fide newspaper" (S.D.N.Y. 5/15/78, CCH Fed. Sec L. Rep. IV 96440).

[14] SEC Rel. IA-563, (Jan. 10, 1977).

clients are residents of the state in which the adviser maintains its principal office and place of business and which does not furnish advice or issue analyses or reports with respect to securities listed or admitted to unlisted trading privileges on any national securities exchange, (2) any adviser whose only clients are insurance companies (a 1970 amendment removed the exemption for advisers to investment companies only), or (3) any adviser who during the course of the preceding 12 months has had fewer than 15 clients and who does not hold himself out generally to the public as an adviser nor acts as an adviser to any investment company registered under the Investment Company Act.

Registration and Qualifications

Registration under the Advisers Act is a relatively easy and straight forward process (See Rules under Section 203). It is accomplished by filing Form ADV with a fee of $150. Form ADV is relatively simple and contains questions relating to the basic business of the adviser as well as information regarding certain principals of the business. However, the SEC has recently amended Form ADV to require substantial additional information regarding the adviser's business, procedures, investment methods, and the qualifications of an expanded number of personnel of the adviser including individual investment managers.[15]

Expanded Form ADV is described in detail later in this chapter.

Pursuant to Section 203 of the Act the SEC now requires information on the adviser's basis of compensation, the nature of the business including the manner of giving advice or rendering analyses or reports, and a balance sheet.

The Act provides that the SEC must act on the registration application within 45 days by granting the application or by instituting a proceeding to determine whether registration should be denied (Section 203(c).)

The SEC sponsored proposed amendments to the Advisers Act which were introduced in Congress in 1976. These were reported favorably by the Securities Committee to the Senate but were not voted on. The SEC has not subsequently sought passage of these amendments although it is currently conducting a staff study which may result in another legislative initiative. Among other things they would have given authority to the SEC to promulgate rules for qualifications of investment advisory personnel and for financial capacity for advisers. They included three proposed studies involving (1) whether excluded entities such as banks should continue to be excluded from the Act, (2) whether statutorily authorized self regulatory organizations would

---

[15] SEC Rel. IA-664, (Jan. 30, 1979).

be appropriate and feasible in the advisory area and (3) the interrelationship of federal and state regulation of advisers.

BOOKS AND RECORDS

Required by Section 204

Section 204 of the Act contains the general requirement that investment advisers shall keep records, furnish copies thereof and make and disseminate reports all as prescribed by the SEC. In addition, advisers are subject to periodic, special or other examinations by SEC representatives.

Registered investment advisers must maintain 13 categories of books and records listed in Rule 204–2.[16] The first 11 categories are straightforward and not unusual except for certain definitional problems (e.g., "general public distribution" in Item 7). However, items 12 and 13 are somewhat unusual in that a purpose of this recordkeeping requirement would seem to be to prohibit so-called "scalping"—trading by advisers or their personnel on inside (nonpublic) information—or "frontrunning,"— investment actions before the transaction is made for or recommended to clients. Item 12 requires the maintenance of records of securities transactions of the investment adviser, or employes involved in the investment process, for their own accounts. Item 13 requires the same information for advisers and personnel in a business other than advising investment companies or other advisory clients, e.g., publishers. Records prescribed by Rule 204–2 relate to the following:

1. Cash receipts and disbursements.
2. Asset, liability, reserve, capital, and income and expense accounts.
3. Memoranda of each order given by the adviser for the purchase or sale of any security, and instructions received from clients concerning securities or orders, including identification of the person recommending the transaction and the person placing the order.
4. Checkbooks, bank statements, cancelled checks, and cash reconciliations.
5. Bills or statements relating to the business.
6. Trial balances, financial statements, and internal audit working papers.

---

[16] The recent revision to Form ADV added a requirement that disclosure statements (i.e., brochures) furnished pursuant to the new brochure rule be maintained under the recordkeeping rule (Rule 204–2(a)(14), SEC Rel. IA-644, January 30, 1979; see note 26 below). Moreover, a new recordkeeping category was added in connection with the new rule on cash referral fee payments (Rule 204–2(a)(15), SEC Rel. IA-688, July 12, 1979; see footnote 35 infra).

7. Originals of all written communications received and copies of all written communications sent by the adviser relating to

    a. recommendations and advice;

    b. funds or securities received, disbursed or delivered;

    c. placing or execution of orders, except unsolicited market letters and other communications of general public distribution not prepared by or for the adviser, and the names and addresses of persons to whom notices, circulars or advertisements are sent if there are more than ten distributees; however, if such is sent to persons named on any list, the list and the source shall be maintained.

8. A list of discretionary accounts.

9. Powers of attorney or other documents granting discretionary authority.

10. Written agreements.

11. Copies of notices, circulars, advertisements investment letters or other documents recommending the purchase or sale of a specific security, distributed directly or indirectly to ten or more persons (other than investment supervisory clients as defined, or persons connected with such investment adviser). A memorandum indicating the reasons for such recommendation shall be retained if such reasons are not contained in the communication.

12. A record of transactions in securities in which the adviser (or any advisory representative as defined) has or acquires any direct or indirect beneficial ownership, except transactions in accounts over which there is no influence or control, or in United States obligations. Advisory representatives are defined as partners, officers, directors, employees who make recommendations or participate in the determination of recommendations and employes with access to recommendations, as well as persons controlling the adviser or affiliated persons as defined. If adequate procedures are instituted and reasonable diligence used to obtain reports, failure to do so shall not violate the Rule.

13. This item is comparable to 12 and is applicable to advisers primarily engaged in a business other than advising registered investment companies or other advisory clients.

Additional records are required of advisers which have custody or possession of securities or funds of any client, including:

1. Purchases, sales, receipts and deliveries of securities and other activities of such accounts.

2. A separate account for each such client showing detailed transactions.

3. Copies of confirmations of all transactions.
4. Records of client interests in each security.

Finally, every adviser who renders any investment supervisory, (defined in Section 202(a)(13) as continuous investment advice based on individual needs) or management services (not defined) shall keep additional records for such accounts, including:

1. Records showing separately for each such client the securities purchased and sold and related information.
2. For each security in which any such client has a current position, information from which the adviser can promptly furnish the name and interest of such client.

Other Requirements—ERISA

Of major interest to advisers managing assets of qualified employe benefit plans is Part 4 of ERISA relating to fiduciary responsibility. Among other things, this contains a requirement that investment manager must be appointed by a named fiduciary, and the named fiduciary must have authority under the plan to make the appointment.[17] Particularly in the case of smaller plans, it may be advisable for the adviser to review the plan for this authority. An interesting question is what is the potential liability of an adviser who is not appointed by a named fiduciary who has been given this authority in the plan documents.

The question of the coverage of the ERISA prudent man rule in Section 404, and the proposed Department of Labor regulations thereunder will be covered in detail in other chapters of this book. However, there is some uncertainty as to the scope and coverage of these regulations, which to date have not been the subject of any judicial determinations.[18]

There are several other issues applicable to advisers under ERISA such as the providing of brokerage and advisory services to a plan. These are discussed in relevent sections below.

There are several practical issues relating to advisers of ERISA accounts relating to recordkeeping and asset mix.

As to recordkeeping, it appears that the records required to be kept under the Advisers Act may not protect the adviser when the prudence of its investment decision is questioned. The adviser may wish to keep records on companies in which it invests and retain its files for some period even after the security is sold so that it can reconstruct the facts taken into account when the investment was made,

---

[17] See Section 402 of ERISA.

[18] See Department of Labor, "Proposed Regulation Relating to the Investment of Plan Assets under the 'Prudence' Rule," 43 FR 17480 April 15, 1978. (The regulation was adopted in modified form effective July 23, 1979. 44 FR 3722 (July 26, 1979).)

if necessary. Consideration also should be given to keeping minutes of investment meetings and having at least one internally prepared memorandum dealing with the purchase of the security showing that total reliance was not made on outside research. An internal research department also seems to add a measure of protection.

The area of asset mix is one of some difficulty. There appears to be little judicial interpretation on the requirement of diversification by type of security to amplify the diversification requirement of ERISA, and investment managers have to be concerned that under the Conference Committee Report on Section 404 of ERISA some minimum commitment to fixed income securities is required. The Committee Report states: "Ordinarily the fiduciary should not invest the whole or an unduly large proportion of the trust property in one type of security . . ."

If an ERISA plan is managed by only one investment manager, she or he may be required by this language to make a minimum commitment to fixed income securities, even though the client desires maximum exposure to equities. A meaningful commitment to fixed income securities would seem to be required, but there is no definition of "meaningful." The same question can arise where there are multiple managers and the client directs that asset mix be determined by the adviser as though it were managing the entire trust. Where there are multiple managers, of course, an adviser can be selected to manage a specified type of security—separate equity and fixed income managers. In the case of larger plans, the expectation with respect to asset mix often is provided in the agreement. Internally, advisers usually refer to specific limitations imposed by the client or otherwise as investment restrictions, and less restricted directions (with no numerical or percentage) as investment guidelines.

Institutional Investment and Beneficial Ownership Disclosure

The SEC has recently adopted new rules applicable to filing and disclosure requirements relating to beneficial ownership.[19] Disclosure of beneficial ownership originated with the Williams Act of 1968, which requires disclosure of beneficial ownership of more than 5 percent of certain equity securities. Since this disclosure generally relates to contests for control, beneficial ownership includes the power to vote. The new rule adopts a definition of the term "beneficial ownership" which also includes the power to dispose of a security. Securities in portfolios managed by affiliates are aggregated for reporting purposes. The threshold for reporting remains at 5 percent ownership. A short form report has been adopted for institutional investors which do not

---

[19] SEC Rels. 34-14692 and IC-10212 (April 28, 1978).

invest for control. The long form (13D) must be filed within ten days after the acquisition, but the short form (13G) need be filed only within 45 days after the end of the calendar year, and more than 5 percent "beneficial ownership" must exist at the end of the calendar year. This requirement imposes additional recordkeeping and reporting requirements and is especially relevent to larger advisers.

The SEC has also adopted new rules, pursuant to the direction contained in Section 13(f) of the Securities Exchange Act, which was added by the Securities Acts Amendments of 1975. These new rules establish filing and reporting requirements for institutional investment managers.[20] They apply to institutional investment managers which advise accounts aggregating over $100 million and is designed to gather data on the impact of institutional investors upon the securities markets. A subsequent amendment requires that Form 13F be filed quarterly rather than annually by such institutional managers within 45 days after the end of each quarter (except the fourth), and after the end of the calendar year.[21] The form requires disclosure of the name of the issuer, the title of the issue, the class of the issue, CUSIP number, number of shares or principal amount in the case of convertible debt, and the aggregate fair market value of each equity security held. There is an exemption for holdings of less than 10,000 shares if the market value of the security is under $200,000.

The new rule applies to exchange traded and NASDAQ quoted equity securities, a list of which is available. To be required to report, these securities must aggregate $100 million at the end of a calendar month. A separate statement is required for accounts beneficially owned by natural persons, since information concerning them is kept confidential. Otherwise, the information assembled is public. The SEC will issue lists of institutions and the securities they control, and lists of securities, showing which institutions control them and the amounts controlled by each. Voting power does not trigger reporting, as it does under the beneficial ownership rules described above. Again, this imposes substantial new recordkeeping and reporting requirements, but because of the threshold of $100 million, the rule applies only to the medium sized and larger advisers.

INVESTMENT ADVISORY CONTRACTS

Topics Covered

Section 205, in addition to covering fees, as discussed later in the chapter, requires that contracts contain a provision prohibiting assignment without the consent of the client, and requires notification to clients of changes in membership of investment advisory partnerships.

---

[20] SEC Rel. 34–14852 (July 31, 1978).
[21] SEC Rec. 34–15461 (December 19, 1978).

However, where other than a minority partnership interest has changed, or if there has been a transfer of a controlling block of a corporate adviser's voting securities, then the client must consent to the continuance of the agreement, since such transfers constitute an assignment as defined in Section 202(a)(1). While not required, it is obviously preferable to obtain such consents in writing.

The investment advisory contract can be a simple power of attorney or a lengthy contractual document. For ERISA accounts, a recital of appointment by a named fiduciary is advisable. Topics to be covered could include the following.

1. identification of the parties;
2. extent of investment discretion permitted;
3. the advisory fee (how computed, when billed);
4. a provision with respect to settlement procedures (where assets are held by a bank as trustee or custodian the provision would be that the adviser direct securities purchased to be registered in the name of and delivered to the bank or its nominee, and that all proceeds from the sale of securities be delivered to the bank or its nominee, but where the adviser has possession of securities Rule 206(4)–2 is applicable);
5. possibly a provision dealing with the frequency and content of reports supplied by the adviser;
6. for ERISA accounts a representation that the adviser is registered under the Advisers Act;
7. a termination provision;
8. a provision specifying the state whose law is applicable;
9. prohibition against assignment by the adviser without consent of the client; and
10. a provision is sometimes included stating the investment objective of the account.

In some cases the adviser agrees to abide by the investment guidelines and investment restrictions furnished by the client from time to time. Attorneys representing ERISA clients often require a provision dealing with the standard of care to be exercised by the adviser, simply incorporating into the agreement the ERISA prudent man rule.

Particularly with respect to small clients, the SEC is concerned that the agreement not amount to an express or implied waiver of the client's rights under the securities laws. It is unclear whether such an agreement may include a gross negligence test to determine the adviser's potential liability to the client.

Investment Objectives and Restrictions

Some agreements require the adviser to abide by a set of investment restrictions which can be measured arithmetically. Very seldom will two or more clients arrive at exactly the same set of investment restrictions. Thus, considerable effort may be required to monitor the restrictions. These restrictions are similar to investment company fundamental policies.[22] The typical mutual fund fundamental policy will not require the sale of a security because of changes in market values subsequent to purchase. The mutual fund concept is to add the cost of a security being purchased to the market value of current holdings in determining whether or not a particular test is violated.

Where a private client bases the test strictly on market value, then a sale may be required in order to meet the test. For example, if a client prohibits holding more than 10 percent of the assets of the account in any one security, then after acquiring say a 6 percent or 7 percent position, a sale may be required when the issue constitutes more than 10 percent. Monitoring of these restrictions may be complicated and time consuming. A number of the following tests can be based on either cost or market value:

1. Maximum percentage of the account to be invested in one industry.
2. Maximum percentage of the account to be invested in one company.
3. Minimum requirements for an issuer, such as market capitalization, minimum sales or minimum earnings.
4. Prohibition against purchasing stock of the employer.
5. Maximum percentage of the account to be invested in equities.
6. Maximum percentage of the account to be invested in fixed income securities.
7. Maximum percentage OTC stocks.
8. Minimum commerical paper ratings.
9. Size of banks issuing certificates of deposit.
10. Maximum percentage of the account to be invested in foreign securities.
11. Minimum bond ratings and instructions with respect to maturities.
12. Prohibitions against purchasing restricted stock, using leverage or purchasing warrants.

It is also unclear as to the extent of the adviser's liabilities if one of these tests is violated.

FEES FOR INVESTMENT ADVISORY SERVICES

Section 205(1) prohibits registered advisers from receiving compensation on the basis of a share of capital gains or capital appreciation,

---

[22] See ICA Sections 8(b) 1 and 2, and 13(a).

thus prohibiting the typical hedge fund fee arrangement.[23] Performance fees are prohibited where the client is a qualified employe benefit trust or an account of $1 million or less. Where a performance fee is permitted there must be a "mirror image" provision providing for a reduction of fees of the adviser as well as an increase in the fees of the adviser. The rules (205–1 and 2) provided detailed definitions of investment performance, investment record, and other applicable terms which are used for performance fees.

MARKETING INVESTMENT ADVISORY SERVICES— DISCLOSURE

Advertising

The general requirements for advertising are contained in Rule 206(4)–1 under Section 206, the antifraud section. However, Rule 206(4)–1 provides limited guidance as to prohibited advertising under Section 206(4), and covers only testimonials, past specific investment recommendations, and uses of charts and formulas to determine which securities to buy or sell. Otherwise, the only guidance given is the general admonition to avoid untrue statements of a material fact or statements which are otherwise false or misleading. The Rule makes it a fraudulent, deceptive, or manipulative act, practice, or course of business within the meaning of Section 206(4) for any investment adviser (registered or not), directly or indirectly, to publish, circulate or distribute any advertisement:

---

[23] On June 19, 1979, the SEC proposed Rule 205–3 exempting from the prohibition of Section 205(1) of the Act fees based on a share of net capital gains or net capital appreciation of the funds of a "business development company" if certain conditions are met. (SEC Rel. IA-680) Business development companies, often called venture capital companies, acquire securities by private placement in other companies which are typically relatively small unseasoned companies in the development stage. There are extensive conditions which must be met under the rule relating to the business, assets, and securities holdings of the business development company, and the business, assets, and type of securities issued by the portfolio company.

Comments on the proposed rule have been critical and, among other things, questioned whether the rule may result in requiring registration as an investment adviser of companies not now registered. Some comments urged that such business development companies should not be subject to registration. The question of required registration depends upon several factors including whether the business development company is considered as one client for persons investing in it or whether each investor in it should be counted individually under the exception in Section 203(b)(3). There is an additional issue whether such company is holding itself out as an adviser under that Section. It seems likely that the comments and reconsideration by the SEC will result in a modified proposal which will be released for comment rather than adopted in final form. It is also likely that the proposal will consider the question of the factors important in determining whether registration is required.

1. Which refers to any testimonial of any kind concerning the investment adviser or concerning any advice, analysis, report or other service rendered by the adviser.
2. Which refers to past specific recommendations of such investment adviser which were or would have been profitable to any person. However, certain advertisements are not prohibited if they set forth or offer to furnish a list of all recommendations made by such investment adviser within at least the prior 12 months at a minimum if such advertisement, and such list:

   a. Identifies the securities, the date and nature of each recommendation, the market price at that time, the price at which the recommendation was to be acted on, and the market price as of a recent practicable date; and
   b. contains a cautionary legend indicating "it should not be assumed that recommendations made in the future will be profitable or will equal the performance of the securities in this list".

3. Which represents that any graph, chart, formula, or other device being offered can in and of itself be used to determine which securities or when to buy or sell, or which represents that such presentation being offered will assist any person in making decisions, without prominently disclosing in such advertisement the limitations thereof and the difficulties with respect to its use.
4. Which contains any statement that any report, analysis or other service will be furnished free or without charge unless such actually is or will be furnished entirely free without conditions or obligations.
5. Which contains any material misstatement or is otherwise false or misleading.

Advertisements are defined as any written communications addressed to more than one person, or any presentation in any publication or by radio or television which offers (1) any analysis, report or publication concerning securities or to be used in making determinations as to which security or when to buy or sell; or (2) any graph, chart, formula, or other devise to be used in making determinations as when or which security to buy or sell; or (3) any other investment advisory service with regard to securities.

There are a number of difficulties in making simple representations with respect to past performance because of the following complexities:

1. Use of the mean of all accounts or a segment of accounts ignores the fact that there may be significant size differences—the $100,000 account and the $10,000,000 account are treated equally.
2. Weighting performance by size of account implies that performance correlates with the size of accounts which is often not true.

3. Weighted and unweighted averages may not take into account the deviation of performance around the mean.
4. There may be differences, even subtle differences, in objectives of accounts which make them irrelevant for a particular presentation.
5. While the timing of contributions and withdrawals may be taken into account, arithmetically, by using time weighted returns, there are other more subtle effects. For example, a very large cash addition or cash withdrawal could dramatically change the percentage of the account invested in equities and the percentage of cash reserves and lead, in turn, to different performance results.

Reflecting a new SEC approach to rulemaking, using general concepts rather than lengthy and detailed requirements, exhibited previously in various changes to Investment Company Act rules, the SEC has taken action in the advertising area. On March 8, 1979 the SEC withdrew its Statement of Policy on investment company sales literature, which has been severely criticized, and has requested public comment on a proposed interpretive rule concerning false and misleading sales literature.[24] Thus it seems unlikely that much additional guidance on advertisements under the Advisers Act will be forthcoming in the near future.[25]

---

[24] On March 8, 1979, the SEC announced the withdrawal of its Statement of Policy on investment company sales literature which was a lengthy, complex, technical, and much criticized document. (Sec. Act Rel. 6034).

At the same time the SEC requested public comment on proposed Rule 156 an interpretative rule concerning the use of false or misleading investment company sales literature. After receiving comments on the proposal, the SEC has now adopted Rule 156, in modified form, on October 26, 1979 (Sec. Act Rel. 6140). The final rule contains three parts. The first restates the general antifraud prohibitions against using sales literature that is materially misleading in connection with the offer or sale of securities, and provides a general definition of the term "materially misleading."

The second part explains what is or is not misleading, which depends upon the context in which the statement is made, and lists particular factors which can be used in making such a determination.

The third part provides a rather comprehensive definition of the term "sales literature."

In response to a comment letter by the NASD expressing the concern that the discontinuance of interpretative opinions from the staff could frustrate industry self-regulation, the Commission noted that it has under study a proposal, made by the NASD, to use its exemptive powers to exempt filings under Section 24(b) (copies of advertisements) by companies that meet sales literature filing requirements of self-regulatory organizations.

[25] However, the SEC has adopted a new rule and amended another under the Securities Act allowing expanded advertising in investment company sales literature (Sec. Act Rel. 6116, August 31, 1979). New rule 434d permits radio and television advertising and also advertising in a bona fide newspaper or magazine. Amended Rule 134 allows expanded "tombstone" advertisements by investment companies prior to the effectiveness of a pending registration statement in the form now permitted after registration is effective.

Brochure Rule and Revised from ADV

On January 30, 1979, the SEC adopted proposals under the Investment Advisers Act in revised form[26] which were originally proposed in 1975[27] and reproposed in 1977[28]. The impetus for this proposal began with the SEC Special Study of the Securities Markets in 1963 which raised the specific concern about the possible lack of qualifications of investment advisers and their personnel, especially certain smaller advisers serving small and unsophisticated investors. The concept of a written disclosure statement was articulated in the January 1973 SEC Report on Small Accounts and Investment Management Services and reenunciated in several speeches by Commissioner Sommer.

New Rule 204–3 requires registered investment advisers (or those required to be registered) to deliver a written disclosure statement ("brochure") containing information concerning the adviser's background and business practices, when entering into an advisory contract with a prospective client. The brochure must be delivered either (1) at least 48 hours prior to entering into the contract, or (2) at the time of entering into a contract which provides for the right of termination without penalty within five business days. (Part II of reversed Form ADV, described below, may be used to satisfy the brochure delivery requirement.)

Advisers entering into a contract with a registered investment company, or providing solely for impersonal advisory services of less than $200 are exempt from all delivery requirements.

Advisers providing impersonal advisory services requiring payment of $200 or more must deliver or offer to deliver a brochure to clients at the time of entering the contract.

Advisers must also deliver a brochure to current clients (1) when those clients enter into a materially changed advisory contract, (2) annually (as explained in the next paragraph), and (3) when material changes are made in the brochure (as discussed below).

The rule requires nonexempted advisers, annually to deliver, or offer in writing to deliver without charge, to each of their clients a written disclosure statement meeting the requirements of the brochure rule.

Moreover, any brochure delivered must be amended to correct inaccuracies in certain items and an amendment to Form ADV filed, and the adviser must promptly file an amendment to Form ADV correcting any material inaccuracy in certain other items.

While the brochure rule does not specifically require advisers to furnish a revised brochure to each client every time a material change

---

[26] SEC Rel. IA-664.

[27] SEC Rel. IA-442.

[28] SEC Rels. IA-601, and 602.

occurs, the SEC release states that this obligation is within the adviser's general fiduciary duty to clients. The release adds that, under Section 206 of the Act, advisers have a fiduciary duty to disclose to clients major changes which would particularly affect the investment adviser relationship.

The brochure rule permits specialized brochures by allowing advisers to omit from brochures to clients or prospective clients certain information that does not relate to the type of advisory service for that client.

Finally, the rule specifically states that it is not intended as a "safe-harbor" from other disclosure requirements.

Revisions of Form ADV. Revisions to the SEC registration Form ADV for advisers relate to new information requirements and a reorganization of the Form into Parts I and II.

Part I has been designed to reflect the statutory additions made by the Securities Acts Amendments of 1975, and to obtain so-called "survey" information about the basic characteristics of the advisory industry aimed at making the SEC inspection program more effective.

Part II requires information concerning the background and business practices of advisers, and is the same information required in the brochure. Part II may be delivered to fulfill the brochure delivery requirements.

Schedules A, B, C and D of Form ADV have been amended, as has Form BD of the Exchange Act, to make those schedules identical for registered investment advisers who are also registered broker-dealers.

Form ADV Part I. The following new information, is now required in Part I of Form ADV:

1. An explanation if the registration in any state has been suspended or involuntarily terminated, or voluntarily terminated or withdrawn (Item 3(b)).
2. A history of mergers and acquisitions for ten years (7(b)).
3. An expanded list of statutory disqualifications pursuant to the 1975 Amendments (10).
4. A list of material litigation if the adviser is a defendant (14).
5. Several items in Part I are intended to provide information about the basic characteristics of investment adviser. These include disclosure of: an adviser's custody or possession of securities or funds of a client (12); number of employes (13(a)); the extent, if any, of investment supervisory services (13(b)); are a ranking based on dollar amount, of the adviser's business by type of client, including number of accounts, market value and a numerical listing of accounts by size, both for discretionary accounts and nondiscretionary accounts (15 and 16). (This information, as well as information in Part II, is

required to be updated annually by new Form ADV-S within 90 days after the end of the fiscal year.)

6. An unaudited year-end balance sheet prepared in accordance with generally accepted accounting principles for advisers not required to deliver a certified balance sheet in the brochure (17). (An audited balance sheet as of 15 months prior to filing or delivery, must be included by advisers in the brochure and included in Part II of Form ADV if (1) the adviser has custody or possession of clients funds or securities, or the adviser requires prepaid advisory fees in excess of $500 and six months or more in advance.)

Contents of Written Disclosure Statement Form ADV Part II. Part II of the revised Form ADV requires certain basic information about the adviser and additionally, the same information required in a written disclosure statement, i.e., brochure.

Both Part II and the brochure must contain information concerning the background and business practices of an investment adviser, including (by Item number in Part II):

1. The types of advisory services provided and the fees for such services.
2. The types of clients using the adviser's services.
3. The types of investments with respect to which the adviser generally gives advice.
4. The methods of analysis, types of investment strategies, and sources of information used by the adviser.
5. The standards of education, if any, established by the adviser with respect to person(s) associated with the adviser.
6. The actual education and business experience of certain associated persons.
7. Other business activities of the adviser.
8. Other securities industry activities and affiliations.
9. The adviser's participation, if any, in connection with securities transactions of clients.
10. Any conditions for establishing or maintaining advisory accounts.
11. The nature of the adviser's discretionary authority if any, with respect to advisory accounts, and the adviser's brokerage placement practices.
12. The adviser's process for reviewing accounts.
13. With respect to certain advisers, a certified balance sheet.

A detailed description of this information is as follows:

1. Advisory Services and Fees. This takes the form of a checklist and includes, among others, investment supervisory services, account management services not involving investment supervisory services, the issuance on a subscription basis of a periodic publication relating to securities, and issuance of reports or analyses.

Moreover, information must be supplied concerning basis or bases of compensation, amounts charged (basic fee schedules and an indication of whether fees are negotiable), and when fees are payable. If fees are payable in advance disclosure is required as to what extent, if any, and under what conditions, such fees are refundable. Termination provisions must also be disclosed.

2. *Types of Clients.*   The types of clients required to be listed include individuals or specified classes of individuals, investment companies, pension and profit-sharing plans and banks.

3. *Types of Securities.*   This is a checklist of the types of securities concerning which the adviser generally provides advice.

4. *Methods of Analysis, Sources of Information and Investment Strategy.*   In narrative fashion, the adviser must disclose:

a. method of securities analysis, e.g., fundamental analysis, technical analysis, cyclical analysis or charting;

b. principal sources of information, e.g., financial newspapers and magazines, company prepared information, inspections of corporate activities, research materials prepared by others, or corporate rating services, and

c. types of investment strategies generally recommended or used to implement any investment advice rendered to clients, e.g., long-term purchase (securities will be held at least one year except in unusual circumstances), short-term purchases (securities will generally be sold within one year after purchase), trading (securities will generally be sold within 30 days after purchase), short sales, margin transactions, or option writing, including covered options, uncovered options, and spreading strategies.

5. *Education and Business Standards.*   This item requires disclosure of any general standards of education and business background required of persons associated with the adviser whose functions or duties relate to providing investment advice to clients, other than clerical or ministerial personnel.

6. *Education and Business Background.*   Disclosure is required for each member of the adviser's investment committee, or similar group, of the name, age, formal education after high school, and business background for the preceding five years. An investment committee is described as one which determines or approves what investment advice shall generally be rendered by the adviser to any client or to which clients. If there is no investment committee or similar committee, information must be provided for persons who determine or approve the type of investment advice which will be rendered by the adviser.

7. *Other Business Activities.*   This item relates to other business activities of the adviser including specifically his activities and affiliations in the securities business. This question is largely directed to

advisers who provide advice only as an adjunct to their primary activities in other areas such as insurance or real estate or in addition to an unrelated primary occupation.

8. *Other Securities Industry Activities or Affiliates.* The adviser must disclose, if it offers or sells products other than securities to its clients, information about other securities activities and affiliations.

9. *Participation or Interest in Securities Transactions.* The adviser must disclose whether:

a. As principal, it sells securities to or buys securities from any advisory client;

b. as agent, it effects securities transactions from any advisory client or any person other than an advisory client; and

c. if it recommends to advisory clients or prospective advisory clients the purchase or sale of any security in which the adviser holds a position or interest.

A description is required of the circumstances relating to these transactions and any internal procedures established concerning conflicts of interest in such transactions. The adviser must also disclose any restrictions imposed upon the adviser or an associated person in connection with the purchase or sale for its or their account of securities recommended to advisory clients. This requirement complements the recordkeeping requirements on securities transactions discussed above.

10,11, and 12. Investment Supervisory and Account Management Services. Advisers who provide investment supervisory services or account management services must describe:

a. What conditions, if any, including minimum amount of assets under management, are imposed on accounts (10);

b. The extent, if any, of discretionary authority involved in the supervision and management of accounts (11);

c. The process of reviewing each investment advisory account (12); and

d. Reports regularly furnished to clients concerning their advisory accounts (12).

If an adviser determines or suggests a broker or dealer through which, or the commission rates at which, securities transactions for client accounts are affected, even though not providing investment supervisory or account management services, questions must be answered relating to adviser's brokerage placement practices including the selection of brokers and the amount of transactions (11). (A detailed description of this requirement is contained in Section C below).

13. Balance Sheet. An audited balance sheet must be filed with the Commission and included in the brochure delivered to clients if the adviser *(a)* has custody or possession of clients funds or securities, or *(b)* requires clients to prepay advisory fees in excess of $500 and for six months or more in advance.

Requirement to Revise Form ADV

Registered investment advisers are required to file a revised Form ADV no later than July 31, 1979. This requirement is set forth in amended Rule 204–1(a). Rule 204–1(b) has been amended to require investment advisers to amend the individual items in Part I and II of Form ADV at various times as follows:

a. Promptly after the information becomes inaccurate—Part I, items 2, 4, 6, 10, 12(a) and (b) and 14;

b. Promptly after the information becomes materially inaccurate— Part I, items 5, 7, 8, 9 and 11, and Part II all items except 13 (the balance sheet); and

c. Annually for all other changes.

As will be covered in other chapters of this Handbook, certain states, notably New York, had previously begun adopting concepts, included in the SEC disclosure statement, involving increased information in state filings which must be sent to advisory clients or a notice delivered that it will be sent upon request.

Disclosure of Brokerage Placement Practices

The Securities Acts Amendments of 1975 added Section 28(e) (1) to the Securities Exchange Act. This Section expressly permits investment managers to pay brokerage commissions for transactions in managed accounts in excess of the lowest rates available if they determine that the commissions are reasonable in relation to the value of the brokerage and research services provided. The SEC was authorized to establish rules requiring investment managers to disclose their policies and practices with respect to such commission practices.

Initially there was considerable concern about the interpretation and application of Section 28(e), not alleviated by the SEC's interpretations,[29] but no significant litigation seems to have arisen on the subject following the advent of negotiated rates on May 1, 1975 and the increasingly competitive atmosphere in the brokerage community. While institutions generally remain cautious about practices in this area and have adopted internal guidelines and compliance procedures, the concern seems to have subsided.

On November 30, 1976, the SEC proposed Rule 28e2–1 to require

---

[29] Interpretations of Section 28(e) of the Securities Exchange Act of 1934; Use of Commission Payments by Fiduciaries, SEC Rel. 34–12251 (March 24, 1976).

disclosure of brokerage placement practices by registered investment advisers, investment companies and others. Advisers were to be subject to the rule as "investment managers" if they exercise investment discretion over client accounts and if they determine or suggest brokers or commission rates for the account.[30] In addition, certain registration and reporting forms were to be amended and other rule changes proposed. The primary vehicle for this disclosure was a written disclosure statement to be delivered to new clients before entering into contracts and to all clients annually.

The Commission had previously proposed in 1975, the so-called brochure rule under the Investment Advisers Act, which was reproposed in 1977 along with proposed amendments to Form ADV (see discussion in B, above). The brochure rule would also have mandated the delivery of a written disclosure statement to prospective and existing clients both before contracts were entered into or renewed, and periodically when changes were made. The disclosure document—brochure—and Form ADV were to include certain information about brokerage practices.

By SEC action taken on January 30, 1979, these two separate proposals—the brochure rule and brokerage placement practices disclosure rule—were coordinated. Under the new brochure rule (Investment Advisers Act Rule 204–3,—see discussion above) a written disclosure document is required for certain advisers with expanded brokerage placement information in narrative form (but omitting statistical information required in the amendments described below), which information is also required in the amended Form ADV.[31]

The rationale for omitting the statistical information in the brochure is that it would not be compatible with a general disclosure document such as the brochure.

The new brokerage placement practices release applies only to certain investment companies registered under the Investment Company Act and to certain other types of accounts including H.R. 10 plans, employe benefit plans, and collective funds or separate accounts for the assets of such plans, interests or participations in which are registered under the Securities Act.[32] The disclosure requirements in narrative form are comparable to those under the brochure rule for advisers and additionally require various statistical information about brokerage transactions. These take the form of requirements for additional information in registration statements filed under the Investment Company Act, registration statements for securities filed under the Securities Act, and proxy rules applicable to investment companies.

---

[30] SEC Rels. 33–5772, 34–13024, IC-9547 and IA-554.

[31] SEC Rel. IA-664, note 26, supra.

[32] SEC Rels. 33–6019, IC-10569 and IA-665.

The release announcing the adoption of the requirements for brokerage placement disclosure discusses at length the reasons for the November 1976 proposal, the critical comments received on that proposal and the steps taken to remedy the areas of controversy. The release states:

> In light of the comments received from the public the Commission has made certain modifications from the 1976 Release's proposed rulemaking. As mentioned above, the information which generally has been retained represents matters which—to a greater or lesser degree—are frequently treated in existing investment company disclosure in this area. However, the general quality of disclosure in this area is uneven and, with respect to investment advisers and pooled accounts which are not registered investment companies, insufficient or non-existent. Essentially, the Commission has taken the investment company industry's better practices as the basis for the industry's required standards and for the standards to be required of investment managers. The Commission believes that the disclosure requirements it has adopted are more attuned to current brokerage allocation practices and in some cases elicit disclosure more meaningful than that now being provided.

Required Disclosures—Forms N-1 and N-2. The additional disclosures include revised Item 7 *Brokerage Allocation* in the Investment Company registration Forms N-1 and N-2. This requires the following statistical information:

1. the aggregate dollar amount of brokerage commission paid by the investment company during the three most recent fiscal years;
2. the aggregate dollar amount of brokerage commissions paid during the three most recent fiscal years to any brokerage

    a. which is affiliated with the investment company,
    b. which is affiliated with such affiliate, or
    c. which is affiliated with an affiliate of the investment company, its investment adviser or principal underwriter, disclosing the identity of each such broker and the relationships;

3. the percentage of the investment company's aggregate brokerage commissions paid to each such broker during the most recent fiscal year;
4. the percentage of the aggregate dollar amount of transactions involving the payment of commissions effected through each such broker during the most recent fiscal year; and
5. the reasons for any material difference in the percentage of brokerage commissions paid to, and the percentage of transactions effected through, any such broker, the reasons therefor.

Other required information in the narrative section is a description of how brokers will be selected to effect securities transactions and

how evaluations will be made of the overall reasonableness of brokerage commissions paid, including the factors considered in these determinations.

The instructions to the item require that if the receipt of products
or services other than brokerage or research services, or the receipt
of research services, is a factor in selecting brokers, the products and
services should be specified and the nature of the research services
identified. Moreover, any authorization to "pay up" for brokerage or
research services (i.e., commissions in excess of other available rates)
must be disclosed. The narrative section must also specify whether
any research services furnished by brokers for an investment company
may be used by the investment company's investment adviser in servicing all of its accounts, and, if applicable, that not all such services
may be used for the investment company. Other policies or practices
used for the allocation of research services provided by such brokers
must be explained and the broker must "state if there is directed
brokerage of the investment company's business to a broker because
of research services provided, pursuant to an agreement or understanding, the amount of such transactions and the related commissions."

Comparable amendments are made to Form S-1 (Item 20, *Brokerage
Allocation*), and Form S-8 (Item 9, *Investment of Funds*), relating to
the registration of securities under the Securities Act issued in connection with certain employes' stock bonus, pension, profit sharing, or
annuity plans.

Finally, the proxy rules under the Investment Company Act, Rule
20a–2, are also revised to require comparable information in the proxy
statement of investment companies.

The amendments apply to registration statements and proxy statements which are filed or amended on or after May 1, 1979.

RELATIONSHIPS WITH BROKERS

Broker Referrals and Continuing Relationships

A common practice in the securities industry involves the referral
of clients to investment advisers by brokers. The recent case of *Rolf
v. Blyth, Eastman Dillon & Co.*[33] dealt with the liability of a broker
(Blyth, Eastman) and its registered representative (Stott) for the fraud
of the investment adviser (Yamada) who was recommended to the
client by Stott. This decision is important to investment advisers as
well as brokers since it may influence future referral relationships.

In this case the plaintiff, Dr. Rolf, gave discretionary authority in
1963 to Blyth, Eastman (then known as Eastmann Dillon Union Securi-

---

[33] *Rolf* v. *Blyth, Eastman Dillon & Co.* 424 F. Supp. 1021 (S.D.N.Y. 1977), *aff'd*
570 F. 2d 38 (CA 2 1978), *cert. den.* 47 LW 3391 (12/5/78)

ties) to manage a discretionary account valued at about $400,000. Prior to 1962 Dr. Rolf had nondiscretionary accounts with various brokers. His second discretionary account was maintained with Blyth, Eastman from 1963 until 1969, when the partner managing the account retired because of ill health. When the account was reassigned by Blyth, Eastman to Stott, Dr. Rolf expressed a preference for an investment adviser, and Stott provided the names of two. Dr. Rolf interviewed and selected Yamada who managed his account until 1971. In 1972, Yamada was enjoined by the SEC from engaging in fraudulent and manipulative practices and pleaded guilty to a criminal conspiracy. In 1973 and 1974 Yamada pleaded guilty to other criminal violations.

At the time Yamada was given discretionary authority over the Rolf account in 1969 (at which time Yamada enjoyed a good reputation as an investment adviser), the value of the portfolio was $1,423,000, and was comprised of good quality listed securities. About 10 months later the account consisted mainly of low quality securities and was worth $446,000, of which almost one-half was represented by one restricted stock. The account declined further in 1970, to about $225,000. In early 1971 the SEC investigation of Yamada became public and Blyth, Eastman refused to execute trades for Yamada. Rolf learned of these difficulties, terminated his discretionary account and subsequently commenced suit.

A federal district court found that Yamada fraudulently manipulated stocks in Dr. Rolf's account, actions of which Stott was ignorant. However, the court further found that Yamada's overall management of the account also was fraudulent (within Section 206 of the Advisers Act), as was Stott's "hand-holding," that is, his continued voicing of confidence in Yamada to Dr. Rolf. Continual assurances by Stott of Yamada's competence was characterized as having been made with willful and reckless disregard for whether his statements were true or false.

The Court of Appeals decision included a technical analysis of whether Stott's conduct gave rise to aiding and abetting liability under Section 10(b) of the Securities Exchange Act and Rule 10b–5 thereunder, as concluded by the lower court. The Court concluded that such liability exists, in part because Stott was held to owe a direct fiduciary obligation to Dr. Rolf. Because of this direct fiduciary obligation a recklessness standard was held to be appropriate, rather than the stricter standard of actual intent to defraud. In order to establish Stott's aiding and abetting liability other legal elements were required, including knowledge of the adviser's fraud and substantial assistance in the fraudulent mismanagement of the portfolio. The knowledge requirement was satisfied by proof of reckless conduct, which was essentially the hand-holding of the client without investigation. Stott had knowledge of most trades, was aware that low quality securities were being purchased and for a time was in daily contact with the adviser. The substantial assistance test was held to have been met through processing the orders. For purposes of the appeal, Blyth, Eastman conceded liability for the acts of its agent.

Blyth, Eastman did not apply its suitability or other of its existing internal compliance standards to the Rolf account because investment decisions were being made by an adviser to whom discretionary authority had been granted. The Court of Appeals held that the execution of a trading authorization giving Yamada discretionary authority to effect portfolio transactions in Dr. Rolf's Blyth, Eastman account, did not relieve Stott or Blyth, Eastman of their normal broker fiduciary duties because of the lower court's finding that Stott undertook to oversee the account. Dr. Rolf maintained, and the lower court had agreed, that Stott was involved in the management of the portfolio, since Stott and Yamada were in daily contact, Stott recommended investment ideas to Yamada using Blyth, Eastman research, most trades were executed by Blyth, Eastman, and there was an intent to continue an investment role on the part of Blyth, Eastman after the partner who previously managed the account retired and Yamada was appointed as an investment adviser. The argument that Stott was a mere order-taker was rejected.

In determining how Dr. Rolf's damages should be measured the Court of Appeals disagreed with the lower court's conclusion that only commissions and interest should be awarded, and in remanding the case for reconsideration of damages the lower court was instructed to take into account market losses, after subtracting therefrom the average percentage decline of a well recognized market index during the period in question.

A strongly worded dissenting opinion emphasized that the actual manipulation of prices of securities by the adviser was unknown to Stott, so that at worst Stott lulled Dr. Rolf into accepting Yamada's decisions to purchase unsuitable securities. The dissenting opinion expressed the view that this activity should not constitute aiding and abetting securities fraud. Further, the hand-holding activities of the registered representative and his belief that many of the stocks purchased were "junk" should not lead to liability for fraud. The adviser had an excellent reputation and there were indications that plaintiff, an experienced investor, had an aggressive investment objective.

Apparently because of concern that a broker may be liable for losses occasioned by unsuitable investments purchased by an investment adviser to whom discretionary authority has been granted, the Court of Appeals amended its opinion by adding the following footnote:

> 16A. This decision does not impose liability on a broker-dealer who merely executes orders for unsuitable securities made by an investment advisor vested with sole discretionary authority to control the account. In the present case, the broker-dealer, although charged with supervisory

authority over the advisor and aware that the advisor was purchasing "junk," actively lulled the investor by expressing confidence in the advisor without bothering to investigate whether these assurances were well-founded.

This amendment of the opinion suggests that three elements were present which triggered liability, in addition to the purchase of unsuitable securities.

First, the broker-dealer was charged with supervisory authority over the adviser. However, as a practical matter, a registered representative recommending an investment adviser who is on the broker's approved list generally will work to maintain his relationship with the client after the adviser is appointed. The broker is likely to undertake to oversee the account, expressly or impliedly, in order to continue his client relationship. Thus, the question whether or not the trading authorization insulates the broker if the broker maintains no independent relationship with the client may not have a great deal of practical significance in many referral situations.

Second, the broker-dealer knew the general character of the securities purchased by the adviser—"junk" in this case. Typically the broker will meet this requirement, particularly where, as here, it holds the securities and executes most trades. But as the dissent pointed out, it is virtually impossible for a brokerage firm to have available to it research information on every stock, especially those stocks outside its own selected areas of interest.

Third, the broker-dealer expressed confidence in the adviser without investigating whether these assurances were well founded. It appears that such assurances may not be given on the basis of the adviser's reputation, since Yamada enjoyed a good reputation at the critical times. It would follow then that the broker must be careful in discussing the account with the client, since assurances based on reputation may be translated into a warranty of the merits of the individual securities. Care on the part of brokers in communicating with clients whose accounts are managed by advisers appears advisable, but given the uncertainties posed by the Rolf decision, this care does not guarantee insulation from liability.

It can be suggested that in addition to exercising prudence in the selection of an adviser to recommend, and care in client communications, brokers may wish to satisfy themselves that there is a satisfactory investment advisory agreement between the client and the adviser. In *Rolf* the investment objectives of the client do not appear to have been clearly defined. At one point in the decision the client's objective was characterized as "substantial capital gain in an investment program emphasizing preservation and augmentation of capital," and there were indications of an intent of the client to double his money.[34]

---

[34] Ibid.

Advisers and brokers should consider the following hypothetical situation: there are no investment objectives or policies are articulated clearly in writing; the client conveys the impression that he is an aggressive trader willing to take high risks; the account is managed toward maximum capital appreciation and performs poorly; and the client then takes the position that his objective was preservation of capital, and securities purchased for him were not appropriate for this objective. It is clear that many misunderstandings can be minimized by stating an investment objective in the investment advisory agreement. If the objective is maximum capital appreciation, an intent to follow from time to time specified investment policies can be set forth; short selling, trading on margin, options transactions and the like can be authorized, and intent to use these devices can be stated. (Short selling—an indication of aggressive investment intent—was specifically authorized in Dr. Rolf's trading authorization, but not discussed in the opinions.) The purchase of lower quality issues can be authorized. Definitions of "lower quality" in such terms as market capitalization of the issue can be devised. For less aggressive accounts investment objectives and guidelines could, of course, be stated differently.

This suggestion of careful drafting of the investment advisory agreement is aimed more at the fundamental risk, that is an attack based on fraudulent mismanagement, rather than to the more complicated question of broker-dealer aider and abettor liability. This approach, possibly coupled with broker monitoring of whether or not the adviser is following any stated investment guidelines, and care in communicating with clients may be a reasonable solution to the *Rolf* problem, given the legal uncertainties raised by this case.

Cash Payments for Referrals

This subject is related obliquely to the case of *Rolf* v. *Blyth, Eastman Dillon*, (discussed in detail in Section A above), in that it also deals with the marketing of investment advisory services. On February 2, 1978 the SEC proposed Rule 206(4)–3 under the Advisers Act, which would establish the conditions under which an investment adviser may make cash payments to someone who solicits clients for him.[35] The background for this proposal, stated in the release, is the concept that the potential for conflicts of interest is so great that one solution would

---

[35] SEC Rel. IA-615.

The SEC, on July 12, 1979, adopted Rule 206(4)–3 prohibiting cash referral fee payments by investment advisers, except under certain specified circumstances, to any person who solicits a client for such adviser. At the same time, it adopted a corresponding recordkeeping rule, Rule 204–2(a)(15) (SEC Rel. IA-688).

The Rule, promulgated under Section 206, the general antifraud section of the Advisers Act, is effective September 30, 1979, and differs from that as proposed in both structure and substance. It prohibits cash referral payments by registered advisers (and

be to ban cash referral fees altogether if the solicitor is not an employee of the adviser.

The proposed rule would permit payment of cash referral fees in three circumstances:

1. Where the marketing representative is an employe of the adviser who is either primarily engaged in performing duties relating to the investment advisory business of the adviser or is clearly identified as a sales representative for the investment advisory services of the adviser. Here the prospective client would expect the natural bias of the marketing representative toward the employer.

---

those required to be registered) unless four conditions are met. The first three conditions apply to all payments made in any of three described circumstances. The three conditions are:

1. That the adviser be registered under the act with the SEC.
2. That the solicitor (person receiving the fee for referring a client) not be subject to a statutory bar from the securities business.
3. That the payment be made pursuant to a written agreement.

The three circumstances under which payments can be made (subject to meeting the three conditions noted above) are as follows.

First, that the solicitor is recommending only "impersonal advisory services"—recommendations not based on individual objectives or needs, or furnishing only statistical information. This condition is not met if the solicitor recommends other than impersonal advisory services or if such other services are actually performed for the client. In the proposed rule, these solicitations were exempt but under the new rule must meet the three conditions noted above.

Second, that the solicitation is made by certain persons affiliated with the adviser who disclose their relationship with the adviser. The qualified persons designated in the rule have been expanded from those primarily engaged in sales efforts as provided in the proposal, to partners, officers, directors, or employees of the adviser or entity owned, controlled by, or under common control with the adviser.

The third circumstance is the so-called third party solicitor situation. In this case there must be a written agreement between the adviser and the solicitor containing (a) permissible solicitation activities, (b) an undertaking by the solicitor to perform according to the adviser's instructions and in compliance with the Advisers Act, and (c) a required delivery by the solicitor, at the time of solicitation, of a brochure and the solicitation disclosure described below.

The required brochure is the brochure that the adviser must deliver to a prospective client before entering into a contract required by the recently adopted Rule 204–3 (brochure rule).

The solicitor's written disclosure must contain (a) name of the adviser, (b) nature of the relationship, (c) that the solicitor will receive compensation, (d) the terms of the compensation arrangement, and (e) whether the client will pay a specific charge or a higher advisory fee because the client's relationship with the adviser results from the solicitation.

Finally, the prospective client must receive from the client, at the time of entering into the contract, a written acknowledgment, signed and dated, that the client has received the brochure and the solicitor's disclosure.

The adviser must make bona fide efforts to ascertain that the solicitor has complied with the written agreement with the adviser, and have a reasonable basis for belief that compliance has occurred.

Additionally, a new recordkeeping item has been added to Rule 204–2 (item 15), requiring that the adviser keep copies of the client acknowledgments and the solicitor disclosure statements delivered to clients.

2. Where the services are impersonal, involving written materials or oral statements which are not individually tailored, or statistical information which does not comment on the investment merits of particular securities, or a combination of the two.
3. Others, where a series of conditions are met:

   a. The solicitor is not the subject of a SEC order barring or suspending the right of the solicitor to be associated with an investment adviser or who has engaged in certain prohibited conduct, or has been the subject of a specified type of injunction.
   b. During the course of the solicitation the prospect receives a written document containing various disclosures, such as the name of the solicitor, the name of the adviser, the nature of the relationship between the adviser and the solicitor, and a description of the compensation to be paid to the solicitor. Any additional charge to the prospective client resulting from the solicitation, such as a higher advisory fee than other clients might be charged, must also be disclosed.
   c. The adviser has the duty to supervise the solicitation activities of the marketing representative as though he were the adviser's own employee. The release suggests that this obligation can be prescribed in the contract between the adviser and the solicitor.
   d. At least annually, if additional referral fees are to be paid, the adviser must furnish the client a new disclosure statement, which includes a description of all compensation the solicitor received during the preceding contract period.

The release concludes with two paragraphs discussing a related subject—broker referrals and direction by the adviser of the client's brokerage business to the broker-dealer as compensation for the referral. Thus, in addition to uncertainties created by *Rolf,* the SEC has expressed concern about the practice, as follows:

> A solicitor who has a pre-existing relationship with the prospective client, e.g., a registered representative of a broker-dealer, may, depending on the nature of his relationship with his client, have fiduciary obligations to such client which require him to make a reasonable attempt to find the investment adviser best suited to the particular client. So that it is clear that this obligation continues to exist even if the solicitor complies with all provisions of the Rule, paragraph (d) of the Rule expressly provides that the standards set forth in the Rule are not intended to relieve any solicitor of any fiduciary or other obligation applicable to such person in connection with the solicitation activities covered by the Rule.
>
> It may be difficult for investment advisers who direct their client's brokerage transactions to particular broker-dealers as compensation for client referrals to disclose to their prospective clients meaningfully and in a manner which can be evaluated the existence of such arrangements.

In addition, investment advisers and broker-dealers have statutory and common law obligations to their clients which may preclude their participating in an arrangement which, among other things, might require an investment adviser to direct a client's transactions to a particular broker-dealer, irrespective of the broker-dealer's ability to execute the transaction competently and at an appropriate cost.

Therefore, in certain circumstances, it may be a fraudulent course of business, within the meaning of Section 206(2) of the Act (15 U.S.C. 80b–6(2)), for an investment adviser to use client commission dollars for this purpose and this rule proposal only addresses the applicability of the Act to those investment advisers who make *cash* payment to individuals who solicit clients for them.

The Commission is in the process of reviewing its position with respect to various uses of client commission dollars which in the past have been common in the securities industry, but are now prohibited. When the review is completed, the Commission will consider whether it is appropriate to amend this rule so that it explicitly addresses the applicability of the Act to investment advisers who use directed brokerage as compensation for client referrals. However, the Commission wishes to emphasize that nothing which is stated in this release or this rule proposal should be taken as an expression of its views on the question of whether directed brokerage can be used in this manner. [footnotes omitted, emphasis in original and paragraphs supplied]

The proposed rule has not yet been adopted.[36]

PROHIBITED TRANSACTIONS—FRAUD

General

Section 206 contains general antifraud provisions comparable to those in the other federal securities acts. However, unlike other federal securities laws which provide a more detailed statutory framework, under the Advisers Act many activities must be labeled as fraud in order to be prohibited. In addition, there are multiple fraud provisions. Activities so labeled include the following:

1. Misleading advertising, but there is no detailed guidance as to what is misleading. (Rule 206(4)–1.)
2. Inadequate supervision of sales.
3. Excessive trading, i.e. churning.
4. Failure to make special disclosure where the advisory fee exceeds 2 percent of the assets under management.
5. Mass merchandising of small accounts, which is inconsistent with the concept that individual service will be given.
6. Use of hedge clauses in the advisory agreement which leads the

---

[36] See note 35, supra.

client to believe that one has waived one's rights under the securities laws.[37]

7. Holding client's cash or securities without complying with Rule 206(4)–2.

These provisions relate to all investment advisers, not only those who are registered or required to be registered, but also nonregistered investment advisers. Several of these activities are considered in more detail below or in earlier sections of this chapter.

Dealing with a Client as Principal or Broker

The antifraud section of the Advisers Act, Section 206, prohibits certain transactions by investment advisers with their clients without disclosure of the adviser's capacity to the clients. Specifically, Section 206(3) in effect provides an investment adviser must disclose to a client in writing before the completion of any transaction described below and obtain the consent of the client to such transactions.

The transactions covered are (1) An adviser acting as principal for her own account to knowingly sell any security to or purchase any security from a client; or (2) while acting as broker for a person other than such client to knowingly effect any sale or purchase of any security for the account of that client. Excluded from the Section are transactions with a customer or a broker or dealer if such broker or dealer is not acting as an investment adviser in the transaction.

An early Commission release sets forth the policy of this Section and its application.[38] This pronouncement begins with the concept that investment advisers are fiduciaries and are required under common law to serve the interest of clients with undivided loyalty, and a breach of this duty may constitute violations of the antifraud provisions of the federal securities laws including Section 206 of the Advisers Act.

In interpreting Section 206(3) the release states that the written disclosure to the client must contain, at a minimum (1) the capacity in which the adviser proposes to act, (2) the cost to the adviser of any security proposed to be sold, or if a purchase and the adviser knows or is reasonably certain of the price of resale a statement of that price, and (3) the best price which could be effected elsewhere if more advantageous to the client. The total amount of the cost to the adviser or resale price (or total profit) should be disclosed in dollars, not merely by a formula or a percentage or a maximum per share.

The interpretation continues by stating that even though Section 206(3) applies only to registered investment advisers (an amendment

---

[37] See SEC Rel. IA-58 (April 18, 1951).

[38] SEC Rel. IA-40 (Jan. 5, 1945).

in 1970 made it applicable to all investment advisers registered or not), Section 17(a) of the Securities Act and Sections 10(b) and 15(c) (1) of the Exchange Act (general anti-fraud provisions comparable to Section 206) could be applicable to all investment advisers in such circumstances.

Finally, it is noted that the disclosure must be in writing, although the consent need not be, and a blanket disclosure in a general agreement would not suffice in the opinion of the SEC representative. (It would be prudent, of course, to obtain the consent in writing.)

Custody or Possession of Clients' Funds or Securities

Various requirements are also imposed under Section 206 setting conditions and limitations on the custody or possession of clients funds or securities. Unless these conditions are met, the adviser cannot take any action with respect to the funds or securities without violating Section 206 and Rule 206(4)–2 thereunder. The conditions are:

1. All securities are segregated and identified and held in safekeeping.
2. All funds are in clients-only bank accounts, the accounts are in the name of the adviser as agent or trustee, and separate records for each account are maintained with sufficient details regarding transactions therein.
3. The client must be notified immediately of the details of the maintenance of the funds and securities, and any changes, in writing.
4. At least quarterly, statements showing the funds and securities, and all transactions, must be sent to each client.
5. Independent public accountants must verify the funds and securities by actual examination annually without notice. A certificate thereof must be filed with the Commission after each examination.

Adviser and Personal Securities Transactions

In 1970, Congress added Section 17(j) to the Investment Company Act, prohibiting affiliated persons of investment advisers, or principal underwriters, for investment companies from engaging in fraudulent, deceptive, or manipulative acts, as may be defined by Commission rules, relating to the purchase or sale by such persons of "any security held or to be acquired by a registered investment company." This Section was added because of conflicts identified in the 1963 Special Study and the 1966 Report on Public Policy Implications of Investment Company Growth. In addition to the general prohibitions, the Commission may require the adoption of codes of ethics by investment companies, and investment advisers and principal underwriters thereto.

In 1972 the SEC released proposed Rule 17j–1 designed to implement Section 17(j) but withdrew it in 1976 following extensive objections to it. In 1978, a revised proposed Rule 17j-1 was announced.[39]

This proposal contains anti-fraud provisions relating to the trading by certain affiliated persons in securities held by or being considered for purchase by investment companies (these provisions are substantially identical to the earlier proposal). In addition, the proposal requires the adoption and enforcement of codes of ethics by investment companies and advisers and principal underwriters to such companies, to prevent violations of the antifraud provisions. (Again, this was the same as the earlier proposals.) Finally, a category of persons designated as "access persons" must report personal securities transactions to their employer. Access persons include directors, officers, or employees involved in the investment decisions making process. (This requirement was similar to the earlier proposal with some differences as noted below.)

The new proposal does not contain specific trading prohibitions, as did the earlier proposal, but it is left to the companies to determine such prohibitions and incorporate them in their own codes.

Independent directors of investment companies need not report their securities transactions unless such directors had actual knowledge that, within the prior 30 days, the securities had been purchased or sold by the investment company or such purchase or sale by the investment company had been considered. The concern here is that the Commission wants to avoid discouraging highly qualified individuals from serving as independent directors.

Companies adopting codes need not report violations of the codes to the SEC but must keep records of violations and actions taken. The rule would become effective six months after adoption. Codes which are adopted must be filed with the investment company form N-1R.

Inside Information

The subject of "inside information" emerged as a most important area of potential legal concern for investment managers in the late 1960s and has continued to be one of significance since that time. Based on the historical evolution of the inside information doctrine and its application to changing circumstances it will likely continue to be a timely subject for the foreseeable future.

---

[39] SEC Rel. IC-10162 (March 20, 1978).

On September 12, 1979, the Securities and Exchange Commission approved proposed Rule 17j-1 in modified form (520 BNA *SRLR* A-14, 9/19/79; *The Wall Street Journal,* 9/13/79 p. 3). Before the effective date of the rule, which has not been announced, the commission plans to promulgate specific prohibitions to be contained in the code of ethics required to be adopted by investment companies and their advisers and principal underwriters.

The inside information doctrine falls within the ambit of Section 10(b) of the Securities Exchange Act and Rule 10b–5 thereunder. Rule 10b–5 is a general antifraud provision and prohibits (1) schemes to defraud, (2) material misrepresentations and ommissions, and (3) fraudulent courses of business. Rule 10b–5 has been held to apply to proxy statements, reports filed with the SEC, prospectuses, company annual reports, and private communications among other things. As will be covered in another chapter of this Handbook it was thought to apply to non-contributory negotiated employee pension plans as held by a Court of Appeals in *Daniel* v. *International Brotherhood of Teamsters.* However the Supreme Court reversed this holding.[40] Finally, Rule 10b–5 applies to analyst's research and recommendations, and actions by securities professionals including investment managers.

Inside information is defined as the disclosure and sue of material nonpublic information. This broad definition has been applied to a variety of circumstances. An examination of several judicial and SEC decisions will illustrate its impact. In an early SEC decision, *Cady Roberts & Co.*,[41] the SEC sanctioned a broker who received information from a director that the quarterly dividend of Curtiss Wright had been cut. The broker received this information before it was publicly disseminated and traded on it.

The opinion of the Commission noted that knowledge of the corporate action—the reduction of the dividend—was not arrived at as a result of perceptive analysis of material public information, or of nonmaterial, nonpublic information (which is not considered to violate Rule 10b–5). The principle that this kind of perceptive, evaluative analysis and resulting transactions is not a violation of Rule 10b–5 has been subsequently called the "mosaic" theory.

Analysts obtain information from a wide variety of sources; some of it is material and public and some nonmaterial and nonpublic; some is written and some oral. Analysts may assemble the information, evaluate it, fit it into a mosaic model and reach conclusions. These conclusions may be very significant—in fact, if the company had communicated them to the analysts, they might be material inside information. But the analysts are considered free to act, since this nonmaterial nonpublic information does not fall within the inside information doctrine. Expressed in a variety of ways, this position has been generally recognized by the Securities and Exchange Commission and by courts which have considered the issue.

In 1968, two landmark events occurred. The first was the Second

---

[40] *Daniel* v. *International Brotherhood of Teamsters, Chauffuers, Warehousemen and Helpers of America,* 561 F. 2d 1223 (CA 7 1978), *rev'd* 46 LW 3526 (2/21/78)

[41] *In re Cady, Roberts & Co.* SEC Rel. 34–6668, (Nov. 8, 1961); 40 SEC 907 An earlier SEC release received little notice.

Ward LaFrance Truck Corp., 13 SEC 373 (1943).

Circuit Court of Appeals decision in *SEC* v. *Texas Gulf Sulphur*,[42] where the court issued an injunction against Texas Gulf Sulphur based upon a misleading press release which failed to disclose a vast mineral find. Furthermore, the court found that officers, directors and certain employes of Texas Gulf Sulphur were insiders and violated the inside information doctrine when they traded on the information about the mineral find before it was public. Moreover, the Court found that two of these insiders (who were classified as "tippers") conveyed this information to friends and relatives who traded ("tippees"). These employes were held liable for the trading profits of their tippees. In one circumstance, the information conveyed was that Texas Gulf Sulphur was "a good buy."

The second event in 1968 was the SEC administrative action against Merrill Lynch, 14 of its employees and 15 of its institutional customers. Merrill Lynch, as managing underwriter for a pending offering of convertible debentures of Douglas Aircraft, properly had been told about significant unpublished losses sustained by Douglas which adversely affected the interim earnings and the projected earnings for the year. The SEC alleged that Merrill Lynch representatives in turn improperly conveyed this information to certain of its institutional customers who traded Douglas stock before the information was public.

The SEC sanctioned Merrill Lynch and its employes, pursuant to an offer of settlement,[43] and the case against the institutional customers proceeded to a hearing and an SEC decision. In the decision, the Commission found that all but two of the institutional customers had received the inside information from Merrill Lynch and traded on it. These institutions were sanctioned by the Commission for this conduct.[44]

A spate of judicial and SEC decisions followed.

In *Glen Alden*[45] the corporation was enjoined by a court for violations of Rule 10b–5 based upon the selective disclosure of five-year revenue and income projections, which showed marked increases, to a small group of analysts and investment managers.

The *Faberge* case involved two separate proceedings. The first was a court proceeding for an injunction by the SEC against Faberge and two of its officers which resulted in an injunction by consent of the defendants.[46] The violation involved the selective communication to

---

[42] *SEC* v. *Texas Gulf Sulphur*, 401 F. 2d 833 (CA 2 1968) *cert. den. sub nom. Coates* v. *U.S.*, 394 U.S. 976 (1969)

[43] *In re Merrill Lynch Pierce Fenner & Smith*, Admin. Proc. 3–1680, (Aug. 27, 1968); SEC Rel. 34–8459 (Nov. 25, 1968); 43 SEC 933

[44] *In re Investors Management Company*, SEC Rel. 34–9267 (July 29, 1971); 44 SEC 633

[45] *SEC* v. *Glenn Alden*, Consent decree, CCH 92280 (S.D.N.Y. 1968)

[46] *SEC* v. *Faberge, Inc.*, SEC LR-5548 (Oct. 2, 1972).

a number of analysts and investment managers by the financial vice president of Faberge, before it was publicly disseminated, that Faberge had experienced its first quarterly loss in many years.

The second proceeding was an SEC administrative action against several brokers and investment advisers. Investment managers and analysts from these organizations had heard directly from the financial vice president about the loss, or head of the loss through a chain of communications beginning with those who had talked with the financial vice president.

All were found to have violated the inside information doctrine. Some were found censurable prior to a hearing and others who proceeded to a hearing were censured by the SEC.[47]

In *SEC* v. *Lums*,[48] the President of Lums had conveyed to a broker sharply reduced earnings estimates and the broker in turn conveyed them to two portfolio managers at IDS, both of whom sold large blocks of Lums stock. IDS consented to an injunction, as did the managers, and agreed to adopt compliance procedures to prevent the misuse of inside information, Lums its president and the broker were enjoined. The broker's employer was found not to have violated Rule 10b–5 because it had in existence compliance procedures to prevent the misuse of inside information which it took steps to enforce as a part of a regular program.

One of the most interesting cases is the recent decisions in *SEC* v. *Bausch & Lomb*. In a suit for an injunction the SEC alleged that the chairman of Bausch & Lomb had selectively disclosed revised earnings estimates to analysts from several brokerage firms. To a degree unmatched by predecessor cases, its issues involved vital aspects of the research process followed by securities analysts.

The major issue was whether an analyst acted on analytical judgment resulting from the collection and analysis of information and facts, which, though undisclosed, were not material, reaching a determination on those coupled with his experience and knowledge of the company, or whether he was the recipient of material, nonpublic, inside information and acted on it. The SEC, courts, and others have repeatedly stated the former is permissible, while the latter is not.

This is commonly called the mosaic theory which maintains that it is permissible for an investment professional (or others) to obtain nonmaterial nonpublic information, use it in their mosaic or model and trade in the securities on the conclusions which are material to the user. This is true even though communication of the conclusion to the professional would have been material inside information.

All of the defendants, which included the brokerage firms and cer-

---

[47] *In re Faberge, Inc.*, SEC Rel. 34–10174 (May 25, 1973); SEC Rel. 34–10835 (June 10, 1974).

[48] *SEC* v. *Lums, Inc.*, 365 F. Supp. 1046 (S.D.N.Y. 1973)

tain individuals, consented to injunctions (or in the case of two individuals, to be bound by the injunctions against their employers), and the case continued to trial against Bausch & Lomb and its chairman. The lower court found that there had been no disclosure of material inside information to the analysts even though the information received resulted in a mosaic with a material conclusion, that is earnings would be down. In one instance the court found that a revised earnings estimate had been communicated but in that case the information had not been acted on. The Court of Appeals sustained the decision on appeal by the SEC, but did not reach the question of materiality in all of the findings by the lower court. Rather it held that those facts which had been conveyed were either not material or were already publicly known and that the SEC had not proved that other facts had been conveyed.[49]

The final installment thus far in the long line of inside information cases[50] is the Administrative Law Judge's decision in an SEC administrative proceeding against five investment advisers and Ray Dirks, the man at the center of the drama through which the Equity Funding fraud came to light. The Administrative Law Judge (ALJ) in his opinion[51] found that Dirks and the five investment advisers had vio-

---

[49] *SEC* v. *Bausch & Lomb, Inc.*, Injunction by consent against Faulkner, Dawkins & Sullivan. Two employes agree to abide by injunction.

SEC LR-7263 (Feb. 10, 1976) The employes agreed to consent to SEC censure.

SEC Rel. 34–13210, 11 SEC Docket 1561 (Jan. 27, 1977); 420 F. Supp. 1226 (S.D.N.Y. 1976), *aff'd*, 565 F.2d 8 (CA 21978); *see* note 26 *infra*.

[50] In May 1979, the Supreme Court agreed to consider the case of the first criminal conviction for misuse of "inside information," and heard arguments in the case in early November 1979. *U.S.* v. *Chiarella*, 588 F.2d 1358 (C.A. 2 1978), *aff'g.* 450 F. Supp 95 (S.D.N.Y. 1978); *cert. gr.* 99 S. Ct. 2158 (May 14, 1979). This case involves an employee of a financial printer who discerned the identity of the parties in several tender offers and a merger, even though they were disguised in the documents which his firm was printing. He used this information before it became public to trade in the securities of the companies, in violation of his company's policy, realizing profits after the transaction became public. He agreed to an injunction and disgorgement of his profits in an enforcement action by the SEC (SEC L.R. 7935, May 25, 1977), and was subsequently indicted and convicted for criminal violations of Section 10(b), and Rule 10b–5 thereunder, of the Securities Exchange Act. The conviction was upheld by the Second Circuit Court of Appeals.

The securities industry is vitally interested in this decision not only because it is the first criminal conviction for misuse of "inside information," but involves so-called "market information" which relates to the market price of securities rather than the financial condition or operations of the company, and was not learned from an inside source revealing confidential information. The Securities Industry Association has filed an amicus curiae brief expressing its fear that the broad application of such a rule would be an inappropriate disruption to the securities market and the work of market professionals. The SEC has responded in an amicus brief to ameliorate these concerns.

[51] *In re The Boston Company Institutional Investors, Inc.*, Admin. Proc. File No. 3–5068.

On September 1, 1978, an SEC administrative law Judge found that all five respondent investment advisers had violated Rule 10b–5 by trading on inside information. Four were censured although the fifth was not as not being required in the public interest. The individual respondent, Raymond Dirks, was suspended for 60 days for selectively communicating inside information, a finding which he is appealing to the full commission.

lated the rule against trading on inside information. Dirks was suspended from association with any broker or dealer for 60 days (a finding which is being appealed) and four of the advisers were censured. The fifth adviser, the Dreyfus Corporation, although found to have violated the law, was not censured because the ALJ determined it was not necessary to do so in the public interest.

All of the advisers had received information from Dirks, who during a three week period in March 1973 had been told about a massive fraud at Equity Funding first by a former employe, and then by several other former employes and consultants to the corporation as well as one present employe.

The ALJ found that all of the advisers had used this information, before it was public, in effecting sales of Equity Funding stock. However Dreyfus had partially disclosed some of the information to its purchaser and had in the interim adopted compliance procedures to prevent the misuse of inside information.

While most of the decided cases, including those discussed above, are SEC administrative actions which have usually resulted in relatively mild sanctions, or suits for injunctions by the SEC to prevent future violations, investment managers should not be misled. Administrative actions in serious cases can result in revocation of an adviser's registration or the barring of individuals from employment in the securities industry. Moreover, civil suits have resulted in large monetary judgments or settlements for violations of the inside information doctrine.

Corporate Projections

On November 7, 1978, the Securities and Exchange Commission reached completion of a project which has been under study and undergoing numerous variations since the early 1970s.

In Securities Act Release 5992, the SEC adopted Guides for the disclosure of projections of future economic performance in registration statements under the Securities Act of 1933, and filings, including proxy statements, under the Securities Exchange Act of 1934, as well as for projections made outside these filings.

The statement by the Commission encourages, but does not require, SEC registered issuers to publish projected financial information both in filings with the Commission and otherwise.[52]

---

[52] Coincident with the adoption of a new "going private" rule for public companies (SEC Rel. 33–6100, August 2, 1979), the SEC proposed amendments to that rule which would require disclosure of projections for a company involved in a going private transaction. Any projections must be summarized which relate to revenues, income, or earnings per share prepared by such company or on its behalf during the preceding 18 months which had been furnished to lenders or to persons who prepared reports, opinions, or appraisals "materially related to the transaction." The SEC also requested comments on (1) whether the disclosure should extend to projections relating to current or future periods made within the prior five years whether furnished to outsiders or not, (2)

While encouraging the voluntary public disclosure of projections the Guides state practices which should be followed in making projections in the areas of (1) who can project, (2) disclosure of assumptions, (3) items to be projected, (4) third party review, (5) revisions and updating of projections, (6) time period for projections, (7) discontinuance and resumption, (8) tax shelters, and (9) projections required by regulatory authorities.

Simultaneous with the adoption of the Guides, the Commission proposed a "safe harbor" rule for projections.[53]

The SEC adopted generally the approach taken by the SEC Advisory Committee on Corporate Disclosure which studied various aspects of corporate disclosure beginning in early 1976, culminating in its final report issued November 3, 1977. Among many other recommendations, the Advisory Committee made several recommendations for significant changes in the SEC projections policy. Generally, the Committee recommended that the Commission issue a public statement encouraging companies voluntarily to disclose management projections in filings with the Commission and elsewhere. In making this recommendation, the Advisory Committee noted that its position on specific aspects of projection disclosure would permit wide latitude to companies issuing projections and stated that the Commission should review and monitor projection disclosure to determine the utility to investors of such information and the cost to issuers.

Neither the Advisory Committee's Report nor the SEC's release dealt specifically with forecasts by other than corporate management or someone acting on its behalf.

The question of forecasts by analysts and portfolio managers has, however, been the subject of discussion from time to time with the SEC especially in the informal meetings during 1972 which preceded the SEC hearings on projections in late 1972. Among other groups participating in those informal discussions, the American Institute of Certified Public Accountants and the Financial Analysts Federation

whether the costs of compliance outweigh the benefits to investors and the public interest, and (3) whether the proposal would have an adverse effect or be burdensome on competition. (SEC Rel. 33–6101, August 2, 1979).

[53] SEC Rel. 33–5993 (Nov. 7, 1978).

A "safe harbor" rule was adopted by the SEC on June 25, 1979. (SEC Rel. 33–6084) The rule provides that "forward looking statements" made in filings with the SEC, or in annual reports to shareholders required by the Securities Exchange Act, will not be fraudulent (e.g., false or misleading) unless they were made without a reasonable basis or disclosed other than in good faith. The rule covers statements containing or relating to (1) revenues, income, earnings per share, capital expenditures, dividends, capital structure, and other financial items, (2) management's plans and objectives for future operations, (3) future economic performance in management's discussion and analysis of the summary of earnings, and (4) assumptions underlying or relating to the foregoing matters.

The new rule expressly excludes investment company projections from its "safe harbor." The effective date of the rule was July 30, 1979.

have at various times addressed the question of forecasting generally, and in the latter case forecasts by securities analysts and investment managers. While the SEC expressed interest in this process, they have not proceeded with the subject but rather considered the efforts of these organizations as important background to their consideration of the issue of projections by public corporations.

There have been a number of cases decided which involve the legal standards for projections, under Section 10b and Rule 10b–5 of the Securities Exchange Act, relating primarily to registered representatives of brokers.[54] These cases establish the proposition that projections made in good faith, founded on a reasonable basis, will not be actionable. However, if they are not, Rule 10b–5 may be violated.

LIABILITY

Implied Private Actions under the Investment Advisers Act

In early 1977, the Court of Appeals for the Second Circuit held in *Abrahamson* v. *Fleschner* that a private right of action is implied by the Advisers Act.[55] Although the Advisers Act was enacted in 1940, no appellate court had implied a private right of action for damages under this statute until this case.

The plaintiffs were limited partners in a hedge fund and the partnership agreement gave the general partners authority to invest in any kind of security, to sell short, to purchase commodities and to utilize leverage. Yet, as in *Rolf* (discussed above) there was some confusion about investment objectives. Prior to making their investments in the partnership, plaintiffs were told that the partnership would have a conservative investment policy, and conservative policies were suggested in reports to the limited partner investors. The complaint was based on the high percentage of the portfolio invested in restricted securities, up to 88 percent. When the plaintiffs first learned of this, from a footnote in an annual report, it was too late to withdraw from the partnership that year, and withdrawal had to be delayed until the end of the following fiscal year. The lower court did not reach the merits of the claims under the Advisers Act, and dismissed the complaint because plaintiffs had realized a profit on their overall investments.

Whether or not to allow a private suit for money damages under

---

[54] *SEC* v. *F. S. Johns & Co.*, 207 F. Supp. 566 (D.N.J. 1962); *see Dolgow* v. *Andersen*, 53 F.R.D. 664 (E.D.N.Y. 1971), *aff'd* 464 F. 2d 437 (CA 2 1972), action against issuer.

[55] *Abrahamson* v. *Fleschner*, 392 F. Supp. 740 (S.D.N.Y. 1975), *rev'd* 537 F. 2d 27 (CA 2 1975)

568 F. 2d 862 (CA 2 1977) *reh. den.* 1/6/78; *cert. den.* 5/16/78

a federal statute revolves around technical legal arguments, essentially relating to the intent of Congress. The court observed:

> There are compelling reasons why the courts have been particularly willing to recognize private rights of action under the antifraud provisions of the federal securities laws. Those provisions are designed to protect specific classes of injured parties. Moreover the SEC—the agency charged with administration and enforcement of the federal securities laws—does not have sufficient resources alone to enforce the many provisions of the statutes. Absent judicial recognition of private rights of action, the federal securities laws most assuredly would fail to provide the effective regulation over the securities industry which Congress intended [at page 872].

The court then turned to a U.S. Supreme Court decision for specific guidance:

> In *Court* v. *Ash,* the Supreme Court suggested that the following factors be considered in determining "whether a private remedy is implicit in a statute not expressly providing one":
>
> > "First, is the plaintiff 'one of the class for whose *especial* benefit the statute was enacted' . . .—that is, does the statute create a federal right in favor of the plaintiff? Second, is there any indication of legislative intent, explicit or implicit, either to create such a remedy or to deny one? . . . Third, is it consistent with the underlying purposes of the legislative scheme to imply such a remedy for the plaintiff? . . . And finally, is the cause of action one traditionally relegated to state law, in an area basically the concern of the States, so that it would be inappropriate to infer a cause of action based solely on federal law?"
>
> We believe that each of these factors point unmistakably toward recognition of an implied right of action under Section 206 of the Advisers Act [citations omitted].

A vigorous dissent made a number of arguments leading to the opposite conclusion, including the legislative history of the Advisers Act, which was "designed as a threshold attempt to effect a compulsory census of investment advisers, and not as a pervasive regulatory scheme." The dissent noted that Congress has the unique ability to set the limits on civil actions for damages.

An observation in the dissenting opinion with regard to damages is significant in light of the willingness of the majority of the court of appeals to be somewhat innovative in computing losses, which often happens in securities cases. In remanding the case for trial on the issue of damages, the following guidance was given in the majority opinion:

> This is not to say, however, that a plaintiff may recover for losses, but ignore his profits, where both result from a *single* wrong. In determin-

ing on remand whether plaintiffs have sustained any damages from the alleged fraudulent investments, the district court should determine, first, at what point defendants' representations became fraudulent due to the increasing proportion of portfolio investments in unregistered securities. The court should compute the total on all holdings of unregistered securities due to changes in price *after* that date. Finally, the court should determine what proportion of FBA's holdings was inconsistent with representations that the partnership was in a most conservative posture, and the other representations made to the limited partners. The proper measure of damages then would be that part of net losses incurred on unregistered securities after the point when the defendants' representations became fraudulent which stems from the portion of those investments inconsistent with defendants' representations [Footnote omitted, emphasis in the original].

The U.S. Supreme Court has declined consideration of *Abrahamson.* In early 1978 the Court of Appeals for the Fifth Circuit agreed in *Wilson* v. *First Houston Investment Corp.* with the holding of the majority in *Abrahamson,* but a strong dissent agreed with the dissenting opinion in *Abrahamson.*[56] The claim in *Wilson* involved representations that a computer analysis of the stock market would lead to elimination of investments not meeting certain standards, and that the computer system was not being utilized sufficiently; massive losses in the account were realized. Citing the dissent in *Abrahamson* with approval, the dissenting opinion in *Wilson* views congressional intent as follows:

> No legislation states that a person shall have a right to action in the federal courts under these circumstances. Yet, eminent jurists of the United States Court of Appeals for the Second Circuit have, like my brothers today, discovered the need for a private cause of action and, in a gesture somewhat patronizing of the Congress, have determined to complete the work of that body by reading one into the Act.

A petition for U.S. Supreme Court review of this decision is presently pending.

The latest installment in this important securities law story is represented by the very brief opinion in *Lewis* v. *Transamerica Corp.,* where the Court of Appeals for the Ninth Circuit agreed with *Abrahamson,* and the dissent again agreed with the dissent in *Abrahamson.*[57] The Supreme Court agreed to consider the *Lewis* decision, arguments held and rearguments scheduled, so that it appears that this significant issue may be resolved in the near future.[58]

---

[56] *Wilson* v. *First Houston Corp.,* 566 F. 2d 1235 (CA 5 1978); *reh. den.* 569 F. 2d 1155

[57] *Lewis* v. *Transamerica Corp.,* 575 F. 2d 237 (CA 9 1978); *cert. gr.* 47 LW 3317

[58] On November 13, 1979, the Supreme Court held that there is a limited private remedy under the Advisers Act. In *Transamerica Mortgage Advisors, Inc.* v. *Lewis,* (No. 77–1645, 48 L.W. 4001, 11/13/79), the Court upheld in part the Court of Appeals

SEC Administrative Powers

Section 203(e) specifies the conduct which can be the subject of disciplinary sanctions by the Commission. After appropriate notice and opportunity for hearing the Commission may (1) deny registration to, (2) censure, (3) place limitations on the activities, functions or operations of, (4) suspend for a period not exceeding 12 months, or (5) revoke the registration of an investment adviser.

Comparable powers are provided over associated persons (as defined in Section 202(a) (17)), by Section 203(f). Such activities include:

1. willful false or misleading statements or material omissions in any filing with or proceeding of the SEC;
2. conviction within the last ten years of a felony or misdemeanor which involves *(a)* the purchase or sale or any security, *(b)* taking a false oath, *(c)* false reports, *(d)* bribery, *(e)* perjury, *(f)* burglary, or any conspiracy to do such, or which *(g)* arises out of the conduct of the business of a broker, dealer, investment adviser, or other specified businesses, *(h)* involves embezzlement, fraudulent conversion, misappropriation of funds or securities or similar conduct, or *(i)* involves the violation of other specified sections of federal law;
3. a permanent or temporary injunction, judgement, or decree of any court from acting as an investment adviser or in other specified capacities;
4. the willful violation of the Securities Exchange Act or any rules thereunder;
5. aiding and abetting such violations; or
6. being subject to a Commission order currently effective, barring or suspending the right of such person to be associated with 'an adviser.

For purposes of Section 203 a person shall not be found or have reasonably failed to supervise any other person if (1) procedures have

---

for the Ninth Circuit by ruling that contracts may be rescinded under Section 215 of the Act in actions by a private individual, but reverses by holding that no private action for damages is provided for a violation of Section 206.

Both the Fifth Circuit and the Second Circuit Courts of Appeals, in addition to the Ninth Circuit, had held that the Advisers Act implies a private right of action for damages.

In a five to four decision the majority of the Court held that by its terms Section 215 implies a remedy for voiding an advisory contract when its provisions or its performance violate the Act. In addition to recission, restitution and injunctions against performance are available. However, the Court was unwilling to read into the statute, when it finds the words and the legislative intent silent, a private right of action for monetary damages. It rejects arguments that it would be desirable and useful for such a private right of action to be implied and decides, in view of the silence and the SEC's powers to bring injunctive suits and administrative actions, and the criminal penalties under Sections 203, 209, and 217, that these represent the extent of the remedies under the Act to enforce Section 206.

been established, (2) a system established for applying such procedures which would be reasonably expected to prevent and detect violations, and (3) the person has reasonably discharged the duties and obligation for which she or he is responsible under such procedures and system without reasonable cause to believe that they were not being complied with.

A right of review of SEC action is provided by Section 213 which involves the appeal of a Commission order to a federal court of appeals.

Criminal violations of fines up to $10,000 and not more than two years imprisonment are provided by Section 217.

The SEC has been granted investigatory and enforcement powers under Section 209. This Section details the powers and procedures of the SEC in investigations, including the power to subpoena witnesses and records.

Commission records and Commission examinations or investigations and the results thereof may be made public under Section 210, and to hearings and records thereof made public under Section 212.

Chapter 24

Legal Limits on Investing: with Reference to State Regulations

JOHN L. CASEY

Senior Vice President-Law
Scudder, Stevens & Clark
New York, New York

I wish I were able to provide a reference work in which investment rules were martialed in such a way that we could easily establish which apply to each particular type of managed account: a book which would permit us as managers to look up the answer in the same way we look up a telephone number in a telephone book. However, while some ordinances are clear in form and specific in application, many involve matters of judgment and discretion. Even those which appear clear and stable can be changed by a legislature or by a court case. As a result, no attempt will be made to provide the equivalent of a loose-leaf service of current statutory powers and limits. Rather, benchmarks will be identified which help us ask the right questions; problems once identified are well on the way to solution.

In that effort, we will proceed inductively, starting with a case study of a personal trust with individual family trustees who hire a professional manager. From that vantage point it becomes possible to touch on the more complex rules for accounts such as retirement funds established for employes of states and municipalities, investment companies, and other savings institutions. Substantively, we are to see what a trust is, how to go about analyzing its terms and objectives, what the prudent man rule means as to different kinds of investments and as to conflicts of interest, how legislatures have tried to set out lists of "OK securities" (lists which have not improved investment results or protected the manager). Finally, the impact on investment managers of current ideas of corporate good citizenship and social investing is explored.

Our focus is principally on state laws, both statutory and common

650

law. Underlying the discussion is the conclusion that logic does not necessarily control and the manager must continually come back to the controlling instructions. As Dean Erwin Griswold of the Harvard Law School used to say, "I don't care how you feel—what does the Internal Revenue Code say?" The pursuit of abstract knowledge will be limited. Our more practical concern is on how to reduce the risk of an inadvertent violation of some regulation.

We live in a world of illusions. Reference points we are using can become irrelevant; good insights can seem amusingly old-fashioned. No one can bathe in the same river twice, as Dorothy Sayers pointed out. It may look the same—but the river moved on, with its silt and water. Yet if I have moved with the river, my frames of reference have gone.

As on any grand tour, it can help to have an architectural overview. To do so here, please read through the summaries which appear at each section head. Then come back to read the chapter with the details about plinths and posterns.

APPROACHING A COMMON TYPE OF TRUST

> What is a trust? The job of an investment manager for a trust versus an individual account? How does the manager go about establishing the guidelines and having them readily available in the future?

Portfolios come in many different guises. The simplest is an individual's personal investment portfolio. There, objectives (income, stability of capital, growth of capital) can be determined and investment tools (cash, short-term bonds, long-term bonds, equities) identified without too much legal and regulatory reference. When that individual creates a personal trust—or many individuals share in a common vehicle such as a mutual fund or retirement plan account—it is a whole new ball game, and a great deal of attention must be paid to the regulatory area.

Personal trusts are widely used investment vehicles and their analysis follows a pattern which can apply to more complex structures.

What is a Trust?

A trust consists of three elements: (1) the trust property, (2) one or more beneficiaries, and (3) one or more trustees (managers). The *property* can include cash, securities, real estate or intangibles such as an account receivable. *Beneficiaries* may be one or many, simultaneous or successive, known and unknown. The family trusts with which we are most familiar designate a current (known) income beneficiary and a class of persons who will, if they are then living, receive the remainder at the death of the income beneficiary. The *trustee (invest-*

ment manager) may be a trust company, family member, broker, professional investment manager, friend, or lawyer. Trustees may be amateurs or professionals. The trustees named in a document may split their role with an outside investment manager.

A trust may be revocable and amendable; or it may be irrevocable. It may be a *living trust* (created by a trust agreement executed by the trustor/grantor during lifetime), be a *testamentary trust* (created by will) or be defined by law.

Making the Review

In each case there is a set of governing terms and the first job of a manager is to identify and review them. In a testamentary trust we start with the will; in a living trust, with the trust indenture. For a custodian of securities of a minor under a Gifts to Minors statute, it is the text of the Act in the state in question.[1]

To assist in such a review of the controlling document (and subsequent retrieval of the information) a checklist form is often essential. That analysis and review is no less essential to individual trustees of a typical family trust than to a trust company or to an outside investment manager employed by the trustees. The answers to the checklist should be kept in a convenient place as a source of easily available information for the future—so that the mental obstacle of having to dig through the trust agreement will not inhibit compliance. The checklist which appears as Exhibit 1 contains key specific items for a particular trust plus a set of general signals. Answers to specific points such as whether the trust can invest in foreign securities or nondividend paying stock obviously are helpful for a manager to have nearby. Some more subtle points are touched also. The form, through the reference to taxation of gains, income need and tax bracket of the income beneficiary, reminds the outside investment manager and the trustee that there is a theoretical (and perhaps real) conflict to be balanced between a life beneficiary's interest in highest income and the remainderman's interest in capital appreciation. The rules of trust investing are not identical to those for an individual where no trust is created. Another section of the form mentions accounting and release procedures. That reminds us that liability, if any, can go on indefinitely unless and until there is an accounting by the trustee and a release by the affected parties. The reference on the bottom reflects the fact that in any form, shorthand expressions tend to be used. That is fine so long as the expressions mean the same thing to each reader. Cross references to other frames of reference become easy to forget. So the meaning of terms ought to be memorialized and readily available to a future manager.

---

[1] See *Gifts of Securities or Money to Minors—A Guide to Laws in 50 States*, Securities Industry Association, 20 Broad Street, New York, N.Y.

Exhibit 1

OPERATION GUIDE
FIDUCIARY ACCOUNT

Title:

To Be Delivered to New Account Manager
on Reassignment of Account

_____ Executors   Unamendable Agreement with
                             Trustees   Will of

_____ Who Died
                             Dated _____ Currently f/b/o _____

_____

(Remainder—e.g. family, charity, trustor)

Investment Control:

Income Need   (Income beneficiary)
Tax Bracket   (Income beneficiary)   Management Fee Chargeable to PRINCIPAL?
                                                            How charged?
Investments: Can We Accept DISCRETION?
                                                            Do We?
Specific Restrictions: Informal RELEASE Provision?
New Purchases   Practice?
    Mutual Funds:
    Foreign Securities:
    Dividend Requirements:
    Speculative:
    Diversification Rules:
Standards for Retention: Allocation of
Securities Excluded from Management: Stock Dividends:

Disposition of Income: Proxy Voting:

Invasion of Principal:

Custody: TAXES:
State Law Controlling Administration: Gains Taxable to:
Successor Fiduciary:
                                           Other Income Taxable to:

Attorney: Year Ends _____

Special Comments: (1) Invest Any Cash above Minimum Working Balance of $_____
                   (2) Procedure for Carrying out Transactions:

(Continue special comments on other side if necessary.)

Analyzed by_____ Checked by _____
                        Date: _____
(Please refer to _____ for guidance in use of this form.)

In your own checklist, other information would be added and some dropped from the form. However, I would suggest that there is a special virtue of having a one-page summary.

We have deliberately omitted some points from the form. It does not cover actuarial assumptions for an employee benefit plan, for example, or power to lend securities or borrow money. Omissions are: (1) to remind us to use our heads about new developments and (2) to suggest we document unusual actions. There will always be questions not answered on a *précis* and, indeed, not foreseen specifically in the underlying agreement. Some omissions of this sort may be laid at the step of the individual scrivener but some, more accurately, will result from a universal lack of second sight. New techniques evolve to meet new circumstances and situations. After all, the purpose of appointing a trustee is to appoint a trusted agent to be the trustor's representative on the spot in the future. To paraphrase Professor Barton Leach: to regulate events 20 years from today the judgment of a mediocre mind on the spot is immeasurably preferable to the guesses of the wisest person living today.

THE BASE CASE

> Introducing Al and Bea Cosmo, Trustees; Dee Cosmo and her children, beneficiaries of the Cosmo Family Trust. Unbundling the prudent man rule into *permissible* and *appropriate* investments. Risk, opportunity and tradition must all be weighed.

For our case study we postulate a trust with a variety of investments, an income beneficiary, a class of remaindermen, and family members as trustees. The trustees are Al and Bea Cosmo, the income beneficiary is Dee Cosmo, the remainder interests are the children of Dee. The governing document is the will of Inez Jordan. In reviewing the will for purposes of the checklist, some other items leap out, such as who has investment control, and the allocation of stock dividends. Other items such as the taxability of gains and income require the input of a tax adviser. The income needs of the life beneficiary must come from a conversation with her.

What are the Investment Powers?

When it comes to the investment section, a combination of will-reading and legal advice will be required.

As indicated in the partially completed checklist (Exhibit 2), we have assumed that the law of Massachusetts applies to the construction. We also will take it that there is an absence of specific prohibitions or suggestions on investments in this will. Legal counsel's advice is likely to take into account the early Massachusetts case of *Harvard College* v. *Amory*,[2] in which the court said that a trustee:

> shall conduct himself faithfully and exercise a sound discretion. He is to observe how men of prudence, discretion and intelligence manage their own affairs, not in regard to speculation, but in regard to the perma-

---

[2] 9 Pick, 446,461 (Mass. 1830).

Exhibit 2

OPERATION GUIDE
FIDUCIARY ACCOUNT

Title: *Cosmo Family Trust*

To Be Delivered to New Account Manager
on Reassignment of Account

Al & Bea Cosmo ~~Executors~~ Trustees ~~Unamendable Agreement~~ with Will of

Inez Jordan Who Died ~~Dated~~ *3/1/'79* Currently f/b/o _____

Dee Cosmo — Then to her, Children
(Remainder–e.g. family, charity, trustor)

Investment Control: *Trustees*

Income Need (Income beneficiary) *Low*
Tax Bracket (Income beneficiary) *High* Management Fee Chargeable to PRINCIPAL? *Yes*
How charged? *50:50*

Investments: Can We Accept DISCRETION? *Yes*
Do We? *Yes*
Specific Restrictions: *None*   Informal RELEASE Provision? *Yes*
New Purchases   Practice? *Annual*
Mutual Funds:
Foreign Securities:
Dividend Requirements:
Speculative:
Diversification Rules:
Standards for Retention: Allocation of *Income*
Securities Excluded from Management: Stock Dividends:
Disposition of Income: *Dee Cosmo*   Proxy Voting: *Trustees*
Invasion of Principal:

Custody: *First National Bank (Bunker Hill)* TAXES:
State Law Controlling Administration: *Mass.*   Gains Taxable to: *Trust*
Successor Fiduciary: *Edward Cosmo*
Other Income Taxable to: *Dee*

Attorney: *Flair, Gybe & Howe (Karen Larkin)* Year Ends *12/31*
Special Comments: (1) Invest Any Cash above Minimum Working Balance of $ *1,000*
(2) Procedure for Carrying out Transactions:

(Continue special comments on other side if necessary.)

Analyzed by _____ Checked by _____
Date: _____
(Please refer to _____ for guidance in use of this form.)

nent disposition of their funds, considering the probable income, as well as the probable safety of the capital to be invested.

That leading case continues to play an important part in American life. Along the same lines, the New York Court of Appeals, later, held in *King* v. *Talbot*:[3]

[3] 40 N.Y. 76, 85–6 (1869).

... the just and true rule is that the trustee is bound to employ such
diligence and such prudence in the care and management, as, in general,
prudent men of discretion and intelligence in such matters, employ in
their own like affairs.

Interestingly enough, however, as Professor Scott[4] points out, peer
prudence in Massachusetts was much more flexible than in New York:
common stocks were frowned on in New York. That such a difference
in views can exist in different states—or times—should be kept in mind.
Similar differences in result can exist between one state and another
today.

   **Conventional and Less Conventional Investments—What is "Pru-
dent"?**   Good faith, diligence, discretion, intelligence, and prudence
of a manager are characteristics mandated by the Massachusetts Court.
Income, safety, long term investing, and "peer reference" are points
made about the trustee's actions. All are within the expression the
prudent man rule. The rule provides flexibility and permits positive
initiatives to be taken. But it also contains cautionary signals. Remember that a trustee's prudence is questioned when there are losses. And
at that point, everyone's hindsight is clear. Under such circumstances,
what if the trustee observed other prudent investors and rejected their
conclusions? It would be a bad result if the law required conformity.
And it does not. It may, however, require extra evidence of care from
a contrary-minded investor.

   That may put a premium on the selection process that is established.
I personally find it helpful to think of selection as involving two stages:
the first a determination of the *permissible* universe of securities; the
second, a selection of permissible securities in light of their *suitability
or appropriateness* to the needs and objectives of this particular account. For example, most trusts would have power to purchase U.S.
Treasury obligations (Treasurys are permissible trust investments). But
would 100 percent investment in them fit the needs of these beneficiaries?

   In our case study, the Inez Jordan will does not contain specific
prohibited investments, nor a list of permissible investments, either,
for that matter. Sometimes you can look to a statute for guidance on
the point. But not here. The guideposts are more imprecise: investments which are traditionally permitted (higher quality, fixed income
and equity securities); investments traditionally thought of as not for
trusts (puts, calls, defaulted bonds, unmarketable securities).

   The judgment on suitability involves an immersion in the facts. The
Investment Advisers Act of 1940 says " 'Investment supervisory services' means the giving of continuous advice as to the investment of

---

   [4] Austin Wakeman Scott, *The Law of Trusts,* 2d ed. (Boston: Little Brown & Co.,
1956), Section 227.5.

funds on the basis of the individual needs of each client."[5] To me that means the manager must think of (1) the investment's risk, (2) the ability of the beneficiary to accept risk, (3) the investment's objective, and (4) the beneficiary's defined objective.

When made, an unconventional investment may seem quite appropriate. If the opportunity does not work out, will the investment seem to have been speculative and not permissible? Think of some points close to home. Is the decline of the value of the dollar a special basis for investment abroad? Are foreign stocks permissible? Could the portfolio use covered call options to shift gains from one year to another for tax purposes? What of the notion that options are speculative? The answer will be to consult the trust's counsel or to consult a briefing memorandum prepared with the help of the manager's own general counsel. Moreover, changed facts change results and as time passes, frames of reference are continually modified. Hence, old interpretive advice by legal counsel should not necessarily be relied on without periodic confirmation.

The Court in *Harvard College* v. *Amory* (quoted above) established the standard by which a fiduciary is judged today.[6] One hundred fifty years later, with only modest changes, it has been reiterated by the Congress in the Employee Retirement Income Security Act of 1974 (ERISA). ERISA, Sect. 404 directs the fiduciary to "discharge his duties with respect to a plan solely in the interest of the participants and beneficiaries and ... for the exclusive purpose of providing benefits ... and defraying reasonable expenses of administering the plan." In discharging these obligations, the fiduciary is to exercise "the care, skill, prudence, and diligence under the circumstances then prevailing that a prudent man acting in a like capacity and familiar with such matters would use in the conduct of an enterprise of a like character and with like aims."[7]

BALANCE, DIVERSIFICATION, CONCENTRATION

Portfolio balance and security diversification: forms they take and roles individual securities play. Two theories of bond investing. Index funds

---

[5] Section 202(a)13. The New York Stock Exchange and the National Association of Securities Dealers have "Know Your Customer" rules (NYSE Rule 405; NASD Rules of Fair Practice, Article III, Section 2). See also SEC Rule 15c2–5. See Harvey E. Bines, *The Law of Investment Management* (Boston: Warren, Gorham & Lamont, 1978) Section 401(2); Tamar Frankel, *The Regulation of Money Managers*, vol. 2 (Boston: Little Brown & Co., 1978) p. 672 ff.; Chase Investors Services of Boston et al. IA Rel. No. 449/3–28–75 SEC File No. 304635.

[6] See Mayo A. Shattuck, "The Development of the Prudent Man Rule for Fiduciary Investment in the United States in the Twentieth Century," *Ohio State Law Journal* (Autumn 1971).

[7] See: Department of Labor Release, "Investment of (ERISA) Plan Assets Under the 'Prudence' Rule," *43 Federal Register 7480* (April 25, 1978).

versus concentration. Prudence: the portfolio overall versus the individual selection.

A Balanced Portfolio

The traditional investment approach of trustees has been through a balanced portfolio, dividing assets between short-term reserves, longer-term fixed income securities and equities. Each category has a function as does their interplay.

Emergencies.   Short-term reserves provide capital for emergencies as well as current income. Relative stability of that capital can be achieved.

Income.   Income needs of the client should be identified and anticipated. The senior security market may offer opportunities to achieve those needs: short, medium and long maturities, convertibles and non-convertibles, preferred stocks and different credits—all offer fixed income.

It is obvious to professionals that bonds fluctuate in market value (indeed, sometimes much more than stocks), although amateurs may focus on the fact that if the issuer is solvent, the bonds will be paid out at maturity. The combination of attitudes has led certain institutional managers to establish a sort of dollar-cost-averaging system with a "ladder of maturities" so that as the years pass, bonds mature rather than being sold and new reinvestments are made in long maturities. Other managers work with a dynamic bond policy shifting between bonds of different qualities and different maturities in light of relative price attraction.

If the ladder technique is followed, there should be documentation that the choice was based on something more than a desire to avoid showing realized losses. If the dynamic policy is followed, the documentation should deal with any benefits to the manager (commissions and spreads from the turnover) and whether the conflicting interests of income beneficiary and remaindermen were balanced.

Some explanation of the volatility of bonds should be made to any client who is innocent of the curves in the road to a fixed payout.

Capital and Income.   The Cosmo trustees have to serve two potentially conflicting goals—they have one income client (Dee Cosmo), and several principal clients (the Cosmo children). One tool to consider: equities of companies with growing earnings as increasing dividends and capital appreciation may both flow from such investments.

Peer Reference.   This traditional balancing of different kinds of investment must be kept in mind inasmuch as a court in the future will, in judging a manager, at least start with what other professional investors were doing at the time. The basis of any departure by the manager from this balanced approach should be well documented and communicated to those who might object.

Diversification

Interrelated is the traditional concept of diversification within these broad categories of investment—diversification by issuer, industry, earnings cycle, credit, quality, and maturity.

The Restatement of Trusts makes the point that the following should be considered in selecting securities: safety of principal; the amount and regularity of income; marketability; maturity; probable duration of the trust; probable condition of the market at the termination of the trust or on maturity of the security; the nature of the diversification and balance of securities; the requirements of the beneficiaries, especially with regard to income; assets of the beneficiaries, including earning capacity; and the impact of taxes.[8] These tests suggest at the outset that a trustee is unwise, indeed, to adopt a philosophy which thoughtlessly rejects diversification and balance.[9]

Concentration and Indexing

The principle of diversification of investments within a category has independent validity. Diversification is certainly used in typical balanced portfolios. One can also see managers who concentrate in equities in turn diversify the equities. Indeed, in the case of many large institutional accounts, separate investment managers are given specific areas and asked to concentrate—*A* manages the short-term reserves, *B* the fixed income portfolio, *C* the equities, *D* the international investments, and *E* small company investment. Each would normally diversify the segment.

Some students of investing have taken the concept of diversification to the "drily logical extreme" of suggesting that information, analysis, and judgment are less desirable than mechanical and very, very wide diversification, involving hundreds of stocks. This argument[10] has resulted in assorted numbers of indexed portfolios. It has always been possible (and, since the advent of complex electronic data processing machines, easy) to create a fund which mirrors with some exactitude

---

[8] Sections 227, 228.

[9] *"Taxes on Investments Which Jeopardize Charitable Purpose," Internal Revenue Code,* Section 4944.

[10] John H. Langbein and Richard A. Posner "Market Funds and Trust-Investment Law," *American Bar Foundation Research Journal,* vol. 1 (1976); and "The Revolution in Trust Investment Law," *American Bar Association Journal,* vol. 62 (July 1976), pp. 887 ff.

a public index of securities (never quite exact, as commissions always have to be incurred for adjusting purchases and sales). Is index fund investing by a trustee permissible? Prudent? Certainly, one purpose of indexing on a random basis is that occasionally an included stock which other professionals thought of as doomed turns out to be a winner. But what if the anticipated risk occurs? Will a court conclude that the selection of the mortal friend was a speculative act?

Individual Security Selection and Portfolio Construction

Is the intellectual underpinning for overall portfolio construction a defense to a challenged loss of an index security? Is each selected investment to be defended on its own? There is a lot of traditional law to say that each investment must stand on its own as a prudent selection. It may well be that mechanistic indexing by a trustee is safe only if there are sophisticated investors who give informed consent.

Whether or not one agrees with the academic work which led to the extreme conclusion of indexing, it unquestionably supports a choice by a manager of diversification; and against putting all your eggs in one basket and watching the basket.

Sometimes market timing is given a keystone role by a manager. Traditional adjustments between the ingredients of a balanced portfolio in light of relative long-term attraction of different kinds of securities are often called investment policy moves. Timing services are short-term oriented and tend to involve significant and abrupt shifts from one segment of the market to another. The fundamentalist Boston investment counsellor, David L. Babson, in an address of October 19, 1978, criticized such moves as follows:

> Over the years, the market forecasters have had results as dismal as those of the politicians and professors who have tried to "fine-tune" our economy. Yet, for more than four decades, the major part of the investment literature has been—and still is—devoted to "timing," a fancy term for guessing the trend of the stock market.

Courts have rarely if ever held a manager liable for a good faith judgment which resulted in lost opportunity. Losses have been the complaint. Then can a trustee who makes unauthorized investments net gains against losses? Courts have traditionally judged the prudence of each investment on its own. Is this judicial approach consistent with the modern approach to investing? Professional managers increasingly focus on the interrelation of securities in a portfolio: can company *A*'s earnings cycle balance the cycle of *B* and help even out risk? The New York Court of Appeals in *The Bank of New York* v. *Spitzer*[11] in

---

[11] 349 N.Y.S. 2d 747, aff'd in re Bank of New York 364 N.Y.S. 2d 164; See also *Stark* v. *U.S. Trust Co.*, 445 F. Supp. 670 (1978).

1975 affirmed the traditional approach that each security must individually meet the test of prudence and an overall increase in the value of the portfolio will not excuse a single imprudent investment. But with a twist:

> The record of any individual investment is not to be viewed exclusively, of course, as though it were in its one watertight compartment since to some extent individual investment decisions may properly be affected by considerations of the performance of the fund as an entity, as in the instance, for example, of individual security decisions based in part on considerations of diversification of the fund or of capital transactions to achieve sound tax planning for the fund as a whole. The focus of inquiry, however, is nonetheless on the individual security as such and factors relating to the entire portfolio are to be weighed along with others in reviewing the prudence of the particular investment decision.

Query: Would a mechanically indexed portfolio meet the *Spitzer* test?

WHEN TRUSTEES RETAIN A PROFESSIONAL INVESTMENT MANAGER

> Delegation by the Cosmo trustees of investment responsibility. Conflicts of interest. Selecting broker/dealers. Personal securities restrictions. Individualized versus tandem account management.

Al and Bea Cosmo, the trustees in our base case are not investment experts. After reading this chapter, they conclude that they need professional investment assistance. Even if trustees are in the business, there are often compelling reasons for their wanting to shift investment decisions to an experienced outsider. There may be potential conflicts of interest between the trust and the trustees, so that an objective decision maker is desirable. By such a barrier, the trust may gain freedom to invest which the family's own conflicts of interest such as potential access to inside information, otherwise would have limited. Such a blind trust approach has successfully been used to insulate persons in public office from investment decisions. Or the trustees may realize how much time can be required to provide continuous investment supervision, with the need to respond promptly to details like a tender offer, a call date on senior securities, a U.S. Treasury advance refunding offer, a discrepancy in records, a failure of a bank or broker to settle an executed transaction on the correct date, as well as a myriad of more substantive matters. Or the motive may be the maintenance of peace between different interests in the family, by shifting a decision to a Solomon-like nonrelative.[12]

---

[12] Several important noninvestment questions must be resolved. Can the trustees hire an independent investment adviser? Will the advisory fee be paid from the trust assets? From the trustees' commissions? From the income beneficiary's flow of funds? Is the proposed fee permitted under the Investment Advisers Act of 1940? Can the

The relationship of trustees and an investment adviser may be structured in different ways. Whatever the understanding, it should not only be clearly set forth in writing at the outset but also periodically reaffirmed: the alternative is disaster.

The simplest relationship is where the trustees establish the investment objectives and policies of the trust and make the investment decision, receiving purely advisory recommendations from the adviser. Such advice may be periodic or continuous, but the trustees retain their responsibility as investment managers. Another approach is where there is a split of specified functions between the designated trustee and the retained investment manager. The trustee may set investment policy and direct the adviser to select and arrange the purchase and sale of specific securities within broad limits. In such a case of divided responsibility, who is to do what should be clearly spelled out in writing. In unusual cases, the governing instrument may give the trustees power to delegate full investment responsibility to the outside firm. In the Cosmo Family Trust case, we will assume that the trustees prefer that relationship and that under all the circumstances the advisory is willing to accept the delegation and become the investment manager.[13] In making the judgment that it will accept such delegation the manager must examine the responsibilities which will be entailed. It is useful to say that the manager steps into the trustees' shoes. That is true but it is a half truth. The manager can be held to a higher standard by virtue of its experience and skill than the trustees would have been. And professional managers who are inexperienced and unskilled may not be permitted to defend themselves on the basis of limited skill. Any professional manager who hangs out a shingle tends to incorporate minimum standards as to its ability, experience and fair dealing.[14]

Other phrases for fair dealing are "good faith," "lack of conflict of interest," and "fiduciary office." Tomes have been written on the sub-

---

investment decisions be shifted from the designated trustees to an outsider? Is the investment adviser permitted to give investment advice to this client under state and federal regulation? See Meredith M. Brown, *Federal v. State Regulation of Investment Advisers: The Heightening Battle for Corporate Control,* (New York: Law Journal Seminars Press, Inc. 1978) p. 77. Compliance with all regulatory procedures is assumed in this article. We also assume that the advisory fee is properly to be paid in equal amounts from income and from principal.

[13] The term *investment manager* is defined in ERISA section 3(38) as a professional fiduciary "who has a power to manage, acquire or dispose of any assets of a plan."

[14] In re *Estate of Killey* (Pa., 326 A2d 373,375)" . . . one who procures his appointment as trustee by representing that he has greater skill than that of a man of ordinary prudence will be held to have such skill as he has represented. See Restatement, 2d, Trusts §174." See *Duker & Duker,* 6 S.E.C. 386, 388–9 (1939) re representation of fair dealing. Note that the proposed Federal Securities Code of the American Law Institute would add to the prohibited practice of "fraud," that of "unfair dealing" (Sec. 915(B)). *Cf.* Meredith M. Brown, "Principal Changes Which Would Be Effected Under the Proposed Federal Securities Code in the Federal Regulation of Investment Advisers" *The Business Lawyer,* vol. 34 N0. 1 (November 1978) page 395.

ject and attempted to provide answers. In line with our approach, a few questions will be asked:

1. Broker Selection. What standards must the manager follow in designating brokers to execute trades for the trust? May an affiliated broker be designated? Is there a different answer if the trade is a principal trade with the affiliated broker acting as dealer? What if the broker is not affiliated with the manager but is a family member or provides benefits to the manager?[15]

2. Personal Securities Transactions of the Manager. The basic principle is that client transactions must come first. Trades of a fiduciary are often scrutinized with great suspicion. Certainly it is improper for an investment adviser registered with the SEC to engage in "scalping"[16] which is a technique of buying in advance of transactions placed for the customers and selling after the market impact of customers is completed. If the manager as a market maker acquires an inventory of the security in advance of recommendations, is that improper scalping or desirable market stabilizing? Can disclosure to the client solve the problem? What is adequate disclosure? What is informed consent?

3. Parallel Management of Accounts. A professional adviser will at a particular time often be attracted to a small number of securities and negative on a small number. If the adviser manages a series of accounts in a uniform way (a model account and mirror accounts), there may be problems of great seriousness as far as a manager's potential liability is concerned.[17]

FAMILY OBJECTIVES AND THE INVESTMENT VEHICLES IN THE COSMO TRUST

Investment goals of income beneficiary versus remainder. A family resolution. Looking at the net result after taxes and expenses. Applying general guidelines of balance and diversification. Transaction costs. A small

---

[15] SEC Release No. IA–615 (February 2, 1978), "Requirements Governing Payments of Cash Referral Fees by Investment Advisers"; SEC's "Statement on the Future Structure of the Securities Markets," (February 2, 1972); John L. Casey, " 'Finders Fee' Compensation to Brokers and Others," *The Business Lawyer* vol. 31, No. 2, (January 1976) page 707; *In re Investors Research Corp.*, et al. SEC Release No. IA–627 (May 1, 1978). It should be noted that since February 1, 1979 broker-dealers cannot execute certain exchange transactions for institutional accounts with respect to which they or their affiliated investment adviser have discretion. Securities Exchange Act of 1934, Sec. 11(a). See as to dealer trades *Trustees of Hanover College* v. *Donaldson, Lufkin & Jenrette* (settled before trial—Civil No. 71–C686, S.D. Ind. 1971).

[16] *SEC* v. *Capital Gains Research Bureau, Inc.*, 375 U.S. 180 (1963).

[17] Harvey E. Bines, *The Law of Investment Management* (Boston: Warren, Gorham & Lamont, 1978). Section 303; American Law Institute proposed Federal Securities Code regulating "mini" accounts; John L. Casey, "Regulatory Speedtraps for the Investment Adviser," Securities Regulation Service (New Jersey: Prentice-Hall 1979), Para. 1,102; *Troyers* v. *Karcagi*, U.S.D.C., S.D.N.Y., 1979, Sweet, J. (Current) Fed. Sec. L. Rep. (Illinois: Commerce Clearing House) Para 96, 929.

local company engaged in building windmills. Deferred compensation. Income producing real property.

Now that we have established that the trustees will be shifting investment responsibilities to an outside professional, we shall take a look at some specific types of property and seek to apply the Bobsey Twins of permissibility and appropriateness.

The Cosmo Trust has been funded by the executors of Inez Jordan's will with shares of a local business, a stream of deferred compensation income, income producing real property, a cache of long-term municipal bonds, Treasury obligations, savings accounts and securities of well known companies. Investment decisions will necessarily be interrelated. Thus, a preliminary decision on the size and composition of a liquid reserve may have to be modified by the subsequent analysis of the relative attractiveness of other securities.

We will start our analysis with a discussion of family objectives and then go on to the broad categories of reserves, other traditional portfolio components, real estate, local business interests, and the deferred compensation.

Family Objectives

These assets are to benefit a mother during her life and her children after her death. The mother, Dee Cosmo, has a limited need for income. If excess income is paid to Dee, her transfer to her children may incur transfer (gift and estate) taxes; moreover, Dee is in a high income tax bracket. Any excess payment to her is unlikely to reach her children without erosion. Her income needs may well be met by personal investments, other trusts, social security, and the income via the deferred compensation and real estate holdings. If so, is there a way of using trust income to benefit the remaindermen of the trust? When consulted on the point, the trust's legal counsel advises that the estate tax on transfer of the trust remainder at the death of Dee Cosmo will be zero, that any taxable undistributed gains would be taxed during the life of the trust to the trust as a separate taxpayer, that all dividend and interest income is to be paid out to Dee as income beneficiary during her lifetime and, accordingly taxed to her, not to the trust.

The estate tax-free character of the transfer to the remaindermen in the future is intriguing. It certainly offers planning possibilities which can affect the manager's investment decisions. It may be appropriate for the family overall if greater capital risk is accepted by the trustees in seeking greater opportunity. The remaindermen bear the added risk but it may make sense because they (the next generation) can receive estate tax-free any accumulation of property and gains. Can income be accumulated in the trust or effectively assigned by the income beneficiary? Indirectly that result might be achieved if low-dividend-paying, high-earnings growth securities are selected instead of high yielding bonds. Such a plan to benefit the remainder interests may be what Dee Cosmo's objective is, especially if it shifts assets from her to her children without gift or estate tax. Moreover, if income is capitalized, the trust's capital growth could provide a base for future income for Dee if she should then need it.

It is not too soon to get the facts about the persons who may receive the remainder. A basic client information form to assist in that search appears as Exhibit 3.

Reserves

We start off with identifiable reserves: Treasury securities and savings accounts. They may have been suitable to the decedent's situation. But are they appropriate in the trust? What is the purpose of liquid reserves in this account? Are they to fund the purchase of stocks and bonds at more attractive prices? A perpetual form of portfolio balance (leaning against the wind)? To capture high short-term interest rates? To meet tax liabilities? Are they really liquid? The answers to such questions will guide the manager to amount-quality-maturity conclusions.

Assuming that the amount is correct, are the vehicles the correct ones? Savings accounts and Treasury securities are permissible investments for trustees generally—but are they really appropriate for this trust? Commercial paper, bankers' acceptances, and money market mutual funds are alternatives to be checked. However, switches should not be precipitous: the consequences should be considered, including income tax results and transaction costs.

For example, do the trust's Treasurys include "flower bonds" which are sold at a discount in the market (often a substantial discount) but can be used at face value to pay estate taxes? In the base case, we are advised that Inez Jordan's estate tax return has been filed but not audited, so there is a potential tax deficiency and "flower bonds" previously owned by Inez might be relevant. If so, those Treasurys are both "reserves" and "long bonds." Whether or not there are "flower bonds," the potential tax obligation should be taken into account in constructing the portfolio. How likely is a deficiency? What is the range? Should not the manager designate specific reserves to meet any known or knowable payments and invest them in short-term instruments of high quality?

Long-Term Municipals

Tax exempt bonds are a traditional tool for income and are permissible trust investments generally. Are they appropriate here? Dee's tax

Exhibit 3

BASIC DATA SHEET

Date:
Date to Be Rechecked:
Social Security or Tax ID
Number:_____

Client Name_____

Address_____

Other Address
and/or Copies to:_____

_____

Minimum/Maximum
Equity Position _____%_____%

Account Objective_____

Income Need from Portfolio _____ Tax Bracket_____

Tax Year_____Who Prepares Tax Returns _____

Starting Value of Account_____Equity Proportion____Date_____

When Account Is to Be Appraised_____

Degree of Discretion_____   Who Receives Copies of Advices _____

_____

Custody Arrangements (organization and individual)

_____

Advisory Fee (method of computation
and source of payment)_____

_____

Brokerage Arrangements _____

_____

Individual:

   Date of Birth:

   Names, Assets (and DOB) of Family Members:

   Major Source of Income (proportion relative to portfolio income)

   Checking Account   Name:
                      Number:

   Expectancies: Related Clients:

bracket is relevant. It bears on the manager's decision whether to invest in lower yielding tax exempt or higher yielding taxable income securities, as income which is tax exempt to the trust retains that tax exempt character on distribution. But her need for income is a key point. Are long bonds needed at all? The account review form says that the income beneficiary has a low need for current income. More probing is required.

Discriminating between Issues of Securities; Mutual Funds

Assume municipal bonds are an appropriate area for Cosmo Trust investment. Obviously, municipal bonds are not fungible: they have individual credit worthiness, marketability, volatility, and maturities. They have been known to default or have maturities deferred. If a high need for trust income were to develop, can low quality municipals be selected to achieve a higher yield? Are such "junk bonds" a permissible trust investment in the applicable state? The usual safety tool for low quality securities is diversification. Cautions: (1) diversification is often not a defense if an imprudent security has been selected; and (2) some states favor bonds of their own state as against those of other states which may limit the possibilities of a diversified "junk bond" portfolio.

Price must always play an important part in investment selection. The cost of a round trip in a shift of bonds can be quite high because of bid-offered spreads. There is a special penalty attached to the ownership of odd lots of municipal securities. The "round lot" of municipals may be $100,000. The arithmetic works out this way: a diversified portfolio of ten round lot municipals is $1 million. That suggests a very large balanced portfolio. The need for such substantial assets led to the use of common funds of various sorts, both bank common trust funds and municipal bond mutual funds, as large pools permit trading economies (narrower spreads between the bid and asked), wide diversification of credits, and flexibility in shifting maturities.

Bank common trust funds are not registered as securities and have no prospectuses. As a result, the management expense is very low but they cannot be offered to the public and are available only as an internal tool to a bank trustee. In our case study, we have family trustees and even if they hire a bank as custodian and adviser, they would not have the common trust option. They would, however, have the option of purchasing mutual fund securities. Or would they? The issue will depend on state law. Can trust property be pooled with other assets? Can investment responsibility be delegated to a third party by the trustees? The traditional answer to both questions has been "No" where the document is silent. But trustees may be permitted to delegate and pool via a mutual fund. The issue was dealt with specifically by the New York Legislature a number of years ago when it concluded that New York trustees with broad investment powers could invest in shares of appropriate investment companies. The current text of the act (Estates, Powers, & Trusts Law; Section 11–2.2(b)(1)) reads as follows:

> A fiduciary holding funds for investment may invest the same in securities of any management type investment company registered pursuant to the federal investment company act of nineteen hundred forty, as amended, in any case in which . . . the . . . instrument creating or defining the investment powers of the fiduciary authorizes the investment of such funds in either of the following: (A) Such investments as the fiduciary may, in his discretion, select. (B) Generally in investments other than those in which fiduciaries are by law authorized to invest trust funds.[18]

Can the Cosmo's investment manager also manage the mutual fund in question? Would that be self-dealing? Would there be a double fee? It should be obvious that the adviser ought not to be receiving fees for the same work from both the investment company and from the Cosmo Trust. The Department of Labor has dealt with the questions of whether a double role of this sort is a prohibited transaction under ERISA. Conclusion: If the investment is otherwise appropriate, the fee is approved by an independent fiduciary and no double fee is charged, the use of no-load (no sales charge) mutual funds is permissible.[19] ERISA is not binding on the Cosmo Trust but the reasoning may have some interdisciplinary effect.

If a move from the inherited municipals into a mutual fund is permissible and is indicated, what are the costs of such a move? Even if the mutual fund is a "no-load" fund so that there is no purchase cost of its shares, there will be costs involved on the sale side. Accordingly, there should be a valid investment reason for incurring the sales expense. Commission payments, whether in the form of agency fees or spreads between the bid and the asked in an over-the-counter transaction, like prospective taxes, involve dollars of the trust and belong to the beneficiaries.[20]

---

[18] In some states there is no statutory provision regarding investment of funds by a fiduciary; some have adopted the prudence rule by judicial decision, some by statute, some specify a percentage limit to nonlegals, some treat conservators or guardians differently from trustees, some require prior approval and some have had constitutional prohibitions against investment by fiduciaries in corporate securities. As to a trustee's power to invest in mutual fund shares, consult Investment Company Institute, 1775 K Street, N.W., Washington, D.C. 2006.

[19] *Transactions Between Investment Companies and Employee Benefit Plans,* Dept. of Labor, Prohibited Transaction Exemption 77–4. Cf. purchase of shares of Real Estate Investment Trusts.

[20] As is the case of taxable securities, municipal bonds can involve taxable gains and losses. Depending on the applicable tax law, "cost" may be based on estate tax value in the estate of the decedent or based on original cost. This detail, like sales commissions or spread, must be part of the investment decision. A potential ping-pong effect can

Stocks Generally

First Question: Which securities is the investment adviser to have responsibilities for following on a continuous basis? Often inherited securities are a mixed bag and include certain securities which are not well known. Are any stocks to be excluded from the adviser's responsibility in this case? Will the trustees have full responsibility for such excluded stocks? If the trustees do not wish continuing responsibility, what will be done? Should the trustees set a rational timetable for sales of such securities so that only supervised securities will, after a period, be in the trust? A joint decision by the trustees and the manager as well, perhaps, as the interested members of the family is desirable and the conclusions should be in writing.

Second Question: There must be an analysis of the holdings, issue by issue. Is each stock permissible? Does each stock meet the general rules of "prudence"?

Third Question: Overall, what sort of risk and opportunity is involved? What risk and opportunity are indicated as appropriate in the Cosmo family situation? Do they match?

Rationality is a key element of the preliminary decisions which will be made one by one with respect to the portfolio. Perhaps that is obvious. Nonrational processes such as the intuition of an experienced professional, using computer-selection programs and technical analysis have an important part, however, in the final decision: performance will be keyed to the skilled selection of securities. That is the third wave. The process of narrowing the field to permissible securities, then identifying appropriate securities from that list of permissibles, is an essential start but finally comes the added value which cannot be learned in any book.

The Local Business

As part of the mixed bag of decedent's securities, the Cosmo trustees have acquired shares of a windmill and energy storage company about which only limited information is available—a local business with a limited over-the-counter market.[21] This is an investment of which the

---

be involved where an executor or testamentory trustee sells securities of a decedent. The manager may be establishing an estate tax value by selling securities within six months of the date of death of the decedent. Is that concern applicable in the Cosmo Family Trust case study?

[21] Often such shares turn out to have been acquired in a private placement from the issuer. Legal counsel must be consulted as to how and whether the trustees may sell such securities. They may have to be sold with a prospectus or "dribbled out" in ordinary brokers' transactions, or sold to another "private placement" investor. Note that it is important to check with the lawyer when deciding the final details of a proposed transaction, and again before the transaction is processed.

investment manager, when hired, had no special knowledge. If no knowledge is developed about this investment and there is no support for a decision either to sell or to retain the security, must it be sold in any event? Or can the shares be retained indefinitely? Must there be specific retention language in the governing instrument? Is an appropriate court order necessary? In the absence of adequate clarification the trustee and investment advisor may both have the worst of all worlds—some responsibility for anything that does not work out well. It would seem that if the situation does not admit of a prompt sensible decision supported by research, the beneficiaries' consent or that of a court, or both, are almost certainly desirable.

Do the trustees themselves have special knowledge of the local corporation? If so, it is quite possible that that knowledge grows out of an existing relationship. If so, is the relationship as private investors or as officers or directors of the corporation? The potential conflict of interest problems must be identified and dealt with as well as the knotty problem of the trust's using insider information which the trustees have in their capacity as officers or directors.[22]

Deliberate Retention or Sale

Let's say the company is an investment which the family wishes the trustees to retain. Can they? The company involves many of the aspects of impermissible investments: nonincome producing, new and untried, small, limited marketability. Can there be an adequate exculpation for the manager? If so, how should supervision be pursued? By a participation through a directorship? Is there power under the Jordan will? Can the director be indemnified?

The investing process moves step-by-step from (1) collection of adequate raw material (information); (2) its processing (analysis); (3) its application in light of the objectives, limitations, and needs of the persons involved (suitability); and (4) if action is to be taken, disinterested and optimum implementation (execution through clearance and settlement). This sequence applies to the windmill investment just as to the Fortune 500. So, (1) collect information and establish a method of keeping it current, (2) do the analytical work to support a conclusion as to future prospects, (3) make a judgment which is adequately documented concerning the desirability of retention versus sale by this trust at this time, and (4) time carefully any liquidation.

---

[22] The rule is clear that a person with material inside information may not use that as the basis for personal investment action nor that of friends or business customers. What if a trustee or investment manager, in an excess of caution, declines to use information which may be "material inside information" but which, with the benefit of hindsight, turns out to have been material or nonpublic? A decision made in good faith should be supported by the courts.

As in the case of a listed security, any liquidation would have to be handled in a way which is professional and disinterested. Thus giving the transaction to a trustee who is in the brokerage business would, on its face, appear to be biased rather than professional.[23] But what if Bea Cosmo, one of the trustees, is the best broker? Is that dual role prohibited? In general, trust law prohibits dual roles. In this instance, the trustees are members of the same family as those beneficially interested and disclosure and informal consent to the dual role might be the answer. In any event, from a practical point of view any conflict of interest is exacerbated by silence but defused by consent.

Advisory Fees for a Small Business

Is the fee that will be charged by the manager for supervision related to the value of assets under supervision? If so, is the manager also charged with the valuation of the assets? For assets quoted on a national stock exchange, the valuation is relatively mechanical. When the security is that of a small company whose shares are traded in a thin over-the-counter market, there is a conflict between the manager's self-interest in a higher value and fee and the trust beneficiaries' interest in a lower fee. The potential for misunderstanding could be eliminated by naming a disinterested appraiser or agreeing to a flat fee rather than one related to assets.

If the trustees are to have responsibility and the adviser no responsibility for the windmill corporation, it will be a rare trustee who does not ask some "free" input from the investment manager as to the outlook for solar energy, small companies, or the local region. Any obligation should be spelled out at the outset. But not only then. It should also periodically be restated during the relationship so that there is no misunderstanding and any omission will not result simply from a failure to define who has charge of the ball. Even if there is no direct supervision by the manager (and no fee), the value and type of the investment and any prospective dividend income to be received is to be taken into account by the investment manager when looking at the appropriateness of other assets.

Deferred Compensation

The stream of anticipated deferred compensation income is a prospective source of income for the beneficiary. The consequences in

---

[23] There is a long series of cases on broker selection, both under state trust laws and under the federal securities laws. The manager should be familiar with the line of cases on the obligation of the manager with respect to the reduction of brokerage commissions, beginning with *Moses* v. *Burgin*, 445 F.2d 369 (1st Cir., 1979), and including the issue of recapture for advisory clients of the underwriting spread on new issues (see S.E.C. Release No. 34–15020, File No. SR-NASD-78–3: August 3, 1978).

terms of income to Dee Cosmo and the taxes which will result[24] (who will pay?) must all be reflected as the portfolio is constructed. Of all the investments indicated, is this nonchangeable? It is not really a fee paying asset supervised by the investment manager as it flows through the trust out to the income beneficiary. Not only must it not be ignored, it is a kingpin in terms of portfolio construction. And someone must keep track of it, insure timeliness of payments and identify developing risks and potential alternatives, if any.

Real Property as a Trust Investment

The income producing real property consists of a vacant lot leased for parking and an inner city store on lease. Assume a managing agent for the property. Is the parking lot a permissible investment in this state? Does the store have a long-term lease and a high-risk tenant? Is this a property where capital value is deteriorating although current return is attractive? If so, would retention benefit the income beneficiary and penalize the remaindermen's capital? Are the properties saleable? These are all trustee questions. Also, take into account the income flow and the way the taxes on it will be computed and paid in selecting investments generally.

SPECIFIC INVESTMENT RESTRICTIONS FOR OTHER FUNDS INCLUDING INSTITUTIONS

> The next concentric circle. Personal trust investments limited by statute. Legislative pronouncements for retirement funds of public employes. Limits for investment companies and other savings institutions. Foreign investments. Do standards differ for retaining versus acquiring a security? Client guidelines—a follow-up compliance form and the obligation of a professional to decline an impossible assignment.

Investment vehicles for savings include personal trusts, public and private charitable foundations, employee benefit retirement trusts (including non-ERISA plans such as those for government employes), investment companies, insurance companies, banks, and thrift institutions like savings banks. The Cosmo trust involved no specific investment restrictions. While such flexibility is typical of personal trusts today, it was not always so even as to such trusts. The other vehicles generally still involve specific restrictions of many kinds. Some restrictions are imposed by the account itself. Others represent a legislative attempt to cause prudent investing by specifically defining which investments are permissible. All tend to be built on past loss experience. From the manager's point of view a list of permissible investments

---

[24] Keep in mind the somewhat complex income tax treatment of "income in respect of a decendent."

cannot be transcended. On the other hand, such a list does not necessarily provide a safe harbor; the global rules of prudence, conflicts of interest, suitability, balance, and diversification would still apply.

New York Trustees

An easy place to start in identifying typical restrictions is to look to the New York statute which, until quite recently, controlled investment by executors, trustees, and guardians (Personal Property Law, Section 21). It contained precisely such a "legal list." The statute listed obligations involving the full faith and credit of the United States, certain federal agency bonds, obligations of New York State and its municipalities, obligations of certain municipalities other than New York City (provided, for example, that the issuer had a population of at least 10,000 inhabitants and that the issuing entity had power to levy taxes on real property), certain revenue bonds and Canadian obligations, bonds and mortgages on unencumbered New York real property worth at least 150 percent of the loan, certain savings bank deposits, and public housing authority obligations. The section went on to add that, in addition, some investments in "nonlegals" was permissible if the securities were of American corporations and the aggregate did not exceed 35 percent (later 50 percent) of the aggregate market value of the fund. Bonds would qualify as permissible nonlegals only if they were issued by a common carrier or issued or guaranteed by a corporation, some of whose securities were registered with the SEC. Common or preferred stocks other than bank or insurance company stocks were eligible only if currently fully listed and registered upon a national securities exchange. Finally, the umbrella guide: investment could be made only if the specified types of securities selected were "such securities as would be acquired by prudent men of discretion and intelligence in such matters who are seeking a reasonable income and the preservation of their capital."

There were continued (and effective) pressures in New York for change—to add new permitted securities, to increase the maximum stock percentage to over 50 percent where market values had reached a higher percentage, to permit investment in mutual fund shares, to scrub the legal list in favor of a flexible standard of prudence. Ultimately, the New York trustees legal list was repealed in favor of a "prudent man rule." But it would be careless for a current trust manager to treat the history as of interest only to the archivist. Repeal means that the specific restrictions are no longer mandated. It does not mean that the public policy in favor of investments of that type is obsolete. A manager should be familiar with the legislative history, with prior specific restrictions, and not go blithely ahead assuming an old test is without any relevance. For example, look at the current prospectus of any registered investment company and review the Investment Restrictions section. Each equity security may have to meet minimum standards such as the continuous payment of dividends for a prior period of five years, the issuer in business at least ten years, a maximum of 5 percent invested in any one holding, a maximum of 5 percent in private placements, a maximum of 10 percent in any one industry. The prospectus reflects historic concerns of the SEC and of state securities administrators as to the protection of investors. It also reflects concerns of Congress via provisions of the Internal Revenue Code concerning diversification and transaction requirements for a regulated investment company as well as provisions of the Investment Company Act.

Public Retirement Funds and Investment Companies

While there has been some talk of a federal PERISA (Public Employes Retirement Income Security Act), local legislatures and state common law now are in charge. Investments which a fund can make for the benefit of retiring public employes are often set out in detail by the local legislature. The legislature is apt to begin with structuring the administrative organization, often with separate boards for the separate employe classifications, and then centralizing administration or supervision. For example, New York City has separate fire, police, city employes and teacher funds, with separate trustees. Administrative help is provided by the office of the City Comptroller, an official chosen by the voters in a general election of public officials. A similar structural pattern exists in Washington State which provides a useful case study. Washington State Retirement System has had a detailed legal list imposed by statute including these stock limitations:

1. "corporations created or existing under the laws of the United States or any state, district or territory";
2. total investment in preferred or common stocks not to exceed 25 percent of the portfolio;
3. no more than 5 percent of a portfolio company's outstanding common stock;
4. no more than 2 percent of the fund, based on cost, invested in the common stock of one portfolio company;
5. only stock traded on a national securities exchange; exceptions—preferred stocks, stocks of banks and insurance companies, and Washington State corporations;
6. cash and/or stock dividends paid in eight of the last ten years and, in the aggregate, supported by earnings; and an earned dividend in each of the last three years.

Even with such a list, there are still questions. For instance, in determining 5 percent of outstanding stock, how do we treat convertibles?

Must we treat them as though they were converted?[25] Incidentally, a 1977 law added a standard of "judgment and care under circumstances then prevailing" of "men of prudence, discretion, and intelligence." Has the new prudence section added flexibility or only accountability?

At one time some public retirement systems invested in municipals. There was a self-help aspect. And the legislatures gave their imprimatur. When pressures increased to improve retirement benefits and the yield spreads between municipals and corporates became obvious, there was an investment shift toward maximizing the total return over the long term. There remains, generally, a statutory power for a public fund to invest in municipals, however, as we read in connection with the purchase by the public employe retirement system of the City of New York of Municipal Assistance Corporation (MAC) bonds (a New York State agency) at a time critical to the City of New York. That is, municipals are permissible. Whether it is prudent for a manager to select a particular issue depends on the facts. It should be noted that while there is an overlap, the interest of current worker/plan-contributors and the interest of plan beneficiaries may differ considerably in a particular situation.

Less dramatic than the "big MAC" question, but more common, is underfunding: legislatures have a self-interest in maximizing long term rates of return: they then have the alternative of improving retirement benefits for public employes or of decreasing future appropriations. What if they choose improved benefits without making adequate appropriations and without realistic rates of return? Should the investment manager accept that assignment? If so, at what point and to whose attention should the contradiction be called?

Insurance Companies and other Savings Institutions

In addition to trusts of various kinds, personal and corporate, and investment companies, the major savings institutions are savings banks, commercial banks, thrift institutions of various kinds, and life insurance companies. They offer different opportunities to the investors and different regulatory patterns are imposed. Mutual savings banks pay interest (at regulated rates) to depositors and invest the savings mainly in real estate mortgages, government securities (federal and state) and certain corporate bonds. Their permissible investments are specified by statute and subject to limits. Investment may be made directly; or indirectly through an SEC-registered investment company wholly owned by savings banks. The fund investments are limited to those which are legal for savings banks. It is not uncommon now to permit savings banks to invest also in equities through a diversified registered

---

[25] Cf. Securities Exchange Act Section 13(d) and rules issued under it.

investment company. Credit unions are somewhat similar in deposit structure but make loans generally to members (investors) of the credit union.

Investments by insurance companies are also generally regulated under one or more state laws. Typically, the statute creates a state insurance department with a superintendent who has power to issue orders and regulations. A distinction is made between reserve investments and the regulation of investments for separate accounts. We tend to think of separate accounts as being akin to trusteed investments. That is true as a competitive matter, but the insurance statute is relevant for investment of both reserves and separate accounts. For example, Section 81(13) of the New York Insurance Law focuses on common stock investing of reserves. Among other things, portfolio companies must be banks, insurance companies, or registered under the Securities Exchange Act of 1934 and have had certain earnings over a seven-year period; no more than 5 percent of a company's outstanding shares can be acquired and no more than 1 percent of assets are to be invested in a single company. Upper limits of total stock investment (relative to assets and surplus) are also prescribed. The statutory permission to establish separate accounts (Section 227) contains some exemptive language from the reserve restriction and some higher percentages. These can change. So ought not the investment manager to ask the insurance company client to spell out the perimeters of investment authority with specificity at the outset and amend them if and when laws change? This is a complex area and it is important to clarify whether it is the client or the manager who should stay on top of changes in the law. (This need to clarify roles applies to any complicated area or relationship, of course.)

Dividend Limits

Investment by many regulated institutions may be limited to stocks which have a specified dividend record and a record of earnings which support the dividend. While the dividend test sounds like a reasonable one, it can have unforeseen circumstances: for example, a fashionable high technology company which contains and reinvests its earnings may be barred; a Fortune 500 company may not currently earn the dividend it is paying, owing to a strike. Is that a disqualification? What does the statute say?

Foreign Investments

Many regulated funds cannot make foreign investments. The exact language of the particular prohibition must be studied. As we have seen, in the Washington statute investment in stocks of U.S. corporations was required: a stock of a corporation incorporated abroad was not a permissible investment. Sometimes the test is not as to the corporation but as to the security—is it traded in the U.S.? What of a corporation which is incorporated in the United States but whose earnings are entirely derived from abroad? Is that within the spirit of the prohibition? What of a foreign corporation whose earnings are 100 percent from the U.S. and whose shares are traded on a U.S. exchange? If a corporation's shares are traded in the United States on the American markets, it is easy to assume that they are not foreign securities. But if a foreign security has been improperly purchased, the investment manager may have to make up any loss. And in a large fund, losses can be large, indeed. It is important to set up a procedure so that the likes of Schlumberger, Alcan, and International Nickel, as well as Broken Hill Proprietary, SONY and DeBeers ring a special cautionary bell for the person managing the account of a public fund or of any account where there may be limited authority to invest abroad. Check the statute's exact language. Also, be on guard even if authority to invest abroad has not been proscribed: public funds often cannot purchase over-the-counter industrial securities. Are securities traded on a foreign exchange permissible?[26]

Paraphrasing Dean Griswald: forget logic, what does the statute say?

The Controller of the Currency (Opinion 9.4070—See Handbook for National Trust Examiners) reads:

> Investment in speculative assets is not proper in investing trust funds under the prudent man rule and might expose the bank to liability in the event a loss should be sustained, unless such investment is specifically authorized by the terms of the governing instrument.
>
> Although not an all inclusive list, the following investments can usually be deemed speculative:

Art Objects	Precious Metals
Euro-dollars	Rare Coins
Foreign Companies	Selling Short
Foreign Currencies	Stock Options (see Options)
Jewels	Venture Companies
Oil and Gas Exploration	Warrants
Paintings	

Retention of Securities which Do Not Meet Standards for New Investments

What of a security which is proper when purchased but then changes its character? A company may pass a dividend. An industrial company

---

[26] In ERISA, the test is not incorporation or trading market but the location of the "indicia of ownership": Foreign securities may be purchased but must be within the jurisdiction of the U.S. courts.

might sell out its assets for cash and become an investment company. It might become a subsidiary of a foreign corporation. Or the stock may increase enormously in value and dominate the portfolio. It might decrease in value and be high risk or undersized. A diversified company may spin off to its shareholders a small subsidiary which would not fit the traditional standards of marketability. Both permissibility and prudence questions must be considered. Do the stated restrictions apply to the time the investment is made? Even if the permissibility test is at the time the investment is made, prudence involves a current focus which must not be ignored.

Unrealistic Assumptions

Can we as managers automatically accept the guidelines, limitations, or actuarial assumptions which are given to us? Not blindly. The manager is the expert and must exercise good faith. Unrealistic assumptions can cause dreadful results: they can mislead a plan sponsor into allocating too little money to meet the pension needs of its faithful employes; or they can induce the investment manager to take improper risk in an effort to achieve an unrealistically high goal. The answer of the investment manager is incomplete if it is only "whatever you say, boss." Whether or not there is a legal liability, being a professional means that the fiduciary should speak up, and even forego the assignment as a matter of principle if the guidelines do not make sense. That concept of professionalism applies generally.

To make sure everyone is on the same channel is a joint project of institution and manager. A specific set of guidelines from one institution to its manager reads as follows:

> While it is understood that the trustees wish the investment counsel to have freedom to maximize opportunities, recognition must be given to the fiduciary responsibility resting jointly with the trustees and investment counsel. Therefore, the investments of the trust shall observe the following limitations (percentages refer to the trust's market value at the time of the transaction; obligations of the U.S. Government or its agencies are excluded):

> *All Investments*

> 1. Maximum of 25 percent in the securities of any one industry.
> 2. Maximum of 12 percent in the securities of any one company, but no more than 8 percent in the equities of any one company.
> 3. Maximum of 5 percent in the securities of issuers having a record of less than ten years operations, including the record of any predecessor.
> 4. Transactions in puts, calls, or any form thereof are not permitted.
> 5. Short sales and purchase of securities on margin are not permitted.

6. Real estate investments must receive prior finance committee approval.
7. Purchase of employer securities is not permitted.

Common Stocks

1. Minimum of 90 percent of the stock fund must be listed on the New York Stock Exchange or American Stock Exchange or must be banks,

Exhibit 4

CLIENT _____

SECURITY ANALYSIS SHEET

SELL _____

Date of Recommendation _____

BUY _____

Where

STOCK _____ Price _____ Traded _____

SHARES OUTSTANDING _____   Approx. Average Weekly
Volume over Last Year
including OTC (over-
the-counter) _____

If OTC, Principal
Market Makers _____

DIVIDENDS

Current Declared   Current Yield _____
Annual Rate _____$_____   Percent
                                                          Pay Out ____

Dividend Months _____   Divs. Est. Current Year _____ _____
                              Last Four Years _____ _____
Next Ex Dividend Date _____
                                                      _____ _____
                                                      _____ _____
                                                      _____ _____

OUR EARNINGS ESTIMATES   Earnings Last Five
                                      Years   _____
Current Year _____
                                                 _____
Next Year 19__: _____
                                                 _____
Average Rate of
Earnings Growth: Last 5 Years _____ Last 10 Years _____   _____
(percent per annum)
                                                 _____
Estimated Rate of
Future Earnings Growth _____ Number of Years _____

        Rating _____

      Not Rated _____

SPECIAL COMMENTS:

insurance companies, and financial companies, traded over-the-counter.

2. Minimum market value of $100 million on outstanding shares.
3. Minimum number of shares outstanding of two million.
4. Maximum of 5 percent of an issuer's outstanding shares.
5. Restricted (investment letter) stock is not permitted.
6. Regular dividends are currently being paid.

Fixed-Income Securities

1. Bonds to be rated A or better by either Moody's or Standard & Poor's, except that convertible bonds may be rated Baa or BBB.
2. Private placements must receive prior finance committee approval.
3. Convertible preferred stocks may be purchased only if the company's common stock qualifies.

Securities not meeting the above criteria on the date of adoption of these guidelines or later because of a subsequent change in rating, market value or classification need not be sold.

After an investment disaster, when everyone knows that the investment turned out badly, the investment manager is on the spot. Clear guidelines such as these can help enormously in avoiding misunderstandings. They may be too elaborate in many situations. A minimum need is some contemporary documentation—made at the time of the decision and explaining its rationale—whenever a decision seems outside the mainstream. Exhibit 4 is another approach. It was prepared for an account with special earnings and dividend requirements for the stocks.

While Exhibit 4, as drafted, deals with stocks, bond purchases also can be subject to specific limits. Even high grade securities may lack a market with the result that when a crisis comes, the owner cannot control the situation. Although there are no statutory or stated restrictions, the purchase of a less than easily marketable long term bond might be questioned except in the case of a large trust which will terminate after the bonds' maturity.[27]

---

[27] In the Kansas Banking law, an investment security must be "a marketable obligation," i.e., it must be saleable under ordinary circumstances with reasonable promptness at a fair value. Section 17–11–6 adds "the purchase of investment securities in which the investment characteristics are distinctly or predominantly speculative or the purchase of securities which are in default whether as to principal or interest is prohibited."
Consider these questions:
1. Investment companies are barred from acquiring securities of companies deriving significant income from the securities business. They can lose their flow-through tax qualification if too many capital gains are realized from the sale of securities held for less than three months. They may lack power to purchase and sell puts, calls, straddles,

NEW RESTRICTIONS: SOCIAL-IMPACT INVESTING

The ethical investor. Noninvestment proxy issues and noninvestment investment selection. Whose political views control? Can a manager pursue a private hobby horse? Priorities, costs, and results. The need to identify and resolve inconsistent client instructions.

Background

Investment counselors have been generally alert to client attitudes, causes and prejudices in defining objectives and determining ways to achieve them. In the case of an individual client who disliked tobacco or liquor or gambling, the counsellor would make a point of excluding such stocks from consideration for the client's portfolio. Securities of companies manufacturing products which could offend the moral sensibilities of the particular client could easily be identified in normal cases; they were probably few in number and their omission did not materially limit the universe of potential investment alternatives. So also with institutional clients.

With developing concepts of social investing for institutions and corporate responsibility for portfolio companies, new dimensions have been added: the number of topics is virtually unlimited; the "good" companies may not be identified easily; the omission of "bad companies" can materially alter the investment result. Such issues can involve for the investment manager all the points developed above in this chapter: the need to know the client, to define permissible investments, to agree on what kind of diversification can be achieved, and a fiduciary responsibility to speak up if client instructions as to means are inconsistent with instructions as to goals.

---

warrants, and restricted securities. What of covered calls? Is a preferred stock with warrants attached the same as a convertible? Or barred?

2. Is an interest in a REIT a real estate investment or a stock? Technically, it is neither.

3. The FCC limits holdings of radio broadcasting, TV, CATV companies, and of COMSAT by individuals and groups. Are the restrictions relevant?

4. The CAB regulates the group ownership of stock in an airline. Is that a matter of concern?

5. If one investor or a group of investors beneficially owns over 5 percent of the outstanding equity, a filing with the SEC is required of the beneficial owners under Section 13d of the Securities Exchange Act. This section (sometimes called "The Williams Act") is the federal takeover disclosure statute. Is a client willing to undertake the expense of that filing? Who are the beneficial owners? What is a group? Now beneficial ownership of shares of its clients is attributed to any manager who has or shares in voting power or power of disposition of shares.

6. The manager also should be familiar with restrictions applicable to any category of investors which includes the client. Of general application to all citizens of a state are limits growing out of state Blue Sky laws. Securities administrators restrict the sale of new issues to their constituents: normally public offerings of new issues must be registered and cleared in that state. There is no federal preemption.

The philosophic underpinning for social action by shareholders was spelled out after World War II during the trials of Axis war criminals in Nuremberg. The courts there dealt with a similar interplay of corporate action and the moral responsibility of individuals who had carried out the corporate decisions, concluding that it was no defense that the person charged with crime was "just carrying out orders" from the corporate entity. Individual liability in less heinous circumstances is on the rise: an executive's personal responsibility is not to bribe public officials on behalf of the corporate employer, or falsify records or defraud investors or fix prices: the executive can go to jail. Lawyers and accountants can be held as coconspirators with their clients. Legal sanctions of this sort provide a practical basis for executive, lawyer, or accountant to say "no" to a proposed improper act. But Nuremberg did not deal with violations of the statutory law: quite the contrary. It dealt with an ethical obligation to say "no" even to the government when the government was wrong.

The ability of social action groups as voters-in-concert to lobby with government bodies over issues of ethical significance is nothing new. What is new, is that many groups now see their shareholder role as one to be measured in ethical terms. In that vein, certain antiwar groups sought, as shareholders, to make use of the machinery of corporate government to prohibit U.S. companies from making weapons during the involvement of U.S. armed forces in the Vietnam war. Specifically, the concept was to put to a vote of the shareholders of a Defense Department contractor the proposition that their corporation cease making weapons of destruction.

Current Issues

Once the technique of bringing ethical issues to shareholders was worked out, issues of air pollution, product danger for consumers, racial discrimination, and discrimination against women moved to the forum of the annual meeting.

Corporate Responses

One widely discussed political shareholder issue currently involves the Republic of South Africa. Political issues tend to be stated simplistically and can have strong partisans. So also here. The basis of the South African controversy is the extent to which outsiders should oppose racial discrimination in that country and the desirable or undesirable effect on that country's people of the presence of American business. The Republic of South Africa is a large, prosperous, sophisticated, and complex country with a national identity going back to 17th century settlers. Most multinational U.S. companies can be expected to want to do business there, all other things being equal.

With these various concerns in mind, a set of principles was developed by the Rev. Leon Sullivan, a black Baptist minister who is a director of General Motors. The Sullivan principles guide U.S. companies doing business in South Africa along directions taken toward desegregating companies and public facilities in the U.S. since World War II. Many U.S. companies have adopted the Sullivan principles and many non-U.S. corporations doing business in the Republic of South Africa have adopted similar codes reflecting a conclusion that their presence makes a positive economic and social contribution to that country and its people. On the other hand, some investors have announced a policy of divestment of shares of certain or all companies doing business in South Africa.

Another portfolio development: certain labor unions are urging that members' pension funds be invested to create local jobs or to boycott businesses that are antiunionization or that, sunbelt or multinational, are "exporting jobs."[28]

Shareholder Response

Shareholders can support a management's decision, challenge it, or terminate the relationship. Yale University's analysis is contained in *The Ethical Investor: Universities and Corporate Responsibility,* (Yale University Press, 1972). As described by the Investor Responsibility Research Center, Inc.:[29]

> The report contains fairly detailed guidelines for the voting of stock owned by the university. Among the more significant points are the following: (1) maximum economic return is the exclusive criterion for purchase and sale of stock in all normal circumstances; (2) Yale will not purchase or retain securities for the purpose of approving or disapproving of corporate conduct; (3) Yale will not vote its shares on any resolution that advances social or political causes unrelated to the conduct of the business; (4) Yale will vote for resolutions that seek to eliminate or reduce social injury caused by a company's actions, if it has been demonstrated that the activities do cause social injury, and if the resolution provides a reasonable and effective means of reducing or eliminating social injury; (5) Yale will exercise other shareholder rights—for example, introducing or soliciting support for shareholder resolutions attempting to elect or defeat directors, engaging in litigation—only in exceptional circumstances where a finding has been made that company activities have caused grave social harm (6) Yale will sell its stock rather than exercise

---

[28] Barber and Rifkin, "The North Will Rise Again; Pensions, Politics and Power in the 1980's" (1978; Hearings Conducted by the Senate Judiciary Subcommittee on Citizens and Shareholders Rights and Remedies, Sen. Howard Metzenbaum, D. Ohio, Chairman; Resolution of Councilman Thomas R. Brush of Cincinnati dated January 4, 1979).

[29] "Proxy Voting by Institutional Investors: Six Case Studies" (Yale University Press, January 1979).

extraordinary shareholder rights if it appears that Yale could not modify a company's activity or that modifications would have a highly unfavorable economic impact; (7) Yale will take no action pursuant to the guidelines if it appears that such action will impair the capacity of the university to carry out its education mission. . . .

Another response is that of the Minnesota State Board of Investment as to retirement funds of teachers, state and public employes, police officers, judges, and funds which benefit schoolchildren. In March of 1977, it adopted a written policy that provided in part:

> Whereas, it has become increasingly apparent that the standards of prudence and responsibility should be considered in light of this additional criterion; and social and environmental policies of the corporation in which the state owns or contemplates owing investment; and
>
> Whereas, the investing in an enterprise which is flagrantly violating the law or stubbornly ignoring public policy constitutes implicit endorsement of those policies; and the investment board is of the opinion that government cannot in good faith support such activity without abrogating its duties to the citizens; and
>
> Whereas, it is the investment board's opinion that corporations which do not take the welfare of society and its members into consideration, jeopardize their own financial stability, and in today's world risk depreciation of their investment value . . .
>
> If voting stock in such corporation is held by trust funds administered by the investment board, it may be voted in a manner calculated to ameliorate the existing problem . . .

Minnesota's attitude is summarized in a statement made by State Treasurer Jim Lord on September 28, 1977:

> We have discovered that in the long run, our beneficiaries' interests are not, in fact, promoted by short-range investment policies which destroy our environment, corrupt public officials, and encourage world disorder by legitimitizing nondemocratic and oppressive political regimes.

Somewhat more specific and addressing the issue of portfolio content as well as proxy voting is a position paper of the Roman Catholic Archdiocese of Cincinnati to guide its investment committee:

Proxy voting:

> to use its voting rights as stockholder to effect and influence changes in values and to encourage actions which will benefit all persons, particularly in Third World countries.

Portfolio content: refusal to own

> —Companies whose activities consist primarily in the manufacture of materials and weapons designed to destroy human life;
> —Companies which, by reason of their activities, cause injury to consumers, employes, and others by violation of laws established to protect

health, safety, and human rights, particularly if these violations take the form of discrimination or exploitation of people, the environment or natural resources;

—Companies which manufacture or provide products or services contrary to the moral teachings of the Church.

Any exception to be made, will be considered only for the purpose of bringing pressure to bear in the hope that the policies of administration might be modified or of giving prophetic witness by raising the conscience level of the public in such matters.

The Investment Manager's Response

By definition, an investment manager, whether trustee or outside professional, is an intermediary: the managed assets belong to someone else.

When sociopolitical issues are presented in a proxy statement, what are the rights and responsibilities of the investment manager? The first question is, what is the estimated impact on earnings and market, short and longer term, of the proposal? Is it significant? If significant and negative, can the proposal be supported? If no significant investment impact can be discerned, should the manager abstain? Should the votes be passed on to the true owners? How and at what cost? Should the managers of, say, a cancer research society vote routinely against a course of conduct which may cause cancer? SEC Chairman Harold Williams campaigns for an offset to the inertial power of management by encouraging institutional intermediaries to speak up more about companies in which their clients invest. He has stressed the availability of tools in addition to the Wall Street rule of "support management 100 percent or sell the stock," tools like disagreement letters, press conferences and adverse votes on certain issues. His view seems to be: more input will not adversely institutionalize or "establishmentize" American business, but will make everyone more alert. So far so good. But beware of usurpation of power by intermediaries!

Has the client given social investing instructions? If not, may the investment manager consider issues which are without identifiable investment impact? The following analysis of Ian Lanoff, the ERISA Administrator on February 5, 1979, should be kept in mind:

> While fiduciary considerations such as investment performance may not properly be sacrificed in order to advance the social welfare of a group or region, an investment is not impermissible under ERISA solely because it has social utility. If the socially beneficial investment meets objective investment criteria which are appropriate to the goals of the portfolio, it may be considered in the same manner as other investments which meet these criteria.
>
> In other words, what the pension plan fiduciary needs to determine about an investment is not, first, whether it is socially good or bad, but

how the proposed investment will serve the plan's participants and beneficiaries. The stability of a company's labor relations, the political situation
in a country in which the investment is located or with which a company
does business, and the effect that the public view of a company's social
commitment may have on the profitability of a company are all factors
which may properly enter into the evaluation of an investment.

If after evaluating other factors, two investments appear to be equally
desirable, then social judgments are permissible in determining which
to select. The point is that social judgments may not properly be substituted for any factors which would otherwise be considered in a given
case.

Is the trustee or outside investment manager making social investment decisions? To make the decision requires either a determination
that *(a)* social investing takes precedence over investment return or
(b) social investing will occur only if consistent with equivalent investment results. Is there legal authority to make either decision?

If a trustee makes the decision to invest socially and an outside
manager is asked to implement it, the manager must conclude that
the social investing instruction is authorized (that is, the trustees have
power to give the instructions) and that the instruction is consistent
with the investment objective the investment manager is asked to
achieve; e.g., that a diversified portfolio be constructed.

At some point, a list of restrictions can involve "Catch 22": the
limit of opportunities that the investment manager is given may make
achievement of the investment objective of the client less likely.

J. A. Livingston, in his nationally syndicated Business Outlook column in the *Philadelphia Inquirer* and other newspapers, commented
on the risks of a limited investment universe as follows:

> To me, it's a question that has been answered. If a baseball manager
> trades off some of his top players, it's "mathematically possible" for him
> to win as many games as before, but the probability of doing so would
> be reduced. So it is if an investor sells off stocks of companies that have
> performed preeminently in the past; he has a mathematical chance of
> doing as well as formerly, but the probabilities have been reduced.

An individual's personal political hobby horse can be supported.
But can a fiduciary trim the investment universe to suit personal objectives? In the pre-social investing world, such personal subjective choices
were a breach of a fiduciary obligation. They often involved money
for the fiduciary. Is personal power unrelated? Few, yet, seem concerned about the conflict of interest spectre in the social-investing
area. Perhaps because the goal is a better world, rather than self-interest. But an investment manager should be loathe to subordinate investment considerations of clients to private views on social investing in
the absence of extremely clear, credible and consistent instructions
from the client.

Chapter 25

Professional Self-Regulation

W. SCOTT BAUMAN

The Colgate Darden School of Business Administration
University of Virginia
Charlottesville, Virginia

As is the case in other occupations that are considered to have important responsibilities in terms of the public interest, the professional conduct of investment managers, portfolio managers, and investment advisers is the subject of laws, regulations, rules, and standards. The subject of this chapter is the regulations and standards that are imposed on investment managers by the profession itself. National and state regulation is the subject of preceding chapters in Part 4.

Many occupational groups advocate lofty sounding professional standards of conduct. Much fewer groups however, have made the necessary commitment to establish a professional self-regulatory system that recognizes and enforces standards of conduct which reasonably protects clients and the public interest. Evidence suggests that the investment management industry is making a significant commitment to a self-regulatory system. The Financial Analysts Federation (FAF) and The Institute of Chartered Financial Analysts (ICFA), two associated organizations, are recognized in the United States and Canada as the professional associations composed of the largest number of practicing investment managers, investment advisers, and security research analysts. Its members are referred to as financial analysts. Both of these organizations have been active, both separately and jointly, for many years in developing a professional self-regulatory program.

EDUCATIONAL STANDARDS

The ICFA was formed in 1961 with the following purposes and programs:

— To administer a study and examination program for candidates which guides financial analysts in mastering a professional body of knowledge and in developing analytical skills, and which tests analysts for a reasonable level of competency.

— To award the professional designation, Chartered Financial Analyst (C.F.A.), to persons who meet stipulated standards of competency and standards of conduct for the professional practice of financial analysis; and to permit persons to retain the C.F.A. designation who continue to meet stipulated standards.

— To sponsor and enforce a *Code of Ethics* and *Standards of Professional Conduct*.

In 16 years (1963–78), the Institute administered 25,935 C.F.A. candidate examinations (consisting of three 5¼ hour tests which must be taken sequentially), and awarded the C.F.A. designation to 5,570 financial analysts who successfully completed both the program and at least four years of practice. Another 2,000 analysts are registered in the candidate program. The members of the Institute are the C.F.A. holders. The C.F.A. meets certain educational requirements and master a body of knowledge that are briefly described in Chapter 1 of this handbook.

The FAF was formed in 1947 and is composed of approximately 14,500 members in 51 constituent financial analyst societies located throughout the U.S. and Canada. Regular members are called FAF Fellows. To become a FAF Fellow, a financial analyst must successfully complete the C.F.A. level I examination and meet stipulated standards of professional conduct.

Still another organization, The Investment Counsel Association of America (ICAA) is composed of members who are investment counsel firms. This organization awards the Chartered Investment Counselor (CIC) designation to investment counselors who successfully complete the CIC examination, have five years of eligible experience, and who meet the ICAA *Standards of Practice*.

STANDARDS OF PROFESSIONAL CONDUCT

Once a financial analyst becomes a FAF Fellow or a C.F.A., he or she agrees to practice in conformance with a *Code of Ethics* and *Standards of Professional Conduct*. The standards of both the FAF and the ICFA are virtually the same. The FAF version of the code and standards follows:

Code of Ethics[1]

WHEREAS, the profession of financial analysis has evolved because of the increasing public need for competent, objective, and trustworthy advice with regard to investments and financial management; and

---

[1] Financial Analysts Federation Articles of Incorporation By-Laws, Code of Ethics, Standards of Professional Conduct as revised May 13, 1979.

WHEREAS, those engaged in this profession have joined together in an organization known as The Financial Analysts Federation; and

WHEREAS, despite a wide diversity of interest among analysts employed by brokers and securities dealers, investment advisory organizations, investment companies, investment trusts, pension trusts, banks and insurance companies, and other institutional investors and investment entities, there are nevertheless certain fundamental standards of conduct which should be common to all engaged in the profession of financial analysis and investment management and accepted and maintained by them; and

WHEREAS, the members of The Financial Analysts Federation adopted a Code of Ethics and Standards on May 20, 1962, which have been revised from time to time; and

WHEREAS, The Financial Analysts Federation now provides for individual membership in it and requires that all of its member societies adopt its Code of Ethics and Standards of Professional Conduct and requires that all members of member societies comply with them.

NOW, THEREFORE, the members of The Financial Analysts Federation hereby adopt the following Code of Ethics and Standards of Professional Conduct:

A financial analyst should conduct himself with integrity and dignity and encourage such conduct by others in the profession.

A financial analyst shall conduct himself and encourage the practice of financial analysis in a manner that shall reflect credit on himself and the profession.

A financial analyst should act with competence and strive to maintain and improve his competence and that of others in the profession.

A financial analyst should use proper care and exercise independent professional judgment.

Standards of Professional Conduct

A. Compliance with Governing Laws and Regulations

1. The financial analyst shall have and maintain knowledge of and shall comply strictly with all applicable federal, state, and provincial laws as well as all applicable rules and regulations of any governmental agency governing his activities. The financial analyst shall also comply strictly with applicable rules and regulations of the stock exchanges and of the National Association of Securities Dealers if he, or his employer, is a member of these organizations.

2. The financial analyst shall take steps to assure that his employer is aware of the existence and content of the Code of Ethics and of these Standards of Professional Conduct.

3. The financial analyst shall not knowingly participate in, assist, or condone any acts in violation of any statute or regulation governing securities matters, nor any act which would violate any provision of the Code of Ethics or these Standards of Professional Conduct.

4. A finanicial analyst having supervisory responsibility shall exercise reasonable supervision over subordinate employees subject to his control,

with a view to preventing any violation by such persons of applicable statutes, regulations, or provisions of the code of Ethics or Standards of Professional Conduct.

5. The financial analyst shall not communicate or act on information if to do so would violate the laws and regulations relating to the use of material inside information. When the financial analyst acquires inside information, unless the analyst is in a special or confidential relationship with the issuer and receives the information in that capacity, which information in his judgement is of a material nature, he shall, when appropriate, make reasonable effort to achieve public dissemination of such information by the issuer involved.

6. When, in the course of practice, the financial analyst has encountered evidence that illegal acts have occurred, he is encouraged to report such evidence to an appropriate governmental or self-regulatory authority.

B. Investment Recommendations and Actions

1. The financial analyst shall have a reasonable and adequate basis for investment recommendation and action. He shall maintain appropriate records to support the reasonableness of such recommendation and action. He shall distinguish between facts and opinions in the presentation of investment recommendations.

2. The financial analyst, in making an investment recommendation or taking investment action, shall exercise diligence and thoroughness. Any such recommendation or action shall be supported by appropriate research and investigation.

3. The financial analyst shall, in preparing for general public distribution a research report that is not directly related to a specific portfolio or client, indicate the basic characteristics of the investment involved. The financial analyst shall use reasonable judgement to determine the applicable current relevant factors.

The financial analyst shall, when making an investment recommendation or taking an investment action for a specific portfolio or client, consider its appropriateness and suitability for such portfolio or client. In considering such matters, the financial analyst shall take into account *(a)* the needs and circumstances of the client, *(b)* the basic characteristics of the total portfolio, and *(c)* the basic characteristics of the investment involved. The financial analyst shall use reasonable judgement to determine the applicable current relevant factors.

4. The financial analyst shall not, in the preparation of material for distribution to his employer, associates, customers, clients, or the general public, copy or use in substantially the same form material prepared by other persons without acknowledging its use and identifying the name of the author or publisher of such material. The analyst may, however, use without acknowledgement factual information published by recognized financial and statistical reporting services or similar sources.

5. The financial analyst shall scrupulously avoid any statements, oral or written, which guarantee any investment.

6. The financial analyst shall act in a manner consistent with his obliga-

tion to deal fairly with all customers and clients when *(a)* disseminating investment recommendations, *(b)* disseminating material changes in prior investment advice, and *(c)* taking investment action.

C. Compensation

1. The financial analyst shall inform his customers, clients, and employer of compensation arrangements in connection with his services to them which are in addition to compensation from them for such services.

2. The financial analyst shall make appropriate disclosure of any consideration paid to others for recommending his services.

3. The financial analyst shall not undertake independent practice for compensation in competition with his employer unless he has received written consent from both his employer and the person for whom he undertakes independent employment.

D. Disclosure of Conflicts

The financial analyst, when making investment recommendations, or taking investment actions, shall disclose to his customers, clients, and employer and material conflict of interest relating to him and any material beneficial ownership of the securities involved which could reasonably be expected to impair his ability to render unbiased and objective advice. The financial analyst shall also comply with all requirements as to disclosure of conflicts of interest imposed by law and by rules and regulations or organizations governing his activities and shall comply with any prohibitions on his activities if a conflict of interest exists.

E. Priority of Transactions

The financial analyst shall conduct himself in such manner that transactions for his customers, clients, and employer have priority over personal transactions, that personal transactions do not operate adversely to their interests, and that he act with impartiality with respect to customers and clients. Thus, if an analyst has decided to make a recommendation as to the purchase or sale of a security, he shall give his customers, clients, and employer adequate opportunity to act on such recommendation before acting on his own behalf.

F. Relationships With Others

The financial analyst shall act in a highly ethical and professional manner in his dealings with the public, his clients, his employees, his associates and fellow analysts. The financial analyst shall conduct himself in a fair and businesslike manner in all competitive business situations and shall adhere to the high standards of business conduct expected of all financial analysts. The financial analyst shall not use his business position to influence fellow analysts improperly on matters relating to their professional analysts organizations and shall respect the right of individual analysts to hold varying viewpoints.

These standards identify competent and ethical practices that investment managers and security research analysts are expected to follow and that serve to protect the interests of investors.

ENFORCEMENT OF STANDARDS

One of the most difficult elements of a self-regulatory program to administer is the enforcement of professional standards. The way in which the FAF and the ICFA enforce their standards are described in *Rules of Procedures* which sets forth in detail how conduct complaints are submitted, how they are investigated, and how disciplinary sanctions are imposed on members.

The first formally imposed sanction on a member by the profession was approved by the ICFA in 1974. Since that time, the FAF and the ICFA have imposed sanctions on approximately 18 members— sanctions which have included revocation of the C.F.A. charters, suspension, public censure, private censure, and private admonishment. As compared with other older and larger professions, this is a remarkable record of disciplinary leadership for a private self-regulatory program.

CONTINUING EDUCATION

Because of dynamic changes that have and undoubtedly will continue to occur in the profession, investment managers need to engage in continuing education. As was mentioned in Chapter 1, investment managers and analysts are well educated with the majority having at least one if not two college degrees. It was also mentioned that the vast majority of employer institutions support continuing education of their professional staff through professional society meetings, conferences, and seminar programs.

The FAF and the ICFA sponsor many conferences and seminars for their membership, some in collaboration with university schools of business administration, and publish periodicals including the *Financial Analysts Journal* and *The C.F.A. Digest.* An associated organization, *The Financial Analysts Research Foundation,* commissions and publishes studies and papers which are intended to improve the practice of investment management and research analysis.

Although considerable progress needs to be made in the future, the investment management industry does have a comprehensive professional self-regulatory program which serves to protect the public interest.

REFERENCES

Earp, M. H. and Gillis, John G. eds. *Professional Standards of Practice*, Charlottesville, Va.: The Financial Analysts Research Foundation, 1978.

Bauman, W. Scott. *Professional Standards in Investment Management,* occasional paper. Charlottesville, Va.: The Financial Analysts Research Foundation, forthcoming.

Part Five

Management by Type of Account

Management of Pension Fund Portfolios

PATRICK J. REGAN

Vice President
BEA Associates, Inc.
New York, New York

Employee retirement plans have more than $500 billion in assets and are the largest single factor in the capital market. Until the 1960s, though, they were considered a "sleeping giant," with low portfolio turnover and large holdings of blue chip stocks and high grade bonds. Since then, pension funds have been a vanguard in applying the new investment techniques described in this book, in particular the setting of investment objectives, performance measurement, active bond management and index funds. Retirement benefits and employer contributions continue to increase at a 15 percent annual rate, so it is not surprising that servicing the needs of pension plans has become a growth industry, employing thousands of investment managers, consultants, actuaries and attorneys. The efforts of the latter three groups, in conjunction with the Employee Retirement Income Security Act of 1974 (ERISA), virtually assures that the portfolio manager will be given a set of investment guidelines and objectives. But such guidelines are often confusing and contradictory, and the manager should really understand the financial position of the plan and the sponsor before attempting to structure the portfolio.

The major problem for the investment manager is the arcane language used by actuaries to describe retirement benefit plans. Plans may be public or private, single or multiemployer, defined benefit or defined contribution, final pay or career average pay, integrated with Social Security or not, etc. In addition, plans may have different funding methods, actuarial assumptions, asset valuation methods, and amortization schedules. With so many variables, how can an investment manager begin to ascertain the needs of a retirement plan?

697

THE SIZE AND GROWTH OF PENSION ASSETS

The Securities and Exchange Commission conducts an annual survey of aggregate retirement plan assets. At the end of 1977, the combined assets were $501.5 billion (at cost, not market), of which $221.9 billion or 44 percent were held by public pension funds and $279.6 or 56 percent were held by private pension plans.[1] Among the public plans, three-fifths of the assets were held by retirement plans for state and local employees. Such assets were primarily invested in corporate securities, with bonds favored over stocks. In contrast, the two-fifths of the public fund assets held by plans administered by the U.S. Government were invested almost entirely in Treasury securities.

At the end of 1977, the total assets of the nongovernment or private pension system were $279.6 billion, with 35 percent held by insured pension plans and 65 percent held by noninsured pension funds. The difference between the two types of plans lies primarily in the funding arrangement. For an insured pension plan, retirement benefits are underwritten by an insurance company, and the employer (in the case of a noncontributory plan) pays the annual premium on the insurance contract. But if the plan is of the noninsured or self-insured variety, there is no insurance contract and contributions are placed into a trust, the assets of which are then invested. When people talk about the impact that pension funds have had on the stock market, they are usually talking about private noninsured plans, which tend to invest more than half of their assets in stocks.

Table 1 is based on the SEC data and shows that throughout the 1970s, the aggregate portfolio of private noninsured pension funds has held (on a market valuation basis) 60 percent to 70 percent of its assets in common stock, 20 percent to 25 percent in corporate bonds and the remainder in cash, government securities, mortgages, and real estate. This is in contrast to the two previous decades. In the 1950s, stocks increased from 20 percent to 50 percent of the aggregate portfolio and continued their upward climb until 1972, when they reached 73 percent and corporate bonds slipped to a low of 17 percent of the portfolio. At the end of 1977, the aggregate portfolio was 56 percent stocks, 24 percent corporate bonds and 20 percent other assets. In the latter category, the major growth has been U.S. Government securities, which account for a larger share of the portfolio than mortgages, real estate, cash, preferred stock, and other assets combined.

The table shows that the book value of the pension assets has been growing by nearly 10 percent a year for a decade, and was $181.5

---

[1] "Survey of Private Noninsured Pension Funds, 1977," *S.E.C. Statistical Bulletin*, vol. 37, no. 5 (May 1978).

Table 1
Asset Mix and Unrealized Gains or Losses in Private Noninsured Pension Fund Portfolios (1969–1977)

	1977	1976	1975	1974	1973	1972	1971	1970	1969
Asset mix									
Common stocks	56%	62%	60%	56%	68%	73%	68%	62%	63%
Corporate bonds	24%	22%	24%	28%	21%	17%	21%	24%	22%
Other assets	20%	16%	16%	16%	11%	10%	11%	14%	15%
Total assets	100%	100%	100%	100%	100%	100%	100%	100%	100%
Unrealized gains or losses (in billions of dollars)									
Common stocks	+$3.88	+$15.12	+$4.02	−$16.72	+$8.41	+$38.82	+$23.82	+$13.76	+$11.94
Corporate bonds	− 2.83	− 1.21	− 3.29	− 4.23	− 2.63	− 2.01	− 2.91	− 4.77	− 6.31
Other assets	− .99	− .42	− .27	− 1.08	− .61	− .04	− .43	− 1.30	− 1.61
Total unrealized gains (losses)	+$0.06	+$13.49	+$ .46	−$22.03	+$5.67	+$36.77	+$20.48	+$ 7.69	+$ 4.02
Book value of pension assets	$181.51	$160.41	$145.17	$133.73	$126.53	$117.53	$106.42	$97.01	$90.58
Unrealized gains or losses as a percent of book value	+0.0%	+8.4%	+.3%	−16.5%	+4.5%	+31.3%	+19.2%	+7.9%	+4.4%

billion at the end of 1977. The table also shows that while the difference
between the aggregate market value and the cost of the securities
fluctuates considerably, common stocks account for nearly all of the
volatility. Unrealized gains were a record $38.8 billion in 1972, a mere
$4 billion in 1975 and 1977 and a $16.7 billion unrealized loss in 1974.

While some of the change in asset mix is due to unrealized gains
or losses in stocks, much is due to poor market timing. For example,
David R. Atkinson of Morgan Stanley & Co. examined the quarterly
pension fund cash flow figures of the postwar period and concluded
that "it can be argued that when the largest factor in the equity market
devotes maximum cash flow to stocks, the market is at or near its
top and, conversely, when the percentage going into equities is near
its low point, the market is close to its bottom."[2] He pointed out that
as stock prices rose and bond prices fell between 1952 and 1967, the
percentage of pension fund cash flows directed into equities rose from
30 percent to 60 percent. Since then, the figure has been very volatile,
rising above 140 percent in 1969, 1971 and 1972, but plunging below
20 percent in 1974, 1977, and 1978, when historically high bond yields
offered a strong alternative to stocks.

QUESTIONS FOR THE INVESTMENT MANAGER

Given that pension assets are large and growing and that the asset
mix tends to mirror the fluctuations of stock prices, how can an investment manager tailor a portfolio to the needs of an individual plan?
In most cases, he will be one of several managers handling parts of
the fund, so the responsibility for establishing the overall asset mix
rests with the plan trustees. However, the manager can gain a clear
understanding of the financial status of the plan and the sponsor by
asking a few relevant questions.

1. Is the Plan Sponsor a Government Entity, a Labor Union or a Corporation?

State and local governments generally have a conservative bias in
their investment approach. Most of their retirement plans are contributory, and investment losses ultimately have to be made up by the
taxpayers or the active employee members. Because of this risk aversion, bonds are the single largest asset category in state and local retirement plans. Even though the plans are exempt from taxes, municipal
securities of the sponsor are sometimes held in the portfolio for political
rather than investment reasons.

[2] David R. Atkinson, "Factors Favoring Both A Cyclical and Secular Bull Market
For Equities" (Morgan Stanley, September 6, 1978).

Union plans tend to have a conservative bias for another reason. If the assets of the fund were depleted because of poor investment results, the union might have to reduce pension benefits for retirees. Thus, it is not surprising that union plans often favor fixed income vehicles like mortgages and bonds over stocks.

Corporate retirement plans tend to be more aggressive. The plans are usually noncontributory and the companies can afford to take greater risks than the unions or municipalities.

Top management views pension contributions as a labor cost and any losses on the investment portfolio can be made up from pretax profits. On the other hand, favorable investment performance benefits the shareholders, as the company contributions can be reduced.

2. Is It a Defined Benefit or a Defined Contribution Plan?

As the name implies, a defined benefit plan is one in which the retirement benefits are defined by a formula and the contribution can vary, depending on investment performance. As already noted, pension plans are of the defined benefit type, and superior investment results can lead to lower contributions. In contrast, profit sharing plans are of the defined contribution type and superior investment results do not affect the sponsor. The contribution is usually a specified percentage of pretax profits or payroll. Such plans are most often found in nonunionized growth industries and sometimes the bulk of the portfolio is invested in the company stock. The Sears Profit-Sharing Plan, which at $3 billion is the largest in the nation, is a striking example. For many years, more than three-quarters of the portfolio has been invested in Sears stock.

If an investment manager is going to structure a portfolio for a profit sharing plan, it is important to know the estimated cash flows into and out of the fund and whether or not the portfolio is being used to buffet the price swings of a core holding such as the company stock. If members can easily transfer money out of the profit sharing fund, the manager will have to structure liquidity into the portfolio. Over the longer run, one should focus on the maturity of the work force and the expected growth and profitability of the company and the industry.

Liquidity is not as important in a pension fund, since contributions generally exceed benefits and the liabilities are very long term in nature. In fact, some pension fund trustees choose to ignore liquidity and concentrate on matching the maturity or the "duration" of their bond portfolios to that of the plan liabilities. This method of matching pension assets and liabilities is called "immunization" and is discussed in Chapter 9.

3. How Mature is the Plan and How Will This Change in the Coming Years?

As the work force reaches maturity, the need for a conservative portfolio with sufficient liquidity increases. There are several ratios for measuring the maturity of the plan but two of the most common are the average "attained" age of active members in the plan and the ratio of active to inactive members. For a growth industry like semiconductors the average attained age of plan members might be 35 or 36 years, and the ratio of active to inactive members could be in excess of ten to one. The portfolio of such a plan could be managed aggressively, since contributions will exceed benefits for many years and any portfolio losses could presumably be made up by the company without severely affecting profits. Most companies are not in this enviable position. The typical plan has three or four active members for every inactive members, the active work force grows by 1 percent or 2 percent a year, and the average attained age remains constant, in the 40–41 years of age category. Contributions generally exceed benefits by 50 percent to 60 percent but it is not easy to make up portfolio losses, as contributions tend to be around 20 percent of pretax profits. Sponsors in this position generally favor a conservative asset mix of 50 percent to 70 percent equities, with the balance in fixed income vehicles like corporate bonds, government securities, mortgages, and guaranteed insurance contracts.

Companies in mature industries like steel often have an attained age of 45 or more, with two or fewer active members for every inactive. The active work force may be declining and the inactives can grow dramatically when antiquated plants are shut down. Mature companies are sometimes risk-averse and unwilling or unable to pursue an aggressive investment policy because the amortization of large unfunded pension liabilities can require contributions that sometimes exceed pretax profits.

While the age distribution of plan members may be exceptionally young or old today, the profile can change greatly over a 10–20 year period. The key is the growth of the active work force. Most companies have a long range planning department that can estimate the growth of the business and the active work force needed to support that growth. If this figure is plugged into a pension simulation model that incorporates normal employee turnover, disability and mortality, the active-to-inactive ratio can be projected for a decade or more and the portfolio manager will have a better insight as to how the growth and liquidity needs of the plan will change over time.[3]

---

[3] See the Appendix for a list of firms that offer pension simulation models and pension planning services.

4. How Conservative are the Funding Methods and Actuarial Assumptions Used to Compute the Pension Costs and Liabilities?

Strictly speaking, this should not affect the structuring of the portfolio, but it is essential to an understanding of the financial status of the plan.[4] Generally, companies that use conservative accounting methods use conservative actuarial assumptions and funding methods. The funding method affects the timing of pension costs while the actuarial assumptions determine the total amount of money that must be accumulated. Funding methods fall into one of two categories—accrued benefit methods and projected benefit methods. The former reflect benefits as they accrue year by year whereas the latter project benefits that are expected to be earned over the working lives of the plan participants. The principal accrued benefit method is the unit credit method, which produces the least conservative pension figures. The most popular of the projected benefit methods is the entry age normal method, with contributions made in level annual amounts, often as a fixed percentage of payroll. When a similar projected benefits method is applied on an aggregate basis for all members as a group, it is called the aggregate funding method, which is most conservative and results in higher annual contributions during the early years of a plan. Under this method unfunded past service costs are handled differently. With the unit credit and entry age normal methods, the pension contribution has two components—normal service costs incurred in the current year and the amortization of unfunded past service costs. With the aggregate funding method, unfunded past service costs are not identified separately but are included as part of the normal costs, which are spread over the remaining working lives of the participants.

It is important to know how rapidly the unfunded past service costs are amortized, since they can grow rapidly with the signing of new labor contracts or because of large portfolio losses. Unfunded past service costs are generally amortized over periods of 25 to 30 years, although the Internal Revenue Service allows them to be amortized over periods as short as ten years. Under ERISA, experience gains or losses, such as those generated by the investment portfolio, must be amortized over periods of not more than 15 years. The law requires that experience gains and losses be determined at least once every three years and that market values be reflected in the portfolio valuation. While some sponsors quote the portfolio holdings at year-end

---

[4] For a detailed discussion of funding methods, actuarial assumptions and asset valuation methods see Jack L. Treynor, Patrick J. Regan, and William W. Priest, Jr., *The Financial Reality of Pension Funding Under ERISA* (Homewood, Ill.: Dow Jones-Irwin, 1976). © 1976 by Dow Jones-Irwin, Inc.

market values, many use a three- or five-year moving average or use cost plus a portion of unrealized gains or losses. Before the investment manager structures the portfolio he should know how gains and losses are going to be handled in the actuarial valuation.

The pension liability figure is the present value of benefits that are expected to be paid. As such, it involves a lot of unknown variables, like the expected investment return on the portfolio, the expected level and growth of salaries and benefits, mortality, disability and turnover. These estimates are called actuarial assumptions and they are determined by the sponsor and the actuary, based on recent experience and future projections. Most plans are of the "final pay" variety, where the retirement benefit is a function of the individual's final or highest three or five year's earnings. Although wages and salaries have been growing at a 7 percent to 8 percent annual rate for several years, most companies apply earnings growth assumptions in the 4 percent to 6 percent range. The expected investment returns or interest rate assumptions are in the 5 percent to 7 percent range, even though government securities and high grade bonds have been yielding much more than that. There should be a close correlation between interest rates and the rate of growth of earnings and salaries, since both are affected by inflation. Short-term interest rates are heavily influenced by the policies of the Federal Reserve Board but long-term rates reflect the long-term expectation for inflation plus a risk premium of 200 to 300 basis points. Wages and salaries tend to grow at the same expected rate of inflation plus a 100 to 200 basis point premium for worker productivity. Hence, it is not surprising that the typical company has a wage and salary growth assumption that is a bit less than its investment return assumption. This is illustrated by Table 2. Michael Clowes of *Pensions & Investments* conducted a study of the pension assets of the 100 largest employe benefit plans in late 1977. Table 2 is based on actuarial data he gathered on 39 of those major companies.[5] The companies are ranked in order of their investment return assumptions. The median expected return was 6 percent, but the figures ranged from Armco Steel's 8.5 percent to the conservative 4.75 percent assumption of IBM and United Air Lines. Although the median expected annual growth of wages and salaries was 5 percent, the range was 2.25 percent to 8.4 percent. As shown by the table, there were some cases where the salary assumption exceeded the investment return assumption and there were other cases where the investment assumption was several hundred basis points above the salary assumption. These spreads are important and the mistake that many people make it to focus on the investment return assumption. Until the late 1960s,

---

[5] *Pensions & Investments* (January 2, 1978). The Clowes study and this table were discussed in Patrick J. Regan, "Pension Funds Grapple With the Asset Mix Decision," *Financial Analysts Journal,* (May-June 1978).

Table 2
Investment and Salary Growth Assumptions of Major Corporate
Pension Plans

Company	Investment Return Assumption	Salary Growth Assumption
Armco Steel	8.5%	6.0%
Exxon	7.5	6.0
B. F. Goodrich	7.0	7.0
TWA	7.0	6.0
Bethlehem Steel	7.0	4.0
Standard Oil Calf.	7.0	4.0
U.S. Steel	7.0	Range 3.5 to 4.0
Westinghouse	7.0	N.A.
American Cyanamid	6.5	N.A.
Eastman Kodak	6.25	5.0
Citibank	6.0	Range 3.3 to 8.4
Sun Co.	6.0	5.5
Union Carbide	6.0	5.3
Gulf Oil	6.0	Range 2.3 to 8.3
Minn. Mining & Mfg.	6.0	5.0
Mobil Oil	6.0	5.0
General Dynamics	6.0	Range 3.5 to 6.0
Chrysler	6.0	3.0
General Motors	6.0	3.0
Republic Steel	6.0	2.5
E. I. duPont	6.0	N.A.
Ford	6.0	N.A.
General Electric	6.0	N.A.
Goodyear	6.0	N.A.
International Harvester	6.0	N.A.
Travelers	6.0	N.A.
Commonwealth Edison	5.5	6.5
Consolidated Edison	5.5	Range 4.0 to 6.0
Cities Service	5.5	5.0
Sperry Rand	5.5	4.5
International Paper	5.5	3.5
RCA	5.0 to 6.0	N.A.
United Technologies	5.5	N.A.
Mountain States Tel	5.0	3.5
Pacific Northwest Bell	5.0	3.5
Western Electric	5.0	3.5
Texaco	5.0	3.0
IBM	4.75	N.A.
United Airlines	4.75	N.A.

Source: *Pension & Investments* (January 2, 1978).

most companies were using return assumptions of 4 percent or so. In recent years, plan sponsors have boosted those assumptions to the 6 percent to 7 percent range, raising the salary growth assumptions in tandem to keep pace with inflation. A 1 percentage point boost in the investment return assumption reduces pension costs and liabilities by 15 percent to 25 percent. However, raising the salary assumption only carries about two-thirds the impact of changing the invest-

Table 3
Relative Growth of Pension Costs and Unfunded Liabilities

	1973	1974	1975	1976	1977
Growth of pension costs	14.5%	19.5%	14.7%	20.5%	8.5%
Pension costs as percentage of payroll	NA*	6.5%	6.7%	6.8%	6.7%
Pre-tax profits per dollar of pension contribution	$7.00	$5.45	$4.41	$5.45	$4.88
Unfunded past service costs as percentage of net worth	15.0%	19.0%	24.0%	25.5%	26.0%
Unfunded vested benefits as percentage of net worth	0.0%	5.0%	5.5%	7.5%	8.0%
Unfunded vested benefits as percentage of pension assets	NA*	29.0%	17.0%	24.5%	28.0%

* NA = not available.
Source: *1978 BEA Pension Survey*. Based on median figures from a sample of 40 major corporations.

ment assumption by a similar amount, since the former only affects the liability owed to the active workers while the latter affects all plan members. Thus, the more mature the plan and the lower the ratio of active to inactive members, the more a sponsor can benefit by raising both the investment return assumption and the salary growth assumption by the same absolute amount.

The investment manager who obtains answers to these questions will have a good idea of the plan's needs. But he should also consider the financial position of the sponsor. If the industry is mature and cyclical, if pension contributions are large relative to payroll and pretax profits and if unfunded liabilities are large relative to pension assets and net worth, the sponsor may not be able to afford to pursue an aggressive investment policy. Table 3 shows some average cost and liability figures for a sample of 40 major corporations over the last five years.[6] Retirement costs are a labor expense, and the key ratio watched by actuaries is pension costs as a percentage of payroll. The figures shown in the table indicates that this ratio is very stable, falling in the 6 percent to 7 percent range for major companies. However, these payroll figures were taken from annual reports and include all employees, some of whom are not covered by pension plans. If you relate pension contributions to "covered" payroll, the figures fall in the 9 percent to 12 percent range. Another important ratio is pension contributions as a percentage of pretax profits, which shows how sensitive the company's bottom line can be to changes in pension contributions. Adding the two components together and dividing by the

---

[6] The table is based upon the annual *BEA Pension Surveys* compiled by BEA Associates, Inc. This table appeared in Patrick J. Regan, "Why the Sudden Concern Over Pension Costs and Unfunded Liabilities?" *Financial Analysts Journal* (January-February 1978).

pension contribution yields a pension coverage ratio. As shown by the table, the average company reports about five dollars of pretax profit for every dollar of pension contributions, for a coverage ratio of six to one.

The final factor to be considered is the magnitude of the unfunded liabilities. These unfunded past service costs and unfunded vested benefits should be related to pension assets (for another coverage ratio) and to net worth, since there could be potential claims against the sponsor in the event of a plan termination. As shown by the table, unfunded past service costs had stabilized at 26 percent of net worth at the end of 1977, with unfunded vested benefits at 8 percent of net worth and 28 percent of pension assets. Most pension plans are well funded, but an examination of the methods and techniques used in the calculation of the data will be needed if the figures are unusually large. As a benchmark, about one company in twenty will have (1) pension contributions rising by 40 percent or more in a given year; (2) pension contributions totaling more than 11 percent of total payroll or 20 percent of covered payroll; (3) unfunded vested benefits in excess of 30 percent of net worth or 100 percent of pension assets; or (4) unfunded past service costs equal to more than the average of the last three year's pretax profits.

SUMMARY

In sum, an investment manager can gain a better understanding of the investment needs of a retirement plan by considering the type of sponsor, the type of plan, projections regarding the growth and maturity of the work force, the magnitude of the cost and liability figures and the methods and techniques used to compute those numbers. This data can then be related to the financial position of the sponsor. With the sponsor's risk tolerance and risk preference against this background, the investment manager can structure a portfolio that is more or less aggressive than its typical account, which itself will change with the manager's perception of the capital markets.

APPENDIX

Companies Offering Pension Planning Services

There are many firms that offer pension planning services. Actuaries focus on the projection of pension liabilities while brokerage firms like A. G. Becker and Merrill Lynch concentrate on the measurement of investment results. Among the companies that offer pension simulation models, which project liabilities as well as assets, are the following:

William A. Dreher
Peat, Marwick Mitchell & Co.
345 Park Avenue
New York, N.Y. 10022

Rogers, Casey & Barksdale, Inc.
1234 Summer Street
Stamford, Connecticut 06905

Wilshire Associates Inc.
100 Wilshire Boulevard
Santa Monica, California 90401

Among the firms that offer related pension consulting services are
the following:

The Boston Company, Inc.
One Boston Place
Boston, Massachusetts 02106

Buck Pension Fund Services, Inc.
Two Pennsylvania Plaza
New York, New York 10001

Callan Associates, Inc.
601 California Street
San Francisco, California 94108

Collins Associates
567 San Nicolas Drive
Newport Beach, California 92660

Evaluation Associates, Inc.
25 Sylvan Road South
Westport, Connecticut 06880

Gifford Fong Associates
233 Wilshire Boulevard, Suite 303
Santa Monica, California 90401

Hewitt Associates
100 Half Day Road
Lincolnshire, Illinois 60015

Kwasha Lipton, Inc.
429 Sylvan Avenue
Englewood Cliffs, New Jersey 07632

Meidinger & Assoctes, Inc.
2440 Grinstead Drive
Louisville, Kentucky 40204

Frank Russell Co., Inc.
1100 Washington Plaza
Tacoma, Washington 98402

Chapter 27

Municipal and State Pension Plans

THOMAS P. BLEAKNEY

Vice President and Consulting Actuary
Milliman & Robertson, Inc.
Seattle, Washington

In 1976 Louis M. Kohlmeier prepared an excellent monograph for the Twentieth Century Fund regarding conflicts of interest in managing the investments of public pension funds.[1] He discusses a number of examples of conflict of interest, such as a pension fund of a governmental unit purchasing the securities issued by the unit, or employing brokers and banks having political or other ties to the officials managing the fund.

These and other topics are dealt with at some length in Kohlmeier's work, but it is noteworthy that he begins his summary chapter with a dissertation on a much more subtle conflict of interest, that involving the funding of a public employe retirement program. Although this topic may seem somewhat afield from the main thrust of Kohlmeier's theme or from this, a text on management of investments, a discussion of funding helps to put in focus the characteristics which set public pension funds aside from other investment funds, and particularly from private pension plans.

FUNDING

The question of whether to fund private plans in the United States is academic. Federal law now requires private pension plans to set aside adequate assets on a regular basis to pay for retirement benefits

---

[1] Kohlmeier, Louis M., *Conflicts of Interest: State and Local Pension Fund Asset Management* (New York: The Twentieth Century Fund, 1976).

more or less as they accrue. The actual process can be quite complex, dependent upon the actuarial cost method being used by the plan, but the goal of any acceptable funding method under the federal law must be the same: to assure adequate funds at retirement to pay for all of the benefits accrued.

This concept—setting aside funds during active employment to build up the funds needed to pay benefits after retirement—is called "funding." The contrasting concept, "pay-as-you-go financing," causes the costs of the pension plan to be incurred only as the benefits are actually paid out. Although theoretical arguments can be made for pay-as-you-go financing, they have become moot for private pension plans under federal law.

This is not the case in the public sector. At the time of this writing there is no federal legislation requiring funding of public pension systems. Although most such systems in the United States practice funding to some extent, this is by no means a universal characteristic, with the financing of a number of major public systems at or near the pay-as-you-go level.

There are many classic arguments for funding. Funding gives an employee assets to look to as a source of the benefits accrued under the pension plan. Funding charges to the proper accounting period the retirement benefits accrued during that period. A corollary of that argument is that funding is a discipline on the employer to prevent promising more benefits than can be afforded. Another argument is that funding reduces the cost to the employer of the pension plan, since the return on investments pays part of the cost of the benefits that are ultimately disbursed.

If these arguments become sufficiently persuasive to the plan sponsor, adequate funding will occur. For a public retirement system, the governing statute or municipal ordinance may specify a method of financing the system so as to require funding. Even where funding is not actually required by law, it may become so ingrained as a matter of practice that it is essentially unthinkable that funding will not occur.[2] In these instances, the investment manager can count on the assets of the pension fund growing in a predictable manner for an extended period of time. Dependable growth simplifies the management of pension funds, since disinvestment is rarely required and liquidity is therefore not a significant consideration in setting investment goals.

Unfortunately, economic circumstances may cause some sponsors of public pension plans to cut back on scheduled contributions to the

---

[2] Continued funding may even create legal rights preventing future discontinuance. The Pennsylvania Supreme Court, in *Dombrowski* v. *Philadelphia,* 431 Pa. 199, 245A.2d 238 (1968), ruled that an employee has a contractual right to have the retirement system covering him or her properly funded, and that such funding therefore could not be curtailed.

pension fund. This type of uncertainty adds to the challenge faced by the investment manager of a public pension fund, since the possibility exists that assets of the fund must be sold at some time to pay for the benefits then coming due.

Even public pension systems with long traditions of funding are not completely free from such hazards. For example, in Washington State the two largest retirement systems have a long history of adequate funding, as a result of statutory requirements, reinforced by continuing pressure by public employe groups to maintain sound retirement systems. During a period of economic slump in the state in the early 1970s, however, the governor proposed converting the financing of the systems to a method closely approximating pay-as-you-go. A consulting actuarial firm was retained and issued a report stating that "there is nothing morally wrong or actuarially unsound in the plan." The governor's budget office argued that elimination of funding would pose no harzard to promised benefits, since the state's perpetual life and general taxing authority prevent any default on its commitment to pay pensions as they become due.

The governor's proposal did not prevail. What did emerge, though, were some object lessons about public pension systems and the environment in which they operate. The primary lesson for an investment manager is of a basic distinction between private and public pension plans. Sponsors of private pension plans do not have the option of abruptly cutting off contributions to their funds. Because of the sovereignty of the state, however, a change of heart of the sort discussed above can result in legislation overriding existing funding policy.[3] When this happens, the investment manager faces a disruption in expected cash flow and either drastically reduced levels of investment or actual disinvestment.

The investment manager must also be aware of how quickly public opinion can shift, and be prepared to deal with the change. In the Washington example, the state's leading newspaper was impressed with the governor's arguments in 1971, saying "that no irreparable harm would come from the Legislature's accepting [the governor's] . . . recommendations." It took just three years for that paper to change its tune. As part of the paper's review of the public pension problems which had their genesis in the furor surrounding the governor's proposals, that same newspaper called for pension reform and decried the unfunded debts of the public pension funds.

There is another point to be made from the Washington situation. One of the arguments used by the governor was that certain social

---

[3] As pointed out in footnote (2), employees may have implied contractual rights as a safeguard against such legislative action. However, enforcement of those rights through litigation may consume much time, during which the investment manager faces the problems discussed in the text.

advantages would be gained by not funding. By avoiding the increase in taxes needed to pay for pension commitments, money would not be frozen into investments, a large portion of which would be out of state. This argument implies a form of socially useful investing—pay-as-you-go financing leaves money with the taxpayers for their use, rather than locking it up in investments allocated to pension needs. The topic of socially useful investing is discussed in greater detail later in this chapter. First, though, a broader view will be taken of investments held by state and local retirement systems.

INVESTMENTS HELD BY PUBLIC SYSTEMS

Table 1 presents a summary of the asset mix of public employee retirement systems in the United States in 1977, based upon data compiled by the Bureau of Census. Although the state-administered systems represented less than 7 percent of the total systems counted by the Bureau of Census, they held more than 75 percent of the assets and covered more than 85 percent of the membership.

It is noteworthy that over 10 percent of the assets of locally administered systems are invested in state and local bonds. In many instances, these bonds are those issued by the municipality or other political

Table 1
Assets of State and Local Retirement Systems, 1977

	In billions		
	State-Administered	*Locally-Administered*	*All Systems*
Federal bonds	$ 9.5	$ 2.7	$ 12.2
State and local bonds	0.6	3.0	3.6
Total government bonds	$10.1	$ 5.7	$ 15.8
Corporate bonds	45.4	11.5	56.8
Mortgages	10.2	0.7	10.9
Corporate stocks	21.7	6.2	28.0
Other	7.5	4.5	12.0
Total	$94.9	$28.6	$123.5
	As percent of total		
Federal bonds	10.0%	9.4%	9.9%
State and local bonds	0.6	10.5	2.9
Total government bonds	10.6%	19.9%	12.8%
Corporate bonds	47.8	40.2	46.0
Mortgages	10.7	2.4	8.8
Corporate stocks	22.9	21.7	22.7
Other	7.9	15.7	9.7
Total	100.0%	100.0%	100.0%

Note: Because of rounding, detail may not add to totals. Each public system's figures are as of its fiscal year ended in first half of 1977 or last half of 1976.
Source: U.S. Bureau of Census, 1977 Census of Governments.

subdivision for whose employees the retirement system is maintained. A well-publicized example of such a situation can be found in New York City, where 30 percent of the assets of the city's retirement systems are state and local bonds, according to the census report. Most of these are in Municipal Assistance Corporation bonds issued to help save the city from bankruptcy. Although there are some vestiges in other communities of investments in municipal bonds by local pension funds, the census report indicated that only in Montana were such holdings of any substance. In Montana, 36 percent of the investments of the scattered, local public pension funds were in state and local securities. Outside of Montana and New York, no other state had more than 5 percent of the assets of its locally administered systems invested in state and local government securities.

The New York City situation was certainly unique at the time of the 1977 census, and it is to be hoped that it will remain so. Nevertheless, the question of investments by a municipality's pension fund in securities issued by the municipality deserves further comment. At least three substantial objections can be raised to the practice:

1. Purchase of local bonds (particularly revenue bonds) by a retirement fund may be a subsidy of an otherwise unsupportable municipal venture.
2. Substantial holdings of local bonds might aggravate the burden of extricating a community from a fiscal problem if the community's tax resources become sorely pressed and it defaults on its bonds.
3. Yields on municipal bonds tend to be significantly lower than yields on other investments, due to the tax-free status such bonds possess when they are held by private investors.

With respect to the last point above, it is axiomatic that any investor wishes to obtain the maximum yield on an investment with reasonable safety. The importance of this to public employe retirement systems can be emphasized by comparing investment return with the taxes required to support the systems. For this purpose, it is interesting to analyze the investment return of the systems covered by the 1977 Census of Governments (compare Table 1). The total investment return for the 1977 fiscal years of these systems, excluding capital gains, was $7.7 billion. Based on the average assets of the respective systems, the total earnings and annual rates of return on investments were as shown in the following table:

	Earnings on Investments (in billions)	Annual Rate of Return
State-administered systems	$6.17	7.19%
Locally-administered systems	1.58	6.04
All systems	$7.74	6.93%

During the same year, the total governmental contributions to support the systems was $12.37 billion. If it were possible to increase the rate of yield by 1 percent, the earnings on investments would have increased by $1.12 billion, or over 9 percent of the governmental contribution to the plans. Such an increase in yield in all systems may be incompatible with the maintenance of appropriate safety of principal, but it does not seem unreasonable to hypothesize that the locally administered systems could have brought their rate of yield up to the level attained by the state-administered systems. If this had occurred, an additional $300 million of earnings on investments could have been generated for those systems or, again, about 9 percent of their total level of employer contributions.

In some public systems, particularly the smaller ones, the potential for increasing investment return and thereby reducing future taxes has probably been the victim of bureaucratic neglect. Too often, however, this stereotype of governmental mismanagement has been misapplied to well-managed investment funds of public systems. It is particu-

Table 2
Assets of United States Retirement Plans

	In billions		
	Public Retirement Systems		*Private Pension Plans*
	1967	*1977*	*1977*
Federal bonds	$ 6.7	$ 12.2	$ 18.6
State and local bonds	2.4	3.6	—
Total government bonds	$ 9.1	$ 15.8	—
Corporate bonds	20.3	56.8	41.7*
Mortgages	4.8	10.9	2.5
Corporate stocks	2.4	28.0	98.0
Other	2.7	12.0	11.9
Total	$39.3	$123.5	$172.7
	As percent of total		
Federal bonds	17.0%	9.9%	10.8%
State and local bonds	6.1	2.9	—
Total government bonds	23.2%	12.8%	—
Corporate bonds	51.7	46.0	24.1*
Mortgages	12.2	8.8	1.4
Corporate stocks	6.1	22.7	56.7
Other	6.9	9.7	6.9
Total	100.0%	100.0%	100.0%

Note: Because of rounding, detail may not add to totals. Each public system's figures are as of its fiscal year ended in first half of given year or last half of previous year. Figures for private plans are as of June 30.

* Figures for corporate bonds held by private pension plans may include small holdings of state and local bonds.

Sources: U.S. Bureau of Census, *1977 Census of Governments;* Security and Exchange Commission, series Q-320, *Statistical Bulletin* (various issues).

larly instructive to view the overall picture, both with respect to changes that have occurred in recent years, and in comparison with the investment practices of private pension plans.

INVESTMENT TRENDS

Table 2 summarizes the distribution of assets of public and private pension plans in 1977, and of public funds ten years earlier. A significant trend towards more aggressive investment practices is evident for public systems during the ten-year period. The government bond segment, as a percentage of the total assets, has dropped nearly in half, to slightly over one-eighth of the total. This represents a continuation of a trend which had been evidenced earlier. In 1960, for example, government bonds comprised more than half of the total assets of all state and local retirement systems.

As discussed earlier, there is one exception to the movement away from government bonds among the public systems. The locally administered systems continue to have substantial holdings of state and local bonds. During the ten years ended in 1977, that category of investment showed an increase in dollar amount (although declining as a percentage of the total investment). However, it must be emphasized that the statistics presented in Table 2 are heavily influenced by New York City's portfolio. If the assets of the New York City retirement systems were omitted from both studies, the holdings of state and local bonds by public retirement systems would be as follows:

	1967	1977
	In billions	
State-administered systems	$0.7	$0.6
Locally-administered systems	0.3	0.1
All systems	$1.0	$0.7
	As percent of total	
State-administered systems	2.5%	0.6%
Locally-administered systems	4.4	0.5
All systems	2.9%	0.6%

The much more aggressive investment posture of state and local systems is evident from the enormous growth in the corporate stock segment shown in Table 2. In dollar amounts, the decade ended in 1977 showed more than a tenfold increase in such securities. As a percentage of the total portfolio, the increase was nearly fourfold, from 6 percent to nearly 23 percent. Unfortunately, this was not a good period for common stocks, with the result that some rethinking of this philosophy has occurred. Nevertheless, it is clear that common stocks are in the investment portfolios of these systems as a permanent and major fixture.

Another trend that is evident from Table 2 is the enormous growth in the dollar-value of the investments held by state and local systems. In 1977, public retirement systems held over three times the assets they held in 1967, representing an annual growth rate of over 12 percent. During the same period, the assets of private pension plans grew from $68 billion to $173 billion, an annual growth rate of about 10 percent. In common stocks, the annual rate of growth of public systems was 28 percent, compared to a 12 percent growth rate for private plans in the same category.

Such rates of growth in the public sector cannot continue indefinitely, but even at a reduced rate they have become a major factor in the national economy. Questions have been raised concerning the financial power held by the public retirement systems, and of potential problems associated with having such securities controlled by the boards and administrators of public pension systems. Although such questions are largely beyond the scope of this text, they will undoubtedly be discussed with increasing frequency in the coming years.

INVESTMENT POWERS

The recent growth in assets of public pension systems has accompanied a trend away from rigidly defining the investment powers of these systems and towards allowing their investment managers greater discretion in performing their duties. Unfortunately, statistics quantifying this trend are not readily available, but a 1974 survey carried out by the Chase Manhattan Bank cast some light on the nature of the trend.[4] Of the 161 funds responding to the survey, 51 percent indicated they had the authority to delegate some portion of their investment power. Of these 51 percent, the majority had the right to delegate full investment discretion if they were so inclined.

Arguments can be made on both sides of whether a public pension fund should have the right to delegate its investment discretion. Administrative expenses will generally be lower where investments are managed in-house. One specific way for a large system to save such expense is to set up index funds, such as have been established in the states of New York and Washington. Such funds are designed to parallel the theoretical portfolios used as guides to the performance of the stock market. Since managing an index fund becomes largely mechanical, with little or no discretion, the professional investment manager is not needed where such a fund is used.

---

[4] *Public Pension Funds—A Financing Survey* (New York: The Chase Manhattan Bank, 1974).

Another reason for internal fund management reflects the fiduciary responsibilities of the members of a board governing a public pension system; it could be argued that fulfillment of such responsibilities requires the board to retain all investment discretion. Still another argument for managing a public system's investments in-house is that the system, and particularly the board, are responsible to the taxpayers, but that such responsiveness does not readily extend to discretionary fund managers.

That very point is one of the prime arguments to be used for delegating discretionary authority. If the board has passed along investment discretion to an outside manager, the manager is shielded to some extent from the counterproductive pressures to invest in securities of local interest which may be more risky or lower yielding.

Certainly a major argument for outside investment management is that the quality of the investment decision is likely to be improved. Most public employe retirement systems are too small to maintain an adequate investment staff. Thus they might be better advised to allocate the same portion of their administrative budget to retain part-time investment counsel as would be needed to hire full-time persons of lesser professional expertise. Moreover, even in larger systems, attracting personnel of top professional quality may be difficult because of civil service restrictions, the adversities which accompany a job in the spotlight of public criticism, and possible limitations on a person's professional future.

As discussed earlier, the Chase Manhattan survey revealed a trend towards greater delegation of investment authority. Even more revealing of the liberalization of investment authority were the survey's statistics regarding the trends in authorized investments in common stocks. These statistics are summarized in Table 3. Particularly significant is the fact that the percentage of the surveyed systems authorized to invest more than 20 percent in common stocks went up sixfold in the ten years ended in 1974, from 14 percent to 84 percent. Similarly,

Table 3
Authorized Common Stock Investments of Responding State and Local Retirement Systems

Percentage of Total Portfolio	1964	1969	1974
20 percent or less...........	86%	59%	16%
21–40 percent	6	17	41
41–60 percent	5	18	16
61–80 percent	—	2	7
More than 80 percent	3	4	20
	100%	100%	100%

Source: *Public Pension Funds—A Financing Survey* (New York: The Chase Manhattan Bank, 1974).

the percentage authorized to exceed 40 percent went up over fivefold, from 8 percent to 43 percent. If the group responding to the survey can be considered typical of the entire public employee retirement system universe, a major share of the shackles placed on investment managers has been removed.

This is not to say that all of the restrictions have been removed. It is still common to find detailed specifications regarding investment powers in the statutes governing public employee systems. For example, the largest accumulation of investments under a single management among the nation's public employe retirement systems is that of California's two major systems, with assets of about $16 billion. These funds are subject to three tiers of restrictions:

1. *Constitutional:* For example, common stocks may not aggregate more than 25 percent of the fund, and must be of corporations qualifying by, among other things, paying cash dividends in eight of the ten years preceding investment.
2. *Statutory:* Generally the statutes allow the same investments as are authorized for savings banks in the state, but with several specified exceptions.
3. *Administrative:* Categories of acceptable investments of the systems are spelled out by board resolutions, including details of acceptable bond ratings, property standards and credit risks for mortgages, restrictions on commercial loans, etc.

Similar provisions in some state laws restrict investments to those authorized for life insurance companies doing business in the state. Probably the most common type of provision, however, is one specifying a long legal list. Such detailed specifications reflect legislative concern for the safety of the principal of the pension funds and are intended to assure conservative investment practices. This very concern, however, may work to the disadvantage of the fund by placing the investment manager in a straight jacket and unduly restricting the fund from taking advantage of changing investment opportunities.

In some instances, such heavily-structured restrictions on investments are designed to protect pension systems from making poor investments because of inexpertise. State laws for this purpose are common in states having a number of small systems, with correspondingly small (or nonexistent) investment staffs. Another approach to dealing with such situations is to set up a centralized investment authority. Certainly among the most successful examples of such an approach is that used in Wisconsin. The State of Wisconsin Investment Board manages the investments of nearly all of the major public employee retirement funds in the state. The assets are commingled so that the responsibility of the Board is that of managing a single multibillion dollar fund. Combining the various investment functions into a single entity provides the economies of size needed to develop a professional investment staff.

Just one of the many advantages of centralizing investment authority is exemplified by the cash management methods used by the Wisconsin Board. Because of the immense size of the fund and the nature of its cash flow, the fund has a multimillion dollar float which can be used for investment purposes. The additional income available to the funds from just this single source is measured in the hundreds of thousands of dollars per year.

POLITICAL CONSIDERATIONS

It is not unreasonable to speculate that the investment managers of some public systems welcome a highly-structured statutory investment authority, to shield them from the political repercussions of poor performance in a more discretionary environment. This is but one of the many manifestations of politics on the investments of public employee retirement systems.

Any analysis of public and private pension plans must take note of the major distinction between them that is the result of political considerations. In the private sector, aggressive investment managers will generally have the opportunity to explain the dips and valleys in their investment results. If they are doing a good job in the long run, they need not be concerned about short-term deficiencies. In the public sector, on the other hand, investment managers must constantly be looking over their shoulders at what the public may say about a market decline that temporarily drives down the value of the funds they are managing.

Nowhere is Monday morning quarterbacking more evident than in the public sector. It is the right of the public to know, and the newspapers and other segments of the media are always ready to oblige, particularly when results have been poor. Obviously, this phenomenon has its good features, in keeping those responsible for investments on their toes, but it also has its drawbacks. Chief among the latter is the artificial restriction imposed on the more venturesome of investments. Managers influenced by the prospect of adverse publicity and public criticism tend to opt for the safe route. In the environment of the 1970s, at least, the safe route has been favorable, at least to the extent that fixed income securities outperformed equities. How this will work out in the long run, of course, each must judge personally.

SOCIALLY USEFUL INVESTING

Political influence is one of the attributes of the gold fish bowl in which investments of public pension funds operate. Another might be labeled "socially useful investing." For example, public funds in some states have been urged to adopt a policy prohibiting investment in firms operating in some countries of southern Africa, because of their racial policies. One such state is Oregon, where the Oregon Investment Council was ordered by the State Board of Higher Education to sell all of the Board's investments in companies operating in southern Africa. Although the Board operates an endowment fund, not a pension fund, the issues are clearly related to pension issues, since the Investment Council also invests for the Public Employees Retirement Fund of the State.

The Oregon Board's prohibition was directed at companies employing more than 50 persons, earning more than $500,000 from business operations, or having fixed assets or loans in excess of $500,000 in southern Africa. The Attorney General disputed the Board's order, stating that the Board does not have the powers to direct such investments or sales. Its powers are limited to guidelines concerning the proportion of the funds to be invested in common stock and other investments, along with general recommendations regarding investment objectives. However, the Investment Council itself has the ultimate discretion to buy or sell, subject to the statutory prudent-man rule. At the time of this writing, the Attorney General's opinion has been disputed and is headed for resolution in the courts.

Obviously this type of problem is not limited to public plans. Pressures to alter business practices have been brought by stockholders and even purchasers of the products of the corporations whose stock is being boycotted. Similarly, large, private pension funds, particularly those with some degree of public visibility, are subject to similar pressures. Nevertheless, the bulk of the activity along this line has been, and undoubtedly will continue to be, in the area of public funds, for several reasons:

1. Public pension funds generally involve elected officials in their management. Those who would attempt to bring about social changes through investment pressure will find elected officials prime targets. Their votes will generally be a matter of public record, and can become a campaign issue if the particular social goal is sufficiently attractive to the voters.
2. Appointed board members are also in the public eye. Although the pressures are not as direct, such board members do not have available the same cloak of anonymity as, for example, would be available to a trustee of a private pension plan.
3. A large number of pension board meetings are held in public. "Sunshine" laws mandating open meetings have become common. Actions taken at open meetings are known immediately. Moreover, pressures can easily be brought at such public meetings by atten-

dance of a large number of activists interested in a particular issue.
4. Pension funds involving higher education faculty are particularly susceptible to pressures. Traditionally, the college campus has been the forum for discussion of many of the issues which become translated into actions of social nature. As a consequence, pension funds (as well as endowment funds) of colleges and universities are logical targets for those trying to bring about social changes.

The tactic of selling or failing to buy securities issued by a company being boycotted is one method which tries to bring about social change by investment practices. Another method involves the exercise of stockholders' privileges on issues held by a pension fund. For example, the stockholders in a company may be asked to vote on a potential merger with another company. If the social practices of the second company has some taint, pressure may be exerted on the board directing a public pension fund to cast the votes of the stock held by the fund against the merger, regardless of the potential investment advantage that might otherwise arise.

Upon occasion, specific issues of a social nature will be brought to a stockholder vote, often as a result of stockholders' initiative. For example, stockholders of International Business Machines Corporation, the largest common stock holding of public employee retirement funds, have been asked in recent years to vote on limiting the company's charitable contributions involving animal experimentation, restricting sale of computers in South American (and, in a separate resolution, South African) countries where the equipment may be used for abridging human rights, and changing the corporation's rules regarding political activities of its employees. Pressures can be brought to cast the proxies of a public pension fund for or against an issue, regardless of the effect the vote might have upon the potential investment value of the stock.

One rather interesting approach to the question of how proxies should be voted is the concept of enforced neutrality. This was proposed by a legislator in California following controversial proxy voting on common stock controlled by the Board of Regents of the University of California. If the bill had passed, it would have required that all proxies be voted 50 percent in favor and 50 percent against each measure.

Another form of socially useful investing mandates investments in the state or community of the pension fund. Such funds might be in the form of low-rate mortgages to encourage the local homebuilding industry and to provide better housing for the area's citizens. The investments might also be for marginal industries which need support that would not be available in the general investment market.

A type of local investment discussed earlier was that by New York pension funds in securities bolstering New York City's finances at a time when the city was approaching bankruptcy. Some would not classify this type of investment as a socially useful investment, although its purpose is similar to that of encouraging local industry or providing improved living conditions for local citizens—a subsidy out of pension funds for the local community.

Sometimes the pros and cons of such actions are difficult to sort out. The New York City investments were apparently needed to save the city from financial disaster which, in turn, could have resulted in unemployment for those employees whose pensions are involved. However, the financial managers and ultimately the boards must weigh carefully their responsibilities in all social investments. One salient commentary on the topic appeared as an editorial in *Pensions & Investments,* July 15, 1974:

> [A socially-related investment decision may make] sense from an investment point of view, on the ground that a management which acts in a socially irresponsible manner may be irresponsible in other ways also, and additionally, if the management is fending off social responsibility groups, antitrust and antipollution suits, etc., it won't be running the company well.
>
> Nevertheless, we think that pension funds thinking of dropping stocks for reasons of social conscience should consider their actions very carefully. How does such an action fare under the prudent man rule and the exclusive benefit rule? We don't know, but it's something to consider.
>
> Pension funds should bear in mind that their primary concern is to achieve the best possible rate of growth of assets so as to guarantee the promised pensions. If applying pressure on corporations for more socially responsible behavior through a boycott of the company's stock is likely to affect the fund's performance, then we feel there are better ways of influencing corporate behavior . . .
>
> [There are] two different but related issues . . . [Who] should say how the shareholder voting rights controlled by the funds should be voted? . . . [Should] some of the funds . . . be set aside for social betterment purposes, such as low-cost housing[?]
>
> On the first question, we see no need for legislated guidelines or a new board to make proxy decisions. We feel that fund trustees, because of their familiarity with the investment needs of their fund, and with the affairs of the companies whose stocks are represented in the fund, can handle the decisions probably better than a group of outsiders.
>
> On the second question, we feel the best way for pension funds to directly serve the cause of social betterment is by investing in the most efficient and productive enterprises in the economy, thus contributing to economic growth . . . [This] will insure adequate pensions for pension plan members. And insuring that the nation's retired workers have an adequate retirement income is an important social responsibility too.
>
> Only after that responsibility has been fulfilled should pension funds turn their attention to other relevant social causes.

SUMMARY

The issue of socially useful investing is only one of the problems faced by investment managers of public employee retirement systems. It and other problems grow from the open environment in which public funds operate and from the political pressures that can be brought to bear on the investment manager. Another challenge to the investment manager is the lingering threat of unscheduled reduction of employer contributions, altering investment plans, and possibly even requiring unexpected disinvestment.

Another distinguishing characteristic of public pension funds is the aura of regulation and restriction of investment authority which is common among statutes governing public funds. Although there has been a trend towards more aggressive investments in recent years, public pension funds are still more conservatively invested than private pension funds.

Despite these restrictions (or perhaps because of them), public pension funds appear to have fared reasonably well in comparison to private pension funds. One indication of this can be found in the results of a continuing sample made of the funds it monitors by Merrill Lynch, Pierce, Fenner & Smith. For the five years ended in 1977, the median annual rates of return, on a market-to-market basis, of the public pension fund sample and the total sample were as follows:

	Public Pension Funds	All Funds
Bonds	6.7%	6.5%
Equities	−2.6	−3.2
Total	3.3%	0.0%

Obviously, the public pension funds were fortunate to be more heavily invested in bonds during this period, and this element was reflected in more favorable total returns. However, the better returns were also produced in the separate segments of the portfolios as well as the totals. To the extent these sample results transfer to the entire universe of pension plans, the investment managers of the public pension funds can look to their results with a substantial degree of satisfaction.

BIBLIOGRAPHY

Kohlmeier, Louis M. *Conflicts of Interest: State and Local Pension Fund Asset Management.* New York: The Twentieth Century Fund, 1976.

Pension World. "Annual Survey of State Retirement Systems." (Ongoing report, usually August or September issue each year.) Atlanta, Georgia.

Public Pension Funds: A Financing Survey. Greenwich, Connecticut: Greenwich Research Associates, n.d.

Securities and Exchange Commission. *Statistical Bulletin.* Washington, D.C.: U.S. Government Printing Office, ongoing report.

U.S. Department of Commerce, Bureau of the Census. *1977 Census of Governments.* vol. 6, Topical Studies, no. 1. Washington, D.C.: U.S. Government Printing Office.

U.S. House of Representatives, Committee on Education and Labor. *Pension Task Force Report on Public Employee Retirement Systems.* Washington, D.C.: U.S. Government Printing Office, 1978.

Chapter 28

Life Insurance Company Investments

J. ROBERT FERRARI*

Vice President and Chief Economist
Prudential Insurance Company of America
Newark, New Jersey

Life insurance companies are one of the most important institutional sources of financial capital in the U.S. economy, with $352 billion of assets at the end of 1977. The importance of the industry in the capital markets arises out of its broad range of financial security products that attract personal savings. The investment function involves the channeling of these accumulated funds into the financial markets in a manner that will earn the most advantageous returns consistent with the insurer's contractual obligations. The purpose of this chapter is to describe some of the basic operating, organizational, and regulatory aspects of the investment process in the leading life insurance companies.[1]

LIFE INSURANCE AND SAVINGS

The "whole life" policy and other cash value forms of life insurance create a reservoir of funds from accumulated premiums and investment income, which acts as a reserve to meet future contractual obligations. More specifically, the pool of funds arises because premiums

---

The author is indebted to Catherine Randazzo, Economist of the Prudential, for her assistance in the preparation of this paper.

[1] Life insurance is sold by about 1,750 companies in the United States; many are small companies operating in specific regions of the country. Aspects of this chapter dealing with company operating characteristics apply primarily to medium and large size companies that operate on a national basis, and account for the predominant share of invested assets in the industry.

paid during the early years of the contract exceed the initial outlays for benefits and expenses. In later years, when mortality costs mount and exceed periodic premium payments, the shortfall is made up by earlier premium surpluses and the investment income earned on this reserve. Group pension plans are another major reserve-generating product, and these products have experienced dynamic growth in the last 20 years. Unlike Social Security, which is based largely on an inter-generational transfer of funds, insured pension plans generate a large reserve of funds because of their actuarial funding of benefits to be paid in the future. Thus, pension plans, and related thrift and profit-sharing plans, represent an important vehicle through which private savings are accumulated in life insurance companies.

Savings through life insurance companies differ from savings in other thrift institutions (e.g., savings and loan associations and commercial and savings banks) because they are generally associated with long-term contractual arrangements and tend to be more stable and less subject to immediate withdrawal. Life insurance cash values are pay-able on demand as policy loans, and in periods of tight money these low-interest rate loans become a very convenient source of funds for policyholders. But, in general, life insurance savings are less return sensitive because they are committed to a broad financial security ar-rangement in which the savings element is only incidental to the basic purpose of securing permanent death protection with a level premium, even though the mortality risk increases with age.

Since the early 1960s, a significant development in the life insurance industry has been the introduction of "separate accounts" for the pur-pose of investing pension funds. These separate accounts are not subject to the same regulatory restrictions as the general account, which is the term used to describe the primary portfolio used for life insurance products and pension plans involving group annuity contracts. The initial impetus for separate accounts was to increase the industry's investment flexibility in providing common stock investments for pen-sion plans, since most states impose very stringent limits on the propor-tion of a company's general account that can be held in stocks. Now, however, we find insurers offering pooled separate accounts in publicly traded bonds, private placements, short-term money market instru-ments, real estate mortgages and properties, and even single client accounts especially tailored for larger employers. Several of the largest life insurance companies have been very aggressive in creating and marketing separate account products, but for the industry as a whole separate account assets represented less than 5 percent of total assets at the end of 1977. Because of the relatively small size and specialized nature of separate accounts, the predominant emphasis of this chapter is on general account investments.

SOURCES OF FUNDS FOR INVESTMENT

The sources of funds available for life insurance company investment are generated by both the insurance and investment operations. Investable funds from insurance operations are simply the difference between cash receipts (premiums, pension and annuity considerations, and other deposits); and cash disbursements (death and disability claims, pension and annuity payments, dividends, commissions, taxes, operating expenses, etc.). The investment portfolio itself produces sizable investable funds in two ways: (1) returns on assets from interest, dividends and realized capital gains, and (2) turnover of assets due to maturities, repayments, calls, and sales. Funds from turnover represent reinvestment of existing assets rather than net new funds, and normally account for 40 percent or more of the investable funds in the large companies. Annual investable funds from insurance and investment sources in recent years has averaged over 11 percent of total assets. The absolute magnitude of these cash flows, which in the largest companies exceed $4 billion a year, present a significant investment task.

The volatility of certain cash flow variables, particularly policy loans, optional mortgage repayments and group pension deposits, calls for a systematic forecast of investable funds as a logical starting point in the investment planning process. Most life companies prepare investable cash flow forecasts, typically for the next 12 to 24 months, with the techniques ranging from simple extrapolation to sophisticated forecasting models employing statistical relationships of cash flow variables with economic and financial variables. These projections are used to (1) determine in advance the allocation of funds among investment media and operating departments, (2) ensure the availability of funds for scheduled take-downs of forward commitments, (3) determine desirable minimum cash liquidity balances, and (4) indicate the need for investment in temporary, short-term investments or, alternately, the need for the possible sale of investments or borrowing.

INVESTMENT OBJECTIVES

Distribution of Assets and Liabilities

The investment objectives of life insurance companies are determined in large measure by the nature of the liabilities that arise from the wide variety of financial security products sold to the public. This is based on the fundamental principle of financial management that a firm's assets be structured in a form and with maturities reasonably consistent with the liabilities. A summary of the combined balance sheet for the life insurance industry is shown in Table 1 in order to

Table 1

1977 Balance Sheet Information
for the
Life Insurance Industry

	Amounts (in millions)		*Percentage (percent)*
Assets:			
Cash		2,130	0.6
Investments		330,671	94.0
Government securities	23,555		6.7
Corporate bonds	137,555		39.2
Corporate stocks	33,763		9.6
Mortgages	96,848		27.5
Real estate.............................	11,060		3.2
Policy loans	27,556		7.8
Other miscellaneous assets		18,921	5.4
Total assets		351,722	100.0
Liabilities:			
Reserve liabilities..........................		281,040	79.9
Health insurance reserves	8,329		2.4
Life insurance reserves	167,281		47.5
Annuity and pension reserves	100,888		28.7
Other	4,542		1.3
Accumulated policy dividends		10,427	3.0
Policy dividends payable		5,839	1.6
Mandatory securities valuation reserve		3,486	1.0
Other liabilities		27,313	7.8
Surplus.................................		21,669	6.2
Capital (stock companies)		1,948	0.5
Total liabilities and surplus		351,722	100.0

Source: Life Insurance Fact Book, 1978, American Council of Life Insurance. These data include $17.4 billion of assets, liabilities, and surplus of separate accounts.

give a more detailed picture of the asset-liability mix likely to be found in a fairly typical company.

The largest component of the life insurance industry's liabilities are the reserves which underly the contractual obligations to policyholders, individual and group annuitants, and beneficiaries. State laws generally prescribe the mortality tables, interest rates and methods for calculating these reserves. The composition of reserves has changed over time, reflecting change in the life insurance product. Although total reserves have increased steadily, the growth of pension business has been more rapid than that of life insurance, and consequently the proportion of reserves for annuity contracts has been rising.

A liability account closely related to investment operations is the Mandatory Securities Valuation Reserve (MSVR), which is established to cushion surplus against capital losses or market value declines on corporate debt instruments and preferred and common stocks. (The MSVR will be discussed further under "Insolvency Risk.")

The assets of a life insurance company are mostly investments of the funds accumulated under the outstanding contracts. As shown in Table 1, roughly 94 percent of the industry's assets are investments, predominately long-term corporate securities and mortgages. Other miscellaneous assets, which account for about 5 percent of the industry's total assets, include mostly accrued investment and premium income, and also investment in real estate joint ventures.

Basic Investment Characteristics

As already noted, reserve liabilities accumulated through level premium life insurance and insured pension plans constitute the bulk of the liabilities of a life insurance company. These liabilities are associated with contractual, long-term agreements in which the company promises to pay fixed-dollar amounts and guarantees a fixed rate of interest on policy reserves.

Accordingly, the bulk of the assets should be investments with similar characteristics, that is, they should be long-term, fixed-dollar instruments with yields at least equal to the rate guaranteed in the outstanding contracts. The majority of asset holdings are, in fact, long-term investments, although average maturities are usually shorter than the average duration of the insurance and pension liabilities, which are associated with contracts that may be in force 50 years or more. Thus, assets may turn over several times during the life of the outstanding contracts, and a secular decline in interest rates could result in reinvestment at yields lower than rates guaranteed in policies issued in earlier years. The risk can be minimized by dividend adjustments, conservative margins in interest rate assumptions, and new guaranteed rates. However, due to the secular rise in interest rates in the last 20 years or more, insurers have had no problems earning a return sufficient to cover the rate guaranteed in the life insurance contract.

Life insurance companies still face, however, the risk of not earning a competitive return on investments. The actual rate of return on reserves accumulated with life insurance policies, and the rate earned on the contributions accumulated in an insured pension plan, are key competitive elements. An insurance company that can earn the highest yield on investments may be able to reduce the net cost of insurance below that of its competitors through lower premiums and/or higher policyholder dividends. The competitive yield has become even more important as insurance companies have moved aggressively into the pension and thrift plan business, where their investment-oriented contracts compete directly with other financial institutions for savings dollars.

The Risk-Return Trade-Off

The primary objective of investment policy is to place funds in instruments which earn the highest returns consistent with a level of risk that insures safety of principal. This trade-off between return and risk is of great importance in a life insurance company, because the integrity of the insurance and pension contract is based on a tradition of relatively conservative investment management. Public policy has dictated high fiduciary standards for insurance and annuity reserves, and the essence of broad investment policy is to strike a balance between earning the highest possible returns for policyholders and the level of risk consistent with an appropriately conservative investment portfolio.

A prudent-man view has always executed a strong influence on investment policy, but the very conservative practices of the past have been relaxed somewhat as greater emphasis has been placed on higher returns as an investment objective. While a great reluctance to significantly increase risk still prevails, companies have demonstrated willingness to sacrifice some apparent safety of principal by the acquisition of investments with slightly higher risk but also higher expected returns. Examples are the shift from home mortgages to mortgages on income-producing real estate, development of real estate, and larger proportionate investment in common stocks. Many companies also have invested more aggressively in private placement corporate debt, accumulating sizable portfolios of such instruments with overall risk characteristics equivalent to those associated with a Moody's Baa rating.

In attempting to more aggressively seek higher returns, insurers have relied a great deal on diversification to minimize the risk involved with this strategy.

The companies spread bond and mortgage investments over a wide quality spectrum, and also diversify by industry and geographic location. A fairly steady flow of funds for new long-term investments, and the prevalent use of repayment schedules on bonds and mortgages, have the effect of producing significant diversification of loan maturities in the total portfolio as of any given time. Diversification into real estate and common stock has been a significant development but these investments still account for a relatively small proportion of assets.

INVESTMENT RISK

Insolvency Risk

Legal insolvency, which is a primary concern to life insurance companies, exists when admitted assets (valued under the rules of the state insurance laws) are less than the reserves and other liabilities required by law. In the insurance literature, this concern for maintaining solvency has often been used to emphasize "safety of principal" as a key investment objective. This traditional view, however, often fails to clearly distinguish between the risk on individual investments versus the aggregate risk level of the entire investment portfolio. It is the portfolio view that is relevant to the issue of insolvency risk, since it allows consideration of overall financial margins of safety and diversification techniques.

The risk of insolvency is a function of the accounting relationships that are closely associated with the life insurance industry's unique asset and liability requirements and surplus limitations. In this regard, it is a contingency related not necessarily to real economic values, but rather to an inability to meet certain legal standards or regulations. New York State Law limits participating policyholders' surplus to an amount not greater than 10 percent of legal policy reserves and other policy liabilities.[2] For a mutual company, this law implies a maximum surplus of about 9 percent of assets. Life insurers not similarly regulated as to surplus are permitted to have a larger proportionate amount, but competition and the relative size of the mutuals operating in New York resulted in an industry capital and surplus to asset ratio of 6.7 percent in 1977. With surplus limited to such small proportions, there is little margin for large independent fluctuations in the values of either assets or liabilities. Since the liabilities are determined actuarially, they are relatively stable and predictable. Therefore, the primary insolvency risk—that is, the condition of zero or negative surplus—relates to the possible loss of asset values.

The market value of investment assets can fluctuate with changes in interest rates and business conditions; therefore, valuation of assets at market would be incompatible with restrictive surplus limitations and greatly increase the risk of legal insolvency. Additionally, since life insurance companies generally do not have to sell securities when markets are depressed, there is no point in marking down undefaulted securities that will be held to maturity and repaid at par. In order to avoid the ebbs and flows of surplus values that would be caused by valuing all assets at market, the state insurance laws allow most investments to be valued in the annual statement at stabilized values. More specifically, the National Association of Insurance Commissioners (NAIC) promulgates annual procedures to determine which bonds and preferred stocks can be carried at amortized values.[3]

---

[2] This limitation reflects the public policy view that excess income from operations should not unduly accumulate as surplus, but should be paid out roughly coincident with its accrual in order to achieve a more equitable distribution to each generation of policyholders.

[3] Amortization is the gradual increase or decrease from cost to reflect the approach of payment at par on the maturity date.

.Mortgage loans on real estate also can be valued at amortized values reflecting the gradual repayment of principal, although they are not included in the procedures for valuation of securities. Investment real estate is valued at depreciated cost. Bonds and preferred stocks in default or failing to pass certain minimum financial tests, impaired real estate, and all common stocks are valued at an "association value," which in most cases is market value. An imputed market value may be used when an actual market does not exist for certain securities. Mortgage foreclosure results in acquisition of the underlying property and its transfer to the real estate account until sale.

Regulations also provide for a Mandatory Securities Valuation Reserve (MSVR). This is a reserve liability separate from surplus to be used to absorb realized investment gains and losses, and fluctuations in the annual statement values of securities. The amount of the MSVR is established by annual formula contributions based on a percentage of bond, preferred stock and common stock assets, plus a crediting of realized and unrealized gains and losses, up to a certain total reserve maximum. While the contribution formula and the maximum varies by asset class and by quality rating of the fixed-income securities, the following rules will generally apply to the major portion of a company's portfolio:

Asset Class	Annual MSVR Contribution (as percent of asset class)	Maximum MSVR Value (as percent of asset class)
Bonds	.10%	2%
Preferred Stock	.25	5
Common Stocks	1.00	33⅓

Once the maximum MSVR is reached, contributions cease and capital gains "spill over" into surplus. The common stock component of the MSVR is designed to be much larger than the bond and preferred stock (B&PS) component because common stocks are valued at market and subject to much wider valuation swings. The B&PS component is intended more to absorb capital losses or write-downs of fixed-income securities in default or no longer in good standing, in which case they are required to be valued at market rather than amortized value.

It is instructive to review the operation of MSVR in the last ten years, since the difficult financial market conditions that prevailed during much of this period at times produced sizable capital losses, most of them unrealized, that were absorbed by the MSVR. This industry data presented in Table 2 show the decline in the B&PS component of the MSVR resulting from the 1969–70 recession, and include substantial write-downs by a number of large life insurance companies in the carrying value of holdings of Penn Central obligations. The reserve

Table 2

Life Insurance Industry Mandatory Security Valuation Reserve at Yearend 1968–1977 by Major Reserve Component (amounts in millions)

	Bond and Preferred Stock Component		Common Stock Component	
	Amount	Percent of Maximum	Amount	Percent of Maximum
1968..........	$1,193	N.A.	$2,151	N.A.
1969..........	1,090	58%	1,345	66%
1970..........	729	37	1,296	61
1971..........	752	34	2,154	77
1972..........	755	33	3,236	90
1973..........	753	31	1,355	42
1974..........	559	22	74	3
1975..........	752	26	683	24
1976..........	1,234	38	1,776	51
1977..........	1,580	45	1,121	35

Source: American Council of Life Insurance, based on a sample of 158 companies for 1968–73, 153 companies for 1974–75, and 149 companies for 1976–77.

then recovered only slightly before being hit again by unusually large capital losses on bonds during the 1974–75 recession, including the sizable write-down of Pan American Airline bonds required under the discretionary authority of the NAIC Valuation Committee. In 1974, 40 companies out of the sample of 153 providing the statistics for Table 2 exhausted their B&PS component of the MSVR, and absorbed some losses with surplus. In order to more quickly rebuild the depleted reserve, in 1975 the companies were required to double their annual contribution to the B&PS component until it reached 50 percent of the maximum. As a result of this "double dip" feature and improved financial conditions, the B&PS component has been built-up substantially since 1974.

The common stock component also fell as a result of the market's decline in the 1969–70 recession. It then recovered and peaked in 1972, when the annual contributions to the reserve plus the capital gains on stocks brought the common stock component close to its maximum (33⅓ percent of common stock holdings). The decline of stock prices in 1973 and 1974 exhausted the common stock component in 118 of the 153 sample companies, and some common stock losses were charged to surplus. Losses were so great that the surplus of the 153 sample companies was reduced by 11 percent. The surplus might have remained impaired even after the market recovered sharply, because the MSVR rules require that the unrealized and realized capital gains on stocks must be credited to the MSVR until the maximum reserve value is reached. Under a special one-time provision, however, the NAIC allowed net capital gains for 1975, 1976, and 1977 to be used initially to restore the incursions of surplus resulting from common stock losses in 1973–74, before flowing into the MSVR. Although the appropriate size of the common stock component is subject to debate, the reserve produced by current MSVR provisions did provide substantial protection during the 1973–74 stock market decline, which was greater than any downturn since the depression of the 1930s.

Liquidity Risk

In life insurance companies, as in other businesses, the primary liquidity risk is the probability that funds will not be sufficient to meet obligations as they become due. A casual observer might conclude that life insurers were relatively illiquid in 1977, because less than 1 percent of the industry's assets were in cash and bank deposits and only 2 percent were in short-term securities. However, a more careful cash flow analysis indicates that liquidity is no particular problem for most companies. In *The Investment Process,* James E. Walter wrote "For the larger and more mature companies at least, the danger of technical insolvency is, generally speaking, negligible in that inflows are expected to exceed outflows for the foreseeable future, maturities are well distributed, a portion of assets is readily marketable, and a tremendous reservoir of unused borrowing power exists." This statement, written in the early 1960s, is still applicable today. History shows that even at the depth of the Great Depression, in 1932 and 1933, most life insurance companies maintained a net cash inflow, and for this reason did not have to liquidate assets in those depressed markets.

For the well-established life insurance companies, a cash shortage sometimes does arise due to an overly ambitious schedule of forward investment commitments. This situation usually is easily remedied by renegotiation of delivery dates, temporary borrowing or, if necessary, sales of marketable securities.

The Special Problems of Inflation

Life insurance companies also face some potentially serious adverse consequences from high and accelerating rates of inflation. Under such conditions, nominal interest rates are pushed to high levels, because of the increased inflation premiums incorporated into rates and/or because of anti-inflationary monetary policy responses. When this occurs, life insurance companies are vulnerable to disintermediation in the form of policy loans, which are readily available at below market rates. In the tight money years of 1966, 1969–70, and 1973–74, from 30–50 percent of the industry's new investment funds from life insurance reserve growth were absorbed by increases in policy loans. Further reducing investable cash flow during these periods was the sharp decline in prepayments on existing mortgages.

More fundamentally, the market interest rates in recent years associated with high and accelerating inflation rates have risen much faster than the portfolio yields on the long-term fixed-asset holdings of the life insurance companies. This had made it difficult for the investment element of life insurance to compete with returns on open-market instruments and institutional savings alternatives. This condition has no doubt contributed to a decline in the share of savings going into cash value life insurance, although this has been offset by the rapid growth of the industry's individual annuity and group pension reserves.

Investment responses to inflationary developments have taken a number of forms. In the period from 1966 to approximately 1971, there was a sharp increase in the use of income and equity participation features, or so-called equity kickers, with bond and mortgage investments. Because of the reduced predictability of investable cash flow and wide swings in interest rates, companies have become more cautious in their practice of making investments in forward commitments at rates established far in advance of the actual disbursement of the loans. In 1974–75, for example, many insurers held back on commitments because of the uncertainty surrounding inflation expectations, and in anticipation of higher nominal interest rates. Efforts also were made to reduce loan maturities in order to lessen the risk of changes in future financial conditions. Some companies have attempted to reduce the threat of disintermediation through policy loans by instituting higher contractual policy loan rates on newly issued policies.

The notion that stocks were a hedge against inflation offers at least partial explanation for the steady rise in the proportion of life insurance company general account assets in common stocks in the 1950s and 1960s. Faith in stocks as an inflation hedge has been weakened by the poor overall market performance in the last decade and the deep market decline in 1973–74, but interest in the total return and inflation-hedge aspects of equity investments is still prevalent in the private pension field. This interest has spurred the growth of separate accounts for investment in common stock and real estate equities. Some companies also have been active in the purchase of development of real estate for the general account, because of the inflation protection these investments offer.

COMPANY ORGANIZATION

Life insurance companies in the United States typically are organized as one of two forms, stock or mutual companies. Over 90 percent of the approximately 1,750 life insurance companies in the United

States are stock companies. Mutual companies, however, are generally older and larger than stock companies, and even though far fewer in number they represent about three-fifths of the assets in the industry. A stock company is a form of life insurance corporation owned by stockholders. A mutual company has no stockholders and no capital stock and, instead, is owned by the policyholders. As a general rule, the primary objective of the stock company is to earn profits for its stockholders, whereas the basic purpose of a mutual company is to provide to its owner-policyholders insurance protection and financial security products at as low a price as possible. In reality, many aspects of management and organization tend to be similar for either type of insurer, and the typical insurance or pension client often does not know or care whether a given company is a stock or mutual. In fact, it is said that a mutual company's objective also is to earn profits, but because there are no stockholders such profits accrue to the benefit of policyholders, either through additions to surplus or dividend distributions to policyholders.

In recent years, life insurance companies increasingly have become part of holding companies, a form of organization generally utilized to facilitate diversification. A stock company may be a subsidiary to an "upstream" parent entity chartered as a general business corporation, but mutual companies, because of their ownership characteristics, must form a "downstream" holding company that is a subsidiary of the insurer. But, by and large, whether or not a life insurance company is affiliated with a holding company does not seem to have any significant effect on the manner in which it is operated.

The internal organization of a life insurance company is usually along functional lines broadly categorized as marketing, administration and investments. The marketing area logically includes the individual life or agency, group pension and group insurance departments, and related actuarial, claims and underwriting organizations. The administration function covers a wide spectrum, including personnel administration, computer operations, accounting, legal, public relations, etc. The investment area typically consists of three major departments that specialize in (1) mortgages and real estate, (2) corporate debt (i.e., public bonds, preferred stock and private placements), and (3) common stocks. The latter two departments are sometimes combined into a securities department or division. Depending on company size and/or management style, the investment area may also include treasurer's, economic research, asset management and investment accounting services departments.

Each of the major investment departments is staffed by a team of portfolio managers and analysts who study the economy and the financial markets, evaluate investment opportunities, and prepare detailed investment proposals that require eventual approval by the finance committee of the board of directors. The departments then are responsible for monitoring the performance of each investment that is made.

While most insurers rely heavily on mortgage correspondents and investment bankers, a few large companies make major use of their own field staff of lending specialists. In the corporate finance area, such decentralization facilitates lending to small and medium size regional firms. Regional real estate offices offer the advantage of dealing directly with prospective borrowers and real estate developers, plus a first-hand knowledge of geographic location and conditions that are critical elements in mortgage lending and the purchase or development of property.

REGULATION OF LIFE INSURANCE INVESTMENTS

Life insurance has long been considered a business "affected with the public interest," and this has led to close supervision and regulation by the several states. Life insurance company investment policy is influenced to a large extent by the insurance regulations of the state in which a company is domiciled. Although such laws are the responsibility of the individual states, there is a good deal of uniformity largely attributable to the role of the National Association of Insurance Commissioners (NAIC) in the formulation of investment statutes. Also, there is a high degree of geographic concentration among the companies, so the bulk of the industry's invested assets are regulated by a relatively small number of states. The New York State Insurance Law is particularly pervasive because of its extraterritorial provisions which require companies licensed to do business in the state, but not domiciled there, to "comply in substance" with New York regulations. For these reasons, the following summary of the provisions of only a few important insurance states, and notably New York, is generally representative of the regulatory ground rules that are applicable to the great majority of investment decisions.

One of the most fundamental provisions of the insurance law is illustrated by the New York requirement that no investment or loan shall be made by a domestic insurer "unless the same has been authorized or approved by the board of directors or by a committee thereof charged with the duty of supervising or making such investment or loan." This general limitation is important because of the potential effect on investment policy of the relative aggressiveness or conservatism of directors or finance committee members.

Aside from this broad requirement, there are many specific state insurance provisions applying to investments which generally have three primary objectives: (1) insuring the safety of the assets underlying the reserve liabilities, (2) guaranteeing diversification of the investment portfolio, and (3) limiting the control of an insurer over any firm in which it invests. The first objective is achieved through qualitative limitations, which establish certain criteria for allowable investment outlets. The second and third objectives are achieved through quantitative restrictions, which generally limit the amount of investment in any one type of asset or any one institution.

Qualitative Restrictions

The qualitative regulation of life insurance investments involves the specification of eligible classes of investment, and criteria to establish the minimum quality for investments within the eligible categories. Allowable investments fall into the general categories of: (1) obligations of the federal, state, and local governments, (2) fixed income corporate securities (bonds and preferred stocks), (3) common stock, (4) real estate mortgages, (5) real estate, (6) foreign investments (of the same kind, class and grade permitted in the U.S.), (7) miscellaneous categories such as equipment trust obligations and tangible personal property, and (8) otherwise ineligible investments allowed under so-called "leeway" or "basket" provisions.

The laws further specify conditions that must be met by each individual investment within each of the eligible types. For example, earnings tests aimed at ensuring a safe margin for earnings in excess of fixed charges are applied to corporate debt depending on the secured or unsecured status of the issue. Earnings tests are also used to establish the eligibility of preferred and common stock. Until the law was relaxed in 1972, New York law prohibited investment in the common stock of nonfinancial companies that were not listed on a recognized national exchange. Eligible first mortgage loans are defined by a specified loan-to-value ratio, which is typically 75 percent of the appraised market value of the mortgaged property, except that a mortgage loan on real property improved by a one-to-four unit dwelling, including a residential condominium, may amount to 90 percent of market value.

Quantitative Restrictions

Significant regulatory limitations are imposed on the amount that can be placed in certain investments even though they meet the qualitative requirements for eligibility. The New York Law will be used to illustrate the specific nature and order of magnitude of the more important amount and percentage limitations that are applied.

No limit is placed on the aggregate amount of government bonds and eligible corporate debt obligations held by an insurer. No life company, however, is allowed to invest more than 5 percent of its admitted assets in the debt obligations of any one institution. Other quantitative limitations specify that life insurance companies can hold only 20 percent of the total preferred stock, issued and outstanding, of any one corporation and this amount cannot exceed 2 percent of the life insurer's admitted assets.

New York State Law specifies that life insurance companies may hold up to 5 percent of a single corporation's outstanding common shares, although these holdings cannot exceed 1 percent of the insurer's admitted assets. Additionally, regulations limit total holdings of common stocks to 10 percent of admitted assets or 100 percent of surplus, whichever is less. Life insurance companies usually have surplus of less than 10 percent of assets, so the surplus restriction in most cases determines the applicable limit on common stock holdings. Aside from this provision, many investment officers feel the requirement that common stock be valued at market value, combined with surplus being limited to a relatively small percentage of assets, places a practical limit on the proportion of stock holdings.

Mortgage lending not only is restricted as to the loan-to-value requirements, but is also limited in total to 50 percent of the insurers admitted assets. Investment in mortgage participation loans is limited to 15 percent of admitted assets. The amount of real property an insurer can purchase as an income producing investment is restricted to 10 percent of assets, with the maximum in any one parcel limited to 1 percent.

The law also allows investments in tangible personal property of up to 2 percent of the insurer's admitted assets, and up to 1 percent of assets may be invested in any foreign country, other than Canada (up to 10 percent in Canada). In addition, there is a general leeway or basket provision, whereby investments not otherwise eligible are allowed up to a limit of 4 percent of an insurer's admitted assets.

In 1962, New York State Law permitted life insurance companies to establish separate accounts for use with group contracts under qualified pension, profit sharing, or annuity plans. These provide for a separate portfolio segregated from all other investments (termed the "general account") of the company, which are not subject to all of the quantitative limitations applied to the general account. The impetus for the separate account development was inability of insurers to compete with other financial institutions in the pension markets, because of the stringent limits imposed by the states on the proportion of general account assets that insurers can hold in common stocks. By 1971, all the states permitted separate accounts to be established. Although the first separate accounts were portfolios invested primarily in common stocks, separate accounts are now used to offer a variety of other investment media to pension clients.

LIFE INSURANCE COMPANY TAXATION

Life insurance company income taxation is extremely complicated because the tax formula takes into account unique aspects of the business stemming from the long-term nature of the insurance contract and the related actuarially determined reserve liabilities, which must be invested to meet future claims. Congress also has a goal of maintaining the competitive balance between stock and mutual companies by limiting the deduction for dividends paid to policyholders. The effects of the tax formulae are to create four different tax situations, which can vary from company to company, and within one company from year to year. For this reason, a detailed discussion of the very complex Life Insurance Company Income Tax Act of 1959 is beyond the scope of this chapter, but there are important elements influencing investment policies that deserve some mention.

The main feature relevant to investments is the determination of that portion of net investment income which is to be taxed. The 1959 Act recognizes that life insurance companies are required by law to maintain policyholder reserves to meet future claims, that they add a large portion of their investment income to these reserves, and that these income increments reserved for policyholders should not be taxed. The Internal Revenue Code provides a formula for determining the policyholders' share, or nontaxable portion, of investment income. However, the high level of interest rates in the last decade was not foreseen at the time the formula was adopted, and its application has had the unintended effect of producing a highly progressive tax in recent years, due to the widening gap between the actuarially assumed interest rates used in calculating life insurance reserves and the earned rates on invested assets. As a result, companies are now paying a much higher marginal tax rate on incremental investment income (in some companies, the rate exceeds 40 percent) than in the past. Thus, there is a greater incentive to consider investments with tax-sheltered income (for example, common and preferred stock, municipal bonds, and real estate) and with capital-gains features.

The amounts of certain of these investments are, of course, limited by the state insurance laws as described above. In addition, enormous competitive pressures to (1) lower the cost of insurance by passing along to policyholders each year sizable investment earnings, and (2) offer a high "new money interest rate" on fixed-income contracts for pension plans, put a limit on the proportion of investments featuring tax-deferred income, or capital gains potential at the expense of current income.

SPECIAL FEATURES OF LIFE INSURANCE INVESTMENTS

Forward Commitments

The relative stability of cash flow for investment has given rise to the widespread use of the forward commitment technique in the industry for the acquisition of long-term assets. A forward commitment is an agreement by the life insurance company to deliver to the borrower a specified sum of money, at a specified interest rate, for a specified period of time, on a specified date ranging anywhere from one month to several years into the future.

The forward commitment is not unique to the life insurance industry, but insurers developed the practice earlier than did other institutional investors. All major life insurance companies use forward commitment agreements to purchase or acquire corporate debt instruments, mortgages, and real property. Its use is particularly widespread in the market for commercial and industrial mortgages, and directly- or privately-placed corporate bonds.

Forward commitments involving corporate debt securities normally provide funds for long-term capital needs. The forward commitment process allows borrowers to plan the amount and timing of their capital expenditure programs more effectively. At the same time, it allows the lending insurer to establish a schedule of future long-term investments, with disbursement dates that are geared to a relatively predictable flow of investable funds.

The forward commitment technique is particularly adaptable to commercial and industrial mortgage markets. Long planning and construction periods are necessary for most commercial and industrial properties, and a forward commitment can be tailored to ensure the availability of the long-term permanent financing when the property is at or near completion. Indeed, a commitment for the permanent mortgage financing is usually a prerequisite for the shorter-term construction loans and other interim borrowing usually arranged with a bank or other lender.

The forward commitment process is a crucial part of life insurance company investment planning, requiring careful analysis of financial and economic conditions. Life insurance companies regard forward commitments as binding agreements which have approval by the finance committee of the board of directors. It is necessary, therefore, to insure that the volume of future commitments be coordinated with the amounts and timing of investable funds. Thus, effective use of the forward commitment process requires a projection of cash flow for one or more years into the future. Interest rate forecasts also are required for a successful forward commitment program. For example, if interest rates are expected to rise in the near term, funds should not be committed aggressively at current interest rates. Conversely, if interest rates are expected to fall, a heavy volume of commitments at current interest rates is desirable. Investment officers may build-up or draw down the cash position in order to pursue a commitment strategy based on interest rate timing.

Life insurance investment planning also must consider the proportion of commitments to be allocated to mortgages and to private placements. Changes in the spread between the yield on mortgages and the yields on corporate securities are the primary determinant of these decisions. However, staff considerations and diversification goals usually dictate a minimum allocation to each outlet.

Private Placements

A private or direct placement is the sale of a security through direct negotiation between the purchaser and the issuer. Private placements in recent years have accounted for more than 40 percent of the total dollar volume of new corporate bond financing, and in roughly 90 percent of all of these private placement arrangements the purchasers (or lenders) have been life insurance companies. In addition to this important role in the total long-term corporate debt market, private placements are sometimes the only source of long-term debt financing for small and medium size companies, which typically do not have access to the public market.

The agreement on a private placement has more detailed terms than on a public issue. The lender negotiates with the borrower not only the interest rate and maturity, but also operational rules which the borrower agrees to follow. The borrower and lender agree on maximum amounts of additional financing and spending that can be undertaken without prior consent of the lender. The loan agreement may set a minimum amount of working capital. Other provisions may restrict the borrower's use of bank credit, expenditures on long-term leases, and expansion or merger activity.

In addition to containing terms or covenants that are designed primarily for the protection of the lender, private placements also are tailored to accommodate specific needs of the borrower. In this regard, a private placement is a much more flexible financing instrument than a publicly issued security containing standard features that are extremely difficult to change after issue. Private placement financing for long-term projects will normally incorporate a forward commitment agreement, sometimes with a number of periodic takedowns as funds are expected to be needed instead of a single sum disbursement. The terms of a private placement are more easily changed than with a public issue because there are fewer lenders to contact, and they are in direct association with the borrowers and in a better position to evaluate changing needs. If a borrower's financing needs grow, the loan agreement may be "rolled over" into a new and larger deal. Private placements also offer the advantage of being exempt from registration with the SEC. The borrower, therefore, saves the time and expenses of registration. Since there is a time lag involved in SEC registration, in periods of rising interest rates the borrower entering the public bond market could be faced with a higher interest rate after SEC registration. The rate on the private placement, however, is established when the lender and borrower first reach agreement, and is not increased if rates rise between the time of commitment and disbursement. Conversely, if interest rates in the public market fall, the borrower is still expected to pay the original negotiated rate.

Private issues are not rated by the standard rating services, but the data available on life insurance company holdings of private placements indicate that the average quality is approximately equivalent to Moody's Baa or Standard and Poor's BB. The major life insurance companies are able to take advantage of the higher yields on these medium grade securities, because the risks inherent in each individual investment are offset by the insurers' ability to diversify broadly. Risk is also controlled by limiting the loan maturities, which reduces the likelihood that the borrower's position will unexpectedly deteriorate during the time the loan is outstanding. The typical final maturity of life insurance company private placements is about 15–20 years, but sinking fund or scheduled repayment requirements bring the typical "average life" down to 10–15 years.

In addition to the higher yield because of their generally lower quality, private placements also tend to have a higher yield than public issues of equivalent quality. This historically has averaged about 50 basis points (½). In very recent years, however, the spread has narrowed significantly during periods when life insurance companies had unusually large investable cash positions. The higher yield on privately placed bonds does not reflect greater probability of losses, but rather three characteristics of the private issue. First, the borrower pays an interest rate premium because the issue is not readily marketable, since there is a very limited secondary private market. Also, private borrowers are willing to pay a premium for the flexibility and confidentiality of the private placement. Lastly, many smaller borrowers are not widely known and, thus, have limited access to the public markets.

HISTORICAL INVESTMENT BEHAVIOR

Some valuable insights can be gained by observing the investment behavior of the life insurance companies during the last half-century or more. The investment responses of the companies to a varied sequence of major wars, an economic depression and periods of unprecedented prosperity, and their actions and innovations to strengthen their competitive position vis-a-vis other thrift institutions, provide useful indications of the objectives, attitudes, and economic role of these important institutions.

General Account Investments

Table 3 contains the percentage distribution of the major categories of general account assets of life insurance companies in various pivotal years over the last six decades. These serve to illustrate the investment behavior of the companies during various past economic and political climates, and in modern times.

Investment holdings of life insurance companies during the relatively prosperous years leading up to World War I were predominately in corporate bonds and mortgages. In 1917 these two categories accounted for about two-thirds of total assets. Railroad mortgage bonds dominated the corporate bonds category, representing over 30 percent of total assets. The height of railroad development occurred in the very early 1900s, and insurers played a major financial role because of their desire for these bonds secured by real property. Mortgages are one of the oldest forms of debt instrument, and had comprised a major proportion of invested assets since the very early years of life insurance in the late 1800s.

United States entry into World War I stimulated a significant move by life insurers into federal government securities. This resulted from the financing demands arising out of the war effort, some shrinkage in private lending opportunities, and a significant rise in interest rates on long-term Treasury bonds. By 1920, government securities had risen to 18.4 percent of assets, and the relatively high yield and unequaled safety of federal obligations continued to make these loans attractive into the early 1920s.

The virtually uninterrupted economic prosperity of the 1920s caused insurance companies to deemphasize government investments, in order to satisfy surging private demand for both debt and mortgage financing. Mortgages rose to over 40 percent of assets, as insurers played a major role in financing the high level of construction activity in both residential and nonresidential construction, and in the expansion of farm mortgage credit up to the mid-1920s. The declining relative importance of railroad bonds was largely offset by the growth in public utility debt financing, particularly in the electric companies.

The changes that took place in the distribution of assets during the 1930s are largely explained by the depressed economic conditions of this decade. The market for corporate bonds and mortgage financing shrank significantly in the Great Depression, and at times the demand for capital by private business was almost wholly absent. The federal

Table 3
Distribution of General Account Assets of U.S. Life Insurance Companies

Year	Government Bonds	Corporate Bonds			Mortgages	Stocks		Real Estate	Policy Loans	Misc. Assets	Total Assets (billions)
		Railroad	Public Utility	Industrial and Misc.		Preferred	Common				
1917	9.6%	30.5%	1.9%	0.8%	34.0%		1.4%*	3.0%	13.6%	5.2%	$ 5.9
1920	18.4	24.3	1.7	0.7	33.4		1.0	2.3	11.7	6.5	7.3
1930	8.0	15.5	8.6	1.9	40.2		2.8	2.9	14.9	5.2	18.9
1935	20.4	11.3	9.1	2.5	23.1		2.5	8.6	15.2	7.3	23.2
1945	50.3	6.6	11.6	4.3	14.8		2.2	1.9	4.4	3.9	44.8
1960	9.9	3.1	14.0	22.0	34.9	1.5	2.7	3.1	4.4	4.4	119.6
1977	6.9	1.2	9.5	29.3	28.9	2.9	3.9	3.1	8.2	6.1	334.4

*Breakdown between preferred and common stocks not available before 1947, but the bulk of stock investment up to that time was preferred stock.
Source: *The Life Insurance Fact Book, 1978*, American Council of Life Insurance.

government initiated large-scale relief and public works programs to expand employment opportunities, and as a result government demand for funds became the dominant factor in the capital markets. In contrast to the general economic stagnation, life insurance companies enjoyed continued growth and positive investable cash flow. The companies managed to find some outlets for funds in the corporate bond markets, particularly in the public utilities, but many portfolio managers faced with a persistent increase in assets turned to the U.S. government securities markets. Consequently, at year-end 1935, over 20 percent of the industry's assets were invested in government securities. In addition to the shrinkage of the bond market, many corporate borrowers fell into default with regard to interest and/or principal. Since the life insurance companies had played such a significant role in financing railroad development, they were particularly vulnerable to the rash of railroad bankruptcies during the Depression. Many companies, however, had the wherewithal to retain the railroad bonds in their portfolio, and the actual record of realized losses was quite small compared to the incidence of railroad failures and the principal amounts involved.

Mortgage defaults also were widespread in the 1930s, and life insurance companies found themselves reluctant owners of the underlying real estate in many situations where foreclosure could not be reasonably avoided. Farm mortgages, which had been an important investment outlet for life insurance companies in the prior decade, were particularly hard hit since the impact of the Depression on farm income and property values was much greater than on urban income and real estate. Part of the decline in the percentage of assets in mortgages was offset by real estate acquired through mortgage foreclosures and in 1935 real estate was approaching 9 percent of assets.

In the years prior to the Depression, life insurance companies traditionally had little interest in common stocks, or were not allowed by law to invest in common equities. Consequently, they did not suffer directly from the infamous 1929 stock market crash and the subsequent two-and-one-half years of general market decline.

The investment behavior of life insurance companies during World War II was dominated by the financial requirements of the federal government. Taxes were not sufficient to pay for the bulk of war expenditures, and more than half of the required funds came from federal deficit financing. A large portion of these government borrowings were used directly or indirectly to finance plant and equipment used by private business for wartime production. This resulted in a drastic shrinkage of corporate demand for long-term external funds. Mortgage activity also declined during the war, because general shortages of building materials caused curtailment of nondefense construction.

The participation of life insurance companies in war financing and the relative absence during the war of private outlets for capital are reflected vividly in the 1945 asset distribution. Government securities represented more than half of total assets, while corporate bonds and mortgages declined to lows of 22.5 percent and 14.8 percent, respectively. General prosperity in agriculture and industry, and the fear of postwar inflation created a strong demand for real estate, and life companies were able to dispose of the backlog of real estate from the depression. By 1945, real estate was down to less than 2 percent of assets.

The years immediately following World War II were mainly characterized by a gradual liquidation by the insurers of their large government security holdings. These proceeds, along with steady growth in investable funds, were used to finance the bond and mortgage demands of the postwar economic expansion. By 1960, the government securities share had dipped below 10 percent. Motivated by the relatively high yields on real estate loans, insurers were major participants in the post World War II housing boom. As a result, mortgages recovered to the relative importance they held before World War I, accounting for almost 35 percent of assets in 1960.

An even more fundamental shift in the distribution of assets occurred in corporate bonds. Railroad bonds had declined to a minor position by 1960. The share of public utility bonds peaked in the early 1950s, but still accounted for 14 percent of assets in 1960. Perhaps the most striking feature of investment behavior of life insurance companies in the 15 years following World War II was the intense emphasis on industrial and commercial corporate bonds. The proportion of assets in this category rose from a little over 4 percent at the end of the War to 22 percent by 1960, which was an especially dramatic increase because it occurred during a period when the asset base also was growing rapidly. This important participation by the life insurers in the corporate debt market was a response to the tremendous demands of commercial and industrial corporations for debt financing. It was during this period that the use of the private or direct placement technique became widespread. Liberalizations during the 1950s of the statutory limitations on common stocks, and a less conservative attitude toward equity investments, led to an increase in acquisitions of common stock. By the early 1960s common stock had climbed to about 3 percent of assets.

Since 1960, the proportion of the industry's assets in public utility bonds has continued to decline. However, the industrial and miscellaneous bond category has increased steadily, and in 1977 accounted for almost 30 percent of total assets. It is noteworthy that these instruments, most of which are private placements, have now surpassed mortgages as the major asset category of the life insurance companies. Since the mid-1960s, the companies have allocated increasing proportions of investable funds to corporate debt because of strong business demands for funds, attractive private placement yields, and extended periods of slack mortgage demand brought about by three periods of extreme financial tightness in 1966, 1969–70 and 1974–75. Also, in each of these tight-credit episodes the companies experienced a sharp increase in policy loans, which reduced the investable funds that would otherwise have been available for their traditional outlets. Policy loans at year-end 1971 were over 8 percent of assets, a significant increase from the early 1960s.[4]

In addition to the decline in relative holdings of mortgage loans, there has been a dramatic change within this category resulting from the deemphasis of home mortgages. Since the mid-1960s the industry has been disinvesting in home mortgages as repayments have exceeded new investments. Mortgages on one- to four-family residences accounted for only 15 percent of all mortgage holdings in 1977, versus about 60 percent 20 years earlier. This shift to mortgages on apartments, commercial buildings, and industrial properties stemmed directly from the significant erosion of the yield attractiveness of home mortgages that resulted from statutory limits on mortgage rates, growth of the specialized mortgage lending thrift institutions, the increased role of Federal credit agencies, and other factors.

Common stock holdings had increased to almost 4 percent of assets by 1977, but increases in this category are constrained by the legal limits and valuation requirements discussed previously.

Separate Account Investments

A discussion of life insurance company investment behavior would not be complete without recognizing the introduction and growth of separate account investments in the last decade. Table 4 shows the amount and percentage distribution of separate account assets in 1967, and the most recent year for which data are available, 1977. Since separate accounts were legalized and introduced only in the early 1960s, they were not a significant factor ten years ago. The assets in these accounts, however, have grown dramatically and amounted to over $17 billion in 1977. Not surprisingly, the bulk of the assets (over 63 percent) are in common stocks, because many of these accounts were initiated so that insurers could increase the amount of equities they could legally hold for pension clients. The figures indicate, however, that separate accounts are now being used to offer a variety of other investment media, notably public bonds, private placements and real estate, and this trend and the rapid growth of separate accounts is expected to continue.

---

[4] This policy loan proportion is still far below those in the earliest years of this historical survey, but today private pension reserves, which do not contain policy loan provisions, account for a significant portion of insurance company general account assets.

Table 4
Distribution of Separate Account Assets of U.S. Life Insurance Companies

Year	Corporate Bonds	Corporate Stocks	Mortgages	Real Estate	Cash and Other Assets	Total Assets (in billions)
1967	9.4%	88.1%	1.2%	—	1.3%	$ 1.2
1977	26.3	63.4	1.5	4.6	4.2	$17.4

Source: The Life Insurance Fact Book, 1978; American Council of Life Insurance.

The money management and investment advisory aspects of the separate account development represent a marked departure from traditional general account investment practices that are tied so closely to the particular nature of life insurance liabilities and regulations.

Chapter 29

Fire and Casualty Portfolios

KARL ZERFOSS, JR.
First Vice President
Kemper Financial Services, Inc.
Chicago, Illinois

Insuring property is a competitive business, subject to many influences and to regular cycles (from the impact of inflation on claims). Casualty insurance companies contract with their customers to repair or replace property when losses are claimed. They take in premiums before the loss and invest these funds for a return. Thus casualty insurers have two sources of income: (1) *underwriting,* or the excess of premiums over claims, and (2) *investment income,* or the return on assets held, in effect, pending losses.

Our mission here is to explore the casualty company investment process and how it is affected by (*a*) the particularities of the property insurance business, and (*b*) current and prospective developments in the U.S. economy and capital markets.

THE ENVIRONMENT

We would describe the investment environment for fire and casualty portfolios under three headings. First, the property insurance business itself is volatile and cyclical, due mainly to the variability of underwriting results, illustrated in Table 1. This volatility or cyclicality of underwriting results may produce changes in the corporate tax position and variation between taxable and tax exempt income.

Second, the overall economy is cyclical, producing regular swings in the prices of various types of capital. Cycles in economic activity and common stock prices need no illustration. Nor do the cyclical

Table 1
Underwriting Profit or Loss (pretax) as Percent of Earned Premiums

		1951....	0.24	1961....	0.28	1971....	2.85
1942....	3.43	1952....	3.08	1962....	0.02	1972....	3.44
1943....	7.42	1953....	5.00	1963....	−1.89	1973....	0.78
1944....	3.37	1954....	5.50	1964....	−2.81	1974....	−5.60
1945....	1.47	1955....	3.49	1965....	−3.19	1975....	−8.34
1946....	−5.78	1956....	−1.75	1966....	0.70	1976....	−3.43
1947....	−1.44	1957....	−4.33	1967....	0.07	1977....	1.65
1948....	4.99	1958....	−1.05	1968....	−1.17	1978....	2.39
1949....	9.51	1959....	0.74	1969....	−2.07		
1950....	4.00	1960....	0.64	1970....	−0.72		

Source: Best's Aggregates & Averages; estimate Kemper Financial Services.

variations and secular trend of interest rates. There is, however, less recognition of the large swings in bond prices that can occur in a single year. Table 2 shows the wide variation in yields and equivalent prices of new AA utility offerings since 1964. Price variations of 18 percent or even 10 percent cannot be neglected under the belief that "bonds are safe."

Table 2
Offering Yields on New Issues of 30-Year "AA" Rated Electric Utility Bonds

	Low	High	Range	Approximate Percent Price Change
1964	4.40%	4.50%	.10	1%
1965	4.40	4.80	.40	5
1966	4.87	6.15	1.28	9
1967	5.05	6.65	1.60	18
1968	6.40	6.85	.45	3
1969	7.00	8.85	1.85	14
1970	8.25	9.25	1.00	7
1971	7.00	8.25	1.25	11
1972	7.25	7.60	.35	3
1973	7.35	8.50	1.15	10
1974	8.05	10.40	2.35	18
1975	8.85	10.10	1.25	7
1976	8.10	9.20	1.10	7
1977	7.80	8.45	.65	6
1978	8.65	9.55	.90	8

Source: "Analytical Record of Yield and Yield Spread," Salomon Bros, Kemper Financial Services.

Finally, inflation is overlaid on the property insurance industry cycle and the cycles of capital prices. Rising inflation causes both rising long-term interest rates, or falling bond prices, and escalating claims.

GENERAL APPROACH

How, in this multicyclical and inflationary world, are property and casualty portfolios to be managed? The general approach we recommend is: (1) set investment objectives related to the financial condition and book of business of the specific insurance company, (2) devise an asset-mix range which fits these objectives, and (3) establish maximum authorities for individual security holdings.

This general procedure will result in a well defined investment program and ensure that the board of directors or its finance committee remains well-informed. It even provides the legal framework for the board to maintain ultimate control and responsibility for investment decisions while retaining outside investment counsel.

INVESTMENT OBJECTIVES

We specify the objectives of investing casualty company assets as: to stay in business and to earn a profit. More specifically, the objectives are:

(*a*) to protect the capital and surplus accounts of the business, for it is the capital which enables the company to write business;
(*b*) to maintain liquidity necessary to meet all cash obligations and contingencies;
(*c*) to offset inflation in claim liabilities with rising income and asset values;
(*d*) to comply with all legal requirements and restrictions; and
(*e*) to maximize investment return after taxes.

There are, clearly, conflicts between these objectives. Surplus or principal value must be risked to some extent to increase investment returns from the so-called riskless level of short-term government securities. Liquidity may reduce return. Common stock bought to rise along with escalating claims may perversely fall in value.

The balance of assets and objectives is therefore of critical importance. In the final analysis, the proper balance is a matter of judgment for each board of directors. Each casualty insurance company has unique characteristics for which individual solutions must be found if these objectives are to be met. These characteristics include:

—the types of insurance written,
—underwriting policies and results,
—anticipated income tax position,
—statutory investment requirements,
—surplus position,
—internal corporate restrictions, and
—accounting and reporting requirements.

THE MIX OF ASSETS

The principle we would suggest be followed in setting an asset mix for any specific casualty portfolio is this: various liability and capital categories should be matched or funded by different types of assets.

For example, a liability of specific or firmly estimated size due to be paid in ten years may properly be matched with a long-term bond, while a dividend payable in three months should be backed by cash equivalent.

For the purpose of determining a proper asset mix for a property insurance company, we would use the following classification of assets:

(a) *Ready assets:* cash and money in the course of collection, short-term (under one year) investments, bonds maturing within three years.
(b) *Long-term fixed assets:* bonds maturing after three years, mortgages, preferred stocks.
(c) *Discretionary assets:* common stocks (including those of affiliate companies), real estate equity, other equity investments.

With this classification, the simplest method of handling convertible bonds or convertible preferred stocks is to include them in long-term fixed assets. Division of convertible securities into their fixed income and equity components could be done, but would seem unwarranted in view of the approximate nature of the whole process of asset mix determination.

One set of asset mix guidelines or rules is shown in Table 3. Any

Table 3
Property-Liability Companies Asset Mix Guidelines

Match These Liabilities	*With These Assets*
Primary Allocation:	
Loss and loss expense	35 percent Ready Assets
	35 percent Long-Term Fixed Income Assets
	30 percent Discretionary Assets
Unearned premium	75 percent Ready Assets
	25 percent Discretionary Assets
Dividends declared	100 percent Ready Assets
Other expense	100 percent Ready Assets
Surplus (including	
voluntary reserves)	10 percent of admitted assets in Ready Assets
	Balance—⅓ Long-Term Fixed Income Assets
	⅔ Discretionary Assets
Secondary Allocation:	

Deduct three times current annual investment income from Ready Assets and add this amount to Long-Term Fixed Income Assets.

Deduct two times current annual underwriting cash flow from Ready Assets and add this amount to Long-Term Fixed Income Assets.

Source: Kemper Corporation.

set of rules must be applied with common sense, and with full consideration of the specific company's situation. In Table 3 the particular split of assets to match the important loss and loss expense reserves is based on an expected payout of 35 percent of these reserves within three years, 35 percent in three to five years and 30 percent beyond five years. In any specific case, this allocation should be based on the particular book of business being considered. Other factors affecting these guidelines include surplus. Very strong surplus compared to premiums written, will permit more discretionary assets, while thin surplus relative to writings urges caution. The certainty of underwriting profits will also be a factor: great certainty permits assumption of more investment risk. The adequacy and certainty of reserving practices also enters the allocation. If you consistently underestimate your reserves in interim periods, take fewer investment risks or change your operating procedures.

The secondary allocation in Table 3 reflects one method of recognizing the beneficial effect of cash flow on portfolio liquidity.

In practice, the portion of assets in the discretionary and long-term fixed income categories derived from guidelines such as these should be regarded as maximum. If the guidelines indicate 60 percent of total assets in long-term bonds, this percentage should be held only when investment considerations indicate this is wise. In a highly inflationary period when interest rates are rising and bond prices falling, the long-term bond category should be switched to short maturities to the extent possible, for investment, not liability matching purposes. Bond management is discussed further below. Similarly, common stocks should only be held in the guidelines amount when the outlook for stocks appears very attractive.

State regulatory restrictions must, of course, be observed. These vary according to the state in which the insurance company is domiciled, but generally include maximums for common and preferred stocks and the securities of any one issuer. The National Association of Insurance Commissioners (NAIC) limits nonamortizable and certain nonearning assets, in effect producing an investment quality restriction. New York state presents a number of special problems.

In determining asset mix, the investment manager should consider not only the current balance sheet but also the likely situation one or more years in the future. To do this, future underwriting results, investment income and maturities and other factors affecting cash flow must be estimated. When the present asset mix is compared to the desired mix one year hence, the asset categories into which to direct future cash flow are indicated.

Finally, to protect surplus and thus the business itself against strongly declining securities markets, guideline asset allocations should be checked. Surplus should remain at or above 25 percent (or your objective) of net premiums written if all of the following declines should occur:

—20 percent in common stock market value,
—25 percent in preferred stock value,
— 5 percent in long-term fixed asset market value, and
—25 percent in real estate and other discretionary asset values.

The minimum surplus/net premiums ratio is strictly a judgment call. More conservative boards or finance committees may want to use a minimum ratio higher than our 25 percent, perhaps as high as 40 percent. Further, the minimum ratio used may depend on your view of security market price levels: use higher ratios when you believe securities markets are more vulnerable.

We would not argue the eternal validity of the specific numbers used in these guidelines. In fact, these asset-mix parameters lean toward being overly conservative. What is important is to use a similar process to set a maximum mix for each specific casualty insurance company's book of business.

INVESTMENT PRINCIPLES

The following is a description of investment principles peculiar to property insurance company investing.

Bonds should be Actively Managed

Many insurance companies do not attempt to actively manage their fixed income portfolios, but merely invest cash flow as available and hold bonds to maturity. In this buy-and-hold method, new cash is invested at prevailing interest rates and the chief concern is portfolio income or yield. Since accounting convention decrees that bonds are carried at amortized book value for statement purposes, neglect of bond market price changes has been traditional.

We think this approach is inappropriate for an inflationary environment. The high volatility of interest rates and their rising levels since the mid 1960s (see Table 2) makes it imperative that close attention be paid to the prospects for interest rates. This is the only way to obtain higher total returns during periods of rising interest rates. The key factor in the pattern of generally rising rates and the high volatility has been the level of inflation over recent years, and current prospects in this regard are not encouraging.

Total investment return is the sum of two kinds of economic returns from investment: (1) *income* (yield); and (2) *appreciation* or *depreciation* (change in capital values). Consideration of capital value changes as well as current yield can increase the total investment return and help preserve capital values from inflationary erosion.

How does active management, concentrating on total return, improve on results based on a buy-and-hold philosophy? The basic observation is that interest rates do change over time (see Table 2). As a hypothetical example, assume that bond X varies in price and yield as shown in Figure 1, after being issued at par at the beginning of year one at 9 percent.

Over the five-year period buy-and-hold manager A obtains an average coupon yield of 9.0 percent on cost, but interest-on-interest reduces average annual total return to about 8.9 percent assuming A bought U.S. Treasury Bills with bond X interest payments. If A started with $1,000,000 it would end with $1,531,136.

An active manager, B, holds bond X only when it is rising in price and holds U.S. Treasury Bills when bond X is falling. The average annual total return for B is about 12.2 percent and his $1,000,000 initial investment becomes $1,777,526. The active manager, albeit with oracular vision of the future, has the advantage of 3.3 percent per year, or $246,390 for five years.

The active manager, B, forecasts the change in interest rates and bond prices and acts accordingly. While few if any investment managers can forecast perfectly, portfolio shifts in the general area of turning points can be routinely made. The manager need only have an interest rate forecast and a bond portfolio positioned for the greatest advantage. As the economics and markets change, the portfolio must change. The high probability of sale however requires most bonds in the portfolio to be highly marketable.

Although insurance companies can carry bonds at amortized value, it is not valid to compare book yields with total rate of return. On an 8 percent coupon bond purchased at par which declines to a price

Figure 1

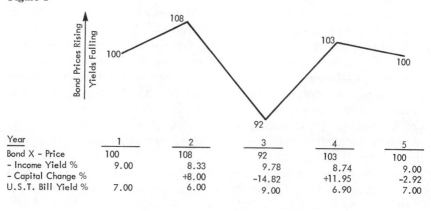

Year	1	2	3	4	5
Bond X – Price	100	108	92	103	100
– Income Yield %	9.00	8.33	9.78	8.74	9.00
– Capital Change %		+8.00	-14.82	+11.95	-2.92
U.S.T. Bill Yield %	7.00	6.00	9.00	6.90	7.00

of 95 as interest rates rise to 8.5 percent, the portfolio has suffered a real loss of 5 percent vis-a-vis the alternative of having held the amount in short-term paper and then investing it at 8.5 percent. The 5 points is merely the present value of ½ point per year over the life of the bond, and therefore it is the present value of the real loss to the portfolio. Even with due regard to the importance of statutory and financial reporting requirements and the impact of trading gains and losses, the potential for incremental gain through a program of active asset management is so great that we believe investment policy should permit as much active management as is prudently possible. This incremental return, incidentally, can give a company an important competitive advantage in the pricing of its insurance products.

In order to obtain a relevant assessment of total rate or return it should be measured over a full economic cycle. We would not place much weight on book yield or realized gains or losses, although we appreciate the impact they have on reported earnings. The important point is that any reduction of current income brought about through the sale of long bonds and reinvestment in short-term paper is likely to be temporary, and more than compensated for by the preservation of capital.

Tax Management

Anticipation is the key ingredient in successful tax management, which is after all, the maximization of after-tax return. Property insurance investment managers must anticipate the underwriting cycle. Simplistically, all income should be tax-exempt or mostly so when underwriting is profitable and taxable when underwriting losses are large enough to shelter investment income. When operations are always profitable there is little problem: maintain the maximum tax shelter consistent with return. In the usual case, however, underwriting profits and losses alternate and some switching between taxable and tax-sheltered income is desirable.

A major conflict may arise due to the similarity of the cycles in tax-exempt yields (because of inflation) and underwriting profits. A possible dilemma is illustrated in Figure 2.

In years 1, 2, 3, and 4, operations are profitable and taxable, calling for tax-exempt income. But inflation and other cyclical influences during these years may be causing tax-exempt yields to rise and bond prices to fall.

Your dilemma as investment manager is this: the choice to reduce taxes by holding long tax-exempt securities in years 1, 2, and 3 will cause capital erosion; the choice to maintain capital values by holding short-term (taxable) securities will cause payment of higher taxes. We

Figure 2

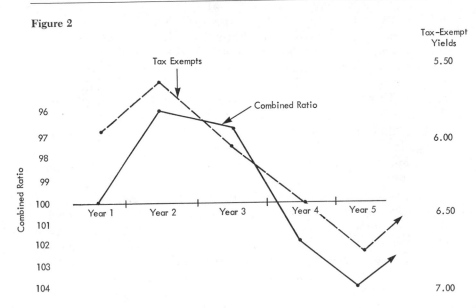

believe most insurance investment managers are overly concerned
with taxes, often neglecting the more important capital considerations.
In recent years, bond markets have been volatile enough to overwhelm
tax considerations.

In the example of Figure 2, we would switch from long tax-exempt
bonds to short taxables in year 2. This increases the tax bill in years
2, 3, and 4 but preserves capital. Switching back into tax-exempts in
year 4 or 5 avoids large bond losses and positions the portfolio for
coming price appreciation. You can do the arithmetic, but capital and
future income benefits will far outweigh the taxes paid.

Realize Common Stock Gains

Since bonds are carried at amortized value and not market value,
a decline in bond prices does not affect surplus for statuatory or rating
purposes. However, converting unrealized losses to realized losses does
impact surplus and net profit and may be undesirable from a business
standpoint whatever the investment merits. Here the common stock
portfolio is helpful. By realizing common stock profits regularly, bond
losses may be taken and the effect on net profit neutralized. Common
stock profits offset the (realized) bond losses in surplus. In just a few
years of offsetting bond losses with common stock profits, book value
(amortized cost) of a substantial portion of a bond portfolio may be
brought close to market value, and this will enhance the ability to
switch asset mix for investment purposes at little cost to surplus.

Diversification and Quality

Active portfolio management requires a highly marketable portfolio in order to effect asset switches quickly at low cost. For this reason, we would recommend limiting bond quality to a BBB rating or better. For the same reason, the size of individual bond holdings should not be so small as to inhibit trading. Government holdings which do not have an upper limit in size for credit purposes, can be held in large amounts. A good rule for high quality state general obligations and corporates is a minimum of $250,000 and a maximum of 2 percent of assets. A lower maximum should be set for lower quality issues.

For common stock holdings, the maximum equity exposure should be divided into 25–50 equal parts or units. Most individual holdings should be about unit size to avoid excessive dependence of portfolio return on one or a few specific stocks. Stocks of smaller companies and high reward-high risk items should be held in partial unit size and collectively should not exceed 15–20 percent of the maximum equity position.

ORGANIZING THE INVESTMENT FUNCTION

The property insurance company investment function may be entirely within the company, supplied entirely by an outside, unaffiliated investment manager or some combination of these. The insurance company must make a "make or buy" decision in a fashion very similar to that of a manufacturer. Volume (or in this case, size of total assets) is the critical factor.

The typical practice has been to have an internal staff. In our opinion, internal management is the efficient method for companies with sizeable assets, say $200 million and above. Smaller companies, lacking adequate staff, have been unable to pursue an active investment strategy as outlined in this chapter. As a result, these companies have been:

—unable to maximize tax-exempt income,
—excluded from common stock investment or limited to long-term holdings of "good stocks," and
—unable to vary bond maturities or pursue other active fixed-income security strategies.

The results are low income and total returns, depreciated equity values in yesterday's "good stocks," and inflexible portfolios filled with low coupon bonds. Many larger companies have pursued inactive strategies with similar poor results on a grander scale.

Whether a company chooses the inside or outside manager approach, the required staff and investment expertise is substantial. We believe a minimum staff would include three experienced fixed income specialists to handle tax-exempts, taxable bonds, preferred stocks and short-term securities and four common-stock specialists, even if the majority of security analysis is accepted from brokerage firms and others outside the firm. Real estate mortgages could possibly be handled by one of the fixed income specialists, but fixed income securities with equity participations would require another person. Thus, we believe that a staff of seven or eight, plus a chief investment officer, is minimal for pursuing active investment strategies.

For those companies retaining outside investment management, special legal requirements normally apply. Most state insurance codes place investment responsibility with the carrier's board of directors. While assignment of this responsibility may be made internally to a finance committee or executive committee, counsel is often wary of full delegation outside the company. For this reason, outside investment advice is often obtained on a nondiscretionary basis.

Nondiscretionary investment management, where the unaffiliated advisor must obtain prior approval of all transactions, is slow, cumbersome, and generally undesirable. Market opportunities, essential in all securities, may be missed. A legally acceptable alternative is for the insurance company board of directors (or finance committee) to give the advisor complete discretion in transactions within closely specified limits. Such limits or authorities would deal with asset mix limits, quality, size of individual holdings, and perhaps maturity.

Chapter 30

Portfolio Management– Guidelines for a Commercial Bank*

EDWARD M. ROOB

Senior Vice President
First National Bank of Chicago
Chicago, Illinois

and

THOMAS A. VAUGHN

Vice President
First National Bank of Chicago
Chicago, Illinois.

Investment policies vary widely among commercial banks, due to differences in size, location, and loan and deposit history. Policies also can and do differ even among banks that are quite similar in these areas because portfolio management is an art and not an exact science.

Thus, the purpose of this chapter is not to espouse or promote any particular investment policy as being the "best possible" one. Rather, it simply is an attempt to point out certain basic factors which should be considered by any bank that is attempting to develop a sound investment program.

Some of the factors mentioned below may appear almost too elementary and obvious to warrant much thought or discussion. However, it is precisely because these factors seem so rudimentary that they are overlooked and neglected by many bank managements. Successful portfolio management starts with a step-by-step analysis along the lines suggested below.

* Reprinted with permission from *The Bankers' Handbook*, revised edition, edited by William H. Baughn and Charls E. Walker, Dow Jones-Irwin, Homewood, Ill., 1978.

INVESTMENT OBJECTIVES AND THE CONSTRAINTS

The first step is to establish and/or recognize your investment objectives and the constraints under which you operate. Portfolio policy obviously must be made in the context of a bank's total needs and requirements; it cannot operate in isolation. Thus, a careful inventory should be made in each of the areas discussed below.

Assess the Bank's Overall Risk Position

Guidelines, Ratios, Measurement Methods. Unfortunately, there are no nice, neat empirical formulas and measuring devices for determining the proper loan/deposit ratio, correct level of capital, and so on for any given bank. Take the matter of capital adequacy as an illustration. Recently, one of the leading bank stock analysts (Harry Keefe of Keefe, Bruyette & Woods, Inc.) stated, "I personally don't know what is the proper capital-asset ratio for a bank and from what I have read, nobody else does either." Therefore, we recommend that each bank management be guided by the following two factors in analyzing the characteristics and conditions of its own bank.

1. Compare your bank's overall makeup with other banks similar in size, structure, location, and so on. Comparisons with industry averages or with banks greatly different in size and/or general composition can be greatly misleading. An obvious example would be a small country bank located in a one-crop locality attempting to "copy" a large city bank in is asset-liability mix, investment strategy, and so forth.
2. Each bank management also needs to decide the asset/liability structure and ratio levels it is "comfortable" with. Variations in ratios among banks that are quite alike in size, location, type of customer, and so on are permissible and should not become a matter of concern, provided that these variations are kept within reasonable limits. For instance, a particular bank may determine to maintain a capital-asset ratio of 7 percent, even though the average for other highly similar banks is 8 percent.

Loan Portfolios and Deposits. Analyze the loan portfolios and the deposits in terms of compositing past history and future trends:

1. The composition of these accounts; i.e., the kinds and amounts of loans and deposits, the types of customers served.
2. Past history (paying particular attention to the volatility of these accounts); both with respect to cyclical as well as seasonal variations.
3. Developing estimates of the type and magnitude of probable future trends.

Capital Position. Review your bank's capital position in relation to its current capital structure and its ability to support future growth and/or a changing asset mix.

1. Evaluate the adequacy of the bank's current capital structure.
2. Try to determine the ability of the current capital account to support your bank's projected future growth and/or a changing asset mix. (As an example, a bank with a 7 percent capital-asset ratio earning 10 percent on its capital, and having a 50 percent dividend payout and an annual asset growth of 12 percent will find that its 7 percent capital ratio will drop to 5.1 percent at the end of five years.)

Investment Personnel and Effort. Evaluate both the amount of "in house" investment expertise available and the effort applied to the bank's investment account. Lack of investment personnel and effort can be partially (but not fully) overcome through using the investment services of large correspondents and various other advisory sources.

Study Liquidity Requirements versus Income Needs

Every portfolio manager faces the mutually exclusive choice between yield and liquidity. This is the classic "trade-off" problem in bank portfolio management.

In analyzing this problem, it is best to begin by trying to make a careful distinction between the liquidity portion of the investment account and the earnings portion. Then, attempt to determine how much emphasis the bank desires to place on each portion.

Estimate the probable impact of future bank growth and other developments on liquidity and earnings requirements.

Analyze the Pledging Requirements to Secure Public Funds

Assess the bank's past and present pledging needs in terms of types and amounts of securities required.

Determine the amount of safety margin desired (i.e., the amount over and above both the required average monthly or yearly balance and the peaks for each pledge account). Again, it will be necessary to estimate the probable future requirements.

Evaluate the Bank's Overall Tax Position, Both Current and Future

Develop a suitable forecast of your bank's asset/liability mix and earnings. Study the possible tax impact of leasing operations, foreign tax credits, transfers to loan-loss reserves, tax-loss trading in the investment accounts, and so on.

Consider possible future legislation and its effect on the tax position.

For example, states and municipalities are trending toward the imposition of local income taxes, and in-state or local municipal issues may or may not be exempted from such taxes.

Failure to adequately assess future tax requirements may mean having to sell or swap large amounts of bonds in a depressed market.

PORTFOLIO STRATEGIES

Once the bank's investment needs and constraints have been clearly established and agreed upon, the next step is to begin developing appropriate and specific portfolio policies and strategies. Unless the proper foundation has been laid, bank investment policy becomes a haphazard, "fly by the seat of your pants" process. Correct investment decisions then come about as a matter of pure luck rather than from studied judgment.

"Three-Part" Portfolio Strategy

Divide the portfolio into a liquidity account, an income account, and a "swing" account.

1. Under this technique, it becomes much easier to readily identify those securities held specifically for long-term investment and those held primarily for liquidity purposes.
2. The traditional portfolio subdivision of a government account, municipal account, and a corporate or other securities account fails to provide an accurate picture of this liquidity-income distinction. Likewise, length of maturity can be misleading because under certain circumstances (as for example in anticipation of rising interest rates) a large portion of the earnings or income account might be held temporarily in short-term issues. The real distinction should be the purpose for which the securities are held, and the liquidity-*income*-"swing" segmentation brings this out most clearly.
3. The "swing" portion of the portfolio is the cushioning factor between the liquidity portion and the earnings portion. Funds are shifted into and out of this portion depending upon market conditions and outlook.

This type of portfolio strategy requires a clear understanding of the difference between liquidity, marketability, and safety.

1. *Liquidity.* Measures the ability to quickly convert a security into cash at a price reasonably close to its current book value.
2. *Marketability.* Measures the relative ease of buying or selling large amounts of a particular security without unduly affecting its market price.

3. *Safety.* Measures the relative degree of creditworthiness of a security; i.e., the ability and willingness of a borrower to meet principal and interest payments when due.

The distinction among these terms is quite important from a portfolio management viewpoint. As a practical illustration, a security such as an intermediate term Treasury note has the highest level of safety and marketability, but it still may not provide very much true liquidity if the current market price is well below book value.

Type of Investment, Diversification, and Quality

The higher a bank's overall risk position (as determined under the section discussing overall risk position), the lower should be the risk exposure in the investment account. For example, a bank in a town heavily dominated by one company should attempt to offset the high relative risk in its loan and deposit accounts by reducing risk as much as possible in its bond investment account through means of greater diversification—emphasizing higher rated issues, and increasing the holdings of governments and short-term municipals.

Diversification. Proper diversification is a very necessary component of sound bank investment policy. However, diversification often is carried too far. Generally speaking, banks' portfolios tend to be over-diversified rather than underdiversified.

Most people generally think of overdiversification in terms of having too many different credits in the portfolio (i.e., holding a large number of widely dispersed state and municipal issues). However, over diversification also can result from holding too many maturities of a given issuer; for instance, holding a dozen different Treasury Bill issues when two or three would be just as suitable.

Quality. The investor should recognize that both credit quality and ratings are relative. A bond with an Aaa rating should not be considered as being an issue which has no credit risk associated with it, but merely that it has greater basic strength and creditworthiness than lesser rated bonds in the opinion of the rating agency. Remember, bond analysis and rating leans heavily upon subjective matters; only a part of the analytical process can be based upon objective measures.

Undue emphasis should not be placed upon quality. Certainly, nothing destroys the performance of a portfolio like a default in principal, but there are many gradations in quality between the highest grade municipals and those relatively few that represent a serious risk of default. Remember, quality entails a cost (namely, an income give-up).

The rating services are not infallible. A local bank may be just as qualified to rate the credits in its region as is a national rating agency.

Portfolio Maturity Structure

The "Ladder" Portfolio

1. This technique derives its name from the fact that approximately the same number of bonds mature at regularly spaced intervals. A simple illustration would be a portfolio with maturities ranging from one to ten years with about 10 percent of the bonds coming due each year.
2. Under this type of system, the proceeds from maturities are reinvested at the longest end of the maturity schedule. (In the previous illustration, this would call for reinvestment in ten-year issues.)
3. The ladder portfolio does offer several advantages:
   a. It requires less investment expertise and management than other types of maturity schedules.
   b. It has a certain degree of "built-in" liquidity because a relatively constant number of bonds mature each year.
   c. It avoids "gambling" on changes in interest rates since maturity proceeds always are simply reinvested at the long end of the ladder.
4. The disadvantages of the ladder concept are:
   a. It will lead to poor investment decisions in certain kinds of markets (such as maintaining the ladder structure when the market seems to be calling for a general shortening, lengthening, and so on).
   b. It tends to operate against yield maximization; over the course of an interest rate cycle, it merely will match the average yields available.
   c. Like many "formula" techniques, a major drawback is that it is overly rigid and restrictive.

The "Dumbbell" or "Hourglass" Portfolio

1. In this type of portfolio system, funds are invested mainly in short and long maturities; there are few, if any, intermediates. Obviously, the short-term segment is the liquidity portion and little emphasis is placed upon income in this part of the portfolio. However, maximization of income is the major objective in the long-term portion.
2. The long and short portions are not held at fixed amounts as is the case under the "ladder" system. Rather, the percentages invested in either short-term or long-term securities will vary, depending upon management's assessment of the market.
3. The advantage of this system are:
   a. A potentially high return since the portfolio manager is able to take advantage of market swings.
   b. A substantial degree of liquidity since a significant portion of the account may be invested in short-term issues.

4. The "dumbbell" technique is not without its disadvantages. The major ones are:
   a. It calls for a great degree of investment expertise and intuitivity due to the higher risk nature of this type of maturity structure and the difficulty of correctly calling market movements.
   b. It requires a continual willingness to trade and take losses when necessary.
   c. It may be difficult to trade large amounts of the investments as quickly as the anticipated market movements demand.

The "Cyclical" Portfolio

1. This type of portfolio concept calls for shortening the maturities when interest rates are likely to rise and for lengthening maturities whenever yields are expected to decline.
2. This concept is ideal in theory but is hard to implement because of the following two factors:
   a. First, there is the difficulty of being able to accurately forecast interest rate movements (and then to be able to trade a large enough portion of the account within the required time frame).
   b. Second, despite the introduction of liability management techniques, bank portfolios still are confronted to some extent by the "classic yield trap." Loan demand and interest rate cycles tend to coincide, thereby creating a dual problem. When loan demand is high, the portfolio has no money to invest in the high yielding bonds. When demand it slack, the portfolio is under pressure to increase profits by extending maturities at the wrong time.

Combinations and "Modified Ladders." In view of the disadvantages listed for each of the above-mentioned portfolio maturity structures, most banks tend to use a combination of these techniques. Perhaps the system most widely used is one which could be termed a "modified ladder" portfolio. Under this system, a bank maintains a reasonable level maturity schedule but allows itself enough flexibility to take some advantage of market swings or other possible future developments. In other words, this even ladder can be "bent out of shape" in order to maximize earnings, improve liquidity, or meet other needs and requirements.

SWAPPING

Swapping is a technique whereby one or more issues are sold and the proceeds are used to purchase other investments in order to take advantage of varying yield spread relationships between quality grades, maturities, and types of investments.

Prior to the late 1960s, most bank portfolios engaged in relatively little swapping. Bond management activity consisted primarily of "buying and holding to maturity." The elimination of bank portfolio capital gains benefits in 1969 removed former trading restrictions so that considerable progress has been made in the direction of active portfolio management through techniques such as swapping.

Yield Pick-Up Swap

This type of swap involves the replacement of one security by another offering a higher yield but similar in all other aspects such as

Exhibit 1
Example of Typical Yield Pickup Swap

Sell: $1,000,000 (par value) U.S. Treasury 5⅞ percent due August 31, 1976 at 98.375 to yield 7.70 percent

Buy: $1,060,000 (par value) Treasury bills due August 24, 1976 at 7.32 percent (discount yield) to yield 7.82 percent (coupon equivalent)

Assumption: settlement date of trade is September 16, 1975

1. If the 5⅞ percent Treasury notes are held to maturity, then the holder would receive $1,000,000 in principal plus $58,750 in interest for a total on August 31, 1976 of $1,058,750.
2. If the 5⅞ percent Treasury notes are sold and the proceeds are reinvested in $1,060,000 par value of Treasury Bills due August 24, 1976, then the results would be as follows:

Sale price of 5⅞ percent notes (98⅜)	$ 983,750
Accrued interest	2,582
Total proceeds of sale	$ 986,332
Purchase price of bills	986,072
Remaining funds	$ 260
Maturity proceeds of bills to be received on Aug. 24, 1976	$1,060,000

3. The two advantages of making this swap are as follows:

First advantage:

Maturity proceeds of bills	$1,060,000
Maturity proceeds of notes	1,058,750
Advantage of swap	$ 1,250

Second advantage:

Maturity date of bills	8/24/76
Maturity date of notes	8/31/76
Advantage of swap	7 days*

---

* That is, we are able to obtain our proceeds seven days earlier and thereby can reinvest these proceeds for this period of time and thereby obtain an added advantage.

quality and maturity. As the name implies, the objective is to increase the total return over the life of the security. An example is shown in Exhibit 1.

The Substitution Swap or Replacement Swap

In a substitution or replacement swap, the portfolio manager continuously analyzes the spread relationships among groups of similar types of securities. A swap is made whenever the yield spread between two highly similar bonds reaches some extreme limit (as a result of temporary market imbalances). The portfolio manager hopes to obtain a profitable "reversal" of this swap at a later date when the spread returns to a more normal historical level. This technique usually is referred to as an *arbitrage*.

The major obstacle to the substitution swap is the absolute necessity to give up yield to maturity when required. However, this yield give-up is only temporary. A substitution swap may require giving up nominal yield for a short while with the intention of eventually being able to increase the total real return. An example is shown in Exhibit 2.

Exhibit 2
Example of Typical Substitution Swap*

Sell: U.S. Treasury 6¾ percent due May 31, 1977 at 98.03125 to yield 7.97 percent
Buy: U.S. Treasury 6⅞ percent due May 15, 1977 at 98.3125 to yield 7.95 percent

1. Above trade results in a small yield give-up.
2. However, this trade is made on the basis of past yield spread relationships between these two issues.
3. Past records indicate that the widest spread between these two issues occurred when the 6¾s yielded 15-basis points more than the 6⅞s while the narrowest spread resulted in the 6⅞s yielding 3 basis points more than the 6¾s.
4. Thus, on the basis of past history, a portfolio manager should sell the 6¾s and buy the 6⅞s whenever the spread relationship narrows with the intention of reversing the swap when the hoped-for spread widening occurs at some later date.
5. In our example, this is precisely what occurs. In 30 days, the following swap was made:

Sell: U.S. Treasury 6⅞ percent due May 15, 1977 at 98.28125 to yield 7.97 percent
Buy: U.S. Treasury 6¾ percent due May 31, 1977 at 97.84375 to yield 8.10 percent
Result: Although a ½₂nd loss (0.03125) was sustained on the 6⅞s, the 6¾s were purchased at a price ⁶⁄₃₂s lower (0.1875) than they were originally sold at, thereby resulting in a net profit of ⁵⁄₃₂s (0.15625) or $1,562.50 per million par value.

---

* This swap was based upon actual market prices which existed during August and September 1975.

The Intermarket Swap

This type of swap attempts to take advantage of changing yield spread relationships between various segments of the bond market. These segments can be differentiated by: (1) type of issue (example—Treasuries versus Agencies); (2) quality (example—Aaa versus A rated general obligation municipals); or (3) coupon rate, and so on.

The changing spread between these segments may represent either a temporary market aberration (which will revert to more normal levels in the near future) or the beginning of a new trend or market structure.

As an illustration of a changing market structure, consider what might be expected to occur during a period of high interest rates. First, the supply of government agency securities will tend to increase sharply because, among other things, disintermediation in the savings and loan industry will require increased borrowings by the Federal Home Loan Banks (FHLB); also, Federal National Mortgage Association (FNMA or Fannie Mae) will see the need to supply funds to the housing market. At the same time, the supply of U.S. Treasury issues will diminish since high interest rates normally are associated with a good economy and increased government tax receipts (and therefore less direct Treasury borrowing). Finally, banks will have less money for investment due to strong loan demand. All of these factors will tend to cause the spreads between Treasuries and Agencies to widen significantly. This widened spread relationship can be expected to reverse when interest rates decline because: (1) issuance of new agency financings will lessen; (2) direct Treasury borrowings will increase as the economy moves into a recession; (3) banks are able to obtain more money for investments due to a decline in loan demand and also by increasing their issuance of certificates of deposit (CDs).

An unusually clear intermarket swap opportunity arose in late 1973. At that time, the yields on Government National Mortgage Association (GNMA or Ginnie Mae) "pass-throughs" rose to very high levels relative to government Agency issues, because the primary buyers of the pass-throughs (savings and loans institutions) were experiencing a deposit drain. Many bank portfolio managers bought these securities since they believed that major pension funds soon would pick up the purchasing slack left by savings and loan associations and the unusually large spread between the pass-throughs and the Agencies would narrow sharply. This is precisely what occurred and those portfolios which had swapped into pass-throughs at the correct time realized a 50 to 70 basis point spread reversal.

The Yield Anticipation Swap

In a yield anticipation swap, the portfolio manager attempts to predict bond yields for some future period of time and then makes swaps based upon this prediction. For example, if yields are expected to decline sharply (and bond prices to rise) in the near future, the portfolio manager would be inclined to swap short maturities for longer maturities because he would want to "lock in" the current high level of yields for as long as possible (and also to seek some capital appreciation).

Needless to say, predicting future rates with any degree of accuracy and consistency is an endeavor fraught with danger. Therefore, yield anticipation swaps have a high degree of risk.

Tax-Loss Trading

A tax-loss trade is simply a swap in which the bonds that are sold are disposed of at a loss. Thus, any of the various types of swaps listed above would fall into the tax-loss category if the sale side of the swap resulted in a loss.

Exhibit 3 presents a simplified tax-loss trade involving two municipal bonds. For ease of explanation, we have ignored transaction costs and made the assumption that the coupon rate, maturity, and quality of the bonds sold and bought are exactly the same. The tax rate is assumed to be 50 percent.

At first glance, there seems to be no advantage to making this swap, merely an exchange of comparable securities. Coupon income stays the same. The future gain is exactly equal to the current loss and the tax consequences offset each other. However, there is an advantage. Today's tax liability has been reduced and the offsetting tax increase will not be incurred until a later date. In effect, we have the use of the cash saved through decreasing the tax liability, at no cost.

In high-rate periods, investment policy should aim for tax loss trades to eliminate low-yield, high-cost holdings and replace them with higher yield current issues, particularly since taxable earnings would tend to be relatively high at these times.

Every portfolio manager should be fully familiar with the federal tax implications of selling and buying like bonds when a loss is incurred on the sale and the sale and repurchase dates are on the same day within a short period of time. Reference should be made to Section 1091 of the Internal Revenue Code which lists the "wash sale" rules and regulations.

Gain Trading

In taxable securities, a profit is the same whether taken now or over time by holding to maturity. In low-rate periods, investment policy should aim for profit taking and shortening of maturities.

Gain trading municipals, however, converts tax-exempt income into a taxable capital gain. There can be reasons for profit taking in municipals (as, for example, at times when the portfolio manager believes bond prices are due to fall and it will be possible to buy the same bonds back more cheaply at a later date). But we should recognize that the tax mechanics work against gain trading in municipal securities.

Open-Ending

This term *open-ending* can refer to one of two investment techniques.

Exhibit 3
Example of Municipal Bond Tax-Loss Trade

Sell: $100,000 par value ABC City 4 percent due October 1, 1985 at 7.00% (78.68)
Buy: $100,000 par value XYZ County 4 percent due October 1, 1985 at 7.00% (78.68)

Original cost of ABC bonds	$100,000
Proceeds of sale	78,680
Gross loss	$ 21,320
Tax savings (50%)	10,660
Net loss	$ 10,660
Maturity value of XYZ bonds	$100,000
Original cost	78,680
Gross gain	$ 21,320
Tax on gain (50%)	10,660
Net gain	$ 10,660

Value of Trade: Depends upon rate at which the $10,660 tax saving can be reinvested until October 1, 1985. If the tax savings are used to purchase additional XYZ County bonds (the most common type of trade), then the advantage of this trade amounts to $6,590 as shown below.

Issue	*Amount*	*Coupon*	*Maturity*	*Yield*	*Original Cost*	*Price*
Sell:						
ABC City	100,000	4.00%	10/ 1/85	4.00%	$100,000	$78.68
Buy:						
XYZ County	113,000	4,000%	10/ 1/85	6.09%	$ 88,908	$78.68

Comparative Statistics	*Sell*	*Buy*	*Change*
Average coupon	4.00%	4.00%	0.00%
Average yield	4.00%	6.09%	2.09%
Average maturity	10.00 yr.	10.00 yr.	0.00 yr.
Annual coupon income	4,000	4,520	520
Annual amortization	0	0	0
	4,000	4,000	4,000
Annual accretion	0	1,205	1,205
Annual return	4,000	5,725	1,725

Loss on Sale:	
Book value of present holdings	$100,000
Sale proceeds	78,680
Gross loss	$ 21,320
Tax savings	10,660
Net loss	$ 10,660
Funds Available For Reinvestment:	
Sale proceeds	78,680
Tax savings	10,660
Funds available for reinvestment	$ 89,340
Cost of bonds purchased	88,908
Remaining funds	$ 432
Break-Even Calculations:	
Annual return on present holdings	4,000
Net loss on sales (annualized)	1,066
Amount to be recovered annually	$ 5,066
Funds available for reinvestment	89,340
Break-even yield	5.67%

Exhibit 3 *(continued)*

Supplemental Information

Time Needed to Recover Loss.
Increased annual return of $1,725 recovers net loss of $10,660 in 6.18 years.
This is 3.92 years prior to the average maturity of the present holdings.

Additional Return on Swap:

Increased annual return	$ 1,725
Average maturity of present holdings	10.00 yr.
Gross increased return	$17,250
Less: net loss	10,660
Net increased return	$ 6,590

1. Advance refunding of maturities or executing the buy side of a swap considerably before executing the sale side. (This is done when interest rates are expected to decline and bond prices to rise).
2. Temporarily keeping maturity proceeds in very short-term highly liquid assets (or cash) or executing the sale side of a swap before completing the buy side. (This procedure is used when rates are expected to rise and prices to fall).

IMPROVING RETURNS ON GOVERNMENT SECURITIES PORTFOLIOS

Repurchase Agreements ("Repos")

A sale under an agreement to repurchase is comparable to a collateralized borrowing. In a repurchase agreement, a portfolio manager will sell certain of his holdings and agree to buy back these same securities on a specified date. The portfolio must pay interest at the agreed Repo rate, but the coupon interest continues to accrue to the portfolio.

The advantage of a repurchase agreement is that the portfolio manager receives cash (i.e., is able to borrow) often at a rate lower than other costs of funds. As an example, let us assume the 30-day term funds rate is 7 percent while the 30-day Repo rate is 6.5 percent. Under these circumstances, the portfolio manager could capture the 50-basis point spread by doing a Repo at 6.5 percent and then selling the money he raised at a rate of 7 percent.

Resale Agreements ("Resales")

A purchase under an agreement to resell is comparable to a collateralized loan. This technique may be used as an interim investment of excess funds for the portfolio.

Lending of Government Securities

Lending government securities is another avenue for increasing a bank's investment income with very little risk. A portfolio manager simply lends a security to a government securities dealer and, in return, receives similar collateral with a market value of 102 percent of the loaned security. The bank earns a 0.5 percent fee for such a loan.

The portfolio does not give up any pledging ability while lending securities since the securities it receives as collateral are of like pledgeability. In addition, a bank may wish to lend securities rather than do a Repo if it is unable to reinvest the cash obtained in a repurchase agreement at a significant yield spread. The lending process currently allows 50-basis points in additional portfolio earnings.

Liability Management

As previously mentioned, bank portfolio management in the past called for selling portfolio securities to meet liquidity needs resulting from deposit drains and strong loan demand. This usually occurred at times when investment opportunities were the most rewarding. On the other hand, a large amount of excess funds generally was available for investment when yields were least attractive and income was needed. Time after time, banks found themselves caught in this "yield trap."

The purpose of liability management is to meet demands for funds by purchasing liabilities (Federal Reserve funds, certificates of deposit, and so on) rather than by selling assets (i.e., portfolio securities). This relatively new technique doesn't simplify the total asset/liability management problem but it does change bank liquidity concepts and frees the portfolio to some extent from its predestined cyclical fate of prior years.

These factors have liberalized investment policy and brought about a new recognition and awareness that a bank is a money processor or dealer. A bank's raw material is money in its marketable form.

AUTHORITY AND CONTROL PROCEDURES

The establishment of a clear, concise authority and control procedures is a highly essential part of portfolio policy. Without sound authority and control procedures, it becomes difficult both to chart future courses of action and to properly assess past performance. By all means, adopt a written investment policy.

Reasons for Having a Written Policy

There are two principal reasons for having a written investment policy:

1. Portfolio constraints, goals, and objectives become clear only when the persons involved in their development and implementation have agreed in their precise wording.
2. A written policy also provides a continuing understanding of these constraints, goals and objectives.

The Elements of an Investment Policy

The following elements should be incorporated in every investment policy:

1. In order to effectively react to changing economic and market conditions as well as new bank constraints and goals, every policy must have a sufficient amount of built-in flexibility and should be reviewed periodically. This factor should help to allay fears that a written policy will become too restrictive.
2. To provide for delegation of authority while maintaining control. In our opinion, this can best be accomplished through establishing a senior investment committee and appointing one bank officer to act as investment portfolio manager. Ideally, the duties and responsibilities of each should be as follows:
   a. Senior Investment Committee
      (1) Should be composed of members of senior management and/or the board of directors.
      (2) Should be ultimately responsible for establishing policy and the basic investment parameters and guidelines.
   b. Portfolio Manager
      (1) His role should involve the active day-to-day management of the investment accounts.
      (2) Should be able to recommend specific investment programs and major courses of portfolio action to the senior investment committee.
      (3) Must have sufficient freedom of action to operate effectively. The senior committee must not hinder the managers functioning with an unrealistically tight, rigid policy.
      (4) Even if the person responsible for the daily management of the portfolio has other nonportfolio related duties, the first and primary responsibility must be the investment account.
3. To develop suitable methods of investment performance measurement and establish the type and frequency of reviews, the report formats, and so on.
4. Do not confuse the investment account with a trading position. Recognize the basic difference in the outlook of these two areas.
   a. The trader must concentrate on the very short-term aspects of the market. One needs a "feel" for what the market is likely to do during the next two to three days.

    b. The portfolio manager should be looking to the longer term and must avoid the temptation to be caught up in the momentary trading sentiment.

5. For these reasons, strong consideration should be given to completely separating the portfolio account from the trading function because:

    a. Both must be allowed the necessary freedom to operate most effectively. Otherwise, one's gain may well be the other's loss.

    b. It avoids the temptation to bury trading mistakes in the portfolio.

CONCLUSION

In recent years, bank portfolio management has been confronted with new and greater problems. Bond prices and interest rates have become much more volatile, banks have expanded their activities into new areas of operation, and attention has been focused on managing liabilities as well as assets. These changes have begun to raise many searching questions about portfolio management in general and various investment techniques and strategies in particular.

We do not claim that the guidelines discussed in this chapter will provide all the answers to bank portfolio-related questions. Neither do we feel that following these guidelines and principles will guarantee a superior investment performance. We do believe, however, they will provide a solid framework within which a bank may more surely and easily achieve improved investment results.

Chapter 31

Interest Rate Futures and the Management of Bank Portfolios

MORTON LANE

President
Discount Corporation of New York Futures
Chicago, Illinois

One of the most exciting developments in American Security Markets in the past few years has been the birth and rapid growth of "financial instrument futures." Commencing in 1975 with the introduction by the Chicago Board of Trade of a Government National Mortgage Association (GNMA) futures contract, and followed by contracts in U.S. Government Treasury Bills and Treasury Bonds, activity in interest rate futures has grown to be a significant and apparently permanent feature of interest rate landscape. Repeating their successful introduction of stock options and currency futures, the two Chicago Futures exchanges: the Board of Trade (CBOT, historically specializing in grain futures) and the Chicago Mercantile Exchange (CME, historically specializing in livestock futures) have demonstrated that the principles of risk management and risk taking have a universality which can be applied to a variety of markets hitherto unexposed to the concept of futures trading. Table 1 shows trading activity and open interest in the new financial futures markets as compared with trading activity in the "cash" market for the last few months of 1978, and serves as testament to this point.

Both the activity and the open interest in these contracts suggest that such markets cannot be lightly dismissed. Further evidence of the successful nature of these markets is provided by figures from the Comptroller of the Currency and the Commodities Futures Trading Commission. The Comptroller of the Currency, responsible for authorizing the entry of national banks into the futures market for legitimate hedging activity, reports that 35 national banks have been approved for entry and that the list of applicants increases daily. The Commodities Futures Trading Commission reports in their monthly

Table 1
U.S. Treasury Bills

	Trading Volume (daily average)		Market Size	
	Bill futures volume*	Dealer activity in Treasury Bills‡	Open interest all Bill futures*	Bills under one year,§ ownership of marketables
Sep.	$4,472M	$5,867M	$34,676M	$160,936M
Oct.	$4,757M	$6,709M	$49,046M	$161,227M
Nov.	$6,899M	$7,022M	$53,831M	$161,548M

	Trading Volume (daily average)		Market Size	
	Bond futures volume†	Dealer activity in bonds over 10 years‡	Open interest in bond futures†	Ownership of bonds over 20 years§
Sep.	$302M	$ 994M	$1,469M	$25,439M
Oct.	$418M	$ 897M	$2,760M	$25,425M
Nov.	$454M	$1,314M	$3,576M	$14,521M

* CME.
† CBOT.
‡ Federal Reserve Bulletin Dealer Transactions.
§ Treasury Survey of Ownership.

analysis that a large percentage of Treasury Bill and Bond futures trading is conducted for the purpose of legitimate hedging of interest rate risks. This last point is important, for it belies the unspoken fear of some bankers that the Chicago activity in interest rates has been no more than a speculative excess which would soon pass away. To be sure, speculation is involved, for participation in the debt markets has meant a great deal of risk in recent years, but risks cannot be hedged away unless there are people prepared to assume such risks. The financial instruments futures markets, therefore, provide a meeting place for two opposite types of people: risk takers and risk averters. The exchanges stand between the two parties guaranteeing the contract on a day-to-day basis. Far from avoiding the futures markets, therefore, banks find themselves increasingly drawn to markets where they can prudently hedge interest rate risks.

EXISTING AND PLANNED FINANCIAL INSTRUMENT FUTURES—HOW THE CONTRACT MARKETS WORK

At the time of writing, the following markets and contracts exist for banks to conduct their hedging activity.

Chicago Mercantile Exchange (International Monetary Market—IMM—subdivision)

1. Three-month Treasury Bill contract (contract size $100 million)
2. One-year Treasury Bill contract (contract size $0.25 million)

Chicago Board of Trade (CBOT)

1. GNMA contract
   (a) with collateralized deposit receipt (contract size $0.10 million)
   (b) with certificate delivery (contract size $0.10 million)
2. Treasury bond contract (contract size $0.10 million)
3. 90-Day commercial paper (contract size $1.00 million)

American Commodity Exchange at the Amex (American Commodities Exchange or ACE)

1. GNMA contract (with certificate delivery, contract size $1 million)

At the same time the following contracts are planned, proposed or under discussion at various exchanges:

1. Euro-dollar time deposit contract (IMM)
2. Euro-dollar CD contract (CBOT)
3. 30-day commercial paper (CBOT)
4. 90-day Treasury Bills (ACE, Commodity Exchange, Inc. of New York, COMEX)
5. One-year Treasury Bill (COMEX)
6. 2-year note contract (COMEX)
7. 4-year note contract (IMM, CBOT, ACE)
8. Domestic CD contract (ACE, IMM)

Details of the various contracts and the way they are traded can be obtained directly from the exchanges involved or from brokerage firms who constitute clearing members of those exchanges. However, it may be instructive to follow through the mechanism involved in a particular contract in order to illustrate the way in which nearly all the contracts are organized. The example we choose is the mechanism used by the IMM in the conduct of trading the 90-day bill contract.

Suppose that XYZ National Bank wants to hedge a risk which involves buying a 90-day Treasury Bill for delivery in September (six months in the future say). To execute that order through the futures market, the bank will call its broker (a clearing member of the exchange subject to the rules of exchange, the scrutiny of the Commodity Futures Trading Commission and the requirements of the Commodity Exchange Act of 1974) who may inform the bank that the September contract traded last at a price of 90.50 (equivalent to a discount of 9.50), and may also inform him where the contract is currently bid and offered in the pit (the pit is the floor location where trading activity takes place). Unlike a dealer's market in government securities, the bid and offer do not represent the broker's bid or offer—they only

Figure 1

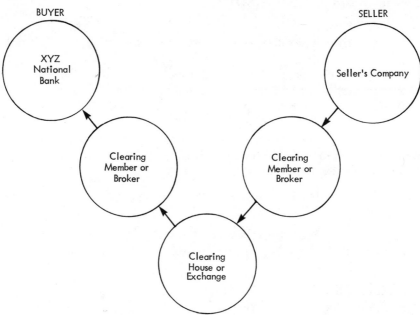

reflect last bids and offers given in the pit by public outcry. All futures
are traded in a single physical location not over a telephone network
as in government securities markets. If the price is appropriate, the
bank will instruct its broker to enter into a contract by buying the
September option. The broker or its agent will then enter the pit
and buy the September contract as instructed. Telephone confirmation
will be given to the bank and it will be "long one September contract."

At the end of the trading day and before the next day's trading
begins, the following activity takes place. The clearing members (brokers) who are the buyers and sellers of the contract inform the clearing
house (the exchange) of the details of the contract, e.g., price, quantity,
date, etc., and as long as there is agreement on all details, the clearing
house will "clear the trade" and the contract is complete. XYZ National
Bank has a contract to buy, with the exchange standing as a guarantor
of the contract. It's not necessary to know who the opposite party is
since the exchange stands legally between the two. Next, the exchange
will request from the clearing member of both buyer and seller, a
margin deposit as a sign of good faith. These requests are passed on
to the parties involved, and XYZ Bank has to send its margin (in cash,
bills, or letters of credit) to its broker who passes them through to
the exchange.

XYZ National Bank may now hold the contract until delivery, taking possession of the specified 90-day bill in exchange for funds, or can divest itself of the contract by selling in the pit, reversing the process above.

There is one further element to futures trading which differs from the government market. That is, while XYZ National Bank holds the contract, its value will be marked-to-market at the end of each trading day. If the price rises, the Bank will experience a profit on the contract and be credited with the appropriate funds that same day! The exchange will deduct from the short or seller's margin the appropriate funds and credit these to the long. At no time are funds unavailable from profitable trades, and at no time is credit extended to losing positions. Daily settlements ensure rigorous and continual surveillance of positions. To banks who have been concerned with recent failures of well publicized "forward" transactions, the procedure of daily settlement on regulated futures exchanges is a great reassurance.[1]

Commercial banks using interest futures for hedging purposes have two main areas in which hedging can be conducted: the asset portfolio and the liability portfolio. In the following section we detail examples from each portfolio to illustrate the versatility of futures trading.

EXAMPLES OF HEDGING SITUATIONS FOR COMMERCIAL BANKS

Asset Portfolio

1. An asset which was acquired so that its maturity coincided with the use of the funds may have to be liquidated earlier than expected due to the rescheduling of projects; therefore, it has interest rate exposure for the amount of time the maturity of the asset exceeds the funding date. This rising interest rate exposure can be hedged against by selling futures contracts to cover the maturity exposure.

2. A bond trader who has structured a trading position to express his risk, suddenly acquires an additional position sold to it by a bank client, and now has more risk than he wishes. He may divest himself of this risk by selling a like amount of futures contracts against the excessive position.

3. A bank portfolio manager whose portfolio is repo'ed or loaned out on a term basis may suddenly wish to reduce exposure to rising interest rates but is unable to sell securities since they are repo'ed or loaned out. The manager can achieve the same result by selling an appropriate amount of futures contracts.

4. A portfolio manager who anticipates a large inflow of funds at

---

[1] The term "futures" transactions is understood to mean contract transactions on regulated exchanges. "Forward" transactions are understood to mean private transactions between parties without independent regulation or surveillance.

a future date, but who expects interest rates to fall before the funds are received may hedge against the opportunity loss by buying future contracts in anticipation of the investment of the funds.

Liability Portfolio

1. A liability manager (a borrower) who expects interest rates to rise and, therefore, wishes to extend the maturity of his liability portfolio can achieve a similar result by selling futures contracts to add to the position. If rates do rise, the profit on the short futures position should equal that which would have been achieved by a longer maturity in the cash market.

2. A liability manager who wishes to raise funds for a short period of time, say three months, and who would also like to conserve on reserve requirements, can sell six-month obligations and divest oneself of the interest rate exposure on the remaining three months by buying interest futures contracts to cover the last three months use of the funds. The manager would thereby achieve a three-month liability as well as conserving on reserve requirements by issuing beyond six months (a saving, which could be as much as 2 percent).

3. A liability manager who feels that his portfolio is too long due to an expected fall in rates can hedge against opportunity loss by buying futures contracts and shortening effective maturity. Prior to the availability of futures contracts it was impossible for banks to reduce liability exposure and retain the use of funds, since reduction of exposure could only be achieved by buying cash assets against the liability.

Clearly, futures contracts can be used in a variety of ways in commercial banks for hedging interest rate risk. In some situations the futures contract merely augments exiting procedures of banks. In others, such as the liability portfolio, the futures contracts present some exciting new possibilities. In order to illustrate these possibilities further two numerical examples are given below.

A Numerical Example; Asset Portfolio

Consider the case of a portfolio manager who on September 21, 1978, was confronted with a portfolio with an average maturity of 12 months, and who believes that rates will rise and wishes to reduce exposure by 75 percent. Further, the yield curve facing the manager on September 21, 1978 is;

3 mos.	*6 mos.*	*12 mos.*
8.04 (discount)	8.10 (discount)	8.08 (discount)

The traditional way to achieve risk reduction would be to sell existing securities, and purchase three-month bills at 8.04 percent. Over the course of the next three months, the manager would have received a bond equivalent portfolio yield of 8.32 percent. In the process, one may have to take losses into the income statement and involve oneself in the purchase and sale of the whole portfolio.

Alternatively, one could have hedged the last nine months of exposure by selling three 90-day T-Bill futures and keeping the existing portfolio. On September 21, 1978, the appropriate 90-day T-Bill contracts covering the maturity spectrum were as follows:

Dec. 78	*March 79*	*June 79*
91.84	91.79	91.74

Three months later on December 20, 1978, these contracts were priced at:

Dec. 78	*March 79*	*June 79*
90.69	90.38	90.21

Had the portfolio manager kept the portfolio and hedged the last nine months of risk by shorting these three contracts, profit on the short on December 20, 1978, would be: $115 + 141 + 153 = 409$ basis points; each point valued at $25. The loss would equal $10,225 per $1 million face value of portfolio. We may approximate the loss on the portfolio by the value of the nine-month T-Bill on December 20, 1978, which was 9.62. Thus the 12-month T-Bill on September 21, 1978, at 8.08 (discount) became a nine-month T-Bill on December 20, 1978, valued at 9.62 discount, thus generating a loss of 154 basis points. Since each nine-month basis point is valued at $75, this is a loss of $11,550. However, the yield on a 12-month T-Bill at 8.08 percent discount is worth 40 bond equivalent basis points more than the three-month T-Bill at 8.04, so that over the three months an additional $990 more income was received on the existing portfolio.

Thus, the traditional versus hedging analyses are as follows:

Traditional Method	*Futures Method*
1. Sell portfolio whose maturity is 12 months	1. Keep existing portfolio whose maturity is 12 months.
2. Buy three-month T-Bills	2. Sell three 90-day T-Bill futures
3. Yield received over three months equal to T-Bill yield	3. Incremental yield received on portfolio over and above 90-day T-Bill rate—$990
	4. Profit on futures short—$10,225
	5. Loss on existing portfolio—$11,550
	6. Net loss on transaction—$335

In this example the hedge was not a perfect hedge, since it did not achieve the exact financial results of the alternative method. However the difference is small enough to illustrate that the major risk exposure was covered at very small costs. An experienced hedger would probably not have hedged by selling a strip of three consecutive futures but would have sold three of the most expensive of the futures, i.e., three of the June 1979 contracts. Had this been done, the above analysis would have turned the cost of the hedge from a small loss to a profit of $1,250 per million of face value portfolio. However whether or not a small profit is made on the transaction, the analysis illustrates that simple asset hedging through futures can work very efficiently.

A Numerical Example; Liability Portfolio

The case of hedging bank liabilities with Treasury Bill futures is a little less exact than the previous case of hedging government assets with a Treasury contract. Treasury contracts and CDs are different instruments and one does not provide a perfect hedge for the other. Nevertheless, the futures contracts can provide a partial hedge and other interesting features can be brought to light.

Consider the case of a liability manager who on December 11, 1978, wished to raise funds for a short period. At that time he could borrow as follows:

90-day rate	*180-day rate*
10.55%	11.05%

Suppose that it decides to issue 180-day paper but the next day receives information which causes it to expect rates to soften and wishes to half its newly-acquired exposure. It could *(a)* buy back another bank's 90-day CD or *(b)* it could buy a 90-day Treasury Bill future against the latter half of its exposure. Had it done *(b)* it would have purchased a contract with a maturity close to the maturity of the CD, i.e., the March 1979 Treasury Bill contract, at a price of 90.76.

By January 10, 1979, however, rates were as follows;

March contract	*180-day CD*
90.45%	11.32%

In other words, rates rose instead of softening. The manager, nevertheless, locked in his cost because he gained 27 basis points on the issue CD and lost only 31 basis points on the long of its 90-day T-Bill future. Not a perfect hedge but one where a major part of the exposure was locked in.

There is one other aspect to this hedge which makes it worthy of consideration, and that involves reserve requirements. Had the original issue been in 90-day CDs the net cost to the bank would have been the 10.55 percent, i.e., the 90-day rate plus 8 percent reserve requirements, a further 84 basis points. However, since a 180-day CD was issued, only 4½ percent requirements or a further 52 basis points extra were required. In other words, for similar three-month risks the bank conserved some 32 basis points on reserve requirements. Although the points spread between 90-day and 180-day rates on December 11, 1978 would not appear to justify the 180-day-futures transaction purely for this reserve requirement reason, it is obviously an important element to consider in making such calculations and can cause considerable benefit in periods of flatter yield curves.

It should be repeated again however, that Treasury contracts can only provide a partial hedge to bank liabilities. Explicitly the futures contract can provide an insurance against that component of CD rates represented by Treasury rates. T-Bill futures contracts can provide no hedging facilities for the fluctuations in the spread between bills and CDs, i.e., the credit risk component. For example, between January 10 and February 9, 1979, T-Bill rates fell 23 basis points, but CD rates dropped 77 points. The T-Bill/CD spread narrowed from 115 basis points to 61 points, i.e., 54 points. In the above 77-point drop in CDs, only 23 points was a hedgeable risk by T-Bill futures contracts. The remaining 54 points could not be hedged with existing contracts. Only when CD futures contracts are available and traded on the exchanges will it be possible to conveniently hedge the credit risk components of bank liabilities.

ARBITRAGE

There is one final area where banks may be involved in the futures markets, and that is the area of "arbitrage" (see Glossary). Obviously, the futures market is a market segmented from the cash market, i.e., there are participants in the futures market who do not have access to the markets and there are participants in the cash market who do not have access to futures. When this is the case, the two markets can get out of line, with excess supply or demand developing temporarily in either market. The role of the arbitrageur is then to supply excess demand in one market and hedge in the other. The transfer of demand between markets is thereby done at low risk and the arbitrageur takes his profit for performing an economic function. It is this arbitrage process which allows the futures market to provide a good hedge and banks themselves may wish to take part in this process.

The analysis of arbitrage situations is similar to that of hedging except that it involves questions of "cheapness" or "dearness" of futures contracts—the initiation of both sides of the transaction—and it therefore must also include financing cost calculations. Exactly how cheapness and dearness may be determined is perhaps best illustrated by numerical example. Consider the situation as it existed at the close of business on March 28, 1979, the cash and futures markets were as follows:

Cash market rates

3 mo.	6 mo.	12 mo.
9.42%	9.39%	9.23%

Futures market rates (90 day bills)

	June	September	March	December
price	90.64	90.71	90.76	90.82
percent	9.36%	9.29%	9.24%	9.18%

Now by observation, it is clear that all futures contracts are higher in price (i.e., lower in yield) than any cash instruments with corresponding maturity dates. It was also further known that the cash market had risen some four points from the previous day, whereas the futures rose 7–8 points. If equilibrium existed previously, excess demand was developing in the futures market. Should the arbitrageur therefore sell futures and buy cash instruments against them on a hedged basis? More properly what reward existed for the arbitrageur and what risks did he take?

There are many ways to evaluate this question and no one way is the proper way. However, one useful observation around which such analysis can be built is to observe that at delivery of a contract it must equal exactly the prevailing three-month T-Bill. Consider for example, selling the September contract against the six-month T-Bill. In order to hedge on an equal risk basis, two September contracts would have to be sold against one six-month T-Bill, i.e.;

Futures	*Cash*
Sell two September 1979 contracts (specifically, December 20 three-month T-Bills) at 90.71 (9.29 percent)	Buy six-month bill (specifically, September 27 bill) at 9.39 percent

Now if the arbitrageur were to hold the above position until the delivery of the September contracts on September 21, he would have to substitute his holdings of September 27 T-Bills for delivery of the December 20 T-Bills required on the September contract. The rate at which he could make that substitution is a critical part of his costs. For example, if between now and June 21 he were to "roll"[2] progressively from one weekly six-month T-Bill (i.e., the six-month T-Bill is issued every week) to the next for an average yield loss of one-half a basis point per week, the cost would be 6 basis points (i.e., 12 weeks between March 28 and June 21). By that time, however, he would be long (in the cash market) and short in the futures market, exactly the same in December 20, 1979 T-Bills, hence perfectly hedged.

Between June 21 and delivery on September 21, however, he would have to *(a)* finance its holding of the December 20 bill and *(b)*

---

[2] A weekly T-Bill roll is the name given by traders to the process of switching between T-Bills of adjacent maturity. Specifically, a trader holding the six-month T-Bill issued at last week's auction will keep his holdings current by switching or rolling to the new six-month T-Bill issued at this week's auction.

periodically adjust his hedge ratio[3] so that the maturity exposure of his futures contract equaled the remaining life of the December 20 T-Bill. Since he would have to go from a hedge ratio of 2:1 on June 21 to 1:1 on September 21, it can be assumed that the average hedge ratio would be 1.5. The profit on this part of his transaction would therefore be the difference between long and short cost at delivery, i.e.;

—short September 9.39 percent at 90.71 or 9.29 percent;
—long at 9.39 percent, less −0.5 "roll" for 12 weeks produces a long at 9.33;
—profit 4 basis points multiplied by average hedge ratio of 1:5;
—profit on transaction 6 basis points.

The final component of the analysis is the rate at which the cash bill must be financed. If it can be assumed that the bill at a 9.23 percent will have positive carry then the above transaction is clearly profitable. If, however, no positive carry be expected then the profits are only equal to six basis points. It will remain for the arbitrageur to make this risk-return judgment.

The above analyses provide a formal method of making bill arbitrage judgments over the period till delivery of the contract. However, it is not usually necessary to wait until delivery for an arbitrage justified by this method to show a profit. The profit may be made within days or weeks depending on the strength of the segmented demands. In the above example, profits were available within a few days. On April 2 prices were as follows:

September Contract	*Six-month T-Bill*
90.48 (9.52 percent)	9.51 percent
Profit on long −12 points	
Profit on short +23 points	

Thus arbitrage profit is net + 11 points or $550 per $1 million less the cost of financing the six-month T-Bill from March 28, 1979 to April 2, 1979, and this would be zero if the "when-issued" Bill were used.

CONCLUSION

The interest rate futures markets have grown considerably since their inception in 1975. With this growth has come depth, liquidity, and a growing awareness on the part of commercial banks about the advantages of using future contracts for hedging purposes. Interest rate futures can provide an alternative method of conducting traditional bank hedging activity (often with more facility than in the cash market). More important however, is the fact that interest rate futures

---

[3] The hedge ratio is the number of contracts held per $1 million of cash position.

provide the banks with new methods of hedging. Liability managers can now hedge their distant maturity risk and preserve the immediate or short-term use of funds. As the variety of contracts grows, this particular use of the market will probably become more easily transacted because of new liability instruments. Banks can therefore participate from the asset and liability portfolio. Also, if they wish to become involved on their trading desks they can become one of the instrumentalities for keeping the cash and futures markets in line through arbitrage. Altogether, the possibilities for banks are exciting and something that they can't afford to overlook.

Chapter 32

Personal Trust Management

JOHN R. BOYD
Vice President
Seattle First National Bank
Seattle, Washington

A prerequisite to personal trust management is the analysis of the personal financial condition of an individual or a family. Questions such as current income, source of income, federal income tax bracket, age, dependents, health, place of residence, and size of capital are all questions that must be examined carefully before an investment program can be undertaken. The establishment of investment objectives and maintenance of this statement of objectives is one key to successful investment results. Each individual's portfolio must be invested in accordance with his or her personal financial requirements.

There are four basic sectors of the capital markets in which the assets of discretionary trust funds for individuals are most commonly invested:

1. Cash equivalents (U.S. government obligations maturing within one year, commercial paper).
2. Fixed income securities (corporate obligations, municipal bonds).
3. Common stocks.
4. Real estate.

Each of the above sectors of the capital markets have varying volatility marketability, and return characteristics. The importance of the investment objective is that it creates a plan from which a portfolio manager can select an appropriate mix of assets. The most significant asset of some nondiscretionary portfolios is an interest in a closely-held business, partnership, or joint venture. These assets, although many times are very valuable, are not readily marketable and therefore require ongoing management unless they are to be sold to third parties or liquidated. The evaluation and operation of a closely held business requires an entirely different set of skills than the management of equity or fixed income portfolios.

And in still other personal portfolios there are valuable nonincome producing assets such as collections of art, stamps, or coins. These assets may be held by an individual for capital appreciation as well as personal enjoyment, but in an estate or a trust established for another individual they may be inappropriate and should be appraised and liquidated. So complete personal trust management services requires not only a thorough knowledge of marketable assets, but special skills in the management of other more exotic or unique investments.

TRUST INSTITUTIONS

Some trust institutions are chartered by the individual states and others by the federal government. The State Bank Commissioner regulates state banks and the Controller of the Currency regulates national banks. There are over 2,000 nationally-chartered bank trust departments and approximately 2,000 state chartered trust institutions. They vary in size from some New York banks which have several billion dollars under management to smaller state institutions with less than $10 million in manageable trust assets. Trust departments of major banks and trust companies currently have under management in excess of $330 billion in assets and serve over 1.3 million customers. Of that $330 billion, $143 billion is made up of approximately 800,000 personal trusts and estates of individuals. Banks administer approximately $150 billion in personal trusts, $13 billion in estates, and $75 billion in agency accounts. In 1977 the average personal trust account was approximately $200,000 in size and the average estate was $110,000. Both large and small trust departments offer a variety of service which includes custodial services and in many instances a full line of investment management services, including in-house mutual funds for both bonds and stocks, management of real estate and in some cases the management of closely-held businesses. In addition, trust departments manage guardianships, probate estates, and provide investment management for charitable accounts.

TYPES OF PERSONAL TRUST

A trust is an arrangement by which an individual confers legal title to property to another person or institution who agrees to manage that property for one or more third parties. The individual creating the trust is called the "trustor." The institution holding the legal title is known as the "trustee" and the person(s) who derive(s) the future benefit from the trust is the beneficiary. A trust for an individual may be created by a will, by agreement between the trustee and the trustor, or by a court order. There are three primary types of trusts for individuals:

1. The testamentary trust is created under the will of an individual.
2. A living trust is established in the individual's lifetime.
3. Life insurance trust, which is funded with the proceeds of life insurance policies.

An individual can become a trustee. However, the vast majority of trusts are managed by institutions, particularly arms of commercial banks. The major advantage of using a corporate entity versus an individual is that the trust institution has a continuing life.

A trust is a very flexible instrument meeting the needs and requirements of an individual; the trust agreement between the trustee and the trustor can be made to accomplish many goals simultaneously. The trust instrument can be changed by the person creating the trust to meet changing requirements of a particular individual or family.

The best known trust service rendered by banks is the settling of estates. The trust department probates a will when designated executor. The will may provide for a trust to follow so that the remaining assets after the probate period are distributed into a trust account which once again could have varying terms and conditions based upon the desires of the deceased. (The testamentary trust is created under the terms of a will.)

There are two types of living trusts—the revocable and irrevocable. A revocable living trust is established during the individual's lifetime and the terms and conditions can be changed by the trustor at any time during the trustor's lifetime. The irrevocable trust, on the other hand, once established cannot be changed. The primary motivation for establishing such a trust is that it provides substantial tax savings under certain circumstances. In addition, some bank trust departments act as guardians in the case of a minor or a legally incompetent person. Normally these relationships are created by court order.

Trust institutions charge fees for the management, custody, and record keeping of individual trusts, charging a fee normally based on a certain percentage of assets with certain minimums. As the portfolio gains in value, therefore, the trust institution will receive a higher management fee.

ORGANIZATIONAL STRUCTURE
OF TRUST DEPARTMENTS

The organizational structure of a trust department varies from bank to bank. There are normally five positions or functions in an investment organization within a trust department of a bank or a trust company:

1. The Trust Administrator

This person has the assigned responsibility for meeting with the client and compiling the biographical and financial data necessary to begin the construction of an investment objective. The investment objective is a process in which all of the relevant personal data is compiled and analyzed and from these facts an investment program is planned. In addition, the trust administrator tends to the individual requirements of a client.

2. The Portfolio Manager

The individual who is responsible for making the actual investment selections for the client is the portfolio manager. She or he works with the trust administrator in establishing the investment objective and then proceeds to develop a program which will make a disposition of assets between cash equivalents, stock, and fixed income instruments. If the client's assets are not of sufficient size to buy individual issues of corporate or municipal bonds, many trust departments offer commingled investment funds. These funds are made up of many individuals, commingled to allow the purchase of larger individual denominations and a greater number of issues than could be purchased by any one individual acting alone. The same is true for common stock and real estate commingled funds. The portfolio manager has the responsibility to monitor on a day-to-day basis the progress of the portfolio and to make adjustments from time to time as the agreement between the client and the trust organization allows. Some instruments permit the portfolio manager to use full discretion and other instruments limit in varying degrees the discretionary actions of the trust company.

3. The Security Analyst

In many trust departments the security analyst has the responsibility of developing the information from which buy and sell recommendations on industries as well as specific companies are made. The analyst works from a broad range of written material including annual reports and other stockholder information, as well as research produced by brokerage houses and other financial institutions. In many instances the security analyst conducts personal interviews with management of the company under investment consideration. The security analyst makes recommendations either directly or through committees to the portfolio manager who will select the appropriate individual stocks and bonds for a particular account.

4. The Securities Trader

The securities trader is responsible for executing the individual bond and common stock purchases or sales. The portfolio manager gives the securities trader purchase and sale orders. It is the trader's job to attempt to get the most advantageous price in the market place.

The above individual positions are present in one form or another in virtually all trust institutions.

A significant element in the success or failure of the investment performance of a trust company is its investment strategies and investment philosophy. Many trust departments are known primarily as equity investors because they invest the majority of the assets under their care in common stocks. Some trust departments have attempted to take a balanced approach between cash, common stocks, and fixed income instruments, attempting to time moves between the sectors of the capital market as their investment forecasts and strategies suggest.

In most instances the very process of constructing the investment objective indicated the portfolio mix by asset type most appropriate for an individual trust account. An individual may have a relatively modest need for current income but is looking for longer term capital appreciation. A portfolio manager may place the client's assets primarily in common stocks and real estate with some fixed income securities and a cash equivalent reserve. Other clients who have the same income requirements but are in a higher federal tax bracket may be placed in low yielding common stocks and municipal bonds along with a cash reserve. So in a very direct sense, the investment objective of the individual and the investment philosophy of the organization will determine the portfolio mix of a personal trust account. Depending on the specific organization the investment overview, forecasts, and/or strategies could be determined by one person. In some trust companies several people serving on an investment committee determine the overall strategic direction of the investment effort, and in still other organizations the responsible investment officer reports to an investment committee what actions have been taken. There appears to be no specific correlation between investment performance and the type of organizational structure which is utilized by a trust institution. There are some organizations in which one person dominates the investment strategy and others that are very participatory and decentralized, with a majority of the trust departments falling somewhere between these two extremes. The basis of selection of a trust organization for a particular individual would be a combination of the length and quality of the investment performance record, and an analysis of their stated investment philosophy as well as the degree of personal service required by the family in question. In most trust departments the trust administrator, portfolio manager, and security analyst work as a team to provide coordinated professional and consistent advice to the individual trust client.

INVESTMENT STANDARDS FOR TRUSTEES

For many years the basic standard utilized by organizations for investing personal funds was the prudent man rule. This standard derived from a 19th century Massachusetts court case which held that a fiduciary (the high standards required between trustor and trustee) could invest the funds of others as a prudent man would do, while taking into consideration the circumstances of a particular account. The Massachusetts State's Supreme Court in *Harvard College* v. *Amory*, ruled: "All that can be required of a trustee to invest is that he shall conduct himself faithfully and exercise a sound discretion. He is to observe how men of prudence, discretion, and intelligence manage their own affairs, not in regard to speculation, but in regard to the permanent disposition of their funds, considering the probable income, as well as the probable safety of the capital to be invested." The above principle with regard to personal trust investing was adopted in various forms by most state legislatures. Between that time and 1974 no meaningful body of law was passed and in many of the very occasional lawsuits filed the prudent man rule test was the only real standard applied by the court. The prudent man test really is an after-the-fact inquiry, asking if the action(s) taken by an investment advisory (fiduciary) on behalf of another would be action(s) that the hypothetical prudent man would have taken in like circumstances. In 1974 ERISA (Employee Retirement Income Security Act) was passed (see Chapter 22 for details) and there are some implications that the standards which apply under ERISA to the management of pension funds may also apply to the management of individual trust accounts. In any event, trust companies consistently have adhered to the prudent man rule for the last 40 years.

Prior to World War II trust departments, when investing for individuals, had a tendency to invest almost exclusively in fixed income securities. Many trust clients in that period had one large single block of stock in a company that was either controlled by or managed within a family and in some instances was publicly held. Income derived from dividends was either distributed to beneficiaries or placed into fixed income instruments by trust organizations. During the 1950s interest rates began to rise and bond prices fell causing trust organizations to reconsider this predominately fixed income preservation of capital philosophy. In the late 1950s and early 1960s trust institutions began to purchase more common stocks on the basis that U.S. corporations had a tendency to increase dividends on an annual or biannual basis and that dividend return plus some capital appreciation would be higher than an investment in a bond which had fixed interest payment until maturity. By the middle 1960s trust institutions had embraced the total return concept which essentially suggested that a dollar of dividend, interest, and/or rental inome was really the same as a dollar of capital gains. This philosophy was solidified to some degree by the U.S. tax code which dictated that capital gains were taxed at a lower rate than dividend income in most individual trusts with dividend-paying common stocks and corporate bonds over $1 million. In the late 1960s many financial institutions spun off a portion of their trust investment departments primarily to manage retirement funds; however, a number of these trust organizations also managed individual funds. During the 1970s the stock market performance overall had not been strong and with the passage of ERISA in 1974 a more balanced approach to trust investing developed.

ERISA encourages diversification and some trust organizations initiated commingled funds for real estate as well as purchasing common stocks of corporations in Japan, Canada, and several of the European common market countries. The search for consistently superior investment performance has not diminished but rather broadened. Over the last 40 years many trust organizations have developed the following tools and strategies.

First, investment forecasts which are an attempt to determine the basic level of economic activity for any period and to refine this economic forecast into a forecast for the movement of interest rates and the stock market as measured by one of the broadly accepted indexes such as Standard & Poor's 500. Once the broad framework of an investment forecast has been made, then the trade-off between the projected rates of return for the four sectors of the capital market can begin. Cash equivalents, fixed income securities, common stocks, and real estate portions of an individual's portfolio usually change slowly with time. However, individual asset turnover within a broad category of the capital market may be much more rapid. It is not uncommon for a fully discretionary equity portfolio to have turnover as high as 30 percent a year. (Eight or ten years ago some investment advisors were advocating a turnover of as much as 100 percent in any given year; however, this investment advice was given in periods of rapidly rising equity prices.) Real estate on the other hand may have a very small anticipated turnover, not only because of the rather high transaction cost associated with selling and buying real estate, but also because a specific and finite piece of property in many instances requires considerable preparation before a sale or purchase can be consummated. A further refinement of the investment strategy is an attempt to determine the relative attractiveness of industries within the Standard &

Poor's 500 and the absolute attractiveness of individual equities. The capital asset pricing model has indicated that diversification among common stocks and corporate bonds is an important element to minimizing market risk. However, the problem still remains for personal trust investors of combining the appropriate time horizon with an anticipated rate of return, thereby giving the portfolio a specific breakdown between income and capital gains while meeting personal objectives. This is where the investment objective is a catalyst between the investment requirements of a portfolio and the personal needs of a client.

The fundamental research and the analysis which goes into economic forecasting, interest rate forecasts, and the analysis of individual investment opportunities largely determines the performance characteristics of a personal trust operation. The investment process is continuous and, therefore, investment performance is the result of a series of decisions by several different types of professionals. The economist, the security analyst, and the portfolio manager must all interrelate effectively in order to identify investment alternatives that provide the optimum risk-reward relationship. One investment style may produce above average investment results in a short time frame and not in another, so the prospective client in search of a trust institution should review ten-year investment results in an attempt to determine whether that organization has demonstrated a consistent application of an investment process. In short, there is no precise formula which will satisfactorily guarantee investment decisions. In some instances the prospective client divides his assets between different trust investment organizations, placing some assets with a trust group that specializes in fixed income management, placing other assets with real estate managers, and still others with a trust department that works primarily in common stocks. This avenue of diversification is practical only for the very large asset pools of $5 million or more. However, there are clearly identifiable procedures by which a client can determine whether a trust institution has exercised good judgement in meeting one's personal unique financial requirements.

CUSTODIAL AND RECORD KEEPING SERVICES

An important element of a successful trust organization is the ability to effectively communicate with its clients. A critical part of this communication is the rather mundane area of record keeping. As well as providing a secure place for the safekeeping of securities, a trust institution is expected to provide at least the following information to clients:

a. a cash summary chronologically showing all income and principal receipts and disbursements,

b. an asset list (with cost and market values),

c. a summary of transactions, and

d. Performance evaluation for the preceeding period (usually one quarter) with comparative data to commonly used indexes.

In addition, many trust organizations provide supplementary data for the client which would include but not be limited to a written or oral summary of the previous period's portfolio strategy and account activity, a forecast of macroeconomic activity and the summary of basic investment strategy—and in some cases the trust institution provides written industry and company reports of investments held in a particular client's trust account. Once again, the above types of information vary between trust departments and as would be anticipated smaller accounts (under $1 million) probably would not receive some of the material mentioned above. Most trust departments of banks do provide a safekeeping capability with periodic asset summary reports mailed to their clients.

As part of the financial planning process, outside professional advisors are generally utilized by a client of a trust department. Attorneys for the drawing of wills, accountants for the determination of an appropriate tax plan, and life insurance consultants are generally consulted. The selection of the appropriate trust department will be determined primarily by the size and proposed disposition of the assets of an individual or family, as well as the philosophy of the trust department. There are some trust companies that do not manage closely-held businesses or real estate. The size of a trust would determine whether commingled investment funds would be used for the disposition of fixed income, common stock, or real estate assets. The determination as to when the various commingled funds are used vary between trust departments. However, it is very difficult to build a fully diversified marketable municipal bond portfolio with less than $700,000 or a corporate portfolio with less than $500,000 which would suggest an account size of approximately $1.5 million.

Another element to be reviewed by the client of the trust institution is the amount of transaction costs as well as management fees incurred in his account. In many instances the commingled fund is the most inexpensive method to obtain effective diversification.

CASE STUDIES

The following are two examples of investment programs recommended for two families.

Case 1

Current Situations. Professional man; age 52 with earned income between $90,000–$120,000 a year; a wife, age 48; three children, age 16–20; own their own home worth $200,000; owes $30,000 on a sailboat and $7,000 in miscellaneous debt. The family's spending requirements are approximately $3,800 to $4,200 per month. The wife has trust assets of approximately $600,000 and a life income in an additional $1 million of assets with her three children as equal remaindermen. The husband has approximately $250,000 in stock and bonds.

Analysis. What is the optimum portfolio of securities and what investment program would most likely meet the financial conditions of the family?

The family has very little debt and the husband's income is adequate to meet the current income requirements of the family; however, with three children near college age, a heavier cash requirement will develop. The wife's $1 million trust fund is to be distributed to her three children; therefore, it would be recommended that a very high percentage of this fund be invested in dividend-paying common stocks, perhaps up to 80 percent. The $600,000 fund which is her separate property, could best be invested 60 percent in municipal bonds—which generate tax-free income, with an additional 20 percent in common stocks, and 20 percent as a cash reserve. The 20 percent to be invested in common stocks could be invested in a common stock trust fund which would provide diversification and a lower management fee. Because the family has a net worth in the neighborhood of $2 million, approximately 10 percent ($200,000) cash reserve should be maintained. These monies could be left in a combination of savings, C.D.s and tax-free project notes with maturities not to exceed a year. As the couple reaches retirement age, it is possible that their current cash flow requirements will decline as their children are educated and leave home and their savings rate will probably move up correspondingly. An investment program should be initiated for excess funds and would be the quarterly purchase of municipal bonds as well as common stocks. Another strategy central to the income side would be to lower income taxes; therefore tax shelters should be explored by the family's investment advisor. Direct investment of real estate or oil and gas funds would be possibilities. The core of this investment program is a strong portfolio of common stocks.

Case 2

Current Situation. Husband 65 years old; wife 63; two children age 35 and 32; income of $65,000 a year; $40,000 salary, directors fees and dividends from an unregistered closely-held preferred stock issue; a 40 percent stock ownership in a closely-held business which acts as a manufacturer's distribution company and a fabricator as well as a custom producer of certain steel products. The business has a net worth of $3.5 million and an annual revenue stream of $11 million with an approximate $300,000 after tax income. The husband is the chairman; one daughter is president and CEO; and a son-in-law is a vice president of this closely-held company. Forty percent of the stock is held in trust for the two children and 20 percent is held in the wife's name. The husband holds $200,000 of investable assets outside of the business. The couple owns their own home as well as a vacation cottage with total value of $260,000.

Analysis. What is the best way to invest the funds of this family? The major source of cash flow for the three working members of the family is the closely-held business and the major assets of the family are in the stock of this business. The question becomes one of the desires of the majority stockholders (the husband and wife) as to the disposition of the business. They may elect to sell to a third party for cash, notes and/or stock, or a combination of the three. However, this may not be to the best advantage of the two working children. The husband and wife may elect to sell the business to the children on a favorable determination basis thereby creating an annuity which would ensure an adequate cash flow for their retirement years. In dealing with closely-held businesses, the most significant question is one of current market value as well as ongoing operating management.

These are very subjective questions which an individual family and their investment advisor, lawyer, and tax consultant will have to answer once the family has arrived at its particular objectives.

Of the $200,000 held jointly by the husband and wife $50,000 should be invested in cash equivalents, with maturities not to exceed one year, and the remaining $150,000 could be placed in municipal bonds. The family has a significant equity position with its closely-held business, therefore, common stocks, although offering diversification and marketabilitty, still have variable rates of return. It, therefore, would appear to be prudent to invest any free cash in fixed-income obligations of high quality.

SUMMARY

The effective management of personal trust accounts requires a thorough understanding of the current financial situation of an individual. Effective personal trust management also requires a periodic review of the personal circumstances of a family, as well as the disposition of assets. Probably the most important single ongoing consideration in the management of personal trusts, other than changes in conditions in the capital markets, is the family's tax situation. The whole process of bringing together the investment philosophy of a trust organization to meet the personal financial needs of a family is the key to long-term client satisfaction. The trust instrument is a flexible document which can meet the needs of several individuals or families simultaneously and provide the investment advisor with varying degrees of discretion and flexibility. In the future the search for superior investment results will continue and the portfolio manager will have better and more refined tools to assist in obtaining the desired financial goals for individuals.

APPENDIX

The following is a checklist of questions for examining individual trust portfolios:

1. Personal characteristics

    a. Age
    b. Health
    c. Geographic locations
    d. Personal pursuits
    e. Occupation
    f. Marital status

2. Financial considerations

    a. Income
    b. Source of income
    c. Capital
    d. Types of capital—instruments in which capital is invested
    e. Tax bracket
    f. A complete listing of bonds, common stocks, real estate, closely-held business
    g. Valuable or unusual items, such as art
    h. Recreational properties
    i. Vehicles

3. Future sources of income

    a. Future anticipated changes in economic status
    b. Anticipated changes in income requirements
    c. Additional sources of capital

The purpose of such a check list is to determine the current assets and tax information as well as future income requirements in order to prepare a personal financial objective from which investment strategies can be prepared.

Chapter 33

Managing Investment Company Portfolios

NORTON H. REAMER

President
The Putnam Management Company, Inc.
Boston, Massachusetts

WHAT IS AN INVESTMENT COMPANY?

An investment company is a trust or corporation whose only business is investing in securities on behalf of its shareholders. Investment companies have many different objectives and come in many different forms but they all have certain things in common. They all pool the resources of their shareholders to select a portfolio of securities which are chosen in order to provide the shareholders with income, appreciation, safety of principal, or some combination of the three. None of them engage in the other kinds of businesses with which companies are normally associated. They don't manufacture products, operate stores, sell insurance, lend money, etc.

Another feature investment companies have in common is that they all rely on professional investors to select or manage the securities in their portfolios. Some investment companies offer continuous management by professionals who not only select the securities but supervise them day by day and replace them with other securities when they believe it appropriate to do so. These investment companies are commonly known either as mutual funds or closed-end funds.

Mutual funds, or open-end funds as they are sometimes called, stand ready to repurchase the shares of their investors or sell new shares at any time. This is why they are called "open-end." The so-called closed-ends funds are more like normal corporations. Once they issue their shares they neither repurchase them nor sell more in the usual course of business and their investors must dispose of their shares to other buyers rather than to the fund itself when they want to sell.

The professional investors advising yet another kind of investment company, called a unit trust, merely select a portfolio of securities at the outset and then make no changes in the following months and years except when a legal event affecting one or more of their investments requires it.

The history of investment companies extends back to the 1820s when a precursor of the investment company as we know it was founded in Belgium under the name of "Societé Generale de Pays-Bâs pour favoriser l'industrie nationale." By the 1860s, British and Scottish investment trusts were being established.[1] To this day the Scottish investment trusts, which are still very much alive and active, retain a certain mystique concerning their investment acumen—at least with investors here in the United States.

While there were various types of investment companies formed in the United States before 1900, it was not until the 1920s that the investment company movement in this country started in earnest. During that period two important developments occurred side by side. In 1924, the first modern mutual funds were established beginning with the formation of Massachusetts Investors Trust in Boston. These funds were for the most part very conservative and survived the stock market crash and great depression of 1929–33 although the value of their holdings was much reduced. However, another type of trust which came into great vogue at around the same time did not survive the crash; this was the leveraged closed-end trust set up to speculate in the booming stock market of the late 1920s. When the bubble burst in 1929 many of these speculative trusts were swept away, their shareholders losing most or all of their investment.

Today, however, the investment company industry consists of over 700 mutual funds, at least 75 closed-end funds and scores of unit trusts (see Table 1). All of these funds taken together have assets totaling over $80 billion.[2] These investment companies are designed to meet a wide range of investment objectives, own a variety of securities and take several different forms. Let's discuss some of these forms in detail.

Open-end investment companies or mutual funds were described briefly earlier, but this most popular form of investment company deserves more complete treatment. Mutual funds generally sell shares to the public on a continuous basis, although some may suspend sales of shares at times for special reasons unique to them. Shares are normally sold through a distributing company closely affiliated with the fund on an exclusive basis. The distributing company may levy a sales

---

[1] *1979 Mutual Fund Fact Book,* Investment Company Institute, p. 10.

[2] *Investment Companies 1979,* Weisenberger Financial Services, pp. 5–6.

Table 1
Growth of Investment Company Assets since 1940

Year	Mutual Funds	Closed-End Companies	Total
1978	$58,144,400,000	$6,116,700,000	$64,261,100,000
1977	51,479,800,000	6,283,700,000	57,763,500,000
1976	54,174,600,000	6,639,046,000	60,813,646,000
1975	48,706,300,000	5,861,300,000	54,567,600,000
1974	38,545,599,000	5,294,000,000	43,839,599,000
1973	49,310,700,000	6,622,700,000	55,936,700,000
1972	62,456,500,000	6,742,800,000	69,199,300,000
1971	58,159,800,000	5,324,300,000	63,484,100,000
1970	50,654,900,000	4,024,200,000	54,679,100,000
1969	52,621,400,000	4,743,700,000	57,365,100,000
1968	56,953,600,000	5,170,800,000	62,124,400,000
1967	44,701,302,000	3,777,100,000	48,478,402,000
1966	36,294,600,000	3,162,900,000	39,457,500,000
1965	35,220,243,000	3,514,577,000	38,734,820,000
1964	30,370,300,000	3,523,413,000	33,893,713,000
1962	22,408,900,000	2,783,219,000	25,192,119,000
1960	17,383,300,000	2,083,898,000	19,467,198,000
1958	13,242,388,000	1,931,402,000	15,173,790,000
1956	9,046,431,000	1,525,748,000	10,572,179,000
1954	6,109,390,000	1,246,351,000	7,355,741,000
1952	3,931,407,000	1,011,089,000	4,942,496,000
1950	2,530,563,000	871,962,000	3,402,525,000
1948	1,505,762,000	767,028,000	2,272,790,000
1946	1,311,108,000	851,409,000	2,162,517,000
1944	882,191,000	739,021,000	1,621,212,000
1942	486,850,000	557,264,000	1,044,114,000
1940	447,959,000	613,589,000	1,061,548,000

Source: *Investment Companies 1979*, Wiesenberger Financial Services, p. 12.

charge (a "load" fund) or sell shares at the exact value of the assets represented by the shares with no sales charge (a "no-load" fund). Where a sales charge is made, it can range up to 8½ percent of the offering price of the shares. A major fraction of this amount is normally allocated to a broker-dealer, who makes the final sale to the public. Alternatively, the distributor in some cases has its own sales force which deals with the public directly. Here, all of the sales charge is retained to defray the considerable cost of maintaining a sales organization in the field.

The justification for this sales charge in the face of no-load funds, which have none, is that it pays for the professional sales advice which the broker-dealer or salesperson provides in making the prospective purchaser aware of the fund and in helping to select the correct fund to meet one's investment objectives. In fairness to both sides of the question, this service is often rendered extremely well. But at other times, the sales charge may not be diligently earned if the broker or salesperson sells an inappropriate fund to a client.

No-load funds sell primarily via advertising and word-of-mouth. This helps to explain why the mutual fund industry is still dominated by load funds which represent about 80 percent of total assets exclusive of money market funds. Nevertheless, during certain periods some no-load funds may attract a considerable quantity of assets. This is especially true if their performance is good enough to attract buyer attention. In the case of these no-loads, investors must usually take the initiative to select and purchase the fund which meets their objectives.

In addition to selling shares, mutual funds stand ready to repurchase, or redeem, these shares from shareholders who have decided to dispose of them for one reason or another. This is a valuable feature of the open-end mutual fund because it guarantees that shareholders will be paid exactly the value of their portion of the securities held in the fund, without uncertainty as to whether someone will buy the shares and whether the buyer will pay what they are really worth. This feature of mutual funds is virtually unique in the world of commerce. How many other products do you own which you could resell to the original vendor at their exact current value on any business day?

Virtually all open-end or mutual funds deal with a closely-affiliated management company as well as a distributing company. This management company is, in effect, an investment advisor who makes investment decisions on behalf of the fund. Management companies vary widely in size and presumably also in skill, given the wide range of performance which has been achieved by funds with similar objectives. Adequate size helps because there are many different functions which a management company must undertake, but it is no guarantee of good results.

There is a third major function to be fulfilled for a mutual fund. This is an administrative or service function in keeping the account and portfolio records, transferring shares which are sold or redeemed, paying dividends and other distributions, answering shareholder inquiries, etc. All of these functions may be performed by a third, closely-affiliated company known as a service or administrative company, or some of the functions may be performed by a bank or other vendor.

In most cases, all three functions, sales, investment management, and administration are carried on by one fund group which in effect sponsors the fund with the public. There is one other group of people to be considered, however, and their importance to the fund shareholder can hardly be over emphasized. This group is the board of trustees, or directors of the fund. The role of the fund's trustees (if it is a trust) or directors (if it is a corporation) is crucial because it is this group of people who have the ultimate fiduciary responsibility for protecting the interests of the fund's shareholders. They are elected directly by the shareholders and determine who shall manage, sell, and administer the fund. As a result, they have the responsibility of determining if these service organizations are doing a good job. If they feel they are not, they can either direct that the service be improved or recommend a replacement.

Historically, many fund boards of trustees or directors did not function very independently from the distributor-manager-administrator, but this has been changing in recent years. Now the independence of these boards is often real as well as theoretical.

Closed-end funds have total assets amounting to about 15 percent of the total of open-end funds and their capital structure is much like that of a normal business corporation. They issue common shares to the public and they may undertake bank loans or sell bonds or preferred stocks to investors. In the early days of the closed-end fund highly complex capital structures were popular, with all the desirable and undesirable effects of leverage introduced by senior securities. Since 1940 the number of funds using senior securities has declined steadily so that today the only significant type of leveraged closed-end fund is the dual-purpose fund described later.

As mentioned above, closed-end funds normally do not redeem their shares or sell new ones, although, like a business corporation they may do either from time to time. As a result, the shareholder has to purchase or sell shares in the open market with the effect that shares of closed-end funds rarely sell at exactly the value of their underlying assets. At times in the past, closed-end funds have sold at premiums over their actual net asset value but more frequently they have sold at discounts (see Figure 1). Premiums have presumably been based on the enthusiasm of shareholders for either the management of the fund, its portfolio, its capital structure or some combination of the three. The reason for closed-end funds selling at a discount is more difficult to determine but in recent years there has been a persistent tendency for investors to be unwilling to pay full value in the open market for financial assets held by intermediaries.

Most of the older open-end funds are common stock funds and are managed by their own staffs. Some are diversified in that they own securities in a substantial number of companies with no one or few of their investments dominating the fund. Others are either more limited in their investment universe (for example, Japan Fund) or more concentrated in their holdings (for example, National Aviation & Technology Corp. with 30–40 percent in airlines and another 40–50 percent in aerospace and technology).

In more recent years, the majority of new closed-end funds have been oriented toward income and have consisted primarily of bonds. These funds have for the most part been issued by large financial institutions, principally insurance companies. In the view of some, issu-

Figure 1
Ratio of Market Price to Net Asset Value for a Group of Closed-End Funds

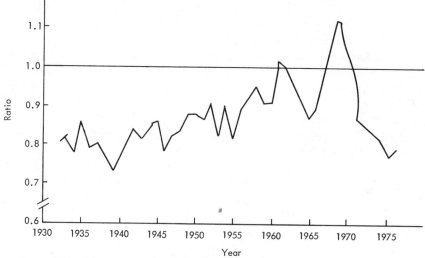

Source: 1933–1972: William F. Sharpe and Howard B. Sosin, "Closed-end Investment Companies in the United States: Risk and Return," *Proceedings, 1974 Meeting of the European Finance Association,* B. Jacquillat, ed. (Amsterdam: North-Holand Publishing Co., 1975); 1973–1975: updated by using data for eight funds (Adams Express, Carriers and General, General American Investors, Lehman, Madison, Niagara, Tri-Continental, and U.S. and Foreign).

ing shares in a closed-end fund for purposes of income investing is somewhat controversial in that it creates an additional aspect of principal uncertainty (the premium or discount) in an investment which is presumably intended to be low in risk.

In 1967, another closed-end fund phenomenon burst upon the scene. This was the *dual-purpose fund* and all of the eight funds now in existence were sold in that single year. These funds were composed of two classes of securities, capital shares which were entitled to all of the appreciation or depreciation; and income shares, which received all the income. Typically, the ratio was 50/50, i.e., each class had a claim on twice the appreciation or income that would otherwise have been expected. One effect was to give the capital shares 2:1 leverage. Dual-purpose funds were previously well known in England but their initial interest in this country was dashed by the poor stock market performance of the 1969 to 1974 period, which turned the leverage of the capital shares from a potential advantage into an actual disadvantage. In the eyes of many, however, this original concept is far from discredited.

The variable annuity is a product which is often related to an investment company. It is an adaptation of the older concept of a fixed annuity in an attempt to offset inflation for the annuitant. In the case of a fixed annuity, the insured purchases a contract in which an insurance company promises to pay a fixed sum each month, either for life or over a predetermined period. In the case of a variable annuity, the purchaser buys a certain number of units which entitle one, typically, to payments for life, but of variable amounts dependent upon the performance of an underlying portfolio, usually of common stocks. If the stocks rise, the monthly payments grow, if the stocks fall, they decline.

The impetus to variable annuities came from the great postwar bull market in common stocks, but since their introduction, stocks have not performed nearly as well and the linkage of their performance to inflation has been tenuous at best. As a result, the great popularity once predicted for the variable annuity has not developed and their assets represent only about 3 percent of the total of the industry.

The final major form of investment company is the so-called *unit trust*. These trusts have become increasingly popular in recent years and have been widely developed and marketed by investment dealers and brokers. The unit trusts are almost exclusively oriented toward income and limited to taxable or tax-exempt bonds. They typically have a long but limited life and while the securities are presumably selected with care, they are not continuously managed in the manner of either a closed or open-end fund. While a custodial fee is paid, there is no management fee and this tends to enhance the income offered to the shareholders when the fund is first sold.

The sponsor of this fund is compensated via a markup on the securities placed in the fund and/or a small underwriting commission. A resale market for the holder of a unit trust is usually maintained by the sponsor. However, both the existence of this market and the level of prices paid are solely at the sponsor's discretion.

The advantage of a unit trust is its typically higher yield at the outset. The disadvantage is the lack of continuous management and the somewhat greater uncertainty as to liquidity.

VARIETY OF OBJECTIVES AND TYPES

Over the years investment companies have been developed to meet virtually every conceivable investment need. This section will outline the principal classes of objectives and types of funds (see Table 2).

When looked at in terms of the major kinds of investment objectives which an individual or institutional investor might have, the number of necessary choices is quite limited; however, the variety of vehicles which have been devised to meet this limited number of objectives is remarkably complex.

Basic investment objectives can really be expressed only with respect to two variables: return and risk. Returns come in two forms:

Table 2
Classification of Mutual Funds by Size and Type (as of December 31, 1978)

Size of Fund	Number of Funds	Combined Assets ($000)	Percent of Total
Over $1 billion	8	$11,139,700	19.1
$500 million–$1 billion	17	11,536,000	19.8
$300 million–$500 million	21	8,333,100	14.3
$100 million–$300 million	87	14,824,600	25.5
$50 million–$100 million	79	5,747,300	9.9
$10 million–$50 million	234	5,916,600	10.2
$1 million–$10 million	128	636,500	1.1
Under $1 million	26	10,600	0.1
Total	600	58,144,400	100.0

Type of Fund	Number of Funds	Combined Assets ($000)	Percent of Total
Common stock:			
Maximum capital gain	103	$ 4,619,300	7.9
Growth	143	12,649,500	21.8
Growth and income	80	13,209,800	22.7
Specialized	23	732,800	1.2
Balanced	25	3,811,400	6.6
Income	119	8,904,400	15.3
Bond and preferred stock	11	1,119,600	2.0
Money market	59	10,462,700	18.0
Tax-free municipal bonds	37	2,634,900	4.5
Total	600	58,144,400	100.0

Source: *Investment Companies 1979*, Wiesenberger Financial Services, p. 43.

income and capital appreciation (or depreciation). Risk is more difficult to define, but in recent years most concepts of risk have centered on the degree of uncertaintly or variability of a future return. Typically, the more return you are seeking, the more risk you must accept. This last concept is so obvious that it hardly seems worth repeating and yet some of the most grievous errors in investing, whether in investment companies or otherwise, are committed through ignoring this very simple principle.

Given these basic objectives, most investment companies can be divided according to (1) ways in which they seek their return (through income, capital appreciation or some combination of the two), and (2) the degree of risk or uncertaintly they accept to achieve this return (high risk, low risk, or somewhere in between).

At risk of oversimplifying, funds can largely be divided into three broad classes:

1. Common stocks
    a. Aggressive growth (including the use of small companies and leverage)
    b. Long-term growth
    c. Growth and income
    d. Income (including option-income funds)

2. Mixed common stocks and fixed-income securities
    a. Balanced
    b. Convertible securities
    c. Income (mixed portfolio)

3. Fixed income securities
    a. Corporate bonds
    b. Government bonds
    c. Tax-exempt bonds
    d. Short-term securities

This list covers the vast majority of funds, but there are still some specialized classes which should be identified, although some may be construed as falling within one of the categories listed above (see Table 3). These include:

1. funds which invest internationally;
2. funds which invest in a single or limited number of industries such as insurance stocks, bank stocks, or public utilities;
3. Real estate investment trusts, which invest primarily in real estate loans, mortgages, or in properties themselves; and
4. tax-free exchange funds, which investors were able to purchase with appreciated securities without incurring a tax liability.

Table 3
Distribution of Mutual Fund Assets Calendar Year End, 1964–1978 (in millions of dollars)

Year	Total Net Assets	Net Cash and Equivalent	Corporate Bonds	Preferred Stocks	Common Stocks	Municipal Bonds	Long Term U.S. Government	Other
1964	$29,116	$1,329	$2,149	$ 687	$24,951	NA	NA	NA
1965	35,220	1,803	2,554	595	30,268	NA	NA	NA
1966	34,829	2,971	2,915	505	28,438	NA	NA	NA
1967	44,701	2,566	2,959	755	38,421	NA	NA	NA
1968	52,677	3,187	3,408	1,675	44,407	NA	NA	NA
1969	48,291	3,846	3,586	1,190	39,669	NA	NA	NA
1970	47,618	3,124R	4,286	1,143	38,540	NA	NA	$525
1971	55,045	2,601R	4,910	1,206	45,891	NA	NA	437R
1972	59,831	2,598	5,068	993	50,735	NA	NA	437
1973	46,519	3,426	4,196	623	37,698	NA	NA	576
1974	34,062	3,357	3,611R	426	26,103	NA	NA	565R
1975	42,179	3,209	4,766	506	33,158	NA	NA	540R
1976	47,582	2,352	6,977	655	37,158R	NA	NA	440R
1977	45,049	3,274	6,475	418	30,746	$2,256	$1,295	585
1978	44,980	4,507	5,545	405	30,678	2,550	1,093	202

Percentages

1964	100.0%	4.6%	7.4%	2.4%	85.6%	NA	NA	NA
1965	100.0	5.1	7.3	1.7	85.9	NA	NA	NA
1966	100.0	8.5	8.4	1.4	81.7	NA	NA	NA
1967	100.0	5.7	6.6	1.7	86.0	NA	NA	NA
1968	100.0	6.0	6.5	3.2	84.3	NA	NA	NA
1969	100.0	8.0	7.4	2.5	82.1	NA	NA	NA
1970	100.0	6.6	9.0	2.4	80.9	NA	NA	1.1%
1971	100.0	4.7	8.9	2.2	83.4	NA	NA	0.8
1972	100.0	4.3	8.5	1.7	84.8	NA	NA	0.7
1973	100.0	7.4	9.0	1.3	81.0	NA	NA	1.3
1974	100.0	9.9	10.6R	1.2R	76.6	NA	NA	1.7R
1975	100.0	7.6	11.3	1.2	78.6	NA	NA	1.3
1976	100.0	4.9	14.7	1.4	78.1	NA	NA	0.9R
1977	100.0	7.3	14.4	0.9	68.2	5.0%	2.9%	1.3
1978	100.0	10.0	12.3	0.9	68.2	5.7	2.4	0.5

NA—Not available.
R—Revised.
Source: Investment Company Institute, *1979 Mutual Fund Fact Book*, p. 30.

FEATURES AND SERVICES OF INVESTMENT COMPANIES

One of the attractive aspects of the open-end investment company approach to owning securities is the variety of special features and services which are provided to make different aspects of investing more convenient.

The investor has a multitude of ways to control the form and amount of one's investment. One can begin by utilizing the services of the investment company to hold one's shares. In this way, one is provided with a regular record of one's holdings without having to take possession of certificates with the various complexities of storage and transmittal so required. The investor may also establish either a voluntary or involuntary (contractual) plan for purchasing shares on a regular basis. In addition, most mutual funds are part of a group with a variety of funds offering differing objectives. For a small sum the investor may exchange his fund shares for those of another fund in the group and thereby adjust his holdings to any change in his objectives or expectations.

Open-end funds also offer a variety of plans for distributing income and capital gains. Most pay quarterly dividends from income earned and the shareholder may elect to receive these in cash or have them reinvested in additional fund shares. Similarly, realized capital gains are paid out, normally once a year, and can be taken in cash or automatically reinvested. With the growing interest in income in recent years, more funds have begun to offer monthly payment of income dividends. This is particularly useful to shareholders who wish to coordinate the receipt of fund income with their regular pattern of expenses. An older form of monthly distribution is the monthly cash withdrawal plan. Under this plan the shareholders specify in advance the amount of distribution they wish to receive each month and shares are liquidated to provide this amount. All income dividends and capital gains distributions are credited to the account and will partially or completely offset withdrawals.

In addition to various plans for purchase and exchange of shares, and a variety of distribution programs, most funds now offer a number of retirement plans such as Keogh plans, individual retirement accounts (IRAs) and corporate pension and profit sharing plans.

Cash Reserve Funds

The advent of funds which invest in short-term money market instruments, so-called cash reserve funds, have introduced some additional features such as the ability to write checks against a mutual fund account, the ability to wire funds into and out of a fund, a nonfluctuating net asset value (for a conservative cash reserve fund) with

any variation absorbed in the income generated by the fund, the decla-
ration of daily dividends (although payments are still made monthly)
etc.

With recent high short term interest rates these cash reserve funds
have enjoyed spectacular growth in investor popularity. By late 1979
they had grown to over $40 billion in assets and in doing so changed
the pace of the investment company industry. Their impact on other
forms of savings such as mutual savings banks and savings and loan
associations has been marked as well.

LEGAL, TAX AND REGULATORY ISSUES

An investment company is normally organized in one of three legal
forms. The most popular is the corporate form, the trust form is also
frequently used. Much less common but still used in certain specialized
applications is the partnership form. In general, the indefinite life and
limited liability of the corporate form makes it the preferred method
of organization, but certain tax factors may make the trust form desirable, particularly for the many investment companies organized in
Massachusetts.

Virtually all investment companies are operated so as to benefit
from Subchapter M of the Internal Revenue Code. By paying out at
least 90 percent of their interest and dividend income, investment
companies are seen to be "conduits" by the Internal Revenue Service.
Accordingly, they pay no taxes on all income and realized gains paid
out and the shareholder thereby avoids an additional layer of taxation
which would be experienced if the investment company were viewed
by the IRS as a conventional corporate entity. The investment company
does have to pay a tax on any income or gain it retains and so in
practice virtually all investment companies pay out all income and
realized gains (except for a limited income carry-over provision) each
year. The shareholder must, of course, declare and pay taxes on all
income and gain received in a given year, whether or not the payments
are taken in cash. Reinvestment of dividends does not eliminate their
taxability to the shareholder.

Regulation of investment companies is broad and deep, i.e., they
are regulated by several different agencies in several different ways.
They are also regulated under a number of different federal laws. A
brief summary of the principal aspects of investment company regulation follows.

The Securities Act of 1933 is addressed to the registration of securities and requires that issuers provide complete and accurate information to prospective purchasers. The effect of this law on open-end
funds is enhanced by the fact that these funds are in continuous registration in order that they may continuously offer shares to the public.

In addition to determining what funds must tell prospective shareholders, the Act limits false or exaggerated claims. Obviously, none of this protects the shareholder against adverse market developments or bad investment judgment by the management of the fund, or prevents one from purchasing an inappropriate fund for one's purposes. All it assures is that the shareholder will receive a prospectus having a certain minimum amount of accurate information.

The Securities Exchange Act of 1934 regulates, among other things, the operations of securities salespeople, including those who sell investment company shares. The act also permits the Securities and Exchange Commission to impose certain standards upon brokers and dealers and sets requirements for the solicitation of proxies which affects investment companies.

The Investment Company Act of 1940 is the major regulatory law affecting investment companies. It was promulgated to prevent abuses which had occurred in the 1920s and 1930s. It should be stressed, however, that there was (and continues to be) a high degree of cooperation with the SEC by the investment company industry in drafting and administering the Act.

The Investment Company Act regulates the conduct of directors, the management and the underwriters of investment companies; their structure and operations; financial practices and accounting; and assets and reserves. It also discourages excessive concentration of power, irresponsible persons in management, and changes in policies without the consent of shareholders.

In 1970 the Investment Company Amendments Act was passed. This updating of the 1940 act set new requirements with respect to fund sales charges and management fees. The Act had a major effect on contractual plan sales charges which reduced the appeal of contractual plan sales to fund underwriters and salespeople. In fact, the SEC had sought stronger legislation than was finally passed by Congress.

This long list of federal regulations affecting investment companies is by no means the end of the regulatory story. Funds are also governed by State Blue Sky laws. In certain cases, these set very strict standards governing the offering of securities to the public which have considerable impact on investment company operations.

Finally, most investment companies are subject to the "self regulatory" control of the National Association of Securities Dealers (NASD). The NASD administers a Statement of Policy concerning advertising and sales materials presented to the public.

One additional group should be mentioned although it is not a regulatory body. This is the Investment Company Institute (ICI) which attempts to serve funds, their investment managers, underwriters, and shareholders via providing information, research, legislative and regulatory activity, etc. This industry trade group was founded in 1941.

It is an active organization with broad membership and participation among funds, fund distributors, investment managers, and administrators.

INVESTMENT MANAGEMENT OF INVESTMENT COMPANIES

Like investment management organizations serving other types of clients, investment company managers come in a wide variety of styles and sizes. These organizations and their investment approaches merit examination, however, not only because they manage nearly $60 billion in open and closed-end fund assets but also because several organizations which were originally limited to managing only open-end funds have become major factors in the management of portfolios for other major institutions, especially corporate pension funds. Major fund organizations currently manage billions of institutional assets in addition to the fund assets under their control.

In part, the success of these organizations may be a result of their extensive experience in operating in a "goldfish bowl" with respect to performance reporting and measurement. Fifteen years ago, when many investment counselors and banks still provided only limited and fragmentary performance data to their clients, mutual funds were calculating performance precisely and in accordance with regulatory standards for wide publication and discussion, not only for shareholders, but also in various services which compiled and published the data for a broad audience of professionals to examine.

This stress on performance has led to some excesses in fund investment activities, but it has also led to the building of strong investment staffs at the major fund groups which have formed the basis for increased competition for banks, insurance companies, and investment advisors.

TYPES OF ORGANIZATIONS

A fully staffed fund investment management activity might typically be organized as shown in Figure 2. In certain ways the layout of the organization chart may seem obvious, but it deserves considerable discussion in understanding the organizational issues confronting not only mutual fund investment managers but also investment managers of all kinds.

We might begin by discussing an aspect not covered by Figure 2; The "investment committee" or "investment policy committee." This committee exists in virtually every investment organization of any size and it has a key role to play in the investment company structure as well. Membership varies from organization to organization, but typically the chief investment officer will chair the investment policy com-

Figure 2
Organization Chart of a Modern Large-Scale Investment Company Investment Management Organization

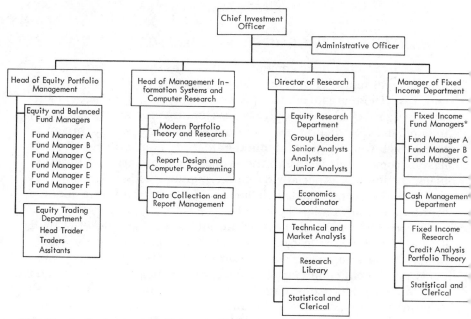

* Fixed income fund managers do their own trading.

mittee (IPC). Other members will normally include the heads of equity and fixed income portfolio management, the director of research, the economist or economics coordinator, and the head of the market analysis department. In addition, there may be some of the senior equity and bond fund managers, and the head of fixed income research.

The investment policy committee has some functions which are generally agreed upon, and some which vary from organization to organization. Most observers would agree that the IPC is responsible for setting the basic investment policy of each fund under management, subject, of course, to the concurrence of the fund's directors or trustees, who have the final authority to act on behalf of the shareholders. If the IPC believes the basic policy of a fund should be changed and the fund directors concur, it may well be necessary to change the wording of the fund's prospectus. This may in some cases even require a vote of the fund's shareholders.

Most of the time, however, the investment policy committee confines its policy-making activities to interpreting the intent of the fund's prospectus and adapting that intent to the ever-changing investment environment. Within this responsibility most observers agree that the IPC of a fund organization is responsible for setting the fund's current strategy on a regular and continuous basis. To do this, most IPC's meet at least quarterly, but more usually weekly or monthly; sometimes as freqeuntly as daily. At their meetings devoted to strategy setting, they will normally consider economic and political developments, equity and credit market developments and trends, and fundamental and technical reports and forecasts of various sectors, industries, and companies.

The output of these meetings will usually be expressed in terms of the proper mix of bonds, stocks, and short-term reserves to be held in the portfolio. In addition, the investment policy committee will usually deal with such issues as maturity structure, quality, and sector emphasis in the bond portfolios and bond funds which are under management. With respect to equity oriented funds the guidance will normally deal with issues of stock growth classification, quality, industrial sector, and industry. Risk exposure concepts will normally be articulated as well.

The role of the investment policy committee in individual stock and bond selections is subject to more disagreement. Few would dispute the assertion that the IPC has the full responsibility for all stocks and bonds which are selected. The question is more one of how it can best discharge that responsibility. This leads us back to the organization chart in Figure 2.

The chart prominently displays both equity and fixed income fund managers. Some organizational commentators would contend that these managers should work exclusively or largely from an approved list of securities selected by the investment policy committee or a subcommittee of this group (a stock selection committee?). Others might advocate selection directly by the fund managers. In either case, the role of the research department (equity or fixed) would be of crucial importance.

Those who advocate greater fund manager discretion do so in the belief that committees lack the deep involvement necessary to make the best decisions in a timely fashion. An individual fund manager knows what is going on and has the incentive to act upon that information. Others might point out the possible greater prudence and care of depending on the group decisions of highly qualified people. The right answer probably depends on the type of individuals involved, the kind of fund objective, and the circumstances. This author prefers the fund manager system in the belief that it leads to more decisive and timely action.

In fact, the open- or closed-end mutual fund manager is almost uniquely suited to bearing a high degree of security selection responsibility because there are very few conflicting demands upon the fund manager's time. Unlike the managers of pension portfolios, endowments, personal trusts, etc., the fund manager is importantly insulated from the client—the fund shareholder—by one or more layers of marketing activity. To some, this insulation is an undesirable feature creating the risk of a loss of perspective. However, in the opinion of this author, this slight risk is much more than offset by the additional time available to the fund manager and the reduced concern over being "second guessed" by a knowledgeable and highly visible client.

Figure 2 makes the equity analyst seem quite removed from the equity fund manager but that should not be the case. There should be an ongoing close working relationship between the two. Not only that, but the flow of information should move both ways with the manager requesting work and counsel directly from the analyst, and providing the analyst with ideas and leads.

Most large fund organizations have very active analyst groups in terms of field research. Company contact is frequent and in-depth and is supplemented by contacts with suppliers and general industry sources. In addition, large fund investment organizations execute sufficiently large orders in substantial enough volume to draw considerable supplementary support from the research departments of a wide variety of Wall Street brokerage firms.

Let's now return to Figure 2 to discuss some additional features of the modern investment company investment organization. Notice the prominent role assigned to the management information systems-computer group. While this chart may go farther than most actual organizations have at this stage, the trend toward management sciences becoming a major activity of fund and other investment organizations has now been clearly set in motion. The functions described in this segment of the chart are worth dwelling upon. They divide into three basic responsibilities:

1. research and development of advanced portfolio management techniques,
2. design of reports and programming, and
3. data collection and the management of reports and other data services.

The importance of these functions is growing to the point that they are becoming a major support activity of modern fund investment organizations.

In recent years, fixed-income fund management has become increasingly important as the investment company shareholder has focused more and more on high income and safety, and less on equities and possible capital gain. Whereas five to ten years ago many investment companies might have contented themselves with one bond manager and an assistant to handle cash reserves, today they are moving toward having:

a. specialized fund managers committed to various kinds of bond funds;

b. cash management departments geared to maximizing the returns available from reserve positions and reserve funds, which often amount to hundreds of millions of dollars;

c. growing fixed income research efforts which must cope with credit analysis of lower-rated issues and new modern portfolio theory concepts which are developing as rapidly in the fixed-income as in the equity sector of the market.

Returning now to the investment policy committee, there is a last function to discuss. This is the committee's role as the focal point of review and control of performance. Investment companies have come to realize that, like any other goal-oriented enterprise, they must organize to monitor the achievement of their goals and set up procedures to correct any shortfalls. This has projected the IPC, or a subcommittee, clearly into the role of reviewing the performance, structure, procedures, and plans of each fund and its manager on a regular basis and assuring that corrective action is taken when required. This review and control process is just as crucial a function of the senior investment committee and the chief investment officer as the establishment of policy or the setting of investment strategy.

One final role of the fund investment organization should be mentioned, this is the administrative, as well as investment, management of its affairs. The five line officers listed at the top of the chart in Figure 1 will normally be the principal administrative as well as investment officers of the fund investment operation. They may be supplemented as shown in Figure 1 by an administrative officer as well. This group, which may constitute an executive, management, or administrative committee, should function individually as well as collectively in the following areas: setting organizational objectives and policies; staffing, compensation, and other personnel functions; assuring development of new products and services; evaluating the performance of the investment operations in their various functions; etc.

INVESTMENT STYLES

Even within each of the three investment objective classes described earlier, there are a variety of investment styles which can be and are applied by different fund investment organizations. While we might try to describe each style within each objective category, these descriptions would soon become redundant. Instead, we may be able to draw some generalizations for equities management and some for fixed income management.

With respect to the management of *equities,* certain major approaches can be identified:

1. Growth Stocks.   There is a significant group of investment company organizations whose basic investment style commits them to investing a substantial percentage of their equity assets in so-called growth stocks. These growth stocks are the common stocks of companies which are growing in per-share earnings at rates which are substantially above the average of all companies in the market because of a dominant position in a key high-growth industry, product, or service. They typically have high returns on invested capital and rapid sales growth and they often are involved in technological or otherwise innovative businesses.

The fund which invests in this kind of stock must be prepared to pay a premium price earnings multiple and to accept lower yield, but other than that it may chose from a wide range of quality grades and degrees of aggressiveness. Like any specific form of investing, growth stocks investing has produced handsome returns in some periods (for example, 1971–72) and substantial performance lags in others (1975–76).

2. Growth in Earnings.   Some funds make the distinction in their investment style between investing primarily in growth stocks and investing primarily for superior earnings growth. While certainly we must acknowledge an overlap in these two styles, it is possible for a fund organization to select securities with rapid earnings progress in prospect because of cyclical or other unusual developments but which are not traditional growth stocks.

3. Young and Aggressive Growth Companies.   There is a family of smaller growth funds which emphasizes companies which are smaller, earlier in their growth cycle, and more volatile both in their fundamental business operations and in stock price performance.

4. Large Seasoned Major Companies.   Some funds emphasize investment in companies which meet certain standards of size or established industry position. These funds emphasize so-called "blue chip" companies because of their presumed quality and safety.

5. "Value" Investing (Low Multiple).   These are funds which emphasize value in their investment selections, focusing on stocks with low price earnings multiples in the belief that these "cheap" stocks will prove to be undervalued in the market place.

6. "Value" Investing (High Yield).   While some investors buy common stocks with high yield simply to benefit from the above-average income stream, some funds buy them as a better way to achieve superior total return.

7. "Value" Investing (Contrary Opinion).   These are always individual stocks, and even whole industry groups, which are out of favor in the market place at a given time. These are so-called contrary opin-

ion stocks which, if selected carefully, have the potential to offer not only the rewards which recognize fundamental progress, but also certain additional appreciation when the stock returns to investor favor.

These seven styles in equity investing are by no means all-inclusive. They merely list the major approach used by open- and closed-end equity funds today. There can be as many variations on these themes as there are fund organizations and fund managers. In fact, there are other issues of equity investment style which might also be properly addressed in this section.

8. Concentrated funds.   Investment styles can also be differentiated with respect to diversification or concentration of holdings. Funds differ in their attitude toward being focused on a limited number of industries and companies or having broad exposure to the economy and the stock market. As a result, some funds are highly concentrated and represent an investment program which will be less like the stock market in its performance. In some years, they may do much better than the market; in other years noticeably worse.

9. Fully Invested Funds.   Either by stated policy or by inclination, some fund managers follow a practice of being generally fully invested at all times. In so doing, the fund organization may be adopting the position that its job is to invest in common stocks, not short-term securities or other reserves, or it may simply be accepting the notion that correctly timing the stock market is too difficult to undertake with any appreciable expectation of success.

10. Market Timing.   Some fund managers believe they can anticipate market price movements well enough to attempt to raise and lower cash reserves in order to cushion the performance of their fund when a declining market is expected and allow it to become more volatile when an advancing market lies ahead. This is a controversial practice because accurate stock market forecasting is regarded by many as an impossible task. However, those who attempt to market time to a greater or lesser degree generally insist that the rewards of success are so high, and the penalties of ignoring the market cycle so great, that to remain fully invested at all times is foolhardy.

11. High- and Low-Turnover Funds.   Quite aside from considerations of market timing, funds can vary widely in their rate of turnover depending on their approach to stock selection and their patience in waiting for rewards. Some funds have turnover as low as 10–15 percent per year. While others, with similar objectives, may have turnover of over 100 percent per year. While various commentators often express strong opinions on the subject of turnover, this author knows of no study which has established any positive or negative correlation between turnover rates and performance.

Fixed income funds have differing investment styles as well. Since the major objective of fixed income funds is the production of as high a yield as safety will allow, the first basic differentiation in style is whether the fund invests in higher or lower quality securities. Bonds are the dominant security in fixed income funds in that preferred stocks have dividend taxation features which make them more favorable for corporations to own and therefore relatively less attractive to investment companies and individuals. Within the spectrum of bond quality, however, there are several different styles:

12. Medium- to High-Quality Bond funds.   These are open and closed-end funds which hold primarily bonds rated A to AAA. They can be considered to take only limited credit risk to achieve their income goals.

13. High-Yield Bond Funds.   These funds emphasize credits in the BBB to B range. They may go a little higher or lower under certain circumstances. They have, therefore, elected to take more risk of default in order to increase their yield to the highest possible levels.

Investment companies also have different ways in which they manage their fixed income portfolios with respect to turnover.

14. High-Turnover Bond Funds.   Relatively high turnover in bond funds is a comparatively new phenomenon borrowed from the managers of some corporate pension funds. Here the bond manager takes advantage of some swaps of less advantageous bonds into better-placed ones to enhance total return. The manager also moves more aggressively to position the fund for developments in the credit cycle by changing average maturity, quality, and the sectors which one is emphasizing at a given time. This style of management is generally limited to the medium to higher quality funds, because lower quality funds often lack the marketability to permit active trading without unacceptable sacrifice of principal value.

15. Low-Turnover Bond Funds.   Traditionally most bond funds have positioned themselves to meet a dividend which was promised to the shareholder, and have traded their holdings relatively little unless concern about the underlying safety of a holding arose. In the generally-declining bond markets of the 1960s and early 1970s, this led to the occurance of large discounts from par value in the funds' holdings.

RISK CONTROL AND MODERN INVESTMENT TECHNIQUES

The developments of modern portfolio theory are beginning to affect the management of investment company portfolios as well as pension funds and other large professionally managed funds. The movement began in the late 1960s with the first applications of risk analysis and control to fund portfolios. The concept of *beta* first appeared at this time. It meant volatility or variability of a security or portfolio and this notion became the best available approximation for risk (see Figure 3).

Figure 3
Fund Objectives Compared with Risk 1960–1969

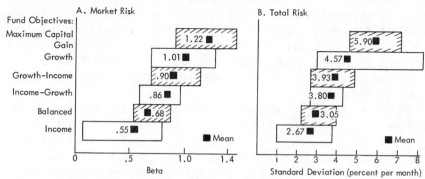

Source: John G. McDonald, "Objectives and Performance of Mutual Funds, 1960–1969," *Journal of Financial and Quantitative Analysis*, vol. 9, no. 3 (June 1974), p. 316.

Once the beta or volatility of a fund could be measured it could be controlled either by holding cash reserves or by replacing higher beta stocks with lower beta stocks. Most fund managers have come to recognize that cash reserves are more effective and predictable in lowering portfolio volatility than replacing a stock with another of presumably lower beta.

Then in the early to mid 1970s there was a rebirth of interest in valuation techniques among fund managers and a number of old and new techniques came into wide use. Of these the most popular is the discounted stream of future dividends model which attempts to value a common stock as a function of the analysts' forecast of expected dividend payments many years into the future converted to a present value.

The efficient market theory was slow to dawn in the fund industry because the concept was not only unpalatable to the industry's hundreds of money managers, but also has thus far proven to be of only limited sales interest. First Index Investment Trust, the only index fund which is publicly available, had assets of $66 million at the end of 1978.

During the last ten years the computer has come into wide use as an investment tool in the fund industry. Many security data bases have been built, both within individual fund groups and as services available for sale to investment companies and others. These have not only aided the securities analyst and fund manager by making data more readily and conveniently available, but they have formed the basis for a wide variety of screening techniques aimed at uncovering undervalued securities.

The ability to assemble large amounts of data for evaluation has permitted a variety of developments in modern portfolio theory to take real form. The use of beta or volatility analysis mentioned above would be difficult without the availability of the computer. Similarly, the calculation of such measures as alpha (the return achieved by a security or portfolio which is not explained by its risk alone) is greatly facilitated. Even the capital market line, the measure of reward available in the market place for accepting greater risk, can be computed rapidly, accurately, and frequently using the computer. These and many other techniques are aiding the management of investment company portfolios today.

Still another new investment tool which is coming into use among fund managers is the application of advanced data analysis and processing techniques to "optimize" portfolios. Optimization means structuring a portfolio in the most efficient manner, reflecting the nature of each of its holdings, to contribute to the achievement of the manager's expressed objectives. The ability of managers to optimize their portfolios more effectively is the product of considerable progress in the ability of researchers to subdivide each security, and therefore each portfolio, into a variety of characteristics which can be analyzed. The fund manager can then build up or reduce the amount of this characteristic present in a fund.

It is probably obvious, but still bears emphasizing, that the contribution of greater data processing power and more advanced theoretical techniques to fund management is likely to grow dramatically in the years ahead.

Still another application of modern techniques is present in a new investment area which promises to have major importance not only in the fund business but in pension fund management as well. This is the internationally-diversified portfolio. In the last few years, the ancient concept of diversifying ones assets geographically has reached a level of sophistication undreamed of even by the "gnomes of Zurich" only a few years ago.

Today international fund managers are using a concept which was discovered by a variety of academics in the 1960s to achieve the promise of higher returns at lower risk. This seemingly impossible trade-off of risk and return is made feasible by the low degree of correlation which exists between different national stock markets. The result is that a worldwide fund can diversify away some of the risk which exists in a portfolio confined to only one market (the U.S. for instance) while not reducing its expected return. In fact, of course many economies and markets outside the U.S. have grown more rapidly and offered higher returns than our market, but even without this favorable experience, there are advantages to international diversification.

Not only are a few funds beginning to take advantage of this concept of investing but in some cases they are using computer programmed diversification models to assist them in determining how much to invest in each market. One such fund, the Putnam International Equities

Fund, uses the following four criteria in its model: return expectations, correlation, variability, and transactions costs.

SELECTING AN INVESTMENT COMPANY

The bewildering array of open and closed-end funds presents the prospective investor with a complex job in choosing the one or two in which to invest. But there are a few rules which can help.

The most important decision the investor has to make is to define personal investment objectives. It is not enough, of course, just to define one's return preference. We each have varying ability and willingness to accept risk and uncertainty as well. They still aren't giving away something for nothing, and if the possible return is high, usually the risk will also be high. Once having made a candid assessment of need for income, capital gain objective and, most important, risk tolerance, the investor's next step is to examine the possible range of fund choices. A broad outline of this range is listed in Table 2.

Next, however, the investor needs to get down to specifics. One needs the details of each fund and information about its performance history. Probably the most comprehensive source of both kinds of information is Weisenberger Financial Services, a division of Warren Gorham & Lamont, Inc., 870 Seventh Avenue, New York, New York 10017. Weisenberger not only publishes quarterly performance data on the vast majority of funds but also publishes an annual investment company survey providing a wealth of data on the investment company industry and specific funds.

When it comes to analyzing performance, there are many surveys which appear in the financial press, the most widely-known probably being in *Forbes* magazine. However, most of these surveys are not comprehensive enough to support detailed study. One regular survey which is comprehensive but may be more difficult to obtain, is the work of Lipper Analytical Services of 5 Carol Road, Westfield, N.J. 07090.

Past performance numbers alone do not tell the whole tale, of course. It may be laughable to say so but what the investor would really like to know is what future performance numbers will be. The only way to gain a clue as to this is to know something about the organization which manages the fund in which you are interested. For example, while a large, well-established fund group hardly guarantees excellent performance: it does indicate the likelihood of a certain continuity of management.

The investor should study the management organization in as much detail as possible. In addition to the fund prospectus, which is required reading concerning fund objectives, etc., it is desirable to read past fund quarterly and annual reports if possible. A telephone call or visit to the management organization would be desirable. However, most investors not only lack the time and resources to make such a contact, but they would be hard pressed to come up with the right questions to ask.

Finally, once the fund has been selected, it is important to retain a perspective on the proper time horizon for expecting results from the investment. Funds should not be evaluated over weeks and months, they should be judged over several years. Only over this period can the effectiveness of management be fairly determined.

As a last caution, an odd fact of investment company investing is that like so many other areas of investing, the majority of buyers choose the most popular fund "at the top" and then sell later and under more depressed conditions. In order to avoid "buying high and selling low," it is essential that the investor keep realistic objectives and risk tolerances ever in view.

Chapter 34

Educational Endowment Funds

J. PETER WILLIAMSON
The Amos Tuck Graduate School of Business
Dartmouth College
Hanover, New Hampshire

HAZEL A. D. SANGER
Vice President
Thorndike, Doran, Paine & Lewis
Atlanta, Georgia

INTRODUCTION

The purpose of this chapter is not to give advice to portfolio managers on how to invest endowment funds; it is simply to acquaint managers with the institutional framework that they must be prepared to deal with. Endowment funds are different. This is a fact easily overlooked by a portfolio manager to whom "tax exempt" means pension funds. The world of educational endowments is a significant one, and endowment funds have unique features. Furthermore, portfolio managers will discover that working with trustees and investment committees of colleges and universities can be more complex than working with pension plan sponsors.

Probably the most significant difference is that the financial knowledge and experience of the majority of trustees and administrators of eleemosynary institutions is not easily translated to the specialized problems of running an endowment fund. Because investment results are a more familiar topic, and more frequently reported, there can be a tendency to focus on that issue to the exclusion of spending policy

827

or gifts, both of which are generally more important in determining future values of the endowment fund. Even at institutions where the board, and particularly the finance or investment committee, includes bankers, investment bankers, or investment counselors, with an impressive level of financial expertise, this expertise is not always integrated with an understanding of the complexities of endowment funds. There are of course exceptions, notably at the very largest institutions, where it is possible to have a financial staff of considerable depth and degree of specialization. At institutions where the trustees have widely different professional and business backgrounds, this is unquestionably a valuable asset in the overall guidance of their institutions, but it also means that, without extensive preparation on the peculiarities of endowment funds, there is often no common point of reference. The first job of the investment counselor, therefore, is to attempt to discover whether there is such a point of reference, and, if not, to assist the institution in developing one. How to do so will be discussed at greater length later.

Another difference, adding complexity to the first, is that over the term of an investment counseling relationship with one institution, there is probably both a greater number and a wider range of people with whom the counselor may deal. This arises from the turnover of trustees, committee members and committee chairmen. At some institutions a portfolio manager can count on seeing the same faces at committee meetings, year after year, but at others there may appear to be new committee members or a new chairman at almost every meeting. In addition, reporting relationships are frequently not as clearly defined as with a pension fund. The investment manager may be reporting directly to a committee, to a committee chairman, to an administrator, or to all of these. As people with different interests and personalities assume new responsibilities, there is sometimes an undefined shift in the reporting relationship which will require special attention. Institutional policies are obviously created by people; given different backgrounds and attitudes, turnover on committees can result in more shifts in both investment and spending policies than would be the case with most pension funds. The investment manager will therefore have a heightened obligation to explain the implications of any changes in policy, and to see whether they are acceptable.

A third difference is the constraint of time. Not only does the supervision of the endowment fund generally take a small part of a trustee's time, but when trustees gather for meetings, which is frequently when the portfolio manager is requested to appear, there are usually many other committee meetings on the agenda, some of more pressing importance. Unless it is possible to schedule separate meetings at another time, discussions of investment policy and of the portfolio must neces-

Table 1
The 25 Largest College and University Endowment Funds (June 30, 1977)

Institution	Market Value ($ millions)	Income ($ millions)
1. Harvard University	$1,227	$64.4
2. University of Texas at Austin	989	95.5
3. Yale University	563	26.3
4. Stanford University	456	24.1
5. Princeton University	434	19.3
6. Massachusetts Institute of Technology	337	14.9
7. University of Rochester	299	10.4
8. Columbia University	288	30.4
9. University of Chicago	279	14.7
10. Northwestern University	246	14.2
11. New York University	243	14.3
12. Rice University	240	14.7
13. Washington University	231	9.7
14. Rockefeller University	185	9.5
15. Johns Hopkins University	177	9.1
16. Emory University	164	7.4
17. Dartmouth College	157	8.3
18. California Institute of Technology	155	10.2
19. Cornell University	154	7.6
20. University of Michigan	116	6.0
21. Vanderbilt University	116	6.3
22. Carnegie Mellon University	112	6.3
23. University of California, Los Angeles	111	6.0
24. University of Notre Dame	110	5.4
25. Wellesley College	110	6.0

sarily be more concise than they would be with corporate officers administering a typical pension fund.[1]

The market value of all college and university endowment funds was $16.3 billion in 1977, according to the National Center for Educational Statistics. Thirty one institutions had endowments of $100 million or more, and they accounted for half of the dollar total. Another 77 institutions had $25 million or more and accounted for a quarter of the total; a further 123 had $10 million or more, 599 had between $1 million and $10 million, and almost 900 institutions had endowments worth less than $1 million. Table 1 shows the top 25 endowments as of June 30, 1977.

As the table indicates, the largest endowments are almost all found at private universities. State universities, with the exception of the

---

[1] The functioning of investment committees is discussed in some detail in *Funds for the Future*, Report of the Twentieth Century Fund Task Force on College and University Endowment Policy, with a Background Paper by J. Peter Williamson (New York: McGraw-Hill Book Company, 1975). Conflicts of interest on boards of trustees, a subject the investment manager should not ignore, are discussed in Chris Welles, *Conflicts of Interest: Nonprofit Institutions* (New York: Twentieth Century Fund, 1977).

universities of Texas, California, and Michigan are generally only mod-
estly endowed.

Pure endowment, or *true endowment* as it is sometimes called to
emphasize its difference from quasi-endowment, refers to funds that
have been given to an institution on condition that the principal be
invested and preserved in perpetuity, to produce an income that may
be spent for support for the institution (or in some cases added in
part back to the principal).[2] *Term endowment* is like true endowment
except that the principal becomes expendable at some future time.
Quasi-endowment or *funds functioning as endowment* describes funds
that belong to an institution and are not subject to any donor's stipula-
tion that the principal is to be preserved, but that the board of trustees
has decided to treat as endowment. Because the decision is the board's,
and not that of a donor, the board may change its position and spend
all or part of the quasi-endowment.

Quasi-endowment is a particularly valuable resource, as a source
of funds in emergencies and sometimes in implementing spending
policies such as those described later. As a part of understanding the
financial position of an institution, and the risks that may appropriately
be taken in investing its portfolio, it is important for a manager to
know how much of the endowment is true endowment, and how much
is quasi-endowment, and whether the board regards them differently
when setting policy. The trustees of some institutions are disposed
to take greater risks in investing quasi-endowment than they will take
with true endowment, since they are not held to the same legal obligation to preserve principal.

Sometimes *restricted* is used to identify true endowment, since the
principal is not available for spending, and *unrestricted* is used to identify quasi-endowment. But it is preferable to reserve these words to
distinguish between endowment that is restricted to the support of
certain activities—the purchase of books for a college library, for example—and endowment that is unrestricted and may therefore be used
to support any activity of the institution. Unfortunately it is often unclear from planning documents and financial statements just what is
meant by restricted and unrestricted, but it is important that the portfolio manager become familiar with the meaning and magnitude of the
restrictions since this will have a bearing on the appropriate portfolio
policy. For example, the income demands made on a restricted fund
may depend upon whether the purpose to which the fund is restricted
is important or relatively unimportant. The word *designated* is used
to describe endowment that the trustees, rather than a donor, have
decided to dedicate to the support of a particular activity.

---

[2] Some useful definitions of terminology and a general guide to endowment fund
reporting are contained in *College and University Business Administration* (Washington,
D.C.: National Association of College and University Business Officers, 2d ed. 1974).

There are other classifications of endowment that a portfolio manager should be aware of. Sometimes a portion of an endowment is held in trust by others. This means that a donor, rather than making an outright gift to the institution, has decided that someone else is to hold and manage the funds and remit the income to the institution. It is generally not possible for the institution to replace the outside trustees who manage these funds, and it may even be difficult to develop an overall investment policy to embrace them, although in most cases they are managed by bank trust departments and do in fact have a reasonably predictable income flow. Because the institution does not have access to the principal, these funds should not be included in any calculation of spending on a total return basis—a topic to be discussed below.

Gifts to educational and charitable institutions are sometimes accompanied by stipulations as to how the money will be invested, and there are frequently unwritten rules with respect to securities the institution will not sell, based upon consideration for past and future donors. It is important that the portfolio manager clearly understand these rules and give some thought in advance to how they may affect investment performance and the way in which a manager will be judged. We will come back later to the matter of measuring investment performance.

All of the classifications we have discussed will be reflected in the financial reports of the institution and to some extent in the investments of the endowment. Colleges and universities follow what is called fund accounting. For every fund there is a set of financial reports.[3] For example, Table 2 shows an excerpt from the balance sheet for Dartmouth College as of June 30, 1977. As the table suggests, these funds may be further subdivided, and Table 3 shows the components within the endowment fund.

At one time it was customary to invest each fund separately, with its own portfolio of stock and bonds. Fortunately most institutions have consolidated many small funds into pooled funds for investment purposes. A pooled fund serves much as a bank common trust fund does, with the individual funds set up by gift representing shares in the pool. Table 3 lists eight pools and the aggregate of the separately invested funds.

A few statistics relating to educational endowment funds may offer

---

[3] Ibid. Also, the investment manager should be aware of the Industry Audit Guide prepared by the Committee on College and University Accounting and Auditing, *Audits of Colleges and Universities* (New York: AICPA, 1973). Proposals for changes in reporting are contained in the FASB Discussion Memorandum, *An Analysis of Issues Related to Conceptual Framework for Financial Accounting and Reporting: Objectives of Financial Reporting by Nonbusiness Organizations* (Stamford, Conn.: Financial Accounting Standards Board, 1978). A Research Report preceded the Memorandum: Robert N. Anthony, *Financial Accounting in Nonbusiness Organizations* (Stamford, Conn.: FASB, 1978).

Table 2

DARTMOUTH COLLEGE
Balance Sheet of
June 30, 1977
(in thousands of dollars)

Current Funds:

Unrestricted	(1,576)
Restricted by college or donor	
Unexpended gifts	2,897
Unexpended investment income	1,857
Unexpended other funds	4,118

Loan Funds:

U.S. Government advances	4,708
Other advances	518
College loan funds	2,746

Endowment and Similar Funds:

Endowment	65,718
Quasi-endowment	55,541
Net realized gains	24,165
Life income funds	12,274

Plant Funds:

Unexpended	1,294
Renewals	118
Retirement of debt	490
Investment in plant	75,225
Total	$250,093

some perspective in judging the importance of endowment to a particular institution. The ratio of endowment income to total revenue for current operations is one measure of importance. In 1977, for 91 private colleges and universities responding to a questionnaire, the median ratio was 7.7 percent; the highest was 68 percent and the lowest was less than 1 percent.

Table 3
Endowment and Similar Funds of Dartmouth College as of June 30, 1977
(thousands of dollars)

	Book Value	Market Value
Pool Fund 1	111,102	110,956
Fund 2	5,438	5,442
Fund 3	3,108	3,071
Fund 4	4,744	4,667
Fund 5	917	952
Fund 6	895	915
Fund 7	4,120	4,151
Fund 8	585	584
Separately invested funds (endowment)	21,072	21,178
Separately invested funds (life income)	5,718	5,547
Total	$157,698	$157,463

Annual endowment income per student is another useful measure of importance. For the 91 institutions the median was $585; the lowest was $25 and the highest was $5,000.

We referred above to the importance of quasi-endowment. Of the 91 institutions, only 81 reported the percentage of endowment that was actually quasi-endowment. The median was 26 percent; the lowest was zero percent and the highest was 88 percent.

ORGANIZATION AND DECISION MAKING

The board of trustees of an educational institution or a charity has the ultimate responsibility for all of the institution's operations and policies. The boards of most charities are self-perpetuating, while trustees of educational institutions may be appointed for life, or elected by alumni, or, in the case of state universities, they may be political appointees. There is generally a budget committee and an investment committee of the board of trustees, although sometimes both functions are combined in a finance committee.

The investment committee will be charged with the direct responsibility for the endowment funds. This responsibility generally includes the establishment of investment policy and objectives, the hiring and monitoring of portfolio managers, and the approval of custodial and sometimes brokerage arrangements. The investment committee may or may not have the last word on the contribution the endowment will make to the operations of the institution.

The fiduciary responsibilities of trustees are generally defined by reference to the prudent man standard. However, in the increasingly large number of states which have adopted the Uniform Management of Institutional Funds Act, trustees' powers and responsibilities in relation to the management of the endowment fund are defined as follows (this is from the Model Act; some states have slight variations):

> SECTION 6. [Standard of Conduct]. In the administration of the powers to appropriate appreciation, to make and retain investments, and to delegate investment management of institutional funds, members of a governing board shall exercise ordinary business care and prudence under the facts and circumstances prevailing at the time of the action or decision. In so doing they shall consider long- and short-term needs of the institution in carrying out its educational, religious charitable, or other eleemosynary purposes, its present and anticipated financial requirements, expected total return on its investments, price level trends, and general economic conditions.

The last sentence provides a useful framework for both the trustee committee and the investment manager in looking at the endowment fund overall and at what it may be expected to contribute to the institution; in fact, to place it in context.

In many institutions the internal administrative staff manage investments that are related to institutional activities, such as loans to faculty or students. Some institutions manage their security portfolios internally as well. Questionnaire responses of 124 colleges and universities with endowments aggregating $8.8 billion in 1977 indicated a median value of 10.5 percent of endowment assets managed internally. Where external portfolio managers are used, a variety of working arrangements can be found. At one time it was customary for the investment committee itself to make all final decisions, with the portfolio manager serving as no more than an advisor. In some cases this procedure was based upon a belief that the trustees could not legally delegate the purchase and sale decisions. At the present time, few trustee committees operate in this way. Not all committees give full discretion to the portfolio manager, although 80 of the 124 institutions referred to above said that they did grant full discretion within a set of guidelines. Some committees require that the manager work from an approved list, and reserve to themselves the authority to add to or subtract from the list.

SETTING INVESTMENT OBJECTIVES

It is particularly important that the investment objectives and policies be written down, both to encourage continuity of policy, and to ensure that the implications of the policies are recognized.[4] A committee may well be reluctant to tackle this subject, which can be complicated and will probably require some background discussion of investment theory as well as—for the trustees—some time-consuming examination of the institution's priorities. It can be helpful for the committee to use a questionnaire to determine priorities since this is the simplest way to identify fundamental differences of understanding or opinion among the committee members, and therefore to determine what they must discuss to reach a consensus. The investment manager should encourage discussion among the trustees against a background of material that will help them to make realistic decisions. He should, for example, provide material on the relationship of both historical and expected returns to inflation, since inflation is clearly a predominant concern. He should be prepared to examine the question of acceptable levels of volatility, since return objectives will almost certainly be penalized if trustees are presented with unanticipated per-

---

[4] *Funds for the Future.* Another useful reference is Burton G. Malkiel and Paul B. Firstenberg, *Managing Risk in an Uncertain Era: An Analysis for Endowed Institutions* (Princeton, N.J.: Princeton University, 1976). A third reference is J. Peter Williamson, *Performance Measurement and Investment Objectives for Educational Endowment Funds* (New York: The Common Fund, 1972).

formance figures which create an undesirable reaction. If the investment organization has the capability of producing simulations, these
can be extremely helpful in the discussion process, to discover which
outcomes would be more acceptable than others.

The manager should summarize what he sees as the most important
objectives and constraints, to be used as a basis for discussion with
the committee. The ideal statement of investment objectives is one
which has been worked on jointly by the committee and the investment
adviser. If the institution already has such a statement, the manager
should raise for discussion any objectives that he considers unrealistic.
If the committee is not interested in writing a statement of objectives,
the investment manager should write down to the best of his understanding what appear to be appropriate objectives and make sure that
everyone on the committee has a copy.

As committee members or administrators change, he should review
the objectives, to make sure that there are no changes in the institution's circumstances, as well as to make sure that the new members
of the committee understand the basis from which the manager is
working. A written statement of objectives which has been actively
discussed will help the investment committee, since it will now have
defined standards against which to judge the manager's performance;
it will also help the manager since he will not have to guess at an
appropriate policy. Investment performance will of course continue
to be important, but within the limits of what is appropriate for the
institution. For example, an investment manager directed to produce
a level of income denominated in dollars should not be blamed if he
has not at the same time beaten the market. Neither should the manager get credit if the marketplace has moved to favor the stocks in
the portfolio: the investment policy has been set to meet the needs
of the institution, not in an attempt to beat the market. The more
straightforwardly this issue is faced, the less chance there will be for
confusion later. If an external performance measurement consultant
is involved, one with an ability to compare funds with similar objectives
will clearly be preferable. Many trustees will have other investment
relationships; care must be taken, as with all investment responsibilities,
that policies are set and results measured within the context of what
is appropriate for that institution.

The starting point in setting objectives is a statement of what role
the endowment is expected to perform. While many boards of trustees
have not articulated their concept of endowment's role, probably most
would agree with a hope or expectation that the endowment will serve
future generations of students about as well as it is serving the present
generation, that it will continue to generate a spendable income that
will hold its own with inflation and purchase a constant set of goods

and services over future years.[5] This is about equivalent to an expectation that the endowment will grow at the rate of inflation. The Harvard University goal is stated as follows:

> The objective of the Harvard Endowment Fund is to invest in such a manner as to create a stream of investment returns which treats equitably, in inflation adjusted dollars, all generations of students and the public as beneficiaries of the various Harvard programs, and does so at a level of risk which is prudent. Harvard's investment horizon must consider current needs as well as the needs of one hundred years from now.

It is important to realize that inflation in higher education may have been as much as 1½–2 percent a year higher than inflation in the economy generally, and in the long run will probably continue to be higher than general inflation, simply because of a lack of the productivity increases found in industry.

G. Richard Wynn has probably studied inflation in higher education as carefully as anyone. He has explained the causes of inflation rates that exceed those for the economy as a whole, and reported for 1964–73 an annual rate of inflation for a sample of liberal arts colleges that was 1.7 percent above inflation measured by the Consumer Price Index. As even he has noted, however, recent years may appear to contradict the lesson of history.[6] A price index for higher education is calculated annually by Kent D. Halstead from the Department of Health, Education, and Welfare.[7] In Table 4 his figures are shown for 1971–77, under *Per HEW*. They can be compared to the Consumer Price Index (which in the table has been adjusted to start at 100 in 1971), and the comparison indicates that over the seven-year period inflation in higher education was actually slightly less than inflation in the economy as measured by the CPI.

But the reason for this lies in the slow increase in personnel compensation in higher education, especially since 1974. The last column in the table shows what the Higher Education Price Index (HEPI) would have been if personnel compensation (which makes up about 70 per-

---

[5] A useful reference on the financial status and financial needs of higher education generally is William W. Jellema, *From Red to Black? The Financial Status of Private Colleges and Universities* (San Francisco: Jossey-Bass, 1973). Two older studies, still useful for their analytic content are Howard R. Bowen, *The Finance of Higher Education* (Berkeley, California: Carnegie Commission on Higher Education, 1968), and William G. Bowen, *The Economics of the Major Private Universities* (Berkeley, California: Carnegie Commission on Higher Education, 1968).

[6] Much of Wynn's analysis is summarized in G. Richard Wynn, "Inflation in the Higher Education Industry," *NACUBO Professional File*, vol. 6, no. 1, (National Association of College and University Business Officers, 1975).

[7] The original publication in the series is D. Kent Halstead, *Higher Education Prices and Price Indexes*, DHEW Publication no. (OE) 75–17005 (Washington, D.C.: U.S. Government Printing Office, 1975). Supplements have been published for 1975, 1976 and 1977.

Table 4
Inflation in Higher Education

Fiscal Year	Consumer Price Index	Higher Education Price Index	
		Per HEW	Per Hourly Earnings Service Workers
1971	100.0	100.0	100.0
1972	103.6	105.6	107.2
1973	107.7	111.2	113.5
1974	117.3	119.0	123.1
1975	130.4	129.2	134.2
1976	139.6	137.8	143.7
1977	147.7	146.7	155.1

cent of the total Index) had risen as fast as average hourly earnings for service workers. The number in the column "Per Hourly Earnings Service Workers" would have represented the HEPI, for an average rate of increase of 7.6 percent, or 0.9 percent faster than inflation in the CPI.

Squeezing personnel compensation cannot go forever. And history suggests that the decline in the relative purchasing power of this compensation will have to be made up at some future time. Higher education personnel lost a total of about 5.5 percent in purchasing power from 1971 to 1977. It therefore seems only prudent to assume for the future a rate of inflation for higher education of at least 0.5–1 percent above the rate of inflation in the Consumer Price Index, and perhaps also to anticipate an additional one-time 5–6 percent compensation increase, in considering what objectives must be met if the endowment fund is to be able to serve the future as well as the present.

The four most important factors that will determine the future value of the endowment fund to an institution are:

1. the investment returns to the fund,
2. the gifts to the fund,
3. the spending rate of the fund (the actual dollars spent—whether from income only or from income and principal—as a percentage of the fund's market value); and
4. the rate at which inflation experienced by the university exceeds that in the economy at large.

It is useful to express this as a formula in which the rates are expressed as percentages of the market value of the endowment portfolio:

$$RTR + G - SR - EIP = REG$$

RTR = the total rate of return of the portfolio in real, or inflation-adjusted, terms

G = the rate of gift additions

SR = the spending rate

EIP = the excess of the institutional inflation rate over the general inflation rate, or the educational inflation premium

REG = the resultant real growth rate of the endowment fund

Thus, a real total return in the portfolio over time of 3 percent, added to a gift rate of 2 percent, will total 5 percent. An institution with a spending rate of 5 percent and facing an internal inflation rate of 2 percent above the general inflation rate will therefore probably see the endowment fund decline by approximately 2 percent in value over time. Obviously there will be very wide ranges around some of these numbers; but the exercise is nevertheless worthwhile in focusing attention on the central issues.

The portolio manager can help to establish what are reasonable performance expectations, and what risks must be taken in aiming at, for example, 3 percent real return a year. If balancing the equation seems to call for an unreasonably high rate of investment performance then something will have to give. Greater effort or fund raising may raise the gift target; otherwise either spending must decline or the trustees must give up an expectation that the endowment will keep up with inflation.

The formula can of course be rearranged to focus on any element in the decision. For example, if the committee members have firm views about the long term real growth objective of the endowment—REG—and an acceptable asset mix—implied by RTR—expressing the formula as

$$RTR - REG - EIP + G = SR$$

will help to determine a sensible spending rate.

Rate of return targets are generally expressed in nominal terms, but there are two good reasons for preferring real terms. The first is that it helps to focus on the issue of positioning the fund with regard to inflation. A suggested expectation of a 9 percent nominal return will be more challenging to an investment committee when it is translated into a zero real return expectation and will probably lead to more careful consideration of the asset mix. The second reason is that future expectations can be more easily compared to past experience, as inflation changes, if they are expressed in real rates.

Keeping up with inflation in providing spendable income is probably the most widely acceptable growth objective. This is equivalent to setting REG equal to zero. Some institutions will, or should, see a different role for their endowments. In some cases endowment is the key to improving quality, and endowment income will be expected to finance new programs and new facilities. In other cases, trustees may be expecting endowment not only to maintain its own purchasing power but to make up the loss of purchasing power in other revenue sources. A small private college, for example, competing with tax-supported institutions, may be unable to raise tuition at as high a rate as inflation. Endowment income may be expected to fill the gap.

Of course it is quite possible that these expectations are unrealistic. A portfolio manager may be able to help the trustees to arrive at realistic assumptions. In the discussion process, it is important to realize that some factors in the equation are either more predictable or more controllable than others.

Real Total Return

Capital market returns and the asset mix will together determine the real total return of the endowment fund. Capital market returns are essentially unpredictable and outside the control of the investment committee. The asset mix, on the other hand, is totally controllable. The asset mix decision should depend on two main considerations:

1. the target level of growth of the fund: if the asset mix is set because of current income needs, this nevertheless has implications for the long-term growth of the fund; and
2. the degree of volatility that is acceptable in the fund: the level of the spending rate, the rate of gift additions and the degree of budget support provided by the endowment fund are all significant factors in deciding this, as well as the risk tolerance of the investment committee.

Spending

The spending rate is totally controllable. This, of course, is quite different from saying that spending in dollar terms is predictable. The alternative approach, of spending a figure set in dollar terms, will of course mean that the spending rate as a percentage of market value is uncontrollable, since it will be determined by fluctuating market values.

Gifts

After the asset mix and the spending rate, the gift rate is the next most controllable item. There is obviously an element of randomness in the experience of any institution, but there is probably some long-term correlation between effort and returns.

Table 5
Fiscal 1975, 1976, and 1977 Gifts to Endowment as a Percent of Average Market Value

	Fiscal 1975 Median Institution	Fiscal 1976 Median Institution	Fiscal 1977 Median Institution
Market value			
Over $50 million	2.0%	3.1%	2.3%
$10 to $50 million	2.3	2.2	3.1
Under $10 million	3.1	5.1	6.7
Private institutions	2.3	2.4	3.0
Public institutions	3.6	4.7	3.7
All reporting institutions	2.6%	2.7%	3.1%

Fund raising is a topic beyond the scope of this chapter, except that its importance to the long-term value of the endowment fund cannot be stressed too much; and it should therefore be considered in setting endowment fund objectives as much as it is in budget planning. Table 5 may offer some guidance with respect to reasonable expectations. It is based on the 1977 survey (the most recent published) of the National Association of College and University Business Officers (NACUBO).

Educational Inflation Premium

It is almost totally outside the institution's power to control this, although its impact may be reduced by organizational changes which may in turn affect the quality of the institution. It is difficult in any case for most institutions to have a clear idea to what extent their internal rate of inflation differs from the general rate of inflation in the economy, or even from published indexes of inflation in education.

The *Stanford University Statement of Goals, Objectives and Policies* covers all the four major determinants by describing the goals of the endowment fund in these terms:

> Follow a spending rule (payout rate) [in this case, 5 percent of a 36-month moving average of market value] that maintains the purchasing power of endowment income and protects the real value of endowment principal.
>
> *a.* An increase in the spending appropriation that over time equals the average institutional inflation rate, to offset the impact of inflation on Stanford's operating budget.
>
> *b.* An expected long-term real total return of between 5–7 percent and a nominal return that reflects inflationary expectations. With a 6 percent inflation assumption, this suggests a nominal return of between 11–13 percent over the next three to five years. In addition to this investment objective, we look for additions to endowment through capital gifts of between 2–2.5 percent a year.

Following any discussion of these major topics in the Statement of Objectives, there should be a list of investment policies defining the types of assets that the trustees consider appropriate, and either the levels or acceptable ranges for the debt-equity ratio, for volatility or variability, for diversification and for liquidity. Investment constraints should list restrictions on turnover, quality standards for stocks or bonds, and any specific companies or areas of investment that are to be avoided. Finally, standards of measurement should be described, as well as the length of the measurement period.

SPENDING POLICY

Spending policy is an important part of the preceding equation, and since the rules governing spending from endowment are unique and complex, the subject is worth some discussion.

Until the mid-1960s, almost all educational institutions were content to follow the traditional legal rules for trusts in determining the amount to be spent from true endowment. They simply spent the income that came in the form of dividends, interest, royalties, and the like, no more and no less. But experience of the earlier 1960s suggested that this practice, while sanctioned by a long tradition, might not be the most sensible. Inflation rates were quite modest, so it appeared that only modest growth in the endowment was necessary to maintain purchasing power. At the same time, common stocks with low dividend yields had shown substantial appreciation. Referring back to the equation that balances the sources and the uses of endowment, it appeared that spending dividends only from a low-yield common stock portfolio meant spending too little currently and saving too much for the future. It meant penalizing the current operations of the institution for the sake of enhanced operations sometime in the future. It is easy in the late 1970s to look back critically at a belief that common stocks could be counted on to provide appreciation well in excess of inflation. But while the dissatisfaction with the traditional rule may have been inspired by misconceptions about the stock market, it was a proper dissatisfaction and one that is just as appropriate today, under quite different market conditions. In the early 1960s an institution heavily invested in common stocks and spending only the dividends on those stocks appeared to be spending too little and saving too much to offset inflation. These days an institution heavily invested in fixed income securities and spending all of the interest on those securities is almost certainly spending too much today, and saving too little to compensate for inflation. This is because in inflationary times a portion of the higher current income from bonds is compensation for probable erosion of the purchasing power value of the investment and should not be spent, but reinvested.

Commenting on the traditional rule that income yield is the appropriate amount for spending, the treasurer of Yale University said in
his report for 1965–66: ". . . it is only by coincidence that yield will
be a correct balance between the present and the future. Some institutions in their particular circumstances ought to save some yield; others
in theirs ought to spend something beyond yield." If an institution is
committed to spending income yield, no more and no less, then it
can achieve an appropriate balance between spending and saving only
by an asset allocation policy that makes portfolio income yield equal
to the appropriate spending amount. The income target can be adjusted on an annual basis, or an attempt can be made by reserving
income to increase control over the income flow from year to year.
In both cases, however, this means that spending policy essentially
drives investment policy. Those who were unhappy in the 1960s with
the traditional rule believed that it is better not to have spending
policy determine investment policy. And so there developed what is
often referred to as the total return approach.

There are two aspects of a total return approach. One involves investment policy.[8] An institution that invests for total return may have
no particular target income level in mind, since a dollar of income
may be treated as equivalent to a dollar of appreciation. In accordance
with the provisions of the Uniform Management of Institutional Funds
Act, quoted above, a total return spending policy means spending what
is considered to be a prudent portion of the total return on the
endowment.[9] This may or may not include a transfer from principal;
but if it does, the principal should only be withdrawn from the net
of the fund's realized and unrealized appreciation over historic cost,
i.e., the value of the fund at the time of the gift. This accumulated
appreciation figure must therefore be carefully watched as transfers
are made and as volatility and asset mix decisions are made about
the overall fund. Most trustees probably wish to attempt a balance
of current spending and growth to maintain purchasing power, although clearly there may be circumstances in which the trustees feel
it is legitimate to favor the present or the future in setting policy for
the fund. Some of these were mentioned earlier. For an institution
holding a predominantly equity portfolio in the mid-1960s, a total return spending policy generally meant spending somewhat more than
the dividend yield, diverting some of the appreciation on the portfolio

---

[8] Investing for total return was put forward in 1969 in a highly influential publication
of the Ford Foundation, the so-called "Barker Report": *Managing Educational Endowments* (New York: Ford Foundation, 1969, 2d ed. 1972).

[9] The legal aspects of the total return spending are discussed in two Ford Foundation
publications: William L. Cary and Craig B. Bright, *The Law and the Lore of Endowment
Funds* (New York: Ford Foundation, 1969) and *The Developing Law of Endowment
Funds: "The Law and the Lore" Revisited* (New York: Ford Foundation, 1974).

into current spending. For an institution with more emphasis on fixed-income securities today, a total return spending policy would call for spending considerably less than the interest income and reinvesting a portion to maintain purchasing power.

Unfortunately, total return spending is associated in many people's minds with spending more than income. And it is remembered as having led many institutions to overspend from their endowments in the late 1960s and 1970s. What went wrong was not the adoption of a total return spending approach but application of the approach on the basis of much too optimistic expectations with respect to the performance of the stock market.

In fact, the major virtue of a total return approach to spending is that it provides a discipline, by ensuring that no more than a limited percentage of the fund (whether more or less than its income) is consumed in any period. It can also help in dealing with the question of how to balance present and future needs. The discipline may at best be inconvenient at times, as many trustees and investment managers found when they faced the prospect of a reduced contribution from the endowment fund to the institutional budget as the results of the years 1973 and 1974 were brought into the formula calculation of the amount available for spending. At worst, it may be disastrous, if the fund raising effort is seriously impaired by alumni reaction to a decline in endowment fund values. Some institutions, in reaction to the poor experience of the mid-1970s—both in terms of asset values and spending levels—have abandoned a total return approach and returned to spending income only, raising their fixed income holdings at the same time, to provide higher levels of income and lower volatility of principal.

Perhaps paradoxically, the greater the percentage of fixed income in a portfolio, the more useful a total return spending formula becomes. A spending formula developed on the basis of long term estimates of return from capital will make it easier to hold spending down to an appropriate level. And applying this approach to a fund with a large fixed income component and therefore low volatility, will produce less variability in spending than would arise from a fund heavily invested in equities. As for the merits of spending only income at high levels of equity exposure, this is a safer policy from the point of view of the budgeting process, since the typical institutional quality portfolio is unlikely to produce declines in income from year to year; and in fact, can probably be relied upon to produce increases. The corollary of course is that the trustees must be prepared to accept consequently higher levels of volatility of the principal value. This approach contrasts strongly with that advanced in the late 1960s, when trustees were dealing with endowment funds with high levels of untapped capital appreciation, to which total return spending approaches

gave them access. With total return spending, the challenge for a portfolio manager and an investment committee who are agreed upon
the long-run investment merits of a predominantly equity policy is
to determine how predictable are those levels of realized and unrealized capital appreciation and, simultaneously, how much volatility the
budget can bear. If the endowment fund contributes only a very small
amount to the budget, much greater volatility may be acceptable than
if the institution is heavily dependent upon the endowment. All of
this has to be taken into consideration and actively discussed with
the trustees.

A number of institutions are using a total return spending policy
today. Those that do not, and simply spend only from income received,
whether they spend all or try to maintain major reserves for smoothing
spending flows, generally have a dollar income target at which the
portfolio manager must aim. It may be important to keep this limitation
in mind when judging the performance of the manager. Occasionally
the target is expressed as a yield percent rather than a dollar income
level, but this makes little sense for the manager or the institution
because fluctuations in value will require constant shifts in asset mix.
Institutions that have adopted a total return spending policy generally
do not impose a strict income target on the manager, although some
have chosen never to spend more than income earned and therefore
will probably indicate a minimum income target. On the other hand
some are willing to spend more than income, but have been forced
to set a minimum income target because a combination of past spending at too high a level and poor investment performance have eliminated the appreciation reserve. Even where a total return spending
policy is followed, investment policy and spending policy cannot be
completely independent; both will require constant reassessment. It
is therefore important that the portfolio manager and the investment
committee understand the relationship between the two.

A total return spending policy demands some mechanical device
for setting the budgeted spending year by year. Working with the
equation we have seen above, a budget committee or an investment
committee usually establishes the appropriate amount for spending
in terms of a percent of market value. In recent years the most popular
figure has been 5 percent. Now if an institution were to spend each
year 5 percent of the market value of its endowment at the beginning
of the year, the result would be an intolerable fluctuation in spending,
because endowment values fluctuate significantly in the market place.
So some sort of smoothing formula is necessary.[10] There are many

---

[10] Formulas for spending, and a general discussion of the establishment of a spending
and an investment policy, are contained in Richard M. Ennis and J. Peter Williamson,
Spending Policy for Educational Endowments (New York: The Common Fund, 1976).

Figure 1
The Trade-off between Stable Spending and Protecting Growth in an Endowment

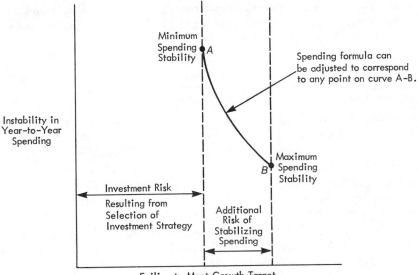

Source: Spending Policy for Educational Endowments, The Common Fund, 1976.

such formulas in use, but a widely used example is: spend in any fiscal year a fixed percentage of the average market value of the endowment at the end of the five preceding fiscal years. A five-year basis appears to maximize the trade-off between keeping the spending reasonably stable and at the same time not imposing too much of a penalty on the future value of the endowment.[11] Some institutions will average quarterly values rather than annual values; some will use three or four, rather than five, years. Some will introduce a time lag between the averaging period and the budget year, or set a year to year percentage increase in income, so that the spending amount can be determined somewhat in advance of the year in which it is spent. Whatever the formula, the objective is to stabilize spending. Now the connection between spending policy and investment policy comes up again. The more fluctuation there is in the value of the endowment fund, the more the reliance that must be placed upon the spending formula to bring about stable spending. And what may not be quite so obvious is that the greater the demand for stable spending the greater the risk that the endowment will not achieve its growth objective. Figure 1 shows in graphical form the trade-off between stability of spending and risk that growth will be insufficient.

---

[11] Ibid., pp. 38–40.

ASSET STRUCTURE

In 1977, NACUBO questionnaire results from 108 colleges and universities with aggregate endowment of $6 billion, reported this median classification of assets:

Equities	59 percent
Bonds	28 percent
Short-term investments	7 percent
Miscellaneous	Remainder

Mention has already been made of securities that for one reason or another are not to be sold out of a portfolio. A few institutions reported a significant percentage of these noncontrolled equities (the highest percentage was 63 percent and the second highest was 31 percent). But the median was zero percent, so most institutions presented no problem to a portfolio manager. In any case, the simplest approach is to segregate the assets.

There appears to have been a small deliberate shift out of equities in recent years. Table 6 is based upon responses to the NACUBO questionnaire from 98 colleges and universities over the five years 1973–77. The first four columns show the average distribution of all the reported assets. The next two columns show the equity and bond percentage components that would have resulted from market movement alone, assuming equities followed the S&P 500 Index and bonds followed the Salomon Brothers Long-Term Corporate Index. The final column reports the change in the equity percentage that was apparently the result of a conscious shift.

Table 6
Asset Distribution for 98 College and University Endowment Funds, Aggregating $6.9 Billion at June 30, 1977

	Reported Percentages				Percentages Due to Market Movement		Deliberate Change in Equity Ratio
	Equities	Bonds	Liquid Assets	Other	Equities	Bonds	
June 30, 1973	65.7%	20.2%	8.0%	6.1%	—	—	—
June 30, 1974	59.7	20.9	12.8	6.6	63.3%	20.3%	−3.6%
June 30, 1975	61.0	24.1	9.1	5.8	61.4	20.6	− .4
June 30, 1976	60.8	27.3	7.5	4.4	62.9	23.1	−2.1
June 30, 1977	57.4	30.3	8.6	3.7	58.9	29.2	−1.5

Stocks, bonds, and short-term investments make up the bulk of almost all endowment funds. Two other general classes of assets may be important, however. One class consists of investments related to the activities of the institution. Many colleges and universities make loans to faculty, frequently residential mortgage loans. Some institutions have quite substantial portfolios of student loans, particularly if the institutions are qualified lenders under government guaranteed and subsidized programs. Investments in faculty and student housing, and in real estate held largely for expansion purposes, can account for significant portions of an endowment. All of these investments (except perhaps some of the real estate) are revenue producing, although their rates of return may compare unfavorably with what is available in the investment marketplace. Usually investments of this sort are administered by a financial officer of the institution, and their investment results will not affect the performance of the portfolio manager. However, in devising an overall policy for the endowment assets it may be necessary to take these investments into consideration.

A second special class of assets includes a number of investment vehicles that educational institutions and charities have become interested in, particularly in recent years. Real estate is perhaps the most obvious. The experience of the last decade or so has suggested to many institutions that real estate offers an effective inflation hedge. A few universities with large endowment funds operate substantial real estate portfolios on their own. But many institutions with quite impressive endowments—in the hundreds of millions of dollars—are still too small to hope to be able to establish well diversified real estate portfolios and to manage those portfolios effectively. A few real estate investment trusts have been made available to endowment funds. Unfortunately, tax laws forbid the commingling of pension fund and endowment fund money in real estate trusts. So the very large trusts that are available to pension funds are not available to endowment funds. The writing of call options and securities lending are two other activities that a number of institutions have turned to in recent years. Securities lending has proved profitable for some institutions, although competition has driven the profits down. Option writing seems to have led to mixed results. Some institutions are quite pleased while others have been very disappointed.

Educational institutions are perhaps more vulnerable than almost any other class of investor to complaints that their portfolios do not meet appropriate social objectives. Partly as a result of the demonstrations and protests of the late 1960s over investments in corporations that seemed to be assisting in the conduct of the Vietnam War, many institutions set up committees to review portfolio holdings and advise on the voting of proxies, with a view to fulfilling appropriate social objectives or at least not promoting objectionable ones. The Investor Responsibility Research Center Inc., in Washington, D.C., is an organization many colleges and universities rely on to conduct research on corporate practices and to provide information on the basis of which a committee may recommend avoidance of certain investments or respond in a particular way to proxy solicitations.

Although some institutions have had written statements of social responsibility for many years, the issue of whether to retain investments in companies doing business in South Africa is a good example of one of the more serious questions that trustees and therefore investment managers will face from time to time. On the South African issue, reactions from trustees have varied from acceptance of a firm legal opinion by a major state university system's legal counsel that it is the obligation of the trustees to maximize the assets under their control and not to use the endowment fund to make any political statement, to a vote for total divestiture by the regents of another state university. Since these issues are generally more moral than legal, the problem for trustees is to balance the demands of one part of their constituencies against the certain disadvantages of loss of diversification in the portfolio, and the probable disadvantage of lower returns. Most institutions that have clarified their positions have decided against divestiture but are prepared to assume a rather more active role in voting proxies and in putting pressure on companies, for example, to endorse the Sullivan principles in their South African activities. While the investment manager will obviously carry out whatever policy the trustees set, his responsibilities during the process of discussion will be to provide supplementary information about companies in the portfolio upon request and to make sure that the trustees understand the investment risks associated with any extreme position.

SUMMARY

The investment counselor or manager serving a college or university must be prepared to deal with an entity quite different from a pension fund. Adapting to the needs and idiosyncracies of trustee investment committees will require considerable care and effort. The legal status of endowment and the varieties of endowment funds—*true, quasi-* and *term, restricted* and *unrestricted*—are important, as are the fund reporting practices of educational institutions.

Setting objectives is a particularly difficult and important activity, because of the varying needs and circumstances of different institutions and the varying background and expertise of trustees and financial officers.

Understanding the causes of inflation for an educational institution, and estimating the inflation rate for a particular college or university is especially important to the establishment of investment objectives and a spending policy. Long-run inflation is almost certain to exceed inflation in the economy generally and this must be taken into account in achieving an appropriate balance among investment results, gift receipts, growth and spending. Although spending policy itself is outside the responsibility of the investment manager it has an important bearing on investment objectives, and the manager can be satisifed with the objectives only if they are consistent with spending levels and growth objectives.

The portfolios of most colleges and universities are not as a rule significantly different from those of other non-profit institutions. The manager may have to be more sensitive to social issues, however, and prepared to deal with requests for reshaping a portfolio to reflect social responsibilities.

Part Six

Money Market Portfolios

Chapter 35

The Mathematics of Interest Rates, Swaps, and Futures

SUMNER N. LEVINE
State University of New York
Stony Brook, New York

Interest rates and yields are expressed in a number of different ways depending on the type of investment instrument and the purposes of the calculation; a situation which may result in considerable confusion. This chapter provides a unified view of rate calculations and presents techniques of expressing rates on a common basis for purposes of comparison. Applications are given to swaps, yield curve analysis and futures.

All of the calculations described below, including compound interest, can be performed quickly and conveniently on a number of inexpensive hand calculators.

EXPRESSIONS FOR RATES

Interest payments may differ as to timing, whether simple (paid out) or compound (reinvested), and whether a 360-day or 365-day year is employed as a basis. For example, simple interest may be paid out when a debt is initiated (discounted debt), during the life of the debt or when the debt matures. U.S. Treasury Bonds and notes use a 356-day year, while federal agencies use a 360-day year.

Interest as a Discount

U.S. Treasury Bills, bankers acceptances, and commercial paper are sold at a discount on a 360-day basis. The relationship between the purchase price and the discount rate is given by:

$$p = v\left(1 - \frac{d \times t}{360}\right)$$

where

p = the purchase price
v = the face value payable on the maturity date
d = the annual discount rate
t = the time in days to maturity

Example: A newly issued 3-month (91-day) Treasury bill paying $10,000 on maturity is selling at a discount rate of 8.04 percent. What is the purchase price?

$$p = \$10,000\left(1 - \frac{.0804 \times 91}{360}\right) = \$9,796.77$$

Interest Paid on Maturity

Certificates of deposit (CDs) maturing within a year, and certain (but not all) repurchase agreements, pay simple interest on the date of maturity. Assuming a 360-day year, the interest, I, is given by the usual expression for simple interest,

$$I = \frac{v \times s \times t}{360}$$

where s is the annual interest rate and the other symbols have the same meaning as above.

Relationship between Discount Rate and Rate at Maturity

The relationship between the discount rate and the rate at maturity is easily obtained. Consider two investments of equal maturity. One is a discount instrument and the other an instrument paying interest on maturity and both are based on a 360-day year. The returns-per-dollar-invested (R) over the period of t days, are given by the following:

(a) discount instrument

$$R = \frac{v}{v - \dfrac{v \times t \times d}{360}} = \frac{1}{1 - \dfrac{t \times d}{360}}$$

(b) interest paid on the maturity instrument

$$R = \frac{v + \dfrac{v \times s \times t}{360}}{v} = 1 + \frac{s \times t}{360}$$

The returns will be equal provided the discount rate satisfies the expression

$$d = \frac{1}{\dfrac{360}{s \times t} + 1} \times \frac{360}{t}$$

or the rate to maturity satisfies

$$s = \frac{1}{\dfrac{360}{d \times t} - 1} \times \frac{360}{t}$$

Using the above, it is possible to select between the two instruments on the basis of return per dollar invested.

Example: Compare the 90-day commercial paper offering 8 percent discount rate with a 90-day CD offering 8.1 percent on maturity. The discounted paper provides a return expressed as an interest rate paid on a maturity basis of

$$s = \frac{1}{\dfrac{360}{.08 \times 90} - 1} \times \frac{360}{90} = 8.16\%$$

Hence, the rate for the commercial paper exceeds that of the certificate.

Compound Rates

When interest is retained in an investment and interest accumulates on the interest and principal, it is said to be compounded. The total amount of compound interest is determined by the number of compounding periods per year, n, and the rate per period k. If an amount P is invested, then at the end of c periods, there accumulates an amount F given by

$$F = P (1 + k)^c$$

and at the end of a year consisting of n periods

$$F = P(1 + k)^n$$

It is customary to express k in terms of the annual *nominal* rate given by

$$r = nk$$

Example: The sum of $100,000 is invested in a time deposit which compounds quarterly (n = 4) at a period rate k of 2 percent. The amount at the end of three quarters is

$$F = \$100,000 \ (1.02)^3 = \$106,120.80$$

and at the end of the year

$$F = \$100,000 \ (1.02)^4 = \$108,243.22.$$

The nominal rate paid is 4×2 percent or 8 percent nominal per year.

When interest is compounded daily, n equals 365 or 360, depending on how the year is defined.

When interest is compounded once per year, the rate is referred to as an *effective* rate and is designated here by i. The relationship between the effective rate and the equivalent nominal rate r is given by

$$(1 + i) = (1 + k)^n = \left(1 + \frac{r}{n}\right)^n$$

or

$$i = \left(1 + \frac{r}{n}\right)^n - 1$$

The effective rate is very useful for comparing and selecting between different compound rates.

Example: Compare a nominal rate of 8.1 percent compounded quarterly with a rate of 8 percent compounded daily. Converting to effective rates, we have

$$i \text{ (quarterly)} = \left(1 + \frac{.0810}{4}\right)^4 - 1 = 8.35\%$$

$$i \text{ (daily)} = \left(1 + \frac{.0800}{365}\right)^{365} - 1 = 8.33\%$$

The quarterly compounded investment provides a slightly greater return over the daily compounded rate.

Converting a Discount Rate into a Compound Rate (Bond Equivalent Yields)

In comparing yields on U.S. Treasury bills to government bonds and on other occasions, it is helpful to convert a discount rate on a 360-day year to a semiannual compounded rate based on a 365-day year. As discussed below, Treasury bonds and notes pay simple interest semiannually on a 356-day basis.

The daily compounded rate (r') corresponding to a discount rate is given by the expression:

$$v\left(1 - \frac{d \times t}{360}\right)\left(1 + \frac{r'}{365}\right)^t = v$$

where d is the discount, or on solving for r';

$$r' \text{ (daily)} = 365 \left\{ \left(\cfrac{1}{1 - \cfrac{d \times t}{360}} \right)^{1/t} - 1 \right\}$$

The daily compound rate r' can be converted to a semiannual rate r since

$$\left(1 + \frac{r}{2}\right)^2 = \left(1 + \frac{r'}{365}\right)^{365}$$

or on substituting the above for r'

$$r \text{ (semiannual)} = 2 \left\{ \left(\cfrac{1}{1 - \cfrac{d \times t}{360}} \right)^{365/2t} - 1 \right\}$$

The last expression is also referred to as the *bond equivalent* yield of a discount instrument.

Example: What is the annual daily compound rate and the semiannual compounded (bond equivalent) rate of a 180-day 8 percent bill?

$$r' \text{ (daily)} = 365 \left\{ \left(\cfrac{1}{1 - \cfrac{.08 \times 180}{360}} \right)^{1/180} - 1 \right\}$$

$$r' \text{ (daily)} = 8.23\%$$

$$r \text{ (semiannual)} = 2 \left\{ \left(\cfrac{1}{1 - \cfrac{.08 \times 180}{360}} \right)^{365/2 \times 180} - 1 \right\}$$

$$r \text{ (semiannual)} = 8.45\%$$

BOND RATES

Bonds and long-term notes pay simple interest semiannually with each payment A equal to

$$A = \frac{v \times C}{2}$$

where

v is the face amount of the bond
C is the coupon rate.

The total return will depend on the price, the coupon rate, and the rate at which the coupon payments are reinvested, as discussed below.

Return when Coupon Payments are not Reinvested

If a bond maturing in n years with coupon rate C is purchased at a price P (including accrued interest) and the coupon payments are not reinvested, then the total amount available when the bond matures is $v + 2nA$ where v is the face amount. The semiannual compounded rate of return r is given by

$$P\left(1 + \frac{r}{2}\right)^{2n} = v + 2nA = v + nCv$$

on introducing the expression for A given above. There results on solving for r

$$r = 2\left\{\left[\frac{v}{P}(1 + nC)\right]^{1/2n} - 1\right\}$$

Example: A \$1,000 bond bearing 7 percent coupons and maturing in 30 years is purchased at \$980.00. The coupon payments are not reinvested; what is the semiannual compounded rate of return on maturity?

$$r = 2\left\{\left[\frac{1000}{980}(1 + 30 \times .07)\right]^{1/60} - 1\right\}$$

$$r = 3.87\%$$

Return when Coupon Payments are Reinvested

When coupon payments are invested semiannually at a compound rate $q/2$ for each semiannual period, the amount available on maturity is given by[1]

$$v + A\,(F/A,\, q/2,\, 2n)$$

where

$$A = \frac{C \times v}{2}$$

and the compound interest factor is

$$(F/A,\, q/2,\, 2n) = \frac{(1 + q/2)^{2n} - 1}{q/2}$$

The above annuity factor can be quickly obtained using a hand business calculator.

---

[1] For a discussion of compound interest factors see Chapter 36 in S. N. Levine, *Financial Analyst's Handbook*, (Homewood, Ill.: Dow Jones-Irwin, 1975). © 1975 by Dow Jones-Irwin, Inc.

The expression for the semiannual compounded rate of return at maturity is now given by

$$r = 2\left\{ \left[\frac{v}{P}\left(1 + \frac{C}{2}(F/A,\, q/2,\, 2n) \right) \right]^{1/2n} - 1 \right\}$$

Example: Consider the above 7's bond maturing in 30 years and purchased at $980.00. The coupon payments are now reinvested at 6 percent compounded semiannually.

$$r = 2\left\{ \left[\frac{1000}{980}(1 + .035\,(F/A,\, 3\%,\, 60)) \right]^{1/60} - 1 \right\}$$

so that

$$r = 6.51\%$$

If the bond were purchased at par, then under the same circumstances

$$r = 6.45\%$$

Example: If the 7's 30-year bond is purchased at par and the coupon payments are reinvested at 7 percent compounded semiannually, then use of the above formula shows that

$$r = 7\%.$$

We note from the above examples that when coupon payments are not reinvested, then the return from the 7's bond, even with appreciation of principal, is less than that from a 4 percent time deposit. To obtain a 7 percent nominal *compounded* return, the coupon payments must be reinvested at 7 percent, for a bond purchased at par.

Yield to Maturity

When the coupon payments are reinvested at the same rate as r ($q = r$ in the above expression) the rate is called the yield to maturity *(YTM)*. This was the case in the previous example for the 7's bond purchased at par and for which the coupons were reinvested at 7 percent. In general for bonds purchased at par the *YTM* is just the coupon rate. However, when the bonds are purchased at a price other than par, this is not the case. For bonds purchased at less than par, the *YTM* is greater than the coupon rate and for bonds purchased at more than par, the *YTM* is less than the coupon rate. Generally bond yields are quoted in terms of the *YTM*. Note, again, that the compounded return from the bond will not be the same as the *YTM* unless the coupon payments are reinvested at a compound rate equal to the *YTM*. To find the *YTM*, the above equation for the compound return must be solved by trial and error for r. To do this, it is convenient to rewrite the equation in the form (with $r = YTM$);

$$-P + \left(\frac{C \times v}{2}\right)\left(p/A, \frac{r}{2}, 2n\right) + v\left(p/F, \frac{r}{2}, 2n\right) = 0$$

where the present value functions are

$$(p/A, r/2, 2n) = \frac{(1 + r/2)^{2n} - 1}{r/2\,(1 + r/2)^{2n}}$$

$$(p/F, r/2, 2n) = \left(1 + \frac{r}{2}\right)^{-2n}$$

and

$P =$ purchase price plus accrued interest
$v =$ face value due on maturity
$C =$ coupon rate.
$n =$ years remaining to maturity

Details for the solution of the equation are given elsewhere.[2] However, in practice, the *YTM* is found from the yield tables.[3]

A useful approximation is

$$YTM = \frac{(C \times v) + (v - P)/n}{(v + P)/2}$$

where n is the years to maturity.

ANALYSIS OF MONEY MARKET INVESTMENTS[4]

The analysis of money market investments requires estimates of how long the funds will be committed and the behavior of the yield curve over the investment period.

It is helpful to express all money market rates (discount and interest) on a common yield basis, namely interest earned per dollar invested per year:

$$Y = \frac{P_2 - P_1}{P_1} \times \frac{360}{t_1 - t_2}$$

where Y is the yield assuming a 360 day year.

$P_1 =$ purchase price of the instrument
$P_2 =$ sales price of the instrument
$t_1 =$ days to maturity on purchase
$t_2 =$ days to maturity on sales.

---

[2] Ibid.

[3] Yield tables are published by the Financial Publishing Co., Boston, Mass.

[4] For details, see chap. 36.

For a discount instrument of face value v and discount rate d held to maturity ($t_2 = 0$) we have

$$P_1 = v \left(1 - \frac{d_1 \times t_1}{360}\right)$$

$$P_2 = v$$

so that

$$Y_d = \frac{360 d_1}{360 - d_1 t_1}$$

In the case of an interest-bearing note with rate s_1 paid on maturity, we have

$$P_1 = v$$

$$P_2 = v \left(1 + \frac{s_1 t_1}{360}\right)$$

and

$$Y_s = s_1$$

However, instead of investing in debt which matures over the required time horizon, yields may often be improved by investing in longer term debt with the intent of liquidating it prior to maturity. For example, suppose that funds are to be committed for 90 days, then 180-day or 270-day paper may be purchased and sold 90 days later. This strategy requires a prediction of interest rates three months after the time of purchase. If a money market investment is purchased at time to maturity t_1 and sold at time to maturity t_2 when prevailing rates are d_2 (or s_2), then the yield for this discount instrument is readily obtained:

$$P_1 = v \left(1 - \frac{d_1 t_1}{360}\right)$$

$$P_2 = v \left(1 - \frac{d_2 t_2}{360}\right)$$

therefore

$$Y_d = \frac{d_1 t_1 - d_2 t_2}{360 - d_1 t_1} \times \frac{360}{t_1 - t_2}$$

Similarly, for an interest bearing instrument we have

$$P_1 = v$$

$$P_2 = \frac{v \left(1 + \frac{s_1 t_1}{360}\right)}{\left(1 + \frac{s_2 t_2}{360}\right)}$$

hence

$$Y_s = \frac{s_1 t_1 - s_2 t_2}{360 + s_2 t_2} \times \frac{360}{t_1 - t_2}$$

Example: Given the following data and yield estimates for banker acceptancies *(BA)* and repurchase agreements *(RP)*, select the best 90-day investment.

	Current 90-day rates	*Current 180-day rates*	*Estimated 90-day rates Three Months hence*
RP (%)	5.50	6.02	5.75
BA (% discount)	5.40	5.90	5.60

The yields for the 90-day paper held to maturity are:

$$Y_{RP} = 5.5\%$$

$$Y_{BA} = \frac{360\,(.054)}{360 - (.054)\,(90)} = 5.47\%$$

The estimated yields for 180-day paper held for 90 days are

$$Y'_{RP} = \frac{(.0602)\,(180) - (.0575)\,(90)}{360 + (.0575)\,(90)} \times \frac{360}{90} = 6.20\%$$

$$Y'_{BA} = \frac{.059\,(180) - (.056)\,(90)}{360 - (.059)\,(180)} \times \frac{360}{90} = 6.39\%$$

Evidently, purchase of the 180-day *BA* would be the preferred investment under the given assumptions.

Break Even Analysis

The above analysis depends on the assumptions concerning future interest rates. In order to gauge the limits of the analysis, it is recommended that a break even study be carried out. As an example, suppose that the decision is between selecting the 90-day *BA* or the 180-day *BA*. The question arises as to how high the discount rate would have to rise in order to select the former over the latter. The discount rate which sets the projected 180-day yield equal to the 90-day yield is called the break even rate, found from

$$\frac{.059\,(180) - 90d_2}{360 - (.059)\,(180)} \times \frac{360}{90} = \frac{360\,(0.54)}{360 - (.054)\,(90)}$$

or

$$d_2 = 6.49\%$$

If 90-day rates remain below 6.49 percent, then the 180-day *BA* is preferred, otherwise the 90-day *BA* provides the higher yield. Thus, the decision depends ultimately on the analyst's judgment concerning interest rates.

ANALYSIS OF BOND SWAPS

The replacement, in a portfolio, of one bond issue by another is referred to as a *swap*. Swaps may be done *(a)* to replace a bond by a nearly identical issue providing a higher yield to maturity (substitution swap), *(b)* to replace a bond by another bond providing a higher compounded rate of return (yield pick-up swap), or *(c)* to minimize losses in anticipation of a shift in the yield curve (rate anticipation swap). Other types of swaps are discussed by Homer and Leibowitz.[5]

The yield pick-up swap can be analyzed straightforwardly using the previously given expressions for the compounded rate of return on bonds.

Example: A portfolio holds a 4's bond, maturing in 30 years, priced at \$671.82. Should this bond be swapped for a 6's, 30 year bond selling at par? Assume the bonds will be held to maturity.

Using the formulas for the compound rate of return and assuming a reinvestment rate of 7 percent, the following results are obtained:

For the 4's bond

$$r = 2 \left\{ \left[\frac{1000}{671.82} (1 + .02 \times 196.517) \right]^{1/60} - 1 \right\}$$
$$r = 6.76\%$$

since

$$(F/A, 7\%/2, 60) = 196.517$$

For the 6's bond

$$r = 2 \left\{ [1 + .03 \, (196.517)]^{1/60} - 1 \right\}$$
$$r = 6.54\%$$

We conclude that the swap should not be done since there would be a loss in overall yield if the bonds are held to maturity.

The rate anticipation swap is, as indicated, considered if the manager anticipates a change in the term structure of interest rates. For example, if the manager expects a relative increase in long-term rates, then he would consider shortening the maturity of the portfolio. If long-term rates are expected to fall, then consideration might be given to lengthening the maturity of the portfolio. As might be expected, rate anticipation swaps are highly speculative.

---

[5] S. Homer and M. Leibowitz, *Inside the Yield Book* (Englewood Cliffs, N.J.: Prentice-Hall 1972).

Example: An issue of 8's bonds maturing in 30 years is currently selling at par while one year T-Bills are selling at 5 percent discount. It is expected that the bonds will be liquidated in three years. It is anticipated that long-term rates will increase to 10 percent in three years, (with the bond priced at $814.34) while T-Bill rates will increase to 5.5 percent and 6 percent at the beginning of the second and third years, respectively. Should the bond be swapped for the T-Bills and the latter rolled over for three years? Assume a 7 percent reinvestment rate for the coupon payments.

The compound rate for the bonds if liquidated in three years is

$$r = 2 \left\{ \left[\frac{814.34}{1000} + .04 \, (F/A, 3.5\%, 6) \right]^{1/6} - 1 \right\}$$
$$r = 2.47\%$$

Note that in this case the proceeds from the bond and interest are worth $[814.34 + (.04)(1000)(F/A, 3.5\%, 6)]$ at the time of liquidation.

To calculate the semiannual compounded rate for the T-Bills, the discount rates are first converted to interest on maturity rates (s) of 5.26 percent, 5.79 percent, and 6.32 percent for the current, second, and third years, respectively, using the relationship

$$s = \frac{d}{1-d}.$$

The semiannual compounded rate is found from

$$\left(1 + \frac{r}{2}\right)^6 = (1 + s_1)(1 + s_2)(1 + s_3)$$

or

$$r = 2 \left\{ [(1 + s_1)(1 + s_2)(1 + s_3)]^{1/6} - 1 \right\}$$

so that

$$r = 2 \left\{ [(1.0526)(1.0579)(1.0632)]^{1/6} - 1 \right\}$$

hence,

$$r = 5.70\%$$

Under the above assumptions, the swap from bonds to T-Bills seems well justified.

INTEREST RATE FUTURES

This section considers the application of interest rate calculations to interest rate futures. Further details are given in Chapter 31.

The future contract is a contract for the delivery of a specified amount of commodity at specified price at a designated date. The commodities underlying the interest futures contract are high-quality debt instruments paying a designated interest rate. When interest rates rise, the market price of the debt instrument decreases and vice versa.

There are currently five types of contracts traded:

1. Three-Month Treasury Bills. Each contract represents $1,000,-000 face value of U.S. Treasury bills with a three-month (13-week) maturity. They are quoted in terms of discount rates *(d)* or the International Monetary Market (IMM) index given by $(1 - d)$.

2. One-Year Treasury Bills. Each contract represents $250,000 face value of U.S. Treasury bills with one-year maturity. They are quoted on a discount rate basis or the IMM Index.

3. 90-Day Commercial Paper. Each contract represents $1 million face value of high grade (A1, S&P, or P1 Moody) commercial paper maturing in 90 days. They are quoted on a discount basis.

4. U.S. Treasury Bonds. Each contract represents $100,000 face value of bonds with a coupon rate of 8 percent and maturing in 15 years or more. They are quoted in percentage of the face value in $\frac{1}{32}$ of a point. Thus a quote of 99–04 signifies $99 + (\frac{4}{32}) = 99.125$ percent.

5. GNMA (Ginnie MAE) Certificates. Each Ginnie Mae (Government National Mortgage Association) pass-through certificate contract represents $100,000 principal value of a package of Veterans Administration and Federal Housing Administration guaranteed 30-year mortgages. Each certificate has a stated interest rate of 8 percent or equivalent. Although the original maturity of the mortgages is 30 years, the average life is 12 years due to prepayment of the underlying mortgages. They are quoted on the same way as Treasury bond futures.

The following examples illustrate the use of T-Bill hedges.

Example: On December 1, an investor expects a cash flow of $1 million in six months, with the sum to be invested in T-Bills. The investor can fix the T-Bill rate of 8 percent discount by taking a long position in 90-day T-Bill futures: December 1—buy a 90-day June future contract at 8 percent discount. Delivery value equals:

$$\$1,000,000 \left(1 - \frac{d \times 90}{360}\right) = \$980,000$$

Outlays are:

1. Security deposit (margin) $2,000
2. Interest lost on security
     deposit at 7 percent for 180 days   70
3. Roundturn commission   50
         Total $2,120

Two situations will be considered on June 1.

1. June 1 T-Bills are at 6 percent:

Sell contracts	$987,500
Gain on contracts	7,500
Security deposit returned	—
Actual Cost	(120)
Net gain	$ 7,380
Net cost of June 1 T-Bills	$980,120
Net discount rate June Bills	7.95 percent

2. June 1 T-Bills at 10 percent:

Sell contracts, Delivery value....	$975,000
Loss on contracts..............	($5,000)
Investment cost	(120)
Net cost of June T-Bills	$980,120
Net discount rate	7.95 percent

The use of a short sale of T-Bill futures is illustrated by a borrower who plans on January 1 to sell $1 million of prime 90-day commercial paper on September 1. In order to protect oneself against a rise in rates over those prevailing on January 1 (7 percent), the investor can short commercial paper futures.

January 1, borrower sells a September 90-day commercial paper contract at 7 percent discount.

Delivery value	$982,500

Outlays are:

1. Security deposit	$2,000
2. Interest on deposit @ 6 percent for 8 months	80
3. Roundturn commission	50
Total	$2,130

Suppose that interest rates increase to 9 percent on August 31 at which time the borrower decides to close her position.

On August 31 borrower buys back commercial paper contracts at 9.00 percent discount	$977,500
Gain in contract................................	5,000
Security returned	—
Actual net cost	(130)
Net gain in contracts	4,870
Net income from sale of 90-day commercial paper	$982,370

The net profit from the short sale offsets the drop in price of the commercial paper.

Chapter 36

Managing a Liquidity Portfolio*

MARCIA STIGUM

Money Market Consultant
New York and London

The money market, which is a wholesale market for low-risk, highly-liquid, short-term IOUs, is a huge and significant part of the nation's financial system. In it banks and other participants trade hundreds of billions of dollars every working day. Yet the market is one about which people who have not operated in it know surprisingly little.

This chapter deals with the principles of running a liquidity portfolio, that is, of investing in money market instruments. Because the money market is so unfamiliar to many, the chapter starts with a brief section on the instruments traded in the market. This section is followed in Part 2 by a description of the dealers who make the market. As an integral part of their operations, money market dealers acquire and finance substantial holdings of securities; so a discussion of their operations inevitably touches on important aspects of managing a liquidity portfolio. Other aspects as well as a discussion of how liquidity portfolios are and should be run by investors, such as banks, savings institutions, and corporations, is contained in Part 3.

PART 1—THE INSTRUMENTS IN BRIEF

Here's a quick rundown of the major money market instruments. Don't look for subtleties; just enough is said to lay the groundwork for a discussion of portfolio management.

Dealers and Brokers

The markets for all money market instruments are made in part by brokers and dealers. *Brokers* bring buyers and sellers together for

---

* Adapted from: Marcia Stigum, *The Money Market, Myth, Reality and Practice* (Homewood, Ill.: Dow Jones-Irwin, 1978). © 1978 by Dow Jones-Irwin, Inc.

a commission. By definition, brokers never position securities. Their function is to provide a communications network that links market participants who are often numerous and geographically dispersed. Most brokering in the money market occurs between banks and between dealers in money market instruments.

Dealers make markets in money market instruments by quoting bid and asked prices to each other, to issuers, and to investors. Dealers buy and sell for their own accounts, so assuming a position is an essential part of a dealer's operation.

U.S. Treasury Securities

To finance the U.S. national debt, the Treasury issues several types of securities. Some are nonnegotiable, for example, savings bonds sold to consumers and special issues sold to government trust funds. The bulk of the securities sold by the U.S. Treasury are, however, negotiable.

What form these securities take depends on their maturity. Those with a maturity at issue of a year or less are known as *Treasury Bills,* or for short, *T-Bills* or just plain *bills. T-Bills* do not bear interest. An investor in bills earns a return because bills are issued at a discount from face value and redeemed by the Treasury at maturity for full face value. The amount of the discount at which investors buy bills and the length of time bills have to be held before they mature together imply some specific yield that the bill will return if held to maturity.

T-Bills are currently issued in three-month, six-month, and one-year maturities. In issuing bills the Treasury does not set the amount of the discount. Instead the Federal Reserve auctions off each new bill issue to investors and dealers, with the bills going to those bidders offering the highest price, i.e., the lowest interest cost to the Treasury. By using the auction technique, the Treasury lets prevailing market conditions establish the yield at which each new bill issue is sold.

The Treasury also issues interest-bearing *notes.* These securities are issued at or very near face value and redeemed at face value. Notes have an *original maturity* (maturity at issue) of one to ten years. Currently the Treasury issues two- and four-year notes on a regular cycle. Notes of other maturities are issued periodically depending on the Treasury's needs. Interest is paid on Treasury notes semiannually. Notes, like bills, are typically sold through auctions held by the Federal Reserve. In these auctions bidders bid yields, and the securities offered are sold to those dealers and investors who bid the lowest yields, that is, the lowest interest cost to the Treasury. Thus the coupon rate on new Treasury notes, like the yield on bills, is normally determined by the market. The only exceptions are occasional subscription and price auction issues on which the Treasury sets the coupon.

In addition to notes, the Treasury also issues interest-bearing negotiable *bonds* that have a maturity at issue of ten years or more. The only difference between Treasury notes and bonds is that bonds are issued in longer maturities. In recent years the volume of bonds offered by the Treasury has been small. The reason is that Congress has imposed a 4.25 percent ceiling on the rate the Treasury may pay on bonds. Since this rate has for years been far below prevailing market rates, the Treasury is able to sell bonds only to the extent that Congress authorizes it to issue bonds exempt from the ceiling, something that Congress does only sparingly. Currently Treasury bonds, like notes, are normally issued through yield auctions.

Banks, other financial institutions, insurance companies, pension funds, and corporations are all important investor in U.S. Treasury securities. So too are some foreign central banks and other foreign institutions. The market for government securities is largely a wholesale market and, especially at the short end of the market, multimillion-dollar transactions are common. However, when interest rates get extremely high, as they did in 1974 and again in 1979, individuals with small amounts to invest are drawn into the market.

Because of the high volume of Treasury debt outstanding, the market for bills and short-term government securities is the most active and most carefully watched sector of the money market. At the heart of this market stands a varied collection of *dealers* who make the market for *governments* (market jargon for government securities) by standing ready to buy and sell huge volumes of these securities. These dealers trade actively not only with retail accounts but also with each other. Most trades of the latter sort are carried out through brokers.

Governments offer investors several advantages. First, because they are constantly traded in the *secondary market* in large volume and at narrow spreads between the bid and asked prices, they are highly *liquid*. A second advantage is that governments are considered to be free from credit risk because it is inconceivable that the government would ever default on these securities short of destruction of the country. Third, interest income on governments is exempt from state taxation. Because of these advantages, governments normally trade at yields below those of other money market instruments. Municipal securities are an exception because they offer a still more attractive tax advantage.

Generally yields on governments are higher the longer their *current maturity*, that is, time currently left to run to maturity.[1] The reason is that the longer the current maturity of a debt security, the more its price will fluctuate in response to changes in interest rates and therefore the greater the *price risk* to which it exposes the investor.

---

[1] A five-year note has an *original maturity* at issue of five years. One year after issue it has a *current maturity* of four years.

T-Bill Futures Market

In talking about the market for governments, we have focused on the *cash market,* that is, the market in which existing securities are traded for immediate delivery. In addition, there are markets in which Treasury Bills and bonds are traded for future delivery. In these markets contracts are actively traded for the future delivery of three-month bills having a face value of $1 million at maturity and of government bonds having a par value of $100,000.

Federal Agency Securities

From time to time Congress becomes concerned about the volume of credit that is available to various sectors of the economy and the terms at which that credit is available. Its usual response is to set up a federal agency to provide credit to that sector. Thus, for example, there is the Federal Home Loan Bank System which lends to the nation's savings and loan associations (S&Ls) as well as regulates them, the Government National Mortgage Association (GNMA) which funnels money into the mortgage market, the Banks for Cooperatives which make seasonal and term loans to farm cooperatives, the Federal Land Banks (FLB) which give mortgages on farm properties, the Federal Intermediate Credit Banks (FICB) which provide short-term financing for producers of crops and livestock, and a host of other agencies.

Initially all the federal agencies financed their activities by selling their own securities in the open market. Today all except the largest borrow from the Treasury through an institution called the Federal Financing Bank. Those agencies still borrowing in the open market do so primarily by issuing notes and bonds. These securities (known in the market as *agencies*) bear interest, and they are issued and redeemed at face value. Instead of using the auction technique for issuing their securities, federal agencies look to the market to determine the best yield at which they can sell a new issue, put that yield on the issue, and then sell it through a syndicate of dealers. Some agencies also sell short-term discount paper that resembles commercial paper.

Normally agencies yield slightly more than Treasury securities of the same maturity. There are several reasons. Agency issues are smaller than Treasury issues and are therefore less liquid. Also, while all agency issues have *de facto* backing from the federal government (it's inconceivable that the government would let one of them default on its obligations), the securities of only a few agencies are explicitly backed by the full faith and credit of the U.S. government. A third disadvantage of some agency issues is that interest income from them is not exempt from state taxation.

The agency market, while smaller than that for governments, has in recent years become an active and important sector of the money market. Agencies are traded by the same dealers who trade governments and in much the same way.

Federal Funds

All banks that are members of the Federal Reserve System are required to keep reserves on deposit at their district Federal Reserve Bank. A commercial bank's reserve account is much like a consumer's checking account; the bank makes deposits into it and can transfer funds out of it. The main difference is that, whereas a consumer can run the balance in his checking account down to zero, each member bank is required to maintain some minimum average balance over the week in its reserve account. How large that minimum balance is depends on the size and composition of the bank's deposits over the previous two weeks.

Funds on deposit in a bank's reserve account are referred to as *Federal funds,* or *Fed funds.* Any deposits a bank receives add to its supply of Fed funds, while loans made and securities purchased by it reduce that supply. Thus the basic amount of money any bank can lend out and otherwise invest equals the amount of funds it has received from depositors minus the reserves it is required to maintain.

For some banks this supply of available funds roughly equals the amount they choose to invest in securities plus that demanded from them by borrowers. But for most banks it does not. Specifically, because the nation's largest corporations tend to concentrate their borrowing in big money market banks in New York and other financial centers, the loans and investments these banks have to fund exceed the deposits they receive. Many smaller banks, in contrast, receive more money from local deposits than they can lend locally or choose to otherwise invest. Because large banks have to meet their reserve requirements regardless of what loan demand they face and because excess reserves yield no return to smaller banks, it was natural for large banks to begin borrowing the excess funds held by smaller banks.

This borrowing is done in the *Federal funds market.* Most Fed funds loans are overnight transactions. One reason is that the amount of excess funds a given lending bank holds varies daily and unpredictably. Some transactions in Fed funds are made directly, others through New York brokers. Despite the fact that transactions of this sort are all loans, the lending of Fed funds is referred to as *a sale* and the borrowing of Fed funds as a *purchase.* While overnight transactions dominate the Fed funds market, there are also some lending and borrowing for longer periods. Fed funds traded for periods other than overnight are referred to as *term* Fed funds.

The rate of interest paid on overnight loans of Federal funds, which is called the *Fed funds rate,* is the main interest rate in the money market, and all other short-term rates are benchmarked from it. The level of the Fed funds rate is pegged by Federal Reserve activity.

Eurodollars

Many foreign banks will accept deposits of dollars and grant the depositor an account denominated in dollars. So too will the foreign branches of U.S. banks. The practice of accepting dollar deposits outside of the United States began in Europe, so such deposits came to be known as *Eurodollars.* The practice of accepting dollar deposits later spread to Hong Kong, Singapore, the Middle East, and other centers around the globe. Consequently today a *Eurodollar deposit is simply dollars deposited in a bank outside the United States,* and the term *Eurodollar* has become a misnomer.

Most Eurodollar deposits are for large sums. They are made by corporations—foreign, multinational, and domestic; foreign central banks and other official institutions; U.S. domestic banks; and wealthy individuals. With the exception of call money,[2] all Euro deposits have a fixed term, which can range from overnight to five years. The bulk of Euro transactions are in the range of six months and under. Banks receiving Euro deposits use these dollars to make loans denominated in dollars to foreign and domestic corporations, foreign governments and government agencies, domestic U.S. banks, and other large borrowers.

Banks participating in the Eurodollar market actively borrow and lend Euros among themselves just as domestic banks borrow and lend in the market for Fed funds. The major difference between the two markets is that, in the market for Fed funds, most transactions are on an overnight basis while in the Euromarket interbank placements (deposits) of funds for longer periods are common.

For a domestic U.S. bank with a reserve deficiency, borrowing Eurodollars is an alternative to purchasing Fed funds. Also, for a domestic bank with excess funds, a Euro *placement* (i.e., a deposit of dollars in the Euromarket) is an alternative to the sale of Fed funds. Consequently the rate on overnight Euros tends to track closely the Fed funds rate. It is also true that, as one goes out on the maturity scale, Euro rates continue to track U.S. rates, though not so closely as in the overnight market.

Certificates of Deposit

The maximum rate banks can pay on savings deposits and time deposits (a time deposit is a deposit with a fixed maturity) is set by

---

[2] Call money is money deposited in an interest-bearing account that can be called (withdrawn) by the depositor on a day's notice.

the Fed through *Regulation Q*. Essentially what Reg Q does is to make it impossible for banks to compete with each other or with other savings institutions for small deposits by offering depositors higher interest rates. On large deposits, $100,000 or more, banks can currently pay any rate they choose so long as the deposit has a minimum maturity of 30 days.

There are many corporations and other large investors that have hundreds of thousands, even millions of dollars they could invest in bank time deposits. Few do so, however, because they lose liquidity by making a deposit with a fixed maturity. The lack of liquidity of time deposits and their consequent lack of appeal to investors led the banks to invent the *negotiable certificate of deposit,* or *CD* for short.

CDs are normally sold in $1 million pieces. They are issued at face value and typically pay interest at maturity. CDs can have any maturity longer than 30 days, and some five- and even seven-year CDs have been sold (these pay interest semiannually). Most CDs, however, have an *original maturity* of one to three months.

The quantity of CDs that banks have outstanding depends largely on the strength of loan demand. When demand rises, banks issue more CDs to help fund the additional loans they are making. The rates banks offer on CDs depend on their maturity, how badly the banks want to write new CDs, and the general level of short-term interest rates.

The bulk of bank CDs are sold directly by banks to investors. Some, however, are issued through dealers, often for a small commission. These same dealers also make an active secondary market in CDs.

Yields on CDs exceed those on bills of similar maturities by varying spreads. One reason for the bigger yield is that buying a bank CD exposes the investor to some credit risk—would he be paid off if the issuing bank failed? A second reason CDs yield more than bills is that they are less liquid.

Eurodollar Certificates of Deposit

A Eurodollar time deposit, like a domestic time deposit, is an illiquid asset. Since some investors in Eurodollars wanted liquidity, banks accepting such deposits in London began to issue Eurodollar CDs. A *Eurodollar CD* resembles a domestic CD except that instead of being the liability of a domestic bank, it is the liability of the London branch of a domestic bank or of a British bank or of some other foreign bank with a branch in London.

Many of the Eurodollar CDs issued in London are purchased by other banks operating in the Euromarket. A large proportion of the remainder are sold to U.S. corporations and other domestic institutional investors. Many Euro CDs are issued through dealers and brokers who also maintain a secondary market in these securities.

The Euro CD market is younger and much smaller than the market for domestic CDs, but it has grown rapidly since its inception. For the investor, a key advantage of buying Euro CDs is that they offer a higher return than domestic CDs. The offsetting disadvantages are that they are less liquid and that they expose the investor to some extra risk because they are issued outside of the United States.

Commercial Paper

While some cash-rich industrial firms participate in the bond and money markets only as lenders, many more must at times borrow to finance either current operations or expenditures on plant and equipment. One source of short-term funds available to a corporation is bank loans. Large firms with good credit ratings have, however, an alternative source of funds that is cheaper, namely, the sale of commercial paper.

Commercial paper is an unsecured promissory note issued for a specific amount and maturing on a specific day. All commercial paper is negotiable, but most paper sold to investors is held by them to maturity. Commercial paper is issued not only by industrial and manufacturing firms but also by finance companies. Finance companies normally sell their paper directly to investors. Industrial firms, in contrast, typically issue their paper through dealers.

The maximum maturity for which commercial paper can be sold is 270 days, since paper with a longer maturity must be registered with the SEC, a time-consuming and costly procedure. In practice, most paper sold is in the range of 30 days and under.

Since commercial paper has such short maturities, the issuer rarely will have sufficient funds coming in before the paper matures to pay off his borrowing. Instead he expects to *roll* his paper, that is, sell new paper to obtain funds to pay off the maturing paper. Naturally the possibility exists that some sudden change in market conditions, such as when the Penn Central went "belly up" (bankrupt) might make it difficult or impossible to sell paper for some time. To guard against this risk, commercial paper issuers back all or a large proportion of their outstanding paper with lines of credit from banks.

The rate offered on commercial paper depends on its maturity, on how much the issuer wants to borrow, on the general level of money market rates, and on the credit rating of the issuer. Almost all commercial paper is rated with respect to credit risk by one or more of several rating services: Moody's, Standard & Poor's, and Fitch. While only top-grade credits can get ratings good enough to sell paper these days, there is still a slight risk that an issuer might go bankrupt. Because of this, yields on commercial paper are higher than those on Treasury obligations of similar maturity.

Bankers' Acceptances

Bankers' acceptances (BAs) are an unknown instrument outside the confines of the money market. Moreover, explaining them isn't easy because they arise in a variety of ways out of a variety of transactions. The best approach is to use an example.

Suppose a U.S. importer wants to buy shoes in Brazil and pay for them four months later, after he has had time to sell them in the United States. One approach would be for the importer to borrow from his bank; however, short-term rates may be lower in the open market. If they are, and if the importer is too small to go into the open market on his own, then he can go to the bankers' acceptance route.

In that case he has his bank write a letter of credit for the amount of the sale and then sends this letter to the Brazilian exporter. Upon export of the shoes, the Brazilian firm, using this letter of credit, draws a time draft on the importer's U.S. bank and discounts this draft at its local bank, thereby obtaining immediate payment for its goods. The Brazilian bank in turn sends the time draft to the importer's U.S. bank, which then stamps "accepted" on the draft (that is, the bank guarantees payment on the draft and thereby creates an *acceptance*). Once this is done, the draft becomes an irrevocable primary obligation of the accepting bank. At this point, if the Brazilian bank did not want cash immediately, the U.S. bank would return the draft to that bank, which would hold it as an investment and then present it to the U.S. bank for payment at maturity. If, on the other hand, the Brazilian bank wanted cash immediately, the U.S. bank would pay it and then either hold the acceptance itself or sell it to an investor. Whoever ended up holding the acceptance, it would be the importer's responsibility to provide its U.S. bank with sufficient funds to pay off the acceptance at maturity. If the importer should fail to do so; its bank would still be responsible for making payment at maturity.

Our example illustrates how an acceptance can arise out of a U.S. import transaction. Acceptances also arise in connection with U.S. export sales, trade between third countries (e.g., Japanese imports of oil from the Middle East), the domestic shipment of goods, and domestic or foreign storage of readily marketable staples. Currently most BAs arise out of foreign trade; the latter may be in manufactured goods but more typically it is in bulk commodities, such as cocoa, cotton, coffee, or crude oil, to name a few. Because of the complex nature of acceptance operations, only large banks that have well-staffed foreign departments act as accepting banks.

Bankers' acceptances closely resemble commercial paper in form. They are short-term, noninterest-bearing notes sold at a discount and redeemed by the accepting bank at maturity for full face value. The major difference is that payment on commercial paper is guaranteed by only the issuing company. In contrast, bankers' acceptances, in addition to carrying the issuer's pledge to pay, are backed by the underlying goods being financed and also carry the guarantee of the accepting bank. Consequently bankers' acceptances are less risky than commercial paper, and thus sell at slightly lower yields.

The big banks through which bankers' acceptances are originated generally keep some portion of the acceptances they create as investments. The rest are sold to investors through dealers or directly by the bank itself. Major investors in BAs are other banks, foreign central banks, corporations, and other domestic and foreign institutional investors. BAs have liquidity because dealers in these securities make an active secondary market in them.

Repurchases and Reverses

A variety of bank and nonbank dealers act as market makers in governments, agencies, CDs, and BAs. Because dealers by definition buy and sell for their own accounts, active dealers will inevitably end up holding some securities. They will, moreover, buy and hold substantial positions if they believe that interest rates are likely to fall and that the value of these securities is therefore likely to rise. Speculation and risk taking are an inherent and important part of being a dealer.

While dealers have large amounts of capital, the positions they take are often several hundred times that amount. As a result, dealers have to borrow to finance their positions. Dealers, using the securities they own as collateral, can and do borrow from banks at the dealer loan rate. For the bulk of their financing, however, they resort to a cheaper alternative, entering into *repurchase (RP or repo for short) agreements* with investors.

Much of the RP financing done by dealers is on an overnight basis. It works as follows. The dealer finds a corporation or other investor who has funds to invest overnight. He sells this investor, say, $10 million of securities for roughly $10 million, which is paid in Federal funds to his bank by the investor's bank against delivery of the securities sold. At the same time the dealer agrees to repurchase these securities the next day at a slightly higher price. Thus the buyer of the securities is in effect making the dealer a one-day loan secured by the obligations sold to him. The difference between the purchase and sale prices on the RP transaction is the interest the investor earns on his loan. Alternatively, the purchase and sale prices in an RP transaction may be identical; in that case the dealer pays the investor some explicit rate of interest.

Often a dealer will take a speculative position that he intends to hold for some time. In that case he might do an RP for 30 days or longer. Such agreements are known as *term* RPs.

From the point of view of the investors, overnight loans in the RP market offer several attractive features. First, by rolling overnight RPs, investors can keep surplus funds invested without losing liquidity or incurring a price risk. Second, because RP transactions are secured by top-quality paper, investors expose themselves to little or no credit risk.

The overnight RP rate generally lies below the Fed funds rate. The reason is that the many nonbank investors who have funds to invest overnight or very short term and who do not want to incur any price risk have nowhere to go but the RP market, because they cannot (with the exception of S&Ls) participate directly in the Fed funds market. Also, lending money through an RP transaction is safer than selling Fed funds because a sale of Fed funds is an unsecured loan.

On term as opposed to overnight RP transactions, investors still have the advantage of their loans being secured but they do lose some liquidity. To compensate for that, the rate on an RP transaction is generally higher the longer the term for which funds are lent.

Banks making dealer loans fund them by buying Fed funds, and the lending rate they charge—which is adjusted daily—is the prevailing Fed funds rate plus a one-eighth or one-quarter markup. Because the overnight RP rate is lower than the Fed funds rate, dealers can finance their positions more cheaply by doing RP than by borrowing from the banks.

A dealer who is bullish on the market will position large amounts of securities. If he's bearish, he will *short* the market, that is, sell securities he does not own. Since the dealer has to deliver any securities he sells whether he owns them or not, a dealer who shorts has to borrow securities one way or another. The most common technique today for borrowing securities is to do what is called a *reverse RP* or simply a *reverse*. To obtain securities through a reverse, a dealer finds an investor holding the required securities; he then buys these securities from the investor under an agreement that he will resell these same securities to the investor at a fixed price on some future date. In this transaction the dealer, besides obtaining securities, is extending a loan to the investor for which he is paid some rate of interest.

An RP and a reverse are identical transactions. What a given transaction is called depends on who initiates it: typically if a dealer hunting money does, it's an RP; if a dealer hunting securities does, it's a reverse.

A final note: The Fed uses reverses and RPs with dealers in government securities to make adjustments in bank reserves.

Municipal Notes

Debt securities issued by state and local governments and their agencies are referred to as *municipal securities*. Such securities can be divided into two broad categories: bonds issued to finance capital projects and short-term notes sold in anticipation of the receipt of other funds, such as taxes or proceeds from a bond issue.

Municipal notes, which are important money market instruments, are issued with maturities ranging from a month to a year. They bear interest and minimum denominations are highly variable, ranging anywhere from $5,000 to $5 million.

Most muni notes are general obligation securities; that is, payment of principal and interest is secured by the issuer's pledge of its full faith, credit, and taxing power. This sounds impressive but, as the spectacle of New York City tottering on the brink of bankruptcy brought home to all, it is possible that a municipality might default on its securities. Thus the investor who buys muni notes assumes a credit risk. To aid investors in evaluating this risk, publicly offered muni notes are rated by Moody's. The one exception is project notes, which are issued by local housing authorities to finance federally sponsored programs, and which are backed by the full faith and credit of the federal government.

The major attraction of municipal notes to an investor is that interest income on them is exempt from federal taxation and usually also from any income taxes levied within the state where they are issued. The value of this tax exemption is greater the higher the investor's tax bracket, and the muni market thus attracts only highly taxed investors—commercial banks, cash-rich corporations, and wealthy individuals.

Large muni note issues are sold to investors by dealers who obtain the securities either through negotiation with the issuer or through competitive bidding. These same dealers also make a secondary market in muni notes.

The yield a municipality must pay to issue notes depends on its credit rating, the length of time for which it borrows, and the general level of short-term rates. Normally a good credit can borrow at a rate well below the yield on T-Bills of equivalent maturity. The reason is the value to the investor of the tax exemption on the municipal security. A corporation that has its profits taxed at a 50 percent marginal rate would, for example, receive the same after-tax return from a muni note yielding 3 percent that it would from a T-Bill yielding 6 percent.

PART 2—THE MARKET MAKERS: DEALERS AND OTHERS

Within the money market there reigns at any time a single price for any instrument traded there. That this should be the case is startling. Money market instruments, with the exception of futures contracts, are traded not on organized exchanges but strictly over the counter. Moreover, money market participants, who vary in size from small to gargantuan, are scattered over the whole United States—*and* throughout Canada, Europe, and elsewhere on the globe. Thus one might expect some fragmentation of the market, with big New York participants dealing in a noticeably different market from their London or Wichita counterparts. However, money market lenders and borrowers can operate almost as well out of Dearborn, Michigan, Washington, or Singapore as they can from Wall Street. Wherever they are, their access to information, bids, and offers is (time zone problems excepted) essentially the same. That the money market is in fact a single market is due in large part to the activities of the dealers and brokers who weld the market's many participants into a unified whole, and to the modern techniques of communication that make this possible.

The Dealers

Money market dealers are a mixed bag. Some are tiny, others huge. Some specialize in certain instruments, others cover the waterfront. One is also tempted to say that some are immensely sharp and others not so sharp, but the not-so-sharp players have short careers. Despite dealers' diversity, one can generalize about their operations.

Activities. The hallmark of a dealer is that he buys and sells for his own account, that is, trades with retail and other dealers off his own position. In addition, dealers engage in various activities that come close to brokering.

The prime example of the latter is commercial paper dealers. Each day they help their customers borrow hundreds of millions of dollars from other market participants. Commercial paper dealers' responsibilities are: (1) to advise their clients on market conditions, (2) to ensure that their clients post rates for different maturities that give them the lowest possible borrowing costs, and (3) for a ⅛ commission, to show and sell that paper to retail. Positioning is part of a commercial paper dealer's operation but only marginally so. Paper dealers will position any of their clients' paper that is not sold, but do so only on a small scale because they are careful to ensure that their clients post realistic rates. A second reason is that commercial paper dealers as a group feel that it is not in their best interests or in that of their clients for them to position large amounts of paper. Commercial paper dealers do, however, stand ready to bid for paper bought from them by retail and thus make a secondary market in paper. Such activity leads them at times to position paper, but the amounts are small. Thus commercial paper dealers act more like brokers than dealers.

Dealers also act at times like brokers in the CD market. A bank that wants to do a large program in one fast shot may call one or more dealers and offer them an 05 (5 basis points) on any CDs they can sell to retail. Finally, smaller dealers who are hesitant about the market or who are operating outside their normal market sector at times act more or less as brokers, giving a firm bid to retail only if they can cross the trade on the other side with an assured sale.

As noted, however, brokering is not what dealing is all about. The crucial role dealers play in the money market is as market makers, and in performing that role they trade off their own positions.

Part of the dealers' role as market makers involves underwriting new issues. Most large municipal note issues are bought up at issue by dealers who take them into position and sell them off to retail. In the market for governments there is also underwriting, though of a less formal nature; frequently dealers buy large amounts of new government issues at auction and then distribute them to retail.

In the secondary market dealers act as market makers by constantly quoting bids and offers at which they are willing to buy and sell. Some of these quotes are to other dealers. In every sector of the money market, there is an *inside market* between dealers. In this market dealers quote price *runs* (bids and offers for securities of different maturities) to other dealers, often through brokers. Since every dealer will *hit* a bid he views as high or take an offering he views as low, trading in the inside market creates at any time for every security traded a prevailing price that represents the dealers' consensus feeling of that security's worth.

Dealers also actively quote bids and offers to retail. In doing so they consistently seek to give their customers the best quotes possible because they value retail business and they know that other shops are competing actively with them for it. This competition between dealers ensures that dealers' quotes to retail will never be far removed from prices prevailing in the inside market. Thus, all the money market's geographically dispersed participants can always trade at close to identical bids and offers.

Profit Sources. Dealers profit from their activities in several ways. First, there are the 05s and ⅛s they earn selling CDs and commercial paper. Particularly for firms that are big commercial paper dealers, these commissions can be substantial, but in total they represent only a small part of dealers' profits.

A second source of dealers' profits is *carry.* Dealers finance the bulk of their long positions (muni notes excepted) in the repo market. Their

RP borrowings are of shorter maturity than the securities they position. Thus their financing costs are normally less than the yields on the securities they finance, and they profit from *positive* carry. Carry, however, is not a dependable source of profit because, when the yield curve inverts, carry turns negative.[3]

A third source of dealer profits is what might be called day-to-day trading profits, buying securities at one price and reselling them shortly at a slightly higher price, or shorting securities and covering in at a slightly lower price.

The sources of profit mentioned so far suffice to pay dealers' phone and light bills—to cover their overhead. Dealers earn really big money on position plays, that is, by taking into position huge amounts of securities when they anticipate that rates will fall and securities prices will rise or by shorting the market when they are bearish.

Being willing to position on a large scale is characteristic of all dealers, although the appetite of some shops for such *speculation* is stronger than that of others. One might argue that positioning done specifically to speculate as opposed to positioning that arises out of a dealer's daily trading with retail and other dealers is not an inherent part of being a market maker. But such speculation serves useful functions. It guarantees that market prices will react rapidly to any change in economic conditions or in demand, supply, or rate expectations. Also the profits dealers can earn from correct position plays are the prime incentive they have for setting up the elaborate and expensive operations they use daily to trade with retail and each other. In effect position profits help to oil the machinery that dealers need to be effective market makers.

To the above it might be added that dealers possess no crystal balls enabling them to perfectly foresee the future. They position on the basis of carefully formulated expectations. When they are right, they make huge profits; when they are wrong, their losses can be staggering.

Dealer Financing

The typical dealer is running a highly levered operation in which securities held in position may total 500 or 600 times capital. Some dealers rely heavily on dealer loans from New York banks for financing, but as one dealer commented: "The state of the art is that you don't have to." RP money is cheaper, and sharp dealers rely primarily on it to meet their financing needs. For such dealers the need to obtain RP money on a continuing basis and in large amounts is one additional reason for assiduously cultivating retail customers. The corporations,

---

[3] The yield curve is said to be *inverted* when short-term rates exceed long-term rates.

state and local governments, and other investors that buy money market instruments from them are also big suppliers of RP money to the dealers.

A good bit of dealer borrowing in the RP market is done on an overnight basis. One reason is that the overnight rate is the lowest RP rate. A second is that securities "hung out" on RP for one night only are available for sale the next day. Nonbank dealers have to clear their RP transactions through the clearing banks, which is expensive. As a result they also do a lot of *open repos* at rates slightly above the overnight rate. Open or demand repos have an indefinite term, and either the borrower or the lender can each day terminate the agreement.

Banks prefer to do overnight repos with customers who will permit them to safekeep the securities bought. This saves clearing costs and ensures that the bank will have the securities back early enough to repo them the next day or to make delivery if they have been sold. To make RP as convenient an investment as possible, some banks have minimum balance arrangements with customers, under which any excess balances the customer holds with them are automatically invested in RP. In effect what such a bank is doing is getting around Reg Q and paying the customer interest on any demand deposits he holds in excess of the compensating balance the bank requires him to maintain.

The financing needs that nonbank dealers do not cover in the RP market are met by borrowing from the banks at the dealer loan rate. In financing, bank dealers have one advantage over nonbank dealers— they can finance odd pieces they do not RP by buying Fed funds.

Interest Rate Predictions

The key rate in the money market is the Fed funds rate. Because of the role of this rate in determining dealers' cost of carry, the 90-day bill rate typically settles close to the funds rate, and other short-term rates key off this combination in a fairly predictable way. Thus when a dealer positions, he does so on the basis of a strongly held view with respect to where the Fed is going to peg the funds rate; *and every long position he assumes is, in particular, based on an implicit prediction of how high funds might trade* within the time frame of the investment.

Confidence Level in Positioning

Positioning is a form of gambling, and the dealers most skilled in this art attempt first to express their expectations about what might occur in terms of probabilities of various outcomes and second to estimate the payoff or loss that a given strategy would yield if each of these outcomes were to occur. Then on the basis of these numbers, they decide whether to bet and how much to bet.

Probabilists who have theorized about gambling like to talk about a fair gamble or a *fair game*. A fair game is one that, if played repeatedly, will on average yield the player neither gains nor losses. For example, suppose a person plays the following game: A coin is flipped; if it lands heads up, he wins $1; if it lands heads down, he loses $1. The probability that the coin will land heads up is ½. So half the time he bets our player will lose $1; half the time he will win $1; and his *expected winning* or *return*, if he plays the game repeatedly, is *zero*.

There is nothing in it for a dealer to make a fair bet. What one looks for is a situation in which expected return is *positive;* and the more positive it is, the more one will bet. For example, if a dealer believed: (1) that the probabilities that the Fed would ease and tighten were 60 percent and 40 percent, respectively, and (2) that a given long position would return the $2 if the Fed eased and would cause one to lose $1 if the Fed tightened, then *expected* winnings would be

$$0.6 \times \$2 - 0.4 \times \$1 = \$0.80$$

In other words, the gamble is such that, if the dealer made it ten times, expected winnings would be $8. That degree of favorableness in the bet might suffice to induce the dealer to position. If the game were made still more favorable, for example by an improvement in the odds, then one would gamble still more.

All this may sound theoretical, but it is the way good dealers think, explicitly or intuitively; and such thinking disciplines them in positioning. As one dealer noted: "The alternative is a sloppy operation in which a dealer runs up one's position because one sort of likes the market now or runs it down because one doesn't like the market."

Quantifying thinking about the market also helps a dealer provide retail with useful suggestions. Most customers can find fair bets on their own. What they appreciate is a dealer who can suggest to them a favorable bet, that is, one on which the odds are out of synchronization with the payoff, and the expected return is therefore positive.

In quantifying expectations and payoffs and acting on them, fleet-footedness is of the essence. Everyone is playing the same game, and the market therefore frequently anticipates Fed actions.

The Maturity Choice

We suggested above that the more favorable the gamble a dealer is faced with, the more securities he's likely to position. There is, however, one more wrinkle to the dealer's positioning decision. A classic part of a bullish strategy is for a dealer to extend to longer maturities. The reason is that the longer the maturity of the securities he positions, the more price play he will get. To illustrate, suppose that a dealer believes that the probability that the Fed funds rate will fall by ¼ is 70 percent and the probability it will rise by ¼ is 30 percent. If the dealer positions the 90-day bill, which has a yield that is likely to move roughly as many basis points as the Fed funds rate does, he will be making a bet on which his potential gains and losses per $1 million of securities positioned are a little over $600. If alternatively—to make the example extreme—he invests in ten-year governments, his potential gains and losses will be in the range of $2,000 per $1 million even if a ¼-point move in the Fed funds rate is assumed to move the yield on these securities only 4 basis points. Whether he positions 90-day bills or long governments, the dealer is making a favorable bet. However, positioning the longer securities is *riskier* because, if rates rise, the dealer will lose much more owning them than he will owning bills.

Dealers are very conscious that extending to longer maturities exposes them to greater *price risk*. They also tend to think that extending to longer maturities exposes them to greater risk for another reason: namely, the predictability of long-term rates is less than that of short-term rates. Short rates relate directly to Fed policy; long rates do so to a lesser extent because they are also strongly influenced by the *slope* of the yield curve. Thus the dealer who extends must be prepared not only to predict wiggles in Fed policy, but also to predict shifts in the slope of the yield curve—an art that is separate from and, in the eyes of many dealers, more difficult than successful Fed watching.

Shorting.   When dealers are bullish, they place their bets by positioning securities: when they are bearish, they do so by shorting. One might expect that the quantity of securities a dealer would short, if one believed that the probability of a fall in securities prices was 80 percent, would be as great as the quantity of securities he would position if he believed that the probability of a rise in securities prices was 80 percent. But in fact dealers will, at a given confidence level, short smaller amounts of securities than they would position. There are several reasons. First, the only instruments dealers can short are governments and agencies; other instruments such as commercial paper, BAs, and CDs are too heterogeneous with respect to name, maturity, and face amount to short. Second, shorting securities tends to be more cumbersome and expensive than going long because the short seller has to find not only a buyer, but also—since the shorted securities must be delivered—a source of these securities.

In recent years it has become increasingly common for dealers to *reverse* in securities shorted rather than to borrow them. One reason is that the reverse may be cheaper. When a dealer borrows securities, he gives up other securities as collateral and pays the lender a borrowing fee, which typically equals ½ of 1 percentage point but may be more if many people want to go short at once. On a reverse the dealer obtains the securities shorted by buying them from an investor with an agreement to repurchase. In effect the dealer is extending a collateralized loan to the owner of these securities. The owner takes the loan because one needs cash or, more typically, because one can reinvest the loan proceeds at a higher rate, and the reverse thus becomes part of a profitable arbitrage.

Whether a dealer borrows securities or reverses them in, he has to make an *investment*—in the first case in collateral, in the second case in a loan to the institution on the other side of the reverse. To figure which investment would yield more, one compares the rate one could earn on the collateral *minus* the borrowing fee with the reverse rate. For example, suppose a dealer has some short-dated paper yielding 5.25 percent to use as collateral. If one did so, one would own that paper at 5.25 percent minus the 0.5 percent borrowing fee, that is, at an effective rate of 4.75 percent. If the reverse rate were 4.90 percent, one would do better on the reverse. A dealer's overall cost on a short is (1) the interest that accrues on the securities shorted (rise in value in the case of a discount security) over the period the short is outstanding, *minus* (2) the yield on the offsetting investment one makes.

A dealer who borrows securities to support a short can never know with certainty how long he can have those securities because borrowed securities can be called by the lender on a day's notice. If, alternatively, a dealer reverses in securities for some fixed period, he knows he will have the securities for that time. Thus a dealer who anticipates maintaining a short for some time may choose to cover through a reverse rather than a borrowing not only because the reverse is cheaper, but also because it offers certainty of availability.

RP and Reverse Book. A large dealer who is known to the street can borrow more in the repo market and at better rates than can a small dealer or a corporate portfolio manager. Thus large dealers find knocking at their doors not only customers who want to give them repo money, but also would-be borrowers who want to reverse out securities to them because that is the cheapest way they can borrow. In response to the latter demand, large dealers have taken to doing repo and reverse not just to suit their own needs but also as a profit-making service to customers. In providing that service, the dealer takes in securities on one side at one rate and hangs them out on the other side at a slightly more lower rate; or to put it the other way around, dealers borrow money from their repo customers at one rate and lends it to their reverse customers at a slightly higher rate. In doing so, the dealer is of course acting like a bank. And dealers know this well. As one noted: "This shop *is* a bank. We have customers lining up every morning to give us money. Also we are in the business of finding people who will give us securities at a little better rate than we can push them out the repo door. So we are a bank taking out our little spread, acting—if you will—as a financial intermediary."

Strategies to Earn Position Profits

We have said that a dealer will position if she is bullish, that she will short securities if she is bearish. There are some subtleties to be added. Let's turn first to *tails*.

Figuring the Tail. As noted, dealers sometimes finance securities they position with term RP, for example, finance with 30-day RP a security with three months to run. Whenever they do so, they are creating a future security and betting that they can sell it at a profit. In judging the attractiveness of this bet, dealers always rely on an explicit prediction of where funds will trade and what yields spreads will prevail at the time the term RP comes off.

The easiest way to explain what is involved is with an example. Assume a dealer is operating in an environment in which the 90-day bill is trading at a rate ⅛ below the Fed funds rate. Assume also that Fed funds are trading at 4⅞, the 90-day bill at 4¾, and 30-day term RP at 4½.

If in this environment the dealer were to buy the 90-day bill and finance it with 30-day term RP, he would earn over the 30-day holding period a positive carry equal to

$$4\tfrac{3}{4} - 4\tfrac{1}{2}$$

or a profit equal to ¼ over 30 days. He would also have created a *future* 60-day bill, namely, the unfinanced *tail* of the 90-day bill purchased.

If he thought, as dealers do, of the carry profit over the initial holding period as raising the yield at which he in effect buys the future security, then by purchasing the 90-day bill at 4¾ and RPing it for 30 days at 4½, he would have acquired a future 60-day bill at a yield of 4⅞.[4] The ¼ carry, which is earned for 30 days, adds only ⅛ to the yield at which the future security is effectively purchased because the latter has a maturity of 60 days, which is twice as long as the period over which positive carry is earned.

Faced with this opportunity the dealer would ask himself: How attractive is it to contract to buy a 60-day bill at 4⅞ for delivery 30 days hence? Note the dealer would precisely break even, clearing costs

---

[4] Note that the *higher* the yield at which a discount security is purchased, the *lower* the purchase price. So buying the future security at 4⅞ is, from the dealer's point of view, better than buying it at 4¾.

ignored, if he were able to sell that future bill at a rate of 4⅞. Thus, contracting to buy the future bill will be attractive if he believes he can sell the future bill at a rate lower than 4⅞.

The dealer's answer to the question he has posed might run as follows: Currently the yield curve is such that 60-day bills are trading ⅛ below the rate on 90-day bills. Therefore, if the 60-day bill were to trade at 4⅞ one month hence and if yield spreads did not change, that would imply that the 90-day bill was trading at 5 and Fed funds at 5⅛, that is, at a level ¼ above the present rate. I do not believe that the Fed will tighten or that yield spreads will change in an unfavorable way, therefore I will trade.

If the dealer were correct and the Fed did not tighten and yield spreads did not change, he would be able to sell 30 days hence the future 60-day bill he had created at 4⅝, which is the rate that would be the prevailing rate at that time on the 60-day bill, if his predictions with respect to yield and yields spread were correct.[5] In doing so, he would make a profit equal to ¼ (the purchase rate 4⅞ minus the sale rate 4⅝) on a 60-day security.

Of course, the dealer's predictions might prove to be too favorable. Note, however, he has a built-in margin of protection. Specifically, if he is able to sell his future bills at any rate above 4⅝ but still below 4⅞, he will make some profit. If, on the other hand, rates or rate spreads move so unfavorably that he ends up selling his future 60-day bill at a rate above 4⅞, he will suffer a loss.

For the benefit of those who like to look at dollar numbers rather than yields, we have reworked the example just presented in dollars in Table 1. Recall the 60-day bill was assumed to be trading at a rate ⅛ below the rate on the 90-day bill, at 4¾ − ⅛ or 4⅝.

In deciding whether to buy securities and finance them for some period, dealers invariably "figure the tail," that is, determine the effective yield at which they are buying the future security created. On a discount security, this yield can be figured approximately but quite accurately as follows:

$$
\begin{pmatrix} \text{Effective yield} \\ \text{at which future} \\ \text{security is} \\ \text{purchased} \end{pmatrix} = \begin{pmatrix} \text{Yield at} \\ \text{which cash} \\ \text{security is} \\ \text{purchased} \end{pmatrix} + \cfrac{\begin{pmatrix} \text{Rate of} \\ \text{profit} \\ \text{on carry} \end{pmatrix} \times \begin{pmatrix} \text{Days} \\ \text{carried} \end{pmatrix}}{\begin{pmatrix} \text{Days left to maturity} \\ \text{at end of carry period} \end{pmatrix}}
$$

Applying this formula to our example, we get:

$$
4\tfrac{3}{4} + \frac{\tfrac{1}{4} \times 30}{60} = 4\tfrac{3}{4} + \tfrac{1}{8} = 4\tfrac{7}{8}
$$

---

[5] Recall the 60-day bill was assumed to be trading at a rate ⅛ below the rate on the 90-day bill, at 4¾ − ⅛ = 4⅝.

Table 1
Figuring the Tail: An Example*

Step 1: The dealer buys \$1 million of 90-day bills at a 4¾% rate of discount.

$$\text{Discount at which bills are purchased} = \frac{d \times t}{360} \times F = \frac{0.0475 \times 90}{360} \times \$1,000,000$$
$$= \$11,875$$
$$\text{Price at which bills are purchased} = F - D = \$1,000,000 - \$11,875$$
$$= \$988,125$$

The dealer finances the bills purchased for 30 days at 4½%.

$$\text{Financing cost}\dagger = \frac{0.045 \times 30}{360} \times \$1,000,000$$
$$= \$3,750$$

Step 2: At the end of 30 days the dealer owns the bills at a net cost figure. Determine what yield this cost figure implies on the future 60-day bills created.

$$\text{Net cost of future 60-day bills} = \text{Purchase price} + \text{Financing cost}$$
$$= \$988,125 + \$3,750$$
$$= \$991,875$$

$$\text{Net discount at which future 60-day bills are owned} = F - \text{Net cost}$$
$$= \$1,000,000 - \$991,875$$
$$= \$8,125$$

$$\text{Rate at which future 60-day bills are purchased}\ddagger = \frac{360 \times D}{t \times F} = \frac{360 \times \$8,125}{60 \times \$1,000,000}$$
$$= 0.04875$$
$$= 4\tfrac{7}{8}\%$$

Step 3: Future 60-day bills created are sold at a 4⅝% discount rate. Calculate dollar profit.

$$\text{Discount at which bills are sold} = \frac{d \times t}{360} \times F$$
$$= \frac{0.04625 \times 60}{360} \times \$1,000,000$$
$$= \$7,708$$

$$\text{Profit} = \textit{Net} \text{ purchase discount} - \text{Discount at sales}$$
$$= \$8,125 - \$7,708$$
$$= \$417$$

Step 4: Figure the annualized yield on a bank discount basis that \$417 represents on a 60-day security.

$$d = \frac{360 \times D}{t \times F} = \frac{360 \times \$417}{60 \times \$1,000,000}$$
$$= 0.0025$$
$$= \tfrac{1}{4}\%$$

---

* Let
$$d = \text{rate of discount (decimil)}$$
$$t = \text{days to maturity}$$
$$F = \text{face value}$$
$$D = \text{amount of discount}$$

Then
$$D = \frac{d \times t}{360} \times F$$

† Actually less than \$1 million has to be borrowed, so the dealer's approach to figuring the tail is only an approximation, but it is a close one.

‡ Solving the equation
$$D = F\left(\frac{d \times t}{360}\right)$$

for *d*, gives us
$$d = \frac{360 \times D}{t \times F}$$

Risk. A dealer who engages in the sort of transaction we have just described incurs a rate risk. He might end up with a loss or a smaller profit than anticipated because the Fed tightened when he did not expect it to; because bill rates rose relative to the Fed funds rate; and/or because a shift in the yield curve narrowed the spread between 60- and 90-day bills. Thus whether a dealer who thinks such a transaction would be profitable actually decides to take the position and the size in which he takes it will depend both on the level of confidence he has in his rate and spread predictions and the magnitude of the risk to which he thinks it would expose him.

The same sort of transaction could also be done in other securities: BAs, commercial paper, or CDs. If the instrument purchased and financed were CDs, the risk would be perceptibly greater because supply is more difficult to predict in the CD market than in the bill market, and CDs back up faster than bills. One way a dealer can and sometimes does reduce the risk associated with a future security he creates by putting a security he or she owns out on term RP is by selling bill futures as a hedge.

Relative Value. Every rational investor wants maximum return, maximum liquidity, and minimum risk. When he shops for securities, however, he finds that the real world presents him with nothing but trade-offs between these properties. Securities offering higher rates of returns tend to be riskier and/or less liquid than securities offering lower rates of return. This is as true in the money market as elsewhere, and it is the reason money market dealers think first of *relative value* when they position.

If the spread at which one security is trading relative to another is more than adequate to compensate for the fact that the higher-yield security is riskier and/or less liquid than the lower-yield security, the higher-yield security has greater relative value and should be positioned in preference to the lower-yield security. If alternatively the spread is inadequate, then the lower-yield security has greater relative value and should be positioned in preference to the higher-yield security. Clearly when dealers talk about relative value, they are really talking about credit risk management and liquidity management.

Relative value considerations arise not only in choices between different instruments but also in choices between different maturity sectors of the same market. A dealer might ask whether one should position six-month or one-year bills. If the yield curve were unusually steep out to one year, and the dealer expected it to flatten, then the year bill would have more relative value than the six-month bill.

Arbitrages

Strictly defined, the term *arbitrage* means to buy at a low price in one market and simultaneously resell at a higher price in another market. Some arbitrages in this strict sense do occur in the money market. For example, when a Canadian agency bank accepts an overnight Eurodollar deposit from a U.S. corporation and resells the funds at ⅛ markup in the Fed funds market, it is engaging in arbitrage in the strict sense of the term. Another example of pure arbitrage would be a dealer who reverses in collateral for a fixed period and RPs it at a lower rate for precisely the same period, that is, a matched transaction in repo.

Money market participants use the term *arbitrage* to refer not only to such pure arbitrages, but also to various transactions in which they seek to profit by *exploiting anomalies* either in the yield curve or in the pattern of rates established between different instruments. Typically the anomaly is that the yield spread between two similar instruments is too wide or too narrow; that is, one instrument is priced too generously relative to the other. To exploit such an anomaly, the arbitrager *shorts* the expensive instrument and goes *long* in its underpriced cousin; in other words, he shorts the instrument that has an abnormally low yield relative to the yield on the instrument in which he goes long.

If the arbitrager is successful, one will be able to unwind one's arbitrage at a profit because the abnormal yield spread will have narrowed in one of several ways: (1) the security shorted will have fallen in price and risen in yield, (2) the security purchased will have risen in price and fallen in yield, or (3) a combination of the two will have occurred.

In the money market, yield spread arbitrages are often done (1) between identical instruments of similar maturity (one government is priced too generously relative to another government of similar maturity) and (2) between different instruments of the same maturity (an agency issue is priced too generously relative to a government issue of the same maturity).

Note that in a strictly defined yield spread arbitrage (the long and the short positions in similar maturities), the arbitrager exposes himself to *no market risk.* If rates rise, the resulting loss on his long position will be offset by profits on his short position; if rates fall, the reverse will occur. Thus the arbitrager is not basing his position on a prediction of the direction of market rates, and he is concerned about a possible move up or down in interest rates only insofar as such a move might alter yields spreads in the money market.

An arbitrage in the purest sense of the term involves *no* risk of any sort since the sale and purchase are assumed to occur simultaneously or almost so. An arbitrage based on a yield spread anomaly involves, as noted, no market risk. But it does involve risk of another sort; the arbitrager is in effect speculating on yield spreads. If he bets that a given spread will narrow and it widens, he will lose money.

Thus, even a strictly defined yield spread arbitrage offers no locked-in profit.

Most money market dealers, are active players of the arbitrage game. They have stored in a computer all sorts of information on historical yield spreads and have programmed the computer to identify anomalies in prevailing spreads as they feed data on current yields into it. Dealers use the resulting "helpful hints to the arbitrager" both to set up arbitrages themselves and to advise clients of profitable arbitrage opportunities.

Anomalies in yield spreads that offer opportunities for profitable arbitrage arise due to various temporary aberrations in market demand or supply. For example, if the Treasury brings a big four-year note issue to market, it might trade for a time at a higher rate than surrounding issues because investors were loath to take the capital gains or losses they would have to in order to swap into the new issue. In this case the cause of the out-of-line yield spread would be, for the time it persisted, that the new issue had not been fully distributed. Alternatively, an anomaly might be created by a particular issue being in scarce supply.

Example of an Arbitrage.   Here's an example of an arbitrage *along the yield curve* based on supply conditions. The Treasury, markets a new two-year note at the end of each month. In contrast it offers three-year notes only in connection with quarterly financings; thus a new three-year note comes to market at most once a quarter.

In late January 1978, the yield curve in the two- to three-year area was relatively flat, partly because the Treasury had not offered a new three-year note for three months. The market anticipated, however, that the Treasury would include a three-year note in its February financing and that this new offering would widen yield spreads in the two- to three-year area. Thus buying the current two-year note and shorting the current three-year note appeared to be an attractive arbitrage.

Here's how one dealer did this arbitrage. On January 30, for settlement on January 31, she bought the current two-year note, 7 1/2 N 1/31/80, at a yield to maturity of 7.44. At the same time he shorted the current three-year note, 7 1/8 N 11/15/80, at a yield to maturity of 7.51

The current two-year note was trading at a dollar price of 100-3+, and the yield value of $\frac{1}{32}$ on it was 0.0171.[6] The current three-year note was trading at a dollar price of 99— 1, and the yield value of $\frac{1}{32}$ on it was 0.0127. The smaller yield value of $\frac{1}{32}$ on the three-year note meant that, for a given movement up or down in interest rates, the three-year note would move 135 percent as far up or down

---

[6] The + in the quote equals $\frac{1}{64}$.

in price as the two-year note would.[7] This in turn meant that, if the arbitrage were established on a dollar-for-dollar basis, that is, if the amount of three-year notes shorted equaled the amount of two-year notes purchased, the arbitrage would expose the dealer to market risk. In particular, if rates should fall while the arbitrage was on, the dealer would lose more on his short position in the three-year note than he would gain on his long position in the two-year note. To minimize market risk, the dealer set the arbitrage in a *ratio* based upon the yield values of $\frac{1}{32}$ on the two securities. Note that this procedure insulated the arbitrage against general movements up or down in yields but not against a relative movement between yields on the two securities.

Table 2 shows how the arbitrage worked out. The dealer bought for January 31 settlement $1.35 million of the current two-year note and financed these securities by RPing them at 6.65 percent. Simultaneously she reversed in $1 million of the three-year note at the lower 6.20 reverse repo rate and sold them. Sixteen days later, when the Treasury was offering a new three-year note in connection with its February financing, the dealer was able to unwind his arbitrage, which he put on at a *seven-basis-point* spread, at a *nine-basis-point* spread (Step 2, Table 2). The dealer's total return on the arbitrage was, as Step 3 in Table 2 shows, $375 per $1 million of securities arbitraged.

Risk: The Unexpected Occurs. When a strictly defined yield spread arbitrage fails to work out, the reason is usually that something unexpected has occurred. Here's an example. On several occasions in the spring of 1977, the old seven-year note and the current seven-year note, whose maturities were only three months apart, traded at a 10-basis-point spread. This made no sense since it implied that, at the seven-year level, the appropriate spread between securities differing by one year in maturity was 40 basis points—an impossible yield curve. One dealer successfully arbitraged this yield spread three times by shorting the high-yield current note and going long in the old note. On his fourth try the unexpected occurred. In his words: "We stuck our head in the wringer. We put on the 'arb' at 10 basis points and, while we had it on, the Treasury reopened the current seven-year note. That did not destroy the productive nature of the arbitrage but it did increase the time required before it will be possible to close it out at a profit. The costs of shorting the one issue and being long in the other (especially delivery costs on the short side) are high so at some point we will probably have to turn that arbitrage into a loss trade. Had the Treasury reopened some other issue, we would have

---

[7] The calculation is

$$\frac{0.0171}{0.0127} = 135\%.$$

Table 2
An Arbitrage along the Yield Curve

Step 1:   Set up the arbitrage for settlement on January 31, 1978.

    A. *Buy* $1.35 million of the current two-year note, 7½ N 1/31/80, at 100- 3+ (7.44 yield).

Principal......................	$1,351,476
Accrued interest	0
Total purchase price	$1,351,476

    Repo these securities at 6.65.

    B. Reverse in and *sell* $1 million of the current three-year note, 7⅛ N 11/15/80, at 99-1 (7.51 yield).

Principal......................	$ 990,312
Accrued interest	15,155
Total sale price...............	$1,005,467

    Reverse rate 6.20.

Step 2:   Unwind the arbitrage for settlement on February 16, 1978.

    A. Sell out the long position in the two-year note at 99-28 (7.57 yield).

Principal......................	$1,348,312
Accrued interest	4,475
Total sale price...............	$1,352,787

    Pay financing cost at 6.65 repo rate for 16 days: $3,994.

    B. Cover the short position in the three-year note at 98-22 (7.66 yield).

Principal......................	$ 986,875
Accrued interest	18,304
Total purchase price	$1,005,179

    Receive return on reverse at 6.20 for 16 days: $2,770.

Step 3:   Calculate net return on arbitrage:

Return on short position in the three-year note:

Sale price	$1,005,467
Purchase price	−1,005,179
Income on reverse	2,770
Total return	$ 3,058

Return on long position in the two-year note:

Purchase price	$−1,351,476
Sale price	1,352,787
Cost of repo	− 3,994
Total return	$− 2,683

Net return on overall arbitrage:

Return on short position	$3,058
Return on long position	−2,683
Net return on the arbitrage	$ 375

made $20,000 bang. Instead we're looking at a $40,000 paper loss."

The arbitrage in this example comes close to being a strictly defined yield arbitrage. Many money market arbitrages do not. Dealers will often go long in an issue of one maturity and short another issue of quite different maturity. An arbitrage of this sort resembles a strictly defined yield spread arbitrage in that it is a speculation on a yield spread. But it is more risky than such an arbitrage, because if interest rates move up or down, the price movement in the longer-maturity security will normally exceed that in the shorter-maturity security; thus the arbitrage exposes the investor who puts it on to a *price risk.*

Dealers are not unaware of this, and they attempt to offset the inherent price risk in an arbitrage involving securities of different maturities by adjusting the sizes of the two sides of the arbitrage, as in the arbitrage example above. If for instance the arbitrage involves shorting the two-year note and buying the seven-year note, the arbitrager will short more notes than he buys. Such a strategy, however, cannot completely eliminate market risk because a movement in interest rates may be accompanied by a change in the slope of the yield curve.

Bull and *bear market arbitrages* are based on a view of where interest rates are going. A bull market arbitrager anticipates a fall in interest rates and a rise in securities prices. Thus he might, for example, short two-year Treasuries and go long in ten-year Treasuries on a one-for-one basis, hoping to profit when rates fall from the long coupon appreciating more than the short coupon. If alternatively the arbitrager were bearish, he would do the reverse: short long governments and buy short ones.

An arbitrage can also be set up to profit from an anticipated change in the slope of the yield curve. For example, an arbitrager who anticipated a flattening of the yield curve might buy notes in the seven-year area for high yield and short notes in the two-year area, not necessarily on a one-to-one basis. If the yield curve flattened with no change in average rate levels, the seven-year note would appreciate, the two-year note would decline in price, and the arbitrage could be closed out at a profit.

Money market practitioners are wont to call any pair of long and short positions an arbitrage, but it is clear that as the maturities of the securities involved in the transaction get further and further apart, price risk increases, and at some point the "arbitrage" becomes in reality two separate speculative positions, one a naked long and the other a naked short.

Money market arbitragers normally put on both sides of an arbitrage simultaneously, but they rarely take them off simultaneously. As one dealer noted: "The compulsion to *lift* a *leg* [unwind one side of an arbitrage before the other] is overwhelming. Hardly anyone ever has the discipline to unwind both sides simultaneously. Instead they will first unwind the side that makes the most sense against the market. If, for example, the trader thinks the market is going to do better, he will lift a leg by covering the short."

The persistence with which dealers and their customers arbitrage every out-of-line yield spread they find has an important impact on the money market; it ensures that spreads relationships never get far out of line or, to put it another way, that the differences in the yields on instruments of different types and maturities mirror quite consistently differences in the relative values of these instruments.

Hedges. A dealer in long coupons exposes himself to a sizable price risk every time he goes long or short. Yet in the course of servicing customer buy and sell orders, he inevitably has to do so. Frequently, a trader who, in such securities, has no particular view on where the market is going will hedge any position put on his book by customer business. For example, if a customer sells the trader $1 million of thinly traded long bonds, he will short a nearby issue until one can unwind both his long and short positions at what one considers reasonable prices.

The Clearing Banks

We have described the role of dealers as market makers in the money market. Other institutions that play a vital role in this process are the banks that clear trades for dealers in governments, agencies, and other money market instruments. In acting as a clearing agent, a *clearing bank* makes payments against securities delivered into a dealer's account and receives payments made to the dealer against securities delivered out of its account. It also safekeeps securities received by a dealer and makes payments into and out of the account that the dealer holds with the bank. Finally, a clearing bank provides dealers with any financing they require at its posted *dealer loan rate*.

Fails and the Fails Game. If, on the settlement date of a trade, a seller does not make timely delivery of the securities purchased, delivers the wrong securities, or fails in some other way to deliver in proper form, the trade becomes a *fail.* In that case the buyer does not have to make payment until proper delivery is made, presumably the next day; *but* he owns the securities as of the initially agreed-upon settlement day. Thus, on a fail the security buyer (who is *failed to*) receives a one-day free loan equal to the amount of the purchase price, that is, one day's free financing. And if the fail persists, the free loan continues.

Dealers often play some portion of their financing needs for a fail; that is, they estimate on the basis of past experience the dollar amount of the fails that will be made to them and reduce their RP borrowing accordingly. If their estimate proves high, more securities will end up in their box at the clearing bank than they had anticipated, and that bank will automatically grant them a box loan against that collateral. Note that a dealer who plays the *fails game* is in effect using his clearing bank as a lender of last resort.

The Brokers

Brokers are everywhere in the money market. They are active in the *interdealer* markets in government, agencies, CDs, bankers' acceptances, repo, and reverse, and in the *interbank* markets for Fed funds and Euro time deposits. The volumes of funds and securities they broker each business day are staggering. Unfortunately, because few statistics on brokered trades are collected, it is impossible to put precise dollar figures on these amounts. It is possible, however, to give a few suggestive numbers. On an active day one of the top Fed funds brokers, who is in competition with nine other brokers, may broker over $6 billion of funds! Currently about 70 percent of interdealer trades in governments and agencies is done through brokers. Brokers could not survive without a huge volume of trades because the commissions they receive per $1 million of funds or securities brokered are extremely small.

The Service Sold.   Much of what a broker is selling to his clients is a fast information service that tells the trader where the market is—what bids and offers are and how much they are good for. Speed of communication is thus crucial to a money market broker, and each has a board of direct phone lines through which he can contact each important trader he services by merely punching a button. Over those lines brokers constantly collect bids and offers throughout the day. They pass these on to other traders either by direct phone calls or over display screens, referred to throughout the industry as *CRTs*—short for cathode ray tubes.

Usefulness of Brokers.   In recent years brokerage has been introduced to many sectors of the money market in which it previously did not exist; and in those market sectors where it did exist, the use of brokers has increased dramatically. One reason is that the number of dealers in all sectors of the market has expanded sharply; as a result, it has become increasingly difficult for a trader to know where other traders are quoting the market and to rapidly disseminate his own bids and offers other than through the communications network provided by the brokers.

Another reason brokers are used is anonymity. A big bank or dealer may operate in such size that simply by bidding or offering, he will affect either market quotes or the size for which they are good. A second reason anonymity is valued by traders is the "ego element."

In the words of one dealer: "Anonymity is very important to those giant egos on Wall Street. When they make a bad trade, they just do not want the whole world to watch them unwind it at a loss."

Communications

In a discussion of the makers of the money market, ignoring the phone company, Telexes, CRTs, computers, and other communications facilities would be a serious omission. Without Mother Bell and her foreign counterparts, the money market would be utterly different. That the money market is a single market that closely approaches the economist's assumption of perfect information is currently due in no small part to the fact that New York brokers and traders are one push of a direct-phone-line button away from the Bank of America and often only a four-digit extension from London, Singapore, and other distant spots.

Phones, while ubiquitous, are not enough. Giving and receiving quotes over the phone takes more time than money market participants have, thus the growing role of CRTs.

Only a few years ago the only way money market participants could get current quotes was by calling brokers and dealers. Moreover, to get a range of quotes they had to make several calls because no quote system covered the whole market. In 1968 a new organization, *Telerate*, began to remedy this situation by quoting commercial paper rates on a two-page, cathode-ray-tube display system; it then had 50 subscribers. From this modest start, the system was quickly expanded because people wanted more information. Today several hundred pages of information on credit market quotes and statistics are available to Telerate subscribers.

PART 3—THE INVESTORS: RUNNING A
SHORT-TERM PORTFOLIO

Money market investors include a wide range of institutions: commercial banks, S&Ls, insurance companies of all sorts, mutual savings banks, other financial institutions, federal agencies, nonfinancial corporations, international financial institutions such as the World Bank, foreign central banks, and foreign firms—financial and nonfinancial.

One might expect most institutional portfolios to be managed with considerable sophistication, but "the startling thing you would find, if you were to wander around the country talking to short-term portfolio managers [bank and corporate], is the basic underutilization of the portfolio." These are the words of the sales manager of the government department in one of the nation's top banks. Another dealer described portfolio management practices similarly, but in slightly different terms: "Most portfolio managers would describe themselves as 'conservative,' by which they mean that the correct way to manage a portfolio is to look to your accounting risk and reduce that to zero. The opportunities thereby forgone are either ignored or more frequently not even perceived." Most short-term portfolios are poorly managed, many are not managed at all. Before we talk about that, let's look first at how a liquidity portfolio should be managed.

Contrast of a Portfolio Manager with a Dealer

As noted dealers' biggest profits result over time from well-chosen position plays, and a crucial ingredient in a successful dealer operation is therefore the ability to manage well a highly levered portfolio.

Much of what we said about how a good dealer manages his portfolio applies to bank and corporate portfolio managers as well. There are, however, important differences in perspective between the two. First, a dealer is likely to be *much* less risk averse than the typical manager of a liquidity portfolio because it is the dealer's job to speculate on yields and yields spreads, whereas the portfolio manager's job is first to ensure that the funds invested will be available whenever the firm needs them and only second to maximize the return earned. A second difference in perspective is that, whereas the portfolio manager has free funds to invest, the dealer has no such funds, and a decision to invest is therefore always based on a view of the market. A third difference in perspective is the time horizon. A dealer often buys securities on the expectation that he will be able to resell them at a higher price within a few hours or a few days. The portfolio manager, in contrast, is normally looking for instruments that he would be comfortable holding for some longer period—how long depends on the type of portfolio.

The Parameters

A liquidity portfolio is always managed within certain investment *parameters* that establish limits with respect to: (1) the types of instruments the portfolio may buy; (2) the percentage of the portfolio that may be invested in any one of these instruments (in T-Bills the limit might be 100 percent, whereas in CDs, which are less liquid, it might be much lower); (3) the kind of exposure to names and credit risk the portfolio may assume (which banks' CDs and which issuers' commercial paper it may buy and how much of each name it may buy); (4) how far out on the maturity spectrum the portfolio may extend; and finally (5) whether the portfolio may short or repo securities.

The investment parameters within which every liquidity portfolio operates are set by top management. Because senior management delineates the portfolio manager's playing field and thereby the kinds of winnings—return on investment—that he can seek through managing the portfolio, it is important that management take time to learn what the game is about before establishing such guidelines. Another input in this decision should be an evaluation of the kind of money that the firm is likely to have to invest short term: How big is it likely to be? How variable will it be? A third important input is the firm's management style. There are swinging corporations and there are very conservative corporations, and that difference should be reflected in their styles of portfolio management. A fourth factor is the caliber of the personnel the firm hires to manage its short-term portfolio. Investment parameters are meant to limit the portfolio manager's freedom of judgment, and inevitably they will at times prevent him from pursuing strategies that he correctly believes would increase return. For example, tight restrictions on the amount a portfolio manager could invest in BAs might prevent the manager, when BAs were trading at an attractive spread to bills, from making a profitable swap out of bills into BAs. The more qualified the personnel the firm anticipates hiring to run its liquidity portfolio, the wider guidelines should be set and the greater the latitude the portfolio manager should be given to exercise judgment.

Managing a Liquidity Portfolio

In large institutions a portfolio manager is often given several portfolios to manage—one for the firm itself, another for its financing sub, still others for self-insurance funds, and so forth. With respect to each portfolio, the manager must ask: What are the size, variability, and predictability of the money I am investing? The answer depends in part on the purpose for which the funds are held. For example, the short-term portfolio of a manufacturing firm that experiences big seasonal fluctuations in cash flows, as auto firms and food packers do, will be more variable and less predictable in size than a portfolio supporting a self-insurance fund. A second element in the portfolio manager's evaluation of the sort of money he is investing is the cash forecasts the firm gives him—their frequency, the periods for which they are available (these might be tomorrow, the next week, the next month, and the current quarter), and the confidence that historical experience suggests he can put in these forecasts. The portfolio manager's assessment of the sort of money he is investing tells him how long he is likely to be able to hold securities he buys and thus the planning horizon—30 days, 90 days, one year, or longer—upon which he should base investment decisions.

Relative Value. Once the portfolio manager has determined a planning horizon, one asks, just as a dealer does: *Where is relative value?*

The answer to this question requires knowledge, experience, and feel for the market.

On a purely technical level, the portfolio manager first has to face the problem that yields on money market instruments are not quoted on comparable bases. The problem is not just that yields on discount securities are quoted on a discount basis while yields on interest-bearing instruments are quoted on another basis. There are, in addition, all sorts of other anomalies with respect to how interest accrues, how often it is paid, whether the security is U.S. or Canadian (Canadian CDs trade on a 365-day-year basis, domestic CDs on a 360-day-year basis), whether it is a leap year, whether a security happens to mature on a holiday, and other factors. These anomalies are, moreover, *not* reflected in the yield to maturity figures on dealers' quote sheets.

A number of portfolio managers, who run such large sums of money that the cost is justified, have developed sophisticated computer programs that permit them to calculate yields on a wide range of securities on a comparable basis. One such portfolio manager noted: "I developed a program that incorporated a day algorithm which I got from a mathematician. I wanted the computer to know when a weekend occurs and to skip it in evaluating yield on a Friday trade I do for regular settlement. I also wanted the computer to recognize that in agencies July 31 is a nonday [in terms of interest accrued], that February 29 exists whether or not it actually does, and so too does February 30; there's an arbitrage from February 28 to March 1 in agencies, and I want the computer to recognize this. The computer also knows a Canadian security from a U.S. security."

In evaluating the relative value of different instruments, being able to calculate their yields on a comparable basis is just a starting point. In addition, the portfolio manager has to have a good feel for the *liquidity* of different instruments, under both prevailing market conditions and those he foresees might occur. This can involve subtle distinctions. The manager of a large portfolio commented: "I buy only direct issue [commercial] paper that I know I can sell to the dealers—GMAC but not Prulease. It's a question of liquidity, not quality. Also I buy paper from dealers only if they are ready to take it back."

To determine relative value among different instruments, the portfolio manager must also have a good feel for *yield spreads:* what they are, and how and why they change. This too involves subtleties. Here's an example given by one investor: "Lately the six-month bill has been trading above Fed funds. I ask, 'Why?' The technical condition of the market has been excellent with little supply on the street [in dealers' hands]. So the six-month bill should have done better, but it didn't. The reason is that we've got a pure dealer market. The retail buyer, who is scared and going short, is simply not there."

Finally, to determine where relative value lies among different *maturity* sectors of the market, the portfolio manager must explicitly predict interest rates *and* the slope of the yield curve over at least the time span of his planning horizon. Such predictions will be based on a wide range of factors, including a careful tracking of the Fed's stated objectives and whether it is currently achieving these objectives.

Relative value, in addition to depending on the factors we have enumerated, may also be a function in part of the temperament of the portfolio manager—whether he has the psychology of a trader, as a number of top portfolio managers do, or is more inclined to make a reasoned bet and let it stand for some time, an attitude characteristic of other successful portfolio managers. As one investor noted, it makes a difference: "The nine-month bill will, except in very tight markets, trade at yield levels close to the corresponding long issue, which is the one-year bill. So if you are looking for the most return for your dollar on a buy-and-hold strategy, you buy the nine-month bill and ride it for three months. If, however, you want to trade the portfolio— to buy something with the idea that it will go down a few basis points— you are better off staying in the active issue, which would be the current year bill."

Credit Risk.   Most companies, when they have money and are trying to increase yield, will start reaching out on the credit spectrum— buying A-2 or P-2 paper.* A few do so in an intelligent and reasoned way, devoting considerable resources to searching out companies that are candidates for an upgrading of their credit rating to A-1 or P-1 and whose paper thus offers more relative value than that of A-1 and P-1 issuers.

The average firm would, however, be well advised not to take this route. As the sales manager of one bank dealership noted: "We tell a company doing this: 'It's the wrong thing for you to do because you do not know how to do it. You have no ability to track these companies. Also their financial statements are not worth very much and you of all people should know this because you know what you do to your own.' They sort of look at us with jaundiced eyes, and say, 'Oh, yes, I guess that's so.' "

The ablest portfolio managers tend as a group to steer clear of credit analysis. As one of the sharpest commented: "We are not interested in owning anything that does not have unimpeachable credit because, on an instrument that does not, credit will tend to dominate the performance of the instrument more than interest rates. Also, I am a one-man band, and I simply do not have time to evaluate credit risk."

Among large-portfolio managers, the exception to this attitude is most often found in those in insurance companies, who are a different

---

* Commercial paper is rated by several rating services. A-2 and P-2 paper are a grade off top-rated A-1 or P-1 paper.

breed. They are far more comfortable than most with credit exposure. This is an offshoot of their purchases of long corporate bonds. Because of these purchases, insurance companies portfolio managers follow the financial condition of many corporations and consequently can and do knowledgeably buy lesser-grade commercial paper that other portfolios would not touch.

Maturity Choice. While a good portfolio manager can, as many do, refuse to get into credit analysis, he *cannot* avoid making explicit interest rate predictions and basing his maturity choices upon them. As one portfolio manager pointed out: "The mistake many people make is to think that they do not have to make a forecast. But buying a 90-day bill and holding it to maturity *is* making a forecast. If you think that rates are going to move up sharply and soon, you should be sitting in overnight RP; and then when rates move up, you buy the 90-day bill."

Making rate predictions is important not only because an implicit rate prediction underlies every maturity choice a portfolio manager makes, but also because good portfolio managers feel as a group that the way yield on a large portfolio can most effectively be increased is by positioning correctly along the maturity spectrum—by recognizing which maturity sectors of the market are cheap (have relative value) and which are expensive, and buying or shifting accordingly.

Riding the Yield Curve. The best way to illustrate the kind of dividends yielded by maturity choices based on an explicit prediction of how interest rates might move is with a few concrete examples. Let's start by illustrating how a technique commonly used to raise return—namely, *riding the yield curve*—must be based on an explicit prediction of where Fed funds might trade. The idea of riding the yield curve is to increase return by buying a security out on the shoulder of the yield curve and holding that security until it can be sold at a gain because its current maturity has fallen and the yield at which it is currently trading has consequently decreased. Note that the main threat to the success of such a strategy is that short-term rates might rise across the board.

Assume that an investor has funds to invest for three months. The six-month (180-day) bill is trading at 5.41 and the three-month (90-day) bill is trading at 5.21 (Figure 1). The alternatives the investor is choosing between are: (1) to buy the 90-day bill and mature it and (2) to buy the six-month bill and sell it three months hence. To assess the relative merits of these two strategies, the investor does a *break-even analysis.*

On $1 million of bills, a 90-day basis point (a basis point earned for 90 days) is worth $25.* If the investor bought the six-month bill,

---

* The calculation is as follows:

$$\left(\frac{0.0001 \times 90}{360}\right) \times \$1,000,000 = \$25.$$

Figure 1
Yield Curve in an Example of Riding the Yield Curve

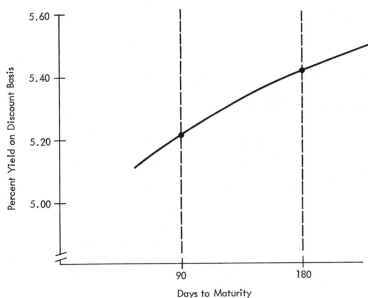

he would earn 20 basis points more than if he bought the three-month bill. Thus, he could sell out the six-month bill after three months at a rate 20 basis points above the rate at which he bought it, that is, at 5.61, and still earn as many *dollars* on the investment as he would have if he had bought and matured the three-month bill (Table 3). Therefore the rate on the three-month bill three months hence would have to rise above 5.61 before holding the six-month bill for three months would pay out fewer dollars than buying and maturing the three-month bill.

How likely is this to occur? Note that because of the slope of the yield curve (a 20-basis-point drop between the six-month and three-month bill rates), the rate at which the three-month bill trades three months hence would be 5.21 if no change occurred in interest rates, 40 basis points below the break-even rate of 5.61. Thus the investor has 40 basis points of protection and the question one has to ask in making a choice is: How likely is it that the Fed will tighten in the next three months so sharply that the three-month bill will rise 40 basis points, from 5.21 to 5.61? If the answer is that it is highly unlikely, then one would buy the six-month bill and ride the yield curve.

Note that the investor who buys the three-month bill and matures it will earn $13,025 on each $1 million of bills bought (see Table 3). If, alternatively, one opts to ride the yield curve and does so successfully (i.e., buys the six-month bill and is able, because the Fed does not in

Table 3
Dollar Calculations of Return in Example of Riding the Yield Curve

I. Buy $1 million of 90-day bills at 5.21 and hold to maturity.

Face value	$1,000,000		Discount at purchase	$13,025
—Purchase price	986,975		—Discount at maturity.....	0
Return	$ 13,025		Return	$13,025

II. Buy $1 million of 180-day bills at 5.41 and sell at break-even yield of 5.61.

Sale price	$985,975		Discount at purchase	$27,050
—Purchase price	972,950		—Discount at maturity	14,025
Return	$ 13,025		Return	$13,025

III. Buy $1 million of 180-day bills at 5.41 and sell at 5.21.

Sale price	$986.975		Discount at purchase	$27,050
—Purchase price	972,950		—Discount at maturity	13,025
Return	$ 14,025		Return	$14,025

fact tighten, to sell out at 5.21), one will earn $14,025, which exceeds $13,025 by $1,000. This $1,000 equals the extra 40 90-day basis points one earns: 20 because the six-month bill is bought at a 20-basis-point spread to the three-month bill and 20 because one is able to sell it three months later at a rate 20 basis points below the rate at which it was bought.

Actually the investor riding the yield curve in our example has more protection than we indicated. The reason is that, when he buys the six-month bill, he invests fewer dollars than when he buys the three-month bill. So on a *simple interest basis,* he would earn an annualized rate of return of 5.35 if he bought and matured the three-month bill, whereas if he bought the six-month bill at 5.41 and sold it as the break-even level of 5.61, he would earn an annualized return, again on a simple interest (365-day-year) basis, of 5.43, which is greater.[8] To earn an annualized return of only 5.35 on the funds invested in the six-month bill, the investor would have to sell it out after three months at a discount of 5.68, which is 47 basis points above 5.21. The first break-even calculation we made on a dollar-return basis is intuitively easier to follow, but this second more refined calculation is the one the investor should make if he is interested in maximizing yield.

Another Maturity Decision.   Here's a second example of how a conscious prediction of interest rates over the investor's time horizon can help an investor increase yield. When it appears that the Fed might tighten, the reaction of many portfolio managers is to retreat in panic to the base of the yield curve. Whether doing so is wise depends on

---

[8] The formula is:

$$\text{Annualized return on a simple interest basis} = \left(\frac{\text{Dollar return}}{\text{Principal invested}}\right) \div \left(\frac{\text{Days held}}{365}\right).$$

the opportunities available and on how fast and how far the Fed is likely to tighten.

In April 1977, it was felt that the Fed was tightening. Funds were trading at 4¾ and no one was sure where that rate was going. It was the feeling of the market that a ¾ point move was needed and that 5½ would probably be the top side, but some in the market suggested 5¾. Just prior to this period, six-month BAs had risen in yield from 5.20 to 5.85 because of a lack of demand on the part of investors; the yield on three-month BAs was 5.45. At this point a portfolio manager with three-month money to invest faced a choice. One alternative, assuming he was managing an S&L portfolio, would have been to adopt the bearish strategy of selling overnight Fed funds in anticipation of eventually getting a 5½ overnight rate.[9] Alternatively, he could have decided to buy six-month BAs and sell them after three months.

Using the same sort of break-even analysis illustrated in the previous example, one investor facing this choice concluded that if he bought six-month BAs at 5.85, one could after 90 days sell them at 6.30, and do as well as if one had invested in overnight Fed funds and the Fed funds rate had in fact immediately moved to 5½.[10] In other words, he could sell six-month BAs three months hence at 85 basis points above the rate at which three-month BAs were then trading and still earn as many dollars as by rolling funds overnight at 5½. That 85 basis points of protection seemed more than sufficient, so he bought the six-month BAs. As things turned out, the Fed's target for funds was only 5¼–⅜, so the BAs turned out to be by far the better investment. An investor who did not use this analysis would, however, have probably missed this opportunity.

Asymmetric Positions of the Investor and the Issuer. The two maturity-choice examples we worked through involved a choice between riding the yield curve and making an alternative investment: in one case buying and maturing the three-month bill, and in the other case rolling funds in the overnight market.

With respect to riding the yield curve, it should be noted that the bank liability manager issuing CDs or a firm issuing commercial paper is playing precisely the opposite ball game from the investor—one is trying to minimize interest costs, the other to maximize return earned. If the issuer of paper finds that, from a cost point of view, it makes sense to roll three-month CDs, then the investor should be buying

---

[9] The alternative facing a corporate portfolio manager would have been to invest in overnight RP at a slightly lower rate.

[10] The calculation assumes that the same number of dollars would have been invested in both instruments. It also allows for the fact that the investor of large sums in Fed funds gets in effect daily compounding of interest. The Fed funds rate is quoted on a 360-day-year basis.

six-month paper and riding it for three months rather than rolling three-month paper.

Stability of Return. As one good portfolio manager after another will note: "Real money is to be made by positioning correctly along the maturity spectrum—by making conscious market judgments and acting on them."

Such positioning does not, however, guarantee *steady* high return. One reason is that sometimes the portfolio manager will be wrong in rate predictions. A second reason is well described by one manager: "If you can invest out to two years and you feel strongly that rates are going to fall, you might choose to have an average 9- or 12-month maturity—not everything out in the longer spectrum. If you are correct and the market rallies, the proper response is to shorten the portfolio— not just to sit there and hold this apparent book yield, but to recognize it. The reason you sell is that the market eventually gets to a point where you think it has reached a peak and might go lower. If after you sell you decide that you were wrong and believe—on the basis of a new rate forecast—that rates are likely to go still lower, you buy in again long term."

It's hard to produce a stable income pattern with that sort of portfolio management, and thus it would be criticized by some. But the basic assumption is that the firm is a going concern. Therefore, the portfolio manager's primary goal should be long-term profitability, not stability of income.

In this respect the track record of the World Bank's liquidity portfolio is interesting. The managers of this portfolio are constantly making maturity choices of the sort described above. In February 1977, their treasurer noted that over the previous 29 months, they had earned on their dollar portfolio a high average return, 9.32 percent, but their monthly annualized returns had fluctuated from a low of −0.67 percent in one month to a high of almost +32 percent in another.[11]

As that track record suggests, in evaluating the performance of a managed portfolio, monthly figures are meaningless. A portfolio manager needs to look at his average record for six months or longer to get a true feel for performance.

Time Horizon and Maturity of Securities Purchased. In the example we gave of why the return on a managed portfolio is likely to fluctuate from month to month, the portfolio manager—believing that rates were likely to fall—might well have well have extended maturity into the two-year area. In this respect it's important to note that such an extension does not imply that either the portfolio manager's planning horizon or interest rate forecast extends anywhere near two years. It simply implies that he is confident that rates will fall during some

---

[11] *The Money Manager*, February 14, 1977, p. 3.

much shorter time period and is willing to sell and realize a gain once this occurs.

Good managers of short-term portfolios, in which the maturity parameters are widely set, frequently buy Treasury notes and other longer-term instruments in the hope of realizing short-term gains. Said an ex-portfolio manager: "If I liked the market, I'd buy a ten-year bond even if I needed the money tomorrow." That's an extreme example, but this portfolio manager had the inborn instincts of a good trader, which he eventually became.

Changing Relative Value. The search for relative value is not a one-time affair. The money market is dynamic; changes in demand, supply, expectations, and external events—from announcements of the latest M1 figures to changes in tax laws—are constantly having an impact on it. And as they do, yield spreads and rates change. Thus relative value may reside in one sector today, in another tomorrow.

A good portfolio manager must reassess his position each day, asking not only whether expectations with respect to interest rates have changed, but also whether transitory anomalies have arisen in spreads or distortions in rates from which he could profit.

One cause of transitory rate distortions is overreactions by investors. Said one portfolio manager: "When I saw that huge five billion M1 figure last Thursday, I started buying, knowing that in a few days the market would come back. This sort of overreaction has been much more common since '74, in part because there are so many more players in the market today."

Here's an example of another transitory rate situation from which a corporate portfolio manager could benefit. Capital gains are taxed as ordinary income for banks, at the capital gains rate for corporations. Thus a longer-term municipal note selling at a discount from par offers a double-barreled tax advantage to a corporation but not to a bank.[12] Banks, however, are such big investors in this market that at times discount muni notes are priced to the bank market rather than to the corporate market. When they are, a corporation can earn a much higher after-tax return on such notes than it could from taxable securities of comparable maturity and risk.

Tracking changes in relative value takes time and effort but, as a portfolio manager gains experience, it becomes almost second nature. Also a portfolio manager can rely on the dealers for help. Once a portfolio manager recognizes that a change in relative value has occurred between instruments or maturity sectors, his response should be to *swap* or *arbitrage*.

As one portfolio manager with wide parameters observed: "Arbitrating a portfolio is one way to make money, whether it's a complete

---

[12] This assumes that the corporation is in a position to benefit from tax-exempt income.

arbitrage or a swapping arbitrage between sectors of the market. Money market instruments oscillate in relative value for very good reasons; and as you get experienced, you can with not too much time keep asking why one sector of the market is out of line with where it should be—the latter judgment being more than an extrapolation of a historical average. Once you have convinced yourself that the reason is transitory, then not to own the instrument that is undervalued and be short in the other instrument that is out of line is foolhardy."

Extension Swaps. One very simple swap strategy many portfolio managers use is to *extension swaps.* They pick a maturity sector of the market they like, say two- or three-year governments, and then, for example, adopt the strategy of *extending* (lengthening maturity) a few months whenever they can pick up five basis points and of *backing up* (shortening maturity) a few months whenever that costs only three basis points. If market conditions are such that many such swaps can be done a portfolio manager can pick up basis points this way. Note that, whereas a 90-day basis point is worth only $25 per $1 million, a three-year basis point is worth $300.[13]

A similar practice used by some investors in bills to pick up basis points is to roll the current three-month or six-month bill each week when new bills are auctioned. If conditions are such that new bill issues, which the market has to absorb, are priced in the auction cheap relative to surrounding issues, then by rolling his bills the investor may be able to pick up each week two or three $25 or $50 basis points by doing this. A second advantage of this strategy is that it keeps the investor in current bills which are more liquid than off-the-run issues.

In swapping and trading generally, "it's important," as one portfolio manager noted, "to know what dealer will deal in what and who will make the best markets. Say a bank has a big writing program and uses the dealer community—Becker, Sali, and Goldman. The bank sells the dealers 70 million, and they resell them to retail. If I have some of that bank's CDs, I would not go to Goldman, since I know their customers are stocked up on those CDs. Instead, I would go to some fourth dealer whose customers are light in that bank's CDs."

Leverage. Like a dealer, a portfolio manager can repo securities one owns.[14] If the portfolio is that of a fair sized bank, the portfolio

---

[13] The calculation is

$$3(0.0001 \times \$1,000,000) = \$300.$$

[14] Jargon in this area is confusing. Dealers talk about "doing repos" when they are financing their position and about "doing reverses" when they are borrowing securities. Some portfolio managers who use repurchase agreements—just as dealers do—to lever, talk about doing repo, others talk about doing a reverse (i.e., reversing out securities). We have opted to use the word *repo* when the initiative comes from the side wanting to borrow money, and *reverse* when the initiative comes for the side wanting to borrow securities.

manager will probably be able to repo securities directly with retail customers. If, alternatively, the portfolio is that of a corporation or other institution that does not have direct contact with suppliers of repo money, the portfolio manager can always RP securities with the dealers, who will in turn hang them out on the other side.

The ability to repo securities can be used by a portfolio manager in various ways. If an unanticipated short-term need for cash arises at a time when the portfolio manager has established a position he wants to maintain, he can bridge that gap by borrowing RP money instead of selling securities. Said one corporate portfolio manager: "We never fund to dates. We fund to market expectancy—what we think is going to happen to interest rates. We can repo the portfolio so we never have problems raising money for short periods. If we have to raise money for a long period of time to meet a portfolio embarrassment [securities in the portfolio can only be sold at a loss], that means we made an error and had better face up to it."

Another way a portfolio manager with wide parameters can use the RP market imaginatively is to buy a security, finance the first part of its life with term RP, and thereby create an attractive future security. That is a technique of portfolio management, a corporate manager can use as well as a dealer, and some do.

Still another way a portfolio manager can use the RP market is to out and out lever the portfolio—buy securities at one rate, turn around and RP them at a lower rate, and then use the funds borrowed to buy more securities. Or the portfolio manager can simply buy securities for which he has no money by doing a repo against them at the time of purchase. A portfolio manager who uses this technique commented: "I repo the portfolio as an arbitrage technique everyday and probably run the biggest matched sale book in American industry. We RP anything we can, even corporates. In doing RP, I am either financing something I have or buying something I don't have any money for. We take the RPs off for quarter ends because they might comprise the aesthetics of our statement." Avoiding repos across quarter ends is common among those corporations that use repos, so it is impossible from looking at financial statements to determine whether a corporation uses repos to borrow.

To the corporate portfolio manager who can use repos, it is, in the words of one," the most flexible instrument in the money market. You can finance with repo, you can borrow using it, and you can ride the yield curve using it—buy a two-month bill, put it out on repo for a month, and then sell it or do a 30-day repo again. And you can use repo to create instruments; put a six-month bill out on a two-month repo, and you have created a four-month bill 2 months out."

Despite the many and reasonable ways in which the ability to borrow in the repo market can be used, it is rare for a corporate short-term portfolio manager to be able to hang out any of the portfolio on repo.

In large banks, the practice of RPing the government portfolio is almost universal. Such a bank views its government portfolio as a massive arbitrage rather than as a source of liquidity. Among smaller banks, practices with respect to the use of repo vary widely.

In a discussion of the use of the repo market by portfolio managers to borrow, a distinction should be made between portfolio managers who are using the market consciously to borrow and lever, and those who are, so to speak, coaxed into doing reverses. As noted, when dealers want to short securities they will often cover their short by reversing securities. If the security is not one that is readily available, the dealer will go to a broker of repo who knows what securities various banks, S&Ls, and other institutions have in their portfolios. The broker will attempt to get an institution that holds the needed securities to reverse them out by showing that institution an attractive arbitrage. Such a transaction looks like an ordinary repo but the initiative comes not from the institution that is borrowing but from the dealer who wants to cover a short. Many banks, S&Ls, and other institutions that would never use the repo market to borrow to meet a temporary cash need or to lever will reverse out securities that they intend to hold indefinitely, probably to maturity, to pick up basis points on an arbitrage.

Use of the T-Bill Futures Market. Portfolio managers who are free to use the T-Bill futures market are currently in the distinct minority, but for those who can, it offers an array of opportunities to lock in yields, arbitrage, hedge, and speculate. And a few portfolio managers use futures contracts extensively as one more tool of portfolio management.

Shorting Securities. It's unusual for the manager of a corporate portfolio to have authorization to sell securities short but not as rare as it used to be. The ability to short securities can be useful to a portfolio manager in a number of ways. For one thing, it permits one to arbitrage as dealers do—going long in an undervalued security and short in an overvalued security—as a speculation on a yield spread. A few corporate portfolio managers do this quite actively.

There are, as one portfolio manager noted, also tax reasons for shorting: "Say you have ballooned maturities in part of your portfolio out to ten years. You were right on the market and have only 30 days to go to get a long-term capital gain. But you think the market might back up and you want to take some of the risk out of your position. To do so is easy—you short something similar. In the corporate tax environment, the tax on long-term capital gains is 30 percent, while the tax on ordinary income is 48 percent. With that sort of 18-point advantage, you have to be badly wrong on the short not to come out ahead shorting." For banks there is no incentive to short for tax purposes because their long-term capital gains are taxed as ordinary income.

Still another reason a corporate portfolio manager might want to short is because borrowing through a short seems less expensive than selling an attractive investment. Said one portfolio manager: "If we decided, yes, the market is in here [in a given maturity sector], then we would look for the cheapest thing [the instrument with most relative value] on a spread basis—CDs, BAs, or bills—and buy that. Even though bills might yield less than, say, Euro CDs, we might buy them because the spread on Euros into bills was too tight. We'd make the decision to buy or not and then buy the cheapest thing. When we made the decision to sell, we would sell the most expensive thing. But we could not short so we were sort of up against it at times when we had to sell. I had already bought the cheapest thing around, so generally I have to sell something cheap. It bothered me a lot not to be able to short when we needed cash, but perhaps it would have raised questions with strockholders."

The Big Shooters. We have drawn in this chapter a distinction between dealers and portfolio managers that is perhaps too sharp. There are in the U.S. money market a number of huge liquidity portfolios taking positions that rival those taken by more than one dealer and a few of those are very actively managed. The people who run these portfolios utilize every tool of portfolio management that the dealers do—from creating future securities and figuring tails to shorting to do speculative arbitrages. Some also trade their positions as actively as a dealer. Said an individual who ran one such portfolio: "I sometimes bought securities today that I knew I would have to sell for cash the next day. I might even buy if I was bullish for the next few hours—I have bought securities on the day cash was needed and sold them later in the day if I thought the market would go up a couple of 32nds." The major differences between portfolios of this sort and a dealer operation are first that retail business is important to a dealer, and second that, whereas dealers are highly levered, a leverage ratio of 3:1 is highly unusual and probably top side for a liquidity portfolio.

Marking to Market. In well-run short-term portfolios, it is common practice to mark the whole portfolio to market each day. The objective of running a portfolio is to maximize over time not interest accrued, but *total financial return*—interest earned plus capital gains realized minus capital losses realized. A portfolio manager who has this objective will, if he buys a two-year note with a 7 percent coupon and then finds that yields on the two-year have risen to 8 percent, view his decision to have bought the 7 percent coupon as a serious mistake. Moreover, if he anticipates that rates will rise still further, he will sell out that security at a loss (convert one paper loss into a realized loss) and wait to recommit long-term until he thinks rates have stabilized.

The use of this tactic in portfolio management calls for a willingness to book capital losses, and that willingness is a hallmark of every good portfolio manager. Realizing losses is, however, difficult to do psychologically; it is something a trader must discipline oneself to do. One advantage of marking a portfolio to market each day is that it helps get the focus of those who buy and sell for the portfolio off book value. As one portfolio manager noted: "If market value declines today and you book to market, tomorrow you start at that market value. And your gain or loss will be a function of whether tomorrow's price is better than today's." Said another: "If you mark to market, the past is gone. You've made a mistake, and the point now is not to make another one."

Tracking Performance. Active management can substantially increase yield on a short-term portfolio. "You can as much as double yield on a short-term portfolio," said one practitioner of the art, "by arbitraging sectors and by changing maturities in response to interest rate forecasts."

In an institution where the short-term portfolio is actively managed, there are always people in top management who understand the credit market and who are therefore comfortable with creative management of the institution's portfolio. It is also the case that the focal point in management of the portfolio is on yield earned rather than on when money is needed. In other words, the portfolio manager's main concern in investing is with where relative value lies, not with when he needs cash; specifically he does not *fund to dates*—buy three-month bills because he needs money three months hence.

Performance in every liquidity portfolio managed to maximize return is carefully tracked. A key element in this tracking is marking the portfolio to market so that the return-earned calculation incorporates not only realized, but also unrealized capital gains and losses.

Once performance is tracked, it is compared against a variety of yardsticks. A portfolio manager might, for example, compare his performance with what he could have achieved had he followed any one of several naive strategies: rolling overnight funds, rolling three month bills, or rolling six-month bills. If the portfolio invests longer-term funds, the yardstick might be the yield on two-year notes or on three-year notes.

Another standard often used is the performance achieved by various money market funds, each of which runs in effect a large-liquidity portfolio.[15] Comparisons between the performances of two portfolios are, however, difficult to make. One has to ask about the differences in the parameters: in maturity restrictions, in percentage restrictions, and in name restrictions. Also differences in the time flow of funds through two portfolios may affect their relative performances.

Still another approach used in evaluating performance achieved is

---

[15] A money market fund is a mutual fund that invests in money market instruments.

to compare actual results with the optimal results that could have been achieved. In other words, to ask: How high was the return we earned compared with what we could have earned if our market judgments had always been correct?

Tracking performance and comparing it against various yardsticks are important not only because they give the portfolio manager a feel for how well one is doing, but also because they give management some standard against which to evaluate his performance. As one portfolio manager noted: "I'm a money market specialist working for an industrial concern so it's hard for management to evaluate what I do unless I give them some frame of reference."

In a few rare cases, the portfolio manager is not only judged, but also paid, according to how well he performs. That sort of arrangement is typically found only in a corporation or a bank that has a large short-term portfolio and has recognized that, to get professional management, it has to hire a street-oriented person who will never do anything but run money or work at a related job.

The Way It's Done

We have discussed so far how a rather elite minority of portfolio managers who have wide latitude in what they may do and who possess the skill and judgment to make good use of that latitude manage their portfolio.[16]

Most liquidity portfolios—be they owned by corporations, banks, S&Ls, or other institutions—are managed without much sophistication; perhaps it would be more correct to say they are barely managed at all. The problem is often that top management has never focused on the question of what portfolio management is all about and how it should be done. In the case of corporations, management will often adopt the attitude: We're in the business of manufacturing, not investing. Having done that, they fail to apply to the management of their short-term portfolio the principles of management that they daily apply to the whole corporation. Banks and S&Ls that daily, in the course of their normal business operations, assume carefully calcualted credit risks are quite capable of simultaneously running their securities portfolios according to the guiding principle: buy Treasuries and mature them.

Restrictive Guidelines. The failure of top management to be interested in and to have knowledge of what managing a liquidity portfolio

---

[16] One observer in a position to know puts the number of really well-managed liquidity portfolios in corporate America at half a dozen. If people on the street (Wall Street, that is) were asked to compile their lists of those six corporations, no one would fail to mention Ford, which has portfolios universally viewed as being aggressively and astutely managed. Another portfolio that consistently gets kudos from the street is that of the World Bank.

involves almost invariably results in the establishment of extremely tight guidelines on what the portfolio manager may do, guidelines that reflect, as one portfolio manager noted, "the attempt of a bunch of guys who know nothing about securities to be prudent."

Tight guidelines make it impossible for a portfolio manager to use almost any of the strategies of portfolio management discussed earlier in this chapter. In particular, tight maturity guidelines can create a situation in which a portfolio manager has almost no leeway to rasie yield by basing his investments on market judgments. For example, one giant U.S. corporation, which has volatile cash flows, will not permit its portfolio manager to extend further than 30 days; that still leaves him some room to make choices but none are going to be very remunerative because he is working at best with $8 basis points.[17] Not atypically, there is no one in the corporation who cares and no one who tracks performance.

Another problem with tight guidelines is that they are sometimes written in terms of amounts rather than percentages. This can make a large portfolio difficult to manage and may also lead to a false sort of diversification. An extreme example of such guidelines is provided by a corporation that went so far as to limit the amount of T-Bills its portfolio could hold.

The Accounting Hang-up.   The failure of top management to understand or interest itself in the management of the liquidity portfolio also results in what might be called the *accounting hang-up.* Specifically, it has created a situation in which the majority of portfolio managers, all of whom would describe themselves as *conservative,* believe that the correct way to manage a portfolio is to reduce their accounting risk to *zero.* In other words, they attempt to run the portfolio in such a way that they will *never* produce a book loss.

This obviously means that they can never take market risk of any sort: they can't do swaps that would produce a book loss regardless of how relative value shifts; when they need cash, they can't decide what to sell on the basis of relative value; they can't arbitrage; in fact, they are literally reduced to rolling overnight money and buying securities they intend to mature.

To appreciate fully how the decision never to take a loss restricts a portfolio manager, it is necessary to understand that when a portfolio acquires a discount security, such as bills or BAs, the accountant accrues each day interest income on that security at the discount rate at which it was purchased, so when the security is redeemed at maturity for full face value, all of the difference between the purchase price and

---

[17] The calculation:

$$0.0001 \times \frac{30}{360} \times \$1,000,000 = \$8.33.$$

the face value (i.e., the discount at purchase) will have been accrued as interest. This seems reasonable enough but it means, for example, that if a portfolio manager buys six-month bills at 5.41 and resells them three months later at 5.61, that is, at a rate *above* that at which he bought the bills, *he will have incurred a capital loss even though in dollar terms he has earned money.* Table 4 spells out the mathematics of this. Note that by buying the six-month bill at 5.41 and holding it for 90 days, the portfolio has earned $13,025 and the $500 capital loss occurs only because the accountant has accured $13,525 of interest over the holding period.

Table 4
Accounting Treatment of $1 Million of Six-Month Bills
Bought at 5.41 and Sold Three Months Later at 5.61

Book value at purchase	$972,950
+Interest accrued over 90 days	13,525
Book value at sale	$986,475
Price at sale	$985,975
−Book value at sale	986,475
Accounting capital gain (loss)	($ 500)
Price at sale	$985,975
Price at purchase............................	972,950
Actual gain	$ 13,025

The yields and maturities in this example were purposely chosen so that they are identical with the yields and maturities used in the example of riding the yield curve presented earlier in this chapter (see Table 3). Once these numbers are seen in the context of that example, it is clear that the unwillingness to take an accounting loss (to expose the portfolio to an accounting risk) rules out even the most basic investment strategy based on market judgment, namely, riding the yield curve. In this respect, note that in our example the portfolio manager who rode the yield curve stood to gain—if interest rates did not rise—an extra $1,000 of return, *and* a lot of protection against losing in terms of dollars earned but *not* against incurring an accounting loss.

Portfolio managers preoccupied with accounting losses and gains are encountered by dealers frequently. Said one: "It cracks me up when someone comes to me with BAs or bills and says, 'What's your bid?' and I say, '5.60,' and he says, 'I can't sell because I bought at 5.50 and I can't take a loss.' It makes no sense if he has held the instrument for awhile, but I do not question people any more. I figure they just don't understand the concept. Still it's crazy, if you have to generate cash, to say that you cannot sell the instrument it is best to sell because you cannot take a 10-basis-point loss." Said another dealer: "I talk to portfolio managers about this problem and encounter nothing but resistance. They do not care if they could earn more money, they are just not going to take a loss. It's an organizational, not a rational constraint."

The whole accounting problem applies not only to discount securities, but also to CDs and other interest-bearing securities, because the accountant accrues interest on them just as he does on discount securities; in addition, he amortizes over the time to maturity the premium on coupons purchased at a price above par and accretes the discount over the time to maturity on coupons purchased at a discount from par.

A Negative Sum Game.   The aversion to book losses and the failure to track performance that are characteristic of many institutions create a negative sum game for the portfolio manager. If he invests on the basis of market judgment, he ends up in a position where, if his judgment is wrong, the resulting losses—even if they are losses only by accounting standards—will be highly visible and criticized, whereas if his judgment is correct, the resulting gains will not be perceived by senior management.

The obvious response of the portfolio manager put in this position is to make no attempt to predict interest rates and to invest so as to avoid all market risk. If such a portfolio manager reaches for yield at all, one does so by buying P-2 paper or Euro CDs because they offer relatively high yields without ever asking whether they have *relative value.* Such portfolio managers think of themselves as sophisticated because they know a lot about many different markets, *but* when they need cash three months hence, they buy a three-month instrument instead of making a conscious market decision.

Opportunity Cost.   The typical "conservative" portfolio manager thinks of himself as never having lost a penny or at least as not having lost very many, and his accountant will confirm that this is so. But in fact an institution with a portfolio run on the principle that it funds to dates and never takes a market risk incurs a large *opportunity cost,* namely, the earnings forgone because the responsibility to manage funds in the portfolio has been renounced. An example is provided by the illustration of riding the yield curve given earlier in this chapter. The portfolio manager who rides the yield curve with a lot of basis points of protection built into the gamble does not have to be right more than half the time to noticeably increase yield. Thus, to refuse to do so in order to avoid the risk of an accounting loss implies a cost, one that is no less real because it is not perceived by most institutions.

There is also a more subtle aspect to opportunity cost. As one portfolio manager commented: "Most people you talk to will buy a six-month bill and hold it to maturity and say that they are not taking any risk because they know what they are going to earn. That is farcical. They *are* taking a risk, one that is not measured by the accounting system but is measured in terms of opportunity cost. And the institution may in reality be affected by this risk. If rates rise sharply and the money invested could have been used elsewhere, there is a cost to having bought those securities. Either the institution has to finance them somehow or it may be forced into other business decisions that are suboptimal."

It is easy to find examples of common portfolio practices that can be pursued only at a considerable opportunity cost. One such practice is to say that if money is needed in 30 days, cash on hand should be invested in a 30-day instrument even though predictable cash flows will more than suffice to cover that need. Another is to invest a large amount of money in short-term instruments when it is clear that most of that money is not going to be needed in the short run or even in the long run. A corporation that pursues such a strategy, as some triple-A credits do, is paying a large premium year in and year out to ensure that it can survive even a severe credit crunch without mild discomfort.

With respect to the opportunity cost associated with the latter policy, one sales manager noted: "If stockholders realized what was going on in some corporations with cash holdings that are large relative to their total assets, what amount of money it is costing the company to not manage money, you might have some stockholder suits. I found one company that could go no longer than 90 days; they had a roughly $500 million portfolio; and the average life of their investments was about 60 days. They could never buy and sell, never swap. I figured that in 1976 the fact they could not extend to the one-year area probably cost them 1½ to 2 percent in yield. On half a billion that could add significantly to the bottom line [$10 million if the increase in yield was 2 percent]. And there was *no* call for the funds."

It is sometimes suggested that the reason some large corporations do not manage their portfolios is that they have too much money; that is, it is not possible within the confines of the money market to actively manage $3 or $4 billion. Sums of that magnitude are, however, actively managed; the World Bank's $6 billion portfolio is a prime (and not unique) example.

As noted, there is an opportunity cost to not managing money. The counterpart is that it costs money to have someone manage a portfolio, consequently there is some level below which benign neglect—rolling commercial paper or investing surplus cash in a money market fund— is the preferable alternative. That cutoff point is hard to pinpoint; estimates put it anywhere from $10 to $30 million. Somehwere up from that, between $50 and $100 million, there are solid benefits to be reaped from having someone watch the market on a daily basis.

For the firm at the opposite pole, one with hundreds of millions to be managed in one or a number of portfolios, the optimal solution may be one that a few institutions in this position have adopted—namely, to hire a professional, set wide guidelines, monitor put pay performance, and on an incentive basis. A side benefit of doing so is that the same individual can be used, as is done in many corporations, to manage the parent's or its financing sub's commercial paper operations. Anyone who can manage a short-term portfolio well can manage a commercial paper operation equally well, since the latter is nothing but a *negative* portfolio.

Ignorance of opportunity cost and extreme risk aversion are not the only reasons why many large institutions have failed to opt for professional management of their portfolios. Another is that they would have to pay a professional money manager in toto what a senior executive earns. A third reason is that corporations, especially if they are headquartered in outlaying places, have difficulty attracting and holding street-oriented people.

For a large corporation that wants to aggressively manage its portfolio, the commonly practiced alternative tactic of having one fast-track rookie do the job for awhile and then train another to do it does not always work out. Said a portfolio manager who traveled that route: "Trading is an art form which I could not succeed in teaching my peers who had come through the system as I did. I would have done better to take on some kid hustling on the streets of Marrakech."

Part Seven

Computer Techniques

Chapter 37

Computer Construction of Optimal Portfolios

PAUL R. SAMUELSON
Director of Portfolio Analysis
The Ford Foundation
New York, New York

Programs are now widely available on time-sharing computer facilities to construct optimal stock portfolios along the lines suggested by modern portfolio theory.[1] This chapter will define the general type of problem, which these programs are designed to solve. The most important versions of these programs will be introduced and their applications presented within a static framework. More realistic applications of these programs to revise portfolios through time will then be considered. This chapter will also examine enhancements to the portfolio construction programs to make them more useful to portfolio managers. Finally the type of judgment required by portfolio managers to implement the transactions indicated by the programs will be explored.

THE CONSTRUCTION OF AN OPTIMAL PORTFOLIO AT A SINGLE POINT IN TIME

A rather formal definition of the problem is required for several reasons. First, the definition prescribes both the type of appropriate solution techniques and the type of solution, in this case portfolio. Second, the explicit recognition of important assumptions allow one to see the impacts on the solution, when these assumptions are relaxed. Third, portfolio construction is an adequately complicated process that

---

[1] This chapter assumes a fuller analysis of modern portfolio theory. The reader might refer to Chapter 4.

Exhibit 1
The Efficient Frontier

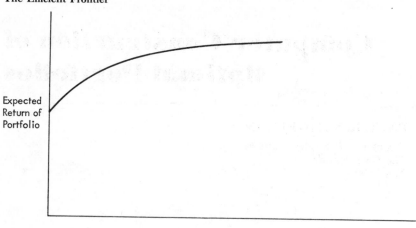

Expected
Return of
Portfolio

Variance of Portfolio

one needs to include only relevant attributes of portfolios and limit alternatives among solution techniques.

This section will assume for convenience a single period framework. This means that the portfolio is constructed at a single point in time and is expected to stay fixed until the end of the period. In a slight variation, the portfolio might be revised from its current holdings by trades executed immediately (or on one particular day), although not necessarily without cost.

The second section introduces a multiperiod framework. This section will also assume that important attributes (risk, return, etc.) of the portfolio can be valued relative to one another in an explicit manner. An expression called an objective function (or utility function), combines quantified values of the attributes. This way of describing a portfolio has not yet been fully accepted by portfolio managers. Frequently, managers have defined their portfolios either by the particular stocks held, or by their particular style of management: growth stocks or hedge fund. Because an objective function combines the important attributes of a portfolio into a single expression, one can compare in a simple fashion very different portfolios.

Investors always prefer more rather than less expected return on their portfolio, and generally prefer less rather than more risk. This chapter only discusses portfolio construction programs, which explicitly include the trade-off between return and risk. These programs often consider other attributes of portfolios. Yield, industry concentrations, company concentrations, and the transaction costs (required to generate the new portfolio) are often factored into the trade-off.

Many programs ignored by this chapter may prove useful to portfolio managers in different cases. One program constructs capitalization or equal weighted portfolios. Another program fills industry categories with the most recommended stocks. Since none of these programs take risk into account, they use very simple rules and provide essentially trivial new portfolios.

Among the included portfolio construction programs, the most common objective function trades off expected return and risk, defined as the variance of return. In terms of efficiency, a frontier can be constructed of portfolios with maximum returns for a given level of variance (see Exhibit 1). If one assumes that a risk-free asset (such as treasury bills) is available, then one is really interested in the trade-off of excess return for the portfolio (its return above the risk-free rate) and variance.[2] In general, investors seek to achieve the largest value of:

$$\mu_p - \lambda_v \sigma_p^2$$

where

$$\mu_p = \text{excess return on portfolio}$$
$$\sigma_p^2 = \text{variance of portfolio}$$
$$\lambda_v = \text{investor's trade-off.}$$

The portfolio manager must supply expected excess returns on stocks which are candidates for the portfolio. The expected return for the portfolio consists of the sum of the returns on the stocks weighted by their proportions in the portfolio:

$$\mu_p = \sum_{n=1}^{n} h_n \mu_n$$

---

[2] The notation follows that of Rosenberg (1977). Below is a list of symbols in order of appearance. Symbols with an additional subscript of "t" indicating period t have not been included.

$\mu_p = $ excess return on portfolio
$\sigma_p^2 = $ variance of portfolio
$\lambda_v = $ investor's trade-off.
$\mu_n = $ excess return on stock n
$h_n = $ proportion of portfolio in stock n
$V_{mn} = $ covariance of stocks m and n
$\beta_n = $ beta of stock n
$\mu_m = $ excess return of market
$\alpha_n = $ nonmarket return of stock n
$\sigma_m^2 = $ variance of market
$\omega_n^2 = $ nonmarket variance of stock n
$\omega_p^2 = $ nonmarket variance of portfolio
$\hat{\beta}_n = $ estimated historical beta of stock n
$\hat{R}_{mn} = $ estimated nonmarket covariance between stocks m and n
$Y_i = $ loading of the portfolio on factor i
$F_{ij} = $ covariance of factors i and j
$\gamma_k = $ loading of the portfolio on industry k
$\delta_n = $ active position (portfolio proportion minus market proportion) in stock n
$\sigma_n^2 = $ specific variance of stock n

where

$$\mu_n = \text{excess return on stock } n$$
$$h_n = \text{proportion of portfolio in stock } n.$$

The variance of the portfolio will equal the sum of the covariances between stocks m and n, weighted by their proportions:

$$\sigma_p^2 = \sum_{m=1}^{N} \sum_{n=1}^{N} h_m h_n V_{mn}$$

where

$$V_{mn} = \text{covariance of stocks } m \text{ and } n.$$

In examining the equations for portfolio excess return and variance, one can recognize immediately that the latter requires many more forecasts. Programs attempt to break down return and risk forecasts into components, in order to reduce the total number of forecasts required. Virtually all programs begin by assuming some version of the capital asset pricing model. According to this model, the returns to a stock can be attributed to its beta (or volatility) times the market's excess return, plus its nonmarket return, frequently referred to as an alpha or relative mispricing:

$$\mu_n = \beta_n \mu_m + \alpha_n$$

where

$$\beta_n = \text{beta of stock } n$$
$$\mu_m = \text{excess return of market}$$
$$a_n = \text{nonmarket return of stock } n.$$

This relationship is frequently represented by a security market line, where the slope of the line indicates the excess return of the market and the distance from the line indicates the stock's nonmarket return (see Exhibit 2).[3] Similarly a stock's variance can be partitioned into market and nonmarket components:

$$\beta_n^2 \sigma_m^2 + \omega_n^2$$

where

$$\sigma_m^2 = \text{variance of market}$$
$$\omega_n^2 = \text{nonmarket variance of stock } n.$$

With a more complicated formulation a portfolio's variance may also be constructed

$$\omega_p^2 = \sum_{m=1}^{N} \sum_{n=1}^{N} h_m h_n R_{mn}$$

---

[3] This concept was first implemented by Wells Fargo Investment Advisors.

where

$$\omega_p^2 = \text{nonmarket variance of portfolio}$$
$$R_{mn} = \text{nonmarket covariance of stocks } m \text{ and } n.$$

In current practice, the portfolio manager supplies certain inputs to the portfolio construction program, and the vendor supplies others. The manager always supplies the objective function designating the trade-off between risk and return. One may also add values for other portfolio attributes to the objective function. Penalties are enacted for transaction costs (as a percentage of purchase or sale price) and deviations from beta and yield targets. Alternatively, one may constrain the portfolio's attributes, placing maxima or minima on risk, yield or turnover.

The manager always supplies forecasts of nonmarket returns for stocks, which contain one's recommendations for all stocks under consideration (unless one pursues a passive strategy). These are one's justification for being a portfolio manager; one usually forecasts the excess return of the market also. Finally, the portfolio manager supplies constraints on concentrations in individual stocks and industries.

The vendor of the program almost always supplies the estimates of risk. Estimating the risk of individual stocks has not yet become a function of research analysts or portfolio managers. Analysts have too narrow a context for comparing risk across different types of stocks. Also, they tend to equate their degree of ignorance or uncertainty about a stock with its riskiness (variance of return). Portfolio managers do not generally have the time to concentrate on risk, as it diverts from their attention to returns. Therefore the vendor estimates the market's variance and the market risk, nonmarket variances and covariances of stocks.

Exhibit 2
The Security Market Line

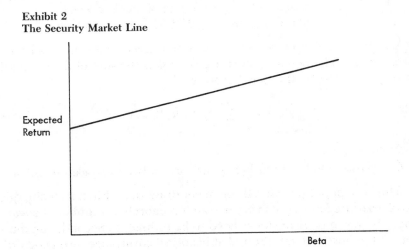

The output of each portfolio construction program is a new optimal portfolio. This portfolio has a new set of stock holdings and a higher value of the objective function than the existing portfolio. Depending on the vendor, portfolio analyses of the existing and optimal portfolio are produced, as well as a list of required trades.

Currently available portfolio construction programs differ primarily in their estimation of portfolio nonmarket risk. The programs have secondary differences in their objective functions, formats for forecasts of nonmarket returns, specification of trading costs and allowable constraints on stock positions (as well as technical differences in solution algorithms). There are only two vendors, Barr Rosenberg Associates of Orinda, Ca., and Wilshire Associates of Santa Monica, Ca., who devote substantial resources to maintaining optimization programs, available through time-sharing to clients.

Gifford Fong Associates of Santa Monica, Ca., and Canavest House, LTD of Toronto, Canada, also offer less complete models. Two versions of the single-index model, one by Sharpe and the other by Elton, Gruber, and Padberg (described below) are available in the public domain, and can be installed relatively easily on a computer. In Exhibit 3, the main features of available programs are outlined.

The first type of program, called for convenience the historical model, estimates a full historical covariance matrix of stocks, considered candidates for the portfolio. The last 60 months of stock excess returns are regressed against the market's excess returns:

$$\mu_{nt} = \hat{\beta}_n \mu_{mt} + \alpha_{nt}$$

where

$\mu_{nt} =$ excess return of stock n in period t

$\mu_{mt} =$ excess return of market in period t

$\hat{\beta}_n =$ estimated historical beta of stock n

$\alpha_{nt} =$ nonmarket return to stock n in period t.

Covariances are constructed from nonmarket returns of all pairs of securities. The portfolio's nonmarket risk is the sum of these covariances, weighted by the position sizes:

$$\omega_p^2 = \sum_{m=1}^{N} \sum_{n=1}^{N} h_m h_n \hat{R}_{mn}$$

where

$\hat{R}_{mn} =$ estimated nonmarket covariance between stocks m and n.

This type of program has three major drawbacks. First, its technique involves brute force by its very nature. An enormous number of covariances between pairs of stocks need to be estimated. Second, one must accept the heroic assumption, that historical covariances are good esti-

Exhibit 3
Portfolio Construction Programs

	Model of Non-market Risk	Source Risk Estimates	Solution Technique	Objective Function	Portfolio Attribute Constraints	Other Constraints	Formats for Nonmarket Return Formats
Full-Service Commercial Time-Sharing							
Barr Rosenberg Associates	Multiple factor	Fundamental risk	Quadratic program	Includes risk, return yield, beta, transaction costs	Beta, turnover	Individual stock	Rigid
Wilshire Associates	Multiple factor or historical	Fundamental or historical	Quadratic program	Risk, return, and transaction cost	Beta, yield, P/E, turnover	Industry and individual stock	Flexible
Less Complete Commercial Time-Sharing							
Canavest House Ltd.	Single	Fundamental	Linear program	Return and transaction cost	Beta, yield, turnover	Industry and individual stock	Flexible
Gifford Fong Associates	Historical	Historical	Quadratic program	Risk and return	Turnover	None	None
Public Domain Programs							
Sharpe	Single	Risk estimates not supplied	Linear program	Risk, return, and transaction costs	None	Individual stock	Rigid
Elton, Gruber & Padburg	Single	Risk estimates not supplied	Closed form	Risk, return, and transaction costs	None	None	Rigid

mates of future covariances. The errors are necessarily large, as covariances fluctuate greatly over different periods. This type of program has become increasingly less popular. It is expensive to run and very hard to control.

The second type of program, usual called the single index model, assumes that all nonmarket returns of stocks are independent of one another.[4] While this assumption is clearly false, it may lead to better portfolios, than using inaccurate (and frequently misleading) estimates of covariances. These programs often use regressions of the last 60 months of stock returns to estimate a stock's beta and its nonmarket risk (the standard error of estimate of the equation). In a second alternative, the total variance of a stock is estimated from the price of an option selling against it and a rather simple formula. Then, this total variance is divided into market and nonmarket portions (using an historical beta estimate). In a third alternative (discussed below), the beta and nonmarket risk can be estimated from accounting data.

The portfolio's nonmarket risk is the sum of the nonmarket risk (variances) of stocks, weighted by their position sizes:

$$\omega_p^2 = \sum_{n-1}^{N} h_n^2 \, r_n^2$$

where

$$r_n^2 = \text{estimated nonmarket variance of stock } n.$$

This type of program should work quite well with some kinds of investment strategies and quite badly with others. If a manager determines one's estimates of nonmarket returns (i.e., one's recommendations) based primarily on factors unique to each stock, this type of program will produce accurate estimates of the portfolio's nonmarket risk and of the contributions of each stock to the portfolio's risk. If a manager bases one's recommendations on similar characteristics across stocks (such as growth rates, or leverage), the program will underestimate the nonmarket risk of the optimal portfolio and misestimate in magnitude and in direction the contributions of stocks to portfolio risk. Basically, this type of program is "blind" to the risks of betting on similar kinds of stocks. This short coming may be partially off set by limiting concentrations in particular stocks and kinds of stocks. These constraints again entail only second-best solutions. This type of program has been quite popular for its simplicity and relative cheapness to run.

Barr Rosenberg, attempts to use current accounting data on firms to construct fundamental rather than historical estimates of risk. It is well beyond the scope of this chapter to explain in any detail (see

---

[4] See Sharpe (1963 and 1974) and Elton, Gruber, and Padberg (1975 and 1977).

Chapter 6) how betas are estimated for individual stocks. In a brief summary, accounting, price, and volume information are collected for each stock in six categories: (1) market variability containing price and volume data, (2) low valuation and unsuccess containing earnings and book value, (3) growth orientation containing dividend information and earnings-price ratio, (4) earnings variability containing earnings changes, (5) immaturity and smallness containing capitalization and asset information, and (6) financial risk containing leverage and cash flow coverage. Exhibit 4 lists the items contained in each category. The values for each stock are normalized about an average value for stocks in a large universe. Then, an equation was estimated in several steps to explain beta estimates across many securities and many (monthly) time periods by the combinations of individual items (and the membership of stocks in one of 39 industries). For each stock, current values of the items are then used to attempt to forecast a fundamental beta. A similar procedure is performed to forecast specific

Exhibit 4
Rosenberg's Categories of Accounting Items

Market Variability
1. Historical beta estimate
2. Historical standard error
3. Historical beta squared
4. Historical standard error squared
5. Square root of (historical beta times standard error)
6. Bayesian adjustment for beta
7. Share turnover, last quarter
8. Share turnover, last 12 months
9. Share turnover, last five years
10. Ratio of volume to standard error
11. Current stock price
12. Stock price range, last 12 months

Low Valuation, Unsuccess
1. Growth in earnings per share
2. Indicator of recent earnings change
3. Relative strength measure
4. Negligible E/P indicator
5. Book-price ratio
6. Average tax rate
7. Indicator of dividend cuts
8. Return on equity

Growth Orientation
1. Average payout
2. Current Dividend yield
3. Dividend yield, last five years
4. Zero dividend yield indicator
5. Growth in total assets
6. Changes in capital structure
7. Earnings-price ratio
8. Normalized earnings-price ratio
9. Earnings-price, last five years

Earnings Variability
1. Variance of earnings
2. Extraordinary items
3. Variance of cash flow
4. Earnings covariability with U.S. corporate earnings
5. E/P Ratio Covariability with market E/P

Immaturity and Smallness
1. Total assest
2. Market capitalization
3. Net plant/gross plant
4. Gross plant/book value
5. Number of years listed on exchange
6. Earnings history indicator

Financial Risk
1. Leverage at book value
2. Leverage at market value
3. Debt/assets
4. Uncovered fixed charges
5. Cash flow/current liabilities
6. Current asset/current liabilities
7. Earnings dilution
8. Tax adjusted monetary debt

risk of stock, that part of a stock's total risk, which can not be explained by its beta, membership in an industry, or response to group factors.

Rosenberg developed an ingenious and elaborate method to account for group factors.[5] For each of the six categories, he estimated an equation to construct a risk index (from the individual items), which would respond to the factors effecting similar kinds of stocks. For example, stocks with high financial risk would tend to have high leverage and low ratios of current assets to liabilities. They would have a positive loading (or value) on the risk index for financial risk and would tend to have returns similar to the index (all else being equal). Stocks with low financial risk would have a negative loading on the index and tend to move in the opposite direction. Historical covariances between the risk indexes are also estimated.

In order to estimate portfolio risk (as opposed to the risk of individual stocks), the program first estimates the beta, six loadings on the risk indexes and specific variance for each stock. The program then estimates the average loading for the portfolio (based on a capitalization weighted average of the stocks' loadings) on each index. The portfolio's market risk is estimated in a standard fashion—averaging the stock's betas. The nonmarket risk is the sum of covariances between the six risk indexes, variances attributable to membership in 39 industries (averaged for the portfolio) and variances specific to individual stocks:

$$\omega_p^2 = \sum_{i=1}^{6} \sum_{j-1}^{6} y_i y_j F_{ij} + \sum_{k=1}^{39} y_k^2 I_k^2 + \sum_{n=1}^{N} \delta_n^2 \sigma_n^2$$

where

y_i = loading of the portfolio on risk index
F_{ij} = covariance of risk indexes i and j
y_k = loading of the portfolio on industry k
I_k^2 = variance of industry k
δ_n^2 = active position (portfolio proportion minus market proportion) in stock n
σ_n^2 = specific variance of stock n.

The imagination and power of this approach manifests itself in the construction of the risk indexes and the response of stocks to the factors behind the indexes. This approach definately captures more of the nonmarket risk inherent in strategies selecting "good" kinds of stocks rather than "good" stocks of all kinds. However, this simplified representation of nonmarket risk for the portfolio can still be blind to the risks of particular strategies, and produce significant misestimates. This

---

[5] See Rosenberg (1977), for an extended analysis of the multiple factor model.

type of program is certainly the most "robust" of the three for handling most types of portfolio strategies.

The future development of portfolio construction programs may proceed in several directions. The "bottom line" for evaluating the effectiveness of new programs, will be their ease and accuracy in generating estimates of market and nonmarket risk. In estimating market risk (or betas) of individual stocks, a simpler equation needs to be found. The best equation would allow analysts to forecast (rather than use current) values for leverage, growth rates, earnings fluctuations and payouts, in order to arrive at a forecast beta. The risk indexes also need to be simplified and rationalized to construct better estimates of portfolio nonmarket risk. There may be two divergent paths. On one hand, risk indexes appropriate for any type of portfolio strategy may be developed. On the other hand, special purpose indexes may be constructed, which are blind to the risk of many strategies, but accurate in a few.

THE REVISIONS OF AN OPTIMAL PORTFOLIO THROUGH TIME

This section relaxes the assumption that the portfolio is constructed within a single period framework. It will introduce four overlapping periods which define the time horizons for different parts of the investment process. Clearly the dissection of problem into discrete parts distorts the continuous and multifaceted character of portfolio revisions. However, if one can tolerate extra complication, this type of analysis can suggest the judgment needed by portfolio managers to implement revisions.

One can define the four periods briefly. The planning horizon, extending over many years, defines the times, over which the portfolio's attributes matter. The decision interval, usually two to four weeks, refers to the period, during which the manager's desired trades are held fixed. The projection horizon, typically six to twelve months, represents the relevant future period for forecasts of stocks' returns. Finally, trades are executed during the trading interval, lasting anywhere from several days to several months.

A portfolio manager usually establishes a long planning horizon with his client: frequently five to ten years with pension funds, and possibly longer with individuals. One develops objectives, typically involving the maximization of ending period portfolio value, subject to minimizing periodic contributions (or maximizing periodic withdrawals) and minimizing the variability of portfolio value.

The portfolio manager actually makes periodic decisions at least as frequently as monthly. The time between each decision can be called the decision interval. Each time the portfolio manager revises the portfolio, one needs to translate the investor's planning objectives into values for portfolio attributes, along the lines of a single period objective function. If one assumes that the investor prefers more expected return and less risk, then the manager wants to construct a multiperiod objective function, which maximizes the sum of the portfolio attributes in each decision interval:

$$\sum_{t=1}^{T} \mu_{pt} - \lambda_{vt}\,\sigma_{pt}^2$$

where

μ_{pt} = portfolio expected excess return in period t

σ_{pt}^2 = portfolio variance in period t

λ_{vt} = investor's trade-off in period t.

The portfolio manager has one strong reason and one weak reason for not treating the current decision interval as a single period problem, and ignoring future decisions intervals. First, the trade-off of portfolio attributes will be a function of time and the size of the portfolio at that time. Although one will revise the portfolio mainly because of changes in investment opportunities (particularly changes in forecasts of nonmarket returns), the manager will also need to account for changes in trade-offs of attributes.

Dynamic programming provides the best solution to how the trade-offs may change at different decision intervals. This type of program attempts to take directly into account a series of decisions. Truly optimal decisions are defined assuming that all other decisions following from it are optimal, contingent on knowing the portfolio size and investment opportunity sets at future times. However, this type of program is not yet working in practical application. One can only infer certain qualitative implications for adjusting trade-offs through time. If one maintains a constant trade-off (i.e., λ_{vt} remains fixed for all time periods), one will maintain a fixed level of investment in risky assets, despite changes in the level of wealth. If one wants to maintain a constant proportion of investments in risky assets, then one needs to decrease λ_{vt} with increases in wealth and increase λ_{vt} with decreases in wealth. However, the exact adjustments for different levels of wealth are not easy to anticipate.

The portfolio manager can take more obvious actions, in response to a second reason for recognizing future decision intervals. The investor may be concerned about particular changes in investment opportunities, which would adversely affect one's total portfolio. For an individual, one's total portfolio consists of stocks, other financial assets and one's source of employment (often called human capital). A company's total portfolio consists of its pensions fund and business activities. If possible, the portfolio manager wants to purchase a financial asset, presumably a stock, which hedges the risk of these other assets. Often these stocks may be hard to find. As an example, a security analyst involved with high technology stocks might wish to invest in utilities. When technology stocks fall, along with her salary, she may be partially bailed out by her investments in utilities. As another example, one would clearly suspect that car sales go down when gasoline prices go up. Therefore, an automobile manufacturer's pension fund might be especially attracted to oil stocks.

A portfolio manager projects nonmarket returns for stocks over a longer period than one's decision interval. Forecasts of nonmarket returns usually assume a six to twelve month's "work out period." Therefore, a manager will frequently update forecasts of returns and change decisions over overlapping projection periods. Estimates of stocks' nonmarket returns change from three different causes. First, expected nonmarket returns may actually become realized nonmarket returns: undervalued stocks may appreciate and overvalued stocks may depreciate. Second, new information of material interest (not already discounted in the price) may arise about a stock. Third, a portfolio manager (or analyst) may correct one's forecast of nonmarket returns, based on revised analysis of the same information about a stock. Instability of forecasts of nonmarket returns carries no problems if trades are executed costlessly and instantly. The current portfolio based on old recommendations becomes the new optimal portfolio based on new recommendations.

Because there are positive costs to trading, frequent changes in recommendations (particularly arising from the analysts' changes of mind) cost money. Currently available portfolio construction programs create an optimal portfolio at a discrete moment in time. They can not anticipate changes in return estimates.

Portfolio managers have discovered that portfolios with very similar attributes (particularly in terms of expected excess return and risk) can be constructed with completely different stocks. Small changes in expected returns for individual stocks, can also change dramatically the size of their desired holdings in the optimal portfolio. For example, two utilities stocks may appear virtually identical to the optimization program, except for differences in their nonmarket return forecasts. If the forecast on one increases relative to the other, the program will no doubt double the desired position in the favored stock and erase the position in the other.

Portfolio managers, accustomed to betting on favorite stocks are often dismayed that one stock substitutes so readily for another, in the mind of the optimizer. It again requires a leap of faith for the manager to believe in good portfolio attributes rather than good stocks.

If managers understand better the source of sensitivity of optimal portfolios to changes in inputs and the reasons for easy substitution of stocks, they can actually use these properties to advantage. In particular, managers can run sensitivity tests varying particular estimates of nonmarket returns (or as is frequently done, the magnitude of estimates of all stocks' nonmarket returns) to construct a range of portfolios. They may then revise their current portfolio toward this series of targets rather then one optimal portfolio.

The manager may also want to partition a stock's nonmarket return estimate in a fashion similar to the partitioning of it contribution to nonmarket portfolio risk. Within the framework of the multiple factor model, stock returns can be divided into bets on the risk indexes, on industries and on factors unique to individual stocks. This partitioning may help the manager to understand the similarity of stock's return attributes (and risk attributes) as seen by the portfolio construction program.

Finally, the manager may also wish to rank trades, based on their marginal contribution (or impact of 1 percent transaction), to the objective function. Actually this is a standard feature of one of the portfolio construction programs. A manager then has a set of priorities for implementing trades.

The portfolio manager does have a means of controlling the instability of optimal portfolios through time and the associated magnitude of portfolio revisions, caused by changes in forecasts of nonmarket returns. He can introduce direct recognition of expected transaction costs. As discussed in the first section, expected transaction costs are the sum of commissions, taxes (on a sale these may be large if capital gains must be realized) and adverse price impacts. These costs must be amortized over a period of time, in order to compare the cost of a swap, with expected price workouts. Because transactions costs have been estimated as averaging anywhere from 50 basis points to 150 basis points (before amortization), portfolio managers have spent considerable efforts in measuring costs of actual transactions and estimating costs for different types of trades. Sophisticated cost calculations often depend on size of trade as a percentage of daily volume in the stock, or on the estimated liquidity of the stock. Optimization programs are now refined enough to accept even nonlinear formulations of trading costs.

Yet improved estimates of expected trading costs can help a portfolio manager only so much. He, along with his trader, must actually implement the transactions indicated by the optimization program. In reality, commissions and price impacts vary considerably for similar trades. Also, trades do not all take place instantly or even quickly (and some don't even take place at all). One can define still another interval, the trading interval, as the period following the receipt at the trading desk of requests for trades, terminated by their completion or cancellation. In the simplest case, the trading interval is shorter than the decision interval. The portfolio manager will revise his estimates of nonmarket returns, run the program, and submit a list of trades to the trading desk. The trader will then execute those trades before the manager's next decisions. In the more frequent case, the trader executes the bulk of trades requested, but some remain undone, when the portfolio manager submits new requests. Then the trading interval exceeds the decision interval and can easily overlap several intervals.

Portfolio managers have found that they need to use some flexibility in revising trade requests based upon different rates of execution. There appear to be no easily quantified rules for doing this. For example, the portfolio manager may have a negative nonmarket return estimate on a stock. The result of the portfolio optimization (even when taking into account expected trading costs) indicates selling out the position. The manager submits the sell request to the traders, but the trade is delayed in execution. During the delay, the portfolio presumably absorbs the "real" cost of the stock declining (assuming the portfolio manager was correct). The portfolio also absorbs the "opportunity" cost of not buying and holding the desired new stock. Further but less significantly, other trades become less optimal (and basically contribute more nonmarket risk to the portfolio) because they originally made sense, assuming that all other purchases and sales were made.

Clearly, the portfolio manager, faced with an unexecuted sale, would prefer to execute a "second best" solution, selling more of the "next worse" stock (or stocks). He needs a substitute transaction, which can at least be executed and at a reasonable cost. However, he can ordinarily only sell what he already owns. For purchases, it appears much easier to substitute a request for one stock instead of another. Again, the portfolio manager needs to be flexible with his priorities of stocks to purchase.

Essentially, any portfolio construction program provides a "global" solution to the problem of revising a portfolio. The program has to assume that all inputs, particularly estimates of nonmarket returns and trading costs, are equally valid. The portfolio manager, on the other hand, may discover that some estimates on an individual basis are not valid. He, then, will almost certainly need to make "local" adjustments in the size or terms of executing particular trades, from the desired trades indicated by the global solution of the program.

Portfolio construction programs are currently being used in two easily discernible applications for actual portfolio revisions. Managers are implementing "passive" strategies, either imitating index returns or constructing "naive" portfolios for different tax bracket investors (such as high-yield portfolios for tax-exempt investors and low-yield for taxable). Managers are also implementing "active" strategies, revising portfolios frequently through time, based on changes in return forecasts of stocks.

There are very different concerns in using portfolio construction programs in the two applications. The use of programs to implement passive strategies is clearly easier. Higher standards and increased competition reflect this. The objective function of index fund clients involves simultaneously minimizing nommarket risk and trading costs. The managers do not forecast nonmarket returns, but do need to estimate expected trading costs. In the simplest situation, managers hold virtually all the stocks in an index. Only the relative capitilizations of the stocks in the index are necessary to determine the desired holdings at a point in time. Any of the three types of portfolio construction programs—using historical, single index, or multiple factor models—will arrive at this same conclusion. At periodic intervals (usually monthly), the program generates transactions, which primarily reinvest cash generated by dividends to bring all holdings to market weights. In package programs negotiated with brokers, trades are executed immediately at a fixed commission cost and with no price impacts (as their price is determined by the day's close). This type of portfolio revision executes itself mechanically, with almost no judgment required of the portfolio manager.

In more complicated situations, managers imitate index returns, holding considerably fewer stocks than are contained in the index. Fewer stocks are held either because of the small size of the fund (many positions would not equal one round lot) or to reduce transaction costs. When revising the portfolio, the manager attempts to bring its attributes closer to the index (i.e., reduce its nonmarket risk) while minimizing costs of trades. The manager must input into the program one's best estimates of trading costs of individual securities. Again, it does not matter very much, which of the three versions of the program one uses. However, one almost certainly wants to receive, besides a listing of "optimal" revisions, substitute revisions, conditional on actual trading costs differing from expected. In implementing trades, one may shift to a pattern of incremental trades on a stock by stock basis through time, if that appears to be cheaper than a package trade with a broker. The manager's judgment becomes directed toward cheap trading and secondarily toward maintaining the desired portfolio attributes.

Portfolio managers implementing naive strategies, tilting their portfolios toward particular yield or beta targets, must be much more careful about the quality of their inputs (stocks betas and yields) and about the model of nonmarket risk used in the portfolio construction program. The single index and historical full covariance estimates of nonmarket risk will almost certainly lead to underestimates of nonmarket risk for the portfolio and to incorrect proportions of individual stocks. Again, the manager may focus one's efforts on accomplishing trades among a list of close substitue stocks.

Obviously, portfolio managers pursuing "active" strategies use portfolio construction programs in a variety of ways. In fact, most managers do not use these programs directly to determine portfolio revisions. Often managers use the program to construct an optimal portfolio based upon current estimates of nonmarket returns for stocks, without considering transaction costs. This type of exercise, while providing some indication of the direction of desired trades, primarily serves to check the reasonableness of the estimates of return. Based upon seeing the implications of the estimates reflected in the optimal portfolio, the manager then revises one's estimates.

In another type of exercise, portfolio managers construct "paper" portfolios, which are revised at periodic intervals using current return estimates and realistic trading cost estimates. The "simulated" portfolios typically have several versions either with different portfolio attributes or with different return estimates. This exercise provides fairly realistic estimates of returns to particular active strategies. The revisions in the paper portfolio also provide a neat comparison to the revisions taking place in the actual portfolio.

Some portfolio managers actually do use these programs as their primary means of determining portfolio revisions. Determining appropriate values for portfolio attributes for particular investors (i.e., the objective function) usually involves considerable initial effort but infrequent revision (annual perhaps). Second, arranging for frequent updating of return estimates involves still more effort, both to maintain the mechanics and maintain the quality (which may of course not be the portfolio manager's problem at all). Maintaining realistic trading cost forecasts requires on-going judgments. On one hand, the manager needs to revise one's estimates of the expected holding period for stocks (or the time over which trading costs will be amortized). On the other hand, one needs to improve one's estimates on particular stocks of expected commissions and price impacts. These are direct inputs into the portfolio construction program.

The manager has the opportunity to add the most value to the process of active management in implementation of the output of the program. One needs to use one's judgment in making local adjustments to the indicated trades, based upon small changes in the validity of the inputs to the program. In particular, one needs close coordination with one's traders. As stated earlier, actual trading costs will differ considerably from those expected. Suggesting substitute trades can achieve portfolio attributes more quickly and cheaply. Also, one needs to add flexibility to the process, by responding to particular changes in return estimates (frequently caused by new information or sharp unexplained price movements) with adjustments in desired transactions.

The focus of judgment for the portfolio manager equipped with an efficient portfolio construction program will change. One will spend less time in repeating the work of the program—to determine portfolio revisions conditional on desired portfolio attributes and estimates of returns, risk, and trading costs. One will spend more time adjusting actual revisions for material changes in stock recommendations and trading conditions. The challenge to a portfolio manager appears clear. One must understand the important features of one's portfolio construction program and the requirements for feeding it. One must have the courage to believe in one's inputs—especially forecasts of return. Finally, one needs to use all one's skill and imagination to achieve in the portfolio, the attributes indicated by the portfolio construction program.

REFERENCES

Elton, Edwin J.; Gruber, Martin J.; and Padberg, Manfred W. "Simple Criteria for Optimal Portfolio Selection." Working paper no. 51, Salomon Brothers Center for the Study of Financial Institutions. New York: Graduate School of Business Administration, New York University, 1975.

Elton, Edwin J.; Gruber, Martin J.; Padberg, Manford W. "Simple Rules for Optimal Portfolios Selection: The Multigroup Case." *Journal of Financial and Quantitative Analysis.* (September 1977) 329–45.

Ferguson, Robert. "Active Portfolio Management." *Financial Analysts Journal.* (May–June) 63–72.

Fisher, Lawrence. "Using Modern Portfolio Theory to Maintain an Efficiently Diversified Portfolio." *Financial Analysts Journal.* (May–June 1975) 73–85.

Rosenberg, Barr. "Security Appraisal and Unsystematic Risk." Working paper no. 58, Research Program in Finance. Berkeley: Institute of Business and Economic Research, University of California, 1977.

Rosenberg, Barr, and Rudd, Andrew. "Portfolio Optimization Algorithms: A Progress Report." Working paper no. 42, Research Program in Finance. Berkeley: Institute of Business and Economic Research, University of California, 1976.

Sharpe, William F. "A Simplified Model for Portfolio Analysis." *Management Science* (January 1963) 277–93.

Sharpe, William F. "Imputing Expected Security Returns from Portfolio Composition." *Journal of Financial and Quantitative Analysis* (June 1977) 463–72.

Treynor, Jack L., and Black, Fischer. "How to Use Security Analysis to Improve Portfolio Selection." *Journal of Business* 46 (January 1973, no. 1) 66–86.

Chapter 38

Commercially Available Computer Services

ARTHUR WILLIAMS III

Vice President
Merrill Lynch, Pierce, Fenner & Smith
New York, New York

The use of computers by investment managers has moved out of its infancy and will likely reach adulthood in the 1980s. This growth, which was rather unspectacular in the 1960s and early 1970s, is gaining momentum from a number of sources: reduction in cost of computation, development of data and data base management systems, proliferation of financial modeling languages, models and statistical packages, improvement in telecommunication techniques, and development of sophisticated output formats which use cathode ray tube visual screen, CRTs and graphics. It is well known that the cost of making a given computation on a computer has been reduced by about 99 percent in the last 25 years. In comparison with other costs the reduction of course is considerably greater. The microcircuits which made these cost savings possible have also permitted development of small computers which are also priced at 1 percent of the costs of their predecessors. The second area, data, is equally crucial. A computer may be very efficient at crunching numbers but unless it has numbers to crunch it will not fulfill the required need. There is no lack of information being created in the world today. The need, rather, is to capture this data in computer form and also, which is less obvious, to have computer software which makes it possible to *access* the data (as distinct from manipulating the data once it has been accessed). Important progress has been made in capturing and managing data, with numerous time-sharing vendors having developed enormous data bases, and other suppliers providing data in convenient machine readable form. Once the user has the computation power and the data, one then needs

939

software for manipulating this data. Here again, considerable progress has been made with the development of modeling languages which make it relatively easy to establish the programs required, and of specific models which allow the user to change the numerical data being used in a specific set of formulas. For the user who wishes to develop his own models, there are statistical packages which make it possible to calculate growth rates, do regressions, etc., without going to the trouble of programming the calculation techniques. Development of CRTs has permitted rapid and efficient input and output methods. Clearly it is possible for a computer to fill a screen with information more rapidly than this information can be printed on any normal printer. This makes it possible to create special format screens in which clerks "fill in the blanks" when entering data, and also permits rapid response from the computer to requests from the user. Development of graphic packages has also enhanced usability of computers since graphics make some data more interesting and understandable, and permit saving of time and the expense of the artist's efforts. Finally, in order for the whole process to be economical, users of time-sharing facilities in remote locations must have economical telecommunication systems such that telephone line charges do not make the cost of usage prohibitive. Fortunately, development of satellites and improved transmission and data handling techniques have made vast improvements in this area also possible.

Undoubtedly one of the most important factors leading to increased utilization of computers by the investment manager and other computer users is time-sharing, or the ability to use a given computer system by more than one person more or less simultaneously. (The terms "on-line" and "interactive" are synonomous with time-sharing.) This development has made possible sharing of not only computer hardware but also data and software applications. A second benefit deriving from time-sharing is the ability to achieve results immediately. In the traditional "batch" system the user transcribes data and programs onto keypunch sheets which are then used by keypunch operators as the basis for creating cards. Cards are then fed into the computer and programs executed to read this information and perform the necessary calculations. In this environment if either the user or the data entry clerk made a single error, the user would not be aware of this until the following day. In a pure on-line environment the user inputs data and programs directly into computer files and executes programs. He is then in a position to verify data and check any errors. Because computers are expensive and tend to be underutilized at night, a hybrid system has developed for most production work. Data is entered through time-sharing facilities and the programs are executed at night for delivery the next day. In this way data entry can be checked with computer programs which verify accuracy, and yet the use of the computer's computational facilities is reserved until evening when demand is less.

A factor exercising a strong influence upon increasing use of computers is the training students receive in universities and business schools in this area. Most graduates today are unafraid of computers and have had hands-on experience with them. Further, they have been trained in the quantitative techniques which are most applicable to computer problems. The largest factor inhibiting use of computers is (along with cost) lack of familiarity with what can be done and how it can be done. There are still barriers which prevent the average investment manager, regardless of his level of intelligence, from being able to sit down at a terminal and begin to work without a reasonable amount of training. However, these roadblocks are falling as users become more knowledgeable and systems simpler, and by 1990 the vast majority of investment managers will be using computers in their daily operations.

ORGANIZATION

This chapter is divided into three parts: introduction, list of services, and list of firms providing services. For instance, the first area discussed is economics. The introduction summarizes how computers are used in economic analysis. The "list of services" itemizes by firm available economic data, analysis, and software. Readers finding a particular service of interest may turn to part three which lists the name, address, and contact of the firm. Generally speaking, the criteria for inclusion were that the service must be available in the marketplace to investment managers and must involve either computer programs or data in computer-readable form. Information or software which is available on-line is noted, indicating that investment management could have access to this service merely in installing a computer terminal in its office. A summary of the formation included is provided below.

Economics

Few areas are better suited to use of computers than the field of economics. There are masses of data from numerous sources, much of which is readily available in computer form. Further, there are endless ways to combine this information in order to better understand historical and future relationships. Data is available on countries, regions, industries, monetary and industrial sector, and demographics. Sources include federal and foreign governments, international agencies, and private and government agencies within various countries.

Portfolio Strategy

With development of historical data on rates of return and uncertainty or variability of these rates of return it has become possible to apply statistical techniques to establishing probabilities of future events based upon past history. The most common of these is the Monte Carlo simulation which, in effect, involves throwing darts at a board containing possible outcomes to see the probability of each resulting. In this process, and in others, it is possible to develop not only expected rates of return but also probabilities and consequently a relationship can be developed between risk and return.

Common Stock Analysis and Management

The combination of data available on price histories of common stocks as well as information on fundamentals, together with various theories on the relationship of individual stocks to the market, has permitted creation of models and optimizations. It is possible to look at a stream of estimated dividends and find the rate of return which equates these future dividends with the current stock price. Stocks can then be ranked according to expected return or a relationship can be established between the expected return and some estimate of the stock's risk. The most common optimization is one which attempts to establish a portfolio with a given beta (sensitivity to market) or yield yet which would closely track the market index by minimizing nonmarket or specific risk. In this way an investment manager could take its list of approved purchases and establish various portfolios which will meet client needs. This technique is used to create index funds but index funds are only one case of an optimized portfolio (namely the one which has a beta and other characteristics like the market).

Financial data bases can be used in two ways. First, it is possible to take a list of companies and extract certain data about them. For instance, an investment manager might want to know the price, price/earnings ratio, and yield of each stock on his approved list. On the other hand, criteria can be established and a data base screened for stocks which fit these criteria. For instance, a manager whose style is to own companies with high yields and high ratios of book value to market value might screen the data base for companies which are noteworthy in each category. He then uses this list as a basis for further research.

Fixed Income

Because bonds are so subject to mathematical analysis it is surprising that computers have not been more frequently applied in this area.

However, with increasing interest in fixed income investing there is a great though recent interest developing. One of the greatest needs has been for prices. Since most bonds are not traded on exchanges and many bonds do not trade frequently enough to establish prices the need has arisen for computer-based models to take market information and from it create prices for many bonds. A number of suppliers are active in this area. The next step in the process, once price data became available, was to combine it to create price indexes showing rates of return of the bond market and various sectors. Considerable progress has been made in this area in the last few years. As price information is maintained for longer periods of time it becomes possible to measure historic relationships to see how current markets differ from those in the past. In terms of future projection, the impact of specific forecasts can be measured precisely as they relate to a particular portfolio, and the impact of changes on the portfolio can also be measured. Along a similar line, simulations can be made as to how portfolios can be structured to meet differing client needs for liquidity, income, and risk.

International

Because of geographical and language barriers the use of computers for international investing seems promising. A surprising number of services are already available in this area, particularly relating to economic developments. On the other hand, lack of accounting standards and limits on data published on specific companies tend to inhibit use of quantitative techniques for common stock analysis.

Accounting

While certainly computers have been used by investment managers, particularly bank trust departments, for accounting for portfolios, this area suffered from being an early application and it is surprising how many accounting systems are just achieving reliable results as the decade of the 1980s approaches. Portfolio accounting is the process of creating a record of the securities held in a portfolio as of a point in time and the changes occurring in a portfolio during a given period. The former are called position or evaluation statements (evaluation if they contain market valuations) and the latter are called cash or transaction statements. Development of accounting techniques has suffered for two reasons. First, the investment manager who is not also the custodian does not have accurate information on a daily basis as to dividend and interest income credited to the account or of contributions by the fund sponsor. Secondly, there is a lack of standards. For instance, bonds can be valued with or without accrued interest, convertible bonds can be classified as equities or bonds, and short-term instruments can be segregated as cash equivalents or included with other fixed income investments. A recent development in the area of accounting is the on-line facility which enables the manager to see his portfolios on a daily basis either on CRT or on a terminal printout. Some services even offer real time reports which are updated continuously similar to the prices on stock market quotation machines.

Performance Measurement and Portfolio Audit

These services are sometimes offered in conjunction with accounting reports, though the more sophisticated analyses involving risk measurement and comparisons with other portfolios are typically provided separately. The more analytical of these services attempt to distinguish among the impact of the securities markets, the risk policy of the fund, and the manager's contribution through selection and timing. Portfolio audit services verify receipt of income and execution prices, monitor uninvested cash, and provided other information related to financial control.

News and General Business Information Services

Just as numerical data bases of economic, company and securities price information have developed, similarly a number of organizations have created the ability to maintain computer files of the written word. Some of these services provide on-line news reporting or analysis, and others act as libraries which can access millions of pieces of information on an enormous number of subjects.

Real Estate

While most investment management organizations are not involved in real estate management, nonetheless there appears to be growing emphasis in this area and there are some services available to those managers who wish to account for real estate transactions and measure or simulate the impact of the structure of real estate deals.

LIST OF COMMERCIALLY AVAILABLE COMPUTER SERVICES

The following lists commercially available firms with a description of the data bases and services. The various organizations are listed in the following order, by topics shown.

    I. *Economics*
       Data
       Analysis and simulation

II. *Portfolio strategy and simulation*
III. *Common stock analysis and management*
    Income statement and balance sheet
    Prices
    Dividends
    Industry data
    Betas
    Annual meeting announcements
    Analyst coverage
    Analysis and software
IV. *Fixed-income Securities analysis and management*
    Prices
    Maturity, call, and related features
    Analysis and software
V. *International information*
VI. *Accounting*
    Bank trust portfolio
VII. *Portfolio Performance Measurement and Audit*
    Rates of return
    Analysis and software
VIII. *News and general business information services*
IX. *Real estate*

I. Economics

Data

ADP Network Services, Inc.*—Chase Econometrics; CENSUS of coal Mines Data Base (Coal mines and operations) from McGraw Hill's Keystone Coal Industry Manual; FDIC; FSLIC

Business International Corporation*—Data base of 20,000 economic time series on 130 countries, emphasis on national accounts statistics, but including data on trade, labor force, and population; prices; production, and consumption of selected commodities. Includes short term forecasts on approximately 20 variables for each of 35 major economies, updated on a regular schedule. Available on-line via GE's Mark III computer network.

Chase Econometrics*—Historical data bases covering: finance (3,000 series based on Federal Reserve Bulletin), flow of funds (4,000 series showing financial flows between sectors), wholesale prices (2,700 monthly commodity prices), consumer prices (1,500 monthly series), U.S. macroeconomy (9,000 series), Business Conditions Digest, energy statistics, regional industrial and personal income data, agriculture and passenger car industry, international (statistics on 150 countries, OECD International data with 15,000 economic series); Forecast data bases showing estimates for major series covered in historical data bases, Instat on-line news service.

---

* Available on-line.

Citibank*—Citibase (formerly maintained by National Bureau of Economic Research) 3,500 time series on U.S. economy updated daily, including financial, industrial, demographic, income, government and foreign data; Forecasts of selected series, DATABASE financial information on 3,000 corporations.

CompuServ*—Citibase; Federal Deposit Insurance Corp. (FDIC); Federal Savings and Loan Insurance Corp. (FSLIC).

Computer Science Corporation*—Citibase.

ComputelSystems Ltd.*—Subset containing 25,000 series from CANSIM (TM) database on Canadian economy and related areas of U.S. economy (data maintained by Statistics Canada).

Comshare*—1970 Census of Population and Housing with updated estimates by region, population characteristics and income; Citibase; Subset of 25,000 series from CANSIM (TM) data base on Canadian economy and related areas of U.S. economy.

Control Data*—Citibase; Technotec data base for exchanging technological information through a worldwide time-sharing service; SIBYL/RUNNER time-series data analysis and forecasting program.

Data Resources*—Historical databases including over four million time series covering U.S. national, state and local, and international macroeconomic, financial, flow of funds, industry, prices, and other economic variables. Special data bases include Conference Board, DRI Capsule, Compustat, Value Line, Standard and Poor's, Bank of America Money and Credit Statistics (BAMACS), DRI Industry Financial Service Pro Forma, Government Agency Yield, DRI LDC Country Monitoring, FDIC, Cost Forecasting, Steel, Energy including Platt's and Oil and Gas Journal, Petrochemical, Forest Products, Paper and Pulp, Consumer, Insurance (Best), Agriculture, Transportation, Automotive, Japan, Canada DRI EEC Country; IMF, World Bank, OECD (Trade Series A and C, NIA, MEI, ENERGY); on-line news, data analysis, and forecast memos daily.

Economic Information Systems Incorporated—Detailed files on the 120,000 manufacturing establishments that account for 95 percent of U.S. industrial output and the 280,000 nonmanufacturing establishments that account for 80 percent to 85 percent of output in nonmanufacturing sectors; establishment file includes data on employment, sales and share of market, and SIC; input-output file contains information on the volume of purchases of more than 1,000 products and services by consuming industry, establishment, and parent company.

General Electric*—Currency exchange, Citibase, A. D. Little, Dept. of Commerce, UCLA Business Int'l. (130 countries, 20,000 time series) Bank of Japan, Nomura Securities data base; SIBYL/RUNNER; 1970 census of population and housing.

Interactive Data Corporation*—Chase econometrics; Europrospects International Data Base (covering U.K., Belgium, Netherlands, France, Germany, and Italy), U.S. macroeconomy, interest rate, and exchange rate data; FSLIC balance sheet and income statement data on 4,000 savings and loan associations; FDIC balance sheet and income statement data on 14,000 banks; Ohio Economic Data Bank (15,000 time series), National Assn. of Homebuilders housing and mortgage model and data bases; Jaffee and Rosen housing-mortgage model and data bases; Ward's AutoInfoBank of car and truck deliveries, production, inventories, and shipments.

Informatics*—Citibase.

Insco Systems*—Citibase.

International Monetary Fund*—International financial statistics: 17,000 time series on exchange rates, international liquidity, reserves, money supply, exports and imports, inflation, etc.; annual data begins in 1948, quarterly in 1957 and monthly in 1964. Direction of trade: 44,000 series showing direction of imports and exports by country for 160 countries. Balance of payments: 39,000 time series on balance of payment components and aggregates for 110 countries annually from 1967. Government finance statistics: 16,500 time series showing central government revenues, grants, expenditures, lending, financing, and debt for 90 countries for last six years.

International Monetary Fund*—Data on about 150 countries on trade, finance, prices, national income, and demographics.

Lockheed Information Systems*—Historical and forecast information from PREDICASTS, Inc., on national, regional, industry, and international time series; Economic Information Systems data bases on industrial plants and nonmanufacturing organizations providing sales figures in millions, share of market, and employee size; Disclosure, Inc. data base of all 11,000 public companies filing reports with the Securities and Exchange Commission including 10K, 10Q, 8K, proxy statements, registration statements, prospectus, annual reports to shareholders, listing applications, N1R, and N1Q reports.

MJK Associates*—Daily and historical futures and cash prices for commodities and currencies.

Merrill Lynch Economics*—Historical data covering 11,000 series of economic, financial, industry, and demographic data; 4,500 series of producers prices; 12,000 series with state and SMSA detail. Forecasts for 850 macroeconomic variables; auto, truck, and carpet industry; age-income demographics; News Comment daily commentary on economic indicators released the previous day.

National CSS*—Merrill Lynch Economics; FSLIC; FDIC; regional data on California.

On-Line Systems Inc.*—Citibase.

Predicasts Inc.*—Historical data and forecasts on macroeconomic, industry, company, and product data.

Rapidata*—Telerate Historical data (10,000 series on currency exchange rates, money market instruments outstanding, dealer inventories, commercial bank, Federal Reserve & U.S. Treasury data); International Monetary Fund; Citibase; Federal Reserve Bank of San Francisco data base (13,000 series on bank reserves, money supply, and credit market conditions); Market statistics data base (demographic and economic factors for U.S. counties and metropolitan composites).

Remote Computing Corporation*—FSLIC, daily and historical prices for commodities and currencies.

Service Bureau Company*—Citibase; FDIC data base on 14,000 banks; FSLIC data base on federally insured savings and loan associations; Robinson-Humphrey data on 125 banks; DRI Capsule Data Base— over 3,700 time series on U.S. economy updated daily; NCUA— over 20,000 credit unions with four years of historical data.

Scientific Time Sharing Corporation*—Citibase; International Financial Statistics (IMF).

I. P. Sharp Associates Ltd.*—Citibase; price data; Canadian banking, demographic, and economic data; IMF 2,000 series on U.K.; Actuarial Data Base of mortality and projections of actuarial data including salaries; foreign currency data base.

Statistics Canada*—Canadian Socio-Economic Information Management System (CANSIM) data base of 250,000 series on Canadian national accounts, prices, labor, industry, capital and finance, agriculture, demographic, and other areas.

Time Sharing Resources*—Citibase; 3,900 series on wholesale prices; Business Conditions Digest data base; FRB index of production and flow of funds; IMF data base.

Tymshare*—Citibase.

Analysis & Simulation

ADP Network Services, Incorporated*—Econometric models.

A. G. Becker Inc.—Sector Analysis: econometric analysis of industry performance

(The) Boston Company—Economic software packages relating the economic environment to the investment outlook for industry groups.

Chase Econometrics*—Industry and macroeconomic models including financial, international, foreign exchange, industrial production, agriculture and fertilizer models.

CompuServ*—Financial modeling; time series forecasting.

Control Data Corporation*—Financial modeling; time series forecasting.

Data Resources*—Extensive national, state, and local; industry, international econometric models and forecasts including macroeconomic, financial, industry (including 81 industry DRIFS income statement and balance sheet key concept forecasts; banking and interest rates, cost forecasting, steel, energy, petrochemical, forest products, paper and pulp, consumer, insurance, agriculture, transportation, and automotive). All models and forecasts are fully documented and available on line and in periodic printed text. Econometric Programming System (EPS) including databanking, estimation, model simulation, graphic and reportwriting; Financial modeling.

Economic Information Systems—Software for manipulating proprietary data bases (see *Economic Data*).

General Electric*—Economic, industry, international, and interest rate forecasting models.

INSCO Systems*—Econometric planning Language.

Interactive Data Corporation*—Industry and macroeconomic models; time series forecasting; interest rate forecasting; international modeling; natural gas model which forecasts availability of natural gas and oil in U.S. given regulated prices and other parameters.

Merrill Lynch Economics*—Industry and macroeconomic models including auto, truck and carpet industry models.

National CSS*—Economic modeling system for forecasting, model simulation, regression, smoothing and seasonally adjusting, graphics, and report writing.

On-Line Systems*—"What if" economic forecasting.

Remote Computing Corp.*—Time series forecasting; thrift industry financial planning systems.

Rapidata*—Time series forecasting, industry analysis and forecasting, econometric modeling, state space forecasting, and graphics.

SDC Search Service*—Historical data and forecasts on macroeconomic, industry, company, and product data.

Service Bureau Company*—Time series analysis and forecasting.

Time Sharing Resources*—QED econometric modeling language.

Tymshare*—Industry and macroeconomic models.

II. Portfolio Strategy and Simulation†

Barra*—Conditional forecasting service; simulation of equity-bond portfolio strategy, and performance attribution.

A. G. Becker Inc.—Asset allocation model: includes bonds, stocks, and cash equivalents and interfaces with particular contribution streams.

(The) Boston Company—Asset allocation models, valuation models, full covariance analysis, graphic output, portfolio optimizations.

---

† Excludes consulting services directed at fund sponsors.

Buck Pension Fund Services—Asset return simulator integrated with full pension liability model; allows analysis of investment returns, pension liabilities, and contributions under alternative funding and investment policies.

Canavest House—Portfolio simulation based on capital market forecasts to balance risk and return.

Computer Directions Advisors—Asset allocation model to meet rate of return and risk objectives. Monte Carlo simulation based on Ibbotson-Sinquefield stock and bond distribution projections; market timing model using focus.

Data Resources*—Market timing and asset allocation model: Monte Carlo simulation using 100 simulations per year; allows different inflation assumptions; can be interfaced with other models.

Effron Enterprices*—Asset allocation model, Monte Carlo simulation technique with any number of simulations and any number of years for a study determined by the client. Simulations use clients projections and statistical data available from the investment community. Output presented in tabular and graphic form.

Gifford Fong Associates*—Asset allocation model with multiasset flexibility, graphic output, and full covariance analysis; assets and liabilities handled separately.

Interactive Data Corporation*—Portfolio strategy; services of Barra, Gifford Fong Associates and Wilshire Associates.

InterSec Research Corporation—Simulation of risk-return impact of international equity and debt diversification on domestic portfolio performance.

Rapidata*—Asset allocation model.

I. P. Sharp*—Canavest and simulations.

Wilshire Associates*—Asset allocation model; Monte Carlo simulation with 200 simulations for each of 20 years; includes ERISA minimum and maximum funding requirements and allows use of several actuarial funding techniques and nonlinear liability growth.

III. Common Stock Analysis and Management

Income Statement and Balance Sheet

ADP Network Services*—COMPUSTAT; Value Line, EXSTAT data base on foreign companies; FDIC; Cates Lyons Bankcompare.

A. G. Becker Incorporated—Bank data for in-depth credit evaluation of the billion-dollar U.S. banks, as well as Japanese and Canadian banks; data provided semiannually using mid-year and year-end figures; Markscan: a comprehensive on-line information system providing price trends, yields, ratios, and earnings forecasts on all S&P 500 industry groups and all stocks in the S&P 500, as well as other stocks (more than 1,000 issues in total); consensus estimates provide benchmarks of equity evaluations.

CompuServe*—COMPUSTAT.

Compustat*—(See S&P Compustat below).

Comshare*—Value Line.

Data Resources*—DRI Industry Financial Service Pro Forma; COMPUSTAT; Value Line; FDIC data on 14,000 federally chartered banks.

Financial Data File (Dun & Bradstreet)—Financial statements of over 700,000 public and private firms.

Fund Monitoring Services—Portfolio evaluation by industry and individual assets.

General Electric*—Value Line.

Graphic Management Systems*—Value Line data base and flexible high volume graphics capability.

Indata Services Company—Earnings consensus.

Interactive Data Corporation*—COMPUSTAT; Value Line; I/B/E/S earnings forecasts; FDIC data on 14,000 federally chartered banks; EXSTAT data base of 2,000 U.K. and foreign companies; FSLIC savings and loan data.

Lynch, Jones & Ryan*—Institutional Broker Estimate System (I/B/E/S) weekly and historical earnings estimates of 45 major brokerage firms on over 2,200 companies.

Media General Financial Services—Wide range of price, value and fundamental data on 3,300 common stock issues.

National CSS*—Value Line.

Rapidata*—

Quotron Systems Inc.*—Earnings forecasts.

Service Bureau Company*—COMPUSTAT.

I. P. Sharp Associates*—Financial data on over 200 large Canadian companies.

Shaw Data Services*—Value Line; five-year earnings and dividend growth rates and R^2; quarterly dividends and earnings.

Standard & Poor's—Stock guide data base: information on about 4,500 firms appearing in the S&P monthly Stock Guide.

S&P Compustat*—20 years of annual data on 3,800 companies, 10–12 years of quarterly data on 2,700 companies.

Tymshare*—Value Line.

Value Line*—Annual (since 1955) and quarterly (since 1963) financial data on over 1,600 industrial, utility, transportation, and financial companies; sales and earnings by product line; forecasts of earnings and dividends; three to five years company projections; industry composites; replacement cost accounting data.

Warner Computer Systems*—COMPUSTAT; FDIC; FSLIC.

Prices

ADP Network Services*—Daily and historical prices for ten years on 25,000 securities.

Bunker Ramo*—Real time prices.

Center for Research in Security Prices—Historical price data: monthly prices on every NYSE Common Stock from January 1926 to present; daily closing prices for each trading day for NYSE and ASE Common stocks from July 1962 to present.

Citibank*—Telstat prices via Citiquote.

CompuServ*—Daily and historical prices of stocks, options, and market indexes.

Data Resources*—Daily and historical prices on all exchanges, OTC, stock options, and market indexes.

General Electric*—Daily and historical prices.

Graphic Management Systems*—On-line stock prices and volume with flexible high volume graphics capabilities.

Interactive Data Corporation*—Current and historical prices of stocks, options and market indexes; EXSHARE prices and related information on 5,000 U.K. and 9,000 Europe, Asia, and African securities.

Monchick-Webber*—Real time last sale and quotes for options and related stocks for all option markets; End-of-day also shows volume, range, and other data.

Muller Data Corporation—Daily pricing of all exchange and OTC stocks.

National CSS*—Telstat prices.

On-Line Systems, Inc.*—Telstat prices daily and historical for 2½ years.

Quotron Systems, Inc.*—Real time prices and quotes on all listed stocks; retrieval of string of transactions on individual stock.

Rapidata*—Daily and historical data; market indexes; stocks, London commodities and options.

Remote Computing Corporation*—Daily and historical prices exchange and OTC stocks; option prices; commodity prices; market indices.

Service Bureau Corporation*—Telstat; Monchik-Weber option prices; VALPORT historical prices on 27,000 securities.

I. P. Sharp Associates Ltd.*—U.S. and Canadian exchange prices; current and latest year's prices for options traded on Canadian exchanges.

Shaw Data Services*—Daily prices for five years for all listed and 250 OTC stocks.

Telstat Systems*—Daily and historical prices; market indexes.

Time Sharing Resources*—Telstat.

Tymshare*—Daily and historical prices and market indexes.

Warner Computer Systems*—Six years of daily prices for over 10,000 securities; technical indicators; market indexes.

Dividends

Bunker-Ramo*—Dividends.

Center for Research in Security Prices—Cash dividends and other distributions for every NYSE stock from January 1926 to December 1977, including declared dates, exdates, record dates, and payment dates; type of distribution; tax status, and other details; also name changes, industry code changes, mergers, reorganization, and shares outstanding; from July 1962 to December 1977 similar data available for ASE stocks, plus information on trading halts and bid and ask prices when shares did not trade.

CompuServe*—Telstat dividends.

Data Resources*—Historical and forecast dividends for companies and industries.

Graphic Management Systems*—Dividends on NYSE and ASE stocks.

Interactive Data Corporation*—Dividends and current and average payment ratios on all listed and 250 OTC stocks.

Muller Data Corporation—Dividends and dividend notification.

Quotron Systems, Inc.*—Dividends.

Rapidata*—Telstat dividends.

Shaw Data Services*—Dividends on all listed and 250 OTC stocks.

Telstat*—Dividends.

Warner Computer Systems*—Indicated annual dividend rates; exdividend dates; holder of record dates; and payment dates.

Betas

Barra*—Fundamental betas on 4,800 companies.

Becker Securities—Betas.

A. G. Becker Incorporated—Predictive (technical) betas on over 3200 stocks using daily data; updated monthly.

CompuServe*—Monthly betas on 6,000 common and preferred stocks based on month-end prices.

Data Resources Incorporated*—Fundamental betas on 750 companies; Value Line betas.

Gifford Fong*—Technical betas using Kalman Filtering techniques on 6500 stocks updated monthly.

Interactive Data Corporation*—Barra, Merrill Lynch, Value Line, Wilshire Associates, Gifford Fong.

Merrill Lynch*—Monthly betas on 6,000 companies starting 1971.

Shaw Data Services Inc.*—Alphas, betas, R^2, relative strength, dollar trading volume for all listed and 250 OTC companies.

Value Line*—Betas and standard deviations on 1,600 companies.

Wilshire Associates*—Fundamental betas on 6500 stocks updated quarterly.

Annual Meeting Announcements

Interactive Data Corporations*—Proxy service on NYSE, ASE, PSE, and MSE stocks.

Analyst Coverage

Nelson's Directory of Securities Research—Data on brokerage firms providing research coverage of corporations, corporations covered by brokers, and analysts covering industries.

Industry Data

ADP Network Services*—Cates, Lyons & Co. bank data base; coal industry company and mine operations Data Base from McGraw-Hill's Keystone Coal Industry Manual.

Cates, Lyons & Company, Inc.*—Financial data on 250 banks and bank holding companies from data in annual reports, 10K's "lead bank" regulatory reports, and press releases; eight-page profile on each bank, 23 ratio "summary grid," peer-group composites.

Chase Econometrics*—Fertilizer, nonferrous metals; insurance and agricultural industry forecasts.

Data Resources*—DRI Industry Financial Services forecast of key balance sheet and income statement variables. Special models for banking, cost forecasting, steel, energy, petrochemical, forest products, consumer, insurance, agriculture, transportation, and automotive.

Economic Information Systems—Value of shipments, market potential, and share of market of all establishments and parent companies with sales of $.5 million in each of 800 industries (identified at a four-digit SIC level of detail) covering the manufacturing, mining, agricultural, construction, transportation, communications, utilities, trade, finance, business services, and nonprofit sectors of the economy.

Federal Deposit Insurance Corporation (FDIC)*—Balance sheet and income statement data on 14,000 banks.

Federal Home Loan Board/Federal Savings & Loan Insurance Corp (FSLIC)*—Balance sheet and income data on 4,000 federally insured savings and loan associations.

(The) Information Bank*—On-line retrieval of news and articles on standard industry groupings.

Interactive Data Corporation*—Natural gas model which forecasts availability of natural gas and oil in U.S. given regulated prices and other parameters; Chase Econometrics.

Lynch, Jones & Ryan—I/B/E/S earnings estimate data for 12 major
sectors and 66 industry groups.

McGraw-Hill Mining Informational Services—Metal and nonmetallic
mining, smelting, and refining industry. E/MJ Census of Mines
Data Base of companies and mine-plant operations, world-wide.

Merrill Lynch Economics*—Auto, truck, and carpet industry data and
models.

National CSS*—Merrill Lynch Economics; FDIC.

Service Bureau Company*—FDIC; FSLIC; NAIC—a data base of all
U.S. insurance companies—some information is by total company,
some by state and some by line of business; BANKANAL—a data
base of historical data on over 160 bank holding companies.

I. P. Sharp Associates Ltd.*—Balance sheet, income statement, and
traffic statistics reported to the Civil Aeronautics Board.

Ward's AutoInfoBank*—Data on deliveries, production, inventory, and
shipment of U.S., Canadian, and imported cars and trucks.

Warner Computer Systems*—FDIC and FSLIC.

Analysis and Software

ADP Network Services, Incorporated*—Financial modeling and
screens using Compustat and Value Line; PERFEX portfolio
weighting versus S&P 500, MERGE proforma income statement
and balance sheet for merged companies.

Barra*—Services to measure common stock risk, sources of return and
impact of multiple managers; index fund management portfolio
analysis; portfolio optimization.

A. G. Becker Inc.*—Index matching software; Equity Portfolio Review
Service: Analyzes and profiles equity portfolios & provides comparison with a representative background. Homogeneous Stock
Grouping Analysis: Classification of securities into broader than
industry groups to facilitate diversification analysis.

(The) Boston Company—Portfolio analysis, manager analysis, data base
screens and custom reports, growth analysis, risk measurement,
graphics, modeling, forecasting and simulation, analytical option
reports and technical charts.

Buck Pension Fund Services—Common stock analysis measures risk
and returns of individual securities, single portfolios, and multiply
managed portfolios.

Campbell (Walter) Associates—Research and consulting for planning,
development, investment, and acquisition projects—screens and
analysis using some 40 to 50 independent data base sources of
publicly and privately held companies; company and industry profiles, topical reports, and surveys.

Canavest House, Incorporated*—Portfolio optimization through better understanding and use of client's forecasting ability; security ratings; buy sell recommendations based on risk-return trade-off.

Citibank*—ENTERPRISE financial modeling system.

CompuServe*—Using COMPUSTAT data base provides screens, custom reports, standard financial reports, graphics and modeling, financial forecasting and simulation; software can be used on customer's data as well.

Computer Directions Advisors—Portfolio analysis through Focus package.

Data Resources, Incorporated*—Financial analysis system for analyzing company and industry data using COMPUSTAT and Value Line data bases; portfolio optimizations.

Effron Associates*—Provide standard and/or custom designed reports of investment characteristics of clients' portfolios by asset segment. Summaries and detailed analyses utilizing more than 60 investment indicators are available. Industry segment analysis, profile analysis of investment characteristics of a portfolio and static versus actively managed portfolio analysis over time are also available.

Evaluation Associates—Breakdown of major characteristics in individual and aggregate portfolios; sources of portfolio and market returns.

Gifford Fong Associates*—Optimization which maximizes R^2 for a given beta.

Graphic Management Systems*—Using customer's COMPUSTAT data can provide screens, custom reports and graphics; includes custom charts of company and industry performance relative to S&P indices; can incorporate customer's earnings estimates.

Huggins & Co. Inc.—Risk-reward and portfolio analysis including industry breakdown versus S&P 500.

Indata Services Company—Impact of multiple managers; risk-reward analysis; expected stock prices.

Interactive Data Corporation*—Company and industry analysis; analyst evaluation systems; options and arbitrage; data base screens; proforma financial statements; Barra, Gifford Fong, Merrill Lynch, and Wilshire optimizations and index fund packages.

Merrill Lynch*—Index fund management system; screens and analyses using Compustat and Telstat data bases.

Monchik-Weber Associates*—Options Moniter provides real time market data, sophisticated analyses, theoretical values, and strategy rankings via disply terminals; POLAR on-line reporting system.

Rapidata*—PROBE statistical analysis, graphics, screens, arbitrage Remote Computing Corp.*—Option Accounting System.

Service Bureau Corporation—Options management system; screening and comprehensive report generation including custom reports, standard financial reports, graphics, ratio analysis, trend analysis, forecasting and industry comparative analysis using the following data bases:

COMPUSTAT; EURABANK (foreign banks); EXSTAT (European companies); NAIC (U.S. insurance companies); LRDB (Life insurance rates); FDIC; FSLIC; NCUA; OPTIONS; and TELSTAT.

I. P. Sharp*—Canavest optimizations.

Shaw Data*—On-line displays of screens and analyses using Value Line and Shaw Technical data bases; company, industry and customized analyses.

Shearson Hayden Stone—Screens and analyses using COMPUSTAT.

Standard & Poor's—Data base screens and reports on 4,500 companies listed in Stock Guide.

Standard & Poor's COMPUSTAT—Screens and analyses using COMPUSTAT data base.

Time Sharing Resources*—QED financial modeling language.

Tymshare*—Screens and analyses using Value Line data base.

Warner Computer Systems*—Software to analyze COMPUSTAT data base; customized reports, financial reports and data base screens generated by use of proprietary software; STATPACK and SPSS software available for statistical analysis on user's own data bases. Financial modeling and forecasting capability provided by Proforma II modeling system.

Wells Fargo—Portfolio models and optimization using discounted dividend cash flow model.

Wilshire*—Index fund management system; inventory fund system; portfolio models and optimization.

William O'Neil and Company—Charts and statistical data on customer's portfolio.

Wismer Associates*—Management information and accounting system for common stock portfolios; daily pricing, and appraisal.

IV. Fixed Income Securities Analysis and Management

Prices

ADP Network Services, Inc.*—Daily and historical prices.

CompuServe*—Daily and historical prices, discount corporate data.

Data Resources Incorporated*—Daily corporate, government, and money market instrument prices.

Effron Enterprises*—Data on convertible bonds and convertible preferred securities along with relevant investment information on each security and its underlying common security.

Interactive Data Corporation*—Corporate listed and OTC bonds, government bonds and 1.1 million municipals of 38,000 issuers; indexes; foreign bond pricing; EXSHARE international bond prices;

Europrospects monetary data on six major countries; Merrill Lynch bond indexes.

Merrill Lynch*—Daily and historical prices on governments, corporates, and municipals; includes private placements and equipment trust certificates; monthly indexes on 35 subsectors of corporate and government bond market.

Muller Data Corporation—Municipal prices; listed corporate prices. Municipal Securities Evaluation Service Inc. (subsidiary of J. J. Kenny)—Municipal evaluations daily and historical.

National CSS*—TELSTAT prices.

On-Line Systems*—Current and historical TELSTAT bond prices for 2½ years.

Rapidata*—Rates on domestic money market instruments, Treasury and agency bonds, Canadian and Eurodollar certificates; listed and OTC bond prices; custom bond data bases.

Remote Computing Corporation*—Daily and historical prices.

Service Bureau Corporation*—Listed corporate bond prices; municipal bond prices.

Telstat Systems*—Daily and historical prices.

Time Sharing Resources*—TELSTAT prices.

Warner Computer Systems*—TELSTAT prices; descriptive information on bonds; S&P and Moody's ratings.

Maturity, Call and Related Features

Data Resources*—Retirement Features Data: sinking fund, call, and conversion data.

Interactive Data Corporation*—Called-bond notification; sinking fund, call, and conversion data.

Analysis and Software

ADP Network Services*—Daily dealer prices with three year's history on 750 bonds; screens and spread analysis including deviations from traditional relationships.

Barra*—Fixed income analysis; model of investment risk.

A. G. Becker Incorporated—Bond Portfolio Review Service: analyzes and profiles bond portfolios against a representative background, with reports provided semiannually; Bond Computer Service: offers on-line research techniques, current and historical performance studies, statistical analysis, and market sector reviews; the data base is composed of more than 1,000 actively traded issues quoted by Becker traders twice daily.

(The) Boston Company—Credit analysis reports, bond screens, fixed income portfolio analysis and graphics, portfolio structure analysis, yield spread history charts.

Buck Pension Fund Services—Fixed-income analysis measures risk and return of individual securities, single portfolios, and multiply managed portfolios.

Campbell (Walter) Associates—Research and consulting services; screens and analyses of debt securities.

Canavest House—Bond management service: assistance in bond mix decision, yield curve forecasts, optimal risk-return trade-off.

CompuServe*—Bond portfolio management system; money market management system; CUSIP search; pricing retrieval.

Computer Directions Advisors—Portfolio analysis using Focus group and bond yield curve shift model.

Data Resources*—Interest rate forecasting and flow of funds analysis.

Effron Enterprises*—Provide general and/or custom designed reports of the investment characteristics of clients' portfolios; sector, quality, yield to maturity, years to maturity are some of the features available for analysis; screens for convertible securities data.

Evaluation Associates—Breakdown of portfolio sectors; sources of return.

Fund Monitoring Services—Bond Analysis Report (B.A.R.) Graphically Presented.

Gifford Fong Associates*—Fixed income simulations to measure effects on portfolio of shifts in yield curve; bond optimization system.

Huggins & Company—Simulation of portfolio performance under different scenarios; measures impact of swapping activities including gain or loss of each transaction.

Indata Services Company—Performance analysis with accrued interest; sector analysis.

Interactive Data Corporation—Credit analysis; fixed income yield studies; Blue List screening system; Gifford Fong Associates and Wilshire simulations.

Lipper Analytical Distributors—Fixed income fund analysis by maturity, quality, and sector.

Merrill Lynch—Portfolio structure analysis; risk and risk adjusted return.

Municipal Securities Evaluation Service, Inc. (Subsidiary of J. J. Kenny)—Municipal bond portfolio statistical analysis and screens.

Rapidata*—Spread analysis, arbitrage, screens and graphics.

Remote Computing Corporation*—Liquidity Management System for trading in, reporting on, and auditing fixed income and mortgage backed securities.

The Service Bureau Company*—ASSET & SLIMS—fixed income portfolio evaluation and analysis system that contains interest reporting, accretion and amortization, market pricing and swap analysis.

Shaw Data Services*—On-line portfolio management system shows valuation and distribution and dollar weighted averages of current yield, yield to maturity, coupon, maturity, quality and sector; Horizon analysis based on client-supplied forecasts of term structure.

Standard & Poor's*—Blue List offerings and price changes; bond guide data retrieval on 5,700 bonds; financial data on fixed income securities.

TELSTAT—Inhouse municipal bond pricing service; CUSIP lookup system.

Warner Computer Systems*—Bond Inventory System.

Wells Fargo—Bond portfolio management systems.

Wilshire Associates—Analysis of sources of return.

Wismer Associates*—Cash management system includes accounting, cash flow forecasting, optimal decision simulation, swaps, arbitrage, and historical data base.

V. International Information

ADP Network Services, Incorporated*—IMF; Chase Econometrics; 25,000 series on more than 100 countries; EXSTAT data on 2,000 companies.

A. G. Becker Inc.—Data for credit analysis on Canadian and Japanese banks.

Campbell (Walter) Associates—Consulting and research; bond screens; news and text retrieval.

Business International Corporation*—See entry under Economics.

Canavest House, Inc.*—Return projections on 150 TSE stocks using dividend discount model.

Computel*—Canadian Indicator Time Series Service containing 18,000 time series from the CANSIM system.

Chase Econometrics*—28,000 international series; including IMF; 15,000 OECD series; forecasts of 300 variables for each of 12 countries and for foreign exchange rates for nine currencies.

Data Resources Incorporated*—DRI Canada (subset of CANSIM system); Japan-Macro (Japanese data); OECDMEI (main economic indicators of OECD countries); IMF (monetary data on 110 countries); EECEUROPE (macroeconomic data on EEC countries plus U.S. and Switzerland); EXRATE (price and exchange rate data on 15 major countries); International Financial (BAMACS) Forecasts.

FIND/SVP—News and text retrieval from international data bank.

General Electric*—Currency exchange, Bank of Japan and Nomura Securities data base.

(The) Information Bank*—News and abstracts from *Financial Times* (London), *Wall Street Journal, N.Y. Times,* and other publications.

International Monetary Fund*—See entry under *Economic Data.*

InterSec Research Corp.*—Simulation of impact of overseas equity and debt diversification on risk and return of domestic portfolios;

20 years of stock market and exchange rate data for ten countries; eight years of bonds, bills and CPI data for ten countries; international indexing strategies.

Interactive Data Corporation*—Chase Econometrics; EXSTAT financial data on 2,000 European and Australian companies: 160 annual balance sheet and profit and loss items starting 1971; updated weekly from Extel Statistical Services Ltd., London; Europrospects economic data base on six major countries; EXSHARE data on prices, dividends, capital changes and related information on 14,000 foreign securities (includes equities, fixed interest securities, preferential capital, loan stocks, debentures, warrants, unit trusts, insurance and property bonds, Eurobonds, offshore and overseas funds, government stocks, and convertible securities).

Lockheed Information Systems*—International data on countries and industries including forecasts; Foreign Traders Index listing manufacturers, service organizations, agent representatives, retailers, wholesales/distributors, and cooperatives that import U.S. goods or represent U.S. firms abroad.

Predicasts Inc.*—2500 composite economic time series on foreign countries.

Rapidata*—IMF data

Scientific Time Sharing*—IMF data.

SDC Search Service*—International data on product and technological development, countries, and industries.

Service Bureau Company*—EURABANK—1000 non-U.S. banks with up to four years of historical data. EXSTAT—2000 European and Australian companies with six years of annual data.

I. P. Sharp Associates Ltd.*—Bank of Canada data on money supply and prices of money market instruments and bonds; 24,000 time series from CANSIM; IMF financial data, UKCSO data base of 2,000 series on United Kingdom; financial data on over 200 of Canada's largest companies; daily and historical prices from Canadian stock exchanges on stocks and options; Canavest optimization.

Statistics Canada*—CANSIM data base of 280,000 time series covering economic and demographic facets of Canada; also includes Bank of Canada (financial), Quebec Bureau of Statistics (economic), and Canadian Housing and Mortgage data; MINIBASE contains up to 25,000 series subset of main base; some hard copy and machine-readable retrieval capabilities.

Time Sharing Resources*—IMF international time series.

VI. Accounting

Bank Trust

Comshare (Trust Marketing Division)—Trust accounting and management information systems; bond and coupon payment, and reconcilement; benefit check production; participant accounting for Trasops and for defined contribution plans.

SEI*—Trust-Aid on-line, real-time trust management and accounting system; security movement and control, automatic fee processing, cash management, ERISA reporting, pension payment processing, pricing, performance measurement, dividend and interest processing and reconcilement.

The Service Bureau Company*—St. Joseph Personal Trust System— On-line trust management and accounting system.

Wismer Associates*—Trust accounting and managment information system, portfolio appraisals, participant statements, pricing, performance measurement.

Portfolio

Automatic Data Processing*—Portfolio accounting on-line.

(The) Boston Company—Portfolio accounting and appraisal.

Bradford Trust—Portfolio accounting.

CompuServe*—Money market management and accounting system; portfolio accounting.

Data Resources*—Portfolio accounting and appraisal.

Digital Information Corp.*—Securities Management System provides installed computer with software and data for inhouse portfolio accounting.

Effron Enterprises*—Portfolio accounting and appraisal service available on-line—includes information on each type of security (i.e. stocks, bonds, options, cash, etc.) for each transaction; dividend, cash position and broker analysis are some of the available reports; also available is an interactive portfolio monitoring and evaluation service which can be used on-line or delivered in hard cover reports.

Indata Services—Weekly portfolio accounting.

Interactive Data Corporation*—Portfolio accounting and appraisal; estate valuations.

Lloyd Bush & Associates—Data base management system with computational system built in so each record can access its own unique set of calculations and central data base retrieval.

Lynch, Jones & Ryan—Options management system.

Merrill Lynch—Bond portfolio appraisal; options management and accounting system.

Municipal Securities Evaluation Service Inc. (Subsidiary of J. J. Kenny)—Municipal bond portfolio valuations.

On-Line Systems*—PERVAL portfolio accounting.

Rapidata*—Portfolio valuations and accounting on-line.

Remote Computing Corporation*—Liquidity Management System for fixed income and mortgage backed securities; options accounting system; SPECAN portfolio analysis system.

SDC Search Service*—Retrieval of citations to accounting literature from 1974 to present on Accountants Index produced by American Institute of Certified Public Accountants.

SEI Corporation—Portfolio accounting.

Service Bureau Corporation*—Valport portfolio accounting; SLIMS—Fixed income portfolio accounting, market pricing, and evaluations.

Shaw Data*—On-line portfolio accounting including portfolio analysis, portfolio ranking, and performance measurement.

Standard & Poor's*—Fixed income portfolio accounting.

Telstat—Valuation of portfolios and large securities files; computerized back-office accounting system for use with minicomputer by investment advisory firms.

Time Sharing Resources*—Interactive portfolio monitoring and evaluation system.

Tymshare*—Accounting; estate valuations and appraisals.

Wismer Associates*—Cash, modified cash, and accrual basis accounting; amortization and accretion of premiums, discounts, and deferred gains and losses on swaps; handles fixed income, equities, mortgages, and mortgage backed securities.

VII. Performance Measurement and Portfolio Audit

Rates of Return

A.D.P. Network Services*—Market indexes.

Center for Research in Security Prices—Monthly common stock returns including or excluding dividends for each NYSE common stock from January 1926 to present; completely adjusted daily returns for each common stock listed on the NYSE or ASE from July 1962 to present.

CompuServe*—Market indexes.

Computer Directions Advisors—Bank commingled funds, mutual funds and insurance companies; market indexes.

Data Resources*—Market indexes, DRI Financial Service.

Effron Enterprises*—Universe containing performance statistics on plan sponsor portfolios managed by professional money management firms; identification of each plan sponsor is kept anonymous but money management firms are identified by name; market indexes included in universe.

Evaluation Associates—Investment manager profiles with performance of investment managers, data bases of fund and manager performance, and market indexes.

Hamilton, Johnston—Bank commingled funds, mutual funds, insurance company equity pools, market indexes.

Interactive Data Corporation*—Market indexes; Computer Directions Advisors data base.

Lipper—Mutual fund performance and analytical data on open and closed end equity and fixed income funds.

Merrill Lynch—Bank commingled funds; bond indexes on 35 subsectors of corporate and government bond market.

Rapidata*—Market indexes.

Rogers, Casey & Barksdale—PIPER pooled bank fund returns and market indexes.

Service Bureau Company*—Market indexes

Telstat*—Market indexes

Tymshare*—Market indexes.

Warner Computer Systems*—Market indexes.

Analysis and Software

Automatic Data Processing*—Portfolio audit and performance measurement.

Barra‡—Analysis of sources of common stock portfolio return and impact of multiple managers.

A. G. Becker Inc.—Funds Evaluation Service: Analyzes characteristics and performance results of more than 4,000 managed funds representing nearly 1,000 managers. Comparisons include those based on fund type, manager type and fund investment policy.

Trust Administrative Control Service: portfolio audit

(The) Boston Company—Performance measurement, portfolio review
  · versus strategy and guidelines.

Buck Pension Fund Services—Analyses risk and return for single and multiply managed portfolios; identifies returns due to policy and value added by money management; monitors risk exposure and diversification.

Callan—Performance measurement, portfolio audit.

CompuServe*—Performance measurement, portfolio audit.

Computer Directions Advisors—Performance measurement; inhouse performance measurement.

Digital Information Corp.*—Performance measurement and audit system installed on minicomputer in customer's office.

Effron Enterprises—Performance measurement, portfolio audit; analysis of all types of securities; customized reports.

Fund Monitoring Services—Performance measurement in two formats for fund sponsors and investment counselors; Fund Audit Verification Service; customized reports.

Gifford Fong Associates*—Bond measurement which partitions total return into various components

Graphic Management Systems*—Performance measurement with extensive graphic capability.

---

‡ Excludes services directed solely to sponsors.

Huggins & Co. Inc.—Time and dollar weighted returns; risk adjusted analysis;

Indata Services—Time weighted returns by stock, industry and sectors; money manager impact analysis; comparison with common stock, commingled taxed, commingled nontaxed, fixed income, pension and endowment, and taxed funds.

Interactive Data Corporation*—Performance measurement; portfolio audit; Gifford Fong Associates and Wilshire Associates services.

InterSec Research Corp.*—Risk adjusted performance measurement for international equity and debt portfolios.

Merrill Lynch—Performance measurement; portfolio audit.

Rapidata*—Time weighted rate of return; portfolio audit.

Service Bureau Company*—VALPORT performance measurement.

Shaw Data Services*—On-line performance of total, equity, fixed income, and cash sectors.

Telstat—Inhouse system for measuring return, risk and performance versus market indices which are supplied monthly on magnetic tape.

Timesharing Resources*—Interactive performance measurement system.

Tymshare*—Performance measurement; portfolio audit.

(The) Vanguard Group of Investment Companies*—Performance measurement with custom report formats, including risk analysis and comparison with market indices and PIPER data base.

Wilshire Associates—Performance measurement.

Wismer Associates*—Performance measurement.

VIII. News & General Business Information Services

Bunker Ramo*—On-line news display.

Campbell (Walter) Associates—Consulting and research assistance; retrieval of bibliographic abstracts, news items, text, and reports on companies, industries, and business topics.

Chase Econometric*—INSTAT on-line economic news service.

Data Resources*—Retrieval of selected economic news releases, weekly Domestic and International news summaries, Weekly Money and Credit Memos and Economic Commentary Memos.

Dow Jones News Services*—On-line retrieval of data using broad variety of terminals operated from customer's office.

Dun's Market Identifier (Dun & Bradstreet)—All U.S. and Canadian firms by industry, branch, plant, number of employees, sales size, credit rating.

Economic Information System—Information on consumption of products by establishment, location, company, industry, and geographical region; share of market and line of business information; accounts for 95 percent of industrial output in U.S.

Editec*—The Electric Library—Access to 80 data sources and 50,-000,000 articles from 200,000 journals and 3,000,000 books; lists and summarizes data; helps secure full copies of required information; periodic updating available.

FIND/SVP—Data retrieval, special research, 10K reports, periodic updating; Wall Street Research Report Clearinghouse provides analyses of companies and industries; business library contains 10,000 subject files and 7,000 company files; access to over 100 major computer information data banks.

(The) Information Bank—On-line data base and information retrieval system containing abstracts and bibliographic information from some 62 business, financial, general interest and specialized publications including The New York Times, The Wall Street Journal, Washington Post, Financial Times (London) and Business Week. Accompanying products include a real time news summary; microfiche of the full text of New York Times material; off-line printouts of abstracts; creation; processing and maintenance of proprietary data bases. Also included is statistical data on corporate earnings reports, and expanded vocabulary in business and financial area. Data base contains over 1.5 million abstracts dating back to 1969 and, for *The New York Times,* is current to four days.

Lockheed Information Systems*—News items covering business, economics, and many other major areas of interest; accessing over 100 data bases in science, technology, business, agriculture and economics.

Merrill Lynch Economics*—News Comment daily commentary on economic indicators released the previous day.

Money Market Directories*—Names, addresses, and other details on fund sponsors and investment managers.

Predicasts*—Lockheed Dialog System and SDC Search Service.

Quotron Systems Inc.*—On-line news display.

SDC Search Service*—On-line interactive retrieval on data bases covering science and technology, industry and economic trends and forecasts, management, social sciences, government reports and actions, and many other disciplines. Approximately 20 million citations on-line.

Ward's AutoInfoBank*—Data on deliveries, production, inventory, and shipments on U.S., Canadian, and U.S.-imported cars and trucks.

World Trade Center Information Center—Data retrieval and research using computer data bases and other sources.

IX. Real Estate

Coopers & Lybrand*—Real estate project evaluation (for evaluating real estate investment proposals, with and without replacement reserves); Mortgage analysis (level payment required to amortize the interest and principal of a specific mortgage, with ability to handle changes in interest rates and repayment terms); available on General Electric time-sharing.

Decisionex, Inc.*—QUICK computer model for simulating real estate investments results under varying conditions; available on Burroughs Corporation and Informatics time-sharing networks.

Interactive Data Corporation*—Real estate simulations.

List of Firms and Services

Firm Name	*Services Offered*
ADP Network Services 425 Park Avenue New York, NY 10022	Economics Common stock analysis Fixed income analysis International Accounting Performance measurement
Barra 12 El Sueno Orinda CA 94563	Portfolio strategy Common stock analysis Fixed income analysis Performance measurement
A. G. Becker Inc. 2 First National Plaza Chicago, IL 60603	Economics Portfolio Strategy Common stock analysis Fixed income analysis International Performance measurement
(The) Boston Company One Boston Place Boston, MA 02106	Economics Portfolio strategy Common stock analysis Fixed income analysis Accounting Performance measurement
Bradford Trust Company 70 Pine St. 10th Fl. New York, NY 10005	Accounting
Buck Pension Fund Services, Inc. 2 Pennsylvania Plaza New York, NY 10001	Portfolio strategy Common stock analysis Fixed income analysis Performance measurement
Bunker-Ramo	Common stock analysis News and general information

Firm Name	*Services Offered*
Bush, Lloyd & Associates One Battery Park Plaza New York, NY 10004	Accounting
Business International Corp. One Dag Hammarskjold Plaza New York, NY 10017	Economics International
Callan Associates 601 California St. San Francisco, CA 94108	Performance measurement
Campbell (Walter) Associates 89 Hunnewell Newton, MA 02158	Common stock analysis Fixed income analysis News & general information International
Canavest House Inc. P. O. Box 13 Commerce Court East Toronto Canada	Portfolio strategy Common stock analysis Fixed income analysis International
Cates, Lyons, & Co., Inc. 74 Trinity Place New York, NY 10006	Common stock analysis
Center for Research in Security Prices Graduate School of Business University of Chicago 5836 Greenwood Avenue Chicago, IL 60637	Common stock analysis Performance measurement
Chase Econometrics Associates, Inc. 555 Cityline Ave. Bala Cynwyd, PA 19004	Economics International News and general information
Citibank Citishare Citicorp Center 153 E. 53rd St. New York, NY 10043	Economics Common stock analysis
Coopers & Lybrand 1251 Avenue of the Americas New York, NY 10020	Real estate
CompuServe 1211 Avenue of the Americas New York, NY 10036	Economics Common stock analysis Fixed income analysis Accounting Performance measurement

Firm Name	Services Offered
Computer Directions Advisors, Inc. 8750 Georgia Avenue Silver Springs, MD 20910	Portfolio strategy Common stock analysis Fixed income analysis Performance measurement
Computer Science Corp. 650 North Sepulveda Blvd. El Segundo, CA 90245	Economics
Computel Systems, Ltd. 1200 St. Laurent Blvd. Ottawa, Ontario K1K3B 8	Economics International
Comshare-Trust Marketing Division 1700 Market St. Phila, PA 19103	Accounting
Control Data Corp. HQWØ5I 8100 34th Ave. South Minneapolis, MN 55440	Economics
Data Resources, Inc. 29 Hartwell Ave. Lexington, MA 02173	Economics Portfolio strategy Common stock analysis Fixed income analysis International Accounting Performance measurement News and general information
Decisionex, Inc. 1200 Post Road East Westport, CT 06880	Real estate
Digital Information Corp. 5455 Buford Highway Suite A-105 Doraville, GA 30340	Accounting Performance measurement
Dow Jones News Service 22 Cortlandt Street New York, NY 10007	News and general information
Dun & Bradstreet 99 Church Street New York, NY 10007	News and general information
Editec, Inc. The Electric Library 53 West Jackson Blvd. Chicago, IL 60604	News and general information

Firm Name	*Services Offered*
Economic Information Systems, Inc. 9 East 41st Street New York, NY 10017	Economics News and general information
Effron Enterprises, Inc. P. O. Box 17 White Plains, NY 10604	Portfolio strategy Common stock analysis Fixed income analysis Accounting Performance measurement
Evaluation Associates, Incorporated 25 Sylvan Rd. Westport, CT 06880	Performance measurement
Federal Deposit Insurance Corporation (FDIC) DRSS 550 17th St. N.W. Washington, D.C. 20429	Common stock analysis News and general information
Federal Home Loan Bank Board (FSLIC) Informations Systems Div. 1700 G Street N.W. Washington, D.C. 20552	Common stock analysis News and general information
FIND/SVP 500 Fifth Avenue New York, NY 10036	International News and general information
Fong (Gifford) Associates 233 Wilshire Blvd. Suite 303 Santa Monica, CA 90401	Portfolio strategy Common stock analysis Fixed income analysis Performance measurement
Fund Management 78 East 56th St. New York, NY 10022	Common stock analysis Fixed income analysis Performance measurement
General Electric Co. 301 North Washington St. Rockville, MD 20850	Economics Common stock analysis International
Graphic Management Systems 20 East 46th St. New York, NY 10017	Common stock analysis Performance measurement
Hamilton, Johnston & Co., Inc. One Palmer Square Princeton, NJ 08540	Performance measurement

Firm Name	*Services Offered*
Huggins & Co., Inc. 1401 Walnut St. Philadelphia, PA 19102	Common stock analysis Fixed income analysis Performance measurement
Informatics, Inc. 1500 Broadway New York, NY 10036	Economics Common stock analysis
(The) Information Bank (Subsidiary of The New York Times Company) 1719A, Route 10 Parsippany, NJ 07054	Common stocks International News and general information
Indata Services Co. 644 Danbury Road Suite One Georgetown, CT 06829	Common stock analysis Fixed income analysis Accounting Performance measurement
The INSCO Systems Corporation State Highway No. 66 Neptune, NJ 07753	Economics
Interactive Data Corporation 22 Cortlandt Street New York, NY 10007	Economics Portfolio strategy Common stock analysis Fixed income analysis International Accounting Performance measurement Real estate
International Monetary Fund Bureau of Statistics 700 19 St., N.W. Washington, D.C. 20431	Economics International
InterSec Research Corp. 122 East 42 Street New York, NY 10017	Portfolio Strategy International Performance measurement
Lipper Analytical Distributors, Inc. 74 Trinity Place New York, NY 10006	Fixed income analysis Performance measurement
Lockheed Information Systems 3521 Hanover Street Palo Alto, CA 94303	Economics International News and general information

Firm Name	*Services Offered*
Lynch, Jones & Ryan 20 Exchange Place New York, NY 10005	Common stock analysis Accounting
McGraw-Hill 1221 Avenue of the Americas New York, NY 10020	Economics Common stock analysis
Merrill Lynch One Liberty Plaza New York, NY 10080	Economics Common stock analysis Fixed income analysis Accounting Performance measurement News and general information
Media General Financial Services P. O. Box 26991 Richmond, VA 23261	Common stock analysis
MJK Associates 2343B Homestead Road Santa Clara, CA 95050	Economics
Monchik-Weber Associates 111 John Street, 10th Fl. New York, NY 10038	Common stock analysis
Money Market Directories, Inc. 818 East High Street Charlottesville, VA 22901	News and general information
Muller Data Corporation Data Division 25 Broad Street New York, NY 10004	Common stock analysis Fixed income analysis
Municipal Securities Evaluation Service, Inc. (Subsidiary of J. J. Kenny Co. Inc.) 55 Broad Street New York, NY 10004	Fixed income analysis Accounting
National CSS, Inc. 187 Danbury Road Wilton, CT 06897	Economics Common stock analysis Fixed income analysis
Nelson Communications Directory of Sec. Research Information 551 Fifth Avenue New York, NY 10017	Common stock analysis

Firm Name	Services Offered
William O'Neil & Co. 11915 La Grange Ave. Los Angeles, CA 90025	Common stock analysis
On-Line Systems Inc. 115 Evergreen Heights Dr. Pittsburgh, PA 15229	Economics Common stock analysis Fixed income analysis
Predicasts Inc. 11001 Cedar Avenue Cleveland, OH 44106	Economics Common stock analysis International News and general information
Quotron Systems, Inc. One Battery Park Plaza New York, NY 10004	Common stock analysis News and general information
Rapidata 20 New Dutch Lane P. O. Box 1049 Fairfield, NJ 07006	Economics Portfolio strategy Common stock analysis Fixed income analysis International Performance measurement
Remote Computing Corp. 1076 East Meadow Circle Palo Alto, CA 94303	Economics Common stock analysis Fixed income analysis Accounting
Rogers, Casey & Barksdale Inc. 1234 Summer Street Stamford, CT 06905	Portfolio strategy Performance measurement News and general information
Scientific Time Sharing Corporation 7316 Wisconsin Ave. Bethesda, MD 20014	Economics Common stock analysis International
SDC Search Service 2500 Colorado Avenue Santa Monica, CA 90406	Economics International Accounting News and general information
SEI Corp. Valley Forge Executive Mall #7 680 E. Swedesford Road Wayne, PA 19087	Accounting

Firm Name	*Services Offered*
Service Bureau Corp. 500 West Putnam Avenue Greenwich, CT 06830	Economics Common stock analysis Fixed income analysis International Performance measurement Accounting
Shaw Data Services, Inc. 122 East 42nd Street New York, NY 10017	Common stock analysis Fixed income analysis Accounting Performance measurement
Sharp (I.P.) Associates Ltd. 145 King St., West Toronto, Ontario M5H 1J8	Economics Portfolio strategy Common stock analysis International
Shearson Hayden Stone 1 New York Plaza New York, NY 10004	Common stock analysis
Standard & Poor's Compustat Services, Inc. 7400 South Alton Court Englewood, CO 80112	Common stock analysis
Standard & Poor's Corp. 345 Hudson Street New York, NY 10014	Common stock analysis Fixed income analysis Accounting
Statistics Canada CANSIM R. H. Coats Building 23rd Floor, Area L Ottawa, Canada L1AOZ8	Economics International
Telstat Systems, Inc. 150 East 58th Street New York, NY 10022	Common stock analysis Fixed income analysis Accounting Performance measurement
Time-Sharing Resources, Inc. 777 Northern Blvd. Great Neck, NY 11022	Economics Common stock analysis Fixed income analysis International Accounting Performance measurement
Tymshare, Inc. 260 Madison Avenue New York, NY 10016	Economics Common stock analysis Accounting Performance measurement

Firm Name	Services Offered
Value Line 711 Third Avenue New York, NY 10017	Common stock analysis
Vanguard Group of Investment Companies P. O. Box 1100 Valley Forge, PA 19482	Performance measurement
Ward's Auto Info. Bank 28 West Adams Detroit, MI 48226	Common stock analysis News and general information
Warner Computer Systems, Inc. 605 Third Ave. New York, NY 10016	Common stock analysis Fixed income analysis Performance measurement
Wells Fargo 475 Sansome Street San Francisco, CA 94111	Portfolio strategy Common stock analysis Fixed income analysis
Wilshire Associates 100 Wilshire Blvd. Suite 308 Santa Monica, CA 90401	Portfolio strategy Common stock analysis Fixed income analysis Performance measurement
Wismer Associates, Inc. 6355 Topanga Canyon Blvd. Woodland Hills, CA 91367	Portfolio strategy Common stock analysis Fixed income analysis Accounting Performance measurement
World Trade Center Information Center Lobby One World Trade Center New York, NY 10048	News and general information

BIBLIOGRAPHY

Daniells, Lorna M. *Business Information Sources.* Berkeley, Calif.: The University of California Press, 1976.

Information Market Place, 1978–79. New York, N.Y.: R. R. Bowker Company.

Interactive Computing Directories. Boulder, Colo.: The Association of Time-Sharing Users Inc.

Part Eight

Stock Market Indexes

Chapter 39

Stock Market Indexes

SUMNER N. LEVINE
State University of New York
Stony Brook, New York

The Dow Jones Industrials and the Standard & Poor's 500 Indexes are often used as benchmarks for evaluating performance. However, the limitations of these indexes should be clearly recognized, as discussed below.

The DJI Index is calculated by adding up the prices of each stock listed in Table 1 and dividing the sum by a factor which currently has the value of 1.465 on November 12, 1979.[1]

The S&P 500 Index stocks are listed in Table 2, together with their percentages of capitalization of the total index. The S&P Index is an arithmetically weighed index given by

$$I_{sp} = \frac{\sum\limits_{i} P_{it} \times N_{it}}{f \sum\limits_{i} P_{ib} \times N_{ib}} \times 10$$

where

P_{it} = the current stock price of a company
P_{ib} = the base period stock price of a company
N_{it} = the current number of shares of a company
N_{ib} = the base period number of shares of a company
f = a factor used to adjust the index for changes in capitalization.

The base period values for the S&P Index are the averages for 1941 to 1943.

---

[1] Further details are given in the *Financial Analyst's Handbook*, vol. 1, (Dow Jones-Irwin, 1975), Chap. 35. (Homewood, Ill.: © 1975 by Dow Jones-Irwin, Inc.)

Table 1
Dow Jones Industrials

Allied Chemical
Alcoa
American Brands
American Can
American Telephone & Telegraph
Bethlehem Steel
Dupont Corp
Eastman Kodak
Exxon
General Electric

General Foods
General Motors
Goodyear Tire
Inco Ltd
International Business Machines (IBM)
International Harvester
International Paper
Johns Manville
Merck & Co
Minnesota Mining and Manufacturing (3M)

Owens-Illinois
Proctor & Gamble
Sears, Roebuck
Standard Oil of California
Texaco
Union Carbide
U.S. Steel Corp
United Technology
Westinghouse
Woolworth, F.W.

It is evident from the above that the stocks with the largest capitalization exert the greatest effect on the S&P Index. Indeed, the top 40 companies have a greater effect than the remaining 460 stocks combined.

The fact that the DJI and the S&P indexes reflect the price performance of a handful of highly capitalized issues can result in a very misleading perception of the behavior of the market as a whole. A decline in the price of 30 or 40 highly capitalized issues could offset price increases of hundreds of smaller issues.

A more revealing index of broad market performance is the Equal Investment Index.[2] This index assumes equal investments of $1,000 in each stock of the New York or American Stock Exchanges. The base period is January 11, 1973. With this index each issue has the

---

[2] Published weekly in *The Financial Weekly* Richmond, Va.: Media General Financial Publications.

Table 2
S&P 500 Index Stocks

	Rank	Percent Capitalization
INTL BUSINESS MACH	1	7.090
AMERICAN TEL&TELEG	2	6.362
EXXON CORP	3	3.714
GENERAL MOTORS COR	4	2.498
GENERAL ELECTRIC C	5	1.665
EASTMAN KODAK	6	1.547
ROYAL DUTCH PETROL	7	1.385
SCHLUMBERGER, LTD	8	1.326
STANDARD OIL INDIA	9	1.326
STANDARD OIL CO CA	10	1.243
MOBIL OIL CORP	11	1.228
TEXACO INC	12	1.067
MINNESOTA MINING &	13	1.053
SEARS ROEBUCK & CO	14	1.043
PROCTER&GAMBLE CO	15	1.035
DU PONT DE NEMOURS	16	1.023
ATLANTIC RICHFIELD	17	0.975
SHELL OIL CO	18	0.843
PHILLIPS PETROLEUM	19	0.802
CATERPILLAR TRACTO	20	0.797
FORD MOTOR CO	21	0.796
COCA-COLA CO	22	0.792
DOW CHEMICAL CO	23	0.779
MERCK & CO INC	24	0.772
GULF OIL CORP	25	0.759
XEROX CORP	26	0.719
AMERICAN HOME PROD	27	0.659
JOHNSON & JOHNSON	28	0.645
PHILIP MORRIS, INC	29	0.642
GENERAL TELEPHONE	30	0.591
HALLIBURTON CO	31	0.587
HEYERHAEUSER CO	32	0.575
LILLY ELI & CO	33	0.573
BANKAMERICA CORP	34	0.558
GETTY OIL CO	35	0.532
CONTINENTAL OIL CO	36	0.529
TENNECO	37	0.452
CITICORP	38	0.447
K MART	39	0.443
GEORGIA-PACIFIC CO	40	0.441
AVON PRODUCTS INC	41	0.440
BOEING COMPANY	42	0.433
BURROUGHS CORP	43	0.429
UNION PACIFIC CORP	44	0.428
SMITHKLINE	45	0.427
REYNOLDS R J INDS	46	0.427
INTL TEL & TEL COR	47	0.425
HEWLETT-PACKARD CO	48	0.394
UNION CARBIDE CORP	49	0.386
AMERICAN ELEC PWR	50	0.373
UNION OIL CO CALIF	51	0.363
AETNA LIFE & CAS C	52	0.363
PACIFIC GAS & ELEC	53	0.357
PFIZER INC	54	0.346
COMMONWEALTH EDISO	55	0.340

Table 2 *(continued)*

	Rank	*Percent* *Capitalization*
BRISTOL-MYERS CO	56	0.336
PEPSICO INC	57	0.334
DEERE & CO	58	0.333
INTERNATIONAL PAPE	59	0.332
AMERICAN EXPRESS C	60	0.324
RCA CORP	61	0.320
US STEEL CORP	62	0.312
DIGITAL EQUIPMENT	63	0.311
UNILEVER N V	64	0.308
SUN CO.	65	0.301
WARNER LAMBERT CO	66	0.301
EMERSON ELEC CO	67	0.298
PENNEY J C INC	68	0.294
BEATRICE FOODS CO	69	0.292
ALUMINUM CO OF AME	70	0.291
TEXAS INSTRUMENTS	71	0.286
ABBOTT LABS	72	0.286
SOUTHERN COMPANY	73	0.285
MORGAN J P & CO IN	74	0.284
MONSANTO CO	75	0.273
NCR CORP	76	0.270
MCDONALDS CORP	77	0.264
WESTINGHOUSE ELEC	78	0.263
SPERRY RAND CORP	79	0.253
SOUTHERN CALIF EDI	80	0.253
GENERAL FOODS CORP	80	0.253
TRAVELERS CORP	82	0.252
AMAX INC	83	0.248
CITIES SERVICE	84	0.246
SCHERING PLOUGH CO	85	0.244
TEXAS UTILITIES CO	86	0.241
DRESSER INDUSTRIES	87	0.239
ALCAN ALUMINUM LTD	88	0.238
TELEDYNE CORP	89	0.235
DUKE POWER CO	90	0.233
REVLON, INC	91	0.232
CONS EDISON NY	92	0.230
RAYTHEON CO	93	0.230
FEDERATED DEPT STO	94	0.227
CONNECTICUT GEN IN	95	0.226
INCO LTD	96	0.224
CBS INC	97	0.218
KELLOGG CO	98	0.218
SUPERIOR OIL CO	99	0.216
PUBLIC SERVICE EL&	100	0.215
CONTINENTAL CORP	101	0.213
HONEYWELL INC	102	0.210
POLAROID CORP	103	0.206
AMERICAN BRANDS	104	0.206
COLGATE PALMOLIVE	105	0.206
KRAFTCO CORP	106	0.203
MIDDLE SOUTH UTILI	107	0.199
GENERAL MILLS INC	108	0.197
RALSTON PURINA	109	0.196
AMERICAN CYANAMID	110	0.195
CPC INTERNATIONAL	111	0.192

Table 2 *(continued)*

	Rank	Percent Capitalization
DISNEY WALT PRODTN	112	0.191
GOODYEAR TIRE & RU	113	0.189
BAXTER TRAVENOL	114	0.188
UNION CAMP CORP	115	0.188
ROCKWELL INTL CORP	116	0.187
TRANSAMERICA CORP	117	0.181
MCDONNELL DOUGLAS	118	0.177
PHILADELPHIA ELECT	119	0.177
GANNETT COMPANY	120	0.176
AMP INC	121	0.176
ANHEUSER BUSCH INC	122	0.175
VIRGINIA ELECTRIC	123	0.175
INTL HARVESTER CO	124	0.175
FLORIDA PWR & LT C	125	0.175
SAFEWAY STORES INC	126	0.173
ENGELHARD MINERALS	127	0.172
CAMPBELL SOUP CO	128	0.172
BAKER INTL	129	0.170
MOTOROLA INC	130	0.166
CHAMPION INTERNATI	131	0.164
KIMBERLY CLARK COR	132	0.163
CONTINENTAL ILL CO	133	0.163
SEAGRAMS LTD	134	0.163
GRACE W R &CO	135	0.163
CARNATION CO	136	0.162
BETHLEHEM STEEL CO	137	0.161
CENTRAL & SO WEST	138	0.159
TIMES MIRROR CO	139	0.158
CHASE MANHATTAN CO	140	0.157
TEXAS EASTERN TRAN	141	0.156
UNITED TECHNOLOGIE	142	0.156
UNITED TELECOMMUNI	143	0.155
LOUISIANA LAND & E	144	0.152
BOISE CASCADE CORP	145	0.151
TRW INC	146	0.150
STERLING DRUG, INC	147	0.150
DETROIT EDISON CO	148	0.149
INA CORP	149	0.149
CORNING GLASS WORK	150	0.149
MANUFACTURERS HAND	151	0.148
TEKTRONIX INC	152	0.147
AMERICAN BROADCAST	153	0.146
AMER HOSPITAL SUPP	154	0.145
SANTA FE INDUSTRIE	155	0.144
MCA INC	156	0.144
OHIO EDISON CO	157	0.143
INGERSOLL RAND CO	158	0.142
HEINZ H J CO	159	0.141
ALLIED CHEMICAL CO	160	0.140
OWENS CORNING FIBE	161	0.140
WESTERN BANCORPORA	162	0.139
ARMCO STEEL CORP	163	0.138
COLUMBIA GAS SYSTE	164	0.136
HERCULES INC	165	0.134
NORTHERN NATURAL G	166	0.133
NIAGARA MOHAWK PWR	167	0.132

Table 2 *(continued)*

	Rank	Percent Capitalization
UNITED STATES FID&	168	0.131
BLACK & DECKER	169	0.131
INTL FLAV & FRAG	170	0.131
CROWN ZELLERBACH	171	0.129
PPG IND INC	172	0.129
DANA CORP	173	0.128
CONTINENTAL GROUP	174	0.128
BORDEN INC	175	0.127
HOUSEHOLD FINANCE	176	0.127
KAISER ALUM & CHEM	177	0.127
BENDIX CORP	178	0.127
TIME INC	179	0.126
F M C CORP	180	0.126
AMER NAT RES	181	0.125
INTL MINERALS & CH	182	0.125
LINCOLN NATL CORP	183	0.125
PEOPLES GAS CO	184	0.125
PANHANDLE EAST PIP	185	0.123
NABISCO	186	0.123
NORTHWEST INDS	187	0.123
ST PAUL COS INC	188	0.122
DELTA AIR LINES	189	0.121
NORTON SIMON INC	190	0.121
INTEL	191	0.121
FIRESTONE TIRE&RUB	192	0.121
GILLETTE CO	193	0.121
MARTIN MARIETTA	194	0.120
SOUTHERN PACIFIC C	195	0.120
TEXTRON	196	0.120
WINN-DIXIE STORES	197	0.118
LITTON	198	0.117
SEARLE G. D. & CO	199	0.117
INLAND STEEL CO	200	0.117
KENNECOTT COPPER C	201	0.117
CHESEBROUGH-PONDS	202	0.116
N L T CORP	203	0.116
SOUTHERN RAILWAY C	204	0.115
TEXASGULF INC	205	0.114
JEFFERSON PILOT CO	206	0.114
ST REGIS PAPER CO	207	0.114
GULF & WESTERN	208	0.113
BALTIMORE GAS&ELEC	209	0.113
PITTSTON CO	210	0.113
KNIGHT RIDDER	211	0.113
NORFOLK & WESTERN	212	0.113
CONSOLIDATED NAT G	213	0.112
MELVILLE CORP	214	0.112
SOUTHERN NAT RES	215	0.112
TANDY CORP	216	0.111
FIRST CHICAGO CORP	217	0.111
NORTHN STS PWR MIN	218	0.109
AMERICAN CAN CO	219	0.109
SCOTT PAPER CO	220	0.108
HILTON HOTELS CORP	221	0.108
N L IND	222	0.108
EL PASO CO	223	0.107

Table 2 *(continued)*

	Rank	Percent Capitalization
MISSOURI PACIFIC	224	0.106
METRO GOLDWYN MAYE	225	0.106
PUBLIC SUC CO IND	226	0.106
CIT FINANCIAL CORP	227	0.105
UAL INC	228	0.104
STANDARD BRANDS IN	229	0.104
SAFECO CORP	230	0.102
WHIRLPOOL CORP	231	0.101
GENERAL AMERN OIL	232	0.100
GENUINE PARTS CO	233	0.100
EATON CORP	234	0.100
WOOLWORTH F W CO	235	0.099
NEWMONT MINING COR	237	0.099
CONTINENTAL TELEPH	237	0.098
WALKER HIRAM G&W	238	0.098
CARRIER CORP	239	0.098
GOULD INC	240	0.097
REYNOLDS METALS CO	241	0.097
NATIONAL STEEL COR	242	0.096
MESA PETROLEUM	243	0.096
FIRST INTL BANCSHA	244	0.096
BECTON DICKINSON	245	0.096
LUCKY STORES	246	0.095
MCDERMOTT J RAY	247	0.095
DAYTON-HUDSON	248	0.095
CAPITAL HLDG CORP	249	0.095
MEAD CORP	250	0.094
TIMKEN CO	251	0.094
CHRYSLER CORP	252	0.094
NORTHWEST BANCORPO	253	0.093
HEUBLEIN INC	254	0.093
ECKERD (JACK)	255	0.092
MCGRAW HILL INC	256	0.092
CELANESE CORP	257	0.092
NORTHWEST AIRLS IN	258	0.091
BORG WARNER CORP	259	0.091
ROADWAY EXPRESS IN	260	0.091
CENTRAL TEL & UTIL	261	0.091
PHELPS DODGE CORP	262	0.090
PILLSBURY CO	263	0.090
CAPITAL CITIES COM	264	0.090
PERKIN-ELMER CORP	265	0.089
LOUISIANA PAC CORP	266	0.089
ENSERCH CORPS	267	0.089
OWENS-ILLINOIS INC	268	0.088
GARDNER-DENVER CO	269	0.088
KROGER CO	270	0.088
AMERICAN GEN INS C	271	0.088
ST JOE MINERALS CO	272	0.087
CHEMICAL NEW YORK	273	0.087
COMBUSTION ENGINEE	274	0.085
SQUARE D CO	275	0.084
CONTROL DATA CORP	276	0.084
DOW JONES CO	277	0.084
RELIANCE ELECTRIC	278	0.084
MELLON NATL CORP	279	0.083

Table 2 *(continued)*

	Rank	Percent Capitalization
POTLATCH CORP	280	0.082
JOHNS MANVILLE COR	281	0.081
INTERCO INC	282	0.081
AMERICAN STANDARD	283	0.081
CHESSIE SYSTEM INC	284	0.081
SANTA FE INTERNATI	285	0.080
MAY DEPT STORES CO	286	0.080
COOPER INDS INC	287	0.080
DOME MINES LTD	288	0.080
NATIONAL DISTIL&CH	289	0.080
PACIFIC LTG CORP	290	0.080
BURLINGTON INDUSTR	291	0.079
CLARK EQUIPMENT CO	292	0.078
BENEFICIAL CORP	293	0.078
AHMANSON H F & CO	294	0.078
ASARCO CO	295	0.078
HOLIDAY INNS INC	296	0.077
FIRST CHARTER FINL	297	0.077
WARNER COMMUNICA	298	0.077
BURLINGTON NORTHER	299	0.076
UNITED STATES GYPS	300	0.075
COORS ADOLPH CO	301	0.074
WISCONSIN ELEC PWR	302	0.074
CHUBB CORP	303	0.074
MARRIOTT CORP	304	0.074
HUGHES TOOL CO	305	0.073
HOUSTON OIL MINERA	306	0.073
ESMARK INC	307	0.073
QUAKER OATS CO	308	0.072
WILLIAMS COS	309	0.072
CROWN CORK&SEAL IN	310	0.072
WESTVACO CORP	311	0.071
HOSPITAL CORP	312	0.070
DIAMOND INTERNATIO	313	0.070
CNA FINL CORP	314	0.069
MASONITE CORP	315	0.067
MCGRAW EDISON CO	316	0.067
ALLIED STORES CORP	317	0.066
NEW ENGLAND ELEC S	318	0.066
REPUBLIC STEEL COR	319	0.065
ARMSTRONG CORK	320	0.065
GENERAL SIGNAL COR	321	0.065
GREAT WESTN FINL C	322	0.063
TEXAS GAS TRANSMIS	323	0.062
AMSTED INDS INC	324	0.062
BRIGGS & STRATTON	325	0.061
WALTER JIM CORP	326	0.060
BECKMAN INSTR	327	0.060
HOMESTAKE MNG CO	328	0.059
CHAMPION SPARK PLU	329	0.058
JOY MFG	330	0.057
BANKERS TRUST N Y	331	0.057
SEABOARD COAST LIN	332	0.057
EASTERN GAS & FUEL	333	0.056
GENERAL DYNAMICS C	334	0.056
ARA SERVICES, INC	335	0.055

Table 2 *(continued)*

	Rank	Percent Capitalization
MACY RH&CO	336	0.055
PULLMAN INC	337	0.054
METROMEDIA INC	338	0.054
BUCYRUS ERIE CO	339	0.054
FRUEHAUF CORP	340	0.054
LIGGETT GROUP	341	0.053
COX BROADCASTING C	342	0.053
AMERICAN AIRLINES,	343	0.052
PITNEY-BOWES, INC	344	0.052
SUNBEAM CORP DEL	345	0.052
I C INDS INC	346	0.051
FIRST NATL BOSTON	347	0.050
ALLIS CHALMERS	348	0.050
FOSTER WHEELER COR	349	0.050
HUMANA	350	0.050
THOMAS & BETTS COR	351	0.049
BLUE BELL INC	352	0.049
CYPRUS MINES CORP	353	0.049
MAYTAG CO	354	0.049
REVCO D. S. INC	355	0.049
MAYER OSCAR & CO	356	0.049
CARTER HAWLEY HALE	357	0.048
YELLOW FGHT SYS IN	358	0.048
CENTEX CORP	359	0.048
CRANE CO	360	0.048
AMF INC	361	0.048
DR PEPPER CO	362	0.048
CONSOLIDATED FREIG	363	0.046
SCHLITZ JOS BREWIN	364	0.046
IDEAL BASIC INDS	365	0.046
RAMADA INNS INC	366	0.045
TWENTIETH CENTY FO	367	0.045
ACF INDUSTRIES INC	368	0.043
BRUNSWICK CORP	369	0.043
CHURCH FR CHK	370	0.043
EMERY AIR FGHT COR	371	0.043
AMERICAN STORES CO	372	0.043
REXNORD INC	373	0.043
LIBBEY-OWENS-FORD	374	0.042
SEDCO INC	375	0.042
NATL SEMICONDUCTOR	376	0.042
CUMMINS ENGINE INC	377	0.042
NATIONAL GYPSUM CO	378	0.042
GOODRICH B F CO	379	0.042
ZENITH RADIO CORP	380	0.041
HOWARD JOHNSON CO	381	0.041
ECHLIN MFG CO	382	0.041
WRIGLEY WM JR CO	383	0.040
LONE STAR INDUSTRI	384	0.040
JEWEL COS INC	385	0.040
EVANS PRODS CO	386	0.040
PAN AM WRLD AWYS	387	0.039
CLOROX CO	388	0.039
HERSHEY FOODS CORP	389	0.039
CAMPBELL RED LAKE	390	0.039
GENERAL CABLE CORP	391	0.038

Table 2 *(continued)*

	Rank	Percent Capitalization
BROWNING FERRIS	392	0.037
ASA LTD	393	0.037
GERBER PRODUCTS CO	394	0.037
CINCINNATI MILACRO	395	0.036
WHEELABRATOR-FRYE	396	0.036
SINGER CO	397	0.036
AMERICAN MTRS CORP	398	0.035
ASSOCIATED DRY GOO	399	0.035
OKLAHOMA NATURAL G	400	0.033
SCOTT FORESMAN & C	401	0.033
RITE AID CORP	402	0.033
FLINTKOTE CO	403	0.033
TRANE CO	404	0.032
EX-CELL-O CORP	405	0.032
FAIRCHILD CAMERA	406	0.032
IOWA BEEF PROCESSO	407	0.031
N C N B CORP	408	0.031
HUDSON BAY MNG SML	409	0.031
WESTMORELAND COAL	410	0.030
MASSEY FERGUSON LT	411	0.030
HELLER WALTER E IN	412	0.030
DENNEYS INC	413	0.030
BROWN GROUP INC	414	0.029
HOBART CORP	415	0.029
AMER MEDICAL INTL	416	0.029
CONE MLS CORP	417	0.029
FIRST PA CORP	418	0.028
UNIROYAL INC	419	0.028
STEVENS J P & CO	420	0.028
PUREX LTD	421	0.028
GREAT ATL & PAC TE	422	0.027
COLUMBIA PICTURES	423	0.027
TAFT BROADCASTING	424	0.026
HARCOURT BRACE JOV	425	0.026
WEST POINT PEPPERE	426	0.024
OUTBOARD MARINE CO	427	0.024
READING BATES OFFS	428	0.024
AKZONA INC	429	0.024
MARSHALL FIELD & C	430	0.023
BROOKLYN UN GAS CO	431	0.023
SPRINGS MLS INC	432	0.023
MACMILLAN INC	433	0.022
FEDERAL PAPER BRD	434	0.022
MILTON BRADLEY CO	435	0.022
AMSTAR CORP	436	0.022
CHICAGO PNEUMATIC	437	0.022
PEABODY GALION	438	0.021
INTERLAKE INC	439	0.021
MARYLAND CUP CORP	440	0.021
KAUFMAN & BROAD IN	441	0.020
BARD C. R.	442	0.019
CROUSE & HINDS	443	0.019
FLEETWOOD ENTERPRI	444	0.019
BROWN CO	445	0.019
SKYLINE CORP	446	0.019
NATIONAL CAN CORP	447	0.019

Table 2 *(concluded)*

	Rank	Percent Capitalization
SHERWIN WILLIAMS C	448	0.018
GRUMMAN CORPORATIO	449	0.018
COPELAND CORP	450	0.017
PABST BREWING CO	451	0.017
ROYAL CROWN COLA C	452	0.017
BEMIS INC	453	0.017
FIRST MISS CORP	454	0.016
GENERAL PORTLAND C	455	0.016
REEVES BROS INC	456	0.016
COCA-COLA BOTTLING	457	0.016
ST LOUIS-SAN FRAN	458	0.015
STOKELY VAN CAMP	459	0.015
CLUETT PEABODY & C	460	0.015
U S HOME&DEV CORP	461	0.015
QUESTOR CORP	462	0.014
NATIONAL MEDICAL	463	0.014
GIDDINGS&LEWIS INC	464	0.014
MEREDITH CORP	465	0.014
REVERE COPPER BRAS	466	0.014
WARNER & SWASEY CO	467	0.013
ACME CLEVELAND COR	468	0.012
BEKER INDS CORP	469	0.012
ENVIROTECH	470	0.012
GLOBAL MARINE INC	471	0.012
MCLEAN TRUCKING CO	472	0.012
UMC INDS INC	473	0.011
JONATHAN LOGAN INC	474	0.011
NOHASCO CORP	475	0.011
HANDLEMAN CO DEL	476	0.010
NORTH AMERN COAL C	477	0.010
WHEELING PITTS STE	478	0.010
GENESCO INC	479	0.009
KOEHRING CO	480	0.008
ROPER CORPORATION	481	0.008
WHITE MTR CORP	482	0.008
FABERGE INC	483	0.008
FEDDERS CORP	484	0.008
LOWENSTEIN M & SON	485	0.007
BELDEN CORP	486	0.007
BROWN & SHARPE MFG	487	0.007
REDMAN INDUSTRIES	488	0.007
WARNACO INC	489	0.006
GINDS INC	490	0.006
AMALGAMATED SUGAR	491	0.005
ALBERTO CULVER CO	492	0.005
ALPHA PORTLAND IND	493	0.005
HOLLY SUGAR CORP	494	0.004
MACKE CO	495	0.004
MONARCH MACH TOOL	496	0.004
MUNSINGWEAR INC	497	0.003
IDEAL TOY CORP	498	0.003
TONKA CORP	499	0.002
KROEHLER MFG CO	500	0.002

Source: Standard & Poor's, August 1979.

same dollar value proportion of the total market investment. The index is given by

$$I_{EI} = \frac{1}{N} \sum_{i=1}^{N} \frac{P_{i,}(t+1)}{P_{i,}(t)} \times \text{(previous period index)}$$

Where $P_i(t)$ is the price of the ith issue at the beginning of the period, $P_{i,}(t+1)$ is the price at the end of the period, and N is the number of issues on the exchange.

A comparison of the above indexes is shown in Table 3. The discrepancies are evident. During the periods shown

Table 3
Percent Change in Indexes, 1977–1979

Period	EI Index			Other Indexes	
	NYS	*ASE*	*Combined*	*DJI*	*S&P 500*
January 1977 to January 1978	.4%	17.8%	6.5%	−19.3%	−12.6%
January 1977 to January 1979	21%	64%	36.9%	−12.0%	− 2.0%

there was a bear market in the more heavily capitalized issues, as indicated by the DJI and S&P 500 indexes, but a bull market in the less heavily capitalized stocks.

Glossary[1]

Abnormal Performance Index (API). An abnormal performance index measures the behavior of stock prices not explained by their normal relationships to general market movements. The normal relationship of the return on a security to the return on the market is described by the market model:

$$R_i = a_i + \beta_i R_M + e_i$$

where R_i is the return on the security, R_M is the return on the market, a_i and β_i are parameters, and e_i is a random variable with an expected value of zero. Abnormal behavior will result in values of e_i different from zero and nonrandom.

Accretion (of a discount). In portfolio accounting, a straight-line accumulation of capital gains on discount bonds in anticipation of receipt of par at maturity.

---

[1] Note that the material in this glossary is under copyright and cannot be reproduced without the permission of the publisher. We wish to acknowledge the following as copyright holders for the glossary material: Weisenberger Investment Companies Service, Dow Jones Books, Dow Jones-Irwin, and Richard D. Irwin, Inc. In addition, those entries marked by * are copyrighted by and reprinted with the permission of the New York Stock Exchange, Inc.

The Sources are: *The Commodity Futures Trading Commission Act of 1974,* Committee on Agriculture and Forestry, United States Senate, (U.S. Government Printing Office, Washington, D.C. 1974), pp. 134–37; John A. Prestbo, ed. *The Dow Jones Commodities Handbook, 1976* (Homewood, Ill.: Dow Jones Books, 1976), pp. 155–60; Jack Treynor, Patrick J. Regan, and William W. Priest, Jr., *The Financial Reality of Pension Funding Under ERISA* (Homewood, Ill.: Dow Jones-Irwin, 1976), pp. 141–44; *Glossary: the Language of Investing,* The New York Stock Exchange, Inc. (May 1978): Marcia Stigum, *The Money Market, Myth, Reality and Practice,* (Homewood, Ill.: Dow Jones-Irwin, 1978), pp. 549–66: James H. Lorie and Mary T. Hamilton, *The Stock Market, Theories and Evidence* (Homewood, Ill.: Richard D. Irwin, 1973), pp. 267–76; Wiesenberger Investment Companies Service, Thirty-Eighth Annual Edition, 1978 Boston, Mass.: Warren Gorham & Lamont, Inc.), pp. 83–88.

Accrued Interest. Interest due from issue or from the last coupon date to the present on an interest-bearing security. The buyer of the security pays the quoted dollar price plus accrued interest.

Accumulation Plan. An arrangement under which an investor may make regular purchases of investment company shares in large or small amounts. Automatic reinvestment of dividends and distributions is usually provided. (See also **Contractual Plan** and **Voluntary Plan**.)

Actuarial Assumptions. The assumptions—about such matters as mortality rates among employees and pensioners of a pension-sponsoring organization, turnover rates among employees, rates of wage inflation, and investment return on pension fund assets—used by actuaries in reckoning the cost of, and accordingly the required annual contributions to, a particular pension plan (See **Mortality rate, Turnover rate, Investment return,** and **Pension cost**.)

Actuarial Cost Methods. The particular formulas and techniques used by actuaries to determine the amounts and incidence of annual contributions required for adequate funding of particular pension plans. (See **Funded Benefits**.)

Actuarial Gains (losses). Also called **Experience Gains (losses)**. The effect on actuarially calculated annual contributions of (1) deviations between actual prior experience (with respect to mortality, turnover, investment return, etc.) and the actuarial assumptions employed; or of (2) changes in actuarial assumptions.

Actuarial Valuation. The process by which an actuary estimates the present value of benefits to be paid under a given pension plan and, on that basis, calculates the amounts of annual contributions or of accounting charges. (See **Present Value**.)

Agencies. Federal agency securities.

Agency Bank. A form of organization commonly used by foreign banks to enter the U.S. market. An agency bank cannot accept deposits or extend loans in its own name; it acts as an agent for the parent bank.

All-in Cost. Total costs, explicit and other. Example: The all-in cost to a bank of CD money is the explicit rate of interest it pays on that deposit *plus* the FDIC premium it must pay on the deposit *plus* the hidden cost it incurs because it must hold some portion of that deposit in an noninterest-bearing reserve account at the Fed.

All or None (AON). Requirement that none of an order be executed unless all of it can be executed at the specified price.

Alpha (α_i). Alpha is the constant term in the equation relating risk premium on an asset to the risk premium on the market. Its *expected* value is zero, but is actual value may differ from zero. It is this possibility that explains investors' efforts to identify under- or overvalued securities, i.e., those with nonzero alphas.

Amortization. Accounting for expenses or charges as applicable rather than as paid. Includes such practices as depreciation, depletion, write-off of intangibles, prepaid expenses and deferred charges.*

Annuity. A contract, usually issued by an insurance company that provides an income for a specified period of time such as a number of years or for life. (See also **Variable Annuity.**)

Arbitrage. A technique employed to take advantage of differences in price. If, for example, ABC stock can be bought in New York for $10 a share and sold in London at $10.50, an arbitrageur may simultaneously purchase ABC stock here and sell the same amount in London, making a profit of 50 cents a share, less expenses. Arbitrage may also involve the purchase of rights to subscribe to a security, or the purchase of a convertible security—and the sale at or about the same time of the security obtainable through exercise of the rights or of the security obtainable through conversion.*

Asked. The price at which securities are offered for sale.

Assumed Investment Rate *(AIR).* This is the rate which must be assumed for the purpose of setting premiums and statutory reserves for a guaranteed minimum death benefit. The premiums are those which flow into a separate account.

Balanced Fund. An investment company that at all times holds bonds and/ or preferred stocks, in varying ratios to its holdings of common stocks, in order to maintain relatively greater stability of both capital and income.

Bank Discount Rate. Yield basis on which short-term, noninterest-bearing money market securities are quoted. A rate quoted on a discount basis understates bond equivalent yield. That must be calculated when comparing return against coupon securities.

Bankers' Acceptance (BA). A draft or bill of exchange accepted by a bank or trust company. The accepting institution guarantees payment on the bill.

Bank Line. Line of credit granted by a bank to a customer.

Bank Wire. A computer message system linking major banks. It is used not for effecting payments, but as a mechanism to advise the receiving bank of some action that has occurred, e.g., the payment by a customer of funds into that bank's account.

BANs. Bond anticipation notes are issued by states and municipalities to obtain interim financing for projects that will eventually be funded long term through the sale of a bond issue.

Basis Point. $\frac{1}{100}$ of 1 percent.

Basis Price. Price expressed in terms of yield to maturity or annual rate of return.

Bearer Bond. A bond which does not have the owner's name registered on the books of the issuer and which is payable to the holder. (See: **Coupon Bond, Registered Bond**)*

Bearer Security. A security whose owner is not registered on the books of the issuer. A bearer security is payable to the holder.

Best-Efforts Basis. Securities dealers do not underwrite a new issue, but sell it on the basis of what can be sold. In the money market, usually refers to a firm order to buy or sell a given amount of securities or currency at whatever best price can be found over a given period of time; can also refer to a flexible amount (up to a limit) at a given rate.

Beta Coefficient (β). The beta coefficient measures sensitivity of rates of return on a portfolio or on a particular security to general market movements. If the beta is 1.0, a 1 percent increase in the return on the market will result, on average, in a 1 percent increase in the return on the particular portfolio or asset. If beta is less than 1.0, the portfolio or asset is considered to be less risky than the market. Beta is the regression coefficient of the rate of return on the market in the market model equation,

$$R_i = \alpha_i + B_i R_M + e_i.$$

An estimate of the beta coefficient of a portfolio is a weighted average of the betas of the portfolio's component assets.

The Beta Factor *(R_z).* In Sharpe's capital asset pricing model, the expected risk premium on an asset depends on the expected risk premium on the market multiplied by the asset's beta coefficient.

In a more elaborate model (attributable to Black, Jensen, and Scholes), the expected return on an asset depends also on the expected return on a portfolio not correlated with the market *(R_z)* multiplied by $(1 - \beta)$. This second factor is called the beta factor.

Bid. The price offered for securities by one who wishes to buy them.

Block. A large amount of securities, normally much more than what constitutes a round lot in the market in question.

Blue Sky Laws. Laws of the various states governing the sale of securities, including mutual fund shares, and the activities of brokers and dealers within the particular state.

Book. A banker, especially a Euro banker, will refer to one's bank's assets and liabilities as its "book." If the average maturity of the liabilities is less than that of the assets, the bank is running a *short* or *open* book.

Book-Entry Securities. The Treasury and the federal agencies are moving to a book-entry system in which securities are not represented by engraved pieces of paper but are maintained in computerized records at the Fed in the names of member banks, which in turn keep records of the securities they own as well as those they are holding for customers. In the case of other securities where a book-entry system has developed, engraved securities do exist somewhere in quite a few cases. These securities do not move from holder to holder but are usually kept in a central clearing house or by another agent.

Book Value. An accounting term. Book value of a stock is determined from a company's records, by adding all assets then deducting all debts and other liabilities, plus the liquidation price of any preferred issues. The sum arrived at is divided by the number of common shares outstanding and the result is book value per common share. Book value of the assets of a company or a security may have little or no significant relationship to market value.*

Break-Point. Dollar-value level of a purchase of mutual fund shares at which the percentage of the sales charge becomes lower. Typically, a sales charge schedule contains five or six break-points.

Bridge Financing. Interim financing of one sort or another.

Brokers' Loans. Money borrowed by brokers from banks or other brokers for a variety of uses. It may be used by specialists and to help finance inventories of stock they deal in; by brokerage firms to finance the underwriting of new issues of corporate and municipal securities; to help finance a firm's own investments; and to help finance the purchase of securities for customers who prefer to use the broker's credit when they buy securities. (See: **Margin**)*

Bullet Loan. A bank term loan that calls for no amortization. The term is commonly used in the Euromarket.

Buy Back. Another term for a repurchase agreement.

Callable Bond. A bond that the issuer has the right to redeem prior to maturity by paying some specified call price.

Call Money. Interest-bearing bank deposits that can be withdrawn on 24-hours notice. Many Euro deposits take the form of call money.

The Capital Asset Pricing Model. The capital asset pricing model describes the way prices of individual assets are determined in markets where information is freely available and reflected instantaneously in asset prices—that is, efficient markets.

Prices are determined in such a way so that risk premiums are proportional to systematic risk, which is measured by the beta coefficient.

Capital Gains Distribution. A distribution to investment company shareholders from net long-term capital gains realized by a regulated investment company on the sale of portfolio securities.

Carry. The interest cost of financing securities held. **Negative Carry.** The net cost incurred when the cost of carry exceeds the yield on the securities being financed. **Positive Carry.** The net earned when the cost of carry is less than the yield on the securities being financed.

Capital Market Line. The capital market line in the Sharpe model is the ray from the risk-free rate of return (R_f) that is tangent to the efficient frontier of risky assets. It describes the relationship between expected rates of return on efficient portfolios and risk as measured by σ_p. All efficient portfolios lie on this line if lending and borrowing are permissible at the (same) risk-free rate.

The mathematical relationship is

$$E(R_p) = R_f + \left[\frac{E(R_M) - R_f}{\sigma_M} \right] \sigma_p.$$

The slope of the line,

$$\left[\frac{E(R_M) - R_f}{\sigma_M} \right],$$

is the reward per unit of risk. (for notation see symbols at end of glossary)

Capitalization. Total amount of the various securities issued by a corporation. Capitalization may include bonds, debentures, preferred and common stock and surplus. Bonds and debentures are usually carried on the books of the issuing company in terms of their par or face value. Preferred and common shares may be carried in terms of par or stated value. Stated value may be an arbitrary figure decided upon by the directors or may represent the amount received by the company from the sale of the securities at the time of issuance. (See: Par)*

Cash Equivalent. Includes receivables, U.S. Government securities, short-term commercial paper and short-term municipal and corporate bonds and notes.

Cash Flow. Reported net income of a corporation *plus* amounts charged off for depreciation, depletion, amortization, extraordinary charges to reserves, which are bookkeeping deductions and not paid out in actual dollars and cents. (See: **Amortization**).*

Cash Management Bill. Very short-maturity bills that the Treasury occasionally sells because its cash balances are down and it needs money for a few days.

Cash Market. Traditionally this term has been used to denote the market in which commodities were traded against cash for immediate delivery. Since the inception of futures markets for T bills and other debt securities, a distinction has been made between the cash markets in which these securities trade for immediate delivery and the futures markets in which they trade for future delivery.

Certificate of Deposit (CD). A time deposit with a specific maturity evidenced by a certificate. Large-denomination CDs are typically negotiable.

Characteristic Line. A characteristic line relates the return on an asset or portfolio to the return on a market index. The slope, β, measures volatility, or sensitivity to market movements.

Claimant. A person, whether employed or retired, with claims, recognized as valid by his or her employer or by law, to specific benefits under some pension plan.

Clear. A trade is carried out by the seller delivering securities and the buyer delivering funds in proper form. A trade that does not clear is said to **fail**.

Clearing House. The part of all futures exchanges (usually a separate corporation with its own members, fees, etc.) which clears all trades made on the exchange during the day. It matches the buy transactions with the equal number of sell transactions to provide orderly control over who owns what and who owes what to whom.

Clearing House Funds. Payments made through the New York Clearing House's computerized Clearing House Interbank Payments System. Clearing house debits and credits are settled in Fed funds on the first business day after clearing.

Close. The end of the trading session. On some exchanges, the "close" lasts for several minutes to accommodate customers who have entered buy or sell orders to be consummated "at the close." On those exchanges, the closing price may be a range encompassing the highest and lowest prices of trades consummated at the close. Other exchanges officially use settlement prices as the closing prices.

Closed-End Investment Company.   An investment company with a relatively fixed amount of capital, whose securities are traded on a securities exchange or in the over-the-counter market, as are the securities of operating business corporations.

Closed-Up Fund.   An open-end investment company which for one reason or another has discontinued the sale of its shares to the general public but still stands ready to accept redemptions.

Coefficient of Variation $\left[\frac{\sigma_x}{\bar{x}}\right]$.   The coefficient of variation is the standard deviation divided by the mean, or

$$\left. t\sqrt{\frac{\Sigma\,(x_i - \bar{x}\,)^2}{N}}\; \right| \; \bar{x}$$

It is a measure of the *relative* spread of a distribution about its means. Coefficients of variation can be compared, since they are relative measures.

For example, if the standard deviation of a distribution of rates of return were 2 percent, and the mean were 5 percent, the coefficient of variation would be 0.02/0.05 or 0.4 percent.

Collateral Trust Bond.   A bond secured by collateral deposited with a trustee. The collateral is often the stocks or bonds of companies controlled by the issuing company but may be other securities.*

Commercial Paper.   An unsecured promissory note with a fixed maturity of no more than 270 days. Commercial paper is normally sold at a discount from face value.

Commission.   The fee charged by a broker for making a trade on behalf of customers.

Commission House.   A firm that specializes in executing buying or selling orders for customers in spot or cash and/or futures markets for a commission or does not itself deal in futures or actuals.

Compounding.   Compounding is the arithmetic process of finding the final value of an investment or series of investments when compound interest is applied. That is, interest is earned on the interest as well as on the initial principal.

Conduit Tax Treatment.   Term used to describe the method by which regulated investment companies and their shareholders are taxed. The company is considered simply a "conduit" or channel which serves to pass investment income and realized capital gains through to the tax-paying shareholders and, therefore is not itself also taxed on such income and gains.

Continuous Compounding.   The annual rate of return compounded continuously is the natural logarithm ($\log_e$) of the ratio of the value of the investment at the end of the year to the value at the beginning.

For example, if the wealth ratio were 1.1, is natural logarithm would be 0.09531. The annual rate of return compounded continuously would be 9.531 percent. This is easily converted to an annual rate of return compounded annually using the formula $e^x - 1$, where x is the annual rate compounded continuously.

If the period is other than one year, the annual rate compounded continuously can be found by dividing the logarithm of the wealth ratio by the number of years in the period.

Contract. In the case of futures, an agreement between two parties to make and in turn accept delivery of a specified quantity and quality of a commodity (or whatever is being traded) at a certain place (the delivery point) by a specified time (indicated by the month and year of the contract).

Contractual Plan. A type of accumulation plan under which the total intended investment amount is specified, with a stated paying-in period and provision for regular monthly or quarterly investments. A substantial portion of the sales charge applicable to the total amount to be invested usually is deducted from the first year's payments.

Contributory Plan. A pension plan under which the employes covered contribute some stipulated part of the funding of the benefits they are to receive.

Correlation Coefficient (ρ). A simple correlation coefficient is a measure of the degree to which two variables move together. If the relationship is causal, it can be interpreted as a measure of the degree to which knowing the value of one variable helps to predict the value of the other.

The coefficient is the square root of 1 minus the unexplained variance of one variable, given its relationship to the other, divided by its total variance. Symbolically, for the variables, x_i and x_j

$$\rho_{ij} = \sqrt{1 - \frac{s_{i \cdot j}^2}{s_i^2}}$$

The square of the correlation coefficient is the coefficient of determination. It measures the percentage of the total variance of i explained by its relationship to j.

Correspondent. A securities firm, bank or other financial organization which regularly performs services for another in a place or market to which the other does not have direct access. Securities firms may have correspondents in foreign countries or on exchanges of which they are not members. Correspondents are frequently linked by private wires. Member organizations of the NYSE with offices in New York City may also act as corresponents for out-of-town member organizations which do not maintain New York City offices.*

Coupon. (1) The annual rate of interest that a bond's issuer promises to pay the bondholder on the bond's face value. (2) A certificate attached to a bond evidencing interest due on a payment date.

Coupon Bond. Bond with interest coupons attached. The coupons are clipped as they come due and are presented by the holder for payment of interest. (See: **Bearer Bond, Registered Bond**)*

Covariance (Cov$_i$j). Covariance is a measure of the degree to which two variables move together. A positive value means that on average, they move in the same direction. The covariance is related to, but not the same as, the correlation coefficient. It is difficult to attach any significance to the absolute magnitude of the covariance.

Symbolically, the covariance between two variables, x_i and x_j, is

$$\frac{\Sigma (x_i - \bar{x})(x_j - \bar{x}_j)}{N}$$

The covariance is also equal to $\rho_{ij}\sigma_i\sigma_j$, so its magnitude depends not only on the correlation, but also the standard deviations of the two variables. Stated alternatively, the correlation coefficient is the covariance standardized by dividing it by the product of σ_i and σ_j.

Cover. Buying futures contracts to offset previous selling. "Short covering" often results in market prices rising despite what appear to be sufficient reasons for prices to fall.

Cumulative Preferred. A stock having a provision that if one or more dividends are omitted, the omitted dividends must be paid before dividends may be paid on the company's common stock.*

Current Yield. Coupon payments on a security as a percentage of the security's market price. In many instances the price should be *gross* of accrued interest, particularly on instruments where no coupon is left to be paid until maturity.

Cushion Bonds. High-coupon bonds that sell at only a moderate premium because they are callable at a price below that at which a comparable noncallable bond would sell. Cushion bonds offer considerable downside protection in a falling market.

Debenture. A bond secured only by the general credit of the issuer.

Deferred Variable Annuity. An annuity contract which provides for annuity payments to commence at some future date.

Defined Benefit Plan. See **Pension Plan.**

Delivery. The tender and receipt of the actual (cash) commodity, or of warehouse receipts covering such commodity, in settlement of a futures contract.

Delivery Month. The specified month within which a futures contract matures and can be settled by delivery.

Delivery Point. The place(s) at which the cash commodity may be delivered to fulfill an expiring futures contract.

Depository Trust Company (DTC). A central securities certificate depository through which members effect security deliveries between each other via computerized bookkeeping entries thereby reducing the physical movement of stock certificates.*

Deviation, Residual *(x$_i$ −$\bar{x}$)* or *(e$_i$)*. A deviation is the amount by which a particular value differs from some other value such as the average, or mean. Deviations can also be related to values, such as normal trend values, or to theoretical values one would expect on the basis of an historical relationship among the variables. This type of deviation is usually called a residual. Deviations from the mean are used to compute the variance and standard deviation of a distribution. A deviation from an expected value, given the existence of a relationship with one or more other variables, is the error term in a regression equation. In the two variable case, $y = a + bx + e_i$, e_i is a residual (which is a random variable with a mean of zero).

Diminishing Marginal Utility of Wealth. Marginal utility is the amount of additional satisfaction associated with an additional amount of something such as money or wealth. If successive increments in satisfaction decline as the level of wealth increases, there is diminishing marginal utility. This implies risk aversion, because, at a given level of wealth, the gain in utility associated with some increment in wealth is less than the loss in utility associated with a decrement of the same amount of wealth.

Direct Paper. Commercial paper sold directly by the issuer to investors.

Direct Placement. Selling a new issue not by offering it for sale publicly but by placing it with one or several institutional investors.

Direct Purchase Fund. A mutual fund whose shares are purchased directly from the fund at no, or a low, charge; investor generally must deal directly with the fund, rather than through an investment dealer or broker.

Discount Bond. A bond selling below par.

Discount Securities. Noninterest-bearing money market instruments that are issued at a discount and redeemed at maturity for full face value, e.g., U.S. Treasury Bills.

Discretionary Accounts. A trading account in which the customer puts up the money but the trading decisions are made at the discretion of the broker or some other person.

Dispersion. Dispersion is the spread of a distribution about its average, or mean value. The greater the spread, the greater the variability. It can be measured either absolutely or relatively. Common absolute measures are the standard deviation, the variance, and the semi-interquartile range. The most common measure of relative dispersion is the coefficient of variation (the standard deviation divided by the mean).

Diversification. Diversification is the spreading of investments over more than one company or industry to reduce the uncertainty of future returns caused by unsystematic risk.

Diversified Investment Company. Under the Investment Company Act, a company that, in respect to 75 percent of total assets, has invested not more than 5 percent of its total assets in any one company and holds not more than 10 percent of the outstanding voting securities in any company.

Documented Discount Notes. Commercial paper backed by normal bank lines plus a letter of credit from a bank stating that it will pay off the paper at maturity if the borrower does not. Such paper is also referred to as *LOC* (letter of credit) *paper.*

Dollar Bonds. Municipal revenue bonds for which quotes are given in dollar prices. Not to be confused with "U.S. Dollar" bonds, a common term of reference in the Eurobond market.

Dollar Cost Averaging. An automatic capital accumulation method that provides for regular purchases of equal dollar amounts of securities and results in an average cost per share lower than the average price at which purchases are made.

Dual-Purpose Fund. A type of investment company, introduced to the United States from England in early 1967, which is designed to serve the needs of two distinct types of investors: (1) those interested only in income and (2) those interested solely in possible capital growth. Has two separate classes of shares.

Edge Act Corporation. A subsidiary of a U.S. bank set up to carry out international banking business. Most such subs are located within the United States.

Efficient Frontier. The efficient frontier is the locus of all efficient portfolios. If neither lending nor borrowing is allowed, it is that part of the boundary of the feasible set that includes only efficient portfolios of risky assets. If lending and borrowing are permissible, the efficient frontier is the ray drawn from the risk-free rate to the point of tangency on the efficient frontier of risky assets. This line is called the capital market line.

Efficient Market. An efficient market is one in which prices always fully reflect all available, relevant information. Adjustment to new information is virtually instantaneous.

Efficient Portfolio. An efficient portfolio is one that is fully diversified. For any given rate of return, no other portfolio has less risk, and for a given level of risk, no other portfolio provides superior returns. All efficient portfolios are perfectly correlated with a general market index, except portfolios with beta coefficients above 1.0 and which do not achieve that relatively high risk by levering an efficient portfolio. Such portfolios lie on the curved frontier of portfolios consisting exclusively of risky assets.

Equipment Trust Certificate. A type of security, generally issued by a railroad, to pay for new equipment. Title to the equipment, such as a locomotive, is held by a trustee until the notes are paid off. An equipment trust certificate is usually secured by a first claim on the equipment.*

Equivalent Bond Yield. Annual yield on a short-term, noninterest-bearing security calculated so as to be comparable to yields quoted on coupon securities.

Eurobonds. Bonds issued in Europe outside the confines of any national capital market. A Eurobond may or may not be denominated in the currency of the issuer.

Euro CDs. CDs issued by a U.S. bank branch or foreign bank located outside the United States. Almost all Euro CDs are issued in London.

Eurocurrency Deposits. Deposits made in a bank or bank branch that is not located in the country in whose currency the deposit is denominated. Dollars deposited in a London bank are Eurodollars. German marks deposited there are Euromarks.

Eurodollars. U.S. dollars deposited in a U.S. bank branch or a foreign bank located outside the United States.

Exchange Privilege. The right to exchange the shares of one open-end fund, or class of fund, for those of another under the same sponsorship at nominal cost or at a reduced sales charge. For tax purposes, such an exchange is considered a sale and new purchase.

Ex-dividend. A synonym for "without dividend." The buyer of a stock selling ex-dividend does not receive the recently declared dividend. Every dividend is payable on a fixed date to all shareholders recorded on the books of the company as of a previous date of record. For example, a dividend may be declared as payable to holders of record on the books of the company on a given Friday. Since five business days are allowed for delivery of stock in a "regular way" transaction on the New York Stock Exchange, the Exchange would declare the stock "ex-dividend" as of the opening of the market on the preceding Monday. That means anyone who bought it on and after Monday would not be entitled to that dividend. When stocks go ex-dividend, the stock tables include the symbol "x" following the name.*

Exempt Securities. Instruments exempt from the registration requirements of the Securities Act of 1933 or the margin requirements of the Securities and Exchange Act of 1934. Such securities include governments, agencies, municipal securities, commercial paper, and private placements.

Expected Rate of Return. The expected rate of return on an asset or portfolio is the weighted arithmetic average of all possible outcomes, where the weights are the probabilities that each outcome will occur. It is the expected value or mean of a probability distribution. For example, the expected return on a portfolio, $E(R_p)$, is the weighted average of all possible returns, R_i, each weighted by its probability. Mathematically, $E(R_p) = \Sigma p_i R_i$.

Ex-Rights. Without the rights. Corporations raising additional money may do so by offering their stockholders the right to subscribe to new or additional stock, usually at a discount from the prevailing market price. The buyer of a stock selling ex-rights is not entitled to the rights. (See: **Ex-dividend**)*

Extension Swap. Extending maturity through a swap, e.g., selling a two-year note and buying one with a slightly longer current maturity.

Fall. A trade is said to fail if on settlement date either the seller fails to deliver securities in proper form or the buyer fails to deliver funds in proper form.

Feasible Set. The feasible or attainable set includes all individual securities and all combinations (portfolios) of two or more of these securities available to the investor within the limits of the capital available to one.

Federal Credit Agencies. Agencies of the federal government set up to supply credit to various classes of institutions and individuals, e.g., S&Ls, small business firms, students, farmers, farm cooperatives, and exporters.

Federal Deposit Insurance Corporation (FDIC). A federal institution that insures bank deposits, currently up to $40,000 per deposit.

Federal Financing Bank. A federal institution that lends to a wide array of federal credit agencies funds it obtains by borrowing from the U.S. Treasury.

Federal Funds. (1) Noninterest-bearing deposits held by member banks at the Federal Reserve (2) Used to denote immediately available funds in the clearing sense.

Federal Funds Rate. The rate of interest at which Fed funds are traded. This rate is currently pegged by the Federal Reserve through open-market operations.

Federal Home Loan Banks (FHLB). The institutions that regulate and lend to savings and loan associations. The Federal Home Loan Banks play a role analogous to that played by the Federal Reserve Banks vis à vis member commercial banks.

Fed Wire. A computer system linking member banks to the Fed, used for making interbank payments of Fed funds and for making deliveries of and payments for Treasury and agency securities.

Fiduciary. A person who is vested with legal rights and powers to be exercised for the benefit of another person.

Filter Rules. A filter rule is a simple mechanical rule for deciding to buy or sell assets. An x percent filter rule for investing states that if the price of a security rises at least x percent, buy and hold the security until its price falls by x percent from a subsequent high. The security should then be sold or sold short until the price rises by x precent from a subsequent low.

For example, if the filter is 5 percent and the price of Security A rises from a low of 100 to 105, the security should be purchased. If the price rises to 110 and then declines to 104½, the stock should be sold or sold short. This position should be maintained until the price rises by 5 percent above a subsequent low. The filter need not be the same percentage for buy and sell signals.

Fixed Annuity. An insurance contract guaranteeing that the annuitant will receive a specified number of dollars each month, even if the insured outlives his life expectancy.

Flat Income Bond. This term means that the price at which a bond is traded includes consideration for all unpaid accruals of interest. Bonds which are in default of interest or principal are traded flat. Income bonds, which pay interest only to the extent earned are usually traded flat. All other bonds are usually dealt in "and interest," which means that the buyer pays to the seller the market price plus interest accrued since the last payment date.*

Float. The difference between the credits given by the Fed to banks' reserve accounts on checks being cleared through the Fed and the debits made to banks' reserve accounts on these same checks. Float is always positive, because in the clearing of a check, the credit sometimes precedes the debit. Float adds to the money supply.

Floating-Rate Note. A note that pays an interest rate tied to current money market rates. The holder may have the right to demand redemption at par on specified dates.

Flower Bonds. Government bonds that are acceptable at par in payment of federal estate taxes when owned by the decedent at the time of death.

Forward Market. A market in which participants agree to trade some commodity, security, or foreign exchange at a fixed price at some future date.

Forward Rate. The rate at which forward transactions in some specific maturity are being made, e.g., the dollar price at which DM can be bought for delivery three months hence.

Funded Benefits. That portion of the total benefits, including those not yet vested, estimated as having to be paid under a pension plan that is, as of a given date, covered by funds already accumulated for future payment of benefits.

Funded Vested Benefits. That portion of total vested benefits covered by accumulated funds. (See Vested Benefit.)

Futures. Contracts calling for a cash commodity to be delivered and received at a specified future time, at a specified place and at a specified price.

Futures Contract. Contracts for the purchase and sale of commodities for delivery some time in the future on an organized exchange and subject to all terms and conditions included in the rules of that exchange.

Futures Market. A market in which contracts for future delivery of a commodity or a security are bought and sold.

General Obligation Bonds. Municipal securities secured by the issuer's pledge of its full faith, credit, and taxing power.

Geometric Mean (M_g). The geometric mean is the nth root of the product of n observations. It is the correct measure to use when averaging annual rates of return, compounded annually, over time.

In calculating the average of rates of return, it is necessary to take the geometric mean of wealth ratios in order to allow for negative rates. The average rate of return is then the geometric mean minus one. For example, if the annual rates of return for two years were 10 percent and 8 percent, the average annual rate of return would be

$$\sqrt[2]{1.1 \times 1.08} - 1$$

or .0899. If the annual rates for two years were 100 percent and -50 percent, the average annual rate of return would be

$$\sqrt[2]{2.0 \times 0.5} - 1 = 0.0.$$

Gini's Coefficient of Variation. Gini's coefficient of variation is the mean difference between all possible pairs of observations divided by the mean. Symbolically, it is:

$$\sum_{i=1}^{N} \sum_{j=1}^{N} \frac{(x_i - x_j)}{N} / \bar{x}$$

where

$$i \neq j.$$

Glass-Steagall Act. A 1933 act in which Congress forbade commercial banks to own, underwrite, or deal in corporate stock and corporate bonds.

Hedge. To reduce risk, (1) by taking a position in futures equal and opposite to an existing or anticipated cash position or (2) by shorting a security similar to one in which a long position has been established.

Hedge Fund. A mutual fund or investment company which, as a regular policy, "hedges" its market commitments. It does this by holding securities it believes are likely to increase in value and at the same time is "short" other securities it believes are likely to decrease in value. The sole objective is capital appreciation.

Hypothecation. The pledging of securities as collateral—for example, to secure the debit balance in a margin account.*

Immediate Variable Annuity. An annuity contract which provides for annuity payments commencing immediately rather than at some future date.

Incentive Compensation. A fee paid to an investment company adviser which is based, wholly or in part, on management performance in relation to specified market indexes.

Income. *Gross*—total amount of dividends, interest, etc. (but not capital gains), received from company's investments before deduction of any expenses.

    Net—balance of gross income after payment of expenses, fixed charges and taxes. Also referred to as net investment income.

Income Fund. An investment company whose primary objective is current income.

Incubator Fund. A colloquial term used to describe an investment company which operates as a private fund before first offering its shares to the public.

Indenture of a Bond. A legal statement spelling out the obligations of the bond issuer and the rights of the bondholder.

Indifference Curve. An indifference curve represents combinations of, say, risk and return, that are equally valued.

    For risk averters, indifference curves are convex from below when return is measured on the vertical axis and risk on the horizontal axis. The shape varies with the risk-return preferences of the individual.

Individual Retirement Account. A tax-saving retirement program for individuals, established under the Employee Retirement Income Security Act of 1974.

Initial Margin. Customers' funds put up as security for a guarantee of contract fulfillment, and as defined by the rules of the exchange.

Insured Plan. A pension plan under which benefits are to be paid by a particular insurance company on the basis of an insurance contract between that company and a pension-sponsoring employer.

Insured Redemption Value Plan. An insurance program designed to protect investors against loss in long-term mutual fund investments.

Internal Rate of Return. The internal rate of return is analogous to the familiar yield to maturity on a bond.

The internal rate of return is the rate of discount which makes the net present value of an investment equal to zero. In the case of a bond, if

$$P_o - \sum_{t=1}^{N} \frac{I_t}{(1+i)^t} + \frac{P_N}{(1+i)^N} = 0,$$

where P_o is the initial price, P_N is the terminal price, I_t is the interest in year t, i is the internal rate of return.

Intrinsic Value. The intrinsic value of an asset is the value that asset ought to have as judged by an investor. Discrepancies between current value and intrinsic value are often the basis of decisions to buy or sell the asset.

Inverted Market. A futures market where prices for deferred contracts are lower than those for nearby-delivery contracts because of heavy near-term demand for the cash commodity. Normally, prices of deferred contracts are higher, in part reflecting storage costs.

Investment Company Amendments Act of 1970. First comprehensive amendment of the 1940 Act in three decades. The Act establishes new standards for management fees, mutual fund sales commissions and the periodic payment of contractual plan sales commissions.

Investment Management Company. Organization employed to advise the directors or trustees of an investment company in selecting and supervising the assets of the investment company.

Investment Performance Index (IPI). An investment performance index differs from a price index in that it takes into account cash dividends and other distributions to shareholders.

Investment Return. The combination of yield (interest, dividends, rents, royalties, and other income) and capital gains (or losses) resulting from investing and trading a pension fund's assets. (See **Pension Assets.**)

Issuer. With reference to investment company securities, the company itself.

Junk Bonds. High-risk bonds that have low ratings or are actually in default.

Keogh Plan. A tax-saving retirement program for self-employed persons and their employees. (Also known as H.R. 10 Plans.)

Last Trading Day. The day when trading in an expiring contract ceases, and traders must either liquidate their positions or actually make or accept delivery of the cash commodity. After that, there is no more futures trading for that particular contract month and year.

Least-Squares Regression Line. A least-squares regression line minimizes the sum of the squares of the vertical deviations of observations from a line drawn through them.

For example, if a regression line is fitted to points representing pairs of values of x_i and x_j, the equation is

$$x_i = a + bx_j$$

The squared vertical distances of the actual values of x_i from the theoretical values, given its relationship to x_j are minimized. The mean values of x_i and x_j will always be a point on the regression line.

Legal List. A list of investments selected by various states in which certain institutions and fiduciaries, such as insurance companies and banks, may invest. Legal lists are often restricted to high quality securities meeting certain specifications.*

Letter Stock. See Restricted Security.

Leveraged Lease. The lessor provides only a minor portion of the cost of the leased equipment, borrowing the rest from another lender.

Life Annuity. Monthly payments made for the life of the annuitant regardless of how long he or she lives.

Limit, Limited Order, or Limited Price Order. An order to buy or sell a stated amount of a security at a specified price, or at a better price, if obtainable after the order is represented in the Trading Crowd.*

Limit Move. The maximum that a futures price can rise or fall from the previous session's closing price. This limit, set by each exchange, varies from commodity to commodity. Some exchanges have variable limits, whereby the limit is raised automatically if the market moves by the limit for a certain number of consecutive trading sessions.

Living Trust. A trust instrument made effective during the lifetime of the creator; in contrast to a testamentary trust, which is created under a will.

Lock-Up CDs. CDs that are issued with the tacit understanding that the buyer will not trade the certificate. Quite often the issuing bank will insist that the certificate be safekept by it to ensure that the understanding is honored by the buyer.

Long. A trader who has bought futures or options, speculating that prices will rise.

Long Bonds. Bonds with a long current maturity.

Management Investment Company. A broad term covering all mutual funds and closed-end investment companies which change their portfolio holdings from time to time. The exceptions are a few funds that have fixed lists of holdings, and contractual plans; these are defined by the investment company as unit investment trusts.

Margin. The amount paid by the customer when he uses his broker's credit to buy a security. Under Federal Reserve regulations, the initial margin required in the past years has ranged from 50 per cent of the purchase price all the way to 100 per cent. (See **Brokers' Loans, Margin Call**)*

Margin Call. A demand upon a customer to put up money or securities with the broker. The call is made when a purchase is made; also if a customer's equity in a margin account declines below a minimum standard set by the exchange or by the firm (See **Margin**)*

The Market Model. The market model describes the relationship between the rates of return on individual securities or portfolios and the rates of return on the market.

For example, for a particular security i, the relationship can be written as follows:

$$R_i = a_i + \beta_i R_M + e_i$$

where R_i is the rate of return on i, R_M is the rate of return on the market, a_i and β_i (beta) are parameters, and e_i is a random variable with an expected value of zero.

The model is useful for isolating "abnormal" stock-price behavior from that due to the influence of several market conditions.

Market Order. An order to buy or sell a stated amount of a security at the most advantageous price obtainable after the order is represented in the Trading Crowd. (See **Limit Order, Stop Order**)*

The Market Portfolio. The market portfolio includes all risky assets in proportion to their market value. In the capital asset pricing model, it is the optimum portfolio of risky assets for all investors. Graphically, it is located at the point of tangency of a ray drawn from the risk-free rate of return to the efficient frontier of risky assets.

Matched Book. If the distribution of the maturities of a bank's liabilities equals that of its assets, it is said to be running a *matched book.* The term is commonly used in the Euromarket.

Mean Absolute Deviation. The mean absolute deviation is the average of the absolute values (the signs are disregarded) of the deviations of a group of observations from their expected value. Symbolically it is

$$\frac{\Sigma |x_i - \bar{x}|}{N}.$$

where N is the number of observations.

Median. The median of a distribution is the value that divides the number of observations in half. If the distribution is normal, the mean and the median will coincide. If the distribution is not normal and has positive skewness, the mean will exceed the median. If the skewness is negative, the mean will be below the median.

Money Market. The market in which short-term debt instruments (bills, commercial paper, bankers' acceptances, etc.) are issued and traded.

Money Market Fund. A mutual fund whose investments are primarily, or exclusively, in short-term debt securities, designed to maximize current income with liquidity and capital preservation.

Monthly Investment Plan. An arrangement for regular purchases of stocks listed on the New York Stock Exchange, possible through member firms. Minimum investment is $40 monthly or quarterly. Automatic dividend reinvestment is rpovided, if desired.

Mortality Rate. Death rate—the proportion of the number of deaths in a specified group to the number living at the beginning of the period in which the deaths occur. Actuaries use mortality tables, which discriminate death rates by age and sex, and sometimes also by occupation or other characteristics. The mortality tables currently being used differ very widely.

Mortgage Bond. Bond secured by a lien on property, equipment, or other real assets.

Multicurrency Clause. Such a clause on a Euro loan permits the borrower to switch from one currency to another on a rollover date.

Multiple Correlation. Multiple correlation is a measure of the relationship between one variable (the dependent variable) and two or more other variables (the independent variables) simultaneously. It is an extension of simple correlation to include more than one independent variable.

Municipal Bond Fund. Unit investment trust or open-end company whose shares represent diversified holdings of tax-exempt securities, the income from which is exempt from federal taxes.

Municipal (Muni) Notes. Short-term notes issued by municipalities in anticipation of tax receipts, proceeds from a bond issue or other revenues.

Municipals. Securities issued by state and local governments and their agencies.

NASD. The National Association of Securities Dealers, Inc. An association of brokers and dealers in the over-the-counter securities business. The Association has the power to expel members who have been declared guilty of unethical practices. NASD is dedicated to—among other objectives—"adopt, administer, and enforce rules of fair practice and rules to prevent fraudulent and manipulative acts and practices, and in general to promote just and equitable principles of trade for the protection of investors."*

NASDAQ. An automated information network which provides brokers and dealers with price quotations on securities traded over-the-counter. NASDAQ is an acronym for National Association of Securities Dealers Automated Quotations.*

Nearby Contracts. The futures that expire the soonest. Those that expire later are called deferred contracts.

Negotiable Certificate of Deposit. A large-denomination (generally $1 million) CD that can be sold but cannot be cashed in before maturity.

Nominal Return. The nominal return on an asset is the rate of return in monetary terms, i.e. unadjusted for any change in the price level. The nominal return is contrasted with the real return which is adjusted for changes in the price level.

Non-Diversified Investment Company. A company whose portfolio may be less fully diversified than is required by the Investment Company Act for qualification as a diversified investment company.

Non-Qualified Plans. Retirement plans which do not meet the requirements of Section 401(a), 403(a) or 403(b) of the Internal Revenue Code or of the Self-Employed Individuals Tax Retirement Act.

Normal Cost. That portion of the annual contribution assigned, under the actuarial cost method used, to liabilities for benefit payments derived from years of employment subsequent to inception of a pension plan. (See **Past-Service Cost.**)

Normalized Earnings. Normalized earnings are the earnings one would expect in a "normal" or mid-cyclical year. There is no general agreement about the best way to normalize earnings, but it is not uncommon to use a moving average for three, four, or five or more years. Normalized earnings are sometimes called "steady-state" earnings.

Note. Coupon issues with a relatively short original maturity are often called *notes.* Muni notes, however, have maturities ranging from a month to a year and pay interest only at maturity. Treasury notes are coupon securities that have an original maturity of up to ten years.

Offset. Usually, the liquidation of a long or short futures position by an equal and opposite futures transaction. Open positions can be offset at any time during the life of a futures contract.

Oil Drilling Fund. In some ways, oil drilling participation funds resemble mutual funds and are frequently sold by the same investment firms. However, they are not registered under the Investment Company Act and differ from mutual funds in the way they invest, the purposes for which they invest and the market for which they are designed.

Omnibus Account. An account which a member of one exchange has with, usually, a clearing member or another exchange and for which the first member is not required to disclose the names or other information concerning the one account, which actually represents the accounts of a number of customers of the first member.

Open Contracts, Open Interest. The obligation entered into by a party to a futures contract either to buy or to sell the commodity specified. The obligation is "open" until it is settled by an offsetting transaction or by delivery.

Open-End Investment Company. An investment company whose shares are redeemable at any time at approximate asset value. In most cases, new shares are offered for sale continuously.

Open Repo. A repo with no definite term. The agreement is made on a day-to-day basis and either the borrower or the lender may choose to terminate. The rate paid is higher than on overnight repo and is subject to adjustment if rates move.

Opportunity Cost. The cost of pursuing one course of action measured in terms of the forgone return offered by the most attractive alternative.

Option. A right to buy (call) or sell (put) a fixed amount of a given stock at a specified price within a limited period of time. The purchaser hopes that the stock's price will go up (if he bought a call) or down (if he bought a put) by an amount sufficient to provide a profit greater than the cost of the contract and the commission and other fees required to exercise the contract. If the stock price holds steady or moves in the opposite direction, the price paid for the option is lost entirely. There are several other types of options available to the public but these are basically combinations of puts and calls. Individuals may write (sell) as well as purchase options and are thereby obliged to deliver or buy the stock at the specified price.

There are also listed call option markets on the Chicago Board Options Exchange, the American, Midwest, Pacific and PBW Stock Exchanges. These differ from the over-the-counter market in that trading is limited to selected issues, expiration of contracts is standardized at four dates during the year, exercise prices are set at multiples of 5 below 50 and multiples of 10 above 50, and option prices are determined through a continuous competitive auction market system.*

Optional Distribution. A payment from realized capital gains and/or investment income that an investment company shareholder may elect to take either in additional shares or in cash.

Original Maturity. Maturity at issue. For example, a five-year note has an original maturity at issue of five years; one year later it has a current maturity of four years.

Overbought. A term used to express the opinion that prices have risen too high too fast and so will decline as traders liquidate their positions.

Oversold. Like "overbought," except the opinion is that prices have fallen too far too fast and so probably will rebound.

Paper. Money market instruments, commercial paper, and other.

Par. (1) Price of 100 percent. (2) The principal amount at which the issuer of a debt security contracts to redeem that security at maturity, *face value*.

Par Bond. A bond selling at par.

Participant. Any person covered by a pension plan, both those still employed and those already retired and receiving pension benefits.

Participating Preferred. A preferred stock which is entitled to its stated dividend and, also, to additional dividends on a specified basis upon payment of dividends on the common stock.*

Pass-Through. A mortgage-backed security on which payments of interest and principal on the underlying mortgages are passed through by an agent to the security holder.

Past-Service (or Prior-Service) Cost. That portion of the annual contribution assigned, under the actuarial method used, to liabilities for benefit payments attributable to years of employment prior to the inception of a pension plan. (See **Normal Cost.**)

Pension Assets. The securities and other property purchased with cash contributions to a pension fund, and with investment returns on the fund, and presumably available—upon sale at prevailing market price and so converted into cash—for payment of pension benefits as they fall due.

Pension Benefit Guaranty Corporation. Also designated PBGC, the Guaranty Corporation, or the Corporation. A U.S. government agency, set up under ERISA within the Department of Labor, with a board of directors consisting of the Secretaries of Labor, Commerce, and the Treasury, intended to insure that participants in pension plans covered by ERISA will receive all benefit payments to which they are entitled under their respective plans, within certain limits defined by ERISA. The Guarantee Corporation is empowered by the act to collect premiums and attach the corporate assets of pension-sponsoring companies in order to be able to pay benefits under terminated plans.

Pension Costs. The sum of a pension-sponsoring company's annual contributions to a pension fund over the life of the plan being funded. For noncontributory plans, the ultimate cost equals the total benefits paid plus the expenses incurred in administering the plan, minus the investment return on fund assets (or plus negative returns), plus the net cost to the company of losing the use of such funds in the company's operations, or the net cost to the company of borrowing money to pay required contributions. Actual pension costs will *not* coincide with actuarially computed costs, and the two may differ greatly.

Pension Liabilities. The sum of the obligations to pay stipulated benefits to plan participants over the life of the plan. The nature and measure of such liabilities were a major subject of discussion in this book.

Pension Plan. A systematic way of providing retirement income. Pension plans differ from other kinds of retirement plans (e.g., profit sharing plans, variable annuity plans, savings plans and deferred compensation plans) in that retirement benefits are defined by specified formulas (which relate benefits to such variables as length of employment, average or terminal compensation, and employment category). Retirement benefits are almost always paid out of funds accumulated through annual contributions and investment return on the funds accumulated rather than paid as current expenses of the plan-sponsoring organization. Pension plans may be public (namely, that provided by the U.S. social security system), civil service (for employes of federal, state, and local governments and for career military personnel) or private (for employes of profit-seeking organizations and nonprofit organizations, such as churches). Private pension plans may be either insured or noninsured. In insured plans, benefits, in stipulated amounts, are paid to retired employees by an insurance company to which the employer has paid stipulated premiums (or has made lump-sum payments—that is, bought annuities) for particular employees. In uninsured pension plans, insurance companies are not involved. Instead, the assurance that the provisions of the plan will be fulfilled is made the responsibilities of trustees (hence the designation "trusteed plans" for uninsured plans). This book is concerned primarily with uninsured, therefore trusteed, pension plans of profit-seeking companies. The term "pension plan," without further qualification, will mean just such plans.

Pension Portability. The ability of an employee, covered under a pension or profit-sharing plan, to move one's interest in such a plan from one employer to an Individual Retirement Account.

Pension Rollover. An employee's opportunity to take distributions from a qualified pension or profit-sharing plan and, within 60 days of the distribution, reinvest them in an Individual Retirement Account, or the further privilege of an employee at a later date to transfer the funds in the account to an employer who rehires one.

Pension-Sponsoring Organization. A company, or other organization, which establishes a pension plan, and supplies all or most of the required funding.

Pit. The areas on exchange floors where futures trading takes place. Pits usually have three or more levels and are common mainly in Chicago; in New York the trading areas are more often called rings and consist of open-center, circular tables around which traders sit or stand. Pits normally accommodate more traders than rings.

Plus. Dealers in governments normally quote bids and offers in 32nds. To quote a bid or offer in 64ths, they use pluses; for example, a dealer who bids 4 + is bidding the handle plus $\frac{1}{32} + \frac{1}{64}$, which equals the handle plus $\frac{3}{64}$.

PNs. Project notes are issued by municipalities to finance federally sponsored programs in urban renewal and housing. They are guaranteed by the U.S. Department of Housing and Urban Development.

Point. (1) 100 basis points = 1 percent. (2) One percent of the face value of a note or bond. (3) In the foreign exchange market, refers to the lowest level at which the currency is priced. Example: "One point" is the difference between a sterling price of $1.8080 and $1.8081.

Preferred Stock. A class of stock with a claim on the company's earnings before payment may be made on the common stock and usually entitled to priority over common stock if company liquidates. Usually entitled to dividends at a specified rate—when declared by the Board of Directors and before payment of a dividend on the common stock—depending upon the terms of the issue. (See: **Cumulative Preferred, Participating Preferred**)*

Premium. The amount by which a preferred stock, bond or option may sell above its par value. In the case of a new issue of bonds or stocks, premium is the amount the market price rises over the original selling price. Also refers to a charge sometimes made when a stock is borrowed to make delivery on a short sale. May refer, also, to redemption price of a bond or preferred stock if it is higher than face value. (See: **Discount Bond, Short Sale**)*

Present Value or Worth. The present value of a payment or payments is the actual value discounted at an appropriate rate of interest. The discounting reflects the productivity of capital and the risk premium. For example, the present value of a share of stock, V_o, is the stream of future earnings discounted to perpetuity, or,

$$V_o = \sum_{t=1}^{\infty} \frac{E_t}{(1 + i)^t}$$

where E_t are the earnings in period t and i is the rate of discount.

Price Risk. The risk that a debt security's price may change due to a rise or fall in the going level of interest rates.

Prime Rate. The rate at which banks will lend to their best (prime) customers. The all in cost of a bank loan to a prime credit equals the prime rate plus the cost of holding compensating balances.

Principal. (1) The face amount or par value of a debt security. (2) One who acts as a dealer buying and selling for one's own account.

Probability Distribution. A probability distribution is a distribution of possible outcomes with an indication of the subjective or objective probability of each occurring.

Profit-Sharing Retirement Plan. A retirement program to which a percentage of the gross profits of a corporation (or of the earnings of a self-employed person under a Keogh Plan) is contributed each year; the eventual benefits are not predetermined as in the case of a pension plan.

Prudent Man Rule. An investment standard. In some states, the law requires that a fiduciary, such as a trustee, may invest the fund's money only in a list of securities designated by the state—the so-called legal list. In other states, the trustee may invest in a security if it is one which a prudent man of discretion and intelligence, who is seeking a reasonable income and preservation of capital, would buy.*

Qualified Plans. Retirement plans which meet the requirements of Section 401(a), 403(a) or 403(b) of the Internal Revenue Code or the Self-Employed Individuals Tax Retirement Act.

Random Selection. Random selection is similar to picking stocks by throwing darts at a stock listing.

Technically, random selection means that each element in the relevant population has a known and positive probability of selection. For example, if an index were based on 10 randomly selected stocks from a population (list) of 1000, the stocks could be selected with equal probabilities or, say, with probabilities proportional to the market value of the outstanding shares of each of the 1000 firms.

Random Walk. A random walk implies that there is no discernible pattern of travel. The size and direction of the next step cannot be predicted from the size and direction of the last or even from all the previous steps. If one wanted to find a random walker, the best place to look would be the starting point.

Random walk is a term used in mathematics and statistics to describe a process in which successive changes are statistically independent. The serial correlation is zero.

The changes are a random variable with an expected value of zero.

RANs. Revenue anticipation notes are issued by states and municipalities to finance current expenditures in anticipation of the future receipt of nontax revenues.

Redemption Price. The price at which a bond may be redeemed before maturity, at the option of the issuing company. Redemption value also applies to the price the company must pay to call in certain types of preferred stock. (See: **Callable**)*

Red Herring. A preliminary prospectus containing all the information required by the Securities and Exchange Commission except the offering price and coupon of a new issue.

Refunding. Redemption of securities with funds raised through the sale of a new issue.

Registered Bond. A bond whose owner is registered with the issuer.

Registered Investment Company. An investment company that has filed a registration statement with the Securities and Exchange Commission under the requirements of the Investment Company Act of 1940.

Regression Analysis. Regression or correlation analysis is a statistical technique for estimating the relationship between one variable (dependent variable) and one or more other variables (independent variables).

The relationship estimated, usually a least-squares regression equation, is often used to predict the value of the dependent variable, given the values of the independent variable, or variables.

Regression Coefficient. A regression coefficient indicates the responsiveness of one variable to changes in another. If the relationship between two variables is described by a straight line, the regression coefficient is the slope of the line.

The regression coefficient between rates of return on an asset and rates of return on the market is called the beta coefficient.

Regulated Investment Company. One that has elected to qualify for the special tax treatment provided by Subchapter M of the Internal Revenue Code; not to be confused with registration under Investment Company Act of 1940.

Regulation D. Fed regulation currently requiring member banks to hold reserves equal to 4 percent of their net borrowings over a 28-day averaging period from foreign offices of other banks.

Regulation M. Fed regulation currently requiring member banks to hold reserves equal to 4 percent of their net borrowings from their foreign branches over a 28-day averaging period. Reg M also requires member banks to hold reserves equal to 1 percent of all Eurodollars lent by their foreign branches to domestic corporations for domestic purposes.

Regulation Q. Fed regulation imposing lids on the rates that banks may pay on savings and time deposits. Currently time deposits with a denomination of $100,000 or more are exempt from Reg Q.

Regulation T. The federal regulation governing the amount of credit which may be advanced by brokers and dealers to customers for the purchase of securities. (See: **Margin**)*

Regulation U. The federal regulation governing the amount of credit which may be advanced by a bank to its customers for the purchase of listed stocks. (See: **Margin**)*

Reinvestment Privilege. A special service offered by most mutual funds and some closed-end investment companies through which dividends from investment income may be automatically invested in additional full and fractional shares. Reinvestment specifics provided by the individual funds.

Reinvestment Rate. (1) The rate at which an investor assumes interest payments made on a debt security can be reinvested over the life of that security. (2) Also refers to the rate at which funds from a maturity or sale of a security can be reinvested. Often used in comparison to "give up" yield.

REIT. Real Estate Investment Trust, an organization similar to an investment company in some respects but concentrating its holdings in real estate investments. The yield is generally liberal since REIT's are required to distribute as much as 90% of their income. (See: **Investment Company**)*

Repo. See **Repurchase Agreement.**

Repurchase Agreement (RP or Repo). A holder of securities sells these securities to an investor with an agreement to repurchase them at a fixed price on a fixed date. The security "buyer" in effect lends the "seller" money for the period of the agreement, and the terms of the agreement are structured to compensate him for this. Dealers use RP extensively to finance their positions. Exception: When the Fed is said to be doing RP, it is lending money, that is increasing bank reserves.

Reserve Requirements. The percentages of different types of deposits that member banks are required to hold on deposit at the Fed.

Restricted Security. A portfolio security not available to the public at large, which requires registration with the Securities and Exchange Commission before it may be sold publicly; a "private placement"; frequently referred to as "letter stock."

Revenue Bond. A municipal bond secured by revenue from tolls, user charges, or rents derived from the facility financed.

Reverse Repurchase Agreement. Most typically a repurchase agreement initiated by the lender of funds. Reverses are used by dealers to borrow securities they have shorted. Exception: When the Fed is said to be doing reverses, it is borrowing money, that is, absorbing reserves.

Revolver. See **Revolving Line of Credit.**

Revolving Line of Credit. A bank line of credit on which the customer pays a commitment fee and can take down and repay funds according to his needs. Normally the line involves a firm commitment from the bank for a period of several years.

Reward-to-Variability Ratio. The reward-to-variability ratio is the risk premium on an asset per unit of risk as measured by the variability or standard deviation. Sharpe used this measure to rank mutual funds.

Right of Accumulation. The application of reduced sales charges to quantity purchases of mutual fund shares made over an extended period of time. Exact provisions vary among the funds that offer this privilege and reference should be made to individual prospectuses.

Risk Aversion. Risk aversion means riskiness matters and is disliked. A risk averter will hold a portfolio of more than one stock in order to reduce risk for a given expected return.

    Technically, the utility function of a risk averter will depend on rate of return *and* risk and will not be linear. This implies diminishing marginal utility of wealth.

    A risk-averse investor will incur additional risk only if he *expects* a higher rate of return.

Risk-Free Rate of Return (R_f). The risk-free rate of return is the return on an asset that is virtually riskless. For example, Treasury bills maturing in one year have a precisely predictable nominal rate of return for one year. The risk premium on an asset is the rate of return in excess of the risk-free rate. The risk-free rate is normally used in portfolio theory to represent the rate for lending or borrowing.

Risk Neutrality. Risk neutrality means risk doesn't matter. A risk-neutral investor cares only about rate of return and would hold a portfolio of one asset—the one with the highest expected rate of return. Risk neutrality implies constant marginal utility of wealth. The utility function for such an investor is linear. It is represented by the equation $U = a + bE(R)$, where U is the utility of the return on an asset and where $E(R)$ is the expected return on the asset.

Risk Premium $(R_i - R_f)$. The risk premium on an asset is the actual return minus the riskless rate of return. In Sharpe's capital asset pricing model, the risk premium for any asset is proportional to its beta—the measure of sensitivity to general market movements.

    If R_i is the rate of return on an asset, and R_f is the riskless rate, $R_i - R_f$ is the risk premium.

Rollover. Reinvest funds received from a maturing security in a new issue of the same or a similar security.

Round Lot. In the money market, round lot refers to the minimum amount for which dealers' quotes are good. This may range from $100,000 to $5 million, depending on the size and liquidity of the issue traded.

Round Turn. The completion of both a purchase and an offsetting sale, or a sale and an offsetting purchase.

Runs. A run is a sequence of changes in the value of a variable, all having the same sign. The number of runs in a sequence of changes is the number of reversals in sign plus one.

For example, if price changes are classified as zero, positive, or negative, a sequence of $++-++0--$ would include five runs.

Sampling. Sampling is the process of selecting a subset of a population. It may or may not be random. The usefulness of a sample depends upon its representativeness, or the degree to which one can make inferences about the excluded population on the basis of the sample.

Savings and Loan Association. National- or state-chartered institution that accepts savings deposits and invests the bulk of the funds thus received in mortgages.

Savings Deposits. Interest-bearing deposit at a savings institution that has no specific maturity.

Secondary Market. The market in which previously issued securities are traded.

Separate Account. This account is completely separated from the General Account of the insurance company, since its assets are generally invested in common stocks.

Serial Bonds. A bond issue in which maturities are staggered over a number of years.

Serial Correlation *(p).* Serial correlation measures the degree to which what happens next is related to what happened previously.

Serial correlation is measured by the simple correlation coefficient between two variables, one being the successive value of the other. Serial correlation can also be measured with lags. For example, a change in the price of a stock can be serially correlated with the change before the last one as well as with the last one.

Shareholder Experience. A measure of the investment results which would have been obtained by an actual mutual fund shareholder. Differs from Management Record because of the inclusion of the sales charge, when applicable, and may make different assumptions regarding the treatment of income dividends and capital gains distributions. Is usually expressed in terms of a hypothetical $10,000 investment.

Short Bonds. Bonds with a short current maturity.

Short Coupons. Bonds or notes with a short current maturity.

Short Covering. Buying stock to return stock previously borrowed to make delivery on a short sale.*

Short Position. Stocks sold short and not covered as of a particular date. On the NYSE, a tabulation is issued once a month listing all issues on the Exchange in which there was a short position of 5,000 or more shares and issues in which the short position had changed by 2,000 or more shares in the preceding month. Short position also means the total amount of stock an individual has sold short and has not covered, as of a particular date.*

Short Sale. A person who believes a stock will decline and sells it though he does not own any has made a short sale. For instance: You instruct your broker to sell short 100 shares of ABC. Your broker borrows the stock so he can deliver the 100 shares to the buyer. The money value of the shares borrowed is deposited by your broker with the lender. Sooner or later you must cover your short sale by buying the same amount of stock you borrowed for return to the lender. If you are able to buy ABC at a lower price than you sold it for, your profit is the difference between the two prices—not counting commissions and taxes. But if you have to pay more for the stock than the price you received, that is the amount of your loss. Stock exchange and federal regulations govern and limit the conditions under which a short sale may be made on a national securities exchange. Sometimes a person will sell short a stock he already owns in order to protect a paper profit. This is known as selling short against the box.*

Sinking Fund. Indentures on corporate issues often require that the issuer make annual payments to a sinking fund, the proceeds of which are used to retire randomly selected bonds in the issue.

SIPC. Securities Investor Protection Corporation which provides funds for use, if necessary, to protect customers' cash and securities which may be on deposit with a SIPC member firm in the event the firm fails and is liquidated under the provisions of the SIPC Act. SIPC is not a Government Agency. It is a non-profit membership corporation created, however, by an Act of Congress.*

Skewness. Skewness is a measure of the asymmetry of a distribution. A normal distribution is symmetrical and has no skewness. If there are more observations to the left of the mean, the skewness is positive; if more to the right, negative.

Split Funding. An arrangement which combines investment in mutual fund shares and purchase of life insurance contracts such as under an individual Keogh Plan.

Spot Market. Market for immediate as opposed to future delivery. In the spot market for foreign exchange, settlement is two business days ahead.

Spot Price. The price at which the physical commodity is selling.

Spread. (1) Difference between bid and asked prices on a security. (2) Difference between yields on or prices of two securities of differing sorts or differing maturities. (3) In underwriting, difference between price realized by the issuer and price paid by the investor.

Standard Deviation. The standard deviation is a commonly used measure of dispersion. It is the square root of the variance. It is based on deviations of observations from the mean and is therefore in the same units as the observations. A measure of relative dispersion is the standard deviation divided by the mean (the coefficient of variation). This is often useful in comparing distributions that differ substantially in the magnitude of the numbers.

The formula for the standard deviation, σ, is

$$\sqrt{\frac{\Sigma (x_i - \bar{x})^2}{N}}$$

For a probability distribution,

$$\sigma = \sqrt{\Sigma P_i [x_i - E(x)]^2}$$

Statistical Independence. If two variables are statistically independent, the correlation between them is not significantly different from zero. That is, the changes in the two variables are unrelated. Knowledge of the changes in one is of no value in predicting the other.

For example, the weak form of the efficient market hypothesis asserts the statistical independence of successive price changes. Current prices reflect and impound all of the implications of the historical sequence of prices so that a knowledge of that sequence is of no value in forming expectations about future price changes.

Stop-Loss Order. An open order given to a brokerage firm to liquidate a position when the market reaches a certain price so as to prevent losses from mounting. Sometimes market price trends are accelerated when concentrations of stop-loss orders are touched off.

Stop-Out Price. The lowest price (highest yield) accepted by the Treasury in an auction of a new issue.

Straddle. The usually simultaneous purchase of one futures month and the sale of another either in the same or different commodity or exchange.

Subchapter M. The sections of the Internal Revenue Code that provide special tax treatment for regulated investment companies.

Subordinated Debenture. The claims of holders of this issue rank after those of holders of various other unsecured debts incurred by the issuer.

Swap. (1) In securities, selling one issue and buying another. (2) In foreign exchange, buying a currency spot and simultaneously selling it forward.

Swap Fund. See **Tax-Free Exchange Fund.**

Systematic Risk. Systematic risk is the volatility of rates of return on stocks or portfolios associated with changes in rates of return on the market as a whole. It can be estimated statistically from the market model. The percentage of total variability that is systematic is given by the coefficient of determination and the degree of responsiveness to market movements is measured by beta.

Tail. The difference between the average price in Treasury auctions and the stop-out price. (2) A *future* money market instrument (one available some period hence) created by buying an existing instrument and financing the initial portion of its life with term RP.

TANs. Tax anticipation notes issued by states or municipalities to finance current operations in anticipation of future tax receipts.

Tax Anticipation Bills (TABs). Special bills that the Treasury occasionally issues. They mature on corporate quarterly income tax dates and can be used at face value by corporations to pay their tax liabilities.

Tax-Free Exchange Fund. An investment company organized to permit investors holding individual securities selling at appreciated prices to exchange such securities, without payment of capital gains tax, for shares of the fund.

Term Fed Funds. Fed funds sold for a period of time longer than overnight.

Term Loan. Loan extended by a bank for more than the normal 90-day period. A term loan might run five years or more.

Term RP (Repo). RP borrowings for a period longer than overnight, may be 30, 60, or even 90 days.

Thin Market. A market in which trading volume is low and in which consequently bid and asked quotes are wide and the liquidity of the instrument traded is low.

Tight Market. A tight market, as opposed to a thin market, is one in which volume is large, trading is active and highly competitive, and spreads between bid and ask prices are narrow.

Time Deposit. Interest-bearing deposit at a savings institution that has a specific maturity.

Time-Weighted Rate of Return. The time-weighted rate of return is a weighted average of the internal rates of return for subperiods dated by the contribution or withdrawal of funds from a portfolio. To calculate it, one needs to know the value of the portfolio at the time of each cash inflow or outflow and the dates on which these occur. Rates of return on mutual fund shares are time-weighted rates of return.

Total Return. A statistical measure of performance reflecting the result of acceptance of capital gains in shares, plus the result of reinvestment of income dividends.

Trading Limit. The maximum price movement up or down permitted in one trading session under the Rules of an Exchange.

Treasury Bill. A noninterest-bearing discount security issued by the U.S. Treasury to finance the national debt. Most bills are issued to mature in three months, six months, or one year.

Turnover Rate. The rates at which a firm's employes, and their several categories, are fired, quit, or otherwise terminate their employment, thus limiting their eligibility for benefits under the firm's pension plan.

Turnover Ratio. The extent to which an investment company's portfolio is turned over during the course of a year. For a closed-end company, the total of purchases and sales of securities (other than U.S. Government obligations and short-term notes) is divided by two and then divided by average assets. For a mutual fund, a rough calculation can be made by dividing the lesser of portfolio purchases or sales (to eliminate the effects of net sales or redemptions of fund shares) by average assets.

Underwriter. A dealer who purchases new issues from the issuer and distributes them to investors. Underwriting is one function of an investment banker.

Unfunded Benefits. That portion of total pension obligations not covered by accumulated pension funds.

Unfunded Vested Benefits. That portion of liabilities for fulfilling vested benefits not covered by accumulated pension funds.

Unit Refund. Monthly payments made to an annuitant during one's lifetime. At one's death, a lump sum payment is made to the designated beneficiary of the remaining value of the account.

Unmatched Book. If the average maturity of a bank's liabilities is less than that of its assets it is said to be running an unmatched book. The term is commonly used in the Euromarket. Equivalent expressions are open book and short book.

Unsystematic Risk. Unsystematic risk is the variability not explained by general market movements. It is avoidable through diversification. Only inefficient portfolios have unsystematic risk.

Utility Function. A utility function describes the relationship for an individual between various amounts of something such as wealth and the satisfaction it provides.

If one's preferences are known, his utility functions can often be approximated by precise mathematical equations. The signs and values of its derivatives indicate the direction and magnitude of changes in utility associated with changes in the amount of the good possessed.

Variable Annuity. An annuity contract under which the dollar payments received are not fixed but fluctuate more or less in line with average common stock prices.

Variable-Price Security. A security, such as stocks or bonds, that sells as a fluctuating, market-determined price.

Variable-Rate Loan. Loan made at an interest rate that fluctuates with the prime.

Variance (σ^2). The variance of a distribution is a measure of variability based on squared deviations of individual observations from the mean value of the distribution. Its square root, the standard deviation, is a commonly used measure of dispersion.

The formula for the variance is,

$$\sigma^2 = \frac{\Sigma (x_i - \bar{x})^2}{N}$$

If the distribution is of future outcomes that are not known with certainty, the variance is a weighted average of the squared deviations and the weights are the probabilities of occurrence. That is,

$$\sigma^2 = \Sigma P_i [x_i - E(x)]^2$$

Vested Benefits. Those pension benefits, claims to which are inalienable, under terms of particular pension plans and, since enactment of ERISA, under provisions of that law.

Volatility. Volatility is that part of total variability due to sensitivity to changes in the market. It is systematic and unavoidable risk. It is measured by the beta coefficient.

Efficient portfolios have no additional risk, and volatility is the only source of variability in rates of return.

Voluntary Plan. An accumulation plan without any stated duration or specific requirements other than the minimum amounts which may be invested at one time. Sales charges are applicable individually to each purchase made.

Wealth Ratio $\left(\frac{W_t}{W_o}\right)$. A wealth ratio is the terminal value of an investment divided by its initial value. It is used in calculating rates of return.

    The wealth ratio is expressed as W_t/W_o where W_t refers to the terminal value and W_o to the initial value. The annual rate of return compounded continuously is

$$\log_e \frac{\left(\frac{W_t}{W_o}\right)}{n},$$

where n is the number of years in the period. The annual rate of return compounded annually is $e^x - 1$, where x is the annual rate compounded continuously.

Weighting. Weighting is the specification of the relative importance of each of a group of items that are combined. For example, stocks included in indexes may be equally weighted or weighted according to value.

When-Issued Trades. Typically there is a lag between the time a new bond is announced and sold and the time it is actually issued. During this interval, the security trade *wi*, "when, as, and if issued."

Yankee Bond. A foreign bond issued in the U.S. market, payable in dollars, and registered with the SEC.

Yield Curve. A graph showing, for securities, that all expose the investor to the same credit risk, the relationship at a given point in time between yield and current maturity. Yield curves are typically drawn using yields on governments of various maturities.

Yield to Maturity. The rate of return yielded by a debt security held to maturity when both interest payments and the investor's capital gain or loss on the security are taken into account.

SYMBOLS USED IN GLOSSARY

$E(x) = $ The expected value of x also represented by $\bar{x}$

$\beta_i = $ The beta coefficient

$\sigma_i^2 = $ The variance of the ith asset (stock)

$\sigma_M^2 = $ The variance of the market

$\sigma_P^2 = $ The variance of the portfolio

$\sigma_i = $ The standard deviation of the ith asset

$\sigma_M = $ The standard deviation of the market

$R_P = $ The portfolio return

$R_M = $ The market return

$\rho_{im} = $ The correlation coefficient between the ith asset and the market

$COV_{ij} = $ The covariance between the ith and jth assets

$N = $ The number of observations

Index

A

Abrahamson v. *Fleschner,* 645
Absolute expected returns, 402
Account balance, 459
Account management, 35
Active portfolio management, 9–10, 225
  business cycle analysis, 243–61
  composite index, 269–70
  versus passive management, 283–86
  security analysis, 229–43
  selection, 229–43
  technical analysis, 230, 261–81
  timing, 229–31, 243–81
  trading costs, 293–99
Advertising, 617–19
Advisory account, 22
Affiliate system of investment management organization, 47
Agency account, 22
AICPA; *see* American Institute of Certified Public Accountants
Allocation, 459
American Commodities Exchange, 779–81
American Institute of Certified Public Accountants (AICPA), 544–45
  Committee on Investment Companies, 554–56
  corporate projections, 644–45
Apartment buildings, 349
Arbitrage, 785–87, 889–95
  bull and bear markets, 894
Asset mix
  cause of changes, 405
  definition, 404–5
  determination of, 407–9
Assignment, 385
Average correlation models, 192
Average present-valued time, 326

B

Bank of New York v. *Spitzer,* 660
Bank Administration Institute (BAI), 447–48
Bank trust department, 55–57, 791–94
Bankers' acceptances, 875–76
Bankruptcy prediction, 339–40
  discriminant analysis, 339

Banks for Cooperatives, 870
Bar charts, 266
Barbell portfolio, 332
Barr Rosenberg Associates, 926–30
Baseline portfolio, 496–506
  communication between sponsor and manager, 505–6
  evaluating departures from, 500–503
  management activity, 498–99
  sources of return, 503–4
Bayesian adjustment, 211
Bear market, 249, 251, 257–59
Becker Funds Evaluation Service, 140
Becker Securities Corporation 750, 463
Becker universe, 401
Benchmark yield curve, 307–8
Beneficial ownership, 613
Beneficiaries, 651
Beta, 822–23; *see also* Portfolio beta predictions
  portfolio, 67–68, 457
Beta coefficient, 7, 138, 144, 456–58
Beta risk measurement concept versus Value Line performance, 136
Blue Sky laws, 814
Bond
  beta, 335
  call provisions, 320–21
  duration, 326–29
  price volatility, 309, 319
  sinking fund provisions, 321
Bond beta, 335
Bond portfolio management, 305–42, 474–506
  active management, 475–96
  bankruptcy detection, 339–40
  baseline portfolio management, 496–506
  benchmark yield curve, 307–8
  beta, 335
  coupon, 411
  dumbbell portfolio, 332–33
  duration, 326–29
  economic credit analysis, 317
  expected return, 308
  immunization, 323–30, 337–39, 341–42
  interest rate anticipation, 309–11
  laddered portfolio, 332–35

Bond portfolio management—*Cont.*
  maturity, 409–10, 317–18
  nonlinearity, 335–37
  objectives, 318
  performance measurement, 483–86
  price volatility, 319
  quality, 410–11
  return functions, 330–32
  risk, 318–24
  sector-quality-coupon selection, 311–15
  sector transactions, 412
  swapping, 315–17
  yield volatility, 320
Bond theory, 305–7
Branch type investment organization, 46–47
Breakeven analysis, 862, 902
Breakeven time, 325–26
Brochure rule, 620–25
  brokerage placement practices disclosure, 626
Broker, 867–68, 896–97
Broker referrals and relationships, 628–35
Brokerage firm investment advisory department, 59
Brokerage industry, 604
Brokerage placement practices disclosure, 625–28
Brownian movement, 82, 84, 86
Bull market cycle, 249, 251–57
Business cycle
  bear market, 249, 251, 257–59
  bull market, 249, 251–57
  critical factors, 275–80
  forecasting, 243
  investment cycles mirroring, 273–81
  investment timing, 243–61
  stock prices, 246
Buy and write strategy, 394–95
Buy call and Treasury Bill strategy, 393–94
Buy-long-and-hold strategy, 333–34

C

In re Cady Roberts & Co., 639
Call
  buy call and T-bill strategy, 393–94
  definition, 385
  purchasing, 390, 394
  selling, 391–92, 394
Call risk, 320–21
Canavest House Ltd., 926–27
Capital asset pricing model (CAPM), 8–9, 202–10, 335
  world market investment portfolio, 366
Capital market line, 460–61, 464–70
Capital market research, 33
Carry, 880–81
Cash flow, 459
Cash flow impact, 459

Cash market, 870
Cash reserve funds, 812–13
Cash surrender value, 30
Casualty insurance portfolios; *see* Fire and casualty insurance portfolios
Certificates of deposit, 872–73
Certified Public Accountant (CPA), 11
C.F.A. Digest, 692
Chain of command system, 36
Chartered Financial Analyst (CFA), 11, 606
  candidate study program, 12, 117–20
  competency standards, 12–16
Chartered Investment Counselor, 605, 688
Chartist, 75–76
Chase Manhattan Bank, survey of public pension funds, 716–18
Chicago Board of Trade, 777, 779
Chicago Mercantile Exchange, 777–78
Clearing banks, 895–96
Closed-end fund, 24–25, 55
  bonds, 805–6
  dual purpose fund, 805–6
  investment companies, 801–2, 805–6
  leveraged, 802
  real estate, 353–55
Closing transaction, 385
Commercial bank portfolio management, 761
  arbitrage, 785–87
  asset portfolio, 781–85
  diversification, 765
  futures market, 777–85
  government securities, 773–74
  hedging, 778–85
  income account, 764
  investment policy, 774–75
  liability management, 774, 782–85
  liquidity account, 764
  objectives, 762–64
  quality, 765–66
  repurchase agreements, 773
  swapping, 767–73
  swing account, 764
Commercial paper, 874–75
Committee system of decision making structure, 37
Commodities Futures Trading Commission, 777–79
Commodity Exchange Act of 1974, 779
Common factor risk, 458
Common stock evaluation, 231–43
  models, 234–43
Common stocks
  beta coefficient, 7
  investment returns, 420, 423–25
  portfolio fund allocation, 6–7
Comparative institutional approach to market efficiency, 73–74
Comparative position statement, 551, 559

Computer construction of optimal portfolio, 921
  construction programs, 926–31, 935–38
  historical model, 926–27
  multiperiod framework, 931–38
  single index model, 928–31
  single point in time, 922
Computer Directions Advisers, Inc., 228
Computers, 823–24
  accounting, 943–44
  commercially available services, listed, 944–75
  common stock analysis and management, 942
  economic analysis, 944
  fixed-income investing, 942–43
  information services, 944
  international investing, 943
  performance measurement, 944
  portfolio audit, 944
  portfolio strategy, 942
  real estate investing, 944
Concentrated investment funds, 821
Concentration, 460, 659
Conflict of interest, 575–76
  consent, 577–78
  disclosure, 577–78
Consent, 577–78, 580
Consumer Price Index, 425
Contrary opinion, 262–63
Conversion of puts to calls, 385, 395–96
Core-noncore portfolios, 299–302
Corporate projections, 643–45
Correlations of stock movements, 184–93, 280
  models, 189–93
Correspondent type of investment organizations, 47
Court v. *Ash*, 646
Covariance, 172–74
Covered call writer, 385
Covered put writer, 385
Cross-sectional beta, 456
Currency risks, 369–74
Current income, 545, 559
Current ownership income, 552–56
Current value income, 551
Custodian bank, 385
Cyclical portfolio, 767

D

Daniel v. *International Brotherhood of Teamsters*, 639
Dart board fund, 106–7
Dealer loan rate, 895
Dealers, 867–69
  activities, 879–80
  arbitrage, 889–95
  extending to longer maturities, 884–85

Dealers—*Cont.*
  figuring the tail, 886–88
  financing, 881–82
  hedging, 895
  inside markets, 880
  interest rate predictions, 882
  positioning, 882–84
  profit sources, 880–81
  relative value, 889
  risk, 889
  RP and reverse book, 885–86
  shorting, 884–85
Decentralized style of decision-making structure, 38
  superstar system, 39
Decision-making structure, 36–39
  chain of command system, 36–37
  committee system, 37
Default risk, 321–22
Deferred fixed annuity, 29
Designated endowment, 830
Development properties, 350
Diefenbach study, 524–26
Direct placement, 742–43
Disclosure, 577–78, 580, 620
Discount bonds, 478–79
Discounted stream of future dividends model, 823
Discriminant analysis, 339
Diversification, 458–59
  trust investments, 659
Dividend, 676
Dollar-weighted rate of return, 453–54
Dow Jones Industrial Average, 463, 979–80
Dow theory, 97
  price charts, 263–69
Dual purpose funds, 24, 805–6
Dumbbell portfolio, 332–33, 766–67
Duration of bond, 326–29, 337, 341–42

E

Earnings per share (EPS) announcements, 111–12
Economic forecast, 232
Economic research, 33
Educational endowment funds, 827
  asset structure, 846–47
  board of trustees, 833
  classification, 830
  fund accounting, 831
  gifts, 831, 839–40
  inflation, 835–36, 840–41
  investment committee, 833
  objectives, 834–41
  real total return, 839
  social objectives, 847–48
  spending policy, 841–45
Efficient frontier, 179–84

Efficient market, 8–9
  definition, 70–71
  requirements for, 72–75
Efficient market-random walk hypothesis
  active portfolio management, 284–85
  beating market averages, 151–52
  beta versus portfolio performance, 144–45
  beta versus Value Line performance, 136
  block trade, 118–21
  Brownian movement, 84, 86
  dart board fund, 106–7
  EPS announcements, 111–12
  EPS forecasts versus market price changes, 130–33
  expectations, 150–51
  explainable outliers, 95–96
  filters, 97–98, 100
  implications of theory, 156
  legal barriers to efficient markets, 104–6
  low P/E portfolios versus high, 122–24
  low P/E portfolios versus random selections, 126–27
  mutual funds versus random portfolios, 131–35
  new information studies, 114–16
  news reporting lag, 112–14
  next move concept, 83–85
  pension performance consistency, 140–41
  performance measured by securities market line, 146–48
  psychological limitations, 125–26
  random numbers, 88–91
  rebalancing, 91–93
  reflecting barrier concept, 98–100
  relative strength strategy, 100–104
  research advice versus performance, 127–29
  risk versus investor returns, 142–44
  runs, 93–95
  secondary distribution, 116–18
  security analysis, 148–50
  semistrong form, 79–80, 108–21
  serial correlation, 81–84, 87–88
  splits, 109–12
  stock price gyrations versus intrinsic value, 141–42
  strong form, 80, 121–55
  Value Line rankings versus performance, 135–36
  weak form, 78–79, 81–108
Efficient portfolios, 5
Elton, Gruber and Padberg portfolio construction program, 926–27
Employee Retirement Income Securities Act of 1974 (ERISA)
  administrative exemptions, 599–600

Employee Retirement Income Securities Act of 1974—*Cont.*
  diversification rule, 591
  equity portfolios performance, 445–46
  exclusive purpose rule, 589
  exculpatory provisions, 593–94
  fiduciary standards, 568, 571–72, 574, 585–94, 657
  indicia of ownership rule, 591
  individual account plan exception, 592
  liability for fiduciary breaches, 592
  loyalty, 578
  mandatory provisions, 586–89
  monitoring execution costs, 507
  permissive provisions, 586–89
  prohibited transactions, 576, 584, 594
    fiduciary conduct restrictions, 595
    general transactions, 595
    property restrictions, 596
    specific transactions, 595
  solely in the interest rules, 589
  statutory exemptions, 598
  transactional analysis, 600–602
  transitional rules, 598
Employee retirement plans, 28–29, 697
  assets, 698
  companies offering services, 707–8
  corporate, 701
  defined benefit, 701
  defined contribution, 701
  ERISA; *see* Employee Retirement Income Securities Act of 1974
  maturity, 702
  municipal and state; *see* Municipal and state pension plans
  pension costs and liabilities, 703–7
  portfolio management, 27, 29, 59–60
  private, 698
  public, 698, 709
  state and local government funds, 700
  union, 701
Environment for investment, 6–8
Equity Funding stock fraud, 642–43
Equity market
  annual appreciation, 431
  compared to real estate returns, 427–28, 432
  rates of return, 63
Equity portfolio
  company selection, 416
  industry portfolio, 414
  management styles, 413–14
  performance measurement; *see* Equity portfolio performance
  sector portfolios, 416
Equity portfolio performance, 445
  benchmarks for comparative analysis, 462–63
  comparative analysis of returns, 463–64
  control, 472–73

Equity portfolio performance—*Cont.*
correcting performance, 470–73
history of measurement, 447–48
management trends, 470
optimization, 472
other measurements, 459–60
period of performance, 451
return and diversification relationships, 470
return measurement, 452–55
risk measurement, 456–59
simulation, 472
sponsor objectives, 449
subdivision of funds, 449–50
Equity real estate investment trusts (EREITS), 431
annual returns, 433–37
performance evaluation, 433–36
risk-adjusted performance evaluation, 437–40
Equivalencies, 386
ERISA; *see* Employee Retirement Income Securities Act of 1974
Escrow receipt, 385–86
Ethical Investor: Universities and Corporate Responsibility, 683
Eurodollar certificates of deposit, 873–74
Eurodollars, 872
Excess return, 243
Excess return to beta index, 195–96
Exchange rates, 369–74
forward premium or discount, 371
spot rates, 371
Exclusive benefit rule, 589
Executions
measuring costs, 513–16
model for evaluation, 511
monitoring costs, 507
trading costs, 508–11
transaction costs, 511, 516–17
Expected returns, 405–7
Expiration cycle, 387
Expiration date, 387
Explainable outliers, 95–96
Extension swaps, 908

F

Fails and fails game, 895–96
Federal agency securities, 870–71
Federal Financing Bank, 870
Federal funds, 871–72
Federal Home Loan Bank System, 870
Federal Intermediate Credit Banks, 870
Federal Land Banks, 870
Federal regulation of investment managers, 605
advertising, 617–19
brochure rule, 620–25
corporate projections, 643–45

Federal regulation of investment managers—*Cont.*
ERISA, 612–13
fees, 6
fraud, 635–38
inside information, 638–43
Investment Advisers Act of 1940; *see* Investment Advisers Act of 1940
investment advisory contract, 614
liability, 645–48
marketing of advisory services, 632–35
registration and qualification, 609–10, 621
SEC disciplinary sanctions, 648–49
SEC filing and disclosure requirements, 613
Federal Reserve System, 870
Fiduciary, 597–98
Fiduciary law, 567
investment technology, 572–73
loyalty, 575–78
public interest, 579–80
preventive measures for manager, 580–81
disclosure and consent, 580
documentation, 581
exculpatory clauses, 580
investment objectives, 580
knowledge of laws affecting client, 580
standard of reasonable care, 568
whole portfolio approach, 572
Figuring the tail, 886–88
Filters, 97–98, 100
Financial Accounting Standards Board (FASB), 544
Statement No. 33, 544–45
Financial Analysts Federation (FAF), 605
Code of Ethics and Standards of Professional Conduct, 606, 688–92
continuing education, 692
corporate projections, 644–45
enforcement of standards, 692
Financial Analysts Journal, 605, 692
Financial Analysts Research Foundation, 692
Financial instrument futures, 777
Fire and casualty insurance portfolios
asset mix, 753–55
bond management, 755–57
common stock, 758
diversification, 759
investment income, 750
objectives, 752
organization of investment function, 759–60
tax management, 757–58
underwriting, 750
First Index Investment Trust, 823
Fisher effect, 370

Fixed-income fund
  investment style, 821–22
  management, 818–19
Flower bonds, 478, 665
Forbes magazine, investment company
    surveys, 825
Form ADV, 609, 620–25
Formal retirement fund, 27–29
Forward commitment, 741–42
Forward discount or premium exchange
    rates, 371
Fraud, 635–38
Full capitalization approach to portfolio
    construction, 288–93
Full-laddered strategy, 333–34
Fully-funded pension fund, 28
Fully invested funds, 821
Fundamental analysis, 77–78
Fundamental beta coefficient, 458
Futures market, 777–85

G

Gain trading, 771
General market analysis, 262–63
Gifford Fong Associates, 926–27
GNMA; *see* Government National Mort-
    gage Association
Goldman Sachs
  business cycle and stock market per-
      formance evaluations, 247–48
  common stock evaluation model, 242,
      244–45
Gordon model of common stock evalua-
    tion, 237
Government National Mortgage Associa-
    tion (GNMA or Ginnie Mae)
  futures contracts, 777
  interest rate calculations, 865–66
  money market instrument, 870
  pass-throughs, 482, 770
Growth stocks, 820

H

Harvard College v. *Amory*, 569, 654, 657,
    794
Harvard University, endowment fund,
    836
Hedging
  currency risks, 373–74
  dealer, 895
  financial instruments futures, 777–85
  markets and contracts, 778–81
High-and-low-turnover funds, 821
High-turnover bond funds, 822
High-yield bond funds, 822
Higher Education Price Index, 836–37
Historical beta coefficient, 456
Hotels and motels, 351
Hourglass portfolio (dumbbell portfolio),
    332–33, 766–67

I

Immediate fixed annuity, 29–31
Immunization of portfolios, 323–30
  mathematically, 341–42
  pension funds, 701
  studies, 337–39
In the money, 387
Income beneficiary, 25
Independent organization, 43
Index fund, 8, 72, 823; *see also* Passive
    equity management
  choosing index, 286–88
  management methods, 290–91
  market inventory fund, 302–4
  pooled, 299
  trading costs, 293
Indexed portfolio, 659–60
Indicator Digest, 269–70
Individual factor risk, 458
Industrial buildings, 348–49
Industry index models, 190
Industry portfolio, 414
  weights, 414–16
Industry research, 33–34
Inflation
  higher education, 835–36
  interest rates, 370
  linkage between exchange rates, 370
  real estate, 346
Information coefficient analysis (ICA), 532–
    42
  case studies, 535–38
  evaluation, 541–42
  portfolio management, 538–41
Information effect, 510
Inside information, 579, 638–43
Institute of Chartered Financial Analysts,
    11, 605
  continuing education, 692
  purposes and programs, 687–88
  standards of professional conduct, 688
Institutional investors, 603–4
Insurance companies, 29–31
  investment operation, 57–59
Inter vivos trust, 25
Integrated organization, 40
Interest rate anticipation, 309–11
Interest rate anticipation swap, 316
Interest rate calculations
  bond rates, 857–60
  breakeven analysis, 862–63
  compound rates, 856
  converting discount to compound rate,
      856–57
  as discount, 853
  futures contracts, 864–66
  money market investments, 860–63
  paid on maturity, 854

Interest rate calculations—*Cont.*
  relationship between discount rate and
    rate at maturity, 854
  swaps, 863
Interest rate cycle risk, 319
Interest rate futures, 777–88
Interest rates in international markets,
    370–71
  Fisher effect, 370
  forward premium, 371
  inflation rates, 370
Intermarket swap, 316, 481–83
Internal analysis; *see* Technical analysis
Internal Revenue Code of 1954 (the Code),
    585
  exclusive benefit rule, 589
  prohibited transactions, 594
International diversification, 359
  correlation of foreign to U.S. markets,
    361–63
  currency risk, 369–74
  efficiency of foreign markets, 378
  exchange controls, 380
  exchange rates, 369–74
  expected returns, 363–69
  foreign stock market size, 375–78
  market segmentation and integration,
    366–69
  performance measurement, 379–80
  portfolio risk, 374–75
  risk reduction, 360
  risk-return tradeoff, 379
  taxes, 380–81
Intrinsic value, 387
Investment accounts; *see* Portfolio
Investment adviser
  definition, 607
  exclusions, 608–9
Investment Advisers Act of 1940, 574,
    656
  antifraud provisions, 635–38
  brochure rule, 620–26
  broker referrals, 628–35
  brokerage placement practices, 625–28
  coverage, 607–8
  definition of investment adviser, 607–9
  disclosure, 578, 620–25
  ERISA, 608
  Form ADV, 609, 620–25
  investment advisory contracts, 614–16
  marketing services, 617–20
  private right of action for damages, 645–
    47
  proxy rules, 628
  qualifications, 609–10
  recordkeeping, 610–12
  registration, 609–10
  regulation of investment managers, 605
  SEC administrative powers, 648–49
Investment advisory contracts, 614–16

Investment advisory services publications,
    60
Investment company, 53–55
  closed end funds, 801–2, 805–6
  definition, 801
  internationally diversified portfolios, 824
  investment management of, 815
  mutual funds; *see* Mutual funds
  objectives, 807–11
  optimization, 824
  organizational form, 813, 815–19
  regulation, 813–15
  risk control, 822–23
  selecting, 825–26
  services, 812
  styles of investment, 820–22
  taxation, 813
  unit trust, 802
  valuation techniques, 823
Investment Company Act, 577–78, 584
  proxy rules, 628
  regulations, 605, 814
  Section 17, 577
Investment Company Amendments Act of
    1970, 814
Investment Company Institute (ICI), 814
Investment company performance mea-
    surements, 543
  comparability to other performance
    measures, 546–51
  current income data, 551–56, 559
  price level changes, 556–58
  tax considerations, 560–61
  timing problems, 561–63
Investment counsel, defined, 605
Investment Counsel Association of Amer-
    ica, Inc., 605
  Standards of Practice, 688
Investment counsel firm, 53
Investment counseling, 62–63
Investment cycles, 273–81
Investment forecast, 795
  trusts, 795–96
Investment fund restrictions, 673–86
  dividend limits, 676
  foreign investments, 676–77
  insurance companies, 675–76
  New York statute, 673–74
  public retirement funds, 674–75
  social impact investing, 681–86
Investment management
  control of program, 9–11
  definition, 3
  environment, 6–8
  federal regulation; *see* Federal regula-
    tion of investment managers
  objectives of investors, 4–6
Investment management firm, 53
Investment management law, 567

Investment management organizational
structure, 32
affiliate system, 47–48
branch type, 46–47
correspondent system, 47–48
decision making, 36–39
multipurpose or integrated organization, 40–43
operational functions, 32–36
size of organization, 48
specialized organization, 43–45
unitary organization, 45–46
Investment manager
definition, 604
federal regulation; *see* Federal regulation of investment managers
professional standards, 605
qualifications, 11–22
Investment objectives, 61
evaluating policy and operations, 68–69
risk control, 63–69
risk tolerance of investor, 67
Investment policy committee, 815–17, 819
The Investment Process, 734
Investment time horizon, 403
Investor Responsibility Research Center,
Inc., 847
Irrevocable personal trust, 26

K–L

King v. *Talbot,* 655
Korschot study, 526–29
Kuhn-Loeb Bond Index, 463
Laddered portfolio, 332, 766–67
Land as real estate, 351
Legal barriers to efficient markets, 104–6
Leverage, 351–52, 908–10
Leveraged closed-end trust, 802
Lewis v. *Transamerica Corp.,* 647
Life insurance annuity, 30
Life insurance companies
assets, 727–29
company organization, 735
forward commitments, 741–42
fund sources, 727
general account investments, 744–48
inflation, 734–35
insolvency risk, 731–34
investment objectives, 727
liability, 727–29
liquidity risk, 734
mutual companies, 735–36
private placements, 741–42
programs, 29–31
regulation, 737
risk-return tradeoff, 730
savings, 725–26
separate account investments, 748–49
stock, 735–36
taxation, 740

Life tenant, 25
Line charts, 266
Lipper Analytical Services, 825
Liquidity, defined, 764
Liquidity effect, 510
Liquidity portfolio management
accounting, 914–16
arbitrage, 907–8
credit risk, 901–2
investment parameters, 898
manager contrasted with dealer, 898
marking to market, 911–12
maturity choice, 902, 904–7
opportunity cost, 916–18
performance tracking, 912–13
relative value, 899–901, 907–8
restrictive guidelines, 913–14
riding yield curve, 902–4
shorting securities, 910–11
swapping, 907–8
Liquidity premium theories, 331
Living trust, 25
Load mutual fund, 23–24
Long term corporate bonds, investment
return, 421, 423–25
Long term government bonds, returns,
420, 423–25
Loss-constrained portfolios, 476–80
Low-turnover bond funds, 822
Lowry's Reports, 138–40

M

Management account, 22–23
Management company, 53–55
Management fees, 285
Management information system-com-
puter group, 818
Mandatory Securities Valuation Reserve
(MSVR), 728–29, 732–34
Market analysis; *see* Technical analysis
Market inventory fund, 302–4
Market line, 149
Market model, 186
Market portfolio, 8
Market risk, 8, 456
Market segmentation hypothesis, 331
Market sensitivity, 456
Market timing, 821
Market-timing effects, 465–66
Marketability, 764
Marking the market, 911–12
Massachusetts Investors Trust, 802
Mean return, 160, 163–64
*Measuring the Investment Performance of
Pension Funds,* 447
Medium-to-high-quality bond funds,
822
In re Merrill Lynch Pierce Fenner & Smith,
640

Merrill Lynch, Pierce, Fenner & Smith, common stock evaluation model, 234–43
Modern portfolio theory
  correlations, 184–85
  efficient frontier, 179–84
  mean return, 160, 163–64
  performance measurement of portfolio, 446–47
  portfolio analysis, 184
  portfolio choice problem, 160–63
  portfolio selection criteria, 193–200
  risk, 160, 165–71
  riskless lending and borrowing, 177
  single index models of stock movement, 185–89
  variance, 165–77
Money market, 867
  clearing banks, 895–96
  communications, 897
  dealers; *see* Dealers
  inside market, 880
  instruments; *see* Money market instruments
Money market instruments
  bankers' acceptances, 875–76
  certificates of deposit, 872–73
  commercial paper, 874–75
  Eurodollars, 872
  federal agency securities, 870–71
  federal funds, 871–72
  municipal notes, 878
  repurchase agreements, 876–78
  reverse RPs, 877–78
  T-Bill futures market, 870
  U.S. Treasury securities, 868–69
Mosaic theory, 639, 641
Moving averages, 266–69
Multiindex models, 189–92
Multipurpose organizations, 40–43
Municipal bonds, 665
Municipal and state pension plans, 709
  Chase Manhattan Bank survey, 716–18
  funding, 709–12
  investment powers, 716–19
  investment trends, 715–16
  investments held, 712–15
  political considerations, 719
  socially useful investing, 719–22
Municipal notes, 878
Mutual funds, 23, 53–55; *see also* Investment company
  administration, 804–5
  cash reserve funds, 812–13
  classification by size and type, 808
  distribution of assets, 810–11
  load fund, 803–4
  no-load fund, 803–4
  organizational form, 813

Mutual funds—*Cont.*
  trust investment, 667–68
  trustees, 804–5

N

National Association of Insurance Commissioners, 731, 737, 754
National Association of Real Estate Investment Trusts (NAREIT), 430
  price index, 431
National Association of Security Dealers (NASD), 814
Negotiable certificates of deposit, 873
Net management effect, 465–66
Neutral hedge, 387
New information studies, 114–16
New York State Insurance Law, 737, 739–40
New York Stock Exchange Composite Index, 463
News reporting lag study, 112–14
Next move concept, 83–85
No-load mutual fund, 23–24
Non-insured pension plan, 28
Nonmarket risk (standard error), 456, 458

O

Office buildings, 348
Open-end investment company, 23, 801
  real estate, 353–55
Open-ending, 771, 773
Opening transaction, 387
Optimal portfolio, 195–200
  computer construction, 921
  cutoff rate, 196–98
Optimization, 824
Option valuation, 387–88
Options
  accumulating position, 390–91
  class, 385
  objectives, 385
  overriding, 394–95
  overvalued, 388
Out-of-the money, 387
Overriding, 394–95
Overvalued option, 388

P

Parent company-subsidiary company organizational structure, 48
Party in interest, 597
Passive equity management, 9–10
  versus active management, 283–86
  asset allocation, 302
  choosing index, 286–87
  core-noncore portfolios, 299–302
  definition, 282
  market inventory fund, 302–4
  performance, 286

Passive equity management—*Cont.*
  pooled versus individual portfolios, 298–99
  portfolio construction, 288–93
  risk-return considerations, 285–86
  trading costs, 293–99
  trading strategies, 293
Pension funds; *see* Employee retirement plans
Performance tracking, 912–13
PERISA (Public Employee Retirement Income Securities Act), 674
Personal trusts; *see* Trusts
Point and figure chart, 266, 268–69
Pooled pension common trust fund, 29
Portfolio
  fund allocation, 6–7
  individual/family type, 22–27
  return on, 171–72
Portfolio accounts, 22
Portfolio adjustments, 399
  asset mix, 404–5, 407–9
  bonds, 409–12
  equity, 412–18
  expected returns, 405–7
  fixed-income portfolio changes, 409–12
  objectives change, 400, 403
  results expected, 401
  risk tolerance, 402–4
Portfolio beta predictions, 202–20
  Bayesian adjustment, 211
  capital asset pricing model, 202–6
  error estimation, 210–12
  fundamental descriptors, 215
  manager-generated, 457
  traditional method of estimating, 206–10
  varying parameter regression, 209–10
Portfolio choice problem, 160–63
Portfolio geometric mean return, 469
Portfolio immunization; *see* Immunization of portfolios
Portfolio manager, 792
Portfolio objectives, 4–6
Portfolio plans, 8–9
Portfolio reallocators, 126
Positioning, 882–83
Predictive ability
  Diefenbach study, 524–26
  information coefficient analysis, 532–42
  Korschot study, 526–29
  measurement, 523
  Value Line method, 529–32
Premium, 388
Price charts
  bar charts, 266
  Dow theory, 263–65
  line charts, 266
  moving average, 266–69

Price charts—*Cont.*
  patterns, 265–66
  point and figure charts, 266, 268–69
Price volatility of bonds, 319
Private placement, 742–43
Professional self-regulation, 687–92
Profit sharing plans, 701
Property and casualty insurance portfolios, 31; *see also* Fire and casualty insurance portfolios
Proxy rules, 628
Prudent-man rule, 25, 569–70
  ERISA, 589–90
  trusts, 656, 794
Pure endowment, 830
Pure expectation theory, 316, 330–32
Pure yield pickup swap, 315, 476–80
Put
  buying, 392–93
  definition, 388
  selling, 391, 395
Putnam International Equities, 824–25

Q–R

Qualifying employer real property, 597
Qualifying employer security, 596
Quasi-endowment, 830
Random numbers, 88–91
Random walk hypothesis; *see* Efficient market-random walk hypothesis
Rate anticipation, 486–88, 493–96
Rate anticipation swap, 863
Real estate investment trusts (REITS), 347, 350
  investment portfolio, 429
  management, 429
  price index, 430
  systematic risk, 431–32
Real estate portfolio management, 345
  capitalization rate, 357
  commingled funds, 353–55
  diversification, 346, 353
  high quality property, 348–49
  high risk property, 349
  income, 346
  income value formula, 356
  incremental value, 347
  inflation protection, 346–47
  intrinsic value determination, 351–52
  leverage, 352–53
  liquidity, 347
  manager, 355–56
  performance evaluation, 356–57
  stabilized net income, 357
  staffing, 353
Real estate portfolio returns, 426–40
  equity real estate investment trusts, 431–40
  index appreciation, 430–33
  index trends, 426–29

Real estate portfolio returns—*Cont.*
investment trusts, 429–30
risk-adjusted performance evaluation, 437–40
traditional performance evaluation, 437–40
Real realized income, 545
Realized income, 545
Rebalancing, 91–93
Record management, 35–36
Reflecting barriers concept, 98–100
Reinvestment risk, 322
immunization, 324
REITS; *see* Real estate investment trusts
Relative strength strategy, 100–104
Relative value, 889–901, 907
Repurchase agreements (Repos), 773, 876–78, 881–82
Resale agreements (Resales), 773
Research information
defined, 521–22
predictive ability measurement studies, 523–42
Residual risk, 188
predicting, 214
Restaurants as real estate properties, 351
Restricted endowment, 830
Restricted option, 388
Retirement plans; *see* Employee retirement plans
Return on investment
definition, 452
dollar-weighted, 453
time-weighted, 453
Reverse repurchase agreement (reverse RP), 877–88
Revocable living trust, 25
Risk
bond portfolio management, 318–24
call, 320–21
dealer, 889
default, 321–22
equity portfolio performance measurement, 455–59
immunization, 323–24
interest rate cycle, 319–20
reinvestment, 322–24
Risk-adjusted returns, measurement of, 469
Risk premium, studies of, 332
Risk tolerance, 402–3
Riskless asset, 177–78, 180–82
Rolf v. *Blyth, Eastman Dillon & Co.*, 628–32
Roll Effect, 308, 313, 315
Rule system of decision making structure, 38
Runs, 93–95

S

Safety of a security, 765
Sales forecast, 232
Salomon Brothers Corporate Bond Index, 463
Salomon Brothers Long Term Corporate Bond Index, 305, 490
Salomon Brothers Total Return Index, 484
Salomon Brothers Total Return Index for Mortgage Pass-Through Securities, 491
Scalping, 576, 663
Sears Profit-Sharing Plan, 701
SEC v. *Bausch and Lomb*, 641
SEC v. *Faberge, Inc.*, 640
SEC v. *Glen Alden*, 640
SEC v. *Lums*, 641
SEC v. *Texas Gulf Sulphur*, 640
SEC Advisory Committee on Corporate Disclosure, 644
SEC Report on Small Accounts and Investment Management Services, 620
SEC Special Study of the Securities Market in 1963, 620
Secondary distribution, 116–18
Sector portfolio, 416–18
Sector-quality-coupon selection, 311–15
Sector swap, 481–83
Securities Act of 1933, 605
Release 5992, 643
Securities Acts Amendments of 1975, 614, 625
Securities Exchange Act of 1934, 576
brokerage placement practices disclosure, 625
filing and reporting requirements, 614
inside information, 639
investment company regulation, 814
regulation of investment managers, 605
Section 28(e), 577
Securities and Exchange Commission, 578
brochure rule, 578
corporate projections, 643
Investment Advisers Act of 1940, 607, 609
Securities trader, 793–94
Security analysis, 229, 231
economies of scale, 156
efficient market theory, 148–51, 156–57
sales analysis and forecasts, 231–34
Security analyst, 793
Security beta coefficient, 457–58
Security research, 33–34
Security selection effects, 465, 467
Self-regulation of investment managers, 687–92
Sensitivity (delta factor), 388
Separation theorem, 180
Serial correlation, 81–84, 87–88

Series of options, 388
Sharpe portfolio construction program,
    926–27
Shopping centers as real estate investment
    properties, 349
Shorting, 884–85, 910–11
Single index model of stock movements,
    185–89
Single-purpose organization, 43–45
Social impact investing, 681–86
    educational endowment funds, 847–48
    investment managers responsibility,
        685–86
    municipal and state pension plans, 719–
        22
    Sullivan principle, 683
Sources of Return in Corporate Bond Port-
    folios, 504
South Africa, 682–83, 721
Special purpose buildings as real estate in-
    vestment, 351
Specialized organization, 43–45
Spectral analysis, 86–87
Splits, 109–12
Standard of reasonable care, 568–75
Standard and Poor's 500 Index
    Composite, 463
    equity portfolio performance measure-
        ment, 463
    market inventory fund, 302–4
    passive equity management, 282–83,
        286–93
Standard and Poor's 400 Industrial Index,
    463
Standard deviation of portfolio, 456
Stanford University Statement of Goals,
    Objectives and Policies, 840
Statistical research, 34
Stock market indexes
    Dow Jones Industrials, 979–80, 990
    Equal Investment Index, 980, 990
    Standard and Poor's 500 Index, 979–90
Stocks; *see* Common stocks
Straddle, 389
Stratified sampling approach to portfolio
    construction, 288–93
Striking price, 389
Substitution swap, 317, 480–81, 769
Sullivan principle, 683
Swapping, 315–17, 767–73
    interest rate analysis, 863–64
    intermarket, 769–70
    liquidity portfolio management, 907–8
    substitution, 317, 480–81, 769
    tax-loss trading, 771
    yield anticipation, 770
    yield pickup, 768
Synthetic put, 389
Systematic risk, 8, 431–32, 456

T

Tax-loss trading, 771–72
Taxes, 389
Team system of decision making structure,
    38
Technical analysis, 75
    composite index, 269
    contrary opinion, 262–63
    general market analysis, 262–63
    investment timing, 261
    price charts, 263–69
    random walk theory, 270–73
    stock selection techniques, 262
Term endowment, 830
Testamentary trust, 25–26
Time-weighted rate of return, 453–54
Total dollar value, 460
Total return spending, 842–45
Trading costs
    commission, 509
    market impact, 510
    spread, 509–10
    transaction cost, 511
Trading effect, 467–68
Traditional mean model of stock move-
    ment, 192
Transaction, 460
Transaction costs, 285, 293–99
    benchmark prices, 511–12
    equity portfolio performance measure-
        ment, 460
    operationally defined, 511
    reducing, 516–17
Transactions management, 35–36
Treasury Bills, 868
    equity portfolio performance measure-
        ment, 462–63
    inflation, 422
    interest rate calculation, 865
    return on investment, 420, 423–25
Treasury bonds, 865, 869
Treasury notes, 868–69
Trust(s)
    balanced portfolio investment approach,
        658
    bank trust department, 791–94
    beneficiaries, 651, 791
    case studies, 797–99
    capital market investment, 789
    checklist, 652–55
    defined, 651, 790
    ERISA standards applicable, 794–95
    irrevocable, 791
    life insurance trust, 791
    living, 652, 791
    mutual funds, 667–68
    portfolio construction, 660–61
    professional manager, 661–63

Trust(s)—*Cont.*
  property, 651
  record keeping services, 796–97
  revocable, 652, 791
  stocks as investment, 669
  testamentary, 652, 791
Trust administrator, 792
Trust indenture, 652
Trust institutions, 790
Trustee, 651–52, 654–57, 790
  investment standards, 794–96
Trusteed pension program, 28
Trustor, 790
Turnover, 460

U

Uncovered writer, 389
Underlying security, 389
Undervalued option, 389
Uniform Management of Institutional
  Funds Act, 833
Unit trust, 802
Unitary organization, 45–46
Unrestricted endowment, 830
Unsystematic risk, 456

V

Vacant properties as real estate invest-
  ment, 350
Value investing, 820
Value Line Composite Average, 463
Value Line Investment Survey, 135–36,
  228–29

Value Line method of measuring pre-
  dictive ability, 529–32
Value Line One-Year Performance Rank-
  ings, 529
Variable annuity, 806–7
Variable hedge, 390
Variance, 165
  combination of assets, 167
  portfolio, 172–77
Varying parameter regression, 209
Venture capital funds, 24
Volatility coefficient, 516

W

Weisenberger Financial Services, 825
Wells Fargo Investment Advisers, 282
Will, 652, 654
Williams Act of 1968, 613
Wilshire Associates, 926–27
Wilshire 5000 Equity Index, 463
Wilson v. *First Houston Investment Corp.*,
  647

Y

Yield curve
  analysis, 313–15
  riding, 902–4
Yield curve anticipation, 488–92
  snap-ups and snap-downs, 489–92
Yield illusion, 487–88
Yield pickup swap, 768
  interest rate analysis, 863
Yield spread, 900–901

DUE

F